THE PSYCHOLOGY PROBLEM SOLVER®

REGISTERED TRADEMARK

A Complete Solution Guide to Any Textbook

Staff of Research & Education Association
Dr. M. Fogiel, Chief Editor

With Contributions By
Don Sharpsteen, Ph.D.
Associate Professor of Psychology
University of Missouri at Rolla

Research & Education Association
61 Ethel Road West
Piscataway, New Jersey 08854

THE PSYCHOLOGY
PROBLEM SOLVER®

Printed in the United States of America

Library of Congress Control Number 2003092656

International Standard Book Number 0-87891-523-0

PROBLEM SOLVER is a registered trademark of
Research & Education Association, Piscataway, New Jersey 08854

WHAT THIS BOOK IS FOR

For as long as psychology has been taught in high schools, many students have found it difficult to understand and learn because of the broad scope of the subject and the complex interrelationships of the mental processes and behavior. Despite the publication of hundreds of textbooks in this field—each one intending to provide an improved approach to the subject over previous attempts—students continue to be perplexed. As a result, psychology often becomes a course taken only to meet school or departmental curriculum requirements.

In a study of the problem, Research & Education Association found that students' difficulties with high school psychology stem from five basic causes:

(1) No systematic rules of analysis have been developed which students may follow in a step-by-step manner to solve the problems they will typically encounter. This is brought about by the multitude of conditions and principles that may be involved in a psychology problem; often, the student is faced with a number of possible methods for solving a problem. To prescribe an approach to be followed for each of the possible variations would involve wading through an enormous number of rules and steps—a task that could become more burdensome than solving the problem directly, with some accompanying trial and error—to find the correct solution route.

(2) Psychology textbooks currently available will usually explain a given principle in a few pages written by a professional who has special insight into the subject matter which is not shared by students. The explanations are often written in an abstract manner that leaves students confused as to the application of the principle. In addition, the explanations given are not sufficiently detailed or extensive to make students aware of the wide range of applications and different aspects of the principle being studied. The numerous possible variations of principles and their applications are usually not discussed, and it is left for the students to discover these for themselves while doing exercises. Accordingly, the average student is expected to rediscover that which has been long known and practiced, but not published or explained extensively.

(3) Usually, the examples that accompany the explanation of a topic are too sparse and too simple to enable students to obtain a thorough grasp of the

principles involved. The explanations do not provide sufficient basis to enable students to solve problems that may be subsequently assigned for homework or given on examinations.

The examples are presented in abbreviated form, leaving out much material between steps and requiring students to derive the omitted material themselves. As a result, students find the examples difficult to understand—contrary to the purpose of presenting examples in the first place.

Moreover, examples are often wordy and confusing. They do not state the problem and then present the solution. Instead, they pass through a general discussion, never revealing what is to be solved for.

Examples also do not always include diagrams/graphs, wherever appropriate, and thus students do not obtain the necessary training to draw diagrams or graphs to simplify and organize their thinking.

(4) Students can learn this subject only by doing the exercises themselves and reviewing them in class. We believe students need to obtain experience in applying the principles so that they can see the many different ramifications that stem from each.

In doing the exercises on their own, students find that they are required to devote considerably more time to psychology than to other subjects with comparable credits. This is because they are uncertain about the selection and application of the principles involved. Moreover, all too often they find it necessary to discover the "tricks" not revealed in their textbooks or review books which make it possible to solve problems easily. As a result, students find themselves spending a great deal of time resorting to trial and error to solve problems.

(5) When reviewing the exercises in the classroom, instructors typically have students take turns writing solutions on the blackboard or on a computer, and explaining them to the class. Presenters often find it difficult to explain the solutions in a manner that both holds the interest of the class and enables their classmates to follow their line of thinking. Furthermore, the students being addressed are too busy copying the material from the board to properly take in all of the oral explanations and focus their attention on the methods of solution.

This book is intended to aid high school psychology students in surmounting the difficulties we've described by supplying detailed illustrations of the solution methods which are usually not apparent or readily available to students. We illustrate those solution methods by selecting the very problems that are most often assigned for class work and given on examinations. The problems are arranged in order of complexity to enable students to learn and understand a particular topic by reviewing the problems in sequence. The problems are illustrated with detailed step-by-step explanations, to save students the large amount of time that is often needed to fill in the gaps that are usually found between steps of illustrations in textbooks or review/outline books.

The staff of REA considers psychology a subject that is best learned by allowing students to view the methods of analysis and solution techniques themselves. This approach to learning the subject matter is similar to that practiced in scientific laboratories, particularly in the medical field.

In using this book, students can review and study the illustrated problems at their own pace; they are not limited to the time allowed for explaining problems on the board in class.

When students want to look up a particular type of problem and solution, they can readily locate it in the book by referring to the Index, which has been extensively prepared. It is also possible to locate a particular type of problem by just glancing at the material within the boxed portions. To facilitate rapid scanning of the problems, each problem has a heavy border around it. Furthermore, each problem is identified with a number immediately above the right-hand margin.

To obtain maximum benefit from the book, students should familiarize themselves with the following section, "How to Use this Book."

To meet the objectives of this book, staff members of REA have selected problems usually encountered in assignments and examinations, and have solved each problem meticulously to illustrate the steps that are particularly difficult for students to grasp. Special gratitude is expressed to them for their efforts in this area, as well as to the numerous contributors who devoted their time to this book.

The difficult task of coordinating all our contributors' efforts was carried out by Carl Fuchs. His conscientious work deserves much appreciation. He also trained and supervised art and production personnel in the preparation of the book for printing.

Finally, special thanks are due Helen Kaufmann for her unique talent in rendering those difficult border-line decisions and in making constructive suggestions related to the design and organization of the book.

HOW TO USE THIS BOOK

This book can be an invaluable aid to students in psychology as a supplement to their textbooks. The subject matter in the book is developed beginning with heredity, culture and behavior, learning, and cognition, and extending through sensation, perception, motivation, development, personality, behavior pathology, therapies, and social psychology. Extensive sections are also included on testing and measurement, methodology, and statistics. In addition, there is a particularly helpful section to guide students in writing experimental reports by providing a series of examples. A glossary of over 2,000 items not found in the usual textbooks also adds to the usefulness of this book.

Each chapter of the book is accompanied by a series of short answer questions to help in reviewing the study material and preparing for exams.

HOW TO LEARN AND UNDERSTAND A TOPIC THOROUGHLY

1. Refer to your class text and read the section pertaining to the topic. You should become acquainted with the principles discussed there. These principles, however, may not be clear to you at the time.

2. Then locate the topic you are looking for by referring to the "Table of Contents" in the front of this book.

3. Turn to the page where the topic begins and review the problems under each topic, in the order given. For each topic, the problems are arranged in order of complexity, from the simplest to the more difficult. Some problems may appear similar to others, but each problem has been selected to illustrate a different point or solution method.

To learn and understand a topic thoroughly and retain its contents, it will be generally necessary for students to review the problems several times. Repeated review is essential to gaining experience in recognizing the principles that should be applied and for selecting the best solution technique.

HOW TO FIND A PARTICULAR PROBLEM

To locate one or more problems related to a particular subject matter, refer to the Index. In using the Index, be certain to note that the numbers given refer to problem numbers, not to page numbers. This arrangement of the Index is intended to facilitate finding a problem more rapidly, since two or more problems may appear on a page.

If a particular type of problem cannot be found readily, it is recommended that the student refer to the "Table of Contents" and then turn to the chapter that is applicable to the problem being sought. By scanning or glancing at the material that is boxed, it will generally be possible to find problems related to the one being sought, without consuming considerable time. After the problems have been located, the solutions can be reviewed and studied in detail. For this purpose of locating problems rapidly, students should acquaint themselves with the organization of the book as found in the "Table of Contents."

In preparing for an exam, it is useful to find the topics to be covered on the exam from the "Table of Contents" and then review the problems under those topics several times. This should equip the student with what might be needed for the exam.

Max Fogiel, Ph.D.
Program Director

CONTENTS

CHAPTER 1

THE SCIENCE OF PSYCHOLOGY

BASIC CONCEPTS AND HISTORY

● PROBLEM 1-1

What is psychology?

Solution: Broadly defined, psychology is the study of the behavior of living organisms. Most psychologists today agree with this definition, although many expand upon it. Some psychologists further describe it as the study of experience-- that which occurs inside an individual which may or may not be reported by him. Other psychologists object to such an inclusion. They believe that inner experience is too subjective to be studied with scientific laws. The existence of such varied approaches add to the complexity of the field.

Psychology has acquired a multitude of definitions throughout its history. At one time, it was considered to be the study of the mind. This definition was changed when it was agreed that the mind is not entirely open to scientific analysis. The workings of the mind can only be known through the observation of the behavior it controls. Recent efforts to make the discipline more objective and scientific have resulted in the definition of psychology as the study of behavior. The next step in understanding psychology is to define behavior.

Behavior refers to any observable action or reaction of a living organism. Psychology is the study of several levels of behavior, each of which is of special interest to various types of psychologists. For example, some psychologists focus on the behavior or actions of nerve cells, sweat glands, and adrenal glands. Other psychologists concentrate on behaviors that exist on a higher level such as aggression, prejudice, or problem solving. Thus the field of psychology is complicated by its several subspecialties, each of which has its own set of approaches.

A key word in the definition of behavior is "observable." Behavior refers to movement, activity, or action that is overt. Some behaviors are more easily observed than others.

1

An EEG machine is needed to observe brain wave movement, whereas aggressive behavior can be witnessed with the naked eye.

To explain and understand behavior accurately, one must go beyond the mere reporting of observable movement. Four fundamental characteristics must be taken into account. These are: the organism, motivation, knowledge and competence. Differences in behavior are explained in terms of differences in one of these factors. The first factor, the organism, refers to the living biological entity--a human being or lower animal--and its biological characteristics and limits. Behavior cannot be studied properly without accounting for the organism's biological capacity. Its nervous system, endocrine system and other biological structures must be examined. Knowledge of its biological history and heredity are also necessary.

Motivation must also be accounted for in the study of behavior. Motivation is the immediate cause of behavior. Psychologists define it as the immediate forces that act to energize, direct, sustain, and stop a behavior. To understand behavior, we must examine its motivational underpinnings.

In psychology, the word "cognition" is often used in place of "knowledge"--that is, what the organism knows. To examine a particular behavior in its proper perspective, one needs to understand the organism's perception of his environment and what he knows, thinks, and remembers.

Competence is the fourth factor necessary in the understanding of behavior. Competence refers to the skills and abilities of an organism--how well he can perform a certain task.

Psychology is not as simple as it first appeared. The science of behavior is very complex. Psychologists today need a basic understanding of other scientific fields, such as biology, physics, chemistry and linguistics. In studying psychology, one will also encounter sociology, anthropology, economics, political science and the other social sciences. To thoroughly evaluate behavior, the psychologist must be familiar with all of these areas.

● **PROBLEM 1-2**

Discuss the three basic goals of psychology.

Solution: The three basic goals of psychology are: to measure and describe behavior, to predict and control behavior, and to understand and explain behavior.

Much of a psychologist's work involves measuring and describing. This is a necessary process in understanding and manipulating a phenomenon. Such concepts and processes as I.Q., anxiety, learning, attitudes, and abilities must be measured. To accomplish this, psychologists have developed tests or techniques for measuring.

Measuring devices must have two characteristics. First, they must be reliable. This means an individual's score or rating should not vary with repeated testing. For example, an intelligence test which yields highly different scores each time the same individual takes it, is useless. Second, a measuring device must be valid. This means it should measure what it is designed to measure. An I.Q. test, for example, would not yield an accurate measure of an individual's level of anxiety. All techniques for measurement and description of behavior should be reliable and valid.

The second major goal of psychology is to predict and thereby to control behavior. Prediction is based heavily on measurement. A psychologist can accurately predict a student's performance in school if he has some measurement index of his intellectual capacity. Tests are given in a variety of situations in order to predict behavior: for college entrance, job placement, and to facilitate one's vocational choice.

Prediction is related to modification and control. Behavior change is often the primary goal of the psychological practitioner. A psychotherapist attempts to change abnormal behavior; an industrial psychologist tries to modify or improve employee work habits; a prison psychologist wants to correct deviant behavior in the inmates; and the marriage counselor wants to modify the behavior of a husband and wife to improve their relationship. Before a psychologist can alter behavior, he must have a thorough knowledge of his subject(s) through reliable and valid measurement techniques by which he can predict their behavior.

The third and final goal of psychology is to understand and explain behavior. The psychologist attempts to draw conclusions from what he has observed. He tries to formulate hypotheses which are consistent with known facts. There are many phenomena related to behavior which have yet to be explained. Basic psychology is an attempt to understand and explain significant issues in human behavior which have far-reaching implications.

● **PROBLEM** 1-3

Trace the development of psychology from ancient times to the establishment of experimental methods in the late nineteenth century.

Solution: Psychological notions can be traced to ancient times, when man first began to think abstractly and raise questions about himself. Since the beginning, man has asked such questions as: How do we experience the world around us? What is the relationship between our experience of the world and our bodily functions? How do we learn things? What accounts for differences in behavior and temperament among people?

The science of psychology, as well as other sciences such as physics, chemistry, and biology, was rooted in philosophy--the oldest science. The ancient Greek philosophers--Aristotle, Plato, Socrates--who first observed and interpreted their en-

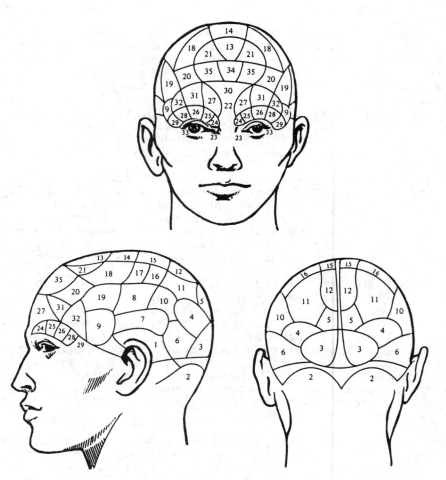

Phrenology was an attempt to assess characteristics of various
areas of the skull. Phrenologists used charts such as the one
shown above as guides.

vironment, attempted to organize their findings in an orderly
fashion. The philosophers were the first to recognize that
human beings have, in addition to a physical body, some kind
of nonphysical equipment or apparatus used for thinking. They
called this "thinking apparatus" the "psyche." Over the
centuries, this word has meant such things as "spirit," "soul,'
"form," and sometimes "function." The most popular equivalent
evolved into "mind." The suffix "-ology" means "the study of.'
Therefore, for many centuries psychology was considered to be
the study of the mind.

The philosophers saw the mind as an entity or structure,
an element with no physical substance. The mind's functions
were thought of as "mental," as compared to the physical functions of the body. The most important question that arose
from this idea was: What is the relationship between the
mind and the body?

The French philosopher René Descartes (1596 - 1650) was
very interested in this "mind-body problem" and was influential
in the trends of thinking concerning it. He firmly believed

4

in "dualism," a philosophical concept which states that man has a dual nature--one mental and the other physical (in contrast to "monism" which holds that only one type of nature exists). To answer the question of how the mind is related to the body, Descartes developed a concept known as "interactionism." According to this concept, the mind affects the body and vice versa. This interaction occurs in the pineal gland, a small gland in the lower center of the brain. Descartes believed that it was through this pineal gland that the mind, with its functionings of reasoning and willing, caused the body to perform its various functions.

In the eighteenth century, certain individuals described the various functions of the mind as independent "faculties." Every "mental" activity in which man engaged such as thinking, loving and hating, was the work of a particular area of the mind or faculty. Thus, any aspect of behavior could be explained by attributing it to the function of its respective faculty.

In the early nineteenth century, some scientists, such as Gall and Spurzheim, attempted to analyze the mind's functions by examining the size and shape of the skull. (By this time, scientists commonly agreed that the mind was inside the head.) Gall and Spurzheim attempted to study the mind's functions through a science called phrenology, which involves the examination of the conformations of human skulls. They believed that a person with a prominent faculty, as observed in his behavior, would likewise have a large development in that part of the skull, just above where the faculty was located. For example, if they found someone to be highly generous, they would then examine that individual's skull, and if an unusual bump was found on some part of his head, they would label that region the "generosity" region of the mind. This notion seems absurd in light of today's knowledge, but phrenologists were generally earnest scientists who were highly regarded during their own time.

By 1850, the field of mental philosophy had truly evolved into the distinct science of psychology. Experimental methods had begun to be devised in order to examine various psychological phenomena.

● **PROBLEM 1-4**

Discuss the trends in problems and methods in the history of psychology.

Solution: The earliest historical records indicate the extent of man's curiosity about himself. Since the beginning, man has asked questions about himself, his experiences, his environment, and the relationship among the three. Man's approach to the many problems raised by these questions has shifted from the study of (or the attempt to study) the inner processes of the mind to the study of observable behavior. Whereas early psychologists were concerned with measuring and understanding mental processes, latter-day psychologists have directed their attention to the study of overt behavior.

The most important trend in the methodology of psychology has been an increase in the use of empirical methods--methods that rely on observation--as a basis for theorizing. This system is opposed to theorizing based on intuition. Before psychology employed scientific methods, beliefs about the mind and behavior were based mostly upon speculation, making psychology a sub-field of philosophy. Psychology did not become a scientific field until the nineteenth century when it became empirical, possessing biological underpinnings and an experimental superstructure.

Before the establishment of modern science, empirical methods were used by philosophers. Beginning with the ancient Greeks, philosophers observed and interpreted their environment and tried to organize their findings in an orderly way. Philosophy is the father of all modern sciences. Chemistry, physics, and biology all trace their roots to philosophy, which developed specialties in each of these areas. The field of mental philosophy evolved into psychology.

The discovery of the experimental method prompted the separation of the specialties from philosophy. The experimental method differs from naturalistic observation in that, during experimentaion, the scientist creates the conditions whereby a process will occur and can be observed; usually this is done in a laboratory. Physicists and chemists were the first to discover and use the experimental method. These physicists and physiologists were the first to apply the experimental method to problems of a psychological nature. These problems included color vision, hearing, and brain functions. Eventually, however, psychologists recognized that psychology should develop its own experimental methods for studying its own unique problems in order to develop as a distinct science.

Most psychology historians pinpoint the beginning of experimental psychology to 1860, when Gustav Fechner (1801-1887) published a book entitled Elemente der Psychophysik (Elements of Psychophysics), which was concerned with the measurement of sensory experiences. Wilhelm Wundt (1832-1920) established the first laboratory of psychology at the University of Leipzig in Germany in 1879. The establishment of Wundt's laboratory launched a movement in which experimental laboratories of psychology were built in several locales. The first formal laboratory established in the United States was at John Hopkins University in 1883. Only a few years later, psychology laboratories were erected in most of the universities in the country.

SCIENTIFIC INVESTIGATION

● PROBLEM 1-5

Discuss the role of theory in psychology.

Solution: To arrive at a theory is one of the primary objectives of science. Science makes its greatest strides when theories are formulated which can summarize observations and predict what will happen in new situations.

A theory has three important functions in the science of psychology. First, it can serve as a scientific shorthand by summarizing and generalizing observations. In psychology, some principles summarize literally hundreds of observations. The principle of reinforcement (the strengthening or weakening of behavior as a result of reward or punishment) is one such example.

A second function of a theory is that it acts as a predictor, forewarning the experimenter about what to expect in certain situations. Prediction is the ultimate objective of all science. A theory need not, however, be entirely comprehensive. It can present only the important features of a particular area. A theory is not always entirely accurate. Several theories in science have been found to be erroneous or misleading.

A third important function of a theory is that it acts as a guide in collecting further observations in research. The concept of reinforcement began as a theory and was responsible for a multitude of experiments related to reinforcement. Theories serve as the basis on which scientists decide what steps to take next in making observations. Through continued experimentation, errors can be found in a theory. If errors are found, the theory is modified. If no error is found, the theory is kept intact and used as a guide for further experimentation.

● **PROBLEM 1-6**

List and describe the scientific characteristics of psychology.

Solution: As a science, psychology is defined through three basic characteristics: it is empirical, systematic, and it employs measurement techniques.

The term empirical refers to data that are collected through methods of observation and experimentation. Psychology as a science does not base its data and theories upon intuition or opinion. Observations and experiments are conducted which can be repeated by other psychologists. The psychologist obtains data and makes quantitative measurements which can be verified by other psychologists.

As a science, psychology is also systematic. Observations must make sense and must be capable of being summarized economically into principles. These principles can be either a system of classification or precise laws that state the order or relationship among observed phenomena.

Measurement is another scientific characteristic of psychology. The various sciences are usually ranked according to which has the most precise measurements. Physics is usually thought to be the most "scientific" of the sciences; its measurements are very precise. Because most psychological problems are so complex, it is not always easy to devise methods of measurement to solve them. However, psychologists employ numerous devices for behavior measurement, such as

intelligence tests. Psychologists are constantly working at
devising and improving tests that measure the complex realm
of behavior.

Define the following: induction, deduction, hypothesis, null
hypothesis, and operational definition.

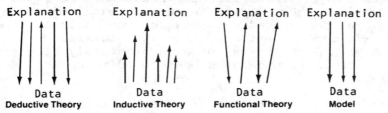

Four modes of theory construction in psychology. While all
theories use both data and explanation, they differ in their
emphases upon each and in how each modifies the other.

Solution: In the development of a science, a circular path
is followd by the researcher, wherein he begins with observations, formulates tentative principles, then makes further
observations. The beginning of the circle is called induc-
tion--the researcher induces or formulates tentative principles based on observations he has made. In induction, the
scientist attempts to summarize his observations. The next
part of the circle is called deduction. In deduction, the
researcher deduces or makes predictions about observations he
has not yet made. The reasoning here is that if the inductive
analysis is correct, predictions can be made with a degree of
certainty. Whether or not the predictions are correct, further analysis is needed. If the predictions are wrong, the
results are analyzed again and a new deduction is tested.
Even if the original deduction is confirmed, the researcher
analyzes his findings. The confirmed deduction itself will
often suggest other predictions. In science, especially psychology, there are no final answers.

    In experimentation, investigators form what are known as
hypotheses and null hypotheses. A hypothesis is similar to
induction. It is an educated guess about a particular phenomenon based on informal observation. For example, an experimenter might hypothesize that if an infant receives a great
deal of attention from his mother, his cognitive development
will be affected. Often, however, a hypothesis is expressed
negatively, that is, as a null hypothesis. The null hypothesis for our previous hypothesis would be: if an infant receives
a great deal of attention from his mother, there will be no
effect on cognitive development. If a researcher did find a
relationship between the variables of maternal attention and
cognitive development, he would reject the null hypothesis.

    In scientific research, the scientist uses operational
definitions to define concepts. An operational definition is
one in which a concept is defined in terms of measurable and
observable operations. In other words, a concept is described
in terms of the operation that was used to measure it. For

example, intelligence can be defined operationally as a score obtained on an intelligence test. Intelligence is often defined in psychology as that which intelligence tests measure. An operational definition is a more precise way of defining a concept.

● **PROBLEM** 1-8

Distinguish between data and inference. How is this distinction significant in the analysis of mental processes?

Solution: Data refers to the recorded results of an experiment or observation. Data are reported in terms of the procedures used to carry out a particular experiment or observation and in terms that describe the behavior of the subject(s). Data are public in that all those who observe the same experiment or make the same observation will report the same results. Data are stable; any investigator who repeats an experiment or observation, should obtain similar data.

Data take various forms. Data are measured in terms of a test score, a period of time taken to complete a certain task, or a physiological measure. An example of data collection would be the following: A researcher interested in classroom attentiveness observes a particular class of students. He notes that some students are slouched in their seats, yawning, and gazing out the window while others are sitting up straight in their desks looking directly at the teacher. These observations, which the researcher records, are his data. This information is in terms of observable behavior. It involves no assumptions or guesses.

Often, however, a researcher makes inferences based on his data. He may infer from a student's yawning that he is bored and inattentive. Likewise, he may infer that a student sitting up is attentive. An inference can be defined as an assumption about structures and processes which cannot be directly observed. The researcher in this example must make inferences about classroom attentiveness based on his data of observable behavior. He must draw certain conclusions because attentiveness cannot be observed directly.

Since many mental processes do not lend themselves to direct observation, the investigator in psychology must rely upon inferences based on data.

● **PROBLEM** 1-9

List and describe the important methods of investigation in psychology.

Solution: Psychologists use several methods to study behavior. The method used depends on the type of behavior under investigation. The major methods of psychology are: the individual case study, naturalistic observation, tests, interviews and surveys, and experimentation.

In the individual case study or the case history method,

9

a single individual is examined intensively in order to examine a problem or issue relevant to that person. This method is often used in the assessment and correction of abnormal behavior patterns. In a case study, the psychologist often uses a number of procedures such as collecting biographical data on the individual, administering psychological tests, and conducting interviews with the subject. Sigmund Freud used the individual case study method of investigation.

Naturalistic observation refers to the systematic observation of a certain event or phenomenon in the environment as it occurs naturally, without any intervention on the part of the investigator. The researcher avoids manipulation if he believes that it would adversely affect the basic characteristics of the particular phenomenon. If laboratory investigation interferes with the natural occurrence of the phenomenon, then the psychologist would prefer to witness it in its natural environment. For example, certain behavior patterns of monkeys, such as mating behavior, might differ in a laboratory setting. Hence, the psychologist would try to observe this behavior as it occurs in the monkeys' natural habitat.

Numerous psychological tests have been designed to assess certain aspects of behavior. These tests attempt to measure such factors as intelligence, anxiety, and leadership ability. All of these tests consist of a number of questions. When the test is graded, the person receives a composite score which should reflect his typical behavior in normal circumstances.

As previously stated, the interview is used in conjunction with the case study method. Interviews may be structured or unstructured. Structured interviews, in which individuals are asked to respond to a number of pre-formulated questions, are most often given when the psychologist wants to collect information from a group of people. An unstructured interview is usually used in the intensive study of an individual. Here the direction of the interview is guided by the individual's responses and the examiner's hypotheses concerning the underlying rationale of these responses.

Surveys are similar to psychological tests and interviews in that individuals are asked to reply to a series of questions or items. In a survey, however, the purpose is not to test or analyze a specific aspect of a person or group. The surveyor wishes to learn an opinion, attitude, or belief on a particular issue. Newspapers and public opinion polls conduct surveys to obtain the public concensus on a certain topic.

In experimentation, the psychologist examines a specific phenomenon in a controlled laboratory environment. Here, he can rule out all extraneous and distracting variables and manipulate, with precise equipment and procedures, the conditions he wishes to examine.

In experimentation, the researcher examines cause and effect relationships between a changing variable and a certain behavior. For example, if a psychologist wishes to examine the effect of early isolation on social development, he might place a monkey in isolation during the first few years of its life. The monkey would be placed in a controlled environment. The animal would receive everything necessary for physical survival, but it would not come into contact with other monkeys. After a certain number of years, the monkey would be placed in a cage with other monkeys who were not deprived as he was. The psychologist would then note the animal's reactions. Hence, the psychologist is attempting to determine the effect of a variable--early isolation--upon a certain behavior--social interaction.

● **PROBLEM** 1-10

Discuss the advantages and limitations of the experimental method of investigation.

NOW RELAX AND
ACT NATURAL

Solution: The most important advantage of the experimental method is that it allows for direct cause-effect conclusions from the data. If there is proper control in a particular experiment, that is, variables other than the independent variable are kept constant, and it is observed that the dependent variable changes as the independent variable changes, then the experimenter can conclude that the relationship between the independent and dependent variables is causal. In nonexperimental research methods, causal relationships cannot be drawn. In a case study, an investigator might learn that a neurotic person had an unhappy childhood, but the researcher cannot conclude that the unhappy childhood necessarily caused the neurosis.

Often in nonexperimental methods, a correlational approach is used. Here, a statistic called a correlation coefficient is employed to determine the strength of a relationship between two or more variables. For example, an investigator could interview or survey a cross section of neurotic individuals. For each person, there would be two scores, one which indicates neurosis, and another which may indicate an unhappy childhood. A correlation of zero would mean that the existence of neurosis is not related to an unhappy childhood. A positive correlation indicates a positive relationship between the two variables--the greater the neurosis, the more unhappy the childhood. A negative correlation indicates an inverse relationship--as one value increases, the other value decreases. For example, one infers that the more neurotic the individual, the less unhappy his childhood. But the correlational approach does not allow one to draw causal conclusions. Unlike what the experimental method does, it only gives an indication of the strengths or weaknesses of a relationship between two factors.

Another advantage of the experimental approach is that it can be repeated, not only by the researcher who devised it, but by anyone who has the proper equipment. Repetition of an experiment under controlled conditions reduces doubt if similar observations are made each time it is performed. Agreement among different observers is an important advantage. In addition, repetition makes experimentation convenient. Since the conditions are artificially produced, an experiment can be performed at will without having to wait for conditions to be just right as in naturalistic observation.

Three important limitations exist in experimentation. The first is that experimentation cannot always be used. Areas such as human eugenics and selective breeding are not experimentally explored for ethical reasons. Also, people and animals are not always willing to cooperate with the experimenter.

A second important limitation of the experimental method is that it is artificially arranged by the scientist. Often, a psychologist acts on hunches or suspicions which may lead to error. Sometimes he might select a variable that he believes is significant but which in reality is not. The experimenter must constantly guard against erroneous conclusions drawn from experiments which are artificially arranged.

The third limitation of experimentation is that it sometimes interferes with the factor it attempts to examine. In many situations, it is extremely difficult and sometimes impossible to control all irrelevant variables. Experiments utilizing human subjects are especially difficult, since people who know they are being studied sometimes do not act like their normal selves during the experiment. Such factors have to be seriously considered in any psychological experiment.

SCHOOLS OF THOUGHT

● PROBLEM 1-11

Describe the structuralist school of psychological thought.

Wilhelm Wundt

Solution: Structuralism, the first theoretical school in psychology, evolved primarily from the work of Wilhelm Wundt, who
established the first laboratory of psychology at the University of Leipzig, Germany in 1879. Wundt believed that the
proper object of study for the science of psychology was the
content of the conscious mind. Wundt was influenced by the
physical scientists of his time, who were successfully employing the experimental method and the atomic theory of matter in their work. The atomic theory of matter stated that
all complex substances could be separated and analyzed into
their component elements. Wundt embraced this theory, believing that such analysis should be applied to psychological
phenomena. He wanted to divide the mind into compartments or
mental elements in order to identify and analyze them. Wundt
made one of the first attempts towards "structuralism," as
this school of thought came to be known.

To analyze mental elements, Wundt used an experimental
method called introspection, whereby a subject reported as
objectively as possible the contents of his own mind. In one
procedure, a subject would report his experiences in connection with certain stimuli. For example, he might be presented
with a light, a sound, or an odor and asked to describe it in
detail. After the subject examined and reported his inner
experiences, his verbal report would be analyzed and categorized in order to determine the number and types of mental
elements that it contained.

Wundt concluded that there were three basic mental elements: sensations, images and feelings. Sensations are experiences of stimuli perceived through the senses; images are
sensation-like experiences produced by the mind, and feelings
are the emotional aspects of an experience.

The major drawback of structuralism was that it focused
on the structure and activity of the mind rather than on overt
behavior. Psychologists today are still concerned with mental

13

activities, but are primarily interested in how these activities influence behavior. Another drawback of structuralism is that it is not an objective approach since it relies on individual subjective verbal reports. Such data do not lend themselves to scientific study. Behavior, on the other hand, can be observed objectively and its analysis yields scientific data. Despite its limitations, structuralism dominated psychology for many years in the United States and Europe.

● **PROBLEM 1-12**

Discuss the functionalist school of psychological thought.

Solution: In the late nineteenth century, a number of schools of psychological thought were established. One school, functionalism, was influenced by Darwin's theory of evolution. Whereas the structuralists were concerned with the components of the mind, the functionalists were interested in the mind's activities and the reasons for the various activities. The functionalists promulgated the idea that behavior and mental processes are adaptive--that is, they enable an individual to adapt to a changing environment. They recognized the connection between the mind and behavior. In addition, they studied mind-body interactions, and examined how the mind interacts with other bodily organs and systems in adapting to the environment. The functionalists also identified and studied the stream of consciousness, which they believed to characterize human behavior.

As far as methods are concerned, the functionalists did not reject the introspection of the structuralists, but they preferred the observation of behavior; they emphasized the total activity of the individual. The most important contribution of the functionalists to the development of psychology was the introduction of the concept of learning--adaptation to the environment--to psychological examination. The most influential proponents of functionalism were William James (1842-1910) and John Dewey (1859-1952). James' book, The Principles of Psychology, is a famous summation of functionalist ideas.

● **PROBLEM 1-13**

Describe the behavioristic school of thought.

Solution: Behaviorism originated in the United States and developed from the ideas of John B. Watson (1878-1958). Watson rejected the functionalists' acceptance of the introspection method of analysis. Watson believed that the only data applicable to the scientific field are data assimilated on outward behavior. Watson asserted that behavior is affected by certain stimuli in the environment and that the major component of psychological study should be the identification of stimulus-response relationships. Watson rejected the idea of the mind as an existing structure that can be objectively analyzed. Watson began a stimulus-response (S-R) school of thought which later branched out into several areas.

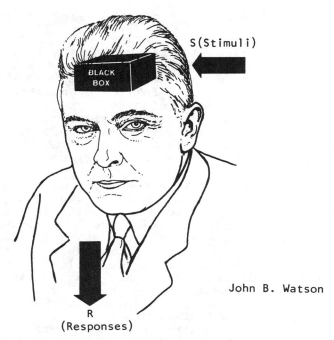

S(Stimuli)

BLACK BOX

R
(Responses)

John B. Watson

Behaviorism possesses other important characteristics. One is an emphasis on conditioned reflexes--simple learned responses to stimuli--which this school of thought classifies as the building blocks of behavior. Another characteristic is the stress on learned as opposed to unlearned behavior. Behaviorism denied the existence of instinctual or inborn tendencies. According to Watson, all of man's behavior is the result of the conditioning of reflexes. Watson believed that a man can be trained to perform any type of task or fulfill any occupational position. Behaviorism also emphasized animal behavior, holding that no important behavioral differences exist between man and animal and that man can learn a great deal about his own behavior by studying the behavior of animals. Watson and his followers initiated a great deal of animal experimentation which has continued up to the present day.

The behaviorist school initiated new schools of thought called neobehaviorist schools. These were prominent during the late 1930's and the 1940's. Leaders of these schools included Tolman (1932), Hull (1943), and Guthrie (1952), who attempted to formulate general theories of behavior on the basis of animal experiments. The neobehaviorists wanted to prove that predictions from their theories were more accurate than those posited by non-behaviorists. Often, the predictions of behaviorist theory resembled those of other theories of psychology. Henceforth, behaviorists have devised more specific, smaller-scale theories from which unique predictions can be drawn.

● **PROBLEM 1-14**

Describe the characteristics of gestalt psychology.

Solution: Like functionalism and behaviorism, gestalt psychology was a reaction to structuralism. Gestalt psychology was founded in 1912 by Max Wertheimer and his colleagues K. Koffka and W. Kohler in Germany. At the same time, behaviorism was becoming popular in the United States. The word "gestalt" has no exact equivalent in English, but it denotes a meaning similar to "form," "organization," and "configuration." This definition reflects the gestalt psychologists' emphasis on organizational processes in behavior. Gestalt theory is often associated with perception, since perceptual problems were a main focus of this school, just as learning was emphasized by the behaviorists.

The gestalt psychologists opposed the structuralists' and behaviorists' method of reducing experience into small component parts such as sensations or conditioned reflexes. The Gestaltists believed that behavior and experiences are not compounds of simple elements but rather patterns or organizations. They borrowed this idea from physical science. Physical scientists believe that the whole of a phenomenon is more than the sum of its parts. For example, if one looks at a still photograph, one perceives it as a whole, not the sum total of various features of the picture. The same theory holds true with most objects perceived; the parts or features of the object are somehow organized into perception so that these parts are seen as a unified whole or configuration. The Gestaltists also identified an effect which they called "apparent movement" or the "phi phenomenon," in which movement is perceived in still objects such as neon signs.

The Gestaltists employed a method called phenomenology, whereby a subject uses the introspection technique of structuralism, but with one important difference. In contrast to the structuralists, who believed in trained introspection in order to identify elements of experience, the Gestaltists believed in naive introspection. They wanted to examine what something looked like to an observer, but they did not want the elaboration yielded by the structuralist technique. They held a subject's naive report to be a useful observation. Phenomenology, then, is a method of natural observation in human perception.

The early gestalt psychologists stressed the study of human experience and perception. However, they studied other problems as well, such as those dealing with learning, thought, and problem solving. Kohler, for example, argued that learning and problem solving were organizational processes like perception. He described the "moment of insight" in which the individual suddenly realizes how to solve a particular problem in a problem solving task.

● **PROBLEM** 1-15

Briefly describe the theory of psychoanalysis.

Solution: Sigmund Freud (1856-1939) is the founder of psychoanalysis. He developed the psychoanalytic theory during the years 1885 to 1939. Psychoanalysis is a very complex area. However, some general remarks can be made about it.

Psychoanalysis is not a school of thought in psychology. Psychoanalysis developed outside the psychological laboratory in medical practice as the result of an effort to apply science and medicine to the study and treatment of abnormal behavior. Freud, a Viennese psychiatrist, was dissatisfied with the way psychiatry during the nineteenth century classified mental disorders and pigeon-holed mental patients, offering neither valid explanations for the causes of the diseases nor methods for treatment. In an attempt to resolve this problem, Freud used both empirical (observational) and experimental techniques, although he was limited in the use of both. He could only make observations in the course of treating his patients which did not permit him to experiment in any systematic way. From experience, however, Freud was able to develop a method of treatment and a theory of personality.

Psychoanalysis refers primarily to Freud's method of treatment. In this method, free association is the basic tool. The subject reports whatever comes into his mind.

Freud's theory of personality is of great interest to psychologists. Freud divided the personality structure into three parts: the id, which consists of the basic biological impulses; the ego, which copes with stress in the environment and mediates between the contrasting desires of the id and superego; and the superego, which represents the dictates of one's conscience. Freud's primary tool for investigation was the case study, which included autobiographical material, dream analysis, and the free association of individual patients.

Psychoanalysis during Freud's time was primarily a theory of abnormal behavior, whereas today it is regarded as a method of treatment for mental illness. Psychoanalysis itself has been subdivided into schools such as Jung's analytical school and Adler's individual school.

Many neo-Freudian theories have been developed in recent times. Theoretical views in psychoanalysis continue to change and evolve to this day.

● **PROBLEM 1-16**

Discuss the influence of the five early schools of thought on modern psychology.

Solution: The early schools of thought were important in the development of psychology, but today they have largely disappeared. Few psychologists today would identify themselves as belonging to one particular school, although some have certain biases toward one school, especially when there are alternative theories of explanation regarding a particular phenomenon. But despite the biases, practically all psychologists agree that each school had some beneficial effect on the shaping of psychology as we know it today.

Structuralism was criticized severely by the schools of thought which followed it, but structuralist-type ideas are still found in modern psychology. The famous Swiss psychologist Jean Piaget described changes with age in the structure of the human mind. American experimental psychologists examine how knowledge is organized and describe the structure of memory, by which an individual can recall events. In addition, the principles of association which the structuralists used to describe the formation of complex mental events from simpler elements is still the basis of one of today's learning theories.

The most important contribution of functionalism was the emphasis of learning as an important adaptive process. While functionalism was not a coherent school, its principles were important in stressing the functional or pragmatic significance of the mind.

Behaviorism and gestalt psychology have had the greatest influence on the shaping of modern psychology. The behavioristic concept of learned responses as the building blocks of behavior remains an important principle in modern psychological theory. B.F. Skinner is the most well-known behaviorist today. He has developed both a theory based on this basic behavioristic concept and a method of changing behavior-- behavior modification. These are based on his observation of the effects of reward and punishment on behavior.

The most influential concept of gestalt psychology is the idea that behavior is a continuous, organizational process, the whole of which is different from the sum of its parts. The preference for process analysis over content analysis of behavior is a gestaltist idea that still has a bearing on many aspects in psychology, the most notable of which is learning.

Psychoanalytic thought has been the most lasting of the five schools. Several psychologists today hold some of its principles, although its influence on human behavior theory has greatly decreased since the height of Freud's popularity. Psychoanalysis, however, is still important in certain areas of clinical psychology and forms the basis of some psychotherapeutic techniques.

PSYCHOLOGY AS A PROFESSION

● **PROBLEM** 1-17

Describe psychology in terms of a profession. List and define different types of psychologists.

Solution: In addition to being a science, psychology is also a profession. There are several different types of psychologists, although their activities often overlap. As a field of employment, psychology can be divided into two basic areas. One area consists of scientists or researchers and the other of practitioners. Practitioners are involved in advising and counseling. Scientists devote themselves mainly to research.

There are six primary sources of employment for the psychologist: (1) colleges and universities, (2) elementary and secondary schools, (3) clinics, (4) industry, (5) government and (6) private practice.

Psychologists are categorized according to the type of activity or research in which they engage. These activities include nine basic types, although it is possible for an individual to be active in more than one area.

Experimental psychologists conduct experiments in order to further the research in various areas of psychology, such as learning, motivation, or perception.

Biopsychologists study the influence of biological factors on human and animal behavior. Such factors include genetics, the nervous system, and the endocrine system.

Social psychologists employ scientific research methods in order to study individual behavior in social situations. Social psychologists are concerned with the organism's interaction with others.

The developmental psychologist studies normal behavioral development from conception through adulthood. He deals with the acquisition of various skills through the development of cognition, perception, language, motor abilities, and social behavior.

Educational psychologists are concerned with the process

19

of education. They engage in research to develop new and improved methods of education. They also implement new systems of education.

The personality psychologist studies the individual in order to discover basic underlying dimensions of behavior and to assess persons on the basis of such dimensions. For example, he would determine whether an individual is extroverted or introverted.

Clinical psychologists assess abnormal behavior in order to diagnose and change it. They usually treat hospital inpatients or those whose disorders are so severe that they cannot cope with reality.

Counseling psychologists usually treat people whose disorders are not very serious. They offer advice on personal, educational or vocational problems. Marriage counselors and school guidance counselors fall into this category.

Industrial psychologists work for public and private businesses or the government. They apply their knowledge of psychological principles to such areas as personnel policies, consumerism, working conditions, production efficiency and decision-making. The two basic fields of industrial psychology include Personnel Psychology and Consumer Psychology.

In the area of education or teaching, most psychologists have a Ph.D (Doctor of Philosophy), which requires four to five years of graduate study. Most psychology teachers are employed by colleges and universities, although the number employed by high schools is increasing as more and more high schools are initiating introductory psychology courses in their curriculums.

SHORT ANSWER QUESTIONS FOR REVIEW

Choose the correct answer.

1. Psychology is best defined as (a) the study
    of the mind (b) the study of experience (c)
    the study of behavior (d) the science of mental
    processes

    c

2. In order to accurately explain and understand
    behavior, each of the following must be taken
    into account EXCEPT: (a) motivation (b)
    phrenology (c) the organism (d) competence
    (e) knowledge

    b

3. In psychology, the word "cognitive" refers to
    (a) knowledge (b) learning (c) memory
    (d) reflexes

    a

4. The ability of an organism to perform certain
    tasks is referred to as (a) learning (b)
    knowledge (c) level of maturation (d) com-
    petence

    d

5. The modern psychologist needs to have knowledge
    of (a) biology (b) sociology (c) linguis-
    tics (d) all of the above (e) none of the
    above

    d

6. The two general types of psychologists are:
    (a) scientists and researchers (b) counsel-
    ors and practitioners (c) experimenters and
    educators (d) researchers and practitioners

    d

7. Such factors as genetics and the nervous system
    would most concern the (a) social psychologist
    (b) biopsychologist (c) personality psychol-
    ogist (d) industrial psychologist

    b

8. Personnel policy is the concern of the (a)
    social psychologist (b) industrial psycholo-
    gist (c) educational psychologist (d) ex-
    perimental psychologist

    b

9. In psychology, measurement devices must be
    (a) reliable (b) valid (c) both (a) and
    (b) (d) neither (a) nor (b)

    c

10. An example of data is: (a) a test score
    (b) a hypothesis (c) an idea (d) a conclu-
    sion

    a

11. Intensive examination of a single individual is
    the objective of (a) the survey (b) natur-
    alistic observation (c) the case study (d)
    experimentation

    c

21

SHORT ANSWER QUESTIONS FOR REVIEW

12. The use of a controlled environment is most
    characteristic of: (a) naturalistic observa-
    tion (b) testing (c) the case study (d)
    experimentation

    d

13. The major advantage of naturalistic observation
    is that (a) causal relationships can be drawn
    (b) a controlled environment is employed (c)
    phenomena can be witnessed in their own environ-
    ment without adverse interference from the in-
    vestigator (d) all of the above

    c

14. The most important advantage of the experimental
    method is that (a) a natural environment is
    employed (b) causal relationships can be drawn
    (c) a precise correlation coefficient can be
    determined (d) it can be applied to all psy-
    chological phenomena

    b

15. Theory has the following functions EXCEPT: (a)
    serving as a scientific shorthand (b) acting
    as a predictor (c) guiding further research
    (d) providing a completely accurate view of
    behavior

    d

16. The statement, "intelligence is that which in-
    telligence tests measure," is an example of
    (a) an operational definition (b) introspec-
    tion (c) free association (d) a deduction

    a

17. The statement, "a mother's intake of narcotics
    during pregnancy has no effect on the develop-
    ing fetus," is an example of (a) monism (b)
    a deduction (c) behaviorism (d) a null hy-
    pothesis

    d

18. The first psychology laboratory was established
    by (a) Gustav Fechner (b) Wilhelm Wundt
    (c) Sigmund Freud (d) John Watson

    b

19. The belief that man has both a mental and a
    physical nature is called (a) monism (b)
    dualism (c) interactionism (d) phrenology

    b

20. Examination of the skull was one of the methods
    of (a) monism (b) interactionism (c)
    philosophy (d) phrenology

    d

21. The concept that complex substances can be
    described in terms of their component elements
    is characteristic of (a) structuralism (b)
    functionalism (c) behaviorism (d) Gestalt
    psychology

    a

SHORT ANSWER QUESTIONS FOR REVIEW

22. The following are concerns of functionalism
EXCEPT: (a) mind-body interaction (b)
adaptation to a changing environment (c)
stimulus-response relationships (d) stream
of consciousness

c

23. Animal behavior was emphasized by the (a)
structuralists (b) functionalists (c) behaviorists (d) psychoanalysts

c

24. Gestalt psychology focused mainly on problems
dealing with (a) perception (b) learning
(c) motivation (d) development

a

25. The method the Gestalt psychologists used in
order to observe how an object was perceived
by a subject is called (a) introspection
(b) phi phenomenon (c) apparent movement
(d) phenomenology

d

26. As compared to our modern notion of psychoanalysis, during Freud's time it was regarded primarily as (a) a sub-field of psychiatry
(b). a method of treatment for mental illness
(c) a theory of abnormal behavior (d) a system of observation and experimentation

c

27. The most important contribution of functionalism to modern psychology is (a) the concept
of learned responses as the building blocks of
behavior (b) the idea that behavior is a continuous, organizational process (c) the principles of free association used to describe the
formation of complex mental events from simpler
elements (d) the emphasis of learning as an
important adaptive process

d

Fill in the blanks.

28. _____ can be defined as any observable action
or reaction of the living organism.

Behavior

29. _____ refers to the immediate forces that act
to energize, direct, sustain, and stop a behavior.

Motivation

30. The _____ psychologist studies individuals in
order to discover basic underlying dimensions
of behavior and to assess people on the basis
of such dimensions.

person-
ality

31. In a _____ interview, individuals are asked to
respond to a number of pre-formulated questions.

struc-
tured

23

SHORT ANSWER QUESTIONS FOR REVIEW

32. The _____ method is often used in the assessment and correction of abnormal behavior patterns.

case
study

33. In _____ the investigator does not manipulate the environment of the phenomenon under investigation.

naturalistic observation

34. An investigator would employ a _____ if he wished to learn public concensus on a particular issue.

survey

35. A statistic called a _____ is employed to determine the strength of a relationship between two or more variables.

correlation coefficient

36. It was the discovery of _____ which prompted the breaking off of the specialties within philosophy.

the experimental method

37. Behaviorism began from the ideas of _____ .

John B. Watson

38. _____ is the founder of psychoanalysis.

Sigmund Freud

Determine whether the following statements are true or false.

39. The workings of the mind can only be known through observation of the behavior it controls.

True

40. Behavior refers to all movement or activity of the living organism, both observable and unobservable.

False

41. To say a measuring device must be valid means that it must always yield a subjective measure.

False

42. In experimentation, the investigator interferes with the natural occurrence of the phenomenon under scrutiny.

True

43. The interview is used in conjunction with the case study method.

True

44. The most important advantage of observational research methods is that causal relationships can be drawn.

False

45. A correlation coefficient of zero indicates

SHORT ANSWER QUESTIONS FOR REVIEW

		Answer
	an inverse relationship between two variables.	False
46.	Theory is useful because it summarizes and generalizes scientific observations.	True
47.	Psychology as a science never bases data or theory on intuition.	True
48.	The use of empirical methods helped turn psychology into a scientific field.	True
49.	John Watson believed that the mind can be objectively analyzed.	False
50.	Most modern psychologists consider themselves as belonging to a particular school of thought.	False

CHAPTER 2

HEREDITY, CULTURE AND BEHAVIOR

EVOLUTION AND INNATE BEHAVIOR

● PROBLEM 2-1

List the criteria necessary in order to label behavior "instinctive." Define taxes, reflexes, fixed action pattern, and innate releasing stimuli.

Solution: There are four basic criteria which a behavior must meet in order to be described as instinctive. First, it must be characteristic of a species. This means that the particular behavior must be indicative of the species as a whole and must be either genetically determined or the result of evolutionary development. Second, the behavior must not be a learned behavior; it should occur in an organized fashion, without any prior training or practice. Third, innate or instinctive behavior should be consistent. This means that every time the behavior occurs it should be performed in basically the same manner. Fourth, instinctive behavior should occur in the absence as well as in the presence of stimuli which may elicit it. Instinctive behavior may be elicited by a particular stimulus, but it should continue even after the stimulus is removed. That is to say, instinctive behavior should not be controlled by or dependent on stimuli alone.

Taxes refer to innate tendencies in orientation toward a certain stimulus. An ant attracted to a piece of candy is an example of a taxis. Reflexes, on the other hand, are innate responses to certain stimuli. For example, a human infant's tendency to fan his toes when they are tickled is a reflex (called the Babinski reflex). Neither taxes nor reflexes persist after the eliciting stimulus has vanished; hence, neither is instinctive.

Fixed action pattern (or FAP) refers to a pattern of behavior that is innate and organized. Many researchers believe that in lower animals this pattern of organized behavior is held in check or inhibited until it is released by a stimulus called an innate releasing stimulus. These investigators believe that this innate releasing

26

stimulus triggers the nervous system so that it will express itself in a fixed action pattern. Many believe aspects of social, sexual, and aggressive behavior in lower animals to be instinctive. Instinctive behavior is believed to be much less common in the higher animals.

● **PROBLEM 2-2**

Discuss how the evolutionary heritage of man has shaped human behavior in terms of limits, potentialities, and the development of particular structures.

Solution: Man's evolutionary history has played a large part in determining his behavior and, because of this history, man as a species has developed in a specific way. First, our evolutionary heritage has limited us in many ways. For example, we are limited in what we can perceive. Our sensor organs which receive stimuli, called receptors, are sensitive to only certain types of energy. Because of the nature of our brain structure, we can only process information picked up by our receptors in certain ways. Such limitations shape our behavior. If we could perceive more than we normally can, our behavior would be much different.

Our evolutionary heritage, on the other hand, has given us outstanding potentialities for behavior. For one thing, we are the species most capable of representing the world through symbols. Language is the most important of these. We are able to use meaningful speech and other symbols such as writing because our brains are uniquely organized for this purpose. Indeed, the most important factor that distinguishes man from the lower animals is his ability to use symbols.

Through evolution other functional capacities for behavior have been built into the human brain. Much of our aggressive and emotional behavior is the result of our evolutionary heritage. Studies have shown that stimulation of certain portions of the limbic system--one region of the brain--with small, electrical currents can cause aggressive, emotional tantrums. On the other hand, stimulation of other portions of this same system can inhibit or curtail aggressive behavior. Hence, our potentiality for aggressive behavior and some forms of emotional behavior are linked to some extent to our evolutionary heritage.

Much of our behavior reflects our evolutionary past. All psychological functions which have a direct basis in the functioning of the brain are part of our evolutionary heritage. These include memory ability, learning ability, emotion, sexual behavior, hunger, and thirst.

● **PROBLEM 2-3**

Define maturation. Describe in what way maturation is the basis for much of human behavior.

Solution: Maturation refers to the development of bodily processes and the changes in behavior that result from such development. As certain parts of our bodies grow and develop (mature) related aspects of our behavior also change. As maturation occurs, new behaviors become possible.

The development of most of our basic behavior patterns is the result of maturation, not learning. For example, motor abilities--those that involve the use of limb muscles--mature. Walking, the most important motor development, is an ability that matures rather than something which is learned. Motor skills which lead up to walking occur in a definite sequence. Studies indicate that this sequence holds for all humans. Several studies have also shown that infants who are restricted in movement for a great amount of time (and therefore have no opportunity to practice motor skills) develop them at the same rate as infants who are given a great deal of freedom of movement and opportunity for practice. From this evidence it can be concluded that motor development results from maturation, not learning.

Several human abilities mature: prehension (the ability to grasp objects), language, learning ability and social behavior. Each of these progresses through a sequence of orderly maturational stages.

● **PROBLEM 2-4**

Describe the role maturation plays in the "readiness" or potentiality for a certain ability.

Solution: There are several skills which must be learned. Operations such as reading, writing, game-playing, sewing, and many other skills must be learned. However, even here maturation plays a role, since there is a certain time in the course of development when the individual is ready to learn a particular skill. Maturation underlies the "readiness" or potentiality for learning such skills. Before this readiness is reached in the course of maturation, learning the particular skill is impossible.

There are several kinds of readiness and these are reached at a characteristic age. For example, readiness for learning speech usually occurs around the age of 2 years, while readiness for learning how to read generally occurs at 6 years of age. Readiness comes to maturity fairly abrubtly and when it does, learning occurs rapidly if ample opportunity is provided.

One must remember, however, that rates of maturation differ among individuals. In general, if one ability develops or matures slowly, others will also, although there are exceptions to this rule.

28

INDIVIDUAL GENETIC CONSTITUTION

Define and discuss the function of each of the following:
chromosome, gene, DNA. Distinguish between X and Y
chromosomes. Distinguish between dominant and recessive
genes.

Solution: A chromosome is a microscopic body in the
nucleus of all human and plant cells. It contains the
genes, which are the carriers of heredity. Each mature
human sex cell (sperm or ovum) contains 23 chromosomes.

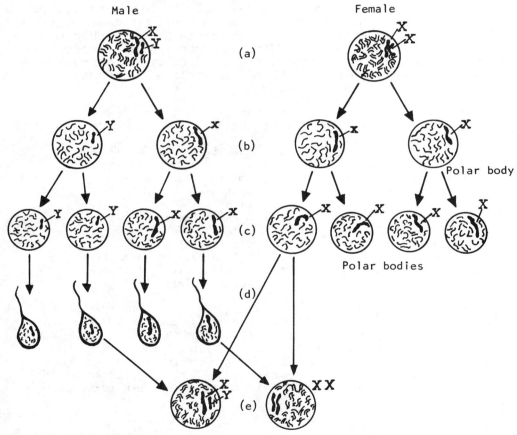

Human gametes and fertilization. (a) Both male and female cells
contain 22 pairs of chromosomes, plus either XY(male) or (XX)
(female). (b) Cell division without duplication of the chromosomes takes place, yielding for the male one X and one Y cell,
and for the female an X cell plus a polar body:(c) and (d). One
further cell division with duplication of chromosomes takes place
leading to four sperm (two X and two Y) in the male and one egg
plus three polar bodies in the female. The polar bodies contain
little cytoplasm and disintegrate later. (e) Egg and sperm unite to form a zygote. The one on the left, containing X and Y
chromosomes, will develop into a male, while that on the right,
with two X chromosomes, will become a female.

Each of the 23 chromosomes contributed by the sperm cell and the ovum at conception is believed to contain between 40,000 and 60,000 genes.

DNA, deoxyribonucleic acid, is a long, chainlike molecule consisting of four chemical bases arranged in an enormous number of combinations. Two strands of this molecule comprise genes and are arranged in the form of a helix (a double spiral). These strands are capable of reproducing themselves as well as crossing over from one strand of the spiral to another, thereby forming new combinations of genetic material. DNA is considered to be the basis of all life.

An X chromosome is a sex chromosome (a chromosome which determines sex) which is produced by both the mother and father. The mother produces only X chromosomes. If the sperm that fertilizes the ovum contains an X chromosome, the offspring will be female. The father in addition to producing X chromosomes also produces Y chromosomes which when joined with the mother's X chromosome would produce a male offspring.

Dominant and recessive characteristics

DOMINANT	RECESSIVE
Normal hearing	Congenital deafness
Normal amount of hair	Baldness
Dark hair	Light hair
Curly hair	Straight hair
Normal color vision	Color blindness
Dark eyes	Light eyes
Poison ivy immunity	Poison ivy susceptibility
Normal amount of skin pigment	Albinism (lack of pigment)
Double jointedness	Normal joints

A dominant gene is one that takes precedence over all other genes for a particular trait. Genes in the fertilized egg occur in pairs. The dominant gene, if paired with a lesser, recessive gene, will determine the trait that will be present in the offspring. The characteristics yielded by a recessive gene will not show up in the offspring, unless it is paired with another recessive gene.

● **PROBLEM 2-6**

Define zygote. What does it mean to be homozygous or heterozygous for a particular trait? Differentiate between monozygotic and dyzygotic twins.

<u>Solution</u>: The term "zygote" refers to a fertilized egg cell. It is the first cell in which the genes of the mother and father are joined together. The word "zygote" itself derives its name from a Greek word which means "yoked" or "joined together."

The zygote contains forty-six chromosomes--twenty-three from the unfertilized egg and twenty-three contributed by the father's sperm cell. After it is first formed, the zygote looks much like the unfertilized egg cell, but this is because the egg is much larger than the sperm cell and it can absorb the sperm cell without showing it.

The zygote soon divides in two, less than two days after fertilization. These cells in turn divide, and the whole process of cell division during the course of prenatal development begins.

Every individual carries two genes for a particular trait--one from their mother and one from their father. A person is homozygous for a specific trait if both genes that determine the trait have the same characteristics. For example, if an individual has two genes that call for brown hair, he has brown hair. To be heterozygous for a particular trait means that the two genes which determine that trait have different characteristics. The resultant trait depends on which gene is dominant. For example, if an individual's genes for eye color consist of a dominant gene for brown eye color and a recessive gene for blue eyes, the individual will have brown eyes.

Monozygotic twins are also called identical twins. In this case, the cells dividing from the zygote separate into two masses. Henceforth, two individuals form. Monozygotic twins have the same heredity and thus the same appearance throughout life. Dyzygotic twins or fraternal twins develop at the same time in the mother, but each individual originates from a separate zygote--two eggs each fertilized by two different sperm cells. As opposed to monozygotic twins, fraternal twins can have differing traits; they can even be of opposite sexes. Fraternal twins develop in separate amniotic sacs whereas identical twins develop in the same amniotic sac and are both bathed by the same amniotic fluid.

● **PROBLEM 2-7**

Define and describe the processes of mitosis and meiosis.

Solution: The process of cell division whereby new cells are formed to replace old ones is called mitosis. The cells in our bodies are constantly undergoing this process--new cells are formed to replace those that are dead or worn out. Worn-out cells are absorbed into the surrounding tissues and fluids. Mitosis occurs most rapidly during a child's growth and when the body repairs an injury; for example, when a person cuts himself, new skin cells are formed to replace the lost skin.

Bodily cells are able to reproduce themselves because DNA, which is found in the chromosomes, has the ability to reproduce new cells. Cell division occurs when a set of chromosomes duplicates itself: another set is formed exactly like the original. This new set separates itself from the

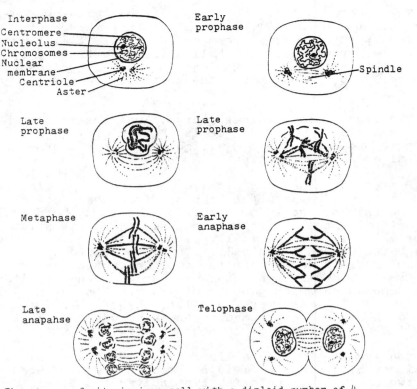

Interphase
Centromere
Nucleolus
Chromosomes
Nuclear membrane
Centriole
Aster

Early prophase

Spindle

Late prophase

Late prophase

Metaphase

Early anaphase

Late anapahse

Telophase

The stages of mitosis in a cell with a diploid number of 4.

parent set and becomes surrounded by a membrane. The new chromosome set and membrane become the nucleus of a new cell.

The process of meiosis is also referred to as reduction division. It is the process by which human sperm and egg cells are formed. Like the process of mitosis, it involves the duplication of chromosomes. However, in the case of sperm and egg cells, a single division results in four new cells rather than two cells. Each new cell contains only half the number of chromosomes found in the original cell. As the cells divide, the number of chromosomes in them are reduced;

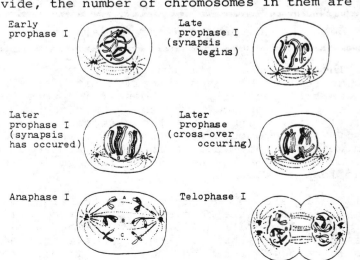

Early prophase I

Late prophase I (synapsis begins)

Later prophase I (synapsis has occured)

Later prophase (cross-over occuring)

Anaphase I

Telophase I

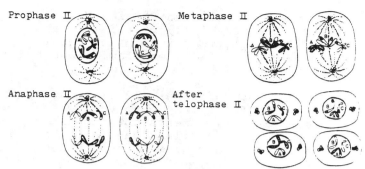

The stages of meiosis in a cell with a diploid number of 6.

hence the name reduction division. Each egg and sperm cell contains twenty-three single chromosomes as opposed to the forty-six chromosomes, or twenty-three pairs of chromosomes, found in other cells. The sperm and egg cells have only half the normal amount of chromosomes in order that, when they join, the resulting new cell contains the right amount of chromosomes. The zygote would be unable to live if it contained any more than forty-six chromosomes.

● **PROBLEM 2-8**

Discuss the influence of heredity on intelligence. Cite the hypotheses of Jensen and Bronfenbrener.

Correlations Between IQ Scores for Persons with Varying Degrees of Genetic Similarity

Identical twins reared together	.87
Identical twins reared apart	.75
Fraternal twins reared together	.53
Siblings reared together	.55
Parents and their children	.50
First cousins	.26
Grandparent-grandchild	.27
Unrelated children reared together	.23
Unrelated children reared apart	.00

Solution: Several studies have indicated that heredity plays a major role in determining intelligence. Hunt (1961), for example, found that the average correlation coefficient of intelligence test scores for identical twins is about .90. (For fraternal twins it is about .65). The study showed that as genetic similarity among individuals decreased, so did the similarity between intelligence test scores. Hence, identical twins had the highest correlation between test scores, while unrelated children had the lowest (.00). The correlations between the test scores in siblings was estimated at .50. Hunt's results clearly support a genetic influence.

Other studies involving twins also show heredity to be a major influence on intelligence. Muller (1925) found that identical twins showed negligible differences in intelligence test scores, even after they had been raised in different environments ("split-twin" studies). In a classic case involving identical twins, Jessie and Bessie, Muller found that Bessie, who grew up in a relatively poor family and had only four year of school, scored two points higher on an IQ test than Jessie, who grew up in an affluent family and had completed high school.

Newman, Freeman, and Holzinger (1937) substantiated Muller's findings. They found that monozygotic twins who were raised in disimilar environments obtained intelligence tests scores which were more similar than were the scores of dyzygotic (fraternal) twins who grew up together.

Arthur Jensen (1969) advanced a controversial theory which holds that heredity is most responsible for an individual's intelligence level. He estimated that the contribution of heredity to intelligence is 80 percent while the environment's contribution is only 20 percent. This estimate was derived from comparisons of intelligence test scores among different racial groups. Jensen found that American Blacks performed less well than American whites and that Caucasians performed less well than Orientals. Jensen argues that the most important environmental influences on intelligence are prenatal; however, differences in test scores between those of different racial and social classes cannot be attributed to environment alone. This conclusion invites racist interpretations and has been hotly debated. According to Jensen's 80-20 ratio of the influence of heredity and environment, it would follow that American whites have more potential for intellectual activities than American Blacks. Jensen also argued that compensatory educational programs are useless.

Urie Bronfenbrenner (1972) has questioned Jensen's 80-20 ratio. He suggests that the twin studies upon which Jensen bases his claims involved too many uncontrolled variables. For example, when Jensen studied the intelligence comparison of monozygotic twins who were raised in different environments, the cultural aspects were really quite similar.

Newman, Freeman, and Holzinger (1937) had previously reached an estimate of 50 percecnt for the amount of genetic influence on heredity. Later on, Fehr (1969) also found a 50 percent or less genetic influence on intelligence.

● PROBLEM 2-9

Define eugenics. Describe Tryon's and Searle's experiments with rats in their attempt to determine the amount of influence heredity has on intelligence.

Solution: Eugenics can be defined as a system of genetic engineering whereby certain individuals are chosen for reproduction on the basis of their genetic traits. This practice of selective breeding was first advocated by Francis Galton, Charles Darwin's cousin. During the last half of the nineteenth century, he was concerned about the diminishing number of gifted men in England, and he believed that only parents who possessed favorable genetic characteristics should be allowed to bear children.

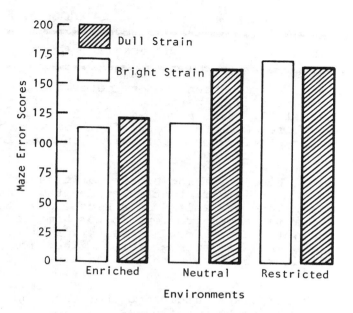

The effects of heredity and environment
on maze learning in rats.

The practice of eugenics with animals is popular and widespread, particularly among farmers who wish to raise superior farm animals.

An experiment conducted by Tryon (1940) at the University of California tested the inheritance of learning ability in rats. Tryon succeeded in producing a strain of bright rats and a strain of dull rats by means of selective breeding. Taking a group of rats, half male and half female, Tryon ran them through a maze and recorded the number of errors each rat made. He mated those the scores showed to be the bright rats and did the same with the dull rats. He subjected the offspring of both the bright rats and the dull rats to the same maze test, again recording their scores. He then mated the brightest offspring of the bright rats with each other and the dullest rats of the dull parents with each other. Tryon continued with this procedure--mating the brightest of the bright rats with each other and the dullest of the dull rats with each other--for a total of 18 generations. After 8 generations he found that the dullest rats from the bright group were brighter than the brightest rats from the dull group. Thus, Tryon showed that eugenics under controlled conditions can produce superior strains of animals and supports the theory that intelligence depends a great deal upon heredity.

Searle (1949), however, tested the same strains of rats and found that neither strain was universally bright or universally dull; that is, those rats who scored well on the maze-running task did not perform well on all types of tasks. In the same way, the dull rats who did poorly at maze-running were not poor at every task. However, those findings do not completely discredit Tryon's findings since Tryon was looking at maze-learning ability alone.

35

Discuss the influence of heredity on personality.

Solution: Twin studies have been used to determine the amount of genetic influence on personality. Rosanoff, Handy, and Plesset (1937) found a case in which a pair of identical twins who grew up in different families were both found to be sexually promiscuous. Both girls entered institutions at the age of twenty.

Lindeman (1969) also found marked similarities between monozygotic twins raised in different environments. In a case of two brothers, one was raised in a secure and stable home while the other was moved from one foster home to another. As adults, they were found to be very similar with regard to attitudes, work and even gestures. They even volunteered for military service within eight days of each other.

A study by Eysenck (1964) indicated that emotional disorders can be caused by genetic influence. It was found that with regard to criminal behavior and alcoholism, identical twins raised in different environments are more likely to display similar tendencies than fraternal twins. However, other studies of monozygotic twins who were raised in diverse environments show that behavior and personality traits differ, thus favoring emphasis on environmental influence. Some studies have even indicated that monozygotic twins who were raised in the same environment often develop differing personality traits. A study done by Shields (1962), for example, reported that in one case study one of the twins (MZ) took a physically dominant role with the other and became a leader.

Discuss the influence of heredity on emotional responsivity for both animals and humans.

Solution: Research has indicated that emotional responsivity can be inherited in animals. Significant differences can be seen in the degree of savageness between wild and domesticated animals. Wild animals such as gray rats, wolves, and lions are innately savage whereas their domesticated counterparts--white rats, dogs, and cats are innately tame. Even if these animals' environments are changed, they still retain their respective potentials for tameness and savageness. A wild animal raised by humans from birth will always remain potentially savage and will never become as tame as a domesticated animal. A domesticated animal released to the wild may become relativity savage, but will remain more "tamable" than animals whose ancestors were wild.

Several experiments have been conducted to detect emotional inheritance. In one study, Hall (1938) tested the level of emotionality in 145 rats by using a device called

an "open field"--a large compartment that usually elicits
fear. Of these rats, Hall mated 7 of the most emotional
females with the 7 most emotional males. Likewise, the 7
least emotional females were mated with the 7 least emotional
males. This inbreeding continued for several generations.
It was found that the offspring of the emotional rats were
a great deal more emotional than the offspring of the unemotional rats. This difference was considerable, even in the
first generation of offspring. In Hall's test of emotional
responsivity, he found that the scores of the emotional offspring were seven times those of the unemotional offspring.

The inheritance of emotions has also been studied in
humans, although not as extensively as in animals because of
practical and ethical considerations. In one experiment, Jost
and Sontag (1944) studied children between 6 and 12 years of
age over a period of 3 years. The researchers measured various bodily states which are known to at least partly reflect
emotion. Among these were skin resistance, pulse and respiration rates, and salivation. For subjects, the researchers
chose pairs of identical twins, pairs of siblings, and pairs
of unrelated children. They wanted to see whether twins
(who have identical heredity) are more similar in emotional
responsivity--as reflected in bodily states associated
with it--than siblings and unrelated children. Using a correlation coefficient (a number between + 1.00 and - 1.00 used
to express the degree of relationship between two sets of
measurements arranged in pairs) the researchers combined the
correlations of the scores on the different measures of bodily
states. It was found that the correlations between identical
twins were consistently higher than those for siblings, and
the correlations for siblings were higher than those for unrelated children. Overall, the relationships clearly showed
that heredity is influential in bodily states associated
with emotion.

● **PROBLEM 2-12**

Name and describe various behavior disorders that can be
genetically inherited.

Solution: Several types of behavior disorders can be inherited through the genes. Brain damage may be inherited
when the body, as a result of genetic inheritance, is not
able to produce enough of the enzymes needed for proper
development.

Hemiplegia and some types of cerebral palsy can be
genetically transmitted. Hemiplegia is a condition in which
one side of the body is paralyzed. Cerebral palsy is a
disorder in which the brain cannot control muscle movement.

Learning disorders and various types of retardation
can be traced to genetic causes. Down's Syndrome, or mongolism, is one such form of retardation. This condition
is most often found in children of very young mothers or
mothers who are over forty years of age. It is caused when
the paired chromosomes in an egg or sperm cell fail to
separate properly when they join to form a zygote. A mongo-

loid child is characterized by a low intelligence level,
an unusual skin fold in the corners of the eyes, a wide
nose, and protruding tongue. A child with Down's Syndrome
has an average life span of ten years.

     With regard to mental illness, Gottesman and Shields
(1966) found a higher concordance between identical twins
who had schizophrenia than between fraternal twins with the
same disorder. This means that of all twin children studied
who had schizophrenia, more individuals of identical pairs
had a schizophrenic twin than the fraternal members.
Gottesman and Shields found the concordance rate for identical twins--that is, the percentage of those twins in which
both members are schizophrenic--to be 42 percent, based on a
sample of 28 pairs of identical twins. They found the concordance rate for fraternal twins to be only 9 percent,
based on a sample of 34 pairs of twins.

     Schizophrenia is one of the most commonly diagnosed
mental illnesses in the United States. It is characterized
by the individual's detachment and inability to relate to
the surrounding environment. Some studies have indicated
that schizophrenia can be, in part, genetically inherited.
But most research cites stress in family life and abnormalities in the nervous system as the major (or at least precipitating) causes.

NATURE VERSUS NURTURE

• PROBLEM 2-13

Distinguish between biological determinism and environmental
determinism.

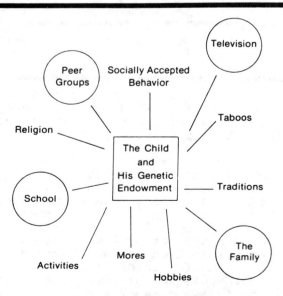

The child's culture interacts with his genetic endowment to
determine the sort of adult he will become.

Solution: Biological determinism refers to the attitude that biological heredity is the only factor that determines differences among individuals. The British scientist Sir Francis Galton published a book in 1869 entitled Hereditary Genius in which he stated that man's abilities are derived from innate intelligence regardless of his surrounding environment. This was a popular view at the time. Parents and teachers were encouraged not to interfere with the natural development of their children. Children should be safeguarded from the harmful effects of the environment rather than be stimulated by it. In other words environmental factors could only hurt the child's development, never help it.

Environmental determinism stresses the importance of cultural influences and other aspects of the environment that influence human development. Theorists of this viewpoint believe that human development can be controlled by manipulating the environment. Today, most "environmentalists" do not deny the importance of genetics in development but sometimes tend to ignore it in their research and writing.

The debate between biological determinists and environmental determinists is still taking place. It is popularly referred to as the nature--nurture controversy.

● **PROBLEM 2-14**

Discuss how nature and nurture interact in human behavior. Define genotype and phenotype. What is meant by the epigenetic approach to the study of behavior development?

Solution: Most psychologists today agree that both heredity and environment, or nature and nurture, interact to determine behavior. Nature, inheritance, sets the potentialities for behavior, while nurture, the environment, determines the extent to which these potentialities will be realized. For example, an individual may be born with a certain potential for intelligence, but whether this potential is fulfilled depends on various factors in the environment: availability of books and schools, encouragement of learning in the home, etc.

Genotype refers to the genetic constitution of an organism; its potential, in other words phenotype, refers to the observable characteristics of an organism; that is; the extent to which its potential is realized. The genotype, nature, does not set fixed genetic limits for behavior. Because the genotype must act through the environment to produce a particular behavior, no such limits exist. The important point is that behavior is not solely dependent upon an individual's genotype, but rather upon the interaction of the genotype with the individual's environment.

The epigenetic approach to the study of behavior development is one which concentrates on the interaction of nature and nurture. The conceptual basis of this approach is that there is an on-going interplay, during the course of development, between behaviors that are genetically controlled and the environment. The result of this interplay is the observed behavior--the phenotype.

One study that illustrates the epigenetic approach is one concerning the accuracy of pecking behavior of seagulls in Eastern North America. Hungry chicks ordinarily peck at the red bills of mother birds in order to make them regurgitate food. Using a controlled laboratory setting, cards on which the mother gull head was drawn were presented to young chicks. Records were kept of the number of times the chicks pecked at the red bill drawn on the card. It was found that on the first day after hatching, approximately 33 percent of the pecks were hits while on the fourth day, after much practice, about 80 percent of the pecks were hits. Here we see that genetics provides the basis or potential for pecking while environmental experience determines the extent to which this potential will be fulfilled. Thus we see the epigenetic approach taken toward this study--the interaction of nature and nurture.

● **PROBLEM 2-15**

Describe the theory of Stern (1956) in the nature-nurture controversy.

Solution: Stern's widely accepted hypothesis on the contribution of heredity and environment with regard to behavior development has been termed the "rubber-band" hypothesis. In it, he models by analogy a genetic trait to a rubber band, and the extent to which the trait develops, to the length to which the rubber band stretches. That is, an individual is born with a certain amount of genetic endowment for a particular trait, and the amount the trait develops depends on the environment. Stern suggests that "different people initially may have been given different lengths of unstretched endowment, but the natural forces of the environment may have stretched their expression to equal length, or led to differences in attained length sometimes corresponding to their innate differences and at other times in reverse of the relation."

● **PROBLEM 2-16**

What is the relationship between the genetic factor and the environmental factor in intelligence?

Solution: It is clear to most psychologists that intelligence is determined by both genetic and environmental factors. The predominant view is that the genetic factors place an absolute ceiling on an individual's intelligence potential, and he may or may not reach this potential, depending on how enriched or deprived his environment is. Thus an individual may have the potential to develop an IQ of 120, but if his learning environment was bad in childhood his IQ may never develop past 105. It is believed that there is a critical period in a person's childhood in which he must develop certain intellectual functions. If this critical period is characterized by emotional, intellectual, social, or physical (e.g., food, shelter) deprivation, then the person's IQ will not develop to its full potential. This is usually an irreversible result; that is, even if the person's later life is enriched, he will not be able to raise his IQ significantly and reach his potential.

There are many instances in which a young child's IQ increases with an improvement in environment. Skeels (1966) conducted a study in which he took very young, girls (under 19.3 months) from an orphanage in which the environment was seriously depressed and placed them in an institution for the mentally retarded. Their IQ's improved from a mean of 65 for the group to a mean of 91.8 during an 18 month period. The cause of the subnormal mean IQ of 65 was the lack of personal attention in the orphanage. The girls had a severe emotional deficit which impaired their intellectual development. In the institution for the mentally retarded, the girls experienced improved caretaking by retarded adult women who had a mental age of five to nine years. These retarded women were attentive and affectionate towards the little girls and this compensated for the previous emotional deficit. Eleven of the thirteen children placed in the institution for the mentally retarded were adopted. Another group of 12 little girls stayed in the orphanage; their mean IQ dropped from 86.7 to 60.5 in two years. None of these girls was adopted, and one of them died.

In another study by Newman et al (1937), it was found that the average correlation of intelligence between identical twins raised in very similar environments was .88; whereas the correlation of intelligence for fraternal twins raised in very similar environments was only .63. This difference between identical and fraternal twins indicates that heredity is an important factor in determining IQ. However, the correlation of intelligence for siblings is only .51-.53; and since any two siblings are as genetically similar as any two fraternal twins the difference in the correlation between the two groups must be attributed to environmental factors. Obviously, fraternal twins are raised in more similar environments than are siblings in general. When the correlation of intelligence for identical twins raised apart from each other was computed it was found that the correlation was .77. The correlation of intelligence for identical twins raised apart was still higher than the correlation of intelligence for fraternal twins and for siblings. This evidence seems to suggest that heredity plays a more important role in determining intelligence than does environment. However, this study was conducted with a small number of subjects and therefore the results are not as impressive or authoritative as they seem.

Thus it can be seen that heredity and environment combine to determine an individual's intelligence. It appears that a child's father's occupation is the most accurate predictor of a child's future IQ. Father's occupation is even more effective in prediction than father's IQ. Psychologists are still actively involved in determining heritability indices for intelligence. A heritability index represents what proportion of the variance of a particular trait in a given population (the individual differences--that is, why

person A has an IQ of 80 and person B has an IQ of 150) is
attributable to hereditary or genetic factors. The higher
the heritability index, the more pessimistic is the outlook for raising an individual's IQ.

Describe Sherman's and Key's (1932) study of the Hollow
Children. What do their findings indicate about the effect
of environment on intellectual development?

Solution: Several studies have indicated that children who
are raised in isolated regions, where they are deprived of
the degree or quality of environmental stimulation which
other children in less isolated areas receive, are intellectually inferior. One famous study concerning this aspect
was done by Sherman and Key (1932) on a group of isolated
mountain children which they call the "Hollow Children."

The Hollow Children lived in various isolated villages
in the Blue Ridge Mountains about 180 miles west of
Washington D.C. Interestingly, these villages had remained
isolated in varying degrees for decades prior to the study.
Sherman and Key chose four villages in the region to study.
Each varied in its amount of contact with the outside world.
For example, Colvin was the innermost village and was the
most isolated. The other villages, in order of most isolation to least, were Needles, Rigby, and Oakton. Each of these
villages varied in the amount of schooling available. The
researchers found that Colvin provided the least amount of
schooling. During the 12 years previous to the study, a
school had been open a total of only 16 months. It was found
that only three of the adult residents were literate. In
Rigby, which was closer to civilization, a school had been
open for 66.5 months during the same amount of time. Many
of the adults here were literate and there was a post office
which provided some contact with civilization. A village
called Briarsville which was located at the foot of the
mountain was much less isolated than the mountain villages and
was used as a control group for the study.

The researchers used various intelligence tests such as
the Stanford-Binet and the Goodenough Draw-A-Man test, to
compare the intellectual ability of the extremely isolated
children in Colvin to the less isolated children in Briarsville. Sherman and Key wanted to see if the environmental
deprivation had any effect on intellectual development. Since
most of the residents of the Blue Mountain area were of common ancestry (English and Scotch-Irish), it was assumed that
the genetic pool was similar for most of the people in the
region. Since heredity as a factor in intellectual development was more or less in check (controled for), the researchers
could more accurately gauge environmental influence as a
factor.

Two significant findings came out of this study. The
first was that scores on the intelligence tests increased as
one moved from the most isolated village to the least isolated.
Hence, the children of Colvin had the lowest scores while the

children of Briarsville, the control group, had the highest.
Secondly, it was found that older children (14 and 15-year-
olds) performed worse than younger children. The very young
children were not significantly below the test norms. This
would indicate that a deprived environment has a detrimental
effect on intellectual development. Both of these findings
suggest that an individual's environment has an important influence on his ability to do well on these kinds of tests.

As a cautionary note: there is no accurate definition of
intelligence. In this study, it was defined as that which intelligence tests measure.

One of Sherman and Key's most important and basic conclusions was that "children develop only as the environment demands
development."

● **PROBLEM 2-18**

Discuss Krech's study with rats as it relates to the influence of the environment on intelligence.

Rats that are raised in enriched environments are
intellectually superior to their less fortunate colleagues.

Solution: David Krech and his associates (1960; 1962; 1966)
in their experiments with rats found that rearing in an enriched environment produces a higher level of intelligence
than rearing which takes place in a relatively impoverished
environment.

In their experiments, Krech and his associates created
two types of environments for the rats: enriched and deprived. A rich environment for the rats was a large, well-
lighted cage that had plenty of toys to keep them occupied
(e.g., marbles, exercise wheels and gnawing or scratching
posts). A deprived environment was a small, dimly lit cage
with none of the toys of the enriched cage. Furthermore, the
deprived rat's cage was lined with tin in order to obscure
his view. As opposed to the enriched rat, the deprived rat
was permitted no contact with humans or other rats.

Krech found that the rats raised in the enriched environment possessed a higher intelligence level (as measured by maze learning ability) compared to the rats who were raised in the impoverished environment. He also found that the chemical composition of the brain of a rat raised in an enriched environment differed significantly from that of a rat reared in a deprived environment. The rats from the enriched environments were found to have more cholinesterase and acetylcholinesterase in their brains than the deprived rats. These two chemicals are believed to affect the transmission of impulses from one brain neuron to another. An increase in the amount of these chemicals in the brain would facilitate learning ability.

Enriched rats also have a larger visual cortex than deprived rats, which would also aid learning. In addition, enriched rats developed brains which were heavier than those of deprived rats.

Krech's studies clearly suggest that an enriched environment is beneficial to a rat's development, and an impoverished one is detrimental. There is every reason to believe that we can safely assume that this conclusion is also true for humans; however, there is a dearth of evidence to support this conclusion.

● **PROBLEM** 2-19

Discuss the rationale behind childhood intervention programs such as Project Headstart. Why did Project Headstart fail? What is the new trend in such programs? What deprivation factors are beyond the reach of these programs?

Solution: Childhood intervention programs were originally developed by U.S. government and private educational agencies acting on the supposition that intelligence is strongly influenced by environment, and therefore poor and culturally deprived people are at a great disadvantage academically. The best known of these intervention programs is Project Headstart. In accordance with the theory of environmental influence, underprivileged children ready to enter first grade--about five years old--were given experience with toys, books, and games with which most middle-class children are familiar. It began as a summer program and lasted eight weeks.

Project Headstart was not completely successful. The children made immediate gains in IQ, but these gains were unstable: the children's IQ's returned to the pre-intervention level as soon as the program ended. Opponents of Headstart, who believed that intelligence is determined genetically, used this information to support racist claims that blacks had less innate intellectual ability than did whites.

Owing to its poor organization, however, Headstart was destined to fail from its inception. It simply was not designed to play an important enough role in the lives of the children. Mainly, the children's experience in the program was isolated from their family environments. The enrichment did not extend to the rest of the family, the unit which has

44

the most significant influence on a child. In addition, an eight-week intervention program cannot compensate for the cultural deprivation a five-year-old minority child has experienced. Intervention programs must begin earlier, last longer, and make more complete changes in a child's life.

The new philosophy of childhood intervention is to involve the mothers of the children in the programs: mothers are taught how to be effective teachers. This kind of intervention has been extremely successful. Children's IQ scores rise, thus lessening the disparity in group IQ's. Moreover, there is a secondary benefit to this kind of intervention. When a mother is involved as the teacher, her self-esteem is raised, her cooperation increases, she becomes closer to her child, and can spread her learning to other mothers in the area.

In view of the new program's positive results, the evidence against the efficacy of intervention programs is insubstantial. Even the best intervention programs, however, cannot affect the pervasive deprivation that exists in poverty areas. Pre-natal care is often inadequate, and nutrition is often insufficient. Self-respect is frequently low. All these factors have negative effects on a child's intellectual development. Nevertheless, even if intervention programs are not completely successful, it cannot be concluded that the environment is not an important factor in the determination of intelligence.

CULTURE AND BEHAVIOR

● PROBLEM 2-20

Define culture. What does Benedict (1934) mean by cultural relativity?

Solution: Culture is a difficult term to define; it encompasses much. We can say that a culture is the sum total of the mores, taboos, traditions, beliefs, value systems, and implicit and explicit standards of behavior that characterize a particular society. A child's culture interacts with his genetic endowment in determining the sort of individual he will become.

There are several means by which a child comes to learn about his culture and the ways in which he is expected to behave. Among these are school, religious institutions, the family, peer groups, and the mass media.

It is cultural characteristics that produce the greatest differences among various races of people, since genetically determined characteristics are actually very similar. People possess more genetically determined characteristics that are similar (i.e., two arms, two legs, a single head) than characteristics that differ (i.e., skin pigmentation, hair texture). It is the environmental, cultural variations which are most outstanding: language, social customs, attire. It

45

is probably the case that a major portion, if not most, of an individual's behavior is determined by the particular culture in which he is raised.

Benedict (1934) believes that human behavior can only be understood and evaluated within the context of its cultural environment. He calls this belief "cultural relativity." Most behavioral scientists today would tend to agree with this viewpoint. Based on cross-cultural research, it is quite clear that certain behaviors which are acceptable in one society may not be acceptable in another. For example, the cannabalism of certain secluded Amazon tribes would not constitute acceptable behavior in the United States, but it is the norm in these South American tribes.

● **PROBLEM 2-21**

Are there cultural differences in intelligence?

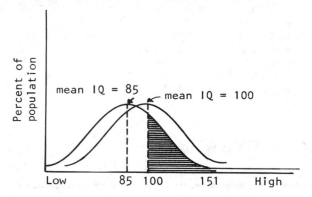

Solution: There is no good evidence that there are cultural differences in intelligence. There are, however, mean IQ differences between subcultural groups. Since IQ tests are designed for use in Western cultures, and there are no good cross-cultural (or cross-subcultural) intelligence tests, it is difficult to make valid comparisons among various cultural and subcultural groups. It seems reasonable that there are really no cultural differences in innate intelligence. Certainly if intelligence is the ability of an individual to deal effectively with his environment, there are no cultural differences in intelligence. People in other cultures deal as effectively with their environments as do people in Western culture. In fact, there is a considerably lower incidence of mental illness in non-Western cultures. (Mental illness is often used as an index for maladjustment to a particular society.)

When mean IQ differences for two separate groups are reported, it is important to realize what these differences mean. Study the graph (shown above) of the distribution of Black IQ scores in the population superimposed on the distribution of white IQ scores in the population: The difference between mean IQ's = 100 -85 = 15 points. 15 points is equal to one standard deviation. A mean IQ difference of 15 points does not imply anything about specific individuals. The shaded portion of the graph represents those blacks who scored above the mean for white people. Approximately 16% of the black population scored above the mean of the white population. Thus, it is not possible to judge an individual's intelligence on the basis of the mean intelligence of his sub-culture. Any one individual may be at the top end of the IQ distribution with an IQ, for example, of 140.

When a group of black infants, whose natural parents' IQ was average for Black's in general was adopted into white middle class professional homes, their group IQ increased to above 105. It is clear that a deprived learning environment has a severely detrimental effect on the development of any child's intelligence.

● **PROBLEM 2-22**

Discuss Mead's (1935) study of three New Guinea tribes. What do her findings indicate about the effect of culture on personality?

Solution: In her studies of three New Guinea tribes, Margaret Mead (1935) found that personality traits, especially those related to dominance, vary depending upon the culture. Mead was particularly interested in the differences between the sexes in each society and found distinct differences in the expected modes of behavior for males and females among the three cultures.

The three tribes Mead studied were the Arapesh, the Mundugumor, and the Tchambuli tribes. She found that both sexes in the Arapesh culture were "placid and contented, unaggressive and noninitiatory, noncompetitive and responsive, warm, docile, and trusting." In contrast, Mead found that both the men and women of the Mundugumor tribe "developed as ruthless, aggressive, positively sexed individuals, with the maternal cherishing aspects of personality at a minimum." In the third tribe, the Tchambuli, she found a "genuine reversal of the sex attitudes of our own culture." Hence, we see three cultures, each with its unique standard for appropriate behavior. In the Arapesh tribe, "feminine" behavior is the norm for both sexes; in the Mundugumor, "masculine" behavior is the norm for both; in the Tchambuli, males are "feminine" and females are "masculine."

When discussing personality as it relates to culture, one should look at the environment of a society, since this largely determines the kind of society which develops. The Arapesh were an agricultural tribe. They inhabited the sterile mountain regions some distance away from the coast of New Guinea. The Mundugumor were cannibalistic. They lived along the banks of a fierce jungle river called the Sepik, which they greatly feared. Like the Arapesh, the Tchambuli were an agricultural tribe. They were a highly artistic people. In this culture, where the appropriate behavior of the sex roles was "reversed," the men were in charge of the artistic activities while the women were engaged in the practical work necessary for survival. While the men spent a great deal of their time practicing various ceremonial dances and experimenting with various art forms, the women gathered food.

From her studies, Mead believed that the development of such personality traits as masculinity and feminity are not dependent on the individual's sex, but rather on his particular cultural environment--the values, beliefs, and standards of behavior of the society in which he lives. This is not to say that everyone in a particular culture accepts and lives by its rules; there are always those individuals who are considered deviant. Yet it has been found that most of the people within a given culture adhere to the accepted modes of behavior, since it is quite often the case that refusal to adhere to norms results in rejection, abandonment, and hostility from the other members of the society.

SHORT ANSWER QUESTIONS FOR REVIEW

Choose the correct answer.

1. All of the following are criteria for instinc-
    tive behavior EXCEPT   (a)   behavior should be
    genetically determined   (b)   behavior should be
    unlearned   (c)   behavior should be unorganized
    (d)   behavior should be consistent   c

2. A moth attracted to a lighted lamp is an example
    of a(n)   (a)   reflex   (b)   taxis   (c)   fixed ac-
    tion pattern   (d)   instinct   b

3. Man's evolutionary history has shaped his beha-
    vior in terms of   (a)   limitations   (b)   poten-
    tialities   (c)   psychological functions which
    have their basis in the brain   (d)   all of the
    above   d

4. Which of the following skills mature?   (a)
    reading   (b)   walking   (c)   game-playing   (d)
    writing   b

5. Which of the following skills is learned?
    (a)   speech   (b)   prehension   (c)   social be-
    havior   (d)   reading   d

6. All of the following are characteristic of DNA
    EXCEPT: (a)   it consists of two chemical bases
    arranged in a large number of combinations   (b)
    the two gene strands are arranged in the form
    of a helix   (c)   the gene strands are capable
    of reproducing themselves   (d)   it is consid-
    ered to be the basis of all life   a

7. Which of the following is NOT true about fra-
    ternal twins?   (a)   they are also called dyzy-
    gotic   (b) each individual originates from a
    different zygote   (c)   they can be of opposite
    sexes   (d)   both develop in the same amniotic
    sac   d

8. Meiosis is similar to mitosis in that   (a)   a
    single cell division results in two cells   (b)
    both involve the duplication of chromosomes
    (c)   each new cell contains the same number of
    chromosomes found in the original cell   (d)
    all of the above   b

9. In most studies on the influence of heredity on
    intelligence, the highest correlations in intel-
    ligence have been found between   (a)   dyzogotic
    twins   (b)   monozygotic twins   (c)   siblings
    (d)   unrelated children   b

SHORT ANSWER QUESTIONS FOR REVIEW

10. Which of the following behavior disorders can be genetically inherited? (a) hemiplegia (b) Down's Syndrome (c) schizophrenia (d) all of the above

d

11. Another term for genotype is (a) nature (b) nurture (c) biological determinism (d) none of the above

a

12. In Sherman and Key's study of the Hollow Children, those children with the lowest intelligence test scores resided in (a) Briarsville (b) Rigby (c) Colvin (d) Needles

c

13. According to Krech's studies, all of the following are true of enriched rats EXCEPT (a) they are more intelligent as shown by their maze learning ability (b) they have more cholinesterase and acetylcholinesterase in their brains (c) they have a smaller visual cortex (d) they have heavier brains

c

14. Culture encompasses all of the following EXCEPT (a) mores (b) traditions (c) genotype (d) value system

c

15. In Mead's (1939) study of the three New Guinea tribes, a reversal of the sex attitudes of our own culture was found in (a) the Arapesh (b) the Mundugumor (c) the Tchambuli (d) all of the above

c

Fill in the blanks.

16. _____ refers to a pattern of behavior that is innate and organized, and is inhibited until released by an innate releasing stimulus.

Fixed action pattern (FAP)

17. _____ refers to the development of bodily processes and changes of behavior as a result of such development.

Maturation

18. _____ are the carriers of heredity.

Genes

19. A mature female produces only _____ chromosomes.

X

20. A _____ gene is one that takes precedence over all other genes for a particular trait.

dominant

21. _____ refers to a fertilized egg cell.

zygote

50

HORT ANSWER QUESTIONS FOR REVIEW

. A person is _____ for a specific trait if both genes that determine the trait have the same characteristics.

homozy-
gous

. _____ twins originate from the same zygote.

Monozy-
gotic or
identical

. The process of Meiosis is also referred to as _____ .

reduction
division

. _____ is a system of genetic engineering whereby certain individuals are chosen for reproduction on the basis of their genetic traits.

Eugenics

. Brain damage is inherited when the body, as a result of genetic inheritance, does not produce enough of the _____ needed by the brain for proper development.

enzymes

. _____ stresses the importance of cultural influences on human development.

Environ-
mental
determin-
ism

. _____ refers to the extent to which the potential of an organism is realized.

Phenotype

. Stern's hypothesis on the contributions of heredity and environment to behavior development has been called the _____ hypothesis.

rubber-
band

. The idea that behavior can only be understood and evaluated within the context of its cultural environment is called _____ .

cultural
relativ-
ity

termine whether the following statements are true
 false.

1. Much of man's aggressive and emotional behavior is the result of his evolutionary heritage.

True

2. The development of most of our basic behavior is the result of learning.

False

3. The zygote contains 23 chromosomes.

False

4. It can be said that Jensen is an ardent supporter of biological determinism.

True

5. In Tryon's study, it was found that the dullest rats from the bright group were not as bright as the brightest rats from the dull group.

False

51

SHORT ANSWER QUESTIONS FOR REVIEW

36. Searle found that rats who scored well on the
    maze running task did not perform well on all
    types of tasks.   True

37. Some studies have indicated that monozygotic
    twins raised in the same environment often de-
    velop different personality traits.   True

38. A wild animal raised by humans from birth can
    become as tame as a domesticated animal.   False

39. Jost and Sontag found that identical twins are
    more similar in emotional responsivity as re-
    flected in bodily states than siblings.   True

40. Gottesman and Sheilds found the concordance
    rate of schizophrenia for identical twins to
    be much greater than that for fraternal twins.   True

41. Sir Francis Galton was a staunch supporter of
    environmental determinism.   False

^2. The genotype sets fixed genetic limits for be-
    havior.   False

43. The epigenetic approach focuses on the interac-
    tion of nature and nurture.   True

44. Lack of personal attention was the primary
    cause of IQ deficiency in the orphanage child-
    ren of Skeel's study.   True

45. In the Sherman and Key study of the Hollow
    Children, it was found that older adolescents
    performed better on intelligence tests than
    younger children.   False

46. One of the most important reasons of the fail-
    ure of Project Headstart was the lack of mater-
    nal intervention in the program.   True

47. The most outstanding differences among people
    are those that are environmental.   True

48. If intelligence is defined as the ability of
    an individual to deal effectively with his en-
    vironment, then it can be said that there are
    no cultural differences in intelligence.   True

49. Mead found that geographical location was not
    an important determinant in the development of
    cultural behavior.   False

SHORT ANSWER QUESTIONS FOR REVIEW

50.   Mead believed that personality traits such as
      masculinity and femininity are for the most
      part dependent on the individual's gender.   False

CHAPTER 3

LEARNING

BASIC PRINCIPLES

● PROBLEM 3-1

Define the term "learning."

Solution: Learning is a relatively permanent change in behavior resulting from conditions of practice or experience. It is important to use the words "relatively permanent" because transient changes in behavior do not indicate that learning has occurred. (Behavior refers to all the activities an organism engages in, including thought and communication.) Transient changes in behavior are usually spontaneously reversible.

The adjustment of the eyes to different light conditions is a transient change in behavior whereas the learning of basic principles of mathematics is a relatively permanent change in behavior. Learning can be easily distinguished from memory in this case. A student who learns basic mathematics principles should be able to derive formulae and solve problems whereas the student who has only memorized formulae and certain problem solving procedures will forget them as soon as he stops regularly retrieving them from his memory.

● PROBLEM 3-2

What is a learning curve?

Solution: The study of learning has often involved the study of performance on various tasks. A learning curve is a quantitative representation of the process of learning as measured by changes in performance. (Performance and learning are not to be considered equivalent. Learning is a process which can be inferred from changes in performance.) A learning curve shows the rate at which improvement in performance takes place for a given task.

Bryan and Harker (1897) were responsible for one of the earliest efforts to quantify the process of learning. They investigated the performance of men apprenticed as tele-

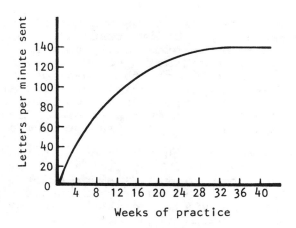

graphers. The graph shows part of their results. Sending ability was measured by cbserving the number of letters per minute the men were able to dispatch.

The curve shows large gains during the early weeks of training. The gains then become smaller and smaller until they finally level off. This type of learning curve, in which improvement slows down after reaching a certain point, is called a negatively accelerated curve.

Many types of learning, though certainly not all, have been shown to be negatively accelerated. The fact that this kind of curve is found in many types of learning has caused some theorists to speculate that all forms of learning follow the same laws.

● **PROBLEM** 3-3

What are the four basic factors in learning?

Solution: The four basic factors in learning are arousal, motivation, reinforcement, and association.

For learning to occur the organism must be in a relatively high state of arousal. No important or significant learning can take place during sleep. An organism must not only be aroused it must also be motivated.

Motivation is important because it allows behavior to be elicited. It is assumed that children learn in a school environment because it motivates them in some way. Some psychologists contend that children learn in school because of an innate need to achieve mastery. Others claim that children learn because they are motivated by the approval or love they receive for success. Thus, motivation and reinforcement are closely linked and are perhaps inseparable.

Reinforcements come in two forms, positive and negative (or reward and punishment). Despite what some educators or parents might feel, positive reinforcement or reward has been shown to be significantly more effective in changing behavior than negative reinforcement or punishment. Some psychologists strongly believe that all learning is reinforced. Sometimes the reinforcements are not obvious; they are nevertheless present. It is important to note that the principle of reinforcement is practically universal in psychology, even among psychoanalysts. However, psychoanalysts do not use the term reinforcement; they speak of the "pleasure principle." The pleasure principle states that an organism acts to increase pleasure whenever possible and to decrease displeasure (pain) whenever possible. Pleasure and displeasure are analogous with reward and punishment.

Association is a factor that is common to most learning situations. The term association implies a connection in time and place between two events. The formation of associations is the function of the brain. It is assumed that a great deal of learning is due to the association of stimuli and responses. Complicated learning often involves chains of stimuli and responses in which even the response can function as a stimulus.

Some psychologists are not convinced that associations between stimuli and responses adequately explain all learning; this does not diminish its importance in accounting for simple learning tasks. Learning that requires abstract conceptualization cannot be explained convincingly by the four factors described. These factors are only helpful in understanding relatively simple forms of learning.

● PROBLEM 3-4

What is a reinforcer?

Solution: A reinforcer is any event which increases the probability of a response in a particular situation.

There are two major types of reinforcers: positive reinforcers and negative reinforcers. Positive reinforcers are stimuli whose presence increase the frequency of the response. Negative reinforcers are those stimuli whose termination increase the frequency of the response. In psychological experiments, food is usually the positive reinforcer and electric shock the negative reinforcer.

It has not been established conclusively what makes a stimuli reinforcing. Different theories of learning hold different beliefs about what qualities reinforcers must have.

It is important to remember that punishment is not a negative reinforcer. Punishment does not result in the frequency of a response becoming greater. In this respect it does not fit our definition of a reinforcer.

● PROBLEM 3-5

Define the following types of reinforcement: positive, negative, primary, conditioned, social, generalized. Give an example of each.

Solution: Reinforcement refers to the delivery of a reward

that will strengthen a particular behavior. Reinforcement
is the effect of a reinforcer--a stimulus which increases the
likelihood that the particular behavior will be performed
again.

There are several ways of describing reinforcement. It
may be either positive or negative. Positive reinforcement
occurs when a reward or pleasant stimulus is administered
after some behavior has been performed. For example, if a
child cleans his room and his parents reward him with extra
spending money, his behavior has been positively reinforced.
Negative reinforcement refers to the removal of an unpleasant
stimulus after a certain behavior has been performed. In
this case, the avoidance or the termination of the unpleasantness is the reward or reinforcer. For example, a child's
parents may forbid him to leave the house until he cleans
his room. If he cleans his room and is allowed out, his
behavior has been negatively reinforced; the unpleasant stim-
ulus--confinement to the house--has been removed. This reinforcement increases the likelihood that the child will
continue to clean his room regularly.

Reinforcement may be either primary or conditioned
(also called secondary). Primary reinforcements satisfy
basic, unlearned drives. Examples of primary reinforcers
are food, drink, sex, and anything that satisfies an instinctual desire. A child who receives candy for good behavior has been reinforced through primary means.

Conditioned or secondary reinforcement occurs when the
reinforcing stimulus is not inherently pleasant or reinforcing, but becomes reinforcing through its association with
other pleasant or reinforcing stimuli. Money is an example
of a conditioned reinforcer. Coins and paper currency are
not in themselves pleasing, but the things money can buy are.
Therefore, an association is made between money, a secondary
reinforcer, and primary reinforcers. Hence, the term "conditioned."

Social reinforcement occurs when the reinforcer consists of feedback from individuals in one's surrounding environment. Examples of this include attention, approval,
affection, indifference, enmity. Each of these social reinforcers strengthen a particular behavior. A child who wins
a game and gains peer approval, for example, is receiving
social reinforcement.

Another type of reinforcer is called generalized.
This includes stimuli which are satisfying or reinforcing
for almost any behavior in any situation. Examples of generalized reinforcers are prestige, power, money, and peer
approval. All of these are reinforcing regardless of the
situation.

● **PROBLEM 3-6**

What is secondary reinforcement?

Solution: Such stimuli as food, water, and shock are known
as primary reinforcers. They are able to be easily used to

Poker chips normally have little or no value for chimpanzees, but this chimp will work hard to earn them once he learns that the "Chimp-O-Mat" will dispense food in exchange for them. The chips are secondary reinforcers.

condition behavior both operantly and classically. Psychologists discovered early that stimuli that are associated with primary reinforcers begin to acquire some reinforcing qualities of their own.

Pavlov demonstrated this by first conditioning a dog to salivate when hearing a metronome (the CS) and then pairing this CS with the view of a black square. The black square soon became a new CS and elicited salivation--in the absence of the metronome (which was now the UCS).

The phenomena of secondary reinforcement is not restricted to the laboratory. The most common secondary reinforcer in this society is probably money. Research which used poker chips to reinforce responses made by monkeys (the monkeys later "cashed in" the chips for food) was successful. This research led to practical applications in mental institutions and in prison systems. The mental patients and prisoners were said to be living in a "token economy."

● **PROBLEM 3-7**

What is generalization?

Solution: After an organism has learned a specific response to a stimulus it will make this same response to stimuli which are similar to the original stimulus. The more similar the new stimulus is to the original stimulus, the more likely it is that the learned response will occur.

Gradient of stimulus generalization

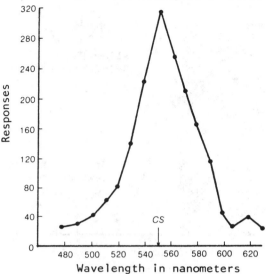

The gradient of stimulus generalization is shown for a group of pigeons trained to peck a button illuminated with a light of 550 nanometers and then presented with test buttons of several other colors, ranging from 480 to 620 nanometers. The graph shows that the closer the test stimulus was to the training stimulus of 550, the more the birds pecked.

This view was supported by research utilizing pigeons. Pigeons were trained to peck at a yellow-green light disk for food. When the response was learned (indicated by consistently correct responses), other colors were used in place of the original yellow-green. The closer the approximation of the new color to the original, along a color wavelength scale, the higher the response rate.

Stimulus generalization occurs independently of any specific training other than conditioning. Examples of such generalizations are common in everyday life. The behavior we have learned in response to honking cars is a common example. Two car horns do not make the same sound, but people learn to respond similarly to all car horns. In these cases, people respond to a general class and not to a particular.

● **PROBLEM 3-8**

What is discrimination?

Solution: Discrimination is the inverse of stimulus generalization. In discrimination, the organism learns to respond differently to similar stimuli. The greater the similarity between stimuli the lesser the probability that the organism will respond differently. Unlike generalization, discrimination must be learned.

Discrimination is not always easy to learn. If an experimenter gives reinforcement to a rat pushing a black

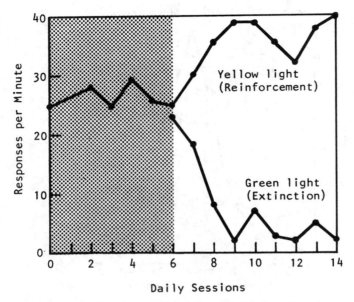

A plot of a pigeon's development in discriminating between two colors. Throughout the fourteen daily sessions the pigeon is rewarded with grain for pecking at the light when it is yellow. Beginning on the sixth day, however, the light is green half the time and the bird's pecking is never reinforced when the light is this color. Steadily, its pecking at the green light decreases while its responding to the yellow light increases.

circle but does not reinforce pushing a white circle, the result could be that the rat, upon continually choosing the white circle, will begin not to push anything at all. Since such research illustrates the importance of early experiences in learning, the need for guidance and help during the early stages is evident.

As in stimulus generalization, examples of discrimination are common in everyday life. Traffic lights are one good example. People learn to respond differently to red, green, and yellow lights; they learn to discriminate.

● **PROBLEM 3-9**

What is perceptual learning? How is it different from response learning?

Solution: Assume that a pigeon is placed in a Skinner box. There is a key in the box. When the pigeon pecks the key it receives a small amount of food. The pigeon will learn to peck at the key more often. This is a standard case of operant conditioning, which is one type of response learning.

Response learning involves the formation of a stimulus-response association. The key (stimulus) becomes associated with pecking the key (response). This relatively permanent association is created through the reinforce-

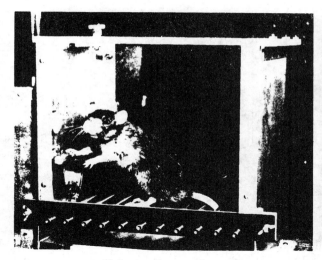

Skinner boxes for use with rats and pigeons.

ment process. The pigeon is rewarded with food if he pecks the key. If the pigeon stopped receiving food for the pecking response, the association between the pecking and the key would gradually weaken, and the frequency of pecking the key would decline sharply.

In contrast to response learning, there is perceptual learning. Perceptual learning refers to relatively permanent changes in the manner of perceiving the world. Perceptual learning involves an association between two stimuli, rather than between a stimulus and a response. Location learning is one kind of perceptual learning. The fact that the pigeon in the Skinner box is readily able to locate the position of the key indicates that it has learned the relationship between spatial stimuli in the box. This learning of stimulus associations which occur apart from the actual responses to the stimuli, is called perceptual learning.

● **PROBLEM 3-10**

How can it be determined if perceptual learning has occurred?

Solution: Response learning, by definition, involves the responses of an organism to stimuli. Responses are observable behaviors. Response learning can therefore be studied by observing the movements and activities of the organism.

In contrast to response learning, perceptual learning involves the formation of relationships between stimuli. The formation of relationships is an internal process. As such, it cannot be directly observed. In order to determine if perceptual learning has occurred, indirect methods of study are required.

One of these experimental methods involves change-

The Lashley jumping stand

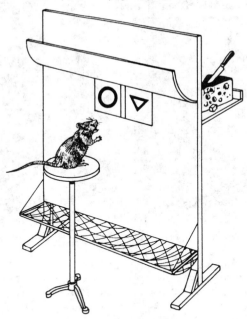

In discrimination studies, the rat must jump from the stand through one door or the other. If he selects the correct door, it opens and he lands on the platform, where he finds food. The wrong choice lands him unpleasantly in the net below.

responses. In this type of experiment, a task is learned by the subject using one specific set of responses. Once they are learned, the organism is prevented from using the same responses again. In order to successfully complete the task, the subject must use a different set of responses.

If the original learning was entirely dependent upon stimulus-response associations, the subject should be rendered incapable of completing the task when he was prevented from using the responses he learned first. If, on the other hand, the subject can complete the task, it can be inferred that it was not only responses that were learned--stimulus relationships must also have formed. The formation of stimulus-stimulus associations, or perceptual learning, enables the subject to alter his responses and then complete the task.

For example: Suppose that a group of rats is trained to swim through a maze in order to obtain food at the end of the maze. The water is then drained, and these same rats are again placed in the same maze. The rats are now able to run through the maze and subsequently obtain the food. What can be concluded?

Assume that the rats in the water-filled maze were learning only a set of specific responses. They would thereby learn the set of movements enabling them to swim in the proper direction. When the water is drained and the rats can no longer use the swimming motions they should not be able to obtain the food at the end of the maze.

Assume, alternatively, that the rats were learning not just a set of movements, but a set of relationships between stimuli. In this case, they would be learning relationships between the features of the maze. This knowledge would enable the rats to develop what has been called a "cognitive map." Disruption of the specific swimming responses would not destroy the cognitive map of the maze and the rats should be able to complete the task with different movements.

If the rats can still complete the maze (when the water is drained), one can infer that perceptual learning has taken place. Although the formation of stimulus-stimulus associations has not been directly observed, the fact that the animal is able to change responses indicates that the original learning consisted of more than just the learning of responses. Experiments with changed-responses provide one method of determining whether perceptual learning has occurred.

● **PROBLEM 3-1i**

Distinguish between association and field theories of learning. Give an example of each.

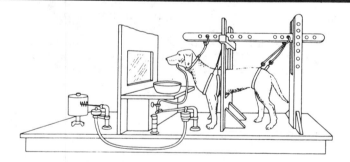

Classical salivary conditioning apparatus used by Pavlov. The apparatus permits the conditioned stimulus (a light) to appear in the window. The delivery of meat powder to the food bowl serves as the unconditioned stimulus.

Solution: Association and field theories of learning are of interest to us today chiefly because of their historical significance in the area of learning. Generally, field theory was the precursor of what we now know as humanistic theories of behavior; while associationism can be seen as the source of subsequent behavioral theories.

The field theory of behavior was first developed by Kurt Lewin and named by analogy to a theory of electricity and magnetism. It emphasizes that behavior does not depend on the organism alone or the environment alone, but on what goes on between the two. In field theory, psychological events, like physical events, are thought to represent a balance and interaction of many forces, and a change anywhere in the system is seen as affecting the whole system. For psychologists applying this theory, behavior is shaped not by individual chains of cause and effect, but by the combination of forces which make up the entire field.

The influence of this theory first became apparent with the appearance of Gestalt psychology with its emphasis on patterns in experience and behavior; according to these psychologists, the whole of experience or behavior is more than the sum of its parts and the parts take much of their character from the whole. Learning was seen by the field theorists as a central process, like seeing. It occurs all at once. Immediate learning consists of seeing the elements of a problem situation in a new relationship. This approach emphasizes "insight" learning rather than trial and error.

The theory of association states that learning consists of the formation of associations between responses and the stimuli which are present when those responses are made. Association is a common phenomenon. Being reminded of an experience by stimuli which were present during the experience is an example. The odor of burning wood may remind one of a Christmas vacation in the North woods. This common phenomenon has been known for a long time, but careful study of the conditions under which stimuli and responses are associated is recent. It really began with Pavlov's now classical conditioning experiments with salivation in dogs.

The association theorists and their descendants see learning as automatic, gradual, and as "forced upon" the organism by the external demands of reward and punishment; the field theorists, or the humanists, tend to see learning as dependent on the consciousness of the relationship involved in a particular situation, on the restructuring of the "field" of the learner.

CLASSICAL CONDITIONING

● PROBLEM 3-12

What is classical conditioning? Include a brief explanation of the principal terms used to describe a simple classical conditioning experiment (CS, UCS, CR and UCR).

Solution: Pavlovian, classical (because of Pavlov's now classic experiments) or, the term preferred by many today, respondent conditioning is a simple form of learning in which a subject is conditioned to respond to a new stimulus with an innate or a previously acquired response. In Pavlov's experiments with the salivating response of his dogs he established the basic methodology and terminology still used today in classical conditioning experiments. He knew dogs would salivate when they tasted food. Pavlov referred to the food as the unconditioned stimulus (UCS) because it naturally and consistently elicited salivation, which he called the unconditioned response (UCR).

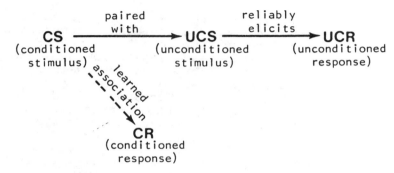

Diagram of classical conditioning.

Pavlov later taught dogs to salivate to light. This was accomplished by presenting a light just prior to presenting the food. After a series of such pairings, the dog would salivate to the light even before food was presented. In this case, the light was a conditioned stimulus (CS) and the salivation to the light was a conditioned response (CR). Pavlov found that he could condition many neutral stimuli to elicit a particular response by repeatedly pairing the neutral stimulus with an UCS.

In classical conditioning, then, the conditioned stimulus (CS) which elicits no response at first, and the unconditioned stimulus (UCS), which consistently evokes a particular response, are presented together to the subject for a number of trials. After some time, the unconditioned stimulus (UCS) can be removed and conditioned stimulus (CS) will elicit a response similar to the unconditioned response (UCR). The subject learns to respond to a stimulus in a way he had not responded before. The subject has been respondently or classically conditioned.

● **PROBLEM 3-13**

Give an overview of the historical development of classical conditioning.

Solution: As early as 1897, Ivan P. Pavlov (1849-1936), a Russian Nobel prize winner for work on the digestive process, virtually discovered the conditioned response and was the first to investigate it systematically. This phenomenon had been observed before but Pavlov was the first to appreciate its significance. Like many great discoveries, it appeared to be an accidental finding and didn't even seem like much of a discovery at the time. While studying the gastric secretions of dogs in his laboratory, Pavlov noticed that the sound of the footsteps of his associate (who fed the dogs) tended to evoke saliva flow in his dogs. What was curious and interesting to him was that the dogs salivated before the food was put in their mouths. It was of such great interest to him that he stopped his work on gastric secretions and began to study what he called "psychic secretions." He soon discontinued working with the footsteps as a stimulus and began to train his dogs to salivate to a tuning fork or a light.

The essential features of the reflex tradition to which Pavlov belonged have their roots in the work of Descartes, who in the seventeenth century introduced the concept of reflex to describe innate muscle responses following sensory stimuli. Later, Sechenov postulated that the brain operated as a mediator in the reflex process. He termed these "acquired reflexes." Pavlov, accepting Sechenov's definition of an "acquired reflex," saw the possible experimental operation for defining and investigating the "psychic" secretions of his dogs.

Pavlov's terminology is still regarded by investigators of learning as including the most basic descriptive units of behavior and are applicable even in learning paradigms other than classical conditioning. Among his contributions was the introduction of the following terms: conditioning, conditioned stimulus, unconditioned stimulus, reinforcement, stimulus generalization, extinction.

J. B. Watson built upon and expanded Pavlov's work. He applied conditioning principles to emotions, mental disease, language, and learning. In learning, Watson employed the concept of conditioning as a central theoretical construct in which complex learning was considered to be simply the chaining of conditioned reflexes.

The decade following Watson's initial writings saw the broad and largely speculative application of conditioning to a wide range of behaviors, extending from individual behavior to social action. During this period "conditioning" became synonymous with "association" until detailed descriptions of Pavlov's work and reports from more recent research conducted in American laboratories began to reveal the complexities of conditioning. At this time, the prevailing and popular views of the conditioning reflex as a unit of habit and as a substitute for association began to come under strong attack from scientific circles. Nevertheless, these initial views of conditioning have had a strong residual influence on American concepts of conditioning. Specifically, there is still a prevalent tendency to regard any phenomenon deemed associative in nature as "classical conditioning." This term, however, should be reserved for the actual theoretical accounting of such learning experiments (though analogs of classical conditioning from everyday experiences are helpful in initially understanding the phenomenon).

The frequent use of "classical conditioning" as a theoretical term without any substantial body of research using Pavlov's method created the illusion among researchers and the public that Pavlov's findings were complete and well substantiated, which was not true. Consequently, there was a relative neglect of research in classical conditioning until recently.

● **PROBLEM 3-14**

What is simultaneous conditioning? What has research indicated about this type of conditioning?

Solution: In the procedure used in respondent conditioning called simultaneous conditioning, the CS is presented continuously. Then, within five seconds of the onset of the CS, the UCS is presented. Finally, both stimuli terminate together. The classical Pavlov experiments in conditioning employ a simultaneous or nearly simultaneous presentation of the CS with the UCS. For example, a ticking metronome (CS) is turned on, and after 3 seconds a bit of food (UCS) is put in the mouth of the dog. The UCS, the food in the mouth, elicits salivation. After several trials or presentations of the CS and the UCS together, conditioning has taken place; the ticking metronome when presented alone will elicit salivation.

Nearly all possible time relations between the CS and the UCS have been used in conditioning research. Of all these various experimental time relations between the CS and the UCS, the simultaneous conditioning setup leads to the quickest and easiest learning of the CR. However, exact simultaneity of CS and UCS does not produce the fastest conditioning. Virtually all experimenters have reported that a delay of about 1/2 a second between the onset of a CS and the onset of a UCS produces the fastest learning. On either side of this interval, learning proceeds more slowly. This time relation, intriguing as it is, has thus far eluded complete explanation.

● PROBLEM 3-15

What is meant by the term "forward conditioning?" Discuss the two types of forward conditioning: trace and delay conditioning.

Solution: The exact temporal relation between the conditioned stimulus (CS) and the unconditioned stimulus (UCS) varies from experiment to experiment in respondent conditioning. The most frequently employed time relation between a conditioned stimulus (CS) and an unconditioned stimulus (UCS) is to present CS-UCS pairings in which the CS continues at least until the moment of onset of UCS. Traditionally, the relationship remains constant between each individual procedure, but intervals between the CS and the UCS are a potential area for research and have in fact been the subject of numerous learning experiments. One type of temporal relation between the CS and the UCS is called forward or temporal conditioning.

In forward conditioning, the onset of the CS precedes the onset of the UCS. Forward conditioning results in strong CS-produced responses. Also in forward conditioning, CR strength increases as the onset of CS occurs closer in time to the onset of the UCS. An optimal time interval exists between the CS onset and the UCS onset. Both relatively long and quite short time intervals between CS onset and UCS onset result in weaker CR's than otherwise.

Two types of forward conditioning are generally distinguished:

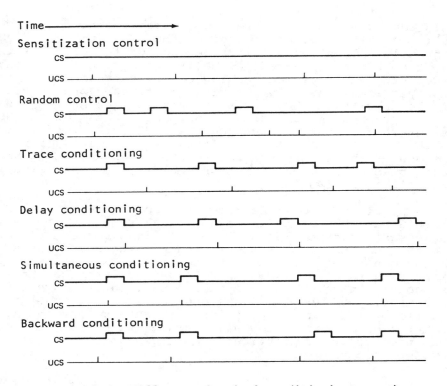

Time——————————————————▶
Sensitization control
CS
UCS

Random control
CS
UCS

Trace conditioning
CS
UCS

Delay conditioning
CS
UCS

Simultaneous conditioning
CS
UCS

Backward conditioning
CS
UCS

Diagrams of the different classical-conditioning procedures.
Upward deflections of the lines represent the onset of a
stimulus, and a flat line means that no stimulus is being
presented.

1. Delayed conditioning: Any procedure by which the CS
   is presented for more than five seconds before the
   start of the UCS is called delayed conditioning. In
   this method, the two stimuli still overlap in time,
   and they still terminate together. After conditioning, the CS elicits the response at about the time
   when the UCS used to occur during conditioning.
   Therefore, any forward conditioning in which the CS
   terminates at the onset of the UCS or later is referred to as delayed conditioning.

2. Trace conditioning: Trace conditioning is forward
   conditioning in which the CS terminates prior to the
   onset of the UCS. In trace conditioning, the CS is
   presented for a brief period of time and is then
   turned off. After a pause, the UCS is presented.
   After trace conditioning, the CR will not follow the
   CS immediately, but will occur at about the same time
   after the end of the CS as the UCS did during conditioning.

● PROBLEM 3-16

Describe a backward conditioning procedure. What is the
usual effect of this kind of conditioning? Include an
explanation of inhibitory conditioning.

Solution: In backward conditioning, the CS is presented after the UCS. Backward conditioning is not very effective, if at all. In fact, backward conditioning procedures typically result in what is called inhibitory conditioning.

In a classical experiment, backward conditioning would take place if a light (CS) would be turned on shortly after the food (UCS) was delivered to the dog. This procedure has shown that "no particular event" (CR) will occur while and/or soon after the CS occurs.

Further, the presentation of a CS without a UCS immediately following impairs future efforts to induce acquisition of typical classical conditioning between that same CS and UCS, and actually decreases the strength of a CR produced by another CS paired with the same UCS. Presenting a light after the food was given to a dog inhibits a future learned response to the light, even if it was presented simultaneously with the food. It would also weaken the response to another stimulus, for instance, a bell presented with the food. This effect is referred to as inhibitory conditioning. To differentiate between this type of conditioning and typical classical conditioning, typical classical conditioning (when a response is actually elicited) is frequently described as excitatory conditioning.

● **PROBLEM** 3-17

What is higher-order (second-order) conditioning?

Solution: Higher-order conditioning is based on secondary reinforcement. Primary reinforcement is the pairing of the conditioned stimulus with the unconditioned stimulus. That is, the conditioned response follows the conditioned stimulus in anticipation of the unconditioned stimulus. The presentation of the unconditioned stimulus following the response is called primary reinforcement. In secondary reinforcement a neutral stimulus is paired with the conditioned stimulus after that conditioned stimulus can reliably elicit the conditioned response. When this is accomplished the new or second conditioned stimulus will elicit the conditioned response even though it was never directly paired with the unconditioned stimulus.

Higher-order conditioning can be exemplified by a Pavlovian experiment. In his original experiment Pavlov used the sound of a metronome as the conditioned stimulus. A few moments after the metronome had been turned on, Pavlov gave the dog meat powder. Soon the dog began to salivate when he heard the metronome. In the higher-order conditioning experiment Pavlov used a card with a black square on it as the second neutral stimulus. He presented the card with the black square to the dog before the metronome was turned on (note: the metronome was already able to elicit the conditioned response). No meat powder followed the sound of the metronome, however. Despite this, the response to the metronome had been so strongly reinforced previously that the card with the black square was able to elicit salivation after only a few pairings with the sound of the metronome. Usually it is not possible to execute a third stage of conditioning since the original conditioned stimulus and the second conditioned stimulus are no longer followed by the unconditioned stimulus; therefore the conditioned response will be extinguished. All conditioned responses are eventually extinguished if they are not reinforced.

Higher-order conditioning is important because it may help explain the complex forms of learning that simple classical conditioning has not accounted for.

● **PROBLEM** 3-18

If, after a conditioned response has been acquired, the procedure is changed so that the CS is repeatedly presented without being followed by the UCS, what is the result?

Solution: Extinction of conditioned respondent behavior occurs when the CS is presented without the UCS a number of times. The magnitude of the response elicited by the CS and the percentage of presentations of the CS which elicit responses gradually decreases as the CS continues to be presented without the UCS. If presentations of the CS alone continue, CR strength declines to at least the level present before classical conditioning was begun.

Everyday experiences illustrate the importance of extinguishing fears soon after they are acquired. Otherwise, the fear may not only become deeply-rooted but it may also generalize to other areas. Soon after a driver is in a car accident he is encouraged to resume driving as soon as possible. A man thrown from a horse is advised to get right back on the saddle before a single incident develops into something more serious.

Extinction of a CR can be seen as a learned response; the change in response to the CS is a relatively permanent one and extinction does not affect responses to a wide variety of stimuli. The extinction process for classical conditioning is quite similar to the process for establishing classical conditioning. Both involve one stimulus, the CS, being followed independently of responding by a second stimulus; for extinction, the second stimulus may be thought of as "no particular event." The offset of a stimulus, the occurence of no particular event, serves as a CS. Then according to the definition of classical conditioning, extinction of the CR is an instance of classical conditioning. Another theory, however, states that extinction is only inhibition of the previously learned response.

● **PROBLEM** 3-19

What observations support the inhibition of response theory of extinction?

Solution: Pavlov believed that CR's were only inhibited during extinction; they were not irretrievably lost. Experiments in which a novel or unexpected stimulus is intro-

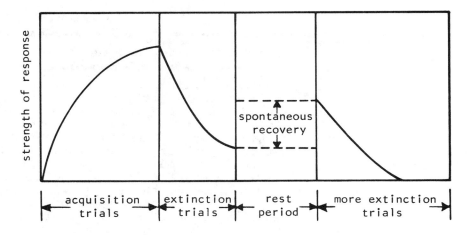

A schematic diagram of the course of acquisition,
extinction, and spontaneous recovery. Within limits
the longer the rest period, the greater the degree
of spontaneous recovery.

duced while the experimenter is trying to extinguish a conditioned response tend to support his belief. These experiments show a temporary increase in the strength of the fal-
tering conditioned response (CR) occurs with the introduction of a novel stimulus. (For this reason, he gave the
name "disinhibition" to the sudden rise in the strength of
the CR undergoing extinction.)

Conditioned behavior can later reappear without additional conditioning, even though extinction had appeared to
be successful. This is known as spontaneous recovery. If
a rest interval follows the extinction of a CR, it will
reappear spontaneously but in a somewhat weaker form. Then,
if conditioning is done again using the same stimuli, the
original response will be strengthened quickly. In
fact, reconditioning is a faster process than original conditioning. As Pavlov argued, the CR is never completely
extinguished, it is only blocked from being actively produced by the new conditioning.

Spontaneous recovery was first studied experimentally
during the extinction of a CR. A CR had been extinguished
and the animal was taken out of harness and out of the experimental situation for a reasonable period of time. When
the animal was brought back to the experimental situation
and presented with the CS, his CR reappeared spontaneously,
though at half its strength prior to extinction. It was
also found that if an animal is continually put through the
cycle of extinction and recovery, the spontaneous recovery
that occurs becomes less and less at each trial. Eventually,
the response will not recover at all.

Though the above discussion supports the theory that
extinction is an inhibition of a learned response, there
is usually no basis for selecting this inhibition of response theory over the counter conditioning theory which
states that the new competing response replaces the original
learned response.

What are habituation, latent inhibition and facilitation?

Solution: Habituation (or adaptation) refers to a decrease
in response to a repeatedly presented or constant stimulus.
The response can be measured either physiologically or behaviorally. An example of habituation is the decrement in
awareness to a loudly ticking clock. When someone enters
the room and notices that the clock is ticking loudly he may
find the clock to be an annoying stimulus. However, after a
short period of time, he will habituate to the loud ticking;
he will not notice the ticking and it therefore will fail
to annoy him further. Of course, the phenomenon of habituation occurs only with fairly innocuous and low-level stimuli; it can even occur in cases involving fairly intense
stimuli, but it will take longer for the organism to habituate.

   Latent-inhibition refers to the decrease in the effectiveness of classical conditioning that results when a subject receives prior, nonreinforced exposure to the conditioned stimulus. For example, if a rat is periodically exposed to a tone but receives no reinforcement for any response, it will habituate to the tone; the rat will learn
to effectively ignore the tone. If the experimenter then
tries to classically condition the rat with the tone he may
not be very successful. For instance, if he wanted to have
the rat associate the tone with the presentation of an electric shock and to respond to the tone by avoiding the particular object that transmitted the shock he would find that
the rat would take much longer to avoid the object than a
rat who had not received prior, non-reinforced exposure to
the conditioned stimulus. This phenomenon is referred to
as latent-inhibition. Latent-inhibition is an important
learning principle in animals as well as people. It is important that a subject not be habituated to a stimulus that
will be used in a learning procedure; the use of such a
stimulus would impair the learning process.

   Facilitation (or potentiation) refers to the increase
in responding that occurs after repeated presentations of a
given stimulus. This process, which has also been called
sensitization, occurs more frequently with aversive stimuli.

   Habituation and facilitation do not cause permanent
changes in behavior. After a period of time has elapsed
since the stimulus was last presented, responding will return to the level it was at before conditioning took place.

OPERANT CONDITIONING

What is operant conditioning?

Solution: Operant conditioning is a learning process in

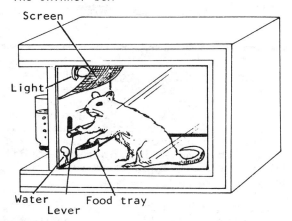

The Skinner box

The experimental chamber called the Skinner box is used for
many studies of operant conditioning. When the rat pushes
the lever, a pellet of food automatically drops into the food
tray.

which the frequency of a specific response is shaped and
maintained by the consequences of the response. The basic
format of the research in this area is to gather information about behavior from the systematic study of the effects of behavior on environment.

This type of conditioning process was formulated
initially in the works of John Watson but the biggest contributor is B. F. Skinner. Skinner began by studying the
variables which are crucial in the shaping and maintaining
of animal behavior. Through careful experimentation Skinner developed guidelines for operant conditioning, and this
work was soon extended to include human subjects.

In the typical operant conditioning process, the organism is signalled to perform a specific response. When
the response is performed the organism is reinforced--it is
given something that it was previously deprived (as food or
water). Through a process known as shaping (or differential reinforcement of successive approximations) the organism learns the exact response required for the reinforcer.
For the specific demonstration of such a process, Skinner
developed an apparatus designed to give a signal to the
organism, a means of responding to the signal, and a method
of delivering the reinforcement. This device is nicknamed
"the Skinner box." The figure gives a general idea of what
such an apparatus looks like.

Skinner also developed an apparatus known as the cumulative recorder. This machine provides a graph of the
total number of responses made in a certain period of time.
The purpose of the recorder is to study the rate of response frequency as a function of both time and noted
events (such as the delivery of reinforcement).

Discuss briefly the historical development of operant conditioning.

Solution: Operant conditioning began with E. L. Thorndike's Law of Effect, which states that responses may be altered depending on the effects they produce in the environment. At about the same time Thorndike was conducting his experiments at Columbia University, Small introduced the maze as a learning instrument for animals. The maze soon became standard equipment for operant conditioning experiments and has probably been used more than any other type of learning problem.

The first systematic study of operant conditioning was made by B. F. Skinner in 1938. He developed an apparatus (now known as the "Skinner box" second only to the maze as standard equipment in learning experiments) which consisted of a small enclosure with a lever device and a food receptacle. A hungry rat was placed in the box, and in time usually pressed the lever by chance, and automatically received food (a reward). After some time, most of the rats learned to make this response (lever-pressing) as soon as they entered the box. This learning was termed operant conditioning because the animal had to perform an operation to get a reward.

Skinner later applied the techniques of OC to the development of teaching machines. In recent years, Skinner's attention has extended to philosophical issues based on his operant conditioning theory, the result being the book Beyond Freedom and Dignity in which he subscribes to the doctrine of determinism. From his laboratory experiments with rats he has come to the belief that societies as well as individuals can be controlled.

In the past two decades the number of operant conditioning psychologists has increased more than in any other area of psychology. As the operant movement grows, the field for research is constantly expanding.

● **PROBLEM 3-23**

Define shaping and chaining, give an example of each.

Solution: Shaping and chaining are principles involved in the operant conditioning theory of learning.

Chaining is a series of responses in which each response leads to the next. Learning the words to a song is an example of the chaining of responses. A person may learn one line and then the next. In this sequence the termination of one line, together with the melody, serves as a stimulus for the next line. In this way, the sequence of responses becomes very important, as one can see by trying to start singing in the middle of a song.

Teaching a rat to press a bar for food pellets.

The rat is first rewarded with food for movements in the general
vicinity of the bar; and then rewarded only when it places its
forepaws on the bar and finally activates the bar by pressing
down on it. During shaping, before the rat begins to press the
bar, the experimenter watches the animal and delivers reinforcement with a manually operated switch.

The chaining of responses is possible only when each
link in the chain is available. If this is not the case,
each response must be established independently.

The shaping of responses is the teaching of behavior
by reinforcing successively closer approximations to the
desired behavior until the desired response is attained.
Teaching a dog to fetch a stick is an example of shaping.
At first, the trainer may reward the dog for just approaching the stick. Then, the reinforcement may be contingent
on picking up the stick, and later, a reward may be given
only for carrying the stick toward the trainer. In this
way, the behavior is shaped gradually until it reaches the
desired form.

● **PROBLEM 3-24**

Discuss four types of partial reinforcement schedules and
their effects on response. Illustrate your answer with
graphs.

Solution: Time plays an important role in operant conditioning. The schedule or rate of reinforcement has a profound effect on the rate of response and must be carefully
considered in any discussion or explanation of operant behavior.

The continuous reinforcement schedule, where each correct response is reinforced, is sometimes used but more commonly, experiments in operant conditioning establish partial
reinforcement schedules which either:

1) Vary the frequency of the reward strictly according
    to time intervals. These are called interval sched-
    ules. The number of responses is irrelevant.

2) Vary the frequency of the reward according to the rate

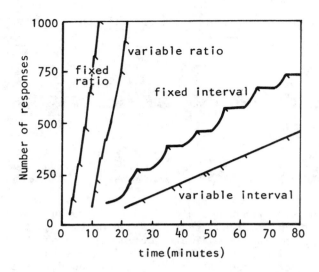

of response. These are ratio schedules. Time is irrelevant.

Within these two types of schedules a reward is administered
on either:

1) A regular basis, called a fixed schedule;

2) Or in an intermittent manner, called a variable
   schedule.

Combinations of these schedules yield four basic kinds of
partial reinforcement schedules:

1) A fixed-ratio schedule: Reinforcement is given after
a set number of responses are emitted. Use of this schedule
produces a strong, durable response pattern, though response
tends to drop off immediately after reinforcement. Pay
given after a certain number of garments are sewn or a certain quantity of baskets of fruit are picked is an example
of a fixed-ratio schedule. The employees work quite rapidly
but there is usually a pause before beginning each section
of work.

2) A variable-ratio schedule: The number of responses
required before reinforcement is given is intermittent and
irregular. This type of schedule produces the highest rates
of performance. Response continues at a high, nearly constant rate, sometimes approaching the maximum physical capabilities of the organism. Slot machines provide an example
of this type of schedule; the gambler never knows when he
will receive the reward. Dishonest gamblers also hook their
victim with this type of schedule; at first the opponent is
allowed to win fairly often. Eventually, however, he continues to play even when he is not winning at all.

3) A fixed-interval schedule: Reinforcement occurs after
a certain fixed period of time. No matter how much work is
done, reinforcement is given after a set period of time.
This schedule has the lowest yield in terms of performance.
However, just before reinforcement time, activity increases.

Most people with salaried positions are reinforced with a weekly or monthly check and are operating on a fixed-interval schedule.

4) A variable-interval schedule: This schedule varies the amount of time that must elapse before a response is rewarded. This schedule tends to have consistent performance but a slightly lower frequency than a variable-ratio schedule. Trying to call a busy number is an example of this type of schedule. No matter how often you try, the amount of time (variable) that the line is busy determines when you will be rewarded (reaching the person you wished to speak with).

The table demonstrates a hypothetical response measure for each of the four above-mentioned schedules and for continuous reinforcement. Though continuous reinforcement is the fastest way to learn, it is least effective for long-term learning because a rigid expectation of reward is set up, and extinction of the learned response will be rapid when reinforcements are eliminated.

● **PROBLEM** 3-25

What is the difference between the trial and error method and the successive method of approximation? Why is the method of successive approximation more efficient for learning motor skills than the trial and error method?

Solution: Learning by trial and error involves the selection of successive acts or behaviors which may or may not lead to the attainment of the goal. An individual performs one act after another until the act is effective in attaining the goal. If the first act doesn't bring about the desired end, it is discarded and another one is tried in its place. Finally, one act or response will be found to deliver the desired goal. The individual has thus learned the appropriate act or response by experience. An example of this form of learning is seen when a small child wants to eat cookies from a box. First he tries to pull the box apart. Next he tries to jump on the box. He may even throw the box on the floor. Finally, he cries for help and his mother comes to open the box. He has learned through trial and error that the most successful way to open the box is to cry for help.

The trial and error method is not efficient for learning complex motor skills because the correct responses may occur very infrequently. It would be very dangerous, for example, to allow a first-time flyer to pilot a plane by trial and error. An effective way of learning motor skills is by the method of differential reinforcement of successive approximations.

This method involves the reinforcement of acts similar to the desired one (an approximation). The method involves differential reinforcement, that is, the same act is not continually reinforced; during each successive trial reinforcement is given only if the subject engages in an act that more closely resembles the desired act. As the training proceeds, closer and closer approximations to the desired goal are required for reinforcement. Learning becomes a series of gradual steps. For the airplane pilot, this means beginning his training on the ground at school, progressing to working controls in a plane on the ground, moving to simple training planes and finally attempting more difficult combat or passenger planes. If he attempted to fly initially in a combat plane, simple trial and error methods would be extremely dangerous.

● **PROBLEM 3-26**

What is autonomic conditioning?

Solution: Autonomic conditioning refers to the operant conditioning of autonomic responses such as heart rate and intestinal contractions. Through conditioning, a subject could alter the rate of an autonomic response. It was known for a long time that autonomic responses could be classically conditioned but it was believed that they could not be operantly conditioned until 1969 when Miller's experiment proved otherwise.

Miller implanted electrodes in the "pleasure centers" of rats' brains. When these electrodes were activated the rat experienced pleasure; that is, he was rewarded. Miller divided the rats into four groups. He monitored the heart rates and intestinal contractions of all four groups. When rats in the first group were observed to have an increased heart rate they were rewarded; that is, the electrode was activated. The second group was reinforced for low heart rate. The third group was rewarded for intestinal contraction and the fourth group for intestinal relaxation. It was found that the four groups' autonomic responses changed remarkably. The first group had a higher heartbeat, the second a lower heartbeat; both had normal intestinal contractions. The third group's rate of intestinal contractions increased while the fourth group's rate decreased; both groups exhibited normal heart rates. Miller's experiment showed that autonomic responses could be operantly conditioned. The experiment encouraged research in a new field. Experimenters are now searching for cures to disorders like high blood pressure through operant conditioning procedures.

● **PROBLEM 3-27**

List and define the three behavior control systems promulgated by Bandura (1969).

Solution: In his attempt to integrate all the knowledge about learning, Bandura (1969) devised a theory stating that behavior is controlled by one of three systems--hence, the derived term "behavior control system." According to the theory, behavior is controlled by external stimuli, by their consequences or by internal (symbolic) processes.

External stimuli that initiate behavior are the first
type of the behavior control system. Reflexive behavior
produced by environmental stimuli falls into this category.
For example, sneezing from dust in the air, or coughing
from smoke inhalation is behavior that is controlled by
external stimuli. In addition, stimuli that come to be
associated with stimuli which directly yield responses
(conditioned stimuli), also produce responses and fall into this category. For example, an individual may blink his
eyes every time a puff of air is blown into them. If a
buzzer precedes every puff of air into the eyes, the person
will eventually come to blink at the sound of the buzzer
alone. In this case, an external stimulus becomes meaningful through the process of classical conditioning. Other
behaviors that are controlled by external stimuli include
responses controlled by stimuli present at the time of
reinforcement or punishment. Through this, a child learns
the appropriateness of certain behaviors. He may be reinforced for a certain behavior in one situation and punished
for the same behavior in another. For example, he comes to
learn that it is acceptable to laugh and scream in a play-
ground but not during a funeral.

The second type of behavior control system that Bandura
describes refers to behavior controlled by its consequences.
Such behavior is the result of operant conditioning. In
this process, an individual emits a behavior that is reinforced, either positively or negatively. However, this
control system does not only include a single act of reinforcement, but all reinforcing feedback that one receives
concerning the appropriateness of the behavior. This feedback will affect future behavior.

The third type of behavior control system is controlled
by internal (symbolic) processes. Man has the ability to
visualize or predict the outcomes and long-range consequences
of various behaviors. Working toward some distant goal such
as a car or house is characteristic of this type of control
system.

This level of behavior is most frequently found in
adults and adolescents since it requires a certain level of
maturation. Infants and pre-schoolers are not capable of
setting long-range goals for themselves. Rule internalization, which is another aspect of this control system, also
requires a degree of maturation.

In theory, human behavior is controlled by one of the
three systems described above, but in practice, most behavior results from a combination of two or all three of these
systems.

CLASSICAL VS. OPERANT CONDITIONING

● PROBLEM 3-28

Describe the differences between classical and operant
conditioning.

Distictions Between Classical Conditioning and Operant Conditioning

Classical Conditioning	Operant Conditioning
Behavior affected is usually experienced as involuntary-for example, reflexes (knee jerk, salivation, eye blink), feelings (fear, anxiety).	Behavior affected is usually experienced as voluntary-for example, actions (bar press), thoughts (plans for action).
Key events (unconditioned and conditioned stimuli) are presented to the organism.	Key events (reinforcement and punishment) are produced by the organism's behavior.
Those events elicit the behavior; that is, they directly evoke it.	Those events control the behavior; that is, they determine how often the organism emits it.
In the absence of key stimuli, the behavior does not occur.	In the absence of specific stimuli, the behavior does occur; the the effect of discriminative stimuli is to alter its frequency.

Solution: Classical and operant conditioning may seem quite similar: both are forms of conditioning, if one withholds the reinforcement or UCS, extinction occurs. Stimulus generalization, discrimination, spontaneous recovery, and higher-order conditioning are properties of both. Indeed the similarities are great; in fact, both types of conditioning are not necessarily mutually exclusive.

The differences, however, are significant. Most of these are procedural in nature.

1. In CC the occurrence of a CR is reflexively forced by the UCS (e.g., salivation); in OC the response is more voluntary (pressing a bar).

2. In CC the UCS occurs without regard to the subject's behavior; in OC the reward is contingent on the occurrence of a response.

3. CC is preparatory or anticipatory; OC serves to emphasize or guide an organism which already has certain critical responses available.

4. In CC the UCS is the reinforcing stimulus that maintains a response through consistent pairing with a previously neutral stimulus, the CS precedes the UCS; in OC the UCS consists of an incentive, positive or negative, that follows the behavior that is the object of conditioning.

5. In CC the UCS occurs or does not occur independently of whether the CR is made; in OC the reinforcing stimulus is response-contingent.

6. CC is more concerned with what makes one respond and OC focuses on how one responds.

7. Elicited responses represent only a small proportion of the behavior of higher organisms. The remaining

behavior is operant.

8. In CC responses are elicited; in operant conditioning they are emitted.

● **PROBLEM** 3-29

Distinguish between classical and operant conditioning, describing a typical experiment involving each. What is higher-order conditioning?

Solution: Conditioning is the term used by psychologists to explain the process by which we develop behavior patterns. Through exposure to certain conditions we develop patterns of response. Careful investigation has made it possible to distinguish between different types of conditioning.

Classical conditioning was the first type to be systematically observed and investigated. Ivan Pavlov, a Russian conducting research on digestion in dogs, noticed that his dogs, who were regularly fed by his assistant, began to salivate at the sight of the assistant (salivation is a response that usually occurs when the actual food is presented). To investigate this phenomenon, Pavlov consistently rang a bell before the dogs were fed. Eventually, after this sequence of events had occurred several times, the dogs salivated to the sound of the bell, even if no food was given. Thus, the dog had learned a new association, that between the bell and the food. Previously, they had salivated only to the food, after conditioning they salivated to either.

Classical conditioning is the process of substituting one stimulus for another to evoke an innate or a previously learned response. A non-laboratory example illustrating this is the response a person has when he meets someone who reminds him of someone else he knows. Most likely, he will have a similar emotional response to the new person as he does to the more familiar person. He has been classically conditioned to respond to the new stimulus as he did to the old.

Another kind of conditioning, observed initially by B. F. Skinner, is operant conditioning. He found that by putting a white rat in a box with a lever that delivered a food pellet when inadvertently pressed, the rat would gradually begin to press the lever more often, even if food was not forthcoming for long periods of time. The rat had learned an association between his response (pushing the lever) and his satisfaction (food pellet).

In operant conditioning the organism learns to "operate" in his environment to either produce, remove or avoid certain stimuli. The outcome of a situation depends entirely on the organism's response. For example, a pigeon will get food if he pecks a key, a rat can escape shock by pressing a lever and a rat can avoid shock altogether by pressing a lever just before it is scheduled to occur again. In all of these

cases, the organism exerts control over his environment.
Rewards and punishments serve to increase or decrease the
probability of a response occurring again. Whenever someone teaches a dog to do tricks, a child to read, ride a bike
or be polite, he may be using operant conditioning. In
these cases he rewards the dog or child for doing what he
wishes with either a doggie bone, a candy or simply his approval. In addition, the immediate pleasurable sensations
received as a person first imbibes alcohol, drugs or has a
cigarette are thought to be instrumental in the development
of habituation to these substances. Thus, certain forms of
addiction can be explained through operant conditioning.

   In summary, classical conditioning is concerned more
with what makes one respond; only the stimulus changes in
classical conditioning experiments, and one learns to give
a familiar response to a new stimulus. Whereas, in operant conditioning a particular behavior occurs at random and
is then either purposely or accidentally accompanied by a
reward which tends to make its occurrence a greater possibility. Experiments in operant conditioning focus more on
how one responds.

   Higher-order conditioning can be observed in both
classical and operant conditioning. In classical conditioning, a dog that has already been taught to salivate
to a bell can, through higher-order conditioning, be taught
to salivate to a tone. The experimenter accomplishes this
by consistently presenting the tone just before the bell.
The dog will associate the tone with the bell and the bell
with the food so that the tone will acquire the power to
elicit salivation.

   Higher-order conditioning is seen in operant conditioning when, as in classical conditioning, an organism
associates one stimulus with another stimulus that has been
reinforced. For example, a rat may first press a lever to
receive food. This food delivery is preceded by a sound.
After the lever-pressing response has been extinguished
(by not presenting food when the lever is pressed for a
number of trials), the organism will press the lever anyway if the sound is presented again.

● **PROBLEM** 3-30

What function does time have in classical and operant
conditioning?

Solution: Both classical and operant conditioning depend
on temporal contiguity--events occurring close to one another in time. In classical conditioning, the CS and UCS
must be in temporal contiguity and in operant conditioning
the reward must follow closely after the desired response.

   The optimal time interval depends on the type of response involved. The interval between response and reward
is relatively shorter for an eye-blink response than it is
for a bar-pressing response.

Though it had been expected that delay of gratification (reward) in operant conditioning would hinder performance, this has not always been found to be true. Some researchers have hypothesized that the delay effect is related to the concept of secondary reinforcement. Experimentation has supported this hypothesis by showing that during the delay an organism is often in the presence of stimuli which have been associated with the primary reinforcement, thus giving no impairment of learning.

AVERSIVE CONTROL

● **PROBLEM** 3-31

What is aversive conditioning? Include a description of escape conditioning and avoidance conditioning (both active and passive) in your answer.

Shuttle box used in training dogs to avoid traumatic shock.
(A tone or a light can be used as a conditioned stimulus.)

Solution: One type of conditioning deals with the administration of aversive or negative stimuli to control behavior. Aversive conditioning or control maintains behavior by withdrawing aversive stimuli. Aversive stimuli are stimuli whose withdrawal increases the rate of responding.

There are two main types of conditioning that employ aversive stimuli to control behavior: 1) In escape conditioning the subject responds in order to terminate an aversive stimulus after it has begun. A rat is given an electric shock whenever he steps on a certain section of his box; as he leaps over a hurdle to another section, he escapes the shock. 2) In avoidance conditioning the subject's response to a neutral stimulus delays the occurrence of an aversive stimulus. For instance, a light is presented and followed in 30 seconds by a shock or loud blast. If the subject emits a desired response during the light flashing the aversive stimulus does not occur.

Eventually, to maintain avoidance behavior, only the neutral stimulus needs to be presented. The aversive stimulus (shock) needs to occur, intermittently, to reinforce the avoidance and maintain the behavior. Whenever the subject fails to respond in time to the neutral stimulus (light) the aversive stimulus (shock) is applied and reinforces responding to the neutral stimulus. A simple human behavior pattern resulting from avoidance condition-

ing is the application of suntan lotion. A sunburn is the
aversive stimulus. If one applies the suntan lotion before
going to the beach, one avoids the sunburn. Should one go
to the beach one day without applying the lotion and receive a sunburn, the motivation to apply the suntan lotion
the next time one thinks of going to the beach will be
greater.

Avoidance conditioning can produce either active
avoidance in which the organism must demonstrate a certain
response--for instance, jumping over a bar or pressing a
lever, or passive avoidance in which the organism must not
respond--not press a lever, or step on a section of the box
--in order to avoid the aversive stimulus.

Few control or aversive conditioning procedures can be
viewed as entirely positive, since an experimenter deprives
an animal of food or drink or administers shocks and imposes
discomfort on it. For this reason, fewer experiments that
use aversive conditioning techniques are reported. Still
it is a fact of life that one is subject to aversive con-
ditioning--lack of food, drink, bad weather, disapproval
of peers and rejection, are all aversive stimuli which
everyone is conditioned to try to avoid or escape from as
soon as possible.

● **PROBLEM 3-32**

Define punishment. How does it differ from negative reinforcement?

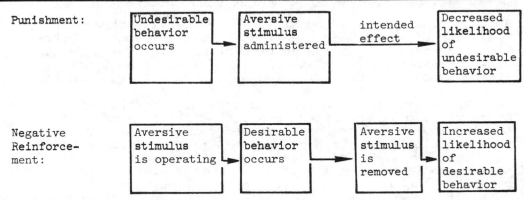

Solution: Punishment is a technique used to decrease the
likelihood of a particular response. It involves the administration of an unpleasant stimulus contingent upon the
occurrence of a certain undesirable behavior. Sending a
man to jail for robbing a bank is an example of punishment.
Robbing a bank is considered an undesirable behavior. Incarceration is an aversive or unpleasant stimulus. By administering the unpleasant stimulus (sending the man to
jail) contingent upon the occurrence of the undesirable behavior (robbing a bank), society hopes to decrease the
strength of this response (robbing banks).

In contrast to punishment, negative reinforcement is

used to increase the likelihood of a certain behavior. In punishment, an aversive stimulus is administered. In negative reinforcement, it is removed. In learning theory terms, negative reinforcement involves the termination of an aversive stimulus contingent upon the occurrence of a desired behavior. Giving a prisoner time off for good behavior is an example of negative reinforcement. The aversive stimulus (incarceration) is terminated if the desirable behavior (obedience to rules and regulations of the prison) occurs, thereby increasing the likelihood of the behavior (obedience).

● **PROBLEM** 3-33

Discuss the relationship between punishment and extinction.

Solution: Extinction and punishment are used with varying success to eliminate particular behaviors. Extinction can operate in both classical and operant conditioning situations. In the former, it involves the presentation of the conditioned stimulus without the unconditioned stimulus. In the latter, a learned response is no longer reinforced. Punishment involves the administration of an unpleasant stimulus following a certain behavior. One might assume that extinction and punishment, if used together, would be more effective in the elimination of behaviors than either one used alone. Experimental evidence has shown that this is not the case.

Consider a typical escape training procedure. An apparatus that contains a starting box, runway, and goal box is used. A gate separates the starting box from the runway. When the gate opens, a shock is delivered from the floor of the starting box and the runway. There is no shock in the goal box. A rat placed in the starting box of such an apparatus will learn to run out of that box when the gate opens, then down the runway until it reaches the goal box. Thus, the animal learns to escape the shock.

To extinguish this escape response, the experimenter can cease shocking the animal when the gate is opened. The first few times that the gate is opened and no shock is administered, the rat will run to the goal. This is because the open gate has been paired with the unconditioned stimulus (shock), resulting in the opened gate becoming a conditioned stimulus. (Running to the goal box is the unconditioned response.) When the conditioned stimulus is presented, it will elicit a conditioned response (running to the goal). After a few trials, however, if the unconditioned stimulus is not present, the conditioned response will be eliminated.

Suppose that, while the conditioned response is being extinguished, the animal is also being punished for running into the goal compartment. In such a situation, the gate would open, and the rat would not receive a shock. As it entered the goal compartment, he would be shocked. It would seem logical to assume that the elimination of the running behavior would be more rapid, that there would be an additive effect between the two procedures. This is not necessarily the case. In fact, it has been found that under certain conditions, the use of punishment in conjunction with extinction may actually decrease the effectiveness of the extinction procedure. This is just one of the many difficulties that have been found in the use of punishment as a technique of behavior change.

● **PROBLEM** 3-34

How effective is punishment in eliminating unwanted behavior?

Solution: Although there is conflicting evidence, it is generally accepted that punishment very often is effective in the elimination of undesirable behavior.

Several studies show that the intensity of the unpleasant stimuli is an important factor. Stimuli which are only mildly aversive usually have no effect; moderately aversive stimuli serve to reduce the rate of responding; and extremely intense, harsh, punishment eliminates the behavior completely and permanently.

It is important to note that punishment does more than suppress a response. Punishment is also a stimulus itself, it becomes associated with responses such as anxiety, fear, and pain. Permanent behavior change is not exclusively a result of harsh punishment. When moderate punishment is supplemented by the opportunity to learn new acceptable responses, permanent change usually occurs. This has been demonstrated in experiments with animals and human beings.

● **PROBLEM** 3-35

What is B. F. Skinner's view on the effectiveness of punishment?

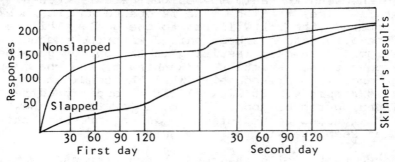

Solution: B. F. Skinner, writing in Science and Human Behavior (1953), described punishment as the "commonest technique of control in modern life." Despite its extensive usage, Skinner believes that punishment is not only ineffective as a means of control, but that it actually works to the ultimate disadvantage of the punishing agency and the individual being punished.

Punishment, Skinner states, certainly does have an immediate effect in reducing the likelihood of a certain response. The short-term effectiveness of punishment is misleading--the suppression of behavior is often a temporary state. As animal experiments have revealed, punishment will not permanently eliminate the behavior.

Punishment then, is not effective in the long run as a means of control. Its use is made even more questionable by the harmful side effects which accompany it. Skinner discusses a variety of "unfortunate by-products" of punishment. Punishment, for example, may develop fear and anxiety in the punished individual. This can lead to interference with the individual's adaptation to daily life. In extreme cases, it may incapacitate the individual. The subject may eventually demonstrate little or no interest in food, sex, or practical or creative activities. The emotional by-products can actually damage the individual's physical health, leading to disorders of the digestive system, allergic reactions or other medical difficulties.

On the other hand, punishment can also damage the controlling agency. The punished individual may counterattack the punishing agent. He may act violently, as teenagers do when they defy authority by destroying school property. The individual doesn't always exhibit violent behavior, he may engage in passive resistance instead. The child who cannot avoid parental control, may become stubborn. The employee who cannot overtly revolt or vandalize, may decrease his production.

Skinner recommends that society seek alternatives to punishment in order to change behavior. Behavior may be eliminated by allowing it to follow its developmental schedule. As children develop, for example, they will normally outgrow certain bothersome behaviors. One should consider, Skinner states, not punishing the child for such behaviors, but allowing them to terminate in accordance with their natural course. Extinction, Skinner claims, is probably the most effective alternative. A parent, for example, should ignore objectionable behavior on the part of the child. The objectionable behavior will gradually cease.

In summary, Skinner believes that civilized man can increase his happiness by eliminating the use of punishment, a technique of control which is both ineffective and harmful.

SHORT ANSWER QUESTIONS FOR REVIEW

Choose the correct answer.

1. Pavlov believed that "neurosis" could be pro-
    duced experimentally by frustrating an animal
    during the process of: (a) reconditioning
    (b) extinction (c) conditioned discrimina-
    tion (d) stimulus generalization

    c

2. Avoidance learning is characterized by (a)
    slow extinction (b) rapid extinction (c)
    response suppression (d) response recovery

    a

3. The instrumental conditioning term "Reinforce-
    ment" is linked closely to the concept of (a)
    latent learning (b) observational learning
    (c) perceptual learning (d) law of effect

    d

4. Immediately subsequent to the elimination of an
    instrumental reward, an animal's responses (a)
    decrease in frequency (b) increase in fre-
    quency (c) the frequency remains constant
    (d) spontaneous recovery occurs

    b

5. When the UCS is presented prior to the CS,
    backward conditioning takes place, this is
    noted for (a) reversal of UCR and CR sequen-
    ces (b) confusion and fear in animals (c)
    powerful conditioning (d) weak conditioning

    b

6. Temporal conditioning (a) is synonymous with
    trace conditioning (b) is synonymous with de-
    layed conditioning (c) is synonymous with si-
    multaneous conditioning (d) presents the UCS
    on a fixed time schedule (e) utilizes a CS
    that is inherently self-rewarding

    d

7. In a case where a person has intense fear of
    small rooms, the room serves as a (a) UCS
    (b) CS (c) CR (d) UCR (e) S(delta)

    a

8. The most classical conditioning can be expected
    to occur (a) when the UCS precedes the CS by
    one-half second (b) when the CS precedes the
    UCS by two seconds (c) when the UCS precedes
    the CS by two seconds (d) when the CS pre-
    cedes the UCS by one-half second (e) when the
    CS precedes the UCS by five seconds

    d

9. Which of the following would be true of instru-
    mental conditioning (a) the response is elic-
    ited by the presence of the unconditioned stim-
    ulus (b) reinforcement increases the frequen-
    cy of the response associated with it (c) there

is trace presentation of CS and UCS (e) there is simultaneous presentation of CS and UCS   **b**

10. Reinforced for lifting one paw during the presentation of a buzzer, a dog now lifts two paws --a case of (a) response generalization (b) stimulus generalization (c) spread of effect (d) classical conditioning (e) second order conditioning   **a**

11. Which of the following most accurately describes negative reinforcement? (a) onset of an aversive stimulus (b) cessation of an aversive stimulus (c) withdrawal of a positive reinforcement (d) extinction (e) punishment   **b**

12. In higher-order conditioning, a former (a) UCS serves as a CS (b) UCR serves as a CR (c) CR serves as a UCS (d) CR serves as a UCR (e) CS serves as a UCS   **e**

13. Partial reinforcement (a) enhances classical conditioning speed and efficiency (b) interferes with classical conditioning (c) interferes with the maintenance of an operantly conditioned response (d) is never used in operant conditioning (e) is never used in type R conditioning   **b**

14. A prerequisite to assuming that an unconditioned stimulus-response connection exists is (a) the UCS must be a reinforcer for the UCR (b) the UCR must be a reflex response to the UCS (c) the UCR must be an innate response to the UCS (d) the CR and UCR must be identical   **a**

15. Second-order conditioning is an important phenomenon because it demonstrates how an originally neutral CS can assume properties of (a) first-order conditioning (b) instrumental stimuli (c) a reinforcer (d) positive reward   **c**

16. The 1920 Watson study in which he paired a loud noise with the presence of an animal to a little boy created _____ in the boy (a) guilt (b) speech (c) fear (d) affection   **c**

17. The reinforcement schedule most likely to lead to a lasting and powerful response is (a) fixed interval (b) variable-interval (c) fixed ratio (d) variable ratio   **d**

SHORT ANSWER QUESTIONS FOR REVIEW

<u>Fill in the blanks.</u>

18. The reinforcement schedule characteristic of
    gambling is _____ .

    variable
    ratio

19. Early in the 20th century, Richard Seman, a
    German scientist, and Sigmund Freud postulated
    the existence of _____ , traces of experiences
    that remain in the nervous system.

    engrams

20. Tolman believed that reinforcement provides
    information to the subject about which acts are
    likely to be punished and which are likely to
    be rewarded (S-S relations); this relation is
    learned, he felt, and retained in the head as
    "cognitive _____ ."

    maps or
    map

21. If a child heard the word "cat" (CS) every time
    he saw (UCR) a four-legged furry animal (UCS),
    he might eventually think "cat" (_____) every
    time he heard "cat."

    CR

22. In the formula S-O-R, which depicts the course
    of learning, S is the stimulus, O is _____ ,
    and R is the response.

    the organ-
    ism or
    person

23. The eyeblink response can be classically condi-
    tioned by presenting a dull light (CS) to the
    human, subject just prior to an air puff (UCS),
    which elicits an eye blink (_____).

    UCR

24. Reversal of the CS→UCS pattern, presenting the
    UCS prior to CS, is called _____ . This se-
    quence results in very weak conditioning.

    backward
    condi-
    tioning

25. A reinforcement (the UCS) in classical condi-
    tioning serves to _____ a response; the rein-
    forcement in instrumental conditioning follows
    the behavior, thereby increasing the probabil-
    ity that the behavior will recur.

    elicit

26. In keeping with Tolman's conceptions about prob-
    lem solving, Bandura distinguishes two catego-
    ries of it: acquisition, the cognitive process
    of registering observations and recalling one's
    own and others' past responses, and _____ , the
    execution of these cognitively acquired re-
    sponses.

    per-
    formances

27. A grown man's fear of dogs after having been
    bitten by the neighbor's animal when he was a
    kid is an example of _____ .

    stimulus
    generali-
    zation

SHORT ANSWER QUESTIONS FOR REVIEW

28. An event that can strengthen the tendency to behave in certain ways is known as a _____ .

reinforcer

29. An involuntary response to a stimulus that usually involves feelings or expectancies is a _____ .

UCR or uncondi-tioned response

30. A stimulus that is able to elicit a particular response without training is called a _____ .

UCS or uncondi-tioned stimulus

31. A very broad term for designating the acquisi-tion of skill or understandings, _____ refers to the processes of perceptual organization, to the relatively permanent effects of practice on understandings, and to change in behavior caused by experience or practice.

"Gestalt"

32. A response to a stimulus originally inadequate to elicit it is called, in learning terms _____ .

CR, con-ditioned response, or condi-tioned reflex

Determine whether the following statements are true or false.

33. According to Bandura's theory of observational learning, performance is closely linked to in-strumental learning.

True

34. An example of a classically conditioned re-sponse is a choice point response in a maze.

False

35. The conditioned response(CR) will disappear (extinction) unless the UCS is reintroduced.

True

36. An event that can strengthen the tendency to behave in certain ways is known as a discrimin-ation.

False
It is known as a rein-forcer

37. Observational learning represents a combination of classical and instrumental conditioning.

False

38. Retention of training in regenerated planaria supports the theory of biochemical changes as the physical foundation of learning.

True

SHORT ANSWER QUESTIONS FOR REVIEW

39. The discrepancies between Thorndike's and Tolman's theories of learning revolve around the paradox of explaining behavior either associationistically (habit) or cognitively (knowledge, expectations).

True

40. The law of effect postulates that the response that is performed most frequently and most recently during a trial is the response most likely to be elicited in the future under similar stimulus conditions.

False
This is the law of Exercise, not the Law of Effect. Students should know the difference

41. The fixed interval schedule of reinforcement is harder to extinguish than the variable ratio schedule of reinforcement.

False

42. In classical conditioning the outcome is controlled primarily by the experimenter, but in instrumental conditioning the outcome is controlled by the subject.

True

43. Animals cannot be taught to overcome the effects of stimulus generalization either through classical conditioning or by being trained in conditioned discrimination.

False

44. Bandura accounts for acquisition through the classical conditioning of perceptual responses.

True

45. An example of a strong conditioned reinforcer is food.

False

46. One of the main differences between an instrumental response and a conditioned response is that the former is not under the subject's control.

False
It is under the subject's control and this constitutes one of the main differences

47. The main difference between classical and operant conditioning is that in classical conditioning you pair the correct response with the un-

SHORT ANSWER QUESTIONS FOR REVIEW

conditioned stimulus until learning takes place
and in operant conditioning you elicit the correct response out of a number of associated responses by rewarding only the response to be
elicited.

True

48. Second order learning is included in the definition higher order conditioning.

True

49. Any object, event, or energy that arouses a
receptor and produces some effect on an organism
is a stimulus.

True

CHAPTER 4

HUMAN LEARNING

GENERAL PRINCIPLES

● PROBLEM 4-1

What are the types of human learning?

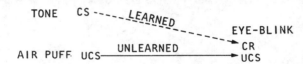

Schematic Diagram of Classical Conditioning of the Eye-Blink Reflex

Solution: Although the number of ways a human being learns is almost infinite, in order to study learning, psychologists have had to construct systems of classification. Human learning can be divided into six general categories: conditioning, motor learning, discrimination learning, verbal learning, problem solving, and concept learning.

Classical conditioning is the learning of a response to a particular stimulus which previously could not elicit that response. Human beings can be conditioned to respond to stimuli in much the same way as animals were in the famous Pavlovian experiments. Pavlov's dogs were conditioned to salivate before food was actually placed in their mouths. By pairing a conditioned stimulus (CS) with an unconditioned stimulus (UCS), a number of responses such as eyelid closure and shock avoidance can be classically conditioned in humans. Usually, conditioning is successful when the required response is very elementary.

Operant conditioning can also be demonstrated in humans. This type of conditioning results in the development of behaviors which operate on the environment to produce some effect. Motor learning, the learning of discrete or continuous motor skills, is one example. Typing and playing darts are discrete tasks. Driving a car is an example of a continuous task. To study motor learning in a controlled and quantitative manner, tasks like rotary pursuit learning and maze learning are employed in experimentation. Rotary pursuit learning consists of learning to keep a small metal stylus in contact with a moving disk. Since measuring the acquisition of a skill usually involves scoring the accuracy of responses, time on target serves as a measure. As time elapses, learning proceeds and the subject is able to keep the stylus on the target for longer periods of time. Once learned, continuous tasks (unlike discrete tasks) are not usually forgotten. For example, one who has learned to ride a bike in childhood may be surprised at how easily he can ride again after a lapse of twenty years.

Another type of learning common to both humans and animals is discrimination learning. It has been found that children learn to discriminate in their daily lives in the same way that animals do during experimentation. Both situations have a general characteristic in common: Two stimuli are always present, either simultaneously or successively, and one of the two stimuli is often rewarded or punished. This is how an infant learns to differentiate between his mother and strangers and between a cat and a stuffed animal. If an infant sees a real cat and a toy cat, he may decide to pet each one. The real cat may reward the infant by purring and cuddling up to him. The toy cat will remain motionless. Thus, there is an absence of reward when the toy cat is touched. The infant has learned to discriminate between the two stimuli.

For human beings, verbal learning is the most significant kind of learning. Verbal learning provides an important link between elementary non-verbal learning processes, language, and thought. All formal and most informal education in older children and adults involves verbal learning. The great majority of experiments which study learning focus on verbal learning.

The nature of verbal associations has been studied through rigorous experimentation. Researchers have approached the study in different ways. In the method of serial anticipation a subject learns a list until he can anticipate the word that follows the one he's looking at; in paired-associate learning a subject learns to associate the first member of a pair (stimulus) with the second member (response); in free learning a subject reproduces a list of words in any order, this shows the experimenter how he organized the material.

Human problem solving is regarded as "thinking." Most human problems are solved through prior verbal learning, although sometimes they are solved by operant conditioning (responses without thought). However, problems are usually stated in words and solved through verbal reasoning. Problem solving progresses through several stages: the problem is stated, evidence for a solution is arranged, an idea emerges, alternatives are evaluated, and the solution is verified.

Concept learning involves distinguishing and reacting to a common aspect in a group of objects. A concept is formed when certain attributes of an object or event can be

95

Equipment Used to Produce and Measure Eye Blinks

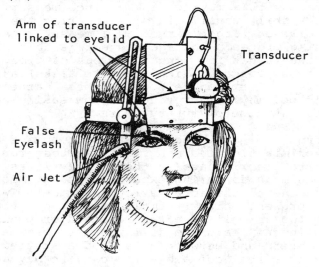

The subject wears a false eyelash which is linked by a thread
to the apparatus to measure the blinks. The tube delivers a
puff of air which serves as the unconditioned stimulus.

abstracted and generalized to other aspects or events.

Human concept learning usually involves attaching verbal labels to the common properties of objects; it can be
viewed as a type of verbal learning. Many of the words
people learn are labels for concepts: boat, stone, vegetable,
man, etc. In each case, the words represent some common
aspect in the objects that can vary in many ways; carrots,
spinach, broccoli, and celery are all vegetables, but they
all differ from one another. Concepts are the tools of
thinking.

● **PROBLEM** 4-2

What are the major factors involved in human learning?
How do they affect the learning process?

Solution: The major factors that influence learning in

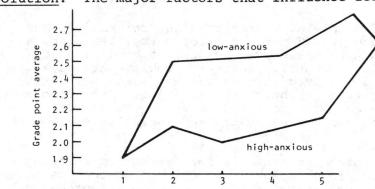

Fig. 1

humans are: intelligence, chronological age, motivation, previous learning and anxiety.

Intelligence, as defined by Thurstone (Thurstone and Thurstone, 1941), is both an underlying intellectual general ability and a number of specific intellectual abilities that a person possesses.

Although they are not foolproof measures, I.Q. scores are used to determine how intelligent an individual is. A person's cognitive ability as measured by an I.Q. score does not always determine his ability for verbal learning. Stevenson (1972) has found that only children with extremely high or low scores on intelligence tests show a positive relationship with high or low verbal learning ability. The relationship is less strong for children with I.Q. scores in the average range.

Chronological age also determines the rate of learning, particularly verbal learning. Children begin to use expressive language at about 18 months and probably understand some language before that. From ages 3 to approximately 20, learning ability steadily increases. Thereafter, it remains fairly constant, dropping slightly until about the age of 50. After 50, the person experiences greater difficulty in learning new material.

Someone with a great desire to learn is said to be highly motivated. Motivation is very important in what one learns and how quickly one learns it. A motivated person will generally learn faster and more efficiently than an unmotivated one. To learn efficiently, a person must intend to learn (intentional learning). However, incidental learning -- learning that is not intended but which results simply from exposure to material -- sometimes does occur. The degree of incidental learning does not approach that of intentional learning in real life situations.

How much a person retains from previous learning will also partially determine the rate of learning in a current situation. Both positive and negative transfer from previous learning can occur. Positive transfer will aid in the learning of new material, while negative transfer will interfere with new learning. The more a person can transfer his previous learning to the new situation, the faster he will learn. This is positive transfer. Negative transfer is said to occur when what one has learned previously makes it more difficult to learn something new. Negative transfer deters the learning process. Zero transfer may occur when there is a combination of positive and negative effects that cancel each other out. This would indicate that previous learning, in a particular instance, neither helped nor hurt in a current learning attempt.

Another major factor involved in learning is anxiety. Anxiety is an emotional state characterized by non-specific fears and various autonomic symptoms. Most people feel anxious when taking examinations. Usually, the more anxious a person is, the lower his performance level on a verbal learning task.

The effect of anxiety is different for different learning tasks. For a simple eyelid conditioning task, anxiety is good: high-anxious subjects condition more rapidly than low-anxious subjects. For many simple tasks, such as discrimination learning, anxiety level makes no appreciable difference. In complicated tasks such as school learning, anxiety seems to be a hindrance. An experiment conducted by Spielberger (1962) found that among students with very high or very low scholastic aptitude, anxiety level had no effect on academic success. However, among students whose scholastic aptitude was between the two extremes, high anxiety resulted in lower grade point averages than did low-anxiety (Fig. 1).

● **PROBLEM** 4-3

Discuss the determinants involved in making a task easy or difficult to learn.

Solution: Experience has shown that almost any task will be more difficult to perform the first time than after it has been rehearsed a few times. Of course, the ease with which it is initially performed depends on the individual, who is subject to such learning factors as intelligence, chronological age, motivation, previous learning and anxiety.

Psychologists have developed two general methods for assessing the difficulty of a task. The first is to present two related tasks in succession and see how the learning of the first one affects the learning of the second. This is called transfer of training. There can be positive, negative, or no perceivable transfer; that is, the learning of the first task can help, interfere or have no effect on the learning of the second task.

The second method involves varying some features of the tasks to be learned and determining how each feature contributes to the ease of learning. For example, in verbal learning there are a number of essential features which affect the rate at which verbal material is learned. These features are: pronunciation, discrimination and meaningfulness. A word that can be easily pronounced is learned more quickly than one that is not.

The things we remember best are those that "stand out" from the routine. For example, if there is a group of six people, five ordinary women and one ordinary man, and one is told to briefly look at the group, he will most likely remember the man in more detail than the women. The person's ability to discriminate is evident here.

The most important feature in verbal learning is meaningfulness. Meaningfulness is responsible for the types of associations evoked by what is to be learned. There are many different kinds of associations and many ways in which they can be related.

What are the best methods of learning?

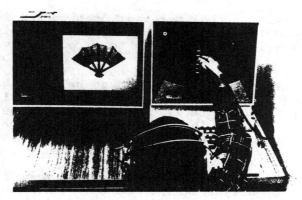

Teaching Machine

Solution: In general, a task is learned quickly and efficiently if it is practiced for short periods of times with
intervals of rest in between. Continuous or massed practice is not so efficient, except for problem solving or inductive reasoning tasks (Hall, 1966).

Practice periods for most tasks should be short, since
the longer they are, the slower the rate of learning. However, they should not be so short that the task is divided
into insignificant units (Kimble and Bilodeau, 1949). In
general, the length of the rest periods should also be
short, since very long rest periods (e.g., 24 hrs) do not
increase the rate of learning significantly. For example,
a person studying a chapter in a textbook will most likely
learn it just as efficiently if he studies for one hour and
rests for one hour, or if he only rests for half an hour.
If certain material is well organized and is known relatively well, mass learning (cramming) is beneficial.

Distribution of practice (dividing practice time into
relatively short intervals and taking rest periods) usually
facilitates motor learning (e.g., typing) to a greater extent than verbal learning (e.g., learning a group of related
words).

Being informed about the results of one's efforts in a
detailed and timely fashion is very useful to both motor
and verbal learning. For example, suppose that two people
are blindfolded and told to hit a ball with a pool cue into
a certain pocket on a pool table. Each may feel around to
determine where the ball is, how he is holding the stick,
etc. One person, immediately after shooting, is told by
how much and in what direction his aim was off. The other
person, after a long interval, is only told that he missed,
or that he didn't miss. After repeated trials, the first
person will do considerably better than the second.

Some knowledge of the results is better than none. If the second person wasn't told anything after his attempts, he probably would have done even worse. Feedback also works as an incentive. A person who knows how he's doing is more inclined to try a task again than is one who is told nothing about his performance or is told too late.

In memorizing verbal material, recitation is vital. A person may read the answer to a question and think that he knows the answer. However, when required to give the answer on a test he may not remember it at all or may be able to give only a partial answer. Had he recited the answer either aloud or subvocally the amount he could have recalled would have been much greater. Reciting to a friend or one-self is better than no recitation at all. If as much as 80% of study time is spent in active recitation, the result is better than when all the time is spent reading (Gates, 1917). This applies to virtually any type of material.

In trying to learn certain material, should one study it as a whole or divide it into parts? This question does not have a clear-cut answer; each method has its advantages and disadvantages.

The "part" method works better when the material to be learned is so long that trying to learn it at once results in cramming (for example, learning a long part in a play). Learning by parts has the advantage of maintaining motivation, since one gets feedback quickly. This method will only work if the parts are linked and learned as a whole; sometimes however, the parts are learned in the wrong order.

A person who ordinarily learns quickly will obtain the best results if the material is meaningful to him and if it is separated into various sections with rest periods at appropriate intervals. One cannot say that one method is always better than another; it depends on the individual and the material to be learned.

In the development of programmed instruction, educators have compiled and implemented the knowledge available on human learning. The programmed texts came first. Then machines which teach certain subjects were created. Today, the programs can be put into a general-purpose computer.

As the name implies, this method requires that a specific procedure be followed. Usually, the student answers questions which gradually become more difficult. After each question is answered, the student is told whether he answered it correctly or not. This, as discussed earlier, is important in keeping the person motivated. When interesting questions or problems are presented to the student, he will usually want to continue working on the task. Unfortunately, some of the programmed texts and machines are not very interesting.

A convenient aspect of the programmed method is that it allows the student to proceed at his own pace. In a classroom situation, the fast learner may get bored, and the slow learner may miss some important concepts. Another positive aspect of the method is that the material is learned in small steps. This is necessary for practically all types of individuals. By going step-by-step, the person grasps concepts the first time around, and is ready to proceed to new steps. Wrong responses are spotted immediately so that the student does not build on misinformation.

● **PROBLEM** 4-5

Are animal conditioning experiments applicable to human beings?

Solution: From the 1930's through the 1950's, theoretical work in American psychology consisted largely of the efforts of the "learning theorists." Their basic orientation is that the principles of learning are very similar throughout the animal kingdom. They constructed general theories about human learning based on their findings on animal learning.

Today, very few psychologists strongly advocate applying the findings of animal research directly to people. Successful demonstrations of applied principles of learning theory are most common when the task for the human being is made very much like the task performed by the animal. Therefore, many studies of eyelid conditioning and shock-avoidance conditioning have been done with human subjects. These experiments have features in common with those performed with animals and seem to follow similar laws.

Under specific laboratory conditions and with specific instructions, certain experiments will yield classical and operant conditioning in human beings. However, demonstrations of human conditioning can be rendered very different from those of animal conditioning if the instructions are changed even slightly. For example, if in a finger-with-

drawal experiment the subject is shocked on the finger after
the conditioned stimulus (CS), a light, is presented, he will
learn to remove the finger immediately after the CS appears.
But if the subject is told to keep his finger on the key,
no withdrawal conditioning will occur in a substantial number of trials. One can remove or create a conditioned response by giving different instructions. In the first case,
if the person is told he's not going to be shocked any more,
the light (CS) will not cause him to withdraw the finger.
On the other hand, if he's told that when a light goes on
he'll receive a severe shock, without any previous training
he'll remove the finger when the light goes on. This illustrates the great importance language has in the learning
and behavior of humans. Since human beings are the most
complex organisms, it is very difficult to devise a general
theory about their learning.

VERBAL LEARNING

How did verbal learning and memory studies begin? What was
Ebbinghaus' contribution to early learning and memory
studies?

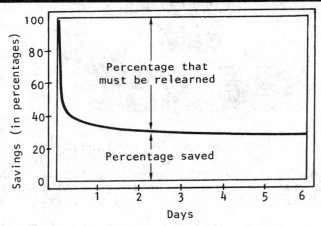

Ebbinghaus's general curve of forgetting. This shows the
savings by percentages in terms of trials needed to relearn
a list of nonsense syllables.

Solution: Hermann Ebbinghaus, a young German philosopher,
was the first to examine learning and memory scientifically.
His experiments in the late 1800's attempted to give an
empirical basis for the study of human learning, memory
and the association theory.

Ebbinghaus' concept of memory was derived from the
British associationists. Memory was thought to be the associations between ideas or events which occurred close in
time. To study learning, Ebbinghaus presented a subject
with a series of items. By counting how many times the
subject had to be exposed to the series before he could com-

pletely recall it, Ebbinghaus had a measure of learning difficulty. Measuring memory was more complicated. How does one measure the memory of a person who can recite a poem one day but cannot recite the poem in its entirety the following day? Ebbinghaus' solution was to require that the subject relearn the material the next day. He recorded how many times it had to be rehearsed before it could be recited once with no mistakes. Memory was measured by calculating the "savings" in relearning.

To control for the fact that different materials vary in difficulty (prose, poetry, numbers, etc.), Ebbinghaus developed nonsense syllables as his material for experimentation. Consonant-vowel-consonant combinations like GAX, WEV, LOM were used in his experiments. These nonsense syllables could all be vocalized as if they were words. They were chosen because they were relatively free of prior associations. Ebbinghaus used himself as his subject. His experimental program lasted for years. He tested himself in one set of conditions after another.

What is the relation between the amount of material and learning time? Ebbinghaus experimented with this problem. Experience shows that a lot of material is harder to learn than a small amount. But how much harder? Ebbinghaus found that in dealing with one to seven digits, a person needs to only hear them once; then, if he is not disturbed, he can hold them in short-term memory. But when the material exceeds seven digits, the time needed to memorize each item increases sharply because the person needs to hear or see the list of numbers several times. The number of trials increases very rapidly as the list is lengthened, and the time required to learn increases correspondingly. Subsequent work by many other investigators has confirmed these findings.

What is the relation between time and forgetting? After learning a list of nonsense syllables, Ebbinghaus would relearn it at some fixed time interval later (ranging from a few minutes to a month). If relearning the list took the same number of trials as was needed for the original learning, he concluded there was no memory of it. If, on the other hand, he could recall the list with no rehearsal, then there was complete memory. He found that massive forgetting began as soon as learning had concluded. Forgetting was very rapid at first and then proceeded more and more slowly. Other researchers have confirmed these findings.

When Ebbinghaus discovered that so much forgetting took place in such little time, he concentrated on finding ways to overcome some of the forgetting. His findings show that overlearning originally, that is, learning the material well beyond the point of correct recitation, leads to superior retention of the material later. A second method of overcoming forgetting is repeated learning. This occurs when material is learned just to the point of recitation the first day, and relearned to this same point each day for a few days.

Both frequency of trials and distribution of practice are important aids to learning and are effective against forgetting. Practice and distribution in combination are particularly effective for superior retention.

Ebbinghaus also made contributions to the field of associative learning. He considered the learning of units of language (such as his nonsense syllables) to be the best example of associative learning. Ebbinghaus' data suggest that associations are formed by relatively automatic (unconscious) processes. Thus, he concluded that such learning is probably more complex than thought and can be the basis for further investigation of the structure of cognitive activities. Ebbinghaus stimulated research in the area of associative learning and provided a theoretical framework for such research.

● **PROBLEM** 4-7

Describe the methods of verbal learning.

Solution: There are four basic kinds of verbal learning: Serial learning, serial-anticipation learning, paired associate learning, and free recall learning.

Serial learning occurs when a list of items is memorized and recalled in a particular order. Someone learning the series of events leading up to the American Civil War must engage in serial learning. In experiments, serial learning is studied with lists of words, numbers or nonsense syllables. The subject is presented with the whole list and each time he attempts to learn the items on it he must recite the list in the correct order. This is sometimes called the study-test method. The subject tries to write down the list in the correct order but does not know whether he is correct or not until the next study trial is presented for him to learn. This method seems to yield better learning results than the serial-anticipation method described below.

In serial-anticipation learning, a list of items, usually nonsense syllables, is also used in experimentation. The items are presented one at a time for a standard time interval -- usually two seconds. The first time the list is presented, the subject will not know what successive syllables are correct. But beginning with the second trial, he is asked to anticipate the syllable that follows the one he is looking at. If the list consisted of Jiz, Mux, Xoy and so on, he would first be shown Jiz and be expected to say Mux. Two seconds later Mux would appear, letting the subject know that he was correct and giving him the cue for anticipating Xoy. A student learning a vocabulary list in order also does this to a certain extent. After a word on the list is covered, the student anticipates what the next one is. This method provides immediate feedback to the student about the accuracy of his response. When he is shown the first item, he guesses the second one. Then he is given the second item so that he can guess the third. This tells him if he was correct on the previous guess.

This is unlike the study-test method, where the correct responses are not known until the next time the complete list is presented.

In paired-associate learning, the subject must learn a list of paired items. The left-hand item of the pair is the stimulus item and the right-hand item is the response item. The subject must learn the pairs so that when given the stimulus item, he can produce the response item. This type of learning occurs in many situations. For example, when someone is attempting to learn a foreign language, there is a stimulus item and a response item. The stimulus item is a word in the foreign language (casa), and the response item is the corresponding word in English (house). When the stimulus term (casa) is seen, the response term (house) is remembered. In experimentation, paired lists of nonsense syllables, words, or numbers are constructed. After the subject learns the list, the response item must be given when the stimulus item is presented.

Free recall learning is the learning and recalling of a list of items. The retrieved items need not be in any specific order. Everything, however, must be remembered. Here, the experimenter's emphasis is on how the responses are organized by the subject. The order the subject chooses in recalling the items demonstrates the type of organization that took place.

Serial-anticipation and paired-associate experiments are the classical methods of studying verbal learning. The formation of simple associations is illustrated by these two methods, since the items used in experimentation hardly have any acquired meaning. The other methods usually involve more meaningful materials.

● **PROBLEM** 4-8

Define paired-associate learning and the methods it uses.

Solution: In this type of learning, the subject attempts to learn a list of paired items. The serial anticipation method is the typical method employed in paired-associate task experiments. In this method, the first item of the pair is presented alone, followed by both items of the pair presented together. For example, if the stimulus word is "boat" and the response word is "horse," the subject is presented with:

boat
boat-horse

The subject's task is to correctly give the response term (horse) before it is given. When the recall method is used, the subject is repeatedly given the pairs and responds by recalling the pairs correctly in serial order.

Psychologists quickly saw the advantages of paired-associate learning over serial learning. Paired-associate tasks are often considered easier than serial tasks because

half of the items do not have to be anticipated; they merely
serve as cues to signal the other half of the items. Also,
in the paired-associate task, an item of the pair serves
only one function: stimulus or response. In the serial
task sequence, the middle item of A-B-C ("B") serves two
functions. It is a response (and feedback item) for "A"
and a stimulus item for "C." Therefore, the paired-associate
task allows for a more exact analysis of the learning which
takes place. The paired-associate task also allows us to
look at the learning of a pair independently of its position
in the list, unlike serial tasks.

Another reason why psychologists favor paired-associate
learning is that its experimental method is similar to nonverbal learning and conditioning experiments. For example,
the left-hand item of the pair serves as a stimulus that
evokes a response (the right hand item). The subjects'
response is reinforced by the appearance of the complete
pair. This is similar to the theory of learning as a conditioned response.

● **PROBLEM** 4-9

What is serial-learning? What two theories account for
serial-learning?

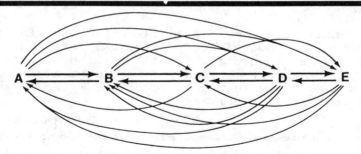

Diagram showing the traditional conception of how the first
five letters of the alphabet would be chained together in
the proper serial order by means of associative bonds.

Solution: Whenever items of a task are learned in sequence, serial learning takes place.   Common serial learning tasks include counting from one to ten, learning the
alphabet and spelling a word. In all of these examples,
it is necessary to learn not only the correct items but
also their correct order.

A popular method used in serial learning experiments
is serial recall. In this procedure, the subject is presented with a list, one item at a time. Then he is required to recall the list in correct serial order. Another popular method used in serial learning experiments
is the serial anticipation method. In this case, the subject first learns a list of items in sequence. Next, he
is presented with the first item on the list and is required to respond by giving the second item before it is
presented. Then, the second item is presented and the
subject is required to give the third item before it is

shown to him, etc. Learning is considered to be complete when the entire list can be correctly anticipated at least twice in succession.

There are two separate theories concerning what cues or stimuli a subject uses in order to learn a serial task. The traditional belief, suggested by Ebbinghaus and others, is that isolated items are linked together by association into associative chains as learning occurs. Direct associations are formed between items next to each other and remote associations are formed between items farther apart. These can be either forward associations (from an earlier item in the chain to a later item) or backward associations (from a later item to an earlier item).

A more recent theory suggests that associations may not be formed between items in the list. Subjects instead learn the proper sequence of items by linking them to a particular position on the list. In other words, the subject learns that A is first, B is second, etc., without linking A to B to C, etc.

● **PROBLEM** 4-10

Discuss the effects of rehearsal and mediation in the verbal learning procedure.

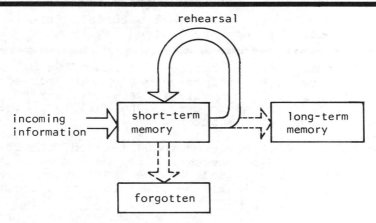

Short and long-term memory diagram

Solution: There are two basic variables that affect verbal learning: rehearsal and mediation.

Rehearsal serves two functions. First, it allows items in short-term memory to be retained. Secondly, it appears to facilitate the transferring of material from short-term to long-term memory.

The total time spent learning is the important factor in rehearsal. The individual presentation rate and the number of trials are not as important.

In most contexts, rehearsal is necessary for learning. The few exceptions seem to be for highly dramatic material (insults), or for material that is originally well organized (nursery rhymes). It is not known how this learning occurs.

The mediating factors, some of which arise in the learning situation itself and some of which are transferred from previous learning, are crucial in the organization of learning. The principle of mediation consists of using a third, implicit term, in order to associate two other items. Mediators are usually subjectively generated items that have something in common with both original items. For example, "party" can serve as a mediator for "democratic" and "birthday."

Mediators in verbal learning do not have to be verbal. Imagery is a better mediational device when an image is evoked, as in the case of concrete-noun paired-associates. However, when an image is not easily evoked, as in the case of abstract words, then it is better to use verbal mediators. If a group of people is told to draw a mediational picture for noun pairs, and another group is told to use verbal mediators, the results would be the following: The subjects who used imagery would recall more of the "concrete" noun pairs, while the subjects who used verbal mediators would recall more of the "abstract" items.

● **PROBLEM** 4-11

Discuss the characteristics of verbal materials that influence how effectively they are learned.

Solution: There are various characteristics of verbal materials which influence how effectively they are learned: list length, item position, meaningfulness, similarity, frequency, concreteness and imagery. The ability to transfer learning is also very important.

The longer the list of items to be learned, the more difficult learning the list becomes. The number of trials necessary increases very rapidly as the list is lengthened, and the time required to learn the items increases correspondingly.

The position of the items is also a very important factor. Subjects learn the first and last items on a list best. This is called the primacy effect and the recency effect, respectively. When a list contains a few items that are different from the majority of items, the different items are learned more quickly. This is known as the isolation effect.

The ease with which we learn something also depends on the meaningfulness of the material. The more meaningful it is, the better it is learned and retained. Meaningfulness of material is derived from how many associations the material can evoke and from the conceptual and hierarchical relations among its items.

Similarity, though it sounds like a single variable,

actually encompasses three variables. Verbal units may be similar in that they look or sound alike, have the same meaning or belong to the same category.

Studies have shown that learning a list of items becomes more difficult as the similarity in meaning or appearance of its items increases. A list containing the words sad, unhappy, depressed, miserable, burdened, withdrawn, gloomy and frowning is a much harder list to learn than a list containing adjectives which are not similar. Likewise, a list containing the words bike, back, buck, bake, book is harder to learn than bike, front, cook, deer, read.

Similarly in appearance, meaning or category between stimulus and response items also inhibits learning in paired-associate task experiments. It has been found that in paired-associate learning, similarity of stimulus items has a greater inhibiting effect on learning than similarity of response items.

Frequency seems to act in the same way as meaningfulness. One is better able to differentiate the acquired characteristics of frequently seen words so that they are easily recalled. If one encounters a word very often, one will learn it quickly and retain it for a very long time.

Concreteness refers to a verbal item's position in a concrete-abstract dimension. For example, "carrot" is more concrete than "vegetable." The more concrete a noun, the better the chances that it will elicit a mental image (imagery). Therefore, it is easier to learn a concrete word than an abstract one.

The type and amount of past learning a person has done affects his rate of acquisition of new material. Transfer of training may be positive or negative. What is learned in one situation is sometimes appropriate to another situation. When previous learning facilitates later learning or performance, it transfers positively. When previous learning interferes, it transfers negatively. Positive transfer will probably take place if the new material is similar to material previously learned. Positive transfer will make the learning of the new material an easier process.

● **PROBLEM 4-12**

What is the serial-position effect and the serial-position curve?

Solution: When engaging in a serial-learning task, some parts of the list are usually easier to learn than others. A serial-position effect usually occurs which makes the items at the beginning of the list easiest to learn, the items at the end of the list the next easiest to learn and the items in the middle of the list the most difficult to learn. When this is plotted by item position, a bow shaped curve, called a serial-position curve, occurs. See Fig. 1.

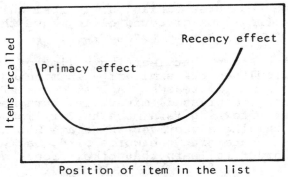

The serial position curve

A common illustration of the serial-position effect occurs when young children try to recite the alphabet. They begin with "A,B,C,D," and end with "X,Y,Z" but the middle is a scrambled assortment of letters.

Psychologists suggest that the serial-position effect is due to a primacy-recency effect. A primacy effect occurs when the items at the beginning of a list are learned faster and remembered better. A recency effect occurs when the items near the end of the list are learned faster and remembered well. If both effects occur, as in the serial position curve, it is called a primacy-recency effect. Two theories have attempted to explain why material is learned this way.

Stimulus-response theory suggests that the middle of a list is more difficult to learn because there is greater interference from various types of associations established during learning.

The Gestalt theory suggests a figure-ground view of the learning task. Items are seen as "figures" against a background. Both ends of the list form distinctive backgrounds that cause the items at each end to stand out so that they are easier to learn, items in the middle of the list are "lost" among other items.

● **PROBLEM** 4-13

What makes a piece of material to be learned meaningful, and how does its meaningfulness affect the rate of learning?

Solution: One of the most important factors in verbal learning is the meaningfulness of the material. An item is made meaningful by the associations it evokes for the subject. These associations vary in their number and in the way they are interrelated. Each item to be learned, a word or nonsense syllable, evokes a number of associations. Some items elicit more associations than others. For example, a subject may associate the item BIK with bike, a Bic pen or bicker. But the item BQR may mean absolutely nothing to him.

The greater the number of associations elicited, the easier it is to learn and retain material because its meaningfulness is increased. If only a very few or no associations are evoked by an item, learning is difficult because the material is less meaningful to the learner. These points were illustrated by Noble (1952a, 1952b). The experimenters constructed a long list containing two syllable English words and two syllable nonsense words. An index of meaning was obtained for each word in the following manner: A group of subjects looked at the list, one word at a time, for 60 seconds, and reported their own lists of associations for each word. An index of meaning was obtained for each item by counting the average number of associations given by the group. Indices ranged from a low of 0.99 associations for the nonsense word "govey" to 9.61 associations for the word "kitchen." On the basis of these indices, three lists of words were constructed. One list had an average "meaningful index" of 1.28, a second had an index of 4.42, and a third had an index of 7.85.

Subjects were then compared on their rate of learning the lists by the serial anticipation method. As required by the method, each word was presented in a specific order a number of times. After the subject learned the list, the first word was presented and the subject had to anticipate the next one. When the following word was presented, he had to anticipate the one after that and so on. The list with the lowest "meaningful index" took almost three times as many trials to learn as the list with the highest index. The list with the intermediate index was between the extremes.

The number of words in each list was the same. The only significant difference was meaningfulness as measured by the number of associations they evoked. Therefore, the more meaningful something is, the easier it is to learn and retain it.

Other variables also affect the meaningfulness of verbal material. A verbal item is more meaningful and easier to learn if it is similar to a word in the subject's language. For example, an English-speaking subject may find the word BIK easier to learn than BQR because the former is similar to the types of words found in his native language.

Meaningfulness also depends upon the familiarity the learner has with an item. An item which has been experienced more frequently will have greater meaningfulness and will therefore be easier to learn. The letters BIK have probably been seen more frequently by English-speakers than BQR.

Also, the more easily an item is pronounced, the greater meaningfulness it has. BIK is easily pronounced as one unit but B-Q-R requires three separate responses.

In paired-associate task experiments, the more meaningful the response item, the faster the learning rate. Meaningfulness can be facilitated by coding material to make it more meaningful. For example, to learn BQR, it might be helpful to create a sentence such as Beautiful

Queens are Rich. As the item takes on added meaning,
learning becomes easier.

How is material organized for meaning? What is clustering?
What are conceptual and associative hierarchies?

Solution: The items on a list, besides having individual
meaning, also have different degrees of association with
each other. When a list has "organization," it is easier to
learn. There are two types of organization: conceptual and
hierarchical. These can appear separately or in combination.
Conceptual organization will be considered first, then a
combination of conceptual and hierarchical organization, and
finally, a strictly associative hierarchy.

    The following are examples of a conceptual list and a
non-conceptual list:

Conceptual list	Non-conceptual list
Mary	peach
surgeon	horse
bicycle	emerald
football	wide
Louise	blue
hemotologist	murder
car	flounder
baseball	arm
Rhoda	gold
cardiologist	airplane
train	book
soccer	whiskey

    The list on the left is comprised of members that
form a limited number of categories: female names, types
of doctors, means of land transportation and sports that
use balls. The members in the list on the right form no
categories. When a subject is asked to recall the conceptual list, he'll recall it according to its categories.
This is called "clustering." If grouping items is possible,
a person will do it because it will aid learning and recalling. Clustering may occur according to conceptual categories, or to conceptual or associative hierarchies depending
on how the items relate to each other.

    In a conceptual hierarchy, the items fall into similar
conceptual categories, but the concepts in turn may be
grouped into categories at a higher level. This makes a
hierarchy of many levels, starting with the concrete and
ascending to the general, more abstract, concepts. For example:

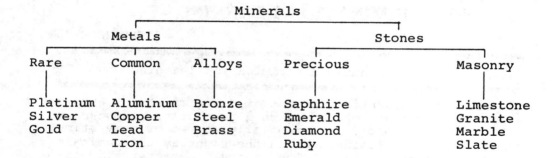

An associative hierarchy is not so effective as a conceptual one but it is helpful. Each word in this hierarchy is meaningful but is arranged by association, not conceptually. For example,

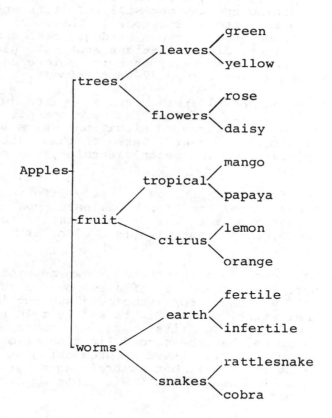

Experiments have illustrated that the meaningfulness of material is derived from the associative value of its individual items and from the conceptual and hierarchical relations among them. The ease with which we learn something depends on the meaningfulness of the material to be learned. The more meaningful it is, the better it is learned and the easier it becomes to retain.

HUMAN DISCRIMINATION LEARNING

What is involved in human discrimination learning?

Solution: The essential feature of discrimination learning is not whether a person can learn a particular response but rather, can he respond differentially to two or more stimuli? Infants learn discriminations in the same way that aminals do during experimentation. The general characteristic involved in both situations is the presence of two stimuli, either simultaneously or successively, where only one of these stimuli is frequently rewarded or punished. In this way, after many occurrences, the infant learns to distinguish between a real puppy and a toy puppy, milk and solid food, etc. If the infant touches both a puppy and a toy puppy, the puppy will reward the infant by responding to his touch, whereas, touching the toy dog will result in an absence of reward (no response). Eventually, the infant learns to discriminate between the two types of dogs, real and toy. It is believed that these discriminations must take place before the acquisition of language; that is, before the infant can attach verbal labels to different stimuli.

Since discrimination learning takes place during daily life, it is difficult to study its development. Therefore, psychologists have constructed situations where it can be studied in a controlled manner. Three of these situations are: probability learning, incidental learning, and reversal learning.

The learning of discriminations in daily life is probabilistic. Both the stimuli to be discriminated and the reinforcements attached to them vary from situation to situation. For example, something white in a glass is probably milk, but not always.

Human beings engage in a phenomenon known as probability matching, where the probability of a response matches the probability of an event. For example, a subject is presented with a panel which has two lights and is told to predict which light will come on first. The experimenter arranges the apparatus so that the second light comes on 75% of the time. The subject will start by predicting at a chance level (50% of the time), but as training progresses he will predict that the second light will come on just about as often as it actually does.

An everyday typical discrimination situation is not only probabilistic, but it also involves multiple cues. The stimulus has more than one aspect which can be discriminated. For example, if a person is told that a certain movie theater is on the corner of 86th Street and Lexington Avenue, he will notice the street signs when he gets there as well as the different things he sees on his way: the coffee shops, people, and other aspects of the environment.

In intentional learning the subject discriminates be-

tween the cues given to him. What he learns is determined
by what he wants to learn, what instructions are given to
him, and what his prior experiences are. Incidental learning refers to the formation of an unintended discrimination.
In the example above, learning that the theater is on the
corner of 86th Street and Lexington Avenue was intentional,
but noticing that there were two coffee shops across the
street and a boutique around the corner was incidental. In
learning discriminations with multiple cues, one learns primarily those that one intends to learn. But depending on
how much attention one is paying to other things, one might
learn much about the other cues.

In reversal learning more than one cue is involved in
discrimination. In this process, after one discrimination
has been established, the subject shifts to a task that is
either the reverse of the first or is the same as the first
but with a shift in the cues utilized. Kendler and Kendler's
(1962) experiment illustrates this: Children were presented
with two cups at a time. The cups were different in both
size and color. On one trial a large black cup might be
paired with a small white cup, or a large white cup with a
small white cup, etc. In the first task, the children had
to choose either large cup regardless of color. In the
second task, one-half of the group was reinforced for making a reversal shift; the small cup was now the correct
choice. The same attribute (size) was relevant, but its
value was reversed. The other half of the group made a
non-reversal shift: another attribute -- color -- became
relevant.

With lower organisms and young children, the reversal
shift is difficult, and the non-reversal shift is relatively
easy. But with older children and adults the opposite is
true. The reason for this is believed to be the difference
in verbal capacity. Young children do not depend upon language in mediational processes to the same extent that
adults do. "Mediation" refers to the process of words,
images or associations, internally aroused, acting as a
link in making discriminations. For example, the mediating
word for the attributes "black" and "white" is "color."
This is an abstract process which children find difficult
or impossible to do. Because young children lack mediational facility, they learn non-reversal shifts more easily
than reversal shifts.

A reversal shift requires "unlearning" and then "reversing" original learning, but a non-reversal shift requires only that the relevant attribute of the first learning be ignored. As his verbal ability increases with age,
the older person is better able to make discriminations
which are linked to a verbal response. The discrimination
task becomes one of classifying attributes according to a
relevant concept (in this example, size). In a reversal
shift, the same concept is required; nothing new has to be
learned. For example, if the mediating concept is size
and the original relevant attribute is "large," the new
relevant attribute would be "small" after a reversal shift.
However, a non-reversal shift for the person with verbal
facility requires that he extinguish his original learning

that size was important and recognize another attribute as being relevant to reinforcement, such as color. Thus, discriminations linked to a verbal response enable those with verbal facility (older children and adults) to learn reversal shifts with more ease.

MOTOR SKILLS

● PROBLEM 4-16

What are the important factors in the acquisition of motor skills?

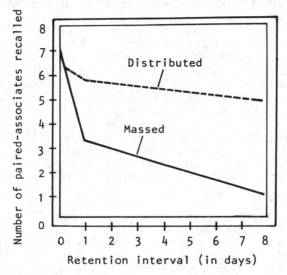

Solution: Many factors are important in the acquisition of motor skills, including feedback, transfer of training, repetition, distribution of practice, reminiscence, whole vs. part learning, coherence, and complexity.

Bilodeau and Bilodeau (1961) stated that "studies of feedback, or knowledge of results (of how a task was performed), show it to be the strongest, most important variable controlling performance and behavior." Learning occurs best when feedback is given. The more frequently feedback is given, the better the performance of the task. In general, there are two types of feedback, primary and secondary.

Primary feedback refers to the response given from the system that the person is operating. For example, in steering a car around a right curve, a person will turn the car to the right. He will notice the effort exerted in his arms while turning the steering wheel, the sway of his body to the left as the car is turned and the line in the middle of the road appearing slightly to the left of the car. These are all forms of primary feedback that the driver receives which tell him he managed the curve in the road.

Secondary, or augmented feedback, is information which does not come directly from the movement of the system. Secondary feedback could be seen in the example above if a passenger in the car remarked "You made that turn nicely." Secondary feedback becomes most important if a person wants to please an observer or if primary feedback is somehow unable to reach him (as when a person has a physical disability).

Transfer of training also affects the acquisition of motor skills. Transfer refers to the influence of previous learning on new learning situations. Positive transfer occurs when previous learning makes new learning easier. Negative transfer occurs when previous learning interferes with the learning of new material. When transfer occurs in motor learning tasks, the effects are almost always positive; this is not true in verbal learning (Briggs, 1969). Even if prior motor learning is not helpful to subsequent learning, it will rarely interfere. There are, of course, exceptions. Negative transfer effects can occur when aircraft controls in different planes are located in the same place but are designed for different tasks. Shifting from one plane to the other could result in an accident due to negative transfer. As is true in verbal learning, the more similar two motor tasks are, the greater the positive transfer will be between them.

Repetition, another factor in motor skill acquisition, refers to the practicing of the task. Repetition will facilitate the learning and development of the skill. The distribution of the practice, or the amount of time spent practicing, will also affect the rate at which a person learns a motor task.

According to Hall (1966), spaced practices (short periods of practice separated by periods of rest) result in more efficient learning than massed practice (continuous practice). Massed practice for long periods of time may lead to fatigue and loss of motivation which result in less efficient learning.

The most efficient method of spaced practice varies two features: (1) the length of the practice period, and (2) the length of the rest period. In general, short practice periods result in more efficient learning of a motor task. Periods should not be so short, however, that the task is separated into meaningless units.

According to Lorge (1930), the longer the rest between practice periods, the more effective a given amount of practice will be. Very long rest periods, however, do not increase the learning rate. Most tasks do not require rest periods of more than a few minutes. Beyond this optimal time, learning rate will not increase.

Short practice periods interspersed with short rest periods seem to be more effective for motor learning than one or two long practice periods with one or two long rest periods.

If a person stops practicing a skill, takes a rest, and begins again, he will usually perform better than he did during the first practice period. This is due to a phenomenon called reminiscence. Reminiscence can occur after spaced or massed practice. Rest periods dissolve fatigue but not the learning of correct responses. This accounts for the fact that reminiscence enhances motor learning.

Whether the motor task is best practiced as a whole skill or in small parts depends upon the particular task. If the skill depends on the integration of components, it is better to practice the skill as a whole. Studies on piano playing suggest that the most efficient learning results when the skill is practiced in its entirety. Practicing parts separately (e.g., right hand vs. left hand) may actually interfere with the learning of the skill. However, if the skill depends on the successful completion of independent components, it is more beneficial to learn each part well before putting them together. Swimming proceeds most rapidly when learned with this strategy. Breathing, arm stroke and kick are learned separately before they are combined into one skill.

Task coherence and task complexity are two final factors important in the acquisition of motor skills. A task is coherent if it is predictable and repetitive over time. Coherence enables one to predict a motor response for the immediate future. Driving a car on a familiar, straight road in good condition is a partially coherent task. At a given speed, the driver knows he will have to make limited adjustments of the brakes or steering wheel. However, driving an unfamiliar car on a narrow, unfamiliar, curving mountain road in poor condition may be less coherent. The driver will not know what to predict next. The more coherent a task, the easier it is learned and the better it will be performed.

Task complexity refers to the number of responses, or elements in a response sequence, that must be made. The less responses necessary, the faster the learning rate. Many simple tasks may be coherent; but this is not necessarily so. If a person were presented with a board of 100 lights, each with a switch which must be activated whenever a light is turned on at random, the task would be simple yet incoherent. It is incoherent because the person cannot anticipate which light will come on at what time. The sequence is not repetitive. Yet it is simple because the motor act requires the switch to be turned in only one of two ways -- on or off. Thus, simple, coherent tasks are easier to learn and perform than more complex or incoherent tasks.

● **PROBLEM** 4-17

What is a perceptual-motor task? What is the role of maturation and culture in the learning of these tasks?

Solution: Running, riding a bicycle, knitting, and writing

are examples of perceptual-motor tasks. These tasks require the performance of integrated, coordinated movements guided by perceptual input. Accomplishment of these skills relies equally on both the perceptual and motor systems.

The many skills one learns in a lifetime which depend upon eye, foot and hand coordination are basically derived from the learning of two complex, basic patterns of motor functioning: bipedal locomotion (walking) and reaching-grasping-manipulation. Although it is "natural" for human beings to accomplish these skills, each individual must learn to coordinate his sensory, nervous and muscular functioning by exercise and practice.

The development of many skills depends upon a combination of maturational limits and cultural determinants. The neuromuscular system of the child must be mature if he is to learn to walk, run and develop other more complex skills. The child's environment must also provide both opportunities and reinforcements for developing the skill.

Elementary patterns of grasping and walking develop from a combination of maturation and learning. Running, jumping, hopping and skipping develop in pre-school years from the walking pattern. During school years both gross (e.g., swimming) and fine (e.g., writing) motor coordination are developed. Children all over the world are developing their motor skills during these years although the manner in which they develop them is culturally determined. A father in Canada may encourage his young son to ice skate while a father in a Pacific Island may decide it is more important for his son to swim. Traditional societies may culturally determine sex differences in motor skill learning. Boys have generally been encouraged to develop gross motor skills such as jumping, kicking and throwing. Girls have traditionally been encouraged to develop fine motor skills such as piano playing or sewing. These sex differences become most apparent in traditional cultures during the adolescent years.

An illustration of how cultural determinants influence the learning of gross motor tasks, is shown in a study by McGraw (1935). McGraw found that children at two years of age could be taught to roller skate. Although they are physically mature enough to learn this skill, few two-year-olds know how to roller skate in our culture because it is not encouraged until a later age.

● **PROBLEM** 4-18

Discuss the phases of learning a perceptual-motor task.

Solution: According to Fitts (1962, 1964), learning a skill involves three stages: cognition, fixation and automation. Cognition involves becoming familiar with the type of task it is, what must be done, what materials are required (if any) and what type of movements must be made. Establishing familiarity and integrating basic responses is the first phase of learning a task.

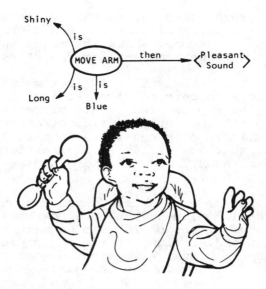

During the fixation phase, one receives kinesthetic feedback (information from the muscles) by performing the task. During this phase one learns to make the task response under appropriate stimulus conditions. For example, learning to use the brake pedal of a car in phase one is expanded to learning to use the brake pedal at a red light but not at a green light in phase two. Verbal mediation is sometimes employed at this stage. In other words, a person may talk himself through the task in order to respond with the appropriate movement. For example, "The light is red so I must stop. I stop by moving my foot from the accelerator to the brake and pressing down."

In learning a continuous motor task, the range of variations in input one must respond to is learned during the second phase. For example, in learning to steer a car, the control of the steering mechanism must be learned: Does the car wander from a straight path or is the car quick to respond to slight variations in the steering wheel's movement?

The last stage of learning a skill involves automation. During this phase, one continues to practice the skill while focusing on the fine details and organizing responses into larger units. For example, if one were learning to type, one would concentrate on increasing the word per minute rate (a detail of the task) and also on the ability to type larger units (words or phrases instead of letters). Verbal mediation is no longer needed. Speed and accuracy improve as automation increases.

● **PROBLEM 4-19**

What is the difference between discrete and continuous motor tasks? Which is easier to remember after an interval of time?

Solution: Motor tasks differ in regard to continuity. A

task may be either continuous or discrete. Discrete tasks consist of a series of movements which are separate from each other. Typing is an example of a discrete task. Rolling the knob to move the paper, striking a key, hitting the carriage return are all separate movements which comprise the task of typing.

Continuous tasks are a series of smooth movements which merge together. The direction, extent and force of continuous movements vary according to the situation. An example of a continuous task is steering a driving wheel in a car. The amount and direction of steering depends upon the continuous turning of the wheel various amounts depending upon the situation on the road.

One characteristic of continuous skills is that they are not easily forgotten. A common example is bicycle riding. Most adults can ride a bicycle without too much difficulty even if the skill was not practiced in twenty or more years. One possible explanation for this is that continuous skills are often practiced. Another reason may be that very little interference from other tasks occurred during the intervals between the exercise of the continuous skill. Learning a new skill, even a similar one, cannot create much interference if the perceptual-motor sequence of the first skill is well-integrated and automated.

The retention of discrete skills is usually not as good. An experiment by Neumann and Adams illustrates this point. Two sets of eight switches each were presented to the subjects. They were required to learn and match corresponding members of the two sets. Retention was measured by the number of trials it took to relearn the task until it could be performed twice without error. Results showed forgetting began after only twenty minutes. Retention continued to decrease for a period of one year. Forgetting of discrete motor skills (unlike continuous skills), is probably a function of interference from other learning.

CONCEPT LEARNING

● PROBLEM 4-20

What are factors which affect concept attainment and how does each affect the learning of concepts?

Solution: There are two basic theories about the mechanisms that describe concept learning performance: the Continuity Theory and the Non-continuity, or Hypothesis-testing Theory. The Continuity Theory, a derivative of the association, stimulus-response theories, asserts that subjects learn a concept gradually through associations between positive and negative instances of a concept, the responses the subject gives, and the reinforcement of a correct response.

The Non-continuity Theory maintains that subjects

form hypotheses about the correct solution rule, test the hypotheses, and learn by trial and error. Recent investigations support the Non-continuity Theory. An important factor which affects concept attainment, according to this theory, is the dominance of cues in the stimuli. This includes the facts that (a) subjects may enter the concept learning situation with a certain set of preferences for which features they will notice (dominance hierarchy), (b) subjects will more quickly learn to classify the stimuli according to a category if all of those categorical instances elicit the same associated response (dominance level), and (c) subjects will be more likely to form hypotheses based on the salient dimensions of a cue (cue salience).

The term "concept" is defined by its critical features -- relevant attributes that specify the stimulus characteristics of the concept, and the rule defining the relationship between the relevant attributes. The latter is the most important cognitive characteristic of concept learning. Therefore, in order for subjects to attain a concept, they must:

- learn what the attributes are;

- code the attributes into the stimulus objects;

- learn to group the objects into various concepts using the rules of logic.

The dominance of a feature for a particular concept contributes to determine how easily the subject learns that concept. Furthermore, the feedback and reinforcement that the subject receives after performance will also affect the rate of concept attainment. It helps subjects identify the underlying features of the stimuli and eventually learn the conceptual structure of the objects examined.

More recently, a third type of theories explaining concept learning performance has been introduced, namely, Information-processing Theories. Basically, they are extensions of the Non-continuity Theory, emphasizing internal, cognitive activities. These theories are based on similarities between man and computers; both accept external inputs, operate on them, and produce a response. Thus, the emphasis of Information-processing Theories is on the selection and organization of information.

● **PROBLEM** 4-21

Distinguish among conjunctive, disjunctive, and relational concepts.

Solution: The strategies people use to learn concepts have been studied in laboratory experiments in which subjects are given concept-learning tasks. In a typical procedure, the experimenter chooses a classification rule to define a concept and presents the subject with a set of stimulus events that specify an object of a given color (red or blue), shape (circle or square), and size (large or small). The subjects are asked to determine the positive instances, or exemplars, of the occurrence of the classification rule. The experimenter then indicates whether or not the response was correct. This procedure is repeated over many trials until the subject is either able to explain the concept or explain the necessary criteria required for a positive instance to occur. For example, if the conceptual problem is a single attribute identification problem, i.e., redness, then all the stimulus events containing the color red, regardless of their other attributes, would be positive instances of that event. The other stimulus events of shape or size would be considered negative instances, or non-exemplars.

More complex concept learning is often referred to in terms of the relations among the attributes defining the concept. These connections are based in logical relationships. Some of these relational concepts are:

Conjunctive - two relevant attributes must be present for the stimulus event to be a positive instance, i.e., red and square, regardless of size. The logical operator is "and", symbolized as $\cap$, referring to "intersection" in set theory.

Disjunctive - the presence of either of two relevant attributes is sufficient for a positive instance to occur, i.e., red or square. The logical operator is $\cup$, referring to "union" in set theory.

Joint Denial - those stimulus events that are not red and not square determine if it is a positive instance. In set theory, this is symbolized as $\bar{R} \cap \bar{S}$.

There are many other relational concepts which are more complex, that also derive from logical relationships. These amount to various combinations of conjunctive and disjunctive rules. For example, a conditional concept is one where a relevant attribute on one dimension (color, shape, or size) depends on the presence of another attribute on a different dimension. In logic this is known as the if-then clause, i.e., if the stimulus event is red, then it must be square.

TRANSFER OF LEARNING

● PROBLEM 4-22

Discuss the variables which determine whether transfer will be positive or negative.

Solution: The degree of similarity of the stimuli and responses in two tasks is one of the most important variables

123

determining whether transfer will be positive or negative. To investigate this variable, Bruce (1933) used paired-associate learning in his famous transfer experiment which has since been replicated by others.

Bruce constructed lists of paired-associate stimulus-response items for two tasks. The condition of the paired-associate lists varied. In one experimental condition, the stimuli of tasks one and two were different, but the responses were identical. In another, the stimuli were identical but the responses were dissimilar. In other conditions, either the stimuli or responses in Task 2 were similar to those in Task 1.

The results of this study show that very strong positive transfer results when the stimuli are similar and the responses are identical. In other words, the more that previous and future learning are similar, the more likely it is that positive transfer will result. In verbal learning, there is some positive transfer even when the stimuli are dissimilar but the response is the same. In general, the more similar the stimuli, the more likely it will be that positive transfer will occur.

Positive transfer may also increase with the amount of similarity between responses in the original and new situation. For example, although the games of tennis and badminton are different, they require similar responses and skills which make learning easier. If, however, two responses are extremely dissimilar, negative transfer will result. For example, airplane accidents occasionally occur because a pilot will transfer a response he made on similar controls on a plane he flew previously to those of a new plane. Although the controls (stimulus) are similar, they require different responses. An accident created in this way is the result of negative transfer.

In summary, some major points concerning stimulus-response similarity found in these experiments are:

1. Learning to make identical responses to new stimuli results in positive transfer.

2. Learning to make new (dissimilar, opposite or antagonistic) responses to similar or identical stimuli results in negative transfer.

3. The amount of transfer, regardless of whether it is positive or negative, is a function of stimulus similarity.

4. Whether transfer is positive or negative is largely dependent upon response similarity.

● PROBLEM 4-23

Discuss transfer of training in everyday life and in formal education.

Solution: Two fundamentally different types of transfer of training need to be understood clearly. Suppose that a comedian has learned that his nightclub audiences roar with laughter whenever he tells jokes that ridicule religion. When he is invited to perform on a college campus, he relies on this kind of joke, and the students laugh uproariously. This is an example of positive transfer. What the comedian learned to do in one situation applies equally well in another. Suppose that the comedian is then invited to perform at a Christian Fellowship convention. His religious jokes, of course, fall flat, and his performance is a miserable failure. This is an example of negative transfer. What worked in one situation is not applicable to another.

Researchers have studied the variables affecting transfer by using paired-associate learning in their experiments. For example, two groups, experimental and control, are compared for the amount of time taken and accuracy in learning a paired-associate task. Each experimental group first learns Task 1 consisting of a list of paired items (A and B). Then the experimental group learns Task 2 which is a second list of paired items (C and D). To see if learning Task 1 helped (transferred) the learning of Task 2, a control group is employed which does not learn Task 1 but must learn Task 2. The two groups are compared to assess which group performed better.

| Experimental group | learn Task 1 | learn Task 2 |
| Control group | Rest | learn Task 2 |

If the experimental group does better on Task 2 than the control group, it can be assumed that the learning of Task 1 transferred positively to the learning of Task 2. This is called positive transfer. If, however, the experimental group does not do as well on Task 2 as the control group, it can be assumed that the learning of Task 1 somehow interfered with the learning of Task 2. This would be an indication that a negative transfer took place. It is also possible for zero transfer to occur. This is seen if the groups do not differ in their performances. This would indicate that the learning of Task 1 did not make any positive or negative difference in the learning of Task 2.

It has been assumed that a certain degree of positive transfer takes place from what is learned in school to what is needed in daily life. Most researchers agree on "transfer of elements," which is the type discussed above. But a general theory called "formal-discipline theory" is questioned. It proposes that only a limited number of mental faculties need to be trained; once trained, they can be used in a great variety of situations. Schoolboys used to study Greek and Euclid, not for their intrinsic value, but because they were supposed to train the mind.

Another theory, the "mental-faculty theory," which

has almost been completely abandoned because experimentation has not supported it, proposes that one could train school children to be neat in their appearance and in their habits by teaching them to be neat in their school-work. Educators have also gradually relinquished the notion that one can instill a general ability through sheer exercise of a particular faculty or habit.

In modern times, educators have found that the greatest amount of positive transfer occurs when school subjects are taught so that students can apply them to everyday life.

MEMORY PROCESSES

● **PROBLEM** 4-24

Briefly describe the three stage theory of memory processing.

Three memory systems

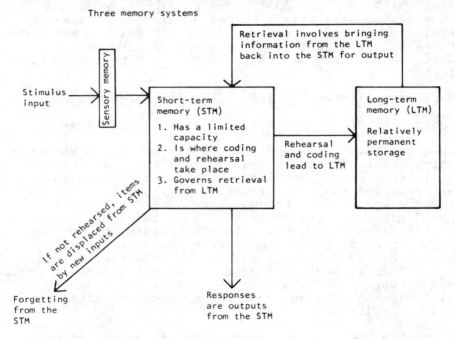

Solution: Our ability to remember depends upon a complex information processing system. Researchers have suggested that there are at least three stages of memory which are distinguished on the basis of storage time. Immediate (sensory) memory lasts for about one second, short-term memory lasts for several minutes, and long-term memory is thought to be permanent. Each memory stage involves different processes and is affected by time, interference and inhibition factors.

Immediate (sensory) memory has been described as a bridge between perception and memory. Sperling's (1960)

and Averbach and Cornell's (1961) experiments have supported the theory of immediate memory, which refers to a
brief afterimage of the stimulus itself. Immediate memory may give one the opportunity to organize and categorize what was seen, which is essential for a more permanent memory.

Short-term memory refers to what a person remembers
for several seconds after an experience. Short-term memory
is a temporary process that holds the trace of an experience for a limited amount of time or until a more permanent trace can be established in long-term memory.
Short-term memory is susceptible to both interference
processes and the effects of time.

Long-term memory is the permanent record of the experience. The storage of items in long-term memory is affected not by the passage of time but by interference
processes. Items enter long-term memory through a rehearsal process which occurs in short-term memory. Items
which are not rehearsed in short-term memory are usually
lost and cannot enter the long-term memory store.

● **PROBLEM** 4-25

Discuss the short-term memory process. What are the differences between visual and auditory short-term memory?

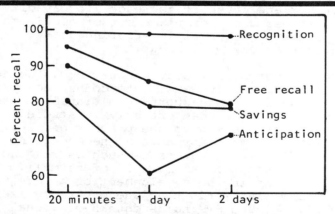

Solution: Short-term memory (STM) seems to be a temporary
store for items or experiences. It lasts for only a few
seconds. STM is not only limited in terms of time but
also in its capacity. It can only hold about seven items
(plus or minus two) of information at a time. This brief
memory span requires deliberate rehearsal to prevent the
memory from decaying over time. For example, if a person
does not rehearse the names of people he met at a party he
will quickly forget them. An item will also be displaced
(forgotten) if STM reaches its capacity level and new items
continue to enter. If, however, an item is considered important enough, it will be rehearsed in STM and transferred
into the more permanent long-term memory.

Although the storage capacity of the STM is only about
seven items, one can increase the amount of material in STM

127

by efficiently regrouping or reorganizing incoming information into "chunks." For example, although a person may not be able to remember 15 individual words, such as list A shown below, he might remember them if they were grouped into five phrases of three words each, as in list B:

List A			List B		
cows	eat	flowers	cows	eat	grass
drink	water	dogs	dogs	drink	water
grass	baby	cries	baby	cries	more
grapes	need	sun	grapes	need	sun
want	more	light	flowers	want	light

STM is highly susceptible to interference. For instance, when a person begins dialing a telephone number but is interrupted in the middle of dialing he either can't continue without looking at the number again or if he can, it is likely he will get a wrong number. Brown (1958) suggests that if there is only a small amount of information in STM (e.g., a telephone number), it will take much interference to disrupt the memory. If, however, a great amount of information is stored in STM (such as directions to a party), even a little interference may disrupt it.

Interference can disrupt STM because there is no time for rehearsal of the item after a response. Information may also be disrupted because the interfering activity could also enter STM and cause it to reach its capacity for stored items. In either case, displacement of old items unrehearsed (or items which the interfering activity prevents from being rehearsed) will occur.

There is controversy over whether human beings have one memory system or separate, interconnected systems for each sense modality. The short-term visual and short-term auditory memories have been extensively studied. Short-term visual memory refers to the process of retaining visually perceived stimuli for several seconds. A poor visual memory may affect important tasks such as reading which requires visual perception and recall of stimuli. Poor visual memory may impair the development of an adequate sight vocabulary (familiar words that one can recognize and read at a glance). Visual STM holds chunks of visual information (as words while reading) until the rest of the information is received and the complete stimulus (the sentence) is processed for meaning. STM also allows recall of the beginning of a sentence after the end has been reached. Comprehension of what is seen (in reading, this is a word or sentence), according to LaBerge and Samuels (1974), occurs partially in STM and is completed when the material is transferred into LTM.

The workings of auditory STM are similar to those of visual STM. Auditory STM is the process that allows one to store the incoming phonemes, words or phrases that are heard (depending upon the size of the chunk) until a pattern is recognized. Kier believes that one understands what one hears when one matches the information stored in STM to what one knows from one's previous experiences. For example, "Dogs sleep" would be perfectly comprehensible to most native English speakers. However, "dua dogs" would present a problem to most English speakers. The word "dua" might be heard clearly, but the listener would probably be unable to understand this word, because it is not associated with a concept within his experience. A traveler to Indonesia, however, might associate "dua" with the Indonesian language's word for "two." Since "dua" is a word he has previously experienced, he might be able to understand the phrase immediately.

People begin to process what they hear for meaning even before all the information has entered STM. In other words, even before one hears a complete sentence, one has already begun to match the information which has entered STM to one's previous experiences, and partial comprehension has taken place.

Like visual STM, auditory STM transfers important information into long-term memory and employs silent rehearsal strategies to keep information from decaying. Poor auditory memory results in poor ability to recall what is heard and an inability to hold more items in STM than the system's capacity will allow. According to Kier, if the system's capacity is two items, a three syllable word will not be processed, or a five word sentence will not be understood.

Visual and auditory STM do not seem to be independent of each other. Items in one memory may be recoded into the other memory. Again using reading as an example, many researchers claim that the visual memory traces people store in the visual STM (for example, the letters d-o-g) as they read, are recoded into a phonological code in the auditory STM (so that they "hear" the sound "dog"). There is also evidence that people who do not process visual and auditory stimuli at the same speeds may be poor readers.

● **PROBLEM 4-26**

Discuss the long-term memory process, including the methods for measuring long-term memory retention.

Solution: In contrast to STM, long-term memory (LTM) is capable of holding large amounts of material permanently. Information that is needed every day, as one's telephone number, vocabulary, one's birthdate, etc., is stored in LTM and retrieved when needed.

Information that has been rehearsed in short-term memory is transferred to the more permanent LTM store. There are three ways to measure the amount of LTM retention: recall, recognition and savings. The recall method requires that the subject reproduce something learned in the past with a minimum of cues. This is the most difficult way to remember information; therefore, the smallest amount of retention is measured with this method. When a student is asked to take an essay examination, for example, the instructor is utilizing the recall method of retention.

The recognition method is another frequently used method of measuring retention. The subject must recognize whether or not he has been exposed to the information before. This method is most frequently used in multiple-choice examinations. There is, however, a chance factor that the student may correctly guess the answer without really remembering the information, thereby inflating the amount of retention measured.

The third method of studying long-term memory retention, and the one most frequently used by psychologists in experimental studies on retention, is the savings method. The subject is required to learn something that he has already learned before. The measure of retention is the difference between the time or number of trials required for original mastery and the time or number of trials required for the second learning. For example, if it took 40 tries to learn a list of digits the first time, but only 20 tries the second time, the savings would be 50 percent. The savings method shows retention long after other methods have stopped showing retained material. In one study (Burtt, 1941), a psychologist read his 15 month-old son passages in Greek each day for three months. When the boy was 8 years old, he was required to learn the same selections in addition to new ones. The results showed that the old selections were learned in less time than the new ones. Therefore, exposure (even in infancy) to complex "nonsense" material resulted in savings at a later date. Although it may be difficult to recall material previously learned, if the opportunity to relearn or use the material again is presented, a considerable amount of savings may be found.

LTM may be disrupted by interference effects. Retroactive inhibition (interference) occurs when the retention of information is interfered with because of activities which occurred after the initial learning. For example, a person who goes to a big party and learns the names of many new people may forget names learned early in the evening because the ones learned later will interfere with the early learning. However, if he forgot the names of the people he learned later in the evening, proactive inhibition (interference) may be taking place. Here, the early learning interferes with the retrieval of material learned later. The less interference effects of any kind, the greater the probability of retaining information.

FORGETTING

● **PROBLEM** 4-27

What is meant by the Decay Theory of forgetting? What are some objections to this theory? What evidence exists to support this theory?

Solution: The simplest theory to account for forgetting is the Decay Theory, also referred to as the Disuse, or Trace Theory of forgetting. This theory postulates that memories progressively fade with the passing of time. Support for the Decay Theory comes from the common notion that memories weaken over time if they are not exercised. The hypothesis has been strengthened by studies of the physiological neural activities that are presumed to occur in short-term memory, i.e., the idea that neural activity progressively weakens over time in a manner analogous to the Decay Theory.

Nevertheless, objections to the Decay Theory outweigh evidence supporting it. Experiments have demonstrated that forgetting is affected by the activities a subject engages in during the time between the learning and the test of retention. If a set period is established between the time material is learned and the time it is tested for retention, the Decay Theory predicts that subjects who remain actively awake will report the same amount of retention. Results show this prediction to be incorrect. This experiment was first conducted by Jenkins and Dallenbach (1924) and was later replicated by others. It was found that those subjects who slept during the retention interval remembered significantly more of the nonsense syllables they had originally learned, than those subjects who remained awake.

Other experimental observations also provide evidence against the Decay Theory. Studies have demonstrated that the nature of the subject's activity preceding the initial learning affects forgetting. It seems improbable that memory decays because of disuse.

● **PROBLEM 4-28**

Describe the Interference Theory of forgetting. What has research indicated in regard to this theory?

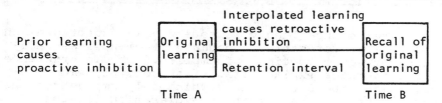

Interference theory

Solution: The Interference Theory states that forgetting occurs because new, conflicting information interferes with an original memory. Forgetting, therefore, does not depend on time, but on the amount of new, interfering information. Accordingly, forgetting involves difficulties, not in memory storage, but in memory retrieval where there is competition between alternative responses at recall. The main emphasis of the theory is on stimulus-response, associative learning principles. For example, suppose a subject associates the stimulus "dog" with two responses, "animal" and "canine." If, on a given test, the subject recalls the "dog"-"canine" association, then, according to the Interference Theory, the association of "dog"-"animal" was difficult for the sub-

131

ject to retrieve because of the competition, or interference. from the "dog"-"canine" association.

Interference theorists study two types of interference: (1) retroactive interference, where old memories in storage are interfered with by new memories (Table 1), and (2) proactive interference, where new memories are interfered with by older memories; memories related to events that occurred prior to the learning of the new information (Table 2).

Table 1: Experimental Design for the Study of Retroactive Interference.

GROUP:		EXPERIMENTAL		CONTROL
STEP 1:		Learn List A		Learn List A
STEP 2:		Learn List B		Rest
TEST:		Retention of List A		Retention of List A

Table 2: Experimental Design for the Study of Proactive Interference.

GROUP:		EXPERIMENTAL		CONTROL
STEP 1:		Learn List A		Rest
STEP 2:		Learn List B		Learn List B
TEST:		Retention of List B		Retention of List B

The Interference Theory is more widely accepted as an explanation for "forgetting," because it emphasizes relationships between competing information. The Interference Theory incorporates explanations of successful memory retrieval, unlike the Decay Theory which only emphasizes the autonomous temporal changes as an explanation for the failures of memory.

Laboratory investigations can easily test the Interference Theory by manipulating a subject's learning history during a limited period of time. For example, two groups of subjects, an experimental and a control group, would be given a list of associations (List A) to study. The control group would then rest during the retention interval, while the experimental group would study a second list of associations (List B). When both groups would be tested for retention of List A, the experimental group would not score as well as the control group; retroactive interference caused their "forgetting," that is, List B completed, or interfered with their retrieval of List A. Many studies have supported the Interference Theory of forgetting.

132

Devise an experiment which would distinguish between Decay
and Interference theories of forgetting. What results
would have to be obtained to support the Decay theory?
To support the Interference theory?

Solution: In order to devise an experiment to distinguish
between the Decay and Interference Theories of forgetting,
the hypotheses of both theories need to be clearly defined.

Step 1: Defining the hypotheses.

The Decay Theory, which states that memories fade
with the passing of time, would expect no difference
in the results of a retention test between subjects
who rest during a retention interval, and subjects
who remain active during the same retention interval.

The Interference Theory would expect a significant
difference in the amount recalled on a retention test,
between the two groups of subjects. Those subjects
who remain active during the retention interval are
expected to suffer interference from the activity
they engaged in after their original learning task.

Following a statement of hypotheses, an experimental
situation should be designed.

Step 2: Experimental design method

Subjects: Two groups of subjects should be employed:
a control group - subjects who rest after
an initial learning task, and an experimental group - subjects who enegage in an
activity after an initial learning task.

Procedure: (a) Present learning task A to the control
and experimental groups.
(b) During a given retention interval
(e.g., 2 hours), allow the control
group to rest, while the experimental
group works on learning task B.
(c) Present a learning task A retention
test to both groups of subjects.

Step 3: Results

If the results of the learning task A retention test
indicate that both groups of subjects recall the same
amount from learning task A, then the findings would support the Decay Theory. The results would prove that regardless of the activities a subject engages in, the mere
passage of time progressively fades memories, thus causing
"forgetting."

In contrast, if the results of the learning task A

retention test show that the experimental group recalls a significantly fewer amount than the control group, then the results would support the Interference Theory. It would provide evidence that learning task B caused response competition, indicating that interference from other memories causes "forgetting."

● PROBLEM 4-30

Compare and contrast Incremental and One-trial theories of learning.

Solution: A commonly accepted notion about learning is that practice, or repetition, strengthens new associations gradually. Thus, "learning" is measured by the change in response strength over practice trials. This "practice makes perfect" approach to learning represents the Incremental, or Gradual Theory of Learning. Nevertheless, this apparently simple notion is complicated by the controversy about whether learning occurs gradually over practice trials and repetition, or whether it occurs all at once on a single trial.

The One-trial Theory, also known as the All-or-none Theory, postulates that the learning of individual associations is either completely learned on one trial, or remains completely unlearned. In other words, it is not the appearance of the learning curve that differs between the two theories, but the interpretation of what the curve represents.

According to the Incremental Theory, the smooth shape of the learning curve represents the subject's gradual learning due to practice and repetition. In contrast, the All-or-none Theory predicts that the curve appears smooth only because the experimenter averages over many subjects and many associations. If, however, the performance of an individual subject on an individual association were to be examined, the learning curve would appear jagged, implying that the subject's performance shifts from a chance level to a perfect performance in one trial.

● PROBLEM 4-31

Have studies on learning supported the Incremental or the One-trial Theory of learning?

Solution: Research conducted to determine whether the Incremental Theory of learning or the One-trial (All-or-none) Theory of learning is correct, generally utilizes paired-associate learning tasks. Studies exist which provide evidence in support of both theories. Neither theory is "correct" in an absolute sense. Yet, psychologists have proposed a number of explanations to reconcile the array of empirical and theoretical discrepancies.

Theoretically, if an experimenter is concentrating on

the behavior of individual subjects, the All-or-none Theory of learning provides the best description of an individual subject's learning curve. The objection to the Incremental Theory is based on the fact that data, when collected from a group of subjects, result in an average, or mean performance for the group; a result that does not correspond to the behavior of any individual in the group.

Although specific instances of learning can be very sudden, this apparent rapid learning may be based on a slowly acquired skill from past experience. In other words, it is likely that the shape of the learning curve for a given task is highly dependent on the knowledge and past experience that the subject brings to the new learning situation. If the learner has little experience, learning may occur gradually. If he has a great deal of experience, learning may appear on a single trial.

The following explanations attempt to resolve the discrepancies between empirical and theoretical findings by asserting that the two theories are complementary:

(1) Two separate learning systems may be available for different learning situations -- gradual learning for simple learning tasks and all-or-none learning for complex learning tasks.

(2) Learning may require many small associations, each learned on a one-trial basis. But the process may appear to be incremental when viewed in its entirety.

(3) Each of the two theories may explain different memory processes: storage and retrieval. Storage in memory may occur in an all-or-none fashion but retrieval from memory may operate on an incremental basis.

Thus, it is possible to think of both theories of learning as being correct. Ultimately, it may depend on the type of learning task involved.

● **PROBLEM** 4-32

What have been the results of studies which investigated the tip-of-the-tongue (TOT) state?

Solution: Studies of the tip-of-the-tongue phenomenon focus on a person's ability to recall words or names. The tip-of-the-tongue phenomenon is probably familiar to everyone: It involves a word or name that one has difficulty retrieving; the search for the word often leaves the person in an uncomfortable state. The evidence that the person knows the word is two-fold: (a) either the person is eventually successful in retrieving the word, or, (b) if a wrong word is presented, the subject in the tip-of-the-tongue state is often able to reject it and can explain its similarity with the target word.

Brown and McNeill (1966) studied this phenomenon in a laboratory setting. They read dictionary definitions of somewhat uncommon words to subjects and asked the subjects to provide the correct word associated with the definitions. Whenever a tip-of-the-tongue phenomenon occurred, the subject was asked to write down words similar in sound or meaning to the target word, the number of syllables, and the initial letter of the word. Brown and McNeill obtained evidence for partial recall; many of the subjects were quite accurate at providing the first letter and the number of syllables in the target word.

Thus, the characteristics of the target word that were recalled by the subject served as cues in tapping the memory for the eventual retrieval of the word. The more phonetic and semantic features the subject was able to think of, the more opportunity the subject had to narrow the words down, eventually producing the one that was defined by a particular feature. This experiment provides evidence that people use semantic and phonetic characteristics associated with a word for the retrieval process in memory. Brown and McNeill concluded that during memory search, generic recall -- general memory -- often occurs before specific recall, the immediate retrieval of the target word.

This study appears to support the Attribute Theory proposed by Underwood. According to Underwood, memory can be thought of as a collection of attributes that serve two different functions: (1) Those attributes that are independent of the actual verbal event, such as when and where the event occurred, serve to discriminate or differentiate between memories. These attributes are called non-associative attributes. (2) Those attributes which define the verbal characteristics of the verbal event serve retrieval purposes. These attributes are called associative attributes.

SHORT ANSWER QUESTIONS FOR REVIEW

Choose the correct answer.

1. Which is true about Hebb's consolidation theory
   of memory trace? (a) it hypothesizes that a
   type of learning consolidation activity occurs
   simultaneously with the learning event, "lock-
   ing in" the memory trace instantly (b) it hypothesizes that a type of learning consolidation activity occurs for minutes and even hours
   after the event (c) it hypothesizes that elec-
   tro convulsive shock impairment of long-term,
   but not recent memory, provides basic support
   for his theoretical position (d) children fit
   this theoretical model but adults do not (e)
   adults fit this theoretical model but children
   do not

   b

2. For a person who has just learned a list of adjectives, the task least likely to interfere
   with this learning would be the learning of
   (a) a list of numbers (b) a list of nonsense
   syllables (c) another list of adjectives (d)
   a list of nouns (e) a list of synonyms

   a
   Numbers
   are the
   most dis-
   tinctly
   different
   from ad-
   jectives

3. The field theorist emphasizes the role of learning in (a) S-R associations (b) drive reduction (c) reinforcement (d) cognitive processes (e) sensory processor

   d

4. One of the primary effects of anxiety on learning is the occurrence of (a) removal of mental blocks (b) more interference with familiar material than with new material (c) reduction in the ability to discriminate clearly (d)
   heightened motivation increasing proficiency on
   virtually any task (e) proactive facilitation

   c

5. The Von Restorff effect applies to (a) serial
   learning (b) task completion (c) prepotent
   stimulus (d) meaningfulness of learned
   material (e) memory span

   c The
   effect is
   that some
   distinct
   quality of
   a stimulus
   in a se-
   ries makes
   the partic-
   ular stim-
   ulus stand
   out from
   others
   (e.g., red

137

SHORT ANSWER QUESTIONS FOR REVIEW

ink blot
against a
background
of blue
ink; a num-
ber on a
word list

6. Which one of the following is more likely to
   enhance learner performance? (a) massed
   practice (b) nonsense syllables (c) distributed practice (d) functional fixedness
   (e) feedback   e

7. Which of the following types of learning constitutes learning by matching an item on a
   test? (a) savings (b) relearning (c) recognition (d) recall (e) reconstruction   e

8. The continuity theory of learning suggests that
   learning (a) is on an all or nothing basis
   (b) is sudden (c) is a gradual process (d)
   continues throughout one's life (e) begins
   at birth   c

9. Which one of the following devices is most
   familiar to paired associates learning experiments? (a) visual cliff (b) memory slides
   (c) memory drum (d) Skinner box (e) pursuit rotor   c

10. The ability to remember material is greatest
    for material that is (a) related to very
    painful experiences (b) opposed to one's own
    viewpoint (c) slightly unpleasant (d) in
    agreement with one's own attitudes and values
    (e) slightly pleasant   d

11. Which one of the following is not specifically
    a retention aid? (a) chunking (b) overlearn-
    ing (c) meaningfulness (d) knowledge of
    results (e) associating a mental picture or
    scene with the verbal material   d

12. A primary difference between escape and avoid-
    ance conditioning is that (a) in escape con-
    ditioning, the aversive stimulus is always re-
    ceived by the subject (b) in escape condition-
    ing, the aversive stimulus is not received by
    the subject (c) in escape conditioning, suc-
    cessive approximation is used (d) in escape
    conditioning, successive approximation is not
    used (e) escape conditioning utilizes re-
    sponse chaining   a

138

SHORT ANSWER QUESTIONS FOR REVIEW

13. For which of the following is retention highest? (a) poetry (b) meaningful material
(c) specific dates (d) motor tasks (e)
concepts and principles

    d

14. Which of the following is a memory storage
distinction espoused by many psychologists?
(a) minimal and maximal (b) subsequent and
consequent (c) perceptual and motor (d)
short term and long term (e) informational
and motivational

    d

15. The point in a learning curve during which no
increase in performance is evident but physiological limit has not yet been reached is called
the (a) asymptote (b) reminiscence (c) latency (d) extinction (e) plateau

    e

16. The earliest studies on record of verbal learning and rote memory were conducted by (a)
Thorndike (b) Pavlov (c) Skinner (d) Ebbinghaus (e) Mowrer

    d

Fill in the blanks.

17. The man who introduced the use of nonsense syllables into verbal-learning experiments was_____.

    Ebbinghaus

18. The aspect of the serial-position effect which
pertains to recall of the first part of a list
is known as the _____ effect.

    primacy

19. The aspect of the serial-position effect which
pertains to recall of the last part of a list
is known as the _____ effect.

    recency

20. In _____ memory, processed information is stored
up to approximately 30 minutes.

    short
    term

21. _____ is a type of memory error by which the individual, unable to remember a particular item,
manufactures an appropriate substitute.

    Confabula-
    tion

22. Retroactive inhibition, interference from learning after acquisition, and _____ inhibition,
interference from previously learned material,
are equally powerful when retention is tested
several days after acquisition.

    proactive

23. According to the _____ theory of forgetting, the
strength of memorized information becomes weaker
due to the passage of time and gradually disappears.

    decay or
    trace

SHORT ANSWER QUESTIONS FOR REVIEW

24. Forgetting material learned immediately before some traumatic event happens to the person is called retrograde _____ .

amnesia

25. Rapid progress on the solution of problem following a rest period is known as _____ .

incubation

26. _____ are things (objects, words, events) that represent something other than what they are, of which they are the referents.

Symbols

27. The theory of forgetting according to which forgetting occurs because learning acquired before or after the information to be recalled interferes with its retrieval is called the _____ theory of forgetting.

interference

28. Freudian psychologists theorize that forgetting represents an _____ effort to rid the self of bad memories; the process by which this occurs is known as repression.

unconscious

29. _____ is a type of memory whereby the individual retains mental images (i.e., pictures) of the learned material.

Idetic or photographic

Determine whether the following statements are true or false.

30. Free recall differs from serial learning in that the latter requires subjects to recall the items in a particular order.

True

31. Resting after practicing a motor task leads to improved performance upon resumption of the task (reminiscence) because massed practice improves recall.

False
Rest reduces interference from work inhibition

32. Most of the evidence suggests that short term and long term memory decay at the same rate over time.

False

33. One major difference between the computer and man with regard to their problem solving abilities is that the computer is faster but more cumbersome.

True

34. The clustering effect deals with the relationship between position and recall.

False

SHORT ANSWER QUESTIONS FOR REVIEW

35. An essay item on an examination requires the retentive skill of recognition.

False
It re-
quires re-
construc-
tion

36. Learning how to learn is essentially a process of establishing learning sets.

True

37. That the ability to remember completed tasks exceeds the ability to remember uncompleted tasks is known as the Ziegarnic effect.

False
The Zie-
garnic ef-
fect is
that uncom-
pleted tasks
are better
remembered
than com-
pleted
tasks

38. A learning technique by which particular stimuli are linked with specific responses is called paired-associate learning.

True

39. Individuals with Korsakoff's psychosis suffer gaps in memory which they fill in with irrelevant or disconnected material.

True

40. Memory and retention mean the same thing.

False
Memory is
a more in-
clusive
category

41. Recall is a measure of retention by which the correct answer is presented to the subject, who must select it from among several alternatives.

False
This is
the defin-
ition of
recogni-
tion

42. The early verbal learning studies concentrated on how subjects learned and maintained meaningful material.

True

43. Once material has been completely learned, overlearning (continued practice) sometimes leads to even greater recall.

True

44. Short term memory may be organized through sound, whereas long term memory may be organized through meaningful categories.

True

SHORT ANSWER QUESTIONS FOR REVIEW

45. Acquisition, extinction, and asymptote are all terms relating to the learning curve.

    True

46. Skinner was the originator of the concepts of conditioned and unconditioned stimuli and conditioned and unconditioned responses.

    False
    It was
    Pavlov who
    was the
    originator
    of these
    terms

47. Dollard and Miller's four fundamentals of learning are drives, cues, responses, and reinforcements.

    True

48. The Whorf hypothesis claims that language patterns are determinants of thought patterns.

    True

49. Mowrer is known for his instigation of the idea of innate competence while Chomsky and Lennenberg are known for their investigations of several principles of psychology.

    False

50. Programmed learning machines such as teaching machines and computer assisted instruction are fairly much in use these days.

    True

51. The man who taught a few pigeons to play ping pong through his techniques of operant conditioning was B. F. Skinner.

    True

52. Recall, reconstruction, recognition and relearning are all methods of measuring retention.

    True

CHAPTER 5

COGNITION

THINKING AND ITS DEVELOPMENT

● **PROBLEM** 5-1

Define thinking. How is it different from learning?
Describe two major types of thinking.

Solution: Thinking is the process by which humans manipulate representations of the world. The processes involved
in thinking are called cognitive processes.

Thinking is more complex than learning. In learning,
stimulus-response associations are acquired. In thinking,
the person applies current perceptions to these associations to further his purposes. While learning involves
stimulus-response relations, cognitive processes involve
stimulus-stimulus relations.

All of the many different kinds of thinking fall into
two major categories: nondirected or associative thinking and directed thinking.

Nondirected thinking has no destination. This category includes reverie: aimless "stream of consciousness"
thinking, free association, mind-wandering and fantasy
(which includes dreaming and daydreaming).

Directed thinking aims toward a goal. It is found in
the processes involved in reasoning (problem solving),
logic (critical thinking), and creativity.

● **PROBLEM** 5-2

List and describe the stages of cognitive development as
defined by Piaget.

Solution: A child's cognitive structure--his repertoire
of schemes (organized patterns of behavior)--changes as he
develops. This development consists of qualitative changes
in sequence or stages. Piaget's stages of cognitive devel-

opment reflect a progression of learning. The characteristics of each stage are dependent on the learning that has
taken place during earlier stages and makes way for succeeding stages.

According to Piaget, there are four basic stages of
cognitive development: sensorimotor, preoperational (which
is subdivided into preconceptual and intuitive stages), concrete operational, and formal operational.

The first stage, sensorimotor, begins at birth and
lasts until the child reaches two years of age. During
this time, the child's behavior is mostly reflexive. His
perception of the world is limited to those things he can
immediately perceive. He cannot abstract; objects which he
is not in contact with do not exist for him. He has no
language ability during the early part of this phase but
begins to acquire it near the end. By the end of the second year he also acquires symbolic intelligence, that is,
he can conceive of objects that are not directly in view.

The second stage of cognitive development is called
preoperational; it lasts from ages two to seven. Because
a great deal of development occurs during this time span,
this stage is often subdivided into the preconceptual
stage that lasts from two to four years and the intuitive
stage that lasts from ages four to seven. The preconceptual stage is characterized by egocentric thought--the
child sees the world only in relation to himself--the activities he performs upon it and the stimulation he receives from it. During the intuitive phase, thinking and
problem solving are based on intuition. The child has not
yet acquired logic nor has he learned the concepts of conservation and reversibility. A child at this stage of development would say that a tall, narrow container of water
holds more water than a short, wide one even if both hold
the same amount of water. This demonstrates the absence
of a notion of conservation. The intuitive child is also
unable to reverse a thought. He cannot, for example,
think of an object as a whole once he has divided it into
two parts. The child's thinking is static. He thinks of
objects as having permanent states; he cannot envision
transformations. He cannot understand that an object can
change its shape without changing in quantity.

The preoperational stage is called such because it precedes the development of operational thought. An operation,
according to Piaget, is a process that changes its object.
The change may be a result of a physical action, of a
thought about an action, or a manipulation of ideas; that
is, thoughts about thoughts. In operational thought, then,
the individual mentally manipulates the environment.

The period of concrete operations lasts from ages
seven to eleven years. At this time, the child can think
logically; he no longer needs to depend on his intuition.
However, his logical thinking is limited to concrete objects or simple ideas he can conceive. Abstract thinking
is still largely undeveloped. The child acquires an understanding of numbers during this stage and is able to

Monopoly à la Piaget

Piaget's stages of cognitive development may be easier to remember if we relate them to a single example. What would
happen at each stage if we played a game of Monopoly with the
child?

Sensorimotor
stage:

The child puts houses, hotels, and dice in
mouth, plays with "Chance" cards.

Preoperational
stage:

The child plays Monopoly but makes own rules
and cannot understand instructions.

Concrete
operational
stage:

Children understand basic instructions and
will play by the rules, but are not capable
of hypothetical transactions dealing with
mortgages, loans, and special pacts and bar-
gains with other players.

Formal
operations
stage:

The child no longer plays game mechanically;
complex and hypothetical transactions unique
to each game are now possible.

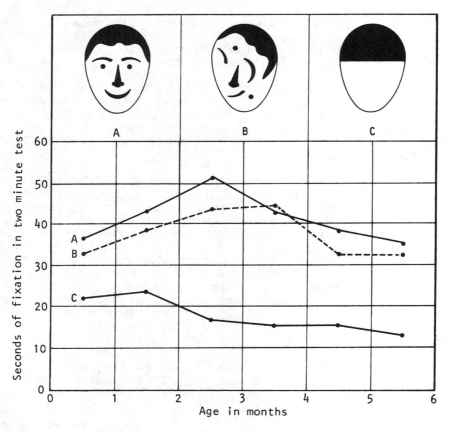

conserve. He develops the ability to think of the reversibility of various processes. However, his sense of
reversibility is limited to actions in the real world,
what Piaget called empirical reversibility. This is different from operational reversibility when the child can
conceive the consequences of a reversed action. Operational reversibility is not acquired until the next stage.

The formal operational period is the last stage in Piaget's system of cognitive development. It begins at the age of 11 and lasts through ages 14 or 15. The child can now think in a completely logical fashion. He can think in the abstract since he is no longer limited to concrete images in his immediate perception. As mentioned before, he is capable of operational thought. In addition, religious beliefs and a sense of idealism are also developed. By 15 years of age, the functional ability of an individual's cognitive structure is fully developed and can handle most logical thinking.

● **PROBLEM** 5-3

Describe scheme, assimilation and accommodation as defined by Jean Piaget.

Solution: The famous French psychologist, Jean Piaget, considers adaptation a basic process in development. A newborn child's behavior is mostly reflexive; that is, it centers on the child himself. Eventually, however, the child responds to external stimuli and must learn to deal with his environment. Piaget calls this learning process adaptation. The child learns to adapt to his surroundings.

Piaget defined two aspects of adaptation: assimilation and accommodation. The newborn infant, however, does not interact with his environment. His behavior consists of reflexive activities such as sucking, looking, crying. Piaget calls these early behaviors schemes (also called schema or schemata).

For the child to survive in the world, however, he must learn to adapt. This involves an interplay between assimilation and accommodation. According to Piaget, it is only through adaptation that people (children as well as adults) interact with their environment. An individual displays assimilation when he uses previously learned responses to new stimuli. A person who has only driven cars with automatic transmissions will not have to learn how to drive from scratch when confronted with a car that has a standard (stick) transmission. Much of what he already knows about driving will aid him in driving the car with the standard transmission. This is assimilation. However, in order to drive the new vehicle he must still learn how to operate the stick shift. He must become familiar with the different methods employed in driving both types of cars. This is accommodation. Thus, assimilation and accommodation interact to produce a new behavior that facilitates adaptation to a different environment.

● **PROBLEM** 5-4

Describe the component process theory of cognitive development. Name and describe the five mental processes necessary in problem solving according to this theory.

Solution: Piaget described cognitive development as a se-

quence of operations through which a child progresses.
American psychologists, however, prefer the component
process theory of cognitive development. The theory is
based on the assumption that a child's cognition develops
as he reaches certain levels of competence in various cognitive skills. As the child gains cognitive abilities,
they are integrated into a general cognitive ability.

The component process theory is concerned with problem
solving. The degree of success achieved is used as an index for measuring cognitive ability. Before a child is
fully competent to solve problems, he must be capable of
using five mental processes: encoding, memory, evaluation,
deduction, and mediation.

Encoding refers to the acknowledgment, understanding,
and labeling of stimuli encoded as images. At this point
in development, the child can imagine a particular object
or sensation--he does not need to perceive it directly.
When he acquires language, words are used in the encoding
process. A child's success at problem solving is contingent on his ability to encode stimuli properly--he must be
able to recognize it and know what it is called.

The next step in the problem solving process is called
memory. The child must be able to remember stimuli he has
encoded and be able to draw on that information when it is
needed to solve a problem. Language increases the child's
memorization capacity to a large degree. Generally, it
is the child's repetition of the words that describe a
particular experience or stimuli that later enables him
to remember the stimuli. Research indicates that the ex-
tensiveness of the child's vocabulary is an important factor in problem solving ability.

The third mental process of problem solving is called
evaluation. At this level the child sets up a hypothesis
and weighs its advantages and disadvantages. The process
of evaluation can begin at age 2.

The next step in the problem solving process consists
of the twin processes of deduction and hypothesis generation. Here, the child draws on hypotheses he has already
made in order to arrive at a decision or make a deduction
when confronted with a problem. For example, a child may
know that both scissors and razor blades can be used to
cut paper. If one of these instruments is not available,
he will use the other. Hence, the hypothesis--both scissors and razor blades can cut paper--leads to the deduction: use one to cut paper; if it isn't available, use
the other.

The last of the problem solving mental processes is
mediation. Mediation refers to the use of various tools
or mediators to facilitate internalization of thought.
Mediators include words, images, and concepts. The use
of mediators is necessary in solving reversal-shift problems where the subject is asked to do the opposite of
what he did in an earlier identical situation. For example, a child is presented with two containers filled

to different levels with liquids of different colors. He
is then asked to choose the container with the greater
amount of liquid. To solve the problem he must disregard
the color of the liquid. Once he learns to do this, he
is asked to select the container with the least amount
of liquid. If the child has good verbal mediation skills
he will do this successfully. He can use words as mediators to tell himself which container has the least amount
of liquid. Children's use of language as a cognitive
tool usually occurs between the ages of 5 and 7.

● **PROBLEM** 5-5

Briefly discuss Jerome Bruner's theory of cognitive
development.

Solution: Jerome Bruner's theory on the development of
thinking recognizes the importance of such factors as
culture, evolution, integration, and language in the cognitive growth of a human organism.

Bruner believes that the development of intellectual
functioning is shaped by technological advances. Certainly, the way people thought a few centuries ago, before
the development of modern industry, is markedly different
from the way people think today. Even during the same
period of time, cognitive development differs between
populations of technically advanced societies and those
that are unsophisticated. Cultural effects are important
in cognitive development in other ways, language being
the most important.

Bruner believes in an evolutionary consistency. He
takes the alloplastic view that individuals adapt to
other persons and objects rather than the autoplastic
view which sees cognitive development as a predetermined
unfolding that is relatively unaffected by environmental
events. In contrast to Piaget, who took the autoplastic
view, Bruner believes that cognitive processes evolved
subsequent to technological advances. In this sense,
technology causes evolution. According to Bruner, the
brain evolved to its large size due to new selection pressures after the introduction of various tools.

Bruner's feelings against pre-determinism in cognitive development are reflected in his belief that movements, perceptions, and thoughts depend upon technique
rather than upon wired-in arrangements in the nervous
system.

Bruner stresses the importance of integration. Inherent in this idea is the notion that there are few simple,
individual adult acts that cannot be performed by a child.
According to Bruner, cognitive maturation results from
the integration of acts and skills and humans need
"blueprints" or plans of higher order combinations. Language, he asserted, is the means by which such plans are
generated, not the other way around.

Bruner believes that humans perceive basically the same objects and events as lower organisms, but the representation and retrieval of such experiences are different. Bruner identified three fundamental ways by which human beings convert immediate experiences into cognitive representations. The first to develop is the enactive mode which is based upon action or movement. For the child in this stage, objects have meaning only with respect to the actions performed on them. A bottle has meaning for an infant only in terms of the pleasurable liquid that can be derived from it. The enactive mode is also important to adult behavior. There are several skills, such as playing a musical instrument or a game, which are difficult, if not impossible, to learn strictly by verbal instruction. This occurs because knowledge of these activities is heavily stored in the enactive mode.

The next mode to develop is called the iconic. In this stage, knowledge of the world is based heavily on images which stand for perceptual events. A picture, for example, may stand for an actual event. While the emphasis is usually on visual images, other sensory images are possible.

The symbolic mode is the last mode to develop. In this stage, language provides the means for representing experience and for transforming it. Most adult thought is in the symbolic mode. Bruner considers the acquisition of language and the development of the ability to think in the symbolic mode to be the chief milestone of cognitive development.

● **PROBLEM** 5-6

What are concepts? How are concepts useful? Describe two types.

Solution: Concepts are symbols or representations of connections between two or more objects, events, or ideas. Concepts summarize or generalize the similarities among various entities.

Concepts are useful; they permit the classification of objects and events so that an overwhelming amount of stimuli can be reduced to manageable proportions. This facilitates thinking at high levels of complexity. Cars, buses, and trucks are dissimilar in several ways, yet they can be described according to their common properties: "motor vehicles."

Concepts are also used to distinguish relations among objects and events so that similarities and differences may be found. As such, they allow for comparisons and contrasts. For example, the concept "bright light" indicates its relation to different intensities of light.

There are two basic types of concepts: simple and complex. A concept is simple when it represents a single stimulus property. For example, a given set of items are either red or not red. When multiple stimulus properties are considered simultaneously a concept is complex.

Complex concepts can be further subdivided into conjunctive, disjunctive, and relational concepts. With conjunctive concepts, the objects represented possess two or more common properties. For example, a motor vehicle is a conjunctive concept because such an object must at least have two attributes--it requires an engine or motor and it must be mobile. Disjunctive concepts are based on entities in which only one property or a combination of properties is necessary to fulfill the concept. "Food" is an example of a disjunctive concept since any digestible item can be considered food; digestibility is the sole necessary property. Comparisons between two properties express a relational concept. To say that "bananas are sweeter than steak," reflects a relational concept.

Concepts can also be categorized as concrete or abstract. Concrete concepts represent concrete objects such as "house" or "bread." Abstract concepts represent ideas such as "love" and "justice."

● PROBLEM 5-7

Discuss three ways in which concepts can be attained.

Solution: Three ways in which concepts can be attained are: through the attachment of labels to entities, through the use of contexts, and through the use of definitions.

The first method is often used, especially by children. By labeling objects and events, children extract the common properties that define certain categories.

New concepts are also acquired through the means of the context in which they appear. In language (which is intimately connected to concept formation), the meaning of an unrecognizable word can be acquired by the way it is used in a particular sentence. If the sentence is to make sense, other words in the sentence may demand that the unrecognized word have certain properties. In such a situation, one may understand the concept of the word without knowing the word. The following example illustrates this: "As she was enceinte, Mary had to make sure that her diet was nutritious until the end of the ninth month." If one did not know the meaning of the word "enceinte," one could probably guess that it means "pregnant" from the context of the sentence.

The attainment of concepts through definitions is the most important. This refers to the verbal description of a concept. This method is often used in the learning of complex concepts.

● PROBLEM 5-8

Define percepts and images. What is the difference between the two? What variables determine the kinds of images a person possesses?

Solution: Percepts and images are two types of internal
pictures. A percept is an internal picture of a fragment
of reality which is bound in a stimulus-response fashion
to the sensations impinging upon the person at the time
it occurs; it is a sensory experience. Such pictures are
subject to transformation and distortion by the person's
past experiences, sets, and expectations.

Images are not directly dependent upon the incoming
flow of stimulation. Images are stored representations
of sensory information that can be recalled by the person
at will. For example, if one thinks of a familiar object,
a picture of it can be seen in the mind. This picture
is not as clear or vivid as the object itself but it is
closer to the objective reality of the object than any
verbal description of it.

Images vary from person to person depending on a number of variables: experiences, interests, and motivations.
The form of images also varies. Visual images are believed
to be experienced more frequently than auditory images.
Only a small minority of people report olfactory, taste,
and neuromuscular images.

● **PROBLEM 5-9**

Define the following: symbol, signal, sign. What symbols does language employ? How are symbols involved in
the process of thinking?

Solution: A symbol is a stimulus that can be substituted
for an actual object or event. It represents or "stands
for" something different from itself. Words are important
symbols. Even a simple sentence can stand for many things,
for example, "We like pizza" symbolizes people, a feeling,
and an object. Numerous aspects of the environment can
be symbolized.

A signal is a stimulus that indicates that another
stimulus is about to occur. A signal may function as a
symbol and vice versa. For example, the word "Danger!"
may be both a symbol for a particular dangerous occurrence
or a signal that something dangerous is coming or is about
to occur.

A sign may be either a symbol, a signal, or both. In
contrast to a signal, a sign usually represents a more
permanent state. For example, on a three-way traffic light
the flashing of a yellow light is a signal that the light
is about to change to red. When it is not part of a three-
way traffic light, a yellow light is usually a sign of
warning.

Words are the most important symbols that language
employs. Other symbols include the hand gestures and facial and bodily expressions used in body language, the
hand movements used in sign language for the deaf and the
system of dots that comprise the Morse Code.

Symbols are important to the development of concepts which, in turn, are an important aspect of thinking, language, problem solving, creativity, and other processes. The study of cognitive processes involves an examination of how symbols of objects and events are related to one another in the thinking of human beings. The emphasis here is on stimulus-stimulus, rather than on stimulus-response relations.

In the cognitive process, symbols other than words may be used. Einstein claimed that he often thought in mathematical symbols. Composers sometimes report thinking of their creations in musical symbols.

● PROBLEM 5-10

What is the difference between convergent and divergent thinking?

Solution: The word "thinking" in this context refers to problem solving. Guilford was the first psychologist to make a distinction between these two types of problem solving. In convergent thinking, a person searches for one solution to a problem,while in divergent thinking a person generates a number of possible solutions. Convergent and divergent thinking are not exclusive of each other. A person can be proficient in both convergent and divergent thinking.

There are two types of problems--those which have only one correct answer and those that have more than one correct answer. A simple arithmetic problem such as, 5 + 3 = 8 can be solved by convergent thinking. There is only one possible answer to this question. Convergent thinking depends upon one's ability to categorize events and objects in a logical manner.

Divergent thinking requires flexibility, fluency of ideas,and originality. The solution of complex chess problems, for example, requires divergent thinking. This is true because there are always many possibilities that a chess player must consider before making his move. He must not only evaluate his opponent's last play, but in deciding what his own move will be he must anticipate all th possible plays his opponent may respond with. The chess master considers numerous possibilities; he exemplifies the highest order of divergent thinking.

Guilford believes that creative thinking is primarily divergent in nature. Creativity involves thinking that is not restricted to any one direction. The creative problem solver is not limited to a small range of possibilities. He is able to imagine many solutions, see new relationships, and invent new meanings for old concepts. Thus, divergent thinking and creativity are closely related. Tests of creativity usually measure divergent production; that is, the number of possible answers to a particular problem an individual can generate.

PROBLEM SOLVING

Describe and give an example of each of the following
types of problems: simple, conceptual, and reasoning.

Solution: Simple problems, sometimes called "one-shot"
problems, are those whose solutions are arrived at through
a relatively small number of uncomplicated steps. At the
outset the person receives all the information he needs
to solve the problem in the form of written or spoken instructions. A simple problem has a specific solution
which the person, upon arriving at, usually recognizes
as correct.

There are various types of simple problems. The majority of them, such as anagrams, rely on language skills
for their solutions. Other simple problems depend on perceptual organization. For example, in the following problem a person might be asked to move only three matchsticks
to convert the figure into a 16 match arrangement of four
squares. The problem requires that the solver utilize
his visual imagery.

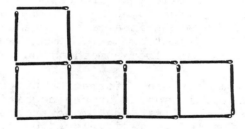

The most sophisticated types of problems require reasoning and logical analysis. A syllogism, for example,
requires the use of logic. Syllogisms are three-step arguments that consist of two premises, both assumed to be
true, and a conclusion. The problem is to decide whether
the conclusion follows logically from the premises. The
following is a syllogism:

    A = B
    B = C
    Therefore, A = C   True or false?

Syllogisms are solved with the rules of formal logic.
These rules, used in the analysis of arguments, determine
whether or not the statement is internally consistent.
The formal logic utilized in solving syllogisms requires
three things: each premise must be considered with all
its possible meanings, all the meanings of the premises
should be combined in all possible ways, and the conclusion
is valid only if it can be applied to every possible combination of the premises.

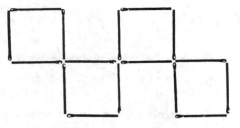

solution to matchstick problem

Describe the following approaches to problem solving:
computer simulation models, algorithms, heuristic methods,
split-half methods.

Solution: Computers today are continuing to solve problems
that would ordinarily take humans an extremely long period
of time. A computer operates by executing the operations
that have been inputted into its system (detailed instructions for handling each component of the problem), which in
turn creates the output of the computer--the solution. Since
computers possess the ability to retain programmed information electronically (they compartmentalize information to
access the bits of information directly), they are able to
operate more quickly than human beings, who are dependent
upon retaining information in a manner in which information
may be stored in different areas (a memory may be recalled
from an object, but also from something entirely different).

Simulation models are information processing systems
designed to duplicate aspects of the cognitive activities
of human beings. The first such model to be employed,
the Logic Theorist (LT), was developed by J. Newell and
H. S. Simon. Most simulation models are limited in that
they can duplicate only certain aspects of human cognitive
behavior such as attitude change or verbal learning. Simon
and Newell (1964), however, observed that all the models
have a great many component processes in common; they incorporated these to develop the General Problem Solver
(GPS). This single model is designed to simulate the entirety of human cognition through use of a great many concepts, heuristics, and strategies that are believed to
underlie human cognition. To the degree that the GPS
approximates human cognition, it provides a general theory
of human cognitive behavior.

The algorithm approach to problem solving involves
methodically considering all the possible alternative solutions to a problem, one by one. This procedure invariably results in a correct solution. Most people, however, would not use this method to solve a complex problem since it may be extremely time-consuming.

A heuristic approach to problem solving is concerned
with narrowing down the number of alternatives to be considered. Heuristics are shortcuts, gimmicks, rules of

thumb, and the like, which people use to reduce the amount of information they must scan in order to find appropriate answers. A card player, for example, does not consider all possible moves at once, only those that are appropriate at a certain point in the game. Newell and Simon have suggested that using general rules which suggest a line of attack appropriate for a solution to the problem may be formulated and followed in a heuristic approach.

The split-half method is another way of speeding the problem solving process. In this approach, the number of alternatives is divided into two groups and each is considered separately. This splitting may be done several times depending on the number or complexity of the alternatives. By what is essentially a process of elimination, the correct solution is eventually reached.

● **PROBLEM** 5-13

List and describe the stages of problem solving as proposed by Johnson.

Solution: According to Donald M. Johnson there are three stages in problem solving: preparation, production, and judgment.

In the preparation stage, the individual assesses the problem: he determines its nature, evaluates the information available and considers the obstacles that may surface.

The production stage involves a search for possible alternative solutions. Most research concerned with simple problem solving concentrates on this stage. The researcher measures the time a subject spends in solving the problem; the length of this interval reflects the subject's involvement in generating alternative solutions.

The third stage of problem solving is judgment. At this level the person evaluates all the possible solutions to the problem and selects the one he thinks has the best chance of being correct.

Some psychologists include a fourth stage in this scheme. They call it the "incubation" period. During this stage the person withdraws from the problem before a solution is found. He may need to engage in some other activity for some time before he can find the solution. Often when the individual returns to the problem he solves it with much ease. One explanation for this is that while the person is away from the problem the unconscious mind continues to work on it. Another explanation suggests that the incubation period allows the individual to "clear his mind," that is, get over any short-sighted or repetitious behavior that is preventing him from finding the solution.

The three basic stages of problem solving do not always occur in a neat, orderly fashion. Depending on the

complexity of the problem, stages may warrant a number
of repetitions. It may be necessary to reexamine the
problem for new information, to repeat stages of production
for different parts of the solution, or to evaluate possible solutions several times in the light of new information.

● **PROBLEM** 5-14

Discuss the role of insight in problem solving. Describe
Karl Duncker's theory.

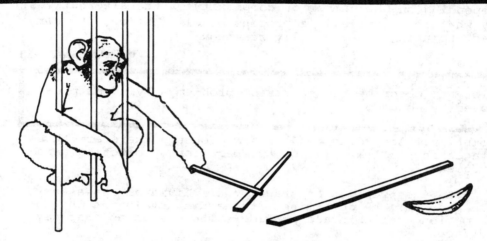

Psychologist Wolfgang Köhler felt that solution of a multiple
stick problem revealed a capacity for insight.

Solution: In contrast to many learning theorists who contend that problem solving involves a long process of trial
and error, other psychologists, most notably Wolfgang Köhler, have claimed that true problem solving requires insight. Köhler believed that problem solving cannot occur
without the planning and foresight characteristic of realistic thinking.

     In a series of experiments with chimpanzees (1926),
Köhler devised an arrangement in which all the elements
necessary for the solution to the problem were in full
view of the animals. The results confirmed his claims
that the arrangement of elements necessary to a solution
determines to a large extent whether or not the solution
will be reached.

     In humans, many psychologists have noted the "aha"
experience in which a person suddenly acquires insight
into how a particular problem should be solved.

     Some psychologists, however, have questioned the
"suddenness" of this process. Karl Duncker (1945) concluded that problem solving most often occurs after an
individual passes through a series of progressively more
specific formulations of the problem, each arising from
the one before it and partly shaped by it. Duncker de-

scribed three components of this scheme. He called
the first stage the general range. Here the person
reformulates the problem in such a way that the direction
in which a solution might lie is suggested. In the second
stage, called functional solution, the individual arrives
at just that. He narrows the range of possibilities to
arrive at a functional solution. At this point he can
assert that when X is achieved, the problem will be solved.
In the last stage of Duncker's series, called the specific
solution, the person finally discovers the means of finding X and solves the problem. If this X did not yield
the correct solution, the individual returns to an earlier stage and resumes the process until a satisfactory
solution is found.

● **PROBLEM** 5-15

Define reasoning. Give two types. What types of errors
can occur in reasoning?

<u>Solution</u>: Reasoning is a cognitive process used in prob-
lem solving when the person incorporates two or more aspects of his past experience. Reasoning is considered
a mediational or mediating process. It refers to the intermediate step that connects an observable stimulus with
an observable response; the reasoning itself is unobservable.

There are two forms of reasoning: programmatic and
generative thinking. Programmatic reasoning occurs when
existing systems of thought are used. Generative thinking occurs when systems of thought are created.

Human reasoning is subject to errors in logic and
distortions. These stem from the "atmosphere effect,"
the semantic effect, prejudices and biases, and the "halo
effect."

The atmosphere effect refers to a tendency to allow
the manner in which statements or premises are phrased
in a logical statement or problem to influence the conclusion drawn by the individual. In a syllogism, it is
the tendency to accept conclusions that are consistent
with the "atmosphere" or context established by the premises of the syllogism. For example, a set of premises
all of the form "All ____ are _____," establishes an
atmosphere for a conclusion of the same form. To illustrate, if one's premises were: "All A's are B's," and
"All C's are B's," one might be led to conclude that "All
A's are C's." By filling the blanks with various words,
it becomes apparent that a conclusion in the same all-
encompassing form does not always follow logically. With
the following premises: "All cars are red," and "All
bicycles are red," one could not logically conclude that
"All cars are bicycles."

The semantic effect refers to a tendency in people
to accept conclusions based on what they know to be fac-
tually correct or on what is consistent with their be-

liefs. If a syllogism read "All gorillas eat meat," and "All primates eat meat," one might accept the conclusion that "All gorillas are primates," even though it does not logically follow from the premises. By substituting "fish" for "gorillas" it becomes more apparent that the conclusion is not correct.

Prejudices and biases are far more common in judging people and events than in solving syllogisms. Prejudice often infiltrates a person's judgments without his realizing it.

The halo effect also permeates the judgment of people and events. It occurs when someone generalizes the quality of one characteristic to other characteristics. For example, people might believe that an excellent singer must also be a talented actor or that a bad singer must necessarily be a terrible actor. In the halo effect, one impression leads to stereotyped impressions about the "goodness" or "badness" of a person or event.

● **PROBLEM** 5-16

What factors account for individual differences in problem solving?

Solution: Among the factors that affect individual differences in problem solving are: motivation and personality, intelligence, background knowledge, memory, and application of knowledge.

An individual's level of desire or drive to solve a problem influences his ability to find a solution. Extreme lethargy or anxiety tends to hinder problem-solving. Frustration tolerance--the ability to proceed despite thwarted efforts to reach a goal--as well as the individual's manner of dealing with frustration also influence success at problem-solving.

Most psychologists agree that people with a high level of intelligence are better problem solvers than those with low intellectual ability. Several factors account for this. Very intelligent people are more likely to test out hypotheses they have formed rather than use a mechanical, time consuming and often unproductive trial and error approach. Intelligent people are more likely to develop insightful solutions; they are not likely to submit to such inhibiting factors as functional fixedness and mental set effects.

Wide background knowledge and extensive formal education give an individual a considerable advantage over those who lack these. Those with more background knowledge can bring together more aspects of a solution. Sometimes, however, those who are self-taught and are not hindered by traditional views and approaches have been able to solve problems which have defied those with extensive formal training.

It has been demonstrated that individuals with good memories are better problem solvers than those with poor memories. Those with better memories have a wider range of facts at their disposal.

Those who can apply previous learning to novel situations are generally better problem solvers. Knowledge can be applied to problem-solving in three ways: directly, without change; transformed in some way; and combined with several sources.

● **PROBLEM** 5-17

Describe some factors that inhibit productive or creative thinking with regard to problem solving.

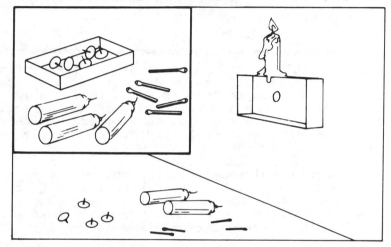

The candle problem. The upper panel shows the equipment available for mounting a candle on a wall. The lower panel shows the solution.

Solution: In problem solving, productive or creative thinking is required when there are no precedents in one's experience for handling a particular problem. Habits, preconceived sets and functional fixedness are all elements that can interfere with creative thought.

Although they may be helpful in solving some problems, past experiences sometimes prevent one from finding new and better solutions. Habits, which are products of experience, are not always conducive to problem solving. For example, if one was to wash some dirty pots with heavy, baked-on food, a scouring pad would be best suited to do the job. If, however, a cocktail glass was then presented for cleansing, one would be well-advised to break the habit of using a scouring pad in exchange for something softer.

Set is an aspect of habit and describes an individual's preparation to receive a particular stimulus. To illustrate set, one could ask a friend to pronounce the

following words: pin, spin, win, bin, tin, sin, line.
Mispronunciation of the last word indicates that the subject has a certain expectancy that this word will sound
the same as the others in the set.

Another effect of experience is functional fixedness.
Here, people are prevented from using certain objects in
innovative ways because of the specific function that has
been attached to them by habit and tradition. For example, many people would not recognize at once all the
functional possibilities for an ordinary shoe box.

CREATIVITY AND ORIGINALITY

● PROBLEM 5-18

Define creativity. What traits characterize creative
individuals?

Solution: Creativity has been defined as the production
of something that is original and socially desirable and
significant. Most psychologists agree that a solution
is novel only if it is new to the person who arrives at
it. That is, regardless of how many others may have proposed the same solution, if an individual arrives at it
independently, it is novel.

So far, no completely reliable method for measuring
creativity has been developed. The best of the creativity
tests is Mednick's Remote Associations Test which is based
on the notion that the novel response which fulfills the
requirements of a particular problem, is an index of creativity.

Another method for evaluating creativity is to study
individuals considered creative. Studies of these people
indicate that, as a group, they show less emotional in-
stability than the general population. They have a tendency to rectify immature, nonconformist behavior with
adult thinking and reasoning ability. They are generally
not as rigid and dogmatic in their views as less creative
people tend to be. Creative people are more likely to
take responsibility for their actions and decisions.

Another characteristic believed to distinguish creative people from the rest of the population is independence
of mind. Because they are less concerned about what others
think of them, creative individuals feel freer to let their
thinking extend over a wider range of possibilities--some
of which may be considered "taboo" by a majority of people.
Hence, creative people are more likely to conceive and/or
develop ideas that seem ridiculous or are unpopular with
less creative people.

Intelligence levels among creative people are fairly
high. However, it has been found that a high level of
intelligence does not correlate reliably with a high score

on a creativity test. Nevertheless, it is generally accepted that highly creative people are highly intelligent; this intelligence is reflected in their enjoyment of novel and complex art work.

● PROBLEM 5-19

Define and distinguish between original behavior and creative behavior.

Solution: Original behavior is displayed when an infrequent response is made. A maximum degree of originality is attained when only one person produces a particular response. Psychologists have noted degrees of originality: the fewer people who produce a certain response, the more original the response.

Creative behavior consists of responses that meet a minimum criterion of originality and are also relevant, practical, or feasible in some way.

The most important distinction between original and creative behavior is in the measurement of each. The measurement of originality is straightforward and fairly reliable--it involves recording the frequency of a given response. Creativity, however, involves a subjective rendering--a judgment by someone. Hence, there is more disagreement over degree of creativity than degree of originality. If two people were to read the same novel, they would be more likely to agree on its originality than on its creativity.

In any situation, there are likely to be more original responses than creative responses. Most people can easily execute an original response. A creative response usually requires more effort. For example, if one were asked to recommend a title for a book, "X = TIN < Q" would be a very original proposal. However, unless this title is directly or symbolically related to the story, it would not be very creative.

LANGUAGE AND ITS ACQUISITION

● PROBLEM 5-20

Define language. List and define its elements.

Solution: Language is the complex arrangement of sounds that have accepted referents and can be arranged to derive meanings. Language is an important tool in thinking. It enables one to explore actual or potential relations among parts of the environment that words symbolize. The units of language include: phonemes, morphemes, syntax, and prosody.

Phonemes are the smallest units of sound in a lan-

Phonemes in general American English and their sounds

Phoneme	Sound	Phoneme	Sound
/ee/	heat	/b/	bee
/I/	hit	/d/	dawn
/e/	head	/g/	go
/ae/	had	/m/	me
/ah/	father	/n/	no
/aw/	call	/ng/	sing
/U/	put	/f/	fee
/oo/	cool	/θ/	thin
Λ	ton	/s/	see
/uh/	the	/sh/	shell
/er/	bird	/h/	he
/oi/	toil	/v/	view
/au/	shout	/th/	then
/ei/	take	/z/	zoo
/ou/	tone	/zh/	garage
/ai/	might	/l/	law
/t/	tee	/r/	red
/p/	pea	/y/	you
/k/	key	/w/	we

guage. They are the single vowel and consonant sounds found in every language. English has 45 phonemes, an average amount in comparison with other languages. Phonemes are the first sounds an infant makes.

Phonemes combine with each other to form morphemes, the smallest units of meaning in a given language. In English, morphemes can be whole words such as "lamp," "chair," and "boy"; prefixes such as "pre-," "anti-," and "de-"; or suffixes such as "-ness," "-ing," and "-ed." There are more than 100,000 morphemes in English; this does not represent an exhaustion of all the possible combinations of the 45 phonemes.

Besides constructing meaningful words, a person must be able to make the proper combinations to express sophisticated thoughts and ideas. Syntax--the grammar rules of a language--is necessary for effective expression and communication. Syntax relies on the ability to combine morphemes into meaningful and grammatically correct sentences.

In addition to these three basic units of language (phonemes, morphemes, syntax), the person also acquires prosody. Prosody refers to the manner of expression. It includes such lingual features as intonation, accents, pauses and other variations in pronunciation that affect the meaning of spoken language.

● **PROBLEM** 5-21

Define surface structure of language and deep structure of language. Give an example of each. Illustrate Chomsky's transformational grammar.

162

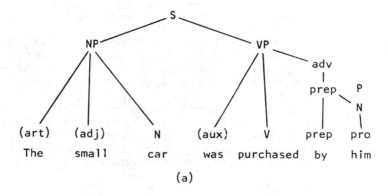

(a)

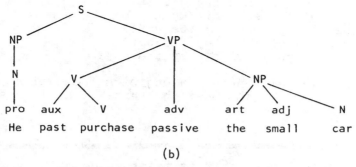

(b)

Surface structure (a) and deep structure (b) of the sentence "The small car was purchased by him." Note that the deep structure is in the form of an active declarative sentence. Two transformations are involved. One of them changes the tense of the verb (represented as an auxiliary in deep structure) and the other one (represented by the adverb, indicating passive tense, i.e., how the purchase was made) changes the sentence from active to passive.

Solution: Language has two aspects or "structures." The surface structure refers to the actual spoken utterances or written material of language. The deep structure refers to the corresponding patterns of meaning that underlie the surface structure. The following example illustrates these two structures:

Mary baked the cake.
The cake was baked by Mary.

Here, the surface structures are different but since the two sentences have the same meaning, they also have the same deep structure. Conversely, two sentences may have identical surface structures but different deep structures, as in the following:

It is drinking water.
It is drinking water.

The deep structures of these sentences could be:

It is water for drinking.

Water is being drunk by it.

Noam Chomsky (1957) was the first to distinguish between surface and deep structures; he constructed a theory
of transformational grammar based on these structures.
He defined the "kernel" of a sentence as the basic declarative thought of the sentence. For example, "The boy hit
the girl" could be a kernel sentence. Through transformational grammar, Chomsky showed how a basic structure
could be transformed into other surface structures which
represent the same kernel. Using the kernel sentence
above, the following transformations could be derived:

The girl was hit by the boy.
The boy didn't hit the girl.
Did the boy hit the girl?
The girl wasn't hit by the boy.
Didn't the boy hit the girl?
Was the girl hit by the boy?
Wasn't the girl hit by the boy?

The kernel sentence along with these eight transformations comprise the basic patterns of English surface
structure.

● **PROBLEM** 5-22

Define semantics. What is meant by denotation and connotation? Describe Osgood's semantic differential.

Solution: Semantics is the study of the meanings of
words. More specifically, semantics is the study of how
meaning is related to the surface structure of language,
that is, how we infer deep structure from surface structure.

There are basically two kinds of word meaning: denotation and connotation. Denotation or denotative meaning is the word's external referent. That is, an actual
car is the external referent of the word "car." Denotations are the concrete meanings of words.

Connotation refers to the verbal associations and
emotional implications of a word. Bar and cocktail
lounge, for example, have similar denotations but very
different connotations.

In the late 1950's, Osgood developed a technique
for measuring the connotative meanings of words called
the semantic differential. It is used to study the dimensions of meaning. Using this method, subjects are
asked to rate a number of individual words on a number
of scales. Each rating scale has seven intervals, or
spaces, between two words that are diametrically opposite
such as "good-bad," "sweet-sour," and "weak-strong."
Words like "table" and "avenue" would be judged by the
subject as belonging closer to one end of the spectrum
or the other or right in the middle.

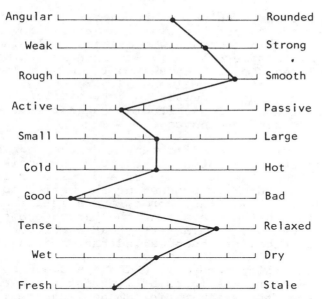

Angular |___|___|___|___|___•___|___|___| Rounded
Weak |___|___|___|___|___|_•_|___|___| Strong
Rough |___|___|___|___|___|___•___|___| Smooth
Active |___|___•___|___|___|___|___|___| Passive
Small |___|___|___|___•___|___|___|___| Large
Cold |___|___|___|___•___|___|___|___| Hot
Good |_•_|___|___|___|___|___|___|___| Bad
Tense |___|___|___|___|___|___•___|___| Relaxed
Wet |___|___|___•___|___|___|___|___| Dry
Fresh |___•___|___|___|___|___|___|___| Stale

A semantic differential profile for the word polite. Subjects rated the word on each of the 10 bipolar scales indicating, for example, exactly where polite fell on the
dimension defined by the words angular and rounded. The
profile shown is an average of a group of 20 subjects. Another similar group produced a profile that was practically
identical to this one.

Three factors or types of rating scales are used in
the semantic differential technique. The first is the
evaluative factor on which the favorableness of a word
is rated. Examples of this type of scale are "good-bad"
and "fair-unfair." The second class is the potency factor which includes such scales as "large-small" and
"strong-weak." The third group, the activity factor,
consists of scales that measure such attributes as
"active-passive" and "fast-slow."

After subjects have rated the words on the various
scales, the words are located on what Osgood termed the
semantic space--a type of graph which reflects how the
words were rated according to the three factors.

Osgood found that groups of people with similar backgrounds and/or interests tend to have similar connotative
meanings for words in their everyday vocabularies. People
from different cultures differ more from one another than
do people from the same culture.

● **PROBLEM 5-23**

Discuss the relationship between language and thought.
Is language necessary for thought? What is the Whorfian
Hypothesis?

Solution: Many psychologists agree that language is an

important tool in thinking but that it is not necessary to thinking. To support their assertion they point to animals and human infants who possess no language skills yet exhibit complex cognitive structures. Studies of deaf children who are exposed to language relatively late in the course of their lives indicate that the development of their thinking processes is very similar to that of hearing children. These studies suggest that cognition can develop without language.

B. Whorf, who studied many American Indian languages, developed the linguistic relativity hypothesis. Whorf concluded that the structure of a particular language influences the thinking process of the native speakers of that language. In other words, one's entire way of thinking depends on the grammar of the language one speaks. This hypothesis, which asserts that cognition is dependent on language, has been called the Whorfian Hypothesis.

Psychologists who oppose Whorf's theories would probably support the ideas of linguistic universalism which stress the similarities among languages. These psychologists might argue that aspects of the environment which are more important to members of a particular culture are reflected in their language and way of thinking. This suggests that thinking precedes language.

Although the controversy has not been resolved, research clearly demonstrates that language and thought are related. In fact, the two appear to be interdependent.

● **PROBLEM** 5-24

Describe the structural theory of language acquisition. Define generative grammar.

Solution: Noam Chomsky is the foremost proponent of the structural or genetic theory of language acquisition. The theory maintains that language acquisition is an innate capacity. The mental organization of humans, according to this theory, is governed by certain innate principles. These patterns provide the basis for all cognitive processes--perception, learning, and thinking. Some psychologists argue that these principles account for the similarity in language development among members of the human species. Lenneberg (1969) agrees with this notion; he concluded that language acquisition in a child is consistently correlated with motor development once the child reaches a certain stage of physical growth.

Those who subscribe to the structural theory--structuralists--believe that the child acquires a set of rules for language which enable him to make an infinite number of utterances, most of which he has never heard before. Considering the speed of language acquisition, a rule strategy seems more likely than a rote learning process.

Evidence supporting this rule learning system can

Milestones in motor and language development

Age (years)	Motor Milestones	Language Milestones
0.5	Sits using hands for support: unilateral reaching	Cooing sounds change to babbling by introduction of consonantal sounds
1	Stands; walks when held by one hand	Syllablic reduplication; signs of understanding some words; applies some sounds regularly to signify persons or objects i.e., the first words
1.5	Prehension and release fully developed; gait propulsive; creeps downstairs backward	Repertoire of 3 to 50 words not joined in phrases; trains of sounds and intonation patterns resembling discourse; good progress in understanding
2	Runs (with falls); walks stairs with one foot forward only	More than 50 words; Two-word phrases most common; more interest in verbal communication; no more babbling
2.5	Jumps with both feet; stands on one foot for 1 second; builds tower of six cubes	Every day new words; utterances of three and more words; seems to understand almost everything said to him; still many grammatical deviations
3	Tiptoes 3 yards (2.7 meters); walks stairs with alternating feet; jumps 0.9 meters	Vocabulary of about 1000 words about 80 percent intelligibility; grammar of utterances close approximation to colloquial adult; syntactic mistakes fewer in variety; systematic; predictable
4.5	Jumps over rope; hops on one foot; walks on line	Language well established; grammatical anomalies restricted either to unusual constructions or to the more literate aspects of discourse

be found in studies on "pivot" and "open" classes of words. Brown and Bellugi (1964) contend that the pivot-open system develops into a more advanced grammar through "differentiation." This process allows pivot words to subdivide into other classes of words (e.g., articles, possessive pronouns) when special rules are adapted for their use.

The generative grammar of a language is the set of rules that determine how the language is structured. The generative grammar is not the same as the proscriptive and restrictive rules of a language. Generative rules are believed to be automatically incorporated into the child's cognitive structure during the early years of development. The human brain has evolved in such a way that this spontaneous acquisition of linguistic rules is one of its natural functions.

Discuss two approaches that can be used in examining early language acquisition.

Solution: One method of measuring language acquisition in the infant involves calculating the number of words in the child's vocabulary. A distinction is needed between active vocabulary and passive vocabulary. Active vocabulary refers to all the words the infant both understands and pronounces. Passive vocabulary includes the words he understands but cannot use when he speaks. When measuring a child's vocabulary acquisition, most psychologists measure the passive vocabulary. To record a child's progress, a researcher might use a normative table. The table would show the age of a child in one column and the average number of words acquired for each respective age in the next column. The problem with normative tables, however, is that they attempt to reflect a child's passive vocabulary, an element that is very difficult to pinpoint. The actual number of words a child knows and understands at a particular time is almost impossible to determine. Yet many researchers have produced tables which they believe to be accurate estimates.

One of the best known normative tables for assessing language acquisition was constructed by M. E. Smith (1926). Smith based his findings on both active and passive vocabulary. He reported, for example, that a child knows one word by 10 months of age, three words by 12 months, 22 words by 18 months, and 272 words by his second birthday. Smith traced language acquisition up to 6 years of age; he reported that at this stage the child has acquired an average of 2,562 words in his vocabulary (passive and active).

Several studies have been performed that use active vocabulary as the sole basis of measurement. These, however, underestimate the child's actual vocabulary.

A second approach in the study of language acquisition is to examine the quality of the acquired language rather than measuring the size of the child's vocabulary. Landreth (1967) believes that linguists (language researchers) see the child not only as a developing being whose language acquisition can be measured but also as a guide who helps them understand the workings of language.

Trace the steps of language acquisition during the infant's first two years of life.

Solution: The first sounds a newborn makes are expressed in his crying. Most of this crying (approximately 90 per-

Measuring visual preference in infants

Switches for recording fixation time
and presenting visual patterns

Observer

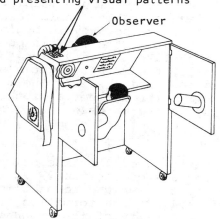

A device used to measure the interest value of different
visual patterns in terms of time spent looking at them. The
subject sits facing a "stage" where patterns are presented.
His view is restricted to the inside of the illuminated chamber.

cent) consists of the utterance of a single syllable--
the sound "a," as in the word "sat."

Crying is the infant's sole means of verbal communication. It is used as a defense and as a signal to communicate his physical needs and discomfort. After a few
months, the infant learns to use crying as a means to attract attention. During this period, the infant is capable of making eight distinctive sounds. Five of these
are often vowels and three are consonants.

As he grows and his mouth cavity develops, the child
begins to express non-crying as well as the crying sounds.
This phase is usually called babbling. Every sound that
a human is capable of making is found in the child's
babbling. Until the age of 6 months, the infant's babbling appears to be random, although some linguists have
found a semblance of order in the type and the number of
phonemes (single sounds) vocalized. Irwin (1949) reports
that the child's babbling contains, initially, vowel
sounds, followed by consonants such as "h," "p," "b,"
"m." The infant repeats these sounds, varying the pitch
and intensity. By the age of 6 months, the infant's
babbling becomes more organized. Sounds are repeated consistently until they are perfected.

Osgood (1957) describes early language acquisition
as a circular reflex. The child makes a sound, hears it,
and repeats it when he hears it. This process continues
in a circular fashion. Simultaneously, the child's
babbling sounds begin to approximate simple morphemes.
The child's environment continuously influences his vocalization. He starts pronouncing phonemes that are
germane to the native language of his community.

The period of babbling leads to a stage called "echolalia," in which the child "echoes" or repeats sounds he hears himself and others make. The child also learns word associations that attribute meaning to his utterances. Often when a parent hears the child make a particular sound, he assumes that the baby is beginning to talk. The parent often responds to the child's communications. For example, if the child repeatedly says "bah bah" in the presence of a ball, the mother might assume that the child is referring to the word "ball." She might present him with his toy ball. Through her action, the mother helps to create for her child an association between the sound "bah bah" and the actual ball. Hence, words gradually acquire meaning for the child.

Most linguists agree that the child pronounces his first word at the age of one year. It is difficult to determine the point at which the babbling sound "bah" becomes the word "ball." The formation of a word is not determined by the quality of its pronunciation, but rather by the speaker's interpretation of the word. "Bah" becomes a word when it first means "ball" to the speaker.

The child's first words usually consist of pairs of identical sounds such as "mama," "dada" or "bye bye." New words quickly follow and the child practices them constantly. Aside from this active use of language, the child also understands a great deal that he can't express. Often, he can follow a command given by a parent. Such commands might include "no no," "lie down," and "come here." These commands, when combined with gestures, help to increase the size of his passive vocabulary.

During his second year, the child's vocabulary, both active and passive, continues to expand, even though his range of syllables remains limited.

At approximately eighteen months, the child begins to put two words together to represent a complete sentence. Braine (1963) explained this phenomenon in terms of pivot words and X words. Pivot words are those which the child uses repeatedly in combination with other words (X words). In the typical two-word sentences of a child at this stage such as, "see ball," "see hat," "see boy"; "see" is the pivot word and the words that accompany it are X words.

By the end of the second year, the child is capable of using syntax in his speech. Several theories in psychology attempt to explain this new ability; however, no single theory is widely accepted.

● **PROBLEM** 5-27

Trace language development during preschool age.

Solution: During preschool age, the language development of the child progresses beyond the formation of two-word sentences. He begins to form three-word sentences and, from this point on, his language and grammar become more diverse and complex. Three-word sentences are formed by combining pairs of two-word sentences. For example, "The big." and "The boy." combine to form "The big boy." During early preschool age the child also learns some ordering rules. He learns to order adjectives by correctly saying a sentence such as, "The two blue cars," rather than "The blue two cars."

During this period, word classes differentiate into subclasses and the child eventually incorporates and uses all the parts of speech in language: noun, verb, adjective, etc..

During the third year, the child learns transformations. He can take a simple declarative sentence and transform it into a command, a question, or a negative. By applying the transformational rules that he has now incorporated, he can transform a sentence such as "He goes," into "Did he go?" or "He did not go." The child is now at a much more advanced stage than in infancy when he merely attached the word "no" to the beginning or end of a sentence to form the negative.

During preschool age, the child learns the proper use of articles as well as the proper time to use singular or plural nouns. He learns that "a box" is correct but "a money" isn't; he begins to understand that "two men" is proper pluralization, not "two mans."

Vocabulary becomes more extensive during the preschool period. By age 4, the child has a vocabulary of well over 1,000 words.

● **PROBLEM** 5-28

Discuss the role language plays in the intellectual development of the preschool child.

Solution: Several studies indicate that the level of linguistic ability in children is related to the level of intellectual ability. As the child's capacity to use language increases, his level of intelligence increases. The increase in intelligence facilitates the further development of language. Research shows that language ability is an important factor in discrimination and dimensional learning. Studies have shown that discrimination learning—the ability to distinguish one object from another—is easier to the subject if the objects are both well known and have names with which the subject is familiar. In addition, attributing names to unfamiliar objects facilitates discrimination in the child.

Pyles (1932) concluded that verbalization facilitates learning. Employing 80 children as subjects, whose ages ranged from 2 to 7, Pyles tested the effect of language on discrimination learning. In her experiment, Pyles presented the children with five different animal forms. Underneath one animal she hid a toy. The child had to select which animal covered the toy. In one situation, the animal forms were named and were familiar to the children. In another variation, Pyles used unfamiliar and unnamed animal forms. In the third variation, unfamiliar forms were used but names were ascribed to each of them. Pyles found that only 54 percent of the children tested were able to distinguish successfully among the five animal forms when they were unfamiliar and unnamed, but 72 percent were able to distinguish among unfamiliar forms when names were ascribed to them. Hence, Pyles concluded that language facilitates learning.

Bruner (1966) has shown that the child's level of thinking is also related to his linguistic ability. In one of his experiments (with Kenney, 1966), Bruner used a tray or matrix of nine glasses of three different heights and widths. In this test of transposition, children between the ages of 5 and 7 were asked to perform one of three tasks: restore the glasses on the tray to their original order; replace missing glasses from the pattern; or rearrange the matrix by transposing glasses of the diagonal corners. The subjects were asked to describe the matrix as they originally found it and the condition of the matrix after they rearranged it. Bruner and Kenney's subjects voiced three types of descriptions. The youngest subjects employed global descriptions. These subjects used words that conveyed size: "bigger," "littler," "gianter," "smaller." Dimensional descriptions were used by older children. A typical dimensionsal description might sound like the following: "This one is smaller and thinner while that one is taller and fatter." Some subjects used a third type of verbal description, labled confounded, because it combined dimensional and global terms; that is, both words of size and dimensional words. Bruner and Kenney concluded that children who used dimensional description were more successful at transposing the glasses than those children who used confounded or global terms. Therefore, language and thinking levels are directly related.

● PROBLEM 5-29

What is the Language Acquisition Device (LAD)? Describe how it works.

Solution: During the third year of life a child learns syntax (the rules of grammar). Chomsky (1957, 1965) proposed a theory to explain the acquisition of syntax. He believes that children are born with a certain "something," a certain gene predisposition that enables them to learn grammar. This is called a Language Acquisition Device (LAD) or an Acquisition Machine (AM). This "something" exists at birth. Chomsky used this concept to explain the relative ease with which the normal child learns grammar. He also uses it to explain why most children make few grammatical mistakes when learning syntax.

Chomsky's LAD theory has not been proved nor disproved. Although some linguists tend to question the theory (presumably for its vagueness), a better explanation has yet to be devised which can account for the rapid acquisition of syntactic rules during the third and fourth years. Imitation is not a good explanation because the child often makes grammatical mistakes which he could not have picked up from others. Rather than mere imitation, the child learns certain rules that become ingrained in his psyche. He knows, for example, that to indicate the plural tense, he should add "s" to the end of a word. He may not know, however, that this is not the correct procedure in every case. He might say, for example, "oxes" rather than "oxen."

Until a better explanation is provided for syntax acquisition, the subject will remain a source of conjecture and debate.

● **PROBLEM** 5-30

Describe the effects the following factors have on language acquisition: gender, twins, bilingualism, stuttering, social class, minority-group membership.

Solution: In the acquisition of language, girls have an advantage over boys. They learn language at an earlier age, often articulate better and generally have fewer speech defects. Some explain this by maintaining that girls have closer and longer interaction with their mothers than boys do. With the advent of television, however, this difference between the sexes has lost importance.

Several researchers have indicated that twins acquire language at a slower rate than other children. They do not receive as much individual attention and the amount of maternal interaction is less. Also, twins have the habit of developing a private jargon between themselves. Hence, they are less likely to learn socially accepted vocabulary and syntax.

Numerous studies have indicated that bilingual children, in general, acquire language more slowly than monolingual (one language) children. Bilingualism develops in immigrant families where native customs are maintained. The child has to confront two distinct cultures. Because the child learns two languages at once, not enough time is allowed for the full development of one. It has been found that the vocabularies of bilingual children are smaller for both languages. In addition, articulation and syntax are generally poor. Often, the bilingual person is not proficient in either language.

In addition to the obvious problem of slow language acquisition, bilingualism can also create emotional and social problems for the child. Speaking English with an accent in front of peers can create serious adjustment problems at school.

Stuttering occurs when the workings of a child's mind (or an adult's) are far quicker than his ability to speak the words necessary to express himself. In children, especially those between the ages of 3 and 4, this feature is normal and expected. The discussion of passive vocabulary noted that a child knows more words than he is able to express. Similarly, when a child stutters, his mind is working at a level too advanced for his limited vocabulary to express adequately. Most psychologists agree that if parents accept stuttering as a normal part of their child's development instead of making the child anxious by drawing attention to it, the stuttering will diminish.

A significant relation has been found between social class and language development. Bernstein (1961) found that teenage boys from middle class families scored higher in verbal tests than teenage boys from working or lower class families. The two classes have different attitudes about the importance of language development. Deutsch found that the language of lower class families tends to be more restrictive when compared to that of higher classes. Often, working class parents will speak to their children in short, clipped phrases with such responses as "yes," "no," and "go away." Hence, the child's speech does not develop beyond this. Also, he is rarely corrected when he makes a mistake in pronunciation, usage or grammar. Because the parents do not appreciate the importance of developing language, the child lacks a good linguistic model. Consequently, these children inherit their parents' indifference to the importance of language development.

Membership in a minority group can also hinder language development. The acquisition of language is particularly slow and difficult for black children growing up in a ghetto. Most of these children learn a dialect called "Black English." The dialect creates problems for them--both lingual and social--when they enter school and are expected to master standard English.

INTELLIGENCE: PIAGET

● PROBLEM 5-31

Discuss Piaget's outlook on intelligence. What is meant by equilibrium? Define structure, functioning, and content.

Solution: According to Piaget, intelligence is not a quantitative object that can be measured in units. Rather, intelligence is manifested in an individual's ability to adapt to his environment. The success with which an individual deals with a situation reflects his intelligence. Intelligence is dependent on the dual processes of assimilation and accommodation in the interplay between subject and environment. Assimilation and accommodation must exist in equal amounts for the individual to behave intelligently. When assimilation and accommodation are in perfect balance, a state of equilibrium exists. Intelligence, therefore, is a striving toward equilibrium, a move toward adapting to a new situation by using previous learning and modifying (accommodating) it so that it can apply to a successful dealing with a problem or a change in the environment. Piaget's view of intelligence is best described by his term "intelligence-in-action," which refers to an individual's interaction with his environment.

In addition to describing intelligence as the manifestation of individual-environment interaction, Piaget also described the cognitive or intelligent aspect of the individual. All humans are born with reflexive behaviors. In a reflex, a particular stimulus produces a particular response; because the stimulus produces this response and no other, Piaget reasoned that an intellectual component must underlie the behavior. He termed this component "structure," and he called the twin processes of assimilation and accommodation "functioning." Structure and functioning are utilized by the individual to interact with the environment. Piaget called the product of this process, that is, the new behavior that is displayed, the "content." As new behaviors are learned, structure is increased, thereby enabling the person to broaden the means by which he interacts with his environment.

SHORT ANSWER QUESTIONS FOR REVIEW

Choose the correct answer.

1. All of the following are types of nondirected thinking EXCEPT (a) free association (b) creative imagination (c) reverie (d) daydreaming

   b

2. Which of the following problems would require divergent thinking? (a) adding a column of numbers (b) deciding whether to turn left or right at an intersection while driving a car (c) choosing the best move in a card game (d) repairing a broken typewriter

   c

3. "Textbook" is an example of which of the following types of concepts? (a) simple (b) conjunctive (c) disjunctive (d) relational

   b

4. The utterance "$\bar{a}$" is an example of (a) a phoneme (b) a morpheme (c) syntax (d) prosody

   a

5. All of the following are morphemes EXCEPT (a) "pre-" (b) "girl" (c) "-ing" (d) "n"

   d

6. The flashing red lights at a railroad crossing are best described as (a) concepts (b) symbols (c) signals (d) signs

   c

7. Using Osgood's semantic differential technique, the rating scale "sour-sweet" would be of which of the following types? (a) evaluative (b) potency (c) activity (d) all of the above

   a

8. Which of the following sentences has the same deep structure as "Mary hit the boy."? (a) "Mary hits" (b) "The boy hit Mary" (c) "Mary can hit" (d) "The boy was hit by Mary"

   d

9. Which of the following is NOT true about the structural theory of language acquisition? (a) Innate principles account for similarities in language development among humans (b) The innate principles account for all cognitive processes (c) Language is acquired more by rule than by rote (d) Environmental factors are more important than genetic factors in language acquisition

   d

10. According to Bruner, the most sophisticated type of description is (a) simple (b) global (c) dimensional (d) confounded

    d

SHORT ANSWER QUESTIONS FOR REVIEW

11. According to Piaget, the child begins to think logically in which period of cognitive development? (a) sensorimotor (b) preoperational (c) concrete operations (d) formal operations

c

12. In which stage does abstract thinking become developed? (a) sensorimotor (b) preoperational (c) concrete operations (d) formal operations

d

13. If one had to learn how to operate an electric typewriter after typing with a manual one for a long period of time, Piaget would call any resultant change in behavior a/an (a) schema (b) assimilation (c) reflex (d) accommodation

d

14. Piaget termed the intellectual component of behavior (a) scheme (b) structure (c) functioning (d) content

b

15. The labeling of stimuli is involved in which of the following mental processes? (a) encoding (b) evaluation (c) deduction (d) mediation

d

16. A child forms hypotheses in the mental process of (a) encoding (b) evaluation (c) deduction (d) mediation

b

17. According to Bruner, the mode which is based most heavily on perception is (a) enactive (b) iconic (c) symbolic (d) alloplastic

b

18. A "clearing of the mind" occurs in which of the following stages of problem solving? (a) preparation (b) production (c) judgment (d) incubation

d

19. Which of the following is the most sophisticated type of problem? (a) long division (b) an anagram (c) a syllogism (d) arranging blocks in size order

c

20. The hiring of a carpenter based on his looks is an example of (a) the atmosphere effect (b) the semantic effect (c) prejudice and bias (d) the halo effect

d

21. All of the following have been known to be characteristic of creative people EXCEPT (a) immature behavior (b) flexibility of views (c) independence of mind (d) less emotional stability than the general population

d

SHORT ANSWER QUESTIONS FOR REVIEW

22. An individual can suggest no use for a paper
    clip other than for holding papers together.
    This is an illustration of (a) functional
    fixedness (b) set (c) habit (d) "Einsel-
    lung"

    a

23. According to Dunker's problem-solving scheme,
    reformulation of the problem occurs in which
    of the following stages? (a) the general range
    (b) the functional solution (c) the specific
    solution (d) none of the above

    a

24. If one had to select a box from a number of
    boxes that weighed the same as a given box, one
    might weight each and every box to find one with
    an identical weight. Such an approach to this
    problem would be called (a) heuristic (b)
    algorithmic (c) GPS (d) split-half

    b

25. Which of the following is NOT true about eidetic
    imagery? (a) It is the ability to produce
    clear visual images that can be scanned for de-
    tails (b) It is the same as "photographic mem-
    ory" (c) It is more common in children than
    adults (d) It may hinder the understanding of
    abstract ideas

    b

Fill in the blanks.

26. _____ is the name of the stage in which the
    child repeats sounds that he hears himself and
    others make.

    "Echolalia"

27. _____ are stored representations of sensory in-
    formation that can be recalled by the person at
    will.

    Images

28. _____ refers to the manner of expression.

    Prosody

29. A _____ may be either a symbol or a signal or
    both.

    sign

30. Chomsky called the basic declarative thought of
    a sentence its _____.

    kernel

31. A child's _____ vocabulary is always larger
    than his _____ vocabulary.

    passive,
    active

32. According to Piaget, the child's behavior is
    mostly reflexive during the _____ stage.

    sensori-
    motor

33. _____ exists when assimilation and accommoda-
    tion are in perfect balance.

    Equilib-
    rium

178

SHORT ANSWER QUESTIONS FOR REVIEW

34. _____ refers to the use of such tools as words, images, and concepts for the internalization of thought.

Mediation

35. _____ describes an individual's preparedness to receive a particular stimulus.

Set ("Einsellung")

Determine whether the following statements are true or false.

36. Thinking and learning are similar in that they both involve stimulus-response relations.

False

37. The semantic differential is useful in determining word connotation.

True

38. Every phoneme that a human is capable of making is found in the child's babbling.

True

39. It has been found that twins and bilingual children acquire language more quickly than non-twins and monolingual children.

False

40. Stuttering is a normal characteristic of preschool children.

True

41. The child acquires symbolic intelligence during the sensorimotor period of cognitive development.

True

42. Operational reversibility is acquired during the period of concrete operations.

False

43. Bruner adopts the autoplastic view of cognitive development that individuals adapt to other persons and objects.

False

44. In the iconic mode, cognition is based heavily upon action or movement.

False

45. New systems of thought are not ordinarily created in programmatic reasoning.

True

46. If an individual arrives at a solution to a problem by himself and others at the same time arrive at the same solution, the solution cannot be called novel.

False

47. The highest intelligence levels do not necessarily correspond to the highest scores on tests of creativity.

True

SHORT ANSWER QUESTIONS FOR REVIEW

48. Experience can be an obstacle to creative
    thinking.

    True

49. The major advantage of computer use in problem
    solving is their perfect memories.

    True

50. In the heuristic approach to problem-solving,
    each and every alternative is considered.

    False

CHAPTER 6

INFORMATION PROCESSING

HISTORY AND COMPUTER SIMULATIONS

● PROBLEM 6-1

Briefly trace the early history of thought and memory.

Solution: Pre-Socratic philosophers made little or no distinction between the study of physical and psychological
phenomena. An examination of the nature of the sense organs
was about as far as psychological thinking penetrated the
"natural philosophy" of that period. Diogenes appears to
have been the first to postulate an information center or
"central sense" for the processing of sensory information.
Later, Plato developed a theory of thinking that was based
upon sensory input. He hypothesized that just as the sense
organs are set to perceive certain aspects of the environment, the thought-organ is set to perceive another, different
aspect of the real world. He believed that the function of
the thought-organ was to deal with a changeless and timeless
all-encompassing whole that lay behind the operation of the
changing sense impressions. The ability to conceptualize
points to the existence of "universals" which are the proper
object of thought. Plato proposed that these "universals"
existed independently of the object itself. Conceptualization occurs when, for example, a person realizes that "cat"
belongs to the general category of "animal." In this case,
"animal" is a "universal."

Aristotle rejected Plato's formulations. He maintained
that universals were not separate or outside of the objects
themselves. Aristotle believed that the mind could not by
itself grasp the universal, but could only know it through
active mental processes. That is, through the apprehension
of many chairs, one would come to know the category "chair."
This point of view still interests psychologists today.
Aristotle also introduced the concept of "association." This
important observation--that thoughts tend to run from one to
another related thought--continues to guide theorists who investigate the nature of thought. Aristotle noticed that
thoughts appeared to become connected by contiguity (occurring
at about the same time), similarity and contrast. From these
observations he developed the laws of association.

The contribution of the Medieval Period has traditionally
been underestimated. The theological overtones of the time
are now believed to have contributed to the legitimization of
the scientific method. The belief that every occurrence could
be explained by general principles was an unrecognized contribution of this period.

Roger Bacon is often credited with being the father of
the scientific method. He worked at Oxford during the late
Middle Ages and was the first to depart from pure description
to a set of rules about how things operated. The 17th century
marked the beginning of what can be called modern psychological
thought. Since then, questions about information input and
the operation of the mind upon it have been studied in many
areas of inquiry which have influenced current experimental
psychology.

Inquiry into memory began with Plato. The Greek philosopher considered memory to be similar to a piece of wax onto
which different impressions were stamped. This conception has
survived time and underlies a number of modern theories that
purport to explain mental operations. Modern theorists however, have found the area of human memory to be much more
complex than Plato anticipated. Some psychologists have proposed the existence of three types of memory, each governed
by different principles: sensory, short-term, and long-term.
The search for the law that explains memory completely is far
from over.

● **PROBLEM** 6-2

With what aspects of human behavior is information processing
theory particularly interested? How does its focus differ
from traditional areas of psychological inquiry such as perception and cognition?

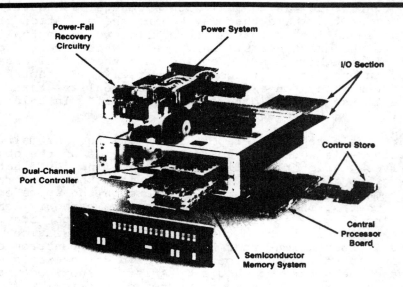

A digital computer

Solution: One of the latest developments in psychology is

the emergence of the field of "information processing." The
term is borrowed from the "information sciences" which include computer programming, systems analysis, and the mathematical theory of communication. To some extent, this new
branch of psychology combines the concerns of the perception
and the cognition psychologists. Both types of psychologists
tackle the question: How does the human mind operate?

The advent of the computer has enhanced the general understanding about how organisms receive information (perception)
and how they process it further before acting on it (cognition). The computer offers psychologists a tangible model
from which they can develop and refine theories about the
operation of the human system.

Since the 17th century, when Descarte proposed that the
mind and body are separate entities, it was believed that
mental operations were unmeasurable. These operations were
thought to be outside the mathematical parameters of time and
space. The lingering influence of this mode of thinking is
receiving its final blows from the models offered by computer
science which demonstrate that information processing procedures are indeed measurable and tangible.

Computer programs have been found to exhibit some remarkable similarities with the thinking process. A computer program tells the machine to execute certain procedures, to combine information according to specified rules, to store some
information, and to retrieve other. The computer model concerns itself with the same type of processes that cognitive
and perception psychologists have been attempting to answer
since long before the development of computer technology.

Despite the similarities, it cannot be said that the
human being is precisely like a computer. Unlike men,
"intelligent programs" are unemotional, inflexible, and cannot be distracted. The complexity of human perceptual and
thinking processes cannot be wholly explained by the simplistic
theories arising from the analogy with the computer. However,
many facets of the organization and operation of human processing have been elucidated by the application of the computer model.

Above all, the computer model has legitimized the efforts
of cognitive psychologists to explain the operation of the
thinking process by the use of schemas or symbols. Previously,
these efforts were often suspect due to the intangible nature
of the "cognitive transformation" processes that were said to
be responsible for learning and memory. Theories that dealt
with measurable physiological processes or overt movements
could be understood. However, the inherently invisible, in-
explicable, and abstract quality of the thought process had
discredited the work of the cognitive psychologists. Many
critics entertained the possibility that these psychologists
were speaking of nothing at all with their schemas and transformations. The introduction of computer programs has changed
this bias.

Because the model of a computer program consists mainly
of symbolic information--just as in the theories purporting

183

to explain the human system--cognitive scientists have received a philosophical reassurance. It was proven that the
flow of symbols can control a tangible machine. The computer
program is a guide for the selection, recovery, combining,
out-putting and storing of information just as is the human
thought process.

In summation, information processing is a broad area
that includes all the procedures that affect the transformation of sensory input, including how it is stored, selected,
reduced, recovered, elaborated, eliminated, and blocked. The
breadth and scope of this new field of inquiry allows for
the treatment of such traditional topics as sensation, perception, problem solving, cognition, imagery, memory and
learning.

● **PROBLEM** 6-3

Borrowed from computer-programming, the "executive routine"
concept offers an explanation for the action of memory.
Explain.

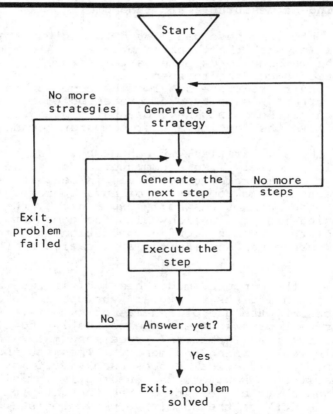

Flow diagram of a computer program designed to serve as a
rudimentary information-processing theory of problem solving. This is the "executive" or general controlling portion of a problem solving program. The computer has a
set of strategies, component activities or subroutines,
and rules for their use. This executive routine tells the
computer how to use them.

184

Solution: Conventionally, memory has been thought of as the
simple associative revival of earlier responses. The problems connected with it have revolved around attempts to discern how the recall mechanism operates. The notion that there
may be a data-processing mechanism that intervenes between
memory and action has been unpalatable to scientists--partic-
ularly those who are stimulus-response oriented--because it
suggests the presence of "a little man in the head" who is
busy searching, selecting, censoring and turning back on
earlier decisions.

The advent of computer programs and their capacity at
solving human information problems has begun to offer a solution to the problem of the "executive" in information
processing theory. Computers may have a program
which is called the "executive routine." Most programs consist of a number of subroutines or independent subprograms.
Usually the transfer from one subroutine to another is included on each subroutine. In some cases, however, when the
choice of operations is more complex, the choice of the next
routine must be transferred to a separate subroutine called
the "executive." All common subroutines are generally ended
by transferring to this executive routine which then decides
the next appropriate action. In this way, the higher
executive routine "uses" the other routines. This executive
does not carry out searches or constructions with the other
routines and it does not include the informaton stored on the
other routines. It often does not even contain many sophisticated processes, but it has final control of the program as
a whole.

This concept may prove to be considerably useful to the
study of memory and its operations. It offers a reasonable
alternative to the simplistic idea that all memory operates
on the basis of association, habit strength or competing
responses, while preventing a regression to the postulation
than an unmeasurable component controls behavior.

● PROBLEM 6-4

Describe a typical information processing sequence model.

Solution: There are many highly sophisticated information
processing models available. The following is a brief and
general outline of the major stages that might be included in
a typical model that explains how the human perceptual and
cognitive systems process the flow of stimulation from the
environment.

Stage 1: Iconic or echoic storage. This stage represents a fleeting experience that is of great importance in
the study of information processing. In the visual realm the
iconic image is that which occurs during a single glance.
Usually lasting approximately 1/15 of a second, iconic storage
consists of a series of successive glances each representing
a small section of a larger object. In hearing, the duration
of different echoic codes are less distinct, but each is a
sample of a larger auditory event.

Stage 2: Image representation or encoding. The momentary sensory experience provides an abundance of information that when combined with other experiences can lead to the recognition of a particular image or sound. For example, momentary glances provide color, texture, density, movement and shape. At stage two this information would be examined and compared. Essential features would be extracted so that the pattern might be recognized as the word "car." By the encoding of this word, other information such as color, brightness and shape can be discarded.

Stage 3: Storage: Short-term memory. It is here that the encoded information resides until it can combine with information coming from the next moment or until it can be transferred to long-term memory. Short-term memory has a limited capacity; it can usually store up to about 8 items.

Stage 4: Storage: Long-term memory. Not all information is finally stored in long-term memory. But whatever memory is not within short-term memory can be said to be in long-term memory where it is available for use as needed. Attention processes play an important role in determining whether information will be transferred from short to long-term memory.

● **PROBLEM** 6-5

The most crucial time for the retention and classification of information is the moment when it is received. Comment upon this assertion and include experimental support for your conclusions.

Solution: Ideas and opinions about people, places, and situations are often tied to first impressions. If a student strikes up a friendship with a person in his astrology class, it is likely that the next time he wants to discuss astrology, this person will come to mind. The person has many other qualities by which other people relate to him. However, the student's first experience caused him to classify the person in the part of his memory associated with astrology.

This type of classification can occur for many different characteristics: one may recall that a person is polite or red-headed or knowledgeable about ice hockey or a writer of poetry. These first impressions, which are used as a basis for classification, serve as rapid retrieval cues. The other information that is stored about the person requires the search effort associated with intentional recall.

When subjects are presented a series of similar words, letters, or numerals and are asked to recall them, they most often do so in temporal order. This appears to indicate that the order in which items are received is a fundamental basis for classification. However, sometimes factors other than the sequence of presentation become important. For example, if a list of items contains different stimuli such as flashes of different colored lights and numbers, recall is facilitated when it occurs by content rather than order. This is also true when letters and numbers are mixed; recall is better when they can be grouped together. When words with similar

186

meanings are presented in long word lists, they tend to be recalled in clusters by category. This suggests that distinctions are made in information at input and that the information is filed in the appropriate category of memory.

● **PROBLEM** 6-6

How can one reconcile the fact that so many different explanations exist for human behavior? Include a brief discussion of the cognitive (information processing), dynamic (motivational), and behavioral (stimulus-response) approaches to the study of psychology.

Solution: The study of human behavior or psychology is an enormous field that encompasses many different approaches to the same problems. When one becomes involved with the study of one particular approach, it can appear that the whole of human action can be explained by only that way of organizing the available information. Each of the various approaches is legitimate and the existence of so many of them helps the student to begin to understand that very little is known about why humans behave as they do. Each of the existing approaches may contain some element of the truth presented from a slightly different perspective than another approach. Consider the following three examples of differing approaches:

The cognitive approach to behavior sees all psychological occurrences as having a cognitive basis. Starting with the tangible, measurable stimulus that acts on the sensory-receiving apparatus of the organism, the cognitive scientist is concerned mainly with tracing the course of this sensory input to eventually determine how the thoughts, memories or beliefs of a person influence his actions and experiences.

The approach of the behaviorist is quite different from that of the cognitive psychologist. The behaviorist is concerned mainly with observable variables. He rejects the existence of inner processes. This type of psychologist believes that hypothetical constructs designed to explain unobservable phenomena are highly questionable and non-objective. He maintains that the science of psychology cannot afford to proceed from such foundations.

Finally, the dynamic or motivational scientist would begin a study of human nature by examining the motives of the person under study. A man's actions are seen to follow from his goals, drives, instincts and needs.

Clearly, human behavior can be examined by all three of the above approaches and yield interesting information. The psychology student should be careful not to adhere blindly to one school of thought. What one group of psychologists cannot explain may be easily accounted for by another group.

● **PROBLEM** 6-7

What are "demand characteristics"? How does the demand characteristic of a perceptual fragmentation experiment influence its outcome?

Solution: In any experimental situation the experimenter must take into account the subject's perception of what the experiment is about and what is expected from him. These "demand characteristics" can greatly influence the results of the experiment. This is particularly true when the sense of the experiment is hard to grasp. In this case, subtle cues from the experimenter may be important to how the subject deals with the situation. If the nature of the task is ambiguous it is also likely that demand characteristics will have an effect on the outcome of the experiment.

One common study in recent years is the study of perceptual fragmentation. In this experiment, figures that divide into various segments are shown on a tachistoscope. After a while, some of the figures disappear entirely. Whenever possible these fragments tend to produce meaningful new patterns rather than nonsensical ones to the subjects. This result was of great interest to theorists who believed that templates were involved in pattern recognition. However, the following experiment appears to disprove this notion. A study was conducted in which one group was given a set of patterns labeled 1, 2, 3, 4, 5, etc., and was told each was a numeral and another group was given the same numbers and told not to expect numerals. The first group tended to see the letters as undergoing far less fragmentation than did the second group who reported the numbers to be meaningless designs.

These results point to the importance of the demand characteristics of the experiment. A subject who is shown letters or numerals under conditions in which they break up and disappear is likely to think that his task is to perceptually keep the letters or numerals together as long as possible. Meanwhile, a subject who is shown meaningless patterns may think his task is to break them apart even further.

For data that is clear of demand characteristics, special controls may have to be designed to measure what impact the perception of the experiment has on the responses of the subjects.

THE CODING OF INFORMATION

● PROBLEM 6-8

Discuss the evidence which supports the theory that there are two different encoding and memory systems--visual and verbal.

Solution: Organisms relate to and organize their environment with two different sets of languages. There is an internal visual language with its own rules, concepts, associations, and memories and there is an audio language with its own particular rules and governing concepts. These two systems do not necessarily overlap entirely. The organism's experiences seem to depend on an intricate interaction between the two systems.

Interesting research that has been conducted on epilep-

tic and brain damaged patients has disclosed that the centers
for visual and verbal information processing may have different locations. It appears that the right side of the brain
is the locus of spatial or visual information handling, while
the left side is responsible for verbal learning and memory.
For example, when information is presented to the left side of
the brain only,the subject is able to describe what he has
been shown. If, however, it is presented to the right side
of the brain, he cannot describe what was seen, but is able
to select the object from a group of other items or to give
some other nonverbal response, such as laughing or gesturing
in response to the item. Normal individuals have also been
tested for this hemispheric dominance through special experiments. Making physical matches between letters occurs faster
when the information is presented to the right side. When the
subjects must deal with names, however, the task proceeds at
a faster rate when the information goes to the left side.
Music is better processed by the right side, while the perception of verbal information is facilitated when it is presented
to the left ear.

Though these processes are controlled separately, their
operations can and do appear to overlap in time. Information
may simultaneously elicit visual associations and associations
to its verbal description.

● **PROBLEM** 6-9

What is iconic coding? How does backward masking help to
prove its existence?

Solution: Coding is an important aspect of the memory systems.
The code refers simply to the form of the representation of
the external impression. Visual impressions are referred to
as "iconic" and auditory impressions as "echoic".

Iconic codes tend to resemble previous experience. They
have been studied by experiments with images (internal
visual representations). For example, if asked to describe
one's mother, one might begin by describing her height, hair
color, and attractiveness. But it's likely that one would
have a visual picture in mind that would contain a great deal
of information that would be difficult to translate into words.
Another example of this phenomenon occurs when one is asked
to imagine a monkey with a banana and a hat. It is very
likely that the picture produced would have the monkey holding
a banana with a hat on his head. Thus the iconic code which
is associated with past visual experiences influences the
nature of the image that is produced. No instruction whatsoever was given about the relationship between the banana, the
monkey, and the hat. Yet, the mind produced an image that was
based on past experience.

Some interesting experiments have been conducted that
have demonstrated that initial information received from, for
example, a letter flashed on a screen, is highly visual.
After the letter is flashed there is a brief period of time
during which the impression can be completely erased by the
flash of a bright light. This time period is about five

seconds, but during this time the image can be read as though the stimulus was still present. This backward masking effect demonstrates that the brief life of memory codes can be easily erased by input that is specific to the given sense modality. It may seem that these memory codes are insignificant to the thinking process. It is more plausible, however, that the iconic impression is acted upon by higher brain functions so that its meaning is constructed from the information that is presented in the code.

● PROBLEM 6-10

How do iconic concepts answer the question of how universals or general categories are represented in human memory?

Solution: A concept is said to be formed when an individual is able to respond to a series of different impressions or events with the same label. There is often a common element in the different events that permits this concept formation. For example, we learn to respond to a number of different two and three-dimensional impressions with the label "man," and to many different four-legged animals as "cat." "Iconic" or visual concept formation appears to be of an abstractive nature. A visual image presented to a person appears to be compared to memories of similar past events and finally stored or assimilated as part of the overall concept of which it is a part. A study done by Bahrick and Boucher demonstrates this aspect of iconic memory.

Subjects were shown lists of visual patterns of familiar objects in common categories such as "tables." One group of subjects was required to name the object at the time of learning and the other was not. Subjects were then tested either immediately after exposure to the lists or six weeks later. They were first asked to recall the name of the particular objects and then they were asked to pick out from a group of similar objects the exact item they had seen. The group that had verbalized the names of the items did much better with verbal recall of what they had seen when they were tested immediately, but when the testing occurred after six weeks, there was no difference in the verbal recall of the two groups. Apparently, the ability to recall after six weeks was strongly related to the calling forth of a visual image and then finding the name that corresponded to the image. It was also discovered that the ability to remember the name of the object was completely unrelated to the ability to select the correct table from the many tables presented.

Further, subjects had an extremely difficult time recognizing the precise table. They seemed to have placed the impression of the table into the general category of "tables" so that the name could be recalled, but not the exact representation of the table. It was concluded from these results that the objects that were seen had become a part of a visual system--or iconic structure--that represented the concept of table.

This ability of the mind to go from the particular to the general reduces the probability that one will be able to remember the exact details of what was seen. However, it does make it possible to handle more information and provides an economical storing mechanism. It also gives a code with which to think. Since the nervous system stores highly abstracted representations of what has been seen or experienced, the existence of iconic concepts, which represent the real world in a derived manner, begins to answer the question of how "universals" (general categories) are represented in memory. It allows one not only to see how the particular would be related to a central concept but also allows one to recognize variability within the different aspects of the concept. These concepts give a basis for the classification of new experiences and provide material for imagery and for reasoning to occur.

● **PROBLEM** 6-11

Visual perception is a constructive process. Discuss.

Solution: Visual perceptions are based on a scanning process of the eyes. Normally, the eyes shift to a new fixation point every second. It is the integration of the information that is collected with each separate eye movement that produces a single impression of a solid object. For instance, as one reads this page, as many as three to four fixations may be occurring for each separate line of type. But one does not experience a confusing melange of visual impressions, one sees a solid, stationary page of print. This act of translating many different "photographs" on the retina into a comprehensible, consistent world has not been studied extensively, though it is one of the most basic and important processes in the human information transformation system. That visual experience is consistent and smooth even though actual physiological experience consists of a rapid succession of constantly changing impressions suggests that visual memory must provide a guideline to help the organism determine what is actually present.

This memory has been conceptualized not as a series of many photographs, but as a schematic guideline to which each new fixation adds additional information. This can perhaps best be understood by comparing it to what is preserved of a sentence when one remembers only its meaning and not the exact words. This visual memory would serve to give consistency and orientation to new visual experiences and help one to correctly interpret ambiguous visual situations.

Perception of movement aids the hypothesis that vision is a constructive process that occurs over time. Movements of the object itself along with movements of the head and eyes change the location of the stimulus that falls on the retina, yet one perceives stable objects. These movements are actually an aid to certain types of depth perception. It must be the integration of retinal information over time that allows one to see a moving object as solid. This same process can explain how organisms integrate the information provided by the many rapid eye movements that occur in the process of vision.

191

What is "eidetic" imagery? Why is it rarely found in adults?

Test picture used to identify children with eidetic imagery.

Solution: Individuals that have the capacity to retain the
details of visual scenes to a greater degree than the
average person are called "eidetikers." These people have
eidetic or, as it is more commonly known, "photographic
memory." This ability occurs most frequently in children.
It is virtually never found in adults in this culture.
Researchers identified children with this ability by asking
them to focus on a screen where an image had just appeared
and to describe various details of the scene. Children who
succeeded at the task were found to have a finely developed
capacity for detail. In a scene with Indians fishing, for
example, the eidetic children were able to tell how many
feathers were in the Indian headdress, describe the numerous
colors in the woolen blanket, and give careful descriptions
of the expressions on the faces of the people in the scene.
During the description process, eidetikers seem to rely on
eye movements. Their eyes scan the empty space as they did
when the original picture was displayed. This seems to demonstrate that the process is primarily visual. The children
were also able to distinguish between "seeing" and "remembering." The only experimental material available deals with
the retention of a visual impression directly after it is
presented, however, anecdotal evidence supports the notion
that some individuals with this capacity can describe a scene
in perfect detail after a number of years.

     Why is this capacity so rarely found in adults? Does
it merely fade with age? Doob conducted a study with native
Nigerians and found that among rural members of the tribe
studied, eidetic imagery was common. However, among urban
members of the same tribe, there were few traces of eidetic

ability. A number of conclusions can be drawn from these
findings. One is that acculturation to the demands of adult
urban or modern life is incompatible with the eidetic capacity. The factually-oriented, scientifically-based value
system of this culture lends very little support to the imagination; vivid imagery has little use and is not supported by
social acceptability. The uneasiness an adult would tolerate in reporting the experience of something that is not
actually present and the influence of this attitude on the
developing child could well explain why children lose this
capacity.

● **PROBLEM** 6-13

Distinguish between perception and imagery or hallucination
as would a theorist who views perception principally as a
constructive process.

Solution: There does not appear to be a sharp boundary between perception and hallucination except in extreme cases.
The commonly accepted definition that perception occurs when
one experiences something that is physically present and that
hallucination occurs when the perceptual experience is of
something that does not physically exist is inadequate. A
man lying in bed dreaming about his alarm clock going off is
still dreaming even though the alarm clock is sitting right
beside him and will, in fact, soon go off. As one sits in
front of a television set, one is surely perceiving the picture of the cowboy shoot-out although neither the cowboys
or the guns or their horses are actually present. Because of
these phenomena, images are definitionally distinguished from
actual perception by the presence or absence of sensory stimuli rather than external objects. If what one sees or hears
is not perceived by one or more of the senses, it is said to
be illusory.

This definition still presents certain problems because
the usual perceptual experiences do not appear to be based
directly and solely on the stimuli received. Rather, they
seem to result from an interaction of the incoming stimuli
and past perceptions in memory store. The usual perceptual
experience appears to be a kind of constructive process whereby the incoming stimuli is integrated with past experiences
to create something that is different from both the present
event and past memories. Imagery differs from normal perception in that it incorporates otherwise irrelevant sensory information, such as an overheated room, to produce a novel or
nonexistent experience, such as dreaming that one is journeying
on a safari in the tropics. The imagery is not just a matter
of opening the file drawers of memory but of constructing new
models with the incoming information. Perception relies
heavily on incoming relevant sensory information, while imagery
relies more on what is already in storage to construct a reality.

● **PROBLEM** 6-14

Discuss echoic memory. How does its nature differ from that
of a tape recorder?

Solution: Because auditory perception takes place over a period of time, some kind of memory must preserve it long enough for speech processing to occur. Although some of the shorter syllables last for only fractions of a second, their characteristic qualities require time for recognition. Not just speech, but all auditory information is distributed over time. No single millisecond has enough information to feed anything useful into the cognitive processing system. If the information that arrived at the auditory channels was discarded immediately, it would be impossible to hear at all. The medium for the temporary storage of auditory information is called "echoic" memory. The maximum duration of echoic memory has been difficult to determine.

This transitory memory decays gradually, and its duration has varied inversely with the difficulty of the task that was used to measure it. Estimates of its duration range from one to ten seconds.

Echoic memory is not entirely comparable to a taped recording of the acoustic environment. The information that enters echoic memory storage has been transformed by the mechanisms of the cochlea and perhaps by other processes by the time the storage stage is reached. Whatever recording does occur, it seems certain that the unit of storage for memory is finer than the segmentation of speech that it makes possible. People do not "hear" exact representations of sound waves. What they hear has been interpreted for coding in echoic memory.

● **PROBLEM** 6-15

How is incoming sensory verbal information abstracted in terms of classification?

Solution: Information that comes into the sense channels and is further processed often goes through an abstracting operation whereby its components are reduced and coded in a condensed form. This requires the interaction of the new information with memory. This is perhaps best exemplified by the written word. Meaningful English words exist on at least three perceptual levels. First, a word is an arrangement of patterns--a visual or auditory code; second, it is a name; and third, it is an abstraction of some perceptual event which derives its meaning from the context in which it is found. Each level of processing requires time and the operation of different cognitive mechanisms. For example, consider the word "fire:" visual stimulation occurs first; word recognition occurs next; finally, its meaning is derived from the context. The context determines whether it is processed as a natural, chemical event or as the action of an angry employer.

These operations are performed on incoming information usually without the organism's awareness. They have been indirectly measured by calculating the amount of time required for them to occur. In one experiment, subjects were shown a pair of items and were asked to determine if they were similar or dissimilar. To indicate their decision, they were asked to press either a key marked "same" or one marked "different." Letters of the alphabet were used as test stimuli. Reaction times were fastest if the identity of the two figures was the same (CC). The next fastest response time occurred when the figures had the same name, but a different form (Cc) and the slowest response came when the letters were in the same class (either both were vowels or both were consonants such as Lc). This type of experiment has made it possible to study the existence of mental operations at different levels of complexity even in a seemingly simple task. The conclusion is theoretically of great importance; the nervous system classifies information over a period of time.

● **PROBLEM** 6-16

How do motor or enactive codes differ from visual or verbal codes. Illustrate with examples.

Solution: Codes in the memory system which store motor activity are called "enactive codes." Because most studies on problem-solving have focused on visual and verbal codes, very little is known about how enactive codes affect thinking.

Researchers have suggested that the movements required to hit a baseball are so complex that it would take just as many operations to program a computer to play baseball as it would to have it play chess. It appears that cognitive scientists have felt justified in ignoring the area because only a minimal amount of attention is necessary to utilize motor skills. Nevertheless, if the science of information-processing is to be complete, enactive codes must be understood.

Experiments conducted with typists have demonstrated the difference between visual and motor codes. A skilled typist can type the alphabet with no problem. However, if he is asked to recite the letters on the keyboard, in their correct order without looking, he can do so only with great difficulty and a high error probability. Subjects report that they locate the letters manually. That is, they do not have visual representations of the letters. This indicates that the skilled typist may have developed a motor code that is separate from any visual code.

There are many motor tasks one can successfully perform while attending to something different. For example, most people can accomplish the following while directing minimal attention to the task: knitting, walking, dressing, etc. Many people are familiar with two methods of finding their way: they can have a mental map construct that can be reproduced at will or they can find their destination without being able to instruct someone else on how to do so. These observations indicate that although motor skills are stored in memory, they can be utilized without directing active, conscious attention to the task.

To date, it is difficult to isolate enactive codes from other codes in the thinking process.

Why is the time required to produce associations to pictures greater than the time required to produce associations to words?

Solution: Generally, one thinks of associations as verbal descriptions. However, it has been demonstrated that associations between objects and actions can occur without verbal links. It was discovered in the early 40's that associations to pictures are different than associations to the names or descriptions of the same picture. Associations to pictures are more often related to the active performance with the object in the picture, for example, "bicycle--ride." Whereas the association to the word is more likely to be a category, "bicycle--transportation." Also, the time it takes for associations to pictures to form is greater than that for words. It has been hypothesized that this is because the picture produces visual associations which have to be transformed into words. This description fits well with the self-reports of subjects who have participated in these experiments.

It has further been demonstrated that visual memories may be clustered in memory by their distinctive physical-spatial properties rather than by their names. Thus, the processing time involved for transforming the visual impression into a verbal impression would include a search for the correct category and the specific name after locating the appropriate visual memory.

LSD used to be called a "psychomimetic" drug because it caused effects similar to those of mental illness. Why has this explanation been refuted?

Solution: The "hallucinogenic" drugs are so named because they often produce hallucinations at least to the extent that the images that are produced are projected into a localized space. However, they are not hallucinations in the true sense of the word since the subjects rarely believe that what they perceive is real. This is not the case with patients suffering from schizophrenia. Patients who have visual hallucinations tend to experience them as true representations of the world around them. Furthermore, almost all the hallucinations effected through the use of LSD and related drugs are visual, whereas the large majority of schizophrenic patients experience auditory hallucinations. That is, the chronic schizophrenic hears voices more often than he sees visions.

The visions that are chemically produced have a novel aspect--unfamiliar, incomprehensible shapes, forms, colors and combinations occur. The formation of these images is probably partly due to visual memory but the drug seems to also produce an overall distortion of the visual world which is greatly aided if the eyes remain closed. The schizophrenic patient, on the other hand, more often sees images and hears

Schizophrenic reactions	Drug-induced "model psychosis"
Mood	
Daydreaming and extreme withdrawal from personal contacts, ranging from sullen reluctance to talk to actual muteness.	Dreaming, introspective state, but preference for discussing visions and ruminations with someone.
Communication	
Speech vague, ambiguous, difficult to follow; no concern about inability to communicate; past tense common.	Speech rambling or incoherent but usually related to reality; subjects try to communicate thoughts; present tense used.
Irrationality	
Great preoccupation with bodily functions; illnesses attributed to unreasonable causes (the devil, "enemies").	Great interest in the vast array of new sensations being experienced; symptoms attributed to reasonable causes.
Hallucinations	
Frequent, very "real" hallucinations, usually auditory and extremely threatening.	Hallucinations predominantly visual; rare auditory hallucinations not so personal or threatening; subjects attempt to explain them rationally.
Delusions	
Delusions common, usually of reference, persecution, and grandeur.	Delusions rare; occurrence probably due to individual personality conflicts.
Mannerisms	
Bizarre mannerisms, postures, and even waxy flexibility manifested by certain patients.	Strange and bizarre repetitive mannerisms rare.

voices with the eyes open. These hallucinations take place in the context of specific affective states and contribute to the delusional preoccupations of the individual. They appear to represent a series of representations taken from visual memory to reproduce a dreamlike state that the patient believes to be real. Therefore, the analogy that was once commonly made between the effects of LSD and the schizophrenic state was misleading.

Of course, all who take drugs do not have similar experiences. The wide-spread differences in the perceptual effects make popular use of the drug dangerous.

MEMORY SYSTEMS AND RETRIEVAL

● **PROBLEM** 6-19

What are memory systems? Discuss the different characteristics of short-term and long-term memory.

Solution: Memory can be divided into two different systems. One system contains all information that is presently active. This is short-term memory. Generally, there is a limited amount of information available in this system as the capacity for immediate processing is quite limited. This can be easily seen when one is having a conversation and cannot remember what one was going to say. Short-term memory is of great importance to information processing theorists because

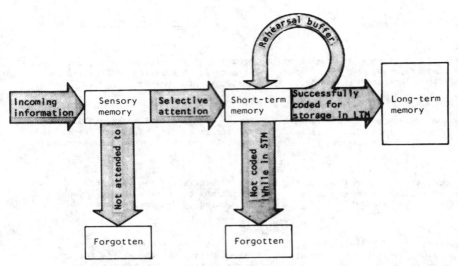

Incoming information → Sensory memory → Selective attention → Short-term memory → Successfully coded for storage in LTM → Long-term memory

Rehearsal buffer

Not attended to → Forgotten

Not coded while in STM → Forgotten

it is this system that relates a current piece of information to previously stored material. Short-term memory can be used to update the information in long-term memory, which includes all memory that is not currently active. Items in short-term memory have a very brief span if they are not sustained by active attention (a process called "rehearsal"). The "memory span" can be demonstrated by hearing a long list of numbers. Immediately after hearing the list, the average retention is eight items. This is the length of the short-term memory span.

Psychologists have theorized that active or short-term memory is supported by an ongoing electrical process in the brain, while long-term memory involves an actual change in the physical properties of brain cells. Material that is in long-term memory can be brought into active memory and will not be lost if it is interrupted. However, it appears that the capacity of the active system is still limited to a brief period of recall even if it is recalling material from long-term memory. This limited capacity of active memory is thought to contribute greatly to the difficulties people have with problem-solving. The human organism is only able to contain and examine a limited amount of information at any one time in the active state.

There are other clear differences between short and long-term memories. Short-term memory is direct and immediate while long-term memory can be slow and difficult. It usually requires effort to put new information into long-term memory. However, the contents of short-term memory, events that have just occurred, have never left consciousness and are accessible. For example, answer these two questions: What is the topic of the preceding paragraph? What did you wear last Monday?

Past events have to be searched for with great effort. The capacity of long-term memory is virtually limitless and therefore, makes it difficult for theorists to study. Researchers have yet to conceive of a method that could account for the extremely rapid retrieval of long-term memory. In reading this page--seemingly without effort--huge demands are being made on the long-term memory system. It must select

meaning from millions or billions of stored items. Yet,
to the reader it is an effortless procedure.

● **PROBLEM** 6-20

What are the two principal explanations for the limited capacity of short-term memory?

Solution: Material in short-term memory has a very short life
span if it is not reinforced by conscious rehearsal (repeating
the information to oneself). Two theories that explain the
brief recall ability of this memory system are the "interference" and the "time-decay" explanations.

The interference model can be understood by assuming
that short-term memory has a set number of spaces in which it
can hold information. When the information that is entering
is greater than the space available, some items are forgotten
or replaced by the new information. Generally, the items that
are forgotten are those in the middle of the list. This is
because what is learned first usually interferes with what
comes later (proactive interference) and what is learned later
usually interferes with what came earlier (retroactive interference). Thus, it is the items in the middle that are most
susceptible to forgetfulness.

Some theorists have also tried to explain the limited
capacity of short-term memory by supposing that the longer an
item stays in memory, the weaker it becomes until finally it
can no longer be recalled at all. This process would be analogous to an electrical capacitator whose charge decays with
time: each unit of time would weaken the traces of the previously acquired information.

The test of these two theories is difficult to devise
because it is very difficult to design an experiment in which
a subject is "doing nothing," which would be necessary to test
for the time decay theory. If the subject is not given a
task to do, he might be rehearsing the material. Therefore,
a perfect memory of the material could be explained by rehearsal or lack of interference. A poor memory also proves nothing,
time decay or interference could explain it, particularly if
another task is given. In experiments that have been designed
to present a task that would involve different material and
not interfere with retention, such as the task of detecting
a weak signal in noise for a subject who had just heard a set
of letters, the results indicate that both theories may be
somewhat correct, but neither exclusively. Thirty seconds
after the material is presented, the subjects retain it quite
well, but after these thirty seconds, the information becomes
very weak--the smallest amount of interference will destroy
it. Therefore, it appears that rapid forgetting in short-term
memory is due both to the passage of time and to interference
from new information. Of course, from one point of view,
time and new information are synonymous to the nervous system
which is continually processing the input from the environment.

What is "rehearsai?" What role does it play in short-term memory?

Solution: Short-term memory is immediate and direct; it has a limited capacity for retention. For example, when a series of numbers is presented only seven or eight will be recalled. This information will also rapidly be lost unless conscious attention is directed to the retention of the information. When attention is directed on the material it can be retained for an indefinite period of time. Information can be kept active in short-term memory through a process of "rehearsal."

Rehearsal appears to serve two main functions. The first, as already mentioned, is to allow material to remain in short-term memory indefinitely. The second appears to be to assist in the transfer of information from short to long-term memory where it can be permanently stored. The capacities of short-term memory affect the amount of information that can be successfully rehearsed. It is a relatively small amount of material that can be remembered and kept alive through rehearsal. Rehearsal does not increase the capacity of the short-term memory system. It appears to work on the decaying information in short-term memory, refreshing it and thereby re-entering it into short-term memory. If there is too much material to be rehearsed, some items will be decayed or forgotten before there is time for rehearsal to revive them.

It is relatively easy to measure the speed of rehearsal and thereby determine how much material can be successfully rehearsed. The rate of silent speech is about equal to that of spoken speech. Experimentation has demonstrated that this rate cannot possibly exceed about ten words per second. Since the average short-term memory span is about eight words, it is easily seen that the capacity of this system is quite limited.

What data support the theory that short-term memory is essentially auditory?

Solution: The auditory nature of short-term memory has been documented by a number of experiments. In one study of "retroactive inhibition" the subjects heard four letters which they were asked to remember. They were then asked to copy eight letters which were presented visually. After this, they were tested for their memory of the four letters they had heard. The ability to recall was significantly impaired if the eight letters they were asked to copy were acoustically similar to the four presented originally. This suggests that visual information is recoded into auditory codes which are subsequently confused with one another in the recall process.

Subjects tend to group what they hear according to a structure—usually a rhythmic one which serves as a series

of cues for the words or letters to be remembered. Any
interruptions in the rhythmic sequence has serious detrimental
effects on recall. For example, Conrad found that when he
presented an eight digit series to his subjects and said
"nought," the retention rate dropped from 73 to 38 percent.
Thus, it appears that verbal stimuli are incorporated into a
rhythmic structure. Furthermore, any stimulus that deviates
from the structure can substantially interfere with rehearsal
(repetition of the items in memory) and produce memory loss.

Another group of studies by Conrad that focused on
errors in immediate recall found that the most common types
of error in recall are the interpolation of one element for
another or the substitution of one for another. What is
important for the study of the nature of short-term memory
is that the substitutions tend to be items that sound like
the original visual stimuli. Wickelgren explicitly has shown
that in active verbal memory letters seen on the tachistoscope
will tend to be confused if their initial phoneme is common,
as for example, F, L, M, N, S and X which all have an initial
/e/. This further substantiates the theory that short-term
memory is auditory or at least linguistic. It is, in short,
inner speech.

● PROBLEM 6-23

What have DeGroot's chess experiments demonstrated about the
nature of long-term memory structures?

Solution: Memory structures are permanent organizations of
related material stored in long-term memory. For these
structures to be developed, attention, effort, and time are
required. However, once the structures are thoroughly committed to memory their retrieval is effortless. The capacity
of these memory structures is unknown. It appears that their
complexity is limited only by their degree of development.
Certain highly gifted individuals, professionals or experts
in a particular field appear to be able to develop quite
complex memory structures. A musician, for example, in playing his instrument does not have to use conscious effort to
produce every note; it has become an automatic process even
though the learning of the memory structures that permit this
unconscious processing may have taken many years of intensive
study and practice.

A series of experiments concerning the memory of master
chess players by DeGroot have produced valuable data on this
particular skill. Studying the ability of novices, experts
and master chess players to remember the position of pieces
on the board, DeGroot allowed each subject to look at a chess-
board for 5 seconds. The pieces were arranged in positions
which occurred during the 20th move of a master level game;
20 pieces were on the board at the time. The master chess
players showed a remarkable ability to remember the position
of the pieces, and if they were incorrect on the first guess,
almost all of them guessed correctly if given only one more
chance. Overall, the masters had 85% correct on the first
trial, while the experts had only 35% correct and the novices
did far worse. To take the study further, DeGroot attempted

to measure the general memory abilities of the three groups and discovered that the master players did not have a great advantage over the other players when the pieces were randomly arranged on the board. The further removed the memory task was from chess, the greater the similarity in the performance of the three groups became.

These findings suggest that the excellent performance of the master players is based on a perceptual ability. The impression of the pieces on the board in the midst of a game makes contact with a highly organized memory system. Just as a reader does not read individual letters or even words, the master chess player does not see and process each individual piece, rather he appears to see a pattern that relates to already existing structures in memory which makes it possible for him to retrieve the correct arrangement of the board. This achievement, which is one of great complexity, occurred with almost no effort. It emphasizes the point that one's present experience is highly influenced by past experience. The chess player "sees" according to his past contact with the chess board and pieces.

● **PROBLEM 6-24**

Distinguish between effortful and effortless retrieval, giving examples of each.

Solution: The retrieval of information from memory is a most important part of the information processing system of humans. Retrieval can be of two kinds: it can occur rapidly with little or no active recall or it can require attention and effort. The first type of recall is "effortless" and occurs generally when the new information presented is identical or close to that which has been previously stored. The recognition of words that is required to read this paragraph is a good example of this type of retrieval. When the new information presented is not identical to that which has been previously stored it requires more effort to remember. Seeing a familiar face does not guarantee that one will remember the name of the person without considerable effort. On the other hand, one might recognize the name of a person and not be able to "place" them or call to mind an image of what they look like. The information stored in the first instance was more strongly of a visual nature, while that of the second was more likely to be primarily verbal. Thus, the new information was in a form that was not identical to what was most strongly stored in memory.

There appear to be stages of information retrieval. For instance, if asked to name the author of "The Goldberg Variations" or to describe the name of the nearest galaxy, some subjects would be able to do so effortlessly, others might require a clue and another group may be able to say immediately that they could not answer. From experiments such as this, it has been concluded that an initial effortless retrieval occurred and that an effortful search of the area of memory that had been retrieved was necessary before the correct answer could be produced. This occurs when the information given is enough to reach a given area of memory but not a specific association.

What is proactive interference and what does it indicate about how information is classified? What is retroactive interference?

Solution: In studying the nature of retention and recall of information, one experiment presents three items to a subject and then distracts his attention for a brief period of time. After the first trial, retention is nearly perfect, but on subsequent trials recall deteriorates. It is thought that this occurs because the items that were stored in previous trials begin to confuse or interfere with the items from the current trial. This effect of prior learned items on the retention of information is called "proactive interference."

The type of item that is presented before a particular item also influences recall. This points strongly to the importance of classification in retention. If, for example, letters are presented for a number of trials and then numbers are presented, the numbers will be recalled with a high level of accuracy for the first few trials. This indicates that the memory of the letters does not interfere with the retention of the numbers and thus that they are likely to be stored in different parts of memory. This tendency for recall to improve when a change in category is made is called "release from proactive interference." Interestingly, some of the categorical changes that produce release from proactive interference are not even noticed by the subjects. This may imply that items are stored in temporal order and that the difference in types of lists is used as a way to avoid confusion so that there is no interfering effect from a letter list when a number list is presented. One explanation for these findings is that different parts of memory handle different types of information and that temporal order is important. Whichever explanation is finally accepted, those findings are important to any theory about the development of memory structures (connected pieces of information which associatively give rise to one another).

A study by Funkhouser showed further how classification at input affects retention. Subjects were shown pictures of simple objects such as chairs and trucks. The subjects were divided into groups. One group was asked to classify the objects by color, another by shape, and a third group was asked to make no classification. When this was completed, a brief distracting task was presented after which the subjects were asked to recall the items they had previously been shown. Some subjects were asked to recall using the same categories by which they had taken in the information; others were asked to recall using different categories. The speed and accuracy of recall for subjects who were permitted to recall using the same categories were far superior to that of the subjects who had to use different categories. This indicates that the classification that is made at the time of input of the material has a restricting influence on the way in which the material can be readily used. It is most accessible if it is associated with the same category; recall of the material becomes slow and laborious if it is needed in a different classification system.

The term "retroactive interference" refers to the effect the last items learned have on the retention of information. Researchers have shown that the last few items learned tend to interfere with the earlier items. Thus, if the effects of proactive and retroactive interference are real, then the items in the middle of a long list should be the least likely to be recalled. This should be true because these items are subject to both proactive and retroactive interference. Experiments on memory have illustrated that this is exactly what happens when a subject is asked to recall a long list: the items at the beginning and at the end have a higher frequency of recall than those in the middle.

SELECTIVE ATTENTION AND PATTERN RECOGNITION

● PROBLEM 6-26

What is attention? Include a description of the "energy" and "analytic mechanism" approaches.

Solution: What is attention? As with so many perceptual processes, its nature is unknown though its measure has been taken and theorized about by a number of researchers. It is the capacity to attend to certain stimuli that has not yet been successfully programmed into any computer that may explain why pattern-recognition machines fall so far short of the human capacity. Traditionally, attention has been explained as a definite allocation of "energy." No distinctions were made in types or degrees of attention; it was all considered part of the same process.

This definition and approach to attention has been basically rejected by information-processing theorists who have tended to explain it as a focusing of analyzing neural mechanisms on a particular portion of the stimulus input field. Thus, when an organism pays attention to something he makes more careful and detailed analyses of the information coming into that part of the sensory receiving apparatus. Processing goes on with more sophisticated and limited mechanisms than he is using for the other incoming information. This analytic model presupposes two levels of attention: focal attention and a preattentive process. The preattentive process provides the material on which focal attention will act. An example of the more generalized activity of preattention is the fact that one can drive a car safely for 15 or 20 minutes without attending to the activity. Should a pedestrian suddenly cross in front of the car, the driver's attention would immediately focus on the mechanics of driving.

● PROBLEM 6-27

Describe the basic approach and results of research on the topics of selective and divided attention.

Solution: In studying the topic of selective filtering it is
important to distinguish between information which is temporarily or permanently "ignored" and information that is the
focus of attention. The two basic approaches to studying
attention are: shadowing studies and listen and report
studies.

Shadowing studies were first conducted by Cherry in
1953. In a shadowing experiment, the subject is requested
to verbally repeat a message aloud as "close behind" the
speaker's voice as possible. The task is often interfered
with by the simultaneous presentation of extraneous auditory
and visual stimuli. When asked questions about the characteristics of the added stimuli, subjects were very vague, suggesting that shadowing is a powerful way of focusing attention on the chosen message. The conclusion derived from
shadowing experiments is that organisms can only attend to
one thing at a time.

In the listen and report studies, the subjects hear the
entire message before attempting to repeat it. No shadowing
is involved and these studies are sometimes referred to as
split-span or divided attention studies. The results from
research in this area is generally in agreement with the
results of the shadowing studies.

● **PROBLEM** 6-28

Describe Broadbent's theory of Selective Attention and the
main problems it has.

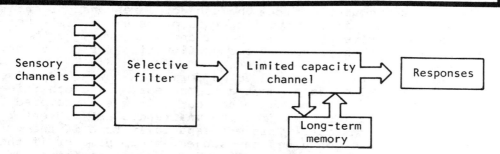

Information flow diagram for Broadbent's filter theory

Solution: The research which formed the basis for theories
of selective attention was conducted by Broadbent in the late
1950's. Broadbent's approach became known as the filter
theory because it generally hypothesized that certain sensory
inputs are rejected (forgotten or not perceived) while others
are "allowed in" for further processing.

According to Broadbent's theory, when several messages
reach the sensory organs simultaneously, they are processed
through a series of parallel channels (this is represented
by the first set of arrows in the figure). They then
enter a selective filter which attunes the sensory organs
to important cues from the stimulus. Only the information
attended to is processed further. It is then directed into
a limited capacity channel where it is retained by the processing system. Information not selected for attention then

205

enters a preperceptual system where it decays.

Cherry's research supports the filter theory and quantitatively follows the workings of the system.

The filter theory is not flawless. Although it adequately explains many concepts, it is criticized for operating on an all-or-none basis. Research has demonstrated that information which is not fully attended to does not necessarily decay. Investigations using shadowing techniques are good examples of this. An alternative line of research has been proposed which attempts to solve the problem of all-or-none learning. It has been suggested that the selective filter acts to "alternate" rather than "block" those inputs which are rejected. In this way, all sensory inputs are attended to but each to a different degree.

● **PROBLEM** 6-29

How does the filter-amplitude theory account for selective attention in hearing?

Solution: Experimenting with selective listening, Broadbent suggested that attention works like a filter that rejects certain input and passes other input along for further processing. The hypothetical filter mechanism can be tuned to any one or number of sensory channels (or types of sensory impressions). It only passes information on for further cognitive processing from channels to which it is specifically tuned. Only information that has passed through the filter can subsequently affect the subject's response or enter into memory. At first, this filter theory seems to fit the data from selective attention experiments, however, further experimentation has produced some difficulties for the theory.

When subjects were asked to perform a shadowing exercise, (repeat a list of words presented to one ear, while other information is presented to the other ear), it was discovered that the rejected messages from the unattended ear did enter the subject's attention. This was especially true if the unattended message contained the subject's own name or if the message presented to the unattented ear included information that would contextually be expected in the message receiving the focus of attention. For example, if the information presented to the ear from which the shadowing was taking place was:

"Looking at the large birch/astronomic figures. . ." while that from the unattended side was simultaneously:

"They could not believe/tree in the corner," the word "tree" was heard even though it came through the unattended side because the subject was expecting it due to the context. One may always be set for one's own name just as one is set for a particular input that corresponds to the context presented. Whatever the theoretical explanation for these interesting findings, it was necessary to modify the filter theory to include them.

Treisman offered the suggestion that the filter mechanism "attenuates" rather than rejects information. That is, the information that comes through the filter is weakened but remains strong enough to be picked up by other cognitive systems that are especially tuned to hear it. This filter-amplitude theory accounts for the introduction of certain types of unattended information into the processing system.

● **PROBLEM** 6-30

A major problem in thinking is maintaining alertness or concentration. What have experimental findings demonstrated about this problem?

Solution: It is difficult to direct the flow of attention for any length of time on one particular subject or source of stimulation. The natural tendency of the mind seems to be to wander. This difficulty of mental concentration has an analogy in sensory perceptual processes. When subjects are presented with a visual stimulus that remains fixed on the same spot on the retina (this is accomplished with special equipment) it disappears after a short period of time.

In one experiment, subjects were asked to attend to a blank screen and told to report whenever they saw a dim light appear. Because the light was so dim it required great concentration on the part of the subjects. Alertness quickly waned, and the more time that passed, the more likely it was that the light would go unnoticed. Even if the rate of sensory input was high (the light was flashed often) the subjects had difficulty maintaining attention. In another experimental situation, subjects were asked to watch the hands on a clock and to attempt to detect when the movements were particularly larger than usual. During this experiment there was much sensory input as the hands were moving quite rapidly, yet performance waned within a matter of minutes. It is difficult to maintain attention even if active involvement occurs. One subject was asked to press a button each time a light came on; his performance also worsened with time.

The nature of the lags in performance is of interest as it was noted that subjects appeared to "turn off" to the task for brief periods of time. If the task was designed to allow for many changes to new stimuli sources, the decline in performance was greatly reduced. The human system is apparently designed to respond most readily to novelty or change in stimuli; concentration requires resistance to this natural tendency.

● **PROBLEM** 6-31

Discuss the theoretical problem of pattern recognition. Why is it an important dimension of information processing theory?

Solution: When a stimulus evokes the same response consistently it has been "recognized" by the nervous system. The problem for psychologists is to describe this process of pattern recognition. One of the reasons this is such a difficult problem is

that many different stimuli can produce the same reaction. An
area that has received a great deal of attention in this regard is the manner in which varying forms of different letters
are consistently recognized. An "R," for instance, is recognized as an "R" in many different hand-and machine-written
forms. It is the ability of the human information processing
system to select the central similarity from the many visual
configurations that are registered that makes pattern recognition so difficult to explain.

To date no machine has been constructed that can recognize the sights and sounds in its environment with the same
accuracy and detail as the human organism. In fact, past
attempts to construct pattern recognition systems have not
even achieved the level of the perceptual systems of primitive
animals. It is difficult to realize the enormous complexity
of this process because recognizing and responding occurs so
quickly and with so much ease that it would seem that the
processes involved must be simple. However, to the scientist
who wishes to draw a neurological map of the processes that
occur from sensation to reaction, the explanation of recognition remains elusive.

● **PROBLEM 6-32**

What are the three major theories of pattern recognition?

Solution: The development of pattern recognition theories
is long and complex. Each theory seemed exciting and promising at its inception but with time and further investigation
proved to be inflexible or too weak to explain the enormous
complexity of the human perceptual system. The three major
theories of pattern recognition are template matching, feature
analysis and analysis by synthesis. Analysis by synthesis is
the latest and most promising of the three theories. To date
it is the most capable of dealing with the problems in this
area.

Template matching theories purport that each pattern is
recognized by noting its similarity with a basic model.
Fingerprinting is a good example of the use of template matching in everyday life. A sample fingerprint may not precisely
match another taken from the same person, but the match will
be reasonably close--close enough to be recognizable. Template matching theorists encounter immediate problems when
trying to explain even simple variations in patterns. People
recognize an "R" even if it is upside-down, very small or
huge. The template theory would have to be expanded to include a new template for every size and orientation to provide even a beginning viable explanation of the capabilities
of the human pattern recognition system. A number of modifi-
cations of the theory have been offered, but generally, the
examination of template theories has led to the development
of a variety of attribute or feature-analysis theories.

The feature analysis theories, of which the most well-
known is probably "Pandemonium," include mechanisms that
easily explain the ability of the nervous system to analyze
small details in sensory input. The cognitive system is

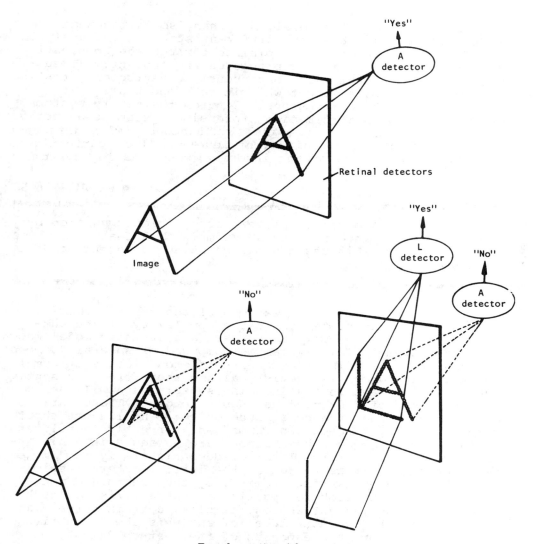

Template Matching

explained as being hierarchically organized in its analysis
of information. At the first level, the "analyzers" determine
if a particular input has certain characteristics or features.
These features are not known but a number have been postulated such as roundness, angularity, the presence of parallel
lines and gaps. It is assumed that there are many analyzers.
No single attribute is required to arouse these analyzers;
they respond to a combination of features. The identification
of the specific feature depends on the combination of input.
More complex data needs to pass to higher levels of analysis,
but even very complex input is thought to be processed by
analysis of features. Compelling though it seems, particularly
in compensating for the weaknesses of template theory, feature
analysis breaks down in a number of situations. For example,
it cannot reveal whether the sounds "noo-dis-plaee" mean "new
display" or "nudist play." It also cannot explain why most
people see a "B" in ßoy but a "13" in 2ß67.

The latest theory of pattern recognition, analysis by

synthesis, is a complex model, but then, so is the human brain. It suggests that the different steps in the analysis of information can only be explained through the combination of sensory analysis, memory processes and thought. It suggests that the organism is continuously constructing, testing and revising theories about what it sees and hears. It places a great deal of responsibility on the memory systems and sees the human information processing system as an active synthesizing process. It works simultaneously with different types of information at different levels. It is currently the preferred explanation of the information processing system.

● **PROBLEM 6-33**

The "Pandemonium" model of pattern recognition suggested by Selfridge in the late 50's is an example of a feature-analysis theory. Discuss its basic design, strengths and weaknesses.

Solution: Oliver Selfridge was one of the first workers in the computer field to recognize the complexity of the pattern recognition problem. He devised a systematic model known as "Pandemonium." This system is composed of several "demons" that operate on the information at different levels of complexity. Each demon is egotistical and therefore incessantly looks for his image in the incoming sensory data. If he finds evidence of his image he shouts loudly. These various levels of shouting produce a pandemonium. The loudest shout is registered by a "decision demon" who correctly identifies the incoming pattern. These demons are arranged in a hierarchical manner. The first level of demon is simply an "image demon" whose job it is to record the initial external stimulus. These images are next examined by the "feature demons." The feature demons look for particular characteristics such as vertical lines, right angles, circles, certain curves and acute angles. At the next level of analysis the "cognitive demons" listen for the responses of the feature demons, on guard for a particular pattern for which each is responsible. The more features a cognitive demon finds that correspond with its particular pattern, the louder it yells. The decision demon who operates at the next level of information processing listens for the loudest yelling and deduces that the pattern represented by that cognitive demon is the one that is most likely occurring in the environment.

This is a flexible system that allows learning to occur (the more trials, the better the cognitive demons are at recognizing their pattern). It also can account for the effects of context with the addition of "contextual demons" at the cognitive demon level. Also, individual neurons have just the type of nature as that described for the feature demons. It is a system that is compatible with what is already known about the way the nervous system processes external signals.

The examination of this theory has revealed that it is probably on the right track as far as there being feature

210

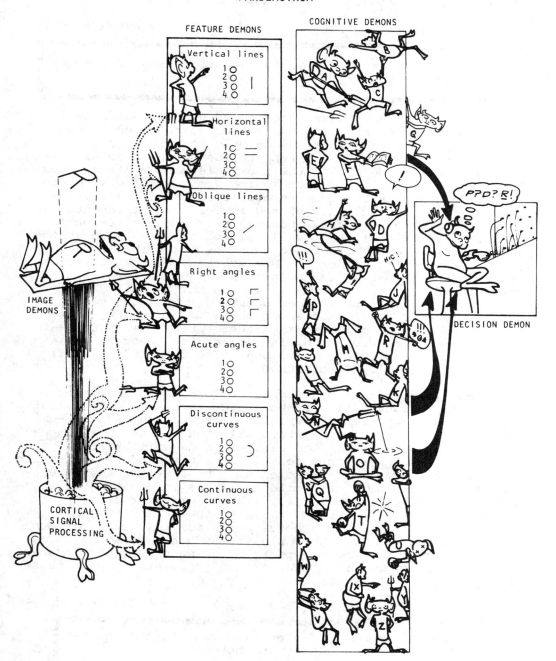

detectors in the human nervous system, but that its specific aspects need refining and enlarging. It has been suggested that there may be analyzers of whole figures rather than just parts, for example. The levels of abstraction are now thought to be much more complex than those outlined originally by Selfridge. A serious criticism of this theory is the fact that it does not account for attention.

OTHER APPROACHES AND APPLICATIONS

● PROBLEM 6-34

What part do "heuristics" play in the processing of sensory information?

Solution: What is perceived and recorded of actual experiences is only a selected representation of the event. Not only do organisms tend to focus on only certain attributes of a given impression, but they tend to record the "representative" or average quality of their experiences. This process is accomplished by "heuristics" which are ways of making complex judgments of situations through the use of reality-simplifying devices. Examples of heuristics are "representativeness" (when asked to make a judgment people often reason from an average situation) and "availability" (judgments about the frequency of an event are based upon the accessibility of such an event in the memory). For example, when asked which occurs more frequently in the English language, words that begin with "K" or words with "K" as the third letter, most people will say that the former occur more frequently. In reality, however, there are about three times as many words with "K" as the third letter than there are words which begin with "K." Because an initial letter is a better retrieval cue than a middle letter, words beginning with "K" are more accessible to retrieval than those with a "K" appearing later.

The way in which impressions are formed of other people offers an opportunity to see heuristics in action. If a list of adjectives is presented describing the person, the subject's final rating of the person will tend to be an average of the adjectives given. The earlier words will be given more weight than those that come later and the adjectives which contradict the overall impression will be disregarded. Therefore, the opinion does not reflect all the information given, but only a reduced amount of it. Thus, memory processes appear to simplify the world. This statement may in itself be an oversimplification. There remain complex human pattern recognition systems that psycholgists do not understand in which material from memory appears to by-pass conscious processing and still make subtle and refined judgments such as those made by a master chess player.

● PROBLEM 6-35

Why are parallel memory codes so important in the understanding of the role of memory in thought?

Solution: Whenever new information is encoded, the internal and external environment in which it occurred is also assimilated. Even when one is specifically concerned with a particular aspect of an event, surrounding input also enters the memory system.

For example, during an interview a person may focus his attention on the interviewer's remarks and reactions. How-

ever, if on some future occasion he tried to remember the
details of the room in which the interview took place, he
could probably do so by calling on the visual or iconic
memories that were stored during the interview. The person's
general impression of the interviewer may be contained in
memory in categories relating to the interviewer's position,
title, and his reactions to the interviewee. The person
would rely on his visual memory if he tried to recall the
interviewer's appearance. This simultaneous storage of
information in memory is called "parallel storage" and is of
prime importance in the study of both memory and thinking.

At any time after an experience, information can be activated from a number of different sources including the
temporal verbal and iconic visual records of what occurred.

Considerable cross-filing and referencing of incoming
information can take place producing temporal memory (the
recall of the sequence of events) in different categories.
Generally, a subject is given a list of letters and numbers
and is told in advance that he will be asked to recall the
items in accordance with their respective categories (letters or numbers), he will recall more readily by category
than by temporal sequence. However, if he is subsequently
presented with varying lists and is asked to select the list
he had previously heard, he will have very little difficulty
doing so. This demonstrates that although the information
was initially coded by category, the temporal memory is accessible to the subject and therefore was coded simultaneously
(in parallel sequence) with the category storage.

● **PROBLEM 6-36**

Outline the basic concepts of the Craik and Lockhart approach
to memory.

Solution: Researchers studying memory observed that rote
learning does not result in as high a probability of recall
as material acquired in context. This led researchers such
as Craik and Lockhart to propose theories involving series
of processing stages.

For Craik and Lockhart, information processing begins
at an initial input level where all information is analyzed
in terms of physical characteristics (a type of sensory
level). At the next stage, processing is concerned with
context, meaning, and recognition. In order to account for
the observable limited capacity of the memory, Craik and
Lockhart have proposed a "limited capacity central processor." This concept is designed to utilize stored information.
The important point is that it is the processor that is limited, not the amount of storage space. Retention in the Craik
and Lockhart model is determined by depth of analysis. Thus,
according to these theorists, there is a hierarchy of cognitive analysis.

Distinguish between rational or logical thinking and intuitive or prelogical thought. How are these two operations thought to interact in the creative process?

Structure of the
Benzene molecule

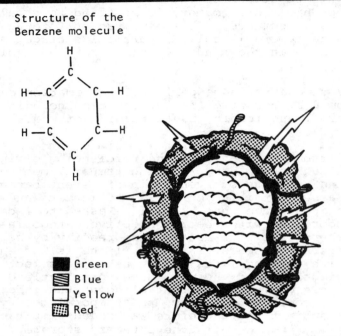

Green
Blue
Yellow
Red

Kehule's dream from which he predicted the structure of the benzene molecule.

Solution: Studies of split-brain patients have generated much interest in the possible existence of two types of thinking. These two types of mental operation go by a variety of different names: rational vs. intuitive, logical vs. prelogical, constrained vs. creative, primary vs. secondary, etc. A principal difference between the two processes is that the first requires conscious attention while the second does not, and that the first is principally verbal while the second is nonverbal.

Numerous reports from scientists, mathematicians, and artists confirm that the solution to a problem may come automatically, with no conscious effort, when a rest period follows a long session of concentration on the problem. Cognitive psychologists are interested in finding whether unconscious processing is more complex and therefore, more creative than the conscious work that preceded the rest period.

Because the prerequisite to an "ah-ah" insight (as this spontaneous problem-solving is sometimes called) is that a great deal of conscious effort has been directed to a particular problem, it seems likely that the two processes—conscious and unconscious—rely on one another. The conscious effort may serve as a retrieval mechanism that activates unconscious sources that may be necessary to produce the cor-

rect solution. This process may require that some time
elapse so that the active half of the mental processing
equipment may rest. There are numerous theories about how
this might occur. What is relatively certain is that the
two processes are interdependent and that the most creative
output occurs as a result of their interaction.

● **PROBLEM 6-38**

Discuss the role of "language frequency" in the recognition
thresholds of words. How does "fragment theory" explain
this phenomenon?

Solution: Reading and word recognition in general have been
one of the most widely studied areas of human perception in
the past century and have generated an abundance of theoretical controversy. The experimental technique that has probably
provided the most information in this area is one that involves the use of the tachtiscope. The tachtiscope is an
instrument that permits visual material to be presented to
a subject for a brief duration--usually less than 1/4 second,
which is the length of time required for a single visual
fixation. Among other uses, this instrument has allowed for
recognition thresholds to be determined.

One result that has been duplicated in experimental situations is the effect of familiarity and specifically of
language-frequency on the recognition threshold of words.
The Thorndike-Lorge, which is a listing of the frequency of
use of English words, is used to determine the frequency of
a given word. The more commonly used words are more easily
and quickly recognized than the rare words even if they have
a similar shape and length. For example, "yet" is recognized
more easily than "yak," and "accept" more readily than "accede."
Many explanations for this phenomenon have been offered. The
most commonly accepted today is the fragment theory.

Fragment theory supposes that when a word is briefly
presented to a subject he only sees a fragment of it. From
this fragment he makes an educated "guess" as to what the
word might be. He is much more likely to choose a familiar
word, one that occurs frequently in common usage, that incorporates the fragment that he saw. Many predictions that can
be made from this theory have been supported by experiment.
Even rare words have low thresholds if there are no similar
common words. If two words have the same general appearance,
the rare word will have a higher threshold and the common word
will be more often offered as an incorrect response to the
stimulus. On the other hand, an equally rare word that does
not have a common word similar to it, will not have such a
high threshold. This theory about word familiarity and recognition belongs to a school of theories that maintain that cognition begins with incomplete stimulus information and proceeds from there to create a structured and meaningful world.

● **PROBLEM 6-39**

How does information processing theory explain rapid reading
for meaning?

Solution: A reader does not usually "identify" each of
the words. That is, he does not pronounce each word silently
to store it in verbal memory. Most adults read word for word
only when the material is very difficult or when the print is
hard to see. Even words of a well-learned phrase cannot be
inwardly repeated more rapidly than at the rate of 600 per
minute. The reading rate of many people is more rapid than
600 words per minute. One explanation of this phenomenon is
the "redundancy" of the English language. It has been observed that English readers can fill-in missing letters and
phrases in the language with remarkable accuracy. This is
the "redundancy effect." Some have estimated the redundancy
of the language at 50 percent. This redundancy is thought
to supplement what the reader sees with information from past
experience so that the meaning can be correctly inferred without having to actually process each word. Because some readers
can read more rapidly than even 1200 words per minute this
explanation has been questioned as inaccurate or at least
incomplete.

It is possible to make an analogy between the recognition of words (without having to give attention to individual
letters) and the reading of sentences (without processing each
individual word). However, there is a higher process involved in the grasping of the meaning of a phrase that is
not necessary for the identification and labeling of a single
word. It is this play of higher cognitive processes that remains an enigma to scientists. Reading can be seen as externally guided thought, and its secrets may remain undis-
closed until the nature of thought itself is understood more
thoroughly. It may be that rapid reading for meaning bypasses
verbal memory altogether by some process yet unknown; it
certainly results in a nonsensory construct-"meaning." At
best, the state of the art in this area remains at the level
of clarifying and expanding the questions that need to be
asked.

SHORT ANSWER QUESTIONS FOR REVIEW

Choose the correct answer.

1. Plato's theory of thinking was based upon   (a)
    sensory input   (b)   auditory input   (c)   tactile
    input   (d)   none of the above   a

2. Computer simulations help explain human   (a)
    perception and cognition   (b)   distractability
    in solving problems   (c)   ability to solve all
    types of problems   (d)   none of the above   a

3. The first stage in the visual information proc-
    essing system is   (a)   short-term memory   (b)
    visual image representation   (c)   iconic storage
    (d)   none of the above   c

4. Master chess players   (a)   have better general
    memory abilities than the average nonplayer
    (b)   are better at remembering the positions of
    pieces haphazardly arranged on a chess board
    (c)   are better at remembering the position of
    pieces on the 25th move of an actual game   (d)
    none of the above   c

5. The computer is least able to match the human
    capacity for   (a)   long-term memory storage
    (b)   selective attention   (c)   executing 'sim-
    ple' arithmetical computations   (d)   pattern-
    recognition   d

6. The following determine(s) a subjects perform-
    ance on a memory task   (a)   demand character-
    istics   (b)   selective attention   (c)   number
    of items to be recalled   (d)   all of the above   d

7. Evidence suggests that spatial or visual infor-
    mation is handled by the brain's   (a)   left
    hemisphere   (b)   right hemisphere   (c)   two
    hemispheres   (d)   none of the above   b

8. It has been hypothesized that eidetic imagery is
    rarely found in the adult urban dweller because
    (a)   the smog in his atmosphere does not facili-
    tate it   (b)   things move too quickly in the
    city   (c)   it would not be socially accepted   c

9. Motor activity is stored in   (a)   enactive
    codes   (b)   visual codes   (c)   verbal codes
    (d)   tactile codes   a

10. Unlike a person under the influence of a psycho-
    mimetic drug, a schizophrenic patient   (a)   be-
    lieves his visions and the voices he hears are

real   (b)   does not need to close his eyes to
sharpen his perceptions   (c)   experiences more
auditory than visual hallucinations   (d)   all
of the above   (e) none of the above

e

11. Material in long-term memory   (a)   may be lost
    if the person is interrupted while retrieving
    it   (b)   is hypothesized to involve on-going
    electrical processes in the brain rather than
    actual changes in the physical properties of
    brain cells   (c)   includes all memory that is
    not currently active   (d)   may include informa-
    tion that never passed through short-term mem-
    ory

c

12. The items that are most likely to be forgotten
    are those at the   (a)   beginning of a long list
    (b)   middle of a long list   (c)   end of a long
    list

b

13. To accurately test the time decay theory an ex-
    perimenter would have to devise a method where
    the subject   (a)   does nothing   (b)   is busy
    with some other task while he waits to be tested
    (c)   rehearses the material continuously as he
    waits to be tested   (d)   cannot anticipate how
    much time will elapse before he is tested

a

14. According to proactive interference, the recall
    of individual items in a list is interfered with
    (a)   by items that come later   (b)   by items
    that came earlier   (c)   if all the items are
    similar   (d)   if all the items are dissimilar

b

15. Material in long-term memory is retained
    through   (a)   rehearsal   (b)   chunking   (c)
    retroactive inhibition   (d)   none of the above

d

16. The "interference effect" is due to the   (a)
    limitless capacity of long-term memory   (b)
    dissimilarity between stimulus items   (c)   lim-
    ited capacity of short-term memory   (d)   time
    interval that elapses between the presentation
    of stimulus items

c

17. Without rehearsal, memory traces in short-term
    memory may last for about   (a)   10 milliseconds
    (b)   100 milliseconds   (c)   1 second   (d)   20
    seconds

d

18. A model in which the internal representation of
    a pattern is structurally similar to the stim-
    ulus pattern is called a   (a)   visual feature

SHORT ANSWER QUESTIONS FOR REVIEW

model (b) constructive model (c) template
matching model (d) none of the above — c

19. A model of visual information processing includes (a) the pattern of light projected onto the retina (b) internal processes (c)
both (a) and (b) (d) neither (a) nor (b) — c

20. A scanning method typically proceeds in English-
speaking subjects from (a) right to left (b)
left to right (c) top to bottom (d) none of
the above — b

21. Verbal short-term memory encodes material in
(a) a visual form (b) an acoustic form (c)
both (a) and (b) (d) none of the above — b

Fill in the blanks.

22. The rapid and brief eye movements that iconic
store is closely related to are called _____. — saccades

23. Symbols humans use in thinking are _____. — images and concepts

24. According to Chomsky's transformational grammar,
there are _____ possible transformations for any
kernel sentence. — eight

25. According to Piaget, the stage at which children
begin to think hypothetically is called the
_____ _____ period. — formal operational

26. When an individual gives the same label to various objects he is said to have formed a(n)
_____. — concept

27. Selfridge's "pandemonium" model of pattern recognition is an example of a _____ theory. — feature-analysis

28. A person who solves problems by considering
every possible solution (rather than eliminating some choices by using rules of thumb) is
said to use the _____ method. — brute force

29. Simultaneous storage of information in memory
is called _____. — parallel storage

30. Material is retained in short term memory
through _____. — rehearsal

SHORT ANSWER QUESTIONS FOR REVIEW

31. The transfer of material from short-term memory to long-term memory is facilitated by the use of _____ devices.

mnemonic

32. A person who glimpses at an object then closes his eyes immediately experiences a(n) _____ .

icon

33. A person capable of _____ imagery can produce clear visual images that can be scanned for details.

eidetic

34. Methods that serve as shortcuts for solving problems are called _____ .

heuristics

35. _____ thinking does not require conscious attention.

Intuitive

36. According to "_____ theory," a subject only sees part of a word when he is briefly presented with it. He then makes an educated "guess" in identifying the word.

fragment

Determine whether the following statements are true or false.

37. In the short-term memory stage, visual information is encoded independently of the construction of a visual image.

True

38. Long term memory is believed to have a limitless capacity.

True

39. Human memory for pictures is lower than the memory capacity for verbal or linguistic material.

False

40. Information never drops out before the organism chooses to either use or ignore it.

False

41. A natural order is followed when viewing a picture.

False

42. Short term memory encodes visual stimulation in a linguistic or conceptual form.

True

43. Decay with time and interference are both responsible for the loss of information from short term memory.

True

44. Functional fixedness helps an organism perceive new ways of looking at objects.

False

45. Structural theorists argue that capacities for

SHORT ANSWER QUESTIONS FOR REVIEW

	cognitive processes are innate.	True
46.	Retrieval involves search and decision processes	True
47.	A person can increase the quantity of material retained in short-term memory by "chunking".	True
48.	Stimuli can never elicit both visual and verbal associations.	False
49.	Associations between objects and actions cannot occur without verbal links.	False
50.	The probability that a particular word in a long list will be recalled is highest when the subject sees it as belonging to a different category from all the other words.	True

CHAPTER 7

STATES OF CONSCIOUSNESS

MIND-BODY PROBLEM AND CONSCIOUSNESS

Discuss the mind-body problem and describe the solutions proposed by: the structuralists, the behaviorists, the Gestalt psychologists, and those who have proposed semantic solutions.

Solution: The mind-body problem has been in existence for more than 2500 years. Ancient philosophers discovered that in addition to his physical body, man possesses nonphysical equipment which he uses for thinking. Having recognized man's physical and mental components, the philosophers asked: What is the relationship between the two?

This question has been tackled throughout the centuries. Many individuals and groups have proposed solutions but to this day there is no definitive solution.

Following the method of chemists, the structuralists believed that the mind could be divided into mental elements and analyzed in its compartments. The structuralists employed the process of introspection for this analysis. In their approach to the mind-body problem, these men adopted the view of psychophysical parallelism. This school of thought, originated by the philosopher Spinoza in 1665, proposed that the mind and body are independent systems that operate parallel to each other but do not interact. Armed with this premise, structuralists proceeded to study the mind directly, ignoring any influence the body may have on its functioning.

John Watson stressed the need to examine observable behavior. His behavioristic school of thought concentrated on observing stimulus-response relations and ignored the "mind" or contents of consciousness. The behaviorists considered the mind and the method of introspection poor bases on which to construct a science. In their solution to the mind-body problem, the behaviorists recognized only the physical nature of man (physical monism) they regarded the mind as merely a description of physical events.

In contrast to the structuralists, who separated mental processes into elements, the Gestalt psychologists regarded all phenomena as wholes. Isomorphism, a key concept in Gestaltist thought, refers to an identity of pattern between two objects or events. For instance, the relationship between a road map and road exemplifies isomorphism. A highway on a road map may be designated as a wide blue line. The actual highway may be wide but it is not blue. The road and the road map share an isomorphic relationship. They are not the same object, but the characteristics of one (such as curves) may be read from the other.

In response to the mind-body problem, the Gestalt psychologists adopted the principle of psychological isomorphism. According to this principle, an isomorphic relationship exists between subjective experience and chemical-electrical processes in the brain. Given this relationship, one should be able to form a "map" of neurological processes by examining conscious experience.

Other psychologists have found semantic solutions to the mind-body problem. Gilbert Ryle and B. F. Skinner don't perceive the mind-body relationship as a problem; they believe the problem is in semantics. Terms referring to mental states ("subjective terms") are learned as part of the process of acquiring language. But language is not subjective. Because it is a means of communication, language by its nature is intersubjective. A mother may observe her child and say "Johnny, you are tired." Soon, Johnny will learn to say, "I am tired." But, according to Skinner and Ryle, Johnny is not reporting the result of an introspective examination, but describing himself in terms that were initially applied to him on the basis of cues (symptoms, behavior situations) observed by his mother. This approach takes the "mind" out of the mind-body problem.

Herbert Feigl proposed an indentity theory as a semantic solution to the mind-body problem. According to this theory, certain neurophysiological terms and phenomenal terms (those of subjective experience), refer to the same process. When someone says "I was scared," he is using a phenomenal term to describe an event. The same event might be described by a psychologist in different terms. The psychologist might say that his body produced a great deal of adrenalin or that his heart rate accelerated. Feigl's solution acknowledges that one reality can be described in different languages.

● **PROBLEM** 7-2

What is meant by the term consciousness?

Solution: To the average person, consciousness refers to wakefulness or alertness. An individual who is conscious

223

is awake and aware of himself and his surroundings. An unconscious person is not aware of anything. In psychology, however, consciousness does not merely refer to an all-or-nothing state of wakefulness. Consciousness refers to the sum total of mental experiences.

Consciousness exists at different levels in a wide range of graded states. These mental experiences include: coma (which results from severe physical injury), dreaming, fatigue or dullness, wakefulness, alertness, full activity and creative thinking, and hyperactivity. Man experiences all but the most extreme of these states in everyday life.

Each state of consciousness contains varying levels of activity. An individual is least active if he is in a coma state of consciousness and most active in a hyperactive state. During waking states, man engages in a wide variety of activities: thinking, talking, looking, listening. Several of these activities may be performed simultaneously. One of the most prominent activities man engages in is talking to himself, carrying out a constant monologue which many equate with thinking.

Davis (1962) established three criteria an individual must meet to be considered conscious. The person must be aware of: 1. self -- he must be able to recognize himself as distinguished from the environment; 2. time -- he must be able to discriminate between the present, past and future; and 3. location in space -- he must have a sense of his location in the external world.

● PROBLEM 7-3

What is the difference between consciousness and awareness? Define automatic behavior.

Solution: In a state of wakefulness, man can be conscious of many things without being aware of them. A person may know that certain objects are present in his environment and that certain events are occurring, but they may not be the focus of his concentration. Therefore, he is conscious of them but not aware of them. He can become aware of them if he directs his attention to them.

William James (1890) spoke of consciousness as a "selecting agency" which chooses to notice certain phenomena in the environment, emphasizing some things and suppressing others.

The best way to distinguish between consciousness and awareness is to apply the concept of automatic behavior. The term "automatic behavior" is self-explanatory: it refers to any behavior that can be engaged in without much concentration and effort. Several activities, such as riding a bicycle, are performed automatically. Motor responses in these activities are automatic because the person does not need to think about them to perform them. When riding a bicycle, the person is conscious of such responses as

steering, pedaling, and braking, but he does not think about
them -- he is not immediately aware of them. He is also not
aware of the cues to which he responds, such as traffic
lights, stop signs, and other vehicles on the road. However, unregistered stimuli may suddenly leap into awareness. For example, a previously unnoticed car may turn
directly in front of the bicycle. The rider will be aware
of the car but his response -- applying the brakes or
swerving to avoid the car -- would be automatic. He would
not have to think about what motor responses to make.

● **PROBLEM 7-4**

Define and describe incidental memory and subliminal perception (subception).

Solution: Two cases in which perception occurs without
awareness are incidental memory and subliminal perception.
In these instances, an individual is conscious but not
aware of stimuli around him. Nevertheless, he can assimi-
late information concerning the stimuli.

Incidental memory refers to the recall of stimuli that
never reached the subject's state of awareness. This
phenomenon was reported by Belbin (1956). In an experiment,
Belbin had his subjects sit in a waiting room where posters
illustrating driving safety practices hung on the walls.
Later, Belbin found that none of the subjects could recall
the information contained in the posters with any accuracy.
However, when the subjects were put in a driving situation
where they could draw on this information, the results
showed that a process of assimilation had occurred in some
subjects. Belbin found that drivers who had seen the posters could apply the safety precautions in the driving situation. Non-drivers, however, had trouble doing this.
This difference between drivers and non-drivers was not
evident in a control group that had not seen the posters.
The drivers in the experimental group, apparently accustomed to heed such safety warnings, continued to do so,
even when they were not aware of perceiving the messages.

In subliminal perception -- also called subception --
a stimulus is presented just below the threshold at which it
can be consciously perceived. To achieve subliminal perception, a stimulus is presented at such high speed or intensity that it is impossible for the subject to recognize.
In the late 1950's, an advertising company that used massive subliminal perception brought the subject before the
public eye. Messages that read "Drink Coca Cola" and "Eat
popcorn" were flashed intermittently at threshold speeds
during the showing of a movie. The company reported a significant increase in the sale of Coca Cola and popcorn.
Unfortunately, carefully controlled evaluations were not
performed, therefore it is impossible to attribute the increase in sales to the technique. This case has spurred
a number of studies on subliminal advertising, but none of
them has found sufficient evidence to support its effectiveness.

Define perceptual defense. Describe McGinnies's study
(1949) and Lazarus's and McCleary's study (1951).

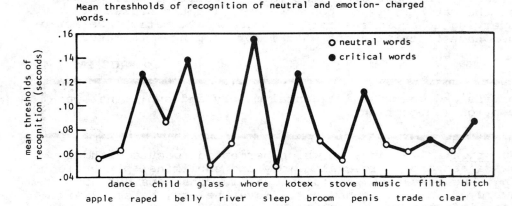

Mean threshholds of recognition of neutral and emotion- charged words.

Solution: Perceptual defense is one example of perception
without awareness.   in this case, a stimulus that is perceived is either totally or partially blocked from awareness.
Freud suggested that this theory holds true for stimuli
that arouse anxiety in the individual. One way to test this
theory is to show whether perceptual thresholds (the lowest
points at which particular stimuli can be perceived) for
such stimuli are higher in the presence of anxiety.

     McGinnies (1949) attempted to prove the theory by pre-
senting a series of words to a group of subjects. The words
were of two types: neutral words and taboo or critical
words. The words were first presented to the subjects at
subliminal speed, then they were presented at progressively
slower speeds until they could be identified correctly.
McGinnies cited two important findings from his study.
First, subjects took longer to identify the taboo words
than the neutral words. Second, galvanic skin responses
(GSR's) were higher for taboo words presented at subliminal
presentation levels (levels at which the subject could not
identify the word). McGinnies concluded that the subjects
were aware of the taboo words but used a perceptual defense
to keep the words out of consciousness. He believed that
the subjects were discriminating without being aware of it.

     McGinnies's study was a subject of heated debates.
His critics argued that word frequency in language had a
powerful effect; the more frequently a word is used in
everyday conversation, the more readily it can be identified. Hence, taboo words would take longer to identify
since they aren't used as often. Furthermore, a subject
might hesitate before pronouncing a taboo word for reasons
of social propriety. This is called the response-suppres-
sion effect.

     In order to avoid the pitfalls of the McGinnies ex-
periment, Lazarus and McCleary (1951) conducted a study

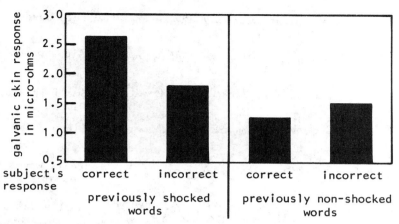

The height of each bar indicates the amount of sweating. When subjects incorrectly identified a previously shocked word, they sweated more than when they misidentified a previously non-shocked word. This is the discrimination without awareness effect.

using nonsense syllables. Employing nonsense syllables prevented the undesirable effects mentioned above from occurring. In the first stage of the experiment, subjects were presented with the nonsense syllables at subliminal levels. Five syllables were accompanied by a mild electric shock. The syllables were then presented at increasingly slower speeds until they could all be identified correctly. The syllables associated with the shock yielded higher GSR's than neutral (unshocked) syllables. But the most important finding of this study, with regard to perceptual defense, was that subjects showed higher GSR's for shocked syllables even before they were able to identify them. Like McGinnies, Lazarus and McCleary concluded that discrimination can occur without awareness. They discovered that man possesses built-in perceptual defense mechanisms that allow him to perceive stimuli without being aware of them.

SLEEP, DREAMS, AND DAYDREAMS

● PROBLEM 7-6

Identify and describe the four stages of sleep. Define and describe Stage 1-REM.

Solution: Only recently scientists have been able to analyze sleep. This was made possible by the invention of the electroencephalograph (EEG) -- a machine that can measure and record "brain waves" -- the brain's recurrent electrical patterns. The changes that these patterns undergo during sleep are recorded by the EEG for researchers to analyze. Based on such changes, scientists have divided sleep into four stages.

Before actual sleep, a subject is in a relaxed waking state with his eyes closed. The EEG illustrates this state

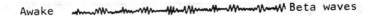

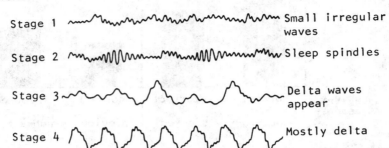

Awake ———————————————— Beta waves

Eyes closed, ————————— Alpha waves
relaxed

Stage 1 ———————————————— Small irregular
waves

Stage 2 ———————————————— Sleep spindles

Stage 3 ———————————————— Delta waves
appear

Stage 4 ———————————————— Mostly delta

Changes in brain-wave patterns associated with various stages of sleep.

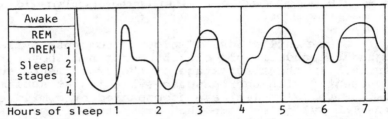

Awake							
REM							
nREM 1							
Sleep 2							
stages 3							
4							

Hours of sleep   1   2   3   4   5   6   7

Typical changes in stages of sleep during the night.

in the form of alpha brain waves or alpha rhythm, a wave pattern of 10 cycles per second. Sleep begins with the onset of Initial Stage 1 EEG. Here, the alpha rhythm is replaced by slower, irregular waves. However, this EEG pattern is not very different from that found in an active, awake person. As the individual falls further into sleep, the wave pattern increases to 14 cycles per second bringing the person into Stage 2 sleep. This stage is characterized by spindles -- sharply pointed waves recorded by the EEG. Larger and slower delta waves appear in Stage 3 of sleep. These waves measure one to two cycles per second. Both spindles and delta waves appear in Stage 3. However, in Stage 4, delta waves predominate. The entire cycle of Stages 1 through 4 is executed four to six times during an average eight hour period of sleep.

Another important stage of sleep is called Stage 1-REM. Eugene Aserinsky found that rapid eye movements (REM's) occur during Stage 1 EEG. These REM's are jerky movements of the eyes beneath the eyelids. REM's are detected and measured by a machine called an electroculogram (EOG). In his research, Aserinsky found that in about 80 percent of the time, subjects who were awakened during these periods reported a dream.

Dreams generally occur during this stage, although dreamlike activity can occur in other stages of sleep. The Stage 1-REM is a period of deep sleep even though its EEG pattern is similar to that of an active, awake individual.

228

For this reason, it has been called "paradoxical sleep."

As each cycle of sleep is repeated, the Stage 1-REM becomes longer. The first one occurs about 90 minutes after sleep has begun and lasts for about 5 to 10 minutes. The stage increases in duration at each 90 minute cycle. As expected, the last Stage 1-REM stage is the longest. During this stage, the sleeper experiences the longest and most vivid dreams. A dream during this stage can last from half an hour to an hour. This last dream is the one that is most likely to be recalled. Quite often, the individual awakens during the last Stage 1-REM.

● **PROBLEM** 7-7

Define hypnagogic state and hypnopompic state. List and define the ego states in the hypnagogic period

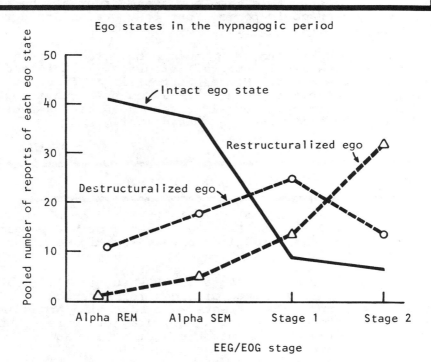

Ego states in the hypnagogic period

EEG/EOG stage

Solution: The hypnagogic state refers to the state one experiences when going from a wakeful state to sleep. This state is highly similar to the hypnopompic state, when one goes from sleep to wakefulness. Some researchers believe that the two states are practically identical.

The limited research in this area has focused on the hypnagogic state. The most recent studies have consisted of experiments in which subjects were awakened while they were in a hypnagogic state and asked to describe their experiences. Based on the subjects' reports, the hypnagogic state has been described in terms of three ego states: intact ego state, destructuralized ego state, and restructuralized ego state. In the intact ego state, the subject remains in contact with his external environment. He can control his mental processes and distinguish between the internal and external world. In the intact ego state, the subject recognizes his location in the outside world. In the destructuralized ego state, the subject loses contact with the external world and a sense of his place in that world. Mental content in this state is no longer reality-oriented. In the restructuralized ego state, mental content is relatively logical and reality-oriented but there is no contact with the external environment.

Investigators have found that reports which indicate the presence of intact ego states are highest at the beginning of the hypnagogic period -- at alpha rhythm. As sleep progresses, however, the incidence of intact ego states decreases. The number of reports of a decentralized ego state is relatively low. The number increases through Stage 1 sleep, then declines at Stage 2 sleep. Very few reports of a restructuralized ego state occur at the beginning of the hypnagogic period, but they gradually increase throughout all stages of falling asleep.

From these results, a trend can be noted. Contact with the external environment is gradually lost as sleep begins and progresses. Mental content is at first logical, it then becomes bizarre and is followed by a stage that exhibits some logic in mental content despite the fact that there is no contact with the outside world.

● **PROBLEM** 7-8

Discuss the effects of sleep deprivation.

Solution: A wide range of effects result from sleep deprivation. Behavioral changes after sleep deprivation can be as mild as simple irritability or as dramatic as bizarre hallucinations.

In a study conducted at UCLA (Pasnau, et al., 1968) four subjects were deprived of sleep for a period of 205 consecutive hours. The effects were both mild and dramatic. One subject, who experienced a very dramatic effect, became hysterical during a psychomotor training task and screamed incoherently upon hallucinating a gorilla.

Prolonged sleep deprivation -- 220 hours or more -- can lead to psychotic-like behavior. Studies have indicated that those who displayed this type of behavior often had traumatic childhoods and neurotic and work disturbances. Other physiological changes that occur as a result of sleep deprivation include a decrease in the amount of alpha brain waves and a low voltage EEG.

● **PROBLEM** 7-9

Discuss the incidence of somnambulism. What explanations have been offered for it?

Solution: Somnambulism, or sleepwalking as it is more commonly called, is reported to exist in 1 to 5 percent of the population. The incidence has been found to be high among males, children, and among those who have suffered from enuresis (bedwetting) and have had a family history of somnambulism.

Psychology offers several explanations for somnambulism. Some psychologists regard it as a dissociative state in which there is a loss of memory and awareness of identity. Others regard it as a dreamlike disturbance of consciousness. Because sleepwalking is more common in children than adults, it is often viewed as an immature habit pattern. If sleepwalking persists into adulthood a more severe diagnosis is applied.

Some researchers consider somnambulism as a symptom of an epileptic state. They have found that a higher frequency of EEG abnormalities occurs among sleepwalkers than non-sleepwalkers.

Psychologists share very different views on the actual condition of sleepwalking. Some psychologists report that it is a state in which the individual is not awake. Others describe it as a state in which the person is not asleep. Psychologists generally disagree about motor ability during this state. Psychologists generally agree that after he awakens, the sleepwalker experiences total amnesia for the somnambulistic incident. A single sleepwalking episode usually lasts approximately 15 to 30 minutes.

● **PROBLEM** 7-10

Discuss the effects of REM deprivation during sleep.

Solution: Dreaming occurs during the Stage 1-REM period of sleep. Aserinsky and Kleitman (1953) reported incidents of increased heart rate and breathing during these periods of rapid eye movements. Other researchers have reported that the body's central nervous system is active during this period, undergoing severe fluctuations in heartbeat and blood pressure.

Studies have been conducted on REM deprivation in which subjects slept but were awakened each time they entered the REM period. A control group was also employed whose subjects were awakened the same number of times as the REM-deprived subjects, but only during non-REM periods. Researchers found that during each successive night of the experiment, the REM-deprived subjects entered into more REM periods. During the day, these subjects appeared more tense, irritable and generally more anxious than the control group subjects. The REM-deprived subjects experienced difficulty in concentrating and remembering. When the experimenters finally allowed the REM-deprived subjects to sleep without interruption, the sleepers dreamed 60 percent more than usual. This additional dreaming has been called "REM rebound."

These studies seem to indicate that man has a need to dream.

Discuss Freud's theory of dreams. Define manifest content, latent content, condensation, displacement, symbolization, secondary elaboration.

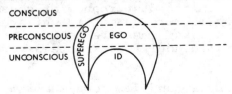

The Relationship of Personality Structures to the Levels of Awareness

Solution: Sigmund Freud was the first major psychologist who considered dreams meaningful. Before Freud's development of psychoanalysis, psychologists believed that dreams consisted of either useless information or the refuse of mental life. Freud used dreams in the design of his psychoanalytic theory. He believed that dreams provide the clearest example of unconscious processes at work. According to psychoanalytic theory, the psychological energy one uses during waking periods is shifted both to the unconscious and to certain perceptual areas of the brain during sleep. When one begins to dream, the external world is almost completely eliminated and replaced by an internal world. The content of dreams is dependent upon the emotions that have been aroused during the previous day. These emotions are associated with the primary sex and aggression drives as well as the repressed memories that center on these drives.

Freud analyzed the dreams of both children and adults. He found that children's dreams often consist of wish fulfillment. These dreams deal with the wishes the child is aware of as well as those which are unconscious. A child who experiences an intense desire to own a particular toy, for example, might dream that he gets it.

In the dreams of adults, motives are not as clear. Although most adults report their dreams to be nonsensical and confused, Freud identified two types of interrelated dream content. First, there is the manifest content of the dream. This is the information about the dream that the individual remembers and can report. Beneath this surface content is a latent content. Latent content consists of unconscious desires which are usually related to the sex and aggression drives. Freud suggested that recognition of these wishes during waking hours may be too painful or unacceptable to consciousness. Therefore, these wishes find expression through dreams.

Even in dreams, however, these unconscious wishes are not expressed directly. Instead, they are expressed in disguised form through what Freud called the dream processes.

Common Freudian dream interpretations and their symbols:

1. Parents- emperors, empresses, kings, queens
2. Children (brothers and sisters)- small animals
3. Birth- water
4. Death- journey
5. Nakedness- clothes, uniforms
6. Male genitals- sticks, umbrellas, poles, trees, anything elongated, pointed weapons of all sorts
7. Erection- balloons, airplanes, zeppelins, dreamer himself flying
8. Male sexual symbols- Reptiles, fishes, serpent, hand or foot
9. Female genitalia- pits, hollow caves, jars, bottles, doors, ships, chests
10. Breasts- apples, peaches, other fruit
11. Intercourse- mounting a ladder or stairs, entering a room, walking down a hall or into a tunnel, horseback riding, and so forth

In this way, the individual's conscience is not aroused.

Freud identified four dream processes by which unconscious desires are disguised in dreams. The first process is called condensation. Here, people and objects are represented with the characteristics of several different familiar individuals and objects. For example, a character in a dream may look like someone one knows, dress like another, speak like a third, and have the name of a fourth.

Freud identified the second dream process as displacement. Displacement involves a reallocation of psychic energy. The elements that figure most prominently in the manifest dream do not have much significance with regard to unconscious drives; hence, they carry little psychic energy. Those elements that are replete with psychic energy are the small details in dreams. Often, these details cannot be recalled.

The third dream process, symbolization, stemmed from Freud's observations that certain dream elements have common meanings for many people. However, most people cannot identify or interpret the latent meaning of these elements.

In the last dream process, secondary elaboration, dream elements are arranged in a certain order to form the whole dream. This process involves the incorporation of a story line or the use of events from the previous day to fill in transitions between the significant dream elements and unify the dream.

According to Freud, the major purpose of the dream processes is to arrange a compromise: to allow the dreamer gratification from unconscious drives yet keep them hidden from a repulsed conscience. Freud's theory is important because it challenged the myth that dreams are insignificant. However, his theory awaits proof. Most of its critics argue that it lacks a scientific method for the analysis of dream content.

Briefly describe two non-Freudian dream theories.

Solution: Carl G. Jung, a Swiss physician, was one of the most outstanding critics of Freud's theory. He believed that it was too restrictive and that it neglected some important aspects of man's dreaming. According to Jung, certain dream elements are characteristic of all people. Jung believed that some underlying personal elements in a dream are common to all people, regardless of cultural and individual differences. These elements are archetypal; they are characteristic of man as a species. For example, if someone were to dream about climbing a mountain, Freud would see this dream as reflective of a past event or wish in the individual's life. Jung, however, would expand upon this interpretation to include a characteristic common to all people. In this case, it would be the desire for achievement, to rise to the top. Jung also believed that a person's personality in his dreams is the opposite of his personality when he is awake. For example, a person who is usually outspoken would be very timid in a dream.

Another non-Freudian theory about dreams holds that dreams are continuous or congruent with thoughts people have when they are awake. Many psychologists agree that problems people worry about while awake are usually the same problems they worry about in dreams. The same needs and desires apparent in wakefulness are also present in dreams. Psychologists have found that subjects who have been deprived of food report more dreams in which food is a major element than subjects in a control group. Hence, the theory that dreams continue the thoughts experienced in wakefulness is dissimilar to Jung's theory that dream thoughts are opposite to waking thoughts, and Freud's theory that dreams represent expressions of unconscious desires which are repulsive or disagreeable to consciousness.

● PROBLEM 7-13

Describe daydreams. How do they differ from dreams?

Solution: A daydream is a fantasy created by an individual during a waking state. In daydreams, a person conjures up images of scenes or events which are extremely gratifying. These images often reflect egoistic desires for power, prestige, wealth or erotic pleasures.

Daydreams are not related to dreams experienced during sleep. Daydreams do not share the same basic characteristics: their content is more closely related to reality and they are usually more logical and coherent. Hence, daydreams can be reported with more ease than dreams.

The important difference between daydreams and dreams is the element of control. Daydreams are controlled by one's waking consciousness, and one can determine the exact nature of the daydream. The mental images and processes are under control. In dreams the mind does not have this degree of control.

Furthermore, in a daydream, the healthy individual recognizes that he is fantasizing whereas in dreams, the individual does not realize that he is dreaming.

HYPNOSIS, POSSESSION, AND OUT-OF-BODY EXPERIENCES

● PROBLEM 7-14

Define hypnosis. How is it induced? Describe neutral hypnosis.

Solution: Hypnosis is defined as a state of consciousness in which the subject experiences a relaxed mental state that lacks the ongoing thought processes which ordinarily occur in normal consciousness. Hypnosis is not a form of sleep. The EEG seen in hypnosis is similar to that of the waking, active state. A subject under hypnosis is completely relaxed, operates his mind and body involuntarily, and is in a state of hypersuggestibility: he readily accepts suggestions from the hypnotist.

Hypnosis is induced while the subject is either sitting or lying down. The hypnotist usually asks the subject to relax and free himself from any stress or anxiety. The hypnotist will suggest to the subject that he is becoming sleepy in order to make him thoroughly relaxed (but not necessarily asleep). The hypnotist builds on those suggestions to which the subject responds early in the session in order to assure the subject that he moves into a deeper hypnotic state. Sometimes, the hypnotist uses a gadget during the induction procedure. This apparatus has no purpose other than to make the hypnotist appear more "scientific" in the subject's eyes, thereby increasing the subject's confidence in him.

In neutral hypnosis the subject is completely relaxed and detached, although still attentive to the hypnotist's suggestions. No suggestions are made about any specific future event. This state arises after the hypnotist's long and repetitious suggestions about sleep and relaxation. Subjects in this state usually describe their minds as being a blank.

● PROBLEM 7-15

Give eight characteristics of the hypnotic state. Define posthypnotic effect.

Solution: The several characteristics indicative of a subject in a hypnotic state include:

1. Passivity. The hypnotic subject is passive rather than active. He passively accepts suggestions from the hypnotist.

2. Attention selectivity. Under hypnosis, a subject often concentrates his attention solely upon the one particular object or event he is told to focus on.

3. Hypersuggestibility. The hypnotic subject readily accepts the hypnotist's suggestions.

4. Distorted perception. Hypnosis can alter perception in several ways. The hypnotist can employ hypoesthesia, in which the power of a certain sense becomes reduced or obliterated. For example, the hypnotist may tell his subject that his vision will become blurred, and the subject will consequently report that his vision is blurred. The hypnotist may also suggest to the subject that he will lose all feeling in his left hand. Consequently, he will report no sensation if his left hand is slapped. Pain can be reduced with this method. The hypnotist can also employ hyperesthesias, wherein one or more of the subject's senses becomes sharper. This method also involves sensing stimuli that are not actually present. The hypnotist, for example, can tell his subject that he sees a wild animal, at which point the subject will envision it and react accordingly

5. Altered awareness. Awareness can be eradicated, heightened, or shifted, depending upon the hypnotic suggestion. A subject can become keenly aware of his bodily processes at the suggestion of the hypnotist, or, at another suggestion, he can engage in an activity without being aware of it.

6. Lack of emotion. A hypnotic subject is completely unemotional, unless he is told to display a particular emotion by the hypnotist.

7. Altered memory. Memory can be altered depending on the suggestions of the hypnotist. Under hypnosis an individual can recall many things which he would not ordinarily be able to remember in normal consciousness. Memory can also be dulled during hypnosis. The hypnotist can even suggest to the subject that he won't remember his own name. A hypnotist will often tell his subject that he will not remember anything that happened during the hypnotic session when he awakens or that he will only remember certain parts of it.

8. Altered identity and regression. Under hypnosis the subject's sense of his personal identity can be changed. Upon the hypnotist's suggestion, the subject can assume the personality of another person and behave appropriately. Age regression is also possible. For example, it may be suggested to an adult subject that he is a four-year-old, in which case he will behave as he believes a four-year-old normally acts.

There have been cases in which hypnotists have told their subjects to regress to a time before their concep-

tion. These subjects have often assumed different personalities, presumably those of people they were in previous
lives. Such celebrated cases as Bridey Murphy have provoked
mass interest in the possibility of reincarnation. However, hypnotists lack the scientific evidence necessary to
assert that reincarnation has in fact occurred. The subjects have given no verifiable information regarding a past
life that they could not have obtained in their present one.

A posthypnotic effect is any phenomenon that occurs in
the hypnotic subject in ordinary, waking consciousness as a
result of a suggestion made by a hypnotist during a previous
hypnotic session. For example, during a hypnotic session
the hypnotist will tell his subject that he will fall asleep
one hour after he awakens from the hypnotic state. As a
result one hour after the subject is awakened from the hypnotic state, he falls asleep without knowing why. Often,
subjects rationalize posthypnotic behavior

● **PROBLEM** 7-16

Discuss some applications of hypnosis.

Solution: Hypnosis is an important experimental tool in
psychology. In addition, it serves important medical and
psychiatric purposes in such areas as dentistry, obstetrics
and psychotherapy. Hypnosis has been applied to almost
every branch of medicine.

Hypnosis has been extremely useful as a pain-killer in
the treatment of terminal cancer patients. Hypnosis has
been found to reduce pain to such a high degree that morphine becomes superfluous. Decades ago, before chemical
anesthetics were available, hypnosis was used widely as an
analgesic in surgery.

Hypnosis is used to relieve stress in a wide variety
of situations and to overcome undesirable habits such as
smoking and over-eating. Hypnosis can even be used to has-
ten the healing process of wounds.

Hypnosis has been found to have a high entertainment
value. In this area it has often been used in an unethical
manner. People enjoy seeing others behave in bizarre ways.
Due to these public displays, many have regarded it as a
form of magic and as a result, hypnotism has attracted much
skepticism. Despite this, scientific experiments have
shown that hypnosis is an altered state of consciousness.

● **PROBLEM** 7-17

Define and describe a possession state. What explanation
has been offered for it in our society? How is it induced?

Solution: A possession state is one in which an individual
believes his own personality or spirit has been displaced
or transcended by another spirit or nonphysical entity

which assumes control of the subject's body.

Those who experience possession states perceive the possessing entity in a variety of ways: as a spirit of a deceased human, an animal spirit or a force from nature. Spiritualist mediums, an important source of information regarding possession states, claim to attain a possession state of a deceased human. In religious sects, there are reports of demonic possession (possession by the devil) and holy possession (possession by the Holy Spirit).

A possession state may be pleasant or unpleasant to the subject. He may either attach great spiritual signif-icance to it or none at all.

Little is known about the true nature of possession states due to a lack of reliable evidence. Even reports by those who have experienced this state are lacking. These people often report amnesia regarding the experience or say they are unclear about it.

The prevalent explanation that society offers for pos-session states is that they result from a fragment of one's unconscious mind which comes forward and takes control of the person's mind and actions. Parapsychologists have of-fered this as a hypothesis in response to mediums who be-lieve they are possessed and can give information about people they've never met. These parapsychologists believe that the possession results from an aspect of the medium's unconscious mind and that the knowledge they have about persons they've never met comes from their ESP abilities.

Possession states can be induced voluntarily or invol-untarily. They can result from mental illness or be in-duced deliberately through various forms and combinations of prayer, drugs, dancing, and trance-inducing techniques.

● **PROBLEM** 7-18

Define an out-of-body experience. Describe a typical ex-perience. What are the psychological and physiological effects of such an experience?

Solution: An out-of-body experience is one in which the in-dividual feels his physical body is someplace other than where his consciousness would lead him to believe. An in-dividual having this experience often reports seeing his own physical body. This experience therefore seems to in-volve a separation of mind and body.

A typical out-of-body experience begins when the indi-vidual is sleeping, dreaming or ill to the point of coming close to death. It can also follow a severe accident where the victim is dangerously close to death. In these cases, the subject suddenly finds himself back in a normal state of consciousness but floating near the ceiling and looking down at his own body. Most subjects report the spontaneity in which this state comes about. Some suddenly find them-

selves in a distant place but others report the sensations
they have felt in traveling to that place. The experience
can last anywhere from a few seconds to several hours according to the reports of individuals who have experienced
this phenomenon. Most people experience the out-of-body
phenomenon only once during their lives.

Not much is known about the effects of an out-of-body
experience. Very little experimental research has investigated the phenomenon. A large part of the existing information comes from reports of those who have experienced
it. Most people find it an ecstatic and highly rewarding
experience. Many report that a belief in life after death
is acquired or reinforced after this experience. Studies
on the physiological effects of the state have monitored
brain wave activity during the actual experience. One subject showed brain wave patterns characteristic of Stage I -
REM sleep. Another showed alpha waves which occur during a
relaxed waking state. Presently, no conclusive statement
can be made about brain wave activity during an out-of-
body experience.

MEDITATION

● **PROBLEM** 7-19

Define meditation. What are its general purposes?

Solution: Meditation is an altered state of consciousness.
Through physical and mental exercises the subject achieves
a state of relaxation and tranquility which allows him to
gain insight into himself and to discover the meaning of
worldly objects. Meditation requires an intense and concentrated effort to rid the mind of daily concerns and
thoughts so that a state of mystical union or transcendence
may be achieved.

Meditation is typically associated with Eastern religions. But Western religions, particularly Roman Catholi-
cism, have also employed its practice. The two most popular types of meditation are Yoga (from the Hindu tradition)
and Zen (from the Buddhist tradition).

The foremost purpose of meditation is the attainment
of truth and permanent happiness. Those who engage in meditation believe that because people are basically hedonistic
-- always behaving in such a way so as to attain pleasure
and avoid pain -- their range of perceptions is narrow.
Thus, people don't see reality as a whole and don't recognize the truth; they live in a world of illusion. As these
illusions build, one becomes severed from himself and
the outside world. As a result, one never achieves eternal
happiness. Meditation techniques are designed to cut
through illusions so that the individual may perceive truth
directly.

The following is a function definition of the term: Meditation is a nonintellectual process that removes a person's

239

illusions so that he may reach a state of consciousness from which he can clearly perceive truth.

● **PROBLEM** 7-20

What are some techniques of inducing meditation? Define mantras and yantras.

A mandala

<u>Solution</u>: Meditation is induced through a variety of special exercises. The meditator usually sits or kneels in a comfortable position that is conducive to relaxation. The setting is normally quiet and simple to prevent distractions. The meditator then concentrates on something. The object of his attention depends on the type of meditation he is engaging in. In Zen meditation the meditator concentrates on his breathing. In Yoga, he may focus his attention on pranayama, which are complex, artificial breathing exercises.

Other focal points for meditation include mantras and yantras. Mantras are sound patterns which can be used for meditation. The meditator generates these himself. He may utter them or imagine them in his mind. A popular mantra is "Om mani padme hum," which comes from ancient Indian.

Yantras, on the other hand, are meditative focal points in the form of visual patterns. A yantra can be a religious object, a burning candle, or a complex design of the cosmos called a mandala.

Concentration on a particular object or process is the key to the induction of all types of meditation. The meditator tries to rid himself of the usual way of thinking and perceiving the world. His aim is to clarify and sharpen his perceptions and awareness in order to arrive at a direct perception of the truth, himself, and the world around him.

● **PROBLEM** 7-21

Describe concentrative meditation, opening-up meditation, and self-remembering. What is the purpose of each? How is each induced? What effect is attained?

Solution: Concentrative meditation is characterized by its one-pointedness. The meditator fixes his attention on a single object for a long period of time. In one form, simple Zen meditation, the subject concentrates on the abdominal movements that occur during breathing. If his concentration should stray from the focal point, concentrative meditation requires that he return it gently because forcing it might distract it even further.

In concentrative meditation awareness exists even though there is no sensory input or mental activity. This awareness, in the presence of mental emptiness or voidness, is a pure one that allows for a clearness of perception not possible in ordinary consciousness. The process lets the meditator arrive at a clear perception of truth. The benefits of successful concentrative meditation are seen in its results. A person who has completed such a session reports feeling refreshed and having a clearer perception of his environment. He feels he is perceiving objects directly and objectively as they really are, not as they seem during ordinary consciousness when certain filters distort them. In addition, desires for certain objects and people are quenched.

Opening-up meditation shares the same purpose as concentrative meditation however; its method of induction and the time when its effects are felt are different. In opening-up meditation, the subject focuses his attention on everything around him rather than on one particular object. He concentrates on all the stimuli affecting him and on his reactions to the stimuli. Because this procedure is very exhausting, sessions in this type of meditation are much shorter than those in concentrative meditation. A clearer perception of oneself and of the environment are experienced immediately, not as an aftereffect as is the case in concentrative meditation.

Self-remembering is a form of meditation similar to opening-up meditation. The premise in self-remembering is that individuals are slaves to the events they experience and to their reactions to these events. People live in a "waking dream" in which their needs and desires are so intrinsic to their person that their perceptions of the environment and of themselves are distorted. Their only escape is their ability to direct a small part of their attention to an awareness that will not bind them. The objective of self-remembering is not only to be aware of oneself and one's environment, but to also be aware of this awareness. Such an acute and total awareness can help the individual attain the freedom of making choices independently and objectively and to overcome the determinism passed onto him from his cultural upbringing.

The difficult technique of self-remembering requires that the person divide his attention into two roles: actor and observer. The actor part observes and is aware of thoughts and events, while the observer is aware of being aware of these thoughts and events.

Success in self-remembering is said to free one from

events that shape one's life and to create such a total
awareness that one can make decisions more freely and assume greater control of reactions to stimuli.

● **PROBLEM** 7-22

Discuss some physiological changes that can occur as a
result of meditation.

Solution: Studies on meditation practitioners have shown
brain wave changes during and/or after meditation. Research on several types of meditation have indicated an increased number of alpha brain waves and, in some cases, the
appearance of theta brain waves. There have also been findings of a lowered metabolism and heart rate in those who
practice meditation.

Many people have found meditation useful as a therapeutic aid, claiming that it allays anxiety and reduces
tension. Meditation as a method of alleviating extreme and
everyday pressure is gaining wide popularity, particularly
in the United States.

People have expressed a great interest in the feats of
expert meditation practitioners. Yogis (those who practice
Yoga) have been known to control involuntary physiological
processes. There have been reports of Yogis who can cease
breathing for remarkable periods of time and who can consume enough water to clean their lower intestine. Until
recently, these reports were largely ignored in the Western
world but they have attracted much attention due to the
growing field of biofeedback research.

SENSORY DEPRIVATION STUDIES

● **PROBLEM** 7-23

Discuss the methods and findings of experimental studies
conducted on sensory deprivation.

Solution: Experimenters who hope to determine the effects
of sensory deprivation try to remove or distort all external stimuli in the subjects' environment. Scientists use
three different approaches to create such an environment.
None of these methods is perfect. Even in the most controlled setting, an individual can still hear the blood
flow near his ears, as well as the sound of his breathing.
He can also feel changes in body temperature and moisture.

In the first experimental approach, the researcher
tries to reduce external stimuli to a minimum. For example,
a subject might be placed in a sound-proof room in which
there is no light. He may wear ear plugs to prevent him
from hearing his own sounds and may even be bandaged to
prevent any tactile stimulation. Often he will be asked to
lie on a bed and neither move nor talk.

In the second approach to sensory deprivation, the
researcher distorts or changes the pattern of sensory input. For example, a constant buzzing sound might be used
to exclude any sounds in the environment. In one experiment, Heron (1961) had his subjects wear translucent goggles
through which light could be seen, but no visual patterns
could be discerned.

A third approach to sensory deprivation involves creating a monotonous environment in which there is little or no
change in stimuli. Wexler and his co-workers (1958) used
this approach in their experiments when they placed their
subjects' arms and legs in rigid cylinders. This apparatus
prevented movement and tactile stimulation.

Differences in methodology have made it difficult to
form broad generalizations about the experimental findings
of sensory deprivation.

Psychologists have often found that after a long period
of time, sensory deprivation can cause trouble in thinking
clearly and concentrating. Subjects in these experiments
often experience a disorganization in thought processes.
Many of these people find it difficult to count beyond 20
or 30.

Prolonged sensory deprivation can cause impaired visual perception. Heron's experiment (1961) showed that objects in the room appeared wavy and moving to the subject's
eyes after he removed his glasses.

Cohen and his co-workers (1961) found that subjects
in prolonged states of isolation and sensory deprivation
generally obtain low scores on tests of intellectual functioning. Although they found that each subject's short-
term memory had increased, the scientists detected decreases in reasoning ability, mathematical reasoning, and
in the ability to abstract and generalize.

Discuss the findings of hallucinatory behavior as a result of sensory deprivation. What relationship has been suggested between this behavior and schizophrenia?

Solution: Scientists have discovered that several types of hallucinatory behavior can result from sensory deprivation. In Heron's (1961) experiment, subjects wore translucent goggles which allowed the penetration of light but did not permit them to view objects clearly. The subjects reported, upon taking the goggles, that objects were hurling toward them and that they saw geometric patterns in the air and movie-like scenes. Many had trouble deciding whether they were asleep or awake.

Bexton, Heron and Scott (1954) also used translucent goggles in their experiment. More than half of their subjects reported the scenes and geometric patterns that Heron's (1961) subjects had experienced. They also saw such images as spots of lights and cartoons. However, when these subjects were asked to engage in activities requiring a great deal of concentration, such as multiplying 3-digit numbers in their heads, the images were minimized.

Zubeck and his associates (1961) studied auditory as well as visual hallucinations. Zubeck's subjects hallucinated bells ringing, dogs barking and typing sounds.

Scientists have suggested that these hallucinations may be related to schizophrenia. In many cases, hallucinations resulting from sensory-deprived environments appear similar to those experienced by schizophrenics. Some researchers have suggested that processes which occur in the schizophrenic patient are similar to those that result in a healthy individual who is placed in a sensory-deprived environment. Rosenzweig (1959) has indicated that both cases involve the disruption of sensory and perceptual inputs. In the case of the schizophrenic, the disruption is internal whereas in the person who existed in the deprived environment, the disruption is external. Both cases involve the same basic process.

● **PROBLEM** 7-25

Describe Spitz's (1945) study of sensory deprivation in a social setting. What do his findings suggest?

Solution: Sensory deprivation often occurs outside the laboratory, most notably in social settings. The effects of sensory deprivation in such an environment were reported by Spitz (1945). He compared the development of children in an orphanage, where there was little sensory stimulation, to that of children who were raised in a nursing home and received a great deal more care and stimulation.

The children in both homes received the same nutrition

and medical care and lived in sanitary environments. The children in the orphanage, however, received less maternal stimulation, which has been found to be a necessary factor in normal development. Here, six nurses cared for 45 babies. In the nursing home, on the other hand, each mother took care of her own child.

The babies in the orphanage received less visual stimulation than the babies in the nursing home. In the nursing home, babies were often taken out of their cribs. From this vantage point they were able to see what was happening in the ward. The orphanage babies were sometimes taken out of their cribs when they were changed or fed. In addition, sheets were draped over the bars of their cribs, preventing them from witnessing any external events. This effect is similar to the one created by the use of translucent goggles in laboratory experiments: light was admitted but objects could not be discerned visually.

Spitz's findings are important because they suggest that sensory and social deprivation during the first few years of life can adversely affect normal development. Spitz found that during the first four months of the babies' lives, scores on tests of development were the same for both groups. However, during the last four months of the first year, the orphanage babies received lower scores on the same tests. This discrepancy in the scores shows that both groups began with basically the same potential, but dissimilarities in their environments influenced differences in test scores.

Spitz found that several orphanage babies became greatly weakened, both physically and mentally. This led to a higher mortality rate among the orphanage children. Spitz also found that most of the nursing home babies were walking and talking by ages two and three whereas only two of the 26 orphanage babies could walk and talk at a comparable period.

BIOFEEDBACK

● PROBLEM 7-26

Describe biofeedback. What are its applications? What are its two major links to the attainment of altered states of consciousness?

Solution: Biofeedback refers to techniques that make information about bodily functions available to a person so that he can regulate these functions. The term biofeedback literally means feedback of biological information.

Any bodily process that cannot be controlled voluntarily is called autonomic. At one point it was believed that such processes as heart rate, blood pressure, and body temperature were autonomic. This view was challenged by Neal Miller and Leo Di Cara (1968) who trained rats to control their heart rate by as much as 20 percent through the tech-

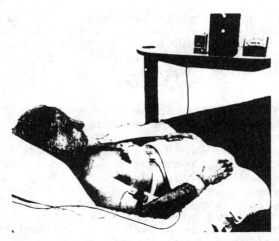

During a biofeedback training session to control heart rate
the patient watches a "traffic sign" with red, yellow, and
green lights which shows him how he is doing. An intercom,
on the left of the table, enables him to communicate with
the doctor and a meter, at right, shows him what percentage
of the time he is accomplishing his task.

niques of operant conditioning. This technique was later
applied to humans. It was found that feedback made voluntary control of autonomic processes possible. For example,
the electrical activity of a particular involuntary muscle
fiber can be amplified electronically and made known to
the subject in the form of a sound. The pitch of this sound
varies according to the amount of activity of the muscle.
Thus, a person can regulate the activity of a muscle which
he ordinarily cannot control.

Biofeedback has other applications as well. The most
notable of these is control of heart rate through use of a
device called a "traffic signal." This device can tell a
subject whether his heart rate is too slow, too fast, or
normal. The traffic signal is basically a box with three
lights -- red, yellow, and green -- in the same vertical
order as a traffic light. Devices which record the subject's EEG and breathing are attached to him and the information is fed into the traffic device. When the red light
goes on, it means that the subject's heart rate is too fast
and that he should lower it. A yellow light indicates that
heart rate is normal and should be maintained. A green
light means that heart rate is too slow and should be increased.

Another application of biofeedback is the control of
brain waves. Biofeedback regulation of brain wave activity
lets the individual learn to relax more. Alpha waves are
the EEG pattern in the relaxed, waking state. Beta waves
indicate a higher electrical activity and characterize an
individual in a mildly stressful state. A subject may be
told that a low tone indicates the presence of alpha waves
and a high tone denotes brain waves of higher electrical
activity. The person can then learn to control the amount
of electrical activity in his brain to reduce stress.

Biofeedback can also be used in the treatment of slow movements and slow reaction times, both of which often accompany old age. Woodruff and Birren (1972) have reported success in training elderly subjects to increase their alpha wave frequency, thus increasing the speed of movements and of reaction times.

There are two major links of biofeedback with the attainment of altered states of consciousness. First, research has shown that biofeedback techniques can be used to induce altered states of consciousness. People who learn to control what are ordinarily autonomic processes often report altered states of mind. Second, biofeedback techniques can be used to attain the same altered states of mind and the same physiological changes that accompany meditation. Among the physiological changes are increases and decreases in the frequency of alpha brain waves.

PSYCHOACTIVE DRUGS

● PROBLEM 7-27

What are psychoactive drugs? List and define the various types according to their function.

Solution: Psychoactive drugs are those that can cause subjective, psychological changes in consciousness. These include alcohol, marijuana, sedatives, stimulants, narcotic drugs, and hallucinogens.

Sedatives or tranquilizers are those drugs that reduce tension and anxiety. Examples of these are resperine and chlorpromazine.

Stimulants or energizers tend to counteract fatigue and produce upswings in mood. Among these drugs are amphetamines ("pep pills"), caffeine, and imipramine.

Narcotic drugs are those that can be used as painkillers. Among these are morphine and heroin. Narcotics are physiologically addictive and dependence on them usually results in a continual increase in dosage.

Hallucinogenic, psychedelic, and psychomimetic are interchangeable terms for drugs whose major feature is the production of hallucinations. These drugs affect the brain functions of perception, cognition (thought processes), and emotion. They may produce pleasurable or depressive reactions and a sense of bodily detachment. Examples of these are mescaline, psilocybin and LSD (lysergic acid diethylamide, or LSD-25).

● PROBLEM 7-28

Discuss the psychological effects of alcohol intoxication with regard to perception, self-awareness, emotions, and motor functioning.

Alcohol Concentration in Blood	Experimental and Behavioral Effects	Amounts of Common Beverages*
.50%	Death likely.	
.30%	Stupor likely.	1 pint whiskey
.15%	Intoxication noticeable to observers: clumsiness, unsteadiness in walking. Reduction of anxiety, fears, impairment of mental functioning. Feelings of personal power. State-dependent memory.	5 cocktails, 28 ounces wine, or 10 bottles beer
.12%	Impairment of fine coordination, some unsteadiness in walking or standing. Feelings of social and personal power.	4 cocktails, 22 ounces wine, or 8 bottles beer
.10%	Legally defined as impaired driving in California.	
.09%	Amplified emotions, lowering of inhibitions.	3 cocktails, 1 pint wine, or 6 bottles beer
.06%	Relaxation, warmth, feeling "high", some impairment of motor acts which require a high degree of skill.	2 cocktails, 11 ounces wine, or 4 bottles beer
.03%	No obvious behavioral effects.	1 cocktail, 5½ ounces wine, or 2 bottles beer

*The alcohol concentrations in the blood for the shown quantities of beverages are based on 150 pounds body weight. Concentrations would be higher for the same amount of beverage consumed by a lighter person and vice versa. A cocktail is specified as containing 1½ ounces of distilled liquor. Wine refers to ordinary table wine, not fortified (dessert) wine.

Solution: With regard to perception, low levels of alcohol intake can produce a slight increase in auditory acuity and pleasant feelings such as warmth and relaxation throughout the body. At higher levels of intoxication, sensory impairment occurs with skills that require fine coordination such as reading. Double vision is likely at very high levels of intoxication.

With regard to self-awareness, alcohol intoxication tends to produce feelings of increased competence and ability rather than a realistic perception of the impairment in mental and motor functioning.

Alcohol intake is known to amplify emotions and to relax and lower inhibitions. At a high level of intoxication, existing anxiety is reduced. Also at high levels, fantasies of personal power arise. Feelings of "socialized power" tend to occur at lower intoxication levels. Here, the individual perceives himself as possessing the ability and power to perform great feats such as saving the world.

It is widely believed that alcohol lowers sexual inhibitions but there is some speculation as to whether this is a direct effect or a culturally mediated effect. That is, looser standards of conduct are applied to those who are defined "drunk" than to those who are sober.

With regard to motor functioning, there is some impairment in motor acts that require a high degree of skill at low levels of intoxication. At high levels there exists clumsiness and an unsteadiness in walking and standing.

Discuss the psychological effects of marijuana intoxication including its effects on perception, emotions, cognitive processes, memory, identity, time sense, performance.

Solution: Marijuana intoxication leads the user to feel that his perception is enhanced, that he perceives the true qualities of objects. The intoxicated person usually finds novel qualities and finds an increased pleasure in all sensory experiences including sexual orgasm. Objects or events that are ordinarily ambiguous to the user become vivid. New and pleasing internal bodily sensations are also felt. To date, there is no evidence that there is any actual lowering of thresholds for any sense receptor. It is possible that these effects may result from altered processing of incoming stimuli.

Most experienced marijuana users report feelings of pleasantness although unpleasant experiences are possible. Both pleasant and unpleasant experiences are considerably amplified during intoxication. Stressful and unpleasant feelings may occur in new users who, after a negative initial reaction, do not continue use.

Cognitive processes also change rapidly during intoxication. Thoughts are perceived to be more intuitive and less bound by ordinary logic. Except at high levels of intoxication, the user feels he is in good control of his thought processes.

Marijuana intoxication produces both state-dependent memory and some overall loss of memory functioning. Memory span is shortened considerably.

One's sense of identity can be greatly altered during intoxication. The user usually becomes more childlike and open to experiences. He becomes more accepting of events, finds it hard to play conventional social games, and has more spontaneous insight into himself.

During intoxication, time is perceived as moving more slowly although some report that time passes rapidly. In addition, there is a keen sense of existing in the present.

There is usually less movement during marijuana intoxication. There is less inclination to move about, and if there is movement, the user perceives it as very smooth and coordinated. Studies have generally found that most motor activities are not impaired by marijuana intoxication in experienced users. Naive users sometimes experience great difficulty in performing relatively easy tasks.

● **PROBLEM** 7-30

What is a psychedelic drug? Discuss the psychedelic experience.

<u>Solution</u>: The term "psychedelic" literally means "mind manifesting" and is applied to any drug whose primary effect is to induce an altered state of consciousness. Among these drugs are LSD (lysergic acid diethylamide), mescaline (the active ingredient of peyote cactus), psilocybin, and a large number of other drugs occurring naturally in plants.

R.E.L. Masters and Jean Houston, two leading investigators of the psychedelic experience, have distinguished four levels in the experience. These are the Sensory level, the Recollective-Analytic level, the Symbolic level, and the Integral level.

In the Sensory level, one finds the beginnings of hallucinations. Colors become intensified, rainbows may form in the air, commonplace objects become great works of art and so on.

In the second, more profound level, Recollective-Analytic, the subject experiences very strong personal emotions which, with proper guidance, could lead to therapeutic experiences in which personal conflicts are resolved. Without such guidance, most subjects' experiences remain at this or the previous Sensory level.

In the next level of profundity, the Symbolic level, the images and hallucinations which the subject experiences are related to such subjects as the history of man, evolution, and rites of passage. If successful at this level, the subject can gain important insights and experiences dealing with the nature of being human.

The last and most profound level of Masters's and Houston's design is the Integral level. This level is seldom reached. If attained, however, the experiences are religious and mystical often including a confrontation with God. The individual may report such phenomena as the death of his ego, a union with God and a rebirth. Because of their extreme profundity, experiences at this level cannot be accurately expressed in verbal terms.

SHORT ANSWER QUESTIONS FOR REVIEW

Choose the correct answer.

1. In their approach to the mind-body problem, the
    structuralists adopted the view of (a) physi-
    cal monism (b) psychophysical parallelism
    (c) the identity theory (d) psychological
    isomorphism   b

2. One of the key concepts the Gestalt psycholo-
    gists employed in dealing with the mind-body
    problem was (a) interactionism (b) physical
    monism (c) psychophysical parallelism (d)
    psychological isomorphism   d

3. Consciousness is best defined as (a) the whole
    range of states of awareness (b) graded states
    of alertness (c) the sum total of mental expe-
    riences (d) all the varying levels of human
    activity   c

4. In a sleeping subject, the EEG first shows the
    appearance of spindles (bursts of activity) in
    (a) stage 1 sleep (b) stage 2 sleep (c)
    stage 3 sleep (d) stage 4 sleep   b

5. The type of brain waves which predominate in
    stage 4 sleep are (a) alpha (b) beta (c)
    delta (d) gamma   c

6. Dream deprivation studies (a) involve allow-
    ing the subjects to sleep until they begin to
    go into REM periods (b) indicate that there
    is some purpose to dreaming (c) indicate that
    such deprivation increases the amount of dream-
    ing when subjects are allowed to resume normal,
    undisturbed sleep (d) all of the above   d

7. The subject remains in contact with his envi-
    ronment in which of the following ego states
    of the hynogogic state? (a) intact (b) de-
    structuralized (c) restructuralized (d) de-
    centralized   a

8. All of the following illustrate the differences
    between consciousness and awareness except (a)
    automatic behavior (b) creative thinking (c)
    incidental memory (d) subception   b

9. An experiment on cats in which the animals were
    allowed to sleep but were prevented from dream-
    ing showed that (a) the cats developed se-
    rious mental disorders and eventually died (b)
    there was no effect on the behavior of the cats

251

SHORT ANSWER QUESTIONS FOR REVIEW

(c) the cats preferred dreamless sleep to sleep interrupted by dreams (d) the cats became better in operant learning situations | a

10. Which of the following is NOT one of Freud's dream processes? (a) condensation (b) displacement (c) personalization (d) symbolization | c

11. The dream process in which one aspect of a dream is a composite representation of several entities in reality is (a) symbolization (b) condensation (c) displacement (d) secondary elaboration | b

12. Which of the following is characteristic of the hypnotic state? (a) heightened emotion (b) clear perception (c) attentional selectivity (d) all of the above | c

13. Studies indicate that those subjects who are most easily hypnotized are (a) weak (b) abnormal (c) intellectually oriented (d) a and b | c

14. Meditative focal points in the form of sound patterns are called (a) mantras (b) pranayamas (c) yantras (d) mandalas | a

15. Opening-up meditation is unlike concentrative meditation in (a) its method of induction (b) its objective (c) major effects (d) all of the above | a

16. Which of the following is NOT a physiological effect of meditation? (a) lowered metabolism (b) decreased heart rate (c) decreased number of alpha waves (d) appearance of theta waves | c

17. Biofeedback can be used in the control of (a) heart rate (b) brain waves (c) reaction time (d) all of the above | d

18. Alcohol is (a) a stimulant (b) a depressant (c) a non-addictive drug (d) none of the above | b

19. Marijuana intoxication (a) has no effect on emotions (b) lengthens memory span (c) makes the subject feel his perception is enhanced (d) generally increases the amount of motor activity | c

SHORT ANSWER QUESTIONS FOR REVIEW

20. All of the following factors are involved in influencing a good or bad trip EXCEPT (a) quality of drug (b) mood of user (c) amount of
experience of drug user (d) none of the above

d

21. Controlled studies have shown that claims of
increased creativity under the influence of LSD
are (a) not substantiated (b) substantiated
(c) true only of good "trips" (d) true for
85% of the cases studied

a

Fill in the blanks.

22. The essence of _____ meditation is "one pointed-
ness" of the mind.

concentra-
tive

23. According to Freud, the dream process that disguises dream material by combining separate
events or objects from reality is called _____ .

condensa-
tion

24. In their solution to the mind-body problem, the
_____ recognized only the physical nature of
man.

behavior-
ists

25. _____ is any behavior that can be engaged in
without much concentration and effort

Automatic
behavior

26. In _____, presented stimuli are below their
threshold values.

subliminal
perception
or subcep-
tion

27. _____ occurs when stimuli that are perceived are
totally or partially blocked from awareness.

Perceptual
defense

28. REMs are detected and measured by a(n) _____ .

electrocu-
logram
(EOG)

29. _____ are sharply pointed waves recorded by the
EEG.

Spindles

30. The state one experiences when going from sleeping to waking is called _____ .

hypnopom-
pic

31. _____ refers to the information one can report
about a dream whereas _____ refers to the unconscious desires underlying the dream content.

Manifest
content;
latent
content

32. _____ involves a reallocation of psychic energy.

Cathexis

SHORT ANSWER QUESTIONS FOR REVIEW

33. The apparent biological clock that operates in a regular, rhythmic fashion in humans is called _____ .

circadian rhythm

34. A technique by which people can observe measurements of bodily processes that are otherwise unobservable is called _____ .

biofeedback

35. The wave pattern of 10 cycles per second which is found during the relaxed waking state is called _____ .

alpha rhythm

Determine whether the following statements are true or false.

36. Somnambulism and sleeptalking do not seem to be related to usual dreaming.

True

37. The primary effect of alcohol intoxication on self-awareness is that it tends to produce feelings of increased competence and ability rather than a realistic perception of the impairments of mental and motor functioning.

True

38. A number of studies have indicated that LSD and other psychedelics cannot be used profitably in psychotherapy as once believed.

True

39. Deikman hypothesized that what happens in contemplative meditation is deautomatization.

True

40. During REM sleep nearly all motor functioning is inhibited.

True

41. LSD promotes two varieties of psychedelic experience, one mystical and one nonmystical.

True

42. Intoxication and delerium are altered states of consciousness.

True

43. Hypnosis is a form of sleep in which there is a lack of all thought process.

False

44. Hypnosis is an effective therapeutic aid in alleviating pain and stress.

True

45. Consciousness demands awareness.

False

46. The EEG pattern of an active, awake person is similar to that of Stage 1-REM.

True

47. According to Freudian theory, the motives be-

SHORT ANSWER QUESTIONS FOR REVIEW

hind adults' dreams are much clearer than those
of children's dream.

False

48. Jung believed that there are certain types of
dreams which all men share.

True

49. Out-of-body experiences evolve gradually.

False

50. Parapsychologists believe that possession states
are derived from a fragment of the unconscious
mind.

True

CHAPTER 8

SENSATION

THE CONCEPT OF THRESHOLD

● PROBLEM 8-1

What do the terms absolute threshold and differential threshold refer to?

Stimuli to be compared:

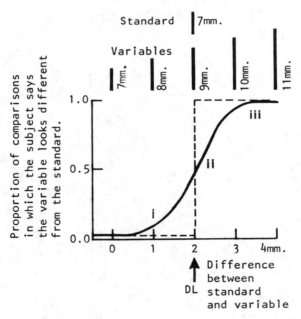

Solution: A basic research problem involving sensory systems concerns "What is the minimum amount of physical stimulation that we can 'experience.'" For example, in the visual system, we would like to know how dim a light can become before we cannot see it anymore. It is believed that there is an 'absolute threshold,' which is defined as the minimum amount of energy needed for a stimulus to be detected by our senses. This threshold differs for each sense. In vision, a minimum amount of light energy must pass through our eyes for us to

256

see a light. In the auditory system, a different minimum, this time of sound energy, is needed for us to hear what someone is saying.

A second important question regarding sensory systems is what is the smallest difference needed to exist between two stimuli before we are able to distinguish between them. For example, how different must two lights be before we can tell that they are each of a different intensity. This minimum difference is called the 'differential threshold' (also the 'difference threshold' or DL). It is not constant, even for a specific sensory system. For instance, if you are in a room with one person talking, you will definitely notice when a second person begins talking. That additional sound energy will be above the differential threshold (DL). However, if you are at a party where one hundred people are talking, if another person suddenly begins to talk, you may not notice that additional voice. In this case, the differential threshold is higher; a greater amount of sound energy is needed in order for the addition to be noticed. However, if a band began playing it would probably be noticed. In general, the greater the intensity of the original stimulus, the greater is the differential threshold. The additional stimulation must carry more energy in order to be noticed.

● **PROBLEM** 8-2

Describe the use of thresholds and their relationship to Weber's law.

Solution: A threshold is basically a boundary which separates the stimuli that elicit one response from the stimuli that elicit a different response. (Many reports of psychophysical studies use the Latin equivalent, limen, instead of threshold).

An example is useful in differentiating among the different types of thresholds. Suppose you present to your subject a low frequency tone through a set of calibrated headphones. If the tone is below a certain frequency (measured in Hz.), the subject's report is "I don't hear anything." If the tone is continually increased it will eventually reach a frequency where the subject reports "Yes, I hear it." The frequency of the tone has now just crossed the lower threshold. This is also referred to as the stimulus threshold and is abbreviated RL (from the German "Reiz Limen"). If the tone is continued to be increased the subject will report that it is getting higher and higher, and by noting these changes a difference threshold (DL) is established. The DL is also referred to as the just noticeable difference (j.n.d.). The j.n.d. is not merely a fixed value but a percentage of a standard value. This proportion is known as Weber's law and is simply stated as "a stimulus must be increased by a constant fraction of its value to be just noticeably different." This proportion is symbolized as:

$$\Delta I / I = K$$

in which I symbolizes intensity and Delta I the increase necessary to yield a j.n.d.

If the tone is continually increased it will eventually reach a level where it cannot be perceived (i.e. - a dog whistle). This upper limit is the terminal threshold (TL).

● PROBLEM 8-3

Describe the three basic methods of measuring and analyzing thresholds.

Solution: It is apparent that the use of thresholds in psychophysics and perception is important. In order to reliably measure and analyze thresholds, statistical methods were developed. There are three basic methods used for this purpose. They are alike in that they all present (for comparison) a constant Standard stimulus (St) and a variable Comparison stimulus (Co). When attempting to establish the RL, the St is zero, the Co is relatively low, and verbal reports are usually limited to "yes" and "no" responses. When establishing the DL, the St is of some strength and the Co may be "greater", "less", or "equal to" the standard.

The above method is the Method of Limits. This is the only direct method of locating a threshold and Co approaches and recedes from St by small increments. It is then appropriately noted at what level subject's responses shift from one type to another.

The second method is the Method of Average Error. In this approach the subject is required to adjust Co to apparent equality with St. This is done numerous times and the average differences in his approximations are computed as the accuracy of his discrimination.

The third, and final, method is the frequency method. In this method each Co is compared with St many times and the relative frequency of responses is noted.

● PROBLEM 8-4

What is the Theory of Signal Detectability and how is it different from the more classical psychophysical view?

Solution: The Theory of Signal Detectability (TSD) is a theory which maintains that the classical view of the "threshold" is an oversimplification. Proponents of TSD argue that anytime a subject reports that a signal is present, the subject is actually telling the experimenter two things: the subject's ability to detect the stimulus (e.g. how good is his eyesight?) and the subject's motivation to detect the stimulus (e.g. will he receive $100 for detecting the signal).

The classical view, however, maintains that the subject is telling the experimenter only one thing: discrimination/ detection/recognition ability. The classical psychophysicists did include "catch trials" (trials where no stimulus was presented) in their experiments, but they used them only to assure that their subject would maintain vigilance. No attempt was made to analyze catch trials systematically or statistically.

Proponents of TSD maintain that it is essential to analyze these "false alarms" to separate "bias" from "sensitivity." Consider the following experiment: a blind man is placed in a room before a light which the experimenter controls. The experiment involves asking the blind man to tell the experimenter whether the light is on (which he is told will be the case 50% of the time) or off (which he knows will be the case the other 50% of the time). The blind man will receive $1 every time he says that the light is on, when it is in fact on. There is no penalty for incorrectly reporting the presence of the light (not unlike the classical psychophysics experiment). The blind man, if he's smart, will of course report that the light is on every trial. He never misses the "signal." He wins $50. By classical methods of data analysis, he can see perfectly.

The TSD, however, takes into account statistically the fact that the blindman made as many "false alarms" as "hits." He cannot see better than chance. He succeeds at the game because of his "response bias." Consider the less extreme case of a situation where a "normal" subject receives $1 for hits, but is penalized $1 for false alarms. But this time he is told that the signal will be present 80% of the time. It may be expected that the normal subject will not say "present" everytime, but probably more than 80% of the time. He will most likely avoid saying a signal is present when he is certain it is not, but reports its presence when there is some chance that it occurred. None of this hypothetical decision making (at least in the latter example) need be conscious. It is not assumed that the subject is lying, simply that given an ambiguous situation (like a detection experiment) the uncertainty of whether a stimulus is present or not is resolved both by sensory discrimination and by motivation/expectation/bias.

The TSD is probably the dominant view in contemporary psychophysics. The fact that a given subject's responses to identical stimulus arrays can be manipulated by expectation and bias is compelling (subjects of course often insist that there was no change in their strategies; they are not lying; the stimulus is ambiguous). It should be noted, however, that even though proponents of TSD can, by employing statistics, separate out the effects of bias from actual sensory ability, the threshold values (actually their range in normal subjects) obtained by classical psychophysicists over the years appear to be remarkably accurate. TSD may thus be seen most profitably as an extention of, rather than a replacement for, the classical concept of threshold.

VISION

● PROBLEM 8-5

List the principle parts of the eye and describe their function.

Solution: The human eye is a complex organ consisting of several parts. The cornea is the outer transparent coating in front of the eye. Its function is to protect the internal parts.

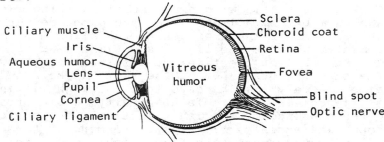

Diagrammatic section of the human eye.

The lens is a transparent tissue that focuses the image by changing shape - thickening for near objects and thinning for distant ones. This process is called accommodation, and is carried out by expansion or contraction of the ciliary muscles. Like the cornea, the lens is curved in shape. It bends and focuses light rays onto the retina.

The retina is the photosensitive curtain of nerve cells located at the back of the eye. Over 120 million photoreceptor cells are found in the retina of each eye. There are two types which are named according to their shape: rods and cones. Rods are found throughout the retina area except in the small central region called the fovea. They are highly concentrated along the outer edge of the retina. Rods are extremely sensitive to light energy, most especially to achromatic (black-white) light and dim light; hence, they facilitate night vision.

Cones are located primarily in the fovea. There are about 6 to 7 million cones in each eye. They require large amounts of light energy stimulation before responding. Cones possess the ability to respond differentially to different wavelengths. They are thus sensitive to color (which is dependent on wavelength); it is through the cones that we perceive color.

The pupil is the round opening in the center of the eye through which light passes to the retina. The pupil appears as the black circle in the center of the eye.

The colored portion of the eye is called the iris. It is the tissue that surrounds the pupil and regulates its size - contracting or dilating in order to adjust the amount of light entering the eye.

● PROBLEM 8-6

Define light and describe its characteristics. How is it measured? What are its primary sources? Define contour and optic array.

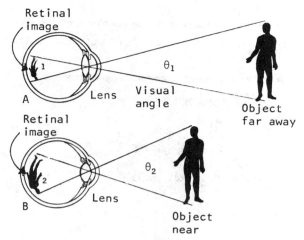

Two examples of optic arrays from objects with their retinal images.
Only lines from the extremeties of the objects are illustrated. In
A the object is far away, so the visual angle is small with an ac-
companyingly small image projected on the retina. Notice that the
lens inverts the image. In B the object is closer, so there is a
larger visual angle and a larger retinal image.

Solution: Light can be defined as that portion of the electromagnetic spectrum of radiation that affects visual receptors. Light has various characteristics including photons,
waves, intensity, and composition. Physicists view light as
having a dual nature. On the one hand they see it as composed of photons - packets of energies. On the other hand, it
is thought to consist of waves which are described by their
wavelengths. Intensity refers to the number of photons of
the light while composition is the number of wavelengths.

One device used for measuring light intensity is a
photographer's light meter which is capable of transforming
physical light energy into a measurable electrical current.

Visible electromagnetic energy; that is, light that can
be perceived, comes from a variety of sources - the sun,
light bulb, fire. But the most abundant source of light is
that which is reflected from object surfaces. Most of the
light that enters the eye is reflected light. The brightness
of an object - how intense it appears to the perceiver - depends on how much light it receives from a light source and
how much is reflected to the perceiver's vision. Light objects reflect almost all the light that illuminates them
while dark objects reflect very little since they absorb
most of the light that falls on them. Because of the fact
that different objects reflect different intensities and
wavelengths of light, the human eye can perceive these differences. Contours also make this possible. Contours are
the borders between areas that reflect different intensities
and wavelengths.

An optic array is a pattern of energy that is reflected
from the surface of an object. An array is best illustrated
by thinking of an object with visible lines or rays projecting from it from every possible surface point to the eye of
the perceiver.

Briefly describe the process of sensory transduction in the visual system.

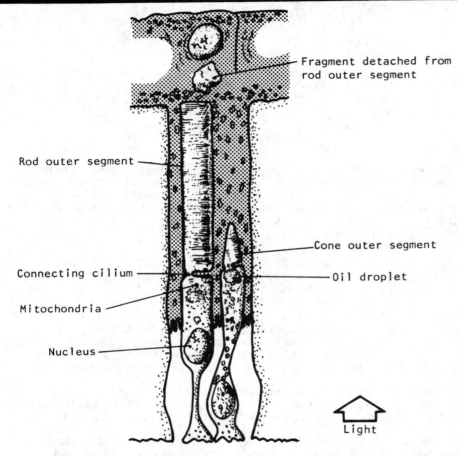

Fragment detached from rod outer segment

Rod outer segment

Cone outer segment

Connecting cilium

Oil droplet

Mitochondria

Nucleus

Light

<u>Solution</u>: Sensory transduction is the process which translates physical information from our environment into electrical information which our brain can "understand." A general outline of sensory transduction in the visual system is as follows.

Light strikes specialized 'receptor cells' in our eyes (on the retina). This causes light-sensitive substances in these cells to undergo chemical changes. These chemical changes cause an electric event called a 'generator potential' to occur. The generator potential then activates nerve cells, which transmit the visual information to our brain.

There are two types of receptor cells in our eye. These are the rod cells and cone cells. The light-sensitive substance in rod cells is called rhodopsin. When light hits rhodopsin, it changes into two different substances called retinene and opsin. There are three types of light-sensitive substances found in cone cells. Each type is sensitive to a different color of light. Thus we speak of blue, green, and red cones. In general, the substances found in cones

are called iodopsin. When the proper frequency of light
hits iodopsin, it undergoes chemical changes similar to those
described above for rhodopsin. These chemical changes are
able to cause an electric event - the generator potential.

Once the physical stimulus from our environment - light
- is in the electrical form of a generator potential, nerve
cells can be activated. These nerve cells then send the information, in an electrical form, to our brain. This is how
sensory transduction in the visual system takes place. It
is unfortunate that the crucial process of how a generator
potential is produced, is not yet fully understood.

● **PROBLEM** 8-8

What are the three main cell layers of the retina? How are
they structurally and functionally interconnected?

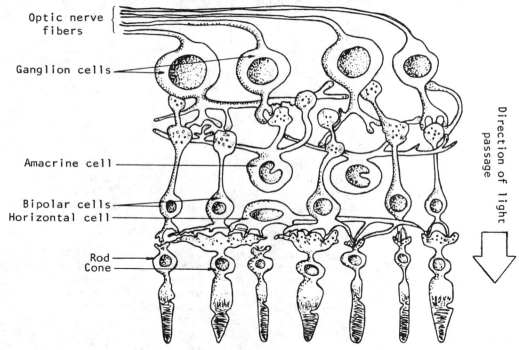

Optic nerve fibers

Ganglion cells

Amacrine cell

Bipolar cells
Horizontal cell

Rod
Cone

Direction of light passage

Solution: The retina is composed of three cell layers - a
transparent layer of ganglion cells, transparent bipolar
cells, and finally, receptor cells. The receptor cell layer
is located on the side of the retina away from the light.
This is why the human retina is called an 'inverted retina';
light must travel through the rest of the retina before reaching the light-sensitive receptor cells.

The receptor cells of the retina function in sensory
transduction; they convert the physical stimulus from the environment into an electrical message which the brain can "understand." This electrical information is then passed through
"horizontal cells" to the bipolar cell layer. Some processing
of the information is thought to take place at the level of
the horizontal cells.

The ends of the bipolar cells are interconnected through amacrine cells. Some information processing is also thought to take place at this level. These cells send visual information on to the ganglion cell layer. Fibers of the ganglion cells make up the optic nerve. The optic nerve then carries visual information up to appropriate areas of the brain.

● **PROBLEM** 8-9

What is the "tricolor" theory of color vision? What is the "opponent-process" theory of color vision? How has recent research provided evidence for both theories?

Opponent-process cells

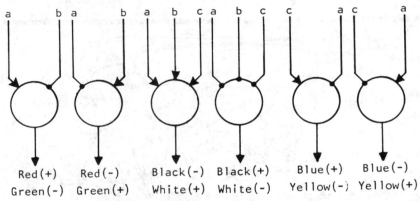

Red(+)   Red(-)   Black(-) Black(+)   Blue(+)   Blue(-)
Green(-) Green(+) White(+) White(-)   Yellow(-) Yellow(+)

Solution: The "tricolor" theory, first proposed by Young, and the "opponent-process" theory, originally called the Hering theory, are attempts to explain how we can see different colors. Recent research has shown that both theories may be correct, though for different levels in the visual system.

The tricolor theory of color vision proposed that there are three types of color receptors in the eye. Each responds maximally to one of three colors - either red, green, or blue. Any color can be produced by properly mixing light of these three colors. For example, mixing yellow and blue light produces white light. Thus every color we see would activate some or all of these color receptors. By interpreting the activities of the different receptors in our eye, our brain could 'know' the colors we are seeing.

The opponent-process theory of color vision stated that there are only two kinds of color receptors in our eye. Each receptor was thought to represent a pair of colors - one red-green, and one blue-yellow. The receptors were thought to respond to these colors in an 'opponent' fashion. This means that they would be excited in response to one of the colors, and inhibited in response to the other. The total amount of activity in these receptors could then be "interpreted" by our brain. It was thought that in this way we see color.

Recent research has provided evidence that each of these theories operates, though at different levels of our visual system. For example, it has been found that there are three types of color receptors in our eye - red, green, and blue cone cells. These, located in the retina, operate along the lines of the tricolor theory of color vision.

However, when these cones send their information to the ganglion cells of the retina, the opponent-process theory appears to be a better explanation. Also, cells in the lateral geniculate body (LGB), a part of the brain that deals with vision, seem to operate according to the opponent-process theory. Four types of opponent cells were found in the LGB. One was excited by red and inhibited by green; another was excited by green and inhibited by red. Similar cells for yellow and blue were found. Thus there is some evidence for both of the above theories operating in color vision.

● **PROBLEM** 8-10

Distinguish between rods and cones with respect to location and function.

Solution: Rods and cones are two types of light-sensitive cells located in the retina. Cones are concentrated mostly in a small region of the retina called the fovea. Rods are most numerous just outside of the fovea.

Rods and cones also differ with respect to their functions. Cones function in our most acute or distinct vision. They are responsible for our vision in the daytime and in bright light. In addition, the cones are the retinal cells necessary for color vision (as they are frequency sensitive).

Rod cells, on the other hand, function mainly in night vision. They are more sensitive to light, and thus will respond to very dim lights that cones cannot respond to. However, rod vision is not as distinct. Also, rods only produce black-and-white images (they are frequency insensitive). This explains why, though we can usually see everything in a dark room, little appears in color, and edges of objects may appear fuzzy.

● **PROBLEM** 8-11

Why is the rod system of vision more sensitive to light than the cone system?

Solution: The retina of our eye is composed basically of three interconnected layers of cells. A layer of receptor cells, which include rods and cones, are connected to bipolar cells. These bipolar cells are in turn associated with a layer of ganglion cells. However, the precise arrangement is different for rods and cones. It is this difference which allows the rod system to be more sensitive to light.

A minimum amount of stimulation is needed for a ganglion cell to begin sending visual information to the brain. This is called the threshold value. In the cone system of vision, one cone connects to one bipolar cell, which is in turn connected to one ganglion cell. Therefore, a single cone must

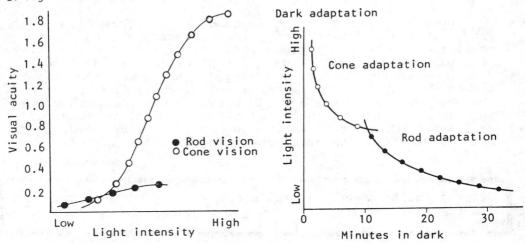

Visual acuity as a function of light intensity

Dark adaptation

receive the threshold value of stimulation in order to activate a ganglion cell. This requires relatively bright light,
and is why cones function in daytime and in bright light vision only.

The rod system of vision is organized differently. Here,
a large number of receptor cells are connected to one bipolar
cell. Also, a number of bipolar cells are associated with a
single ganglion cell. Therefore, stimulation from many receptors is added together by the time the ganglion cell layer
is reached.

This is why the rod system of vision can function at
very low light intensities, while the cone system cannot. In
dim light, a single cone cell does not receive enough stimulation to reach threshold. Therefore, it cannot activate its
ganglion cell. The rod cells do not receive enough stimulation to reach threshold either. However, many rod cells connect to a single ganglion cell. When the small amounts of
stimulation received by each of these rods are added together,
threshold may be reached. Their associated ganglion cell will
then be activated. This summing process involved in the rod
system is called 'lateral summation.' It explains why rod
vision is more sensitive to light than cone vision is.

● **PROBLEM** 8-12

What is lateral inhibition and how does it function in our
visual system?

Solution: Lateral inhibition refers to the process whereby
the activity of one nerve cell inhibits a neighboring nerve
cell from being activated. This process has two major functions in our visual system. It reduces the amount of repetitious information being sent to the brain. In addition,
it serves to sharpen the contrast at edges of objects.

When a uniform patch of light stimulates part of our retina, the cells on which the patch falls are all stimulated

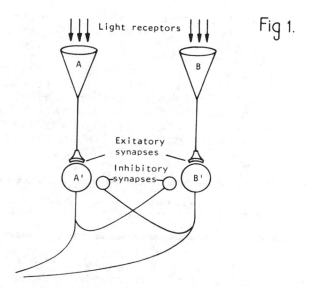

Fig 1.

Light receptors

A

B

Exitatory
synapses

Inhibitory
synapses

A'

B'

equally. Similarly, all cells not being stimulated by the
patch are also in equivalent states. If our eye were to send
information about each of these cells to the brain, most of
the messages would be repetitious. Lateral inhibition eliminates this redundancy. Consider light receptors A and B in
Fig. 1. These send information to ganglion cells A' and B'.
When A' is activated, it inhibits B', and vice versa, in the
process called lateral inhibition. If only A' is stimulated,
it will inhibit B' and also send its information along to the
brain. However, if both A' and B' are stimulated, each will
inhibit the other, and no message will be sent to the brain.
Since A' is stimulated, it will inhibit B'. Since B' is
stimulated, it will inhibit A'. This will occur if we shine
light on both receptors A and B. Thus we see that information about light stimulation will be sent to the brain only
when neighboring receptors are unequally stimulated. In
this way, lateral inhibition eliminates repetitive information.

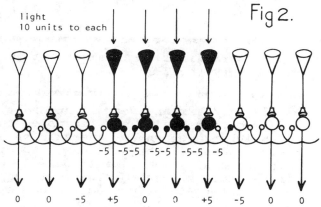

Fig 2.

light
10 units to each

-5 | -5 -5 | -5 -5 | -5 -5 | -5

0   0   -5   +5   0   0   +5   -5   0   0

This process also emphasizes edges of objects. Consider
Figure 2. The darkened spaces are cells that have been stimulated. Each receptor receives, for example, 10 units of
stimulation. These 10 units of stimulation are transferred
to ganglion cells. When stimulated, each ganglion cell inhibits its two neighboring cells. This is the process of

lateral inhibition. If 10 units of stimulation are given, each neighbor will receive 5 units of inhibition. Therefore, if a ganglion cell has two neighbors which are as stimulated as it is, no information will be sent from that cell to the brain. 10 units of stimulation will be cancelled by the two neighbors, each providing 5 units of inhibition. Thus we see that only when two neighbors are unequally stimulated, will information be sent to the brain. This occurs at edges, or boundaries between objects. In this way lateral inhibition sharpens images of edges that are sent on to the brain.

● **PROBLEM 8-13**

Trace the path that visual information takes on its way to the brain. Begin with the retinal receptor cells.

Solution: Visual information, first received by the retina's receptor cells, passes through a number of different cells and undergoes a number of transformations before it reaches the brain. First, the information passes through the cell layers of the retina. That is, it is passed through the bipolar and ganglion cell layers. From the ganglion cells, visual information is carried by the optic nerve into the central nervous system.

About half-way to the brain, the optic nerve reaches an intersection called the optic chiasm (from the Greek letter chi, χ). Here, some fibers from our left eye cross over to proceed to the right side of the brain, and vice versa. Some fibers continue up along the side from which they originate.

Once past the optic chiasm, nerve fibers carrying visual information are called optic tracts. Information from the optic tract is carried to the visual center of the thalamus. This center is called the lateral geniculate body. Finally, the lateral geniculate body relays the information to the visual cortex for final processing.

● **PROBLEM 8-14**

It is said that a topographical arrangement exists in visual cortex. What is meant by this?

Solution: A topographical arrangement is an orderly mapping of a sensory surface on the brain. For example, the existence of a topographic arrangement of the skin on the brain would mean that every point on the skin has a specific corresponding area in the brain; there would be a "map" of the skin in a certain part of the brain. This arrangement is sometimes called a point-to-point projection or correspondence.

There is a topographic arrangement in visual cortex and the lateral geniculate body (LGB), another part of the brain that is involved in vision. In this case, it is the retina of the eye that is represented, point by point, on the brain. A specific part of the retina projects to a particular area of the LGB. This area of the LGB then projects to a specific region of visual cortex.

It follows that if a part of a person's retina is destroyed, there will be corresponding regions in the LGB and cortex which will no longer receive visual information. If an area of one's visual cortex is damaged, that person will be 'blind' in one part of his eye. This is because a part of his retina will have nowhere to "send its messages." Topographical arrangements such as this exist in other sensory systems as well.

● **PROBLEM** 8-15

To which half of our brain does an image in the left visual field project?

Solution: Information from the left visual field projects to the right half (hemisphere) of the brain. This can be seen in the diagram.

Consider first information that enters the left eye. An image in the left visual field would hit the nasal part of your left eye - that is, the side of your eye that is closest to your nose. This information then travels along the nasal fibers of the left optic nerve until the optic chiasm. This chiasm is actually an intersection of the left and right optic nerves.

Nasal fibers cross over to the opposite side of the head from which they originated. This crossing over occurs at the optic chiasm. It means that the nasal fibers of the left optic nerve cross to the right side of the brain at the optic chiasm. Information from the left visual field is carried by the nasal fibers of the left optic nerve, as discussed above. Therefore, information from the left visual field entering the left eye, ends up on the right side of the brain.

A similar analysis can be made for the right eye. Information from the left visual field hits the temporal part of the right eye - that is, the side of the eye further from the nose and closer to the temples. This information is carried along the temporal fibers of the right optic nerve. Temporal fibers do not cross over to the other side of the brain at the optic chiasm. Therefore, information carried by the temporal fibers of the right optic nerve continue to the right side of the brain. Once again we see that information from the left visual field projects to the right half of the brain. Information from the right visual field, similarly, projects to the left half of the brain.

● **PROBLEM** 8-16

What do we mean when we say that our visual system is 50% crossed?

Solution: The retina is the light-sensitive part of our eyes. It sends the visual information it receives from the

environment to our brain, through various nerve fibers.
These fibers are called the optic nerve. Actually, there is
a left and a right optic nerve, one from each of our eyes.
These join in a region called the optic chiasm. Here, half
of the fibers of each optic nerve cross over to the opposite
side of the brain. This is what we mean when we say our
visual system is 50% crossed.

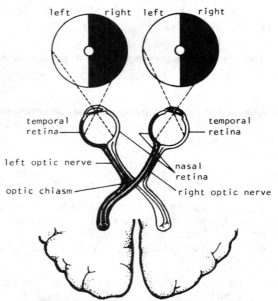

It is the 'nasal fibers' of the optic nerve that cross
over, that is, the fibers that come from the side of your
eye which is closer to your nose. The 'temporal fibers,'
which are on the side of your eye close to your temples, do
not cross. These continue on the same side they were on
when they reached the optic chiasm.

This is illustrated in the diagram. The temporal
fibers of the left optic nerve can be seen continuing on the
left side of the cortex after the optic chiasm. The nasal
fibers of the left optic nerve, however, do not. Rather,
they cross over to the right side of the brain. Here they
continue their path alongside the temporal fibers of the
right optic nerve.

AUDITION

● **PROBLEM** 8-17

What are the three major parts of the ear? Which important
structures does each part contain?

Solution: The three major parts of the ear are the outer,
middle, and inner ears. The outer ear consists of an ear
flap called the pinna, an air-filled tube, and the auditory

tory canal. Sound energy from the environment enters the ear through the pinna and travels down the auditory canal to the middle ear.

Middle ear with ossicles

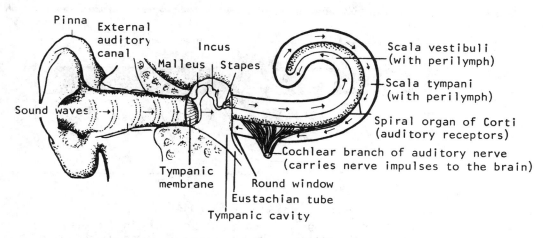

External ear   Middle ear   Inner ear

The middle ear is separated from the outer ear by a thin membrane which is stretched across the auditory canal. This membrane is called the eardrum. Just behind the eardrum are three small bones, the ossicles of the middle ear. The last of these bones is called the stapes. It lies directly in front of the oval window, a membrane which covers an opening to the inner ear.

The inner ear contains two kinds of sense organs. One is concerned with hearing. The other deals with our sense of balance. Only the part of the inner ear dealing with hearing is illustrated. This part is called the cochlea.

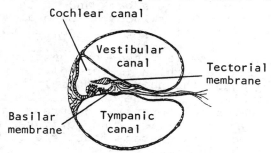

The cochlea consists of three fluid filled canals, each separated from the other by a membrane. These canals spiral around inside the cochlea, which is structured much like a snail shell. The cochlea also contains the organ of corti, which has the receptor cells necessary for hearing. In the auditory system, these receptors are small cells with hairs on their ends. These hair cells are located on a membrane called the basilar membrane. Above the hair cells lies the tectorial membrane. In addition, the cochlea contains the round window, another membrane separating the inner and middle ears. It lies below the oval window which was discussed above.

Briefly describe the process of sensory transduction in the auditory system.

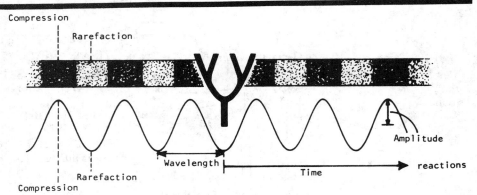

The stimulus for hearing is waves of compression in the air, or more simply, vibrations. The frequency of sound waves determines their pitch. The amplitude determines loudness.

Solution: Sensory transduction is the process which translates physical information from our environment into electrical information which our brain can "understand." The physical stimulus for hearing is sound. Sound is actually nothing more than vibrations, usually of particles in the air.

Vibrations of the air in the auditory canal of one's ear cause the eardrum, a membrane stretched tightly across this canal, to vibrate. The eardrum's vibrations are magnified by three bones located in the middle ear. As the third of these bones vibrates back and forth, it pushes on a membrane called the oval window. The oval window leads to a fluid-filled space inside the ear, called the cochlea.

As the oval window is pushed by bones in the middle ear, the fluid in the cochlea is forced to move. This movement eventually bends the hair of special 'hair cells' located in the cochlea. As these hairs are bent, an electric event called a generator potential occurs. This potential stimulates nearby nerve cells. The activated nerve cells then carry an electrical message about the original vibrations, along to the brain.

● **PROBLEM** 8-19

What is the relationship between frequency and pitch? What is the relationship between intensity and loudness?

Solution: We can distinguish between two tones when they differ with respect to certain variables. One such variable is loudness; one tone may be louder than the other. Another such variable is pitch. Different notes on the piano, for example, may be played equally loud. We would probably still be able to distinguish between them though each note's pitch is different.

Our experiences of pitch and loudness are related to physical aspects of the actual stimulus. For instance, pitch is closely related to the 'frequency' of the stimulus. Sound is basically vibrations of particles in the air. These vibrations are wavelike and are called sound waves. They go up, down, up again, etc. The frequency of a vibration is a measure of how many times it goes up and down in a single period of time, usually a second. If a stimulus goes up and down many times in a second, we say it is a high frequency wave. We generally experience high frequency waves as high-pitched tones. Waves with low frequencies correspond to low-pitched tones.

Similarly, the loudness of a sound is closely related to the intensity of the physical stimulus. Intensity is a measure of the amount of physical energy a stimulus sends to our senses. A high intensity sound sends a great deal of energy to our ear. We experience a high intensity sound as being "loud." Similarly, a low intensity stimulus is perceived as "soft."

However, loudness is not directly related to intensity. Pitch is also not directly related to frequency. Other variables may participate in determining the loudness or pitch of a tone. For example, the intensity of a sound is also important in determining pitch. Increasing the intensity of a sound will often increase its pitch. Frequency may also play a part in determining loudness.

In summary, frequency is very important in determining pitch. Intensity is closely related to experienced loudness. However, other variables are involved in these experiences.

● **PROBLEM** 8-20

What 3 factors are involved in our ability to localize sounds in space?

Solution: Our ability to localize sounds in space involves time factors, intensity factors, and psychological factors (such as our familiarity with the stimulus). This ability is basically due to the fact that we possess two ears which are located on opposite sides of our head. This enables us to localize sounds using time and intensity factors.

It is most likely that one ear will be farther from a sound than the other is. Then the sound will reach one ear sooner than it reaches the second. Therefore, one ear will begin sending messages to the brain before the other. This time difference is noted as the auditory messages reach the brain. The brain can then use this information to determine where the sound came from.

In addition, there are differences in the intensity or strength of a particular sound arriving at the two ears. In order to reach the ear that is farther away, a sound 'passes' the head. This decreases the strength of the sound. Consider the following example. If your mother yells at you and there is a wall between you, the sound will be much less intense than if the wall was not there. In a similar fashion, your head dampens the intensity of a stimulus on its way to the more distant ear. The difference in intensity created is again detected in the brain. The brain can then use this information to localize the original sound.

The above factors provide us with rather reliable information regarding the direction a sound is coming from. This is especially so if the object is to the right or left of us. However, determining the distance of a sound source is more difficult. Psychological factors such as familiarity with the sound become important here. If you heard a church bell and a cricket's chirp of equal strength, you would say the church is much farther from you than the cricket. This is because you know church bells are loud relative to cricket chirps. You are familiar with them from previous experience. Thus if a church bell sounds as strong as a cricket's chirp, the bell must be located farther away.

Psychological factors are also important in determining if an object is above or below us. This is how we determine that the roar of an airplane engine is coming from above us. The sound seems to be coming from all over. However, through previous experience we know that airplanes are unlikely to be beneath us. Therefore, the sound must be coming from above.

● **PROBLEM** 8-21

Briefly outline the path that auditory information takes on its way to the brain.

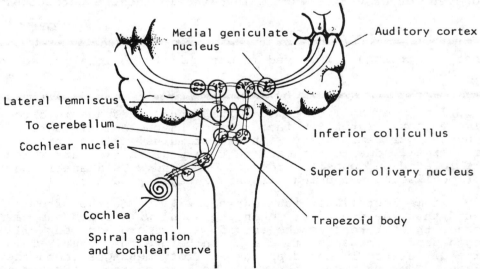

Solution: Physical sounds from our environment are translated into electrical messages in the part of the ear called the cochlea. This electrical message then leaves the cochlea through a group of fibers called the auditory or cochlear nerve. The auditory nerve transmits information about the sounds we hear along to our brain.

En route to the cerebral cortex, the auditory nerve passes through several 'centers' of the brain. First it passes through the cochlear nuclei. These are located at the base of the brain. The nerve then continues upward, passing through the inferior colliculi in the midbrain. Here, half the fibers from each ear cross over to the opposite side of the brain. They then continue on that side until they reach the auditory cortex.

Before the auditory cortex is reached, though, the auditory nerve passes through the medial geniculate body of the thalamus. Finally, auditory information reaches the auditory cortex. Here the information is further processed.

● **PROBLEM 8-22**

Discuss the tonotopic organization of our auditory system.

Solution: The term tonotopic organization refers to the way auditory information is organized in our brain. Specific tones are thought to be represented by specific places in the parts of our brain that deal with hearing. For instance, a low tone may activate cells to the right. A higher tone, on the other hand, may activate cells further left. This is an example of a tonotopic organization.

Different tones create different kinds of vibrations in the air. These vibrations are translated into electrical messages for our brain by special hair cells. These hair cells are located on a membrane called the basilar membrane. The basilar membrane lies in the innermost part of our ear.

It has been found that high tones stimulate hair cells which are closer to the middle part of our ear. Lower tones, on the other hand, affect hair cells farther away from the middle ear. Thus we have a spatial representation of tone at the level of the basilar membrane. This means that a specific tone is represented by a specific place on the basilar membrane.

This arrangement continues in the brain. Specific places on the basilar membrane appear to stimulate specific corresponding places within the brain. Thus there is a spatial organization of tones in the brain. It is thought that this organization enables our brain to distinguish between different tones.

● **PROBLEM 8-23**

Compare and contrast conduction deafness with nerve deafness.

Solution: A person having hearing problems due to malfunctions of the ear has either conduction deafness or nerve deafness. Both kinds of deafness involve some loss of hearing. However, they differ in the particular type of loss. In addition, the reason for the hearing difficulty is different in both cases.

Deafness may result when an ear is not carrying sounds from its outer to its inner parts as well as it should. This is a failure in carrying, or conduction. Therefore, this type of deafness is called conduction deafness. Conduction deafness may result if the bones of the middle ear are damaged. Another cause may be the accumulation of much dirt in the ear. Generally, a person with conduction deafness is equally deaf for both high and low tones. He will probably find that sounds have simply become much softer, as though he had stuffed cotton in his ears.

A person suffering from nerve deafness, on the other hand, will probably have much more difficulty hearing high-pitched tones than low ones. This type of deafness results from damage to the auditory nervous system. This is the part of the auditory system that deals with carrying messages to our brain. Hair cells in the cochlea may be damaged. Hair cells translate sound vibrations of the air into electrical messages our brain can "understand." Specific hair cells respond to specific tones. If some are damaged, the vibrations of certain tones will not be properly translated into electrical messages. Thus a person with nerve deafness cannot hear certain tones, though he may hear others quite well. Nerve deafness is most commonly found among elderly people.

OLFACTION

● PROBLEM 8-24

What are two proposed theories concerning the classification of smells?

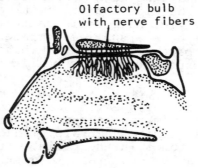

Olfactory bulb
with nerve fibers

Solution: It has been found that there are only three basic colors. That is, all the colors that we see can be described as combinations of the three colors blue, green and red. Researchers have been searching for similar basic categories in the area of smell. Unfortunately, nothing conclusive has been found. Two current theories are discussed below.

One theory concerning the classification of smells proposes four basic categories. This theory includes fragrant, acid, burnt and caprylic as the basic smells. An example of a 'fragrant' smell is that of musk. Vinegar has an 'acid' smell. Roast coffee is an example of the 'burnt' category. Finally, 'caprylic' includes animal odors. There is no concrete evidence for this theory, but its distinctions are sometimes useful.

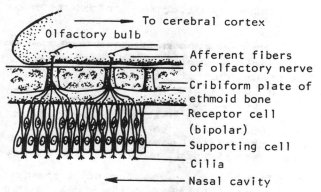

Receptors for the sense of smell(olfaction). Olfactory nerve fibers respond to gaseous molecules.

A second theory of odor classification includes seven classes. This theory distinguishes the following basic smells: camphoraceous, musky, floral, pepperminty, ethereal, pungent, and putrid. The first five categories are thought to be distinguishable in the following way. All substances are composed of particles called molecules. The molecules of each substance have a distinctive shape. The shape of the molecules of a substance is thought to distinguish its odor. For example, a substance may have a minty

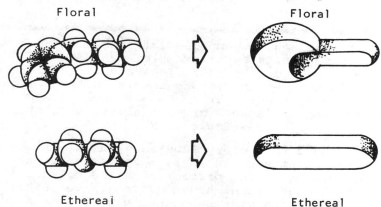

Examples of the molecular shape of two odorous substances, along with their hypothesized receptors.

smell. The molecules of this substance may be square shaped. According to the seven-class theory, all substances with molecules of that shape should smell minty. Any substance which does not smell minty should have molecules of a different shape.

The categories pungent and putrid are distinguished differently. Here, it is the different charges on the molecules that differentiate them. For instance, one molecule may be positive at one end and negative at the other. This pattern would correspond to a particular smell. There is some, but not conclusive, experimental evidence for this theory.

What is the path taken by olfactory information on its way to the brain?

Solution: The olfactory system sends the brain information about odors and fragrances it senses. Actually, what stimulates the sense of smell are small particles called molecules, which enter the nostrils. Once inside, these molecules may touch special long hair cells. These cells translate the physical stimulus of the molecules into electrical information which the brain interprets. These cells relay this information to the brain in the following way.

Olfactory information leaves our nose through bundles of the above mentioned long hair cells. These bundles travel to a brain center called the olfactory bulb. The olfactory bulb is located at the base of the brain. From here, olfactory information travels directly to the part of the cortex that deals with smell. Thus we see that this is one of the simplest of our systems. It is difficult to study, though. This is because the cells which are important are practically inaccessible.

What are three factors that influence our olfactory experience?

Solution: We can easily compile lists of substances which have distinctive smells. For example, many flowers have a specific smell. Also, the odor of garbage is unmistakable. However, we do not yet understand how it is that we can differentiate between these odors. Some factors which are probably involved in 'smell' are: quality, concentration, and rate of flow of the stimulus.

It is thought that every substance has a particular quality which determines its smell. For example, every substance is composed of tiny particles called molecules. The molecules of each substance have a distinctive shape. The shape of the molecules of a substance can be considered a quality of the substance. This quality may be important in determining its smell.

The concentration of a stimulus is also important in determining smell. If ten cans of Lysol were released into one room, the smell would probably be very intense and unpleasant. However, if only a small amount was released, the smell experience would be quite different. The former room was more concentrated with Lysol. This means there was much more Lysol in the same amount of space. So we see that concentration of the stimulus influences olfactory experience.

A third factor involved in 'smell' is the rate of flow of the stimulus. The stimuli for smell are thought to be the gas molecules of the particular substance. Gaseous substances can move, or flow. For example, the wind can be

thought of as simply flowing air. If the molecules of a
stimulus are flowing quickly, the smell will appear strong.
If the molecules are not moving that rapidly, the smell will
seem weaker. Thus, the rate of flow of a stimulus also affects our olfactory experience.

GUSTATION

● **PROBLEM** 8-27

What are the four basic tastes? Where are receptors for
these located?

Solution: Our body responds only to four basic tastes --
sweetness, sourness, saltiness, and bitterness. The cells
which transmit information about these tastes to our brain
are located mainly on our tongue. However, there are some
taste receptors in our throat, also. In addition, the soft
part of the roof of our mouth contains some receptors for
taste.

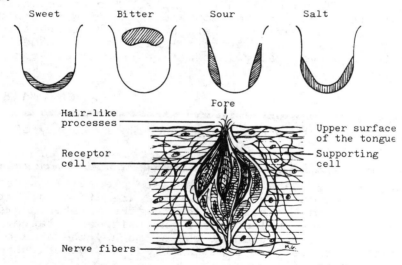

The distribution on the surface of the tongue of taste buds
sensitive to sweet, bitter, sour, and salt. Below, cells of
a taste bud in the epithelium of the tongue.

The taste receptors located on our tongue are organized
in a specific way. Receptors for sweetness are located on
the front of our tongue. Receptors for sourness are on our
tongue's sides. The cells which respond to bitterness are
concentrated in the back part of our tongue. In contrast,
receptors for saltiness range from the sides to the front,
mixed in among the other tastes. Saltiness receptors, however, are slightly more numerous in the front than on the
sides.

● **PROBLEM** 8-28

Summarize what is known about sensory transduction for taste.

Solution: Sensory transduction is the process whereby a physical stimulus from the environment is translated into an electrical message which our brain can interpret or understand. Normally the physical stimuli for our experience of taste are chemical substances such as foods or drinks. Relatively little is known about how these chemical stimuli are converted into electrical messages.

When food is taken into the mouth, it is mixed with the liquid present in the mouth, called saliva. The solution that forms may then flow into one of the many tiny 'holes' in one's tongue called taste pores. Each pore contains slender, hairlike structures. These hairs are part of cells called taste buds, located underneath the taste pore. Taste buds cluster together, forming tiny bumps on your tongue. These bumps are called papillae. The taste buds are the receptor cells for taste.

As a food solution flows into a taste pore, the hairs of the taste buds are stimulated. This somehow causes an electric event to occur. Nerve cells are located at the base of the taste buds. The electric event produced by the taste buds activates these nerve cells. The nerve cells then send electrical information about the original food solution along to the brain. There are three different nerves used to carry taste information to the brain. In addition some of these nerves carry information from other senses, such as touch.

● **PROBLEM** 8-29

What are three factors that influence the intensity of a taste? Explain.

Solution: We say that some foods taste pleasantly sweet; other foods are too sweet. Thus there are different intensities of sweetness. This applies to other tastes as well. Three major factors influence the intensity of a taste. These are the concentration of the stimulus, the area of the tongue's surface that is stimulated, and other tastes present at the same time.

A glass of salt and water which contains only a pinch of salt will not taste very salty. However, one which contains much salt will taste quite salty. The second glass contains a more 'concentrated' mixture. This means it contains more salt in the same amount of liquid. The above salt solutions show that concentration affects the intensity of a taste. The higher the concentration, generally, the more intense is the taste experienced.

Another variable factor is the amount of tongue that is in contact with the stimulus. This can also affect the intensity of a taste. In general, the larger the area of tongue that is stimulated, the more intense is the taste.

In addition, a process called 'contrast' can affect taste intensity. Two different parts of the tongue may be

stimulated by two different tastes at the same time. For
example, one can put a weak sugar and water mixture on one
side of one's tongue, and a weak salt water mixture on the
other. You will find that the salt mixture tastes more intense than it normally would. That is, if the sugar mixture
were not there, the salt mixture would not have tasted as
salty. We see that we can increase the sensitivity to taste
of part of our tongue. This can be done by stimulating another part of our tongue with a different taste. The above
process is called 'contrast.'

● **PROBLEM** 8-30

Certain connoisseurs can recognize hundreds of varieties
of wine by tasting small samples. How is this possible
when there are only four types of taste receptors?

Solution: Taste buds on the tongue and the soft
palate are the organs of taste in human beings. Each
taste bud contains supportive cells as well as epithelial
cells which function as receptors. These epithelial
cells have numerous microvilli that are exposed on the
tongue surface. Each receptor is innervated by one or
more neurons, and when a receptor is excited, it generates impulses in the neurons. There are four basic
taste senses: sweet, sour, bitter, and salty. The
receptors for each of these four basic tastes are concentrated in different regions of the tongue-sweet and
saltly on the front, bitter on the back, and sour on
the sides (see Figure). The sensitivity of these four
regions on the tongue to the four different tastes can
be demonstrated by placing solutions with various tastes
on each region. A dry tongue is insensitive to taste.

        Few substances stimulate only one of the four
kinds of receptors, but most stimulate two or more types
in varying degrees. The common taste sensations we experience daily are created by combinations of the four
basic tastes in different relative intensities. Moreover,
taste does not depend on the perception of the receptors
in the taste buds alone. Olfaction plays an important
role in the sense of taste. Together they help us
distinguish an enormous number of different tastes. We
can now understand how a connoisseur, using a combination
of his taste buds and his sense of smell, can recognize
hundreds of varieties of wine.

● **PROBLEM** 8-31

What are some questions being researched concerning taste
today?

Solution: It appears that there are four basic tastes which
we respond to -- saltiness, sourness, sweetness, and bitterness. Taste researchers today are trying to determine what
the basic chemical component of each of these taste categories is. For example, they would like to learn what substance

281

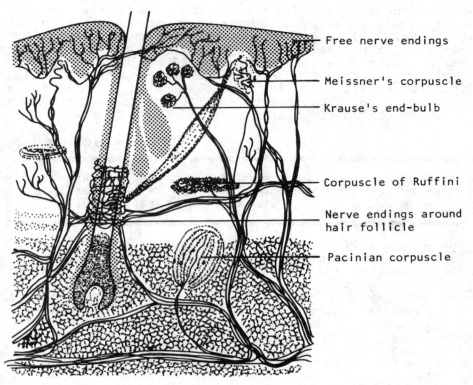

Free nerve endings

Meissner's corpuscle

Krause's end-bulb

Corpuscle of Ruffini

Nerve endings around
hair follicle

Pacinian corpuscle

The skin senses include touch, pressure, pain, cold, and warmth
(and perhaps itching and tickling). This drawing shows some of
the important sensory receptors. There is some specialization
among them: The Krause bulbs are most sensitive to cold;
Meissner's corpuscles, to touch; and Pacinian corpuscles, to
pressure. Free nerve endings are receptors for pain and any of
the other sensations.

is present in all 'sour' foods. This same substance should
not be found in any great quantity in any foods we do not
call 'sour.' This may then be the material (stimulus) to
which our taste receptors for sourness respond. In other
words, this substance may be responsible for the 'sour' taste
of certain foods. No such substance has yet been found for
any of the four tastes.

In addition, other questions are being investigated.
The receptor cells for taste are small hair cells. These
'hair cells' are clustered together in groups. The groups
form little bumps on the tongue called papillae. Researchers would like to know if each papilla is specialized for a
single taste or not. For example, one papilla may contain
only hair cells which respond to sourness. On the other
hand, each papilla may contain all four kinds of hair cells.
Still, they may all be different. For example, each papilla
may contain different amounts of each type of hair cell.

It seems that different parts of the tongue are centers
for different tastes. For example, the back of the tongue
appears to be specialized for bitterness. This provides
evidence for the theory that individual papillae respond to

single tastes only. However, contradictory evidence is also available. The answers have been slow in coming.

CUTANEOUS, EQUILIBRATORY, AND KINESTHETIC SENSES

● PROBLEM 8-32

What receptors are involved in the four skin senses? What stimulus does each receptor respond to?

Solution: Our skin is sensitive to cold, warmth, touch, and pain. These are considered the four skin senses. Psychologists are not certain that specific receptors in the skin correspond to specific skin senses. However, the following distinctions do appear fairly certain.

It seems that free nerve fibers located in the skin are responsible for our temperature sensations. The temperature of our skin is generally slightly lower than that of our blood. Free nerve fibers in the skin respond to changes in the difference between skin and blood temperature. For example, the temperature of our blood is roughly 38°C. The skin temperature of our forearm is usually 33°C. This is a 5° difference. If some ice is put on your arm, the temperature of your skin will be lowered. The difference between your skin and blood temperatures will be increased. The increase is what the free nerves respond to. You will then feel cold. It seems that there are specific nerve fibers responding to either heat or cold.

Pressure, or touch, is another of the skin senses. There are a number of different receptors in the skin that signal that we have been touched. The Meissner corpuscle is one such structure. It is located in the hairless regions of our body. It may be found, for example, in the palms of your hands. The basket nerve ending is located at roots of hairs. It is believed to respond to touch in those body regions that have hair. Finally, small capsules called Pacinian corpuscles are thought to respond when deep pressure is applied to the skin.

The stimulus that the above pressure receptors respond to is the bending or deforming of part of our skin. Therefore, when one first puts a watch on, you feel it. Immediately after, though, you "forget" that it is there. The initial bending of the skin that the watch caused was relayed to your brain by one of the pressure receptors. Therefore, you felt it. However, once the watch is on, your skin remains in the same place. It is no longer being actively bent. The pressure receptors do not respond to this constant pressure. Therefore, you do not feel that you are constantly being 'touched' by your watch.

Pain is the last of the skin senses. It appears that unspecialized free nerve endings in the skin respond to pain. Scientists are not certain exactly what stimulus is needed in order for us to feel pain. It was first thought that

damage to a part of the body causes pain. This is not entirely true. We know that as parts of our body are destroyed,
the body repairs them as quickly as it can. It appears,
then, that we feel pain when our body is damaged faster than
it can be repaired. Thus the 'rate' of body damage, rather
than the 'amount' of body damage, is thought to be the stimulus for sensations of pain.

● **PROBLEM** 8-33

What are the vestibular organs, and how do they operate?

Solution: Our vestibular sense provides us with a sense of
balance. It does this through information about the movements and position of our head. There are two groups of
vestibular organs. These are the semicircular canals and
the otolith organs.

There are three semicircular canals. They are located
in the inner part of our ear. Each one lies in a different
plane. That is, if they were lying on this paper, one canal
would run from top to bottom. Another would run across the
paper. The third canal would run through the paper and out
the back of this book.

The canals are filled with fluid. When our head is rotated, this fluid moves. Which fluid moves depends upon the
particular head motion we make. For instance, we can move
our head up and down. In this case, the fluid in the canal
that is oriented up and down will move. When this fluid
moves, it puts pressure on special cells with hairs that are
located in the canals. These hair cells send information
about our head's movements to the brain.

The canals do not respond to continuous movement. Rather,
the hair cells in the canals respond only to changes in the
rate of motion of the head. Thus when a dancer is spinning,
the semicircular organs are stimulated only when he/she
speeds up or slows down.

The otolith organs are small stonelike crystals. They
are also located in the inner part of our ear. Unlike the
semicircular canals, the otoliths do not respond to movements. Rather, they respond to the actual position of one's
head. If your head is upright, gravity stimulates the otolith crystals in a certain way. They then send this information to the brain. The brain interprets this message and
concludes that the head is upright.

Together, the semicircular canals and the otolith organs
provide one with a sense of balance. You know that you in-
stinctively straighten up when thrown off balance. This
could not be done without the information provided by the
vestibular organs.

● **PROBLEM** 8-34

A person seated on a swivel chair is rotated rapidly. The
rotation is suddenly stopped and the person is told to stand

up. He complains that he feels dizzy. How can you account
for his dizziness?

Solution: The labyrinth of the inner ear has three semicircular canals, each consisting of a semicircular tube connected at both ends to the utricle. Each canal lies in a plane
perpendicular to the other two. At the base of each canal,
where it leads into the utriculus, is a bulb-like enlargement
(the ampulla) containing tufts of hair cells similar to those
in the utriculus and sacculus, but lacking otoliths. These
cells are stimulated by movements of the fluid (endolymph) in

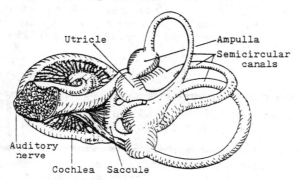

The right semicircular canals and cochlea of
an adult man, shown dissected free of surrounding
bone and seen from the inner and posterior side.

the canals. When a person's head is rotated, there is a lag
in the movement of the endolymph in the canals. Thus, the
hair cells in the ampulla attached to the head rotate, in effect, in relation to the fluid. This movement of the hair
cells with respect to the endolymph stimulates the former to
send impulses to the cerebellum of the brain. There, these
impulses are interpreted and a sensation of dizziness is
felt.

● **PROBLEM** 8-35

When we hold our head upright, there is very little problem
keeping our balance. Yet when our head is turned upside
down, as in a headstand, we still manage to maintain our
equilibrium. How is balance achieved in the latter case?
Discuss your answer in relation to the ear.

Solution: In the inner ear, there are two small, hollow
sacs known as the utriculus and sacculus. Each sac is lined
with sensitive hair cells, upon which rest small crystals of
calcium carbonate (otoliths). Normally when the head is upright, the pull of gravity causes the otoliths to press a-
gainst particular hair cells, stimulating them to initiate
impulses to the brain via sensory nerve fibers at their bases.
Changes in the position of the head cause these crystals to
fall on and stimulate some other hair cells, thereby giving
the brain a different set of signals. The relative strength
of the signals to the brain indicates the position of the
head at any given moment.

When a head stand is being done, the otoliths in the utriculus and sacculus are reoriented by gravity and come to rest on other hair cells. These hair cells are stimulated and send impulses to our brain, informing us that now our head is in a new position. The brain will then transmit the appropriate response to the effectors so that we can maintain our balance even when our head is upside down.

It is important to realize that equilibrium in humans depends upon the sense of vision, stimuli from the proprioceptors, and stimuli from cells sensitive to pressure in the soles of the feet in addition to the stimuli from the organs in the inner ear. This is why in certain types of deafness, in which the cochlea as well as the equilibrium organs of the inner ear are impaired, the sense of equilibrium is still present.

● **PROBLEM** 8-36

What are the receptors for our kinesthetic sense? What specific stimulus does each respond to?

Solution: Our kinesthetic sense gives us information about the positions of the parts of our body. Thus it is important in all movements. A person lacking this sense can still walk. However, he must carefully watch what his legs are doing and where they are, at any and every given time. He cannot 'sense' this. We receive kinesthetic information from nerves that serve muscle spindles, Golgi tendon organs, and possibly, Pacinian corpuscles.

There are free nerve endings surrounding small, specialized muscle fibers called muscle spindles. When a muscle is stretched, these nerves are activated. They then send information about that muscle's activity to the brain. The brain uses this information to determine the position of the part of the body that that muscle is moving.

Our muscles are usually connected to bones. This is how they can move limbs. The fibers which connect muscles to bones, are called tendons. There are special structures in tendons called Golgi tendon organs. This organ has nerve fibers associated with it. When a muscle contracts, tension is put on the tendons. This stimulates the nerve fibers associated with the Golgi tendon organ. They then relay information about the muscle to our brain. The brain again uses this information to determine the relative position of the limbs.

Bones are also connected to one another. The place where two bones connect is called a joint. There are kinesthetic receptors located in the linings of joints. These receptors are believed to be small capsules called Pacinian corpuscles. These can respond to movement. For example, suppose that your lower arm moves. Then, the relative positions of the bones in your upper and lower arms change. This activates Pacinian corpuscles in the joint (elbow). These then relay information about your movements and position to the brain.

SHORT ANSWER QUESTIONS FOR REVIEW

Choose the correct answer.

1. Form vision is most acute in the (a) fovea
    (b) periphery (c) lens (d) cornea   a

2. The "break" in the early part of the dark adap-
    tion curve suggests most nearly that (a) cone
    thresholds are unaffected by a reduction in
    brightness (b) cone thresholds increase in the
    dark (c) rod thresholds have just begun to de-
    crease (d) all of the above   c

3. Dark adaption (a) increases brightness sensitiv-
    ity (b) occurs, paradoxically, in the light
    (c) develops color perception (d) raises the
    visual threshold   a

4. The sensitivity of the eye to light varies with
    (a) wavelength (b) the eye's state of adapta-
    tion (c) the region of the retina stimulated
    (d) all of the above   d

5. Experiments that have been able to restrict a
    specific visual input to a specific location on
    a retina have found (a) increased stimulus
    clarity (b) slight, but not total, fading
    (c) gradual and complete fading (d) partial
    Ganzfeld   c

6. Skin mapping shows that spots of greatest sensi-
    tivity for heat and cold are in (a) different
    places (b) the same place (c) alternating
    locations (d) equidistant from each other   a

7. The two-point threshold is (a) the minimum
    distance between two stimuli necessary for the
    perception of two distinct stimuli (b) the
    minimum elapsed time between two stimuli neces-
    sary for the perception of two distinct stimuli
    (c) the maximum duration a pressure stimulus
    will be perceived when the pressure is at its
    absolute threshold (d) none of the above   a

8. A total number of senses possessed by the normal
    human (a) is known to be five (b) is usually
    taken as the number of different kinds of sense
    receptors (c) is equal to the number of sensory
    trunks in the cortex (d) is not accurately
    characterized in any of these ways   d

9. In perceiving the distance of a sound, a person
    must depend heavily upon (a) complexity and
    resonance (b) dystonia (c) loudness and
    timbre (d) beats   c

287

SHORT ANSWER QUESTIONS FOR REVIEW

10. Sound amplitude is measured on a (a) decibel scale (b) scale of sound volume (c) mel scale (d) none of the above

    a

11. If all frequencies in the sound spectrum are in-volved, the result is (a) a hissing sound with no discriminable form (b) pulsed sounds (c) white noise (d) A and C

    d

12. Auditory J.N.D.'s vary by (a) frequency of tones used (b) intensity of tones used (c) both of these (d) neither of these

    c

13. The term low threshold refers to (a) very low decibel level (b) low level of sensitivity to an incoming stimulus (c) high level of sensi-tivity to an incoming stimulus (d) virtual loss of any sensitivity to an incoming stimulus

    c

14. The illuminance falling on a surface is (a) inversely proportional to the square of the dis-tance from the source to the surface (b) di-rectly proportional to the square of the distance from the source to the surface (c) the natural logarithm of the square of the distance from the source to the surface (d) none of the above

    a

15. Inability to monitor the movements of one's feet and the absence of feedback regarding their posi-tion and relationship to the ground would suggest problems with the (a) labyrinthine sensory sys-tem (b) kinesthetic sensory system (c) vis-ceral sensory system (d) peripheral sensory system

    b

16. Motion sickness (a) is an effect of vestibular stimulation (b) is reduced if the position of the head is fixed relative to the body (c) is not affected by visual illusions of movement, un-pleasant odors or uncomfortable warmth (d) A and B

    d

17. The proprioceptive senses are (a) hidden away in muscles, joints and tendons (b) the kines-thetic sense and vestibular sense (c) A and B (d) neither A nor B

    c

18. The measurements of the sensitivity of smell is not as precise as with vision and hearing because (a) the smell receptors are recessed away from the main path of air through the nasal passages (b) sniffs vary (c) both A and B (d) neither A nor B

    c

288

SHORT ANSWER QUESTIONS FOR REVIEW

19. For the experience of taste to occur, a substance
    must be (a) at least slightly soluble in water
    (b) in contact with receptors located in the
    center of the tongue (c) highly soluble in but-
    ric acid (d) A and B

    a

Fill in the blanks.

20. The primary determinant of hue is _____ .

    wavelength

21. Pigment mixing differs from light mixing in that
    it involves _____ .

    absorption

22. The variation in lens thickness to bring an im-
    age into focus on the retina is _____ .

    accommoda-
    tion

23. The primaries in subtractive color mixing are
    yellow, red and _____ .

    blue

24. A person with a complete lack of cones in the
    retina is a _____ .

    monochro-
    mat

25. The sensation of pain may be invoked by many
    kinds of stimulation. The theory that hypothe-
    sizes that pain is produced by overstimulation
    of any cutaneous receptor is the _____ theory.

    pattern

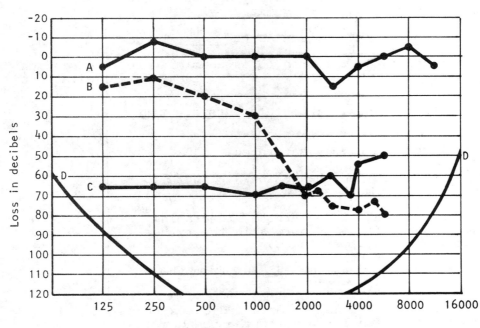

289

SHORT ANSWER QUESTIONS FOR REVIEW

26. Pitch is determined by _____ .

frequency

27. The _____ theory of audition is best suited to explain hearing in the low frequency range.

frequency

28. The overtone accompanying a fundamental tone determines its _____ .

timbre

29. The following is the description of a(n) _____ : an important instrument for studying deafness which consists of a tone generator providing pure tones and which, for each test frequency, reads out the intensity necessary for it to be audible as compared with previously established standards.

audiometer

30. Curve B is the audiogram of a person with _____ deafness.

nerve

31. Curve C is the audiogram of a person with _____ deafness.

conduction

32. In the audiogram, which curve of hearing loss could very likely be gotten from someone over 80 years old!

B

33. In signal detection theory, the measure which indexes the subject's sensitivity and which excludes response bias is symbolized by _____ .

d'

34. Otoliths provide information about _____

tilt

35. Receptors generally referred to as chemical are _____ and _____ .

gustation
olfaction

Determine whether the following statements are true or false.

36. Pastel shades are highly saturated.

False

37. Purkinje shift is the change in wavelength to which the eye is most sensitive.

True

38. One of the commonly demonstrated effects in strong support of the trichromatic theory has been the negative after image.

True

39. The rods are most dense at 15°-20° from the fovea.

True

40. The visual acuity score of 20/10 indicates that a viewer has vision inferior to the standard average subject.

False

SHORT ANSWER QUESTIONS FOR REVIEW

41. A figure frequently used in measurements of visual acuity is the Landott ring.

True

42. The eye is sensitive to wavelength of electro-magnetic radiation ranging from about 400 to 700 millimicrons.

True

43. Pressure, pain, cold and heat are all cutaneous senses.

False

44. The capacity for detecting the direction of in-coming sound is possible only when hearing exists in both ears.

True

45. Auditory receptor cells are located in the coch-lea.

True

46. The 'piano' theory holds that specific nerve fi-bers respond to specific decibel ranges.

False

47. The standard unit for signifying the luminous intensity of a point source of light is the lu-men.

False

48. According to magnitude estimation procedures, the psychophysical relation is exponential.

True

49. The vestibular organs are in the eustachian tube.

False

50. The taste primaries are bitter, sour, bland and salt.

False

CHAPTER 9

PERCEPTION

BASIC PRINCIPLES

● **PROBLEM** 9-1

Differentiate between sensation and perception.

Solution: The major senses of the human organism include seeing, hearing, taste, smell, touch (includes warmth, cold, pain, dryness, wetness, etc.), position, motion, and equilibrium. For each sense we have a sense organ that is affected by a particular type of physical energy. The ear, for instance, is responsive to sound waves. Within each sensory realm there are a number of qualities which recur in varying combinations, such as with the sense of hearing--loud, soft, shrill, resonant,humming, screeching, to name just a few of the qualities that can be discerned by the human ear. The different experiences that we are able to discern within each sensory realm are called "sensations." The sensations are of a tremendous variety, but can all be reduced to a few basic physical variables. Though the eye can see thousands of different scenes, they are all produced by light; though the ear can hear sounds from a siren to a symphony, they are all produced by differing intensity and frequency vibration of sound waves.

Sensations provide us with basic elementary experiences which we further interpret into meaningful events. This interpretation of sensations is a much more complex process than simply registering and reflecting the external world. It involves encoding, storage (memory), and organization of the sensations that are received. It is this process that is called "perception." A very general characteristic of all perceptual experience is to attend to and organize selectively the data that is provided by the sensory system. Precisely how this is accomplished has intrigued scientists, and their research and experimentation has provided an abundant theoretical basis from which the student can explore the mysteries of how we construct our sense-based reality. The problem of explaining how and why we perceive the way we do is one of the most controversial fields in psychology today.

What is the classical explanation of the relationship between stimulation (sensation) and experience (perception)? How has recent research altered the classical view?

Solution: For many years, each type of sensory experience was thought to have particular "receptors" which were most sensitive to certain types of physical energy. At the back of the eye were receptors to respond to light, the ear contained receptors of sound energy, while the skin was thought to be covered with pressure receptors. When a receptor was stimulated it in turn stimulated other nerve cells deeper in the nervous system which in turn stimulated the appropriate "projection area" of the brain.

The process of perception usually occurs so rapidly that it has been difficult to be aware of the complexity of the process and to further examine this classical explanation. Because the mechanisms of a system are often revealed primarily through its errors and distortions, various methods have been devised to study the nature of the perceptual process, mainly through 1) presenting images that are quite difficult to interpret or 2) presenting conflicting images or 3) dealing with images that have no meaning. This research has uncovered information that significantly alters the classical explanation.

Traditionally, the response of the receptors to the sensory input was called "specific nerve energy" because each receptor was thought to act differently from all others. Now, however, it is known that the message we receive depends on the area of the brain that is stimulated rather than on what specific nerve cell brings the message. The receptor cell, rather than responding to the particular physical energy, responds to the information the energy provides which stimulates it to further stimulate a particular area of the brain. This stimulation combines with a memory system containing a record of past experiences which includes the data needed to interpret the signals that have arrived at the brain. The interaction of sensory signals interpreted by the appropriate memory data then produces a subjective perceptual experience.

If you rub your eyes long and hard enough, you would eventually see some type of visual pattern. Explain this phenomenon.

Solution: Most of us who have not had the opportunity to study human psychology or physiology when asked to explain our perceptual processes describe our senses as true reflections of the world around us--the eye might be compared to a camera, the ear to a tape recorder. The senses would be thought to act as recording devices that bring the outside world intact inside for processing and examination. This, however, to the student of the human organism, is a naive understanding. In fact, the sense organs are set to respond to only certain types of physical stimulation which in turn produce the experiences we associate with each of the senses. We perceive only what affects our senses; what does not affect our senses we do not perceive. Thus, there are many aspects of the world around us that exist though we cannot perceive them. Radio waves are an example of a physical property that human organisms cannot perceive.

Interestingly, it is not the nature of the external stimulus so much that determines the perceptual experience we have as it is the area of the brain that is stimulated by any particular sensation. The experience, available to anyone, of rubbing one's closed eyes and producing varieties of light patterns demonstrates the preceding principle. These "pressure phosphenes" are produced even though no light energy has come into the eye. The pressure exerted on the eye stimulates the receptor nerve cells at the back of the retina, which normally respond to light, and their response to this pressure, when communicated to the visual area of the brain, produce the experience of light. An electrical current applied to the eye will produce the same sensation. Also the perception of light can be produced simply by stimulating the appropriate area of the brain with no other sensory basis. In short, we do not experience objects directly. We do not see the image on the retina nor the excitation of a particular nerve within the eye. It cannot even be stated with certainty that we see the final imprint on the visual area of the cerebral cortex. We "see" what our sensory system receives, whether it is a reflection of the world as we normally know it or not.

● **PROBLEM** 9-4

The eye functions very much like a camera. Comment on this assertion.

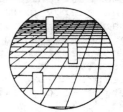

Texture gradients

Solution: As far back as 1600, Johannes Kepler compared the eye to a camera (though at that time he wrote about a darkened chamber with an image in focus on its rear surface). Descartes elaborated on this analogy, and since the 17th century the eye has been compared extensively to the camera. As soon as this model is investigated in depth its difficulties become obvious, yet, it did dominate psychology for many years as a reasonable explanation of visual processes. The idea was that the retina acted as a kind of picture film on which accurate representations of the external world were recorded and stored in the form of memory images for later use.

The fact is that one does not see what is registered on

the retinal image. Retinal images are subject to every small change of position; at every moment the size, shape, and location of external objects is changing on the retina. Yet, our perception of the world is relatively constant. External objects appear rigid, fixed, and stably located in three-dimensional space. Perception and memory are not simply copying processes. It appears that an incoming pattern of light falls on the nervous system in such a way as to provide information to which it is adapted to respond. This information is used to establish orientation in space and for the construction of internal images of external objects.

Recent research seems to indicate that the world we see consists mainly of surfaces (which often appear as "lines") at various angles to each other. A most important aspect of these surfaces is their surface texture. These textures structure the light in such a way that it carries important information to the nervous system about the arrangement of the perceived space. For instance, more distant surfaces are represented more closely together than nearer objects. Consider the example of looking at a highway while driving down it. The highway can most simply be seen, represented as two lines which are perceived as becoming closer and closer as the distance from the car increases. Thus a "gradient of density" falling on the retina informs the subject about the distance of the perceived surface.

The nervous system now appears to play an active role in the reception of light energy rather than the passive recording role it was thought to play when its action was modeled after a camera. In perceiving, complex patterns are taken from the retina and interact with the mental processes of the perceiver so that the inner experience and the external environment are in good correspondence. Rather than windows on the external world the eyes are entry points for a certain quality of information that helps the human organism orient itself to the three dimensional world of space and time.

• PROBLEM 9-5

Color vision is an enigma. Discuss the Young-Helmholtz theory of cone receptors and the opponent-process color theory.

Solution: Isaac Newton can be credited with being the father of modern color theories. His observations with white light falling on a prism that separates the different wavelengths that comprise white light to produce the full spectrum of color (red-orange-yellow-green-blue-indigo-violet) led to the theory that color depends upon the wavelength of the light that strikes the eye. A prism separates out the different wavelengths and arranges them from long to short. Careful examination of this theory has shown that it is too simple to fully explain color vision. For example, there are a number of colors that do not appear in the spectrum, like pink or brown. Also once two wavelengths of light combine, we no longer see the two colors, rather we see a new color, and it is quite impossible for our eye to separate out the colors that went into the production of the new color. A

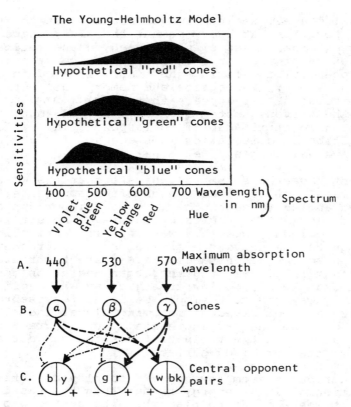

The Young-Helmholtz Model

combination of red and green, for example, produce yellow.
Once we see yellow, we cannot pick out the red and green
wavelengths that combined to produce it.

These facts led to the development of the Young-Helmholtz
theory of primary colors in the mid-nineteenth century. This
theory was widely accepted as an explanation of color vision
for many years. It assumes that there are three kinds of
cones (color sensitive receptors) in the eye, each sensitive
to one part of the spectrum which when stimulated would produce the sensation of one of the three "primary" colors. The
three colors thought to be primary were: red, green and blue.
All other colors were thought to be combinations of these
three. Curiously, when viewed through the prism, these three
colors do not appear pure. The red has an orange tint, the
green, yellow, and the blue, red. It has also been shown
that yellow can be detected in regions of the eye that cannot
perceive red or green. And subjects that are color blind to
red and green can still see yellow.

As early as 1878, Ewald Hering had proposed an opponent-
process theory. In 1955 Hurvich and Jameson extended Hering's
theory and explained color vision from another perspective. In
this system, colors are mixed in complementary pairs: blue
with yellow, red with green and black with white. The judgment of brightness is based on the response of the black-white
mechanism. Colors result from combining blue-yellow and red-
green. While this theory accounts for the facts of color
mixture, for most color-vision defects, for the appearance of
"purity" in color, and for after-images, it has not yet been

substantiated and the mechanism that underlies the color combination process is not yet known. It is a promising theory that hopefully will be tested by physiological investigations in the years to come.

● **PROBLEM** 9-6

Discuss the three attributes of color. Why do red and pink appear to be different colors?

Solution: Our visual system is sensitive to patches of light. We distinguish between different visual impressions generally by three different characteristics: hue, brightness and saturation.

The wavelength of the light determines which "hue" we will perceive. Hue is the generic term that is now applied to what are commonly called colors. Red, orange, yellow, green, blue, indigo, and violet are the basic hues of the spectrum produced by different wavelengths.

When a single wavelength of light is perceived, the hue appears pure or "saturated." As other wavelengths are added, the hue becomes distilled and appears grayer or less saturated. A mixture of wavelengths in which all the wavelengths were equally strong would appear gray. A deep red is a highly saturated red; whereas a pink is a desaturated red. Saturation produces a "red red" or a "green green."

As the intensity of the light increases the light will appear brighter. Brightness is an aspect of both color (chromatic) and black and white (achromatic) vision. Being hueless, blacks and whites do not differ qualitatively but only in their brightness value. The brightness that we perceive is greatly dependent not only on the energy value of the light intensity but on the state of adaptation of the eye (is the pupil contracted for brightness or enlarged for darkness?) Also brightness varies according to wavelength for a given intensity of light. And conversely, the hue and saturation change somewhat if the brightness is altered.

● **PROBLEM** 9-7

Explain the interaction of intensity and frequency in the perception of loudness and pitch.

Solution: A sound's loudness depends on both its intensity and its frequency. The pressure developed in a sound wave leads to an index of the sound intensity. This intensity is commonly measured in decibels. Sounds are measured on a scale from zero for the average least perceptible sound to about 130 for the average pain level. Some representative sounds have the following decibel (dB) values:

pneumatic drill	125	dB
city traffic	90	dB
conversation	60	dB
whispering	20	dB

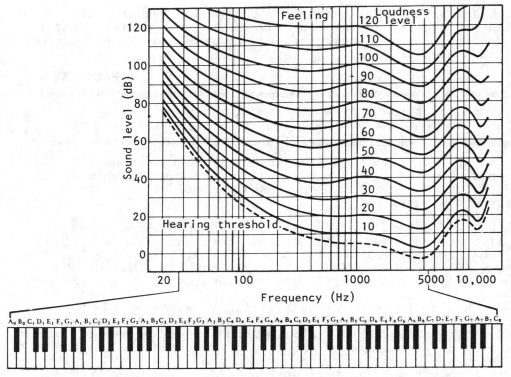

Equiloudness contours from data of Robinson and Dadson (1956).

Frequency is a measure of the number of sound waves per second. The term Herz (Hz) is used for cycles per second of sound vibration frequency.

Sounds originate in the mechanical virbration of objects like piano cords or diaphragms in loudspeakers or vocal cords. These vibrations set up disturbances in the nearby air that are carried through the air as waves. These waves of pressure, called sound waves, are transmitted in the mechanical action of the air molecules which beat repetitively on the ear drum stimulating the receptor cells that produce hearing.

Every sound we hear has some degree of loudness. The principal determinant of loudness is the intensity or sound pressure level of the stimulus. When frequency is constant, intense sounds appear louder than weak sounds. Loudness is determined by the amount of physical movement caused on the moving parts of the ear. The greater the movement, the more the auditory nerve is stimulated and neural impulses are initiated with corresponding vigor.

Pitch is the aspect of sound that is determined mainly by the frequency of the sound waves. Low pitch results from low frequency stimulation and high pitch from high vibration frequency. Though it appears that loudness is due mainly to intensity and pitch mainly to frequency, research has demonstrated that the two attributes of the hearing experience are often dependent on one another. For example when a 8000 Hz tone is raised about 40 dB in intensity, it will be heard as

298

becoming considerably higher in pitch. The change is so great
that it requires a decrease of almost 15% in frequency for the
tone to sound as though it has the same pitch when it is so
intensified. Loudness changes markedly with changes in frequency. Tones between 1000 and 5000 Hz sound the loudest for
a given intensity level. An intensity level that makes a
100 Hz tone barely audible, for example, will be about 40 dB
above sound threshold level for a 2000 Hz tone.

● **PROBLEM** 9-8

Discuss the cues that are necessary to localize a sound source.

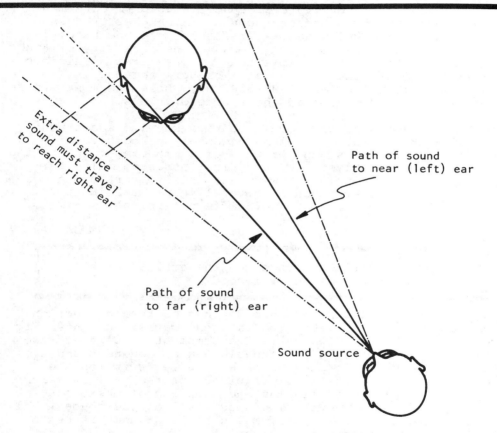

Solution: Though we have two ears, we hear but one acoustical
world. It is through information from both ears (biaural)
rather than one ear (monaural) that we are able to determine
the source, or localize, a sound. Because we take our ability to localize sounds for granted it is difficult to appreciate how much it adds to our auditory experience. Modern
stereophonic equipment makes it possible to have some idea
of how much is added to our sound experience by having sound
localization. If the set is turned from monaural to stereophonic and back again, the difference in the quality of the
sound can be clearly detected. Stereophonic reproduction
allows sounds to be perceived as originating from different
origins and also gives a richer texture of the sound (the
tones become more distinct).

The main cues used to locate the source of a sound are the time and intensity that a tone arrives at each ear. Sounds arrive first at the ear that is closest. The sound also has greater intensity for that ear. The head acts as a kind of shield between the source of the sound and the "second" ear. It has been calculated that the maximum time required for a sound to travel from one ear around the head to the other ear is 840 msec. That, of course, would be for a sound coming from a source located directly to one side of the head. A sound coming from straight ahead would reach both ears at the same time. Time difference cues are mainly used for sounds of low frequency. Sounds of high frequency produce ambiguous time lag cues due to their speed, and the additional cue of intensity difference is used to determine the source of higher intensity sounds. At higher frequencies the shorter sound waves are reflected off the head, thus creating a sound "shadow" whereby the intensity of the sound at the second ear is less than at the first. This cue is used for localizing a sound of a higher frequency. There is a range of frequencies, 1000-5000 Hz, where the most errors are made in the detection of the source of the sound.

Though there is now a small body of knowledge accruing concerning the neural mechanisms necessary to compare signals from the two ears, the problem of explaining localization is far from being solved. We are, for instance, quite far from being able to explain how we are able to sort out a complicated sound pattern such as several people talking at a party and localize the source of different voices.

● **PROBLEM** 9-9

Why is it so difficult to reproduce the quality of a live musical performance on tape or record?

Solution: How we perceive sound depends on the interaction of frequency (rate of vibration of sound waves) and intensity (pressure of the sound waves). The combination of these two aspects of sound produce the experiences of loudness and pitch. A conductor leading an orchestra leads it for the intensities or loudness level required for the hall in which it is performing. When playing back a piece of music at home it is unlikely that the loudness level of the concert hall will be recreated. Therefore, music heard at home is heard at different "loudness contour levels."

Because the intensity is less when music is played back, some of the frequencies that were perfectly audible at the concert, particularly those of a lower level, will fall below the threshold of hearing and will not be heard. Also, as the levels change, the relative loudness at different frequencies changes too. If a piano plays a scale at very high intensity going from high to low notes, in the concert hall all the notes will appear to have the same loudness since at high intensity levels sounds are heard as equally loud. At home when the scale is played back, however, the notes would appear to get louder and louder up to about two or three octaves above middle C, where they would begin to decrease in loudness.

Thus, the main cause of the difficulty of good repro-
ductions lies in the interaction of frequency and intensity.
To receive a true reproduction of a live performance, the
intensity level would have to be the same as it was for the
original performance. Many stereo receivers now have a
"loudness contour" control which increases the relative intensities of both the low frequency and the high frequency
ends of the scale. The effect is to more nearly recreate
the intended "frequency balance" without increasing the overall loudness of the reproduction.

● **PROBLEM** 9-10

How does an individual's perceptual system react to a lack of
sensory input? Discuss the sensory deprivation experiments
and their implications for understanding the nature of the
human nervous system.

Solution: At McGill University in 1959, students were given
the opportunity to participate in a seemingly highly attractive experiment: they were going to be highly paid for doing
nothing. The job they were paid to do was to remain in a
small, bare room with only a cot to lie on. The room was
continually lighted, but they wore goggles over their eyes
which kept them from seeing any patterns; they had cushions
over their ears to reduce sounds and their arms and legs were
wrapped to minimize tactile sensations. They were allowed to
leave the room only to go the bathroom.

These classic sensory deprivation experiments demonstrated that doing nothing, and having virtually no demands
made on the nervous system, was not pleasant as it sounds.
In fact, it turned out to be quite unpleasant. Most students
responded to this treatment initially by sleeping. Sleep
could not go on indefinitely, however, and during the next
phase of the experiment they began to seek stimulation of any
kind. Many subjects found that they began to hallucinate.
All reported that the situation was a negative experience.
Perhaps most telling was the fact that none could endure more
than 24 hours of sensory deprivation, though all had partially
volunteered to stay longer.

More recent sensory deprivation experiments have required
that subjects be suspended nude in a pool of water which is
kept at body temperature to minimize skin sensations, changes
in temperature, and gravitational forces. Subjects report
that they try to direct their attention to any stimulation
whatsoever to reduce the tedium of the experiment. Apparently,
the human nervous system requires a certain minimum amount of
stimulation to function, and certainly to maintain a healthy
mental state.

● **PROBLEM** 9-11

We know less about why certain stimuli are attractive to
humans than we do about what is attractive to fish. Discuss
this statement.

Solution: We do know that certain qualities in people and products are more attractive than others and that subjects usually agree about what is attractive or unattractive. Presently, our knowledge about the specific characteristics that determine attractiveness remains on the level of intuition. This intuition is widely used in advertising and the fashion industry to sell and promote products. Though we might not like to admit it, our own physical attractiveness influences our lives in many ways. Studies have shown that it is an advantage to be attractive: attractive females receive better grades than their unattractive classmates with the same I.Q.s; misbehaving children who are attractive have their misdeeds rated as less serious than the same behavior from less attractive children; attractive females are less likely to be convicted for crimes; attractive people are more likely to be liked by both attractive and unattractive people; and an attractive person is seen as being more likely to hold the same attitude that we do.

Given the importance of attractiveness, it is surprising that we know so little about it. It may be that we have certain innate tendencies to respond favorably to certain characteristics in others, which we label as "attractive." We do not know. We do know that certain animals respond to markings in other members of their species which indicate sex and age and that those markings are predictors of the behavior of those animals. Male fighting fish have, for instance, been trained to perform simple tasks to receive the reward of simply seeing another male fish, which it would normally attack. As yet, we have not isolated such predictive qualities in humans.

NATIVISM AND EMPIRICISM

● **PROBLEM 9-12**

Empiricists vs. nativists: discuss these two points of view and give evidence for both sides.

Solution: The nature of perception is still unclear. For many years perception was explained with a structural (the piecing together of different sensations) or empirical (based on experience) theory. The empiricists believed that perception consisted of individual sensations coming together in different combinations with memories of past sensational experiences. This theory assumes that we don't see shapes, distances or forms at all. We see only points of light arranged in various manners. Some of these arrangements have strong nonvisual memories associated with them which give us the ability to measure distance. Thus, the empiricist theory relies a great deal on learning as an explanation for our experience of the world. The perception of, let us say, a blue pillow would then be a learned experience whereby the mass of blue points of light would combine with the memory of past attempts to grasp or move toward a like object giving size and depth cues. Altogether the visual sensations on the retina and the memory of past muscular actions produce the final impression of the blue pillow.

Recent research has uncovered a number of discoveries that have challenged the empiricist position. Infants can, for example, perceive three dimensionality and distance as soon as they are able to locomote, even though we assume that they had no opportunity to learn such perceptual behavior. Also it is difficult to use the empiricist theory for explaining anything more than simple stimuli. More complex stimuli defy the empiricist explanation. For instance, shapes, colors, movements, as soon as they are examined in different contexts are perceived not as the structuralist explanation would expect, (i.e., points of light) but they are greatly influenced by the background on which they are perceived.

These observations tend to support another school of thought on the nature of perception. The "nativists," as the name implies, believe that human perception is innate. That through millions of years of adaptation, the human nervous system is now equippped with connections that make it automatic for an infant to perceive for example, three-dimensionality, given the correct visual cues. With the state of our knowledge today, it is not possible to determine which of these approaches to perception is most correct. It cannot be clearly demonstrated that perceptual learning occurs early in life and then resists further modification, nor can it be demonstrated that it is innate but subject to modification and new learning. Because of the difficulties involved in examining perceptual processes, especially with infants, it seems that a combination of the two explanations serves us best today. It is likely that we do have some innate perceptual abilities, and also that they can, to some extent, be modified by experience.

● **PROBLEM** 9-13

Discuss the visual cliff and its importance.

Fig. 1

Human infants and newborn animals refuse to go over the edge of the visual cliff.

Solution: For years human space perception has been explained by a "structuralist" approach. Logical elegant and

303

seemingly well supported by numerous experimental findings, this approach can be summarized as follows: the nonspatial visual sensations that contribute to the perception of far and near, left and right, and up and down combine with learned tactile and moving associations to give us the ability to perceive space and distance. Memories of handling various different sized objects and the memory of reaching for such objects at a particular distance combine with visual cues to give a good estimate of how far away an object is. In other words, space perception from the "structuralist" viewpoint is principally a learned phenomenon.

As convincing as this explanation has been, recent experiments have yielded results that present this theory with serious difficulties. The most serious problems from a structuralist perspective come from the results of experiments with infant humans and young animals. Chicks were raised in darkness and thus had no previously learned kinesthetic cues. Placed in a lighted area and placed on pedestals of different heights, the chicks were able to estimate accurately the jump down for each of the heights.

Human infants also seem to use visual depth cues as soon as they are able to move about. An ingenious experiment devised by Gibson and Walk tested this ability. Known as the "visual cliff" experiment, an infant is placed on a large sheet of glass under half of which checked linoleum has been placed (see figure 1). At the edge where the linoleum stops it appears that a sheer drop-off or cliff occurs. The infants avoid that apparent cliff. This experiment and others like it cannot prove that all space perception is innate, but have contributed to the loss of confidence in the earlier idea that space perception must be learned. It presently appears that in space perception, as in so many other areas of human experience, learning combines with innate predispositions to produce mature behavior patterns.

● **PROBLEM** 9-14

Describe the two major theories of perceptual development.

Solution: At present, there are two key theories that attempt to explain how a child develops the ability to distinguish differences among visual stimuli. The points of view of these theories are contradictory. While neither of them has been proven conclusively, there is evidence to support both.

According to one of these theories, children initially perceive parts of objects. That is, they first notice geometrical features of objects such as corners, curves, lines and also spots where lines meet at an angle or intersect in some way. According to Gibson (1969), as the child learns more and more of the distinctive features of objects, they eventually become compiled into a kind of "dictionary." The child sees every specific object as a unique combination of various features. To test this theory, Gibson presented children (ages 4 to 8) with a number of line drawings which resembled printed letters, but were essentially meaningless. Gibson found that errors in identification decreased from age

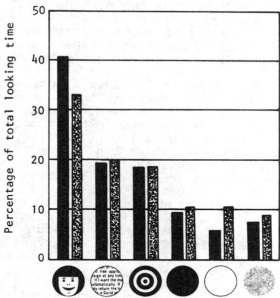

Pattern preference in infants

Importance of pattern rather than color or brightness is
illustrated by the response of infants to a face, a piece
of printed matter, a bull's eye, and plain red, white and
yellow disks. Even the youngest infants preferred patterns.
Black bars show the results for infants from 2 to 3 months
old, gray bars for infants more than 3 months old.

4 to age 8, and that the largest decline occurred in the 5
and 6-year-olds who were just beginning to learn to read. This
then would support the theory that children see objects first
in terms of their parts and that their perceptual ability then
develops as they learn to recognize more and more distinctive
features.

The other major theory of perceptual development in
children argues that a child initially perceives and recognizes "gestalts" or "wholes", and not simply the component
"parts" of the object. Only later on, with more experience,
does the child come to recognize the various parts. According
to Werner (1957), at the same time the child's perception
breaks wholes down into component parts, he is also reinte-
grating the parts into new kinds of perceptions. In these
new perceptions, the parts are separate yet related to the
wholes.

Comparing these two theories, we can see how the first
looks at perception microscopically--an object is perceived
in terms of its parts, while the second theory describes perception macroscopically--objects are first perceived as a
whole greater than the sum of its parts.

PERCEPTION AND THE NERVOUS SYSTEM

● PROBLEM 9-15

Describe how perception is basically studied and the process
of coding.

Solution: Perception is a mental process which by definition is not directly observable. The two methods which scientists most commonly use to study perception are: physiological investigation of the receptors and sensory pathways, and more commonly, verbal reports of subjective experiences of sensation in human subjects and the observable behavior of animals.

The process of perception involves a series of coding operations in which one form of energy is transformed into another type. The energy which is involved can be seen as information which, although changing form, is carrying the same information from start to finish. The first step in the coding process is determining which kind or modality of energy is being utilized (i.e., light, heat, sound, etc.). The second stage in the process is determining where (what part of the brain) the energy is being processed. Each area of the brain and each sense organ responds to stimuli from specific sensory modalities. For example, the eye and optic nerve respond to the stimuli of light (and touch) but do not react to sound or smell. This is, of course, a very simplified view; the degree to which we are able to differentiate among similar sensory stimuli is very precise.

Another concept important in the understanding of sensation and perception is that of the threshold. The threshold is the minimum (or maximum) level of the stimuli which can be perceived by a particular sense organ. Although there are average threshold levels for people in general, each individual may have a threshold which differs somewhat from the norm. On the whole, however, people appear to have remarkably similar threshold levels.

● PROBLEM 9-16

Discuss template matching. How effective is this model in describing human perception?

Solution: Our ordinary experience makes the recognition and classification of the events and objects in our environment seem like an effortless, direct, and simple procedure. The efforts of engineers have, however, demonstrated that the operations involved in recognizing signs and symbols normally encountered are quite complex. In fact there exists no machine that can consistently recognize the objects of its environment with the adaptability and power of the human perception system or even the perception system of primitive animals.

"Template matching" is a logical explanation of how our perceptual system might work. For template matching to occur there must be some representation or template for each of the patterns to be recognized. Recognition occurs when the internal pattern is matched with the external stimulus. This process has been studied mainly with the recognition of words and letters. If, for instance, the letter "R" is presented to the eye, the light-sensitive receptor cells at the back of the eye (retina) are stimulated in a certain pattern corresponding to the letter "R." This pattern of receptor cells is an "R detector" or R template. Yet another pattern would

306

be evoked by the letter "F," and still another for "O." The
pattern evoked is that which most closely resembles the incoming information. This matching system does not require
that all possible templates be examined before the correct
one is selected, it assumes that the closest possible match
will be the most strongly activated.

This seems like a most straightforward explanation of
human pattern recognition however, under more intensive investigation it proves to be too simple and too rigid to explain the powerful and adaptable human pattern recognition
system. Imagine what would happen if the "R" were presented
in a slightly crooked, too large or too small manner. The
template-matching system fails to explain how variations in
the pattern are recognized, unless it supposes that a template exists for each possible size and orientation of all
letters presented. It seems unlikely, then, that templates
could account for human pattern recognition. The variety in
the patterns that must be dealt with poses a considerable
problem for the template explanation. The system would become too unwieldy and complex. Also, this scheme has no means
for recognizing novel versions of patterns for which there is
no template. Humans, as we know, can recognize novel patterns,
and their pattern recognition system requires a more flexible
system than template matching to account for its capabilities.

● **PROBLEM** 9-17

Describe the McCollough Effect. How does it support the
theory that there are colored-line detectors in the human
system?

Solution: In trying to understand the mechanisms underlying
the human visual system, much research and experimentation has
been directed at attempting to prove the existence of specific
detectors for movement and for color. An important source of
information relevant to this research comes from the study
of the aftereffects of strong stimulation. After looking
intensely at a brightly colored light if the gaze is directed
to a smooth white surface the same light will be seen, only
in the complementary color. If the original light was red,
a green light will be seen.

In an attempt to demonstrate that we might have colored-
line detectors in the human visual system, McCollough conducted the following experiment. For 5 minutes subjects were
alternately shown red vertical lines and then green horizontal
lines for about five seconds. Then a pattern of black and
white lines at differing orientations was presented to the
subject. To the subject, the horizontal white lines looked
reddish; the vertical white lines looked greenish; oblique
lines look white. This is the McCollough Effect. The explanation of these results comes from a consideration of
colored-line feature detectors. The strategy used was to
fatigue one set of line detectors, then present a neutral
object (black and white lines). If a complementary set of
features exists, they would show themselves. Thus, if there
are both red and green horizontal line detectors, prolonged

exposure to green horizontal lines would make white horizontal lines appear reddish. If the red vertical line detectors are fatigued, the white vertical lines should appear green, which they indeed do.

The McCollough Effect does demonstrate the existence of two complementary systems sensitive to certain colors. This evidence, while intriguing--particularly when combined with the fact that a small number of colored-line detectors have been recently found in the brains of monkeys--must be carefully weighed. The colored-line detector theory provides an explanation for the existing data and does not contradict any of the available information. However, recently a simpler type of "orientation-device" in the neural system has been postulated which may explain the McCollough Effect even better than the colored-line detectors.

These orientation devices are called "dipoles" and they are simply more sensitive to one input on one side and to another on the other side. For instance, a dipole might be sensitive to red on one side and to green on the other. This account also does not appear to contradict any of the available data and is much simpler in conception than the colored-line detectors theory. It also demonstrates that there is still a great deal to be learned about the visual perceptual system; that much of our knowledge is still at the level of intelligent guesses to explain what has been observed.

● **PROBLEM** 9-18

What are color aftereffects and how are they explained?

Solution: If you stare at a brightly colored image for a while and then look immediately at a white surface, you will see the image again only in the complementary or opposite color to the original image. If you looked originally at blue, you will see yellow; if the original was red, the afterimage will be green; if it was black, it will be white. These color aftereffects offer a clue to the organization of the human perceptual system.

The aftereffect is always the opposite of the original color. This implies the operation of two antagonistic systems working against each other. Since prolonged stimulation of one side of this antagonistic system is required to produce the aftereffect, we can assume that the underlying neural mechanism can be fatigued so that it has a reduced sensitivity to stimulation or at least a reduced ability to respond. Further, we can assume that neural cells are paired so that cells that respond in one way are paired with cells that respond in another, complementary, way. Normally, the output of the pair would be the balance of the two colors. If a blue receptor is paired with a yellow receptor both would respond equally in the presence of white light leading to no color output. In the presence of blue, the blue receptors would fire more strongly, and in the presence of yellow light, the yellow would be triggered with more intensity. If, however, the eye focuses on blue for a prolonged period

308

of time, the blue receptors through fatigue would be unable to respond adequately. If, then the eye looks at white, the yellow receptor would respond normally, but the blue would be inhibited. Since the yellow response outweighs the blue, the white light would be seen as yellow. At the present time this opponent process model is the most common explanation of the mechanisms underlying the aftereffect phenomenon.

● **PROBLEM** 9-19

Discuss the condition known as "masking." How does this phenomenon influence the sound produced by an orchestra?

Solution: The clearness of a visual or audio perception depends not only on its own intensity but also on the other sights or sounds present at the same time. Sensations "mask" one another. For instance, with sound the presence of one sound makes another difficult to hear. Closing of doors, coughing, a baby crying, hand clapping all tend to mask music or speech. To determine the effect of masking, experiments have been conducted to test how much more intense a test sound must be in order to be heard in the presence of a masking sound. It has been determined that if the masking sound contains frequencies within a "critical band" overlapping those of the masked sound, it will effectively block the detection of the original sound. If, however, the two sounds do not share the same frequency range, little masking will occur. The same phenomenon can be observed in visual masking. The extent to which one pattern will decrease the visibility of the other is determined by the degree of similarity in their "spatial frequencies, i.e., a grid pattern of lines close together will effectively mask another grid pattern with lines close together but not a pattern which has lines spaced much further apart.

Masking is taken for granted by musicians. They intuitively know that the lower frequency instruments mask the sounds of the higher-frequency ones and they compensate for this when playing together. The cellos mask the violins, the brass mask the woodwinds, the drums mask the cellos. When the sounds of live music are played back at home the intensity (loudness) is much less than when they are recorded and this in turn changes the masking patterns. The bass sounds are much reduced in level and this makes it possible to follow the fingering of the violin or the guitar. This may not be the virtue that it at first appears to be. To eliminate the masking is to eliminate the sound balance among the instruments that is part of effective group performing.

● **PROBLEM** 9-20

What evidence is there that there are specialized sound detectors for human speech?

Solution: Very little is known about the nature of auditory neural processing. This is partly due to our lack of knowledge concerning auditory patterns. With light energy, it is obvious that lines and contours, angles and movement play an important part in our recognition of patterns around us. But what are analogous features for the auditory system? We do not know.

The nature of human speech makes it appear reasonable to assume that there are specific sound detectors for it. The whole nature of speech seems to be geared to the hearing mechanism. There is evidence that 40% of the neurons in the auditory complex do not even respond to pure tones, but only to more complex sounds such as bursts of noise or clicks. Even 60% of the neural units that respond to pure tones do not do so in a simple way. Some neurons increase their rate of firing when a tone is heard and others decrease their rate of firing. Some respond only when a tone is turned on, others only when a tone is turned off, and others only when the tone is turned on and off and on and off. Some respond only to changes in frequencies and others when stimulated by one tone will cause response to another tone to cease. From this evidence we may infer that the neural units are designed to respond only to unique sounds or patterns of sounds, but at this point we cannot be absolutely certain.

● **PROBLEM 9-21**

Discuss the segmentation problem in speech recognition as it contributes to the pattern recognition theory of human perception.

Solution: The printed word is easy for the nervous system to analyze. Each letter is clearly separated from surrounding letters and each word is separated by an even greater space from surrounding words. It is not difficult to determine the boundaries between letters, words, and sentences when reading; this, however, is not true with speech. When we listen to someone speaking, the words sound distinct and well-defined, but this is an illusion which can be demonstrated by examining the "spoken waveform," a "chart" of the frequency and amplitude of an individual's speech. The spoken waveform shows a combination of inarticulate sounds, ill-pronounced sections, deletions, and contradictions. There is no apparent break in the speech waveform at the beginnings and endings of words. The clear distinction that we hear is apparently put in by some kind of neural analysis, since it is not present in the physical stimulus. This analysis is thought to be done by a pattern recognition system.

Even without access to a recording device of the speech waveforms we can illustrate the objective lack of distinctiveness in speech. When listening to someone who speaks an unfamiliar foreign language the speech seems to come at us in an incoherent stream at an incredibly rapid rate. Even someone who can read the language may have a great deal of difficulty in recognizing the "familiar" words in the speech of a native speaker. The subjective rapid rate of foreign speech is usually an illusion. Since we do not have a pattern recognition and organizing system for the foreign language, the sounds cannot be meaningfully interpreted. Our English pattern recognizing system is inappropriate for the new language.

What is the evidence supporting the idea that we have two
brains rather than one?

Solution: The brain of higher animals, including man, seems
to consist of two fully equipped central processing systems--
the left and the right hemispheres--which are tied together by
a massive set of communication lines called the corpus callosum. Experiments at the University of Chicago in the early
1950's led to the surprising discovering that when this communication line between the two hemispheres is severed, each
hemisphere functions independently, as if it were a complete
brain.

Ordinarily each half of the brain receives only a part
of the information arriving from the sensory receptors. The
left half of the brain receives the information from the
right half of the body and the right half receives input from
the sense receptors of the left half of the body. In a normal
individual, the corpus callosum is used to transfer the missing parts of the message to each hemisphere so that each half
of the brain has a complete picture of the sensory input.

Research on cats whose corpus callosi and optic connectors
were severed, introduced entirely new questions about the
brain mechanism and the split brain phenomenon. When the
cat was working with only one eye (one visual field, actually),
it could respond normally and learn a task; when that eye was
covered, however, and the same problem presented to the other
eye, the animal did not recognize the problem and could not
perform the previously learned task.

It has also been demonstrated that the two brains can
function not only independently, but simultaneously. For
instance, monkeys with split hemispheres can solve independent
problems with each half simultaneously (this has also been
demonstrated with split-brain humans). Recently a great deal
of research has been done on "split-brain" patients. These
are patients who have had the two hemispheres of the brain
severed to control epileptic seizures. These patients appear
at first to be perfectly normal after the operation, but careful experimental techniques demonstrate certain peculiarities
of behavior.

The patient responds normally to any input given to the
right hand or the right eye. If he is, for instance, shown
a cup he will recognize it and describe it as a cup. Objects
presented to the left side of the person produce quite a
different effect. The person is unable to say what he sees.
If asked what he has in his left hand, he responds that the
hand feels numb. However, if the object is put into a bag
with other items, he is quite capable of locating the correct object, but only with the left hand. He is also capable
of showing by gestures the function of the object again with
the left hand. He might for example demonstrate by sipping
what the cup was used for, but he cannot describe it verbally.

In one split-brain subject, the experimenter reported

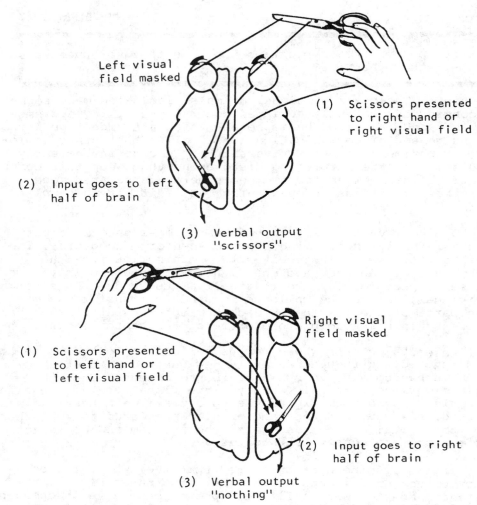

Left visual
field masked

(1) Scissors presented
to right hand or
right visual field

(2) Input goes to left
half of brain

(3) Verbal output
"scissors"

(1) Scissors presented
to left hand or
left visual field

Right visual
field masked

(2) Input goes to right
half of brain

(3) Verbal output
"nothing"

viewing an instance in which the right hand was violently
shaking another person and at the same time the left hand was
coming to the rescue of the person, trying to subdue the right
hand.

The results of these experiments and others like them
seem to indicate that the two sides of the brain have different capacities and functions. But more importantly, the
evidence seems to indicate that separation of the hemispheres
creates two independent spheres of consciousness in a single
organism. These patients literally function in such a way
that the left hand does not know what the right hand is doing.
And given the right experimental conditions respond as if they
were two separate people.

● **PROBLEM** 9-23

What are the functions of the two sides of the brain? Discuss particularly the type of thinking which appears to have
its locus in the right half of the brain.

Solution: In most of the cases of split brain patients--

patients in whom the neural communication lines between the
2 hemispheres of the brain have been severed--it is clear
that language skills develop in the left half of the brain
and the nonverbal skills develop in the right half. Through
the study of brain-damaged individuals, certain other definite functions have been discovered in the two sides of the
brain. Disorders of the right hemisphere produce inability
to orientate in space correctly and dysfunctioning of spatial
or nonverbal thought. Patients retain their speech abilities
with right hemisphere damage. Patients also lose their musical abilities (singing and recognizing tunes and melodies)
when the right hemisphere is damaged. The right hemisphere
can read but it cannot produce spoken words. Therefore, it
does have some language ability but it is not "active." It
can recognize but not produce language. The right half is
quite capable of working with concepts. If a split-brain
person is shown a picture of a large grandfather clock in the
left visual field and told to pick it out of a pile of items
with the left hand, he will pick out a wrist-watch, even
though there are other objects that are more similar in shape
to the grandfather clock. He recognizes that the watch is
functionally the same as the clock.

It is thought that both sides of the brain are responsible
for higher order functions but that the functions are different. The language abilities of the left hemisphere are well
known to us; whereas the visio-spatial abilities of the right
hemisphere are less clearly understood. It has been postulated by Bogen that the functions of the right half of the
brain are intuitive, symbolic, mystical, aesthetic, and synthesizing. It is the performer of the Gestalt-perceiving function,
while the left hemisphere operates in a more logical, analytic,
computerlike fashion. These two modes seem basically dichoto-
mous.

ATTENTION

● PROBLEM 9-24

What happens to memory in the absence of attention? What
role does attention seem to play in memory?

Solution: Our memory is selective. That is, of all the
thousands of sensory impressions that bombard us at any
moment in the day, our attention system enables us to concentrate ourselves on only selected parts of the input--
usually on one set of events. This is fortunate as it prevents us from living a world of chaos. However, sometimes
when we might feel it useful to keep track of several things
at once, we find it difficult to divide our attention. And
it is important that the selective attention mechanism not
be so rigid as to close off all other input but that to which
it is attending. Sometimes other input is important, even
vital to the survival of the organism.

A number of experiments have been attempted to test
whether or not memory of "unattended" sensory information
occurs while attention is focused on some particular task.
One way that this is tested is to have subjects count back-

ward from 100 to one and at the same time present common English words. When the counting test is over, subject's memory for the words is tested. Subjects normally cannot recall any of the words. To test if the words make it even into short-term memory, the subjects are then interrupted immediately after the words are presented and asked if they remember anything. When the experiment is conducted in this manner, the subjects can remember the last few items presented. If, however, even a 30-second delay occurs between the stimulus presentation (the words) and the testing for recall, the words are "lost." It does appear, then, that when attention is concentrated elsewhere, additional incoming information may be processed as far as short-term memory. This further implies that there may be an attentional mechanism required to get material from short-term to long-term memory.

● **PROBLEM** 9-25

How does the active synthesizing process model explain attention?

Solution: Human information processing depends a great deal on the context in which the information is received. Consider the following incomplete phrases:

> Three people were killed in a terrible
> automobile _____(accident)

> Too many people today confuse communism
> with _____(socialism)

> More money buys fewer goods during
> times of _____(inflation)

Though we do not know exactly how the mechanism of attention works, through the study of how the human mind responds to incomplete information, such as the phrases presented above, an active-synthesizing model has been developed. This model supposes that the analysis of incoming sensory signals is done by an active synthesizer which constructs and matches the signals with past experiences, thus allowing for accurate recognition even in the presence of distortions, gaps, inconsistencies, and ambiguities. For the active synthesizing action of attention to process the above sentences consider some of the steps it might have to go through. To let the context of a sentence predict the next word, it must take into account the subject matter under discussion, the grammatical syle, and the grammatical analysis of the parts of the sentence that have already been received. Then it can begin to perceive what possible inputs would be appropriate to the sentence, which would not be, and finally it selects the appropriate word.

This model of an active-synthesizing-attention-mechanism confines the scope of the synthesizer to a very limited, single track at any one time--only one set of signals can receive the action of active attention synthesizing. A passive process also acts simultaneously and continually analyzes all other incoming signals, but the passive action of attention does not allow for the resolution of ambiguities or distortions, nor can it extract complex meanings. For this type of work on incoming sensations, the active process is necessary. The system may switch channels if information coming into the passive channel has general relevance; for instance, if the name of the person receiving the input is registered on the passive channel, the active synthesizing channel may be altered and the attention focus changed by information presented on the passive circuit (this is called the "cocktail party phenomenon"). It is largely by this exercise of attention that the human mind can assert itself against becoming the passive target of random external stimuli.

This is currently a theory that is finding wide acceptance among psychologists as it does explain many of the facets of attention and does not contradict any of the known facts about the attention mechanism. Much of the experimental work that has been conducted to test this theory has been done only with words, word patterns or numerals as these are most easily studied in a laboratory setting.

● **PROBLEM** 9-26

Describe shadowing. How is it used in studies of attention?

Solution: Experimenters interested in the attention process have developed an experimental procedure which allows them to be sure that the attention of the subject is devoted to a single task so that they can study the limits of attention capacity, as well as the mechanisms that are responsible for selective attention and short-term memory. "Shadowing" is the name given to this popular technique for being sure a subject's attention is concentrated on a single task. In a shadowing task, a series of words is read to the subject, and the subject is asked to repeat everything she hears out loud. This repetition is called shadowing. If the material is presented at a relatively rapid rate, this presents a difficult task and requires a good deal of the person's attentional capacities to do. How well the person is attending to the message is determined by how well she does at the shadowing. If the shadowing is too easy for the subject, more difficult material or material presented more rapidly is necessary to insure that most of her attention is directed to the shadowing task. Ideally, the subject will make a small amount of errors, about 10%, so that it can be determined by a change in the error rate if attention to the shadowing task changes.

In a typical experiment, the material to be shadowed is presented to the subject in one ear of an earphone and test material (other information) is presented in the other ear or visually. After the session, the subject would be tested on the material presented to the nonshadowing ear or visually to determine what percentage of the material was retained though it was not attended to.

● **PROBLEM** 9-27

A major goal of advertising is to catch the attention of the audience. One ad gimmick involves having a plane pull a large

sign through the air. Discuss the attention factors being
used in this type of advertisment.

Solution: The conditions that influence the direction of
attention can be placed in two categories: objective and
subjective. When objects themselves directs attention the
objective conditions prevail; when the disposition or character of the mind of the subject directs attention, subjective
conditions are operating. The characteristics of objects
that have been found to be instrumental in the directing of
attention are intensity, size, duration and novelty or contrast. For example, a bright light or loud noise is more
likely to attract attention than a dim light or a soft sound.
A large object is more likely to be noticed than a small one,
and generally, and up to certain limits, a stimulus that lasts
longer is more likely to be attended to than one that is
brief. The most important of all objective characteristics
has been shown to be the novelty of the new stimulus compared to the preceding stimulation.

   Although duration is helpful to attracting attention,
beyond a certain point the sameness of the impression leads
to its being ignored and the attention will automatically turn
to a different stimulus. Change attracts attention. The use
of an airplane pulling a large sign through the air is a device that utilizes this information about the attractive
quality of a novel event. It is unusual to see an airplane
pulling a large sign, and therefore, people are much more
likely to notice it than they are to simply notice an airplane
or a large sign in a more familiar spot, like alongside of
the road.

● **PROBLEM** 9-28

Discuss the role of attitudes and expectancy in attention.

Solution: Besides the external factors of intensity, size,
duration and contrast, attention is highly influenced by
the internal state of the individual. Momentary preoccupations and long term interests are highly instrumental in
determining to what a person will attend in a given situation. If we happen to be thinking of an idea or an object
at the moment, it will attract our attention even under conditions in which it would otherwise go by unnoticed.

   A person's mental attitude is also important in determining the focus of attention. An attitude is a kind of limited
orientation. It will make salient what is relevant to it and
tend to exclude other information. The effect of a mental
attitude or set of expectancies can be seen simply in the
situation where one has a question in mind concerning a particular object or event. The question or mental set will force
the attention to focus on the aspects of the environment that
will answer the question. If one wishes to know the times
trains depart for New Haven, it is likely that the focus of
attention will be on the time-information board and not on
the design of the stonework which surrounds the board. Likewise, if one is curious about the nature of stonework frames,

it is unlikely that train departure times will be noticed at all. Generally, we notice very little for which our mental attitude is unprepared. Though this would seem to limit our experience, it may be essential as it involves a kind of mental economy.

Long term interests and previous education may also influence the direction of attention. In a varied stimulus array, individual's attention may be attracted to stimuli that correspond to their knowledge and experience. Looking through a Sunday newspaper the attention of ten different people may be focused on different sections in different orders, again dependent on their past experience and training.

GESTALT THEORY, CONTEXT, CONSTANCIES, AND ILLUSIONS

● **PROBLEM** 9-29

Discuss Gestalt's Laws of Organization.

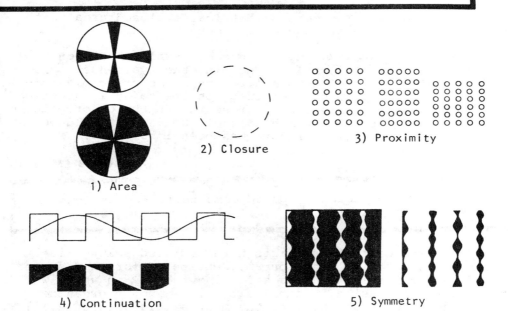

1) Area

2) Closure

3) Proximity

4) Continuation

5) Symmetry

Solution: Gestalt theory followed structuralism as a leading explanation of the human perceptual system. The Gestalt theorists rejected the structural idea that our perceptions were based on an assemblage of separate points of sensation and concerned themselves more with larger units of perception: the forms; figures and the contexts within which they were set. This concentration on the perception of form led to the systematic study of the stimulus determinants of shape and form. From this study emerged a group of "laws" of organization. It is questionable whether they rightly deserve the title "laws" as they are mainly theoretical constructs that yet require further investigation to determine their correctness as explanations of perceptual processes.

There are numerous organizational laws. Five of the

317

most important ones are:

1. Area: The smaller a closed portion of a representation, the more it is likely to look like a figure. The larger the enclosed area, the less likely the eye is to organize it as a whole.

2. Closedness: Areas that are closed are more likely to be seen as figures than are those portions of a representation that have open contours.

3. Proximity: Items that are placed close together are likely to be grouped together in a logical manner. Long horizontal rows of dots are likely to be organized as horizontal lines rather than vertical lines until the vertical line becomes longer than the horizontal, at which point they will be viewed as vertical lines.

4. Continuation: An arrangement that makes the fewest interruptions in a curving or a straight line will be organized as a figure.

5. Symmetry: The more symmetrical a closed area is the more likely it is to be seen as a figure.

These laws have a principle in common which has been called the Minimum Principle. That is, the eye tends to see that which is simplest to see. Though the principles behind the Gestalt approach to perception are today in question, the contribution of this line of research to the description of the cues which determine which part of the visual field belongs to the same object or form has been invaluable.

● **PROBLEM** 9-30

Why is an array of equally spaced dots perceived as rows and columns?

Solution: The Gestalt theorists have compiled a long list of variables that influence our perception of form and shape. One of the overriding factors affecting the way in which we organize an impression is simplicity. We tend to organize ambiguous representations into the most simple pattern available. There are a number of factors that appear to contribute to simplicity which were pointed out by the Gestaltists in the form of "laws" of organization. Though it has been difficult to objectively demonstrate that these "laws" of organization do contribute to simplicity, recent research has begun to make it possible to develop objective standards for recognizing simplicity.

One of the major components of simplicity is proximity. Dots or objects that are placed closely together tend to be grouped together in some kind of meaningful configuration. Columns and rows are organized figures that the eye sees easily and it tends to organize unconnected, yet closely placed objects into a familiar pattern. Whether this tendency to simplicity is inborn or learned, we don't know. We do

know, however, that the nervous system seems to choose to see
the world in the most simple and constant way possible.

● **PROBLEM** 9-31

This diagram is perceived as three squares. There are two
"principles of organization" present, but one is contradicting
the other. Differentiate between the two.

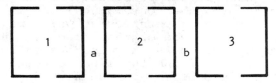

Solution: Gestalt theory, initiated by Max Wertheimer in the
1920's dominated the field of perception for many years.
Today, however, many of its premises are no longer considered
tenable. In spite of this Gestalt theory has made a lasting
contribution to the understanding of form perception and
organization. Concerned with how individuals organize incoming sensations, the Gestalt theorists devoted much study
to form perception and evolved a number of "laws of organization" which could often explain how an individual would organize a particular group of sensations. Five of the most
important factors that were thought to influence the way in
which an object or figure was perceived were: proximity,
area, closedness, symmetry, and continuation of line. Figures that displayed one or more of these principles of organization would be more likely to be seen as a whole rather than
as unconnected parts.

The above figure incorporates two of these principles:
proximity and area. The proximity principle would predict
that objects which are close to each other would tend to be
grouped together and seen as a figure. This would predict
that the shapes "a" and "b" would be perceived. However,
the smaller a closed region, the more it tends to be seen
as figure, and though the two sides of the square are not
completely closed, this principle dominates in our perception of the diagram. The familiarity of the square is probably also a factor in our seeing it instead of figures "a"
and "b."

● **PROBLEM** 9-32

Why does line A seem longer than line B even though they
are the same length?

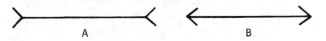

Solution: The figures represented by A and B are classic
Müller-Lyer patterns. They are an example of a perceptual
illusion. The two lines are of the same length though B
appears to be shorter than A. The pervasiveness and strength
of illusions such as this one has contributed to the great

amount of interest in them and investigation of their possible causes. The only way that most illusions or perceptual errors can be detected is by taking an actual physical measuring instrument, like a ruler, and measuring them. Thus far, no reliable means of predicting the effects of illusions or even of anticipating their occurrence has been found, though a number of theories have been set forth.

One theory that has attempted to explain the Müller-Lyer illusion is known as the perspective theory of illusions. According to this theory, the converging lines in line B suggest the depth cue of linear perspective which makes that line appear to be nearer to the viewer than line A. This explains the illusion as being due to the unconscious action of a depth cue. The apparent sizes of the two lines are the same on the retinal image but because of the perspective depth cue, the mind corrects for distance and B looks shorter than A.

● PROBLEM 9-33

(a)   Bat
(b)   B25
Discuss the principle that explains why B in (a) is perceived as the letter B and in (b) one sees the number 13.

Solution: A large part of the interpretation of sensory data is dependent upon information as to what the signal must be, rather than from the information provided within the signal itself. The crucial information is provided by the context in which the sensory signal occurs. The context is the environment in which experiences are embedded. Context supplies the rules underlying the construction of our perceptual world and by so doing tells us what to expect and gives plausible explanations of what we are perceiving. It is because of context that we can miss much of the detail of speech or print but not miss the intended meaning. When reading this paragraph you know much more about what you are reading than the actual words presented. You know that you are reading the English language, that you are reading about psychology and perception. This context gives you many cues about the nature of the messages you will be receiving. Therefore, as your eyes go over the page you can somewhat predict what you will see and you will fill the missing information. These predictions can be so accurate that you may have automatically added the missing "in" of the previous sentence. This ability to use context to correctly interpret sensory information makes the human organism in its perceptual capacities, far superior to any electronic pattern-recognizing computer thus far invented.

In the above example "B" looks like the number 13 in "(b) B25 " because it is seen as part of a numerical sequence, and it looks like the letter B in "(a) Bat" because it is processed as part of the letter grouping that forms the fairly commonly used word "BAT." Many experiments have been conducted that prove the dramatic effects that context can have on perception. For instance, reading and remembering letters is much more difficult if they are laid out in a nonsensical pat-

tern--shygpcylogo--than if the same letters are arranged in a
meaningful pattern--psychology. This same phenomenon can be
observed with a string of words--apples, I, red, who, home,
it, was, brought. The average recall of words presented to a
subject in this order if presented with some background noise
that tends to distract attention will be approximately 50%.
If the same words are presented in a meaningful order--It was
I who brought home the red apples--the recall will be close to
100% even with a greater amount of distracting noise. The
physical information presented is the same in both cases; the
factor determining the recall level would then have to be the
context. Though the power of context is easily demonstrated,
the mechanisms underlying this use of contextual information
are not well understood.

● **PROBLEM 9-34**

The ellipses shown in (a) and (b) are equivalent in size and
shape. Name and discuss the concept which makes (b) appear
more circular.

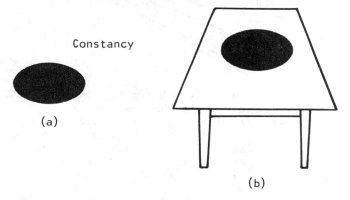

Constancy

(a)

(b)

Solution: In our perception of the world around us nothing
is dealt with in isolation; all contextual information is
taken together. Usually this contextual information fits
together reasonably well. As objects move away, their image
size changes by just the right amount. The relative sizes
and distances are what they should be. If, however, the
artist for art or the psychologist for experimentation
should violate the rules that we seem to unconsciously follow for developing logical constructions, our perceptions
often become inaccurate. It appears that the mind when
piecing together sensory information must produce a consistent image. Therefore, ambiguous or incomplete information will be processed according to the context in which it
is found.

To our vision the table in (b) appears to be three-
dimensional and rectangular due to the linear perspective
produced by the 2 long sides. The eye, therefore, corrects
the elliptical shape allowing for the effect of distance.
With the allowance for the effect of distance the ellipse
appears to be more circular than it did in (a) where the context was the empty space on the flat page that surrounded it.

Why does the lamp post on the left seem smaller than the lamp post on the right despite their physical equality?

Solution: The two lamp posts on the street scene demonstrate the effect of context on the apparent size that we perceive. The three-dimensional street scene gives the appearance of distance. When the viewer looks at the farther lamp post he automatically calculates for distance in judging size. Thus it is not just the retinal image that determines the size we assign to an object, it is the retinal image combined with the apparent distance. We assume the lamp posts are the same size in this scene, but the linear perspective of the street scene provides a depth cue that leads us to see the second lamp post as larger than the first because we assume it is more distant even though they are actually the same size. This phenomenon is an example of a perceptual constancy (size) contributing to an illusion--a "misapplied constancy." This type of perceptual illusion has been studied extensively in an effort to challenge the theory that perceptual learning is based upon past experience. For if it is based upon past experience, we would assume that our experience would teach us to perceive correctly, while illusions such as this seem to indicate that our experience has taught us to see incorrect- ly. Illusions give a strong impression of being correct and can usually only be demonstrated by actual measurement of the objects involved.

● PROBLEM 9-36

A very familiar experience is known as the moon illusion, which occurs when the full moon is on the horizon and it seems much larger than when it is at the zenith (directly overhead). Does this illusion agree or disagree with

Emmert's Law and why? If not, give an example of Emmert's law at work.

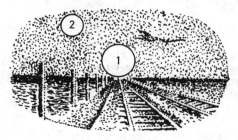
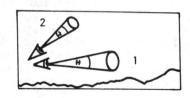

Solution: A phenomenon known as Emmert's Law has fascinating implications when applied to the "moon illusion" experience. To demonstrate Emmert's Law stand in front of a bright window. Gaze at it from a distance of two feet. This should produce an afterimage (when you look away from the bright window you will see the image of the window projected onto whatever surface you look at next). If you project the afterimage from a distance of four feet to a plain white surface you will receive an image that is the same size as the window. If, however, you project the afterimage from a distance of two feet the image will appear to be half the size of the original window image. Formulated as Emmert's Law, the apparent size of a projected afterimage is directly proportional to the distance between the eye and the surface onto which the image is projected.

Because the apparent size of the full moon on the horizon is larger than its size at the zenith this would imply that the reflecting surface of the sky is more distant at the horizon that at the zenith. This effect can be demonstrated in daylight. If you obtain an afterimage from looking at a bright light and then project it onto the sky, it will look larger when it is projected onto the horizon than it will when it is projected overhead.

The most common sense and ancient explanation of the moon illusion today known as the "perspective theory" seems to be one of the most consistent with recent research. The distance cues on the horizon contribute to the illusion by making the moon look farther away when it is on the horizon. The lack of these cues when it is overhead reduce the tendency to correct for distance in perceiving its size.

● **PROBLEM** 9-37

If asked how tall a person across the street is, you can give an accurate estimation. Discuss this perceptual phenomenon.

Solution: Our perceptual system relishes simplicity and constancy. Although, as the distance between the eye and an object increases, the image on the retina undergoes great size changes, we do not perceive this change, and tend to see the object as the same size. We also tend to see large objects as large and small objects as small no matter what their actual apparent size to the eye. A distant mountain may appear on the retinal screen smaller than the tree we are standing next to, but we will still perceive the mountain as larger than the tree.

We are also capable of taking distance into account when we are judging size. Though this calculation occurs automatically, it is usually quite accurate. It is this capacity to judge the size of an object by the combined information from the retinal image and the compensation for apparent distance that makes it possible to look across the street and correctly estimate the height of a person.

Another phenomenon that probably contributes to this ability to estimate size of a person at a distance is "familiar size." This is a traditional depth cue. That is, our familiarity with the usual size of a person helps us to know the approximate distance they are from us. If the person across the street were a child, we would automatically calculate the probable height of the child using our knowledge of the usual size of a child.

● **PROBLEM** 9-38

Normally, one would expect the brightness of an object to increase as more light is reflected from it, however, the perceived brightness of an object also depends on the field that surrounds it. Discuss this phenomenon including a method for its demonstration.

Solution: Just as the loudness of a sound increases as its intensity increases, we would expect that the brightness of an object would increase whenever more light was reflected from it. Experimentation has proven that this common sense prediction is incorrect. As the intentsity of the light falling on a scene is increased, the perceived change of brightness depends on what surrounds the object. If the overall illumination is increased, the intensity of the object of study and the field will increase proportionally and the contrast between the two will remain the same. The brightness of the object, however, does not necessarily increase when the amount of light falling on it is raised. It may get brighter or it may remain the same or it may even seem to lose some of its original brightness. It all depends on the relative intensities of the object and the field.
    In conditions of minimum illumination, when there is no light falling upon the eyes, the resultant perception is of gray, not black as one might assume. We are only able to see blacks when there is some light present and only if there are enough brighter surfaces to provide the contrast that is necessary to produce the experience of black. When there are great brightness contrasts between the object and the field the more light that is added, the darker the object will appear.
    This effect can be demonstrated with the help of a television set as a light source. When the set is turned off, the screen is a gray color in brightness. When the set is turned on, some areas on the screen appear to be intensely

black, much darker than the neutral gray of the set. The set can only intensify the screen. That is, the light beam that effects the face of the tube can only cause light to be e- mitted, it cannot absorb light to create black. The appar- ent darkening of the screen comes about as a result of the contrast mechanisms of the eye.

A procedure that can be used to demonstrate this con- trast phenomenon is to place small samples of a medium gray paper upon backgrounds of white, light gray, dark gray and black. The contrast effect will be experienced in the dif- ferent degrees of brightness that the gray assumes depending on the background. Against the white background, the gray will appear darkest and it will also appear darker when seen against the light gray. Against the dark gray background the medium gray patch will appear lighter than "usual" and on the black it will appear lightest of all.

● **PROBLEM** 9-39

How does Helmholtz's rule explain illusions? How does it account for our interpretation of our own feelings?

Solution: In studying the human perceptual system we quickly learn that it tends to perceive in ambiguous situations, that which is most likely for it to perceive. That is, it tends to see "constants." Usually when this occurs, the perception is correct. However, when it is incorrect the perception pro- duces an "illusion." Helmholtz, in studying the illusion that results from seeing the same color as varying in hues depend- ing on the background on which it was placed, postulated that illusions were based on the same perceptual processes as nor- mal perceptions and were, in fact, only incorrectly applied constancies.

Though this rule is logically appealing, it has proven impossible to make predictions from it without a large amount of information about what is likely or probable. It has, however, proven particularly useful in explaining perceptions about our own internal states and inner experiences. What we perceive as the cause of our feelings is often what is "most likely" to be producing the experience we are having. If we notice an increase in our heartbeat when a particularly attractive person comes into the room and there is nothing else to account for the change in our pulse rate, we may de- cide that we are attracted to or "like" the person, or we may interpret the disturbance as "dislike." This is a self- perception; it involves the labeling of one's internal state and a decision concerning its probable causes based on our past experiences. Our perceptual system plays the odds and usually goes for the favorite.

PERCEPTION OF DEPTH

● **PROBLEM** 9-40

What are depth cues? What is the cue that causes the spherical object to the left to be perceived as two-dimensional and the one to the far right as three-dimensional?

Spherical objects showing the impression of solidity resulting from gradients of illumination (shading).

Solution: The importance of depth cues is well known to
artists, as it is their task to recreate an illusion of an
actual scene or situation. One way that they can do this is
to create a surface that effects the observer's eye in the
same way that an actual scene would. The traditional pictorial depth cues used by an artist are: interposition
(placing one object somewhat in front of another), linear
perspective (converging lines to give an impression of
three-dimensionality), size perspective (identical objects,
one smaller and one larger to convey the image of distance),
familiar size (altering the size of two familiar objects to
demonstrate distance), and shadow distribution (shading used
to produce a three-dimensionality effect).

The spheres above demonstrate the effect of shadowing or
illumination on our perception of the dimensionality of an
object. The shading of the sphere at the far right provides
additional information to the nervous system which produces
the impression of three-dimensionality; whereas the simple
circle outline provides no depth cues and is processed as a
two-dimensional object.

● **PROBLEM** 9-41

Figure A is a classical illustration of reversible figures:
a vase or two profiles. What perception cues are changing
and how does the switching of these cues account for the
continual fluctuation between vase and face profiles?

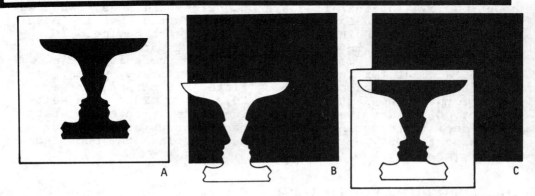

A   B   C

Solution: Usually a contour outlines a single figure in the
real world. In the illustration of reversible figures the
contour line divides two recognizable shapes, which cannot
generally be perceived simultaneously. In looking at
figure A you will note that your perception fluctuates between the vase and the two profiles. If you think you see
them both at the same time, you are either quickly altering

your focus or you see one part of the contour as part of a
dark vase and the other region as part of a white profile.
The shape that is visible is called the "figure" which seems
to be placed between the viewer and the "ground" or the rest
of the picture which lies behind the figure.

In figure B we can see that the vase is the figure. It
is seen as the figure in B due to the physical arrangement of
the black portion of the image. This "interposition cue"
indicates depth and makes the vase appear to be in front of
the black square.

In figure C, however, the profiles appear as the figure.
Again this is due to the arrangement of the squares. This
time the white square containing the profiles intersects the
contour lines of the dark square and the profiles themselves
do the same again giving the impression of distance making
the profiles stand out as figures in a frame in front of the
dark square.

● **PROBLEM** 9-42

This diagram uses four monocular depth cues. Identify and
discuss them.

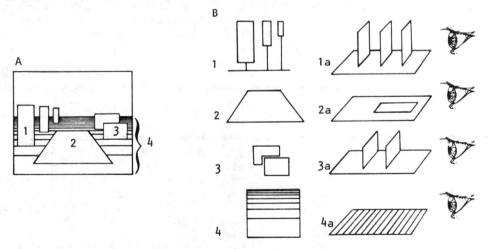

Solution: Monocular depth cues convey to us information
about space through one eye only. These cues are also
called pictorial depth cues since they are employed in paint-
ings to give the illusion of three-dimensional space. Depth
cues that we receive with two eyes are called binocular depth
cues. When an artist tries to create the illusion of three-
dimensionality on a flat surface there are particular aspects
of the scene which must be included in the picture to give
the three dimensional effect. The cues that are conveyed in
the above diagram can be represented as a flat impression
(columns 1-4) or as the tridimensional impression it is meant
to portray (column 1a-4a). The depth cues are as follows:

1. Relative Size. The eye adjusts for three dimensionality with a minimum of cues as it lives generally in

a three dimensional world. Figures become smaller as they are seen at a greater and greater distance. Therefore, the same size rectangle produces smaller tracings as it is viewed at a greater distance.

2. Linear perspective. On the ground the lines of this pictorial trapezoid would be rectangular. Similarly lines that would be parallel on the ground appear to converge on the picture plane. This is the effect called linear perspective.

3. Interposition. When one figure interrupts the outline of another it produces a strong depth cue indicating that one figure is in front of the other though it does not indicate how much distance separates the two figures.

4. Texture-density gradient. A gradient is the rate at which some property changes uniformly from one part of the area portrayed to another. The texture density of this impression becomes denser as it becomes more distant. This effect is achieved on a pictorial plane by drawing the horizontal parallel lines closer and closer together as greater distance is portrayed.

As we can see, it does not take much to present depth information. And a flat surface containing correct depth cues will portray a remakable three dimensional impression if it is viewed holding the head motionless or through only one eye. It is the binocular vision that gives us the cues that the picture is really flat.

● **PROBLEM 9-43**

Binocular vision enhances the perception of depth and distance. Why?

Solution: When we view any near three dimensional object each eye receives a slightly different view because each sees the world from a slightly different position. This produces binocular disparity and double images. Neither of these effects can be produced in pictures without special effects and it is their absence that makes a picture look flat. Without the use of both eyes it is difficult to distinguish between a flat surface representing a three dimensional space and the three dimensional space itself.

When the difference between the views of the two eyes is large a double image effect becomes quite clear. This can be demonstrated by holding a pencil about a foot away aligned with some more distant vertical object and fixing one's gaze first on the pencil then on the more distant object. A double image will be produced if this is done correctly. When the difference between the two eye view is small, the double image can no longer be detected, but the disparity between them still produces a sensitive and powerful depth cue that usually goes unnoticed by us. It is thought that this binocular disparity depth cue is almost certainly innate. We do not appear to learn it and we are not conscious of it as it is occurring.

That binocular difference provided a strong depth cue
was first discovered by Wheatstone in 1838 when he devised
a "stereoscope," an instrument that presents the image of
a scene in two pictures: one from the perspective of each
eye. This produces a remarkably strong spatial, three-
dimensional effect even though one is looking at two flat
surfaces. These devices have contributed much to the study
of the operation of the visual system.

● **PROBLEM** 9-44

Using the Minimum Principle, explain why Figure A is perceived
as two-dimensional and Figure B as three-dimensional.

A   B

Solution: Historically the successor to structuralism as
an explanation of perceptual processes, Gestalt theory,
was principally concerned with the problem of form perception. The Gestaltists developed from their observations and
experiments numerous "laws" of perceptual organization.
These laws are actually an outline of the factors which seem
to influence our perception of space. They can mainly be
summarized by the "law" of simplicity, commonly called the
Minimum Principle. The Minimum Principle states that our
nervous systems is constructed in any given scene, to see
what is simplest to see.

This can be demonstrated by examining the figures.
Figure A and figure B are views of the same cube. Yet figure
A appears to be flat while figure B appears to be three-
dimensional. Why is this? The Minimum Principle would
explain this effect by demonstrating that figure A is simpler
to perceive in two dimensions and figure B is simpler in
three dimensions. Therefore, a pattern would appear to be
three-dimensional if it were simpler to perceive that way,
and two-dimensional if it were simpler to perceive as a flat
impression.

The problem, of course, with this "law" is that "simple"
must be defined and this has proven to be difficult to do
except intuitively. Recent research has attempted to "objec-
tify" simplicity, which may in time make it possible for us
to make predictions about shape and motion perception following objective guidelines for simplicity. It is not yet known,
however, whether our tendency to organize stimuli in the most
simple way possible is innate, but presently the evidence
seems to point in that direction.

PERCEPTION OF MOTION

● **PROBLEM** 9-45

What are movement detectors? Discuss how the human nervous
system processes sensory-movement information.

Solution: Most visual receptor cells are not concerned with distinguishing between moving and stationary objects, though they certainly respond to moving or stationary input. For instance, a moving light will produce changes in the receptor cells corresponding to the location of the light. But this response does not qualify the cells as movement detectors. A movement detector cell or group of cells would ideally respond when an object is moving and at no other time. They might also be selective about the direction and perhaps the speed of the movement. These types of movement detector cells are found in the vision systems of numerous animals--frogs, rabbits and squirrels. These are units of nerve cells that are selectively sensitive to particular types of movement. The frog, for instance has a movement detector cell that responds only to small moving round dark objects--flying-bug detectors! It is currently a working hypothesis that humans also have movement detectors though none have actually been located.

It is thought that movement detectors by themselves would not be able to discriminate between movements caused by the head and eyes and those produced by the actual movements of external objects. Higher brain mechanisms must coordinate the information received from the movement detectors with information from the motor nerves controlling the head and eyes to be able to distinguish changes in retinal patterns produced by the movements of the head and eyes and those of external objects. Our knowledge of the role of higher brain sensory-movement mechanisms is limited. We do know that the movement detector cells or whatever sensory apparatus responds to movement sends messages along to the visual cortex where the cortical processing system receives the information in stages at different cellular levels--simple, complex and hypercomplex. Each analyzes the information received in greater detail. Anything that fails to cause a simple cell to respond will also fail to drive the corresponding more complex cells. The complex and hypercomplex cells simply analyze the information received more thoroughly. For instance, specificity of size or direction might trigger more specific complex or hypercomplex cells. Although the very nature of a motion detector would make it specific to movements in one direction only, hypercomplex cells can sometimes show a specificity to movement in two directions. The movement-detector impulse moves on to more central regions of the brain, but to date investigators have not been able to follow the sensory movement messages any further. The neural mechanisms for extracting movement features appear to be increasingly sophisticated as they enter more deeply into the brain, but we do not yet know the outcome of the voyage of the sensory-movement input.

● **PROBLEM 9-46**

How might the Minimum Principle be applied to the perception of form in motion?

Solution: The Minimum Principle, which states basically that we see what is most simple to see, helps to explain the results of experiments concerning the perception of movement. It appears that we see the arrangement of motions

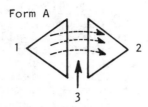

Form A

that involves the least number of changes and which allows
the perceived object to remain as constant as possible. In
form A, for example, if 1 alternates with 2, we could see
two different shapes in different places at the same time,
or we could see one triangle turning over in the third
dimension as indicated by the arrow marked "3". In actual
experiments, subjects tend to see the second movement pattern.

Apparently the view of the triangle rotating in space,
maintaining its angles and sides constant is less complex
to perceive than the two different triangles. This phenomenon allows us to make a number of predictions about the
perception of moving objects. The apparent tridimensionality
of an object is related to its complexity. The simpler a
two dimensional picture, the more likely we are to perceive
it as two-dimensional. The more angles, continuous lines,
and different angles there are within the two-dimensional
picture, the more likely we are to endow it with three-
dimensional properties. Also stationary objects which appear
two-dimensional, become vividly three-dimensional when rotated. The rotation reduces the ambiguity of the flat pattern and provides many cues that make it simpler to perceive
the object as three-dimensional.

● **PROBLEM** 9-47

A movie is a kind of apparent motion. Why is it an apparent
motion and discuss what kind it is?

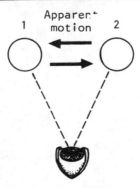

Apparent motion

Solution: Given the correct stimulus the human visual system
perceives motion whether there is any real motion occurring
or not. This is clearly demonstrated by the "phi phenomenon":
A light turned on and off at 1 and 2 produce the impression
that the light is moving from 1 to 2. This occurs with no
actual retinal stimulation of a moving point of light. This
apparent motion is sometimes called stroboscopic motion be-

cause it is so often demonstrated with the use of flashing
lights. This tendency of the perceptual system to perceive
smoothly moving stimuli is the basis of all motion pictures
and television. A series of still pictures is shown in very
brief exposures, called "frames," and the viewer sees motion,
moving pictures. It is virtually impossible for him to see
the individual frames when they are presented in rapid succession.

This makes it possible for filmmakers to manipulate time
and space. An event that usually takes a long time can, by
being shown at very rapid rates, be perceived over a short
period of time. A flower blossoming may take a number of days
but filmed at a slow rate and shown at a normal rate, the
blossoming can appear to take only seconds. "Slow motion"
allows us, conversely, to see activities that are normally
too fast for human vision. Thus, the television viewer of
sports events often is able, through replays and slow motion
shots to perceive the event in much more detail than a spec-
tator actually present. In addition, sequences can be put
together that could never occur anywhere but on the screen
or in the mind of the viewer or the filmmaker. The implications of this imposed reality on the thinking process of
humans are not yet known and remain an area awaiting scientific investigation.

SHORT ANSWER QUESTIONS FOR REVIEW

Choose the correct answer.

1. Persons of average height are "tall to midgets".
   This is an example of (a) linear perspective
   (b) context effects on perception (c) the law
   of dissimilarity (d) none of the above   b

2. Reversing lenses have been used to demonstrate
   (a) the role of cerebral dominance in perception (b) it didn't demonstrate anything (c)
   the effect of linear perspective cues on perception (d) the effect of experience on perception   d

3. Experiments have shown that hungry persons perceive food in pictures to be larger than do sa-
   tiated persons. This finding (a) contradicts
   the principle of size constancy (b) suggests
   that needs can influence perception (c) demonstrates that reinforcing objects are seen as
   larger than they are in reality (d) all of the
   above   b

4. "Visual Cliff" experiments suggest that (a)
   depth perception is innate in certain species
   (b) tactile sensations are an important aspect
   of depth perception (c) depth perception improves with experience with the environment
   (d) A and B only   a

5. An individual who receives normal sight following
   blindness in the early years of life (a) will
   not develop the size constancy aspect of perception (b) will adjust to the visual world almost instantly (c) will experience long-term
   muscle coordination problems because of changes
   in reference points (d) will have to relearn
   auditory and tactile associations necessary to
   accommodate the visual frame of reference   d

6. The autokinetic effect is most commonly demonstrated with which of the following stimuli?
   (a) a spot of light in a darkened room (b)
   lights flashing on and off in a patterned sequence (c) lights rotating around a single,
   central spot of light (d) a steady blue light
   consistently viewed near dusk   a

7. Experiments related to extensive sensory deprivation (a) have never been performed with human subjects (b) have revealed schizophrenic-
   type responses among human subjects (c) have
   revealed hallucinatory responses in human sub-

SHORT ANSWER QUESTIONS FOR REVIEW

jects   (d)   have revealed an overwhelming autokinetic effect

c

8.   Not among stimulus cues involved in depth perception is/are   (a)   light and shadow   (b)   proximity   (c)   relative position   (d)   linear perspective

b

9.   Inverted-glasses experiments demonstrate   (a)
the inability of the human visual system to cope
with the inversion phenomenon   (b)   exaggerated
myopic vision   (c)   the human visual system's
defense response of temporary blindness   (d)
the surprising ability of the human visual system to adjust to the inversion phenomenon

d

10. What of the following most clearly distinguishes
perception from sensation   (a)   observation   (b)
sensation   (c)   learning   (d)   sensitivity

c

11. The motion picture depends for its perceptual
success upon   (a)   the physiological limitations
of the human visual apparatus   (b)   synesthesia
(c)   motion parallax   (d)   the unique capacities
of its optic chiasma

a

12. The rod and frame test is designed to study   (a)
horizontal-vertical illusion   (b)   the Ganzfeld
illusion   (c)   the Holzman illusion   (d)   susceptibility to contextual cues

d

13. Perceptual constancies are primarily a function
of   (a)   reflex   (b)   convergence   (c)   instinct   (d)   learning

d

14. Prominent among monocular depth cues is   (a)
accommodation   (b)   texture-density gradient
(c)   retinal disparity   (d)   retinal polarity

b

15. As a person views a picture one way, he sees
craters. When he turns it 180 degrees, the craters become bumps. The perceptual phenomenon is
due to   (a)   linear perspective   (b)   texture
(c)   relative position   (d)   light and shadow

d

16. The phenomenon which allows recognition of common patterns, although the elements that make up
the pattern are different, is called   (a)   common fate   (b)   similarity   (c)   shape constancy
(d)   transposition

d

17. Figure/ground organization is not a function of
(a)   surroundedness   (b)   preference for white

334

SHORT ANSWER QUESTIONS FOR REVIEW

as figure   (c)   size of the different regions
(d)   symmetry of stimulus   b

18.   In order to guarantee that an observer would not
      be able to use accommodation as a depth cue, one
      would   (a)   permit only monocular viewing   (b)
      use dark conditions   (c)   use a pinhole   (d)
      keep the observer's head stationary   c

19.   Interposition and linear perspective are   (a)
      binocular cues   (b)   oculomotor cues   (c)   extra-
      retinal cues   (d)   pictorial cues   d

20.   Stereoscopes and 3-D movies depend primarily on
      which depth cue?   (a)   accommodation   (b)   dis-
      parity   (c)   convergence   (d)   parallax   b

Fill in the blanks.

21.   Laws of perceptual organization were formulated
      by workers in the _____ school of psychology.   Gestalt

22.   _____ constancy depends on the ratio of reflected
      light between object and surround.   Brightness

23.   A surrounding frame that moves with respect to
      the object it contains produces _____ movements.   induced

24.   As one views a two dimensional representation of
      a large, flat cobblestone area, the perception   texture-
      of distance is attained primarily through _____.   gradient

25.   Koffka and Kohler are Gestalt psychologists; the
      founder of this school and approach to perception   Wertheimer
      is _____ .

26.   The Ames room was specifically designed to test
      _____ constancy.   size

27.   McGinnie's experiments pioneered in the field of   perceptual
      _____ .   defense

28.   The grouping principle that involves movement is   common
      _____ .   fate

29.   In the trapezoidal window experiment, Allport and
      Pettigrew found that Western cultures perceived
      the illusion of a rotating _____ to a signifi-
      cantly greater extent than did other cultures.   rectangle

30.   The _____ illusion involves two lines with arrow   Muller-
      heads on both sides.   Lyer

335

SHORT ANSWER QUESTIONS FOR REVIEW

31. The phenomenon whereby four closely contiguous lines are perceived as a square demonstrates the principle of _____.

closure

32. Misperception of a stimulus: illusion as response in the absence of an external stimulus: _____.

hallucination

33. The Holway & Boring experiment tested several influences of the phenomenon of _____.

size constancy

34. If the visual angle is held constant but the perceived distance is increased, the perceived size of the object _____.

increases

35. A hypothesized effect proposed by Kohler and Wallach to account for displacement effects (figural after effects) has been termed _____.

satiation

Determine whether the following statements are true or false.

36. Concentration on a task may make a person unaware of other stimuli in his vicinity. The basis of this finding is physiological.

True

37. One characteristic of ground which distinguishes it from figure is that it has a lower texture gradient.

False

38. Perception of real movement is not affected by subject fatigue.

True

39. The neurophysiology of attention has been studied in cats. The conclusion from this work is that the central nervous system inhibits the passage of certain sensory impulses.

True

40. A person thinks that he sees a snake moving stealthily through the weeds on a distant hillside. As he gets closer, he discovers that it was only a dark piece of rope. This is a perceptual phenomenon known as delusion.

False

41. Perceptual phenomena have been most prominently explored within the framework of structuralism.

False

42. Depth perception relies heavily on the binocular cue, convergence.

True

43. A subject placed in an elaborate sensory deprivation setting for a renumeration of $20 per day will remain in such a setting indefinitely.

False

336

SHORT ANSWER QUESTIONS FOR REVIEW

44. Divergence is a stimulus-related perceptual phe-
    nomenon believed to be commonly experienced.

    False

45. Dember believes figure reversibility is evidence
    of the fact that change is essential in the main-
    tenance of perception.

    True

46. Restle's adaption-level theory seeks to explain
    the 'moon illusion.'

    True

47. When perceived size remains constant but retinal
    size (visual angle) increases, perceived distance
    increases.

    False

48. The "experience error" as defined by Kohler re-
    fers to the belief that the percept is a copy of
    the proximal stimulus.

    True

49. The phi phenomenon occurs in response to sequen-
    tially flashing lights.

    True

50. That curved lines appear less and less curved as
    you stare at them is known as the Gibson effect.

    True

CHAPTER 10

MOTIVATION

BASIC PRINCIPLES

● PROBLEM 10-1

What is motivation?

NEED → DRIVE → RESPONSE → GOAL
(NEED REDUCTION)

Solution: The field of psychology concerned particularly
with the factors that influence the arousal, direction and
persistence of behavior is called the psychology of motivation. Why does one child perform well in school while
another does not? Why does one person choose to be a
doctor and another a mason? Why is one person attracted
to a life of crime and another to one of altruism? In
other words, why do people behave as they do? These questions demonstrate that motivation is important in human
life. It is only recently that the study of motivation has
been subject to empirical investigations.

The concept of motivation in psychological theory has been
fragmented for decades. It is generally agreed that motives
are energizers of behavior, but how they operate or originate is a continuing source of debate. Each theorist supposes different motivational states. There are the basic
biological drives such as hunger, thirst, and sex. There
are the learned motives such as affiliation, achievement,
competitiveness. There are emotional motives such as
pleasure--from a mild pleasing sensation to ecstasy--and
pain, including anger, fear and frustration. All of these
are potential motivators for behavior.

The research in the area has generally focused on one
particular state. Though motives are studied individually
they are often examined in regard to their interaction
with other processes such as learning, conditioning, perception or social interaction. In addition to the study of
particular motives, there has been increasing interest in
the effect a motivational state has on other psychological

processes such as learning and remembering. This direction
of research has begun to expand and at the same time
connect the varying theoretical schools.

● **PROBLEM** 10-2

Give a brief survey of the history of the psychology of
motivation.

Solution: Interest in the factors that arouse and direct
behavior can be traced back to the dawn of recorded history. Greek philosophers, medieval Christian authors and
Eastern philosophers all addressed the questions that are
today asked by the motivational psychologist. An element
common to many writers and thinkers before the modern era,
which for convenience will be marked by the appearance of
Darwin, was the differentiation between the motivational
forces for animals and for humans. They believed that
animal behavior was controlled by physical forces and that
human behavior was controlled by physical and spiritual
forces. This belief presupposed the existence of both a
physical and a metaphysical reality. The physical was
controlled by external forces, while the metaphysical was
controlled by the individuality, soul, will or reason of
each person.

Other writers in the pre-Darwinian era believed that human
nature is chiefly hedonistic. That is, that the basic
motive behind all behavior is to avoid pain and seek
pleasure. While this type of thinking emerged in ancient
Greece, it was the English movement of the early nineteenth
century represented by Jeremy Bentham and James and John
Stuart Mill that furthered its popularity.

A third approach that preceded the scientific period of
study is typified by the work of Machiavelli and Hobbes.
These thinkers formulated a list of motives which they
believed were mainly responsible for human behavior.
Machiavelli maintained that egotism, fear, love, hunger
and sex were the basis for political leadership. Hobbes
felt that the contradictory nature of man's desires made
it necessary for him to have a strong sovereign to protect
him from himself.

The Darwinian revolution completely changed the nature of
thought on man's place in the world. It destroyed the
distinction between animal and human motivation--both were
said to be motivated by a need to survive. At this point,
the concept of will became superfluous for many thinkers.
The main area of concern became the internal and external
environmental stimuli that give rise to behavior. If will
was to be considered at all, it needed to be considered
from the point of view of its antecedents. It was therefore often eliminated altogether and superseded by the
study of what produced it. These antecedent variables
were of the sort that could be studied in a laboratory or
field setting. This new approach has facilitated the
development of systematic and empirical research in motivation.

Define the cycle represented in figure 1. Discuss the three constructs and why they form a cycle.

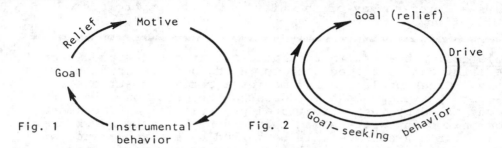

Fig. 1   Fig. 2

Solution: The cycle represented in the diagram refers to a chain of events set off by a drive which may also be referred to as a need or tension. A better diagrammatic representation is shown in figure 2.

Adaptive behavior that is designed to maintain internal and external balance and consistency depends on the satisfaction of drives. Because drives result from tensions or needs, motives for behavior are involved.

Motives for behavior are directed towards the maintenance of homeostasis, meaning, and the establishment of internal and external equilibrium. The process of human adjustment and the criteria for leading a happy and productive life are dependent on the finding and using of acceptable solutions to drives (motives).

Needs and/or tensions arise from primary (basic) drives and from secondary (learned or acquired) drives. Primary drives are the same for everyone. They consist of visceral or survival functions, kinesthetic (activity) functions, and sensory functions (reactions to external stimuli). Secondary drives vary with the individual because they are acquired in the process of growth. Motivations are wound into these drives. That is, the propensity to alleviate a need or tension will give rise to a motive for behavior.

The way an individual handles a motive to seek relief determines the degree to which personal adjustment has occurred and eventually, whether mature or immature behavior results. Attaining relief and/or satisfaction from a need or tension involves the following sequential pattern: there is a motive to seek relief through goal-seeking behavior which is directed towards a goal of satisfaction. For example, until a child reaches two years of age, he seeks relief from wet diapers through crying or other noticeable means. The motive is to seek relief from an uncomfortable feeling through goal-seeking behavior (crying). This is acceptable at this time but eventually the goal-seeking behavior must change. Society expects that by the time the child is about two years old he be toilet-trained. Thus, the motive remains the same but the behavior that brings relief is different.

While the motive for seeking relief from tensions or needs (drive satisfaction) is present since birth, the means and the manner of goal-seeking behavior become increasingly more complex as the individual grows and is influenced by the standards of society. Therefore, the process of development leading to mature, acceptable behavior, requires that the individual adjust his motives so that they are acceptable to society. His behavior must satisfy a personal need and simultaneously comply with societal mores.

● **PROBLEM 10-4**

Make the distinction between primary and secondary sources of drive giving examples of each.

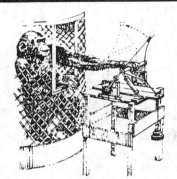

A strong conditioned, secondary reinforcer in daily human life is money. Wolfe showed in an important series of experiments that chimpanzees, too, could learn to use "money." Wolfe showed that they could be conditioned to pull down a heavily weighted handle in order to obtain tokens (poker chips) which could then be inserted into a machine that vended peanuts or bananas. The value of the tokens to the chimps was evident from the fact that they would work for them and save them—and would sometimes try to steal them from one another.

Solution: When speaking about motivational variables a distinction is often made between primary and secondary drive sources. Generally, primary sources of drive are associated with innate bodily mechanisms. These drive sources are sometimes called homeostatic, biogenic or physiogenic. Examples of stimuli having a primary motivational effect are food, water, air, temperature and almost any intense stimuli such as loud noises and electric shocks.

All secondary sources of drive are learned. These are acquired drives--responses that have been acquired in a particular environmental situation. These responses have motivational consequences similar to the primary sources. That is, they influence and direct behavior. Today, much of human behavior is thought to depend upon acquired drives. For this reason, they have been of special importance to the psychologist. These sources of drive include such learned desires as success, power, affection, money, appearance, and security. Some theorists believe that fear, anxiety and certain verbal cues are also learned drives.

In modern culture it is no longer common to experience hunger, thirst or great amounts of pain. What is it then that motivates the great amounts of activity in any large metropolitan area? Acquired drives appear to be central to any explanation of modern life.

● **PROBLEM 10-5**

What is an instinct?

A young wolf raised by humans will howl like an adult in the wild even though it has never heard the cries of other wolves. Behavior that appears to be independent of other learning, as this howling does, is called species-specific behavior.

Solution: It was with the work of Darwin that the concept of "instinct" became important to the study of human behavior. During Darwin's time, the term "instinct" referred to behaviors that were not acquired through learning and experience but that were provided for in the organism's biological structure. It was proposed that on their first appearance, these behaviors are performed, if not perfectly, at least well enough to secure the survival of the individual. This formulation gave rise to a great deal of controversy during the first half of this century between those who adhered to the earlier philosophic idea that instinct was a natural urge to maintain life and seek happiness and those who entertained the possibility that complex behaviors have an innate origin.

The work of William McDougall was especially important in classifying and understanding instincts. McDougall proposed that each instinct is receptive to certain stimuli and contains a disposition to behave in a certain way. He further argued that the receptivity and behavioral components of each instinct might change as a function of learning. He maintained that each instinct has an emotional core that will not change with experience. Therefore, as one became older, an instinct might be activated by different stimuli and produce many different behaviors, but the emotional component will remain the same. He generated a list that paired each instinct with an emotion. For example, flight was paired with fear and pugnacity was paired with anger.

During the early part of the century, hundreds of "instinct" theorists published long lists of new "instincts" and proposed that these were the determinants of the arousal and direction of behavior. There was no attempt to measure

the predictibility of these instincts and the sole
criterion for inclusion in the lists was the opinion of
the particular psychologist who was formulating each list.
It is no wonder that this procedure fell into disrepute.
Consequently, theories about instincts underwent extensive
revisions. Today, it is generally accepted that innate
tendencies interact with experience to produce behavior.

● **PROBLEM 10-6**

What evidence is there to support the theory that an exploratory drive exists in animals and man?

 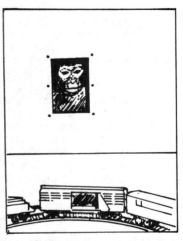

Monkeys will work vigorously for the privilege of viewing an
electric train. Similarly, human children (and adults) find
toys highly enjoyable.

Solution: A wide range of experiments support the idea that
an exploratory or curiosity drive exists. These experiments
have been conducted chiefly with animals. The major finding
can be summarized as follows: In many situations, animals
will prefer to leave familiar surroundings or stimuli in
favor of novel environments or objects. A most commonly
observed laboratory example of this phenomenon is that rats
trained in a T-maze where they can take two routes, simply
for free running purposes, will choose a different route on
alternate trials. This does not appear to be a result of
fatigue. The rats seem to have become tired of experiencing
the same environment. It has also been shown that rats
are more likely to enter a compartment if it contains a
large variety of objects than if it contains only a few or
none at all.

In experiments designed to see whether exploratory behavior
was rewarding or not, the opportunity to explore new situations appeared to have reinforcing qualities. Animals have
learned to choose the arm of a Y-maze that led to a chamber
containing numerous objects. Rats have also learned to
press a bar for more light and to open a door that led to a
different compartment. Novel stimuli quickly lose their

motivating value. That is, after repeated exposure to new
situations or objects, the animal is no longer motivated
to approach and explore them. This appears to further support the theory of an exploratory drive.

There are, however, a number of research findings that indicate that not all novel stimuli elicit exploratory behavior,
particularly in regard to strange objects. Rats, for instance, resist leaving their home cage to explore an elevated runway. Monkeys will not learn to open a door if it
will reveal a dog or the recorded voices of a monkey colony
under attack. A fear drive has been postulated to explain
these findings. However, the circularity that develops when
behavior is explained by either a fear or an exploratory
drive does not have much scientific use. If a strange object is approached, an exploratory drive is used to explain
it. If the object is not approached, the existence of a
fear drive is supported. Overall, it would seem that more
research is needed before the presence of an exploratory
drive can be asserted with certainty.

It is particularly not clear in many of these experiments
whether or not factors such as anxiety or stimulus deprivation
are involved in the behavior that is labeled as "curiosity."
That is, the animal may be motivated by the prospects of
something new, or it may simply be motivated by the possibility of leaving the old environment. It is also likely
and possible that a conceptualization that takes into
consideration both of these factors would, in time, best
explain the behavior patterns of both man and animals.

● **PROBLEM** 10-7

What are the common characteristics of homeostatic or consistency theories? What are some of their shortcomings?

Solution: The idea that behavior has a homeostatic nature
--that is, that it tends to go in a direction that will
restore equilibrium or balance to the organism--has a long
history in many realms besides psychology. The concept
originated in the study of the physiology of the organism.
It was believed that the processes involved in keeping
the body in a consistent state depended on the needs of
the situation. The body was considered an open system that
was constantly interacting with the outside world--at one
moment requiring food intake, at another water, etc.

Three major types of homeostatic or consistency theories
are found in psychology: Heider's balance theory, Osgood
and Tannenbaums' congruity theory and Festingers' theory of
cognitive dissonance. These theories maintain that the
principal motivating force of the organism is to maintain a
consistent physical or psychological state. There is a
good deal of empirical evidence supporting consistency
theorists. Psychophysical research with perceptual constancies has demonstrated that the neurological system
tends to process such stimuli as brightness, color, form,

and size so as to achieve constancy of environmental stimulation. Another type of research that supports these theories is organizational work analyses. It has been found that work behavior tends to be kept at a steady pace despite changes in the external environment such as increased noise level or the introduction of music.

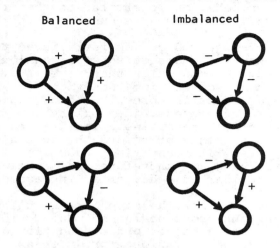

Balanced and imbalanced cognitive structures. Plus and minus signs indicate positive and negative relationships, respectively; arrows indicate the direction of the relationships. The theory states that imbalanced structures tend to change and become balanced.

Despite the support that such theories have accumulated, numerous objections have been leveled against them. Some researchers criticize the theories because they do not account for creativity or for self-destructive behavior. The theories also fail to explain why humans sometimes seek out substances that cannot possibly restore balance in a physiological sense--such as alcohol, tobacco, etc. Researchers also object to the theories on the grounds that they do not account for individual differences in the amount of consistency preferred and in the amount of inconsistency tolerated.

● **PROBLEM** 10-8

What is an acquired drive? Explain how acquired drives are thought to be developed.

Solution: Modern life has made the experience of intense or prolonged pain the exception rather than the rule. This occurrence has caused the assignment of basic drives to the innate, instinctual level of man to lose its strength. In its place, a body of theory has begun to build that explains complex human behavior as a result of acculturation and learning. It is obvious today that human beings are motivated to a large degree by such learned responses or acquired drives as success, power, affection, money, prestige, security, etc. It is clear that these "drives" are learned

since a human infant does not possess these tendencies. To
the scientist, the result of learning is the acquisition of
a response or a tendency to respond. For a drive to be acquired it must elicit a new or altered response that influences the motivational behavior of the organism. The acquisition of these drives can be demonstrated experimentally.
Their effect on behavior is similar to the effects of biologically based drives such as hunger or thirst.

The etiology of acquired drives is believed to begin with a
learned tendency to be discontented or anxious when the
specific object, toward which the drive is eventually directed, is not present. From this viewpoint, cues such as
lack of money, affection, prestige, etc. could acquire,
through a learning process, the ability to arouse an anxiety
reaction with drive properties. The learned anxiety would
serve to motivate behavior toward the acquisition of these
stimulus objects. The resulting reduction of anxiety would
be quite satisfying and therefore, reinforcing. Thus, the
strength of the learned behavior is increased.

As an example, consider the case of the child whose parents
are always anxious about having no money. To this child,
money could become a higher order conditioned stimulus that
could, on subsequent occasions, produce anxiety in him.
The presence of money could actually reduce anxiety in this
child. Thus, in this case, money has all the characteristics
it needs to be considered an acquired drive.

● **PROBLEM** 10-9

Discuss the statement: Fear is an acquired drive.

Solution: Conditioned fear (anxiety) is a well-established
learned motivator or acquired drive. Conditioned fear is a
learned emotional reaction to situations that are believed
to produce painful or harmful stimuli. It is acquired by
the classical conditioning process and has many of the same
effects on behavior as biologically based drives such as
hunger. It will energize behavior and its reduction is
thought to have reinforcing qualities that make it even
stronger as an acquired drive. That fear has energizing
qualities is well supported by everyday experience. It
motivates people in novels, stories, movies and television
to tremendous feats of endurance. It is also true that
fear can function as an inhibitor.

Beginning with the work of Mowrer in the late 1930s, acquired fear has been studied experimentally. Three types
of experiments have contributed to the acceptance of fear
as an acquired drive. The first type of experiment shows
that a response evoked while a conditioned stimulus for
fear is presented is enhanced or augmented. This demonstrates that fear, as a drive, has an activating quality.
The second category of experiments has shown that fear
reduction serves as reinforcement for new learned responses.
Motivational drives must have this capacity to lead to new

learning. The last group of experimental evidence comes
from studies in which the evoking of conditioned fear leads
to the inhibition of the learned response when the fear is
aroused after the reaction. This too is a property of a
motivational drive. Though most of these experiments have
been carried out with animals, there is much evidence that
similar acquired fears and anxieties are important in the
motivational structure of human beings.

● **PROBLEM** 10-10

People work for money: What kind of a goal is money?

Solution: People strive toward two kinds of goals:
extrinsic and intrinsic.

Extrinsic goals, often referred to as artificial goals,
include such things as money, houses, cars and clothes
which can be designated as personal material possessions.
Intrinsic goals, often referred to as innermost goals, are
hopes, aims and desires directed towards self-fulfillment
and a satisfying life. Intrinsic goals reflect such personal
subjective needs as establishing a home, and embarking on
a satisfying career.

Very often people derive the most satisfaction when they
attain their intrinsic goals. However, the fulfillment of
intrinsic goals is often dependent on extrinsic variables
such as money. For example, a potential musician needs
money to secure the necessary preparation and training for
his profession.

The fulfillment of both extrinsic and intrinsic goals is
based on motivation. Motivation is expressed in personal
drives. The individual is not born with motives; he is
born with simple innate equipment which facilitate his
survival. Goal-oriented behavior is based on learning
experiences made possible by this innate equipment.

Since the human being responds to both primary and secondary
(learned or acquired) drives in order to alleviate needs or
tensions, goal-seeking behavior becomes essential to human
adjustment in terms of securing personal happiness and
satisfaction. Through the process of social learning and
adjustment the human being acquires a motivation to attain
self-fulfillment in life.

The fulfillment of intrinsic goals in life are seldom accomplished without the aid of extrinsic goals. Money,
being essential to the accomplishment of intrinsic goals,
becomes a very powerful learned extrinsic motivation and
drives people to work for money.

● **PROBLEM** 10-11

Verbal stimuli may be an acquired source of drive. Discuss.

Solution: Insofar as human motivational systems are thought
to be different from those of animals, it is logical to suppose that the capacity and use of language is a main contribution to the unique motivational mechanisms in humans.
Some theorists believe that from the time verbal behavior
is learned, certain verbal cues may become acquired motivational sources, mainly through the learned responses
that they evoke.

Some verbal cues as, for example, "Hurry up" or "Don't do
that" when spoken by a parent to a child have a marked
motivational effect.   The effect is to produce a general
activation no matter what activity the child is involved
in--eating dinner, cleaning his room, crossing the street.
Because of this ability to energize a wide range of behavior,
these types of motivating words bear a close resemblance to
the acquired source of drive--conditioned fear.   It is
important that these commands be free of specific content
to qualify as learned sources of drive.   "Eat your spinach"
could hardly qualify as a general motivator of behavior.

This theory has been further developed to purport that
individuals learn to administer these motivating words to
themselves.   All people are thought to administer special
self commands during times of stress.   Some individuals
learn to administer words such as "Do your best," "You
must succeed" when they are placed in certain situations.
These would be the individuals that Atkinson describes as
high in need for achievement.   It is easy to observe the
energizing influence the word "hurry" has on someone as he
looks at his wristwatch and learns that he is already 5
minutes late for an appointment.   He will either walk
faster, peddle more quickly, or drive at a higher speed.
Considering the influence of language on human behavior,
it is surprising that so little research has been conducted
in this area.

● **PROBLEM 10-12**

Is sexual behavior an innate or learned motivating factor?
Discuss.

Solution: Though sexual behavior has often been classified
as instinctual, there has been growing interest in the view
that it is at least partially a learned drive.   If it was
completely innate it would not be readily manipulable by
altering the internal or external state of the organism,
which recent experimentation has proven possible.

Though the mating season for animals is thought to be innate, it has been shown that by altering the amount of artificial light to which they are exposed, cats, for instance,
can be made to demonstrate mating behavior in November and
December though their usual season is from February to June.
Experiments have also been done with certain varieties of
fish to demonstrate that the presence of certain external
cues is necessary for sexual behavior to take place.   One

348

type of fish, the stickleback male, displays sexual behavior only at the sight of a female fish with a swollen abdomen. These females contain eggs and when they are seen by the male fish, he begins nest-building behavior. A model of such a female fish also evokes this behavior in the male, while a slim model does not.

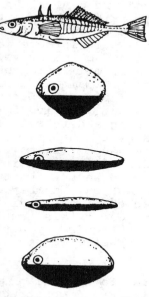

Tinbergen found that a male stickleback will attack any of the bottom four of these models before it will attack the top one, which closely resembles a stickleback in everything but the red belly. The red belly acquired by male sticklebacks during the mating season is a sign for attack that outweighs all other stimuli.

The role of experience in sexual activity also lends support to the idea that sexuality is at least partially learned. While sexually mature rats that have been reared in isolation show normal copulation activity, monkeys and apes with the same background fare poorly. It appears that the position of an animal on the phylogenetic scale is important in determining how much learning influences its sexuality. Though it was for a long time thought of as a primary (or innate) biological drive, sexual behavior is more easily influenced by the learning process than are hunger and thirst, which are essential for the survival of the individual organism. In the higher animals, at least, the survival of the species is somewhat more dependent on the particular experiences of the individual members of the group under study.

MOTIVATION THEORISTS: FREUD, MASLOW, HULL, AND TOLMAN

● **PROBLEM** 10-13

What are the four chief characteristics of an instinct according to Freudian theory?

349

Solution: In Freudian motivation theory, which supposes that all action arises from basic innate biological drives, the term "instinct" is a central and important one. An instinct is characterized by four qualities: its source, impetus, aim and object. There are both internal and external sources of tension. The internal sources originate in the body itself and are generally recurring and consistent. Instincts that originate in external situations are irregular. The impetus of an instinct is the force that energizes the instinct. It is dependent on the intensity of the need that is motivating the drive. The aim of every instinct is to reduce or eliminate the tension that gave rise to it. Sometimes the aim is approached in a number of steps if each step appears to bring one closer to the reduction of the tension. A drive for sex can be somewhat reduced by simply making a date with the object of one's desire. This brings us to the last characteristic of each instinct--its object. According to Freud, the object is anything that will diminish or eliminate the tension. The object that is chosen to reduce the tension-producing stimulation is dependent on a number of variables, not the least important of which is the individual's past learning concerning the reduction of this tension and the expectations associated with the particular situation. This can explain why people have so many strange sexual preferences and obsessions.

Instincts were central to Darwinian theory. Building on this biological basis, Freud constructed a psychodynamic system to explain the scope of human activity.

● **PROBLEM 10-14**

Using Freud's Psychoanalytic Theory, explain why a person is motivated to get himself a drink when he is thirsty.

Solution: Sigmund Freud's theory of motivational processes represents only a limited segment of his life work, but it is a segment on which much of his other work was built. In the Darwinian tradition, Freud believed that behavior was motivated by innate instincts and that those that were most likely to survive were those who could best satisfy those instincts. The instincts were collectively referred to as the "id." Biologically based, they represent basic instinctive life maintaining drives such as hunger, thirst, and life reproducing drives concerning sex. It is these instincts that are the main determinants of human behavior. Each innate need is believed to give rise to tensions and inner stimulations. The reduction of these tensions constitutes the main motive force of the individual. That is, it is the reason for all activity. The individual going for a glass of water is doing so to reduce the tension or inner stimulation that is producing the drive to intake water. The satisfaction of this drive results in a feeling of well-being.

Later in the development of the individual, the "ego" and

the "superego" develop. The ego is the reasoning, "executive," part of the personality structure in the Freudian
system. The superego is the internalized representation
of the parents or social directives for handling the desires
of the "id"--it contains an "ideal" way of satisfying the
basic instinctual drives. The ego functions as a controlling
or balancing agent between the drives of the id and the
constraints of the superego. Anxiety occurs when an individual experiences particularly strong conflicting messages
from the id and the superego. These arise especially in
the area of sexual gratification. One of the ways in which
the ego handles such conflicts is to modify the behavior
so that it satisfies the id and is acceptable to the superego. These instinctual gratifications are called "ego
defense mechanisms."

There are a number of such mechanisms including "regression,"
"compensation," "resignation," "withdrawal," and "conversion." All of these substitute means of gratifying basic
instincts are carried out without the individual knowing
that the ego is trying to arrange for the id to express
itself. Thus, going for a glass of water might actually
be an instance of the defense-mechanism of "conversion."
This is true if the situation that produced the desire for
drink stirred conflicting drives in the individual. For
example, if the subject of conversation is one that touches
too closely on an activity about which he has a great deal
of guilt--having sexual desires for his sister--the desire
of the id to continue talking and the superego's prohibition
against such considerations result in conflict. The ego may
then intervene to produce a desire for water. The ego's
action is satisfactory on two levels: it pleases the
superego by ending participation in the conversation and
it satisfies an instinctual (id) demand.

Freud's motivation theory is basically biological. It has
had a great influence on subsequent theorists and researchers. Freud's imaginative flair often appeals to the modern
day student of motivation and human behavior.

● **PROBLEM** 10-15

Discuss Maslow's hierarchical approach to motivation.

Solution: Abraham Maslow is a chief proponent of the
humanistic school of human behavior. His most widely
discussed and popular theory concerns the hierarchical
nature of man's motivational structure. He set forth a
five-stage model in which the lower, most dominant needs
control the actions of the organism until they are fulfilled,
at which time the next higher needs in the hierarchy become
predominant until they are satisfied, then the next level
of needs come into play and so forth. The 5 levels in his
Hierarchy of Needs, which are best represented in a pyramid
structure, are:

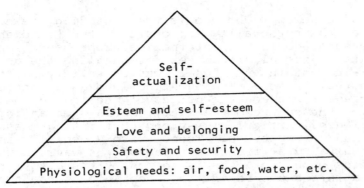

Self-
actualization

Esteem and self-esteem

Love and belonging

Safety and security

Physiological needs: air, food, water, etc.

Most of the time behavior is directed toward lower level needs, the percentage of self-actualizing individuals in the population is thought to be quite small. The higher level needs are expressed more subtley than the lower needs and are thus more difficult to measure systematically.

Theoretically, it is possible to assess a person's dominant needs at any point in his life and to use this information to predict a pattern in his behavior. Maslow's theory lacks strict empirical support. It has been found that an individual's behavior will not reflect his needs unless incentives exist in the environment which promise fulfill-ment of the need. Maslow's contribution to the development of motivational theory will not be known until someone can adequately account for the role of the environment on the expression of motivational needs.

● **PROBLEM 10-16**

How would Maslow differentiate between an individual who was motivated by lower needs and one who was motivated by self-actualization needs?

Solution: Maslow's Hierarchy of Needs theory proposes five motivational levels that direct human behavior in a hierar-chical manner. The most basic needs are physiological, these are followed by safety and security needs, love and belonging, self-esteem and finally, self-actualization needs. As one need is satisfied, the next in the hierarchy becomes the important motivating factor. According to Maslow, there is a marked difference between the behavior patterns of people motivated by lower needs (deficiency-oriented) and those motivated by self-actualization needs (growth-oriented). The deficiency-oriented person can be contrasted to the growth-oriented individual on a number of different behavior characteristics.

The person who is still motivated to satisfy lower needs is characterized by a tendency to be self-centered and concerned with his own needs, to reject his own impulses, to seek goals that are common to many others, to look for gratifica-tions that are relatively short-term and temporary, to seek gratification that results in tension-reduction, to behave mainly on the basis of external cues, and to view others in terms of how they can satisfy his needs.

On the other hand, the growth-oriented person is likely to
be more concerned with the nature of the world at large and
other people than with himself, to be accepting of his
impulses, to attain goals that are individualistic and
unique to him, to be attracted to gratifications that lead
to permanent and long-term change, to behave from internal
rather than external cues, and to view people for what they
are, not as potential subjects he can utilize to satisfy
his needs.

This picture of the self-actualizing individual may be
partly responsible for the increasing number of mental
health therapists who have adopted Maslow's theory or some
variant of it as a goal model for their patients. Self-
actualizing behavior is clearly that of an optimally developed individual. Before Maslow's conceptualization of the
term through his study of exceptional individuals, the
literature was scarce in its descriptions of healthy behavior and heavy in its concentration of pathological
tendencies. It was Maslow who formally introduced to psychology the model of a healthy, optimally functioning
individual. That so many have adopted his theoretical
stance is evidence of the need that existed for the work
he has done.

● **PROBLEM** 10-17

Performance = Drive x Habit is the symbolic representation
of what motivation theorist? Explain this theory including
a discussion of the variables "drive" and "habit."

Solution: Next to Freud, Clark Hull has probably been the
most influential theorist in psychology. Hull's fame stems
from his development of a conceptually tight and mathemat-
ically-oriented theory of motivational processes. He rejected the earlier subjective ideas such as "soul" and
"will" in favor of physically defined and measurable
variables. Hull's basic explanation for behavior was true
to the Darwinian tradition. That is, he believed that man
is basically a survivor. Any life-threatening situation,
according to Hull, prompts man to respond in such a way as
to insure his continued existence. His response may be
innate or learned. Situations that threatened survival
were physically defined as consisting of primary biological
drives such as hunger, thirst, pain, and sex. According to
the theory, stimulation associated with any of these variables arouses behavior that aims to reduce or eliminate the
stimulation. Following from this notion, Hull concluded
that man is motivated to attain a condition with minimal
stimulation. His conclusion was not new. But Hull's genius
was reflected in his ability to evoke precise details to
explain the mechanisms operating in the arousal and activation of behavior.

Hull's theory accounted for the appetitive drives of hunger,

thirst, and sex, and for the aversive drive of pain avoidance. A physiological need was believed to produce a drive
that sought to initiate a behavior that would reduce the
drive and satisfy the need. The behavior the organism employed depended on the degree of success with which the
behavior had reduced the drive in the past. This learned
association between the drive and the behavior that reduces
it is called a "habit."

To explain this process, Hull constructed the formula:
Performance = Drive x Habit or P = D x H. That is, the
strength of the impetus to respond is a multiplicative
function of drive and habit. The formula contains weaknesses which led Hull to revise it. Despite its shortcomings, the formula was important. It was the basis for an
objective and mathematical model of motivation. It stimulated its proponents as well as its opponents to further
research.

● **PROBLEM** 10-18

Discuss what happens when a person is placed in a state of
stimulus or sensory deprivation. How has this research
affected the Hullian view that the human organism is motivated to minimize the amount of stimulation in its environment?

Solution: Early modern motivational theorists, particularly
Clark Hull, hypothesized that man is motivated to achieve a
condition in which he is subject to minimal stimulation, to
insure his survival. This position has attracted much
criticism. Recent work in sensory deprivation has contributed greatly to its demise as a theory. Sensory-deprivation
research has demonstrated that the human organism strives
on moderation. People tend to find environments aversive
when they are either repetitive and predictable or when they
contain a large amount of information or novel stimuli.

Though many people feel it would be a wonderful luxury to
be able to sit and do nothing, experiments with minimal
sensory input have proven this to be untrue. When subjects
are placed in soundproof, uniformly lit rooms with minimal
stimulation for long periods of time, they find the experience to be extremely uncomfortable and unpleasant. After
only a day of such deprivation, subjects show marked dis-
ruptions in their thinking and perceptual processes. Some
even report hallucinations, which appear to be an attempt
by the neural mechanisms to produce some degree of stimulation in the absence of external input. Many report that
they try to focus their attention on whatever stimulation
there is so as to reduce the monotony of the experiment.

Repetitive or unchanging stimulation is equally unpleasant.
Continuous noise ("white noise") has been presented to subjects with much the same result as the deprivation experiments. Humans appear to have a limited-capacity processing
system, a system that is stressed by either an overload or

underload of information. The excess of stimulation produced by large cities and the rapid pace of modern life
have been suggested by some to be the principal causes for
a common malady of modern society--information overload
which was described by Toffler in Future Shock. Though
it may appear that the remedy for this overload is its
opposite or minimal stimulation, it is now known that an
environment that offers a moderate amount of new information
is the optimal one for effective human functioning.

● **PROBLEM** 10-19

What is the activation-arousal theory of motivational processes? How did it serve to compensate for the weaknesses
of Hullian theory?

Monkeys will open locks that are placed in their cage. Since
no reward is given for this activity, it provides evidence of
the existence of stimulus needs.

Solution: The initial premise of the Hullian drive theory
of motivation, which assumed that the strength of a biological drive accompanied by past learning was responsible
for behavior, was weakened when further investigation revealed difficulties with its approach. Two findings that
put Hullian hypotheses in question were the evidence that
organisms sometimes seek increased stimulation, rather than
reduced stimulation and that people continue to show
directed motivated behavior even when there is apparently
no state of need. These findings served as a catalyst for
the development of an approach that would account for the
weaknesses in the original theory.

The new approach, known as the activation, the arousal or
the activation-arousal approach, sets forth the basic
premise that people seek an optimal level of stimulation,
which once achieved, leads to the most effective behavior.
This formulation leaves out the necessity of a biological
deprivation state as a motivating force. It addresses the
problems of drive for increased stimulation and allows for
individual differences in optimal stimulation.

A major problem with this approach is that it has never
clearly defined whether "arousal" refers to a physiological
or a psychological variable. More experimentation is
necessary before the activation-arousal theory can be
forwarded as the explanation for motivational processes.

Tolman showed that learning can occur in the relative absence of internal drive states. What is the name given to this phenomenon and what type of experiments are used to prove it?

Solution: Tolman, a motivational psychologist working in the 1920s, observed that the presence of an appropriate object could arouse a drive or appetite that led to behavior designed to reduce that appetite. This type of motivational process has been labeled as "incentive motivation." Classic examples of this type of behavior are cases where the sight of a pretty girl arouses the sex drive in a male, which had not been active until then, or cases where the smell of hamburgers being grilled as one passes by elicits hunger that previously was not there. Tolman postulated that, in reality, the drive was already somewhat aroused and that the stimuli only served to make it more obvious or hastened the process by which it would come into the individual's awareness. Therefore, this type of "second-order" drive did not have a direct physiological basis, yet it was built upon and determined by "first-order" or physiological drives. Other examples of these types of incentive or second-order drives that were considered included curiosity, imitation, self-deprecation, gregariousness, and assertiveness. To study these drives, Tolman controlled the strength of the primary drives and then recorded the variations that appeared in the strength of the others.

This type of experiment has been performed with rats. In one study, the physiological drive (hunger) was held constant for two groups of rats. Both groups were then placed in mazes. It was found that the group that received bread and milk at the end of the maze performed better than the group that received sunflower seeds. Thus, the characteristics of the goal object were an incentive that contributed to the behavior of the organism. The learning rate depended on the quality of the goal.

Performance = Expectation x Value is the symbolic representation of which theorist and what school of thought? Discuss.

Solution: While Clark Hull was developing his mathematical model of motivational processes, Edward Tolman was working on a different approach to motivational phenomena. Tolman's approach utilized many terms that Hull rejected because of their subjective or cognitive character, such as expectations, demands, values, etc. In Tolman's view, behavior is precipitated by environmental cues, both internal and external, and by a variety of unbalanced situations. The

motivational theories developed by Tolman and a number of
later psychologists are known as expectancy-value theories.
These theories state that behavior is a result of the needs
and demands of a person at any given time and of the quality
of the environment at that particular time as perceived
by that person. Or, more simply, behavior is the result of
the expectancy of attaining what is wished for and the
degree of value attributed to the situation at hand.

The major theoretical components of Tolman's theory were
1) an individual's expectancies of achieving his goal in
a certain environment, 2) the degree to which the goal is
available in the environment and 3) the level of the demand
for the particular goal. These variables could be used to
measure both the persistence and direction of an individual's
behavior. Expectancy-value theory has been used by Vroom
and Porter to explain the commonly observed lack of response
to incentives offered by large organizations of workers
today. They explained that the environment in which many
of today's workers operate is often one with low expectancies
and value-oriented behavior. This is particularly true of
those people in the lower part of the hierarchy, due to
the large size and pyramidal structure of most large organizations. This has been supported by studies in which responsiveness to incentives increased when managers were encouraged and given the opportunity to increase the expectations for reward and success in their employees.

Applications such as these have made this school of thought
appealing and useful to practitioners and psychologists in
many applied areas such as social work, education, industry
and mental health.

ACHIEVEMENT CONFLICTS: MURRAY

● PROBLEM 10-22

Discuss Murray's theory of motivation and what influence it
had on McClelland's development of the Achievement Motivation model.

Solution: Writing and working in the 1930s, Henry Murray
was chiefly a student of personality. He theorized that
human behavior could best be understood by observing everyday life, not by performing laboratory experiments. To
him, motivational processes were a reflection of individual
needs and motives. To the end of conceptualizing these
needs, he devoted much attention and research to supporting
the idea that individual needs observed in everyday life
were viable constructs for studying motivational processes.

The needs studied by Murray had both a directional and an
arousal component. He observed individual differences in
these needs on a relatively complex level. Murray's pioneering work with individual differences in motivational
needs led to the question of how these needs develop. Why
does one person develop the need to harm others, another

the need to be a high achiever, and another the need to be socially active? Another question that his work provoked was, What is the aim of these motives? Hull's work assumed that the force behind all motives was the survival of the organism--biologically based, hunger, thirst, and sex all serve to keep the organism alive and healthy. But what are such motives as affiliation and achievement aimed at achieving?

The work of David McClelland addressed these questions. Essentially, he stated that anything that leads to positive affect produces approach behavior and anything that leads to negative affect produces avoidance behavior. He further explained what gives rise to negative and positive affect. Experiences that represent a moderate discrepancy from past experience along any dimension will lead to positive affect and approach behavior. Situations that involve large discrepancies from past experiences will produce negative affect and avoidance behavior. This view, which he enlarged upon in his work on Achievement Motivation, can be confirmed experimentally. This was a major step for theorists of the expectancy-value school of thought who considered cognitive as well as physical variables to be determinants of behavior.

● **PROBLEM** 10-23

Discuss McClelland's concept of Achievement Motive and the effect of nAch on individual behavior.

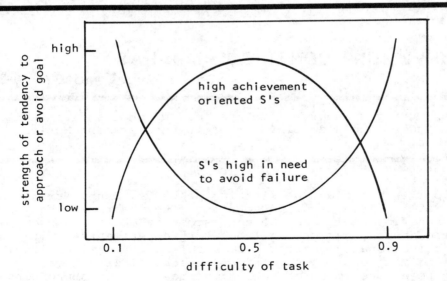

Solution: Why is it that some people are driven to succeed at what they do and others do not appear to have much interest in success or high-level performance? Why are some people unwilling to even undertake a task in which they have a good chance of succeeding? These questions are important, particularly in our success-oriented society. They have been of interest to psychologists for a long time because of their applicability to both work and school performance. The pioneer work in this area was carried out by David

McClelland. He postulated that the achievement motive
develops in some people and not in others because it is a
producer of positive affect for some and of negative affect
for others. An achievement environment produces positive
affect when it produces outcomes that are only moderately
discrepant from those previously experienced, and negative
affect when its results are very different from previous
experience. For example, a person who has scored high on
achievement motivation would be predicted to approach, stay
in, and perform well in situations with opportunities for
achievement. This would occur mainly because achievement
environments are not too different from the environments in
which his previous learning has taken place. Individuals
that measure low on need for achievement would find such
situations negative and tend to avoid them and perform less
effectively in them. Again, mainly because their past
experience did not include much exposure to similar environments.

Since individuals differ in the amount of satisfaction they
receive from achievement, it was further hypothesized that
environments can be measured as providing more or less
achievement opportunities. Achievement-oriented individuals
prefer environments in which there is moderate risk, as
achievement will not be experienced much in low risk situations nor is it likely to occur in high risk situations with
very low probability of success. Feedback on performance
is necessary to the achievement-oriented individual since
it is important for him to know whether he has accomplished
what he has set out to do. Finally, individual responsibility must be provided. The achievement-oriented person
wishes it to be seen as the one responsible for the result.

McClelland further hypothesized from his investigations
that people with a high need for achievement are attracted
to entrepreneurial pursuits for their lifetime occupation
since such activities often afford an environment that contains all the ingredients necessary to produce high achievement stimulation. From this hypothesis, McClelland has
developed theories concerning the economic growth and potential of countries based on the level of achievement-
motivation of their inhabitants.

● **PROBLEM** 10-24

How is Achievement Motive (nAch) measured in both individuals
and countries?

Solution: The traditional method for measuring the motive
to achieve (nAch) is to administer a Thematic Apperception
Test (TAT). The TAT consists of a series of ambiguous pictures which the subject must write stories about. The
experimenter then scores the stories for achievement
imagery. The more achievement-related topics the stories
include, the higher the nAch is inferred to be for the given
individual.

David McClelland wanted to study achievement on a large scale.

He theorized that because high nAch individuals were attracted to entrepreneurial occupations, it followed that
the higher the level of nAch in a country, the greater its
rate of economic growth. Accepting the premise that individual nAch can be measured from a person's literary output
(TAT stories), McClelland measured the nAch of a nation with
a similar procedure. He developed a further dimension of
the methodological approach used to evaluate individual
nAchs.

Assuming that the dominant characteristics of a society would
be most likely to surface in childhood stories and folktales,
McClelland studied the basic themes of these sources for
various nations at different points in their histories.
From this literature he generated nAch scores for the
countries involved and related these scores to the subsequent economic growth or decline of each country. He measured the economic growth by evaluating the use of electric
power and the level of national income. Despite the difficulties that his research approach entailed, McClelland's
results were intriguing. His results supported his hypothesis that economic growth is positively correlated with
need for achievement themes in literature.

Although these results have been supported by other research,
there are also findings that challenge it. Therefore, the
relation between a nation's nAch and rate of economic growth
remains to be confirmed by further research.

● **PROBLEM** 10-25

Fear of failure is closely related to and often interferes
with achievement motivation. Explain this statement.

Solution: The theory of achievement motivation, originally
advanced by David McClelland, has been further developed
by John Atkinson. Atkinson's most recent formulation
describes two basic types of people, both of whom will
respond in an achievement-oriented way, but the environments that will give rise to the greatest achievement behavior will be different for each group. The first group
is comprised of individuals who are more motivated to
achieve than they are to avoid failure; members of the
second group are more motivated by the fear of failure than
by the motive to achieve success. The first group experiences a pleasant affect from success, while the second
group experiences a pleasant affect from avoiding failure.

An important point of consideration for an achievement-
motivated individual is the degree of difficulty of the task
involved. Some tasks have a high probability of success,
such as P = .9, and other tasks have a low probability of
success, such as P = .1. The greatest sense of achievement
is supposedly derived from successful accomplishment of the
more difficult tasks. Atkinson has postulated that individuals who are primarily motivated to achieve will perform
best in situations with tasks of medium difficulty, P = .5.
On the other hand, persons motivated by a fear of failure

would be more likely to be attracted to tasks with an extremely high possibility of failure, P = .05 or with an
extremely high chance of success, P = .95. In both cases
the experience of failure would be mitigated. In the first
because the task was so difficult that almost no one would
be expected to succeed and in the second because chances
of failure are minimal.

The situation that the high fear of failure individual
avoids most is precisely that which the high nAch person
would be most likely to approach--the medium-risk situation,
P = .5. It is assumed that high fear of failure individuals
would avoid all achievement-related tasks if it were possible, but when they find themselves in a situation where
they must work on task-achievement, they will be attracted
to extremely difficult or extremely easy tasks.

These theoretical predictions have produced intriguing, but
confusing results. They have made it apparent that there
is a need for refining and standardizing the measurement
procedures.

BEHAVIORAL AND SOCIAL APPROACHES

● **PROBLEM** 10-26

What is the motive to avoid success? Why is it spoken of
mainly in regard to women?

Solution: Immediately following the first publication of
the nAch studies conducted by David McClelland, it was explained that the data and theory were not applicable to
women. It was suggested that what motivates people to
task-oriented achievement is different for males and females.
It was not until recently that the precise factors that
underlie these differences in motivation were systematically
explored. Matina Horner (1968) conducted a series of experiments at Harvard to explore this question. She concluded
that women with high abilities and high nAchs have "the
motive to avoid success" which is not commonly found in men
with the same attributes.

"The motive to avoid success" is supported by the socialization practices of this society. It results from the idea
that high achievement is incompatible with "femininity."
Therefore, women with high nAchs receive conflicting affects:
they need to be involved in achievement-related endeavors
but they also don't want to challenge society's mores. Thus,
for high nAch women, optimal achievement situations produce
both approach and avoidance behavior. Therefore, the achievement behavior of females is more difficult to predict than
for males. This is because making a prediction would require measuring the approach and avoidance motives as well
as the fear of failure motive.

Intriguing and popular as this theory is, it has not been
easy to replicate the results. One study even showed that

women performed better when their competitors were men rather than women--a finding which contradicts what would be predicted by Horner's research. Evidently, there is much to learn about achievement behavior in women. This area of research is becoming increasingly important today as opportunities for women change dramatically.

● **PROBLEM** 10-27

What experimental evidence is there that brain mechanisms of motivation are responsible for controlling hunger and thirst?

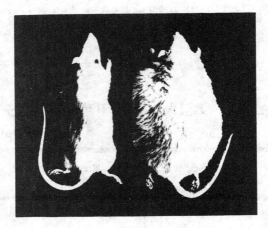

Damage to the hunger-satiety center in the hypothalamus will produce a hyperphagic rat (right) as shown with its normal control.

Solution: If a well-fed animal is placed in a chamber with food that it normally prefers, it will not eat it. If, however, the experimenter turns on an apparatus designed to stimulate an electrode planted in the animal's mid-brain, the animal will proceed to eat. In fact, if the electrode has been properly placed the animal will eat for as long as the stimulation continues. Furthermore, the animal does not just eat anything. His response is identical to that which accompanies the normal biological hunger drive. He is motivated and behaves in the same way as he does when he is hungry. Similar responses have been discovered in a variety of animals for different motivational systems including thirst and reproductive behavior.

While stimulating particular regions of the brain causes an animal to eat, destroying the same region can produce an animal who has no desire for food, even when deprived for long periods of time. Likewise, if stimulating a particular area of the brain causes the animal to stop eating, a lesion in that spot will produce an animal that will not stop eating and appears to be chronically hungry. While psychologists can now control a number of motivational responses through electrical stimulation and surgical procedures, the mechanisms which underlie these responses are still unknown.

How is the esophagus bypass used to study the motivational processes involved in hunger and thirst?

Esophagotomy.

Solution: The digestive system of most organisms is slow, requiring two hours or more to convert a meal into biochemical units for metabolic use. Therefore, many animals, including man, rely on sensing devices that signal when enough food or water has been consumed. These signals come long before a change in the biochemical state can trigger the brain mechanisms to stop eating or drinking.

Some psychologists guessed that a reasonable place for the location of receptors for monitoring the intake of food and drink are somewhere in the mouth or throat area. These researchers designed an experimental device which would help them indicate whether an animal would eat normally even if the food did not reach his stomach. This device is known as the esophical bypass. Theoretically, the animal should eat and drink normally and then stop even though no food or drink has gone further than the mouth and throat. Later, when the consumption motivation system discovers that its estimation had been incorrect, it should again produce eating and drinking behavior in the animal. This is precisely what happens with experimental animals. Placed on a food and drink deprivation schedule and allowed to eat and drink only every 24 hours, the regular habits of the animal are carefully noted. Then the esophagus bypass operation is performed, and once again the animal is placed on the 24-hour deprivation schedule.

A thirsty animal will perform precisely as the theory predicts. He will drink his normal fill and stop. Five or ten minutes later he will drink again, this time more than the first, and then stop. This cycle continues with the amount of water consumed increasing as the deficit increases with time.

A hungry animal, however, will continue eating--sometimes up
to 80% of its body weight (dogs). From these findings, it
is clear that if a mechanism exists for shutting off hunger
it is not in the mouth and throat area. Further experiments
have determined that the feedback mechanism for shutting
off hunger is somewhere in the upper ingestional tract or
the stomach itself.

● **PROBLEM** 10-29

Discuss the role of the reticular activating system in
producing the arousal associated with drive states.

Solution: The normal activation of the brain depends on
the integrity of a loosely packed set of neurons that runs
through the midbrain. This area is called the reticular
activating system (RAS). Investigations of its functions in
the recent past have revealed that it is a sophisticated
and vital part of the central nervous system. It has
abundant and complex connections with other parts of the
nervous system and sends out large numbers of fibers into
the rest of the brain. Communications flow in two directions along these fibers. The RAS receives information
directly from many fibers coming from all parts of the
nervous system. It appears that this area of the brain may
be the central coordinating point for information in the
nervous system.

The most obvious function of this area is that it modulates
the overall activity levels of the brain and therefore
determines the efficiency with which incoming data is processed. Anesthetics have their primary effect by desensi-
tizing this section of the brain, which further supports
the theory that efficient cortical processing depends on
the proper functioning of the RAS. It is this portion of
the brain that appears to produce the activation normally
associated with uncertainty, threat, novelty, conflict,
frustration or other stress-producing stimuli. The activation-arousal of the general system is an important characteristic of such a problem-solving state. It provides the
increased drive level necessary to cope successfully and
effectively with the situation.

● **PROBLEM** 10-30

In a conflict situation what behavioral alternatives does
the organism have at its disposal according to Neal Miller?

Solution: When confronted with a situation that is both
attractive and aversive the organism is likely to experience
conflict. This type of "approach-avoidance" situation was
first systematically studied by Neal Miller. He postulated
that an organism's behavior in relation to a goal with conflicting motives would vary depending on the distance from

the goal and the relative strengths of the approach and avoidance drives. With motives of equal strengths, the further away the organism is from the goal, the more likely it is to approach it. The closer it becomes to the goal, the more likely it is to avoid it, so that a situation is produced that has a stable equilibrium point where the two forces exactly cancel each other. An everyday example of this phenomenon is the person who is attracted to swimming in the ocean. He races to the water's edge and then, if the water is quite cold, he may spend as many as 10 to 15 minutes trying to decide whether or not to go in. Some other variable usually enters--perhaps a friend's coaxing or the sight of a hot dog vendor--to make one or the other of the two motives predominant.

To reduce the conflict for a person in this kind of situation, it is necessary either to increase the positive or approach tendencies of the situation or to reduce the negative or avoidance aspects. This same model has been applied to approach-approach situations in which an individual must make a choice between two equally desirable alternatives, and to avoidance-avoidance situations wherein a person must choose between two equally undesirable decisions.

● **PROBLEM** 10-31

Discuss the role of uncertainty or stress as driving forces in human behavior.

Solution: For as long as a human organism exists in an environment that it considers predictable and normal, it experiences a normal flow or response sequences. However, when something unexpected or threatening enters the environment, the organism becomes alert to the potential problem and mobilizes resources against it. This is subjectively experienced as an arousal or activation state which can range from very high in stress-producing situations to very low in situations with little or no stimulation. The common element in stress-producing situations appears to be a discrepancy between expectations of what will occur and what actually occurs. Uncertainty about one's ability to cope with a forthcoming event, being faced with a situation at a time when it was not anticipated or simply disrupting the normal flow of activity are all stress-producing events.

A famous study, sometimes known as "the executive monkey" experiment, was the basis for some of the current understanding about the activation properties of stress as well as the stress-producing quality of decision-making. Two monkeys were placed in two cages side by side. Each cage had a small box with a button. In one of the cages the box controlled electrical shocks that were administered to both monkeys if the "executive monkey" did not press the bar at least once every 5 seconds. Both monkeys, therefore, received the same amount of shock treatment. However, only one had to remain alert and behave appropriately to avoid the shock while the other monkey lost interest in the box and remained passive. Monkeys were placed in this experimental situation with 6-hour work periods and 6-hour rest periods. During the experimentation, the monkeys did not appear to be any different. Daily physiological tests did not detect anything unusual or abnormal in either monkey. Both had the proper weight and ate normally. However, after 20 days the executive monkey died. The cause of his death was attributed to ulcers. Since both monkeys received the same amount of shocks in the same environment, the painful events were not solely responsible for the stress. It appeared that stress was produced when the monkey had to develop ways of dealing with the threatening situation.

The "executive" monkey on the left has control over the electrical shocks received by both monkeys. The monkey on the right has no control.

The ability to cope with stress varies greatly from individual to individual as does the type of situation that will be perceived as stress-producing. Anything could produce stress--even very minor events. It depends mainly on the condition of the person involved, his past experiences and the availability of personal adaptations to the stress-producing situation. It is the individual's active interpretation of the environment that ultimately produces stress and influences his behavior.

● **PROBLEM** 10-32

What is incentive motivation? What effect have incentives been shown to have on short-term memory?

Solution: The concept of incentive motivation has been

the subject of theoretical debates for decades. It is best understood as an indication that a reinforcement will be given for a particular response. An incentive also has energizing or motivational effects on the organism. It is acquired through interaction with the environment--that is, it is learned from previous experience. Both positive and negative incentives have been used in studies with human subjects. The most common form of positive incentive used is money and the most common negative incentive is loss of money or mild electrical shock.

Much research has been conducted on the effect of incentives on learning and memory. In an experiment with short-term memory, subjects were asked to remember three consonants while engaged in the activity of reading single, random digits on a screen. Altogether, forty consonant trigrams were presented. Ten were presented with one of four colors as background--red, yellow, green or white. These colors served as cues to the reinforcement that would be associated with correct or incorrect recall of the consonants at the end of the trial period. Each subject was well-rehearsed in the color-code incentive which was as follows:

> red -- 1¢ reward for correct response
> yellow -- 5¢ reward for correct response
> green -- electric shock for incorrect response
> white -- no reinforcement for being right or wrong.

The results of this study indicated that at a short retention interval (less than 15 seconds) 80-90% of the trigrams were recalled and incentive had very little influence on recall. However, with longer intervals, the 5¢ reward and the mild electric shock both proved to yield better performance than either the 1¢ reward or the control or no-reinforcement stimuli. Because of the time lag necessary for the effect of the incentive to become evident, it has been hypothesized that its effect may take place during "rehearsal"--the repeating of the words or letters to be recalled. Little is known about how incentive aids memory, the only assertion that can be made is that it helps.

● **PROBLEM** 10-33

What motivational role does anxiety play in verbal learning? How has this typically been measured?

Solution: The motivational effects of an individual's anxiety or arousal state have been studied in a variety of conditions. Much of the research has been conducted in the area of verbal learning because of the accessibility of the data. Two instruments that are often used for determining level of arousal are the Manifest Anxiety Scale (MA) and the Activation-Deactivation Adjective Checklist (AD-ACL).

The MA scale is a self-report inventory in which the subject must respond to statements about himself. An inventory of these responses is taken to determine if an individual is high, moderate or low in relation to group scores on the test. Because anxiety level is thought to correlate with drive level, learning theorists have been particularly interested in the performance of High Anxious and Low Anxious scorers on this measure. Many studies using this instrument have demonstrated that High Anxious individuals do better on verbal learning tasks than do Low Anxious ones.

The AD-ACL is composed of a set of self-descriptive adjectives--each one accompanied by a four-point scale which the individual must complete. A number of the adjectives form a General Activation Scale which is used to determine the High Active and Low Active individuals. The adjectives that are used for the General Activation Scale are words such as "energetic" or "lively." The four point scale is as follows:

```
_____definitely do not feel
_____cannot decide
_____feel slightly
_____definitely feel.
```

Results of studies with this scale have also established a positive relationship between arousal level and verbal learning. The High Active individuals do better on verbal learning tasks than the Low Actives.

In studies that have attempted to compare the different effects of arousal and anxiety, the High Active individuals perform slightly better than the High Anxious group. Overall, experimental results continue to support the theory that any kind of moderate arousal contributes to effective learning.

● **PROBLEM** 10-34

How does equity theory explain aggression?

Solution: Balance or equity theorists assume that inequity or inbalance is a negative tension state which organisms wish to eliminate or reduce. Research in regard to aggressive behavior, both physical and psychological, has produced evidence to support the explanation that inequity is instrumental in causing aggression. In some conditions, individuals perceive that they are receiving outcomes greater than what they deserve or have worked for. This experience produces "inequity"--a tension that results from a familiarity with the basic social norm that indicates that each person receives what he deserves. Inequity often produces a fear that one will be retaliated against for having defied the norm. To reduce this feeling of inequity, a person can follow one of three paths: 1) he can derogate the value of the other person's inputs or 2) he can minimize the other person's inputs or 3) he can deny responsibility for the lack of outcomes that the other person is receiving.

The simplest way to reduce inequity feelings is to justify to oneself that the other person deserves the lower outcomes that he or she is receiving. The easiest way this can be done is to make the person appear as a negative or inferior person. Aggressive behavior toward the individual is initiated with this goal in mind. This is most likely to take place when it is least costly and difficult and when it is most likely to maximize the person's outcomes.

Prejudice and discrimination are explained very well by the equity theory of aggression. The superior status of the prejudiced person is justified by the negative attitudes and behaviors that are perpetrated against the groups that are thought to be inferior.

● **PROBLEM 10-35**

What is cognitive dissonance as explained by Festinger?

Solution: The theory of cognitive dissonance has generated a large amount of controversy and research. Though relatively simple to understand, its implications are widespread and complex. The theory states, basically, that man has many cognitions (attitudes, perceptions) about the world that can have one of three relations to one another. 1) Cognitions can be consonant--they follow from one another and support behavior related to one another. For example, a woman who enjoys cooking, cooks dinner for her family. 2) The cognitions can be irrelevant to one another. This occurs when, for instance, a woman who enjoys cooking telephones her hairdresser. 3) Finally, cognitions can be dissonant. In this case the behaviors that result from the two cognitions are contradictory or at least do not follow from each other. Suppose that the woman who enjoys cooking hires a cook, this means that she will not be cooking much any more. This woman will experience a dissonant state.

The experience of dissonance is a negative one; it produces a motivational state that aims at reducing the dissonance. The greater the dissonance, the more likely it is that behavior will ensue to reduce the dissonance. There are a number of ways in which dissonance can be reduced, many concern the attitudes of the individual involved. The woman who hires a cook may begin to focus on the positive reasons she had for hiring a cook and deemphasize the fact that she herself likes to cook. Dissonance theory predicts that an individual's satisfaction with a decision escalates as any of the following factors is increased: 1) the importance of the decision, 2) the negative side-effects of the decision and 3) the differences between the alternatives the person had to choose from in making his decision.

Cognitive dissonance is an example of a consistency theory and as such has many of the weaknesses and strengths of homeostatic approaches.

● **PROBLEM 10-36**

Discuss the history of the frustration-aggression hypothesis as proposed by Berkowitz.

IT'S ALL **YOUR** FAULT!

If an individual fears punishment for aggressing against the frustrating agent, he may displace aggression onto another target.

Solution: The increase of aggressive behavior in society has attracted the interest of behavioral scientists. The motivation to hurt others has given rise to many theoretical explanations, the most popular of which is probably the "frustration-aggression" hypothesis. Originally, this hypothesis stated simply that aggression was always a result of frustration. Frustration was defined as the interference with the attainment of a certain goal. A one-to-one relationship was postulated between aggression and frustration. It was believed that aggression was always a result of frustration and that frustration always led to a form of overt or covert aggression. As time passed, the theory's weaknesses became apparent and numerous revisions began to take place.

One problem that was quickly pointed out was that there were obvious cases in which aggression appeared to take place with little or no frustration from the object of the aggression. An example is the Jews' persecution in Nazi Germany. Instances were also pointed out where goals were interfered with yet no frustration occurred. Increasingly, the hypothesis has been restated so that aggression is now seen as a likely response to frustration when the expectancy that it will lead to the attainment of the goal is high. Likewise, such a response will be inhibited if the likelihood for punishment for it is perceived as being high. Because of this, high-status persons are less likely to be the objects of aggression (since they hold the power to control rewards and punishments). Lower status or weaker individuals are thus more likely targets of aggression because they do not usually have the means with which to aggress back either economically, psychologically or physically. Therefore, aggression directed against these people is more likely to result in the attainment of a desired goal without undergoing punishment.

Considering all this, the frustration-aggression theory has traveled a long way from its original formulation. It now incorporates the past history and learning of an individual into its explanation and prediction of aggressive behavior

and it is more cognitive in its approach. Aggressive behavior is clearly not the automatic process implied by the
original frustration-aggression hypothesis.

Identify and describe the properties of frustration and discuss whether or not it should be considered a drive.

Solution: Frustration has been defined in many different
ways. For general purposes, the definition of Brown and
Farber, working in the Hullian tradition, is appropriate.
Briefly, they describe frustration as a conflict between
two opposing tendencies: the response originally evoked
by the situation (perhaps connected with the goal in the
situation) and the response evoked by an intervening, frustrating condition. Frustration is the behavior that results
from the interplay of these two opposing responses. It is
commonly agreed that frustration increases the drive of the
existing responses. Therefore, the introduction of a frustrating element into a problem-solving situation is likely
to increase the drive to solve the problem, particularly if
the drive is already strong. Frustration is also responsible
for a change in internal state. This change adds emotional
or affective inner stimuli which may have an invisible
influence on the behavior in the situation.

Operationally, frustration as a concept has a somewhat confusing history, principally because it was used both as a
description of a process and as a product of this process.
To qualify as a motivational drive, "frustration" 1) must
have an energizing as well as a directive and selective
function and 2) the reduction of frustration should act as
a reinforcement in the establishment of learned responses.
Research in the field has supported the concept that these
two properties do belong to frustration as proposed by
Brown and Faber. There do, however, continue to be different conceptual schools of thought.

SHORT ANSWER QUESTIONS FOR REVIEW

Choose the correct answer.

1. Deprivation of a drive causes it to (a) domin-
    ate behavior (b) diminish (c) gradually dis-
    appear (d) change into some other drive   a

2. Maslow's theory of psychogenic needs in the hu-
    man organism states that (a) during the elemen-
    tary school years, social needs assume more im-
    portance than physiological needs b) cognitive
    needs of the child emerge only with considerable
    stimulation in school (c) individual differences
    in relative strength of needs are so great that
    any hierarchy of needs is meaningless (d) the
    hierarchy of needs remains constant throughout
    all of life   d

3. Adequate sexual expression in adult primates re-
    quires (a) early socializing experiences (b)
    sexual training by parents (c) sexual depriva-
    tion in adolescence (d) all of the above   a

4. The affiliation motive develops out of (a) a
    primitive sex drive (b) status needs (c) de-
    pendency needs (d) B and C   c

5. Motivational explanations often add little to
    understanding because (a) human behavior is
    too complex (b) specific conditions for beha-
    vior remain vague (c) most motives are un-
    learned (d) all of the above   b

6. Imprinted behaviors differ from instinctive be-
    haviors mainly in that (a) cues for imprinting
    are more specialized (b) imprinting occurs on-
    ly in lower animals (c) instincts can be modi-
    fied through learning (d) instincts do not in-
    volve instrumental acts   a

7. Of the following, which is true of sexual beha-
    vior in humans? (a) sexual behavior appears
    entirely innate (b) cultural and family pat-
    terns are influential (c) later adolescence is
    a time of sexual maturation (d) sexuality is
    controlled strictly through hormones   b

8. If infant monkeys are deprived of maternal con-
    tact (a) their hunger drive increases (b)
    they refuse to eat or to drink (c) they become
    impaired in sexual functioning (d) none of these c

9. One variable which distinguishes motives from
    simple reinforcers is (a) pleasurable emotions

SHORT ANSWER QUESTIONS FOR REVIEW

(b)   conflict   (c)   avoidance responses   (d)
expectation of change

d

10.   Approach-avoidance conflicts are difficult to
resolve because (a)   the positive and negative
aspects of situations are of equal strength   (b)
a single goal possesses both positive and negative
aspects   (c)   one must choose the lesser of two
evils   (d)   all of the above

b

11.   An acquired motive which has been said to develop
in nearly all individuals is   (a)   hunger   (b)
hoarding   (c)   gregariousness   (d)   aggression

c

12.   The learning theory explanation of acquired motives is based upon   (a)   sublimation   (b)   secondary reinforcement   (c)   cognitive dissonance
(d)   none of the above

b

13.   Freud pointed out that an important influence
upon behavior is   (a)   unconscious motivation
(b)   cognitive dissonance   (c)   level of aspiration   (d)   none of the above

a

14.   Which of the following does not play a role in
hunger   (a)   stomach contractions   (b)   blood
chemistry   (c)   a particular set of nuclei of
the hypothalamus   (d)   none of the above

d

15.   "Drive-reduction" theory holds that the crucial
factor determining what is learned is   (a)   frustration of drives   (b)   contiguity of drive and
stimulus   (c)   reinforcement   (d)   alleviation
of needs

d

16.   If a person's level of aspiration is usually
much higher than his performance level, he experiences   (a)   status enhancement   (b)   failure
(c)   achievement   (d)   reinforcement

b

17.   Which of the following findings are not characteristic of high nAch students?   (a)   they are
more intelligent than low-nAch students   (b)
they have higher PAs than low-nAch students   (c)
they rated their parents more successful   (d)
all of these

a

18.   Which of the following is not a characteristic
of instinctive behavior?   (a)   unlearned   (b)
rigidly patterned   (c)   present at birth   (d)
evident in all members of a species

c

19.   In female rats, maternal behavior is dependent

SHORT ANSWER QUESTIONS FOR REVIEW

upon _____ in the bloodstream (a) prolactin
(b) estrogen (c) ACTH (d) none of the above

a

20. All of the following are what Murray sees as
needs of humanity except (a) N autonomy (b) N
dominance (c) N abasement (d) all of the
above are needs of humanity according to Murray

d

Fill in the blanks.

21. The tendency to return the body to a neutral or
resting state is called_____.

homeosta-
sis

22. The object or condition which satisfies a motive
is called a _____.

goal

23. The psychologist who found a relationship between
a need for achievment, economic growth and children's literature is _____.

David
McClelland

24. A primary reinforcer that is not essential to
immediate survival is _____.

sex

25. When a person must choose between two or more
positively-valued conditions, this is called the
_____ conflict.

approach-
approach

26. An _____ conflict exists when a person is confronted with a choice between two or more nega-
tively-valued persons or objects.

avoidance-
avoidance

27. _____ was the pioneer worker in the field of psychogenic needs; perhaps he is most famous for
having devised the Thematic Apperception Test.

Henry
Murray

28. Perhaps the most fundamental purely psychological need is the need to have others approve of
us and our actions, this is the need for_____.

social
approval

29. Pleasurable internal feelings that result from
accomplishments or behaviors and make it more
likely that these behaviors will occur in the
future are _____ rewards.

intrinsic

30. It has recently been recognized that in an industrial setting giving praise and recognition to
employees _____ motivation.

increases

31. The highest level need according to Maslow's
theory of motivation, the drive to realize one's
potential to the fullest, is called _____.

self-
actualiza-
tion

SHORT ANSWER QUESTIONS FOR REVIEW

32. According to Murray's list of psychogenic needs; the need to get free, shake off restraint, break out of confinement, to resist coercion and restriction, to be independent and free to act according to impulse is the need for _____ .

autonomy

33. The formal model of imprinting, which included the critical period and the permanence of the first attachment was proposed by_____ .

Conrad
Lorenz

34. The study of animal behavior in its natural environment is called _____ .

ethology

35. Objects, such as money and candy, which when given to organisms have the extrinsic effect of increasing the frequency of the behaviors which preceded their presentation are _____ rewards.

extrinsic

Determine whether the following statements are true or false.

36. Among human beings, maternal behavior appears to be instinct based.

False

37. Functional autonomy is when responses to a motive condition may persist even after the original motive condition ceases to exist because the response itself becomes a motive.

True

38. In Harlow's experiment on the affectional drives, baby monkeys were placed in an open-field situation designed to evoke both fear and exploratory behavior when either the milk-giving wire "mother" or the cloth-covered "mother" was present.

False

39. According to Kurt Goldstein, an individual is primarily motivated by a single motive which is called self-actualization or self-realization.

True

40. Maslow believes the needs of man are evil and must be tamed by society.

False

41. The Yerkes-Dodson Law states that the optimal level of arousal decreases with the complexity of the task; high drive states seem best suited for simple tasks, but these may interfere with more complex tasks.

True

42. The experience of thirst involves both dryness of throat cells and low blood plasma concentration.

True

43. Achievement motivation involves either fear of failure or pleasurable anticipation of success.

True

SHORT ANSWER QUESTIONS FOR REVIEW

44. The word "motive" is used in reference to psychological states, "drive" in reference to physiological states, and "incentives" is used in reference to both.

    True

45. Motivation refers only to the degree of vigor or arousal that characterizes our efforts toward a goal.

    False

46. It has been found that acquired drives can be developed in the same way that fear can be learned.

    False

47. High need achievers set extremely high goals on a complex task.

    False

48. Conflicts or inconsistencies among our ideas or our information can give rise to an emotional state called cognitive dissonance.

    True

49. People who score high on achievement on the Thematic Apperception Test do better on a number of tasks than those who score low.

    True

50. Freud and others have prepared rather complete and widely accepted lists of human motives.

    False

51. There is strong evidence to support the hypothesis that self-actualization would emerge strongly if other needs were satisfied.

    False

CHAPTER 11

AROUSAL, EMOTION, AND CONFLICT

MOTIVATION AND PHYSIOLOGICAL CORRELATES OF AROUSAL

● **PROBLEM 11-1**

Discuss the relationship between arousal and motivation.

Solution: Many psychologists regard arousal level as the central aspect of motivation. Various motives have different goals: food, water, shelter, etc. The common element is the arousal of the motivated organism. The more highly motivated the organism, the greater the level of arousal. In theories of human motivation, arousal level is used as a measure, as an indicator, of the strength of a motive. Because of this, arousal level is often considered a central aspect of all types of motivation: emotional, physiological, etc.

   In the association or neobehavioristic theory of learning, the probability of a response is the product of two general factors, one of which is called drive (D), the general level of arousal.

● **PROBLEM 11-2**

Discuss the relationship between arousal level and performance.

Solution: In general, increased arousal level or drive level produces improved performance in animals and humans on simple tasks. Several studies have indicated this to be the case. Bills (1927), for example, found that when tension level is increased in a subject by having him squeeze hard objects, performance was improved for such tasks as memorization, addition, and naming letters. Several animal studies have shown that increased arousal, produced by food or water deprivation, greatly improves performance in learning tasks.

   An extremely high level of arousal, however, can impair performance in situations that require discrimination among cues or responding appropriately at different times. (In

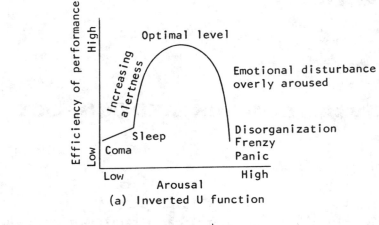

(a) Inverted U function

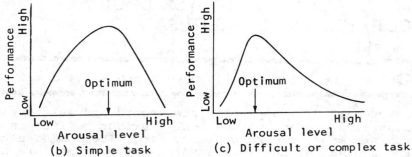

(b) Simple task

(c) Difficult or complex task

(a) The general relationship between arousal and efficiency can be described by an "inverted U" curve. The optimal level of arousal or motivation is higher for a simple task (b) than for a complex task (c).

simpler terms: very complex tasks.) Expressed graphically, the relationship between level of arousal and level of cue discrimination is an inverted U-shape. Up to a certain point, as arousal level increases, so does cue discrimination ability or performance level. This rise in the graph represents an increased ability to discriminate among cues of increasing complexity, as alertness, interest, and positive emotion are increased. After the optimum level--the apex of the inverted U--is reached, as arousal level becomes greater, there is an increase in anxiety and emotional disturbances, and, at the same time, performance declines. This phenomenon is called the Yerkes-Dodson effect after its discoverers.

College students in testing situations who tend to have very high levels of anxiety often do not perform as well as students who have lower anxiety levels. The reason, of course is that insofar as exams are a "complex task" students who are overly anxious are more anxious than the optimal level of anxiety allows.

● PROBLEM 11-3

Describe some methods of arousal measurement.

<u>Solution</u>:   Arousal can be measured in one of several ways.
One method is through the use of an electroencephalogram
(EEG).   Although this machine is most often used to record
brain wave activity during the various stages of sleep, it
can also yield information regarding the state of arousal of
a waking individual.   A person in a relaxed, waking state
usually has an EEG pattern of about 10 cycles per second.
If he is aroused in any way, however, this brain wave pattern will change to what is called an activation pattern,
which consists of fast, irregular waves.   This state of
alertness can be brought on by practically any stimulus--
a noise, a visual pattern, or a task requiring problem-solving
or concentration.   An EEG, therefore, can indicate whether an
individual is in a state of relaxation or arousal.

The EEG pattern, however, does not show the finer distinctions among various states of arousal; therefore, researchers use a number of other measures: heart rate, breathing rate, blood pressure, skin conductance, and pupil size.
Skin conductance and pupil size are especially good indicators.   Even if a small, imperceptible amount of electricity
is passed across an area of skin, the resistance to it decreases (conductance increases) as the arousal of the individual increases.   Pupil dilation occurs when individuals engage in task-solving activities or are presented with interesting or arousing stimuli.   Pupillary responses can be used
to gauge the interest value of almost any stimulus.

● **PROBLEM 11-4**

Name and describe the functions of the major parts of the
autonomic nervous system (ANS).   What changes occur in this
system as a result of increased and decreased arousal level or
emotion?

<u>Solution</u>:   The autonomic nervous system is composed of the
numerous nerves which project from the brain and the spinal
cord to the smooth muscles of various bodily organs.   There
are two major parts to the autonomic system which often, but
not always, work in opposition to each other.   One is the
sympathetic system.   This system increases heart rate and
blood pressure, and distributes blood to exterior muscles.
This system becomes activated when arousal level increases.
The other part, the parasympathetic system, reduces heart
rate and blood pressure and diverts blood to the digestive
tract.   This system is active when arousal or emotional level
is low.   It is ultimately responsible for the build up and
conservation of bodily stores of energy.

When the sympathetic system becomes activated as a result of an increase in arousal level, several physiological
symptoms result.   First, blood vessels in the stomach, intestines and interior of the body tend to contract while those
of the exterior muscles of the trunk and limbs tend to expand.
As a result, blood is shifted from digestive functions to
muscular functions in order to facilitate greater muscular
activity.   Second, more blood is pumped to the muscles through
the circulatory system.   This occurs because nervous impulses to the heart cause it to beat harder and faster, thus in-

Autonomic Nervous System Effects

Organ	Parasympathetic system	Sympathetic system
Pupil of eyes	Constricts to diminish light	Dilates to increase light
Tear glands Mucous membrane of nose and throat Salivary glands	Stimulate secretion	Inhibit secretion Causes dryness
Heart	Slowing, constriction of blood vessels	Acceleration, Dilation of blood vessels to increase blood flow
Lungs, windpipe	Constrict bronchi of lungs to relax breathing	Dilate bronchi to increase breathing
Esophagus Stomach Abdominal blood vessels	Stimulate secretions and movement	Inhibit secretions and movements, diverts blood flow
Liver	Liberates bile	Retains bile
Pancreas		Releases blood sugar
Intestines	Stimulate secretion	Inhibit secretion
Rectum Kidney Bladder	Excitation, expulsion of feces and urine	Inhibition, retention of feces and urine
Skin blood vessels	Dilate, increase blood flow	Constrict, skin becomes cold and clammy
Sweat glands	Inhibit	Stimulated to increase perspiration
Hair follicles	Relaxed	Tensed to make hair stand on end (piloerection)

creasing blood pressure and pulse rate.

Several other autonomic changes occur during a heightened arousal state. Fear, for example, is characterized by such changes as increase in pupil size, drying of the mouth, and the stopping or reversal of stomach and intestinal contractions. During an aroused state, the sympathetic system also discharges two hormones--epinephrine (adrenaline) and norepinephrine (noradrenaline). These are secreted by the adrenal glands located on top of the kidneys. A discharge of epinephrine has several effects on the body. First, in the liver, it helps discharge sugar into the blood in order to make more energy available to the brain and muscles. Second,

380

epinephrine increases heart rate. Third, in the skeletal muscles, it helps discharge sugar reserves so that these muscles can use them more quickly. Finally, it duplicates and strengthens several activities of the sympathetic system on various internal organs. The major autonomic change caused by a discharge of norepinephrine is increased blood pressure caused by constriction of peripheral blood vessels.

Another important autonomic change that occurs during an emotional state concerns a change in galvanic skin response (GSR) or skin conductance. During a state of arousal, the GSR reflects a decrease in skin resistance to the passage of an electrical current.

● **PROBLEM** 11-5

Define emotion in terms of feelings, responses, and motivation.

Solution: Emotion can be broadly defined as a complex state of the organism, generally characterized by a heightened arousal level. The term emotion can be defined in three basic ways: in terms of feelings, responses, and motivation.

Davitz (1969) found that for most people, the term emotion applies to a particular set of feelings. A person feels anger if someone is offensive to him, pleasure if he receives a gift, or fear if a fierce animal is about to attack him. Behavioristic psychologists dislike defining emotion as feelings, since a feeling is a highly subjective state and cannot be measured objectively. As such, they are not likely to yield consistent data; and, in addition, they are difficult to organize. However, much recent work in organizing emotional feeling states has proved encouraging.

Emotion may also be thought of as a response. "Response" in this case refers not only to an overt behavior, but also to an internal process that occurs as a result of a particular stimulus, either external or internal, which is significant to the individual.

Emotion as a response has been viewed in two ways. First, some consider it a response to one's perception and judgment of a particular stimulus situation. For example, if a person perceives and judges a particular situation to be threatening, fear will be the emotional response. Other investigators supporting the (very early) position of William James see emotion as a response to physiological events that occur during a state of arousal. James suggested that emotions are responses to such bodily changes as increased heart rate and respiration.

Emotion can also be viewed in terms of motivation. To some investigators, emotion is identical to motivation. There are two ways to look at emotion in this light. First, emotions are seen as strong motives; an organism is induced or motivated to do something in order to eliminate the motive. In the case of rats, for example, Neal Miller showed that rats learn new responses in order to remove themselves from an environ-

ment in which they had been shocked. The anxiety that motivated them to learn the avoidance response was viewed by
Miller both as an emotion and a motive.

Another view of emotion as motivation, proposed by Sylvan
Tomkins, suggests that motives are important only when they
are energized by emotional excitement or arousal. The motive
specifies a goal associated with a particular physiological
state, but this must be amplified by emotional excitement.
In sexual motivation, for example, the motive is ineffective
unless it is accompanied by emotional excitement.

● **PROBLEM** 11-6

Discuss three indicators of emotion.

Solution: There are three important indicators that are used
to indicate emotion: personal reports, observed behaviors
and physiological indicators.

Personal reports include oral and written reports by
subjects on their experiences. Outward response may not
reveal an individual's feelings or arousal, but it can indicate the type of emotion experienced.

Emotion can be detected from observing behavior. Such
behaviors include gestures, postures, facial expressions,
movements, and other responses which help indicate the emotion
being expressed.

Finally, emotion is indicated by physiological changes.
Changes in heart rate, breathing pattern, blood pressure,
pupil size, EEG pattern, or GSR (galvanic skin response)
indicate arousal level and are often interpreted as an indication of an emotional state.

● **PROBLEM** 11-7

Do different emotional states produce different patterns of
physiological change? Define directional fractionation.

Solution: Research has not supported the idea that different emotional or arousal states yield differing bodily
states. According to Lacey (1967), most individuals show
similar patterns of autonomic response to widely varying
stressful situations.

Some investigators, however, have reported subtle differences in physical reactions among different emotional
states. The most interesting and suggestive of these involves
the phenomenon called directional fractionation. Directional
fractionation can be defined as an autonomic reaction in which
heart rate decreases (as in a parasympathetic reaction),
while other changes occur in an opposite direction, such as
increased skin conductance (GSR) (such as occurs in a sympathetic response). In a normal sympathetic arousal state,
both heart rate and GSR would increase.

In studies where directional fractionation is induced, subjects usually take in external stimuli such as colors and patterns flashed before them or a tape recording of an actor portraying a man dying of injuries. In these situations, however, subjects do not actively react. A normal sympathetic arousal state would result if the individual had to actively react physically or even mentally, as in solving problems.

Despite such infrequent phenomena as directional fractionation, most variations in mood, arousal, or emotion are accompanied by similar bodily states.

● **PROBLEM 11-8**

Describe the following theories concerning the relationship between emotion and bodily states: the James-Lange theory, the Cannon-Bard or emergency theory, and cognitive theory.

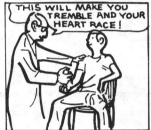

Two of the conditions in Schachter and Singer's experiment on emotion. (A) A subject is misled about the effects he should expect from the adrenaline injection he is receiving. Placed with a companion who joyfully flies paper airplanes around the waiting room, he attributes his state of arousal to a similar mood in himself and joins in. (B) A subject is told exactly what to expect from the injection. Although placed in the same situation as the first subject, he recognizes his physical sensations as the product of the injection and is unmoved by the euphoria of the experimenter's confederate.

Solution: According to the James-Lange theory on the relationship of emotion and bodily states, the individual's perception of his physical reaction is the basis of his emotional experience. The emotional experience occurs after the bodily change and as a result of it. According to William James, if we see ourselves trembling, we are afraid, if we find ourselves crying, we are sad. There is a definite

sequence of events in the production of an emotional state:
1. Perception of the situation that will produce the emotion.
2. Bodily reaction to the situation. 3. Perception of the
reaction and the onset of the emotional reaction as a result.

According to the Cannon-Bard or emergency theory, bodily
reactions do not cause emotional reactions; rather, the two
occur simultaneously. The theory argues that the emotion-
producing situation stimulates nerve cells in certain lower
portions of the brain, which in turn activates the cerebral
cortex and the body structures. Activity received by the
cerebral cortex is felt as emotion, and activity received by
the body structures causes bodily changes characteristic of
the emotion. In the emergency theory, physiological states
which result from lower brain area activity prepare the organism for emergency reactions to threatening, emotion-arousing
situations.

The cognitive theory (Schachter and Singer, 1962) is
somewhat similar to the James-Lange theory, in that it considers felt emotion to be the result of the individual's
interpretation of his aroused bodily state. The main idea
behind the cognitive theory is that bodily states which
accompany many various emotions are quite similar, and that
even when these physiological states do differ, they cannot
be sensed. They may seem different to us because we interpret
them or have cognitions about them, and we feel the emotion
that we believe to be the most appropriate to the arousing
situation. The sequence of events in producing an emotional
state, according to this theory, is: 1. Perception of the
situation that will produce the emotion, 2. An arousal of
a bodily state which is ambiguous, and 3. Interpretation
and naming of the bodily state in terms of our notion of the
external, arousing situation.

● **PROBLEM** 11-9

Describe how a "lie detector" works. How is a lie detection
test conducted?

Solution: A lie detector (polygraph), used to ascertain an
individual's guilt in a crime, is a device that detects and
measures autonomic changes that accompany emotional experience.
There are several variations of the lie detector, but practically all lie detectors measure blood pressure, respiration,
and GSR. The assumption behind the use of the lie detector
is that a person can hide external emotional expression, but
not the involuntary, physiological changes that accompany it.

In a lie detection test, a subject is asked a series of
two types of questions: neutral questions and critical
questions. Neutral questions are those which are designed to
arouse no emotion in the subject. In the case of a suspected
criminal, these questions would not be related to the crime.
They might be simple questions that ask for factual information,
such as, "What is your name?", "Where do you work?", "How tall
are you?", etc. Critical questions are concerned with the
crime and are designed to arouse fear or guilt feelings in the
subject. While the subject is asked both types of questions,

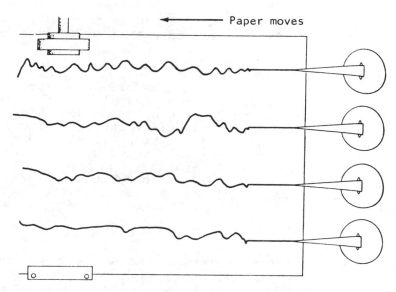

A record from an ink writing oscillograph (polygraph).

a record is made of his physiological responses. After the
test, the examiner compares the responses to the neutral
questions with the responses to the critical questions. If
there is a marked and consistent difference in response between the two types of questions, it is assumed that the subject probably is lying. Similarly, if there is no significant
difference, it is assumed the subject is telling the truth.

It should be noted, however, that such tests are not
always valid. One of the problems of the test lies in the
emotionality of the subject. Some individuals may be so highly
aroused by taking the test that they show strong reactions to
even the neutral questions. Others may show so little emotion that their responses to critical questions may record
the same as those to neutral questions. Hence, lie detection
tests are not always capable of detecting lies.

● **PROBLEM** 11-10

What is a psychosomatic disorder? How is it induced? Give
some examples.

Solution: A psychosomatic disorder is a bodily disturbance
which is induced or aggravated by a psychological stress. The
word "psychosomatic" is derived from "psycho," which means
"mind," and "soma," which means "body."

Many physical changes occur in the body as a result of
aroused emotion or stress. Some of these are desirable,
such as those that mobilize the body's energy and strength
in order to handle an emergency. Others, however, are undesirable, such as those produced by chronic anxiety. When
autonomic changes that accompany psychological stress are
continuous with little or no slackening, actual tissue and
organ damage can result. Even if such continuous autonomic

effects produce no harm, they can make the individual more susceptible to infection and less able to recover from disease.

Research has suggested that many bodily disorders are psychosomatic; peptic ulcers, high blood pressure, asthma, dermatitis, and obesity are some examples. Studies by Brady (1958) have shown that ulcers can be induced experimentally in animals (rats, dogs, monkeys) by exposing them continuously to fear-producing situations. The above disorders are not always induced psychosomatically, however, each can be contracted by individuals who are under no psychological stress. Emotional stress may be only one contributing factor to this disorder, or it may predispose a person to it. It is sometimes difficult to determine whether a disease is wholly or partly psychosomatic.

● **PROBLEM 11-11**

Define general-adaptation syndrome. Name and describe its three stages. What disorders can develop in each of these stages?

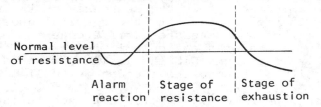

Normal level of resistance

Alarm reaction | Stage of resistance | Stage of exhaustion

The General Adaptation Syndrome. During the initial alarm reaction to stress, resistance falls below normal. it rises again as bodily resources are mobilized, and it remains high during the stage of resistance. Eventually, resistance falls again as the stage of exhaustion is reached.

Solution: "General-adaptation syndrome" is a term used to describe the three stages the body passes through in its reaction to stress. The first stage of this syndrome, or the first stage of bodily reaction to stress, is called the alarm reaction. This reaction consists of the body's usual reactions to heightened emotion—increased heart rate and blood pressure, slowing of digestion and so on. If the individual continues to be exposed to stress, he enters a second stage called resistance. Here, he recovers from the initial stresses of the first stage and attempts to endure it to the best of his ability. If the stress continues even further, and endurance is maintained, a considerable strain is put on the body's resources which may lead to a third stage—the stage of exhaustion. In this stage, the internal resources for dealing with the stress are exhausted, and the body is no longer able to tolerate any further stress. In the course of daily living, the occurrence of this last stage is infrequent. When it does occur as a result of harsh and prolonged emotional stress, death may result.

During the alarm stage, an individual is usually able to

build up resistance to the particular stress that brought on the adaptation syndrome; however, the ability to resist new stresses is decreased. As a result, disorders such as hypertension, ulcers, arthritis, rheumatism, and allergies may occur.

In the second stage of the adaptation syndrome, resistance to the original stress is increased. Because of this there is an over abundance of adrenal secretion. An excess of epinephrine, one of the hormones secreted by the adrenal gland, increases heart rate and blood pressure. Therefore, in this stage, disorders such as hypertension (high blood pressure) and heart disease are possible and likely.

In the third stage of the adaptation syndrome, prolonged stress exhausts the body's resources. This is caused, in part, by an exhaustion of the adrenal hormones. When this occurs, disorders such as rheumatism and arthritis can result.

THE EXPRESSION OF EMOTION

● PROBLEM 11-12

List and describe three major types of emotional expression.

Solution: The three major types of emotional expression are: the startle response, facial and vocal expression, and posture and gestures.

The startle response takes its name from the reaction of the subject. A startle response is usually experimentally elicited by a loud and sudden noise presented to an unsuspecting subject. The entire response occurs very quickly and has the most consistent pattern of any emotional response pattern. The response begins with a rapid closing of the eyes followed by a widening of the mouth. The head and the neck then thrust forward while the muscles of the neck stand out with the chin tilting up. Many investigators believe this to be an inborn response, thus requiring little learning or experience.

Facial and vocal expressions are much less consistent than the startle response. There is wide variety in the facial and vocal reactions of different individuals to the same stimulus. However, there are three different dimensions of emotional expression which can be observed. These are pleasantness--unpleasantness, attention--rejection, and sleep--tension. In pleasant emotions, in general, the eyes and mouth slant upward; in unpleasantness both slant downward. On the second dimension, attention is characterized by wide-open eyes, and often by flared nostrils and open mouth, while in rejection, eyes, nostrils, and mouth are all tightly shut. In sleep, for the most part, there is no facial expression and the eyes are closed. At the other extreme, tension, there is a great deal of emotional expression in the face.

The voice is also an important instrument for indicating emotion. In general, laughter indicates enjoyment; sobbing indicates sorrow; screaming can express fear or surprise; and groans denote pain or unhappiness. A low voice or a break or tremor may indicate deep sorrow. Anger is usually expressed by a sharp, loud, high-pitched voice.

Posture and gestures are the third important means of emotional expression. In happiness or pleasantness, the head is usually held high and the chest out; in sorrow, posture is often slumped with the face tilting downward; in anger, aggressive gestures are often made such as fist clenching; and in fear, the individual either flees or remains frozen in one spot.

● **PROBLEM 11-13**

Define pleasure. Trace its development from infancy to adolescence. What accounts for humor? What situations produce smiling and laughter in adults?

Solution: Pleasure can be defined as a reaction to the satisfaction of a motive or the achievement of a goal. Pleasure is one of the three primary types of emotion. (Fear and anger are the other two.) This definition of pleasure applies to both unlearned or primary motives and learned or secondary motives.

Smiling and cooing are the first signs of pleasure in the infant. This usually indicates that the child is physically comfortable--warm, well fed, and dry. By two or three months of age, pleasure is derived from human faces and friendly voices. Later on, the child expresses pleasure when he executes a new skill such as grasping a toy or when playing a game with someone. As a general principle, it can be said that children derive pleasure from novel, unfrightening situations that are entertaining and offer the child some success in accomplishing something.

Smiling is an expression of pleasure which arises when the child is tickled or stroked. (Because the nervous system needs time to mature, smiling is not possible before the age of two months.) Later it occurs as a response to interesting stimuli. When the affectional drive matures, pleasure is also derived from physical contact with adults--playing with them or holding onto them. When the exploratory drive matures, pleasure is derived from playing with toys and from exploratory activities.

During adolescence when secondary goals have been established, pleasure is mainly derived from social activities and from achievement in academics, athletics, or creative arts.

In adults, smiling and laughter occurs mainly as a result of humor, usually in the form of jokes, riddles, funny stories, etc. There appear to be two situations in which laughter is produced in adults. The first is one in which an individual can express unacceptable behavior in a socially acceptable manner. Adults who laugh at "dirty" jokes can express their preoccupation with sexuality in an acceptable way. Another situation which produces laughter is one in which a measure of incongruity is involved. People laugh when they are led to expect one thing, then something else occurs.

● **PROBLEM** 11-14

Name and discuss fear-producing situations in the course of human development. What factors are involved in the development of fear?

Solution: Situations that elicit fear change throughout development. During infancy and early childhood, fear is caused by the appearance of strange objects or situations that are sudden or unexpected. A sudden loud noise or the appearance of an animal, for example, would elicit fear in the young child.

During middle childhood (ages 6-12), fear is mainly produced by threatening situations--this includes situations which the child perceives as threatening, whether or not they really are. For example, children may be afraid of the dark, of imaginary creatures, or of being left alone. In late childhood, social situations start to become important and the child begins to fear peer ridicule, humiliation, and social threats. Strange, sudden objects and situations become less important as fear-provoking stimuli.

During adolescence and early adulthood, social situations become the most important source of fear. During this period the individual often fears ridicule, exclusion from a group, or speaking to other people. As the person progresses through adolescence into early adulthood, social fears become increasingly important.

There are several factors involved in the development of fear. One way fear is acquired is through conditioning. If a child is bitten by a dog at an early age, he may grow up fearing dogs and possibly other similar animals. A child who suffers a terrifying experience, e.g. being lost in a crowd, might fear crowds as an adult. It is possible for an originally neutral stimulus to become fear-provoking if it becomes associated with a fearful stimulus (classical conditioning). For example, if a parent uses a hair brush every time the child is punished, the hair brush in any situation becomes fearful for the child.

Fear can be acquired symbolically through the child's listening to his parents and their stories. If the child's cognitive ability is sufficiently developed so that he can use his powers of imagination and memory, he can become fearful of people, objects, and situations which he has heard his parents discuss.

Another factor that influences fear acquisition is the child's perception of his environment. As the child develops, he becomes accustomed to various objects and situations. Fear is produced when something unfamiliar or strange appears, such as the face of a stranger or a disembodied face. Again, the arousal of fear is dependent on the child's perception. A child may see a familiar face (his or her mother, for example), but if it is unrecognizable or looks strange to the child, it will induce fear.

● **PROBLEM** 11-15

Describe the causes of anger and the means of expression in children, adolescents, and adults.

Solution: One of the chief causes of anger in both children and adults is interference with goal-directed activity. Restriction of any desired activity will produce anger at any age.

During infancy, any restriction in activity or exploratory motives causes anger as well as the compulsion to engage in tasks required by the parents. Physical constraints such as having to wash, having things taken away, losing an adult's attention, or failure at an attempted task all contribute to anger arousal in infancy and early childhood. In older children and adolescents the causes of anger shift from physical restrictions to social frustrations. Arguments, shunning, sarcasm, bossiness, and thwarting of social ambition are all common causes of anger for teenagers.

Social frustration is also an important cause of anger for adults. Expression of anger, however, is much less overt in adults than in teenagers. Research has indicated that adults more frequently experience annoyance: mild feelings of anger.

Like the causes of anger, expression of anger also changes with increasing age. Infants and young children express through temper tantrums, screaming, bullying, and fighting. Expression is usually direct, immediate, and physical.

In adolescents, expression is subtle and in adults it is even more subtle. Increased social pressure makes physical and direct expression of anger undesirable; hence, expression becomes subtle, indirect, and verbal. Techniques include sarcasm, swearing, gossiping, and plotting.

● **PROBLEM** 11-16

What is an attitude?

Solution: An attitude can be defined as a relatively stable and enduring tendency to react positively or negatively to a particular person, object, situation, or event. The words positively and negatively mean favorably and unfavorably, respectively. An attitude is a tendency to respond emotionally in one direction or another. This direction is based on our preferences and aversions. We prefer things which have given us pleasure in the past and we find aversive those things which have made us angry or fearful. The development of an attitude is contingent upon previous emotional reactions to a certain stimuli (i.e. people, objects, situations) and the subsequent generalization to similar stimuli.

ANXIETY, FRUSTRATION, AND ANGER

● **PROBLEM 11-17**

Describe anxiety. How is it different from fear and anger? What situations give rise to anxiety?

Solution: Anxiety can be defined as a general state of uneasiness or apprehension, the cause of which is ambiguous. This ambiguity is one of the factors that distinguishes anxiety from fear and anger. Anxiety also differs from fear and anger in that it is less intense and more enduring (although it is sometimes possible to suffer from persistent and severe anxiety).

Anxiety can arise in several different situations. First, anxiety can be aroused by mild anger or hostility (since hostile behavior has usually been punished in the past). Because hostile feelings evoke vague fears of punishment, anxiety is aroused. Second, anxiety may occur as a result of fear generalization in which fear learned in one situation arises in similar situations. Third and most important, anxiety may be produced as a result of frustration of motives. Frustration produces anxiety in two ways. First, frustration tends to provoke aggression which leads to fear of punishment for the hostility. Secondly, frustration can cause fear of failure, either in achieving a desirable or positive goal or in avoiding an undesirable or negative goal.

● **PROBLEM 11-18**

Name and describe three major types of frustration.

Solution: Frustration can be classified into three major categories depending on its source. These are environmental frustrations, personal frustrations, and conflict frustrations.

Environmental frustration refers to frustration produced by environmental obstacles blocking the attainment of certain goals. These obstacles may be in the form of objects or people. For example, a flooded road may prevent a driver from reaching his destination

and hence produce frustration. People, especially
those in positions of authority, are also an important
source of frustration, especially for children. Parents,
teachers, and legal authoritative figures often prevent
others from attaining goals.

Personal frustration is the result of being unable
to attain learned goals. Learned goals are those which
the individual comes to regard as important and desirable
as a result of socialization. The individual normally
adopts those goals which are shared by most people in
his society. These may include high scholastic achievement or a good, high-paying job. An individual may
wish to pursue various activities or goals but may
refrain feeling he lacks the necessary ability.
Frustration results when the person feels his goals or
levels of aspiration are too high for his level of
performance. Personal frustration is common in both
children and adults.

Motivational conflict--a conflict of motives--is
the most important source of frustration. Conflict
frustration commonly results from the individual's
desire to engage in a particular activity, but because
of societal attitudes or sanctions against that behavior,
the person refrains. Hence, we have a conflict of motives.
An individual, for example, might like to express his
anger by striking the person he is angry at, but will
experience conflict because he feels social disapproval
will result if he vents his anger. Conflict frustration
is the most deep-seated and persistent of the three
types of frustration, and is usually the most important
source of anxiety.

● **PROBLEM** 11-19

State the frustration-aggression hypothesis. Give
an example that illustrates it.

Solution: Proposed by Dollard, Doob, Miller, Mowrer,
and Sears (1939), the frustration-aggression hypothesis
argues that all aggressive acts are caused by frustration, which is almost always accompanied by anger.
There is strong evidence to indicate that frustration
alone can produce aggression, although it is impossible
to determine whether frustration is a necessary component;
that is, if all aggressive acts require frustration.

An example that illustrates the frustration-aggression
hypothesis would be the case of a pigeon placed in
a Skinner box who has been trained to peck a key in
order to receive grain. If another pigeon is placed
in the box during an extinction period--a period in
which grain is not given for pecking--the trained
pigeon will attack the bystander by pecking at his head,
throat, and especially his eyes. Here, the aggression
was elicited by the frustration that was caused by the
termination of the grain rewards.

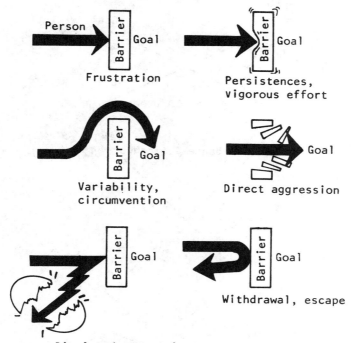

Person → Barrier Goal
Frustration

Barrier Goal
Persistences,
vigorous effort

Barrier Goal
Variability,
circumvention

Goal
Direct aggression

Barrier Goal

Barrier Goal
Withdrawal, escape

Displaced aggression

Summary of reaction to frustration.

CONFLICT

● **PROBLEM** 11-20

> Name and describe the three major types of conflict
> that can cause frustration.

<u>Solution</u>: Conflict frustration--frustration that results
from conflict--is a product of three major types of conflict: approach-approach conflict, avoidance-avoidance
conflict, and approach-avoidance conflict.

An approach-approach is one that occurs in the presence of two positive goals. The individual is attracted
to two equally desirable goals at the same time. For
example, a person may have the opportunity to see a
show or go to a party scheduled for the same night.
The person is torn between the two. Approach-approach
conflicts usually generate the least amount of frustration compared to the other two types of conflict and
are the most easily solved. Usually this type of conflict
is solved by attaining both goals sequentially. In
our example, the individual could solve the conflict
by going to the show first then going to the party
afterwards. More commonly, however, the individual will
make a decision (for example going to the show) and then
rationalize why the decision was correct, thus reducing
conflict anxiety (e.g. the party was probably boring
anyway).

Three kinds of conflict. The graphs represent Miller's
theoretical assumption that the tendency to approach a
desired outcome grows stronger the closer one comes to it
and that the tendency to avoid an aversive outcome grows
similarly but starts later and grows faster.

An avoidance-avoidance conflict occurs when the
individual finds himself facing two negative or undesirable goals. For example, a student would prefer to
watch television rather than study. But if he does
not study he will fail an important exam thereby
incurring parental rebuke and punishment. Thus there
are two negative goals: studying and parental punishment. The student must choose one goal to avoid the
other. Most of the time, however, as in this example,
there is a difference in the undesirability between
the two goals--one is usually less painful than the
other. In this case, studying is less painful to most
people than punishment; hence, the conflict is easier
to resolve.

The third major type of conflict, approach-avoidance
conflict, is the most difficult to resolve. In this
type of conflict, the goal object has both positive
and negative qualities for the individual; hence, he
is both attracted to it and repelled by it at the same
time. Thus, this type of conflict involves making a

sometimes difficult decision. For example, one might
have to decide whether or not to date someone who is
sexually attractive but very rude. Or an employee might
want to ask his boss for a raise but is fearful of
actually doing so. The employee may get the raise
(positive) or he may even lose his job (negative) if
he asks. Approach-avoidance conflicts usually produce
the greatest amount of frustration.

● **PROBLEM** 11-21

Define and describe a double approach-avoidance conflict.

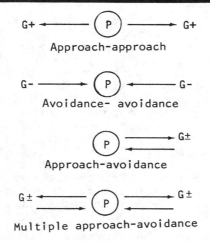

Four types of conflict situation. The "P" represents the
person; "G" represents a goal. The arrows indicate the direction of a behavior called for by a motive relative to that
goal, and the + and - signs refer to the attractiveness or
repulsiveness of the goal.

Solution: A double approach-avoidance conflict is one in
which the individual is caught between two goals both of
which have positive and negative qualities. This is
usually the most difficult type of conflict to resolve.
Often in this type of conflict, the two alternatives are
similar. For example, one might have to choose between two restaurants. One restaurant has good food but
is very expensive, the other is much cheaper but has poor
service. Or one might be faced with deciding which college
to attend. One school has a good reputation but is large
and impersonal while another is small and friendly but has
a lesser reputation. Most of the time, however, double
approach-avoidance conflicts are more complicated than
this, often involving complex social factors which produce
a great deal of conflict and frustration. For example, a
high school student might wish to stay home one evening and
study and thereby achieve high grades and avoid parental
disapproval. However, the student's peers might expect
him to "hang out" with them and the student fears embarrassment at staying home and studying. If he doesn't stay
home and study, however, he will not get good grades and
will invoke his parent's disapproval. Thus each goal--

395

making good grades and going out with friends--has positive
and negative features.

● **PROBLEM 11-22**

Discuss the two types of behavior that can result from an
avoidance-avoidance conflict.

Solution: Two kinds of behavior are likely to result in
the presence of an avoidance-avoidance conflict. One is
vacillation and the other is attempting to leave the field
(the conflict situation).

In vacillation, the individual wavers between the two
negative goals. The strength of a goal increases as the
person moves closer to it. In the case of a negative goal,
the closer one moves toward it, the more disagreeable it
becomes. In addition, as one moves closer toward a negative goal the tendency to withdraw from it becomes greater.
When this happens, however, one is now approaching the other
negative goal which then becomes increasingly disagreeable.
The tendency, then, becomes to move back again. Thus there
is a wavering between the two negative goals. This wavering or vacillating effect can be illustrated by considering
an individual waiting for an elevator and two elevators
arrive at the same time. The person may start to head for
one, then the other, then the first one again, and back and
forth. . . . There is conflict and vacillation until a decision is finally made.

Another behavior that may arise from an avoidance-
avoidance conflict is an attempt to leave the conflict situation (or "field"). Here, the individual tries to run away
from the problem or conflict. A child, for example, in an
avoidance-avoidance conflict in which he must either clean
his room or face punishment may try to avoid the situation
completely by running away from home. Often, however, leaving the field has greater negative consequences than choosing one of the two negative goals. If the child runs away
he will soon become cold and hungry. Most of the time, the
realization of such consequences is enough to prevent someone from leaving the field.

Leaving the field can be done in other ways besides
actually running away. Daydreaming in order to avoid doing
an unpleasant task or using one's imagination to create a
fantasy world in which there are no negative goals to be
faced are other means of leaving the conflict situation.
An extreme way of leaving the field is "regression." Here
the individual "retreats" to early or primitive forms of
behavior in order to avoid dealing with the conflict. An
adult, for example, who does not wish to face a certain conflict might engage in childish behavior to forget and avoid
it. He wishes to return symbolically to an earlier period
of his life when the conflict was not present.

● **PROBLEM 11-23**

Describe approach and avoidance gradients. What is the

difference between the two? What does this difference
indicate about behavior?

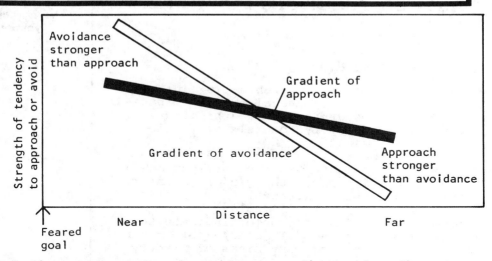

Solution: Approach and avoidance gradients show the
strength of tendencies to approach or avoid positive and
negative goals. Goal strength, that is, the amount a particular goal attracts or repels, grows stronger as one
moves closer to it. As one can see from the figure, the
two gradients differ in that the avoidance gradient is
the steeper of the two. This means that when a person is
far or some distance away from a goal having both positive
and negative characteristics, the positive tendencies or
valences are somewhat stronger than negative ones. In
other words, the individual is more attracted to the goal
at a distance from it than repelled by it. When the
person is near the goal, however, the negative valence is
stronger; the person is more repulsed by the goal than
attracted to it.

     The valences are equal at the point where the two
gradients cross. Here the individual is equally attracted
and repelled by the goal. The person's anxiety is greatest at this point since the amount of conflict is greatest. The person is trapped in an approach-avoidance conflict. The figure shows that the person's initial tendency is to approach the goal, but as he gets closer to it,
the tendency to avoid it becomes stronger. When the
avoidance tendency becomes very strong, the person may
stop some distance from the goal. He is immobile at the
point where the opposite tendencies or valences are equal;
that is, the intersection of the two gradients.

397

SHORT ANSWER QUESTIONS FOR REVIEW

Choose the correct answer.

1. During emotional excitement there is a(n)   (a)
    increase in glycogen in the blood (b)   increase
    in imagery (c)   decrease in breathing rate   (d)
    decrease in blood supply to skeletal muscles   a

2. Cannon's experiments with emotion mainly in-
    volved observations of (a)   the striped muscles
    (b)   heavy activity (c)   the glands of internal
    secretion (d)   fetal kittens   a

3. Introspective studies of emotion indicate that
    emotional awareness is (a)   clear (b)   disin-
    tegrative (c)   full of many kinds of imagery
    (d)   none of the above   b

4. Which of the following is not a true statement
    about emotion? (a)   there are two primary di-
    mentions of emotion (b)   one dimension of emo-
    tion is the qualitative emotion of love-hate
    (c)   one dimension of emotion is the qualitative
    dimension of pleasant-unpleasant (d)   one di-
    mension of emotion is the quantitative dimension
    of intensity   b

5. Another name for the double-bind conflict is
    (a)   approach-approach conflict (b)   avoidance-
    avoidance conflict (c)   approach-avoidance con-
    flict (d)   multiple approach-avoidance conflict   d

6. Emotions (a)   act as goals in themselves (b)
    are unlearned, reflex responses (c)   work
    against cognitive processes (d)   B and C   a

7. Physiologically, emotional response takes place
    (a)   in the brain (b)   in the autonomic nervous
    system (c)   in the muscles and internal organs
    (d)   in all of the above   d

8. Physiological states of bodily feeling appear to
    be interpreted as particular emotions by the in-
    dividual on the basis of (a)   pattern of physio-
    logical activity (b)   instinct (c)   beliefs
    about the situational circumstances (d)   A and
    B   c

9. The first emotions expressed by infants are (a)
    pleasure and anger (b)   pain and rage (c)   de-
    light and distress (d)   anger and fear   c

10. Which of the following conditions indicates a
    hysterical symptom? (a)   blindness in a person

SHORT ANSWER QUESTIONS FOR REVIEW

with normal eyes   (b)   a person trembling after
an accident   (c)   a person crying after the
death of a close relative   (d)   a person screaming in a stalled elevator

a

11. The polygraph measures   (a)   brain waves   (b)
     heart rate, respiration and perspiration rate
     (c)   the truthfulness of an individual   (d)   eye
     movement

b

12. The most important source of frustration for
     human beings is   (a)   obstacles in the environ-
     ment   (b)   personal inadequacy   (c)   goals which
     cannot be reached   (d)   motivational conflict

d

13. The most difficult conflicts to resolve are   (a)
     approach-approach   (b)   double approach-approach
     (c)   avoidance-avoidance   (d)   approach-avoid-
     ance

b

14. The closer one gets to the dentist's office, the
     greater the fear. This is an example of the
     (a)   goal gradient   (b)   functional approach to
     motivation   (c)   intensive approach to frustra-
     tion   (d)   none of the above

a

15. The General Adaptation Syndrome can ultimately
     lead to bodily damage when   (a)   psychosomatic
     diseases fail to protect one from stress   (b)
     adaptive physiological responses fail to occur
     (c)   the adrenal glands return to normal size
     before adaptive responses occur   (d)   one is un-
     able to reduce stress that results in chronic
     bodily arousal

d

16. Which of the following is not true about age
     differences in emotional expression?   (a)   an
     older person is likely to show more restraint
     or control in the expression of emotion   (b)
     an older person's emotional expression tends to
     be more physical   (c)   an older person's emotion-
     al expression tends to be more verbal   (d)   as
     the individual grows older, he can be expected
     to show increasing complexity and differentia-
     tion in his emotional states

b

17. Facial and vocal expressions of emotion are un-
     reliable indicators unless   (a)   the emotions
     are extreme   (b)   they are viewed in context
     (c)   the situations are very simple   (d)   all of
     the above

b

18. Which of the following sources of data leads to

399

SHORT ANSWER QUESTIONS FOR REVIEW

the most reliable identification of specific
emotions? (a) physiological patterns (b) subjective reports (c) instigating situations
(d) overt behavior

c

19. Which of the following is the best conclusion
regarding the frustration-aggression hypothesis?
(a) frustration always leads to aggression, especially in children (b) frustration and aggression lead to similar physiological responses
(c) aggression always occurs as a result of
frustrating circumstances (d) frustration may
lead to aggression or many other coping responses

d

20. In young children, the most general stimulus variable associated with fear is (a) incongruity
(b) pain (c) confusion (d) noise

a

Fill in the blanks.

21. The statement ". . . we feel sorry because we
cry" exemplifies the _____ theory of emotionality.

James-
Lange

22. A short-term tendency to react in a certain way
emotionally is called _____ .

mood

23. The only unlearned emotional response pattern in
human beings is the _____ response.

startle

24. Dollard, Doob, Miller, Mowrer, and Sears have suggested that all aggressive acts are caused by
_____ , which is almost always accompanied by
anger.

frustration

25. A brain operation, which used to be performed to
relieve patients of anxiety and violence is
called _____ .

pre-
frontal
lobotomy

26. A physical disorder that has a psychological
cause is a(n) _____ disorder.

psycho-
somatic

27. The term that psychologists use to apply to the
blocking of motive satisfaction is _____ .

frustration

28. If two conflicting goals are negative, this constitutes a(n) _____ conflict.

avoidance-
avoidance

29. In excited states, the pupil of the eye _____ .

dilates

30. The pilomotor response, commonly known as _____ ,
refers to the fact that hairs move into an erect
position under conditions of stress.

"goose
pimples"

SHORT ANSWER QUESTIONS FOR REVIEW

31. In stressful situations, smooth muscle activity is monitored by the _____ nervous system.

sympa-
thetic

32. _____ and _____ found that both physiological changes and the personal intepretation of the stimulus condition interact to produce an emotional experience.

J. Singer
S. Schachter

33. The most important part of the brain for the integration of emotional expression is the _____.

hypotha-
lamus

34. _____ main contribution to the study of emotional responsiveness is her finding that emotions are a function of the cognitive appraisal of the stimulus situation.

Megna
Arnold's

35. The attribution of human characteristics to objects or nonhuman organisms is called_____.

anthropo-
morphisim

Determine whether the following statements are true or false.

36. The activation or arousal theory of emotion holds that behavioral performance is at its peak efficiency at moderate levels of arousal, with either low or high levels being associated with behavior that is not very efficient.

True

37. Emotions may be differentiated from one another very successfully in terms of bodily reactions.

False

38. Eye movements and other indices indicating arousal show that we are aroused at certain times of the night even when we are asleep.

True

39. Schachter and Singer developed a cognitive theory which has shown that an injection of adrenalin produces anger.

False

40. The analysis of conflict has yielded agreement that we can identify three more or less pure forms.

True

41. Suppression means a total forgetting or denial that a motive exists.

False

42. Frustration always leads to restless behavior and signs of unhappiness.

False

43. The primary emotions cannot be mixed.

False

44. Darwin proposed that the two fundamental characteristics of emotions are survival value and

SHORT ANSWER QUESTIONS FOR REVIEW

signal value.

45. One criticism of James' theory is based on the observation that changes in internal organs often occur relatively slowly in response to external stimuli.

46. In contrast to normal individuals, psychiatric patients may be unaware of the existence of certain strong feelings.

47. The word "emotion" is synonymous with "subjective feeling state."

48. Freud concluded that patients who had hysterical symptoms were suffering from memories that had been actively forgotten or repressed.

49. The study of brain structures is likely to provide information about emotions which can be generalized to many species.

50. Studies of emotionality are closely related to broad ethological and psychoanalytical concepts of emotion.

CHAPTER 12

DEVELOPMENT

BASIC PRINCIPLES

● **PROBLEM 12-1**

Define human development and differentiate between growth and maturation.

Solution: The word development means change. Human development refers to the changes human beings undergo during the course of a lifetime. The actual process of human development cannot be perceived easily. Psychologists can only observe the direction of change and the magnitude of a particular change that has occurred in a given time interval at a particular stage of human development.

Growth refers to changes in the size of the body and its various parts. These changes are quantitative and can be measured by using standardized measurement units. Maturation refers to qualitative changes, changes that are not characterized by an increase in size but by a subtle rearrangement of existing structures. For example, maturational changes in the brain would not be characterized by the addition of new cells but by the rearrangement and organization of interconnections between brains cells already present. Such a change would enable the brain to function at a higher level.

Both growth and maturation are part of the same process of human physical development. Each of these is inseparable; growth has quantitative aspects and maturation has qualitative aspects.

● **PROBLEM 12-2**

List and define three approaches to the study of developmental psychology.

Solution: The three basic approaches to the study of developmental psychology are mechanistic, organismic, and psychoanalytic.

The mechanistic approach originated with John Locke and David Hume. The followers of this school of thought see

the developing human as a passive creature who allows environmental agents to determine the various characteristics
that he will come to possess. Hence, the basic concern here
is to measure the behavioral effects of environmental causes.
Laboratory experimentation is the preferred method of research in the mechanistic approach.

Jean Piaget is the major figure in support of the organismic approach. Here, the emphasis is on the qualitative
differences among various developing structures in the human.
Piaget examines the implications these differences have in
regard to development.

Sigmund Freud is the father of the psychoanalytic approach. The stress here is on sexual and aggressive drives.
Internal development and the influence of environmental influences on development are given equal attention. Much of
Freud's findings are based upon his study of the abnormalities of his patients who underwent psychoanalysis.

● **PROBLEM 12-3**

Briefly trace historical attitudes toward human development
emphasizing the debate between biological determinism and
environmental determinism.

Solution: From the beginnings of Christianity and throughout the Middle Ages, man was believed to be inherently evil.
It was the duty of every individual to redeem himself from
the evil into which he was born. Overcoming temptation and
resisting evil tendencies were the most important lifelong
goals.

At this time, a newborn infant was considered a minia-
ture adult. Hence, it was believed that development was
merely quantitative. A child at birth was thought to be
qualitatively like an adult. The only difference between
the two was physical size. This idea is called preforma-
tionism. Because children were not considered to be very
different from adults, they were expected to behave as a-
dults. When children did not do this, the adults concluded
that their innate evil tendencies were at work. Parents
often punished (sometimes cruelly) their children in order
to purge them of their wickedness.

In the last half of the eighteenth century, J. J.
Rousseau promulgated a theory which opposed the medieval
view. He believed that children are innately good and that
they are naturally endowed with a blueprint for development; hence they are not preformed at birth. Rousseau then
saw that the duty of parents and teachers was to protect
children and create an environment in which their natural
development could occur without interference.

One hundred years later, Granville Stanley Hall expressed the view that individual development parallels the
evolution of the species. This was part of the doctrine of
recapitulation.

The first major figure to stress the importance of environment in influencing human development was John Locke
in the seventeenth century. He believed the child was born

as a blank slate or "tabula rasa" upon which the environmental experiences would determine the course of his development. Locke urged parents to use intelligent, rational
thinking when rearing their children.

J. B. Watson, in 1928, strongly supported environmental determinism. He rejected all ideas concerning inherent
developmental designs. His extreme behaviorism strongly
promulgated the "tabula rasa" concept.

Today, both endogenous (biological) and environmental
factors are recognized as essential in human development.
Biologists are aware that even purely physical changes are
affected by the environment. For example, a developing embryo is affected by the environment existing in the mother's
womb. The pattern of stresses and pulls of gravity are different for each growing fetus. This pattern affects the development of the fetus. This organism-environment interaction is the basis of human development.

A widely accepted theory was introduced by Stern (1956).
He stated that genetic endowment is flexible - like a rubber
band - and that the amount it stretches (develops) is dependent on its interaction with the environment.

● **PROBLEM 12-4**

Discuss Heinz Werner's theory concerning developmental psychology.

Solution: Heinz Werner, educated in Austria, became a specialist in embryology and neurology. He constantly drew
analogies between these fields and developmental psychology.
Like Piaget, he believed that the various aspects of human
behavior are interdependent and that the individual's relationship with his environment is of utmost importance in
development.

Werner devised a concept of developmental change which
he called the orthogenetic principle. This principle states
that every living organism undergoes change in the same direction and passes through certain stages of development regardless of his environment.

Werner saw development as a gradual increase in the
differentiation of behavior. At birth, the individual's
behaviors are fused - Werner called this a syncretic state.
As the child develops, his emotions and behavior differentiate. For example, the generalized excitement of an infant gradually differentiates into feelings of joy and distress. Distress, in turn, differentiates into fear and anger. Werner saw this movement of development from the syncretic to the discrete as a continual process. Behavior is
always becoming more distinct and specific.

Werner also believed that behavior is diffused at first
but that it later becomes more articulated. For example,
when drawing a picture of an object, a child may attempt to
illustrate every one of its angles on the paper instead of
articulating the coordination of the parts.

405

According to Werner, a child's behavior is initially both rigid and unstable. It is rigid when he repeats a specific action and it is unstable when he engages in spontaneous outbursts of anger and joy. As the child develops he learns to distinguish between situations that call for rigid behavior and those that call for spontaneity.

Apparently, Werner was interested in both the early stages of behavior and the progression of behavior from these early stages. The development of behavior from a syncretic, diffuse, rigid and unstable state to a state that is discrete, specific, articulate and allows the person to determine the appropriateness of action in a particular situation helps the child adapt to the complexities of his environment.

PRENATAL DEVELOPMENT AND LABOR

● **PROBLEM** 12-5

Briefly describe the process of fertilization.

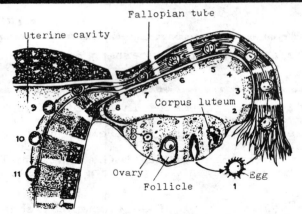

Schematic diagram of the maturation of an egg in a follicle in the ovary, its release(ovulation)(1), fertilization in the upper part of the oviduct(2), cleavage of the egg as it descends the oviduct or fallopian tube(3-7), stages in the development of the embryo in the uterus before implantation (8-10), and implantation of the embryo in the wall of the uterus(11).

Solution: In the female, fertilization occurs in the fallopian tubes that link the ovaries to the uterus. Fertilization results when one of the male's sperm cells enters the fallopian tubes and successfully penetrates, then unites with the outer covering of the ovum. At this point, conception has occurred.

Fertilization normally occurs four to six hours after the sperm has been deposited. Although thousands of sperm cells are deposited, only one successfully completes the long journey through the cervix, up the uterus, and into the fallopian tube to unite with the ovum. The other cells are expelled as waste material.

List and define the three major periods of prenatal development.

Solution: The first major period of gestation (the time between conception and birth) is the preimplantation period. This period lasts about two weeks during which time the zygote (previously called the fertilized ovum) moves down the fallopian tube and implants itself in the wall of the uterus.

The second period is that of the embryo. This period lasts until the eighth week. It begins with the implantation of the zygote into the wall of the uterus. Most of the cell divisions, as well as the formation of all organs, take place during this stage.

The last stage is the fetus, it lasts from the eighth week until birth which occurs about 40 weeks after conception. This period is distinguished by quantitative growth. The fetus can now respond to the most basic kinds of stimulation.

Trace development from the period of the zygote to the embryo.

Solution: After fertilization, the zygote is carried, by currents, down the fallopian tubes and moves toward the uterus. This process takes 7 - 9 days. During this time, cell divisions occur. At the end of this two week period, the zygote contains 64 cells. Because the zygote has received no nourishment from any extrinsic sources, hardly any growth occurs. Hence, the cells are considerably small.

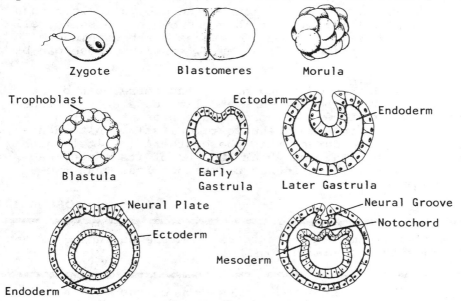

Development during the periods of the zygote and the embryo.

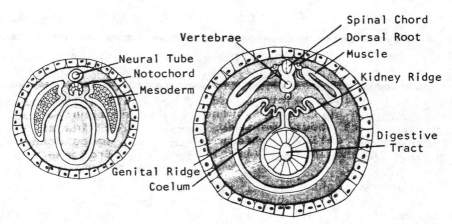

Development during the periods of the zygote and the embryo.
(Continued from the preceding page)

● PROBLEM 12-8

Trace development from the period of the embryo to the fetus.

Solution: Embrionic growth begins when the zygote implants
itself in the wall of the uterus. The embryo secretes enzymes and has tentacle-like growths called "villi" which
enable it to attach to the uterus lining. Here we have the
beginning of the placenta - a flat membrane that links the
embryo to the mother and enables the embryo to derive nourishment from the mother. The embryo's wastes are also ex-
creted through the placenta. Eventually, a structure called the umbilical cord, a long thick cord that attaches the
fetus to the mother, begins to assume the function of the
placenta.

By the end of the first month, the embryo is less than
one inch long and weighs less than one ounce. Massive cell
differentiation has occurred and organs are beginning to
develop. The beginnings of the eyes, ears, and nose can be
discerned.

By the end of the second month, the embryo can be recognized as a human being. Arm and limb buds and external
genitalia are visible. All organs are present at this
point and the entire embryo has curled itself. Although a
great deal happens during this phase, there is little quantitative growth. The embryo at the end of its stage measures between 1 1/2 - 2 inches and weighs less than two-
thirds of an ounce.

● PROBLEM 12-9

Trace the development of the fetus from the beginning of the
fetal stage through birth.

Solution: The fetal period begins between the eighth and
ninth week after conception. By the end of the third lunar
month, the fetus measures 10 centimeters in length and

weighs between three and four ounces. The head comprises about one-third of its entire length.

At this stage in its development, the fetus exhibits various types of movement and it can respond to tactile stimulation. The fetus can arch its trunk or extend its head when touched. Fingernails and eyelids are now beginning to form. The sex is now distinguishable.

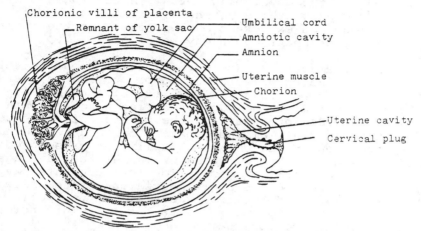

Diagram of advanced fetus shows its membranes and their relationship to the uterus.

After the fourth month, the fetus measures 18 centimeters in length and has completed major development: all of the organs are discernible, the bones have begun to form, the hands can move and grasp, and hair is beginning to grow. Although the fetus is capable of some of the basic kinds of movement, it is not until the fifth month that the mother can feel these movements. The first feeling of fetal movement is called "quickening."

During the fifth month, a soft downy covering called the "laguno" forms over the fetus. The laguno usually grows over the entire body of the fetus and is shed during the seventh month. However, sometimes part of the laguno is present at birth, especially on the baby's back. By the end of the fifth month the fetus is 25 centimeters long and weighs about 9 ounces. Intrauterine movement becomes apparent. Sweat glands begin to develop and the formation of the hair and nails undergoes further development. It is important to note that until this time, the fetus would have had little chance for survival were it born prematurely. If the fetus survives until the twenty-eighth week, its chances for survival outside of the mother's womb are good.

By the end of the seventh month, the mother can give birth and the fetus will survive, although two more months of intrauterine development are desirable.

By the end of the sixth month, the fetus is approximately a foot long and weighs about 20 ounces. Most of the physiological developments have already taken place. From this point until birth, development is primarily quantitative.

What are teratogens? List some examples and describe what effect they have on the developing fetus.

Solution: Teratogens are environmental agents that produce abnormalities in the developing fetus. A teratogen can be a disease a woman contracts during pregnancy, a chemical (drug or hormone) an expectant mother takes, or the radiation to which a pregnant woman may be exposed.

Diseases that can produce harmful effects on the fetus include German measles or rubella, mumps, polio, influenza, and toxemia (blood poisoning). Much attention has been given to the development of rubella during pregnancy since it is the most wide-spread of all the teratogenic diseases. Rubella can cause heart disease, cataracts, deafness, and mental retardation in the child. Toxemia can cause premature birth, result in babies who are smaller than average or it can lead to anoxia - a condition that prevents oxygen from reaching the child's brain. Anoxia can cause epilepsy, mental deficiency and behavior disorders. Mumps, polio, and influenza produce teratogenic effects but these are not as serious as rubella and toxemia.

Within the past twenty years, research has found several drugs to have harmful effects on the developing fetus. These drugs include insulin, tolbutamide, thalidomide, aspirin (large doses), nicotine, heroin, morphine, methadone, and LSD (although research on LSD has been inconclusive.) Pregnant women who are addicted to heroin, morphine, or methadone produce offspring who are also addicted to the drug. Withdrawal symptoms in these children are evident soon after birth. These symptoms include fever, tremors, convulsions, breathing difficulties, and intestinal disturbances. The mother's intake of insulin, tolbutamide (both used for diabetes), and thalidomide can cause various deformities in the fetus. Abuse of the first two drugs can result in death. Excessive intake of aspirin can cause growth retardation and lead to fetal abortion. Nicotine from cigarette smoking increases the fetus' heartbeat. However, there is presently no evidence indicating that smoking causes permanent damage to the heart or circulatory system.

Radiation is the third major type of teratogen. Two sources of radiation are X-rays and nuclear explosions. Large doses of therapeutic radiation have been found to cause spontaneous abortion, defects in the central nervous system, and mental retardation. The bombings of Japan during World War II have shown the effects of nuclear radiation on the unborn child. Pregnant women who were near the explosions gave birth to children that had one or more abnormalities such as dislocated hips, malformed eyes, heart disease, leukemia, and mental retardation. In the case of both therapeutic and nuclear radiation, exposure is most damaging if it occurs during the first twenty weeks of pregnancy.

List and describe some environmental factors, excluding teratogens, that affect prenatal development.

<u>Solution:</u> The interuterine environment of the fetus is relatively stable. However, there are factors that can affect the mother, and in turn, affect the fetus. While there is no direct connection between the nervous system of the mother and that of the child, their physical connection is very close. Hence, factors that affect the physical well-being of the mother will affect the child.

The mother's diet is of utmost importance during prenatal development. Studies have shown that nutritional deficiency can result in mental retardation, rickets, epilepsy, and cerebral palsy. Women on proper diets reduce the chances of premature birth, stillbirth, and miscarriage. This is understandable since the fetus derives its nourishment from the mother. Studies have also indicated that intelligence is dependent on the diet of the mother during pregnancy. Children born to mothers who had enriched diets during pregnancy scored higher on intelligence tests than the children of mothers who didn't.

The mother's age also influences prenatal development. The optimal age for the mother is between twenty-three and twenty-nine years. Studies have shown a higher mortality rate and a greater incidence of mongolism when women give birth while they are above or below this interval. The probability of mental deficiency in the child increases as the woman enters menopause.

Emotional stress in the mother also affects the fetus. Prolonged emotional stress increases hyperactivity in the fetus and increases the likelihood of a difficult labor and delivery.

The attitude of the mother is also important to fetal development. Women who possess poor attitudes concerning motherhood, and women who don't really want their child, will experience a more stressful labor and delivery than those women who are happy and satisfied about their impending role. Often, the mother's attitude toward her unborn child will be the same after the child is born and this will affect the child's development.

Social class is yet another factor that can affect prenatal development. Studies have indicated that mothers who come from low income families have a higher rate of premature births than those who come from higher income families. This correlation between social class and the birth of healthy infants raises moral and social issues.

Briefly describe the process of labor.

<u>Solution</u>: Labor occurs when the fetus, placenta, and other membranes, are separated from and expelled from the mother's body. Labor usually occurs approximately 280 days after the start of the woman's last menstrual period. In the first stage of labor, the cervix (opening to the uterus) enlarges to facilitate passage of the fetus down the birth canal. Contractions occur which exert a downward pressure on the fetus and cause the cervix to widen further. At first the contractions are low in intensity and are spaced far apart, but gradually they increase in intensity and occur closer together.

The actual process of birth is possible once the cervix is sufficiently dilated. In a normal delivery, the baby's head will appear at the opening of the cervix and continue to pass through it until the entire body has been expelled. This stage of labor usually takes about one hour.

The third stage of labor is called the afterbirth. During this time the placenta and other membranes are expelled.

● **PROBLEM** 12-13

Discuss complications that may arise during labor.

<u>Solution</u>: One complication that may arise during childbirth concerns the position in which the child is born. Normally, a neonate is born head first. Sometimes, however, the child may be born in what is called a breach presentation - when the bottom comes out first. Sometimes the neonate may come out feet first or the umbilical cord may come out alongside the head. The physician takes great care to make sure no complications affect the health and well-being of the child and mother.

If a breach presentation occurs and the physician judges the width of the mother's pelvis to be too narrow for a safe birth, he may proceed with a Cesarean section. A Cesarean birth is one in which the child is born by means of a surgical incision in the mother's abdomen and uterus. A Cesarean section might be performed when the head of the fetus is considered too large to easily pass through the birth canal in the mother. In this case, surgical removal might be safer for both mother and child.

The physician may use a surgical instrument called forceps to facilitate the delivery. This elongated, tong-like instrument is placed on the baby's head during delivery. The head can be rotated and pulled by the doctor. This procedure is used if the mother is so heavily sedated that she cannot do the pushing necessary for the birth of her child. Most physicians nowadays avoid the use of forceps because past use has resulted in damage to the newborn's head. When presented with a choice, most doctors favor Cesarean sections over forcep use.

For decades, pain-killing drugs have been administered

to mothers during labor. So far, no study has indicated
that these drugs produce harmful long-term effects on the
child. However, some researchers have concluded that the
behavior of children, whose mothers took medication during
childbirth, is more sluggish during the first few weeks of
life.

Anoxia is another complication that may arise during
childbirth. This condition refers to a lack of oxygen supplied to the neonate. The condition can be caused by either
a rupture of the blood vessels in the brain or by a malfunction in the umbilical cord which prevents it from supplying oxygen to the baby until he is able to breathe on his
own. The elimination of umbilical circulation may occur as
the result of a number of complications. For example, the
cord may become clamped or pinched; oxygen flow may be delayed due to the forcefulness of the contractions, part of
the placenta may become separated from the child and/or the
mother; or excessive bleeding of the mother during labor
may cause a decrease in the oxygen flow to the neonate
through the umbilical cord.

Anoxia can occur before birth if, for example, the
mother is anemic. Because of an iron deficiency in the
blood, the blood cannot carry enough oxygen to the fetus.
The amount of oxygen in the blood of the fetus therefore
is quite low and has an adverse effect on the child's development.

Anoxia is responsible for brain cell damage. It has
been cited to be the cause of some learning and behavioral
difficulties. Cerebral palsy, in which there is arm and
leg paralysis, finger and facial tremors, or an inability
to use vocal muscles, has been traced to anoxia as its
cause.

Anoxia may result in the irritability of the neonate
during the first week of life. It can cause tension in
muscles and a decreased sensitivity to pain and visual
stimulation. Studies concerned with the long-term effects
of anoxia have found that children who suffered from the
disease scored slightly lower on IQ tests than other children during mid-childhood. These children however, may
compensate for this difference in later years.

● PROBLEM 12-14

Define the following: abortion, immature birth, premature
birth, mature birth and post-mature birth. What are some
of the long-term effects of prematurity?

Solution: Abortion refers to the birth of the fetus before
the twentieth week of gestation (prenatal development), when
the fetus weighs less than 500 grams (about 1 pound). No
fetus survives an abortion.

An immature birth occurs when delivery takes place between the twentieth and twenty-eighth week of gestation.
The fetus weighs between 500 and 1,000 grams or 1 to 2

413

pounds. Immature births rarely survive. In an immature
birth, death most frequently results from the incomplete development of the fetus' respiratory system.

A premature birth occurs between the twenty-ninth and
thirty-sixth week. The premature child weighs between 1,000
and 2,500 grams or 2 to 5 1/2 pounds. A child who weighs
this amount at birth is considered premature regardless of
the amount of time he spent inside the womb. The premature
baby has less fat to insulate his body than a mature baby.
He is much more prone to infection and has difficulty breathing since he lacks the muscular strength needed for lung expansion. Premature neonates are placed in incubators after
birth where they receive an adequate supply of oxygen.

Two studies have indicated the long-term effects of
prematurity. One study conducted by Fitzharding and Steven
(1972) found a high incidence of speech defects and learning
problems in school-aged children who were born prematurely.
Despite these difficulties, the children were found to have
a normal IQ. Tutoring and special teaching tools helped
them overcome their learning difficulties.

Scarr-Salapatek and Williams (1973) focused their study
on premature children born to disadvantaged mothers. The
incidence rate of prematurity is higher for mothers from
lower class families than for mothers from other classes.
In addition premature children in impoverished environments
are least likely to overcome difficulties resulting from
the premature birth. The researchers found, however, that
by giving these children additional sensory stimulation and
attention, they were able to overcome many of their handi-
caps.

A mature birth is one that occurs between the thirty-
seventh and forty-second week. A mature neonate weighs at
least 2500 grams or $5\frac{1}{2}$ pounds.

A post-mature birth is one that occurs after the forty-
second week.

INFANCY AND PRESCHOOL PERIODS

● **PROBLEM** 12-15

Define and describe the physical qualities of the neonate.

Solution: A neonate is a newborn infant. The neonate's
skin is wrinkled and the eyelids are closed. The skull
measures slightly less than one-fourth of the total body
length. The body is covered with amniotic fluid. Breathing is audible but sometimes difficult. A neonate's color
may range from blue, because of anoxia (lack of oxygen), to
bright red.

● **PROBLEM** 12-16

Describe the behavior of the neonate and list and define

some of its reflexes.

Solution: Most of the behavior of the neonate is reflexive.
This behavior, however, is not limited to the reflexive behavior his genes provide for him; however, it is safe to
say that none of his behavior is deliberate. The neonate
experiences no real learning. For the most part, he responds to presented stimuli.

Several important reflexes in the neonate have been
discerned and labeled. They include the sucking reflex
which is produced by placing an object in the child's mouth;
head turning which is elicited by stroking the infant's
cheek or corner of the mouth; the Moro reflex which consists

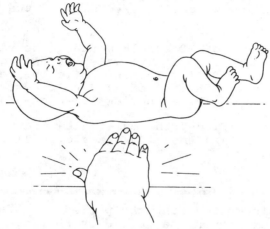

The startle reflex,sometimes called the Moro reflex, is displayed by all human infants. It is a fixed reaction to a
startling event such as a loud noise or loss of support of
the head. The reflex will disappear in the first 6 months
of life.

of the throwing out of the arms and feet and pulling them
back in, it is usually elicited by a loud noise; the Babinski reflex which refers to the fanning of the toes when the
neonate is tickled on the soles of his feet; the Palmar reflex which refers to hand grasping and occurs when an object is placed in the infant's hand. Other reflexes include
swallowing, sneezing, swimming, and stepping.

● **PROBLEM** 12-17

Trace physical growth - height and weight - for the average
male and female child during the period of infancy.

Solution: At birth, the average male neonate measures 20
inches in length and weighs 7½ lbs. The average female
weighs about the same but measures slightly less - about
19 3/4 inches.

At 6 months, the male infant has grown to a height of

26 inches and weighs about 16 3/4 lbs. The female measures
25 3/4 inches and weighs 15 3/4 lbs.

Median Height (in inches) and Weight (in pounds)

	Height		Weight	
Age	Girl	Boy	Girl	Boy
Birth	$19\frac{3}{4}$	20	$7\frac{1}{2}$	$7\frac{1}{2}$
6 mo.	$25\frac{3}{4}$	26	$15\frac{3}{4}$	$16\frac{3}{4}$
12 mo.	$29\frac{1}{4}$	$29\frac{1}{2}$	21	$22\frac{1}{4}$
18 mo.	$31\frac{3}{4}$	$32\frac{1}{4}$	$24\frac{1}{4}$	$25\frac{1}{4}$
24 mo.	34	$34\frac{1}{2}$	27	$27\frac{3}{4}$

By the time the male is a year old, he has grown to a
height of 29 1/2 inches, while the female stands at 29 1/4
inches. The male now weighs 22 1/4 lbs. and the female 21
lbs.

Between the ages of 12 and 18 months, the rate of
growth drops for both sexes. The male has only grown 2 3/4
inches to a height of 32 1/4 inches, while the female grows
only slightly more to a height of 31 3/4 inches. The male
now weighs 25 1/4 lbs. while the female weighs 24 1/4 lbs.

By the end of infancy, the male child stands at 34 1/2
inches and weighs 27 3/4 lbs. The female is 34 inches tall
and weighs 27 lbs.

● PROBLEM 12-18

Trace motor development during the period of infancy. List
the steps of motor sequence as cited by Shirley (1933).
Include prehensile (grasping) development.

Solution: The most important achievement in motor development during the period of infancy is the ability to walk.
A sequence of motor acquisitions precede this: crawling,
sitting, grasping, and climbing.

Research indicates that the sequence of development of
each motor ability is relatively constant although the ages
at which each is acquired varies considerably from one child
to the next.

Shirley (1933) conducted a study in which she found
that a high degree of similarity exists in motor sequence
for different infants. Her sequence for the first 15 months
of life is as follows:

Month	Ability Acquired
0	Fetal posture
1	Chin up
2	Chest up
3	Reach and miss
4	Sit with support
5	Sit on lap, grasp object
6	Sit on high chair, grasp dangling object

416

```
          7                  Sit alone
          8                  Stand with help
          9                  Stand when holding onto furniture
         10                  Creep
         11                  Walk when led
         12                  Pull to stand by furniture
         13                  Climb stair steps
         14                  Stand alone
         15                  Walk alone
```

1. Fetal posture (newborn)
2. Holds chin up (1 month)
3. Holds chest up (2 months)
4. Reaches for object (3 months)
5. Sits when supported (4 months)
6. Sits on lap, grasps object (5 months)
7. Sits in high chair, grasps object (6 months)
8. Sits alone (7 months)
9. Stands with help (8 months)
10. Stands holding furniture (9 months)
11. Crawls (10 months)
12. Walks if led (11 months)
13. Pulls up on furniture (12 months)
14. Climbs stairs (13 months)
15. Stands alone (14 months)
16. Walks alone (15 months)

Most infants follow an orderly pattern of motor development. Although the order in which the children progress from one stage to the next is similar, there are large individual differences in the ages at which various stages are reached. The ages listed are averages.

Shirley believed that the high degree of similarity in motor sequence is related to the cephalocaudal law of development - a law that states that development proceeds from the head toward the feet. Shirley contends that this is a fundamental biological principle of development.

Aside from locomotion, research in infant motor development has concentrated on such abilities as prehension - the ability to grasp. Halverson (1931) found that there are 10 relatively invariable sequential stages. The first stage is the incapability of the infant to make physical contact with the object. The last stage is the culmination of prehensile ability with the infant acquiring an adult-like grasp by the time he is approximately two months old.

● **PROBLEM** 12-19

Discuss the learning that the infant is capable of.

Solution: At one time it was believed that infants could not actively learn since they were incapable of reaching and directly exploring their environment. However, recent research shows this to be untrue. Infants learn particularly well those behaviors which are life maintaining and those which provide them with the opportunity to explore their environment. Both classical and instrumental conditioning can be demonstrated in the infant.

Kaye (1967) conducted a classical conditioning experiment on infants in which a tone was paired with the sight of a nipple: a tone was sounded just before the nipple was presented. It was found that infants as young as 3 or 4 days old associated the onset of the tone with the appearance of the nipple. Hence, they began to suck when the tone was sounded. Even during extinction, when the tone and the nipple were not paired, several infants continued to suck at the sound of the tone by itself.

Siqueland and Lipsitt (1966) showed that infants can be conditioned instrumentally. They increased the probability of head-turning in 3 and 4-day-old infants by using a nipple filled with a sugar solution as a reinforcement. It was found that head-turning was increased as much as three times after 27 rewards. They also found that infants are capable of learning to discriminate. Infants were trained to turn their heads at the sound of a buzzer. The researchers then transferred reinforcement to that of a tone instead. It was found that infants as young as 3 days old could readily reverse their behavior and respond to the tone rather than to the buzzer.

It has been found that young infants are capable of responding to secondary reinforcers. For example, an infant's vocalization and smiling can be increased by tactile or verbal stimulation from the experimenter. Withdrawal of this stimulation decreases the infant's vocalization and smiling.

Describe the perceptual ability of the infant. Define
"visual cliff."

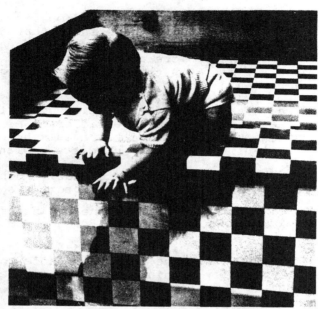

The visual cliff is used for studying depth perception. Subjects who have not developed depth perception typically climb
off the central platform, onto the side that appears deeper.

Solution: Contrary to previous notions, the newborn infant
has several perceptual skills. With regard to vision, for
example, it has been found that infants are sensitive to
light intensity, patterns, and contours. The eyes of a newborn infant can follow a slowly moving object. Infants can
also differentiate various sound pitches as well as certain
odors and tastes.

    Vision takes longer to develop than the other senses.
When the infant first opens his eyes, his visual focus is
relatively fixed at about 9 inches from the cornea - the
approximate distance between him and his mother's face during nursing. Eye muscles are weak, hence, eye coordination
is poor. The infant is unable to change the focus of his
eyes until he is about 2 months of age and he cannot change
the shape of his lens to bring near and far objects into
focus until he is about four months old. The visual acuity
of the average infant is 20/150. This means that an infant
can see objects from 20 feet while an adult with normal vision can perceive the same objects 150 feet away. By the
end of infancy at age 2, however, the child's visual acuity
matches an adult's.

    Depth perception seems to develop by 6 - 8 months at
the same time that the infant begins to crawl. To determine
the existence of depth perception in children a device call-

ed a "visual cliff" is employed. This device usually consists of a raised platform, a part of which is composed of
glass that gives the illusion of a cliff. Depth perception
is noted when the child refuses to crawl from the "solid"
side of the platform onto the glass. This refusal to crawl
"off the cliff" is prevalent in most infants even at their
mothers' inducement.

Several studies have been conducted on visual preference in infants. These studies have shown that infants
spend more time looking at certain stimuli than at others.
For example, infants gaze more at moving objects than at
stationary ones. Their eyes tend to focus on figures with
patterns rather than on those of solid colors.

Infants can also detect the location of certain sounds.
Different frequencies of sound have different effects on
the child. A low intensity sound has a calming effect,
while an extremely loud sound may elicit a violent response.

The neonate is also sensitive to odor. When presented
with an unpleasant odor, the child will turn his face away.

Response to taste is slight in the infant, although
after two weeks he shows a marked preference for sugar over
salt.

Studies indicate that the neonate is able to tolerate
a high level of normally painful stimulation. Hence, sensitivity to tactile stimulation is not great.

By the time the infant is six months old, his perception is quite sophisticated and very similar to that of an
adult.

● **PROBLEM** 12-21

Discuss the importance of maternal stimulation in infant
development. Cite the findings of Spitz, Schaffer and
Emerson, and Harlow.

Solution: Several studies have indicated the necessity of
maternal love or "mothering" for the normal physical, social, and emotional development of the infant.

Spitz (1945) found that institutionalized children have
significantly higher mortality rates than non-institutional-
ized children. In addition, he found that children in institutions display retardation in physical growth and emotional development. Withdrawal, depression and even death
have sometimes resulted. Marasmus or anaclitic depression
refers to the condition that develops as a result of maternal deprivation. Symptoms of this depression include excessive and prolonged weeping, retarded development, sadness
and an increased susceptibility to disease.

Schaffer and Emerson (1964) also studied the effects
of maternal deprivation on the infant. They found that the
mother's responsiveness to the child's crying and the amount
of stimulation she provided for the child comprise the two

420

Infant monkey with artificial mother

key factors in normal emotional development and are the most
important in mother-child interaction.

Harlow (1958, 1959, 1966) conducted one of the best
known studies of mother-child interaction and the effects of
maternal deprivation on infant development. Harlow attempted to study the nature of the attachment between the mother
and infant. He observed that the feeling the infant has for
the mother is derived from the associations he makes when
the mother is present during tension. Through these associations, the infant comes to regard the mother as pleasant.

In his experiments, Harlow used infant monkeys which he
separated from their mothers after birth. In the natural
mother's place, Harlow provided surrogate mothers. In each
monkey's cage, Harlow placed two surrogates. One surrogate
was constructed from bare wire, the other had a soft, terry-
cloth covering. In four cages, the bare wire model possessed a milk bottle with a nipple. In four other cages, the
terry-cloth model had the bottle. Harlow wanted to see for
which model the infant monkeys would develop an attachment.
His prediction was that the attachment would be made to the
model with the milk bottle. The results indicated that the
monkeys always approached the model with the bottle during
feeding time. At all other times though, the monkeys preferred the company of the terry-cloth model. It was also
found that the infant monkey, when hungry, would attempt to
feed from the bottle on the wire mother while clinging to
the terry-cloth mother. Harlow concluded that food-giving
does not render an attachment between mother and child.

Harlow measured attachment in two ways. First, he recorded the amount of time that the infant monkey spent with

421

each model. He observed that during a period of 25 days, the monkeys spent an average of over 12 hours a day with the terry-cloth model while very little time was spent with the bare wire model.

Another method Harlow used to determine attachment was by using a fear-producing stimulus. A fearful object such as a plaster cast of a monkey's head or a toy teddy bear that played the drum was put into the cage. The psychologist recorded the number of times the monkeys ran to each of the models for protection. Harlow found the infant attached itself to the terry-cloth mother when the fearful stimulus was presented, regardless of which model had the milk bottle. If the terry-cloth mother was not present when the stimulus was presented, the monkey's anxiety would increase and cause him to cower in a corner. Harlow concluded that "contact comfort" is an important variable in the formation of mother-child relationships.

In another experiment, Harlow found that monkeys who had been deprived of any surrogate mother, even a terry-cloth model, during the first eight months of life were unable to develop attachments with any surrogate mother. In addition, monkeys who spent the same amount of time in complete isolation were unable to make contact and socialize with other monkeys in close proximity.

Harlow's studies emphasize the importance of maternal stimulation in the healthy emotional and social development of the infant.

● **PROBLEM 12-22**

What does research suggest is the major result of breast-feeding an infant?

Solution: A major part of an infant's early pleasure is derived from oral stimulation and eating. This view, hypothesized by Freudian theorists, also contends that the frustration experienced at this time could significantly affect later behavior. Researchers, attempting to investigate this notion, studied whether or not breast-feeding and the effects of intimate contact with the mother, lead to greater emotional security than bottle feeding. Studies reveal that there is no significant support for this belief.

Researchers today generally contend that the attitude the parents have towards the child during feeding time will have greater long term effects upon the child's development than any specific method used in feeding. Thus, it appears that the most important variable in the feeding of an infant is the warmth or coldness of the feeding parent.

● **PROBLEM 12-23**

Discuss some psychological viewpoints concerning toilet training in infants, especially with regard to the time it should begin. What can be said about the relationship between the type of toilet training a mother administers and her personality?

Solution: Sigmund Freud was the first theorist to recognize toilet training as a significant step in a child's development. Toilet training signifies a child's increased maturity - both physical and psychological - and it indicates a parent's exercise of control over the child's behavior.

Most American children are expected to be toilet trained between the ages of one and a half to two years. In 1957, Sears, Maccoby, and Levin reported that the average age for completion of toilet training is approximately 18 months. Heinstein's (1966) study indicated an average age of 22 months for toilet training completion.

Dr. Benjamin Spock, who is greatly influenced by Freud, suggests in his best-selling book, Baby and Child Care, a need for later toilet training. He believes that children should be allowed the freedom of wetting and messing, and should have some say in determining when training should begin. (Dr. Spock's current advice is less permissive, he believes that children should learn to consider the needs of their parents.)

Toilet training in the United States occurs later than it did a generation ago. A study by Brazelton (1962) indicates that postponing toilet training until the age of two years greatly reduces bed-wetting, soiling, and constipation in late childhood.

Research has indicated that strict, early training usually produces emotional upset in the child and can lead to the problems listed above. Warmth and affection are considered necessary to decrease the likelihood of these disturbances.

Various studies have shown that mothers who start training their children early are usually over-concerned with neatness in all areas. These mothers are more likely to punish their children when their cleanliness standards are not met. Freud and other personality theorists have regarded early, severe toilet training by mothers to be indicative of such qualities as an obsession for cleanliness and orderliness, extreme thriftiness, punctuality, and neatness of dress. These are characteristics of a restrictive mother.

● **PROBLEM 12-24**

Describe three approaches to the study of emotionality. Cite the theories of Watson and Bridges concerning emotional development in the infant.

Solution: Emotionality is a difficult and complex area of investigation. Emotions consist of subjective responses which are not always easily interpreted by an observer. Often, when an adult observes the behavior of an infant, he may ascribe to the child those emotions which can only be produced by adults. Infants cannot directly communicate their feelings. Situations that produce particular emotions in adults cannot be assumed to produce the same emotions in infants. The lower centers of the brain which are respons-

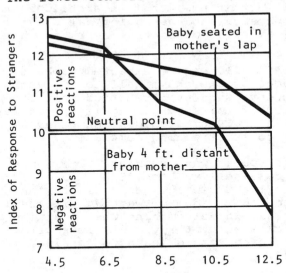

Baby's age in months
(n=16 at each age level)

Under six weeks

Simple dots or angles suffice.

Ten weeks

The eye section alone suffices, the under portion of the face being unnecessary.

Twelve weeks

The eye section still suffices, but the under half of the face must be present even though the mouth is not watched and its movements are only fleetingly noticed. Motion facilitates.

Twenty weeks

The eye section still suffices with wide individual differences. The mouth is gradually noticed. Its movements particularly effective. Wide mouth best. Plastic model of adult effective. Motion facilitates.

Twenty-four weeks

Effectiveness of eyes lessens. Mouth movements generally necessary, the the widely drawn mouth especially. Still no differentiation of individual adult faces.

Thirty weeks

A new stage begins. Attention to face as such lessens, as recognition of facial expression begins, and interest in other children. Progressive differentiation of individual faces.

Stimuli required to elicit smiling response in infants of various stages.

ible for producing emotional reactions are intact and in a state of readiness at birth.

The first major theorist to explore emotional behavior was J. B. Watson (1924). He defined emotion in terms of the situation that produces it. Thus, situations that are dangerous produce fear and situations that are frustrating produce anger. Watson cited three emotions in the infant: fear, anger, and love. He based these findings on the responses infants made to various emotion-producing stimuli. Watson believed that when the infant reacted to a loud noise or felt as if he would be dropped, he expressed fear. A situation in which the infant would be confined would produce anger. Love could be produced by rocking or fondling the infant.

A second method of describing emotions is in terms of observable physical behavior or bodily changes. An individual's violent behavior would indicate anger; flight or retreating would indicate fear; less violent reactions would indicate love.

Some theorists believe that emotions are consciously experienced. When an individual acts fearful he "feels" afraid.

Bridges (1932), in contrast to Watson, believed that an infant possesses one general emotion at birth that can be described only as excitement. This single, diffuse emotion gradually differentiates into specific emotions. By the age of 3 months, the infant is able to display pleasure and dissatisfaction. At 6 months, the child's displeasure has been differentiated into fear, disgust and anger. By the time the infant is a year old, pleasure is differentiated into elation and love. Bridges claims that the emotional range of a two-year-old has differentiated enough so that he can express all the emotions that an adult is capable of expressing.

● **PROBLEM** 12-25

How has the way psychologists view infants changed over the years?

Solution: In the past, psychologists based their observations of infant behavior on comparisons with children and adults. Consequently, infants were viewed as inadequate and passive humans despite the fact that their abilities and sensory functions were not fully developed at this stage. Sleeping is the baby's major task.

Psychologists have recently begun to emphasize the functions that an infant can perform while considering his lack of development and learning abilities. Adaptability and alertness to the environment are just two of the chief functions that psychologists find most babies are able to perform at the infant stage.

Psychologists are also very interested in the individuality of infants. Although infants are heavily dependent

in many ways, they attempt to satisfy their needs in very
individual manners.

Describe the growth changes that occur during the transition
from infancy to preschool age that alter the child's appearance.

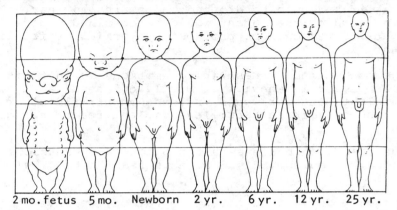

2 mo. fetus 5 mo. Newborn 2 yr. 6 yr. 12 yr. 25 yr.

Changes in form and proportion of the human body during fetal
and postnatal life.

Solution: The period of infancy is generally believed to
extend up to the child's second birthday. A child between
the ages of two and six is considered to be in the preschool
period. During this stage, growth in both height and weight
decreases.

At two years, the average height and weight for a boy
are 34 1/2 inches and 27 3/4 lbs. The average height and
weight for a girl of the same age, are 34 inches and 27 lbs.
respectively.

Much of the infant's fat disappears in the preschool
child. The appearance of fat is greatly diminished by the
facts that fatty tissues are growing at a slower rate than
other tissues and that the increase in height helps compensate for the fat. By age six, fatty tissue is half as thick
as it was during the child's first year. The child gradually begins to look more like an adult. The squat appearance
of an infant is due to his waist being as large as his hips
or chest. The six year old develops a waist that is small
in relation to his shoulders and hips.

Most preschool children lose the protruding abdomen
they carried during infancy. In infancy, the abdomen pro-
trudes because the internal organs are growing faster than
the body cavity. With the increasing rate of growth in
height however, the abdomen recedes.

The proportion of head size to body size decreases
from infancy to preschool age. At birth, the child's head
is slightly less than one-fourth the size of the rest of
the body. By age two, the head is one-fifth the body size,

and by age six, the head is reduced to one-eighth the body size. Thus, the six-year-old's appearance approximates that of the adult's whose head size is about one-tenth of his body size.

● **PROBLEM** 12-27

Briefly describe motor development during the preschool period.

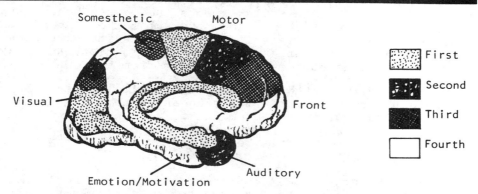

Order of maturation of the various areas of the cerebral cortex. The main sensory and motor areas are labeled, and mature first. Association areas mature later.

Solution: The ability to walk is the child's most important achievement during the course of motor development. By the time he reaches preschool age, his feet have moved closer together while walking and his arms and hands have moved closer to the body. Thus, his balance during locomotion has improved. Eventually, the child also learns to climb stairs, jump, hop and skip.

By the age of 2, the child's grasping ability has also improved. He has become proficient at picking up objects carrying them and carefully setting them down again.

Gesell (1925) described how perceptual-motor development progresses between ages 3 and 5. He found that perceptual and motor skills are interdependent. Gesell reports that a 3-year-old can draw a circle and a straight line whereas a 2-year-old cannot. By the time he is 4 years old, the child can draw a cross and a diamond, these figures are much more difficult to draw. In addition, a 4-year-old can button his clothes. By his fifth year, he can draw a triangle and a prism as well as lace his shoes.

● **PROBLEM** 12-28

Define egocentrism as it applies to preschoolers. What are Piaget's views of the egocentric child in terms of language and moral judgment?

Solution: Egocentrism is a normal stage in human development. In child development, egocentrism refers to the preschooler's primary interest in self. The child is able to perceive and understand the world only from his point of view; he is unable to see a situation as someone else might. This interest in self is not the result of conceit or self-ishness. The child has simply not reached the stage where he can consider the thoughts and feelings of others.

Piaget identified egocentrism in preschool children and was primarily concerned with two aspects of it: language and moral judgment. He believed that the egocentric child uses language primarily for practice and communication with himself. An egocentric child expects the person he's speaking with to know everything about the subject of the discussion. He becomes impatient if he is required to give more details than he feels are necessary. In addition, an egocentric child ignores ideas that differ from his own.

Piaget believed that an egocentric child's moral behavior is the result of his learning and adherence to rules. The child's concept of rules emanates from an authority figure, such as a parent or teacher, whom he believes is omniscient and infallible. This belief leads the child to regard rules as inflexible, sacred, and rigid.

Like Kohlberg, Piaget contended that a preschool child is not capable of achieving a real sense of morality. The egocentric child is only concerned with the outcome of an event rather than with the intention of the actor. If someone accidently breaks one of the egocentric child's toys, he won't forgive that person because he cannot understand or empathize with someone else's feelings or intentions. The child cannot comprehend any system of ethics.

Piaget saw the egocentric child as a very rigid, self-centered individual. However, recent research has revealed that this type of child is more flexible than was once thought. Studies show that preschool children often listen to each other with a significant degree of sympathy. These children have also been found to play together in harmony which naturally requires a certain degree of flexibility. Studies have also indicated that preschoolers may consider moral intentions. As psychologists continue to probe into this area, the concept of egocentrism may come to be redefined in human development.

● **PROBLEM** 12-29

Discuss sex role learning. Is it inherited or learned? Describe two psychological explanations for sex role learning.

Solution: As in most areas of human development, the acquirement of appropriate sex role behavior is both genetically determined and learned. Psychologists, however, have only recently acknowledged this view as plausible. Many sex differences which we now know to be learned were at one time thought to be inherited. The psychological viewpoint has undergone a marked shift from a biological determinist view to a more environmentalist one. Still, sex role characteristics which are inherited cannot be overlooked.

In every animal species, males behave differently from females. Harlow (1962), for example, found that young male monkeys engage in rough play more frequently than female monkeys. Young, Goy, and Phoenix (1964) found that young female monkeys, whose mothers were injected with the male hormone immediately before birth, were more rough or "masculine" in their play.

Psychology offers two theories to account for sex role learning. One theory is based upon the principle of reinforcement. Children are rewarded for behaving in a mode which is considered appropriate for their particular sex and are punished for inappropriate behavior. The other theory is based upon imitation and identification with the same-sexed parent. The child adopts the behavior patterns of the parent of the same sex and becomes as masculine or feminine as the parent. Because reinforcement and imitation are both processes of socialization, sex role learning is a type of socialization.

In their review of evidence on sex differences, Eleanor Maccoby and Carol Jacklin (1971) have discovered that many beliefs about sex differences are unfounded. They contend that sex-related behavior is more often "in the eye of the beholder" than in the behavior of the subject.

The development of sex-related behavior is also dependent upon the parents' interaction with their children. In the United States, sex-stereotyping is common. It begins at birth with the sending of blue cards to announce the birth of a male child and pink cards to herald the arrival of a female. Several studies have indicated that there are marked differences between the way that parents interact with male and female children. For example, three psychologists from Tufts University administered questionnaires to parents of newborn babies. The questionnaire asked them to rate their child on such qualities as size, skin texture, temperament, etc. The study indicated that parents of daughters considered their children to be smaller, softer, and more delicate than parents of males.

In another study, two groups of mothers were chosen to interact or play with a 6-month-old boy. The infant was presented to the first group of mothers dressed as a boy, but he was presented to the second group of mothers dressed as a girl. The mothers who thought that the child was a girl smiled at him more than the other group of mothers. The mothers who thought that he was a girl often selected a doll for him to play with whereas the mothers who thought he was a boy selected a train. Clearly then, sex role differences in behavior are due at least in part to parental expectations and guidance.

● **PROBLEM** 12-30

Describe the process of sex typing in terms of Freudian theorists, social learning theorists, and cognitive theorists.

Solution: Sex typing refers to the process by which the child acquires a number of the masculine or feminine characteristics found in the parent of the same sex. Three major theories attempt to describe this identification process. One is promulgated by Freudian theorists, the second by social learning theorists, and the third by cognitive theorists.

According to the Freudian viewpoint, sex identification occurs with the resolution of the Oedipal conflict. A boy's desire for his mother and a girl's desire for her father is overcome in normal psychosexual development. Through identification with the same-sexed parent, the child reduces the stress involved in the competition for the opposite-sexed parent. In addition, the child experiences vicarious enjoyment from his same-sexed parent's relationship with the opposite-sexed parent.

Imitation is the basis of the social learning theorists' interpretation of sex typing. The child identifies with the parent of the same sex. He imitates the behavior of this parent, thus beginning the process of sex typing. By imitating the behavior of the same-sexed parent, the child adopts characteristics indigenous to his or her particular sex. At the same time, he or she develops a concept of the male and female personalities - what those personalities should be like (the appropriate behavior and mannerisms for males and females). Boys begin to learn that rough or otherwise "manly" behavior is appropriate, and girls learn that dainty, feminine mannerisms comprise proper behavior for them. In social learning theory, behavior appropriate to each sex is reinforced by approval or disapproval. Boys are praised for manly behavior, girls are encouraged to act like ladies. After the child has grasped a set of sex-appropriate behaviors, a sex-typed identity emerges.

The cognitive theory of sex typing has been most notably promulgated by Kohlberg (1971). According to Kohlberg, a sex-typed identity develops before the child's identification with the same-sexed parent occurs. Kohlberg believes that the child first conceives of himself as a boy or girl. This identification process results after hearing his parents refer to him as a boy or a girl and he recognizes superficial traits that distinguish males from females - clothing, hairstyle, etc. This recognition occurs during the preschool period. Later, as the child's concept of sex type is strengthened, he recognizes sex appropriate behaviors and he adopts those behaviors which are appropriate to his sex. At this point, he looks to the same-sexed parent for a role model.

At present, each of these three theories makes valid statements about the development of sex typing. No one theory can, as of yet, be considered better than another.

● PROBLEM 12-31

Define social development. Distinguish between work and

play. List and define three types of play. How does play influence cognition?

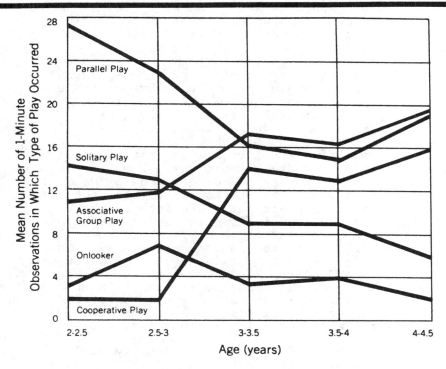

Changes in types of play as a function of age. Solitary, on-looker, and parallel play decrease, while associative and cooperative play increase.

Solution: Social development refers to the development of behaviors the child engages in when he interacts with others. This area of study includes such topics as games, morality, learning the rules of society, and language acquisition.

Work and play are not distinguished by the specific activities they involve since these can be similar. Rather, work and play are distinguished by their end results. Play is engaged in for the pleasure - it is rewarding in and of itself. Work, on the other hand, is engaged in for the purpose of gaining a desired goal. Work can be enjoyable, but enjoyment is only incidental. The goal of most work is the attainment of monetary or material reward.

The child engages in three major categories of play: sensorimotor play, imaginative play, and parallel or coop-erative play which is based on the existence of the inter-action among the players. Sensorimotor play is engaged in during infancy. It involves the manipulation of objects. This manipulation provides the child with pleasurable stim-ulation. Sensorimotor play can consist of motor activities such as crawling, walking, running or waving.

Imaginative play involves games of make-believe. The child may imagine that he is someone or something else; or that the activities he engages in are something other than what they really are; or possibly he imagines that objects that he is playing with are something different than what they appear to be. Daydreaming is a major form of imaginative play. Daydreaming, however, involves no physical activity as compared to the other types of play. It is pure imaginative thinking.

The third type of play consists of two sequential types. Each is named and described in terms of the existance of interaction among the players. The first type, parallel play, begins shortly after infancy. Here, children play side by side but do not interact. They might use the same play materials but any sharing is unintentional. Between the ages of two and five, children begin to act out fantasies, pretending that they are various characters. When children find that they share knowledge of various characters or fantasies with one another, they engage in cooperative play as they act out fantasies together. Any type of play that involves interaction and cooperation among the players is called cooperative. One special type of cooperative play is called sociodramatic play. This type requires that the child's imagination and perception be highly active and alert - quick to pick up cues from the other players. It is comparable to the improvisation of professional actors. Through sociodramatic play, the child learns how to behave in society. In addition, the groundwork is laid for interpersonal relationships.

During the period of cooperative play, quarreling among players arises. This quarreling becomes especially common between the ages of three and four. Such quarreling marks the beginning of competitiveness, a quality which is highly reinforced in preschoolers in this culture.

In addition to teaching the child how to interact socially, play is also an influencing factor in cognition. Sutton-Smith (1967) considered play an activity in which the infant can work through new responses and operations and increase his range of responses. Sutton-Smith called play a mechanism for the "socialization of novelty." Children whose play is varied are given a chance to experience situations which increase their ability to respond appropriately to novel situations that may arise in the future. Children whose play is restricted are less able to respond in unfamiliar situations. Thus, play enlarges a child's repertoire of responses and therby allows him to adjust quickly to new situations.

● **PROBLEM** 12-32

Discuss the importance of the family as a socializing agent. Describe Baumrind's (1967) study of the relationship between the preschooler's personality and the type of discipline he receives from his parents.

Solution: The family is the first important and most powerful socializing agent with whom the child comes into contact. The child receives from the family those things that are necessary for survival; the family fulfills his physiological and psychological needs.

The child learns culture from his family: the rules which govern acceptable and unacceptable modes of behavior in his society. He is introduced to the religion of the family (if any), and adopts the values, beliefs and customs of his parents and siblings. (A distinction should be made here between a nuclear family and an extended family. A nuclear family consists of the parents and children alone. An extended family includes the other relatives. In the United States, the nuclear family is the most characteristic family structure. In this discussion, "family" refers to the nuclear family.)

Baumrind (1967) was interested in the effects of the parent-child relationship on the development of the child's personality. In his study, Baumrind categorized preschool children into one of three personality groups. In the first group, children were friendly, gregarious, and possessed a marked degree of self-control and self-reliance. Children in the second group were withdrawn and generally unhappy. The third group consisted of children who were demanding and who lacked the self-control and self-reliance of the children in the first group. Baumrind found that each child's personality was related to the type of discipline he received from his parents. The friendly, self-controlled children of the first group had parents who were more demanding, controlling, and loving than the parents of the other two groups. The parents of the unhappy and withdrawn children were also demanding, but they exhibited none of the affection that the parents of the first group displayed. The children who lacked self-control and self-reliance had parents who displayed the affection of the first group's parents but who were permissive rather than demanding. Other studies have indicated that children with demanding and affectionate parents often develop into individuals who are independent, self-reliant, and well equipped to handle problems.

● **PROBLEM** 12-33

Discuss the importance of the peer group as a socializing agent. What have studies on the peer group shown about the conformity of the child to its judgments?

Solution: The peer group refers to those children with whom the child associates who are about his same age. Until the age of 5 or 6, the family is the most important influence and socializing agent in the child's life. After this time, the parents still satisfy the child's physical needs, but a great deal of his psychological support comes from his peers. As the child grows older, the influence of the peer group supersedes the influence of the parents. The child comes to learn more about his culture and the rules for appropriate behavior through his friends and associates. Often, a peer group is either a club or a gang and can be described as a sub-culture with its own rules for behavior.

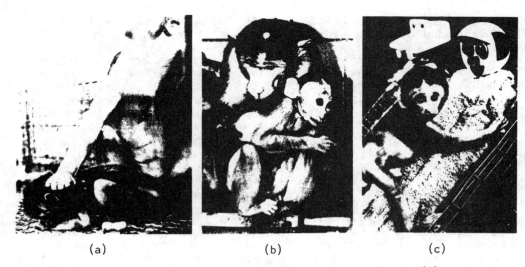

(a)   (b)   (c)

Various forms of maternal and attachment behavior. In (a), the mother is one of Harlow's monkeys who was reared in social isolation. She is pressing her baby's face into the floor of the cage. (b) The monkey mother and baby exhibit a normal relationship. (c) The monkey, reared without its mother, clings to the terrycloth mother.

Several animal studies have indicated the importance of the peer group by demonstrating the harmful effects of its absence. Harlow and Zimmerman (1959) demonstrated that monkeys raised in isolation are incapable of engaging in mature social relations with other monkeys when they are finally brought into contact with them. Male monkeys are incapable of participating in normal sexual relations and females raised in isolation make poor mothers - they cannot display maternal attachment.

Studies have also examined the influence that peer groups exert on the individual and the ways the individual conforms to the group's beliefs, judgments and manner of behavior. Berenda (1950) examined the extent to which children conform to false judgments while they are under the influence of their peers. The study indicated that children conform to false judgments most readily when pressure is exerted by a member of the group they hold in high esteem. Many psychologists, including Piaget, contend that the greatest amount of conformity occurs during middle childhood, when the child is able to take the role of the other; that is, look at a situation from another's viewpoint.

MIDDLE CHILDHOOD AND ADOLESCENCE

● PROBLEM 12-34

Trace perceptual development during preschool age and middle childhood as reflected by search patterns. How do children perceive letters?

434

Solution: Perceptual development reflects changes in gathering information. As the child grows older, he develops organized search patterns which give him prowess in identifying objects. This ability becomes manifest if a child who is blindfolded is able to identify an object placed in his hands by touch. This search method of touch becomes more thorough and systematic as the child grows older. A 3-year-old might just hold an object briefly in the palm of his hand whereas an 8-year-old would run his fingers over the object and extend his thumb and forefinger to try to determine its length. This increase in sophistication of search patterns with increasing age is true for all the senses.

In his analysis of reading methods, E. J. Gibson (1970) found that the object the child searches for is as important as the method he uses to search for it. Studies have shown that 3-year-olds can differentiate between line drawings, and between scribbles and letters, but not between just scribbles or just letters. Five-year-olds can recognize letters but not words, since they ignore the spaces between them.

Children's perceptual skills enable them to employ three different methods to differentiate between letters. These are: openness, curvature and direction. The three methods are acquired at different points in the child's life. Most preschoolers can perceive differences in openness, such as the difference between "o" and "c." But approximately 45 percent of 4-year-olds cannot distinguish letters on the basis of curvature and direction. Through training, however, letter differentiation improves.

• PROBLEM 12-35

Briefly describe physical and motor development during middle childhood.

Age	Height		Weight		Age	Height		Weight	
	Girl	Boy	Girl	Boy		Girl	Boy	Girl	Boy
6 years	45½	46¼	46½	48¼	12	59¾	59	87½	84½
6½ years	47	47½	49½	51¼	12½	60¾	60	93¼	88¾
7 years	48	49	52¼	54	13	61¾	61	99	93
7½ years	49¼	50	55¼	57	13½	62½	62½	103¾	100¼
8 years	50½	51¼	58	60	14	62¾	64	108½	107½
8½ years	51½	52¼	61	63	14½	63	65	111	114
9 years	52¼	53¼	63¾	66	15	63½	66	113½	120
9½ years	53½	54¼	67	69	15½	63¾	66¾	115¼	125
10 years	54½	55¼	70¼	72	16	64	67¾	117	129¾
10½ years	55¾	56	74½	74¾	16½	64	68	118	133
11 years	57	56¾	78¾	77½	17	64	68½	119	136¼
11½ years	58¼	57¾	83¼	81	17½	64	68½	119½	137½
12 years	59¾	59	87½	84½	18	64	68½	120	139

Height (in inches) and Weight (in pounds) at the Fiftieth Percentile for American Children

Solution: The period of middle childhood extends from ages 6 to 12. The child develops significantly during this time. Vast differences in behavior are evident between a 6-year-old and a 12-year-old. The onset of puberty marks the end of the period of middle childhood.

During the period of middle childhood, the child's body experiences a significant increase in both height and weight. However, one can observe a major difference in the rate of growth between boys and girls. From birth until the end of the preschool period, the rate of growth for boys and girls is approximately the same, despite the fact that girls are slightly shorter in height and lighter in weight than boys. This growth rate holds true at the beginning of middle childhood. At the age of 6, girls are about 3/4 of an inch shorter and 2 pounds lighter than boys. By the age of ten, the growth rate of the girl corresponds with that of the boy. The girl soon surpasses the boy in height. At age 12 the female usually becomes slightly taller. Between the ages of 11 and 12, the girl surpasses the boy in weight. She weighs three pounds more by age 13. The boy does not exceed the girl in height until he is 13 1/2 years old nor does he exceed the girl in weight until he is 14 1/2.

Physical growth during middle childhood is also marked by a decrease in the growth of fatty tissue and an increase in the development of muscles and bones. Muscle development is more rapid in boys than in girls. The decrease in the growth of fatty tissue is greater in boys. Girls tend to retain their baby fat longer.

During middle childhood, motor skills continue to develop and improve. By the end of this period, the child can almost completely control his large muscles. Control of small muscles has greatly improved since preschool age.

Significant differences exist between the sexes and their ability to use various motor skills. For example, throughout middle childhood the boy's hand grip is stronger than the girl's hand grip. In a broad jump, boys consistently jump farther than girls after age 7. Such evidence would lead to the conclusion that boys' leg power and arm-leg coordination for jumping surpasses that of the girl. Johnson (1962) found that catching, throwing, kicking, and batting were handled better by boys than by girls. It has been found that boys run faster, throw a ball farther, and jump hurdles better during the period of middle childhood. However, girls surpass boys in some motor skills during this period. Girls have been found to be superior to boys in activities such as cable jumping - an exercise that involves jumping over an object such as a rope when it is held in front of them. Girls also surpass boys in activities that require a sense of rhythm such as hopscotch.

Reaction time plays an important role in the development of motor abilities. Reaction time can be defined as the interval of time between the onset of a stimulus and the beginning of a response to that stimulus. As the child's motor abilities improve, his reaction time improves; it increases as he gets older so that he is able to engage in more rapid activities or activities that require quick action or quick thinking. Whiting (1969) found that the reaction time of a five-year-old is twice as long as an adult's. For example, a five-year-old shows considerable difficulty in catching a ball. As he gets older, however, this skill improves.

Briefly discuss the emotional and social adjustments that occur during middle childhood.

Solution: The period of middle childhood is a relatively calm period in the life of a child. He has resolved the Oedipal dilemma and has learned a great deal about culturally appropriate behavior from his same-sexed parent. By the time he is 5 or 6 years of age, his individuality is, for the most part, established. He has acquired most of the behavioral traits that characterize his personality.

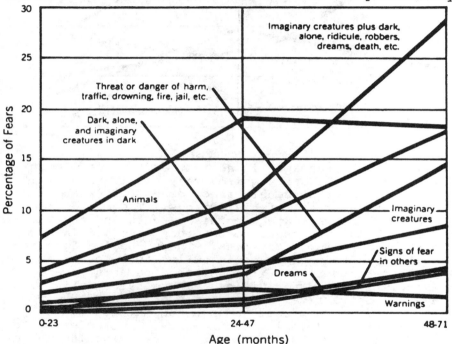

Freud claims that in this period of sexual latency, the child loses interest in sex-related matters. He is freed from the emotional conflicts which arose in earlier "sexual" periods and which will arise again in the future. The child experiences a phase of relative ease and comfort.

The child is still closely tied to his parents at the beginning of this period. They provide for most of his needs. Eventually, however, other influences become important, especially when the child enters school. The teacher in school assumes part of the responsibility for the child's maturation. Parents often feel they can relinquish at least part of their responsibility to an outside agent.

In addition to the teacher, the peer group becomes especially important to the child's learning and social development. As he grows older, he spends more and more time with his peers both in and out of school. The time spent outside the home further diminishes his ties with his parents. The child now wants to be accpeted by his peers, to

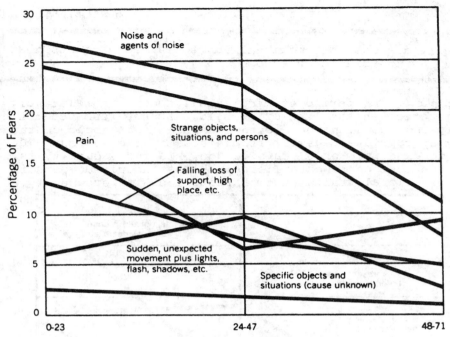

Age (months)

accomplish this he engages in activities that will meet
with their approval. He acquires many skills which increase his sense of personal value, especially when these
skills win the approval of his friends. The child gradually becomes less intimate with his parents and the parents
likewise lose the intense interest they once had in his
daily school and play activities. The so-called "generation gap" could be said to begin during this period as the
child drifts further away from home and parents toward
peer associations and activities. These associations are
not always constructive. For example, the child may become the member of a street gang and he may consequently
involve himself in juvenile delinquency. Surrendering to
peer pressure in this way will often cause disunity in the
home. This does not usually occur until adolescence.

For the most part, the child in middle childhood is a
pleasant, compliant individual with a unique personality.
He is still willing, even eager, to internalize the norms
of his culture.

● **PROBLEM** 12-37

Define morality. Trace moral development as outlined by
Piaget and by Freud.

Solution: Morality is defined as the individual's internalization of rules -- the conventional mores indigenous to his
environment or society.

According to Jean Piaget, morality development manifests itself on two levels: the child's understanding of
rules and his behavior with regard to that understanding.

	Psychoanalytic	Social-Learning	Cognitive-Developmental
Major Theorist	Sigmund Freud	Albert Bandura	Lawrence Kohlberg
Basic Emphasis	Feelings (conscience and guilt)	Behavior (influence of others and stimulus conditions)	Thought (qualitative changes in development)
Mechanism for Acquisition of Morality	Internalization of parental values in the child's superego	Results from conditioning and modeling	Proceeds in orderly stages related to cognitive development
Age of Acquisition	Superego is formed by about age five	Learning continues throughout life; wide individual differences	Ongoing process to adulthood—may fixate at any stage
Cultural Relativity	Morality is culturally relative within a framework of universal psychosexual stages	Morality is culturally relative	Moral values and stages are universal
Agents of Socialization	Parents are central influence	Adults and peers who dispense rewards and punishments and who serve as models are main influence	Persons at next highest stage exert greatest influence
Implications for Education	Education exerts little ifluence	Teacher should serve as good example and should reward appropriate behaviors	Teacher should try to stimulate child by exposing him to moral conflicts and to moral statements at next level

Comparison of the Three Major Theories

From birth until 3 years of age, the child neither understands nor adheres to rules. Piaget lables the next stage the intermediate period, during which the child imitates rules; that is, he imitates the rule-following behavior that he witnesses in others. He still doesn't fully understand rules. This period lasts from ages 3 to 5. By age 7, the child is able to comprehend rules and can adhere to them. He can play games in a social manner. The child can now understand rules and follow them but not until he is about 11 or 12 can he grasp the purpose of the rule or the fact that they can be changed by the mutual consent of the individuals involved.

Piaget also attempted to examine rule understanding through the child's verbalization of his understanding. Upon questioning a number of children about rule origins and their characteristics, he discerned three stages. During the first stage, from birth to 3 years, the child's be-

havior reflects the fact that he has no understanding of
rules. During the next stage, the child believes that
rules are imposed by a high source or authority (such as
God). He believes these rules are timeless and should not
be changed. His behavior, however, is inconsistent with
this belief since he is constantly changing rules in his
game playing. In the next stage he comes to understand
that rules can be changed if agreed to by all the parties
involved.

Piaget also studied the child's understanding of culpability. He was able to delineate two stages. During the
first stage, from birth until 9 or 10 years of age, the
child judges guilt by the objective consequences of the
act. Here, he looks at the quantitative aspects or concrete results as the standard for judgment. For example,
the theft of $100 from a bank would be judged by the child
to be worse than the theft of $95 from a poor family. Af-
ter 10 years of age, however, the child's understanding
of culpability matures; he examines the qualitative aspects
and motives behind the act.

According to Freud, morality is defined by the superego which contains the cultural and religious rules of behavior that the child has adopted. The superego develops
after the phallic stage, after the child has resolved his
dilemma with the opposite-sexed parent (Oedipus or Electra
complex) and begins to identify with the same-sexed parent. Freud believed that the child tries to emulate the
same-sexed parent in every way possible: personality, beliefs, goals, gestures, etc. Therefore, the child also
incorporates that parent's morality -- his sense of right
and wrong. The morals assumed by the superego are in constant conflict with the id. The id wants to fulfill its
primitive desires but is restrained by the superego.

● **PROBLEM** 12-38

Discuss the theory of Kohlberg (1964) on the moral development of the child during middle childhood.

<u>Solution:</u> Kohlberg believes that morality is a decision-
making process rather than a fixed behavioral trait. In
Freudian terms, morality reflects the strength of the ego
which makes compromising decisions between the id and the
superego. Based on this idea, Kohlberg devised a sequential design to explain the development of morality. The
emergence of morality consists of three levels. Each level
consists of two stages of moral orientation.

The first level is called premoral. During the first
stage of this level, the child believes that evil behavior
is that which is punished and good behavior is that which
is not punished. For the child, moral behavior is based
on its subjective consequences. The second stage of level
I is hedonism. The child sees good as something that is
pleasant and desirable, and evil as something that is unpleasant and undesirable. This level of morality is characteristic of the infant and preschooler.

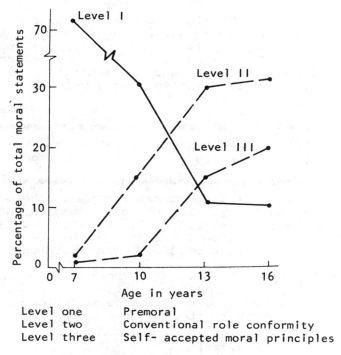

Level one   Premoral
Level two   Conventional role conformity
Level three   Self- accepted moral principles

Mean percent of moral statements on Kohlberg's three levels
made by boys aged 7 to 16

The second level of morality is called morality of
conventional role conformity. At this level one finds that
peer and social relations are important to the child. The
first stage involves the type of morality which will win
approval from parents, teachers, and peers. In other words,
the child recognizes good moral behavior as that which is
praised by society. The second stage of this level refers
to a conformity to laws or to authority figures. Good behavior is characteristic of someone who obeys authority and
society's laws. Both of these orientations reflect the
child's desire to win acceptance and approval and to maintain good relations with whomever he comes in contact.
This level characterizes the morality of the child during
middle childhhod.

The third and highest level of morality according to
Kohlberg's scheme is called morality of self-accepted principles. This level initiates the beginning of the individual's moral standards. The child arrives at an understanding of individual rights, ideals and principles. He
can see beyond the literal interpretation of rules and
laws. He can perceive and distinguish between those laws
that are good and those laws that are faulty. He recon-
nizes democratic principles. An understanding of individual rights and democratically accepted laws are characteristic of the first stage of this level. The second stage
reflects individual principles of conscience. The child
develops notions of right and wrong which take precedence
over the more primitive ways of judging behavior that was
found in the first two levels. This type of morality is
characteristic of the adolescent.

The development of morality is part of the process
of socialization; that is, the learning of behavior that
is appropriate and inappropriate for a particular culture.
In addition, moral development is related to intellectual
development. The child cannot develop a moral system until certain intellectual abilities have developed.

● **PROBLEM** 12-39

Define the period of adolescence. Define puberty and pubescence. What physical changes occur during this period?

Solution: The period of adolescence begins at the onset of
puberty -- sexual maturity. The period of adolescence includes the teen years, ages 13 to 19. Adolescence is an arbitrary segment of a lifespan. It is singled out as a separate period for the purpose of studying development.

Sexual maturity - the ability to bear children defines
puberty. Various physical changes, called pubescence, occur
during the passage from middle childhood to adolescence. Pubescence results in sexual maturity or puberty.

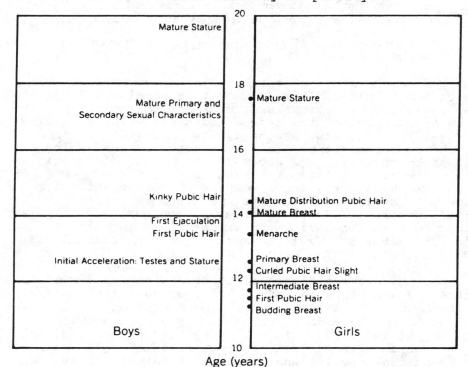

Age (years)

The typical sequence of sexual maturation in boys and girls,
from age eleven to twenty.

The beginning of puberty, or the age at which an individual becomes fertile, is difficult to determine. Many researchers have defined the start of puberty for girls at the
time of their first menstrual period which is called menarche. However, this definition is not entirely accurate
since a girl remains infertile for about a year following

442

the menarche. Pinpointing the start of puberty for boys is
even more difficult although some experts claim that it begins with a boy's first ejaculation. Today, however, most
psychologists agree that the period of adolescence follows
a period of rapid growth or the "growth spurt" which heralds
sexual maturity. Generally, adolescence begins at age 14
for boys and age 12 for girls.

Most of the apparent physical changes that occur during
adolescence are the result of secretions from the pituitary
gland and the adrenal gland. The pituitary gland produces
the hormone called corticotropic which stimulates the cortex
of the adrenal gland. The adrenal gland is responsible for
injecting the two sex hormones, androgen and estrogen, into
the blood stream of boys and girls, respectively. Before
adolescence, more adrogen is produced in males than in females but not enough to effect any visible sex differentiation. However, the onset of puberty changes this balance.
The gonadotropic hormone, produced by the pituitary gland,
starts to act upon the gonads. This action causes the gonads to begin their most important function - the production of sex cells - spermatozoa in the male and ova in the
female. At this time, the gonads also start to produce androgen and estrogen. These sex hormones, together with an
increased secretion of the corticotropic hormone by the
pituitary gland, are responsible for the development of
primary and secondary sex characteristics. Primary sex
characteristics include the enlargement of the genitals or
sex organs. Secondary sex characteristics include the appearance of pubic hair and axillary (armpit) hair, the enlargement of the female's breasts, the lowering of voices
(especially for boys), and the appearance of facial and
chest hair in males.

The pituitary gland produces another hormone called
the growth hormone which is responsible for the growth
spurt - the rapid changes in height and weight that occur
during pubescence. At about age 12, the average height
and weight for a boy is 59 inches and 84 1/2 lbs; for a
girl it's 59 3/4 inches and 87 1/2 lbs. Hence, the female
advantage in height and weight is carried over from middle
childhood to the beginning of this phase. At about the
age of 14, however, the girl loses her edge in growth rate
and by the age of 18, she trails the male by approximately
4 1/2 inches in height and 19 lbs. in weight.

● **PROBLEM** 12-40

Briefly describe motor development in the adolescent.

Solution: One of the most notable characteristics of the adolescent's motor development is his increased physical strength.
The strength results from his rapid growth ("the growth spurt")
and his large amount of physical activity.

Boys, in particular, experience a rapid increase in the
length of their limbs. This is sometimes disadvantageous since
it can cause clumsiness in movement. However, these problems
are eventually solved as the youngster becomes accustomed to
his growing body and learns to use precision and smoothness in

motor activities. The development of this quality is shared by all adolescents. The adolescent's speed of motor performance is greatly accelerated from middle childhood onward. The adolescent acquires keener senses and his reaction time is shorter. Participation in sports aids the development of physical strength and agility and improves reaction time.

Athletic prowess plays an important role in peer relations, especially among boys. An adolescent boy's self-image and self-esteem are highly dependent upon his performance in atheletic events since these bring him peer approval.

● **PROBLEM 12-41**

Discuss some of the psycho-social changes the adolescent undergoes.

Solution: The onset of adolescence effects several psycho-social changes to occur within the individual. Parental influence decreases while peer influence becomes of prime importance. The adolescent feels a greater need to be accepted by his peers. Peer groups provide him with the freedom he needs to experiment with new identities. As the peer group gains importance, so does the adolescent's interest in sex.

In early adolescence, the youth experiences a resurgence of the egocentrism which Piaget posited to be evident during the preschooler period. The adolescent becomes self-indulgent. He is increasingly aware of his appearance for he feels that other people are as preoccupied with his looks as he is. He may, for example, believe that everyone notices his face and is repulsed by his acne. The youth continuously anticipates reactions from others. He also engages in numerous fantasies where he is the focus of attention.

Most adolescents believe that their experiences and feelings are unique, that no one is capable of understanding them.

Although self-esteem sinks at the beginning of adolescence, it gradually stabilizes. It can therefore be said that an average adolescent usually conforms to most norms and has a relatively stable personality.

● **PROBLEM 12-42**

Briefly trace social development during the period of adolescence.

Solution: Two general statements can be made about the adolescent's social development. One is that social skills become increasingly important to the youth as he begins to make more frequent contact with members of the opposite sex. The child progresses from middle childhood, where he sought companionship with members of his own sex, to a more mature stage where he learns the social etiquette necessary to behave appropriately in the adult world.

A second observation that can be made from adolescent social development is that the teenager's parents begin to play less critical roles in his social circle. The child's peers become increasingly important to him.

Lefrancois (1973) derived three general stages of social development which reflect the child's shift of reliance for psychological and emotional support from the parents to friends. During the first stage, the young adolescent is quite dependent upon his parents. They continue to be his chief source of physical, emotional and psychological support. A 12-year-old is likely to seek consolation from his parents if he is upset about something. Hence, the parents' word still holds considerable weight although the extent of dependency is not as great as it was when the child was younger.

The second stage of social development is marked by conflict. After the onset of puberty, the child's peers begin to exert a great amount of influence over him. He is torn between responsibilities to his parents and his desire to be accepted by peers. This conflict usually results in the child's forming an allegiance with his peers. The adolescent wants to spend much more time with his friends and much less time with his parents. During this intermediate stage, conflict arises from a number of factors including parental interference in social life and school work. The parents may criticize the child's friends and tell him whom to associate with. They may also reprimand him about his grades in school. Adding to these conflicts is the fact that the child is financially dependent on the parents and therefore, must succumb to their wishes most of the time. During this period, the adolescent gradually alienates himself from his parents. This alienation continues to grow until the last stage of adolescent socialization.

The third stage of social development is characterized by a relative independence from the parents. This independence does not mean that the adolescent severs all ties with his parents; it simply means that he is now operating in the social realm of his peers whose acceptance continues to be of utmost importance. Although the child spends a greater amount of time with his peers than he does with his parents, he remains either fully or partially dependent on his parents for financial support.

● **PROBLEM 12-43**

Name and describe the various peer groups of the adolescent.

Solution: Before adolescence, children band together in groups of the same sex. These groups are often called cliques. As interest in the opposite sex intensifies with the onset of puberty, the clique usually forms an association with a clique of the opposite sex. Leaders of each group may initiate individual dating between members of the two cliques.

Clique members are bound together by such factors as geographic proximity, educational level, degree of social and personal maturity, similarity of economic and social background and similarity of interests, including sexual interests. One rarely finds examples of heterogeneous adolescent cliques that include individuals whose backgrounds differ greatly in the areas mentioned above.

The crowd, another type of adolescent peer group, is larger and less rigidly defined than the clique. An adolescent must first belong to a clique before he can belong to a crowd. A crowd is composed of individuals with similar social backgrounds and personality types who share an orientation to the future. Every person in a crowd does not necessarily know every other member, but the adolescent can identify each crowd. In school, for example, one can differentiate among the crowds of football players, student government officers, and cheerleaders. As the period of adolescence progresses and interest in the opposite sex increases further, the adolescent identifies less with the same-sexed clique and crowd. In its stead, a clique of couples going steady arises.

The adolescent also develops close, personal friendships while maintaining his "membership" in a crowd or clique. Friendships are more intimate and honest than cliques and crowds. These friendships allow the individual to feel less self-conscious since he doesn't have to worry as much about gaining social approval. He is more open and unafraid to express his fears and doubts. Adolescent friendships are most commonly formed between individuals of similar social and educational backgrounds and of similar interests and personalities.

● **PROBLEM 12-44**

Discuss the psychological impact of physical deviation in adolescents.

Solution: Physical deviation from peers during adolescence can cause a great deal of stress and anxiety. Girls fear being either overweight or exceptionally tall. An adolescent girl experiences a great deal of anxiety if she possesses these qualities. She fears peer rejection and she may develop feelings of inferiority. Similarly, boys are sensitive to excessive shortness and scrawny build. Late sexual maturity may also cause stress to occur in the male or female since it makes them worry about whether they will ever mature.

Girls and boys react differently to early maturation. Girls see early maturation as a disadvantage. They do not like to be ahead of both male and female peers in their physical growth. Social ideas concerning sex roles have been internalized by this time and the female's advanced development over males during this period, leads her to see herself as deviant. This view may cause a great deal of stress in the female. Adolescent boys, on the other hand, see early physical maturation as an advantage. Generally the taller and stronger the boy, the more he is admired by his peers. He is considered more attractive and is usually better at sports. His strength over other boys his own age garners high respect from them.

A study conducted by Jones and Bayley (1950) found that boys who experienced early maturation were more physically attractive, less affected, and more at ease in comparison to boys who matured late.

Adolescents are particularly sensitive about how their physical appearance compares to that of their peers. Very long legs, small breasts and a small number of muscles, are all causes of anxiety during this period. However, as this phase ends, the differences between individuals are reduced until all adolescents of a particular age have matured into adults.

● PROBLEM 12-45

Briefly discuss some of the crises that may arise during adolescence as a result of the quest for autonomy.

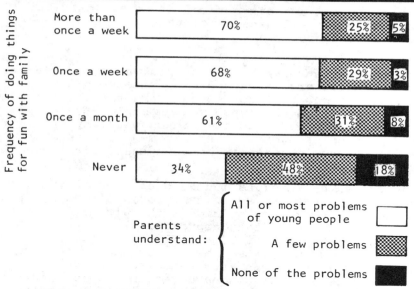

Relationship of parental understanding of young people's problems and the frequency with which the adolescent does things for fun with the family.

Solution: An important aspect of the adolescent period is the severing of ties of dependency with the family. Whether this process happens smoothly or creates a great deal of turmoil depends upon the atmosphere and type of discipline that is exercised in the particular family. For an adolescent who has been raised in a family where reason and warmth prevails, the quest for autonomy should be relatively easy. However, parents who are overly strict make their child's transition from dependence to autonomy a stressful and difficult ordeal. If the parents are unreasonably dominant, the adolescent will become extremely defiant and thereby intensify the conflict that already exists with the parents.

Most psychologists agree that boys have a more difficult time gaining autonomy than girls because girls demand less independence. Psychologists attribute this finding to sex role learning in society. Boys are taught to take an active and dominant role while girls are taught to take a passive role.

If the adolescent is unable to resolve the conflicts that arise from his striving towards autonomy, he may eventually reject and rebel against all of adult society.

Deliquency is one outlet that this rebellion can take. Delinquency occurs often in low income neighborhoods where one finds overcrowded and broken homes as well as inadequate education. Delinquency among boys is often attributed to the lack of an appropriate father figure necessary for identification.

Alienation from soicety and drug abuse may also result from failure to achieve autonomy. Adolescents who are habitual users of hard drugs express strong feelings of isolation, a communication rift with parents, and an inability to "find themselves." These confused adolescents are generally passive and are often referred to as "drop-outs." They have not been allowed to mature from the stage of childhood dependence.

In contrast to these passivists who come from inflexible, authoritarian homes, adolescents who are activists come from homes where parents are permissive and warm. This adolescent has been forced to learn to live independently at an early age. These young people develop personal moral standards and when they reach maturity, they try to make their values work. They attempt to change the "system" by narrowing the gap between their ideals and the reality of society.

The pressures involved in the quest for autonomy may become so great that the adolescent loses all hope, in which case he may attempt suicide - the ultimate "dropping out." Studies indicate that approximately 1,000 young people between the ages of 14 and 21 take their lives every year. Suicide is most often the act of an extremely isolated individual who feels estranged from the rest of the world. He believes that no one cares about his existence; hence, he believes life has little meaning. Psychologist Pamela Cantor lists some of the warning signs of suicide: insomnia, neglect of personal appearance, the giving away of prized possessions and a long-lasting depression.

PIAGET'S THEORY OF COGNITIVE DEVELOPMENT

● PROBLEM 12-46

Briefly trace sensorimotor development during infancy as defined by Jean Piaget.

Solution: Jean Piaget, a famous twentieth century child psychologist, described the period of infancy as the period of sensorimotor development. This period covers the child's first two years of life. The term "sensorimotor" refers to the child's perception (sensori) and physical movements (motor). Piaget divided this period of development into six stages.

The first stage lasts from birth until the child is one month old. The infant's range of activity at this point is limited to looking, sucking, reaching, grasping, crying, and sleeping. But even in this early period, the child's acti-

Piaget's Outline of Cognitive Development

Sensorimotor Period		
Stage	General Development	Object Concept
1. Reflex(birth to 1 month)	Engages basically in reflex activity, especially sucking.	Has none, cannot differentiate self from other objects.
2. Primary circular reactions(1-4 mos.)	Begins to build repertoire of behaviors: bringing hand to mouth to suck on thumb. Repeats what he finds pleasurable.	No differentiation between movement of self and movement of other objects. Disappearance of an object elicits no reaction.
3. Secondary circular reactions(4-8 mos.)	Begins crawling and can reproduce interesting events—pulling a string to shake a rattle; perceives a relationship between his actions and their results.	Anticipates positions of moving objects.
4. Coordination of secondary schemes(8-12 mos.)	Learns to apply previously learned responses to new situations; will lift pillow to find object under it.	Develops object permanence; searches for vanished objects.
5. Tertiary circular reactions(12-18 mos.)	Begins to search for novelty—a period of experimentation. Uses trial and error behavior to attain goals and invents new ways to do things.	Searches for vanished object and takes into account the sequence of places it disappeared to.
6. Internalization of thought (18-24 mos.)	Real beginning of thought. Invents new ways of doing things, not only through actual trial and error but by mental trial and error— by thinking. Can have mental images and think of objects not immediately present.	Can have mental images of objects and their displacements.

vities are not restricted to reflexes alone. By the second week, he generalizes his sucking instinct to rattles and other objects.

During this first month, the infant cannot coordinate his waking activities. For example, he might see a visually appealing object, but he cannot reach for it. The activities of looking and reaching are not coordinated. The further development of the child's activities are thwarted by the fact that sleep dominates much of his life. According to Buhler (1930), a newborn infant sleeps nearly 80 percent of the time.

The second stage of development extends from the age of one month to four months. This stage is characterized by

449

what is referred to as primary circular reactions. This
term is used to describe simple reflexive activities. They
are referred to as primary because they involve the child's
own body. They are called circular because they elicit
their own repetitions. Thumb sucking is an example of this
type of behavior. It begins accidentally: the child happens to put his thumb in his mouth, this triggers the sucking response which gives the child a pleasant sensation and
causes him to repeat the activity. Hence, the behavior is
circular. New behavior in this stage is accidental.

The third stage of the sensorimotor period covers the
period from 4 months of age to 8 months. This period is
characterized by secondary circular reactions and the development of eye-hand coordination. Like the primary circular reactions, these also produce their own repetitions.
However, in this stage, the activities are not performed on
the child's own body. An example of a secondary circular
reaction is the behavior a child engages in when he accidentally causes a rattle to make a noise and then tries to reproduce the result.

The basic underlying principle of both primary and secondary circular reactions is operant conditioning -- the
child continually emits a behavior because the consequences
of emitting the behavior are pleasant (rewarding). The
pleasing sensation the child experiences is a reinforcement.
Each reinforcement increases the likelihood of the behavior's
recurrence. Thus, behavior is purposive because it is emitted in anticipation of a "reward."

The fourth stage in Piaget's developmental theory extends from the age of 8 months to 12 months. During this
period, the child's ability to coordinate behaviors is enhanced. As this occurs, an intentional initiation of behavior replaces the accidental occurrence of new behaviors.
The child at this stage begins to display originality in
confronting obstacles instead of engaging in the repetition
of futile activity. Through generalized assimilation, an
action the child learned in one circumstance is used in a
new situation that is different yet sufficiently similar to
make the action appropriate to both cases.

During this stage there is a great improvement in the
child's imitation skills which are facilitated by a lengthened attention span. The child in this period also acquires
a growing sense of the organization of things with respect
to himself and others. He realizes that objects exist as
entities separate from himself. This realization permits
him to anticipate events that are results of others' actions.

That is, he understands that other people may interact with
an object to produce a result. He also arrives at an understanding of cause and effect. He can recognize signs
that signal an event. For example he knows that a goodnight
kiss signals the onset of an action - going to bed.

The fifth stage lasts from 12 to 18 months and is
marked by tertiary circular reactions. These differ from
the primary and secondary circular reactions in that they

are less rigid; each repetition is modified to some extent. If an action produces a pleasant effect, the child will not only repeat it, but change it somewhat in order to see what other effects might be produced.

All the abilities he learned in earlier stages are expanded and applied to increasingly complex situations. The child becomes systematically adventurous and his interest in novelty is an end in itself. He experiments with new ways to achieve a goal since he is willing to learn by trial and error.

The last stage of Piaget's theory of sensorimotor development extends from 18 months to 24 months or two years. Some psychologists call this stage "toddlerhood" - a transitory period between infancy and childhood. The child takes a great leap in his cognitive development - he can now engage in thought. His ability to reason drastically reduces the number of trial and error tests he must make to solve a problem. He can conceptually narrow his field of possibilities.

The object concept at this stage is fully developed; that is, he knows that objects continue to exist even though he does not perceive them. The child is also capable of imitating objects or people that are not immediately present in his environment. Piaget referred to this ability as "deferred imitation." The child who dresses up in her mother's clothes when the mother is absent is displaying deferred imitation. The child not only internalizes or conceptualizes objects in his mind, but also internalizes the activities related to those objects. Bruner (1966) labels this ability "enactive representation."

● PROBLEM 12-47

Define Piaget's preoperational stage of cognitive development. Name and describe its two substages.

The Conceptual Period of Intelligence

Stage		
1. Preoperational (2-7 yrs.)	a. Preconceptual (18 mos.-4 yrs.)	First such use of representational thought and symbols, such as words, for objects; classification of objects.
	b. Intuitive thought (4-7 yrs.)	Beginning of reasoning, but thinking is fragmented, centered on parts of things, rigid, and based wholly on appearances.
2. Concrete operations (7-11 yrs.)		Can perform mental operations and reverse them. Can add up "all the marbles." Operations are however confined to concrete and tangible objects that are immediately present.
3. Formal operations (12-15 yrs.)		Can form hypotheses, can go beyond appearances to deal with the the truth or falsity of propositions.

451

<u>Solution</u>: According to Piaget, a preschooler's cognitive development is at the preoperational stage. The preoperational stage consists of two substages: The preconceptual which lasts from ages 2 to 4 and the intuitive thought which extends from ages 4 to 7.

In contrast to the intelligence of an infant, a preschooler's intelligence allows him to internalize objects and events in his environment. Whereas an infant understands only what he immediately perceives and can perform activities only on objects immediately present, the preschooler employs symbolism. Symbolism includes the use of symbols and language to represent the world. The child can now think and speak of objects that are not immediately perceived. He develops concepts - actually, "preconcepts," since they are not fully developed. These preconcepts, or the beginnings of cognitive thinking, enable the child to divide objects in the world on the basis of common properties. For example, a preschooler can recognize and name an elephant because of its massive size, gray color, floppy ears, and trunk. However, the preschooler cannot distinguish among different objects of the same class or animals of the same species. For example, a child who sees an elephant in a zoo and later sees another elephant in a circus would probably think that it was the same animal.

The child's reasoning ability during the preconceptual period can be divided into two types: transductive reasoning and syncretic reasoning.

Transductive reasoning occurs when the child bases his inferences on one particular occurrence or on a single attribute of an object. For example, a child might conclude that trucks and cars are the same objects since both have wheels. Likewise, if he sees a chicken lay an egg, he might assume that all animals lay eggs.

Syncretic reasoning reflects the child's constantly changing criteria for classification. This reasoning leads him to classify objects together that are disparate. For example, to distinguish among trucks, cars, and buses, the child would group all the trucks together. But he might also group blue cars with the trucks if one of the trucks is blue. He might also group some red trucks with the buses if some of the buses are red. Hence, the child's ever-changing criteria for classification lead to error.

The next substage of the preoperational stage is called intuitive thought. During this stage, the problem solving ability of the child is based upon his intuition or insight rather than on logical thinking. He is still dependent upon mental images since he is not yet able to see cause and effect relationships. Piaget demonstrated this theory through an experiment where he used a wire with three beads strung onto it. The beads were of three different colors: blue, red, and yellow. Holding the wire vertically, Piaget asked the child to note which colored bead was on top. Piaget then inserted the wire into a hollow cardboard tube and rotated it. As long as the child could imagine the position of the beads inside the tube, he could answer correctly. The child's perceptual capabilities are not developed sufficiently enough as yet, so as to enable the child to base his answer upon the relationship between an odd and even number of turns or half-turns.

Other characteristics of intuitive thinking include heavy reliance on perception and egocentric thinking.

An instance which reflects a preschooler's perceptually dominated thinking is exemplified when the child judges a tall and narrow pitcher to hold more orange juice than a short and wider one despite the fact that both pitchers contain the same amount of liquid. An adult would be less apt to make such an error since his judgments are based on thought more than perception.

Although the child, during the preoperational period, is still somewhat limited in his intellectual ability, (i.e. intuitive rather than logical thinking), he is still capable of performing many tasks and is far ahead of the infant who possesses only sensorimotor intelligence.

● PROBLEM 12-48

Discuss cognitive development during middle childhood as described by Piaget.

Solution: According to Piaget's system of cognitive development, middle childhood is the period of concrete operations.

In Piaget's theory, an operation is a "thought." "Thought" refers to the mental representation of something that is not immediately perceived. During the period of concrete operations, the child is capable of invoking a mental representation or image of an object or an event, but this representation is linked to a mental image of the "concrete" perceptual experience. For example, if someone says the word car to a child in this stage, he will think of a time when he actually saw a car, rather than visualize an imaginary car, one that is divorced from his actual perception.

The period of concrete operations is also characterized by the acquisition of conservation. According to Piaget, conservation refers to the fact that only the addition or subtraction of a portion of an object changes it quantitatively, regardless of its appearance. For example, the child now knows that when a tall glass of water is poured into a smaller but wider glass, the amount of water remains the same. The child has learned to conserve. This stage of learning marks the dividing line between the periods of preoperational thought and concrete operations. The child is now using logical rather than intuitive thinking.

Three important rules of logic characterize a child's thinking during the period of concerete operations. These include identity, reversibility and combinativity. Identity means that there are certain activities which, when performed upon a particular object or situation, leave it unchanged. For example, blowing lightly on a glass of water does not alter it in any way. Reversability refers to the fact that an operation can be undone. The child realizes that the water in the glass which came from a pitcher, can be poured back into that pitcher. Combinativity is a logical law which states that several operations performed on a certain object or situation will yield a completely new object or situation. This law is also called closure. For example, if sugar is poured into a glass of water and then the water is stirred, a new substance, glucose, is produced. Related to combinativity is associativity or compensation. This term refers to the fact that several operations can be combined in different ways to produce the same end product. The child learns, for example, that the water in the glass can be disposed of in several ways: by pouring it down the sink, drinking it, letting it evaporate, etc.

In addition to acquiring a sense of conservation during the period of middle childhood, the child also learns classification. He is able to respond correctly when asked whether a bowl of mixed nuts contained more cashews or peanuts. He understands the concept of subclasses. He also comes to understand the concept of seriation - the arrangement of objects in a certain order following a particular standard. For example, a child during middle childhood would be able to arrange toys of different sizes in a line ranging from the smallest to the largest when asked to do so. In addition, he comes to understand the concept of number. During middle childhood he can comprehend the qualities of both ordinal numbers - numbers designating order (i.e. first, second, third, etc.), and cardinal numbers - numbers that designate quantity (i.e. one, two, three, etc.).

During the period of concrete operations, the child's thinking can deal with real objects and those that are easily imagined. He develops a simple system of logic which permits him to understand conservation. His intellectual development is far beyond that of the sensorimotor infant or the preoperational preschool child. Yet, his thinking is still not as sophisticated as that of the adolescent's whose congitive development is at the stage of formal operations.

● **PROBLEM 12-49**

Discuss cognitive development during adolescence as described by Piaget.

Solution: The stage of formal operations is the final step in Piaget's system of cognitive development. It begins at about the age of 11 when the child begins to free himself from the concrete. He acquires the ability to think about things which are not linked to actual perceptual experiences. His intellectual ability is no longer bound by concrete operations as it was in the previous stage. He can imagine hypothetical states and he realizes that there are many possible solutions to a problem. His thinking becomes increasingly propositional, logical, and idealistic.

A proposition is a verbal statement that is either true or false. Such statements need not be linked to reality. A proposition can also be a hypothesis - a prediction or a possible explanation for some phenomenon.

In propositional thought, the adolescent can consider at once all the possible ways of solving a problem. This ability is fully attained at about the age of 14 or 15. When presented with a particular problem, the adolescent isolates its elements and methodically explores various approaches to its solution. To study this process, Inhelder and Piaget (1958) asked a group of 10-year-olds and a group of 14-year-olds what combination of four different chemicals would produce yellow liquid when a catalyst chemical (potassium iodide) was added. Most 10-year-olds responded by combining only pairs of liquid chemicals. When a correct combination was found, the 10-year-olds would tell the examiner that they had found the solution. It never occurred to most of them that there might be more than one correct solution. The 14-year-olds, on the other hand, saw a wide range of combinations. They combined tubes of chemicals by two's, three's, and four's, until they found a whole range of solutions to the problem. By visualizing and actualizing all possibilities, an individual reaches the level of formal operations. His thinking becomes hypothetical and deductive.

Through the use of propositional thinking, an individual can solve the following problem: If Jack has more oranges than Bill, but less oranges than Sam, who has the most oranges? A pre-adolescent child would have difficulty with this type of problem since it is removed from the realm of concrete perception.

During adolescence, thinking becomes scientific. The adolescent follows the steps of the scientific method which include: formulation of a hypothesis based on certain evidence; critical evaluation of the hypothesis; experimentation; final selection and testing; reporting of results; and conclusion(s). Before adolescence, the child is not capable of thinking in such an organized, systematic way.

The period of formal operations is also characterized by the development of idealism. This idealism relates to the adolescent's ability to deal with the hypothetical - to ponder and compare the real with the possible. Idealism reflects a concern with ideas or ideals over reality. Often this idealism can create a state of discontent as the individual sees how the real world fails to meet his standards of an ideal world.

Adolescent idealism is related to moral development as defined by Kohlberg. The adolescent acquires self-accepted principles with the attainment of formal operations. This attainment is the highest level of morality. The formation of self-accepted principles is not possible before the stage of formal operations. It is only when the child can envision hypothetical states that he can recognize a dichotomy between real and idealized states of

the world. At this time, he can formalize and internalize his own standards of moral behavior -- his self-accepted principles.

AGGRESSION, BIRTH ORDER, AND AGING

● **PROBLEM** 12-50

Trace the development of aggression from infancy to adolescence.

Solution: During infancy, aggressive behavior is evident
in temper tantrums. These tantrums may be caused by: adult
pressure, exhibited in strict toilet training; loss of attention, which is especially apparent upon the birth of a
younger sibling; and excessive stimulation, which occurs
when the infant is fatigued.

As the child becomes older, the example set by the parents' behavior becomes a critical factor in determining his
degree of aggressiveness. Children who observe frequent
and violent outbursts in their parents will develop aggressive behavior. In addition, parental inconsistency, with
regard to punishment leads to aggressive behavior in children. A parent who disapproves of physical aggression yet
uses it to punish the child is likely to produce aggression
in the child. Permissive parents who resort to physical
punishment also produce aggression in children.

During the preschool period, aggression most often
arises from social conflicts that occur during cooperative
play. At this time, the child is unclear about the difference between accidental and intentional aggression. His
egocentric mode of thinking might lead him to believe an
accidental push was deliberate and he will strike back. As
he matures he begins to learn this distinction.

Physical aggression usually decreases with increasing
age while verbal aggression increases.

Boys have been found to be more aggressive than girls
in this society. This factor is due, in large part, to the
cultural stereotypes that designate acceptable masculine
and feminine behavior.

In studying the relationship between childhood aggression and future behavioral development, Kagan and Moss
(1962) found that children from three to six years of age
who were dominant, competitive, and indirectly aggressive
toward their peers, tended to be particularly competitive
as adults.

During middle childhood and adolescence, aggression is
the result of frustration. It can assume several forms
such as rebelling against a figure of authority or engaging
in vandalism. The aggressive behavior can be directed a-
gainst either the person or the object that causes the
frustration, or it can be displaced to another person or
object. For example, a child who bullies a younger sibling

456

may be giving vent to frustration caused by parents who are too strong for him to fight.

The adolescent may suffer from two basic sources of frustration. One of these is the identity crisis where the adolescent has trouble determining his role. The other source includes the sense of depression that arises when he becomes aware of the difference that exists between his actual living situation and the situation in which he would like to live. In this society, a physically mature adolescent must continue to depend upon his parents for economic support because of the cultural demands of schooling. The adolescent's desire to live his life as he pleases without the restrictions of parental dictates, is one of the most common causes of adolescent aggression in this culture.

● **PROBLEM** 12-51

Discuss the relationship between violence on television and the development of aggression in children.

Solution: Television and its effect on the social behavior of children has recently become a major concern not only to psychologists, educators, sociologists, and other professionals, but to concerned parents as well. In 1969, Federal Communications Commissioner, Nicholas Johnson, reported that the average male will have watched television for a full 9 years of his life by the time he is 65 years old. An 18-year-old has spent approximately 22,000 hours watching television.

The children who witnessed an adult model kick and punch a Bobo doll imitate her behavior closely. Children who witnessed a less aggressive model are themselves less aggressive.

Many television critics have argued that when a child views aggressive behavior on television, his own hostile tendencies are increased. These critics believe that as children witness how violence is used to resolve conflicts

and to create a happy and successful conclusion, they themselves use violent behavior to obtain the same happy results. In addition, childrens' tendency to imitate leads
them to re-enact what they see on the television screen.

Some studies have refuted these arguments. Dalmas Taylor found that television violence reduces aggression in
many people. According to Taylor, viewing television violence purges the frustrated person of any hostile feelings
he harbors. That is, witnessing the enactment of violent
behavior permits these people to identify with the aggressor, thereby making them feel as though they had actually
vented their own agression. Bandura's (1969) findings indicate the opposite to be true. He found that exposure to
aggressive models tended to increase the incidence of aggressive behavior.

Critics of television argue that TV viewing increases
passivity in children. They contend that these children
would reap more benefits if they invested the time dedicated to television in more productive activities such as
reading or participating in sports. Himmelweit, Oppenheim,
and Vince (1958), on the other hand, reported that the
children who viewed television in their study had a wider
range of interests than the non-viewers. Schramm, Lyle,
and Parker's study (1961) revealed that children who watched television read as many books as those who didn't. The
controversy about the effects of television violence on
viewers is far from over.

Since television broadcasting has only been in existence for a relatively short period of time, it is still
too early to examine its long-range effects.

● **PROBLEM** 12-52

Discuss the relationship between birth order and personality.
Cite Zajonc's analysis.

Solution: Numerous studies on the relationship between birth
order and personality have led to several generalizations
which psychologists have had difficulty in verifying. Research has been conducted on birth order with regard to scholastic achievement, creativity, aggression, sociability, and
self-esteem.

Many psychologists have concluded that first-borns excel in many ways over latter-born siblings. His high degree
of creativity, curiousity, motivation and competitiveness
makes the first-born a likely candidate for a college diploma
and scholastic honors. The first-born child tends to be more
adult-oriented than his brothers and sisters and is more
likely to suppress agressive tendencies.

First-borns and only children are usually less sociable
than other youngsters -- they tend to feel uncomfortable
around their peers. They often develop language skills at
an earlier age than other children. Studies have shown that
a relationship exists between birth order and the degree of
self-esteem in children who come from families with more

than one child. An only child tends to have the highest self-esteem.

Using a sample of almost 400,000 Dutchmen, Robert B. Zajonc studied the effect of birth order on intelligence. His data indicated that, in general, first-born children are slightly more intelligent than second-born, and second-born children are slightly more intelligent than third-born and so on. However, Zajonc's data also indicated that family size is an influential factor in this relationship. He found that, in general, the larger the family, the less intelligent the children. For example, an only child would be more intelligent than all of the children in a multiple-child family. In addition, the first-born of a large family is more likely to be less intelligent than the latter-born siblings of a smaller family.

Zajonc's data also indicated that the spacing of children critically influences intelligence. In general, the closer in time that the children are born, the lower their intelligence level. Hence, the last-born of a family of three where the children's births are spaced over a period of 15 years would be more intelligent than the second-born of a family of three where the births are spaced over a period of three years.

Zajonc also found that teaching skills to a younger sibling leads to a higher level of intelligence. For this reason, he believed that last-borns were less intelligent than their siblings.-- they had no younger siblings to

teach. He urged parents to try to find younger children in the neighborhood for the youngest child to teach, this way the child will be able to maximize his intelligence.

● **PROBLEM** 12-53

List some symptoms of aging. What happens to cognitive functioning as the individual ages?

Solution: Some of the symptoms of aging include: brain size reduction, deterioration of visual acuity and hearing, a lengthened reaction time, reduced motor control, a poorer concentration ability, and reduced short term memory. Some of these physical disabilities affect conversational ability. Often an elderly person during the course of a conversation will repeat himself unnecessarily or fail to remember something recently said. Feelings of depression and suspicion are common as the elderly become more aware of their disabilities. Psychologists generally agree that the factors that comprise cognitive ability reaches their peak in young adulthood and then taper off.

Green (1969) found that certain abilities decline with age but others improve. For example, spatial skills decline after age 40, but verbal skills improve between the ages of 25 and 64. Whereas muscular strength and speed decline by age 30, intellectual tasks that require the application of well learned material maintain their performance level into the 60's.

SHORT ANSWER QUESTIONS FOR REVIEW

Choose the correct answer.

1. The approach to developmental psychology which
    stresses qualitative differences among various
    developing structures in the human is (a) the
    mechanistic approach   (b)   the organismic
    approach   (c)   the psychoanalytic approach
    (d) the orthogenetic approach   b

2. Which of the following is the correct sequence
    for prenatal development? (a) embryo - zygote
    - fetus   (b) zygote - ovum - fetus (c) embryo
    - fetus - zygote (d) zygote - embryo - fetus   d

3. The major developmental change that occurs during
    the period of the zygote is (a) quantitative
    growth (b) organ development (c) cell
    divisions (d) quickening   c

4. A healthy fetus can withstand birth and survive
    at the end of which of the following months of
    gestation? (a) fifth (b) sixth (c) seventh
    (d) all of the above   c

5. Which of the following is a teratogen? (a) ma-
    ternal diet (b) maternal age (c) emotional
    stress in the mother (d) harmful drugs taken by
    the mother   d

6. The hand grasping action of the infant is called
    (a) Moro reflex (b) Babinski reflex (c)
    Palmar reflex (d) None of the above   c

7. The purpose of the visual cliff is to determine
    the infant's perception of (a) light intensity
    (b) contours (c) distance (d) depth   d

8. The term Piaget used to describe simple reflex
    activities during infancy is (a) primary cir-
    cular reactions (b) secondary circular reac-
    tions (c) tertiary circular reactions (d)
    sensorimotor reactions   a

9. According to social learning theory, sex typing
    results from (a) resolution of the Oedipal
    conflict (b) imitation of the sex-liked parent
    (c) recognition of sex appropriate behavior
    (d) reinforcement of sex appropriate behavior   b

10. The major difference between the intelligence
    of an infant and preschooler is that the pre-
    schooler can (a) internalize aspects of the
    environment (b) make use of symbolism (c)
    make use of preconcepts (d) all of the above   d

SHORT ANSWER QUESTIONS FOR REVIEW

11. According to Piaget, middle childhood is the
period of the (a) sensorimotor stage (b)
pre-operational stage (c) concrete operations
(d) formal operations

    c

12. Manipulation of objects is most characteristic
of (a) sensorimotor play (b) imaginative
play (c) parallel play (d) cooperative play

    a

13. The belief that good behavior is that which is
rewarded and bad behavior is that which is
punished is indicative of which level of morality,
according to Kohlberg? (a) premoral (b)
morality of conventional role conformity (c)
morality of self-accepted principles

    a

14. Which of the following is NOT characteristic of
the period of adolescence? (a) propositional
thinking (b) resurgence of egocentrism (c)
decrease of peer influence (d) increase in
idealsim

    c

15. As an adult ages, which of the following occur?
(a) increase in brain size (b) heightened
short-term memory (c) lengthened reaction
time (d) higher concentrative ability

    c

Fill in the blanks.

16. _____ refers to changes in the size of the body
and its various parts.

    Growth

17. According to the _____ principle, every living
organism undergoes change in the same direction
and each goes through certain stages of development despite their existing environment.

    ortho-
genetic

18. Fertilization occurs in the _____ in the human
female.

    fallopian
tubes

19. _____ is the most widespread of all the teratogenic diseases.

    Rubella
(German
measles)

20. _____ occurs when the oxygen supply is cut off to
the neonate.

    Anoxia

21. The most important motor achievement during infancy is the ability to _____.

    walk

22. Piaget described intelligence during infancy
as _____.

    sensori-
motor

461

SHORT ANSWER QUESTIONS FOR REVIEW

23. _____ is the label given to the condition
brought about by maternal deprivation.

Marasmus

24. _____ refers to the process by which the child
acquires the masculine or feminine characteristics found in the sex-liked parent.

Sex typing

25. _____ occurs when the child bases his inferences
on one particular occurrence or on a single
characteristic of an object.

Trans-
ductive
reasoning

26. The _____ is the first important socializing
agent with whom the child comes into contact.

family

27. The level of morality in which individual moral
standards are established is called, according
to Kohlberg, _____ .

morality
of self-
accepted
principles

28. _____ is sexual maturity.

"Puberty"

29. The propositional, logical, and idealistic
thinking which occurs during adolescence, Piaget
called _____ .

formal
operations

30. A _____ is composed of individuals with similar
social backgrounds and personality types who
share an orientation to the future.

crowd

Determine whether the following statements are true
or false.

31. During the Middle Ages, development was viewed
as being merely quantitative.

True

32. The function of villi is the passage of
nourishment from the mother to the fetus.

False

33. Hardly any growth occurs during the period
of the zygote.

True

34. In spite of all the factors that can adversely
affect prenatal development, the intrauterine
environment of the fetus is relatively stable.

True

35. At present, no study has found pain-killing
drugs administered to mothers during labor to
have harmful long-term effects on the child.

True

36. Infant behavior is limited to the reflexive
behavior coded in the genes.

False

SHORT ANSWER QUESTIONS FOR REVIEW

37. Vision takes longer to develop than the other senses.

True

38. In secondary circular reactions, each repetition of behavior is modified to some extent.

False

39. In Harlow's study of maternal deprivation, infant monkeys clung to whichever surrogate - wire or terrycloth - held the feed bottle.

False

40. Although the physical structures involved in producing emotional reactions are in a state of readiness at birth, infants cannot express emotion.

False

41. Egocentrism is derived from the basic selfishness of the preschool child.

False

42. A child who classifies disparate objects together is displaying syncretic reasoning.

True

43. Intuitive thinking is characterized by a heavy reliance on perception.

True

44. In Bruner's experiment on the relationship of language and intellectual ability, it was found that children who used dimensional description were less successful at transposing glasses in the matrix than those who used confounded or global terms.

False

45. From birth until the end of the preschool period, the rate of physical growth is approximately the same for both sexes.

True

46. During middle childhood, the child has no interest in sex-related matters.

True

47. Studies have indicated that the absence of a peer group can have harmful effects on the developing child.

True

48. One cause of juvenile aggression is parental inconsistency in punishment.

True

49. It has been found that adolescents who are activists most often come from homes where parental authority is strict and inflexible.

False

50. Kinsey reported that males at the time of puberty respond sexually to a wider range of stimuli than girls at puberty.

True

CHAPTER 13

PERSONALITY

GENERAL PRINCIPLES

● **PROBLEM** 13-1

Discuss the functions of a theory of personality.

Solution: Theories are tentative principles set
forth to explain certain observable phenomena. A theory
is by definition speculative and expendable; nevertheless,
it can be quite useful. Findings that do not support a
hypothesis serve to narrow the field of investigation to
more promising alternatives. A theory is useful to scientific investigation if it is relevant to the facts that
have already been observed and if it is capable of generating testable hypotheses. Even the best theories are
only promising ideas in need of more supportive evidence.
This is especially true in psychology.

Theories need to be examined and reexamined to
determine which ones provide the simplest and most economical explanation for the area under study.

Generally, psychological theories of personality
could just as well be called theories of human nature--
the personality psychologist is trying to make sense of
human conduct, to discover the uniformities of character
among individuals, and to devise general principles to
explain particular motives.

It quickly becomes clear to the student of personality that each theorist approaches the area of human
nature with somewhat different assumptions, strategies and
objectives. Each theory needs to be taken as only one
interpretation of human personality. To date, there does
not appear to be a way to empirically test competing
theories for their validity and reliability; some theories
are constructed in such a way that they defy tests that
may confirm their accuracy. Although a study of personality
theories will not yield the ultimate truth about the nature
of human conduct, knowledge of the research and the theoretical bases of those scientists who are interested in and
dedicated to the area offers a strong basis from which to

begin questioning and formulating hypotheses for research
into the nature of human behavior.

A student should approach the study of personality
theories with the knowledge that they are useful, though
expendable guidelines to research and thinking.

● **PROBLEM 13-2**

Distinguish between type and trait theories of
personality. What are some advantages and disadvantages
of these approaches to human nature?

Solution: Historically, the most common way of
approaching personality has been in terms of traits.
"Traits" are enduring and stable characteristics within an
individual that provoke him to action in some consistent
way. Trait psychology represented one of the earliest attempts to introduce order into the multiplicity of human
behavior. It is a simple approach--as it looks for consistencies in behavior.

Examples of traits that have been studied are:
extroversion-introversion (perhaps the most common studied),
submissiveness-dominance, honesty-dishonesty, and intelligence. The dimension of extroversion-introversion was
popularized in the writings of Carl Jung, a psychoanalyst.
One major difficulty with such characterizations is that
they omit a great deal of individual variation around
major types, as well as mixtures that may occur. For
example, an individual is likely, in reading a description
of extroverted and introverted behavior, to find both within
himself.

Another approach to personality which attempted to
isolate particular predicting characteristics of behavior
within an individual was type psychology. This approach
to human behavior dates back to the writings of Hippocrates
and Galen in ancient Greece. According to their temperament theory, individual personality types can be classified
into four categories on the basis of the dominance of one
of four body fluids or humors: the sanguine, the choleric,
the melancholic and the phlegmatic type.

A more modern theorist, Alfred Adler, includes a
typology in his personality theory which relates to this
early temperament theory. Adler developed his scheme of
personality types based on the degree of social interest
and activity level in different personalities. His types
were: (1) The ruling-dominant type (choleric)--this person
is assertive, aggressive and active. He manipulates and
masters the events and situations of his life. While he
has a high activity level, his social interest is low.
(2) The getting-leaning type (phlegmatic)--this type expects others to satisfy his needs and to provide for his
interests. He is characterized by a low social interest
and a low activity level. (3) The avoiding type (melancholic)--this person is inclined to achieve success by cir-

465

cumventing a problem or withdrawing from it. Mastery is achieved by avoiding defeat. He has a low social interest and a very low activity level. (4) The socially useful type (sanguine)--this personality type is said to be the most healthy of all. The socially useful person attacks problems head on, he is socially oriented and is prepared to cooperate with others to master the tasks of life.

The danger with both trait and type theories is that labels of the above kind can be misleading, especially because they tend to disregard situational variables--they ignore the relationship between a person and his environment. They focus exclusively on responses that are too broad. Therefore, their application for prediction is limited except in cases of extremes.

Research that has been conducted to test trait and type theories has shown that traits are not consistent from situation to situation. For example, individuals that were honest in one circumstance were found to be dishonest in another. By ingenious methods, Hartshorne studied a large number of children in a variety of conditions in which honesty or dishonesty could be observed. For example, in one condition they returned their test papers so the children could grade their own papers. Their actual responses were known, therefore, the researchers could determine what, if any, changes were made. While a few children were found who were consistently honest and a few that were consistently dishonest, most varied considerably depending upon the circumstances. The results clearly established that honesty was not a stable trait but varied across situations.

Another criticism of trait or type theory is that any trait attributed to a person by an observer, such as high aggressiveness, is more easily explained as a product of the observer's personal reactions or measuring instrument. This makes the study of traits and types useful to psychologists interested in assessing a person's values and attitudes. The average person is believed to judge others by assigning them traits. The existence of these traits in the person being observed is irrelevant; what is important is the traits the observer chooses to assign. The careful analysis of this attribution process aids the psychologist in studying the person's values and attitudes.

● **PROBLEM 13-3**

What do the results of studies with twins suggest about the influence of heredity on personality?

Solution: Perhaps one of the greatest theoretical debates that takes place among students of human behavior is the degree to which heredity and environment influence individual differences. Traditionally, it has been difficult to devise measures that could assess the effect of heredity without the influence of the environment, since as soon as an infant is born the environment becomes a variable that could influence any measure of behavior.

466

Those who hold that the environment is the major factor in determining individual development contend that where members of a society share certain expectations about a person because he is tall, short, pretty, black, male, female, fat, skinny, and so forth, they then proceed to act toward him in distinct ways which in turn lead him to behave as they expect; thus, what is labeled as hereditary dispositions is only the result of a "self-fulfilling prophecy." The very characteristics that are said to be genetic can be environmentally produced by a social learning process which originates in expectancies. This can be easily observed with sex-typing in some societies.

Studies that have been conducted with identical and fraternal twins have been quite helpful in establishing that there appear to be hereditary determinants of intelligence and psychopathology. Since hereditary factors are constant for identical twins, any variations on their scores on particular measures can be attributed to the environment. This has made identical twins reared apart of special interest to scientists.

Psychological research has demonstrated an interdependency between hereditary capacities and environmental opportunities in determining IQ. Nineteen pairs of twins were studied by Newman, Freeman and Holzinger. The results showed that the greater the educational advantage, the greater the IQ of the twin with that advantage. An observational study by Shields and Slater demonstrated that when both members of twin pairs were neurotic, there was much greater intra-pair similarity in symptoms if the twins were identical than if they were fraternal.

These studies and others like them have made it possible to see that heredity provides a capacity for a wide range of behavior that may then be encouraged or sustained by the environment.

● PROBLEM 13-4

In a family where all male members have been doctors for generations, Peter decides to become an artist. Although his parents claim to love him they are very upset over his choice. How would Rogers explain this attitude shown by Peter's parents?

Solution: Carl Rogers can be counted among the "humanistic" psychologists. Humanistic psychology emphasizes man's capacity for goodness, creativity and freedom; it sees man as a spiritual, rational, autonomous being. Rogers came to understand that an individual's personality was conditioned by his interactions with significant others. The evaluations of his behavior by the adults in his world are assimilated by the child's self-structure. Many behaviors consistent with his parents' conception of what he should be will be praised; while behaviors that are inconsistent with what his parents perceive him to be will be punished or responded to with emotional rejection. Through this process the child learns to experience reality

467

second-hand, as he begins to be guided by the safe feelings
he receives when he is engaged in behavior that is acceptable to his parents. Experience is thus distorted in the
service of maintaining positive regard from his parents.
This positive feedback eventually contributes to a "self"
image that comes to dictate what types of events an individual will permit to enter awareness and what types will
be excluded. Threatening self-perceptions are excluded.

        Through this dynamic we may be able to understand
how Rogers would explain the attitude of disapproval shown
by Peter's parents when they discover that he intends to
become an artist rather than follow the family tradition
of becoming a doctor. In their self-structure is apparently
the idea that they love their son--perhaps even uncondition-
ally. Also part of their self concept may contain the idea
that for male members of their family to be of value they
must be doctors, as this is the way that the other doctors
in the family received positive regard. When they learn
that their son is not going to be a doctor, they discover
that it is difficult to experience feelings of acceptance
and support for him because it is threatening to their own
self-structure. These two perceptions--that they love their
son and that to be of value an individual in the family must
be a doctor--are incongruent and will need to be worked
through, perhaps therapeutically, if a positive solution is
to be found.

● **PROBLEM 13-5**

        What is the double-bind hypothesis as used by
Bateson?

        Solution: A double-bind communication is an example
of what Bateson and his colleagues call "metacommunications."
Literally, this means "along with" or "after" a communication.
It is communication about communication in the sense that
gestures, verbal tone, phrasing and timing may change the
meaning of verbal content.

        The double-bind message contains at least two
messages, sometimes three, all of which conflict with the

apparent meaning of the message. The first meaning is usually a negative injunction: "Do not do that or I will punish you" (typically by some form of withdrawing affection or projecting anger or disapproval). The second meaning is yet another injunction, however, it is accompanied by the message, "Do not see me as threatening you, do not see this command as containing punishment, do not see me as a punishing person." The third meaning is again an injunction that prevents the recipient of the message from escaping from the situation as it implies that love or acceptance will be given if the conflict implicit in the double-bind message is endured. Therefore, no appropriate action is possible.

An example of a typical double-bind message is when a mother asks her child to come sit on her lap, but her voice tone clearly indicates that she hopes he does not. If the child says that the messages are contradictory, he is simply told that they are not. The child is put in a "no win" situation. If he goes to sit on her lap he will receive disapproval. If he does not go sit on her lap, though he wants to, he is denying his own feelings.

This type of disturbed communication has been studied with relation to schizophrenic behavior. Bateson has hypothesized that much of the irrational and disorganized behavior of schizophrenics is the result of exposure during their early years to this type of confusing communication. The possible schizophrenic is required to make some response, but because the messages are contradictory, whatever he does is going to be "wrong." The older a person becomes, the more he internalizes this mode of communications until he begins to accept "can't win" situations as normal to the extent that double-bind communications are automatically present in his response to others' messages even when such messages are simply ambiguous.

● **PROBLEM** 13-6

Discuss Eysenck's theory of personality. Include a discussion of his phenotypic and genotypic basis of personality.

Solution: Originally undertaken to test C. G. Jung's conceptions about the mental disorders of extroverts and introverts, Hans Eysenck's research has produced a theory which bridges two very wide gulfs in personality theory: That between a study of individual differences in personality and the investigation of conditioning and learning; and that between the observable and causal behavior of an individual. Often referred to as biological stimulus-response theory, Eysenck's theory has the advantage of allowing for concrete predictions and tests of its validity.

A brief description of his complex theory can only skim the surface of what his research has produced. His theory may best be described in a hierarchical model. This model includes three levels. At the first observable or phenotypical level, personality types of introversion and

extroversion are measured--usually with pen and pencil
tests. Qualities such as shyness, sociability, activity
and impulsiveness are scored from the results of such tests
as the Eysenck Personality Inventory, the Eysenck Personality
Questionnaire or the Maudsley Personality Inventory. This
essentially descriptive approach came mainly from his early
research with soldiers and airmen and allowed him to determine extreme introversion and extroversion in subjects that
scored consistently high on either of the two dimensions.

The second level of the hierarchy includes performance on laboratory tests such as motor movements, vigilance
and conditioning testing to assess introversion and extroversion. From the hypothetical third level, predictions
about the performance of introverts and extroverts on these
tests are made.

The third level is the causal level for the preceding two levels and for this reason it is classed as the
genotypical level. This basis for personality is conceptualized as a physiological excitation/inhibition balance.
This balance between a tendency to cortical excitation or
to inhibition is seen as an inherited characteristic and is
described as the biological basis for personality. Eysenck
has recently provided a biological refinement of his exci-
tation/inhibition theory. He has pinpointed the ascending
reticular activating system (ARAS) as the basis for cortical arousal or inhibition, and, as a result thereby the
basis for introversion/extroversion since introverts have
more highly aroused ARAS functioning than extroverts.

● **PROBLEM 13-7**

What is the Yerkes-Dodson Law and how might it
contribute to Eysenck's biological model of personality?

Solution: In 1908 Yerkes and Dodson proposed a
general law of motivation which is widely accepted in contemporary psychology by psychologists interested in states
of arousal. Briefly, the Yerkes-Dodson law states that
motivation or arousal may be conceptualized on a continuum
ranging from very high to very low arousal. At the very
low range of arousal the organism is so unaroused that it
falls asleep, while at the very high end of the continuum
its arousal state is so high that its behavior becomes disorganized, fragmented or even frenzied. Optimum performance
is seen to occur in a state of moderate arousal in which the
organism is sufficiently aroused to perform well but not
so aroused as to be distracted or too disturbed to perform
the necessary task. This part of the theory is sometimes
referred to as the "inverted-U hypothesis" because the curve
that is formed when graphically describing the relationship
between arousal level and performance takes the shape of an
inverted-U as illustrated below.

As shown below, as arousal level increases, performance
improves until it reaches a maximum at the height of the inverted-U curve; from that point onward performance level decreases
with increases in the arousal level.

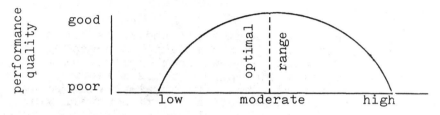

AROUSAL LEVEL

It has also been demonstrated that as task difficulty increases, the optimal level of arousal for highest
performance ratings decreases. That is, the easier the task,
the higher the arousal level needed to produce the best
performance, and the more difficult the task, the lower the
optimum arousal level needed. It is with this aspect of the
Yerkes-Dodson law that the theories set forth in Hans Eysenck's
biological theory of personality can be tested with more
precision and can serve as better predictors of behavior.

Eysenck believes that the introvert/extrovert
dimension of personality has an inherited basis; that it is
measurable by the general level of cortical arousal within
a person and that by measuring this characteristic certain
modes of behavior are predictable.

The Yerkes-Dodson predictions about the relationship between arousal level and performance provide a framework in which to test the hypothesis set forth by Eysenck.
Performance levels should be predictable for introverts and
extroverts if arousal level predicts introverted and extroverted characteristics. Introverts should have the highest
level of arousal while extroverts should have the lowest.
These theoretical predictions have, in fact, been tested
and substantiated by experimentation. This also demonstrates part of the appeal of Eysenck's biologically based
theory of personality--it is readily scientifically testable
and allows for the asking and answering of many questions
about the relationship between cortical arousal and specific
behavior patterns.

FREUDIAN THEORY

● PROBLEM 13-8

List and describe Freud's stages of motivational
development.

Solution: Freud divided the period of motivational
development into five stages. These stages are characterized by the objects that are the goals of the individual
during each particular stage. Freud believed that the primary driving force in an individual's life was the sexual
urge. The stages are therefore especially concerned with
representing changes of sexual gratification in relation to
the child's body. The five stages in sequential order are:
the oral phase, the anal phase, the phallic phase, a latency

period and the genital phase.

The oral phase begins at birth and lasts eight
months. It is characterized by the infant's concern for his
mouth and the gratification he seeks from oral stimuli. The
most obvious oral activity the child derives pleasure from
is eating. Oral stimulation, however, is also produced by
engaging in such activities as sucking, biting, swallowing
and manipulating various parts of the mouth. Freud contended
that these activities are the child's means of fulfilling
his sexual urges. Hence, Eros (the life instinct) makes its
appearance. But Thanatos (the death instinct) is also seen
since quite frequently children destroy objects they come
in contact with, often by biting them.

During this phase, the child's personality is
controlled by the id. He demands immediate gratification of
his wants.

The next stage of motivational development is the
anal phase when the child's central area of bodily concern
is the rectum. Bowel movements become a source of pleasure
to the child. He may defecate often to achieve this pleasure.
This, however, would bring him into conflict with his parents.
The conflict leads the child to develop an ego. He comes
to realize that he cannot always do what he wants when he
wants. He learns that there are certain times when it is
appropriate to expel waste and other times when it is inappropriate. He gradually comes to understand his mother's
wishes and abides by them.

The child's central interest gradually shifts again--
this time to the genital region. This stage is called the
phallic phase and lasts from approximately two years of age
to six. Sexual gratification becomes more erotic during
this time as evidenced by the child's masturbation: actual
manipulation of the genitals.

It is during this stage that the phallus (male
genital) acquires a special significance. Freud believed
that the increased awareness in the male of his sexual
organs leads him to subconsciously desire his mother. In
addition, the male child grows envious and resentful of his
father and wishes to replace him as the object of his mother's
love. This situation is called the Oedipus Complex.

Similarly, a female undergoes a complex wherein she
desires her father and rivals with her mother for her father's
affections. This is called the Electra Complex. This complex involves penis envy on the part of the female child.
She believes that she once had a penis but that it was removed.
In order to compensate for its loss, Freud believed the girl
wants to have a child by her father. Eventually, however,
both the boy and the girl pass through these complexes.
Once this happens, they begin to identify with the parent of
their own sex. This marks the end of the phallic phase and
the beginning of a new one.

The next period, the period of latency, is characterized by indifference to sexually related matters. During

this time, the child's identification with the parent of his own sex becomes stronger. The child imitates his or her behavior--speech, gestures, mannerisms, as well as beliefs and value systems. The child also incorporates more and more of the beliefs and values of his culture. Thus, the super-ego is developing to a greater extent. (It began to develop during the late anal and the phallic stages.) The child comes to distinguish between acceptable and unacceptable behavior in his society.

The period of latency is also marked by the fact that children seek associations (or playmates) of their own sex. Boys prefer the company of boys and consciously avoid girls. Girls prefer contact with other girls and avoid boys. This period of sexual latency lasts five years, from ages six to eleven.

The final stage of motivational development is called the genital phase, which is the longest of the five stages. It lasts seven years from ages eleven to eighteen. This period is similar to the anal stage. There is a renewed interest and pleasure derived from excretory activity. In addition, masturbation takes place and is engaged in much more frequently at this time than during the anal stage.

In the beginning of the genital phase, the person seeks associations with members of his own sex just as in the latency period. But the associations are stronger in the genital phase and Freud believed they are homosexual in nature, even though homosexual activity may not take place. As this period progresses, however, the homosexual tenden-cies are supplanted by heterosexual ones and toward the latter part of this phase, the child makes contact and forms relationships with members of the opposite sex.

Also at this time, the superego undergoes further development and becomes more flexible. In the latency period the superego is quite rigid. The child adopts rules in the most literal sense. During the genital phase, the individual realizes that some rules are less vital than others. Consequently, his behavior will reflect this. He accepts some rules or norms and makes exceptions to others.

● **PROBLEM** 13-9

Explain the terms fixation and regression as used by Freud in his descriptions of human development.

Solution: According to Freud, fixation and regres-sion are the results of abnormal personality development. In his scheme of personality development consisting of different stages, Freud stated that there is a certain amount of frustration and anxiety as the individual passes from one stage to the next. If the amount of frustration and anxiety becomes too great, that is, if there is too much anxiety about moving to the next stage, development may halt and the individual will become fixated at one stage. An overly dependent child is an example of someone who is fixated. Development has ceased at an early stage of development preventing him from becoming independent.

In contrast, regression refers to a retreat to an earlier stage of development. Someone who encounters an intolerable experience and is unable to deal with it may engage in behavior appropriate to someone at an earlier stage of development. Often, regression is used as a means of handling frustration. A six-year-old who reverts to wetting his pants may be expressing his frustration from the loss of parental attention due to the birth of a new sibling. Similarly, a child who displays infantile behavior on his first day of school--crying, thumb sucking, etc.--is regressing.

Regression is usually determined by the earlier fixations of the individual. In other words, the person tends to regress to a stage upon which he has been previously fixated. For example, the child who becomes fixated at a certain stage which results in his overdependence, may become overdependent later in life when faced with an extremely unbearable or frustrating experience. In this case, he is regressing to a point of fixation.

It is important to keep in mind that fixation and regression are relative conditions. An individual rarely fixates or regresses completely. Usually most aspects of an individual's personality will mature normally, but his behavior may be characterized by infantilisms--childish conduct which results from frustrations. Fixation and regression are both related to abnormalities in personality development. Fixation refers to a halting of normal development, whereas regression refers to a return to earlier, less mature stages of development.

● PROBLEM 13-10

Describe the ideas of Freud concerning man's basic instincts and the major components of his personality that are formed during psychosexual development.

Solution: According to Sigmund Freud, man has two basic urges or tendencies. One is survival, the other is procreation. Freud was most interested in the reproductive urge since this one is always being thwarted by the environment. He coined the term "libido" as the source of energy for the sexual urge. It is important to note that Freud considered several behaviors to be sexual in nature, not just the act of sex itself. Activities such as smoking and thumbsucking were considered by Freud to be sexual. He later defined two instincts in man which he called Eros and Thanatos. These are Greek terms that mean love and death, respectively. Eros is the life instinct or the will to live which includes the libidinal urges. Thanatos refers to the death wish or the death instinct. These two urges, according to Freud, compete against each other. It is the life-giving urges of Eros that are most intimately connected with the child's development.

Freud considered personality an expression of two conflicting forces: life instincts and the death instinct.

Freud sees the newborn infant as a simple and selfish being. The infant's personality, he believed, is governed by the id. The id contains all of man's instinctual urges. The infant has no ethical or moral rules; he demands immediate satisfaction of his wants. The infant is pure id--he only feels urges and knows they must be satisfied. He does not understand his environment; he has no idea that due to the nature of his surroundings, instant gratification is not always possible. He only knows, for example, that he is hungry and cries until he is fed. Hence, we have a conflict between the id and reality. This leads to the second level of human personality--the ego. The ego is the intermediary between the id and reality. The ego develops between the ages of eight months and eighteen months as the child acquires an understanding of what is possible. The ego also distinguishes between long-range and short-range goals and decides which activities will be most profitable to the individual. For example, a student might decide he would rather watch television than do his homework. This is a short-range goal. However, he might also realize the long-range goal--that doing his homework rather than watching TV will further his education and possibly lead to a better occupation in the future. The ego in this case might choose the long-range goal since it would be most beneficial to the individual. The long-range benefits are preferred to immediate gratification. Thus, the id and ego work together to determine the individual's goals.

Eventually, the child acquires a moral sense. This is embodied in the third component of his personality called the superego. The superego represents the taboos and mores or rules of the society in which the child lives. It might encompass religious rules as well. The process by which the child comes to learn cultural norms is called socialization. Hence, the development of the superego represents socialization in the child.

The id and superego are often in conflict because fulfillment of many of the id's urges would require behavior that is socially unacceptable.

The superego develops from the ages of eighteen months to six years. It is often described as having two divisions. One is the conscience which consists of the child's internalized rules. The other is the ego ideal, which represents strivings and goals highly regarded by the parents.

● **PROBLEM 13-11**

"The aim of all life is death." What did Freud mean when he said this? Particularly discuss his conceptualization of a death instinct.

Solution: Late in his life Freud reformulated his brilliant and stimulating picture of the workings of the human mind. In his book, Beyond the Pleasure Principle, he proposed that the aim of all life was death and that human behavior was the result of a struggle between the life instinct (Eros) and the death instinct (Thanatos). He observed that the ultimate aim of an instinct was to return the organism to the unstimulable state of inorganic matter, more specifically, to death.

He noted that because it operates invisibly, the death instinct is rarely observable in pure form. It can only be inferred from the observation of its derivatives-- aggressive and violent tendencies. The victory of the life principle over the death principle succeeds by turning the destructive impulses outward toward other people and thus accounts for the aggressiveness in human behavior. The life principle itself serves the death principle. The organism is designed to return naturally to its original state; the self-preservation tendencies of the life principle are designed to insure that the organism eventually die--that it burn out its life energies and return to an inanimate state.

This formulation replaced the primacy of the pleasure principle as the main motivating factor in Freud's system and came as a disturbing shock to some of his followers. Yet, this revised theory was the cornerstone for a completely new model of the mind. Structural in nature, this model included the "ego," the "id" and the "superego"--terms that have become part of the Western understanding of the functioning of man.

● **PROBLEM 13-12**

Define defense mechanism. List and describe some examples.

Solution: A defense mechanism is a process an individual employs to compensate for a desire which cannot be fulfilled because of social taboos. Defense mechanisms

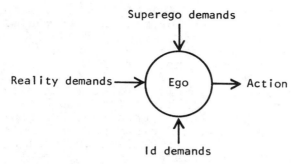

This diagram illustrates Freud's concept of the ego as the
central integrating core of the personality, mediating between inner demands from the id, and the superego and outer
demands from the environment.

are created by the ego in an attempt to deal with the unful-
filled wish by mediating between the id and the superego.
Often, the anxiety which results from conflict between the
id and superego becomes excessive and the individual must
find means of dealing with it. Defense mechanisms are these
means.

　　　　Examples of defense mechanisms include repression,
displacement, reaction-formation, intellectualization, projection, and denial.

　　　　Repression occurs when an individual experiences a
painful incident or event and tries to forget it. He represses the experience by burying it in his unconscious mind.
The unconscious mind is replete with repressed feelings
toward painful experiences. An example of this is an adult
who was once abused by a parent during childhood. The individual tries to forget about the parent or at least those
occasions when the parent abused him.

　　　　Displacement results when an individual wishes to
gratify a desire, but engaging in the activity that will fulfill his desire is socially unacceptable. Hence, the ego
compromises and finds another means of gratification. The
alternate activity may not be as pleasurable as the activity
of his first choice, but it suffices for the time being.
Very often, the desire is unconscious. For example, someone
who constantly desires to engage in sexual activity (a nympho-
maniac) may realize that to constantly gratify her desire may
not be feasible. Hence, she may engage in masturbation. Thus,
one form of behavior is displaced for another.

　　　　Reaction-formation occurs when an individual is
disturbed by his natural feelings toward a particular person,
object or phenomenon. Because of the resulting anxiety, he
consciously tells himself and others that he feels the
opposite of his true feeling. For example, if a person fears
he may be homosexual, he may constantly communicate to others
that he is not. This may be done either verbally or by
engaging in behavior exclusively appropriate for his or her
own sex. A male who fears he is homosexual might engage in
"manly" activities such as fighting or performing various
feats of strength. Likewise, a female who fears lesbian

tendencies might dress in an excessively feminine fashion--
always wearing dresses, jewelry, or makeup. In addition,
people who fear that they are homosexual frequently display
reaction-formation by denouncing homosexuality and
condemning those who are openly homosexual.

Intellectualization is also called rationalization.
It occurs whenever an individual fears that a behavior he
has engaged in might be abnormal. Hence, he searches for ways
or excuses that will "rationalize" his behavior and make it
appear perfectly normal. Intellectualization implies that
the individual is primarily concerned with the intellectual
or rational aspects of his behavior rather than the emotional aspects. For example, an obese person who refuses to
diet, may insist that dieting is unhealthy and that he needs
to eat as much as he does in order to sustain his energy level.

Projection is a defense mechanism where the individual projects or attributes his anxieties or abnormalities to
other people. Returning to the example of homosexuality
given for reaction-formation, a person who fears that he may
be homosexual will overtly deny that he is. In addition, he
will call other people homosexual (even if they are not) in

A Summary of the Major Defense Mechanisms

Name	Description
Repression (denial)	An unpleasant or threatening thought or idea is not permitted into awareness.
Rationalization	A behavior based on an unacceptable motive or cause is explained as resulting from an acceptable motive or cause (e.g., a poor grade explained by poor teaching).
Projection	One's unacceptable motives are attributed to another person. (A hostile person comes to believe that other people are "out to get" him.)
Displacement	A substitution is made, whereby a less threatening target of a motive is substituted for the more natural target (e.g., anger at one's father is "taken out" on one's little brother).
Reaction formation	The individual asserts a motive that is opposite in character to the one that threatens him (e.g., a person threatened by his own fascination with pornography may become a strong advocate of censorship.
Compensation	A personal shortcoming is overcome by an intense effort to become successful in another field (e.g., an unathletic person becomes a sports-writer).
Sublimation	The most direct expression of an unacceptable motive is denied, and related acceptable behavior is substituted (e.g., dancing as a sublimation of sexual motivation).
Identification	One adopts the characteristics of someone who is seen as more powerful or successful in achieving some goal (e.g., boys identify with their fathers because they are more successful and powerful).

478

order to divert attention away from his own fears and allay his anxiety. Also, by calling others homosexual, he reduces the chances that other people will think he is one. Because the individual projects attributes he fears he has, he is displaying projection.

Denial, another defense mechanism, involves a distorted rather than objective view of the world. It often comes about when a person tries to make a particular behavior appear less abnormal or heinous by perceiving the world as a place where everyone or most people engage in the same behavior. Or he may perceive his society as being tolerant or praising of the behavior. For example, someone who always cheats on his taxes may deny that his behavior is wrong because "everyone else does it" or because the government asks for too much money which it doesn't deserve.

Defense mechanisms are defensive in that they protect individuals from anxiety they may not be able to tolerate. These mechanisms may be strong or mild depending on the individual and the anxiety-producing situation.

● **PROBLEM** 13-13

Define the "Oedipus Complex" as it is purported to be experienced by both boys and girls by Freud.

Solution: According to psychoanalytic theory, human development follows a biologically determined sequence. Considering that the search for pleasure is the infant's chief aim, the focus for receiving these pleasurable sensations associated with a generalized sex energy or "libido" begins in the region of the mouth; at about age one and a half to three this focus moves to the anus; and at about age five the sex organs become the main focus for pleasurable sensations. It is during this third period that the "Oedipus Complex" occurs.

This is a crucial stage in psychosexual development. Freud considered it to be instrumental in the eventual development of a strong moral sense. In the boy, the discovery that manipulation of the genitals yields pleasurable sensations and the subsequent admonitions from his parents about engaging in the often taboo activity of masturbation, contributes to the fear that he may be castrated for this misbehavior. His fear is reinforced when he first becomes aware of the female genitals--her lack of a penis convinces him that she has already been castrated.

This "castration-anxiety" becomes connected with the boy's relationship and affection for his mother. As he becomes aware that his mother's attentions are not exclusively his own he begins to experience jealousy and resentment particularly towards his father and any siblings. Freud assumed that the boy's father knows how much the boy would like to be rid of him to have his mother exclusively for himself. Although he develops a submissive and overly loving behavior toward his father, he feels that the all-knowing father may

at any time remove that organ that provides the most pleasure
at this stage in retribution for his angry feelings and
desirous impulses towards his mother. Thus, castration by
the father becomes the overwhelming fear for the boy. He
deals with the problem by repressing his fear, identifying
with his father and developing the "superego," an internal
moral agent incorporated from his parents.

At this same stage of development, the girl child
has a somewhat different experience due to her different
biological construction. For the girl the discovery that
she does not have a penis begins the Oedipus Complex--
sometimes referred to as the "Electra Complex" to distinguish
it from the experience of the boy. The girl also has taken
the mother as her first love-object, but when she discovers
that females lack this vital organ she comes to devalue her
mother and identifies with her father. This may take the form
of imitating masculine behavior or abandoning sexual activity
altogether in an effort to forget her inferiority. The resolution of the Oedipus Complex for the girl was never as clearly stated by Freud as that for the boy. The fear of castration is a decisive motivator for the boy to repress his feelings for his mother and identify with his father and thus
develop strong moral guiding principles. The girl, on the
other hand, has no such strong force for moral development
in her history. Instead, she develops a desire for a penis
substitute--a baby. Her devaluation of her mother and her
jealousy fade with time as she develops the female behaviors
of appealing to the father and desiring a baby as substitutes for the organ she is lacking. This reasoning concludes that girls do not develop a strong moral sense. The
theory has received much attention as a central chauvanistic
cultural influence by adherents of women's liberation.

● **PROBLEM** 13-14

What is the importance of unconscious determinants
of behavior in Freudian theory? How did Freud's conception
of the unconscious differ from the prevailing view of his
time?

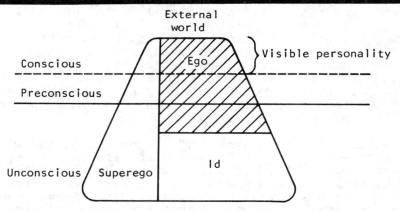

Solution: Initially interested in explaining and
understanding neurosis, Sigmund Freud eventually incorporated
his views on psychopathology into a more general framework

that included normal as well as abnormal behavior. Consistently important in Freud's work was the role of biological and constitutional factors in personality development and functioning.

The fundamental tenet in psychoanalysis as developed by Freud is that behavior is motivated; there are underlying causes for the way in which people behave. He believed that much of behavior was motivated by unconscious drives. In Freud's system, three levels of consciousness were distinguished: the conscious, the preconscious and the unconscious. The conscious consists of events, memories, impulses of which the individual is aware. The preconscious contains memories and drives that can easily be recalled but are not within consciousness at the moment. The unconscious is an explanation for thoughts, memories, emotions, impulses that are out of our awareness. Yet, they influence behavior even though the individual is not aware of their presence.

These unconscious impulses include aggressive and sexual drives, memories of events that were once conscious but that have been repressed because they were too shocking, painful or shameful to admit into consciousness. Unconscious impulses seek expression and often produce dreams. These impulses also explain the bizarre behavior of mental patients--while the contents of consciousness are rational and consistent with events occurring in the present, the contents of the unconscious are independent of logic and unconcerned with the demands of reality.

The concept of the unconscious is thought by some to be one of Freud's greatest contributions to psychological thought. At the time he introduced it, it was a radically new idea. Freud lived during the Victorian era, a period in which sexuality was highly controlled and restrained. His contention that sexual and aggressive impulses were motivators for much human behavior caused a great uproar amongst his contemporaries. Yet his towering conceptions, not the least of which was his description of the processes of the unconscious mind, place him as a pioneer in the history of thought. His contribution to the understanding of individual psychology is evident not only in those who follow his methods but in many other psychological thinkers. Also, his ideas have permeated the social sciences to such a degree that it is even difficult to separate his thinking from what we today accept as common explanations of human behavior.

● **PROBLEM 13-15**

What does Freud claim to be the main function of dreams? How is this function fulfilled?

Solution: To Freud dreams represented attempts at wish fulfillment. He reasoned that the dream is a hallucinatory state that structures events not as they would be in reality, but as the dreamer wishes them to be. When unconscious desires conflict with conscious restraints, however, it is necessary for the "dream work" to pursue devious paths

Dream Analysis

An infantile dream, recalled many years later, points
for Freud to the deep-seatedness and long-lastingness of
psychosexual experiences in the infant years.

A man, now thirty-five, relates a clearly remembered dream
which he claims to have had when he was four years of age:
The notary with whom his father's will was deposited— he
had lost his father at the age of three— brought two large
emperor pears, of which he was given one to eat. The other lay on the windowsill of the livingroom. He woke with
the conviction of the reality of what he had dreamt, and
obstinately asked his mother to give him the second pear;
it was, he said, still lying on the windowsill. His mother laughed at this.

Freud says:

The dreamer's inability to associate justifies the attempt to interpret it by the substitution of symbols. The
two pears...are the breasts of the mother who nursed him;
the windowsill is a projection of the bosom. His sensation
of reality after waking is justified, for his mother had
actually suckled him for much longer than the customary
term, and her breast was still available. The dream is to
be translated: "Mother, give me the breast again at which
I once used to drink." The "once" is represented by the
eating of one pear, the "again" by the desire for the other.

to express the wish. Thus, Freud believed dreams to be an
uncommonly rich source of unconscious material. He maintained
that a skilled observer reviewing the contents of dreams could
discover much useful information in the unconscious mind of
the dreamer. Thus, Freud referred to dreams as "the royal
road to the unconscious."

Because of the disguised nature of wish fulfillment
in dreams, Freud distinguished between the manifest content
of a dream, (the literal content of the dream as experienced
by the dreamer) and the latent content, (the hidden, symbolic, actual meaning of the dream.)

The mental processes that convert wishes and impulses
into the disguised images of the manifest content are called
the "dream work." It is the function of the psychoanalyst
to interpret or undo this dream work, to unravel the manifest content and reveal the more fundamental latent content
from which the dream was derived. The study and interpretation of dream imagery was one of Freud's major contributions
to the study of the unconscious. He believed that a "censorship system" existed at the border of the conscious mind that
was very selective about the impulses it would allow the dreamer to recall to his conscious mind. Wishes that would be
morally unacceptable to the awake dreamer would not be allowed
to appear undisguised in a dream. This distortion by the censorship system made possible the fulfillment of hidden wishes
without too much disturbance to the dreamer. Thus, the only
way that the unconscious could achieve satisfaction for its
strong desires was by evading the censor by masquerading the

Comparison of Three Views of Personality

	Psychoanalytic Theory	Behavioristic Theory	Humanistic Theory
View of human nature	negative	neutral	positive
Is behavior free or determined?	determined	determined	free choice
Principal motives	sex and aggression	drives of all kinds	self-actualization
Personality structure	id, ego, superego	habits	self
Role of unconscious	maximized	practically nonexistent	minimized
Conception of conscious	superego	self-reinforcement	ideal self, valuing process
Developmental emphasis	psychosexual stages	critical learning situations identification and imitation	development of self-image
Barriers to personal growth	unconscious conflicts; fixations	maladaptive habits; pathological environment	conditions of worth; incongruence

unacceptability of its wishes behind the facade of neutral objects or ideas. It is the unconscious and the censor together, therefore, that are responsible for dream content and it is for this reason that their interpretation could contribute so much to the understanding of the dreamer's motivations.

● **PROBLEM 13-16**

Discuss some criticisms of Freud's theory.

Solution: Freud's theories have been repeatedly attacked both by those outside the psychoanalytic circle and those psychoanalysts who differ from him on certain theoretical and practical points. Despite the large number of criticisms, classical psychoanalysis remains the favored approach of most psychiatrists and psychoanalysts--even those that doubt the validity of parts of Freud's theory still use his methods of patient treatment.

The concepts that have been under fire most often have been his views on sex, the unconscious, and the critical determining character of early childhood experience. Because he was living and working in an age in which the mores were unusually strict concerning the expression of natural sexuality, his strong emphasis on sex has been seen by many to be a reaction to this repressive environment. Today, sex is seen as only one of many basic human needs. His assignment of sexual significance to early childhood experience has also suffered severe attack. Cross-cultural studies have failed to confirm the universality of the Oedipus Complex. Also, studies designed to test other hypotheses regarding early parent-child relations have proved inconclusive.

The psychoanalytic method has been criticized because the techniques of free association, dream analysis and transference demand that the patient be relatively healthy to start with, highly motivated to improve and quite skilled at expressing and interpreting his thoughts and feelings. It has also been demonstrated that the lengthy, costly process of psychoanalysis is no more effective than shorter, less costly procedures that are more widely applicable. Again, these criticisms have not prevented classical psychoanalysis from remaining the preferred method of treatment by many mental health practitioners today.

Whatever criticisms might be leveled at Freud, it cannot be denied that he is one of the great modern thinkers. His stimulating and compelling thinking process has served as a source of so much inspiration to students of human behavior that it is difficult to assess the size of his contribution to the study of human nature.

JUNG AND ERIKSON

● **PROBLEM 13-17**

Briefly describe the "collective unconscious" as it was explained by C. G. Jung. Include a description of archetypes.

Solution: In his approach to personality theory, Jung hypothesized that the personality was divided into three major units: the conscious ego, the personal unconscious and the collective unconscious. The conscious ego was the conscious part of personality; the personal unconscious was the contents of the conscious mind that lose awareness; and the collective unconscious was the deeper level of experience which was inherited and detached from anything personal, and so common to all men.

In the depths of the collective unconscious dwelled the primordial images and ideas common to all members of the race from the beginning of life. These are not pre-formed images, they are simply possibilities of action, predispositions to respond to external events in specific ways and potentialities of shaping experience in certain directions. These images were termed "archetypes."

The archetypes act as a model or template to organ-ize an individual's interactions with the world, both inner and outer. They pertain mainly to his emotional reactions. These archetypes are the result of the cumulative effect of perpetually repeated experiences on the human nervous system's development. Events such as the rising and setting of the sun have been experienced by the human race since its inception and through the repetitive subjective emotional reactions to events such as this an internal state is impressed upon the nervous system that dictates a predisposition to react in a certain way. This predisposition to act is trans-mitted to future generations. Thus, the archetypes of the unconscious mind represent a residue of ancestral emotional life.

Jung devoted a large part of his life to studying mythological stories, dreams, fantasies in search of specific archetypal images. He believed that a "mythological tendency" or a predisposition to respond to repeating events by creat-ing a particular type of image to represent them was a real legacy of past generations.

● **PROBLEM 13-18**

What is the "shadow" in Jung's theory? What are the "anima" and the "animus?" What is the "persona?"

Solution: In his theory of personality structure, Jung included the concept of the collective unconscious which refers to the inherited primordial images common to all humans. He called the image of the unconscious "archetypes." There is no limit to the number of archetypes that are possible. Those that appear most frequently in Jungian work include the shadow, the anima and animus and the persona.

The "shadow" represents the repressed, unconscious drives and desires of the personal unconscious; because it is found in all men as their "dark side" it can also be ex-amined as part of the collective unconscious. Mythologically, it is represented by demons, evil spirits, or devils. It is an inferior, undesirable part of personalities that people

prefer not to recognize. It is, however, important to attempt
to recognize and accept it to prevent it from being cut off
from the conscious mind, otherwise the personality would be
incomplete. Extreme discomfort in the presence of another
person may be evoked by a person's projection of his shadow
onto someone else, not realizing that the person is a mirror
of his own weaknesses.

The projected image of the female throughout history
in man's unconscious is his "anima." This internalized
feminine image is based on his real experiences with women
particularly his mother, sister or other family members and
on the collective experience of men throughout history.
The anima determines a man's relationship to women throughout his life. The anima helps a man compensate for his
otherwise one-sided view of his interactions with and perceptions of others. Women have a similar aspect as part of
their unconscious--the "animus." Unlike the anima, the
animus usually contains the images of many masculine figures
which generally represent a rational element for the woman.
In trying to explain the difference in the anima and the
animus, Jung is purported to have said that the anima produces moods in the male and the animus produces opinions in
the female. A danger with these archetypes is that an
individual may become so overwhelmed by them that his or her
masculinity or femininity is threatened.

The "persona" is the front presented to other
people. It is a mask that feigns individuality making the
person and others believe that he is an individual, when
he is actually acting a role through which the collective
unconscious speaks. An individual's persona is therefore
only one theme of the many available from the collective
psyche--it comes into existence to mitigate an individual's
realization of being part of the collective mass of humanity.

● **PROBLEM** 13-19

Contrast Jungian and Freudian theories. Particularly discuss their different versions of the unconscious
mind.

Solution: Due partly to his published acknowledge-
ment that Freud's ideas had been useful in his own clinical
work, early in his career Carl Jung became Freud's hand-
picked successor. Jung had especially found the concept of
the unconscious valuable in his experimental work. At first
Jung agreed with Freud as to what was to be found in the
unconscious mental processes of his subjects--repressed,
unacceptable infantile sexual and aggressive strivings.

As Jung continued his explorations of the unconscious, he found it more and more difficult to accept that
sexual motives were the chief motivator of human behavior.
Freud's principal concept that a pleasure drive rooted in
an individual's childhood sexual experience was the base of
all behavior caused Jung great consternation. Jung felt
that the concept of sexuality should be reserved for extreme
forms of libido only and that the more generalized expressions

of what Freud called libido or sexual drive should be considered in a different framework for better understanding.

The more Jung worked, the more he opposed this point in Freud's conceptual analysis. As his powers of personal perception increased and his professional judgment matured, he discovered forces and content within the unconscious quite unlike anything Freud had ever referred to. Jung's reference point moved from the personal conflict over unacceptable sexual and aggressive motives to transpersonal, universal symbols of the human race's life experiences that transcend the individual's immediate concerns.

Other differences in the two theorists include: (1) Freud viewed libido as the basis of the pleasure principle in humans, Jung observed this energy as one that was able to communicate itself to any field of activity--power, hunger, hatred, religion, or sexuality--without ever being a specific instinct; (2) Freud saw throughout human behavior the dynamics of search for pleasure be it through food, drink or sex, while Jung saw only a "will to live" that through the individual sought to preserve the entire species; (3) Freud found in his patients a damaged reality, Jung discovered instead that life energy had been channeled into a myth-making or fantasy creative process; and finally (4) Freud anchored his ideas in biology--the workings of the body and the mind, but Jung found the roots for his observations in the spirit of his subjects.

● **PROBLEM** 13-20

List and describe Erikson's stages of psychosocial development.

Solution: Erik Erikson, an American psychoanalyst, devised a comprehensive theory for explaining psychosocial development. He believes that human behavior and personality result from a combination of heredity and cultural influences. He divides development from birth to maturity into eight basic stages. Each stage consists of a crisis which indicates a major turning point in the individual's life. This conflict is usually one between individual instinct and the restraining forces of external institutions. The individual must decide between two alternatives--one that is beneficial and another that is detrimental. Success in development is dependent upon successfully choosing the right alternative.

Erikson's stages are: (1) oral-sensory (birth to one-and-a-half years), (2) muscular-anal (one-and-a-half to four years), (3) locomotor-genital (four to six years), (4) latency (six to eleven years), (5) adolescence, (6) young adulthood, (7) adulthood, and (8) maturity.

During the first stage, the oral-sensory stage, the basic crisis centers on the development of either trust or mistrust. An infant is almost completely dependent on others for the fulfillment of his needs. If these needs are con-

sistently satisfied and if he receives love and stimulation
with those he comes in contact with, he will develop a
sense of trust, not only in others but in himself and in
his ability to handle his needs. If, on the other hand,
his needs are not satisfied regularly and he receives little
love, attention and stimulation, he will develop a sense of
mistrust. If the mistrust is severe, the child may become
timid and withdrawn since he has given up hope of ever
achieving his goals. Erikson believes that the development
of a healthy personality is contingent upon the formation of
a basic trust--the individual's belief that his existence is
meaningful.

The second stage of psychosocial development, according to Erikson, is the muscular-anal which occurs in early
childhood. During this period, the basic crisis is between
establishing autonomy and dealing with doubt and shame. The
child who has developed a healthy sense of basic trust begins
to see himself as a separate and autonomous being capable of
doing things for himself. He has now gained some control
of his bodily functions. He begins to assert himself, as
can be seen in his response when asked to do something--he'll
often reply, "no." Erikson believes parents should allow
small children to do some things for themselves and should
encourage exploration so that the child can develop a sense
of autonomy or separateness. In addition, parents should
assist their child in acquiring bodily control in such
activities as walking and bowel movement.

Erikson contends that if parents are overprotective
of their child (i.e., if they don't let him do things for
himself), and are over-demanding with regard to his bodily
functions, the child will develop feelings of shame and self-
doubt. He will be shameful of not living up to his parents'
expectations and will doubt his ability to live as a free,
autonomous being. Individuals who successfully pass through
this stage develop into independent adults who are able to
make decisions for themselves and guide their own lives.

The third stage of Erikson's theory is called the
locomotor-genital stage, which occurs between the ages of four
to six. This period is characterized by the formation of
either initiative or guilt, the development of motor skills
resulting in increased locomotion, increase in language
development as well as imagination and curiosity. Curiosity is especially evident in the child as reflected by his
interest in exploring his (and others') bodies and differences
between males and females. Erikson maintains that this
interest is part of an "infantile sexuality." This includes
an attraction to the opposite-sexed parent. (Note Freud's
influence.) The parent's response to the child's curiosity is an important factor in determining the degree of confidence and initiative the child will develop. A basic sense
of guilt emerges if the child receives a negative or indiffer-
ent parental response to his questions or if he finds himself
in an environment with little to explore. He may become
anxious about asking questions and thereby stifle his
curiosity. A child who receives positive and attentive
parental response will develop a sense of confidence and
initiative. He will feel happy and secure about his

curiosity and will be eager to explore his environment. Successful resolution of this "initiative vs. guilt" crisis enables the child to take initiative and use his imagination in adulthood. He is equipped to deal with new, unfamiliar situations without the restrictions that result from guilt feelings.

The fourth stage in Erikson's scheme is called latency which occurs from ages six to eleven. The basic crisis in this period is industry vs. inferiority. A child develops a sense of industry if he receives attention and praise for various accomplishments. For example, his parents might praise him for drawing a picture well or receiving a good report card or his teacher might commend him for writing the best composition in the class. As a result of such reactions, the child will actively pursue various projects since feedback from others assure him he can successfully execute them. In contrast, a child who fails consistently at various tasks or who receives little or no attention and praise develops a sense of inferiority. He avoids tackling new projects because he feels he will not handle them successfully. He puts little effort and enthusiasm into his work because he believes he is bound to fail. A child who successfully resolves this crisis and develops a sense of industry will come to find enjoyment in his work and will experience a sense of pride in his accomplishments. This attitude is carried into adulthood.

During this stage the child comes to define himself and others in terms of occupations--doctors, lawyers, teachers. The child defines his future self in terms of one such occupation.

Erikson's fifth stage of psychosocial development is adolescence which begins at puberty. The major problem in this stage is the identity crisis. The adolescent keeps asking, "Who am I?" Confusion about his role can cause him much stress and anxiety.

According to Erikson, the adolescent is very fickle about his self-image. This is reflected in constant fluctuations in preferred tastes and in styles of dress and haircut.

In an effort to offset confusion and allay some anxiety, the adolescent may align himself with an individual or group that can provide simple answers to his questions. In his quest for stability, he may devote himself to the guidelines of a teenage gang, a religious group or a political organization. Adopting a lifestyle defined by others and living by others' codes may, however, produce some resentment. He may come to feel that he wants to do what he wants. If, however, the adolescent can't decide what he wants to do, he returns to the identity crisis.

Resolution of the identity crisis occurs when the adolescent receives support from others and is encouraged to seek answers to questions on his own. If he experiments with various lifestyles, he will eventually find one that best suits him. In some cultures, such experimentation

usually lasts until the individual reaches his mid-twenties.
Successful resolution of the identity crisis results in a
positive identity wherein the individual is confident of
himself and his lifestyle.

The sixth stage of Erikson's plan is young adulthood. The basic crisis of this period is intimacy vs.
isolation. At this time, the individual is concerned with
establishing intimate, long-term relationships with others.
If he has successfully resolved the identity crisis, he
will be open and warm toward others, willing to share parts
of himself and respond to others who wish to share themselves
with him. If the identity crisis is not resolved, he will
not be willing to open himself up to others. A person with
an uncertain or unhealthy identity will not want to share
himself with others. Erikson believes that individuals
who refrain from intimate relationships do so because
they fear the emotional risks involved. To support his
statements, he points to hermits who elude intimacy to avoid
being hurt and to pseudo-intimates who have many superficial
friends but never let anyone get close enough for intimacy
to develop. Successful resolution of the crisis in young
adulthood leads to a healthy intimacy with another. A
successful marriage is evidence of this.

The seventh stage of psychosocial development is
adulthood. Here, concern for the next generation is of
major concern. Having passed the stage of intimacy and
concern for only a close few, the individual becomes preoccupied with his children and community. Through such active
concern he avoids stagnation because he receives new stimulation in return. Hence, the basic crisis of this stage is
generativity vs. stagnation. Success in resolving this
crisis is evident in someone who takes an active role in
parental guidance of the next generation and in community
affairs.

The eighth and final stage of Erikson's scheme
is maturity. The basic crisis during this stage is ego
integrity vs. disgust and despair. A sense of integrity
develops if the individual, having looked back on his life,
believes it has been meaningful and relatively successful.
He feels good about his past and is prepared to live the
rest of his life in peace. A feeling of disgust, however,
may arise if the individual sees his life as meaningless,
wasted, and generally unsuccessful. He will feel despair
if he believes it is too late to change or that his personality is so rigid that he can never change it.

THE HUMANIST PERSPECTIVE

• PROBLEM 13-21

What is unique about Gordon Allport's approach to
personality research?

Solution: Allport was the first psychologist to
stress the difference between the nomothetic and the ideo-

graphic methods of study. Nomothetic study involves using large numbers of subjects and generating basic principles of behavior. Ideographic study involves selecting methods of study that will not conceal or blur the uniqueness of a particular individual.

Since Allport did not believe in the validity of general principles he preferred to use the ideographic method. The emphasis upon the importance of personal dispositions (individual traits) as the primary determinants of behavior and as the units of personality leads inevitably to the conclusion that the only effective approach to the study of behavior is a method of studying the individual. Allport never developed a truly effective ideographic method of study but believed that psychologists should begin working earnestly to develop one.

● **PROBLEM 13-22**

What is Allport's theory of expressive behavior? What are three of the important studies he conducted on expressive behavior?

Solution: There are two components of behavior, adaptive and expressive. The adaptive component refers to the function of the act and the expressive component accounts for the individuality of an act. Allport was interested in the individual and the study of expressive behavior --the personal or idiosyncratic component found in even the most stereotyped responses is an excellent method of studying the individual. Allport believed in a general unity underlying personality and therefore he maintained that studying an individual's expressive behavior would lead to an understanding of the central aspects of his personality. Expressive behavior is determined by deeply ingrained personal dispositions (individual traits). Examples of expressive behavior include gait, voice, handwriting, and facial expression.

Allport and Vernon conducted a study designed to measure the consistency of expressive movement. In the experiment, twenty-five subjects were engaged in a variety of tasks in which their expressive movement could be observed. They performed these activities three separate times, each session was followed by a period of four weeks. Allport and Vernon found a reasonably high repeat-reliability (consistency of measure on two different occasions).

The two psychologists then conducted a correlation analysis of the major variables involved in all the tasks. They identified three group factors: the areal group factor, interpreted as a kind of motor expansiveness; the centrifugal group factor, interpreted as an extroversion or outward tendency of expressive movement; and the group factor of emphasis. Group factors have not been clearly described or explained and thus their importance remains unclear. However, the investigators feel that the evidence they collected suggests a generality underlying individual behavior; that there is unity in movement, personality, and mental life.

Allport and Vernon carried out another investigation
involving graphology. The purpose was to determine the extent to which a handwriting sample from a particular individual could be matched with his personality sketch. It
was found that even untrained judges performed at a better
than chance level at this task. Another study was designed
to see if judges could estimate personality accurately on
the basis of voice only. The results of the study showed
that judges were able to relate the voice with both personality characteristics and with certain physical characteristics (age, height, complexion) with better than chance
accuracy. All three studies of expressive behavior cited
above seem to support the concept of unity underlying
behavior.

● **PROBLEM** 13-23

What is Allport's view of the ego?

Solution: Allport did not like to use the term
ego because he did not want to be involved in the confusion
of hypothesizing the existence of an agent inside man's
head that organizes and controls the personality. He
believed that terms like self and ego should be used ad-
jectivally. Thus, he decided to call the self or ego-
functions of the personality the proprium or propriate
function. These functions include bodily sense, self-
identity, self-esteem, self-extension, sense of selfhood,
rational thinking, self-image, propriate striving, cognitive style and the function of knowing.

The proprium develops with time; it is not innate.
It is in this region that the root of consistency in attitudes and intentions is found. There are seven aspects
in the development of the proprium. In the first three
years of life three aspects make their appearance: a
sense of bodily self, a sense of continuing self-identity
and self-esteem. The extension of the self which refers
to taking interest in activities not essential to the
individual's immediate needs and self-image develops between
the ages of three and four. Between the ages of six and
twelve the child develops self-awareness, the understanding
that he can cope with his own problems through reason and
thought. The propriate strivings consisting of long-
range purposes, goals, and intentions develop during adolescence. Even though Allport consistently claims that all
behavior is controlled consciously and influenced only by
contemporary factors, the fact that the proprium is a
developmental phenomenon derived from past experience seems
to imply a direct link with the past.

● **PROBLEM** 13-24

How does Allport's concept of functional autonomy
differ from most other theories of motivation?

Solution: Allport proposed four essential requirements for a theory of human motivation:

1. The theory must acknowledge the contemporaneity
of motives; i.e., whatever moves a person to think or act
moves him now; people are not motivated by their past experiences.

2. The theory must be pluralistic; i.e., it must
allow for many types of motives occurring simultaneously.
Allport was not a reductionist; he did not believe that all
motives could be reduced to one or two organic drives.

3. The theory must invest cognitive processes, such
as planning and intention, with dynamic force.

4. The theory must recognize that each individual
can have a unique set of motives.

Allport's requirements for a theory of motivation
are met by his concept of functional autonomy. While most
theories of motivation stress either organic drives or the
principle of reward as a fundamental basis for action, the
principle of functional autonomy states that a given activity or form of behavior may become an end or goal in itself, in spite of the fact that it was originally engaged
for some other reason. Activities may be capable of sus-
taining themselves without biological reinforcement. An
example of this principle is Allport's explanation for the
reason a man would continue to hunt animals even though he
does not need them for food. A psychoanalyst might say
that this man hunts to satisfy his aggressive instinct, a
behaviorist might say that the man hunts because he is
rewarded with the approval of his peers, Allport would say
the man hunts simply because he likes to hunt.

Functional autonomy permits a relative divorce from
the past of the organism. If an individual is considered to
be driven by desires and intentions that are independent of
earlier motivations, then an individual's personal history
is unimportant in terms of an assessment of his personality
or his motivations. Allport believes that adult motives
supplant the motives of infancy. Furthermore, he maintains
that the maturity of the personality is measured by the
degree of functional autonomy it has attained, i.e., the
degree to which the personality is free of earlier motivations.

Thus, functional autonomy allows for a greater individuality of motives by reducing the importance of biological drives present at birth.

● **PROBLEM 13-25**

What are the fundamental tenets of Allport's theory
of personality?

Solution: The most important tenet of Allport's
personality theory is his stress on conscious motivation.

Allport claimed that in order to understand an individual it is necessary to know what his conscious intentions are; he stressed the ego functions (the proprium) as being most influential in behavior. While the Freudians and even the behaviorists stress the importance of an individual's past in understanding his behavior, Allport regards the past as insignificant in the assessment of an individual's behavior.

Allport maintains that unconscious motivation (repressed wishes and impulses) has no place in a "normal" person's behavior. Only in the case of neurotic and psychotic individuals is unconscious motivation a major factor in determining behavior. Usually, unconscious motivation is closely linked with the individual's past because most of the unconscious strivings are those desires and impulses that were left frustrated, either due to the threat of punishment or to the reality principle in childhood.

A significant extension of Allport's view on this matter is his belief that the difference between a normal and psychologically abnormal individual is qualitative, not quantitative. Most theorists, Freud and Skinner included, regard people exhibiting abnormal behavior as only quantitatively different from those who don't. Therefore, they apply the same principles to the study of both normal and abnormal behavior; Allport's position is radically different on this matter. His view of the normal individual places the elements of motivation at a conscious level and asserts that they are determined by contemporary factors. Skinner, on the other hand, believes that much of an individual's behavior is learned in childhood; Freud thought that an individual's behavior is a result of his childhood experiences.

Behavior therapists and psychoanalysts always search for the source of a current problem in the past. Allport contends that an individual's intentions (hopes, wishes, ambitions, aspirations, and plans) are the most important key to his present behavior. An individual's intentions are best learned by asking him to report them; Allport was therefore critical of projective techniques in personality assessment except when used for people with abnormal tendencies.

The personality structure, according to Allport, is represented largely by traits; these traits motivate behavior. A trait is regarded as a neuropsychic structure which causes an individual to behave in a meaningfully consistent manner. These traits develop as a result of a person's interaction with the environment. There are common traits which are often referred to simply as traits and there is the individual trait which has been referred to as a personal disposition or a morphogenic trait. The common trait is universal to all people or it might be limited to the people in one culture. The individual trait is responsible for a person's uniqueness.

All traits are responsible for adaptive, expressive, and stylistic behavior. Traits and personal dispositions are not clearly observable but are inferred from behavior. A personal disposition represents a generalized predisposition to behavior for an individual (not for the general population). Some dispositions contribute more to an individual's behavior than do others. There are three types of dispositions. A cardinal disposition is so central to an individual's character that almost every action of that person is traceable to its influence. Central and secondary dispositions have less influence, respectively.

Allport's approach to psychology is above all humanistic as opposed to scientific. Allport disdains the application of the principles of natural science to psychology.

● PROBLEM 13-26

Describe and define the structure of personality according to Carl Rogers.

Solution: According to Carl Rogers, the structure of the personality is based on two constructs, the organism and the self. The organism is conceived to be the locus of experience; experience includes everything available to awareness and all that occurs within the organism. The phenomenal field is the totality of experience as perceived by the individual, therefore, it includes both conscious and unconscious experiences. In Rogers' terminology, conscious experiences are referred to as symbolized experiences; unconscious experiences are not symbolized. The phenomenal field is the individual's internal frame of reference; it is his subjective reality. For an individual to act realistically he must determine if his subjective reality, his symbolized experiences, is discrepant with objective reality, the world. If there is a discrepancy, the individual may behave unrealistically and thereby, detrimentally. An individual should strive to reduce the incongruence between subjective and objective realities.

The self is a portion of the phenomenal field. Thus, the self or self-concept refers to the organized and consistent set of perceptions that are self-referential, i.e., that refer to "I" or "me." It also includes the perceptions of the relationships between "I" or "me" and the rest of the world, including other people. This concept of self is usually referred to as a self-as-object definition as opposed to a self-as-process definition. Rogers defines the self as the person's attitudes and feelings about himself; it is not a concept of self in which the self governs behavior and controls adjustment. It is important to note that the distinction between self-as-object and self-as-process is not absolute; there is usually some overlap between the two. In addition to the self, there is an ideal self which represents what the individual aspires to be.

The importance of Rogers' distinction between the organism and the self emerges when the issue of congruence and incongruence is raised. Incongruence between the self as perceived and the actual experience of the organism results in the individual feeling threatened, anxious, and defensive; his thinking becomes rigid and constricted. An individual is considered mature, well adjusted, and psychologically healthy when there is congruence between the actual experience of the organism and the self-image. An example of an incongruence is the existence of hostile feelings together with an individual's self-image of being a nice person. Usually, the result of such a conflict will be a denial of the hostility because it is incongruent with the self-image. The denial results in anxiety and defensiveness. The defensiveness may result in the projection of the hostility to a different target so that it is perceived as something external to the individual. The individual perceives hostility in the treatment he receives from others. Congruence and incongruence also manifest themselves between subjective reality (the phenomenal field) and external reality and between the perceived self and the ideal self. Incongruence between the perceived self and the ideal self results in dissatisfaction and frustration.

The structure of the personality as conceptualized by Rogers is a highly organized and unified system. Rogers rejects atomism and segmentation in favor of gestalt theory. Briefly, gestalt theorists emphasize the "holistic" nature of things in the world. They believe that people perceive things in wholes, not in parts, segments, or atoms.

● **PROBLEM 13-27**

What is Carl Rogers' theory of motivation?

Solution: Carl Rogers' theory of human motivation is based on the assumption that the organism is a purely monistic dynamic system. This means that there is one universal, all-encompassing drive. According to Rogers, the one drive is the desire to "actualize, maintain, and enhance the experiencing organism." The basic tendency is to grow and to expand oneself especially by welcoming new experiences. To actualize means to have a person's real self or essence emerge and to replace any false aspects of his personality. A person's real self includes latent desires and disguised proclivities. A homosexual is self-actualized when he recognizes and accepts his attraction to members of his own sex and acts to fulfill his homosexual inclinations. Obviously, there are often differences between one's self-image (heterosexuality, for example) and one's organismic experience (homosexuality, for example). Both the self and the organism are driven to self-actualize at the same time. The individual must clearly perceive and adequately symbolize choices. Otherwise, he will not be able to discriminate between progressive and regressive ways of behaving; this is essential to achieving the goal of actualization. There is an important cognitive element involved in the drive to actualize. The individual must have some knowledge before he can choose but when he does acquire the knowledge he always chooses to grow rather than to regress. There is no biological necessity requiring the individual to progress.

Rogers speaks of "needs as experienced;" these needs

are all subservient to the basic striving of the organism to
maintain and enhance itself. However, he places special
emphasis on two needs: the need for positive regard and the
need for self-regard. Both are learned needs. Positive
regard refers to the positive assessment an individual receives from other people; the need for positive regard develops in infancy as a result of the love and care a baby receives. The need for self-regard is established as a result
of receiving positive regard from others. These two needs
are not always in congruence and can therefore interfere
with the actualizing tendency.

There are two tendencies to actualize: one to actualize the organism and another to self-actualize. If the
self-image and the organism are in congruence then the actualizing tendency remains unified. Otherwise, the self-
actualizing tendency and the tendency to actualize the organism may each work to the detriment of the other.

● **PROBLEM** 13-28

Explain the development of an individual who is not
psychologically well-adjusted, according to Rogers.

Solution: Rogers believes that though an individual
has the tendency to actualize himself, he is strongly influenced by the environment, especially the social environment.
Rogers' theory is that personal evaluations by others, particularly during childhood, result in a distancing or incongruence between the experiences of the self and the experiences of the organism. If a child experiences unconditional
positive regard, no conditions of worth will develop and the
child's self-regard will be unconditional. If the child's
self-regard is unconditional then the two needs for positive
regard and self-regard will not be at variance with organismic evaluation and the child will be psychologically adjusted.

Usually, a child's actions are evaluated by his parents, often negatively. The child learns to differentiate
between worthy (approved) actions and feelings, and
unworthy (disapproved) actions and feelings. The problem
is that unworthy experiences tend to be excluded from the
self-concept even though they are organismically valid;
this creates an incongruence between the organism and the
self and results in a maladjusted child. The maladjusted
child will experience tension, frustration, and dissatisfaction. The child who excludes certain aspects of his
personality from his self-concept because they have been
disapproved will be unable to self-actualize and therefore
will be unable to completely satisfy his organismic needs
and his latent desires. The child will become defensive
because he has denied certain aspects of himself. This will
have a negative effect on his interaction with other people.
His denied and therefore unconscious impulses will affect
his behavior even though they are not part of his self-image;
the child is not allowed to be what he really is but what
others want him to be. His "true values" are replaced with
spurious values. Thus, an individual's self-concept becomes
increasingly distorted. This situation often can be seen in

maladjusted adults who enhance and support a self-picture that is at variance with reality. It should be noted that Rogers' theory of emotional conflict is very similar to Freud's concept of the id, ego, and superego.

ADLER AND SHELDON

● PROBLEM 13-29

Describe Alfred Adler's theory of personality, pointing out its departures from Freudian theory.

Solution: To Adler the central core of personality functioning is a subjectively perceived sense of inferiority for which an individual strives to compensate by gaining superiority. Because of this, an individual's life-meaning could not be fully comprehended without knowledge of the goal toward which he or she was striving. He further felt that the normal, healthy individual was motivated by a goal that was related to his fellow man, that was rooted in his social interest, while the neurotic personality tended to have goals that were self-centered and egoistic. He felt there were three main life tasks which an individual had to master: vocational, societal and love tasks, and that only a socially useful type of individual with a high degree of activity could successfully master all three tasks.

At the beginning of his psychoanalytic career Adler was a member of Freud's circle of followers. In time, a dispute arose between him and Freud and he withdrew from that circle. Years after the disagreement Adler published a paper citing his differences with Freud's orthodox psychoanalysis. They can be summarized as follows:

(1) The ego: Adler saw the ego, not as a servant to the id's desires but as a creative intelligence attempting to make a healthy adaptation to life.

(2) The Oedipus Complex: Instead of being a purely sexual phenomenon, the Oedipal conflicts were seen by Adler to involve strivings to become superior to the father, to compete with the father.

(3) The significance of dreams: Adler disagreed strongly with Freud's interpretation of the meaning of dreams. For Adler the dream represented an attempt by the dreamer's unconscious to create an emotional state that upon waking would force him to take action that the person would otherwise be reluctant to take. Freud believed that dreams were the fulfillment of unconscious wishes that would be unacceptable in the waking state.

(4) Personality as fragmented: Adler felt that the person, rather than being motivated by states

of biological tension seeking to be reduced, had to be understood as an individual motivated by a drive to grow, to become whole, to be fully what he is. Adler preferred to think of the person as a whole rather than considering the separate parts of his personality.

● **PROBLEM** 13-30

How does the existential perspective explain personality development?

Solution: Among the major contributors to existential thought and therapy are Kierkegaard, Nietzsche, Sartre, Binswanger, Frankl, Laing, May, Tillich and Maslow. The existential psychologist is concerned with a process conception of human nature. Existentialists emphasize the living immediacy of experience. There is, therefore, a focus on the here and now rather than on the past as in psychoanalysis. Man is viewed as a complex of conscious processes, ongoing, changing and constantly striving toward a future state of self-fulfillment. Man is also seen to be unique among living beings in that he can become aware of his strivings.

One of the most important themes to the existential psychologist is the human struggle between being and non-being. This struggle involves not only life and death but full acceptance of oneself versus partial acceptance or rejection of parts of oneself. Being authentic versus being fraudulent is seen to be another major conflict for humans. To be authentic a person needs to be able to be honest with himself, to make commitments to life and to accept the risks and suffering involved in actualizing his full potential. Should a person not do this he will be phony, he will suffer a loss of meaning or alienation from himself. This is seen to be a major source for mental and personality disorders by the existentialist school.

Victor Frankl refers to the neurosis that develops from despair over the apparent meaninglessness of life as the noogenic neurosis. To him the "will to meaning" is more important and central in human life than Freud's "will to pleasure" or Adler's "will to power." This innate search for meaning raises man above the level of a mere robot or stimulus-response mechanism.

Man is thus seen as involved in a continual process of "being" or becoming something in the future--his full potential. Because man can be conscious of his existence at any given time, he also becomes responsible for his existence. Whatever interferes with this process may lead to ontological insecurity or the feeling that one is threatened by non-being.

● **PROBLEM** 13-31

Describe the system of somatotyping as proposed by Sheldon (1940).

Physique, temperament, and psychopathology

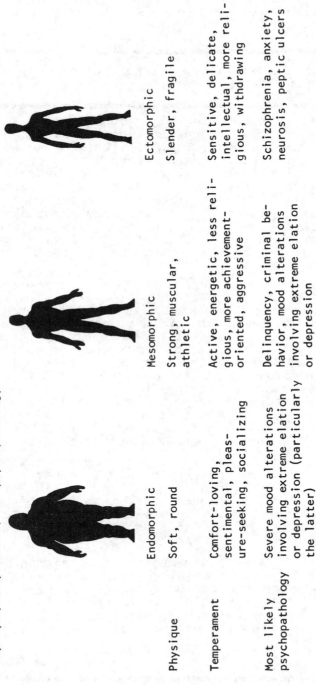

	Endomorphic	Mesomorphic	Ectomorphic
Physique	Soft, round	Strong, muscular, athletic	Slender, fragile
Temperament	Comfort-loving, sentimental, pleasure-seeking, socializing	Active, energetic, less religious, more achievement-oriented, aggressive	Sensitive, delicate, intellectual, more religious, withdrawing
Most likely psychopathology	Severe mood alterations involving extreme elation or depression (particularly the latter)	Delinquency, criminal behavior, mood alterations involving extreme elation or depression	Schizophrenia, anxiety, neurosis, peptic ulcers

500

Solution: Somatotyping is a system that attempts to describe personality in terms of an individual's physique. Sheldon defined three broad categories of body types: endomorph, mesomorph, and ectomorph. Endomorph refers to a soft and fat body; a mesomorph is a muscular, powerful body; and an ectomorph is a thin and frail body. Based on these body types, Sheldon concluded that each had its own peculiar set of personality traits.

An endomorph is characterized by a temperament that is jolly, relaxed, friendly and easy-going. William Howard Taft and Santa Claus are classic examples of endomorphs. A mesomorphic individual is brave, bold, aggressive, and powerful. A number of professional athletes could be considered mesomorphic. An ectomorph is a shy, weak, delicate and socially withdrawn individual.

Most American psychologists ignore Sheldon's findings. Clearly, few people fit into any one particular category. Such a simplistic system is not often useful.

BEHAVIORISM AND SOCIAL LEARNING THEORIES

● PROBLEM 13-32

Define behaviorism and social learning theory.

Solution: Behaviorism refers to a theory that considers only observable behavior. Behaviorists are not interested in mental processes that cannot be observed. B.F. Skinner, the major exponent of behaviorist theory, believes that "emotions" are fictional causes of behavior. This school of thought only measures and analyzes behavior that can be seen--namely, stimuli and responses. Indeed, behaviorist theory is concerned solely with stimulus-response (S→R) behavior.

Behaviorism considers the environment an extremely important influence upon child development. While Skinner has no elaborate or systematic theory of child development, he does see it as a building process. Each new experience adds to a child's dimension and molds him into the person he will eventually become. This view comes as no surprise since behaviorists, with their emphasis on behavior modification and behavioral shaping, see the individual's environment as crucial to his development.

Social learning theory is based on the fact that children imitate. Social learning theory is purportedly related to behaviorism since both involve the principles of operant conditioning (the reinforcement of an unsolicited response). Children's unsolicited imitation is reinforced through various means in social learning theory, either by the child himself or others around him.

Social learning theory is distinguished from behaviorism because social learning theory includes Freudian

concepts. However, it does not include Freud's concepts
of the unconscious and the basic instinctual drives.

Social learning theory is still being developed and
modified. The major components of this theory include the
importance of dependency as the major factor that brings
about socialization, and aggression as an energy that is
channeled into socially acceptable behavior as the child
matures.

● **PROBLEM** 13-33

What implications does the theorizing of B.F.
Skinner and other behaviorists have for personality theory?

Solution: B.F. Skinner has contributed much to
establishing the importance of operant conditioning in
learning and in the application of its principles to
personality development, psychopathology, educational
problems and to other areas. In operant conditioning, the
experimenter waits until the subject makes a desired response
and then rewards him for the response.

This school of thought objects to the postulation
of inner mechanisms as explanations for observable behaviors.
Inner drives of any type whether they be unconscious ids or
self-actualizing impulses are viewed as being equally irrelevant to explaining observed responses once the environmental stimuli controlling those responses are identified.
Thus, from a behaviorist's point of view, postulating
traits or inner drives is merely a redundant statement of
the behavior that has already been observed and serves more
to satisfy the fancy of the theorist than to advance the
knowledge and understanding of human behavior.

Implicit in operant conditioning is that the environment is responsible for the formation of an individual's
pattern of responses that can be labeled as his personality.
Through appropriate environmental control then, healthy
personalities could be programmed. It is, thus, necessary
for behavioral scientists to focus on controlling the
variables in the environment that act on the individual.

In the treatment of psychopathology, reward and
punishment would be seen as the most appropriate means of
altering the aberrant behavior of the patient. From this
point of view, enough punishment administered for unhealthy behavior patterns would eventually serve to remove
that behavior pattern and sufficient reward given for
healthy behaviors will eventually make that behavior pattern
a part of the individual's personality.

● **PROBLEM** 13-34

Describe social learning theory, as formulated by
Bandura and Walters.

Solution: Social learning theory, first described

by Miller and Dollard, is an attempt to combine the principles of social analysis of behavior with principles of
learning taken from the behavior scientist's animal laboratory. Beginning with a criticism of certain aspects of
Miller and Dollard's theory, Bandura and Walters have developed their own social learning theory with the emphasis
on the acquisition of responses through "modeling." Modeling consists of imitating the behavior of another person.
For modeling behavior to occur, the individual must have
the necessary skills to imitate the model and be motivated
to do so.

When accompanied by positive reinforcement, imitation
is an efficient technique for learning the social roles that
are expected of a person in various situations. With an
aggressive, fearful, suspicious, antisocial or hypochondriacal model, however, the individual will not learn socially
useful behaviors. Thus, the quality of models is quite
important in the development of psychologically healthy
responses.

They emphasize that the whole range of learned behavior can be acquired and also modified through modeling
or observational learning as it is also called. Observational learning involves four basic processes: attention
to the model, retention of the relevant model cues, reproduction of the model's performance and reinforcement. Reinforcement may be direct or vicarious. Learning can therefore take place merely by the imitator feeling the model's
rewards and punishments and modifying his own behavior as
a result. Subjects not only imitate their model's behavior,
they also create new behaviors within the same context. For
example, a child who sees an adult slapping a doll will not
only slap it when it is given to him, he may also hit it
with a bat.

The social learning theory of Bandura and Walters
has been applied to psychotherapy, modeled aggression and
tests of competing theories of model-identification. The
recent work has been carried on by Bandura after Walter's
death. Basing his work on established empirical laboratory
principles, Bandura has worked to extend behavior theory
beyond its stimulus-response-reinforcement early days. He
has begun to encompass the less observable but more human
aspect of people--their capacity to interpret and their
awareness of themselves as interpreters of their lives.

● **PROBLEM** 13-35

Discuss the four processes involved in observational
learning according to Bandura and Walters.

Solution: Starting from the premise that most complex human behaviors are learned through verbal transmission
and information and through observation of a skilled model,
Bandura and Walters have devoted much time and research to
the investigation of the process by which learning occurs
through observation. This process is also called "modeling." They have observed four processes through which this

type of learning occurs:

(1) Attention process--Exposure alone does not assure that learning will occur; it is also necessary that the learner pay attention to the model. Several variables have been found to affect learner attention including the distinctiveness and likeability of the model, the past history of reinforcement of the observer for attending to similar models, the psychological state of the observer, and the complexity of the behavior to be modeled.

(2) Retention process--The observer must have the capacity to recall what the model did.

(3) Reproduction process--The observer then must use memory to guide an actual performance. The student driver may recall the steps he observed in learning to parallel park: "Line the front wheels of your vehicle with the back wheels of the car in the space in front of the one into which you are going to park." Even with correct recall the performance will be influenced by the physical abilities of the learner. If a teacher is with the learner and is able to give feedback on parts of the parking process that have been incorrectly retained or for which a particular skill needs to be refined, the learning will take place more rapidly. Thus, abilities and feedback are important guiding processes during a learning experience.

(4) Motivational process--Although an individual may have acquired and retained the observed behavior, he will not translate it into behavior if that behavior is punishing. The student driver will find himself avoiding the need to parallel park if the first few times he tries it other drivers honk impatiently or yell at him for holding up traffic. If, on the other hand, the attempts at parking yield successful results or are reinforced by the encouragement of another person, the learner may be positively motivated to manifest the behavior he has learned.

● **PROBLEM** 13-36

The role of imitation in social learning processes was first systematically observed by Miller and Dollard. Discuss their major conclusions concerning the conditions that affect learning by imitation.

Solution: Experiments with children in different situations in which they were rewarded for imitating a model formed the basis of the conclusions made by Miller and Dollard concerning learning from models. Four types of models were found to be effective in learning situations.

The first type of model is imitated because of the status they are given through "age-grading". Generally, the older a person is the more status and prestige he is accorded. Children rapidly learn to copy the behavior or dress of their older acquaintances because such behaviors are perceived by the child to lead to the greater freedom or independence they think those older than themselves enjoy.

The next type of people that are likely to be imitated are those thought to be superior in social class. Wealth and power are easily discernible cues that greatly motivate the less socially powerful individual to imitate the behavior of those with the more desirable attributes.

Another type of person who is likely to be imitated is one that appears to be particularly intelligent or shrewd. In this sense, intelligence can be defined as the ability to read the environment and adapt quickly in order to obtain the rewards that are possible within the environment. The less intelligent do not learn to read the environment; instead, they copy those who can.

The fourth category of persons that will be readily imitated are specialists who have knowledge and skills due to their special training. In their area of expertise doctors, lawyers, plumbers, carpenters, and psychologists are seen as the interpreters of reality to those who have not had special training.

Of course, not all of these models will appeal to all individuals to the same degree. Generally, however, Miller and Dollard conclude that conditions of life in our society conspire to reward people to match and copy those around them. This tendency, they believe, probably derives strength from the fact that doing the same as others is rewarded in many situations, whereas being different is often a sign of punishment. Also, to be different from those one admires or has learned to feel safe with is a strong source of anxiety. Therefore, copying occurs to reduce unpleasant feelings as the dominant mode of adapting to social life.

SHORT ANSWER QUESTIONS FOR REVIEW

Choose the correct answer.

1. Learning not to respond to stimuli occurs in
    (a) habituation (b) extinction (c) de-
    sensitization (d) all of these (e) none of
    these

    d

2. Moving toward, away from, and against people are
    personality descriptions found in the formula-
    tions of (a) H.S. Sullivan (b) Karen Horney
    (c) Henry Murray (d) A. Adler (e) E. Fromm

    b

3. According to Freud, moral anxiety (a) is
    aroused only when punishment is threatened by
    the real world (b) is experienced by the id
    as guilt or shame (c) is experienced by the
    ego as guilt or shame (d) is experienced by
    both ego and superego as guilt and shame

    c

4. The id derives its psychic energy from (a)
    outer reality (b) the bodily process (c)
    the ego (d) from conflicts (e) the super-
    ego

    b

5. According to Skinner, a drive is (a) a stimu-
    lus (b) a physiological state (c) a psychic
    state (d) a need state (e) none of the above

    e

6. All Tropisms are 1. native rather than learned
    response 2. learned rather than native re-
    sponses 3. orienting responses to stimuli
    (a) only 1 is correct (b) only 2 is correct
    (c) 2 and 3 are correct (d) only 3 is cor-
    rect (e) 1 and 3 are correct

    e

7. Defining personality as "the end product of our
    habit systems" expresses a concept most charac-
    teristic of the psychological orientation termed
    (a) structuralistic (b) psychoanalytic (c)
    gestalt (d) personalistic (e) behavioristic

    e

8. While taking the Rorschach, a subject manifests
    naive verbalizations, unreflective responses,
    concreteness, literalness, and uses many cliches
    to express himself. The examiner would be
    justified in suspecting the operation of the
    defense mechanism of (a) projection (b)
    denial (c) repression (d) regression (e)
    reaction formation

    c

9. Allport, in his personality theory, places major
    emphasis on (a) traits, but not attitudes and
    intentions (b) traits and attitudes, but not

SHORT ANSWER QUESTIONS FOR REVIEW

intentions   (c)   traits and intentions but not
attitudes   (d)   traits, attitudes, and intentions   (e)   attitudes, but not traits or
intentions

d

10. The terms "anima" and "animus" refer to   (a)
the collective unconscious   (b)   the personal
unconscious   (c)   feminine and masculine archetypes   (d)   the shadow archetype

c

11. A person classified as an ectomorph would manifest which of the following types of trait
clusters?   (a)   somatotonia   (b)   somatotype
(c)   morphogenotype   (d)   cerebrotonia   (e)
phenotype

d

12. Multiple abstract variance involves the study of
(a)   trait differences between members of the
same family   (b)   heredity - environment correlations between siblings   (c)   heredity - environment correlations between parents and children
(d)   heredity correlations between siblings   (e)
none of the above

b

13. In the "conflict" type of frustration, the social
factor   (a)   is represented in overt group pressure   (b)   operates through the individual's attitudes and habits   (c)   is frequently present in
group attitudes   (d)   is due to the individual's
feelings

b

14. According to Adler, man is striving for   (a)
self-actualization   (b)   power   (c)   superiority
(d)   leadership   (e)   distinction

c

15. The driving force of mankind according to Adler
is   (a)   inferiority   (b)   incompleteness   (c)
perfection   (d)   self esteem

a

Fill in the blanks.

16. Human beings can learn new behaviors without obvious reward or reinforcement through _____ .

observa-
tional
learning

17. Conflict can be viewed as incompatibility
between _____ and _____ tendencies.

approach
and
avoidance

18. According to phenomenological theory, _____
is in the eye of the beholder.

reality

507

SHORT ANSWER QUESTIONS FOR REVIEW

19. According to Rogers, behavior disorders result
    from the individual's attempts to reduce _____ .

    incongruity

20. The idea that human behavior does not occur
    randomly, but in accordance with intrapsychic
    causes is known as _____ .

    psychic de-
    terminism

21. Because the _____ seeks to gratify its desires
    without delay, it operates on the _____ .

    id, plea-
    sure prin-
    ciple

22. Expressing taboo impulses through creative chan-
    nels is called _____ .

    sublimi-
    nation

23. Cattell developed a test called _____ to mea-
    sure the relative strength of _____ in indi-
    viduals.

    16PF, source
    traits

24. The _____ is characterized by a lack of sexual
    interest.

    latency
    period

25. In social learning theories, an emphasis is
    placed upon _____ as a content of personality.

    measurable
    behavior

26. Primary stimuli which impel behavior to satisfy
    primary needs are called _____ .

    drives

27. A test of _____ is made when the results obtained
    using a new test are compared against results
    which were obtained on previous tests.

    concurrent
    validity

28. A variation on the interview technique is
    _____ .

    field ob-
    servation

29. The most frequent use of psychological tests is
    to diagnose _____ .

    mental
    disorders

30. A fundamental assumption of Kelly's theory is
    that human behavior is determined by _____ .

    personal
    constructs

Determine whether the following statements are true
or false.

31. Psychologists use the term personality to refer
    to the organized, stable, individually charac-
    teristic properties of a person.

    True

32. Personality can be assessed directly.

    False

SHORT ANSWER QUESTIONS FOR REVIEW

33. In personality assessment, the assumption is
generally made that the person being assessed
is truthful and frank.   False

34. Projective tests are most useful in predicting
specific responses in specific situations.   False

35. According to Adler, feelings of inferiority are
the most important motivators of behavior.   True

36. Attitudes are permanent predispositions to react
in characteristic ways.   True

37. Jung assumes that man's behavior is governed by
social instincts.   False

38. The reality principle is obeyed by the superego.   False

39. The portion of the superego which punishes is
the conscience.   True

40. Trait theories try to classify the personality
on the basis of a single category.   False

41. According to Rogers, personality maladjustment
occurs when a difference develops between a
person's self-image and the reality of a
situation.   True

42. A distortion of reality in which an individual de-
ceives himself into believing is called a defense mechanism.   True

43. The psychological mechanism of which fugue is
an example is regression.   False

44. According to George Kelly, revealing a person's
constructs reveals his or her personality.   True

45. What matters in interpreting personality inventories is not the manner in which the subject
delivered his responses but rather to what categories of personality types the subject's responses correspond.   True

46. According to modern theoretical views, only the
ambiguity of the stimulus, and not the ambiguity
of the test situation, determines the stimulus
response.   False

47. The Holtzman inkblot test and the Rorschach are
equally difficult to investigate statistically.   False

SHORT ANSWER QUESTIONS FOR REVIEW

48. According to E. Fromm, transcendence refers to man's need to rise above his animal nature.

    True

49. Skinner's approach is based on the assumption that behavior is unorderly and that man's primary purpose is to control it.

    False

50. Systematic desensitization is a particular kind of counter conditioning.

    True

CHAPTER 14

BEHAVIOR PATHOLOGY

METHOD AND THEORY

● PROBLEM 14–1

> How has abnormal behavior been explained throughout history? How has it been treated?

Solution: Our earliest ancestors believed that abnormal behavior was caused by demons or evil spirits. Ancient skulls have been discovered with holes in them, leading historians and archaeologists to believe that people of ancient times practiced "trephining," a chipping of holes in the skull to let out evil spirits. Later the early Chinese, Egyptians, and Greeks exorcised demons through elaborate prayer rites or even flogging and starvation.

Hippocrates, of the 5th century B.C., was one of the earliest proponents of the "somatogenic hypothesis," which states that something wrong with the "soma" (physical body) disturbs thought and behavior. He also considered emotional and environmental stress to be causes of deviant behavior. Thus, deviant behavior became a matter for physicians to deal with, as well as priests, and as a result treatments became more oriented to physical health. Specifically, Hippocrates believed that the correct balance between the four "humors" of the body -- blood, black bile, yellow bile, and phlegm -- was responsible for mental health. Too much of any "humor" would lead to a particular ailment.

In the Middle Ages the devil was again thought to be responsible for mental illness. The medical model for mental illness of Hippocrates was rejected by the church during this period. The devil was seen as possessing the bodies of sinners and witches. Witch-hunting became an infamous and sad part of our history, and for more than two hundred years the only "treatment" for the mentally ill consisted of public death as "witches."

Witch-burning, 16th-century copper engraving.

Slowly, through the writings of a few more rational and scientific men, such as Robert Burton, who in 1621 wrote The Anatomy of Melancholy, the mentally ill again began to be considered in need of medical attention. This led to the creation of asylums and encouraged a somewhat more humane, if not ideal, treatment for these people. Philippe Pinel was a vital figure in the movement towards humanitarian treatment of the mentally ill. In charge of an asylum during the French Revolution, he began to treat "inmates" (for indeed asylums were little better than prisons before Pinel) as sick human beings rather than beasts. He removed their chains (literally) and they in turn became much more "manageable." When not treated as animals, Pinel's patients behaved as human beings. Pinel believed that the mentally ill should be treated with compassion and dignity, and he achieved some remarkable results by adhering to this principle.

More recently, Kraeplin (1883) distinguished between groups of symptoms (syndromes) in mentally ill individuals. He recognized two major groups of diseases: dementia praecox (an early term for schizophrenia) and the manic-depressive psychosis. These are the predecessors of our current classification system.

In the 18th, 19th, and 20th centuries, an alternative to the early medical somatogenic hypothesis developed. Called a "psychogenic" point of view, it attributed mental disorders to psychic malfunctions. Out of the psychogenic view of mental illness came the pioneering work of Sigmund Freud and the other psychoanalysts of the early 20th century.

Other contemporary psychologists (specifically the behaviorists) feel that there is a need to apply rigorous scientific tests to determine the true causes of, and the effectiveness of cures for, abnormal behavior. They point out that it is difficult, if not impossible, to test psychogenic theories in this way. For example, how can it be determined through experimentation that everyone goes through an Oedipal conflict as Freud asserts? Thus there is now a lively and continual divergence of opinion between the psychoanalysts and the behaviorists in the study of abnormal behavior.

This 15th-century German engraving emphasizes the belief held by medieval Christians that God could protect them from possession by demons.

● **PROBLEM 14-2**

Name and briefly explain three different models used today in the study of abnormal psychology.

Solution: The importance of models, theoretical ways of viewing information, in abnormal psychology cannot be overemphasized. The three predominant models of abnormal behavior are the statistical model, the medical model, and the learning model. The Statistical Model is concerned with distribution of specific behavioral and mental characteristics in the population. Almost by definition, a low frequency of occurrence of a certain characteristic within the general population results in this characteristic being seen as "abnormal." Thus, the statistical model can provide at most a partial description of what we mean by "abnormal."

A more useful model is the Medical Model. The critical assumption here is that abnormal behavior can be likened to a disease. Both somatogenic (originating in the body) and psychogenic (originating in the mind) causes are considered in this model. Both can occur internally (systemic or infectious) or externally (traumatic). Psychoanalytic theory can be considered an example of a psychogenic disease model. There are both systemic and traumatic disease components in Freudian theory. Systemic causes are exemplified by an innately weak "instinct," while traumatic components would include the varied and individually specific effects of external experiences on people.

The third major model in use is a Learning Model, which is closely related to "behaviorism." Here, the crucial assumption is that abnormal behavior is learned behavior and that it is learned in the same way as most other human behavior. In this model the importance of biological and genetic factors is minimized, so that the learning model is primarily psychogenic in nature. B. F. Skinner, an extreme behaviorist, does not refer to internal states (mental processes) at all in his writings, but other learning model theorists do use a "mediational approach" and do consider intervening mental and emotional processes. The viewpoint of these latter theorists is somewhat closer to a disease model of mental illness than Skinner, who rejects the medical models outright.

As yet, there are no overwhelming and conclusive data in support of any one model. Indeed, it is unlikely that any one of the above models will ever be able to fully account for all abnormal behaviors as the behaviors being dealt with, the varied experiences of people, and the people themselves, are so very complex. It may even be that more than one model is useful in explaining the behavior of a given individual. As it so often happens in the early stages of a science, we may eventually discover that each of the proposed models is partially correct and that what is needed is more research and a careful synthesis.

● **PROBLEM 14-3**

Briefly describe three general methods of assessing abnormal behavior.

Solution: Three common general methods for assessing abnormal behavior are the clinical interview, psychological tests, and direct observation. The most basic method of assessing behavior, one that occurs even in everyday life, is the interview. In a clinical interview, the interviewer attempts, through purely conversational techniques, to elicit certain information from the interviewee. The psychologist (just one example of an interviewer -- a pollster is another) probes the interviewee for certain important information. The clinical interview is an assessment technique widely used by professionals who adhere to both medical and learning models, though perhaps for different purposes. A psychoanalyst may be interested in obtaining information about the person's childhood, while a behaviorist may be more interested in learning about the kinds of anxiety-provoking situations in which the person may be currently involved.

A more complicated assessment procedure is the psychological test. The test results are often compared with the results of large groups of people allowing statistical norms to be established for comparisons. Some examples of different types of psychological tests are projective tests such as the Rorschach inkblot test which attempts to reveal unconscious thoughts and feelings, personality inventories such as the MMPI where the subject agrees or disagrees with a great number of statements, and standard intelligence tests.

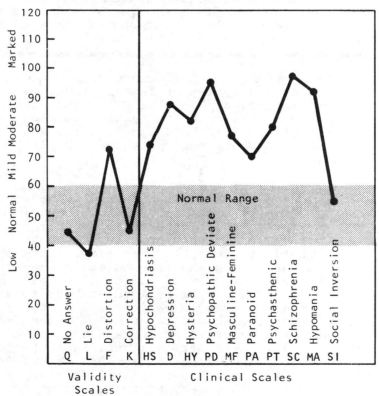

MMPI(Minnesota Multiphasic Personality Inventory)scores of a disturbed individual.

A third method of assessment is through direct observation of behavior. This can be of two kinds. A person's daily behavior may be sampled by an observer who does not attempt to affect the person's behavior. The observation may take place in a natural setting or the laboratory. On the other hand, a person may be asked to react to a situation set up by the experimenter. In this case, behavior is generally assessed before and after the "experimental manipulation."

In summary, three basic methods for assessment of behavior have been detailed. These include: (1) the interview, in which information about a person and his behaviors is elicited through (hopefully) skillful questioning of the person, (2) psychological tests in which information about an individual's personality and behavior must be inferred from written answers to predetermined questions, and (3) direct observation of behavior, which may occur in either a natural or an experimental setting.

● **PROBLEM 14-4**

Behavior disorders are commonly classified by professionals according to categories defined by the American Psychiatric Association in their <u>Diagnostic and Statistical Manual</u> (DSM). This classification system was recently revised to address criticisms of earlier versions of the manual. What were some of the criticisms of the earlier classification system?

Solution: The American Psychiatric Association (APA) has developed a classification system of mental illnesses known as the Diagnostic and Statistical Manual (DSM). The most recent is the DSM-IV-TR. The classification system has been criticized on the grounds that (1) the diagnostic classes are not homogeneous, (2) the system is not reliable, and (3) the system lacks validity.

Whenever a class is formed, the behavior of all its members should be similar along the dimensions distinguishing the classification. That is, there should be some behavioral homogeneity. For example, one of the defining characteristics of an obsessive-compulsive are the intrusive thoughts which the patient seems unable to control. If we were to examine a group of people who had been classified as obsessive-compulsives, we would expect them to all display the symptom of intrusive thoughts. However, many studies have found that knowing what diagnostic category a patient falls into tells relatively little about the actual behavior of the patient. It is commonly found that certain symptoms appear in a number of diagnostic categories, thus making it difficult to predict reliably what the diagnosis will be given the occurrence of a symptom. The problem was that the earlier diagnostic system did not adequately specify how many of these various symptoms must be present or the degree to which they must be manifest in order to make a diagnosis. The second criticism referred to the reliability of the classification (diagnostic) system. Whether or not different diagnosticians will agree that a given diagnostic label should be applied to a particular person is the test of reliability. For a classification system to work, those applying it must be able to agree on what is and what is not an instance of a particular class. There are 3 major reasons why diagnosticians do not always agree: (1) inconsistencies on the part of the patient, such as giving certain information to one diagnostician and not to another, (2) inconsistencies on the part of the diagnostician, such as differences in interview techniques and interpretation of the symptoms, and (3) inadequacies of the diagnostic system, such as unclear criteria. Either too fine a distinction was required or the system forced the diagnostician to choose a category that was not specific enough. In diagnosing abnormal behavior, no infallible measurement device exists; the only means of assessing reliability is whether or not diagnosticians agree.

The third criticism of the classification system was its lack of validity. Whether or not predictions (or valid statements) can be made about a class once it has been formed is the test of validity. Validity has a very specific relation to reliability: the less reliable a category is, the more difficult it is to make valid statements about the category. Since reliability of the earlier diagnostic system was not entirely adequate, by definition, we can expect that its validity will not be adequate either.

● **PROBLEM 14–5**

Describe the five axes of DSM-IV-TR used to describe psychological disorders and their related problems.

Solution: The five axes used in diagnosing mental disorders are 1) clinical disorders, 2) personality disorders, 3) general medical conditions, 4) psychosocial and environmental problems, and 5) global assessment of functioning. All mental disorders are included in axes 1 and 2 (clinical and personality disorders, respectively). Thus these disorders all represent some form of behavioral or psychological dysfunction. The reason for separating personality disorders from other conditions is to discourage clinicians from overlooking them (they are often not as obvious as the other disorders). Axis 1 disorders include schizophrenias, mood disorders, anxiety disorders, dissociative disorders, eating disorders, and others. In contrast to these disorders, personality disorders involve rigid, maladaptive personality traits that are subjectively distressing to the individual or impair his or her ability to get along with others. One might say they involve 'normal' traits and behaviors that are carried to an extreme. The better-known of these ten disorders include the antisocial personality, narcissistic personality, and histrionic personality. The third axis describes medical conditions that caused, exacerbated, or stemmed from the mental disorder; concussions (resulting in amnesia) or cirrhosis (resulting from alcoholism) are examples. Similarly, the fourth axis describes psychosocial or environmental problems that might be related to the mental disorder; for example, divorce or a

death in the family. Finally, an assessment of global functioning describes how well the individual functions in everyday life (e.g., getting along well with others and making good
use of leisure time or being enmeshed in conflictual relationships).

● **PROBLEM 14–6**

Briefly describe the 15 major categories of abnormal behavior from Axis 1 (clinical disorders) of the Diagnostic
and Statistical Manual (DSM-IV-TR) of the American Psychiatric Association.

Solution:

Disorders Usually First Diagnosed in Infancy, Childhood,
or Adolescence is self-explanatory and includes mental retardation, conduct disorders, attention-deficit disorders,
bedwetting, and separation anxiety.

Delirium, Dementia, and Amnestic and Other Cognitive
Disorders involve changes in cognition (e.g., memory loss, an
inability to focus or shift attention, disorientation), specifically that result from medical conditions and/or substances (drugs, toxins, medicines).

Mental Disorders Due to a General Medical Condition include disorders that are generally also listed elsewhere in
DSM-IV-TR but that, for a specific individual, are known or
believed to have their origins in a medical condition (and are
not substance induced).

Substance-Related Disorders include disorders that result from abuse of a drug (e.g., alcohol, nicotine, cocaine),
the side-effects of a medication, or exposure to a toxin.
These would include dependence on, intoxication from, and
withdrawal from various addictive substances.

Disorders in which psychotic symptoms are especially
prominent are described under Schizophrenia and Other Psychotic Disorders. These symptoms include hallucinations (i.e.,
false perceptions), delusions (i.e., false beliefs), disorganized and chaotic speech patterns, and catatonia (a lack of
responsiveness to one's environment).

Mood Disorders are characterized by a disturbance in
mood and include depressive disorders and bi-polar disorders
(which involve alternating between depression, on the one
hand, and states of heightened excitement, optimism, and
arousal, called 'mania,' on the other).

Anxiety Disorders are characterized by fearfulness, apprehension, or even terror. These feelings are often accompanied by shortness of breath, a fear of losing control, the
sensation of being smothered, and palpitations. Anxiety dis-

orders include panic attacks, phobias (intense and irrational fears of objects or situations), and post-traumatic stress.

The Somatoform Disorders category describes disorders involving physical symptoms that cannot be explained in terms of a medical condition, substance use, or another psychological disorder. With conversion disorders, for example, the individual has unexplained symptoms involving voluntary motor functioning or sensory functioning. Thus someone with this disorder might be blind, but the blindness is associated with psychological factors (e.g., stress) rather than neurological ones.

By contrast, Factitious Disorders involve deliberately producing or faking physical or psychological symptoms in order to assume the role of someone who is sick. Moreover, the individual does this in the absence of any external incentives (e.g., winning a lawsuit).

Dissociative Disorders involve the fragmentation of personality; the sense that one part of consciousness, memory, or identity has separated (i.e., "dissociated") from other parts. Amnesia and dissociative identity disorder (formerly known as "multiple personality disorder") are examples of dissociation.

Sexual and Gender Identity Disorders include sexual dysfunctions, which involve disturbances in sexual desire or in the psychophysiological changes of the sexual response cycle and either are distressing to the individual or cause problems within a relationship; paraphilias, in which unusual objects, situations, or activities are the individual's preferred means of achieving sexual gratification; and gender identity disorders, which involve discomfort with being one's own sex and an identification with the other sex.

Eating Disorders involve abnormal eating behavior and unrealistic perceptions of one's body (typically, seeing oneself as fatter than one is). Anorexics diet incessantly and refuse to maintain a normal body weight. Bulimics binge on food and then vomit, use laxatives, fast, or exercise excessively in order not to gain weight.

Sleep Disorders either involve abnormalities in the amount, quality, or timing of sleep, or involve unusual behaviors or physiological occurrences being associated with sleep. Narcolepsy, for example, involves sudden attacks of sleep.

Impulse-Control Disorders Not Elsewhere Classified involve a failure to resist urges or temptations. (This lack of impulse control is evident in a number of disorders described in other categories, as well.) Kleptomania, for example, is characterized by an inability to resist stealing, and pyromania is characterized by an inability to resist setting fires.

Adjustment Disorders involve emotional or behavioral responses (to stressors) that interfere with a person's ability to function normally or are distressing to him or her.

Name and describe four kinds of psychological tests used to assess abnormal behavior. Give an example of each.

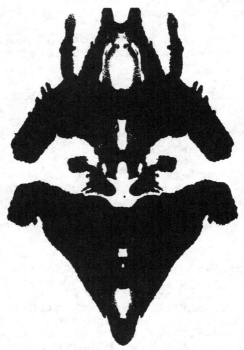

The Rorschach Inkblot Test

Solution: Four commonly used psychological tests are projective personality tests, personality inventories, organic brain dysfunction tests, and intelligence tests. Projective personality tests are exemplified by the Rorschach inkblot test and the Thematic Apperception Test (TAT). In both cases either ambiguous designs (Rorschach) or ambiguous pictures (TAT) are shown to the subject who must respond with a story or description of what he sees in the ambiguous stimulus. The underlying assumption is that because of the ambiguous nature of the stimulus, the subject's response will reveal inner (unconscious) anxieties and motivations. The responses are scored by professionals trained to interpret the responses. Ordinarily, projective techniques are utilized by psychoanalytically-oriented individuals. There are problems with the use of projective tests, especially concerning the lack of reliability (agreement) among interpreters and the test's validity (we never can know, by definition, if the test is actually measuring what it is intended to measure).

Personality inventories, typified by the Minnesota Multiphasic Personality Inventory (MMPI), are standardized tests which present statements to which the subject either

agrees or disagrees. Inventories are used as diagnostic tools
and are especially useful as a relatively inexpensive substitute for the clinical interview. Often included in personality inventories are questions used to detect false responses
to the test, usually statements which almost everyone either
agrees or disagrees with.

Other tests include those used to detect organic brain
dysfunction. Besides X-rays and EEG's (electroencephalogram),
psychiatrists have developed forms of I.Q. tests (for example,
the Trail-Making Test) which are able to detect specific brain
malfunctions.

Standard intelligence tests, such as the Scholastic Assessment Test, are used to predict academic achievement. These
tests are widely used and are generally considered successful
(although there is a feeling that these tests are often culturally biased and thus penalize members of various sub-cul-
tures).

● **PROBLEM 14-8**

Some, though not all, psychologists believe in using
the scientific method for the study of behavior disorders.
What is the basis for "science" in psychology? What
factors are important in the scientific study of psychology?

Solution: A major problem in the study of psychology today
concerns the lack of agreement on theoretical questions and on
solutions to problems among psychologists who adhere to different paradigms or "schools." Many believe that rigorous
scientific research is the only way to gain more complete
answers to the vital questions concerning abnormal behavior.
In this context, science is considered a search for knowledge
through systematic observation and testing of predictions
based on theory and previous research.

There are three important factors to be considered in
the scientific study of abnormal behavior. First, hypotheses,
or claims, must be testable. For example, if it is asserted
that traumatic experiences in childhood lead to problems in
adulthood, this idea must be testable to be confirmed or
disconfirmed by scientific methods.

Second, observations and experiments must be reproducible under the same experimental circumstances by other scientists. This is the concept of reliability.

Certain phenomena, however, are not possible to observe.
For example, a magnetic field is a readily accepted concept in
science, although it is not observable as such. In psychology, inferred or theoretical concepts are resorted to when
necessary. For example, anxiety is a concept, not an observable event, though one can observe trembling and measure an
increased heartbeat.

521

In addition, the inferred concept must be operation-alized, i.e. given an operational definition, a definition based on a set of observable, measurable events. An operational definition of anxiety might include certain psycho-physiological changes occurring during a certain situation (test-taking, for example). Thus we see that the scientific method can be usefully applied to psychology today. Using testable hypotheses, reproducible experiments, and operational definitions of postulated concepts, it is hoped that valid and reliable conclusions regarding abnormal behavior can be drawn.

● **PROBLEM 14–9**

Name and briefly describe four methods of research in abnormal psychology. What are some pros and cons of each method?

Solution: Four major methods of research in abnormal psychology are the experiment, correlational studies, mixed design studies, and single-subject research. The experiment is usually considered the best method for studying causal relationships between events. In an experiment, two groups are chosen randomly. One is designated to be experimentally manipulated (the treatment, condition, that is to be evaluated), while the other condition, called the control group, does not receive the experimental manipulation. The control subjects serve as a basis for comparison. In this way, causes of any changes that occur during the experiment to the first group can be distinctly attributed to the experimental condition. Of course, there are many complex issues involved in experimental design. These will be covered in another chapter.

Using an experiment to study abnormal psychology is quite often not possible due to ethical considerations. It would be highly unethical to create abnormal behavior in human subjects in order to obtain knowledge of its causes. Correlational studies are often used as a less than perfect alternative. Here, the main concern is the relationship of one variable with another. For example, height and weight are usually positively correlated, i.e., tall people tend to be heavier than short people. To obtain this correlation methodically, pairs of observations (such as height and weight of numerous individuals) are obtained. In abnormal psychology it is possible to determine the relationship between social class and schizophrenia, for example. However, even if an extremely high positive correlation between lower-class individuals and schizophrenia were found, i.e., if it were found that schizophrenics had a very strong tendency to be from the lower classes, it could not be stated that one is the cause of the other. Hence the axiom "correlation does not imply causation." This is the main drawback to correlational studies, as the knowledge obtainable from any one study is strictly limited.

In a research method called mixed design, experimental and correlational techniques are combined. The purpose of a mixed design study is to identify precisely to which subjects the experimental condition can best be applied. The different types of populations used are considered the correlational aspects of the study, while the applied conditions or treatments are the experimental factors. One problem with mixed design studies is that they are analyzed statistically as experiments, even though they are partially correlational studies. This can lead to some inappropriate interpretations, such as cause-effect relationships.

The case study, a collection of information on a single individual concerning his or her past, is one common example of single-subject research. Though rather different from the previous techniques, case studies (or "histories") can contribute immensely to our knowledge by providing a detailed description of a particular syndrome. This affords the opportunity to generate many new hypotheses. Another form of single subject research is the single-subject experiment in which an individual is observed methodically before, during, and after an experimental manipulation. Generally, the subject is observed, the subject's experience is manipulated by the experimenter (the experimental condition), and then the subject is observed again in the "pre-condition state." If the subject's behavior returns to the pre-condition state, it is assumed that the experimental manipulation produced the change. The experimental condition is then reimposed to test the reliability of the finding. The major drawback to single-subject research is that findings cannot be generalized.

ANXIETY AND PHOBIAS

● **PROBLEM 14–10**

Describe three methods of assessing anxiety. Why is anxiety a crucial concept in abnormal psychology? Discuss the concept of anxiety as a "construct."

Solution: Anxiety is a crucial concept in the study of abnormal psychology because it is considered to be both a symptom and a cause of varying disorders. Often acute anxiety is considered a disorder in and of itself.

Since anxiety is so important for the study of abnormal behavior, there is a definite need for a way of measuring it in individuals. Three techniques are currently available: self-report, observation of overt behavior, and employing physiological indices.

In the self-report technique, subjects may offer their own subjective impressions of anxiety describing their experience in their own needs. Methodologically, however, this does not allow for comparison between subjects since the subjects give very different descriptions and may have very different standards as to what they mean by "anxious." To overcome these difficulties researchers developed self-report question-

naires to measure anxiety. The Taylor Manifest Anxiety Scale
(MAS) is a commonly used questionnaire of this type. The
statements are taken from the Minnesota Multiphasic Personality Inventory (MMPI), a general personality inventory with
many dimensions. The items which comprise the MAS are those
statements which correlate highly (negatively or positively)
with an independent measure of anxiety.

Overt behavioral measurement usually involves a trained
clinician observing a particular individual's behavior to
determine whether or not the individual appears to be anxious.
This involves a commonsense, and therefore unscientific, measure which is difficult to quantify. Examples of what the
clinician might look for are nail-biting and trembling. Since
anxiety involves a change in the individual's psychological
state, the observer must know what the normal behavior of the
individual is (the so-called "base-rate" of behavior). An
individual who always bites his nails is not considered to be
anxious when he is observed biting his nails. In fact, the
nail-biting might be soothing and the cessation of nail-biting
might in itself result in anxiety. Another example of overt
behavioral measurement is the observation of a discrepancy
between expected and actual performance. If a student normally does "A" work in a class and gets a "C" on a test (assuming that the rest of the class does as expected), then it
could be inferred that the student was anxious at the time
that he took the test. Excessive anxiety usually results in
an impairment of performance.

Finally, physiological changes are known to occur when a
person is anxious. Examples of such physiological changes are
increased pulse rate, rapid breathing, and sweating (this
corresponds to the arousal of the sympathetic nervous system).
Typically, the psychologist will have a base rate measurement
for an individual's physiological functions. These measurements are taken in an environment that does not induce anxiety. When a subject is then in an anxiety-inducing situation,
the meaningful change in the individual's physiological functions is obtained by comparing the new measures with the base
rates. One of the most important physiological measures of
anxiety is the galvanic skin response (GSR), which is the
change in electric potential across the skin surface. The GSR
changes with the increase or decrease in moisture on the skin.
Thus palm sweating, a common indication of anxiety, results in
an increased GSR. The GSR is measured by a galvanometer (the
famous, or infamous lie detector). Electrodes are taped onto
the subject's skin; these electrodes measure electrical potential. The electrodes are connected to wires which are connected to a machine which records the GSR's on a moving roll
of paper with a needle which moves up and down according to
the intensity of the GSR. A large jump by the needle indicates a big change in the GSR; for people who are given a lie
detector test, this is interpreted as a lie, or at least that
they are unusually anxious about answering the question.

Physiological methods used to measure anxiety do not
assess anxiety per se. They actually are measuring certain

definable correlates of anxiety. This is because anxiety itself is a psychological "construct," i.e., an inferred, not observable, phenomenon. The measures of anxiety, considered apart from a specific situation or context, may be meaningless. Rapid heartbeat, for instance, may be an indicator of sexual excitement, not anxiety. Thus, anxiety can be considered a scientific or psychological construct, useful mainly in organizing data and generating hypotheses. As a construct, it is linked to observable behavioral phenomena by the methods of assessment discussed above.

● **PROBLEM 14-11**

Discuss three contrasting explanations of the phenomenon of anxiety.

Solution: Anxiety is construed in different ways by different theorists. The psychoanalytic theory of neurotic anxiety is concerned with overstimulation (overstimulation refers to the existence of many impulses, wishes, and needs that cannot be gratified); learning theorists use a stimulus-response explanation; and other theorists utilize the concepts of control and helplessness.

Freud (psychoanalytic theory) based his final theory of anxiety on the idea that anxiety becomes a signal of future overstimulation. If overstimulation (by id impulses, for example) is allowed to occur, the person may be reduced to a state of extreme helplessness as at birth (which is the prototypical anxiety situation). Anxiety thus signals the ego to act prior to overstimulation.

Neurotic anxiety is the fear of the consequences of allowing a previously punished impulse to be expressed. As an example, a child develops neurotic anxiety when he or she has begun to associate punishment with the satisfaction of a particular wishful impulse. Neurotic anxiety accompanies the continued desire for gratification of this impulse. This kind of anxiety is related to a fear of the loss of love; the child imagines that gratification of a particular impulse will not only yield punishment but loss of love as well. Neurotic anxiety differs somewhat from the kind of anxiety that signals overstimulation.

Behaviorists consider anxiety to be an internal response that may be learned through classical conditioning. A tone, followed by a shock, can be shown to produce fear in rats even when the shock is subsequently taken away. Fear (or anxiety) in this stimulus-response analysis is both an internal response and a drive (which is related to avoidance behavior). However, this type of analysis has not been shown to be useful in dealing with anxious people. Since anxiety is a psychological construct and is not clearly identifiable with any set of behaviors, behaviorists are at a loss to explain it adequately. Many behaviorists reject the concept of anxiety altogether and prefer instead to discuss behavioral manifestations of "internal responses." In fact, B. F. Skinner denied that consideration of "internal responses" has any use and suggested that we should only consider overt behaviors when analyzing "behavioral problems."

One common thread in the psychoanalytic and learning theories of anxiety is the issue of control. The ego cannot control the threat of overstimulation, and the rat cannot control the painful stimulus. Experimental evidence with both humans and animals has demonstrated the importance of feelings of control or helplessness in the development of anxiety. A lack of control, or a perceived lack of control of a particular situation may lead to anxiety.

● **PROBLEM 14-12**

Discuss the anxiety disorders listed in DSM-IV-TR.

Solution: Five general categories of anxiety disorders might be distilled from DSM-IV-TR: (1) Panic disorders, (2) generalized anxiety disorders, (3) phobic disorders, (4) obsessive-compulsive disorders, and (5) stress disorders. In the anxiety disorders, some form of anxiety is either the most predominant disturbance in the clinical picture -- as with panic disorder and generalized anxiety disorder -- or anxiety is experienced if the individual tries to resist giving in to his symptoms -- avoidance of a dreaded object or situation in a phobic disorder, and obsessions or compulsions in an obsessive-compulsive disorder.

The chief features of panic disorders are recurrent anxiety attacks and nervousness. The panic attacks occur at times other than during marked physical exertion or a life-threatening situation. During such an attack, the patient may feel as if he is out of control or about to die, or he may have premonitions of impending disaster. Generally there are many physiological correlates such as rapid heart rate, irregular breathing, excessive sweating, choking, dizziness, or trembling.

Chronic (at least six months), generalized, and persistent anxiety characterizes a generalized anxiety disorder. The anxiety in this disorder is not manifested in the specific symptoms that characterize the other anxiety disorders. In order for a diagnosis of generalized anxiety disorder to be made, the anxiety should manifest itself in at least three of the following six ways: (1) restlessness, edginess, or feeling keyed-up; (2) being easily fatigued; (3) having trouble concentrating; (4) irritability; (5) muscle tension; and (6) sleep disturbance.

Phobic disorders are characterized by strong, irrational fears of specific objects or situations. For example, when a person is extremely fearful of heights, closed spaces, snakes or spiders, provided there is no objective danger, the label phobia is likely to be applied to his avoidance and fear. A person suffering from a phobic neurosis knows what he is afraid of and almost always recognizes that his fear is irrational, but he cannot account for his fear or control it. Two common phobias, both of which are discussed in some detail in DSM-IV-TR, are agoraphobia -- fear of leaving home, and social phobia -- fear of social situations.

Although they are separate symptoms, obsessive and compulsive reactions often occur together as an anxiety disorder. Obsessions are persistent, often unreasonable thoughts that cannot be banished. A person may become obsessed with the idea that he will swear, make obscene gestures, or even commit murder. A compulsion is a persistent act which is repeated over and over. Virtually any behavior can be viewed as a compulsion if the individual reports an irresistible urge to perform it and experiences considerable distress if prevented from doing so.

Stress disorders (post-traumatic stress disorder, acute stress disorder) involve reactions to traumatic events. Those stress reactions might not appear for months or more after the trauma has occurred. Furthermore, the event would have involved experiencing, witnessing, or otherwise being confronted with actual or threatened serious physical injury, or even death, to oneself or others. The individual's response would have included intense horror, fear, or helplessness, as well as dissociation. Typically, the individual also avoids anything associated with the traumatic event.

● **PROBLEM 14–13**

Discuss the theories of phobias that are based on classical conditioning. What are some criticisms of these theories?

<u>Solution:</u> Classical conditioning theory suggests that phobias develop when an object or situation which is not frightening in itself, is paired with a frightening stimulus, with the result that the fear associated with the frightening stimulus comes to be elicited by the previously neutral object or situation. Classical conditioning employs its own terminology to describe this conditioning situation. The frightening stimulus is called the unconditioned stimulus (UCS), and the natural response it elicits -- fear -- is the unconditioned response (UCR). The object or situation with which the unconditioned stimulus is paired is called the conditioned stimulus (CS). After conditioning is established, both the unconditioned stimulus and the conditioned stimulus elicit the same response -- fear. This response, when elicited solely by the conditioned stimulus, is called the conditioned response (CR).

A description of a classic experiment (Watson and Raynor, 1920) concerning the development of phobias may help to make classical conditioning theory easier to grasp. Albert, an eleven-month-old boy, was shown a white rat (CS). At first Albert had no fear of the rat and appeared to want to

play with it. But whenever he reached for the rat, the experimenter made a loud noise (UCS) by striking a steel bar
behind Albert's head, causing Albert fright (UCR). After five
such experiences, Albert became very disturbed (CR) by the
sight of the white rat, even when the steel bar was not
struck. The fear initially associated with the loud noise had
come to be elicited by the previously neutral stimulus, the
white rat. This experiment is summarized in the chart below:

Initial Situation	rat (CS) ⟶ no fear loud noise (UCS) ⟶ fear (UCR)
Conditioning Period	rat (CS) loud noise (UCS) — presented together ⟶ fear
Conditioning Established	rat (CS) ⟶ fear (CR)

     Many learning theorists have elaborated on the case of
little Albert by asserting that the classically conditioned
fear of an objectively harmless stimulus forms the basis of an
instrumental avoidance response. This formulation holds that
phobias develop from two related sets of learning: (1) via
classical conditioning, a person can learn to fear a neutral
stimulus (the CS) if it is paired with an intrinsically painful or frightening event (the UCS). (2) Then the person can
learn to reduce this conditioned fear by escaping from or
avoiding the CS. In this second kind of learning, the response is acquired and maintained by its reinforcing consequences.

     Several criticisms have been made of the classical con-
ditioning model of phobias. First of all, several attempts to
replicate the Watson and Raynor demonstration have failed.
This indicates that the classical conditioning model may not
be as powerful as the Watson and Raynor experiment suggests.
Secondly, clinical reports indicate that phobias may develop
without prior frightening experiences. Many individuals with
fears of snakes, airplanes, and heights tell clinicians that
they have had no unpleasant experiences with any of these
objects or situations. Thus the classical conditioning model
does not appear to account for the acquisition of all phobias.
Thirdly, questions have been raised as to whether laboratory
avoidance behavior in animals (which serve as subjects in most
classical conditioning experiments) and phobic reactions in
humans are really analogous. Avoidance responses learned in
the laboratory are adaptive because they enable an animal to
avoid a noxious stimulus. Phobic behaviors in humans are

maladaptive; they prevent the individual from functioning
normally. Also, it is often dangerous to generalize about
man's behavior on the basis of the behavior of infrahuman
species.

● **PROBLEM 14–14**

Using two classic examples, compare the psychoanalytic and
behavioral conceptions of the onset of phobias.

Solution: Psychologists differentiate between a fear and a
phobia according to the rationality of a particular fearful
response. An irrational, exaggerated fear is usually referred
to as a phobia. Phobias typically have debilitating effects
on an individual's ability to function successfully in his
social environment. Psychoanalytic and behavioral (learning)
theorists explain the onset of phobias employing two quite
different models. Each model has its own classic case history
to refer to when explaining phobic reactions.

Freud (1909) reported the classic case of "Little Hans,"
a little boy who was so afraid of horses that he wouldn't
leave his house. When Hans was three he was reported to have
had an unusually strong interest in his penis. When he was
three and a half his mother observed him playing with his
penis and threatened to "cut it off" if he continued to play
with it. Later, it became evident through conversation with
his mother that he possessed a desire for sexual contact with
her.

Since Hans was not allowed to satisfy his sexual desire
for his mother without punishment, he repressed this desire.
The manifestation of the repression of his sexual attraction
to his mother was (neurotic) anxiety.

Hans first demonstrated his fear of horses six months
after the "sexual incident." He witnessed an accident in
which a horse collapsed on the street and wanted to run home
to his mother.

This information (of course this is a highly simplified
version) was interpreted by Freud to be a demonstration of
Hans' desire to eliminate his father (of whom the horse was a
symbol) so that he could possess his mother. In the accident
that Hans witnessed the collapse of the horse represented a
satisfaction of Hans' unconscious desire to be rid of his
father; the satisfaction of this desire resulted in anxiety
due to the guilty feelings associated with wanting to be rid
of one's father. After Hans saw the collapse of the horse he
ran home; his father was symbolically dead and he could possess his mother.

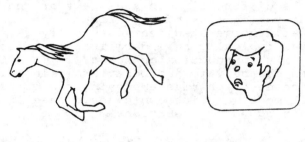

1. The outdoor scene as a neutral stimulus.

2. The falling horse produces fear and anxiety.

3. The association in time between the neutral stimulus and the fear-producing stimulus.

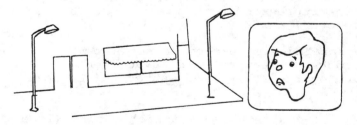

4. A classically conditioned response of fear to the outdoor scene.

Classical conditioning of Little Hans' phobia

Since horses represented his father and the memory of the collapsed horse was a satisfaction of his guilt-provoking desire to be rid of his father and possess his mother, Hans developed a phobic reaction to horses. The possession of his mother was associated with the castration threat which Hans feared. Thus, the avoidance of horses allowed Hans to forget his memory of the collapsed horse (which represented his dead father) and to avoid the ensuing castration anxiety.

Behavioral theories vary in their views of phobias, though they all consider phobias to be learned behaviors. The classic experiment by Watson and Raynor (1920) with Little Albert, typifies the classical conditioning model of the onset

of phobias. Little Albert was an infant when it was demonstrated that he could be conditioned to fear a white rat.
When he first was shown the animal he demonstrated no fear and
seemed to want to play with the rat. But when he would reach
for the rat, the experimenter would cause a loud noise by
striking a steel bar. After five pairings of the sound while
Albert reached for the rat, Albert became very disturbed by
the sight of the rat, even when the sound did not occur. He
thus became afraid of the white rat, a previously neutral
object.

Actually, the fear of the white rat was just the beginning of Albert's phobia. Albert's fear generalized to other
white haired animals, to all small animals of any color, and
finally just to fur itself.

In these two classic cases then, Hans became afraid of
horses due to repressed sexual attraction for his mother and
the consequent fear of castration which was displaced to a
symbol, while Albert became phobic of a white rat and other
associated neutral objects through simple classical conditioning. Evidence, however, suggests that not all phobias are
learned from classical conditioning, nor is it probable that
all phobias are acquired by the symbolic satisfaction of repressed wishes as is suggested by Freudian theory. Thus, neither theory is definitive, but both cases are extremely
important in the historical development of theories of the
onset of phobic reactions.

● **PROBLEM 14–15**

Discuss the modeling theory of phobic disorders and some
criticisms of the theory.

Solution: The modeling theory of phobic disorders assumes
that phobic responses may be learned through the imitation of
others. The learning of phobic reactions through modeling is
generally referred to as vicarious conditioning. Vicarious
conditioning may take place through both observation and verbal instruction.

One study done by Bandura and Rosenthal (1966) demonstrated the effects of vicarious conditioning (observing a
model). Subjects watched a model in an aversive conditioning
situation. The model was hooked up to an array of electrical
apparati. Upon hearing a buzzer, the model feigned pain. The
physiological responses of the subject witnessing this behavior were recorded. After the subject had watched the model
"suffer" a few times, the subject demonstrated an increased
emotional response when the buzzer sounded. The subject began
to react emotionally to a harmless stimulus even though he had
had no direct contact with the noxious stimulus.

Phobic reactions may also be learned verbally through
another's description of what might happen if some activity is
engaged in. For example, a mother may repeatedly warn her

child not to play with matches lest he start a fire and burn himself and his family to death. In this way, the mother is providing a vicarious example through words.

There are a number of faults in the modeling theory of phobic disorders. First, it has been shown that vicarious fear extinguishes quickly. Secondly, phobics who seek treatment seldom report that they become frightened after witnessing someone else's distress. Also many people have been exposed to aversive experiences of others without developing phobias. Thus it seems that the modeling theory fails to provide an adequate model for all phobias.

MOOD DISORDERS

● PROBLEM 14–16

Describe the two major physiological theories of depression.

Solution: These are two major theories concerning what physiological processes may be disrupted to bring on depression. Both theories implicate biochemical factors. The first theory is concerned primarily with electrolyte metabolism and the second with the chemicals involved in neural transmission.

Electrolytes dissolve and dissociate into electrically charged moving particles which carry electric current. Two of the most important electrolytes are sodium and potassium chlorides. The positively charged sodium and potassium particles are distributed differently on either side of the membrane of a nerve cell. There is a higher concentration of sodium outside the neuron and a higher concentration of potassium within it. This difference helps maintain what is referred to as the "resting potential" of the cell. Alterations in the distribution of sodium and potassium produce changes in the resting potential, which in turn affect the excitability of the neuron, that is, whether it is readily excited and thus fired by impulses transmitted from another neuron.

Research has found that in depressed patients there is an elevated concentration of sodium within the neuron. The effect of such a relatively high concentration is to lower the resting potential of the neuron, making it more excitable. Data in addition to those on intracellular sodium levels (e.g. studies which show a higher than normal arousal pattern in the EEGs of depressives) indicate that the depressive's nervous system is hyperexcitable, even though his behavior patterns might make us expect it to be less excitable than that of the normal individual. Not enough is known about the specific relationships between the nervous system and behavior to explain how the apparent hyperexcitability of the depressive's nervous system causes the symptoms of depression. However, the data indicating that the depressive has a greater than normal intracellular level of sodium, and thus a more excitable nervous system, suggests that electrolytes may play a causal role in depression.

The other physiological theory of depression is in almost opposition to the preceding one. This theory suggests that depression results from retardation of the transmission of impulses from one neural fiber to another. It should be noted that whereas the theory discussed previously applies to the entire nervous system, this theory applies only to the sympathetic nervous system and its neurotransmitter norepinephrine. Several pieces of evidence support this theory indirectly. Experiments performed with dogs have shown that "depressed" dogs have low levels of norepinephrine. Drugs that have proven to be effective in treating depression are known to facilitate neural transmission in the sympathetic nervous system by increasing the availability of norepinephrine. Thus it is also conceivable that depression is caused by diminished levels of norepinephrine.

● **PROBLEM 14–17**

Discuss Beck's cognitive theory of depression.

<u>Solution:</u> Many psychological theorists, Freud for example, see man as a victim of his passions, a creature whose feelings exert control over his intellectual capacities. In Beck's theory of depression, the cause-effect relationship operates in the opposite direction.

The basic tenet of Beck's theory is that depressed individuals feel as they do because they commit characteristic logical errors. Beck's position is not that the depressive thinks illogically in general, but that the depressive draws illogical conclusions concerning his evaluation of himself. Thus, an event that would be irritating to a normal person -- for instance, the malfunctioning of a car -- is interpreted by the depressive as an example of the utter hopelessness of life.

These errors in thinking constitute what Beck calls "schemata," or characteristics which determine and structure how the person perceives the world. The depressed person is seen as operating within a schema of self-depreciation and self-blame. Beck describes several logical errors often committed by depressed people in interpreting reality: (1) arbitrary inference -- a conclusion drawn in the absence of sufficient evidence or of any evidence at all. For example, a person concludes that he is worthless because it rains on the day that he hosts an outdoor party; (2) selective abstraction -- a conclusion drawn on the basis of but one of many elements in a situation. A businessman blames himself for the failure of a project, even though he was only one of many people who worked on it; (3) overgeneralization -- a sweeping conclusion drawn on the basis of a single event. A student regards his poor performance in a single class on one particular day as proof of his stupidity; (4) magnification and minimization --

gross errors in evaluating performance. A person believes that he has completely ruined his car (magnification) when he sees that there is a slight scratch on the rear fender, or a person still believes himself worthless (minimization) in spite of several notable achievements.

In order for Beck's theory to be supported, two criteria must be met. First, depressed patients, in contrast to non-depressed individuals, must think in the illogical ways that Beck has enumerated. This point has tentative confirmation, at least in Beck's clinical observations.

Second, it must be shown that the cognitive distortion exhibited by depressives does in fact cause the depressed mood and is not simply a result of being depressed. Beck has found that depression and cognitive distortions are correlated, but a causal relationship cannot be determined from such data, Illogical thoughts could cause depression, as Beck maintains, or depression could cause illogical thoughts. Finally, it could be the case that depression and the illogical thoughts that Beck has observed in depressives are both caused by some third variable, such as a biochemical disturbance, and that the correlation is thus spurious (not causal).

● **PROBLEM 14–18**

What is Freud's psychoanalytic theory of depression? What are some criticisms of this theory?

<u>Solution:</u> Freud's theory of depression stems from his views on development and on the unconscious processes involved in mourning. In order to understand his theory of depression, we must first describe these views.

Freud saw the potential for depression being created early in childhood, specifically during the oral period. During this stage, which lasts through the first year of life, the anatomical location of the sexual instinct is the mouth. The child is presumed to enjoy stimulation of the mouth region through touch and taste and use of muscle. If the child receives too little or too much "oral gratification" in this stage, he may develop an "oral fixation," which may result, according to Freud, in his being overly dependent on other people for the maintenance of his self-esteem.

Freud's view of mourning also plays a role in his theory of depression. Freud hypothesized that after the loss of a loved one the mourner "introjects" the lost person into himself; that is, he identifies with the lost one. Because, as Freud asserted, we often unconsciously harbor negative feelings against those we love, after introjection the mourner becomes the object of his own hate and anger. In addition, the mourner may also resent being deserted by the lost one and may feel guilt concerning real or imagined sins against the lost person. The period of introjection is normally followed by the period of mourning work, during which the mourner recalls memories of the lost one and thereby separates himself from the deceased individual.

The normal process of mourning work may go astray in overly dependent individuals (individuals fixated at the oral stage) and develop into an ongoing process of self-blame and depression. Such an individual does not loosen his emotional bonds with the deceased loved one and instead continues to castigate himself for the perceived faults in the (still introjected) loved one. Thus, the mourner's anger toward the lost one continues to be directed inward upon himself. Using the above analysis Freud maintained that depression is anger turned against oneself.

However, it appears that many people become depressed and remain so without having recently lost a loved one. In order to maintain the viability of his theory in the face of evidence suggesting that this was indeed so, Freud invoked the concept of "symbolic loss." For example, a person may unconsciously interpret a rejection as a total withdrawal of love. A symbolic loss must be worked through in the same way as a real loss. In each case, the unconscious processes of introjection and mourning work are brought into play. In overly dependent individuals, these processes can go astray and result in depression, whether the loss be real or symbolic.

There are several problems in Freud's theory. First, since the person presumably hates and loves the individual he has lost, why is it that only the hate and anger are turned inward and not the love? If the mourner directed his positive feelings concerning the lost one inward, he would be a happy rather than a depressed person. Freud fails to explain why only negative feelings towards the lost one are introjected.

A second difficulty lies in Freud's hypothesis that the seeds of depression are sown in an oral fixation. Freud states that fixation at the oral stage is caused by either too much or too little gratification; however, he gives no indication of how much gratification is enough to prevent fixation. Freud's theory, being nonquantitative, does not adequately deal with the question of what amount of gratification is involved in fixation.

The term "symbolic loss" presents a third problem. This concept is introduced only after the fact, to account for depression in which there has been no loss of a loved one. The concept would not be invoked for people who are not depressed. It is inferred only after a diagnosis of depression and only after no actual object loss can be discerned.

● **PROBLEM 14–19**

Discuss mood disorders as they are described in DSM-IV-TR.

<u>Solution:</u> Mood disorders are characterized by a disturbance of mood accompanied by related symptoms. Mood is defined as a prolonged emotion which colors the whole psychic life and generally involves either depression or elation.

The first subclassification of mood disorders has to do with the predominant mood displayed by the patient. In mood disorders, mood tends to be at one extreme or the other. The patient may be depressed, or he may be manic, or he may exhibit bipolar symptoms -- that is, he may alternate between the extremes of depression and mania. Symptoms of depression include loss of energy, loss of interest or pleasure in sexual activities, feelings of self-reproach, and recurrent thoughts of death or suicide. Some manic symptoms are hyperactivity, decreased need for sleep, loquacity (talkativeness), inflated self-esteem, and excessive involvement in activities without regard to their painful consequences (e.g., buying sprees, foolish business investments, sexual indiscretions, reckless driving). Another symptom of mania is "flight of ideas," which refers to rapid shifts in conversation from one subject to another based on superficial associations. It can be seen, then, that patients with mood disorders may be classified as depressed, manic, or bipolar, depending on which kinds of mood-related symptoms they manifest.

The second dimension along which mood disorders are distinguished has to do with the onset and duration of the individual's disorder. Mood disorders can be characterized as episodic or chronic.

The essential feature of episodic mood disorders is an episode of illness with a prominent and persistent disturbance in mood which is clearly distinguished from prior functioning. Here the onset of the disorder is relatively clear. Episodic mood disorders include major depressive disorder (one or more episodes of depressed mood lasting at least two weeks), manic episodes (at least one week of elevated, expansive, or irritable mood), and bipolar disorder (one or more manic episodes, as well as major depressive episodes).

Mood disorders are classified as chronic when there is a long-standing (at least two years) illness with either sustained or intermittent disturbance in mood. Chronic disorders usually begin in early adult life without a clear onset or specific cause. Generally, the mood disturbances involved in chronic disorders are more prolonged but not so severe as those manifested in episodic disorders.

The chronic mood disorders include dysthymic disorder (two years of depressed mood for more days than not) and cyclothymic disorder (two years of alternating depression and mania). A chronic depressive disorder is characterized by a feeling of sadness. The depressed mood may be either persistent or intermittent and separated by periods of normal mood. These normal periods may last a few days to a few weeks; a diagnosis of dysthymic disorder is not made if there has been a normal period of two months or more.

The essential feature of cyclothymic disorder is a chronic disturbance involving numerous periods during which there are some symptoms characteristic of both the depressive and manic syndromes but not of sufficient severity to meet the criteria for a depressive or manic episode. The manifestations of the two syndromes may be separated by periods of normal mood lasting as long as several months. In some cases the two syndromes are intermixed, or they may alternate.

ALCOHOLISM, ANTISOCIAL PERSONALITY, AND CONDUCT DISORDERS

● **PROBLEM 14–20**

Discuss three different psychoanalytic theories of alcoholism.

Solution: The psychoanalytic view of alcoholism attempts to explain the origin of habitual drinking rather than the maintenance of the behavior. Many of the analytic accounts of alcoholism point towards fixation at the oral stage of development as a precipitating cause. There are, however, several other psychoanalytic theories with different explanations of alcoholism.

One theory by Knight (1937) proposed that the alcoholic's experience with an overprotective mother has created in him a strong need to remain dependent. When this need is frustrated, he becomes angry and aggressive and thus feels guilty about his impulses. The individual then drinks heavily to reduce those impulses and also to punish those who are withholding affection.

Fenichel (1945) argues that being frustrated by the mother turns the young male child toward his father, which produces unconscious homosexual impulses. Later, these repressed impulses compel him to drink in bars with other men. This supposedly allows the alcoholic to obtain some of the emotional satisfaction he has not received from women.

Bergler (1946) emphasized the self-destructive nature of alcoholism. He hypothesized that alcohol addiction is a means of attempting to destroy a bad mother with whom the individual has identified.

● **PROBLEM 14–21**

Describe the characteristics of Korsakoff's psychosis and Wernicke's syndrome.

Solution: Korsakoff's psychosis is a disorder associated with alcoholism which was first described in 1887 by the Russian psychiatrist Korsakoff. The major symptoms of Korsakoff's psychosis are loss of memory for events which have occurred recently, time and space disorientation, and a tendency to make up stories to fill in the forgotten past. Current research indicates that Korsakoff's psychosis probably results from vitamin B and other nutritional deficiencies. Such deficiencies can occur in non-alcoholics, however it is most commonly found in alcoholics as a result of their characteristically poor eating habits. In addition it appears that there are increased vitamin requirements resulting from excessive alcohol consumption.

Wernicke's syndrome is also an alcohol related disorder. very often this disorder is classified with the organic pathologies since it involves pathological changes in the brain stem. The characteristic symptoms are memory loss, confusion, eye dysfunctions, and apathy. It is easily confused with Korsakoff's syndrome and its relation to alcoholism is also through a vitamin (specifically thiamine) deficiency.

Treatment usually consists of increased dosages of the deficient vitamin and an attempt to reduce (if not eliminate) the patient's alcohol consumption.

● **PROBLEM 14-22**

According to Jellinek (1952) what progression does the life of an alcoholic usually follow?

Solution: On the basis of an extensive survey, M. E. Jellinek described the alcoholic as progressing through four stages on the way to addiction. They are: 1) the prealcoholic phase, 2) the prodromal phase, 3) the crucial phase, and 4) the chronic stage.

The prealcoholic phase may last from several months up to two years. In this stage the individual drinks socially and also on occasion heavily to relieve tension. In time the occasions for seeking the effect of alcohol occur with greater regularity.

The prodromal phase is marked by blackouts. The drinker remains conscious and does not appear to be greatly intoxicated, but later he has no recall of what transpired. Alcohol begins to be used more as a drug and less as a beverage. The individual becomes preoccupied with his drinking.

In the crucial phase, the individual has lost control of his drinking. Once a single drink is taken, he continues to consume until he is in a stupor. The individual's social adjustment begins to deteriorate. He begins to drink in the day and neglects his physical health. He might go on a "bender," a several-day period of excessive drinking. At this stage the individual still has the ability not to start drinking, but if he has just one drink, the whole pattern will begin again.

In the final chronic stage, drinking is continual and benders are frequent. The body has become accustomed to alcohol and without it the individual will suffer withdrawal reactions. The individual may suffer from malnutrition and other physiological changes. Having lost his self-esteem, he may feel little remorse about any aspect of his behavior.

● **PROBLEM 14–23**

What did the results of the Oakland Growth Study (Jones, 1968, 1971) indicate about the relationship between personality and the use of alcohol?

Solution: The Oakland Growth Study was a long term research project begun in the 1930's in Oakland California. It consisted of a large sample of children who were studied in great detail and followed up at periodic intervals (studied longitudinally). In the mid-1960's many of these middle-aged individuals were contacted again and interviewed concerning their current alcohol consumption patterns, their reasons for drinking, and their attitudes toward drinking. Based on their answers the individuals were classified into five categories. The information that had been collected on the members during their junior and senior high school years was extensive. Reports on classroom behavior, personality tests, and peer ratings were used. These data were then correlated with adult drinking patterns.

The adult male problem drinkers were characterized in high school as less aware of impressions made on others, less productive, less calm, more sensitive to criticism, and less socially perceptive. It was found that the problem drinkers still retained traits from adolescence such as impulsiveness, extroverted behavior, and a tendency to overemphasize their masculinity. This pattern of poor social adaptation apparent even in high school may have served as the source of stress that induced heavy drinking patterns. The women, with the same pattern of social difficulties were found to be either problem drinkers or individuals who, interestingly, followed total abstinence.

● **PROBLEM 14–24**

What personality characteristics are associated with antisocial personality?

Solution: An antisocial personality (sometimes referred to as "sociopathy") can be viewed as an individual who is basically unsocialized and whose behavior patterns bring him into conflicts with society repeatedly. A group of more distinct characteristics has been formulated by H. Cleckley.

The characteristics Cleckley defines are: 1) average or superior intelligence, 2) absence of irrationality and other commonly accepted symptoms of psychosis, 3) no sense of responsibility, 4) disregard for truth, 5) no sense of shame, 6) antisocial behavior without apparent regret, 7) inability to learn from experience, 8) general poverty of affect, 9) lack of genuine insight, 10) little response to special consideration or kindness, 11) no history of sincere suicide attempts, 12) unrestrained and unconventional sex life, and finally 13) onset of sociopathic characteristics no later than early twenties.

One of the most important aspects of sociopathy is the lack of emotional response from the individual after committing an antisocial act. This lack of shame or guilt can be linked to the sociopath's inability to learn from experience, particularly to avoid punishment. Because the sociopath does not become emotionally aroused easily, he is less likely to suffer from and change his antisocial ways. Many sociopaths have a history of repeated legal and/or social offenses.

The sociopath has little or no regard for social values and norms. They are incapable of significant loyalty to individuals or groups and tend to be selfish individuals.

● **PROBLEM 14–25**

What is a conduct disorder and how is it usually treated?

Solution: A conduct disorder is essentially the childhood equivalent of antisocial personality, although an individual with a conduct disorder doesn't necessarily become an antisocial adult. The primary characteristic of the disorder is repeated violations of other people's rights or age-appropriate social norms. These violations typically involve aggressive, threatening behavior; non-aggressive behavior that causes property damage or loss; theft or lying; and serious violations of important rules.

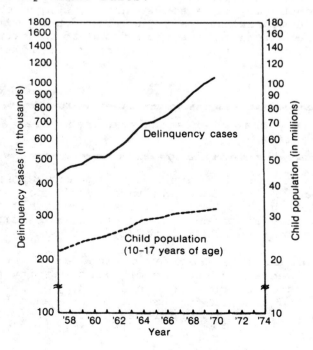

540

Because of the inherent characteristics of the delinquency itself, it is very difficult to correct. The most
successful means of treatment to date has been the development
of therapeutic communities where the delinquents learn societal norms and how to use them. This type of learning situation often includes group therapy. In addition many
psychologists feel that the best and most challenging treatment for delinquency is prevention.

SEXUAL BEHAVIOR

● **PROBLEM 14-26**

Suppose that a young woman agrees to pose nude for a
group of professional photographers. Could the photographers be considered voyeurs in such a situation? Could
the woman be classified as an exhibitionist? Explain your
answers.

Solution: Before arriving at any conclusion, the meaning of
the terms "voyeur" and "exhibitionist" must be explained. A
voyeur is an individual who achieves sexual pleasure through
clandestine "peeping" (as in "peeping Tom"). The element of
risk associated with the conditions of peeping is an important
factor in how the voyeur derives sexual pleasure. Voyeurs are
frequently males who concentrate on watching females undress-
ing or on couples engaging in sexual relations.

Exhibitionism involves the intentional exposure of the
genitals to members of the opposite sex under inappropriate
conditions. The exhibitionist receives gratification from
observing the reactions of the victims, who are involuntary
observers, usually complete strangers.

The photographers would not be considered voyeurs, as
such, because the situation in which they are engaged is neither clandestine nor socially unacceptable. A voyeur only
derives pleasure because of the secret nature of the act.
Furthermore, the woman would not be classified as an exhibitionist because her exposure is conducted in an appropriate
and accepted manner.

● **PROBLEM 14-27**

What is a fetish? Discuss how psychoanalytic and learning
theories would account for the development of fetishes.

Solution: Through cultural and personal preferences almost
any physical object can come to be regarded as sexually arousing. An interest in a particular part of the body would not
normally be considered a fetish, unless this interest is so
strong that the rest of the person is disregarded. A fetish
can be defined as a centering of all or nearly all sexual
interest on some body part or on an inanimate object, such as

an article of clothing. Use, contact, or thoughts about these
objects are a source of sexual excitation for the individual
and can become a dominant force in the individual's life. For
example, a man may be so enthralled with women's feet that he
takes a job as a shoe salesman even though he could qualify
for a better position. The attraction felt by the individual
is involuntary and irresistible.

The inanimate objects that are common sources of arousal
for fetishists are underwear, shoes, stockings, gloves, toilet
articles, and the like. The method or mechanics of using
these articles for the achievement of sexual excitation and
gratification varies considerably, but it commonly involves
kissing, fondling, tasting, or smelling the object. Often
fetishistic objects are used in conjunction with masturbation.

There are several different theories which attempt to
account for fetishistic behavior. Psychoanalytic position is
that fetishes, like other deviations, serve as some sort of
defense mechanism, warding off anxiety concerning normal
sexual contacts. Learning theorists, on the other hand, believe fetishism to be the result of some kind of classical
conditioning experience in the person's social-sexual history.
Sexual arousal may have been elicited by a strong emotional
experience involving some particular object or part of the
body. In an experiment by Rachman (1966) a photograph of
women's boots was repeatedly shown with slides of sexually
stimulating nude females. The subjects eventually came to
exhibit sexual arousal to the boots alone.

● **PROBLEM 14–28**

Describe the four-stage cycle of sexual arousal, as given
by Masters and Johnson (1966).

Solution: After eleven years of study on sexual response in
men and women, Masters and Johnson were able to delineate a
four-stage cycle of sexual arousal for both sexes. The four
stages are: (1) the excitement phase, (2) the plateau phase,
(3) the climatic or orgasmic phase and (4) the resolution
phase.

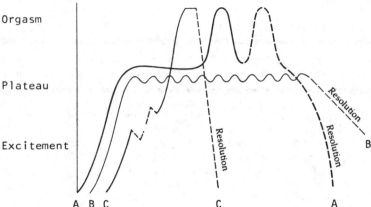

Female sexual response cycle, showing three typical patterns
A, B, and C.

542

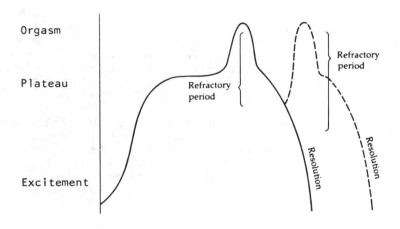

Male sexual response cycle.

The excitement phase is initiated by whatever is sexually stimulating to the particular individual. If stimulation
is strong enough, excitement builds quickly, but if it is
interrupted or if it becomes objectionable, this phase either
becomes extended, or the cycle may be stopped. If stimulation
is continued, it produces increased levels of sexual tension.
This increased tension leads to the plateau phase.

In the plateau phase, if the individual's drive for
sexual release is not strong enough, or if stimulation ceases
to be effective, the woman and/or man will not experience
orgasm. Consequently, he or she will enter a long period of
gradually decreased sexual tension.

The climactic, or orgasmic, phase is a totally involuntary response. It consists of those few seconds when the body
changes resulting from stimulation reach their maximum intensity.

During the resolution phase, there is a lessening of
sexual tension as the person returns to the unstimulated
state. Women are capable of having additional orgasms if
there is effective stimulation during this phase. The resolution period in the male, however, consists of a period which
varies in length among individuals when restimulation is impossible (the refractory period).

● **PROBLEM 14-29**

How did Kinsey investigate homosexuality among men and
women? What differences did he find in the incidence of
homosexuality in men and women?

Solution: In his investigation of homosexuality in men and
women Kinsey used interviewers trained to elicit from individuals self reports of intimate information on present and
past sexual practices. The individuals in Kinsey's study were
chosen to achieve a wide geographic, economic, and

socioreligious distribution. Because the findings indicated that many men and women were neither exclusively homosexual nor exclusively heterosexual, the Kinsey group developed a rating scale. This scale was designed to place the individual on a continuum from zero to six with zero being entirely heterosexual and six being entirely homosexual.

In comparing the sexual activities of men and women, it was found that women indicated a much lower incidence of homosexuality than men. Whereas 37 percent of men had experienced homosexual orgasm after adolescence, only 13 per cent of the women had. Only 3 percent of women had been primarily or exclusively homosexual at any given age period, compared with a figure of 10 percent for men.

In addition, it was found that whereas homosexual men were often highly promiscuous, 71 percent of the women who made homosexual contacts restricted them to either one or two partners.

● **PROBLEM 14–30**

What are some criticisms of the work of Kinsey?

Solution: Kinsey's research on American sexual customs during the 1940's and 1950's was critically received largely, perhaps, because of the controversial nature of the reports. The three major criticisms centered on 1) problems in the interview, 2) sampling problems, and 3) generality of the data.

There are four criticisms of Kinsey's interview techniques. The first being that each interviewer was free to rephrase questions and probe at his own discretion. Because of such latitude in interview procedure, interviewers did not always produce comparable data. It appears that differences in the behavior of the interviewers produced significantly different answers from the respondents. A second concern was that all interviewers for both studies were male. It has often been found that the sex of the interviewer has an effect on what the respondent will be willing to report. For example, more sexual experiences are reported when the interviewer and respondent are of the same gender. A third criticism was that respondents' self reports may have been biased, for example towards attempting to appear normal and to avoid disapproval. The fourth concern was that some questions required that the respondent report retrospectively concerning their adolescence. As a result the reports may have been subject to the distortions that time and experience may impose on memory.

The second major criticism of the reports concerned possible sampling deficiencies. Through lectures and public relations efforts, various groups were asked to participate in the study, but not every member of the groups came to these meetings. In the male sample of sixty-two groups it was found

that members of forty-two of these groups had generally attended college. This suggests greater willingness among men
who have attended college to participate in a study involving
potential embarrassment. But the manner in which the data was
reported precludes an assessment of the effects of this
greater willingness to participate found among better educated
groups. Another problem with the sampling was the intentional
exclusion of nonwhites. Properly speaking, the reports refer
to white Americans.

The third criticism of the reports concerned the
generalizability of the data. Kinsey made sweeping conclusions about men based on responses of less than two hundred
individuals. Kinsey also made numerous highly complex interpretations and evaluations, some of them very prescriptive but
often unsupported by the data. For example, of the 179 males
who engaged in the least amount of sexual activity, Kinsey
asserted that 52.5 percent of all American males were timid or
inhibited individuals, afraid of their own self condemnation
if they were to engage in any sort of sexual activity.

● **PROBLEM 14-31**

How does Freudian theory account for homosexuality?

Solution: The basis for psychoanalytic interpretations of
homosexuality is the concept of heterophobia, (fear of sexual
contact with the opposite sex). This fear is traced back to
events in early life. The Oedipal conflict and its resolution
are regarded as crucial to the direction sexual preferences
take.

In the first years a child is thought to be bisexual,
responding to human contact regardless of gender. Around the
age of four the male child notices differences between his
mother and father. Incestuous wishes by the male child to
replace the father in the mother's affections come to the
fore. The gratification of these sexual desires is thwarted
by the threat of punishment from the father-rival, the para-
mount threat being that of castration. If the boy cannot
resolve the conflict by repressing his desire for his mother
and identifying with his father, he may try to escape from his
Oedipal conflict by avoiding all sexual contact with women.
Women come to represent the young man's unconscious unresolved
incestuous feelings toward his mother.

As he reaches adulthood the conflict may lead the young
man to fantasize that his penis will be injured by insertion
into a woman's vagina. The sight of a woman's genitalia,
because she is without a penis, can trigger castration anxieties. The young man can then have sexual relations only with
another male who, because he does have a penis, will not remind him of the threat of castration.

Describe the Feldman-MacCulloch theory of homosexuality.

<u>Solution:</u> The theory of homosexuality proposed by Feldman and MacCulloch (1971) incorporates both biological and learning elements as conditions in the development of sexual preferences. They distinguish between primary and secondary homosexuals.

Feldman and MacCulloch suggest that there are "male" and "female" areas in the brain of the human fetus which are susceptible to circulating levels of male and female hormones. The brain of the human fetus may be "preset" before birth to foster the development of masculine or feminine behavior in early childhood. If the actual biological and anatomical gender of the child is male and his brain was affected by female hormones, in childhood he will behave in a feminine way, especially if his parents encourage this behavior. However, the predisposition supplied by female hormones will not inevitably make the child a homosexual.

Primary homosexuals are homosexuals with no history of heterosexual arousal or behavior. Because of their hormonal predisposition they lean towards and may be readily conditioned into forming homosexual attachments.

In contrast, secondary homosexuals show conventional development of heterosexual interests into puberty. At some point they have an unpleasant experience with a woman and begin to be afraid of approaching females. They justify their growing fear and avoidance of women by changing their attitudes towards them. Sexual attachments to men, which were previously viewed negatively, now become more appealing and the young man may "experiment."

Finally, the particular subculture in which the person finds himself will markedly affect the extent to which homosexual attractions develop.

SCHIZOPHRENIA AND RELATED DISORDERS

What are the features of schizophrenic behavior?

<u>Solution:</u> The disordered behavior of schizophrenic patients can be organized into disturbances in several major areas -- cognition, perception and attention, affect or emotion, motor behavior, and contact with reality. Usually a patient diagnosed as schizophrenic will exhibit only some of these disturbances. The diagnostician must decide how many problems must be present, and in what degree, to justify the diagnosis of schizophrenia.

Disorders of cognition include thought disorders and delusions. Thought disorder is a behavior that is absolutely essential to a schizophrenic diagnosis. Disturbances in a schizophrenic's thought processes are manifested in his verbal behavior. Usually a schizophrenic will speak incoherently, making references to ideas or images that are not connected. Often he will use neologisms (words made up by the speaker). Thought may also be disordered by loose associations. The individual may have difficulty sticking to one topic, often drifting off on a series of idiosyncratic associations. Another aspect of the schizophrenic's associative problems is the use of clang associations. The patient's speech contains many words associated only by rhyme; for example, "How are you in your shoe on a pew, Doctor?" The words follow one another because they rhyme, not because they make logical sense.

Delusions, another type of cognitive disorder, are beliefs contrary to reality that are firmly held in spite of contradictory evidence. Typically, schizophrenics have delusions of persecution, grandeur, or control. A person with delusions of persecution believes that others are plotting against him. With delusions of grandeur the person believes that he is an especially important individual, such as a famous movie star or Christ reincarnate. Delusions of control involve the person's believing that he is being controlled by some outside force, such as alien beings or radar waves. Delusions may be transient or systematized -- systematized delusions are highly organized delusions which become the dominant focus of a person's life.

Disorders of perception and attention are often evident in the reports of schizophrenic patients. Some mention changes in the way their bodies feel. Parts of their bodies may seem too large or too small, or there may be numbness or tingling. Some schizophrenics remark that the world appears flat or colorless. The most dramatic distortions of perception are called hallucinations, sensory experiences in the absence of any relevant stimulation from the environment. The hallucinations of schizophrenics are not the meaningless patterns of colors and sounds such as may occur during a drug experience. Rather, schizophrenics may hear voices or music, or they may see unreal people or objects. In addition, schizophrenics often have trouble attending to what is happening around them. For example, a schizophrenic may be unable to concentrate on television because he cannot watch the screen and listen to what is being said at the same time.

Three affective abnormalities are often found in schizophrenic patients. In some, affect may be flat; that is, virtually no stimulus can elicit an emotional response. Other patients display inappropriate affect. The emotional responses of these individuals do not fit the situation. The patient may laugh upon hearing that his mother has just died, or he may become enraged when asked a simple question like how he feels. Finally, the affective responses of some schizophrenic patients is ambivalent. A single person or object may simultaneously arouse both positive and negative emotions. A patient may express strong hatred and strong love toward another person at about the same time.

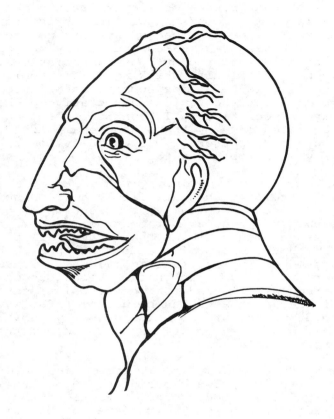

"Ghost of a Flea," based on a hallucination portrayed by William Blake. According to Blake, this flea was in the room and told him that fleas contained the damned souls of blood-thirsty men. Blake, in both his poetry and his etchings, gave many evidences of schizophrenic ideation.

The motor symptoms of schizophrenia are obvious and somewhat bizarre. The schizophrenic may grimace or adopt strange facial expressions. The overall level of activity may be increased, the patient may exhibit much excitement and expend great amounts of energy by running around and flailing his limbs wildly. At the other end of the spectrum these may be catatonic immobility -- unusual postures are adopted and maintained for very long periods of time.

Most schizophrenics have little or no grasp of reality. They tend to withdraw from contact with the world into their own thoughts and fantasies. Usually a schizophrenic becomes unable to distinguish between his own fictitious constructions of reality and what is really happening.

Briefly discuss the following types of schizophrenia:
catatonic, paranoid, disorganized, undifferentiated, and
residual.

Solution: Because of the wide variety of symptoms associated
with schizophrenia, psychologists have found it helpful for
diagnostic and treatment purposes to distinguish among different types of schizophrenia. Classification of a schizophrenic
into one or another of the subtypes depends upon how the psychosis developed and/or upon what kinds of symptoms are predominant in the patient's behavior. It is rare to find a
schizophrenic who fits neatly into one of the subcategories of
schizophrenia. This discussion will cover the types of
schizophrenia listed in DSM-IV-TR.

Disturbances in motor functions are the most obvious
symptoms of the catatonic type of schizophrenia. A catatonic
schizophrenic typically alternates between immobility and wild
excitement, but often one or the other type of motor symptoms
may predominate. In the excited state the catatonic may shout
and talk continuously and incoherently, all the while pacing
back and forth. The immobile state is characterized by physical rigidity, muteness, and unresponsiveness. Despite the
severity of its symptoms, catatonia is more likely than other
forms of schizophrenia to "cure itself" without treatment.

The paranoid schizophrenic is characterized by the presence of numerous and systematized delusions, usually of persecution, but sometimes of grandeur or of being controlled by an
alien force. Auditory and visual hallucinations may accompany
the delusions. Generally, paranoid schizophrenics are more
alert and verbal than other schizophrenics. They tend to
intellectualize, building up an organized set of beliefs based
on the wrong assumptions. Their thought processes, although
deluded, are not as fragmented as those of other
schizophrenics.

The disorganized (or hebephrenic) schizophrenic displays
a variety of bizarre symptoms. Hallucinations and delusions
are profuse and very poorly organized. They typically exhibit
severe regression to childhood behavior which is marked by a
pattern of silliness and absurdity. They may grimace or
giggle wildly for no reason, or they may speak incoherently,
stringing together similar-sounding words and making up words
of their own. They often completely neglect their appearance,
never bathing or combing their hair, and often they will deteriorate to the point that they become incontinent, voiding
anywhere and anytime.

The label undifferentiated is applied to those
schizophrenics who do not exhibit a pattern of symptoms consistent enough to fit one of the other subtypes. For example,
a patient may have highly organized delusions or motor disor-

ders, but not to the extent that he is considered either a paranoid or a catatonic schizophrenic. This particular category has been criticized as being somewhat of a "wastebasket diagnosis" which is applied simply because a patient is difficult to categorize. The patient is, to put it simply, "very crazy," but not in any systematic manner.

The diagnosis of residual schizophrenia is applied to a patient who has had an episode of schizophrenic illness but does not now exhibit any psychotic symptoms, although non-psychotic signs of the illness persist. Emotional blunting, social withdrawal, and communication disorder are common in residual schizophrenics.

● **PROBLEM 14–35**

Describe the process-reactive dimension of schizophrenia.

Solution: The prognosis for schizophrenic disorders depends on many factors. One of the most important is the form in which the onset of the schizophrenic symptoms appear.

In reactive schizophrenia the onset of the symptoms is rapid and sudden. The patient may suffer some pronounced shock, or trauma just before the outbreak of schizophrenia. If the patient was moderately well adjusted before the disturbance, the chances for a recovery are fairly good.

In process schizophrenia the onset of the disorder is slow and the symptoms gradually increase in severity. There was no precipitating trauma and the patient was marginally adjusted. The prognosis for recovery from process schizophrenia is very poor.

● **PROBLEM 14–36**

What is the relationship between social class and schizophrenia? What are the hypotheses accounting for this relationship?

Solution: Several studies have found that schizophrenia occurs most often in the lowest social classes. Although several hypotheses have been offered to explain this relationship in causal terms, further study is needed before a final conclusion can be drawn concerning the role of social class in schizophrenia.

Studies have consistently indicated that the lowest social classes have the highest rates of occurrence of schizophrenia; however, the correlation between social class and schizophrenia does not show a progressively higher rate of schizophrenia as the social class becomes lower. There is a marked discontinuity between the number of schizophrenics in the lowest socioeconomic class and those in others. Many studies found that the rate of schizophrenia was twice as high in the lowest social class as in the next to lowest.

One explanation of the high occurrence of schizophrenia in the lowest socioeconomic classes is that being in a low social class per se may cause schizophrenia. The degrading treatment that people of the lowest class receive, their low level of education, their poor environment, and their lack of opportunity combine to make membership in the lowest social class an experience stressful enough to bring about schizophrenia in many.

Another hypothesis suggests that the problems associated with schizophrenia compel the schizophrenic to become a member of the lowest social class. The cognitive and motivational impairments of schizophrenics reduce their earning abilities to such an extent that they have no choice but to live in privation. In addition, entering a low social class often provides the schizophrenic with a welcome escape from social pressures and intense social relationships.

There is empirical evidence that supports each of these hypotheses. More data must be gathered before the cause of the relationship between schizophrenia and social class is known.

● **PROBLEM 14–37**

Citing specific investigations, discuss what the results of twin studies have suggested about the role of heredity in the development of schizophrenia.

<u>Solution:</u> Concordance is the similarity in psychiatric diagnosis or other traits in a pair of twins. To research the role of genetic factors in schizophrenia, twin studies were designed to find out whether the concordance rate for schizophrenia is greater for identical (monozygotic) twins, than it is for fraternal (dizygotic) twins.

In a major study in Norway, Kringlen (1967) found a 38 percent concordance for identical twins as contrasted with 10 percent in fraternal twins. There were 55 pairs of identical twins and 172 pairs of fraternal twins. Gottesman and Shields (1972) found a concordance rate of 42 percent for identical (MZ) and 9 percent for fraternal twins (DZ) who were hospitalized and diagnosed as schizophrenic. They also found that the concordance was much higher for twins with severe schizophrenic disorders than for those with mild symptoms.

Although the concordance rate for schizophrenia in identical twins is high, the discordance rate is higher. If schizophrenia were solely the result of genetic factors, the concordance rate for identical twins would be one hundred. One must also take into account that since the twins have been reared together, a common environment rather than common genetic factors may account for concordance rates.

In a study by Rosenthal (1970) 16 pairs of monozygotic twins were reared apart from very early childhood. Of the 16 pairs, 10 were concordant and 6 were discordant. The concordance rate of this limited sample was 62.5 percent, a finding that supports the view that a predisposition for schizophrenia is genetically transmitted. Because of the small sample size, however, the data cannot be regarded as conclusive.

Although studies have not proven that schizophrenia is solely transmitted through genetic factors, the findings support the view that a predisposition for schizophrenia may exist. Here it is presumed that certain individuals are more prone to develop schizophrenia if placed under severe stress. However, given a more favorable life situation, the individual's inherent vulnerability may never exhibit itself in the form of schizophrenic behavior.

● **PROBLEM 14-38**

What is a schizo-affective disorder?

Solution: As its name suggests, a schizo-affective disorder may be generally thought of as a combination of schizophrenic and affective disorders. There is controversy as to whether schizo-affective disorders are a subtype of schizophrenia, a subtype of affective disorders, part of a continuum between pure affective disorder and pure schizophrenia, or a separate nosological entity (medical classification). In DSM-IV-TR, schizo-affective disorders are listed as an independent nosological category.

The basic symptoms of a schizo-affective disorder are a depressive or manic syndrome of at least one week's duration that precedes or develops concurrently with certain psychotic symptoms.

Note that an essential requirement for a diagnosis of schizo-affective disorder is that the affective symptoms must develop before or simultaneously with the psychotic symptoms. This requirement excludes those cases in which an affective syndrome appears after the development of a psychosis.

Another requirement for a diagnosis of schizo-affective disorder is that the psychotic symptoms present must be of a type that is not associated with pure affective disorders. The psychotic symptoms that justify a diagnosis of schizo-affective disorder are basically the same as those that justify a diagnosis of schizophrenia. Schizophrenic symptoms such as delusions of losing control over one's thoughts and hallucinations having no content related to depression or mania are symptoms of a schizo-affective disorder when they occur in the context of an affective syndrome.

What is infantile autism? What are its symptoms?

Solution: The word autistic is derived from the Greek word "autos," which means self. Autism refers to an absorption in the self as a means of avoiding communication or escaping reality. Infantile autism, classified as one of the pervasive developmental disorders in DSM-IV-TR, is a childhood psychosis characterized by a very early onset, extreme aloneness, language problems, and bizarre responses to various aspects of the environment.

A child is not diagnosed as having infantile autism unless his age at onset was less than thirty months. It is difficult to determine the exact age of onset unless those who cared for the child during his early years recall accurate information about his behavior as an infant. Often inexperienced parents do not become aware of their autistic child's problems until they observe him in a group with other children.

Usually autistic children show extreme aloneness very early in life. They are often reported to have been "good babies," apparently because they do not place many demands on their parents. They do not fret or demand attention. When they are picked up or cuddled, they may arch their bodies away from their caretakers rather than molding themselves against the adult as normal babies do. Autistic infants are content to sit quietly in their playpen for hours on end, never noticing what others are doing.

After infancy, they do not form attachments with other people, invariably failing to develop cooperative play and friendships with other children. They avoid all social interaction, and as a result they fall rapidly behind their peers in development.

Autistic children are commonly found to have specific difficulties with language. Mutism, a complete absence of speech, is the most prevalent. About fifty percent of all autistic children never learn to speak. When speech does develop, many peculiarities are found. Some autistic children exhibit echolalia -- the child echoes what he has heard another person say. Another abnormality common in the speech of autistic children is pronoun reversal. The children refer to themselves as "he" or "you" or by their own proper names.

Autistic children tend to react to their environment in bizarre ways. One of the most common abnormal behaviors exhibited by autistic children is a refusal to accept changes in their environment. The autistic child becomes extremely upset over changes in daily routine and in his surroundings. A rearrangement of the furniture in the home may trigger a temper tantrum. Besides having a desire for preservation of sameness, autistic children frequently form attachments to odd objects such as refrigerators or vacuum cleaners. They often have a fascination with movement, staring inordinately at moving fans and other spinning objects. Some may show extreme interest in rote memory of things such as train schedules or historical dates.

DISSOCIATIVE DISORDERS AND CONVERSION DISORDERS

● **PROBLEM 14-40**

Discuss the different types of dissociative disorders listed in DSM-IV-TR.

Solution: In dissociative reactions a group of mental processes splits off from the mainstream of consciousness, or behavior is incompatible with the rest of the personality. Five categories of dissociative disorders are listed in DSM-IV-TR: (1) dissociative amnesia, (2) dissociative fugue, (3) dissociative identity disorder, (4) depersonalization disorder, and (5) other dissociative disorders.

Dissociative amnesia involves loss of memory for a period of time, during which the amnesiac cannot remember his name or anything about his previous life, but retains his knowledge of how to function in the world. Amnesia begins suddenly, usually following severe psychosocial stress. The stress often involves the possibility of physical injury or death. In other instances, the stress is due to the unacceptability of certain acts or impulses, such as engaging in a homosexual affair. In still other instances, the individual is in a subjectively intolerable life situation, such as abandonment by a spouse.

The essential features of dissociative fugue are the sudden onset of travel away from one's customary surroundings and an inability to recall one's prior identity. Frequently a person with this disorder will move to a new geographic location and start an entirely new life. This new identity will usually be more gregarious and uninhibited than his prior personality (which is typically quiet and very ordinary). Like amnesia, a fugue is usually precipitated by psychosocial stress. Marital quarrels, personal rejections, and conditions of military conflict or natural disaster are common examples. The duration of most fugues is brief -- hours or days -- although in rare cases a fugue will last many months.

Dissociative identity disorder, the presence of separate and different personalities within the same individual, is perhaps the most dramatic type of dissociative reaction. The individual personalities in this disorder are generally quite discrepant and frequently give the impression of being opposites. For example, the personality of a prim spinster may alternate with that of a flashy, promiscuous bar habituee. Transition from one personality to another is sudden and frequently associated with psychosocial stress. Usually the more persistent or primary personality will remain unaware of the existence of the secondary personality, while the latter is often fully aware of the thoughts and actions of the former.

Depersonalization is characterized by an alteration in the perception or experience of the self so that the feeling of one's own reality is temporarily lost. An individual with this disorder may have feelings of being mechanical or dream-like, or of not being in complete control of his actions. He may have impressions that his extremities have changed in size or that he is perceiving himself from a distance. A diagnosis of depersonalization disorder is made if at least six episodes of depersonalization, each lasting a minimum of thirty minutes, occur within a six week period.

The category of other dissociative disorders is a residual category used for individuals who appear to have a dissociative disorder but do not satisfy the criteria for any of the specific dissociative disorders listed above.

● **PROBLEM 14–41**

What are the psychoanalytic and behavioral theories of dissociative disorders?

Solution: In dissociative reactions a group of mental processes splits off from the mainstream of consciousness, or behavior becomes incompatible with the rest of the personality. The psychoanalytic and behavioral accounts of dissociative disorders are not dissimilar, although each stresses different concepts.

In psychoanalytic theory, dissociative reactions are viewed as instances of massive repression of unacceptable urges, usually relating back to the infantile sexual wishes of the Oedipal stage. In adulthood these Oedipal yearnings increase in strength until they are finally expressed, usually as an impulsive sexual act. The expression of these unacceptable urges means that the defenses against them have failed totally; consequently, a new defense is needed. The unacceptable urges and the stressful event in which they found expression have to be obliterated from consciousness. To do this, the person segments an entire part of the personality from awareness.

Behavioral theory also construes dissociative reactions as an attempt to protect the individual from stress; however, in this theory the concept of repression is not employed and the importance of infantile sexual conflicts is not accepted. Rather, dissociative reactions are viewed simply as an avoidance response used by the individual to escape stressful stimuli.

What is a conversion disorder? What are the psychoanalytic and behavioral theories explaining this disorder?

Solution: In conversion disorders the operations of the musculature or sensory functions are impaired, although the bodily organs themselves are sound. Patients with conversion disorders have reported symptoms such as paralysis, blindness, seizures, coordination disturbance, and anesthesia, all without any sign of physiological cause.

Although there are no physiological causes for the symptoms, in conversion disorder the symptoms are not under the patient's voluntary control.

According to psychoanalytic theory, conversion disorders are rooted in an early unresolved Oedipus (or Electra) complex. The young child becomes incestuously attached to the parent of the opposite sex, but these early impulses are repressed, producing a preoccupation with sex and, at the same time, an avoidance of it. At a later period in the individual's life, sexual excitement or some other event reawakens these repressed impulses, at which time they are converted into physical symptoms that represent in distorted form the repressed libidinal urges.

Ullmann and Krasner (1969) have proposed a behavioral explanation of the development of conversion disorders. In this explanation, the person with a conversion disorder attempts to behave according to his own conception of how a person with a disease affecting his motor or sensory abilities would act. There are two conditions that increase the probability that motor and sensory disabilities can be imitated: (1) The individual must have some experience with the role he is to adopt. He may have had similar physical problems himself, or he may have observed them in others. (2) The enactment of the role must be rewarded. The individual's disability must result in a reduction of stress or in attainment of some positive consequence.

GENETIC AND PHYSIOLOGICAL DISORDERS

Describe the four types of epilepsy.

Solution: Epileptic attacks are generated by a massive discharge by groups of neurons. This discharge causes an increase in brain activity and often results in convulsions.

The grand mal attack is the most severe form of epilepsy. Grand mal seizures are usually described as consisting of four phases: (1) The aura, a warning of the impending

556

convulsion, which may take the form of dizziness, fear, a ringing in the ears, or other peculiar sensations or perceptions. (2) The tonic phase, which is the beginning of the actual seizure, where the muscles of the body become rigid and the patient loses consciousness. (3) The tonic phase gives way to the clonic phase, during which the muscles contract and relax, producing violent contortions and jerking movements of the limbs. (4) As the convulsive movements dissipate, the seizure passes into the coma phase. The individual remains unconscious and the muscles relax. Upon awakening, perhaps almost immediately or perhaps after several hours, the individual has no memory of what happened after the beginning of the tonic phase.

In petit mal epileptic attacks, there is neither an aura nor convulsions. Such an attack is only a momentary alteration of consciousness. The person stops what he is doing and his eyes roll up. There may be a few twitches of the eye and face muscles, but in most cases such seizures are difficult to recognize.

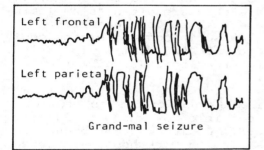

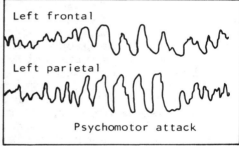

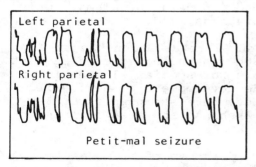

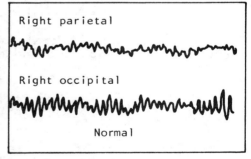

EEG patterns for three types of epilepsy and a normal EEG pattern.

In Jacksonian or focal epilepsy, muscle spasms are limited to particular areas of the body. The location of the seizure depends of course on the area of the brain in which the neurons discharge. For example, a discharge beginning in the visual cortex may produce visual hallucinations.

Psychomotor epilepsy, the fourth kind of epileptic attack, begins with an aura and is followed by a complete loss of contact with the environment; however, during the attack the epileptic appears conscious and engages in some sort of routine or organized activity. The act may be simple, such as chewing, or the epileptic may engage in complex and prolonged activities such as simultaneously groaning and wandering about in automatic fashion. After the attack, the individual has no memory of his actions.

● **PROBLEM 14-44**

List and define the different levels of mental retardation.

Solution: There are five levels of classification of mental retardation: (1) borderline mental retardation, (2) mild mental retardation, (3) moderate mental retardation (4) severe mental retardation, and (5) profound mental retardation.

The person characterized as being a borderline mental retardate has an I.Q. of 68 to 83. With proper training these individuals are able to achieve social and vocational adequacy in adulthood. During school years they are often "slow learners." Although a large percentage fail to complete high school, and can maintain only a low socioeconomic existence, most adults in this group blend in with the normal population. This group is not sufficiently retarded to be eligible for specialized services.

The person with mild mental retardation has an I.Q. of 52 to 67. As children they are eligible for special classes for the educable mentally retarded. Adults in this group can hold unskilled jobs or work in sheltered workshops, although they may need help with social and financial problems. Only about one percent are ever institutionalized.

The person with moderate mental retardation has an I.Q. of 36 to 51. Brain damage and other pathologies are frequent. During childhood they are eligible for special classes for trainable retardates in which the development of self-care skills rather than academic achievement is emphasized. Few hold jobs except in sheltered workshops, and most live dependent on their families.

The person who has severe mental retardation has an I.Q. of 20 to 35. Most are institutionalized and require constant supervision. To be able to speak and take care of ones own basic needs requires prolonged training. As adults they are friendly, but can only communicate on a very concrete level. They engage in very little independent activity and are often lethargic. Genetic disorders and environmental factors account for this degree of retardation.

A person who is a profound mental retardate has an I.Q. below 20. They require total supervision and nursing care all their lives. They can learn little except to walk, utter a few phrases, feed themselves and use the toilet. Many have

severe physical deformities as well as neurological damage.
There is a very high mortality rate during childhood in this
group.

● **PROBLEM 14-45**

What is Down's syndrome? What is its cause?

Solution: Down's syndrome is the most prevalent single-factor
cause of mental retardation. It accounts for 10 to 20 percent
of moderately to severely retarded children.

Children with Down's syndrome seldom have an I.Q. above
50. Their many physical abnormalities are apparent: slanting
of the eyes, flat face and nose, overly large and deeply
fissured tongue, stubby fingers, fingerprints with L-shaped
loops rather than whorls, underdeveloped genitalia, and arms
and legs that are smaller than normal.

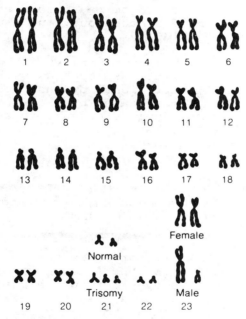

This picture of chromosomes shows an aberration
involving the trisomy of chromosome 21. Most cases
of Down's syndrome, a type of mental retardation,
reveal 47 instead of the normal complement of 46
chromosomes.

Down's syndrome is caused by a chromosomal abnormality.
The vast majority of Down's children have forty-seven chromosomes instead of forty-six. During the earliest stage of an
egg's development the two chromosomes of pair 21 fail to separate. When the sperm and egg unite, chromosome pair 21 has 3
chromosomes instead of the usual 2. This is referred to as a
trisomy of chromosome 21.

Distinguish between acute and chronic brain disorders and the factors commonly diagnosed as the basis of organic disorders.

Solution: Organic disorders are generally characterized by a mental dysfunction in which a structural or biochemical change in the central nervous system is a major factor. Organic brain disorders are classified as being either chronic or acute.

Chronic brain disorders are permanent and irreversible. Syndromes which are commonly connected with chronic disorders include: central nervous system syphilis, severe lead poisoning, senility, and congenital cranial abnormalities.

Acute brain disorders are temporary and can be reversed. Syndromes which are considered to be acute disorders include: alcohol intoxication, mild concussions, and drug poisoning or overdose.

The factors most often connected with organic disorders include: those due to infections (such as syphilis, encephalitis, and meningitis); nutritional dysfunctions (such as vitamin deficiencies); those caused by trauma (such as injuries to the head); aging; tumors; convulsive reactions (such as epilepsy); and the toxic effects of chemical agents such as lead, alcohol, or amphetamines.

What is meant by psychosomatic disorders and what are the general means used for treating them?

Solution: A psychosomatic disorder is one in which an individual's psychological problems are a major factor in an organic pathology. Common disorders which are often psychosomatic in nature are hypertension, migraine headaches, gastrointestinal disorders, and asthma. Psychologists have clearly demonstrated the relationship between psychological stress and ulcers.

Several theories exist as to how symptom selection is made. In dealing with psychosomatic disorders, the four major hypotheses are: the weak-link hypothesis, in which there exists a physiological tendency towards the chosen symptom; the learning hyphothesis, which suggests previous reward for the chosen symptom; the emotional-link, which supports an emotional relationship to specific types of disorders; and the psychoanalytic hypothesis, which sees symptom selection as a function of unresolved conflicts of dependency.

Psychosomatic disorders are no less real or dangerous than disorders with a firm organic base. The treatment is therefore both medical and psychological. The medical treatment is concerned mainly with symptom control and pain relief and the psychological treatment is concerned with determining the cause of the problem and/or preventing its recurrence.

NEUROSES

● **PROBLEM 14–48**

Explain what is meant by the anxiety theory of neurosis.

Solution: The symptoms manifested by neurotics differ widely among individuals. It is generally accepted, however, that neurotic symptoms are a result of inner unresolved anxiety which stirs up conflict within the individual. The symptoms manifested by the neurotic are similar to defense mechanisms in that they usually are in the form of denying and distorting reality, but they differ from the normal defenses because they are rigid and often disrupt daily living.

The symptoms exhibited by a neurotic are usually one of three stages of unresolved anxiety. The symptom can be a normal response to any anxiety, a way to avoid anxiety, or a reaction to the original conflict which caused the neurotic reaction. Very often the symptom is composed of all three levels combined. In the reaction to anxiety, the original conflict is repressed and the anxiety is then expressed psychologically or physiologically. In the case of phobic reactions (i.e., irrational fears) the anxiety is directed to another object which is associated with the original conflict. In the same way, depression is usually the result of the neurotic directing his displaced anxiety back at himself instead of at an external object. The dissociative reaction is an attempt to escape from the conflict by denying one's own identity. In the obsessive-compulsive reaction the neurotic directs his anxiety at changing past mistakes and in conversion reaction the anxiety is channeled into a symptom of physical illness.

● **PROBLEM 14–49**

What factors within the individual are the basis for being able to either withstand conflict or develop neuroses?

Solution: It should be apparent that probably no one is capable of successfully resolving every conflict which arises. Psychologists generally contend that there are two factors which are able to explain why some individuals can tolerate conflicts while others cannot.

The first factor concerns the actual amount of conflict which a person is faced with and can handle adequately. This view was formulated by a research team who studied soldiers who developed neuroses during World War II. The study suggested that there is a direct relationship between the frequency of neurotic reactions and the amount of exposure to stress (combat).

The second factor suggests that the ability to withstand stress is a function of life experiences. Incidence of childhood fears is more frequent in neurotics. It appears that they are more likely to remember these past fears than nonneurotics. It is possible that a neurotic person has had a more insecure childhood than his or her "normal" counterpart, leading to a decreased tolerance level for anxiety. This factor of tolerance combines with the current amount of stress to determine the likelihood of neurosis from resultant anxieties.

It is possible, however, that even an individual with a good tolerance level faced with a severe stress situation may react negatively to such an experience. The result of this is a condition termed "traumatic" neurosis.

● **PROBLEM 14–50**

Why do individuals develop diverse symptoms for similar problems?

Solution: When we looked at the general basis for neurosis it became apparent that a direct relationship existed between the anxiety and the manifestation of the symptom. It was much more of a problem for psychologists to determine why an individual chooses a particular neurotic symptom over another one.

Psychologists have developed three basic hypotheses to account for the process of symptom selection. The learning hypothesis suggests that the idea that the specific symptom selected is a result of general habits learned in the past. This hypothesis contends that if an individual is consistently reinforced upon displaying a certain symptom he will most likely return to that symptom when unresolved conflict arises.

The genetic hypothesis suggests that people are genetically predisposed toward selection of a specific neurotic symptom. It is important to remember here that the selection process is genetically determined. Whether or not a neurosis appears is a function of the environment and not a genetic characteristic.

The developmental stage hypothesis was formulated by Freud and argues that the basis for symptom selection is the individual's developmental level at the time of the original conflict. For example, Freud maintained that conflict repressed during a child's anal stage will develop into an obsessive-compulsive reaction later in life if not otherwise resolved.

Research in this area does not lend definite support to any one of the three hypotheses. As is often the case in psychology, the hypothesis chosen is usually a function of an individual's particular theoretical orientation. Hence, a behaviorist would lend support to the learning hypothesis, the psychoanalyst to the developmental-stage hypothesis, and the psychobiologist to the genetic hypothesis.

● **PROBLEM 14-51**

If a symptom does not succeed in relieving anxiety, does the neurotic discard it?

Solution: A general survey of neurotics would undoubtedly indicate feelings of dissatisfaction with life. The reason for this is that the symptoms manifested by repressed conflicts do not fully separate the neurotic from his anxiety. In many cases the symptoms prove to be a problem in themselves.

Although the symptoms do not always succeed in reducing anxiety and are often troublesome, the neurotic does not discard them. The general contention here is that the symptoms do have the ability to offer some protection from the anxiety and for this reason they are maintained. Additional support for this lies in the fact that once the neurotic is able to avoid experiencing anxiety by manifesting a symptom, a reluctance to change is strengthened each time the symptom is successfully employed. The immediate positive effect of the symptom is more important to the neurotic than any long-term negative consequence.

PSYCHOSES

● **PROBLEM 14-52**

Explain the term "psychosis" and the distinction between functional and organic psychoses.

Solution: Though no longer considered an official category of disorders, the term "psychosis" is nevertheless frequently used to describe severe mental disorders in which thinking and emotion are so impaired that the individual is seriously out of contact with reality and is unable to meet the ordinary demands of life. Deficits in perception, language, and memory are usually so severe that the psychotic has no mental grasp even of ordinary everyday situations. A psychotic individual may exhibit one or more of following symptoms: delusions, hallucinations, emotional disturbances, disorientation, verbal incoherence, and disturbance in nonverbal communication.

An organic psychosis is caused by impaired brain functioning which is attributed to tissue or structural lesions. Organic psychoses may be caused by the circulatory disturbances of old age, disease, accidental injury, or in some cases by prolonged nutritional deficiencies.

A functional psychosis is one which is not accompanied by any apparent pathological changes in tissues or the conditions of the brain. Schizophrenia, the major affective disorders, and paranoid states would typically be considered functional psychosis.

● **PROBLEM 14–53**

Describe and explain the two most common types of functional psychoses.

Solution: The two most common types of functional psychoses are schizophrenia and manic-depressive psychosis. It is estimated that about one-fourth of the admissions to mental hospitals are diagnosed as schizophrenic and about one-sixth are diagnosed as manic-depressive.

Schizophrenia, although it exhibits a wide range of symptoms, is typically characterized by a lack of coherence between the individual's thought patterns and emotions and the observed reactions to his environment.

The manic-depressive psychoses are generally characterized by periodic changes in mood. These changes range from extreme depression to extreme elation. The individual who is in the depressive stage of the cycle is often prone to self injury or suicide. The manic individual, on the other hand, is capable of violence if blocked.

● **PROBLEM 14–54**

What do psychologists generally accept as the causes of functional psychoses?

Solution: At the present time it is not possible to definitely state what the cause of psychosis is. Psychologists doing research in this area generally pursue three lines of evidence.

By studying the family history of psychotic patients, psychologists noted that psychoses can be seen in successive generations. Research tells us that while 0.85% of the general population are diagnosed as schizophrenic, in families where one of the parents is schizophrenic, 16.4% of the children develop schizophrenia. Additional research on this topic indicates a strong hereditary factor in schizophrenia but such results do not rule out environmental factors.

The fact that the environment is a major factor in psychosis is supported by case history data. Cases have been reported on identical twins separated at birth. Life events later appeared to be the basis for one of the twins becoming psychotic and the other remaining normal.

The final line of research pursued by behavioral scientists is biochemical studies. The two basic types of studies done are ones which observe the effect of drugs (such as LSD) on psychotic symptoms and studies which concentrate on the physiological differences observed between normals and psychotics. The studies do give supportive evidence for a metabolic basis for psychosis and recent research indicates direct relationships between manic-depressive disorders and the chemical noepinephrine found in the brain. Relationships between schizophrenia and the neurochemicals serotonin and adrenalin have been shown to exist and research is continuing. However, biochemical factors do not necessarily point to genetic causes of psychosis, because enduring biochemical changes may occur after birth due to environmental factors. In addition, it is conceivable that the biological/physiological anomalies observed in patients are caused by the disorder itself (i.e. the physiological change follows, comes after, the impaired mental and emotional state appears in the individual).

● **PROBLEM 14–55**

What are the general methods currently used in the treatment of functional psychoses?

Solution: Hospitalization is very common among psychotics because of the potential damage they can cause to others and themselves.

The method most often used for treating psychotics is drug therapy. The inadequacy of standard therapeutical techniques to deal with psychosis has led many hospitals to develop a system of maintenance which is designed to control the associated symptoms but does little to actually improve the patient's condition. The use of drug therapy has replaced the more severe methods of insulin shock therapy and electro-shock treatment. The number of psychotics able to be released from mental hospitals is rapidly increasing although psychologists are unsure as to the main aspects of recovery. Statistics concerning release from hospitals may be misleading, however, because many individuals return to hospitalization in time.

Other treatments in addition to drug therapy may include psychiatric interviews, a form of psychoanalysis or psychotherapy; milieu therapy, living in a warm and supportive environment; and social-learning or behavioral approaches, in which specifically appropriate or positive behaviors are reinforced. However, these therapies are used rarely in comparison to medical (drug) maintenance programs, and much research is needed to develop improved methods of treatment.

SHORT ANSWER QUESTIONS FOR REVIEW

Choose the correct answer.

1. Someone with multiple personalities
    would be classified as having
    (a) schizophrenia (b) dissociative
    identity disorder (c) a somatoform
    disorder (d) hypochondriasis
    (e) paranoid personality disorder.

    b

2. Which of the following would most
    accurately describe the delusional
    situation in which a person believes
    others are talking about him?
    (a) delusions of reference
    (b) nihilistic delusions
    (c) hypochondriacal delusions
    (d) delusions of sin and guilt
    (e) delusions of grandeur

    a

3. Rooms seem to "close in" and small
    rooms create feelings of fear that can
    be terrifying. This is a description
    of (a) anxiety reaction (b)
    claustrophobia (c) ochlophobia (d)
    obsessive compulsive

    b

4. A manager of a bank greets people who
    come to his office by shaking hands
    with only his little finger; then he
    excuses himself long enough to wash
    the finger thoroughly in his adjacent
    lavatory. His behavioral symptoms
    indicate (a) schizophrenia
    (b) paranoia (c) pyromania
    (d) delusions (e) obsessive-
    compulsiveness

    e

5. Not part of the symptom nucleus for
    neurosis is (a) inadequacy
    (b) egocentricity (c) fearfulness
    (d) tension (e) high stress
    tolerance

    e

6. A person is completely unresponsive,
    stares blankly into space, and never
    moves. He or she is showing symptoms
    related to (a) paranoia
    (b) hebephrenic schizophrenia
    (c) catatonic schizophrenia
    (d) dyssocial reaction

    c

SHORT ANSWER QUESTIONS FOR REVIEW

7. A lady thinks that she sees a snake
    moving stealthily through the weeds on
    a nearby hill. As she gets closer, she
    discovers it was only a rotten branch
    which had fallen from a tree. This
    perceptual phenomenon is known as (a)
    telekinesis (b) illusion (c)
    delusion (d) hypochondriasis (e)
    hallucination

    b

8. The term "functional psychoses" is
    used to refer to: (a) disorders that
    prevent the individual from achieving
    personality integration (b) disorders
    which stem from the presence of
    physiological defects of the brain or
    central nervous system (c) abnormal,
    nonfunctional behaviors that culminate
    in a decreased level of psychological
    competence (d) disorders of
    primarily psychological origin

    d

9. Mr. Blumkado, a young insurance
    adjuster, developed a peptic ulcer
    after settling a case involving 6.35
    million dollars. A medical doctor
    involved in Mr. Blumkado's disorder
    would look at (a) Mr. Blumkado's
    level of autonomic activity (b) the
    vulnerability of Mr. Blumkado's
    gastrointestinal tract to stress
    (c) Mr. Blumkado's corticovisceral
    control mechanism (d) all of the
    above (e) a and c only

    d

10. Which of the following is not
    characteristic of the neurotic
    depressive? (a) rigid conscience
    (b) considerable stress tolerance
    (c) tendency to feel guilty
    (d) use of symptoms to gain sympathy
    and support from others

    b

11. Hypochondriacal reactions appear to
    occur (a) more frequently among men
    than among women (b) rarely among the
    elderly, unless one has recently
    undergone surgery (c) frequently
    among the elderly (d) along with
    very severe and debilitating psychotic
    disturbances

    c

SHORT ANSWER QUESTIONS FOR REVIEW

12.   The neurotic paradox can best be
        understood when we recognize that the
        neurotic is (a) actually not having
        any problems with stress
        (b) determining whether or not his
        anxieties are realistic (c)
        experiencing immediate relief from
        anxiety as a result of the neurotic
        behavior but in the long run creating
        more stress for himself by doing so
        (d) on the verge of committing
        suicide at one time or another

13.   A key element in the clinical picture
        of paranoia is usually (a) an
        organized delusional system (b) the
        presence of many unsubstantiated
        delusions (c) the experiencing of
        vivid auditory and visual
        hallucinations (d) the general
        "weirdness" of the paranoid behavior

14.   The major affective disorders are
        characterized by (a) extreme and
        inappropriate emotional responses
        (b) severe depression
        (c) withdrawal and emotional
        distortion (d) chronic use of
        depression

15.   Involutional melancholia is
        differentiated from other depressive
        reactions on the basis of (a) the
        increased severity of depression
        experienced by individuals who are
        involutional melancholics (b) the
        tendency for initial appearances to
        occur during the climacteric, and for
        it to become chronic if untreated (c)
        a clinical pattern including
        irritability, restlessness,
        nervousness and insomnia (d) its
        extremely high incidence among
        pubescent girls

16.   The term "schizophrenia" is used to
        include a group of psychotic disorders
        characterized mainly by (a)
        disorganization of the individual
        person's thought process and

perception (b) the individual's
emotional responding becoming
diminished to the point of total
calmness and oblivion (c) a frenzy
of intense social interactions (d)
the individual's sensory-processing
ability becoming diminished

17. The concept of abnormality: (a) can
be easily defined through the use of a
number of diagnostic tools (b) is
clearly delineated from that of
normality through clinical research
(c) has been rejected since cross-
cultural studies revealed that all
standards are relative (d) implies
deviation from a norm that many accept
as a standard for normality

    d

18. The use of the labeling process in the
identification and assessment of an
individual's abnormal behavior pattern
may result in (a) adverse reactions
to the label by both the individual
and society (b) an emphasis on the
underlying psychological structures
which are causing the labeled
individual's behavior (c) a
recognition by the general public of
the inadequacies and limitations of
the labeling process (d) all the
above (e) a and c only

    a

Fill in the blanks.

19. _____ refers to the achievement of
sexual pleasure through clandestine
peeping.

Voyeurism

20. In _____, there is a focus of _____
interest on a bodily part or inanimate
object.

fetishism,
sexual

21. Kinsey found that _____ constituted
just another point along a continuum
of degree of sexual involvement with
same-sex members.

homosexuality

SHORT ANSWER QUESTIONS FOR REVIEW

22. According to Masters and Johnson
(1966) the _____ phase is an
involuntary response.

climatic or
orgasmic

23. According to Masters and Johnson
(1966) the time period during which
restimulation in the male is
impossible is known as the _____.

refractory
period

24. According to Jellinek (1952), the
phase during which the individual has
lost control over his drinking is
called the _____ phase.

crucial

25. The dimension of schizophrenia which
pertains to the patient's prognosis is
_____.

process-
reactive

26. _____ characterizes patients with
extreme mood swings of elation and
depression.

Manic-
depressive
psychosis

27. Neurotic reactions are both _____ and
_____.

maladaptive,
repetitious

28. A crucial criterion for the diagnosis
of schizophrenia is the symptom of
_____ .

hallucinations

29. Blindness in a person with normal eyes
indicates a _____ symptom.

hysterical

30. Pathological behaviors are viewed as
symptoms of a disease or disease-like
process in the _____ model.

medical

31. According to the dynamic model, _____
is a pattern of behavior maintained
for the purpose of avoiding anxiety
and stress.

neurosis

32. A _____ is one in which the person
blocks off large parts of her memory
as a way of avoiding anxiety provoking
associations.

dissociative
reaction

SHORT ANSWER QUESTIONS FOR REVIEW

Determine whether the following statements
are true or false.

33. Functional psychoses are those caused
     by brain damage.   False

34. Phobias are the result of free-
     floating anxiety.   False

35. In conversion reactions, anxiety is
     expressed in the form of physical   True
     symptoms.

36. Any definition of mental illness is
     influenced by cultural standards.   True

37. Compulsive reactions are obsessive
     thought patterns.   False

38. A sociopath is an individual with
     impoverished affect.   True

39. The form of schizophrenia which is
     characterized by childish and   False
     regressed behavior is called
     retrograde schizophrenia.

40. Paranoia is characterized by
     systematized delusions.   True

41. Delirium tremens is an alcoholic
     psychotic reaction.   True

42. Trisomy 21 causes cretinism in
     children.   False

43. Exhibitionism involves the intentional
     exposure of the genitals under   False
     appropriate conditions.

44. A fugue state is one in which the
     individual has amnesia for his past,   True
     but avoids the anxiety associated with
     such a loss of identity by developing
     a new one.

45. A depressive neurotic suffers from
     loss of contact with reality.   False

SHORT ANSWER QUESTIONS FOR REVIEW

46. An antisocial individual is often hedonistic.

True

47. The concordance rate is used to show environmental correlations between siblings.

False

48. Delusions of grandeur are associated with the paranoid schizophrenic.

True

49. Depression reaches psychotic proportions when the person has blackouts.

False

50. In Freudian theory, the Oedipal conflict and how it is resolved is regarded as crucial for determining the direction of sexual preference.

True

CHAPTER 15

THERAPIES

GOALS AND SHORTCOMINGS OF PSYCHOTHERAPY

● **PROBLEM** 15-1

What is the basic goal and logic of psychotherapy and how is this goal generally achieved?

Solution: Psychotherapy is a method of treatment designed to help the patient achieve an effective and satisfactory adjustment. This goal is generally achieved by establishing a positive experience between a therapist and one or more patients or clients. The extensive research and use of different psychotherapies has resulted in the establishing of certain conditions which are believed to be necessary for positive change. Each specific therapy (e.g., client-centered, behavior, psychoanalytic, etc.) has its own set of "strategies" which are based on therapeutic experiences and the underlying theories. In actual practice, the notion of psychotherapy is both a "contrast" between the therapist and client and a highly interpersonal relationship in which skill, empathy and concern are necessary characteristics for the therapist.

● **PROBLEM** 15-2

What are the shortcomings of clinical and scientific evaluations in producing information about the nature of psychotherapy?

Solution: Studies of the outcome of psychotherapy with neurotic patients have shown that about two-thirds of treated adults show marked improvement or recover within two years. These figures are consistent regardless of the type of therapy. The results are not as remarkable as they may seem because the recovery rate of untreated patients is also about 65%. In this context "treated" refers to having undergone a treatment procedure with a trained professional therapist. Many people with neurotic difficulties seek help from nonprofessionals and it appears that this nonprofessional help is about as effective as the treatment procedures used by trained specialists.

These figures may, however, be misleading due to the difficulties inherent in measuring the degree of improvement in these types of cases. A major methodology problem is matching the severity and kinds of problems presented by treated nd untreated patients and by patients who have undergone ifferent types of therapy which may use different labe' or descriptions for the disorders being treated. The lack of valid, consistent criteria for evaluating improvement is another large problem. Some of the criteria that have been used are: the therapist's subjective determination, the client's self-evaluation, changes in the performance on adjustment measurement tests administered before and after therapy. The criteria that have been used in measuring changes in overt behavior include: the absence of symptoms that were formerly present, better use of potentialities, improved interpersonal relationships and improvement in attitudes.

There is evidence that untreated patients show moderate improvement over time. Whereas, treated patients tend to show marked improvement or a marked change for the worse. An inappropriate therapy or therapist can worsen a problem. It is becoming clearer that the therapeutic intervention selected must match the specific type of patient within a given set of circumstances. For instance, behavior therapy appears to be excellent for treating phobic reactions; depressive patients respond best to electroconvulsive shock therapy treatment, and highly educated, mildly disturbed neurotic patients respond best to traditional psychoanalysis. To answer the question, "Is psychotherapy effective?" one needs to consider the type of therapy and the disturbance.

PSYCHOANALYSIS AND LOGOTHERAPY

● PROBLEM 15-3

What are the aims of psychoanalysis?

Solution: Operating within the framework of Freudian theory, the psychoanalyst's goal in therapy is the reconstruction of the patient's personality. To effect this reconstruction the underlying causes for the patient's apparent maladaptive symptoms must be uncovered and explored in depth. In brief, the material of the unconscious mind needs to be brought into the conscious mind so that it no longer serves as a source of anxiety and confusion for the patient.

The psychoanalyst believes that simply curing the symptoms of a particular problem will not relieve the main difficulty for the patient; the underlying conflicting repressed impulses will simply seek expression in some other way. For this reason, it is vital to focus on the source of whatever symptoms there may be.

This type of therapy is long, intensive and usually expensive. The patient is expected to visit the analyst at least four to five times per week for one to two years for a complete analysis to take place. During this time, the psychosexual development of the individual will be retraced through free association and dream analysis. The psychoanalyst will use this information to locate the source of the current problems and to help the patient come to terms with the troublesome unconscious material. When he accomplishes this he will relieve the repression.

In classical psychoanalysis the patient lies on a couch, and the therapist sits out of the client's direct line of sight.

The analyst will then work toward the reconstruction of a new, sounder personality that will be more effective in dealing with life situations and relationships. In psychoanalytic terminology, the ego or rational, mature, conscious part of an individual is strengthened at the expense of the id or irrational, immature and unconscious aspects through a process that makes the unconscious conscious.

● **PROBLEM 15-4**

Describe the basic strategy and treatment procedure of psychoanalysis.

Solution: Although psychoanalysis appears to be a constantly changing area, many of the basic contentions outlined and developed by Freud are still applicable. The basic contention of psychoanalytic theory is that all forms of psychopathology result from the repression of unacceptable drives, inner conflicts (anxieties), and defense mechanisms which reduce the anxiety but do not affect the conflict, thus giving rise to improper psychological development. Instead of dealing with inner conflicts,

the patient represses the conflicts into the unconscious
and is rendered helpless by his own defenses. Psychoanalytic theory then contends that these repressed inner
conflicts are revealed in unconscious actions, dreams,
and pathological symptoms. The basic goal of therapy
therefore is to aid the patient in overcoming this resistance.

Since many conflicts are hypothesized to have been
repressed during childhood, the patient often acts towards
the therapist in the same ways he acted towards his parents
when he was younger. The establishing of this kind of
emotional tie is called "transference."

Freud developed (with Breuer) the technique of free
association. In this process, the patient says anything
that comes to mind and the therapist is able to direct
the flow of associations to the source of the pathology.
In addition to this method of freeing repressed conflicts,
Freud also developed a system for interpreting dreams as
a tool for "entering" the repressed areas of the patient's
unconscious mind. The analytic session itself is designed
to optimally maximize the occurrence of transference. The
therapist, by remaining quiet and aloof, provides the
patient with a "clean slate" on which to transfer the
parental attributions.

The process of transference, the technique of free
association and dream interpretation all serve to give the
patient meaningful insight into the conflicts which are
preventing normal adjustment and corrective change.

● **PROBLEM** 15-5

Define transference. Describe the interaction between
patient and analyst in the transference neurosis.

Solution: One of the purposes of traditional psychoanalysis
is to bring the unconscious, repressed material of the
patient into consciousness. The analytic technique called
"transference"figures importantly in the success of therapy. "Transference" is the name given by Freud to the
tendency of the patient to react to the therapist with
the same childhood emotions he used to experience toward
his parents; one of the main roles of the therapist, therefore, is to serve as a transference object.

This peculiar emotional attachment to the analyst
usually begins to develop during the process of "free association"-- a technique whereby the patient reports whatever
thoughts, feelings or images come to mind, no matter how
trivial or unimportant they seem to be. Because material
from the unconscious is seen as always seeking expression,
this technique is thought to encourage the expression of
this repressed material. Generally, the patient resists
the recall of painful or guilty memories, and it is a further role of the analyst to help the patient overcome this
resistance. In expressing and reliving his past, the

patient transfers to the analyst the hostilities, affections, resentment and guilt he formerly felt toward his parents. Thus, transference brings the problems into the open where they can be analyzed in a rational manner.

These displaced and often intense and inappropriate reactions of the patient to the analyst are referred to as "transference neurosis." It is through the interpretation and examination of this neurosis that the patient learns that his childish reactions are no longer appropriate within the adult world. This frees the individual from childhood fixations and makes available large amounts of energy that were formerly used in repressing the unconscious material.

The resolution of the transference neurosis is one of the most important parts of the cure in classical psychoanalysis. For it to occur successfully, the analyst must be able to maintain the stance of compassionate neutrality. His role is mainly to listen and offer interpretations. He must guard against letting his own personality intrude upon the patient's working out of his problems. It is partly for this reason that all doctors trained as psychoanalysts must undergo psychoanalytic treatment themselves before they begin to practice.

● **PROBLEM** 15-6

How would a Freudian treat agoraphobia? How might a behaviorist?

Solution: There are a number of common phobias. Phobias are intense and irrational fears of particular situations or objects that are recognized by the individual and others to be inherently harmless. For a fear to be considered a neurosis requiring treatment it usually must reach incapacitating proportions. Characteristic of neurotic phobic reactions are feelings of apprehension, heart palpitations, fainting, nausea or fatigue--sometimes panic may occur if escape from the fearful object or situation is not possible.

A widely accepted theory about the origin of phobic reactions comes from Freudian thought. It is believed that the phobia represents a displacement of anxiety from its real source to a symbolic object or situation. This displacement activity allows the repressed anxiety an outlet without threatening the psychological balance of the individual by admitting the true object of the anxiety into consciousness. For example, anxiety associated with sexual temptations may be transferred to a phobic fear of germ contamination. The specific nature of the phobia allows the individual to monitor his exposure to the fear producing situations. Because the anxiety needs periodic outlets, however, it is necessary that the feared object be readily available. It is for this reason that common objects or situations are often selected for fearful reactions--such as high places, open places, germs, crowds, darkness and solitude.

"Agoraphobia" is fear of open places. Adherents of different schools of thought concerning human behavior would approach the treatment of this problem differently. The Freudian therapist would tend to act from the premises stated above. The unconscious source of the irrational fear would need to be brought into consciousness so that the individual could examine the inappropriate responses he was having and come to work out the repressed feelings through his transference relationship with the analyst. Free association, dream analysis and interpretation by the therapist would all probably be utilized by the Freudian attempting to cure a patient of agoraphobia.

A behaviorist, working from a different theoretical basis, would use entirely different techniques. The behaviorist would reject the theory that an inner, buried, unconscious problem was the source of the phobia. Behaviorists tend to act from the premise that the symptom being observed is the problem and the main task is to remove the undesirable behavior. The original cause of the symptomatic reaction is seen as irrelevant.

The techniques a behaviorist might utilize include desensitization, reinforcement, relaxation, shaping, and stimulus generalization. In extinguishing a fear of open places the therapist might first ask the person to relax. Once this is accomplished the behaviorist may expose the phobic person to an open space for a very short time. As he does this, he may continually ask the person to remain calm and give him reinforcement in the form of approval, support and encouragement. At each session the individual would be exposed for longer periods of time to the open space, each time being trained and aided to relax and reinforced positively for relaxation. Eventually, the patient will realize, in the presence of the feared stimulus, that nothing harmful will befall him.

Through this process the individual would learn a more adaptive, reasonable response to the stimulus of open space. He would be conditioned to respond in a new way; his inappropriate behavior would be modified so that it resembled that of a rational adult. Behavior modification is currently considered the most effective treatment for phobic reactions.

● **PROBLEM** 15-7

Explain the concepts of existential neurosis and logotherapy.

Solution: Victor Frankl, a survivor of the German concentration camps of World War II, has focused his theoretical writings and his therapy procedures on his patients' frequent complaints that their lives lack meaning or purpose. This experience of the futile, empty meaninglessness of life--a contemporary disorder--is sometimes called an existential neurosis, characterized by an alienation from society and self. Its key components are the pervasive sense of meaninglessness, loneliness, boredom, apathy, and

lack of direction. Frankl called this collection of symptoms the "existential vacuum" which he attributed in part
to the decline of historical traditions and values, including religion. He believes that this decline in values
has left people with an inner vacuum that has prevented
them from identifying values and a direction in life.

The individual suffering from this modern neurosis
lacks a sense of personal identity and has a tendency to
view himself as an automaton, good for nothing more than
assuming a social role which some other automaton could
just as easily do. These people may even be quite good
at performing their roles in life, but they do so without
real commitment, involvement or purpose. The more obvious
symptoms of the existential neurosis are often precipitated when some obstacle or stress within the environment
interferes with the enactment of the roles they usually
play and reveals their inadequacies.

The treatment that Frankl has devised to treat this
disturbance is called "logotherapy." The purpose of the
therapy is to help the patient find a purpose for living,
a meaning to life. From his experience and work, Frankl
decided that this "will to meaning" was the prime motivator of human beings, and that the "will to pleasure,"
the "will to power" or "self-actualization drives" were
all secondary and of service to the will to meaning. He
believes that man is constantly reaching out for a meaning
to fulfill and that by virtue of his ability to transcend
himself, he is always seeking to serve a cause higher than
himself or to lose his self-preoccupation by loving
another person.

BEHAVIOR THERAPY

● **PROBLEM** 15-8

Describe the different techniques used in behavior therapy.

Solution: Behavior therapy, also called behavior modification, is an attempt to study and change abnormal behavior
by drawing on the methods used by experimental psychologists in their study of normal behavior. Four different
techniques of behavior therapy can be distinguished:
1) counterconditioning, 2) operant conditioning,
3) modeling and 4) cognitive restructuring.

In counterconditioning, an undesired response to a
given stimulus is eliminated by calling forth a new response in the presence of that stimulus. Suppose that a
child has nyctophobia--fear of the dark. Whenever he finds
himself in a dark place (stimulus), he experiences intense
feelings of anxiety (undesired response). The goal of
counterconditioning would be to elicit a new, positive
response in the young client while he is confronted with
darkness. This might be achieved by feeding the child
one of his favorite foods in the dark. In this fashion,

the fear (undesired response) produced by darkness (stimulus) might be dispelled by the positive feelings (new response) associated with eating. Repeated associations of darkness with positive feelings would most likely cure the client of his phobia.

Three frequently used counterconditioning techniques are: a) systematic desensitization b) assertive training, and c) aversive conditioning.

Systematic desensitization, formulated by Joseph Wolpe, is a procedure in which a deeply relaxed person is asked to imagine a series of anxiety-provoking situations, along a continuum. For example, a person who is afraid of taking tests will first be told to imagine the teacher telling the class of an upcoming test; then he'll be told to think of himself studying for the test and finally, he must imagine he is actually taking the test. This procedure may require more intermediary steps, in which the person is told to imagine more scenes before the final one, which is more anxiety producing. The number of additional steps depends on the level of anxiety. The relaxation serves to inhibit any anxiety that might otherwise be produced by the imagined scenes. The imagined scene can be viewed as the stimulus; the anxiety elicited by the scene is the undesired response, and relaxation is the new response. It has been found that the ability to tolerate stressful imagery is generally followed by a reduction of anxiety in similar real-life situations.

Assertive training is helpful to those people who are unable to express positive or negative feelings to others. For example, consider a man who is often treated rudely by a business associate but is too timid to protest or express resentment. Because of his suppressed negative feelings, he experiences anxiety whenever he comes into contact with the business associate. Assertive training assumes that expression of positive or negative feelings can countercondition the anxiety associated with specific interpersonal situations. Applying this assumption to our example, the anxiety (undesired response) elicited by the presence of the rude business associate (stimulus) would be counteracted if the timid man were to express his true feelings to the associate (new response).

Another variant of counterconditioning is aversive conditioning, which attempts to attach negative feelings to stimuli that are considered inappropriately attractive. Imagine that a foot fetishist wishes to be less attracted to the sight or feel of feet. To reduce the attraction, a therapist might give him repeated electric shocks as pictures of feet are presented. The goal of such therapy would be to make feet (stimulus) elicit anxiety (new response) rather than feelings of attraction (undesired response).

Operant conditioning, also known as behavior shaping, is another technique of behavior therapy. The principles of operant conditioning are very straightfoward: behaviors whose frequency it is desirable to increase are rewarded and behaviors whose frequency it is desirable to decrease are either ignored or punished. Operant conditioning has been applied to the populations of many mental institutions in the form of a token economy. Patients are systematically reinforced with plastic tokens that can later be exchanged for goods and privileges. The results of such programs have been very encouraging. Operant conditioning has also been successful in the treatment of children with behavior problems.

A third technique of behavior therapy is modeling, which involves learning by observing and imitating the behavior of others. As an example, examine how modeling would be used to rid a client of a dog phobia. The therapist might expose the client to both live and filmed displays of people interacting fearlessly with dogs. Hopefully, the client would imitate the models he has been exposed to and eventually overcome his fear of dogs. A number of research programs have shown that this kind of learning is helping people acquire new responses in a relatively short time.

Cognitive restructuring, the fourth technique of behavior modification, attempts to directly manipulate the thinking and reasoning processes of the client. Perhaps the best example of a cognitive restructuring procedure is rational-emotive therapy, which has developed from the work of Albert Ellis. Rational-emotive therapy assumes: 1) people cognitively interpret what is happening around them; 2) sometimes these interpretations can cause emotional turmoil; and 3) a therapist's attention should be focused on these internal sentences and not on historical causes. An example of an internal belief which may lead to distress is the notion that it is imperative to be thoroughly competent in everything one does. A person functioning with this idea in mind will view every error he makes as a catastrophe. A rational-emotive therapist would help such a client by first making him aware of the irrational structure under which he is living and then guiding him towards a belief in realistic goals.

● **PROBLEM** 15-9

How is aversion therapy used in treating a patient with a particular fetish?

Solution: A person is said to have a fetish when his or her sexual interest is aroused by an inanimate object, often associated with the attire of the opposite sex such as stockings, shoes, bras, scarves or hats. Some merely collect these items and use them in their sexual imaginings and masturbation activities; others need to have these objects present to have a successful sexual encounter with a member of the opposite sex. Without the fetish object, the person may be incapable of normal sexual response.

Learning theory explains that the fetish object is

accidentally associated with earlier gratifying sexual experiences. The object may have been within the environment during his or her first pleasurable sexual encounter. Each repetition of a successful sexual experience with the object reinforces the connection between the object and gratification and thereby makes it a more effective and attractive stimulus.

To undo this learning process, a behavior therapist might use behavior modification technique of aversive therapy. The procedure used in aversive therapy is the pairing of a stimulus with negative reinforcement so that the patient eventually comes to develop negative associations with the stimulus. For instance, a movie screen might be used to show varieties of the fetish object and the patient, while watching the movie, would receive mild electric shock each time a new image of the arousing object was presented.

This technique has proven to be relatively successful in treating fetishism. However, fetishism is typically associated with a wide range of unusual sexual behaviors which would each have to be treated separately using behavior modification techniques. It is becoming clearer that a combined approach of analytic and behavior modification techniques is the most effective treatment for a variety of behavior disorders including fetishism. Uncovering both the childhood experiences that may have established the fetish and other unusual sexual behaviors would provide the patient with insight about his problem. Once the patient has acquired this understanding, learning techniques, such as aversive therapy, can be more likely to result in a long-term, pervasive change in behavior.

● **PROBLEM 15-10**

Explain the concepts of reciprocal inhibition and systematic desensitization.

Solution: One of the most common procedures utilized by behavior therapists is known as counterconditioning. Counterconditioning is the reinforcing of a behavior which is opposite or aversive to the maladaptive behavior to be eliminated. The most popular method of counterconditioning is called reciprocal inhibition by psychotherapy. This procedure was developed by Joseph Wolpe. A typical psychotherapeutic session of this type consists of: an initial interview, an information talk, basic training sessions, and desensitization sessions.

The training and desensitization sessions consist of a procedure known as systematic desensitization. This technique first teaches the patient relaxation techniques and then sets up a scale on which the anxiety arousing object or behavior is rated according to severity. The anxiety-arousing stimulus is gradually introduced to the patient while the patient employs a relaxation technique upon each presentation of the stimulus. Eventually, the previously anxiety-arousing stimulus is associated with relaxation and the behavior ceases to be maladaptive.

● **PROBLEM** 15-11

What is implosive therapy?   How successful has it been?

Solution: Implosive therapy is a behavioral modification technique based on the idea that repeated exposure to aversive stimuli or disturbing scenes will result in the extinction of the emotional responses associated with the scenes.

After the therapist has acquired information about the conditioned aversive stimuli that stirs the client to anxiety, depression, anger or some other emotionally extreme response, he trains the client in the technique of "imagery." Beginning with neutral situations, such as eating a meal or watching a movie, the therapist describes a setting and asks the client to imagine himself within the situation. This procedure familiarizes the client with the technique and sensitizes him to evoked responses. If the client reacts emotionally during this neutral training, the therapist quickly changes the suggested image.

Once the client understands the procedure, the therapist begins to describe scenes that he knows will evoke strong emotional reactions. The idea is to emotionally "flood" the person by describing the aversive stimuli as vividly and clearly as possible. The client is not allowed to avoid the imagined disturbing scene; he must withstand the repeated exposure if the therapist is to extinguish the associated emotional responses. The client is encouraged to practice the technique between sessions. Therapy is concluded when the aversive imaginings produce little or no emotional response in the client.

These procedures have the advantage that they can be used by skilled individuals at home to extinguish new problem situations. Though it is a relatively new technique, preliminary findings demonstrate that it is highly effective in producing more adaptive responses in individuals experiencing behavior and personality problems.

● **PROBLEM** 15-12

What is a token economy and why is it used in mental hospitals?   What are its benefits and drawbacks?

Solution: Based upon the principles of social learning and motivation theories, a new approach to treating chronic mental patients called "token economy systems" is gaining popularity. Positive reinforcement is used by the entire hospital staff, including the aides, nurses and doctors, to increase the frequency of desired

behavior from the patients. Trained to notice any improvement in behavior and to pay special attention to
normal desirable responses, the hospital personnel reinforce these responses by giving one or more tokens to
the patient. These tokens are used by the patient to
purchase the necessities of each day (meals or a bed
in which to sleep) and luxuries (better living quarters,
new clothes, special reading material, snacks). Thus,
each time a patient makes his bed, has a positive exchange with another patient, arrives on time for meals,
dresses promptly, etc., he receives a token.

The program is especially geared for the individual
patient so that each one can earn the daily necessities
with minimum effort. Essentially, the patients are rewarded for normal ward behavior and for taking care of
themselves. If the patient should resist the system or
make no favorable responses, he may have to miss a meal
or be given a very modest cot to sleep on. No coercive
methods are used within the token economy systems and
apart from mild deprivation, no punishment is administered.
It is believed that ignoring undesirable behavior will
eventually diminish its occurrence.

Thus far, these programs have proven to be very successful for moderating ward conduct; that is, decreasing
bizarre behavior, increasing social interactions, and increasing self-care. However, return to previous behavior
patterns and symptoms have been observed when the reinforcement is discontinued. It appears that the constant
use of the reinforcement techniques outside of the hospital environment need to occur if the positive behavior
patterns are to continue. One alternative that has been
explored in an effort to extend the improvements that are
made in the hospital and eventually increase the discharge
rate of the chronic patients is the development of "halfway houses" within the community where patients live and
work together to reenter community life.

● **PROBLEM 15-13**

What is the major argument against behavioral methods which
treat overt symptoms? How do behaviorists refute this
argument?

Solution: The behavior therapist attempting to effect a
desired change of behavior in an individual operates from
the premise that neurotic symptoms represent persistent
acquired habits that can be extinguished through the
application of learning techniques. No attempt is made
to identify the contribution of childhood experiences or
conflicts to current problems. No investigation of psychological conflicts or attempts to bring insight to the
patient's motives are made. Different techniques are
used for different problems. If one technique does not
work, another is tried. Through systematic desensitization
and counter conditioning, the behaviorist focuses on the
overt symptom. He considers the therapy successful if

the symptom is removed and a more adaptive behavior is learned in its place.

Proponents of analytic therapy particularly oppose this method of treatment. They believe that treatment of overt symptoms without regard to the underlying causes for the maladaptive behavior will only lead to the development of new symptoms. The source of the pathology lies in the hidden conflicting drives of the individual. Without attention to and insight into these repressed conflicts, no real, lasting cure can occur.

The behavior therapist would not attribute the development of nail biting in a patient who had undergone behavior modification treatment for fear of snakes as a result of an inner conflict that had displaced itself from the snakes to the nail biting. Instead, he would probably attribute the behavior to a new learning process whereby the individual had received certain rewards (easing of tension, relief from boredom, etc.) for the behavior pattern. The behaviorist might suggest that it probably began through imitation or that it developed in small degrees until it became a habit quite unassociated with the phobia of snakes.

Some therapists today are beginning to combine the psychoanalytic approach and the behavior modification methods. They see the process of recall and reconstruction of childhood history as an important learning process that will help the patient have a better understanding of the source of his problems. The therapist's focus on the maladaptive behavior patterns because these are the real problem for the patient. From this angle, analytic therapy is regarded as an educational process whose aim is to have the patient unlearn childhood reactions and acquire adult responses. And behaviorist therapy builds on that education by teaching the person an adaptive response that will replace the phobic one through reinforcement.

● **PROBLEM** 15-14

The patient, a psychotic boy, was accustomed to banging his head and slapping his face so vigorously that he had to be kept under restraint. Through the use of behavior therapy, what methods could be employed to eliminate this behavior?

Solution: Techniques of behavior therapy have been found to be highly effective in dealing with the overt, specific symptoms of psychotic patients. Though the treatments do not seem to have long-term curative effects, they are quite effective for modifying immediate maladaptive behavior patterns.

By establishing a base rate of an undesirable behavior, such as the self-destructive behavior of inflicting bodily harm on oneself, selective reinforcement for

behavior patterns in the direction of a desired change
are made. For example, to decrease the incidence of face
slapping and head banging, the therapist might smile and
make an encouraging remark whenever the child refrains
from hurting himself. He might also offer him a more
tangible reward such as money or candy or a hug for re-
fraining from this undesirable behavior. If the behavior
is too extreme, negative reinforcement might be administered as the child begins to hurt himself. A shock or
extreme disapproval from the therapist are examples of
possible negative reinforcers.

The success of such a treatment program is measured
by the amount of decrease in the self-destructive behavior
and the increase in a more desirable behavior pattern.
To be effective, the reinforcement pattern needs to become more and more selective until the hurting behavior
is eliminated. Furthermore, the behavior needs to be
intermittently reinforced even after the new behavior pattern had been learned.

CLIENT-CENTERED THERAPY

● PROBLEM 15-15

What is Rogers' fundamental theory of psychotherapy?

Solution: Rogers contends that people who enter psychotherapy have an incongruence between their conscious
self-image and their real self. This causes them to feel
anxious and to act defensively. The goal of psychotherapy
is to have the client freely explore his thoughts and to
establish a realistic self-image that is congruent with
his real self, the self that is disguised by a set of
parentally or socially imposed values that have no necessary relations to the client's needs. Since the client,
in his normal environment, cannot explore his thoughts
freely without criticism from others it is necessary to
enter into a therapeutic environment.

The Rogerian therapist has the responsibility of
viewing the client with unconditional positive regard
and to be genuine in his acceptance of the client regardless of what the client says or does. The therapeutic
environment must be as unthreatening as possible. The
client must feel free to explore his inner self without
fear of judgment. It is expected that this unthreatening
environment will allow the client to actually experience
the feelings that were denied to awareness because they
were threatening to the structure of the self-image. The
client will find his behavior changing in a constructive
fashion as a result of this new freedom.

Rogerian therapy is often referred to as "humanistic"
because the outlook of the Rogerian therapist is optimistic.
He has faith in the positive side of human nature and believes that there is a potential for every human being to

lead a happy life. The therapist's view is extremely
distant from the client's view of life. This is true because the client is at a low point in his emotional life
and he must draw strength from the therapist to explore
his mind and establish his own values. The therapist is
supposed to inspire confidence. At the same time, the
therapist should not advise or suggest solutions--this
would be counter to the theory of Rogerian therapy. This
is why the therapy is often called non-directive, the
therapist does not direct the client in any way. Because
therapy is client-centered, the client is at the center
of the process; he does the thinking, talking and solving.
The therapist provides the environment in which the client
can work. Rogers prefers to refer to the people in therapy
as "clients" rather than "patients" because of all the
negative connotations of the word "patient."

The results of successful psychotherapy for the client
would be openness to experience, absence of defensiveness,
accurate awareness, unconditional self-regard, and harmonious relations with others.

● **PROBLEM** 15-16

What is self-theory?

Solution: For many years the term "self" was an unpopular
concept because it was vague, ambiguous, and scientifically
meaningless. Many psychologists objected to its usage because they believed that the word "self" was close in
meaning to the word "soul" which had religious connotations
and as such would not be helpful in psychological research.

Rogers initially agreed with this opinion but his
attitude changed after some experience as a therapist.
He found that the self was an important element in the
client's experience. That is, the set of perceptions
that were referential to "I" or "me" played an important
role in organizing the client's experiences. Because
Rogers always contended that it was necessary for the
therapist to understand the client's internal frame of
reference he began to utilize the concept of self. Thus,
self-theory revolves around the usage of the self as an
explanatory concept. Behavior is explained in terms of
self-image. In self-theory, it is recognized that a subjective and imprecise term like self is necessary to refer to a variety of subjective experiences. Rogers also
views the self-image as being central in emotional conflict. An unrealistic self-image will result in maladjustment. Some theorists, like Skinner, would never use
the concept of self as explanatory. Skinner explains
behavior in terms of reward and punishment.

● **PROBLEM** 15-17

What are the research methods that Rogers has used to
explore personality?

Solution: Carl Rogers was the first psychotherapist to suggest that researchers record therapy sessions. It was believed that the accumulation of a set of exact transcriptions would facilitate the intensive study necessary to elucidate the nature of the therapist-client relationship, the changes that occur in the client as therapy progresses, and the changes in the therapist's attitudes towards the client.

According to Rogers, the source of emotional maladjustment is rooted in an unrealistic self-concept. Therefore, through the use of a research method called "content analysis" he attempted to examine the qualitative change in self-reference that occurred during the course of therapy. Rogers established categories into which a client's self-references could be placed. These categories included: positive or approving self-reference, ambiguous self-reference, negative or disapproving self-reference, and references to external objects. The researcher listens to many taped sessions at various points in the therapeutic process and counts the number of references that are made in each category at different times. It was found that during the course of therapy the client's self-references had changed from predominantly negative to predominantly positive. This was only found in clients whose condition had been clinically judged to have improved. This result was inevitable because Rogers practically defined emotional maladjustment as self-disapproval. Therefore, improvement would have to be evidenced by more self-approval.

The method of content analysis can be used with any set of categories. For instance, the categories could be attitudes towards accepting responsibility. It can be seen that the method of content analysis is essentially an idiographic research technique, that is, it focuses on the individual case and not on generating general principles of behavior.

Rogers also originated the use of rating scales for the purpose of measuring process and change during therapy. One of the most interesting scales is the one which measures the therapist's attitudes towards the client. This scale has five stages. Each stage describes the therapist's attitude toward the client in terms of the congruence or lack of it between the therapist's feelings towards the client and the way the therapist acts toward the client. The judges, who included patients and therapists, used only the information available from excerpts of taped sessions. It was found that separate ratings had a fairly satisfactory reliability.

Rogers also uses "Q-technique" for the purposes of research. Q-technique is essentially a method of systematically analyzing a person's attitudes or opinions about anything. Usually, Q-technique is used to measure a person's opinions about himself.

What is the major task of a Rogerian (or client-oriented) therapist?

<u>Solution</u>: The major task of a client-centered therapist is to establish an atmosphere which lets the client be open to experience. By taking the emphasis of therapy away from the search for a cure and focusing on placing the client in a self-developmental and growth situation, the client is able to fully realize his own capabilities and positive characteristics.

A client-centered therapist does not use interpretation to the extent that a Freudian psychoanalyst would; he attempts to be less judgemental and evaluative. Client-centered therapy is the strongest supporter of the need for a client-therapist relationship, the reason being that as the relationship develops the client is less apprehensive about examining his own feelings and behaviors.

● **PROBLEM** 15-19

What basic factor distinguishes client-centered therapy from the more classical therapies?

<u>Solution</u>: The basic factor which distinguishes client-centered therapy from other therapies is that client-centered therapy does not view human nature as self-destructive, defensive, or irrational.

Client-centered therapy, developed by Carl Rogers, views man as the possessor of an innate capacity and motivation towards positive self-fulfillment or actualization. Consistent with this optimistic view of human nature is Rogers' belief that all behavior is selected with the self-fulfillment goal in mind and that although some behavior choices might prove to be self-damaging, the intention is always positive in its orientation.

Another important factor in client-centered therapy is the attempt by the therapist to remain as non-directive as possible during therapy sessions. The ultimate goal is for the client to develop his own solutions to problems.

Also unique to Rogers is his emphasis on researching his own techniques to examine their efficacy.

PHARMACOLOGICAL THERAPY

● **PROBLEM** 15-20

When was the advent of pharmacological therapy in the U.S.?

Solution: The advent of pharmacological therapy began with the introduction of a drug called chlorpromazine in 1952. Chlorpromazine, also known as Thorazine, is a synthetic drug. It was initially used to control violent symptoms in psychotics.

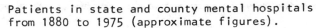

Patients in state and county mental hospitals from 1880 to 1975 (approximate figures).

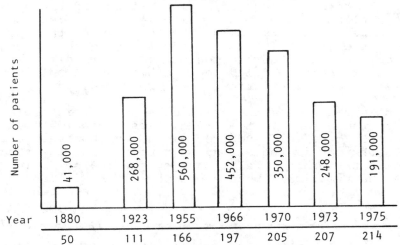

Year	1880	1923	1955	1966	1970	1973	1975
Number of patients	41,000	268,000	560,000	452,000	350,000	248,000	191,000
Population of the U.S. in millions	50	111	166	197	205	207	214

The year 1975 represented the twentieth consecutive year in which the resident population of state and county mental hospitals showed a decline, and this trend is continuing into the 1980s. This decline is considered to be due to a number of factors, including the introduction of major tranquilizing and anti-depressant drugs.

Before the introduction of drugs into therapy, physical restraint was the most common form of patient control. Aside from some barbiturate usage, many patients were also controlled with pre-frontal lobotomies, electro-convulsive shocks, and insulin-shock therapy. The introduction of pharmacological agents into daily use at mental hospitals revolutionized the field of clinical psychology.

● **PROBLEM 15-21**

Describe the development and use of common psychotogenic drugs in use today.

Solution: Psychotogenic drugs cause the production of unusual and exaggerated mental effects. Also known as hallucinogens and psychedelics, these drugs mostly affect the perceptual and cognitive functioning of the individual. The most common examples of psychotogenic drugs are lysergic acid diethylamide (LSD), psilocybin, and mescaline.

LSD is the most widely referred to and most dangerous psychotogenic drug in use today. It is an extremely potent drug (4,000 times stronger than mescaline) and has

been used in a variety of ways since its discovery in 1943.
Its ingestion is accompanied by hallucinations and perceptual distortions; research indicates an impairment of
simple cognitive functions as well.

In the area of psychological research, LSD was once
considered a key to schizophrenia (since it exhibits a
"model" psychosis) and an aid in psychotherapeutic techniques. Both of these contentions have not been substantiated by research and were subsequently rejected. LSD
has been useful in the study of the neurochemical functioning of the brain because of its similarity to serotonin.

● **PROBLEM 15-22**

Discuss the development and use of anti-depressant drugs
in clinical psychiatry.

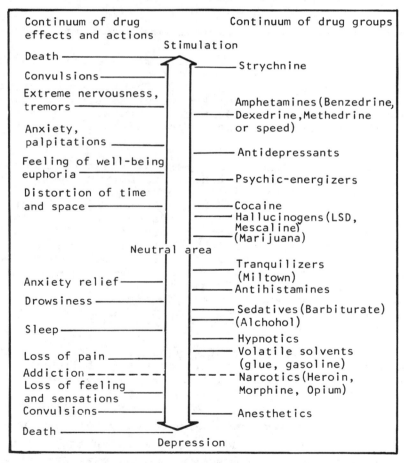

Solution: Anti-depressant drugs have the unique quality
of being able to reverse a state of depression in a mentally
ill person while having no effect on a normal person.
This is what distinguishes anti-depressants from stimulants.
Stimulants cause a reaction in normal people and are not
effective in the treatment of depression.

Anti-depressant drugs were discovered in 1952. A drug called iproniazid, used by I. J. Selikoff to treat tuberculosis, was found to elevate mood. Further investigation concentrated on how this drug functioned. It was finally classified as a MAO (monoamineoxidase) inhibitor. Although some MAO inhibitors are still in use, most treatment of depression is done by the use of safer, more effective drugs called tricyclic anti-depressants.

The research with MAO inhibitors led to the development of the cathecholamine hypothesis of affective disorder which is basically a theory that attributes different forms of psychological disorder to chemical imbalances in the brain.

● **PROBLEM 15-23**

What are the major classes of anti-psychotic drugs and how do they basically function?

<u>Solution</u>: Anti-psychotic drugs, also referred to as tranquilizers, are used to control the symptoms often associated with acute psychotic disorders. Their overall effect is to lower the patient's motor activity and sensitivity--to both internal and external activity. They also serve to reduce the occurrence of delusions and hallucinations in the patient.

The three basic classes of anti-psychotic drugs are: phenothiazines, thioxanthines, and butyrophenones. Phenothiazines, which include chlorpromazine, are the oldest psychopharmaceuticals and are the standard against which all other similar drugs are compared for safety and effectiveness. The main use of phenothiazines has been in the treatment of acute schizophrenics. This type of drug is also used to "maintain" individuals once they are released from mental hospitals. Extensive research by state hospitals and the federal government indicates a very high level of effectiveness. Thioxanthines and butyrophenes are basically derivatives of phenothiazine and are used for the same purposes.

The side-effects of these drugs include low blood pressure, drowsiness and blurred vision. However, the psychotic symptoms that the drugs alleviate are far more serious than their side-effects.

● **PROBLEM 15-24**

Describe the use of drugs in the treatment of anxiety.

<u>Solution</u>: Minor tranquilizers, also referred to as anti-anxiety drugs, are usually prescribed for people with a minor disorder in which anxiety is the main symptom. Anxiety, however, is experienced by everyone. It is only

592

when the level of anxiety reaches such a high state that it is debilitating that direct treatment is necessary.

Sedatives such as barbiturates and alcohol have been used to control the level of anxiety in the past but a class of drugs known as meprobamates was found to be more effective.

Meprobamates were initially introduced to public use under the trade names: Miltown and Equanil. Their popularity was widespread when compared against the use of previous types of barbiturates. This popularity ended with the introduction of a far more effective anxiety control agent: chlordiazepoxide (Librium).

The major problem with this class of drugs is overuse. They are often abused both by the patients and the doctors who prescribe them. This area is also plagued by insufficient knowledge about the drugs' effects on different forms of anxiety.

● **PROBLEM 15-25**

Describe the use of narcotics and the common treatment for their abuse.

Solution: The abuse of narcotics has risen sharply in the U.S. and in other parts of the world. Morphine has been used for centuries and was invaluable in the field of medicine for the control of pain and the development of pain-relieving drugs. It's major problem was that it was addictive; this led to the development of heroin (diacetylmorphine) to treat the addictions. It was soon observed that heroin was also addictive and was twice as potent as morphine. Due to the high recidivism rates of narcotic treatment programs, psychologists realized that in addition to combating the physiological addiction (with drugs such as methadone--Dolophine) it was necessary to combine the drug treatment with social factors such as live-in resident facilities (i.e., Synanon).

● **PROBLEM 15-26**

Discuss alcoholism and the usual steps of rehabilitation for the alcoholic.

Solution: Due to the widespread problem of alcoholism, psychologists have spent much time and energy developing plausible models and treatment programs. Alcoholism is generally divided into three stages: 1) prealcoholic stage--where the drinker finds relief from social and psychological pressure; 2) prodromal stage--where alcohol becomes a drug and the user drinks heavily and frequently forgets what happens during his drinking bouts; and 3) crucial stage--when taking alcohol is a compulsive act accompanied by withdrawal symptoms upon the removal of alcohol

for an extended period of time. It is in this final stage
that the individual is referred to as an alcoholic. The
three personality attributes most commonly associated with
alcoholics are: egocentrism, hostility and dependency.

Aversion therapy is commonly used as part of the treatment
at alcoholic treatment centers. Each time this man takes a
drink, he receives an electric shock.

    Procedures used by rehabilitation agencies such as
Alcoholics Anonymous (AA), generally include: sobering
the person to improve health, making him realize he is
suffering from a disease called alcoholism and giving him
means by which to treat this disease. In the very extreme
cases of alcoholism,electroshock therapy, drug therapy,
or traditional psychotherapy may be utilized.

● **PROBLEM** 15-27

What is the usual course of a manic-depressive reaction?
How is it generally approached therapeutically?

Solution: Manic-depression is considered to be a psychotic
disturbance of an affective nature. Individuals who are
subject to manic-depressive attacks display symptoms that
can be seen as exaggerations of normal reactions. Most
people experience mood changes, but the manic-depressive
experiences extreme mood swings.

    Initial attacks usually occur between the ages of
twenty and sixty, with the optimum age: at about 35.
Patients' first hospital admission for this disorder peak

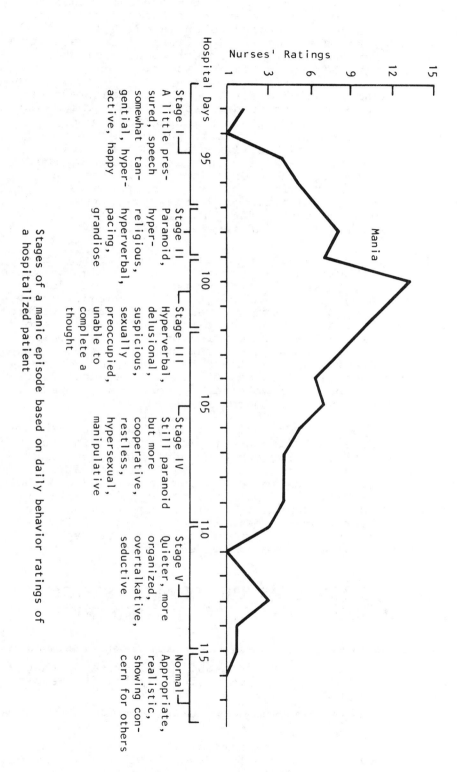

Stages of a manic episode based on daily behavior ratings of
a hospitalized patient

at age forty-five, although many of those admitted at that time have histories of earlier attacks. More women than men experience manic-depression (about 65% of all patients admitted are women). Some feel that this is true because the tendency of men to resort to alcohol when depressed is greater than that for women.

This is a two-sided disorder with the manic and depressive phases occurring at different times. The manic attack is an extreme and exhuberant upswing in mood. Optimistic and confident, the manic person is hyperactive. His speech and his flow of ideas are accelerated. The depressive attack is characterized by the opposite tendencies. The depression precipitates an extreme downswing in effect and gives the person a pervasive feeling of despair or sadness, a slowing of mental and motor activity, fatigue, loss of appetite, restless sleep and a lack of interest in living.

Manic attacks usually occur at an earlier age than depressive attacks, but they do not last as long. A manic attack often lasts for about three months while a depressive reaction may linger for six to eight months. Today, modern drug therapy can bring a manic attack under control within a week, and a depression can be ended within two weeks. The drugs, however, control only the symptoms--if the medication is discontinued, the symptoms return. Once the normal duration of the attack has ended, and drug therapy has been discontinued, the individual usually returns to normal behavior with no aftereffects. However, another attack may occur months or years later.

Lithium is the drug used most often to control manic symptoms. Present studies are trying to determine whether continued use of the drug could prevent further attacks. The results thus far indicate that lithium medication is effective in the prevention of subsequent episodes of both mania and depression. Imipramine, a drug, is sometimes used to control the depressive swing. However, electroconvulsive shock therapy seems to be the current favored treatment for severe depressions because of its speed of action and its greater overall effectiveness.

PSYCHOSURGERY, PSYCHODRAMA, SHOCK, PLAY, GROUP, AND GESTALT THERAPIES

● PROBLEM 15-28

What are the potential benefits and difficulties with psychosurgery and what other type of therapy is often substituted for psychosurgery?

Solution: Psychosurgery, a most drastic form of physical therapy, generally reserved for severely disturbed patients, was pioneered in the 1930s by Moniz and Freeman. This treatment consists of various surgical procedures including the slicing, puncturing, or removal of certain areas of the prefrontal lobes of the brain. The theory underlying this approach was that severing the nerve connections with the thalamus, which was then believed to be the controlling center for the emotions, would relieve severe emotional disturbance.

In certain cases, this procedure turned unmanageable patients into more docile creatures. But in the majority of cases, patients were left with irreversible brain damage. Many were turned into listless, lifeless, insensitive human beings. Thus, psychosurgery has been restricted for use with a limited number of patients. It has been found to be effective in reducing the extreme pain associated with certain forms of terminal cancer.

Other physical therapy treatments for mental patients that are gaining popularity today include electroconvulsive shock therapy and drug therapy. Antidepressant, antimanic, antipsychotic and antianxiety drugs are all in great use today. Since the early 1950s, when psychopharmaceutical drugs were discovered, the care of mental patients has been revolutionized. Though drugs have not been shown to have a curative effect, they are highly effective in dealing with the symptoms associated with a wide range of disorders during their natural course.

● **PROBLEM** 15-29

What is psychodrama and what is its rationale?

Solution: Psychodrama, introduced by a Viennese psychiatrist named J. L. Moreno, is a form of group therapy in which participants act out their feelings as if they were actors in a play.

It is assumed that by dramatizing a role the participant is stimulated to bring forth his feelings and thoughts in a structured form. For example, suppose that a participant is asked to play the role of another group member's father. By acting out this part, the participant is better able to express his feelings and perceptions about his own father than if he were asked to do this directly.

In psychodrama, different kinds of role playing are used to promote the expression of true feelings. For example, the "mirroring" technique is designed for patients who have difficulty expresssing themselves. In this technique, another person, an "auxiliary ego," portrays the patient as he perceives him, thereby furnishing him concrete information on how others view him. Presumably, knowing how others view him will help the participant be more expressive of his feelings and thoughts.

To facilitate the therapeutic role playing, attempts are made to produce a theatrical atmosphere. A real stage is used and an audience is frequently present. At all times, the emphasis in psychodrama is on dramatically expressing true feelings about certain situations.

How effective is electroconvulsive shock therapy in schizophrenia, in depression?

Solution: In the 1930's it was believed that a biological antagonism existed between schizophrenia and convulsions. Therefore, it was determined that the inducement of convulsions in schizophrenic patients might be therapeutic. For some years the drug metrazol was used to induce convulsions in patients. The drug had the disadvantage of causing extreme fear in patients and of being unpredictable about the degree of seizure it caused. In the 1940's, the use of electroconvulsive shock treatment (ECT) came to be widely used because it caused immediate unconsciousness in the patient. Thus, there was no time for a fear reaction and the doses could be controlled so that extreme convulsions could be avoided.

Shock therapy

ECT involves the passage of a 100-volt electric current across electrodes placed at the patient's temples. The current causes immediate unconsciousness and is followed by what appears to be a mild epileptic seizure. Today, prior to administering the shock, the patient is usually given a muscle relaxant to reduce the severity of the convulsions during the seizure. ECT drastically reduces the amount of oxygen in the brain due to the high level of brain activity that occurs during the electroshock which depletes the supply of oxygen and glucose.

It has been shown that, contrary to the 1930's hypothesis that convulsions are an effective treatment for schizophrenia; these treatments are essentially ineffective for schizophrenic patients. However, they have proven to be quite useful in the treatment of depressive patients. The usual procedure consists of 10 to 14 treatments spread over several weeks. The after effects of the treatments include temporary loss of memory, disorientation and confusion. These effects usually disappear within a month or two after the treatments, but are one of the reasons why this type of therapy is resisted by patients.

ECT is one of the most effective and speediest treatments used today for depressive patients. It is more effective than antidepressant drugs which generally require at least two weeks before their effects can be seen. No valid scientific explanation for the usefulness of ECT has been thus far offered. One theory is that the temporary improvement noted after shock treatment may be due to the mobilization of resources to a real threat to existence. A social learning theory suggests that the punishment character of the shock serves as negative reinforcement for the depressive behavior.

● **PROBLEM** 15-31

Explain what is meant by "play therapy."

The therapist presents his young patient with a doll family: father, mother, daughter, and son.

The young patient expresses hostility toward her mother by making the girl doll stamp on the head of the mother doll.

The use of play therapy to permit a child to express her problems.

Solution: Play therapy is a technique which was developed to facilitate therapy with children, though it can also be employed with psychotic patients who are uncommunicative. In play therapy, things such as toys, paint, dolls, clay and blocks are used by the patient as a means of expression. Through play, the patient may convey conflicts and emotions that he is unable to verbalize or perhaps is unaware of. Play therapy is a strong tool that the therapist can use when other methods elicit little information.

What are the major advantages of group therapy over the individual approach?

Solution: In group therapy a professional treats a number of patients simultaneously. Group therapy has gained acceptance not only because of its economic advantages but also because many therapists regard it as uniquely appropriate for treating some psychological problems.

By conducting therapy in groups, a therapist is able to treat more people and charge them lower fees than he would if he were seeing them individually. Thus, from the client's view, group therapy has the advantage of being less expensive than private sessions. From the point of view of many therapists, group therapy is a far more efficient use of professional time than one-to-one therapies since it provides a way to treat more clients.

Proponents of group therapy feel that groups are a uniquely advantageous setting in which to conduct therapy. The social pressures in a group can aid the therapist. For example, if a therapist tells a client that his behavior is childish, the message may be rejected; however, if three or four other people agree with the therapist, the person concerned may find it much more difficult to reject to the observation. Also, clients in group therapy learn to articulate their problems, to listen and to give support to others. Group therapy provides an opportunity for clients to gain insights vicariously when attention is focused on another participant. In addition, many clients are comforted by the knowledge that others have problems similar to theirs.

● **PROBLEM** 15-33

How has general systems theory been applied to family therapy? What is the role of the therapist in family therapy?

Solution: Family therapy is not based upon any particular personality theory or school of thought. In itself it is an approach to human problems. The family is viewed as a patient and the members of the family are treated together. This approach is based on the theory that the individual is a product of his environment and that to produce change within the individual, the environment must first be altered. Specialists from a number of disciplines outside of psychology subscribe to this school of thought. The therapist's orientation determines the techniques and approach that are used in the family therapy sessions. This might involve such diverse aims as uncovering the power structure in the family or improving the communications system.

Most people working with the family approach to therapy seem to agree that the aim of the sessions is to promote differentiation, individuation and growth for each family member. The problems within a family system usually arise because the family members are too close, too emotionally involved with each other. The therapist attempts to help each member as a separate unit who can stand alone.

Family therapy developed from the general systems theory originated by Ludwig von Bertalanffy. General systems theory sees man as an autonomous, creative organism living in an open system. Man's behavior is regulated by his family system. In this view, the whole is more than the sum of the parts. The individual is seen as a responsible participant in his family structure who has a capacity for growth and a potential for change. He must contribute to the improvement of the total system environment. General systems theory also stresses that man lives in a symbolic world of thought and language. Family systems therapy reflects this orientation by stressing communications improvement. Through the study of communication systems, the therapist helps the family members see the subtle communication signals (verbal and nonverbal) that regulate their behavior, and learn how to adopt new, more growth-oriented behaviors.

The general systems approach also includes the concept of "progressive segregation." Individuals pass from a stage of undifferentiated wholeness to a differentiation of parts. The goal of the family therapist is to help each individual emerge as a separate person from the undifferentiated family system.

● **PROBLEM 15-34**

Describe Gestalt therapy and what principles are used in treating neurosis.

Solution: Conceived by Frederick Perls, Gestalt psychology, as its name implies, aims at helping a patient become a whole, integrated person. This theory, which is comprised of a mixture of psychoanalytic and existential concepts, is becoming increasingly popular today. Its main premise is that neurotic behavior or personality disorders are a result of a lack of integration of various apsects within an individual. The painful or undesirable aspects of a disturbed person's personality have not been accepted by him; this leaves him fragmented, confused, and ineffective. The aim of therapy is to bring the self-awareness of the individual to include the presently unacceptable parts. This assimilation process begins to make the person more of a "whole person," which translated into behavior means a more effective, self-reliant, authentic, loving person.

The therapy takes place within a group, but the focus is on the individual. Individuals work through their problem in front of the group when they are ready to do so. Though past experience is seen as important and instru-

mental in determining a person's particular problem, the
solution to these problems is thought to be in the present.
Focus within therapy is on the "now"--the experience of
the individual during the present moment.

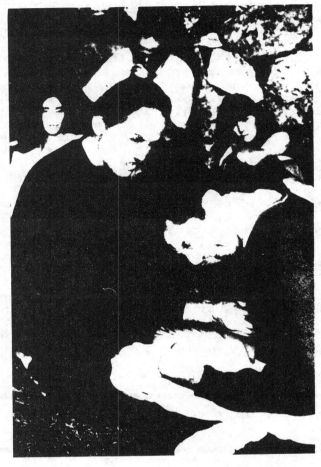

At a gestalt therapy session, the leader(left) encourages a
member to express his pent-up feelings of anger.

Dream and fantasy interpretations are used by Gestalt
therapists. They consider that every object of the dream
or fantasy is a part of the person. Patients are encouraged,
during role playing sessions, to act out the parts of the
people and inanimate objects in their dreams and fantasies.
For instance, if one has a dream about crossing a bridge
in a small car with a friend, one would be asked to play
the part of the bridge, the small car and the friend.

All communication between the therapist and the group
is to be in the present tense. NOW is the most important
concept in Gestalt therapy. The use of the word "I" is
also encouraged so that people will begin to assume more
personal responsibility for their behavior. The tendency
of neurotic patients to avoid unpleasant feelings that
occur is confronted by asking that group members hold onto
the unpleasant emotional experiences. They are then asked

to elaborate on the experience in order to work it out and understand it more fully as part of a self that has been denied or ignored.

NEUROTIC, OBSESSIVE-COMPULSIVE, AND SUICIDAL PERSONALITIES

● **PROBLEM** 15-35

Describe two major types of psychotherapy used in the treatment of neuroses.

Solution: Psychotherapy is the most commonly used treatment for neuroses. Although there are different forms of psychotherapy, a major prerequisite for most is the establishment of an interpersonal relationship between the therapist and patient.

Psychoanalysis, as developed by Freud, is the classic form of psychotherapy. As is seen in the description of the genetic hypothesis of symptom substitution, Freud contended that all neuroses could be traced to repressed conflicts experienced in infancy and early childhood. To determine the nature of the repressed conflict the patient engages in the process of free association. Free association is the means by which repressed conflicts are brought into the consciousness. The analyst is trained to know which parts of the free association are symbols for the inner conflict. As therapy progresses a relationship known as "transference" develops whereby the therapist replaces the parental figures, thus enabling the patient to resolve childhood conflicts. Psychoanalysis is a complex process which is not suited to all individuals.

A different form of therapy called "client-centered" therapy was formulated by Carl Rogers. The basic contention of client-centered therapy is that every person has the potential for a healthy personality and by establishing a close interpersonal relationship with a sympathetic listener (the therapist) the client will be able to resolve his problems. The therapist in client-centered therapy does not advise the client as much as he listens, summarizes and empathizes with the client.

● **PROBLEM** 15-36

Contrast the obsessive-compulsive with the hysterical personality. Include a discussion of the etiology believed to be associated with each.

Solution: Psychopathological behavior is on a continuum from normal to neurotic and psychotic. A personality or character disorder is on the borderline between normal and neurotic behavior. Personality disorders are characterized by a restricted range of maladaptive behavior patterns. These patterns are often displayed in inappropriate situations. For instance, dependence may be continually displayed when self reliance is necessary to hold a job, or aggressive tendencies may be enacted on a bank line where it is more socially acceptable to be passive. This rigidity of behavior leads to poor social adjustment. These individuals do not usually see themselves as having any problem or needing therapy. There are a number of different personality disorders. However, the boundaries between them are not clearly defined and they sometimes serve as a catch-all for disorders that do not seem to fit into other categories.

Two examples of typical personality disorders are the obsessive-compulsive type and the hysterical type. The obsessive-compulsive type is characterized by too much attention to detail and orderliness and by rigid conformity and unnecessary inhibition. This type of person is often irritating to others because of their undue attention to unimportant details and their insistence on perfection. They often lack tolerance and flexibility, but they are usually reliable and efficient. These people lack creativity, spontaneity and have a grim approach to life and work. Their relations with other people are defined along traditional lines and are impersonal.

It is believed that the parents of children with this disorder often have similar traits and that the child destined to develop the obsessive-compulsive character is raised in an environment that stifles frivolity and play and is fraught with much discipline. Emphasis is on industry, work, conformity to rules and regulations, self-reliance and independence.

The hysterical personality type is often found in young women and is characterized by high excitability, self-centeredness, lack of stability and the playing of roles in an insincere fashion. Coquettish behavior is common in this type of personality with a nonresponsive frigidity underlying the flirting. Though most common in women, this pattern is also found in men. Hysterical personalities are heavily dependent on the opinions and stimulation of their social environment to define their identity. Demonstrating a flair for "reading" the emotions and moods of others, hysterics actively pursue the attentions of others by being vivacious, charming, agreeable and seductive. Their own reactions and feelings, however, are shallow, simulated and displayed mainly for manipulative reasons.

The situational causes for this disorder are thought to lie in histrionic parental models, rivalry among siblings for attention, reinforcement of attention-getting behavior and the presence of caretakers during childhood who provided intense though short-lived attention at irregular periods.

Because individuals with personality disorders do not think they need therapy and do not demonstrate an inability to meet the demands of life, these disorders are perhaps the least likely to receive therapeutic treatment.

● **PROBLEM** 15-37

Most suicides do not want to die. Discuss. What are the measures taken by suicide prevention counselors?

Solution: Suicidal behavior qualifies as psychopathological behavior because of the suffering that brings a person to feel that resorting to the prohibited and dangerous expedient of ending one's life is a necessary solution to life's problems. It is thought that most suicides are the acting out of an intolerance for existence rather than a longing for death. The maze of complexities associated with living simply come to weigh too heavily on an individual until it feels reasonable to leave life rather than continue it with so much frustration and suffering.

The incidence of suicide amongst those under twenty-five is quite high and attempted suicide is particularly high in this age group. It is believed that troubled youths use this dramatic move to call attention to a desperate situation in the hope that it will result in improved family or love relationships. For every suicide it is estimated that there are 10 attempted suicides. Even the smallest hints of tendencies toward self destruction are being taken more seriously by mental health practitioners.

Suicide rates vary considerably between societies. Religious taboos and the attitudes of a society toward death are important determinants of suicide rates. However, these factors are not always reliable because the incidence of suicide varies among societies with similar cultures and among the groups within a specific culture. Despite these inconsistencies, it is safe to posit that the cause of suicidal behavior is a combination of social forces, personal characteristics and life stress.

As a rule, the course that a suicide takes begins with the attempt to cope with personal and social needs and expectations in a rational method. If these methods fail, he may seek help from family, friends or therapists. Persistent failure, however, leads to a sense of frustration and futility. At that point, the person's behavior becomes less goal-oriented and more disorganized and confused. Intensified feelings of depression, self-pity, anger and resentment follow. Drugs or alcohol may be resorted to in order to blur the internal confusion. Finally, the person begins to alienate himself from friends and family and he becomes more and more isolated from any social relations. The individual experiences a progressive loss of hope. At this point, it takes very little in terms of failure or frustration to precipitate the suicidal act.

Suicidal acts are often preceded by subtle cries for help. This fact indicates that people who commit suicide

have ambivalent feelings about dying. Suicide prevention
centers base their efforts on the individual's hope to
live, however slight the hope may be.

     The first step the suicide prevention counselor takes
is to determine the risk. He does this by obtaining the
person's age, sex, plan for suicide and his resources. The
counselor then applies the following criteria to the information he has received: with the exception of male blacks,
the older the person, the higher the risk; men are three
times as likely to commit suicide; the more specific and
deadly the method, the greater the risk; and the fewer
people the person can turn to for help, the greater are
his chances of completing the suicide.

     If the counselor finds that the risk of death is very
high he will be more active in trying to intervene. If he
finds the risk to be low, he will try to establish a relationship so as to maintain contact and get information.
He will try to communicate interest and optimism about
finding a solution to the problem. He will then try to
identify and clarify problems. Very often, the suicidal
person is confused about what his problems really are.
The counselor may also make suggestions about possible
solutions.

SHORT ANSWER QUESTIONS FOR REVIEW

Choose the correct answer.

1. The primary goal of therapy is to: (a) change
   an individual's maladoptive behavior (b) help
   an individual achieve more effective coping
   behavior (c) to teach the individual to dis-
   continue making the same mistakes (d) create
   an absolute cure   b

2. The psychological point of view which emphasizes
   unconscious motivation as a factor in human
   behavior is: (a) Client Centered Therapy
   (b) Gestalt Psychology or Field Theory (c)
   Psychoanalysis (d) Stimulus-Response or S-R
   Psychology   c

3. The psychological point of view which emphasizes
   "wholeness" and which is concerned with questions of how one perceives his environment is:
   (a) Gestalt Psychology or Field Theory (b)
   Psychoanalysis (c) Associationism (d) Stimulus-Response or S-R Psychology   a

4. Misperception of a stimulus is to illusion as
   _____ is to hallucination. (a) delusion (b)
   autokinesis (c) response in the absence of
   external stimulus (d) accurate perception of
   an external stimulus   c

5. What is the main difference between Freudian
   psychotherapy and Freudian psychoanalysis?
   (a) Psychotherapy involves more sessions a
   week and lasts longer than psychoanalysis
   (b) Psychotherapy involves less sessions a
   week and lasts longer than psychoanalysis
   (c) Psychoanalysis involves more sessions a
   week and lasts longer than psychotherapy
   (d) Psychoanalysis involves less sessions a
   week and lasts longer than psychotherapy   c

6. Psychotherapeutic methods are most effective
   with (a) neurosis (b) psychosis (c)
   psychopathic personalities (d) alcoholics   a

7. The present day version of behaviorism is known
   as (a) Gestalt psychology or field theory
   (b) functionalism (c) psychoanalysis (d)
   stimulus response or S-R Psychology   d

8. A behavioristically oriented family therapist,
   Huff, has said that the major task of a therapist should be to: (a) punish maladaptive
   family members (b) get the family to switch

SHORT ANSWER QUESTIONS FOR REVIEW

from punishment to reward contingencies (c) reinforce healthy family members in order to help them stay that way (d) organize both positive and negative reinforcement contingencies for the family for the duration of the therapy

c

9. In crisis intervention therapy, the therapist generally: (a) talks about future long term therapy (b) tries to find what the root of the problem is (c) gives immediately needed information and support (d) shocks the patient into facing reality

c

10. Finding out the true role therapy plays in improvement in mental patients is complicated by the fact that: (a) many mentally disturbed patients fail to seek treatment (b) many treatment programs fail to "cure" a patient (c) there is no psychological "model" against which to measure therapeutic gains and setbacks (d) mental disorders often show spontaneous recovery

d

11. Which of the following therapies would be most interested in the way the patient feels about a given problem in his or her life? (a) directive therapy (b) client centered therapy (c) behavior therapy (d) Freudian Psychotherapy

b

12. Transference and resistance are most common in (a) psychoanalysis (b) group therapy (c) behavior therapy (d) phenomenological therapy (e) client centered therapy

a

13. The famous therapist who focused on apparent accidents, slips of the tongue, and the betrayal of id impulses as being unconsciously motivated was (a) Fromm (b) Skinner (c) Freud (d) Adler

c

14. In terms of Freudian psychoanalytic theory, Repression is to suppression as (a) classical conditioning is to instrumental conditioning (b) semiautomatic is to automatic (c) fixation is to regression (d) involuntary is to voluntary

d

15. From a therapeutic standpoint, which one of the following would be considered the most serious? (a) paranoid states (b) obsessive-compulsiveness (c) paranoia (d) anxiety reaction

a

SHORT ANSWER QUESTIONS FOR REVIEW

16. Which of the following would most likely not
be used in the treatment of alcoholism (a)
hospital setting (b) LSD therapy (c)
chlorpromazine (d) family support (e)
Alcoholic's Anonymous

b

Fill in the blanks.

17. "Man's freedom is absolute and it is his own
choices which determine what he shall become
since even refusing to choose constitutes a
choice." The preceeding view is expressed
within _____ psychology.

existen-
tial

18. In almost all cases the major difference, in
terms of credentials, between the Clinical
Psychologist and the Psychiatrist is that the
Clinical Psychologist has a Doctor of Philo-
sophy Degree in Clinical Psychology and the
Psychiatrist has a _____ degree.

Medical
Doctor
or
Medical

19. The method of therapy employing the general
facts and principles developed by Sigmund
Freud is called _____.

psycho-
analysis

20. In psychoanalysis, those associations which
appear to be free wandering but which are
directed by unconscious instinctual drives are
called _____ association. (Hint: the term
was coined by Freud)

free

21. The basic idea behind Gestalt Psychology is
that the whole is greater than _____.

the sum of
its parts

22. During the process of free association or
of associating to dream content, an individual
may evidence an unwillingness or inability to
relate certain thoughts, motives, or experiences. This phenomenon would be called _____
in psychoanalysis.

resistance

23. As a patient and therapist interact, the relationship between them may become very complex
and emotionally involved. Often a person
carries over and applies to the therapist
attitudes and feelings that developed in his
relations with significant others in his past,
perhaps reacting to the analyst as he did to
his father or mother, and feeling the hostility he once felt toward his real father or
mother. This phenomenon would be called _____
in psychoanalysis.

trans-
ference

SHORT ANSWER QUESTIONS FOR REVIEW

24. In _____ therapy, T groups initially focused on the development of human relations and group process skills but have since become much broader in scope.

    sensi-
    tivity

25. A form of group therapy which consists of the presentation of more or less formal lectures and visual materials to patients as a group is called _____ therapy.

    didactive

26. An interesting form of therapy based on role playing techniques in which the patient, assisted by staff members or other patients, is encouraged to act out problem situations in a theaterlike setting is called _____.

    psychodrama

27. Electroconvulsive Shock Therapy has been most effective in the treatment of _____.

    depression

28. An electrical machine which is used in the study of electrical impulses which are correlated with the physiology of the brain and which registers brain waves on the surface of the skull ranging from 100 to 1000 milli-volts is called _____.

    electro-
    encephalo-
    graphy
    (EEG)

29. The fundamental principles underlying _____ therapy are Glasser's principles that abnormal behavior is behaving irresponsibly and that only if people accept responsibility for the consequences of their acts can they adequately cope with their problems.

    reality

30. If a client is lying on the floor, muttering, yelling, twisting and turning, and all the while being urged by the therapist to "get it all out," the therapist is probably engaged in _____ therapy.

    primal

31. Mr. Sachmo has a phobia of dogs. According to behavioristic theory, the best method of ridding Mr. Sachmo of his phobia would be _____.

    systematic
    desensiti-
    zation

Determine whether the following statements are true or false.

32. A form of psychotherapy focusing on the elimi-nation of behavioral symptoms and the learning of new behaviors through classical and instru-mental conditioning procedures is known as family therapy.

    False

610

SHORT ANSWER QUESTIONS FOR REVIEW

33. A school of psychology founded by John B. Watson, which opposed the use of introspection and subjective concepts and advocated the study of overt behavior is the functionalistic school.   False

34. The main assumption behind psychoanalysis is that the personality core elements are established in the first few years of life.   True

35. A method used, usually unconsciously, by an individual to prevent experiencing anxiety in therapy is a defense mechanism.   True

36. In psychoanalysis, a personality marked by orderliness, miserliness, obstinacy, and cleanliness would be classified as an oral personality.   False

37. The Gestalt therapist's view is compatible with the statement: learning is based on specific responses to specific stimuli.   False

38. The psychoanalyst becomes the recipient of affection that the patient felt earlier in her life toward her father. This would be an example of the Oedipus complex.   False

39. The statement "It places an overemphasis upon instinctual behavior" is not a common criticism of psychoanalysis.   False

40. Psychodrama is a form of role playing managerized training technique.   True

41. A primary problem encountered in treating drug addicts, alcoholics, and sociopaths is their contentedness with their present life style.   True

42. Fundamental to all sensitivity and encounter groups is the arrangement of groups into a semicircle and the presence of a therapist.   False

43. According to psychoanalytic theory, the Oedipal complex is successfully resolved when the child identifies with the same sex parent.   True

44. A person smokes a cigarette and, because of an earlier drug administration, becomes nauseous in a technique known as extinction.   False

45. A form of psychotherapy originated by Albert Ellis in which the patient is convinced to stop

SHORT ANSWER QUESTIONS FOR REVIEW

questioning the assumptions that he uses in
thinking about himself and his environment is
called Rational-Emotional Therapy.   False

46. According to Wolpe, a problem which might
     lead to the failure of desensitization train-
     ing in certain individuals is the construction
     of an irrelevant hierarchy.   True

47. Aversion therapy is used primarily as an aid
     to controlling psychotic individuals.   False

48. Transactional analysis generally focuses on the
     individual's overt behavioral responses while
     Gestalt typically deals with intrapsychic
     processes.   True

49. A phenomenological type of psychotherapy that
     focuses upon conscious conflicts and where
     the therapist attempts to lead the patient to
     a realization of his goals by helping him to
     regain a sense of control over his life is
     called existential therapy.   True

50. In therapy, a recent movement in personality
     and clinical psychology focusing upon uniquely
     human experiences in the individual client
     rather than on abstract conceptions of human
     nature is called humanistic therapy.   True

51. A form of therapy in which the therapist serves
     mainly to reflect the feelings expressed by
     the patient, accepting them without evaluation
     is called directive therapy.   False

52. Humanistic-existential therapies are based
     on the assumption that appropriate modifications
     in a person's environment and behaviors may
     considerably enrich his life.   False

53. Assertiveness training has been shown to be
     very helpful in cases involving interpersonal
     difficulties caused by conditioned anxiety
     responses.   True

54. The primary goal of Rogerian or Client Centered
     Therapy is to help a client become willing and
     able to be himself.   True

CHAPTER 16

SOCIAL PSYCHOLOGY

THE FIELD OF SOCIAL PSYCHOLOGY

● PROBLEM 16-1

What is social psychology? What features differentiate
it from other behavioral sciences?

Solution: In the study of human behavior, social psychology focuses particularly on the psychology of the individual in society. More particularly it investigates the influence process of that society as it acts on the individual. To this end, social psychologists may draw from sociology and cultural anthropology, but their primary interest is still the psychological level. This discipline
is not, as many assume, a combination of sociological and
psychological concepts; rather it is a field that has
generated its own unique approach to the analysis of social
processes, based on concepts from the level of individual
psychology to that of wider social behavior.

Social behavior is the main thrust of social psychological research. Through the use of the scientific
method and objective study, a body of knowledge has been
produced that is helping us to understand the underlying
processes in social interactions. Again, the most distinctive feature of social psychology is its emphasis on
individual psychology in terms of individual perceptions,
motivations, and learning to account for the interaction
of the individual and the society of which the individual
is a part.

Within the field of social psychology there are wide
ranges of thought and explanations of social behavior
which run from the psychoanalytic to the behavioristic.
However, there are two main theoretical schools of thought
that can be readily differentiated. The theorists that
concentrate more on the internal processes of the individual and his cognitive processes, are called the cognitive theorists. They believe the human being is an organ-
izer and processor of experience; that his "world view"

contributes greatly to his social behavior. More emphasis is placed on external events by the behaviorists, who tend to adhere to the belief that people are reactors to the events that occur around them. These scientists tend to focus, therefore, on the world external to the individual in explaining his behavior.

The experimental method is the research method used by most all social psychologists, regardless of their theoretical position. At the core of all experiments is the basic question, do changes in one variable (the "independent variable") produce changes in another variable (the "dependent variable")? In this way the body of knowledge coming out of social psychology rests firmly on the scientific method. A question that the student might, however, wish to ask is, "can the scientific method adequately measure all aspects of human psychology?" This is a large question, not to be addressed in this brief space, but one which must be asked by the serious student of human behavior.

● **PROBLEM 16-2**

Give a brief history of the study of social behavior.

Solution: Social psychology, as we know it, is a modern discipline, but the behavior of an individual human being as part of the larger society has been of interest to Man since antiquity. In tracing the history of this interest there can be seen three distinct periods in the development of social psychology as it exists today: the philosophical, statistical and analytical periods.

The philosophical approach to individual behavior in social groupings can be found as far back as 2000 B.C. in the Babylonian Code of Hammurabi. We are more familiar with the more recent thoughts of Aristotle and Plato on the role of man in society. The philosophical approach relied mainly on the power of thought apart from testable data, that is, it relied more on reason or the authority of the writer than on any systematic gathering of factual information. Many of the great thinkers on human nature are part of the "roots" of social psychological thought: Hobbes, Rousseau, Kant, Diderot, Goethe, Freud, Darwin have all contributed to our conceptions of the interaction of society and the individual human being. This philosophical tradition and approach, as we can see dominates the history of social psychology, for the next stage, the statistical or empirical stage, only began approximately 100 years ago with the work of Francis Galton on human genetics.

During this stage in the development of social psychology emphasis was on the description of human traits and the conditions of human society. Generally, it relies upon systematic data gathering to obtain information about the conditions of human nature and life. Galton, inspired by Charles Darwin's views on natural selection, conducted research on the transmission of genius genetically by tracing the history of families whose members had attained great prominence. Also in this tradition is the work of Binet in standardizing tests for human intelligence; Durkheim, who collected statistics on suicide; and the work of the demographists--scientists who study population characteristics. Data gathering had begun.

If the statistical stage began to provide factual descriptive characteristics of human characteristics, then the analytical period, which began at about the turn of this century, is the move toward probing beneath the descriptive data to understand the causal factors in that data. This is the stage in which we find social psychology today. It is now concerned with establishing scientifically valid foundations for what it observes.

● **PROBLEM** 16-3

How can evaluation apprehension be eliminated from social psychological experimental settings?

Solution: It has been argued that most subject's principal desire in an experiment is to look good to the experimenter. (Weber & Cook, 1972). They feel that the typical subject enters an experiment assuming that he is going to be judged on his mental health, intelligence, and moral character. This causes the subject to be apprehensive, and subsequently influences his behavior, perhaps even more than the variable that is of interest to the experimenter.

Because most social psychological experiments take place in a laboratory setting, it is almost impossible to eliminate evaluation apprehension effect. If, however, experimental methodology could be devised that would allow for field (natural setting) experimentation, and the use of "nonobtrusive" approaches, in which a subject is not aware that he is being tested, this effect could be eliminated. Some quite creative experiments have already been devised by social psychologists that completely eliminate this variable. Perhaps inspired by the "Candid Camera" approach, Zimbardo has contributed data on antisocial behavior as it correlates with population density by placing an abandoned automobile on a street in New York City and another on a similar street in Palo Alto, California, and then hiding to record the actions of passersby in the two settings. His subjects never knew, and probably never will know they were part of a social psychological experiment.

Of course, field experiments, such as the one mentioned above, are extremely difficult to conduct usually, and until such time as more expedient methods can be devised that minimize the subject's knowledge that he is being observed, we can expect this factor to influence his behavior and to a certain extent the outcome of the experiment.

● PROBLEM 16-4

A common criticism of social psychological research is that it is not externally valid. Explain.

Solution: All social psychological experiments try to ascertain if a change in one "variable" (description of a quantifiable aspect of a person or object) produces changes in another variable. The variable that is held constant is called the "dependent variable" and the variable that is studied as a possible influencing variable is called the "independent variable." The first question that must be asked in assessing the success of an experimental design is, "was the independent variable alone responsible for the observed outcome of the experiment?" If the answer is yes, then the experiment is what is called "internally valid"; if the answer is no, then the experiment is not worth much from a scientific point of view, as it has failed to isolate any particular causative agent. Many other factors can enter into a psychological experiment and influence the outcome rather than the independent variable, such as the effect of the experimenter, the experimental setting, and apprehension about being evaluated. Because of the nature of what social psychologists study, their experiments are particularly susceptible to these (the interaction of individual and environment) factors.

Once an experiment is established as being internally valid, the next question that must be asked is, "are the results of the experiment generalizable?" If they are, the experiment also can be said to have "external validity." If they are not, the experiment may have discovered something quite interesting about human behavior in a laboratory setting, but not given us much help in understanding it in "real" life. The external validity of a study can be increased by selecting subjects randomly from the group from which one wishes to generalize.

In fact, many social psychological experiments do not appear to be externally valid. This may be due to the necessity of conducting much of the research in artificial settings when the variables of interest concern "natural" human behavior. It is particularly important for the social psychologists, who are concerned with the interaction of the individual and the environment, to develop experiments that are conducted in more natural settings, if they hope to be able to establish external validity in their work.

● PROBLEM 16-5

How is culture a source of social influence?

Solution: In any human society humans are bound to their

culture for a coherent outlook and approach to life. The
essential aspects of a particular culture are precisely what
differentiate one segment of humanity from another. One
need only to travel to a part of the world in which a language other than one's native tongue is spoken to observe
and experience the extent of cultural differences. Oddly
enough, in order to see the way in which our culture influences us, it is generally necessary to experience another
culture.

A culture provides people with a number of ready-made
answers for crucial life problems. It dictates the routine
relationships and social arrangements for survival needs and
the protection and raising of the young. It gives an entire
group of people a means of coping with the world.

Perhaps one of the most subtle, and at the same time
one of the most pervasive, influences of culture on the
individual is the shared perspective or outlook that it
gives members of the same culture. The perceptions, attitudes and values of a society's members are assumed by that
society to be objective or universally accepted, although
this attitude might not be openly expressed.

Through processes of communication, individuals acquire
a sense of common meaning and purpose which contributes
strongly to a particular way of life. In any society, for
instance, there are cultural dictates regarding age and sex.
American society, unlike many other societies tends to be
oriented toward youth, and does not generally hold those
who are older in high regard merely because of their age.
Also, despite the efforts of equal rights legislation, there
is a widespread expectancy that a nurse or a secretary should
be female, and despite the fact that a high proportion of
physicians in many Western cultures are women, in our own
society we tend to think of this as a male role.

Most cultures believe that the earth is round. But
there are vast differences in belief about the nature of God,
the type of government that is best, the manner in which
children should be raised and educated, and the style of
inter-personal relations. We rarely realize how much we
suffer from "cultural provincialism" in our attitudes and
views toward the various aspects of our lives.

Since communication is a central feature of culture, it
is mainly through processes of communication that social
values, attitudes and perceptions are transmitted through
succeeding generations. This social reality that is passed
along through the family and education system influences an
individual's ways of thinking and acting and can have the
effect of very much limiting the type of life a person leads.
Travel, the growth of mass media and higher education all
contribute to the expansion of the limitations a particular
culture can place on its members. Today throughout the
world the phenomenon of "westernization" can be seen taking
place. Effected mainly by the mass media, it is no longer
uncommon to find a fast-food McDonald's in the midst of
Paris, which long represented a culture that would accept no
shortcuts to the production of fine food, nor is it unusual

to see men and women throughout Western Europe in blue jeans
and cowboy boots. Culture, however, is more deeply ingrained
than the external forms of clothing and dining habits, and to
truly understand a man's behavior it is necessary to have an
awareness of the values and attitudes that have become part
of his psychological field through his years of experience
with his particular culture.

CONFORMITY

● PROBLEM 16-6

What is conformity? Distinguish between compliance and
private acceptance.

Solution: The psychological force which causes a person to
act in accordance with the expectations of others is called
conformity. Conformity can also be a change in behavior or
belief toward another person's or group's behavior or belief as a result of real or imagined social pressure. You
walk into a classroom and sit down. You notice that the
twenty-eight other people in the classroom are all wearing
jeans and you are wearing formal clothing. Each time someone looks at you or whispers anything to their neighbor,
you are sure they disapprove of your appearance. You become more and more uncomfortable. You become determined
to never dress that way again for the class. The next day
when you go to class you too are wearing your jeans and feel
much more comfortable. This is conformity.

From this example, it should be clear that the pressure may be imaginary. Perhaps the other students were
actually admiring your courage in wearing something traditional and different. Regardless of the actual thoughts of
the others, your idea that they wanted you to be wearing
jeans (real or imagined social pressure), led you to do
just that (change your behavior).

This real or imagined pressure can lead to a change
in external behavior only or it can lead to a change in
private attitude. In the example given above, it is not
possible to know if "compliance"--a change only in external
behavior--or "private acceptance"--a real attitude change--
has occurred. One method of testing to see if private
acceptance has taken place is to observe if the behavior

618

is maintained in situations in which the group pressure is lacking. Do you still wear a dress or suit when you go anywhere else other than the class? Do you continue admiring attractive, more dressy clothing and secretly believe that the other students are slobs or lazy or must be drugged by advertising to wear clothes that belong on a ranch? You wear your jeans simply to avoid the aggravation of being the focus of their negative judgment. If so, you are complying by wearing your jeans, and your conformity behavior does not reflect a change in your private attitudes.

If, however, you begin to ponder on the advantages of being able to sit wherever and however you want, to run, roll in the grass, climb fences, roller-skate, and so forth, if you are wearing jeans; if you consider the great cost savings you are going to receive by never having to buy anything again but blue jeans and shirts, and the large amount of time you will have once you are liberated from all that shopping to such a point that you don your jeans with a great sigh of relief and set off to class, your conformity behavior is also an indication of a private acceptance of the value of wearing jeans.

Though in this case the distinction between compliance and private acceptance may be clear, it must be realized that in many instances, it is difficult, if not impossible, to tell if conformity behavior implies personal attitude change or not. This is particularly true for laboratory experiments attempting to study these two phenomena.

● **PROBLEM** 16-7

Conformity is generally classified into two types: based upon reward or punishment or based upon a need to know. Distinguish on a more specific plane between the three kinds of responses to social influence.

Solution: The distinction between two general types of conformity presented above can be viewed in a more specialized way which applies not only to conformity but to the entire area of social influence. This more specialized classification is of three types: compliance, identification, and internalization.

Compliance is the mode of behavior exhibited by an individual attempting to gain reward or avoid punishment. This behavior generally ceases once the reward or punishment is not respectively available or avoidable.

Identification is a response to social influence resulting from the individual's desire to be like the person he is identifying with. Such behavior is self-satisfying, it does not require reward or threat of punishment, and the individual loosely adopts the beliefs and opinions of the identifier. It is this last factor which differentiates identification from compliance.

Internalization is a deeply rooted social response

which is based on a desire to be right. The reward here is
intrinsic. Identification is usually the method which introduces a belief or opinion to an individual but once it is
internalized it becomes an independent belief, highly resistant to change.

Some important characteristics of the three types of
social responses are that compliance is the shortest-lived
social response because when the reward availability or
threat of punishment is removed the behavior disappears.
For this reason, compliance is a poor method of social influence. Such continuous reward or threat of punishment is not
necessary for identification but permanence is not assured
since identification values can change with time. Internalization, then, is the most permanent and resistant to change,
and requires little or no reward or threat of punishment.

● **PROBLEM 16-8**

If a group of five people are watching a movie and upon conclusion four of them state that the movie was terrible, what
will the fifth person (who happened to like the movie)
probably say?

Solution: To be able to confidently predict the answer to
such a question requires some knowledge of the concept of
conformity. Although there are numerous factors which go
into the decision to conform or not to conform, the fifth
person would most likely say that it was a terrible movie.
Psychologists basically support two possible reasons for conformity. The first is that the behavior of others might
actually convince the conformer that his initial opinion was
faulty, or it may be that he wishes to gain some reward or
avoid some kind of punishment by conforming. Additional research indicates that seeking reward (i.e., acceptance) or
avoiding punishment (i.e., rejection) is more often the case
since subjects generally do not conform when able to respond
privately. Although nonconformists are idolized by historians and writers, they are not held in such high esteem by
those people to whose demands they refuse to conform, supporting beliefs that society prefers conformity to any nonconformity.

● **PROBLEM 16-9**

Discuss the relationship between conformity and the "unresponsive" bystander.

Solution: Infamous examples of public apathy such as
the murder of Kitty Genovese in the full view of 38 neighbors, caused psychologists to study how impervious to emergencies people have become.

The team of Darley and Latané hypothesized that the
number of people witnessing an emergency situation was a
causal factor in whether or not anyone tried to help. They

hypothesized that this was a direct relationship in that the larger the number of bystanders, the less likely would it be for someone to help. In this respect non-responding is an act of conformity.

Darley and Latané tested their hypotheses in a number of ways and each time the hypothesis was supported: the more people around the less likely one of them would help. One plausible explanation given for this effect is that in such a situation, there is a diffusion of responsibility. The bystanders are hypothesized to feel that in a group setting it is not solely their responsibility to aid the victim. Some factors which cause people to help a victim are: a sharing of a "common fate" situation and a situation where there is no escape, no choice but to help.

● **PROBLEM** 16-10

Outline and explain some of the variables which increase or decrease conformity.

Solution: One of the factors which is causal in controlling conformity is whether or not the opinion of the majority is unanimous. If the subject is presented with one ally, his probability of conforming to the majority is sharply curtailed. In situations where the confederate "subjects" are unaminous in their judgements, there need not be a large number to elicit conformity from the actual subjects. As few as three other people can elicit conformity from a subject and the amount of this conformity remains consistently the same up to sixteen other people. A method which is frequently used to decrease conformity is having the subject make some form of commitment to his initial judgement. Psychologists testing this have found that conformity with prior commitment drops to about 6% from a 25% conformity rate without prior commitment.

Another factor which is causal in the amount of conformity is the kind of individuals who make up the group. A group which consists of experts, friends of the subject, or people similar to the subject (i.e., other students) is most likely to increase subject conformity.

The final factor which is causal in the amount of conformity exhibited by subjects is the self-esteem of the subjects themselves. As might be expected, individuals with low self-esteem are much more likely to conform in a given situation than individuals with high self-esteem in the same situation.

● **PROBLEM** 16-11

Describe the task given to the subjects in the Asch experiments and the results it produced.

Solution: Psychologists generally define conformity as a change in a person's behavior or opinions as a result of real or imagined pressure from a person or group. In attempting to determine which factors are causal in causing a person to conform, psychologists had to set up a situation in which the possible causal factors could be controlled and accounted for.

Asch's task

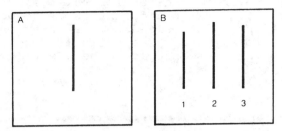

After viewing card A, the subjects must pick the line B that matches.

Asch's results

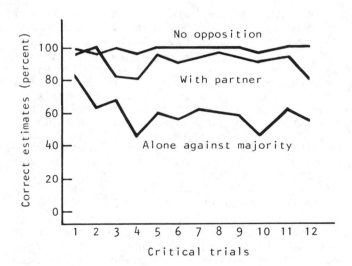

In what is now a classic psychological experiment, Solomon Asch requested subjects to choose which of the three lines (see figure) was the same length as line X. Each subject was on a panel with other "subjects" (confederates of Asch) who all initially gave the same wrong answer. Approximately 35% of the real subjects chose to give an obviously incorrect, but conforming, response. Since there were no explicit rewards or punishments the reason for such conformity could be that in the face of such "overwhelming" opposition the subjects doubted their own perceptions or agreed with the confederates in order to gain group acceptance (or avoidance of group rejection). Asch and his colleagues have repeated this study many times, varying the conditions in attempts to determine what variables play a causal role in decreasing or increasing conformity.

Describe Muzafer Sherif's classic experiment in conformity research. What personality factors have been found to predict whether a person will respond to social pressure by conforming?

Solution: Interested in the effects of group judgments on "the autokinetic phenomenon," Muzafer Sherif conducted in 1935 what has now become a classic experiment in the investigation of conforming behavior. A light projected on the wall of a dark room will appear to move. The movement is, however, due to the movement of the viewer's eyes. The apparent movement is called the "autokinetic phenomenon." Sherif found that individual's judgments of the rate of movement of the light were dramatically influenced by the opinions of others in the group viewing the light. This group pressure also seemed to produce private acceptance, and not just compliance, as the individual determinations of how much the light moved continued to be in keeping with the previous group opinion even when the group was no longer present.

Later experiments in this same area conducted by Solomon Asch found that subjects generally conform about one-third of the time to even an obviously incorrect judgment of a unanimous majority. These results have proved to be highly reliable, and have been obtained in hundreds of studies. In fact, this is one of the most consistent findings in social psychology: people conform one-third of the time to the opinion of a unanimous majority.

What are the personality characteristics that have been found to predict whether or not a person will conform to social pressure? There are three personality characteristics that have proven to be predictive of conformity behavior: 1) An authoritarian person (a person scoring high on the "F Scale" which measures degree of orientation to power) is greatly influenced by authority figures and the more authoritarian a person is the more he or she will conform; 2) People who believe that the circumstances of life are under their control are called "internals," while those that feel that factors beyond their control determine what happens to them are called "externals." As might be expected, externals are more likely to conform than internals; 3) People who are high in need for approval, which is a desire to win the approval of significant others, conform more than people who are low in this need.

Usually people conform because of social pressure, but sometimes it is not necessary to produce conformity. It has, for instance, been proven that a person who supports publicly an opinion that he does not privately accept will often come to change his opinion to be congruent with the publicly expressed one. This is thought to be due to the "dissonance"--a kind of inner discomfort--that is created by the inconsistency between actions and attitudes.

It is important to remember that individual differences coming from personality variables can be changed or even eliminated by different situational factors. In fact, reaction to social pressure seems to be determined mainly by situational factors, while personality characteristics color the nature of the response. It is the interaction of these two variables then, that is most predictive of conformity behavior.

● **PROBLEM** 16-13

What is deindividuation? How has it been tested?

Solution: Social influence also produces movement away from socially acceptable behavior. "Deindividuation" is a state in which a person feels a lessened sense of personal identity and a decreased concern about what people think of him or her. This psychological state can lead to antisocial behavior. Researchers of this phenomenon believe that deindividuation results from feelings of anonymity, lessened responsibility and arousal.

Working from the premise that a large city would produce more anonymity and a lessened sense of responsibility than a smaller city, Zimbardo conducted an identical experiment in New York City and in Palo Alto, California. He placed an apparently abandoned car with the license plates removed and the hood raised on streets in the two cities, and then he and his associates hid in order to observe people's reactions. In New York, within ten minutes a man, woman and child about nine years old came by, and immediately began to remove parts of the car. Within twenty-four hours the car was completely ransacked, the tires were slashed, the windows broken, the doors beaten in. In Palo Alto, the scene was a different one. After seventy-two hours the car remained untouched, except for one passer-by who politely put the hood down when it began to rain.

This experiment supported the hypothesis that the anonymity of a large city gave rise to anti-social behavior. The chances of a person being recognized by someone in a city with a population of 8 million is much less than in a city with a population of 100,000. In a large city there is also a norm of noninvolvement which the New York City vandals probably recognized: people do not get involved in other people's affairs. By the way, the vandals in the New York City experiment were not gangs as might be expected, but were most often well-dressed adults.

There is, however, also evidence that proves that group membership does contribute to deindividuation and subsequent anti-social behavior. It increases a sense of anonymity, gives an individual a feeling of having less responsibility for his or her actions, and the presence of others creates greater arousal.

One Halloween experiment demonstrates: Trick-or-treaters are shown into the dining room after they ring the bell, where they see a table with two large bowls--one full of candy and the other with coins. They are told to take one piece of candy; then the adults leave the room. Of the children who came into the dining room with a group of others, over 60% either took more than one piece of candy or some of the coins. Whereas, if a child was alone, only 20% of the time did he or she violate the request. Apparently, the presence of a group lessened personal responsibility, and in some cases, presented behavior to imitate. Eighty-five percent of the children modeled the first child that approached the table. If he or she committed a transgression (took money or extra candy) the others did also.

To test the role anonymity played in the children's behavior, half the children who entered the house were asked their names and addresses, the others were asked nothing. The names and addresses were slowly repeated by the adults. Almost three times as many unidentified children took more candy or money than those who had identified themselves, whether they were in a group or not.

These results and others like them investigating the nature of anti-social behavior demonstrate what an apparently fragile hold we have on civilized behavior, particularly when urban living which produces conditions most conducive to deindividuation is becoming more and more prevalent.

LEADERSHIP, COMMUNICATION, AND ORGANIZATIONAL STRUCTURE

● PROBLEM 16-14

What is social power? Discuss three types of social power.

Solution: After the great experiments by Asch and Sherif established that people do conform, researchers began to try and determine why. One of the most common explanations is based on the concept of social power. Social power is the ability to change the attitudes or behavior of an individual. There are several different types of social power which have been postulated and studied extensively by French and Raven.

The most complex form of social power is "legitimate" social power in which an individual obeys a person or group because of the power legitimately vested in that person. Obeying a police officer or a court order are examples of being influenced by legitimate social power. Many questions have been raised as to how far this type of power can be allowed to go, particularly in light of the horrors of Nazi Germany. Millions of Jews were murdered by order of the Fuhrer--the legitimate source of social power. Experiments on typical middle-class Americans (Milgram) have also indicated that this tendency to obey a legitimate source of power, even to the point of inflicting harm on others, is alarmingly strong. While legitimate social power is neces-

sary for a society to function effectively, the exercise
of individual conscience must be encouraged as an equal
value to obedience to social power sources.

Another type of social power, "referent" social power,
is an individual's or group's ability to control the behavior of a person or group based on the desire of the
person or group to identify with that source of power. This
type of social influence depends on a person's own desire
to gain satisfaction or approval or personal identity. The
member of the motorcycle gang continues to wear his black
leather jacket with the red eagle even when he is no longer
with his companions because his identity is connected with
being recognized as part of the group. The doctor answers
the call over the loud speaker for a doctor to come for
emergency help, even though he is on his vacation and has
vowed to not work; his idea of the appropriate behavior
for a person in his position--the role of a doctor--is to
be ever ready to respond to the health needs of other people.
This demonstrates the power of the reference group to influence behavior through the identification process.

A third type of social power is "reward" or "coercive"
social power. This is the ability to influence a person's
behavior through having control of the rewards or punishments the person could receive. A child-parent relation
is a classic example of this type of social power at work.
Groups, when administering rewards and punishments to both
compliant and deviant behavior can use quite subtle methods.
Reward can take the form of receiving positive regard and
acceptance from the group members, being made to feel comfortable, being given high status and attention. Punishment might take the form of being ostracized, ignored,
ridiculed, rejected or being given low status.

Though these forms of social power may appear distinctly different, people usually conform because an agent has
more than one form of social power.

● **PROBLEM** 16-15

What are the three classes of variables which increase the
effectiveness of a communication and what factors play a
role in the function of these variables?

Solution: The three classes of variables which increase
the effectiveness of a communication are: 1) the source
of the communication (who says it), 2) the nature of the
communication (how it is said), and 3) the characteristics
of the listeners (who hears it).

The source of a communication is a very important
factor in its effectiveness. The first characteristic
of the source to look at is credibility. Credibility, the
extent to which something is to be believed, is based on
numerous things which include: grooming, manner of dress,
facial expression and tone of voice. People tend to believe people who appear to be expert and/or trustworthy.

To the average person it makes a lot of sense to be influenced by someone with these characteristics. Very often visual impressions are the only things we have to base our impressions on and these are what we use to deem credibility. Trustworthiness is an important characteristic which can be improved upon by: arguing when there is nothing to lose, arguing against one's own self-interests and appearing to not be trying to influence people or change their minds.

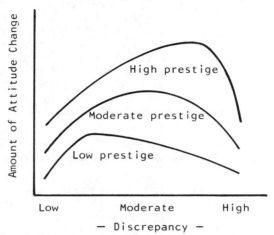

Discrepancy, prestige of the communicator, and attitude change. Maximum change is always produced by the intermediate levels of discrepancy, but the point at which it occurs is determined by prestige, the greater the discrepancy that produces the maximum change.

The nature of the communication (how it is said) is another important factor in communication effectiveness. One area of concern here is the emotional approach versus the reasonable (or logical) approach. Research results generally indicate that a shocking (emotional-based) approach is usually more effective in communicating an idea. As in most areas of psychological reasoning, a great deal of causality depends on the characteristics of the individual to whom the communication is being directed. Self-esteem, for example, is important here in that individuals with low self-esteem are far more affected by the emotional approach than those people with high self-esteem.

The third important factor in communication effectiveness is the characteristics of the audience itself. Individuals with low self-esteem are quicker to be convinced if the speaker appears credible, while high self-esteem listeners are in higher conflict when presented with divergent information from a less than really high credibility speaker. Prior experience of the audience is another crucial factor and some factors which play a role here are: educational level and previous contact with the issue being discussed.

● **PROBLEM 16-16**

As psychologists began to study the effects of mass

communication, they saw the need to distinguish between education and propaganda. Is there a distinction, and if so, what is it?

Solution: The distinction which can be made between education and propaganda is a very fine line. Very often the distinction between the two is dependent on which view you choose to take, since both can often be justified. Most people would say that a geometry text book is an educational tool but very often the examples cited in those books utilize examples of capitalism and free enterprise. They can also indicate biases and prejudices especially in the assignment of sex-roles. Another particularly appropriate example of this is that what the communists refer to as "re-education" we call propaganda or brainwashing.

● PROBLEM 16-17

After World War II there was much speculation about the personalities of those who had committed atrocities. What do the findings of Milgram's studies imply about the personalities of Nazi war criminals?

Solution: In his studies on the nature of obedience, Stanley Milgram discovered that the average middle-class American male would, under the direction of a legitimate authority figure, administer severe shocks to other individuals in an experimental setting.

Briefly, in his experiments two men were told that they would be taking part in an experiment on the effects of punishment on learning. One man was chosen as the learner (who was actually a confederate in the experiment), the other as the teacher. The learner was taken into an adjoining room and strapped into a chair. The experimenter read the instructions to the learner about a word-list he was to learn, loudly enough so that the teacher-subject could hear. The teacher was placed in front of a generator which could administer shocks from 15 to 450 volts to the learner. Under the shock levels were descriptions of the effects of the shock from "slight shock" to "danger, severe shock." The learning session would begin: the first time the learner would give an incorrect answer, a mild shock was administered, and with each subsequent wrong answer stronger and stronger shocks were administered. Even amidst cries from the learner of "Let me out, I've got a heart condition," the teacher would continue administering the shock, though more and more reluctantly.

Out of the forty males that took part in the initial experiments, twenty-six or 65% went all the way and administered the 450-volt shock. This somewhat alarming finding demonstrated the extent to which ordinary people would comply with the orders of a legitimate authority even to the point of committing cruel and harmful actions on their fellow men.

On a television interview, Milgram stated that he would have no trouble staffing a Nazi-style concentration camp with guards from any middle-sized American town. He based this opinion not on his perception of strong anti-Semitism, but on the evidence his experiments had produced concerning the power of legitimate authorities to evoke obedience to their orders. It is therefore likely that the individuals involved in the atrocities of the German concentration camps were of a personality structure not unlike the average citizen in America today--though uncertain and uncomfortable with the nature of some orders--still willing to carry them out in the name of duty or obedience to a superior or someone vested with legal or social power.

● **PROBLEM** 16-18

What is a role? How is it that individuals occupying the same position sometimes play different roles?

Solution: Generally, a group's primary purpose is to achieve some definite goal. To accomplish the goal, positions are established. A "position" is simply where a person falls in the group's hierarchy. "Roles" are the different behaviors an individual displays in connection with a given social position. Therefore, there are behaviors associated with the role of father, the role of employer, the role of student, the role of secretary, the role of teacher. Most people have a multiplicity of roles which must be filled each day.

However, people who occupy the same type of position may play very different roles. Three different roles are possible in any given position in a group depending on the function performed. The "task-oriented" role requires that a person be concerned directly with accomplishing the goal of the group. He relates to people by initiating discussions, seeking opinions and information, organizing activities and directing the group toward the aim. The "maintenance" role requires that the individual playing it be more concerned with the group morale. This person will attend to the personal needs of the group members, including the psychological and emotional needs. The final type of role is the "self-oriented" role; the person who takes this role cares mainly for himself and may even attempt to undermine the goals of the group as a whole if it interferes with his personal desires or needs.

Take a family as an example of a typical group. The father traditionally plays the task-oriented role. He is mainly concerned with seeing that the family is protected and well-cared for physically and financially. The mother plays the maintenance role tending more to the emotional needs of the family, while the children more often play a self-oriented role, looking out for their own interests, with minor concern about the goals of the family as a whole. However, the mother or older children could

629

play the task-oriented role in earning the money to
support the family; the father or older children a maintenance or emotionally supportive role; and either one of the
parents could play a self-oriented role, particularly if
either had alcohol, drug or serious psychological problems.

● **PROBLEM** 16-19

Discuss the "Theory X" and "Theory Y" approaches to human
nature and how they influence managerial style.

Solution: An idea set forth by Douglas McGregor in The
Human Side of Enterprise is that there are two basic philosophical ways of viewing human behavior. He referred to
these two approaches as Theory X and Theory Y. The underlying assumption of these two philosophies is that each
individual has basic beliefs and expectations about what
people are essentially like and how they can be expected
to behave in any given situation. These beliefs and expectations generally have to do with qualities such as
the basic honesty of people, the extent to which a person
will seek responsibility and initiative, and their willingness to work. MacGregor described two different and opposing ways of viewing human nature at work.

The "Theory X" philosophy states that people have an
inherent dislike for work, that they need to be coerced
and controlled, and that they will avoid responsibility
whenever they can. If a particular individual felt that
it was Theory X that accurately described fundamental
human nature, his belief would probably influence his
behavior in interactions. Specifically, if that person
were a manager, his leadership style would be to maintain
tight controls, close supervision, and strict discipline
in order to keep individual members of the work group
from avoiding their job responsibilities. Such managers
would find it difficult to act on the presumption that
workers can be self-motivated, efficient performers
without controls of authoritarian supervision.

"Theory Y," on the other hand, holds that work comes
naturally to people, that they can exercise self-control,
and that they can, under proper conditions, learn to seek
responsibility. A manager holding this point of view would
probably behave differently than did the Theory X manager.
The Theory Y philosophy would most likely lead to an atmosphere of freedom with few controls and reasonably loose
supervision. Admittedly, the Theory X-Theory Y dichotomy
is too simplistic, for most styles of leadership fall somewhere between the two extremes of belief. However, it is
still true that a person's general attitude toward people
will influence the atmosphere that is created in which to
work and the interactions that take place within that environment.

Discuss Fiedler's contingency model of leadership.

Solution: Is there a "best" leadership style? That is, is there a relationship between a leader's style and his effectiveness in getting the group to perform the task at hand? Fiedler, in approaching this question developed a contingency model for leadership. The effectiveness of the leader depended, or was "contingent," upon the inter-action between the leader's style and three situational factors.

His model was developed from his research activities involving managers and supervisors in a variety of organi-zational settings. Using a series of tests to obtain data on the values and attitudes and "style" of each manager, he obtained information in two basic areas:

1. Assumed similarity between opposites—
    This measurement determines the degree
    of similarity between a leader's rating of
    his most preferred coworker and his least
    preferred coworker.

2. Least preferred coworker—This score measures
    the degree to which managers are favorable
    in their ratings of least preferred coworkers.

Someone who rates his least preferred coworker rela-tively favorably, and who does not differentiate signifi-cantly between his most preferred coworker and his least preferred coworker, is called a high-LPC leader. This leader tends to adopt a democratic person-oriented style. A person who rates his least preferred coworker very un-favorably, and who sees a wide differential between the char-acteristics of his most and least preferred coworker, is called a low-LPC leader and tends to adopt a task-oriented autocratic style.

According to Fiedler, the leader who uses the human re-lations style is concerned about the feelings of others and derives satisfaction from a good relationship with his coworkers. The task-oriented individual, on the other hand, is concerned primarily with the task at hand and directs ef-forts toward productivity rather than personal relations.

Fiedler makes the point that a leader's ability to in-fluence the behavior of others is a function of selecting the appropriate style of leadership. The appropriate style may be different for different groups in different situations which brings us back to the three situational fac-tors he believes will have the most significant impact in de-termining the appropriate style of leadership for any given situation: task-structure, leader-member relations and the leader's power. When these three aspects were either very positive or very negative for the leader, a task-

631

oriented, autocratic leader was most effective. When the
situation was intermediate a democratic, person-oriented
leader was more effective.

This model has great logical appeal. For example, if
group members know what they are supposed to do, like the
leader, and the leader has a strong power position, there is
no need to be person-oriented; it would be inefficient and
a waste of time. Also, if group members did not know what
they were to do, did not like the leader and the leader
had a weak power position, it would still seem that a highly
autocratic person would be the most efficient type in that
situation. Attending to the personal needs of the group
members would be a waste of time and interfere with the
accomplishment of the task. A democratic leader will only
prove to be effective in a situation that is moderate in
the three aspects mentioned above, in which either leader
power, task structuring or leader-member relations could be
developed or strengthened. To start with the situation
would need to be moderately favorable to the leader.

While there have been some recent criticisms of
Fiedler's model, it is still widely accepted in management
theory and practice.

● **PROBLEM** 16-21

Contrast the classical and the neoclassical and the modern
approaches to organizational structure. Why is structure
so important to organizational effectiveness?

Solution: One definition of an organization is that it is
a collection of groups each contributing to the purpose of
the organization as a whole. The most important characteristic of an organization is its "structure," that is, the
pattern of relationships among the groups in the organization. It is through structure that an organization coordinates the various independent activities of the groups
of which it is comprised. Without structure, an organization would become chaotic and unproductive. Most organizational theorists and researchers agree that structure is
the single most important characteristic of an organization. However, they disagree as to which structure is the
best and which aspects of structure are the most integral
to effective organizational functioning.

There are three fundamental organizational structure
theories. Classical theory originated around 1900 and was
founded on beliefs that have since been labeled "Theory X"
views of human nature. People were considered to inherently
dislike work and wish to avoid it whenever possible; tightly
controlled working environments in which punishment for non-
performance was the norm were thought to be necessary; and
people were considered to lack ambition or desire for responsibility, but wished to be directed by others and were
mainly concerned with security. It was further believed
that the task to be done should be divided into small units
of operation, in other words, the classicists advocated

division of labor. This should result in workers who were experts in their particular task, but had little knowledge of the final product. The automobile assembly line is a good example of this type of labor division. The classical theorists believed the organization was capable of perfection: that it could be compared to a machine whose design was explained by the organizational chart, and that if the chart was followed without deviation, results would be predictable and profitable.

While the classicists did identify many features of organizational structure, their views of human nature and organizational efficiency have been seriously challenged by the neoclassicists. The neoclassicists adhered more to "Theory Y" theory of human nature in which it is assumed that people like to work; enjoy responsibility with proper rewards; can be self-directing; and have creativity and ingenuity that can be applied to the work. Though the organizational chart was still considered important to the effectiveness of the operation of the organization, very great emphasis was placed on informal organizations within the larger organization that could not be found on the chart. These informal groupings are the natural collecting of people at work. They resemble small groups in their nature. As such, they are concerned with the needs of the individual members more than the needs of the organization as a whole. Sometimes the goals of the informal group are even in conflict with the larger organization. For example, the secretarial group norm produces 3 pages of work per hour, whereas the company expects an output of 5 per hour. Pressure from the informal group will keep a new worker from producing at the expected rate. For this reason, these informal groups need to be considered in the overall picture of management techniques and job performance. Division of labor was seen as repressive to an individual's sense of responsibility and pride in the individual's work and creativity. It was considered that the job of the supervisor was more to motivate the employees than to exercise control over them.

Modern theorists believe that to understand an organization we must look at more than the parts; we must look at the whole or how the parts interact. The hallmark of modern organizational theory is the systems approach. The organization is seen as a living system. What is important to understanding this system is not so much its formal organization or the needs and motives of its workers, but the interaction between the two. The health of this living organization depends on the smooth integration of its parts, its ability to adapt itself to changes in its environment and its continuing growth and "vigor."

ATTITUDES, DISSONANCE, AND PREJUDICE

● PROBLEM 16-22

Does being crowded have a negative effect on humans? What experimental evidence supports this response?

Solution: Currently, 70% of Americans live in urban areas.
The effect of this crowding on human beings has not been
clearly discerned. Though it is assumed that crowding is
bad, there is little hard evidence to prove that this is
so. When crowding research began, it was conducted mainly
on animals. In these experiments, rats, monkeys, rabbits,
and fish all showed pathological behavior as a result of
crowding. For example, the rats became hyperaggressive
and antisocial, some even died of thirst even though there
was a plentiful water supply. These experiments were taken
to prove that crowding would produce the same type of
bizarre effects in humans. However, the experimentation
that has been done on the effects of crowding have yet to
prove that this is true.

     An individual may live in a densely populated area
or spend much of his day in a densely populated situation,
and still not feel crowded. Density is a physical concept,
while crowding is a psychological concept. Density of population does not necessarily lead a person to feel he or
she does not have enough space.

     There is a correlation between density of population
and antisocial behavior, but when other factors are controlled for the difference between densely populated and
moderately populated areas disappears. The other factors
that need to be controlled for are income level and ethni-
city. Poor people and minorities tend to live in densely
populated areas. When the amount of social pathology in
poor ghetto blacks is compared with that of poor blacks in
moderately populated areas,the differences are found to be
equal despite the density of population. In fact, it has
been discovered that delinquency is more correlated with
income than density.

     Because human beings are remarkably adaptable, it may
be that dense living conditions can be adapted to in such
a way that they do not produce pathological behavior. It
is true that in parts of Hong Kong residents have only
thirty-five square feet per person and there does not appear to be any unusual degree of social disorder in that
city. There are many further experiments that need to be
conducted on the effects of crowding before it can be
definitely said that it has a negative influence on humans.

● **PROBLEM 16-23**

Distinguish between an attitude and a value.

Solution: Both attitudes and values can be thought of as
motivational-perceptual states that direct action. Despite this common quality, they have traditionally been
treated distinctively.

     An "attitude" is a person's organization of beliefs
about an object or a situation which precedes and causes
behavior toward that object or situation. The average
adult probably has tens of thousands of attitudes, many

of which he is not even aware. Attitudes usually occur
in clusters or sets around a particular issue or situa-
tion--for example the Viet-Nam War, abortion--supporting
and reinforcing one another.

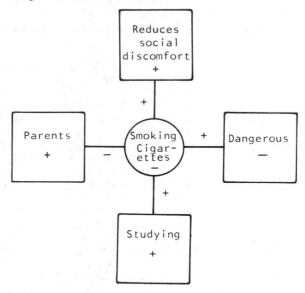

Schematic representation of an attitude toward smoking cigarettes. The core object is surrounded by a cluster of cognitions, which are all related to it. The individual's overall evaluation of smoking cigarettes is determined in part
by its relationship to the separate items in the cluster.

A person's enduring belief about how he should act
and what goals are appropriate and desirable is a "value."
A value can also be seen as the core component of a cluster
of attitudes which directs behavior on a more long-range
basis toward certain goals. Within a culture, a fair degree of congruence is usually found among the ordering
of values. Examples of values (from Rokeach's Value
Survey) are: a sense of accomplishment; a world of beauty;
mature love; pleasure; salvation; wisdom; social recognition; happiness; freedom; an exciting life. Values are
general standards to goals and behavior.

A person generally holds many more attitudes than
values. Values are seen to be culturally linked. That
is, a culture has certain values, not attitudes. In the
United States, for instance, achievement is highly regarded
and is a cultural value that has great influence on the
social goals of many Americans. One of the reasons values
may be more enduring than attitudes is that they serve as
guiding influences for an entire culture.

Attitudes and values are both learned in terms of a
restructuring of the individual psychological field. This
process is a dynamic one since both attitudes and values
are subject to change through the acquisition of new
knowledge. However, attitudes appear to be more susceptible
to apparent change while the basic value underlying them
tends to be resistant to change.

Describe three processes which are considered to be instrumental in the learning of attitudes.

Solution: Often, especially in childhood, learning occurs by imitation without obvious reinforcement or an intention to teach. Hence, children often take on the behavior and the attitudes of their parents. There has been relatively little research on how people acquire attitudes through imitation or modeling (observation of a model of behavior), but it seems reasonable that children acquire many of their attitudes through this process. A father who is often referring to household chores and cooking as "women's work" is likely to produce children who see those activities as more appropriate for women than men. Although the family has the strongest early impact on the formation of attitudes through observation, later on, one's peer or reference group becomes of equal, if not more, importance. Theodore Newcomb's now classic study of Bennington College student's attitudes form their first year through their graduation demonstrated the strong effect a reference group can have on attitudes. Most of the students in their first year held conservative political attitudes, much as their parents did. By the time these same students graduated, they had acquired significantly more liberal attitudes--like those of their classmates.

Attitudes are also sometimes acquired by the process of classical conditioning. If you repeatedly give a person a neutral word and immediately follow it with a word that evokes a strong negative or positive reaction from the person, this will eventually cause the same type of reaction to the previously neutral word. Thus, a person's attitude toward an object or a situation can in part be determined by the connotative meaning the person has attached to it. The connotative meaning is the emotional coloring which is often acquired by some process of nonlaboratory classical conditioning. For example, political candidates with the last name "Kennedy" in the years after the Kennedy administration were thought to have a marked advantage simply because of the positive connotations publicly associated with the name "Kennedy."

The learning of attitudes can also take place through operant conditioning. In operant conditioning, a subject emits a behavior in the apparent absence of any stimulus. If the behavior is reinforced positively, the likelihood that it will be repeated is increased; if it is punished, the chances of it occurring again are lessened. If, after watching a television cartoon in which there were both Caucasian and black children represented, your five-year-old exclaims, "I want a black friend like Johnny," you respond with a smile and a warm assurance that maybe one day he will have such a friend, you have rewarded him with your smile and reinforced his positive attitude toward darker-skinned children. If, on the other hand, you scowl and admonish him for even considering such a thing, telling him that he should "stick to his own kind," you have punished his response, and if others in his environment make similar comments about appropriate playmates, chances are that he will develop negative attitudes about children that are at all different from him in appearance.

Though it may seem that the principles of attitude acquisition are simple, the actual process is quite complex. An adult's attitudes are quite difficult to trace to their source. This is complicated still more by the fact that attitudes can change, even quite significantly in the course of a person's lifetime. There is yet much to be learned in the field of attitude acquisition and change.

● **PROBLEM 16-25**

How does mass communication play a role in the formation of our attitudes and beliefs?

Solution: There is no doubt that mass communication plays a major role in our lives. We are constantly being persuaded by the media to buy certain products, believe certain attitudes, or vote for certain candidates. Such communication is often subtle and very often we don't realize when we are being persuaded. The people responsible for this control of our attitudes and beliefs are not without direction. Much money is spent annually on what is presented to the public and how it is presented. When news stations present violent behavior in their broadcasts they are not trying to harm us but rather entertain us. But as psychologist Elliot Aronson notes, it is this very entertainment which plays so crucial a role in the formation of our attitudes and beliefs. Consumer research indicates that attempts to package and sell products is at first glance very effective. This was also made evident by the "consumer" analyses of the 1968 and 1972 U.S. presidential elections. In both of these campaigns, Nixon was careful to present a better public image than he did in the 1960 television debates between himself and Kennedy. Results of opinion polls concerning the truthfulness of TV commercials indicate that skepticism of such ads goes up as amount of formal education rises and the higher the skepticism, the harder it is to persuade the individual. Another factor which affects our attitudes and beliefs is familiarity. The relationship is that the more familiar an item is, the more attractive it will generally appear to be.

● **PROBLEM 16-26**

What effect does propinquity have on interpersonal attraction?

Solution: The factor that is found to be most predictive of interpersonal attractiveness is propinquity or degree of physical closeness. The closer two individuals are geographically, the more likely it is that they will like each other. A repeated finding concerning mate selection is that individuals find mates who live close by them. One of the indirect justifications for going away to college is to increase the range of contact with possible partners. If you stop and think of who your best friends are, you will probably realize that you and your friend at one time lived or worked near each other.

"Wow! Isn't it great that your house is so close to mine?"

One explanation for this finding is that to avoid dissonance between one's attitudes and one's behavior, it would be necessary to like someone with whom one spent a great deal of time. To test this hypothesis Darley and Berscheid gave women virtually identical descriptions of two people. Then they were told that they would meet and work with one of the two people. Later they were asked to rate how much they liked the two people they had read about. As would be expected from the dissonance theory, the women liked the person they believed they would be meeting and working with significantly more than the person they thought they would never meet.

Another function of propinquity, obviously, is that it makes possible the operation of other factors that can increase attraction such as attitude similarity, which also plays a large role in interpersonal attractiveness. Whether attitudes are actually similar seems less important than whether they are perceived to be similar. Generally, on attitude scales, people rate people they like as having attitudes similar to their own, even if, in fact, this is not true.

● **PROBLEM** 16-27

How does reinforcement theory explain friendship? Contrast this with Heider's balance theory.

Solution: According to reinforcement theory, the most important factor in whether a friendship will develop and
continue is the ratio between the rewards and punishments
(or costs) involved in the relationship. Most people prefer relationships which offer more rewards than punishments. Rewards can take the form of attention, praise,
love, respect or they can be more tangible such as money,
status, good cooking, good conversation. Punishments
could take the form of rejection, ridicule, social disapproval, discomfort, being bullied, ignored, nagged or
more tangibly, our friend might spend our money and time
wastefully.

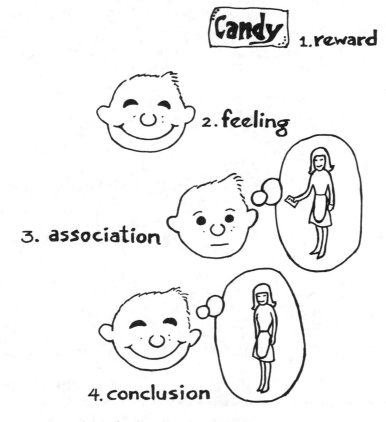

Associating a person with a feeling

Another form of positive reinforcement to friendship
according to reinforcement theory would be similar attitudes. Reinforcement theorists propose that similar attitudes lead to liking and friendship because it is rewarding to have someone agree with us. And it has been
shown experimentally that people react to agreement with
their attitudes just as they react to any other positive
reinforcer (Golightly).

Fritz Heider proposed that the key to understanding
interpersonal attraction was "balance," a harmonious, non-
stress producing state. He also contended that our perception of the attributes of a person controls the way we

behave toward him as well as what we expect from him.
The perceptual factors that are most important in Heider's
theory are constancy and balance. We will tend to see a
person in a set, somewhat unchanging way.

A central function of friendship is to give this
constancy to our attitudes about our friend. This constancy produces a certain psychological economy in that
it is not necessary for us to change our view of our
friend each time we see him or her. It is not necessary
that these attitudes that we form about our friend be
necessarily true. We perceive him or her as being a certain type of person, generally one with attitudes very similar to our own. The need for a balanced psychological environment explains why we tend to see our friends as
people with attitudes similar to our own. People strive
to keep their feelings about important issues and important
people in their lives in balance or consistent.

"We're forming a mutual admiration society. Care to
sign up?"

● **PROBLEM** 16-28

What is the role of psychological inconsistency in the
theory of cognitive dissonance?

Solution: Proposed by Leon Festinger, the theory of cognitive dissonance states that people are motivated to keep
their cognitions--beliefs, attitudes, opinions, values--
consistent. If the relationship between their cognitions
becomes inconsistent, it causes psychological distress
which is called "dissonance." Since this state is quite
unpleasant to most people, it produces a motivation to
change either the attitude or action that is responsible
for the dissonance. The more important the attitudes
and behavior involved in the dissonance-producing situation, the stronger will be the motivation to change

the situation to produce consistency. For example, if
a person believes there is a relationship between smoking
and cancer and continues to smoke heavily, there is a
likelihood that he will experience psychological discomfort
upon realizing the inconsistency between the attitude that
smoking is dangerous to health and life and the action of
smoking.

A key idea is that a person must realize that there
is inconsistency before a true state of psychological inconsistency is produced. Often when there is inconsistency
in beliefs and actions people rationalize their behavior.
The smoker might also hold the attitude that he was the
exception--that while it might be true that the health of
many people is endangered by heavy smoking, his health
would not be. An individual would personally have to experience the inconsistency in his or her cognitions in
order to be motivated to change either attitudes or behavior.

When individuals experience dissonance, they also
actively avoid situations which produce this dissonance.
Festinger conducted a study on smoking habits and attitudes
and discovered that 29 percent of non-smokers, 20 percent
of light smokers, but only 7 percent of heavy smokers
thought that a relationship existed between smoking and
lung cancer. To continue smoking with the strong belief
that it would cause danger to one's health causes dissonance, and as we see from this study is not common. (This
study was done in 1957; today, with more information available on the effects of smoking on health, we might expect
these figures to be different). Dissonance motivates a
person to change, to not remain in the dissonance-producing
situation, or to adopt a new attitude to the situation.

● **PROBLEM** 16-29

Contrast the learning theorists' explanation of the process
of attitude change with that of the consistency theorists.

Solution: Learning theorists contend that for attitudes
to change, rewards or incentives must be offered. Consistency theorists agree that rewards must be offered, but
hold that psychological inconsistency or imbalance is an
equally important factor in producing attitude change.

Both sets of theorists agree with McGuire that the
two most popular and effective ways of producing attitude
change are to present the subject with a persuasive message and to get him or her involved actively in the atti-
tude-change process. Most of us experience persuasive
messages every day in the form of advertising or simply
through the attempts of one of our friends, relations or
associates to engage our cooperation or our support in
some matter. The presentation of persuasive information,
while a necessary step in attitude change, if coupled with
active participation from the subject, is likely to have
much more dramatic effects.

Involving the subject was first observed in traditional psychotherapy. Both Sigmund Freud and Carl Rogers
reported that clients who were actively involved in their
therapy improved much more than clients who sat passively
while the therapist tried to persuade them to change.
Kurt Lewin demonstrated in an experimental effort to get
homemakers to serve unappetizing, yet nutritional parts
of the cow (kidneys, heart), that those that participated
in discussion groups attempting to determine how they could
induce other homemakers to change their eating habits
later were much more likely to serve these meats to their
family than those homemakers who simply passively received
information about why they should serve these meats. (32%
of the active participants and 3% of the persuasive message group later served these organ-meats to their families).

Both learning theorists and consistency theorists
agree that active participation produces attitude change,
Where they disagree is in the explanation of how and why
this occurs. The learning theorists contend that the
greater the reward, the more change of attitude will occur.
The dissonance theorists, however, claim that the less
the reward, the greater the attitude change.

In the case of the homemakers advocating the use of
organ-meats, the learning theorists might structure an experiment wherein the participants would receive monetary
incentives for giving what their peers judged as the most
persuasive talk on why homemakers should consume these
parts of the cow. The best speakers might receive $50,
$25 and $5 respectively for their efforts. The prediction would be that the persons who received the $50 reward
for their presentation would be most likely to serve the
meats themselves because the greater incentive motivated
these persons to be better advocates for the use of the
meats and self-persuasion would be greater and more likely
to produce attitude change.

The dissonance theorists would predict that the
persons who received no reward would be more likely to use
the meat product because the dissonance produced by supporting a subject that one actually was opposed to (most
of the women initially objected to the use of these parts
of the cow) would not be resolved by the idea that one had
done so in order to receive the $50 reward; rather, it
would be necessary to change the attitudes to be more in
keeping with the behavior of researching and speaking
publicly about the great benefits of serving this product.
Thus, the smaller the reward, the greater the attitude
change.

Which of these diametrically opposed views proves to
be correct? Both are correct, but in different situations.
The learning theorists explanation holds true in situations in which the behavior or attitudes involved are
seen as relatively unimportant to the person, while the
dissonance theorists prove correct when the attitudes involved are viewed as important to the person. Sometimes
it is difficult to predict what issues will be important

to most people. The case of whether or not the homemakers should serve organ-meats would probably be less
important than a debate on group marriage for newly-weds.

● **PROBLEM 16-30**

Distinguish between prejudice and discrimination.

Solution: Prejudice is an attitude; it is generally a negative attitude held toward a particular group and any member
of that group. It is translated into behavior through discrimination. Discrimination is action that results from
prejudiced points of view.

It is possible for an individual to be quite prejudiced
and still not discriminate. The Equal Rights Laws that
have been passed in the past decade have helped to reduce
discrimination, but it is less likely that they have reduced
covert prejudice as significantly as they have the more obvious forms of discrimination. However, some evidence exists
that even the prejudicial attitudes of Americans have been
influenced by the laws Congress has passed dealing with
ethnic prejudice prohibiting discrimination in voting, employment and public accommodations. For instance in 1964,
most Americans were opposed to the Civil Rights Act, but
today over 75 percent of the public favors integration.
In areas in the South where they were previously forbidden
to vote, many blacks now hold public office.

In the area of sexism--discrimination based on sex--
the woman manager may have won social position and responsibility, but it does not insure that the other men
and women she works with will be free of the prejudiced
attitudes about women's lack of ability in management, (lack
of rationality, tendency toward dependence and emotionalism)
and other attitudes that may have been acquired and nur-
tured through many years. When discrimination decreases and
prejudice remains, discrimination may begin to take more
subtle forms: not being included in the informal discussions of the other managers, being naturally expected
to prepare the coffee for the meeting, being assigned the
more routine aspects of a particular project, and--an
almost impossible variable to measure--being tuned out or
listened to through the filter of one or another of the
traditional attitudes about women--"she's too emotional,"
she needs to be humored until the bad mood passes," she
can't be serious about business," and so forth. These
are very subtle forms of discrimination that arise from
deeply ingrained prejudiced attitudes.

● **PROBLEM 16-31**

What are generally conceived to be the causes of prejudice
and what contributes to these causes?

Solution: Although prejudice is a complex topic and often

difficult to analyze on an individual level, psychologists have hypothesized that there are basically four causes of prejudice.

The first cause is economic and political competition or conflict. This view basically believes that when any resource is limited, majority groups will vie for domination and acquisition of the resource and in the process form prejudices against the minority group for their own personal gain and advantage. Research has demonstrated a clear link between the level of discrimination and prejudice against a certain group in an area and the scarcity of jobs in that area.

The second causal factor is personality needs. After World War II, researchers began to search for a personality type for prejudice. The major piece of research in this area is by Adorno and his colleagues and is entitled The Authoritarian Personality. The researchers were attempting to find a basis for prejudice within the individual's personality structure. What they succeeded in doing was establishing a relationship between the strictness of parental upbringing and authoritarianism. The authoritarianism was seen as the basis for prejudice and bias. Unfortunately, the relationship (correlational) does not prove that one causes the other but only that they are related. Other researchers have criticized the Adorno research for numerous validation problems, such as poor subject selection.

The third cause of prejudice is viewed as a displacement of aggression. This is commonly referred to as a "scapegoat" theory of prejudice. The general contention is that people tend to displace aggression onto groups which are both visible and unable to fight back. The kind of agression which is displaced upon the group takes the form of socially acceptable methods.

The fourth cause of prejudice is conformity to already existing prejudices within the society or sub-group. Researchers noted that while there appears to be a large difference between the amount of black prejudice in the North and in the South, neither group is distinguishable on the basis of how they score on the Authoritarianism test (the F scale). The problem appears to be caused by accepted beliefs in the particular area of the country. As Elliot Aronson has noted, historical events in the South set the stage for greater prejudice against blacks, but it is conformity which keeps it going.

Although these are accepted as the causes of prejudice, there are other factors which contribute to the formulation and continuation of prejudice. Before outlining these contributions it should be noted that people are most often prejudiced against the group which is directly under them on the socio-economic scale. This gives better insight into the reason for and strength of the contributions. The four contributions are: 1) people have a need to feel superior to someone; 2) people most strongly feel that competition for jobs comes from the next lower level;

644

3) people from the lower socio-economic levels are more frustrated and therefore are more aggressive; and 4) a lack of education on the part of low socio-economic groups increases the likelihood that they will simplify their world by the consistent use of stereotyping. Obviously, no one cause or contribution is the key to prejudice, it being a person-specific problem.

● **PROBLEM 16-32**

What methods are generally viewed as helpful in reducing prejudice?

Solution: An observation of the U.S. today would indicate a definite change in attitudes toward minority groups, but whether or not prejudice is decreasing is not altogether clear.

At one time, psychologists felt that prejudice might be able to be reduced by providing individuals with information contrary to their beliefs. By changing people's attitudes about a certain ethnic group, psychologists believed that you would ultimately change their behavior. This unfortunately was not the case. Public information about a specific group of people usually was only paid attention to by the people of that group. As is seen in the area of cognitive-dissonance, people are not likely to pay much attention to opposite beliefs in important situations.

Another attempted method of change is equal-status contact. The underlying logic of this approach is that although it is difficult to change attitudes by education, it is possible to change attitudes by changing behavior. The application of bringing blacks and whites into direct contact is done with the hopes of showing prejudiced people the faultiness of their ways and to give them a better understanding of the other group. The contact must be equal-status in order to work; unfortunately forced busing and desegregation often fail to meet just this need.

Another method which appears to be highly successful is interdependence. Bringing people together is apparently not enough to decrease prejudice, but bringing them together and setting up a situation in which they must work together is. The factor of mutual interdependence as an agent in the reduction of inter-group hostility has been significantly supported by research in this area. The goal of recent research is to apply this new method in an educational setting where it is needed most.

● **PROBLEM 16-33**

What is the difference between a prejudice and a stereotype?

Solution: Although there are both positive and negative prejudices, most research in this area deals with negative prejudice.

Negative prejudice is a negative, hostile attitude toward a specific group of individuals based on incorrect or incomplete knowledge of that group. Stereotyping is the application of generalized characteristics or motives to a group of people, giving the same characteristics to all the people in the group, regardless of the individual characteristics actually present. Stereotyping is not necessarily an intentional act of derogation; very often it is merely used as a means of simplifying the complex world we live in. However, stereotypes can be dangerous when they narrow our views of actual individual differences. Prejudiced attitudes may then result.

● **PROBLEM 16-34**

How does the study of stereotyping relate to attribution theory?

Solution: Attribution theory rests on a specialized type of stereotyping. Attribution theory basically contends that individuals have a tendency to attribute a cause to any recently viewed behaviors. When viewing an event, the observer uses the information available to him at the time to infer causality. Although there are numerous factors which affect what inference will be made, the major contributors are a person's beliefs, e.g., stereotypes, or prejudices. The process of attribution based on one's prejudices can be described as a "vicious circle." A person's prejudices affect his attributions and his misdirected attributions will then serve to reinforce and intensify his prejudices.

● **PROBLEM 16-35**

What is meant by androgyny in Bem's research?

Solution: Sex role stereotypes are one form of prejudice that pervade our society. People are usually seen as typically "masculine" (aggressive, independent, responsible) or typically "feminine" (passive, dependent, submissive). It has also been assumed that a healthy, normal woman would be "feminine" and a healthy, normal man would be "masculine." Research by Sandra Bem, however, has attempted to establish a sex-typing method that contains elements of both femininity and masculinity. Proposing that psychological health requires that a person have both masculine and feminine qualities, she developed a scale to measure the combination of these characteristics. Individuals that have characteristics of both sexes she called "androgynous."

The scale is called the "Bem Sex Role Inventory." A person is presented with 60 adjectives which are associated with either an extremely masculine or an extremely

feminine person or which can be applied to either sex.
The person is then asked to rate how each term applies to
him or her. A man who states that only the masculine adjectives apply to him is a sex-typed male, the woman who
finds that only the feminine adjectives apply to her is
a sex-typed woman, while those individuals who find that
the neutral words apply more to them are androgynous.
An example of some of the items used in the Inventory are:

Masculine	Feminine	Neuter
Aggressive	Shy	Happy
Dominant	Soft-spoken	Helpful
Forceful	Tender	Secretive
Individualistic	Warm	Solemn
Self-sufficient	Yielding	Truthful

Experiments have shown that men and women who score
quite high on masculinity or feminity also demonstrate high
anxiety and low self-esteem and acceptance. Androgynous
people, however, tend to have high self-esteem. Androgynous
people also tend to be more adaptable, that is, they can
function well in situations which call for typically masculine, independent behavior, as well as those that require
more tender, helpful feminine behavior.

These results point to the possibility of reducing the
strong socialization toward one or the other sex-type role
and encouraging the development of the most positive characteristics of both sexes.

● **PROBLEM** 16-36

"Anatomy is destiny," claimed Sigmund Freud when he
characterized personality differences in men and women.
Discuss.

Solution: This classic phrase "anatomy is destiny" reflects the basic premise in Freud's theory that biological,
anatomical differences in the sexes are responsible for
their personality differences. A central concept in the
different early experiences of boys and girls that contributes greatly to adult personality structure, according
to Freud, is that girls experience "penis envy" upon
discovering that they are differently constructed than
boys which leads to, among other things, feelings of inferiority, jealousy, weak moral sense and desire to have
a baby to substitute for the lack of a penis. Followers
of Freud have developed and refined this basic idea.
Eric Erikson set forth a less psychoanalytic theory, but
one that was still based on anatomy. He felt that due
to their different biological roles men were more motivated to achieve, while women had a greater need to be
accepted by other people.

This position that biological differences explain
the differences in personality of men and women has also

traditionally been supported by examples from the animal
kingdom. Since anatomical and behavioral differences
exist in almost all other species, they must also exist
in humans.

There are obviously differences anatomically in men
and women, but how much do they account for the psychological differences we assign to the two sexes? Let us look
at the facts surrounding this question. Men are generally
larger and more muscular than women at birth; they are
also more aggressive; women are more verbal earlier than
men; men do have better visual, spatial and mathematical
abilities. However, no evidence has been found by the most
recent researchers in this area (Maccoby, et al.) that
girls are more sociable, more suggestible, less achievement-
oriented, or less self-caring than boys. Similarly, there
seems to be no differences between men and women in simple
memory, intellectual, or analytic abilities.

There appears to be much evidence, in fact, that while
in lower animals a great deal of behavior is attributable
to hormones, the influence of biology decreases as one
goes up the phylogenetic scale. Experiences after birth
seem to be much more important in determining a person's
sex-role typing behavior. Studies with hermaphrodites--
people born with both ovaries and testes--have proven most
interesting in this regard. Money, et. al. studied 105
biological hermaphrodites whose parents decided which sex
the child would be assigned at birth and raised him or her
as either a boy or a girl. If anatomy were destiny we
would expect that a large number of these people would
have demonstrated behavior different than that which their
parents assigned them. This, however, was not the case.
Only 5 of the 105 individuals studied deviated from the
sex assigned them by their parents. The decision as to
whether these children would be raised as a boy or a girl,
then, appears to be much more important than the biological
sex in determining behavior.

Margaret Mead's anthropological studies of different
tribes in the South Pacific also puts the biology-as-
determinant question in a weak position. She discovered
tribes in which women were the dominant force, the leaders,
and men were docile, dependent and seductive. If nothing
else, her research has helped to prove that sex-linked
behavior is not universal and therefore does not appear to
be genetically-linked. Rather, stereotyped sex-role behavior seems to result much more from the socialization
practices of a society.

● **PROBLEM** 16-37

Characterize the authoritarian personality.

Solution: "Authoritarianism" is an attitude structure that
gives rise to a persisting orientation to the world built
around the dominant value of "power," whether in terms of

aggressive display or submissive yielding. The person who scores high on the attitude scale that measures degree of authoritarianism will likely have come from a family in which the father was a strong, punishing figure. Maslow was one of the first to describe the authoritarian character structure. According to him it embodies an ideology that views the world in terms of a jungle in which every man's hand is necessarily against every other man's, in which the whole world is conceived of as dangerous, threatening, or at best challenging, and in which human beings are conceived of as primarily selfish or evil or stupid.

Other dominant attitudes of the authoritarian personality are ethnocentrism and prejudice, categorical and conventional thought, superstition and suggestibility, and tendencies opposed to self-examination. Authoritarians also tend to be unperceptive about the feelings or attitudes of others. They are both dominant and submissive--dominant to those perceived as weaker, and submissive to those perceived to be more powerful than themselves.

The F (fascist) Scale that measures the authoritarian personality purports to measure the following nine characteristics: conventionalism (rigid adherence to middle-class conventional values); authoritarian submission (a submissive, uncritical attitude toward the leaders of the ingroup and devotion or obedience to that group); authoritarian aggression (a tendency to be on the lookout for and to condemn, reject, and punish people who violate conventional values); anti-introspection (an opposition to the subjective, the imaginative minded); superstition and stereotyping (the belief in mystical determinants of one's fate and the disposition to think in rigid categories); power and toughness (being preoccupied with leader-follower relationships, identification with power figures, and an exaggerated assertion of strength and toughness); destruction and cynicism (generalized hostility, basic distrust of others); projectivity (the belief that wild and dangerous things are going on in the world); sexual concerns (an exaggerated concern with sexual occurrences).

● **PROBLEM** 16-38

How is the authoritarian personality measured?

Solution: In the late 1940's the American Jewish Congress asked Adorno and his associates to determine if there was a certain personality type that would be responsive to fascist ideology. Adorno then tried to identify people's personality characteristics by first looking at their ideology. To do this, he developed what is now called the California F (fascist) Scale for measuring the "authoritarian personality."

He began with the idea that fascist ideology is comprised of three things: anti-Semitism, ethnocentrism (tendency to reject other ethnic groups than one's own),

and political and economic conservatism. Initially, he
gave separate scales for these items to large numbers
of Americans. He predicted that scores on these scales
would correlate, which they did. Conservatism, however,
had a much lower correlation than ethnocentrism and anti-
Semitism. Next, Adorno collected biographical information
from the people who scored high on the scales and gave
them additional tests until he developed a personality profile for the trait of "authoritarianism."

As it is used today, scores on the F (fascist) Scale
correlate highly with anti-Semitism and ethnocentrism and
correlate moderately with political-economic conservatism.
The F Scale also predicts ethnic prejudice. The F Scale
is an attitude-trait scale. Attitude-trait scales usually
have to do with others in the person's social world.
The responses are taken to be indicative of a characteristic mode of reacting to others. Examples of questions from
the F Scale are:

Obedience and respect for authority are the most important virtues children should learn.
If people would talk less and work more, everybody
would be better off.
There is hardly anything lower than a person who does
not feel great love, gratitude, and respect for his parents.
Human nature being what it is, there will always be
war and conflict.
People can be divided into two distinct classes:
the weak and the strong.
Most people don't realize how much our lives are controlled by plots hatched in secret places.

The first findings from the F Scale indicated that
people with right-wing political tendencies tended to score
highest in authoritarianism. In fact, Adorno's work assumes
that intolerance and authoritarianism exist only among extreme political conservatives. Subsequent research has
shown that it is not only those at the right wing of the political spectrum that tend to demonstrate authoritarian
traits. Rokeach, in his research on dogmatism--a tendency
to be closed-minded, authoritarian, and rigid independent of
any political ideology--discovered that left-wing students
are as closed-minded and rigid in their ideas as the extreme right-wing students.

AGGRESSION

● PROBLEM 16-39

What distinctions are made when defining aggression in
psychology?

Solution: Because the term is used in so many ways, aggression is very hard to define. Mass murderers and successful salesmen can both be described as being aggressive,
but there is obviously a difference between the two.

The defining of aggression in psychology calls for the application of a set of distinctions to aggressive behavior. The first distinction is between harmful versus non-harmful aggression. In this distinction it is the outcome of the behavior which is important. This makes the initial distinction between the killer and the salesman clear. The second distinction concerns the intent of the aggressor. Hitting someone accidentally is not considered aggressive, but hitting someone with the intention of hurting them (even if it doesn't hurt) is. In addition, one final distinction is between aggression which is necessary in the achievement of a goal (as in professional boxing) and aggression which is an end in itself (as in a common street fight).

● **PROBLEM** 16-40

What is the role of frustration in human aggression?

Solution: There are many situations, both painful and un-painful, which can cause aggression. The most common source of aggression is frustration. Research indicates that depriving an individual from attaining something is not enough to elicit frustration. Relative deprivation is what causes frustration. If you don't know something exists, or you know something is unattainable, then you are not frustrated when you don't achieve it. It is when you are able to do something, or feel you deserve something and you are deprived, that frustration arises. This kind of frustration may lead to aggression.

● **PROBLEM** 16-41

What is the frustration-displaced aggression theory of prejudice?

Solution: Based on a psychodynamic or drive view of aggression, the frustration-aggression hypothesis states that frustration toward the accomplishment of some goal produces aggression; if the source of the frustration is near enough and not too threatening, the aggression may be taken out on that person. If, however, the source is either unavailable or too threatening, the frustrated person will displace his aggression onto someone or something else. This someone or something else is called a "scapegoat."

Usually the scapegoat will be someone who is available and nonthreatening (not likely to retaliate). It is believed that much prejudice against ethnic minorities is the result of displaced aggression. Hovland and Sears in a study done in the 1940's discovered a relation between the price of cotton in the South over a 50-year period and the number of lynchings of blacks in the same time period. They discovered that the lower the price of cotton became, the more lynchings took place. They hypothe-

651

sized that the white southerners became frustrated when
the price of cotton fell, as it was their source of liveli-
hood. They could not retaliate against the source, north-
ern manufacturers, therefore, they vented their frustration on the visible, vulnerable black minority.

A problem with this explanation is its implication
that frustration itself is a cause for prejudice. In fact,
aggression and other forms of hostility toward ethnic groups
is increased by frustration only in those individuals who
are already prejudiced.

It has also not been proven that aggressive energy
builds up in a person and must be released onto some object.
It is a theory with about as much experimental evidence
supporting it as there is demonstrating its lack of validity.
As in so many areas in psychological research, there is
need for yet a great deal of experimentation before we can
know with certainty the social-psychological causes of
prejudice.

● **PROBLEM 16-42**

Describe two types of aggression--instrumental and hostile.

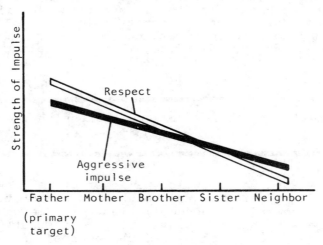

(primary
target)

Feelings of aggression and respect are strongest toward the
primary target. The strength of the aggressive impulse and
of the respect decreases as the distance from the primary
target increases. Since respect declines faster, at some
point the aggressive impulse is stronger. It is then that
the child expresses his anger. The height at which the two
emotions cross determines the strength of the aggression
expressed.

Solution: Aggression, the intentional injury of another
person, is pervasive in the world around us on both a
personal and collective scale. While interpersonal aggression is the most common form, the collective aggression of war and its passive counterpart--participating
vicariously in competitive, violent sport or violence in

the newspapers, television and film--occupy an integral
role in our society today. In the past 150 years more
than 70 million people have died in wars. In the past
15 years, the number of reported murders has increased
120 percent.

Interpersonal aggression, surprisingly, occurs most
often between friends, relatives and acquaintances, and
is much less often associated with robbery or other crimes
than may be supposed. Thus, most aggression is "hostile
aggression." It occurs due to an internal motive state
which results in the intention to harm another person.
This internal state is often what we call "anger."
Another type of aggression, "instrumental aggression,"
does not involve any particular hostility toward the victim, except insofar as he or she is interfering with the
accomplishment of some goal: the aggression is instrumental in the obtaining of some reward. "Crimes of pas-
sion" probably most easily typify hostile aggression:
"Husband kills wife's lover;" while the bank teller who
will not hand over the money and must be eliminated in
order to get the cash is an example of a victim of instrumental aggression.

● **PROBLEM 16-43**

What do the results of most psychological studies of
aggression imply about television programming?

Solution: Today's children spend more time in watching television than in any other activity except sleeping. It is
estimated that over 75 percent of the dramatic shows seen
on television contain violence. What is the effect of
all of this violence on the children who watch it? There
are essentially three viewpoints concerning the effects
of violent television programming.

The social learning theorists claim that television
provides models for aggressive behavior and thereby reinforces already acquired aggressive acts and helps to instill
new ones in the viewers. Because these models are on television they demonstrate that aggressive behavior is rewarded. Also viewing such activity tends to increase the
arousal level of the viewers and thus the likelihood of
being provoked into aggressive behavior.

Another group of theorists believe that the watching
of violence on television has a cathartic effect--through
watching violent individuals on television, the aggressive
energy that builds up in every human is released vicariously. It reduces the aggressive energy level and thus
reduces the possibility that aggressive action will occur.

Finally, some believe that that the effects of television on aggression are unknown, that it has not been
proven that television either reduces or increases the
possibility of aggressive behavior in its viewers.

In fact, the studies that support the cathartic hypothesis are in serious question due to several problems in the experimental design. The majority of experiments conducted in this area have shown an increase in aggression as the result of watching television. It seems particularly true that violent television increases aggression in children that already have aggressive tendencies. However, it is not correct to blame television entirely for a person's aggressive behavior. There are too many other variables. The environment in which a child lives each day, the models of his parents or friends, the rewards and punishments he receives for aggressive behavior all affect the level of aggression. Still, overall it appears that a reduction in violence on television would be likely to produce more good than harmful effects on viewers.

● **PROBLEM** 16-44

Discuss the two main theoretical points of view on the origins of human aggressive behavior.

Solution: Most psychologists believe that aggression is a learned behavior--that aggressive tendencies are learned like any other type of behavior. This social learning theory explanation of aggression supposes that most aggression is learned through operant conditioning, a process whereby a person's actions are reinforced by rewards and discouraged by punishments. Rewards and punishments are thought to shape a person's behavior. If a child is rewarded for random aggressive behavior, the chances are good that the behavior will be repeated. If, however, the child is punished for acting aggressively, the likelihood of that type of behavior occurring again is lessened. Rewards and punishments can be either verbal or physical. The "schedule of reinforcement" has been found to be quite important in the learning of aggressive responses. If a person is intermittently reinforced for aggression, his or her tendency to be aggressive will last longer and be more generalized than if the reinforcement is continuous (Walters & Brown, 1963). This finding is quite important, as a parent will tend to reinforce aggression irregularly, thereby encouraging the continuance of aggressive behavior. For example, a parent will punish aggression directed toward him but will reinforce retaliation against a neighbor child.

Another form of social learning that contributes to the development of aggressive behavior is modelling or observational learning. Bandura & Ross & Ross' research on the effects of modelling on aggressive behavior in children have produced some of the most reliable experimental findings in this area. Modelling is simply a process whereby a person learns a new behavior by watching another person engage in it. A group of nursery school children were exposed to either a live aggressive model, a filmed aggressive model, a cartoon aggressive model, a nonaggressive model or no model. Then they were mildly frustrated and placed in a room with toys. The children

who had been exposed to any of the three aggressive
models were significantly more likely to demonstrate aggressive behavior than those that had been with the non-
aggressive model or no model.   An additional finding is
that an important variable in whether aggressive behavior
will be learned from a model is whether or not the behavior
is rewarded.

A different school of thought concerning the origins
of aggressive behavior does not feel that reward and punishment is related to aggression. Rather, these scientists
think that aggression is an inborn tendency in all animals,
including man. The only reason we are not continually involved in wars is because man uses his intelligence to vent
his aggression and therefore does not always aggress physically. Though Freud originally introduced this idea in
psychoanalytic theory in the 1930's, today this approach to
understanding aggressive behavior has been most supported
by the work of Konrad Lorenz. An ethologist--one who
studies the behavior of animals in their natural habitat--
Lorenz believes that because humans use their intelligence
to aggress, they have never developed natural controls on
aggression against their own species as have other animals
capable of killing their own kind like lions, wolves or
tigers. It has been difficult, however, to experimentally
prove that aggression is innate and physiologists claim
that there is no evidence yet to prove that there is an internal drive to aggression in human beings.

● **PROBLEM** 16-45

What are some of the common methods used to reduce
aggressive behavior and how effective are they?

Solution: There are four basic models of aggression reduction which are commonly in use: punishment, punishment
of aggressive models, reward of alternative behavior, and
the presence of non-aggressive models.

Punishment is probably the first thing that comes to
mind when thinking of how to reduce unwanted behavior.
Research and observation show severe punishment to be
usually temporary in effect and not conducive to the internalization of the desired behavior. Research shows
that children who are reared by strict punishment usually
grow up to be aggressive. This has generally been attributed
to the frustrating effect of severe punishment. Mild punishment is a far more effective tool for reducing aggression.

The second model of aggression reduction is punishment
of aggressive models. The underlying theory here is that a
person who views another person getting punished for a
certain behavior will be vicariously punished as well.
(Possibly the idea behind public executions.) However, in
small group experiments with children, observation of a
model being punished for aggression did not lower the
general level of aggression below that of a control group
which did not observe such punishment.

The third approach to the reduction of aggressive behavior is the rewarding of alternative behavior patterns. This requires ignoring a child when he behaves aggressively and rewarding him when he displays non-aggressive behavior. Although best suited for children, this method sometimes works well with adults, and is based on the idea that the individual is behaving in an aggressive manner to attract attention. The research in this area is highly supportive of this approach. The main success of this method is that it clearly demonstrates that it is possible to train children to respond to frustration in non-aggressive ways.

The fourth and final approach is the presence of non-aggressive models. This is almost a combination of methods 2 and 3 in that it combines the best of both. The supplying of knowledge to the extent that a certain behavior, if acted, would be considered inappropriate, is a powerful control of aggression. By presenting an individual with a situation in which non-controlled people act non-aggressively, the rate of aggressive behavior will drop. This view has been repeatedly supported by research.

● **PROBLEM 16-46**

What are the general contentions as to whether or not aggressiveness is instinctual?

Solution: Whether or not aggression is instinctual is a highly controversial issue. There is a lack of clear evidence concerning the source of aggression in man and most research in this area has been limited to species other than man. Research with lower-order animals (i.e., rats) shows that aggressive behaviors can be inhibited by early experience. This research was extended to the study of humans, where it was found that learning plays a major role in aggressive behavior. However, in humans, aggressiveness is a complex interaction between innate tendencies and learned responses. In searching for an instinctual basis of aggression, scientists have looked for an "aggression center" in the brain. The results of such research indicate that the same physiological stimulus can produce widely divergent responses in man, depending upon previous learning experience. Thus the issue of whether or not aggression has an instinctual basis in man has not yet been resolved.

● **PROBLEM 16-47**

What are some of the theories which support a belief that aggression is necessary?

Solution: The two main approaches to the contention that aggression is necessary are the "survival of the fittest" theory and the "catharsis" theory.

The "survival of the fittest" theory, first expounded by Darwin, was applied to aggression by Konrad Lorenz. Lorenz contends that certain kinds of aggression are necessary for the continued existence of the species. His argument is based on ethnological observation of non-human species. However, although there is supportive evidence to the notion that aggressive tendencies are necessary in lower-level organisms, many social scientists feel that modern man has transcended the need for such an instinct.

The second approach which contends the need for aggressiveness is the "cartharsis" theory. Formulated by Freud, this theory basically supports aggression as a means of releasing inner tension. If this tension were to remain unreleased, mental illness would result. Research does not support this idea and actually has shown the opposite to be true.

● **PROBLEM 16-48**

What is meant by catharsis? How do catharsis theorists claim aggression can be controlled?

Solution: Those who feel that aggression is a drive--a state of excitation that will not subside until its cause is removed--believe that the elimination of aggression depends upon a person's ability to drain or cathart the aggressive energy from his or her system. There is a certain amount of empirical evidence to support this theory that an anger drive will not subside unless it is released through some aggressive activity. Hokanson and Shelter (1961) conducted an experiment in which subjects were insulted and angered and then allowed to either shock the insulter or do nothing. Heart rate and blood pressure measures were taken for all subjects. Those who were allowed to shock the insulter had readings equal to the pre-insult level, while those who were not allowed any aggressive behavior retained high blood pressure and heartbeat readings.

Catharsis theorists believe that aggression can be minimized and channeled into more productive or neutral outlets than retaliating against the cause of the frustration. This is due to the belief that aggressive energy can also be displaced onto another object. Aggressive sports, chopping wood, hammering nails, pounding meat or kneading bread are all examples of activities that can release a certain amount of aggressive energy. This theory is quite popular with non-psychologists and has also been substantiated with experimental evidence. Dobb and Wood (1972) had their subjects insulted by a confederate. The subjects were then given the opportunity to shock someone else or were not permitted to shock anyone. Then the subjects were given the opportunity to shock the person who had insulted them. Those that had shocked someone else shocked the confederate significantly less than those who were permitted no aggressive behavior.

There is also some evidence to support the contention that aggressive energy can be released vicariously through observing someone else aggress against the source of one's frustration. This idea is carried over into support for violence on television and in the mass media as a means of reducing generalized aggressive tendencies. The data supporting this approach is by no means definitive and further research is required before the advocation of violence as a means of reducing violence can be scientifically supported, especially because there exists so much evidence demonstrating that viewing aggression tends to increase aggressive acts.

MOTIVATION: INTERNALITY AND SEX DIFFERENCES

● **PROBLEM** 16-49

Discuss research on "bystander intervention."

Solution: The research of Latane and Darley has been in the forefront of the endeavor to understand "bystander intervention," which refers specifically to taking action to help someone in need. The presence of other people and their relationship to the bystander is a variable which appears to make a difference in the response of the bystander.

In a classic experiment, male subjects heard someone fall, apparently injured, in the room next door. Whether subjects tried to help, and how long they took to do so were the main dependent variables in the experiment. Subjects were placed in one of four conditions: alone, with a friend, with another subject who was a stranger, and with a confederate in the experiment who had been instructed to remain passive at the sounds of the injury.

In the alone situation the subject responded to the need for help 91% of the time; whereas in the company of the passive confederate only 7% of the subjects responded. With pairs of strangers, at least one of the persons intervened in 40% of the pairs, while in the group of two friends at least one person intervened in 70% of the pairs.

percent involvement

The explanation of this finding can be considered in two directions, social influence and diffusion of responsibility. The former suggests that people are susceptible to the apparent reactions of the others present; if other bystanders indicate by inaction that they feel the emergency is not serious, this influences whether the observer will intervene. However, the possibility exists that a state may develop in which each bystander is influenced by the apparent lack of concern of the others, when in fact they may be highly concerned but uncertain and confused. The other explanation regarding diffusion of responsibility suggests that where an individual is alone he feels total responsibility for dealing with the emergency and will bear a good part of the blame if he fails to act. When others are present, the responsibility is diffused, as well as whatever blame may be forthcoming.

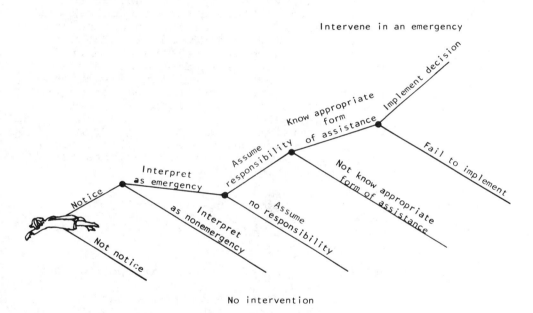

Decision tree analysis of intervention in an emergency.

Another factor which appears to influence bystander intervention is the clarity or ambiguity of the need for help. Clark and Word (1972) looked at how the ambiguity of the situation affects people's willingness to help. In an experiment where a maintenance man walked by a group of students with a ladder into an adjacent room and a few minutes later produced a loud crashing noise, people were slow to come to his rescue if there was any ambiguity as to whether he had actually fallen or simply dropped his materials. However, if his fall was accompanied by a loud groan, "My back, I can't move," the response was quick. Therefore, it appears that two important variables in bystander intervention are how clear it is that help is needed and how much personal responsibility the bystander experiences.

Describe Rotter's Locus of Control scale and what it attempts to measure.

Solution: "Locus of control" as a determinant of individual behavior is predicated on the notion that an important underlying determinant of an individual's action is the degree to which an individual perceives that a reward follows from his own behavior or is controlled by forces outside himself. Lefcourt (1966) described the difference in these orientations: the person with an internal orientation tends to take responsibility for what happens to him, he sees the events of life as having a cause-effect relationship with himself as the cause; the "external" sees the events of life as due to chance or fate or some other factor beyond his control. The difference between people with regard to locus of control is one of degree and it is also situation dependent. In situations with which people have very little experience the generalized tendency measured by the locus of control scale will tend to have considerable effect.

The actual scale consists of twenty-six forced choice items, 13 of which indicate an external orientation* and 13 of which indicate an internal orientation. Examples from the scale are:

*a. Many of the unhappy things in people's lives are partly due to bad luck.
 b. People's misfortunes result from the mistakes they make.

 a. Promotions are earned through hard work and persistence.
*b. Making a lot of money is largely a matter of getting the right breaks.

The asterisked statements represent an external orientation. Items of this kind from the scale have been administered to a variety of different populations for research purposes. Quite consistent findings are found, some of which are: Individuals with high achievement motivation are found to be more internal in their dispositions; males are routinely more internal than females; whites are more internal than blacks; internals are more resistant to influence attempts than externals.

As a part of a person's personality, locus of control is a learned or acquired characteristic and can therefore be changed by new experiences. It is also probably highly dependent on cultural values. In our culture an internal orientation is most highly valued, whereas in India, for instance, the culture would be more likely to favor and reinforce the external world view.

Characterize a person who scores high on internality on the Internal-External Control Scale.

Solution: A high internal on the Internal-External Control Scale might be the ideal achievement-oriented individual; chances are that the person would be a white male, characterized by independence and resistance to influence; successful in whatever he has undertaken; he would prefer tasks that required the use of his own skill to ones relying on chance; he would be more likely to be from the North than the South of the United States; he is likely to be more severe in judging the actions of others than the external; he is apt to judge people on the basis of their accomplishments and to see class differences as attributable to lack of effort on the part of the members of the lower class.

An internal with experiences that reward his efforts will tend to have the internal orientation reinforced. If, however, experiences occur that demonstrate the entrance of "luck" into his life, it is possible that the internal orientation will become more external. For instance, after the lottery for the draft conducted by the Selective Service, a group of internals who scored quite close to each other on the internal-external scale were affected by the number they received in the lottery. Men who "lucked out" became significantly more external than those who would likely be drafted.

Also it is necessary to examine the individual items on the scale to have a more precise estimation of an individual's personal characteristics. For example, it was predicted that political activists would score very high on the internal scale because of their active attempts to change their environment. However, it was found that they have a significant number of external responses on the scale. It was found that these activists were internal on items that measure personal control but external on those that measure system control. There are general shared tendencies among those who score at either end of the internal-external scale, but the scale is not inclusive enough to give a profile of the entire person. Like most other psychological measuring devices, it shows us one aspect of the many-faceted human psychology.

● **PROBLEM** 16-52

What sex and race differences have been found on the Internal-External Control Scale? Discuss.

Solution: Findings on Rotter's internal-external control scale, which attempts to measure how much a person sees his life as subject to personal control (internal), and how much a person tends to see it as controlled by events outside of personal control (external), consistently show that women are more external than men and that blacks are more external than whites. There are two possible explanations for these findings: 1) women and blacks are socialized to believe that they have less personal control over their lives, and 2) they actually do have less personal control over their lives.

A black child is more likely than a white to grow up in a poor, depressed area, to receive less education, to have more trouble getting a job, to be part of a family that is receiving financial aid from the government. The external orientation of the black appears to be an accurate reflection of the way in which society treats them. In fact, it was found that blacks are not external because they believe that luck controls what happens to them. Rather, their externality is based on the belief that society limits their control over their own lives.

The situation for a woman is not dissimilar. Traditional child-rearing techniques include the teaching of sex-typed behaviors that include, for female children, dependency and lack of encouragement in gaining mastery over the environment; the ultimate achievement traditionally has been marriage and family. Also, despite legislation for equal rights, women still tend to be discriminated against in the job market and hold lower paying and lower status jobs than men. In some states, women cannot hold property in their own name or sign legal contracts. Their external orientation, like that of blacks, also may reflect limitations placed on them by society.

● **PROBLEM** 16-53

A projective test is used to measure achievement motivation. Describe this test. What are some of the limitations of this type of test?

Solution: The work of McClelland has contributed most to the development and understanding of the "need for achievement." Growing out of Murray's theory of needs, the need for achievement as defined by him is the need "to accomplish something difficult . . . to overcome obstacles and obtain a high standard. To excel oneself. To rival and surpass others." This need to excel, to succeed, to accomplish, to be successful is considered a secondary need (a need that does not arise directly from physical needs) that motivates people to act just as hunger can motivate them to look for food.

The test that McClelland (1943) used to initially measure the need for achievement (it is often called n Ach) was the Thematic Apperception Test (T.A.T.). This is a test in which people are asked to tell a story about a variety of pictures that they see, answering such questions

as "Who are the people? What has led up to this situation?
What is happening? What will happen? What is wanted?"
It is called a projective test because it is believed that
a person projects his or her feelings and needs into the
pictures. Then the stories are scored and degree of
achievement imagery is assessed by content analysis.

The object in the TAT test is to write a short story about
what is happening in a picture like the one above. You might
try it with this picture. Tell in your story (1) what is
happening and who the people are, (2) what led up to the situation shown in the picture, (3) what the people in the picture are thinking and feeling, and (4) what will happen in
the future. Does your story tell you anything about yourself
and your motives and needs?

There are two major drawbacks to this type of test.
First, the test-retest reliability is not high. That is,
the scores for a person taking the test at different times
vary considerably. The experimenter, then, does not have
a way to know which score is more reflective of the person's n Ach. Situational circumstances appear to have a
strong influence on a person's n Ach. For instance, if
subjects are told that they are going to be evaluated for
their leadership ability, their scores on the T.A.T. are
much higher. This type of variable affects a person's
performance on the test and makes the results somewhat
unreliable. Second, the stories are difficult to score.
A person must be well trained in the system of scoring
devised by McClelland for achievement images.

Even with these difficulties, the n Ach has received
much attention in the past twenty years, and much research
has been conducted based on results from the T.A.T. test.
In behavior science studies it is always useful to investigate the manner in which data is collected before becoming

overly enthusiastic about the results, as the methods for
collecting data, though well-established and long-used,
may not necessarlly stand up to scientific scrutiny. That
such an enormous amount of data has been collected and used
to devise numerous theories and establish correlations
between need for achievement and economic growth, professional and academic success, and many other aspects of
personal and national life, and that n Ach data rests on
the results of an unreliable test, could strike a note of
skepticism into the student of psychology about taking any
results as facts without knowing more about the source of
the data.

● **PROBLEM** 16-54

How do men and women differ in their scores on the need
for achievement? Why might this be?

Solution: While women score as high as men do on need for
achievement as measured by the Thematic Apperception Test,
their need to achieve is directed differently than that
of men. Men's need to achieve is in the realms of intellectual and occupational pursuits, such as achieving a
high academic standing or becoming a doctor or the
president of a company. The need to achieve in women,
however, is more in the fields of homemaking or social
success. This difference in focus is partly explained by
the different programming of men and women in our culture.
Women are traditionally taught to get married and have
children, while men are taught that they are expected to
develop an occupation, a career.

It has also been postulated (Atkinson 1964) that n Ach
is made up of a person's hope for success and fear of
failure. Women do not have high confidence about their
own abilities and therefore women come to display less
need for achievement because they fear they will fail if
they try to excel in something. As men and women grow
older, however, the difference in their scores becomes
greater. A man's need for achievement increases after he
leaves college, but a woman's decreases (Baruch, 1967).

Another theory, set forth by Matina Horner (1972),
is that it is not fear of failure that causes a woman to
shun intellectual and occupational achievement, but fear
of success. Success academically or occupationally is
seen as threatening to men, unfeminine, and likely to lead
to rejection. These conflicting drives cause a woman to
fear success and therefore demonstrate a low need for
achievement. These results have, however, come under
question as it was found that women who are intellectually
and professionally successful show as much n Ach as do men.

Whatever the reasons for the difference in the scores
of men and women, it is well to consider that they may reflect the traditional society stereotypes of a woman and
a woman's place, and that the increasing rejection of traditional sex roles by women may result in the disappearance
of this difference.

Define the motive to avoid success according to Horner.
How did she go about studying this motive in women?

Solution: At Harvard in the early 1970's, Matina Horner set
about studying the attitudes of both men and women to successful members of their own sex in traditionally male-
dominated occupations. She did this by administering one-
line beginning descriptive phrases and having her subjects
complete a story about the person described. The stories
were scored in terms of the consequences of success for
the people in the story. An example of a typical story
beginning is, "Anne finds herself in her last year of
medical school at the top of her class," and "Andrew finds
himself in his last year of medical school at the top of
his class."

About 65% of the women believed that success would
lead to negative results for the women described while
less than 10% of the men described negative results for
the successful men. From these results she postulated
the need to avoid success in women, and later found that
it was particularly prevalent in bright women.

Because of societal expectations that a woman will
not do as well as a man, will marry and occupy a position
to complement him, it was felt that women were in a double-
bind situation, that is, in a situation in which they would
lose out regardless of which choice they made. In this
case, the choice would be whether to maintain the approval
of their peers, and particularly of the males whom they
would be threatening with their high-level intellectual
performance, by performing at a level lower than their
capacity, or to do their best academically and professionally and alienate those around them with their "unfeminine"
behavior. Because of this double-bind situation, Horner
theorized that bright women suffer from a motive to avoid
success in occupational and intellectual pursuits in order
to insure success in emotional and relational pursuits.

Subsequent experimentation, however, has shown that
both men and women feel that a woman who is successful in
a traditionally male-dominated field will encounter negative results. Therefore, her findings may simply reflect
the social stereotyping of male and female roles and may
not be pointing out a motive pertaining specifically to
women. With the loosening of stereotypes about the role
of men and women, further testing will have to occur to
see if this finding will still hold.

● **PROBLEM** 16-56

What are the characteristics of a good manipulator
according to the work of Richard Christie?

<u>Solution</u>: Perhaps it is because we are socially dependent on our interactions with others that such fascination and interest exists in the means by which people exert influence and power over other people. While most of us would like to have our own way as often as possible, we do not want to be manipulated by someone else if we can help it. In the early 1950's Richard Christie became interested in how and in what ways people differed in manipulative tendencies.

The principles of Machiavelli, which are described in <u>The Prince</u>, give advice on manipulating other people, and the term "Machiavellian" has come to be associated with the belief that the ends justify the means and that in order to maintain power one must manipulate people. It was these two tactics that interested Christie, and he sought to discover to what degree they were used by individuals in everyday life. With his associates, he developed a scale based on items drawn from <u>The Prince</u>, such as, "It is wise to flatter important people," "Most people don't know what is best for them," "It is safer to be feared than to be loved." There has been much research using the scale and its subsequent refinements which points to a number of stable findings. Interestingly, scores on the "Mach" scales do not correlate with those on the F (Fascist) Scale which measures degree of authoritarianism, and therefore the two tests measure different tendencies.

Christie proposed (and these positions have been mainly supported by the research) the following four characteristics of an effective manipulator:

1. The relative lack of emotion when dealing with people: Emotional attachments would interfere with manipulation attempts.

2. Lack of conventional morality: In situations in which attainment of power was most important, standard moral practices would need to be seen as an obstacle to the goal. Remember the manipulator holds to the philosophy that "the ends justify the means."

3. No strong ideological commitments: For the same reasons as those stated above, any strong, emotional commitment would tend to reduce the effectiveness of the manipulative type in certain situations that might involve personally important issues. High Mach individuals do very well when asked to speak persuasively on an emotional issue they do not favor.

4. Relative psychological balance: Any gross psychopathology would impede the Machiavellian type from making rational judgments about others with whom he had to deal. That is, his own psychological needs might color his perceptions about those with whom he was interacting.

There is some evidence supporting the idea that people who are involved in roles demanding a good deal of interpersonal contact tend toward higher scores than those who are in impersonal, more distant situations. For instance, in research on intended specialties among medical students, those naming psychiatry and pediatrics scored the highest on the Mach scale and those selecting surgery scored lowest. Of course, this tendency, like most personality variables, does not exist in pure form in anyone. A person may display these tendencies in one situation and be quite different in another.

SHORT ANSWER QUESTIONS FOR REVIEW

Choose the correct answer.

1. The studies of Asch and Crutchfield revealed
    that there was/were (a) little difference
    among subjects in conforming behavior (b)
    considerable differences among subjects in
    conforming behavior (c) no differences among
    subjects in conforming behavior (d) the studies
    did not concern the extent to which subjects
    differed on conforming behavior   b

2. A stationary point of light that appears to
    move in the dark refers to the (a) auto-
    kinetic effect (b) attitude change effect
    (c) conformity effect (d) automated effect   a

3. A group highly influential in determining a
    person's behavior is called (a) family (b)
    peer group (c) reference group (d) church
    organization   c

4. Deutsch and Epstein attempting to demonstrate
    the effect of incentive on non-zero-sum games
    by using real money, found that (a) there
    was increased cooperation among subjects
    (b) there was no effect on subjects (c) there
    was increased competition among subjects (d)
    there was a slight increase in cooperation
    among subjects   c

5. Deindividuation refers to (a) antisocial
    acts (b) disinhibition (c) anonymity in
    a group situation (d) aggression   c

6. The phenomenon that the mere presence of another
    person produces increased productivity is
    called (a) competition (b) social facili-
    tation (c) motivation (d) cooperation   b

7. Research having the purpose of amassing as
    much information as possible about the varia-
    bles concerned is called _____. (a) empirical
    research (b) hypothesis testing (c) experi-
    mental research (d) field research   a

8. Which term is referable to traits that corre-
    late highly with many other characteristics of
    the person? (a) the halo effect (b) logical
    error (c) central traits (d) judgments   c

9. Punishment of a child by the parent for aggres-
    sive behavior in the home will (a) inhibit
    aggressive behavior totally (b) have no

SHORT ANSWER QUESTIONS FOR REVIEW

affect on his behavior because of other role
models   (c)   only inhibit the behavior in the
home and not outside of it   (d)   cause anxiety
neurosis

c

10. The Milgram Experiments indicate that   (a)   the
use of reward and punishment increases compliance   (b)   pressure from the situation increases
compliance   (c)   social pressure increases
compliance   (d)   justification increases compliance

b

11. According to Erikson, the developmental stage
which begins at puberty is characterized by
the polarity of   (a)   intimacy vs. isolation
(b)   ego integration vs. industry   (c)   group
influence vs. individual judgment   (d)
identity vs. role diffusion

d

12. Reactance refers to the process   (a)   by which
increasing external pressure increases compliance   (b)   of counter control   (c)   of deindividuation   (d)   refers to mob behavior

b

13. Displacement of frustration occurs when   (a)
there is no identifiable source of frustration
(b)   source of frustration cannot be attacked
(c)   there is a scapegoat present   (d)   there
is overreaction to a situation

b

Fill in the blanks.

14. _____ is the process by which individuals
learn the basic rules and behaviors of that
society.

Sociali-
zation

15. The psychological explanation of prejudice
stresses _____ and _____.

frustration
and scape-
goating

16. The presence of others in emergency situations
seems to _____ helping behavior.

inhibit

17. Unification of impressions reduces _____.

cognitive
dissonance

18. Where objective or physical standards do not
exist we use _____ as a way to evaluate ourselves.

social
comparison

19. _____ are useful in reducing uncertainty and
anxiety of social confrontations.

Norms

669

SHORT ANSWER QUESTIONS FOR REVIEW

20. _____ theories focus on _____ and the environ-
    mental conditions which affect it.

    Social
    learning,
    behavior

21. _____ involves analyzing the causative rela-
    tionships between environment and behavior.

    Functional
    analysis

22. The observational and imitational processes
    through which behavior is often acquired are
    also called _____ processes.

    vicarious

23. Kelly proposed that interpersonal attraction
    could be analyzed in terms of _____ and _____.

    rewards
    and costs

24. Fear of being _____ is a major factor in
    conformity.

    deviant

25. Group _____ is an important determinant of
    conformity.

    cohesive-
    ness

26. As the discrepancy between a target's initial
    position and the position advocated by a
    received communication increases, the tendency
    toward _____ first increases and then decreases

    attitude
    change

27. The greater the _____ of the communicator, the
    more attitude change is produced.

    prestige

28. Groupthink occurs in highly cohesive groups
    where members are strongly orientated toward
    _____.

    unanimity

29. Social _____ are generalizations about other
    groups.

    stereotypes

30. Dollard's and Miller's model of aggression was
    based on _____.

    conflict

Determine whether the following statements are true
or false.

31. Phenomenology, dissonance theory and Gestalt
    psychology are similar in that they all predict
    behavior on the basis of cognitive structure,
    rather than on the basis of response tendencies

    True

32. Experiments on group behavior indicate that
    deviates from the group norm are generally
    accepted more because they display leadership
    qualities.

    False

33. The term in modern social theory which most

670

SHORT ANSWER QUESTIONS FOR REVIEW

closely approximates Freud's concept of ego
ideal is role model.   True

34. Fromm's concept of the "marketing orientation"
    refers to the undue value society places on
    competition.   False

35. Balance theory deals with the tendency of
    cognitive systems to move from states of in-
    consistency to states of consistency.   True

36. Congruity theory fails to take into account the
    fact that the strength of evaluations is an
    important factor in attitude-change situations.   False

37. In the cognitive consistency model, the inter-
    relatedness of the core object and the surround-
    ing elements means that a change in any one of
    the items tends to produce change in the whole
    system.   True

38. Learning theory would predict that in some
    cases, less incentive for performing a discre-
    pant act produces more attitude change than
    more incentive.   False

39. Dissonance relies on the individual's own
    psychological structure.   True

40. When aggression occurs in the absence of
    anger there is a decrease in the tendency to
    aggress.   False

41. The phenomenon of deindividuation results in
    a weakening of social responsibility and an
    increase in violent behavior in crowds.   True

42. Social facilitation increases the acquisition
    of new skills.   False

43. The effect that anonymity has on conformity
    is primarily due to the individual's conception
    of the consequences of being deviant.   True

44. Role prescription refers to the behavior which
    an individual displays in response to certain
    cues.   False

45. More cohesive groups are more likely to maintain
    a consistent level of performance than less
    cohesive groups but are not more likely to
    have a higher level of performance.   True

46. According to Bandura, observational learning

671

SHORT ANSWER QUESTIONS FOR REVIEW

always occurs in conjunction with reinforcement of the behavior. — False

47. Vicarious processes can result in inhibition and disinhibition of learned behaviors. — True

48. Individuals who score high on machiavellianism are likely to adhere to conventional rules of fairness in competitive situations. — False

49. People affiliate for reasons of social comparison regardless of dissimilarities between them. — False

50. The family is an example of a primary group. — True

CHAPTER 17

ORGANIZATIONAL/INDUSTRIAL PSYCHOLOGY

NATURE OF ORGANIZATION

● **PROBLEM 17-1**

Differentiate between industrial psychology and human factors engineering.

Solution: Industrial psychology (which in recent years has come to be included in the area of organizational psychology) attempts to study human behavior in an industrial or organizational environment. Human factors engineering is an outgrowth or branch of industrial psychology. It is concerned specifically with how people receive information through their senses, store this information, and process it in making decisions. It is also interested in how persons communicate in a man-machine system.

The differences in these two areas can perhaps be best understood by examining the functions of the industrial psychologist and the human factors engineer. The industrial psychologist usually holds a staff position, largely advisory or consultatory, which enables him to apply his talents wherever they are needed. He helps to improve safety programs, and he works with engineers on the human aspects of equipment design. He assists the office of public relations in its interactions with consumers and with the community in which the company operates. He engages in varied programs dealing with mental health of the worker, and he assists management in finding ways to reduce absenteeism and grievances. The industrial psychologist may draw up a plan for the executive development of the newly hired college graduate on one day and discuss the problems of aging employees the next. A psychologist that is more correctly called an organizational psychologist might also be involved with the design and implementation of research projects in areas such as job redesign or enrichment. Communications and management training would also be part of the function of the psychologist concerned with the human factor making its best and most effective contribution to the organization.

The role of the engineer, on the other hand, is concerned with the contriving, designing and producing of structures and machines useful to man. He applies his knowledge of the mechanical, electrical, chemical, or other properties of matter to the task of creating all kinds

673

of functional devices--safety pins and automobiles, mousetraps and mis-sles. Since the ultimate user of these devices is man himself, human characteristics must be considered in their construction. Human mus-cular frailty provided the necessity for and dictated the design of such devices as the lever, the pulley, the screw and hand tools of all sorts. The L-shaped desk for the secretary was designed to bring an enlarged work space within easy reach. The task which confronts the human factors engineer is to describe the special abilities and limi-tations of man in such a way that design engineers can effectively in-corporate the human operator as a component in the man-machine system. This requires knowledge about sensation and perception, psychomotor behavior, and cognitive processes as well as knowledge about the prop-erties of the material world. It is because of the need for this special knowledge about human behavior that this type of engineer is also a psychologist.

As may be evident, the roles of the engineer and the psychologist overlap in working out solutions to a multitude of man-machine problems and together are advancing understanding of human needs in the work environment as well as providing means for meeting them.

● **PROBLEM** 17-2

Discuss Rensis Likert's theory of organization. Include a discussion of the "linking-pin" concept.

Solution: The work of Rensis Likert, director of the Institute for Social Research in Ann Arbor, Michigan, demonstrates that as individual identification with a work group increases, the individual will cooper-ate more with the group and will also be more willing to both give and receive communication within the group, and be more likely to support goals and decisions.

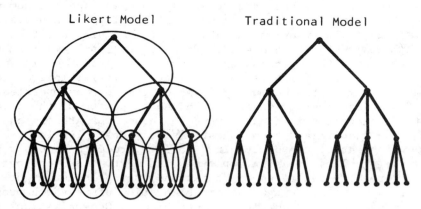

Likert Model   Traditional Model

The Likert Model and the Traditional Form of Organization

From his research, he developed the "linking-pin" concept to pro-vide a method for improving communication and group effort in organi-zations. This concept is based on the idea that management will make full use of the potentials of each of its human resources only when each individual is a fully functioning member of one or more work groups.

674

The linking-pin concept requires that an individual of top management, for instance, be an accepted member of the top management group as well as the middle management group. The key point is that these individuals be accepted as legitimate members of both groups. In this way, the linking-pin concept could be instrumental in bringing about improved communication--not necessarily because more information is available--but because the information that is available is more likely to be accepted when it is communicated by trusted members of the work group.

Carried to its logical conclusion, the application of this concept would provide a network of communications channels throughout the organization. High levels of trust and acceptance among group members would create an atmosphere in which various organizational components could operate in a spirit of cooperation and support.

As might be expected, the most difficult obstacle to the successful implementation of this idea is to find people who will be acceptable to more than one work group. As one crosses hierarchical lines in an organization, one is likely to find large differences in orientation, goals, and attitudes, much more than one finds within a work group. However, an environment which encourages awareness amongst workers of the problems and goals of the other organizational members increases the likelihood of an effective linking-pin arrangement.

● **PROBLEM 17-3**

Differentiate the classical organization theory and the humanistic organization theory discussing the criticisms for both.

Solution: Beginning in the 1900's with the advent of the industrial revolution and the influx of immigrant workers to this country, interest built with regard to the characteristics of the large industrial organization. Previous to this time, it was rare for a large number of workers to be working together under one roof and little was known about what was required to run a large organization effectively.

Efficiency experts like Frederick Taylor were called in by industrialists to describe the components of an effective organization. From an examination of the philosophies put forth in his best known work The Principles of Scientific Management, we can see the genesis of many current management tools and techniques. His work focused on an analysis of the tasks and responsibilities of the first-line supervisor within the organization. He introduced the idea that the planning and executing of work should be separated--the operator should be responsible for the performance, and the management for the planning. It is from his seminal work that what is now called classical organizational theory evolved.

It was not until the 1930's that attention began to be focused on management activities associated with the upper administrative levels (Taylor has been mainly concerned with lower management). This approach, developed by Fayol and others, came to be known as the "functional" school of management (today considered part of classical organizational theory). This approach emphasized the administrative activities of a manager as they are performed at all levels in the organization. By primarily focusing on developing a list of functions that a manager

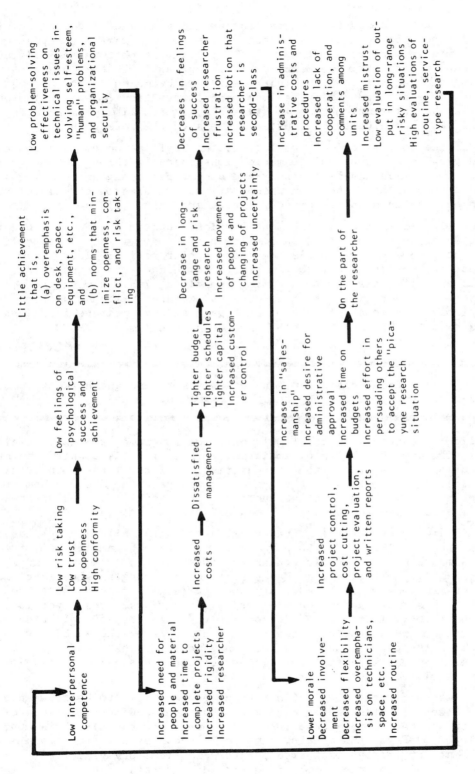

Model of how the values and implicit assumptions of the traditional organization structure depress creative expression.

must perform, this school of thought attempted to develop a series of principles that could be utilized to guide management behavior in all organizational situations.

The general philosophical approach of the classicists included a view of the worker as needing close supervision, a minimum of responsibility and wishing security above all else. It viewed the organization as a machine and put much emphasis on the role of the organizational chart, division of labor, and tight span of control to achieve a logical, well-defined organizational structure.

Though this approach is somewhat out-of-favor today, it still represents a major milestone in the development of a systemized body of knowledge regarding the practice of management, for it represented the first major attempt to develop and apply guidelines for the administration of all levels of the organization.

The views of the classicists on human nature and organizational efficiency have been seriously challenged by the neoclassicists or humanistic thinkers. This school of thought also appears to have had its origins in the 1930's when Elton Mayo and his associates conducted a series of experiments at a Western Electric Plant in Hawthorne, Illinois to test some of the principles of the classical theorists. The results of these experiments were much different than expected from classical theory, and led to the formulation of theories of effective organizational functioning that were in many respects different from that of the classicists.

Of particular importance in the humanistic approach was the role of the human element in the effectiveness of the work environment. The informal organizations that they saw to have a great influence on the quantity and quality of the work done were the natural groupings of people at work. As such, these small groupings are more concerned with the needs of their members than with the needs of the organization as a whole. Because of the influence of this informal group the humanists did not believe that the organizational chart was as important in structuring an effective organization as the classicists. They also believed that a supervisor could supervise many subordinates because individuals were capable of and even performed better if they were given some responsibility for their own activities.

More modern theorists, working with a "systems" approach, tend to believe that it is a combination of the classical and the neoclassical approach which best describes the most effective structure for an organization. They tend to see the organization as a living system, continually changing--both the parts and the whole having to be considered to truly understand the nature of the organization and thus be better prepared to structure it to function effectively.

• PROBLEM 17-4

Discuss Chris Argyris' Personality and Organization Theory.

Solution: Chris Argyris, an organization theorist, has drawn on personality theory to contribute to the understanding of the interaction of the work environment and the individual. In his theory he describes a series of changes an individual goes through from immaturity to maturity.

He indicates that as people grow and develop into mature adults their behavior patterns change to create a more active and independent individual who requires a deeper and broader involvement in activities. The mature adult seeks satisfactions that are complex and moves toward the satisfaction of needs of a higher order than simple safety and security needs of the immature person. This means that the behavior of the mature adult is more difficult to understand than that of the immature person.

Some characteristics he describes of the immature person are: passivity, short span of attention, few manners of behaving, dependence, shallow interests. The mature person is described as being active, having a longer span of attention, many means of behaving, tending toward independence rather than dependence, and having broader and deeper interests.

What makes this theory interesting to organizational theorists is that Argyris tried to consider the importance of taking into consideration immature and mature behavior patterns in understanding the impact of the organization on the individual. When an individual is brought into an organization, he is usually placed in a particular department, given a specific job assignment, told whom he will work for and with, with whom he will communicate, and how he will be evaluated. Though this may not be an accurate description of more advanced organizations, the bureaucratic tendencies of many organizations tend to be addressed to the more immature aspects of an individual's personality. The more humanistic approaches to organizational structure, however, appeal to the more mature sides of the individual and are apt to bring out characteristics in him that will be able to make a greater contribution to the organization.

● **PROBLEM 17-5**

According to P.R. Lawrence and J.W. Lorsch, how is differentiation and integration related to organizational effectiveness? What determines how much differentiation and integration are necessary?

Solution: In 1967, Lawrence and Lorsch, recognizing the inadequacy of existing organizational theory, attempted a study to try to understand what kind of an organization can deal with fluctuating economic and market conditions. They felt that much of the confusion and conflict in organizational theory was a result of the fact that researchers usually conducted their experiments in too limited an environment-- a small segment of a particular organization and often only one particular industry. The researchers decided to attempt a less piecemeal approach to try to develop a more unified theory. They did this by investigating "differentiation" and "integration" in the organizational systems of the plastics, food and container industries firms that had exhibited different levels of success.

By "differentiation" they meant the existence within an organization of differing orientations, points of view, and interests that develop among members according to the task they have to do. To gain insight into the exact nature of differentiation they focused on three factors in the work environment: 1) differences in goal orientation among managers; 2) differences in time orientation; and 3) interpersonal orientation.

The function of developing a state of collaboration in order that differing orientations can be overcome and a unified effort be devoted to attaining organizational goals was called "integration." They felt that the process of integration does not come about automatically through the hierarchy of management, instead, each organization had to develop its own techniques for integration.

The researchers proposed that as the environment of the firm became subject to greater degrees of change--in factors such as technology and market--the firm would exhibit greater degrees of differentiation among its employees and would require more formalized integration policies and procedures. What they discovered was that the demands of the environment played more of a part in predicting differentiation and integration as related to effectiveness than they had initially thought. They found that the state of differentiation in the most effective organizations of the study was consistent with the degree of diversity of the parts of the environment, while the state of integration achieved was consistent with the environmental demand for interdependence.

COMMUNICATION AND DESIGN WITHIN ORGANIZATIONS

● **PROBLEM** 17-6

Discuss the work conducted by Leavitt on communication networks in organizational problem solving situations.

Solution: Many researchers have investigated the effectiveness of various communication networks in problem solving situations. Perhaps the earliest studies in this area were conducted by Bavelas, Smith and Leavitt. In much of this research, communication patterns were set up so as to define the way information flowed between various group members. Then the results of the various communication networks would be measured against such variables as speed of problem solving, morale of the group, accuracy of the solution. From these initial studies there emerged some general guidelines about the attributes of different types of communication networks. Three major types of networks investigated--each with its particular strengths and weaknesses--were: the circle, chain, and wheel patterns.

The circle network is best described symbolically:

 flow of information

This communication flow is more effective than the others in dealing with unique problems that require a creative solution. It produces high group morale, but the speed of performance is slow, the accuracy of the solution is poor, it does not encourage the emergence of a leader and gives no stable form of organization.

The chain network involves the following information flow:

The chain network produces a fast solution with a good accuracy level, though the morale is poor. It produces conditions in which a leader does emerge slowly and which also slowly produces a stable organization.

The final communication pattern, the wheel, is best characterized as follows:

The wheel pattern produces rapid and accurate problem solving, and fosters an environment which quickly produces a strong leader and an immediate and stable organization. The morale, however, is very poor.

Clearly, it would be up to management to determine which communication network best suited the needs of the organization or a given situation. For one problem one type of network would be more effective, and for another problem a different communication flow would produce better results.

● **PROBLEM** 17-7

Define "span of control" and what factors determine the feasible span of control for a manager.

Solution: "Span of control" simply refers to the number of subordinates that report directly to the same superior. Top management's policy regarding span of control at each organizational level will directly impact on a great number of organizational functions. It usually provides a clue to the philosophy and attitudes of top management and also some indication of the nature of the particular industry in which the company functions. In general, the smaller the span of control, the greater the control that can be exercised by a supervisor over his subordinates. The more individuals a supervisor must oversee, the less control he will be able to exert. This is true because each subordinate will generally be more free to act independently; the supervisor does not have to spend as much time providing direction.

Many organizations with wide spans of control have policy statements so rigid that subordinates' behavior is dictated in almost every situation. In this way control and decision making within the organization remain highly centralized even though a large number of subordinates report to the same supervisor. However, it is still true that as the span of control increases it creates an organizational environment in which increasing decision making authority tends to flow to subordinates.

When deciding the appropriate span of control for a given organization, the particular situation and environment in which the organization finds itself must clearly be taken into account. Management must consider a wide variety of factors in order to determine what would be the most effective span of control for a given situation. Perhaps the most important factor influencing span of control is the skill and abilities of the people involved. If the supervisor has strong adiministrative ability and the confidence that experience often brings, he or she will be more able to supervise a greater number of individuals. Also if the subordinate is well skilled and willing to take responsibility for his or her own work activities, a wider span of control is permitted. If, on the other hand, either the supervisor is inexperienced and lacking in administrative ability or the subordinate is inexperienced and unwilling to take responsibility for his or her own activities, the span of control will have to be reduced.

Another important factor in determining an appropriate span of control is the degree to which the work itself requires coordination and interaction. As the necessity for coordination and interaction increases, the manager will need to become more involved in the supervisory function. He or she will need to spend more time with both individuals and groups of subordinates to be sure that activities are coordinated. This necessity will necessarily limit the number of subordinates a supervisor can effectively handle.

Another variable that can affect the span of control is the degree to which the environment is subject to change. A department that is subject to frequent modification of product design, new technologies and variations in policy and strategy will likely need a smaller span of control. The supervisor will be required to give a good amount of time and energy to adapting to the changes and will not have as much time to devote to supervision.

Usually, the smaller the span of control in an organization, the larger the total number of organizational levels and the more hierarchical the organizational structure. As the number of levels within the organization increases, information will normally take longer to move from the operating level up through the organization to top management and vice versa which is a factor to be considered when determining span of control.

Top management's policy regarding the appropriate span of control must strike a balance between the organizational chaos that results from too wide a span of control and the highly bureaucratic and rigid structure that results from too narrow a span of control. It also must be adjusted according to the needs of the particular organization.

● **PROBLEM** 17-8

Departmentalization is the grouping of individual positions and activities into separate subunits of the organization. One type of departmentalization might result in these four subunits: finance, marketing, production and research/development. What basis for departmentalization was used? Compare it to two other bases used for establishing separate departments. Include the advantages and disadvantages of using the different bases.

Solution: The grouping of individuals according to the function they serve in the organization is called "functional" departmentalization. When this approach is used, employees are generally grouped according to the basic corporate functions such as those mentioned in the above question: finance, marketing, production, research/development/engineering, graphics, personnel, etc. Under this type of departmentalization, all individuals within the personnel function would be grouped together in the same organizational department. They do not, however, have to be located in the same geographical area. Departmentalization defines lines of communication and reporting not geographical location. The functional structure allows for greater centralization of authority and decision making than do other structures and also allows for more specialization of talent spread over a wider range of products.

Another type of departmentalization is based upon specific products. Top management isolates certain products and all those employees concerned with the production of that product or products are grouped together in a single department.

A third form of departmentalization is geographically determined. This type of structure is used when top management wishes the locus of control to be concentrated in a specific area or region. These areas may be defined by city, state, section of the country, or even continent. The management of each region would then be responsible for decision making in its entire area. Geographical departmentalization refers to the area in which individuals have responsibility and not necessarily where they themselves are located.

Both product and geographical structures allow for greater attention to specific needs and conditions of specific geographic areas and products. Also, both these organizational forms may provide better training for potential managers due to the greater degree of decentralization and the greater spread of responsibility involved. However, the functional structure is more efficient in that there is likely to be less duplication of effort than in either the geographic or product structure.

● **PROBLEM 17-9**

Compare centralization of authority with decentralization of authority by discussing the advantages and disadvantages of each.

Solution: An organization with a highly centralized authority structure or a tight span of control (a small number of subordinates for each supervisor) allows the maximum control of subordinate activity by the supervisor and therby somewhat insures management control of the time and responsibilities of employees. This type of authority structure contributes to the hierarchical nature of an organization. The flow of information in an organization with many levels is often slow, and communications can easily become confused or inaccurately transmitted. Individuals who are closely supervised are rarely given the opportunity to take initiative and gain broad experience. Thus, employees operating in a highly centralized environment are less likely to be aware of how the organization operates outside of their own defined job responsibility. This tends to limit their development as potential managers as it is more difficult for them to understand the goals of the organization as a whole and the manner in which individual functions contribute to the overall goals.

BASIC FINDINGS	INVESTIGATORS
1. Groups that are less flexible are those with a predominant number of individuals who prefer hierarchical authority social systems.	Ziller (1958)
2. Individuals highly reliant on authority figures in their cognitive processes are less able to reject standard beliefs and develop new belief systems.	Fillenbaum and Jackman (1961)
3. Innovation in organizations is negatively related to the centralization of authority and the demand for hierarchical control.	Guetzkow (1965)
4. People dependent on authority sources for cognitive processing are more resistant to change.	Ehrlich and Lee (1969)
5. The longer people have worked in formal, hierarchical organizational systems, the lower their creativity.	Maier and Hoffman (1961)

Summary of Studies Relating Hierarchical Organization
Systems and Dependency Relationships to Creativity

In a decentralized environment with a wide span of control (many subordinates for each supervisor), employees often have the opportunity to assume initiative and responsibility for their own activities because they have more freedom to act independently. These employees can become involved in a wider range of activities than their specified job function and can become more aware of the workings of the organization as a whole. This experience can be helpful in the development of management's duties. There is, however, a limit to the number of employees a supervisor can supervise, and beyond this limit the manager will no longer be able to function effectively.

In a centralized environment though, employees are not encouraged to take responsibility and familiarize themselves with the operations of the organization as a whole. Advancement is still encouraged through the many levels available in the hierarchical structure of the organization. Generally, advancement to the top is a very lengthy process. Whereas, in the decentralized environment advancement can occur much faster for a particularly competent individual as he or she does not have to pass through as many levels to acquire greater responsibility and will also be able to demonstrate a wider range of qualities and abilities sooner in the less formal work environment afforded by the decentralized structure.

● **PROBLEM** 17-10

"Matrix organization was designed to obtain the advantages while avoiding the disadvantages of functionally specialized departments." Discuss this statement.

Solution: The concept of matrix organization has received much attention in recent years. In the matrix structure, project managers are assigned to a variety of projects, rather than to a single project, the activities of which cut across traditional functional departments. This concept is derived from the project management concept in which an individual is selected to guide the life of a particular project until its completion. Corporations that employ the product management or matrix

683

concept are usually involved in the production of large-scale products
or in projects that require the coordination of many disciplines over
an extensive period of time. The use of this concept began in the aero-
space industry where many projects involve a concentrated effort of
many different areas within the company for a period of months or even
years, at the end of this time all activities associated with the project terminate.

Representation of	Project 1	Project 2	Project 3
Manufacturing	X	X	
Engineering	X	X	X
Marketing	X		X
Finance		X	X
	Team 1	Team 2	Team 3

A Matrix Organization

The communications and coordination problems that arise in a functionally organized environment are much diminished with the use of the
project management structure. These coordination problems stemmed
mainly from the fact that there was no organizational mechanism by which
an individual was singularly responsible for the success of a given
project.

The development of the project management approach, however, was not
without its own problems. The main one, perhaps, was the conflicting
authority structure that developed between the project manager and the
functional department managers. Without clear guidelines on 1) who selects and assigns personnel to the project, 2) who determines how employees charge their time, 3) who terminates workers, and 4) who evaluates
employees for promotions and raises, much confusion and ineffectiveness
can result.

The matrix organization structure purports to solve some of this
authority ambiguity by giving the project managers more authority across
functional department lines. Within the structure at any given time a
series of project managers direct the activities of a number of projects, while the functional line managers allocate their resources in
order to meet the needs of these various projects.

However, both the project management and the matrix organizational
approach give rise to a problem that comes into focus once the project
is completed. If there is no new project, the project manager is usually assigned back to the functional department from which he came. In
many cases, the new job in the functional department will appear quite
routine and dull compared to the project management assignment, which
will result in dissatisfaction and perhaps in the individual resigning
from the company. There may also result a conflict of authority, as
the old project manager must begin to report to a line manager with
whom he previously shared equal status and authority. This type of
conflict is not likely to occur within the traditional functional
departmentalization environment.

Describe what is meant by "index of centrality" and "index of peripherality" in communications research.

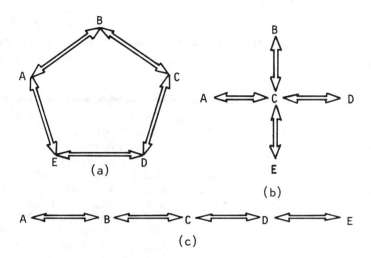

Communication Patterns Used in Small-Group Experiments.
(a) The circle: A decentralized network in which all members
are equally "central." (b) The wheel: A centralized network
in which position C is central and all the others are peripheral. (c) The chain: A moderately centralized network in
which position C is central, positions B and D are intermediate, and positions A and E are peripheral.

Solution: In his investigations of various forms of communications
networks, H. Leavitt developed a mathematical measure of an individual's
position with regard to the communications channels within an organization or group. The two measures he developed were called the "index
of centrality" and the "index of peripherality."

The "index of centrality" provided a measure of the extent to which
a given individual interacts with others. The higher a person scores
on this index, the more that person participates in the communications
that occur. The "index of peripherality" measures the extent to which
individuals are excluded from interaction with others. The higher a
person scores on this measure, the less participation that person has
in the communication flow.

High scores on the index of centrality were always associated with
those in leadership positions. In fact, the leader of a group was always the person who possessed the highest index of centrality. High
scores on the index of peripherality were associated with characteristics
that generally indicate low morale. And individuals with a high peripherality rating were much less satisfied with group membership than
were those who received a high score on the index of centrality.

These two concepts seem to have significant implications for busi-

685

ness management. They suggest possible causes for poor morale and they also point to possible causes for the emergence of informal leaders in the work group, which is so important to effectiveness of the work environment.

PERSONNEL FACTORS

● **PROBLEM** 17-12

Explain Herzberg's two-factor theory. How does it differ from traditional views of job attitudes?

Solution: As a result of research which focused on factors that made employees feel "exceptionally good" and "exceptionally bad," Frederick Herzberg postulated that there are two groups of factors that have a significant impact on worker satisfaction. These are what he calls the "hygiene or maintenance" factors and "motivator" factors. The hygiene or maintenance factors are concerned mainly with t'e environment including company policy and administration, supervision, interpersonal relationships, working conditions, salary, status, and security. The motivational factors are concerned mainly with the job itself. They include achievement, recognition for achievement, the quality of the work itself, responsibility, and growth or advancement.

Herzberg emphasizes that there is a distinct difference between those factors that bring about job satisfaction and those that create job dissatisfaction. From his research he learned that the maintenance factors must be at a certain acceptable level in order to prevent job dissatisfaction, but beyond a certain point, improving these factors did not contribute to job satisfaction. The motivators were discovered to be directly related to degree of job satisfaction. For example, raising a person's salary will keep that person from being dissatisfied with his job, but will not necessarily make him satisfied. Whereas, additional responsibility connected with an article in the company paper reporting on those new responsibilities will tend to raise the person's job satisfaction level.

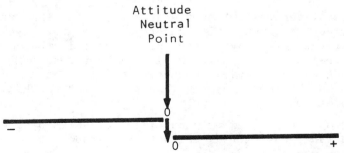

Outline of Herzberg's Job Satisfaction Model

686

As a result of the work done by Herzberg, it became clear that not all changes in the work environment would necessarily lead to an improvement in overall job satisfaction. Because of his research most organizational programs designed to improve the level of job satisfaction within the organization have focused on the motivational factors associated with the job itself instead of on the more traditional factors connected with the environment.

● PROBLEM 17-13

"Overspecialization is the single most important cause of poor management-employee relations." Discuss.

Solution: This statement was made by James C. Worthy who conducted, over a period of 12 years, studies within Sears and Roebuck and Company studying employee attitudes and morales. During this period of time he studied over 100,000 employees. Though this study was primarily to help executives do a better job of handling problems within the organization, its results produced a number of theoretical findings. The principal one being that overspecialization is the main cause of poor management-employee relations.

His evidence suggests that where jobs are broken down too finely there is low morale and also low output. The most sustained efforts are made by those employees who perform the most complex tasks--for instance, salespeople, supervisors, mechanics--and these are the employees who have the highest morale. Because the trend to overspecialization is not limited to individual jobs, but also includes the overspecialization of departments and subdepartments within the organization, the administrative units have had to be expanded with the result that the meaning of the job as a whole has been almost completely destroyed for the employee who has almost no input into the planning and organizing phases of the work.

The overspecialization requires greater and greater supervision and more need for coordination between departments. This leads to another problem--to achieve this coordination management is often forced to construct an elaborate hierarchy of supervisory levels and to develop a wide variety of formal controls. These controls often result in conflict as individual supervisors seek to make a good showing against a specific set of rules possibly at the expense of other departments within the same organization. This type of organization requires a supervisor who is willing to drive others to work; an individual who will pressure others into producing. While this may lead to a high production rate, the costs in terms of human dissatisfaction resulting in job turnover, absenteeism, and grievances leads to actual loss of productivity for the organization.

Worthy concludes that the trend toward increasing size of the administrative unit and the trend toward increasing complexity of the organizational structure are major contributors to the progressive deterioration of management-employee relations. He suggests that a flatter, less complex structure with administrative decentralization tends to create an environment more conducive to improved attitudes, more effective supervision, and greater individual responsibility and initiative among employees.

Define organizational development and discuss its objectives.

Solution: Organizational development is basically a series of programs that have as their objectives the facilitation of change in the organizational climate. The climate of an organization can be thought of as the general perception of the participants of what it is like to be a functioning member of that organization.

As top management has recently become aware through the efforts of organizational psychologists of the complexity of the interactive process between the individual and the organization, it has also begun to realize that traditional management techniques are not enough to bring about effective change. Many of the problems in the organization requiring attention are not so much a function of the structure of the organization, but of the values and attitudes of the individuals making up the organization. It is out of such realizations that organizational development was born. Some of the specific objectives of a program of organizational development might include:

1. A higher level of trust amongst members of the organization including different levels of employees;

2. More desire and openness to working with problems that arise in the work environment;

3. Creating an environment in which authority and decision-making are based upon knowledge and skill and not necessarily on position in the structure of the organization;

4. Improving communication channels between all levels;

5. Raising the level of satisfaction within the organizational environment.

Though specific organizational development programs vary in the details of their design, they all have as their objective the establishment of a feeling of mutual trust in the organization. This trust can be utilized to bring about a more open pattern of communication as well as improve the overall level of support employees offer one another. In this atmosphere of trust, support, and open communication, it is held that individuals will tend to develop better working relationships which will be based on the need to solve organizational problems rather than on the hierarchy of the structure. This leads to more satisfaction with the work to be done as well as greater success in problem solving.

The goals of organizational development are ambitious. They are usually not attempted without much thought and discussion from top management as their implementation often requires a general overall in the inner workings of the organization. Additionally, this type of program is usually conducted by an outside consulting firm with previous experience in organizational development. The outside consultant brings a degree of objectivity that is almost impossible for those individuals who are already members of the organization. This objectivity is particularly important in the implementation of a program that deals directly with people's values and attitudes.

Differentiate subjective procedures, direct measures, and proficiency testing in measuring employee proficiency.

Solution: Determining the proficiency level of individual employees is an important aspect of establishing an efficient work program. There are various methods for ascertaining the proficiency level of employees.

On production jobs, perhaps the simplest and most common method is evaluation based on quantity produced. If Marion produces 120 units per hour and Jack produces only 100, Marion is seen to be more proficient than Jack. Quantity is seen to be the only variable. This is a direct measure technique. It directly measures the on-the-job output of the individual employee. Quantity alone, however, is often an inadequate measure of true productivity. Quality must also be considered for a better measure. If units produces are rejected and subtracted from the output measure the proficiency rating is more meaningful.

An employee can also be tested for particular skills and speed of execution in an off-the-job setting either before beginning a job or after a trial period to measure proficiency. The secretary who is tested for shorthand and typing accuracy and proficiency is an example of an employee undergoing a proficiency test as would be a clerical employee who was required to take a spelling or a math test.

Another factor that is not as easily measured on production jobs is "merit." Merit is a far more general aspect of proficiency than production in terms of items turned out per time unit. Merit includes a variety of characteristics which make a person a valuable employee, such as attitude toward other employees and the supervisor, observance of safety regulations, assumption of responsibility, and the like. Evaluation based on merit is an example of a subjective procedure that does offer a dimension of proficiency that is not measured by direct or proficiency testing.

On nonproduction jobs proficiency is usually always measured by subjective--human judgment--techniques, which although subject to some degree of human error, have proved useful. Evaluating an employee's proficiency by some qualified second party is known as a "merit rating." There are a wide variety of merit-rating systems in use in organizations today each with special features.

Perhaps the most currently popular technique is the "performance review" in which the supervisor and the employee come together to discuss the performance of the employee. This type of interview gives the employee an opportunity to communicate his or her perceptions of the job to the supervisor and can give also a chance for the supervisor to point out strengths and weaknesses in the employee's work.

Another technique for evaluating proficiency is the "critical incident" technique in which there is a determination, through interviews of superiors, of those behaviors which employees exhibit or fail to exhibit that are critical to success or failure in a given job. Once such a list is compiled, supervisors are asked to watch for these behaviors during work performance. If a considerable number of good critical incidents are noted about a worker and a few negative critical incidents have been observed, the person's rating will be high. In this type of rating one receives reports on actual behavior and not just opinions about behavior. It adds an element of objectivity to this subjective technique.

● **PROBLEM 17-16**

Discuss fatigue and its role in accidents on the job.

Solution: Maintaining a consistent work rate throughout an entire day promotes fatigue in a worker. It is for this reason that standard rest periods are generally taken in the mornings and afternoons of a typical work day. The cost effectiveness of giving a worker 15 minutes off each 4 hour work period has proved strong enough so that this is a practice in most all major industrial operations. It has been shown that productivity goes down and accident rate increases as fatigue sets in.

The critical point at which fatigue becomes an accident determinant in any individual has not, however, been ascertained. But it is fairly certain that extreme fatigue will lead to increased accident frequency. In studies focusing on the relation of fatigue to accident rate, caution has been exercised in attributing accidents to fatigue if there was any accompanying change in production rate. The way to separate these two factors was developed by the U.S. Public Health Service in a study in which the production rate was held constant. The technique was to divide the accident index by the production index for a given work period. Results showed that during the earlier hours, production rate was correlated with the accident rate--increase in production brings a higher accident rate. However, this relation breaks down at the end of the day when the accident rate remains high relative to the production rate. This shows the important role of fatigue in relation to accidents and also allows it to be separated from increased production.

It is also believed that overtime is often antiproductive due to the decreased efficiency of the fatigued worker. This understanding has greatly effected the structure of many industries and has led to the development of two or three shifts in order to reduce the need for any individual to work quite long hours for an extended period of time.

MOTIVATION AND JOB SATISFACTION

● **PROBLEM 17-17**

Discuss Maslow's theory and its relevance for employee motivation.

Solution: According to motivational theorists, an individual is constantly acting in order to satisfy a particular need. One motivational theorist, Abraham Maslow stated that these human needs form a hierarchy, and that as the primary needs are satisfied the "higher-order" needs emerge and press for satisfaction. The most basic and fundamental

needs are those that relate to the common physiological drives of mankind: hunger, thirst and sex (though sex is also sometimes associated
with higher needs). It is only after these needs have been satisfied
that the higher needs for safety and security, love, self-esteem and
finally, self-actualization emerge. According to Maslow, a satisfied
need no longer motivates behavior. More specifically Maslow's hierarchy
is:

1. Physiological needs--such as hunger, thirst, sex, physical
   activity.

2. Safety needs--including security from physical and psychological deprivation.

3. Belongingness and love needs--covering relationships of a
   responsive, affectionate and affiliative nature.

4. Esteem needs--the desire for a stable and high evaluation of
   oneself summed up in self respect and the esteem of others.

5. Self actualization--representing the fusion or culmination of
   the other needs in a desire for realization of all of one's
   potentials.

It would be simple to assume that this knowledge could easily be
used for employee motivation. The supervisor or manager would only have
to ascertain what the employee's present specific need was and then arrange circumstances so that that need would be satisfied in return for
the desired work performance. However, due to the complexity of human
nature, it is not always easy to tell what it is that motivates a person.
Money may serve basic physiological needs--food and shelter--or it may be
serving an esteem need as it can be used to purchase objects which enhance
the owner in the eyes of other people. As one moves upward in the hierarchy toward the satisfaction of higher-level needs, the subtleties of
human nature make it more and more difficult to identify how a given
individual may seek satisfaction and what will serve as a motivation.

In the past, business organizations have felt that it was only necessary to satisfy the most basic needs of employees and that was accomplished through the paycheck. Today, however, young workers who have not
been subject to economic hardship appear to take the satisfaction of
physiological and safety needs almost for granted and are often looking
for situations that will provide satisfaction for the higher level needs.
The key question today for organizations then, from this point of view,
is, can they provide workers with higher-level need satisfaction.

● **PROBLEM** 17-18

Discuss the relevance for motivating employees by the results obtained
from reinforcement research.

Solution: Reinforcement theory states simply that the learning of a
task is facilitated when the learner is stimulated by the successful consequences of his or her behavior. Put another way, when an event that
follows the learner's activity results in an increase in that activity,
that event is said to be a reinforcer, and the process involved is
called reinforcement.

Reinforcement can take many forms in an organizational setting.

691

It can be information about successful results or achievement or about progress or improvement, it can be monetary reward, recognition, approval, or the feeling of accomplishment. Another important way in which knowledge obtained from reinforcement research can be applied to the work environment is that the supervisor or trainer should determine the employee's level of aspiration and give him or her practice in setting aspiration levels that are reinforcing and contribute to learning. The performance review is an excellent opportunity for this activity. Both positive and negative reinforcers can be used and are effective in different situations. Positive reinforcing events are effective because they are presented as a consequence of a response. Praise from a superior, feedback that a task has been well done or a good score in a training situation are examples of positive reinforcers. Negative reinforcers are effective because they are withdrawn as a consequence of performing a certain task. Examples include removing an individual from a job he or she dislikes as a result of successful completion of a training course or particular project, and transferring a worker to a new task which is less monotonous than his or her former job for mastering a new skill.

Reinforcement theory has proven that reinforcement is most effective if it occurs immediately after a task has been performed. Waiting until the end-of-the-year performance review or the end of a training session to inform an individual of his or her progress may not be as effective as immediate reinforcement. Investigation of different "schedules" (the timing) of reinforcement is quite rich in possibilities for training and motivation of employees as different schedules yield different characteristics in the behavior acquired. Optimal schedules of reinforcement can be of much practical importance for instance, in arranging pay schedules and the use of bonuses and incentive wages. Good scheduling can contribute to optimal productivity and increased morale.

● **PROBLEM 17-19**

Define job satisfaction and explain how the discrepancy theory determines job satisfaction.

Solution: "Satisfaction" may be defined as the difference between a person's expectations and perceptions about a given situation. If expectations are greater than perceptions an individual will be likely to experience dissatisfaction, the degree of dissatisfaction being related to the extent of the difference between expectation and perceptions.

An example of how this discrepancy theory understands job satisfaction may clarify the above definition. Suppose that two workers, each earning $20,000 a year, are both offered promotions to new jobs at a salary level of $30,000 per year. Assume that worker 1 expects that the new job will make great demands on his time and energy and will require him to change his life style and therefore assumes that an appropriate salary might be closer to $40,000. Worker 2 perceives the new job as not significantly different from the present job in terms of time or responsibility commitment and had expected a salary of $25,000. The same job offer at the same salary level would create two totally different levels of satisfaction for Worker 1 and Worker 2--the difference being directly related to the expectations and perceptions of the two.

As people become better educated and more aware of the opportunities for different kinds of work in their environment, they tend to change their expectations and perceptions. These changes usually increase the overall expectation level of a worker, and can lead to dissatisfaction and frustration even for people in responsible management positions in the organization.

What is most important when utilizing discrepancy theory to determine job satisfaction is to remember that the point of view of the employee is of utmost importance. This point needs to be made because it is perhaps due to the supervisor's failure to ascertain the expectations and perceptions of the employee that much misunderstanding and waste of talent occurs in industry. It is not uncommon for a supervisor to be heard remarking something like, "I just cannot understand Susan. She has a good job with a solid future, but she just won't make much effort." A good job with a secure future may be important in the value system of the supervisor, but it may not matter much in Susan's way of thinking. Her perception of the situation may be quite different. It is the responsibility of the supervisor to devote the necessary time and effort to speaking with his or her employees to determine how they see their job and what they expect from it.

● **PROBLEM 17-20**

Discuss equity theory. When are equity and inequity perceived?

Solution: In a given situation it is possible that one or more of the participants in the situation will perceive that an inequity or injustice is occurring in the distribution of rewards. These inequities may be perceived by individuals despite the fact that there is no inequity that is "objectively" observable by others. Thus, a person's perceptions of the equity or inequity of the situation are of primary importance in considering this explanation of behavior.

An early recognition of the potency of this factor was recognized first by research done by Stouffer and his co-workers during World War II. In this study the paradoxical finding was that army air corps men were less satisfied with promotion opportunities than were those in the military police. This was despite the objective truth that opportunities for promotion were vastly greater in the air corps than in the military police.

This is explained by the fact that the men compared themselves to those equal with themselves. Thus, the high promotion prospects in the air corps induced high expectations, while in the military police far lower expectations for promotion prevailed. Comparing lower ranking men from both groups, greater dissatisfaction is found among the air corps men than the military police, and among the better educated than the less educated. In both instances a greater discrepancy exists between expectation and actual achievement.

In the work situation, a finding that has been repeatedly found is that among those subjects not promoted those who hold high expectations for promotion are more dissatisfied with the "system" than those with low expectations.

In general, an inequity can be thought of, therefore, as the reaction to an imbalance or disparity between what an individual perceives to be the situation and what he or she believes should be the case.

Another factor to consider is that individuals, though they may compare their rewards to others and perceive them to be smaller, may not feel dissatisfied since there is a proportionality between the rewards received as against the investments of each. For example, Patchen found that the satisfaction with their wages, of workers in an oil refinery, was primarily based on the total equity they perceived in wage comparisons, rather than on the actual pay differences alone. Workers were satisfied with their wages if they felt that they were making sufficiently more money than other workers with whom they compared themselves in terms of job responsibility and seniority.

In an actual work situation, equity may be a function of the balance between a person's inputs and outcomes on the job. Inputs include his qualifications for the job and how hard he works, while outcomes include pay, fringe benefits, status, and the job itself. Satisfaction will result when an equitable input-outcome balance prevails.

● **PROBLEM 17-21**

What is a pay incentive program? Describe a commonly used incentive plan.

Solution: Some form of incentive wage is offered to about 60 percent of all industrial workers in the United States. An incentive wage is some form of financial reward used to increase production. A fairly typical type of pay incentive program is based upon job analysis. A job-study engineer is called in to determine the average time it takes the employees to do a particular job. He also determines the most efficient method for performing a particular job. Such factors as fatigue allowance (compensation for the effects of getting tired when a consistent work pace is maintained throughout the day) and the level of skill of the operator are taken into consideration to arrive at the average time for a particular job.

Consider the case of Alice Smith on her job of sealing boxes of cereal in the packing room. Alice's job requires her to put glue on the flaps of the boxes and push them into the sealing belt as they pass down the line. The job has been studied to find both the correct method of doing the work and the average time normally taken to do it. The standard time for this job has been set at thirty-six seconds, or 0.01 hour per box. The rate of 100 boxes an hour means 800 boxes per eight-hour day. However, since Alice can and does seal 125 boxes an hour, or a total of 1,000 boxes, she gets credit for two extra hours for which she receives a bonus of two hours' pay.

At first glance, some kind of incentive system would seem to be an ideal way to step up production and make more money for both employee and employer. However, despite the apparent objectivity of an incentive system based on job analysis, important judgment and value questions enter the picture such as: What is normal job production? What is a fair rate of pay? An overall appraisal of incentive systems in general would probably be that sometimes they work well and probably just as often they do not.

Pay incentives are not always a feasible or effective way of improving employee performance or behavior. Discuss the limiting conditions for this program to be effective.

Solution: Pay incentive programs which reward employees financially for increasing production are not always met positively by employees. When an incentive program fails, the reasons are sometimes psychological. An incentive plan based on job analysis may be met with distrust. The job analyst is often seen as a management person who will set arbitrary rates in order to compel workers to produce more for the same amount of money. Many workers feel that the analyst might establish a standard production rate that is too high. Hence, even though a bonus is provided for exceeding the standard, the extra pay is not worth the effort. Or if the production rate is not too tight and many workers exceed it and thus make more money the company will cut the rate. This suspiciousness may cause workers to hold back on their production rate.

It is also necessary to note that workers also hold down on output in order to protect the less skillful members of their work group. Apparently their loyalties to their fellow workers outweigh the desire for financial gain.

The details of the various incentive systems now in operation are probably of minor importance in determining their success. The important thing is how the worker perceives the system in relation to all of his needs--both material and psychological. The value of incentive pay cannot be viewed in isolation. It appears that work behavior cannot be manipulated solely by the manipulation of money. The prospect of financial gain is only part of the total picture. It is effective only when other basic worker needs are also satisfied.

In which motivation theory are the key concepts outcome, valence, and expectancy? Explain these three concepts in regard to this theory and explain the practical implications for employee motivation for this model.

Solution: Vroom, in his work "Work and Motivation," pulls together a vast literature of theory and facts and emphasizes that there are both motivational and nonmotivational determinants of work performance. A major nonmotivational determinant of a person's performance is his ability to do a task. His performance then is an interaction of his abilities and his motivation.

In essence, Vroom states that an individual's motivation is a function of two factors: (1) the "expectation" that a particular behavior will lead to a desired goal and (2) the "valence" or desirability of the goal. It is the combined strength of these two factors which determines the level of motivation. This is called "Expectancy Theory."

It further predicts that the quantity and quality of work is directly
determined by the perceived value of the rewards offered and the perceived probability that appropriate behavior will lead to these rewards.

To practically apply this model to the work situation, it must be
remembered that the most important variable is the employee's perception of a given situation that has the most significance in determining
his behavior. A manager's perception of the employee's values is likely
to be incorrect due to the difference in the value structures generally
found between management and line levels in an organization. Therefore,
methods must be explored by which the values or goals of the employees
can be ascertained in order that means may be instituted by which the
employee can receive the goals he desires and, at the same time, perform
the desired work for the organization.

Some techniques do exist for determining the desired goals of employees
such as performance reviews, career counseling, and attitude questionaires.
But it is only recently that organizations, through the development of
their Human Resource Development departments, have begun to explore in
more depth the practical application of the work of such theorists as
Vroom.

● PROBLEM 17-24

A person who has had an opportunity to contribute to the establishment
of objectives regarding his or her performance will have a greater degree of commitment and motivation in attempting to achieve those objectives. State and discuss the theory underlying this statement. How
is it implemented practically to motivate employees?

Solution: A great deal of recent research has pointed to the desirability of involving employees in the goal setting and decision making
process of organizations. The increased involvement and participation
of employees in the management process has been attempted through such
programs as job simplification, job enrichment, suggestion plans, and
job redesign. Probably the most popular program designed to involve
employees more actively in management is the goal-setting process
called management-by-objectives.

First explored and explained by Peter Drucker in The Practice of
Management, this program attaches a great deal of importance to mutual
goal-setting between employees and supervisors or between different
levels of management. It is assumed that when employees have the
opportunity to contribute to the organizational goal-setting, they will
be more likely to understand and accept the objectives as they relate
to their own particular work and will be more likely to accept them as
valid and will, therefore, be more motivated to work for them.

The mutual goal-setting process is likely the most important aspect
of the practical application of the management-by-objectives approach.
Either the superior and the subordinate work together to develop a list
of objectives for the subordinate or they work individually on the list
of objectives and later compare their work. Important to the success
of this procedure is that the manager not disregard the input of the
employee and still provide leadership and direction in the final formu-

lation of goals. The manager must be willing to take the time necessary to think through his expectations regarding the subordinate and
must be willing to modify these goals somewhat after interaction with
the subordinate.

This is just the first step in the implementation of this approach.
Once agreed upon goals have been constructed, a specific plan for their
completion must be discussed. This plan sketches out in detail how the
subordinate will proceed and usually includes a timetable for completion of specific goals.

One other condition that must be present in an effective management-
by-objective (MBO) program is a clear definition of the rewards the
subordinate will receive as a result of completing the stated goals.
These usually take the form of pay raises, promotions, additional authority or increased staff help, job title, office space or vacation time.
The specific rewards must be in keeping with the needs and desires of
the individual employee. This aspect of the approach assumes that to
truly motivate a subordinate toward the achievement of certain goals,
the subordinate must see how the reward system within the organization
will tie in with these goals.

Finally, after the implementation of the above steps, a management-
by-objective program calls for a review process at which time both the
manager and subordinate can discuss progress or problems. Reasons for
lack of progress can be discussed at this time and specific steps for
improved future performance discussed. Every effort should be made to
end the session on a positive note so that the subordinate does not
feel a sense of failure or lack of achievement.

If carefully carried out, this process by defining the relationship between performance and rewards enables both manager and subordinate to deal more effectively with the eventual merit and performance appraisal review related to promotions and pay raises. This
contributes greatly to the aims of both the organization and the individual employee.

● **PROBLEM** 17-25

Job enrichment is an approach for redesigning jobs. What does an employer expect to happen by a job enrichment program and what kinds of job
changes are usually made?

Solution: Job enrichment has been called job-redesign-for- motivation,
as it purports to take a routine job and design into it components for
greater satisfaction of higher-level needs of the employees. When a
job is enriched or redesigned for greater motivational factors, the
level of responsibility of the employee is generally increased; the
job is given more "depth." For example, a secretary whose job has been
to type letters, answer the phone, schedule appointments, and open the
mail is then given total responsibility counseling new secretaries in
addition to screening potential new secretaries. The addition of these
tasks significantly raises the responsibility level of the job, gives
the secretary greater independence, and adds planning and organizing
to the work.

Another important aspect of job enrichment is that the employee is granted a greater degree of control over the work situation. This control can take many forms, but it generally includes increasing the worker's power to influence the planning and organization of the work cycle. Also, it requires the worker to use a wider variety of skills. Jobs designed along these lines allow the worker to become more involved with the job as a whole. It is felt that by adding responsibility, independence, and planning and organizing to the job, it will enable the employees to see better how their contribution fits into the needs of the entire organization.

Not everyone is interested in what the theorists describe as a "more meaningful job." For whatever reason, it has been discovered that a number of employees will be resistant to being given greater responsibility and will not cooperate if it is given. For this reason it is quite important to assess both the organizational structure and the needs of the individual employees before embarking on a job enrichment program.

It is also true that not all jobs lend themselves to enrichment. The structure of the entire organization must be taken into consideration before a job redesign program is undertaken. Many assembly line and component-related jobs may be too far removed from the larger company picture to allow for effective design for motivation. Also, if one job is redesigned, it is usually necessary to redesign an entire department because most jobs are quite interrelated. Making the changeover from traditional task-oriented job structures to the process-related jobs that usually arise from job enrichment efforts, can sometimes take a number of years of gradual changes in the responsibilities within a department or organization.

● **PROBLEM** 17-26

List and define four major communication problems in an organization and describe some possible remedies.

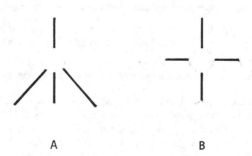

A   B

Hierarchical and autocratic communication networks. These stuctures are identical in terms of who can communicate to whom, as long as the direction of communication is ignored. The pattern on the left looks like a hierarchical structure, because we assume the man on the top can communicate down easier than the others can communicate up.

<u>Solution</u>: In 1953, F.J. Roethlisberger analyzed the principal causes of communication breakdown in organizations. His work still provides a framework for seeking the underlying causes of failure in communication. These are four of the problem areas he found:

1. Struggle for power: When each party feels that it is necessary for the sake of not losing face or status to not give in when there is a misunderstanding, the underlying problem can be a struggle for power. In this situation an individual usually feels that more is involved than a simple misunderstanding. Both sides may feel that they must have their way in order to maintain their position within the organization. Arbitration is one of the best methods of solving this type of communication breakdown. The introduction of an impartial third party has been a technique used by labor and management for many years as a means of working with the struggle for power.

2. Personality clash: Communication breakdown or misunderstanding can result from personality characteristics. Feelings of insecurity, inferiority or aggression may create defense or attack behavior which comes into conflict with the personality of another. In this type of situation it is almost impossible to solve the misunderstanding without raising the self awareness of the individuals involved or transfering one or more of the individual's involved in order to eliminate the interactions that are creating the clash.

3. Social role conflict: This type of conflict arises out of contradictory expectations relating to a particular person in a given role. Because of their sex, nationality, religion, occupation or other characteristics, certain individuals are expected to play certain roles and not others. When a person plays a role that does not fit with another person's idea of who should be playing that role, communication breakdowns can occur. An example might be that the traditional role of women in our society is not consistent with the role of management of an automobile plant. In this situation it may be particularly difficult for male employees to adjust to the woman in the role of manager. Conflicts of this nature can be temporary. It depends much on the ability of the people involved to change their perceptions of another's role. To this end, there is much reeducation occurring within industry today in an effort to implement the Equal Employment Opportunity guidelines in which the government has advised that organizations must not discriminate in their hiring or promotion practices.

4. Genuine communication breakdown: This situation may occur as a result of differing perceptions with respect to a given problem, from a misinterpretation of words or actions, or when one person fails to listen to another. Each individual then reacts according to his interpretation of the situation. It is quite likely that a conflict will arise when this happens since each individual is acting from a different frame of reference. To resolve conflicts of this type it is often necessary to retrace the original statements or actions so that each party becomes aware of the other's intentions and interpertations regarding the original exchange. This gives both individuals a similar frame of reference and improves the chances that the communication breakdown will be resolved.

MANANGEMENT

What are the selection procedures you would use to select a manager?
Discuss your answer.

<u>Solution</u>: The management and leadership research provides some hints in
regard to the personal attributes which may contribute to successful executive performance. However, in general, researchers seeking to isolate
and identify specific "leadership traits" have been unable to provide
much insight into those characteristics that are associated with leadership behavior. At best today, management selection is educated guess
work. However, the research that has been conducted does offer some
possible profitable variables that could be considered for a person attempting to make a reasonable selection of a manager.

Keith Davis, summarizing much research in the area presented four
general traits that are believed to be characteristic of successful
managers:

1. Social maturity and breadth: Leaders are emotionally mature
and have a wide range of interests. They are not easily frustrated and
maintain a high level of self-confidence and self-respect.

2. Intelligence: Leaders tend to have a somewhat higher level of
intelligence than their subordinates.

3. Motivation and drive for achievement: Leaders are found to have
a high drive for achievement and seek more than their followers for
self-actualization or fulfillment of their possibilities.

4. Human relations development: Leaders tend to realize they accomplish goals as a result of cooperation from others. Often they possess a high degree of respect for others as well as empathy and understanding of those around them.

More recent research has demonstrated an interesting new line of
inquiry: that of leadership style. Apparently, different situations
call for different leadership techniques and different leaders have different styles or approaches to leadership. Generally, the models of
leadership can be summarized as "authoritarian," "democratic," and
"laissez-faire." The type of leader that is needed in a particular
organization or a certain department would need to be considered by
those selecting the manager and an assessment of the style of the candidates would need to be made. The role-playing of problem management
situations is a selection technique that allows a selecting committee to
see the style of a particular candidate and might be an effective method
for selecting a manager based on a particular style of leadership.

Compare on-the-job and off-the-job training of management.

<u>Solution</u>: There are few modern corporations that do not have some kind
of management training program for their supervisors and managers.

There are several different types of programs that are currently used in management training.

Probably the most common type of management training is that which takes place through the skills, knowledge, and abilities acquired in actual work experience. This on-the-job training can be a highly effective method of training because the skills learned obviously have direct application to the job at hand. It also has the advantage of being relatively inexpensive as it does not require the development of any formal training program. However, it also has certain limitations. For instance, the young manager may be so concerned with the daily concerns of the job that there is little time to acquire the new skills needed for job advancement. The pressure of the job itself is an interference with the learning process. Thus, a manager with five years of experience on the same job may actually have acquired one year of experience five times over.

Training that takes place at times other than that alloted for the job to be done has the advantage of permitting complete focus on the learning process by the managers or supervisors. There are a number of different approaches to off-the-job training.

The communication of factual information is often accomplished by traditional lecturing and also by programmed instruction. This second method of training is receiving wide-spread use in industry as it combines the advantages of the lecture method (providing much point-by-point information) with the one-on-one learning situation in which an individual's responses are checked for accuracy and special help is administered if necessary.

Case discussions are another approach that is often used in management training sessions. Each participant is provided with a body of information drawn from real-world experience and is asked to examine and analyze the material provided and present and discuss his views of the significance of the case material. Management games and role-playing are also extensively used. Both these methods attempt to set up a situation which represents some aspect of the real world. The participants are able to interact in a dynamic fashion with the invented environments and through this interaction they are able to recognize relationships and concepts which can be applied to real-world situations. Finally, sensitivity training is sometimes included as part of a management training program. This method of training focuses most deeply on the emotions and attitudes of participants and how they influence behavior.

Also available are executive development programs which include mainly formal educational programs whose objective it is to prepare managers to perform more effectively in the future. Perhaps the most important reason for the utilization of executive development programs is the realization on the part of many corporations that many highly talented managers and executives are often lacking in one key area of development--an understanding of the behavioral and interpersonal elements of the job. They have been promoted for their excellence in a particular skill area and they now need to shift their focus from technical to managerial skills. These skills such as communicating, leading, delegating, and motivating are mainly what are dealt with at the executive development programs.

Most training programs will include a variety of these different training techniques depending on the needs of the organization.

● **PROBLEM** 17-29

When organizational decisions have to be made under conditions of uncertainty what approaches does management theory offer for rational decision-making?

Solution: The making of decisions is perhaps the most important function of a manager. Their ultimate evaluation will be determined by examining the important decisions made over a series of time. In most decision-making situations faced by managers, a series of alternatives is available, each of which will have some consequence depending on the occurrence or nonoccurrence of some future condition. Usually there is some risk involved in decision-making--if it were possible to predict with certainty what would occur, the choice between alternate decisions would be a simple one. To aid the decision maker there exists rational, well-defined approaches to the decision-making process which allow an individual to examine a particular set of alternatives with objectivity. Some of these approaches are:

Criterion of Optimism: Under this strategy the manager makes decisions based on complete optimism about the future. He assumes that the most favorable possible conditions will occur and makes decisions accordingly.

Criterion of Pessimism: This approach is just the opposite of the optimistic strategy. In this framework, the manager assumes that the worst will happen and acts accordingly. This approach represents an ultra-conservative approach. Generally, it would not be conducive to long-range growth or profit-making. This strategy would keep a person from taking advantage of profit-making opportunities because of the loss possibilities associated with them. Probably most managers will be neither totally optimistic nor totally pessimistic in their forecasting of the future. It is therefore necessary to introduce other means for arriving at a reasonable decision.

Criterion of Rationality: This approach assigns an equal value to all possible outcomes. The decision maker assigns an equal probability to each possible future occurrence. He then must determine the "conditional value" of the decision, which is determining what the event is worth and multiply that by the probability of its occurring. The strategy selected is the one having the highest "expected value," which is determined simply by multiplying the conditional value by the probability of the event occurring.

A decision maker will, of course, be influenced by his or her value differences and by the varying situations in which a decision must be made. The above approaches do, however, give a firm ground on which initial decision-making can be approached, even under conditions of much uncertainty.

● **PROBLEM** 17-30

Describe the Linear Responsibility Chart (LRC) and its function for management and some of the problems inherent in its use.

Solution: The Linear Responsibility Chart was developed in the early 1950's by S.A. Birn Co. with the purpose of detailing the exact nature of the relationships in a given organization. The relationships described are those between particular individuals in the organization and specific tasks or jobs.

In developing such a chart a manager is forced to think of all the responsibilities of his or her department or division as well as the role of each individual in relation to these jobs or tasks. When such a chart is completed it details the exact responsibilities of each employee as well as how individuals interrelate to accomplish the tasks that are specified. This chart gives a much clearer picture of the organization than can be seen in the simple organizational chart--the relation of each position to every other position with respect to the same job cannot be found on a traditional organizational chart.

Perhaps the most common problem in using the LRC is the amount of time and effort that is required in developing it in the first place. Because it is so detailed, it requires a large amount of managerial time. Some also feel that it is limiting, in that employees are restricted by the responsibilities as listed on the chart; some managers feel it is better for the employee to be able to act when he sees a problem or has an idea regardless of whether it is in an area specifically assigned to him. This type of manager tends to be associated with a "looser" environment in which there is often a more rapid rate of change and for which the well-defined structure of the LRC is not as applicable.

Also, the chart may serve to crystalize authority relationships in the organization that run contrary to the informal status of employees. For instance, on a day to day level employees of two departments may consider themselves to have equal status and to have equal authority. If the organizational LRC chart were drawn up and it happened that one of the departments was placed higher than the other, the informal communications channels that presently exist might be threatened.

Regardless of its problems, in the correct organizational environment, the use of the LRC can bring about a more clear picture of the workings of an organization and a better understanding of its communication and decision-making patterns.

ENGINEERING FOR HUMAN USE

● PROBLEM 17-31

Define displays and discuss their role in human factors engineering.

Solution: In a man-machine system any input element that provides the direct sensory stimulus for the human operator is called a "display." The gas-gauge on a car is perhaps one of the most common and easy to understand examples of a display in a man-machine system. The engineering problem is to determine how to construct displays so that the information required is received quickly and accurately by the machine operator. Thus, the human factors engineer treats the sensory mechanisms of the human being as detector devices.

In designing displays for more complex systems where many inputs must be represented, it is important to provide as much of the relevant information as possible in a single display. For example, the designer of the control panel for an airport flight pattern supervisor has the task of building a display which yields information about the distance of an approaching aircraft from the end of a runway. If this were the only dimension necessary to incorporate into the display, his task would be a simple one. However, to give this information and information about its altitude, heading, or speed of approach in a single simple display is very difficult. Hence, much of the time and effort expended in display design are directed toward finding ways to simplify the presentation of many separate pieces of information and incorporating them into a single meaningful display.

The human factors engineer knows that the human operator serves as a living link between the inanimate parts of the man-machine system. The information obtained from the system displays passes through him, but not in the same way that a message passes through a telephone wire. Such a procedure would be wasteful of man's unique talents as a decision-maker. Instead, the information presented to the operator is assimilated, processed in the light of previously acquired information stored in memory, and evaluated for future action. In many systems the amount and complexity of this processing is incredibly great. In other practical situations, man's controlling acts are quite simple, and if it were not convenient to keep the man around for other reasons, his control functions might well be eliminated.

The design engineer needs to know which tasks are best performed by machines and which are best carried out by a human operator. It is the responsibility of the engineer to be sure that the sensory input channels and the motor output (actions required from the operator) do not become overloaded. Displays are the point at which the man and the machine elements of a man-machine system meet and they can represent the blending of the skill and knowledge of both men and machines of the human factors engineer.

● PROBLEM 17-32

Discuss the work cycle and its four human factors components.

Solution: A work cycle is simply the complete sequence of events from beginning to end necessary to complete a given task. In designing job-task descriptions it is generally imperative to examine the work cycle carefully and completely before drawing up the final description. It is particularly important to go back to the real beginning of the cycle, rather than somewhere along it. For example, the work cycle of flying an airplane mission begins not on the starting ramp but back in the briefing room. It ends when the pilot turns in his flight papers. The start of a maintenance work cycle begins with a work order of some kind and then to the selection of tools and ends with the turning in of a completed work order and the replacement of tools and cleaning of the area of work.

In attempting to describe the work cycle it is a good idea to list the gross tasks in sequence before making a step-by-step description of each task within the larger task. Different persons making the same analysis will have different gross-task titles, as they are quite ar-

bitrary. But the heart of the description is finally in the detailed
activity description of indicator, indication, control response, and
feedback. Skilled individuals will prepare quite similar descriptions
of the same tasks. Task descriptions can be made from direct observation. But they can also be made from blueprint descriptions of equipment or equipment prototypes and information as to how the equipment
should be operated.

All of the work described thus far could be done well by a nonspecial-
ist in human factors, such as an engineer or operations analyst. The
next phase which takes human factors into consideration requires a human
factors specialist. In analyzing the human input into any task, four
psychological functions are usually distinguished. These are: perceptual processes, recall processes, problem solving (decision-making)
processes, and muscular (motor) processes. This division is mainly
made for convenience in analysis. Perceptual processes, for example,
are strongly influenced by recall from previous experience and even
from motor processes. Each task as a whole as well as each specific
activity are studies with each of these functions in mind. The patterns of events likely to produce errors in perception, recall, decision-making, or responses on the machine controls are noted, and the
nature of the expected error is described. In this way, the system is
eventually refined. A "map" is designed that can be used for planning
a strategy for dealing with human factors. From these descriptions
comprehensive plans can be formulated for job design, human engineering of the work environment, proficiency testing, training and training aids, selection procedures, and other areas within the province of
industrial and organizational psychology.

● **PROBLEM** 17-33

The concept of bureaucracy has come to have very negative connotations
today. Discuss those factors you believe are responsible for this
negative attitude.

Solution: In the 1920's Max Weber used a military analogy to develop
what he considered to be the most appropriate approach to developing
effective organization: the bureaucratic approach. He based his approach on the concept that the object carrying out of business could
best take place following defined rules and without regard for persons.
He characterized the effective bureaucratic organization as having
the following features:

1. A clear chain of command throughout the entire organization;

2. A clear definition of duties for each position based upon
   the specific area of responsibility;

3. Clearly defined rules and procedures as to the rights and
   responsibilities of each employee;

4. An impersonal atmosphere;

5. Promotion is based solely on technical competence.

Weber's work laid the groundwork for the initial development of organizational structure in this century and the bureaucratic form is still widespread today--most notably perhaps in the government.

It has, however, met with much recent criticism mainly for its lack of regard of the individual and the tacit assumption underlying the theory on which it is based that human beings are predictably alike and can be factored into an organization in a mechanical manner. The facts, however, have demonstrated that there are individual differences, that humans make errors, that there are exceptions to the rules. As exceptions began to be discovered to the rules, the bureaucratic structure worked with the exceptions by the development of further rules. This has led to some of the confusing and unapproachable rules and regulations in some domains of business and government today. The "red tape" or amount of paper work and time required for some piece of business to pass from one level of the bureaucratic structure to the next has also contributed to the disenchantment with this ideal. The clearly defined job descriptions have detracted from any spirit of cooperation and common problem solving which are today coming to be recognized as vital to the health and continued growth of an organization.

SHORT ANSWER QUESTIONS FOR REVIEW

Choose the correct answer.

1. One name for the study of the design of equipment is (a) human factors engineering (b)
   efficiency design (c) enconomics (d) A and
   C

   a

2. Factors in a worker's environment may influence
   work output by affecting his (a) morale (b)
   motivation (c) physical ability (d) all
   of the above

   d

3. The best definition of human engineering is
   that it is concerned with (a) providing
   therapy using physical methods (b) the design
   of equipment and tasks performed in the operation of equipment (c) the application of
   computers and scientific measuring devices to
   the betterment of human society (d) automated
   instruction methods

   b

4. Which of the following does not determine the
   feasible span of control for a manager? (a)
   profit margin of the organization (b) skill
   and abilities of the people involved (c) degree
   to which the work requires coordination and
   interaction (d) degree to which the environment
   is subject to change

   a

5. The Hawthorne effect refers to the finding that
   (a) increasing the supply of light improves
   performance (b) performance on the experimental task often improves simply as a result of
   the experience of being an experimental subject
   (c) performance can be improved only by improving the working environment (d) increased pay
   is the only effective way of improving performance

   b

6. The means by which information is presented to
   the individual's sensory apparatus is called
   (a) a man-machine system (b) a psychomotor
   function (c) a display (d) control

   c

7. Auditory displays are often valuable as (a)
   controls (b) warning devices (c) psychomotor functions (d) none of the above

   b

8. Controls should be coded (a) distinctively
   (b) auditorily (c) so that they are indis-
   tinguishable (d) in such a way as to guarantee they will be seen

   a

SHORT ANSWER QUESTIONS FOR REVIEW

9. Varying the arrangement of displays and controls
    in complex machinery has led to accidents due
    to (a) machine overload (b) fatigue (c)
    distraction (d) interference of habits   d

10. Which is not a measure of fatigue? (a) errors
    (b) work output (c) food consumption (d)
    physiological changes   c

11. Which of the following is not a component
    factor of a work curve? (a) fatigue (b)
    beginning spurt (c) warm-up (d) error   d

12. The most rapid recovery from fatigue occurs
    (a) before output declines (b) after much
    fatigue has set in (c) at the end of a long
    work-day (d) b and c   a

13. A group leader is most likely to earn "idio-
    syncracy credit" when he (a) deviates immed-
    iately from group norms (b) adheres initially
    to group norms (c) exercises authoritarian
    leadership in the group (d) exercises demo-
    cratic leadership in the group   b

14. Which of the following is not true about
    Management by Objectives? (a) it involves
    setting measurable, concrete performance goals
    (b) it involves subordinate participation in
    the setting of goals (c) it involves organi-
    zational commitment to the program (d) all
    of the above is true about Management by
    Objectives   d

15. Job descriptions are used primarily to (a)
    assure that jobs do not overlap (b) set worker
    characteristics for a specific job (c) deter-
    mine pay scales (d) none of the above   b

16. Job rotation through various parts of a company's
    structure is useful for (a) training new
    managers (b) orienting all new personnel
    (c) relocating dissatisfied employees (d)
    b and c   a

17. Production curves at the beginning and end of
    the day (a) spurt upward (b) spurt downward
    (c) are temporarily depressed (d) are most
    variable   a

18. The effects of fatigue on production may be
    manifested in (a) decreased output (b)
    increased errors (c) both of these (d)
    neither of these   c

SHORT ANSWER QUESTIONS FOR REVIEW

19. Presenting warning signals with a buzzer while
simultaneously giving quantitative information
on a dial system will eliminate (a) overloading (b) inattentiveness (c) machine breakdown (d) habit

a

20. The advantage of using symbolic displays is
that (a) they are more quickly interpreted
(b) they are flexible and accurate (c)
they require no training in order to interpret
them (d) they create a more congenial environment

b

21. Which is not a factor in job satisfaction?
(a) job security (b) working conditions (c)
opportunity for advancement (d) all of the
above are factors in job satisfaction

d

Fill in the blanks.

22. Muscular fatigue has been studied by means of
the _____ .

ergograph

23. The amount of work is the ordinate and amount
of _____ is the abscissa of the work curve.

work time

24. The pioneers of time-and-motion study were an
industrial engineer and his psychologist wife,
the _____ s.

Gibreth

25. McGregor labeled the bureaucratic organization
prescribed by classical theorists _____ and the
humanistic view of organizations _____ .

Theory X
Theory Y

26. Theories that consider the fit between organizational structure and the environment as well as
the fit between structure and employee characteristics are known as _____ theories.

contin-
gency

27. On a _____ question, employees are asked to
select one of several predetermined answers to
a specific question.

fixed
response

28. The term _____ refers to the solidarity among
group members and their attraction toward
membership in the group.

"cohesive-
ness"

29. At _____ Freight performance feedback and praise
have been used to shape and reinforce appropriate job behavior.

Emery Air

30. The three theories which have best explained

SHORT ANSWER QUESTIONS FOR REVIEW

_____ phenomena are drive-reinforcement theory, expectancy theory, and goal theory. — process

31. The type of question most commonly asked on interviews is the _____ question. — open-ended

32. A written statement describing the duties and responsibilities which a job will entail is commonly referred to as a(n) _____. — job description

33. According to the Equity-Inequity Theory, an undercompensated worker who is paid by the piece will _____ productivity and _____ quality. — increase, decrease

34. According to the Equity-Inequity Theory, an overcompensated worker who is paid by the hour will _____ productivity and _____ quality. — increase, increase

35. When the anticipation that a particular behavior will occur appears to be actually causing that behavior, this expectation is called the _____. — self-fulfilling prophecy

36. When expectations regarding behavior are affected by the attractiveness of the person, the _____ effect is at work. — halo

Determine whether the following statements are true or false.

37. Displays are usually designed in the areas of seeing, hearing, or feeling. — True

38. The type of work done does not affect the work curve. — False

39. "Human factors engineering," "human engineering," "psychological engineering," and "ergonomics" are synonymous terms. — True

40. The phenomenon of "end spurt" can be eliminated in an experimental design by informing the subject when he is nearing completion of the experimental task. — False

41. The importance of departmentation is greatest at the uppermost level, at the level immediately beneath that of chief executive officer. This subunit formation is known as primary departmentation. — True

42. Informal communication is sometimes referred to

SHORT ANSWER QUESTIONS FOR REVIEW

Answer

To be covered
when testing
yourself

	as the "grapevine".	True
43.	The results of the Emery Air Freight Study were supportive of the Discrepancy Theory.	False
44.	Process theories are interested in the manner in which needs and situational variables jointly determine a person's behavior.	True
45.	The three most common ways to measure attitudes are interviews, meetings, and questionaires.	True
46.	The first step in developing a selection or placement program is to conduct a job analysis.	True
47.	Training and development are synonymous when referring to planned efforts designed to facilitate the acquisition of relevant skills, knowledge and attitudes by organizational members.	False
48.	Cohesive groups are always more productive than noncohesive groups.	False
49.	Productivity is always the greatest under democratic leadership.	False
50.	Attitudes are learned dispositions, that can be changed; however, many factors must be considered in attempting attitude change.	True

CHAPTER 18

PHYSIOLOGICAL BASIS OF BEHAVIOR

THE CENTRAL NERVOUS SYSTEM

● **PROBLEM 18-1**

Distinguish between the central and peripheral nervous systems with respect to their function and location.

Solution: The central and peripheral nervous systems can be distinguished in terms of location and basic functions. The central nervous system (or CNS) includes the brain and the spinal cord. The brain is, of course, located within the skull and the spinal cord is encased in the bony spinal column which runs down the center of the back. The peripheral nervous system (PNS), on the other hand, consists of nerve fibers which run from the CNS to the periphery, i.e., the hands, feet, internal organs, etc. It includes all parts of the nervous system not encased in the bony skull and spine.

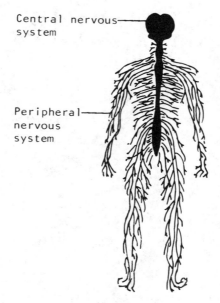

Central nervous system

Peripheral nervous system

The CNS and PNS can also be distinguished in terms of function. The PNS serves mainly as a relay route for information travelling between the central nervous system and the rest of the body. It consists basically of two types of nerves. The first includes the afferent nerves which run from the body to the spinal cord. The second type are the motor or efferent nerves which leave the CNS to travel back to the rest of the body.

The CNS functions as an integrative center. This means that it organizes, collates, and stores information sent to it by the PNS. It consists basically of bundles of nerve fibers composed of axons and dendrites, called pathways, and groups of cell bodies called centers. Pathways are specific in that they transmit only certain types of information to the appropriate centers.

The PNS can also perform some integrative activity. This activity occurs in groups of cell bodies called ganglia. The most important integrative centers of the PNS are two series of ganglia located alongside the spinal column. These are the sympathetic ganglia and the sensory or dorsal root ganglia.

● **PROBLEM** 18-2

What are the three main divisions of the brain? Which major areas does each contain?

Solution: The human brain is considered to have three major divisions; these are the hindbrain, midbrain, and forebrain.

The hindbrain is located at the base of the brain near the beginning of the spinal cord--just above the back of the neck. It contains the major 'primitive' parts of the brain. That is, as man evolved and developed a more complex portion of the brain, this essential portion of the brain stayed much the same, while additional layers were added on to it. The hindbrain includes three major parts--the cerebellum, the pons, and the medulla oblongata. The cerebellum functions in coordinating movements, the pons serves among other functions to connect the two halves of the cerebellum. The medulla is the center for control of breathing and heart rate.

The midbrain lies on top of the hindbrain. It consists of an upper portion called the tectum, and a lower part, the tegmentum. The tectum functions in the visual (sight) and auditory (hearing) systems. The tegmentum contains part of our sleep and arousal system and contains centers for eye movements.

The forebrain is the "highest" portion of the brain, both physically and in degree of complexity. Its major parts include the cerebral cortex, thalamus, hypothalamus, the basil ganglia, and the limbic system. The cortex and

thalamus function in perception, thinking, and learning.
The hypothalamus and limbic systems are important in the
control of motivation and emotion. The basil ganglia plays
a part in motor control, the extrapyramidal motor system,
and emotion. The cerebral cortex is the most complex component of the forebrain, and thus of our entire brain. It
is the center of most of our higher order cognitive processes.

● **PROBLEM** 18-3

Make a diagram of the human brain. Label the principal
parts and list the function(s) carried out by each.

Solution: The human brain is the enlarged, anterior
end of the spinal cord. This enlargement is so great that
the resemblance to the spinal cord is obscured. The adult

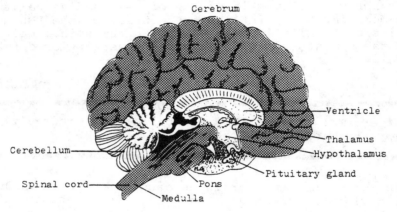

Figure 1. Interior portion of one side of the human brain.

human brain has six major regions: the medulla, pons and
cerebellum which constitute the hindbrain; the thalamus
and cerebrum, both of which are in the forebrain; and the
midbrain.

The most posterior part of the brain, connected
immediately to the spinal cord, is the medulla. Here the
central canal of the spinal cord (spinal lumen) enlarges
to form a fluid-filled cavity called the fourth ventricle.
The medulla has numerous nerve tracts (bundles of nerves)
which bring impulses to and from the brain. The medulla
also contains a number of clusters of nerve cell bodies,
known as nerve centers. These reflex centers control
respiration, heart rate, the dilation and constriction
of blood vessels, swallowing and vomiting.

Above the medulla is the cerebellum, which is made
up of a central part and two hemispheres extending side-
ways. The size of the cerebellum in different animals
is roughly correlated with the amount of their muscular
activity. It regulates and coordinates muscle contraction
and is relatively large in active animals such as birds.
Removal or injury of the cerebellum is accompanied not by
paralysis of the muscles but by impairment of muscle co-

714

ordination. A bird, with its cerebellum surgically removed, is unable to fly and its wings are seen to thrash about without coordination.

The pons is an area of the hindbrain containing a large number of nerve fibers which pass through it and make connections between the two hemispheres of the cerebellum, thus coordinating muscle movements on the two sides of the body. The pons also contains the nerve centers that aid in the regulation of breathing.

In front of the cerebellum and pons lies the thick-walled midbrain. The midbrain is an important integrating region and contains the centers for certain visual and auditory reflexes. A cluster of nerve cells regulating muscle tone and posture is also present in the midbrain. A small canal runs through the midbrain and connects the fourth ventricle behind it to the third ventricle in front of it.

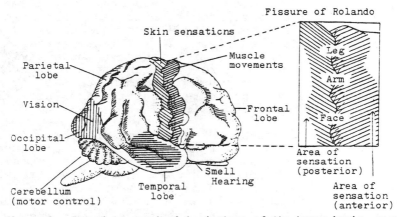

Figure 2. The right cerebral hemisphere of the human brain, seen from the side. The striped areas are regions of special function; the light areas are "association" areas. Inset: Enlarged view of the sensory and motor areas adjacent to the fissure of Rolando, showing the location of the nerve cells supplying the various parts of the body.

The thalamus of the forebrain serves as a relay center for sensory impulses. Fibers from the spinal cord and parts of the brain synapse here with other neurons going to the various sensory areas of the cerebrum. The thalamus seems to regulate and coordinate the external signs of emotions. By stimulating the thalamus with an electrode, a sham rage can be elicited in a cat - the hair stands on end, the claws protrude, and the back becomes humped. However, as soon as the stimulation ceases, the rage responses disappear.

The hypothalamus, located under the thalamus, is a collection of nuclei concerned with many important homeostatic regulations. Electrical stimulation of certain cells in the hypothalamus produces sensations of hunger, thirst, pain, pleasure, or sexual drive. The hypothalamus is also important for its influence on the pituitary gland, which is functionally under its control. Cells of the hypothalamus synthesize chemical factors that modulate the release of hormones produced and stored in the pituitary.

The cerebrum, consisting of two hemispheres, is the largest and most anterior part of the human brain. In human beings, the cerebral hemispheres grow back over the rest of the brain, hiding it from view. Each hemisphere contains one cavity (one contains the first and the other the second ventricle), which is connected to the third ventricle. The outer portion of the cerebrum, the cortex, is made up of gray matter which comprises the nerve cell bodies. The gray matter folds greatly, producing many convolutions of the cerebral surface. These convolutions increase the surface area of the gray matter. The inner part of the brain is the white matter which is composed of masses of nerve fibers.

The cerebrum houses many sensory centers. The posterior part contains the visual center, the stimulation of which causes the sensation of vision. The temporal lobe, located on the side of the cerebrum just above the ears, contains the center for hearing. Running down the side of the cerebral cortex is a deep furrow called the fissure of Rolando (see Figure 2). This separates the motor area of the cortex, which controls the activities of the skeletal muscles, from the sensory area just behind the furrow, which is responsible for the sensations of heat, cold, touch and pressure resulting from stimulation of receptor organs in the skin.

When all the areas of known functions are plotted, they cover only a small part of the total area of the human cortex. The rest, known as association areas, are regions responsible for the higher intellectual faculties of memory, reasoning, learning and imagination, all of which help to make up one's personality. In some unknown way, the association regions integrate into a meaningful unit, all the diverse impulses constantly reaching the brain, so that proper response is made.

● **PROBLEM** 18-4

Briefly describe the cerebral cortex. Include anatomy and function.

Solution: The word cortex means bark, and the cerebral cortex covers the human brain almost as completely as bark covers a tree. It is a gray colored layer of tissue (hence the colloquialism "gray matter" for intelligence), relatively thin, and wrinkled looking. The hilly portion of the wrinkles are called gyri (singular, gyrus). The crevices of the wrinkles, which are the boundaries between gyri, are usually called sulci (singular, sulcus) or fissures.

There are three main fissures running along the cerebral cortex; these are the longitudinal fissure, the central sulcus, and the lateral fissure. The longitudinal fissure runs down the center of the cortex's length. It

divides the forebrain into two halves called cerebral
hemispheres. The central sulcus runs along the width of the
cortex, at about the center. All of the cortex in front of
the central sulcus is referred to as the frontal lobe and is
considered the expressive part of the brain (because it
functions in control of movements and actions). The area
behind the central sulcus is considered the receptive part
of the cortex. This is because it is in this area of the
cortex that receives incoming information from the sense
organs.

The lateral fissure runs along the side of each cerebral hemisphere, intersecting with the central sulcus at two
points. The area below the lateral fissure is called the
temporal lobe. It contains centers involved in audition
(hearing).

The cortex has two additional lobes in addition to the
frontal and temporal lobes discussed above. These are the
parietal lobe, located right behind the central sulcus, and
the occipital lobe, which can be found beneath the back of
the skull. The parietal lobe contains areas such as the
somatosensory cortex. The occipital lobe contains part of
the area of cortex which is involved in vision.

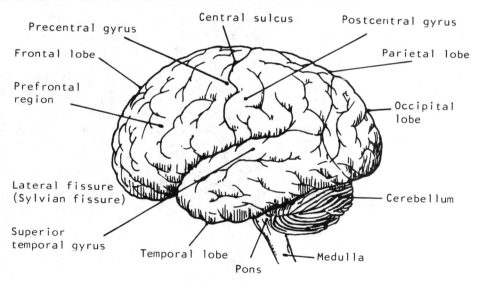

● PROBLEM 18-5

What are simple, complex, and hypercomplex cortical cells?
How do they interact in form vision?

Solution: Simple, complex, and hypercomplex cells are
units of the human brain which deal with form vision. It
is these cells which enable us to discriminate between
circles and triangles, horizontal and vertical lines, etc.
Simple cells of the cortex connect to complex cells. These,
in turn, transfer information to hypercomplex cells.

717

Simple cells are more specific in their response than the other cortical cells. They will respond only to a specific stimulus with one particular orientation and location. For example, a simple cell may respond to straight vertical lines located in the center of the visual field. A stimulus which is in a different place, or one which is not vertical, will not activate this simple cell. Three different simple cells will respond to the letters A, B and C. A simple cell responding to A cannot respond to the letters B or C, and vice versa.

Complex cortical cells also respond only to stimuli with specific shapes and orientations. However, they are not fussy about location. Complex cells will respond to a particular stimulus over a relatively large area of the retina. It follows that a vertical line moving across the visual field would activate many different simple cells in succession. As long as it stays in the vertical orientation, though, it will activate the same complex cells all the way across the retina. Similarly, both stimuli A and B, will activate the same complex cell. Two different simple cells will respond to these same two stimuli. Since simple cells connect to complex cells, several simple cells must feed information to a single complex cell.

Hypercomplex cells receive information from many different complex cells. They respond to particular angles caused by intersections of lines, or specific movements. Figure 1 would cause three types of hypercomplex cells to be activated. Presumably, we perceive objects as triangular when three hypercomplex cells in specific orientations are activated. Thus Figure 1 is perceived as triangular even though its lines are incomplete. The three responding hypercomplex cells were activated through messages from 6 different complex cells, etc. . . This is how simple, complex, and hypercomplex cells interact in form vision. The reader should note, however, that this description is based on one theory of form or pattern recognition. At this point we can not be certain that our visual system operates exactly in this manner. The topic is still being actively researched.

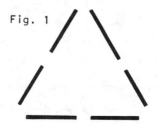

Fig. 1

● **PROBLEM** 18-6

Does a lesion in the auditory area of one cerebral hemisphere necessarily produce deafness in either ear? Explain.

Solution: The two halves of our brain are often referred

to as the left and right cerebral hemispheres. A lesion
in the auditory area of one cerebral hemisphere does not
produce deafness in either ear. This is because each ear
sends messages about what it hears to both cerebral hemispheres. Thus if one hemisphere is damaged, information
from both ears is still received and interpreted by the
second hemisphere.

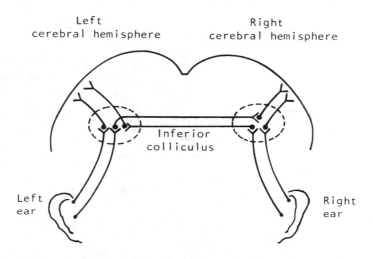

Ipsilateral and Contralateral Travel of Auditory Fibers
(Diagrammatic representation)

Information from each ear travels on the same side of
the brain as it originated as far as the area of the midbrain called the inferior colliculus. Information which
travels in this manner is referred to as ipsilateral. This
means information from the left ear travels along the left
side of the brain. At the inferior colliculus, however, a
change occurs. Slightly over half of the fibers from each
side of the brain cross over to the opposite or contralateral side. The rest of the fibers continue travelling
ipsolaterally. Thus each ear is represented in each half
of our brain. Therefore, damage to one half will not disrupt the functioning of either ear.

● **PROBLEM** 18-7

What is the basic function of the thalamus? How is it
organized?

Solution: The thalamus, a part of the forebrain located
just above the midbrain, functions mainly as a major relay
station of the brain. Information from sensory receptors
which travel through the spinal cord, or information coming from areas of the mid and hindbrains usually arrives at
the thalamus and is then relayed to the appropriate areas
in the cortex.

The thalamus is organized into various centers called
nuclei. Specific nuclei send information to specific areas

of the cortex. For example, the lateral geniculate body is
the visual nucleus of the thalamus. It relays information
to the visual area of the cortex.

It should be noted that the thalamus does not just relay information. Rather, a bit of information processing
does take place at this level. However, the more complicated and final processing occurs in the cerebral cortex.

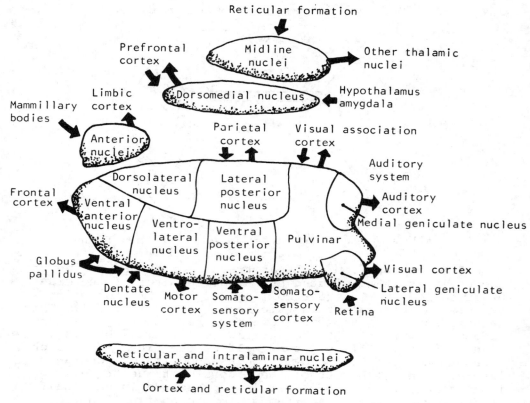

A schematic representation of the thalamus, along with some
of the principal inputs and outputs of the various thalamic
regions.

● **PROBLEM** 18-8

Compare and contrast the thalamus with the reticular activating system.

Solution: Both the thalamus and the reticular activating
system (RAS) are relay stations for information on its way
to the cerebral cortex. However, the similarities end there.
Whereas in the thalamic system, the different sensory systems are kept rigidly separate, the reticular activating
system treats all the senses as one group providing arousal
information. Thus the thalamus has specific nuclei to receive only certain kinds of information. For example, the
medial geniculate nucleus receives auditory information.

These nuclei then send information to specific parts of the cortex; the medial geniculate nucleus sends its information to the auditory cortex. The reticular activating system, on the other hand, is not organized in this way. In the RAS, the same information will activate wide regions of the cortex, and not just specific sensory areas.

In addition, the reticular activating system receives information back from the cortex, forming a loop of activation. The RAS activates the cortex, which in turn activates the RAS, etc. The thalamus usually receives primary sensory information. That is, it receives "raw" information from the senses. It does not receive information which has already undergone processing by the cortex.

● **PROBLEM** 18-9

Distinguish between the white and gray matter of the central nervous system.

Solution: The "white matter" of the central nervous system is actually the nerve fiber pathways. The "gray matter" is simply the collections of cell bodies (called centers).

Nerve fiber pathways consist mainly of axons. In the central nervous system, most axons are myelinated; they are surrounded by a fatty white covering called a myelin sheath, hence their nickname, white matter.

The normal color of a neuron is gray. Thus the centers of the central nervous system appear gray. They consist of cell bodies of neurons, which are neither myelinated nor white.

● **PROBLEM** 18-10

Large deficits of water can be only partly compensated for by renal conservation; drinking is the ultimate compensatory mechanism. What stimulates the subjective feeling of thirst which drives one to drink water?

Solution: The feeling of thirst is stimulated both by a low extracellular fluid volume and a high plasma osmolarity. The production of ADH by the hypothalamus is also stimulated by these factors. The centers which mediate thirst are located in the hypothalamus very close to those areas which produce ADH. Should this area of the hypothalamus be damaged, water intake would stop because the sensation of thirst would be impaired. Conversely, eletrical excitation of this area stimulates drinking. There has been much speculation that, because of the similarities between the stimuli for ADH secretion and thirst, the receptors which initiate the ADH controlling reflexes are identical to those for thirst.

In addition to hypothalamic pathways, there are

also other pathways controlling thirst. For example,
dryness of the mouth and throat causes profound
thirst, which is relieved by moistening. There is
also a learned control of thirst; the quantity of
fluid drunk with each meal is, in large part, a
learned response determined by past experience.

● **PROBLEM** 18-11

What general trends are observed in the evolution of the
brain?

Solution: Generally, the higher an animal is on the
ladder of evolution, the more complex and heavy is its
brain (see Figure 1). In the earthworm, an invertebrate,
the 'brain' is merely a ganglion (a clump of nerve cell
bodies) of about the same size as the other ganglia present
in each segment of the body. Even among the mammals, the
size and complexity of the brain vary to a great extent.
The weight of the brain of a full grown man is approximately
three pounds whereas a gorilla, about four times heavier
than man, has a brain that weighs only one and a half
pounds. This discrepancy in brain weight can account partly for the difference in intellectual capabilities of the
two mammals.

Increasing size is not the only feature seen in the
evolution of the brain. The brains of higher mammals display increasing foldings of their surface. These foldings,
or convolutions, are particularly pronounced in man. By
stimulating various regions of the brain with an electrode,
and observing the corresponding results in behavior, functional mapping of the brains of various mammals has been
achieved. The mapping shows that different regions of the
brain are associated with different functions. There are
the areas for motor functions, somatic sensory functions,
vision, hearing, olfaction, and so forth. The mapping also
shows that the proportion of the total area of the cerebrum
devoted to sensory and motor functions differs greatly
among species. It has been found that, in general, the
more convoluted the surface of the cerebrum (called the
cerebral cortex), the smaller the proportion devoted exclusively to sensory and motor activities. Since, as
mentioned, there is a trend toward increasing convolutions
in the evolution of the brain, we can anticipate that
higher animals have a more convoluted cerebral cortex, and
that at the same time, a smaller proportion of their brain
is involved in sensory and motor functions. This is
supported by the finding that in the cat the sensory and
motor functions occupy a major portion of the cortex,
whereas in man, the area of the cortex devoted to those
functions is relatively small (see Figure 2).

The rest of the brain not associated with motor and
sensory activities contain the so-called associative areas.
These areas are made up of neurons that are not directly
connected to sense organs or muscles but supply interconnections between the other areas. They are believed to

722

be responsible for the higher intellectual faculties of memory, reasoning, learning, imagination, and personality. They are, in short, responsible for the behavioral consequences that most clearly distinguish man from other animals.

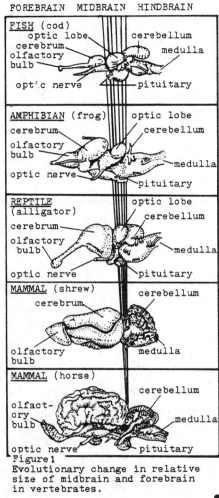

FOREBRAIN MIDBRAIN HINDBRAIN

FISH (cod)
    optic lobe
cerebrum
olfactory
bulb
    optic nerve
    cerebellum
    medulla
    pituitary

AMPHIBIAN (frog)
cerebrum
olfactory
bulb
optic nerve
    optic lobe
    cerebellum
    medulla
    pituitary

REPTILE
(alligator)
cerebrum
olfactory
  bulb
optic nerve
    optic lobe
    cerebellum
    medulla
    pituitary

MAMMAL (shrew)
    cerebrum
olfactory
bulb
    cerebellum
    medulla

MAMMAL (horse)
olfact-
ory
bulb
optic nerve
    cerebellum
    medulla
    pituitary

Figure 1
Evolutionary change in relative size of midbrain and forebrain in vertebrates.

● **PROBLEM 18-12**

What are the two major functions of the spinal cord? Discuss.

Solution: The spinal cord of nervous tissue running from the brain down the back, has two major functions. First, it acts as a messenger, relaying information from the body to the brain and then often back to the body. Second, it directs some relatively simple actions independently without input from the brain.

In its capacity as messenger, the spinal cord is important as it is a path of nerve cells running to and from the brain. Information from the body travels along afferent

nerves to the spinal cord, where it is relayed through specific nerve pathways to appropriate areas of the brain.
The brain considers the information, and if necessary, sends
a message through other spinal pathways to appropriate
muscles and glands to produce any necessary action.

However, not all information from our body must pass
through the brain, though the great majority does. In
simple reflexes, for example, information is passed as usual
to the spinal cord, but the 'decision' for action is made
directly at this level. The knee-jerk reflex is an example
of this. When a specific part of the knee is hit, you kick
out your leg. The command to kick is given without interference from the brain. This can be demonstrated by considering that this and other reflexes are performed even
when the brain is disconnected from the spinal cord. Thus
here the spinal cord must be acting independently.

● **PROBLEM 18-13**

Describe the structures found in a cross section of the
mammalian spinal cord.

Solution: The mammalian spinal cord extends from the
base of the brain and is tubular in shape. Along with
the brain, the spinal cord makes up the central nervous
system of all vertebrates. It has two very important
functions: to transmit impulses to and from the brain,
and to act as a reflex center.

The spinal cord is protected by the vertebral

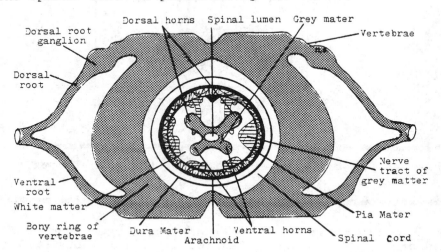

Cross section of the mammalian spinal   cord surrounded by the bony
vertebrae.

column. The vertebral column is composed of segments of
bone, called the vertebrae, connected to each other by
cartilage. The cartilage gives it flexibility, while the
bone gives it strength. It is possible to functionally
divide the spinal cord into five different regions using
the vertebrae as a guide. These are (1) cervical region,

(2) thoracic region, (3) lumbar region, (4) sacral region, and (5) the coccyx. The regions of the spinal cord send out nerves which innervate different parts of the body (see Figure 1).

The spinal cord is surrounded by three membranes: the dura mater, arachnoid, and pia mater. It is a hollow, tubular structure. The hollow portion, called the spinal lumen, runs through the entire length of the spinal cord and is filled with spinal fluid. A cross-section shows 2 regions, an inner mass of gray matter composed of nerve cell bodies, and an outer mass of white matter made up of bundles of axons and dendrites (see Figure 2). The coloration of the white matter region is due to the presence of white myelinated fibers. The nerve cells of the gray matter lack myelin, which is white, and hence the "natural" gray color of nerve cells is seen. Four protuberances of the gray matter are noted. The two anterior processes are called the ventral horns, and the two posterior ones are called the dorsal horns. The axons and dendrites of the white matter carry impulses between lower levels and higher levels of the spinal cord, or between various levels of the spinal cord and the brain.

The spinal cord receives sensory fibers from peripheral receptors at the dorsal root. The cell bodies from which the sensory fibers arise are located in a cluster, called the dorsal root ganglion, in the dorsal root. These sensory fibers pass into the dorsal horns of the gray matter, where they synapse with interneurons and/or motor neurons in the ventral horns. Axons from the motor neurons leave the spinal cord at the ventral root and soon join the sensory fibers, Together they constitute the spinal nerve. Spinal nerves arising from the spinal cord branch to supply various parts of the body except the head, part of the neck, the thorax, abdomen, and the upper and lower extremities.

THE PERIPHERAL NERVOUS SYSTEM

● PROBLEM 18-14

What are spinal nerves and what are their functions?

Solution: Spinal nerves belong to the peripheral nervous system (PNS). They arise as pairs at regular intervals from the spinal cord, branch, and run to various parts of the body to innervate them. In human beings, there are 31 symmetrical pairs of spinal nerves. The size of each spinal nerve is related to the size of the body area it innervates.

All the spinal nerves are mixed nerves, in the sense that all have both motor and sensory components in roughly equal amounts. They contain fibers of the somatic nervous system, which are both afferent (conducting impulses towards the nervous system) and efferent (conducting impulses to effector organs). They also contain fibers of the auto-

nomic nervous system, which are uniquely efferent and
are separable into parasympathetic and sympathetic nervous
systems. Because of this nature, the spinal nerves
function to convey messages from the external environment
to the central nervous system, and from the central
nervous system to various effectors of the body. In
other words, the spinal nerves, as part of the peripheral
nervous system, serve as a link between the central nervous
system and the effector organs.

Somatic fibers of the spinal nerves innervate
skeletal muscles of the body, and are under voluntary

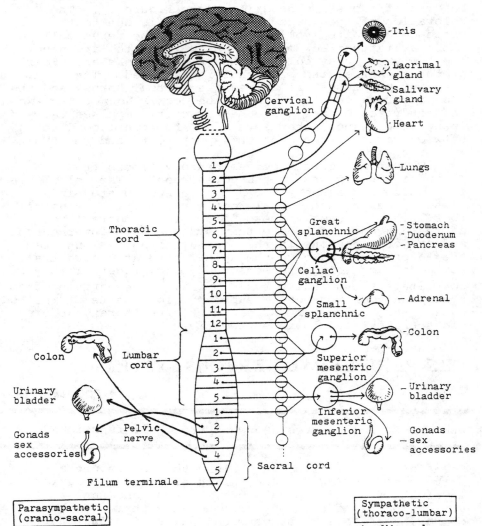

The spinal nerves and their autonomic fibers. The somatic fibers leave
the spinal cord together with the autonomic fibers and then seperate.

regulation. We can bend our arm or leg at will. The autonomic nerves innervate the smooth and cardiac muscles and
glands of the body, and cannot be voluntarily controlled.
We cannot speed up our stomach contractions or heart beat
at will. The autonomic nerve fibers leave the spinal cord
and run for a certain distance with the somatic fibers in

the spinal nerves. Then the two types of fibers diverge
and run to their respective body areas which they innervate.

● **PROBLEM** 18-15

Pilocarpine is a drug that stimulates the nerve endings
of parasympathetic nerves. What effects would you
expect this drug to have on (a) the digestive tract,
(b) the iris of the eye, and (c) the heart rate?

Solution: The parasympathetic system consists
exclusively of motor fibers originating from the brain
and emerging via the third, seventh, ninth and tenth
(vagus) nerves, and of fibers originating from the
pelvic (hip) region of the spinal cord and emerging by
way of the spinal nerves in that region. The parasympathetic system therefore has nerves from two separate
regions - the brain and the pelvic region of the spinal
cord.

        (a) The ninth cranial nerve, the glossopharyngeal,
innervates the salivary gland. It stimulates the
salivary gland to release digestive enzymes. A more
important cranial nerve, the vagus, sends branches to
the stomach, duodenum and the pancreas. This nerve
enchances motility and peristalsis of the digestive tract.
(Motility and peristalsis of the digestive tract should
not be confused with each other. Motility of the tract
causes food to mix and churn but no movement of it.
Peristalsis moves the food down the digestive tract).
It also stimulates the secretion of digestive enzymes by
digestive glands. For example, stimulation of the
pancreas by the vagus nerve causes secretion of the
pancreatic juice. Thus the glossopharyngeal and vagus
together act to promote digestion. When pilocarpine is
present,the parasympathetic fibers are stimulated. The
result is that digestion is facilitated or enhanced.

        (b) The third cranial nerve supplies the muscles
of the iris which controls the size of the pupil of the
eye. Excitation of this nerve causes constriction of
the pupil. Since pilocarpine excites the parasympathetic
system, its presence would cause the pupil to reduce in
size.

        (c) The parasympathetic branch supplying the
heart is part of the vagus nerve. Its action is to
weaken and slow down the heart beat. Pilocarpine introduced into the blood stream would activate the parasympathetic nerve endings, causing the heart beat to slow
and weaken.

● **PROBLEM** 18-16

Describe and give an example of a reflex arc.

Solution: To understand what a reflex arc is, we must

727

know something about reflexes. A reflex is an innate, stereotyped, automatic response to a given stimulus. A popular example of a reflex is the knee jerk. No matter how many times we rap on the tendon of a person's knee cap, his leg will invariably straighten out. This experiment demonstrates one of the chief characteristics of a reflex: fidelity of repetition.

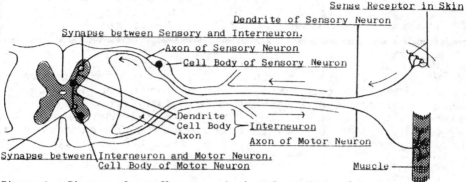

Figure 1. Diagram of a reflex arc, showing the pathway of an impulse, indicated by arrows.

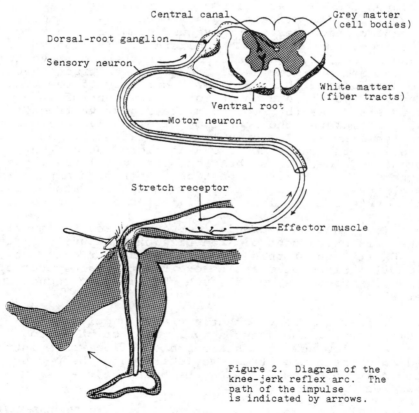

Figure 2. Diagram of the knee-jerk reflex arc. The path of the impulse is indicated by arrows.

Reflexes are important because responses to certain stimuli have to be made instantaneously. For example, when we step on something sharp or come into contact with something hot, we do not wait until the pain is experienced by the brain and then after deliberation decide what to do. Our responses are immediate and automatic. The part

of the body involved is being withdrawn by reflex action
before the sensation of pain is experienced.

A reflex arc is the neural pathway that conducts
the nerve impulses for a given reflex. It consists of
a sensory neuron with a receptor to detect the stimulus,
connected by a synapse to a motor neuron, which is
attached to a muscle or some other tissue that brings
about the appropriate response. Thus, the simplest type
of reflex arc is termed monosynaptic because there is
only one synapse between the sensory and motor neurons.
Most reflex arcs include one or more interneurons between
the sensory and motor neurons (see Figure 1).

An example of a monosynaptic reflex arc is the
knee jerk. When the tendon of the knee cap is tapped,
and thereby stretched, receptors in the tendon are
stimulated. An impulse travels along the sensory neuron
to the spinal cord where it synapses directly with a
motor neuron. This latter neuron transmits an impulse
to the effector muscle in the leg, causing it to contract,
resulting in a sudden straightening of the leg (see Figure 2).

● **PROBLEM** 18-17

Homeostatic regulation of many body functions is not
achieved by the central nervous system but by the
autonomic nervous system. Explain how the autonomic
nervous system can bring about such regulation.

Solution: The autonomic nervous system is divided
in two parts, both structurally and functionally. One
part is called the sympathetic nervous system and the
other is known as the parasympathetic nervous system.
These two branches act antagonistically to each other.
If one system stimulates an effector, the other would
inhibit its action. The basis for homeostatic regulation
by the autonomic nervous system lies in the fact that
the sysmpathetic and parasympathetic systems each sends
a branch to the same organ, causing the phenomenon of
double innervation.

Double innervation by the autonomic nervous
system, together with the action of the endocrine system,
is the basis for maintaining homeostasis inside the body.
If through the stimulation by one system of an organ,
a substance or action is produced excessively, then the
other system will operate to inhibit the same organ,
thus reducing the production of that substance or inhibiting that action. This is basically how the internal
condition of the body is kept constant.

An example will illustrate the above. Both the
sympathetic and parasympathetic systems innervate the
heart. The action of the former strengthens and accel-
erates the heart beat while the latter weakens and
slows the same. When a person is in fright, his heart
beat involuntarily quickens owing, in part, to stimula-

tion by the sympathetic system. To regain the normal
state, the sympathetic system is overridden by the parasympathetic system which decelerates the heart beat.
In the normal condition, the heart receives impulses from
the two antagonizing systems, and it is through a balance
of the two that the proper rate of heart beat is maintained.

● PROBLEM 18-18

What is meant by the autonomic nervous system? What
are its subdivisions and to which of the large divisions
of the entire nervous system does it belong?

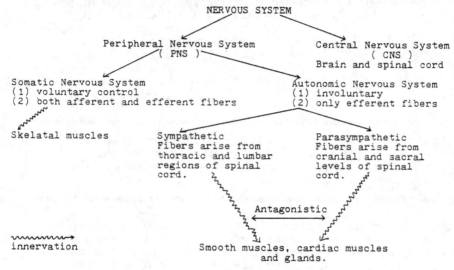

Summary of the divisions and subdivisions of the mammalian nervous
system.

Solution: Nerves from the central nervous system
(CNS) that innervate the cardiac muscles, smooth muscles
and secretory glands form the autonomic nervous system.
Structural and physiological differences within the
autonomic nervous system are the basis for its further
subdivision into sympathetic and parasympathetic systems.
Nerves of these two divisions leave the central nervous
system at different regions. The sympathetic nerves
emerge from the thoracic and lumbar regions of the spinal
cord, and the parasympathetic nerves arise from the
cranial and sacral portions of the spinal chord.

      The autonomic nervous system contains only motor
nerves and is distinguished from the rest of the nervous
system by several characteristics. There is no voluntary
control by the cerebrum over these nerves. We cannot
control our heart beat or the action of the muscles of
the stomach or intestines. Another important characteristic of the autonomic nervous system is that each
internal organ receives a double set of fibers, one set
belonging to the sympathetic system and the other to
the parasympathetic system. Impulses from the sympathetic and parasympathetic nerves always have antagonistic

730

effects on the organs innervated. Thus if one functions to increase a certain activity, the other functions to decrease it.

The autonomic nervous system is part of a larger unit called the peripheral nervous system. The peripheral nervous system contains two types of nerve fibers: the afferent fibers which convey information from receptors in the periphery to the CNS, and the efferent fibers which carry information from the CNS to the effectors. Effectors are tissues or organs which bring about appropriate responses to certain stimuli, both internal (such as from the brain) and external (such as from the environment). Some examples of effectors are the skeletal muscles, cardiac and smooth muscles, and secretory glands. The peripheral nervous system can be divided functionally into two parts. That part which innervates the skeletal muscles is known as the somatic nervous system, and that which innervates the rest is the autonomic nervous system.

● **PROBLEM** 18-19

List the antagonistic activities of the sympathetic and parasympathetic systems.

Solution: Below is tabulated the antagonistic activities of the sympathetic and parasympathetic systems.

Organs innervated	Sympathetic action	Parasympathetic action
Heart	Strengthens and speeds up heart beat	Weakens and slows down heart beat
Arteries	constricts lumen and raises blood pressure	dilates lumen and lowers blood pressure
Digestive tract	slows peristalsis	speeds peristalsis
Digestive glands	decreases secretion	increases secretion
Urinary bladder	relaxes bladder	constricts bladder
Bronchial muscles	dilates passages, facilitating breathing	constricts passages
Muscles of iris	dilates pupil	constricts pupil
Muscles attached to hair	causes erection of hair	causes hair to lie flat
Sweat glands	increases secretion	decreases secretion

In general, the sympathetic system produces the

effects which prepare an animal for emergency situations, such as quickening the heart and breathing rates and dilating the pupil. These alert responses are together termed the fight-or-flight reactions. The parasympathetic systems reverse the fight-or-flight responses to restore an animal to a calm state.

● **PROBLEM** 18-20

Besides their actions, the sympathetic and parasympathetic systems also differ in the neurotransmitter they release. Explain.

Solution: Nerves of the parasympathetic system secrete a neurotransmitter called acetylcholine. For this reason they are usually referred to as cholinergic neurons. Acetylcholine is also the transmitter chemical for synapses between neurons of the peripheral nervous system outside the autonomic system. Nerves of the sympathetic system release noradrenaline, also called norepinephrine, and are thus noradrenergic.

Acetylcholine is a strong base, containing a choline moiety. $[-CH_2CH_2-\overset{+}{N}-(CH_3)_3]$

In exists as a cation (positive ion) at physiological pH (about 7.4). Because of its ability to attach to a membrane and create a reversible change in the membrane's permeability to different ions, acetylcholine released by the presynaptic neuron acts to bring about depolarization and generate an impulse in the postsynaptic neuron. The molecular structure of acetylcholine is:

$$CH_3-\overset{\overset{O}{\|}}{C}-CH_2-CH_2-\overset{+}{N}-(CH_3)_3$$

Noradrenaline has a molecular structure containing a ring moiety:

The closely related compound adrenalin (epinephrine) -

is a hormone released by the adrenal glands, and although its action is similar to that of noradrenalin, it is not a neurotransmitter.

NEURONS AND SYNAPSES

● **PROBLEM** 18-21

What is the basic structure of the neuron? Discuss some variations on this structure.

Solution: It is important to recognize that the term 'typical neuron' is rather vague. Neurons, which are the basic structural and functional units of the nervous systems of multicellular animals, show a great diversity in types. In humans, many types of neurons are present. Nevertheless, often three parts of a neuron can be distinguished: a cell body, an axon, and a group of processes called dendrites.

Essentially, the neuron consists of two parts--the cell body, or soma, and the processes that emerge from the soma. The entire cell is surrounded by a cell membrane which is semi-permeable, that is, it allows some substances to pass through it in certain directions, and others not. The soma also contains a membrane-bound 'nucleus' which directs the cell's activities.

There are two types of processes emerging from the soma --dendrites, which receive information either from other neurons or directly from external stimuli, and axons, which send the information to other neurons, effectors, glands, or muscles. Generally, dendrites are more numerous and are shorter than axons. They branch off the soma much like tree branches do, whereas the axon is usually one long stalk with a bit of branching at its ends.

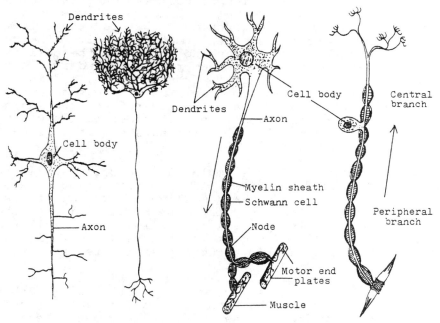

Figure 1. A variety of neuron types in human beings.

The point at which an axon and soma join is called the axon hillock. It is here that an action potential is first generated. The axon itself generally has another covering besides the cell membrane: this is the myelin sheath, a fatty white substance surrounding the axon which is discontinuous along its length; that is, it begins, ends, begins again, etc. The points at which the myelin sheath ends are called the "Nodes of Ranvier". These are important in the propagation of the action potentially along the axon. Towards its end, the axon branches off into smaller, gen-

733

erally bare, fibers that terminate with small knobs called terminal buttons. The terminal buttons hold tiny membrane-bound vessels called synaptic vesicles. These contain the neurotransmitters necessary for the stimulation of near-by cells.

Several variations on this basic structure exist. For one, not all axons are covered by a myelin sheath. These conduct impulses much more slowly than myelinated axons. In addition, the number of dendrites varies greatly among different types of nerve cells. A multipolar neuron gives rise to one axon but many dendrites. A bipolar neuron, on the other hand, has one axon and only one dendrite. Neurons may also vary in the length of their axons and dendrites. In addition, a great variety of dendritic branching can be found among nerve cells.

● **PROBLEM** 18-22

Describe the action potential and how it is generated.

Solution: The action potential is caused mainly by changes in the relative concentration of positive charges inside and outside the cell body. Normally, a nerve cell is negatively charged relative to its environment--that is, there is more positive charge outside the cell than inside it. The reason that these positive charges do not enter the cell is the selective permeability of the membrane surrounding the cell. This membrane lets only certain substances in, and in the 'resting state' of a nerve, it does not allow positive charges outside to enter the cell. Therefore, the inside of the cell is negative relative to the outside, and a relative charge of about -70 millivolts exists. This is called the 'resting potential'.

When a nerve cell is stimulated, the cell usually becomes a little less negative. If the stimulation is enough to cause a charge of about +10 millivolts, we say 'threshold' has been reached. At this point, the permeability of the cell membrane changes radically; it allows almost all the positive charges (i.e., sodium ions) outside the cell to rush in! The cell quickly becomes positive relative to its surroundings, or 'depolarized'.

But this state exists for only a short while. Other positive charges which had been blocked from leaving the cell are suddenly free to leave it. This causes the cell to become negative relative to the outside once again, usually even more negative than it was in the beginning. This is called 'hyperpolarization.' A sodium pump inside the cell then restores it to its original resting potential.

The entire sequence of events discussed above constitutes the action potential. Since when diagrammed it often looks like a spike, it is also called a 'spike potential'. In addition, it is often simply referred to as a 'nerve impulse'.

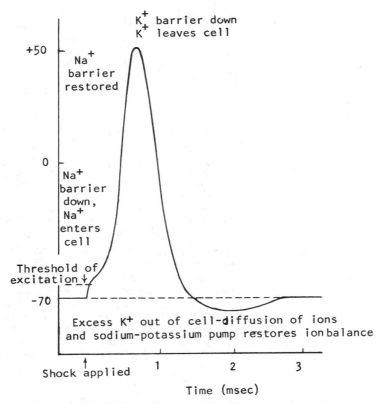

The ionic fluxes during the action potential.

● PROBLEM 18-23

How is an action potential propagated in myelinated and unmyelinated axons? Which type conducts faster?

Solution: Action potentials can be conducted along an axon, propagated, in two different ways, depending on the type of axon. There are two types of axons--myelinated axons and unmyelinated axons. Myelinated axons propagate action potentials by a method called 'saltatory conduction'. Unmyelinated axons conduct them via "passive cable properties".

When an action potential is conducted down an axon by means of the passive cable properties, it is simply created anew at each point of the axon's membrane. The action potential at one point of the membrane stimulates the next point to produce an action potential, and so on down the entire axon membrane. This method of propagation occurs in unmyelinated axons--those that have no covering other than their cell membrane.

Saltatory conduction, occurring in myelinated axons, is very similar, but much faster. The myelinated axon is

735

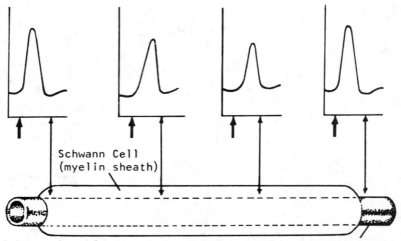

Propagation of an action potential down a myelinated axon.

surrounded by a fatty white covering called a myelin sheath.
This covering contains Nodes of Ranvier--gaps in the sheath
along the length of the axon. In saltatory conduction, the
action potential jumps over the parts of the axon that are
covered by a myelin sheath. So instead of being regenerated
at every point of the axon's membrane as in passive cable
conduction, the action potential is recreated only at the
Nodes of Ranvier. Since the action potential is regenerated
only at the Nodes of Ranvier, this method of propagation is
much faster than propagation by passive cable properties.

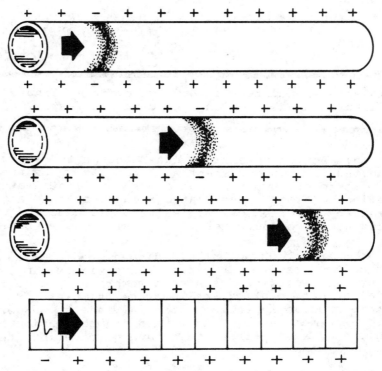

Propagation of an action potential down an unmyelinated
axon.

What is the All-or-None Law? What important implication
does this law have?

Solution: A minimum amount of stimulation is needed for a
nerve cell to begin sending signals. But once this threshold
value is reached, the All-or-None Law states that "the size
of the signal produced is always the same, regardless of the
size of the stimulus." It follows from this law that the
magnitude of the signal produced by a bright red box is the
same as that produced by a dull red box of equal size.

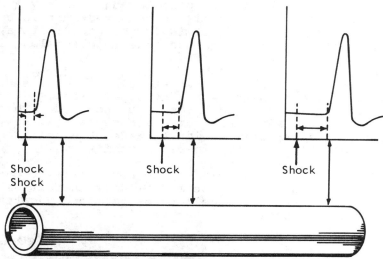

The results obtained when the axon is given a shock that is
above the threshold of excitation. This demonstrates the non-
decremental conduction of an action potential.

This has an important implication concerning how our
system codes for stimuli of different intensities but with
the same general properties, e.g., the two red boxes described
above. If the action potential generated is the same regardless of the particular stimulus properties, differences
in intensity cannot be coded for by differences in magnitude
of the signal. Rather, other factors, such as the number of
such signals produced in a given amount of time, signal the
brain about the intensity of the stimulus. In the example
above the brighter square would cause more signals per unit
time to be sent to the brain than the duller one. In keeping with the All-or-None Law, though, the magnitude of the
electrical changes produced would always be the same.

● **PROBLEM** 18-25

What is an EPSP? What is an IPSP? How do they affect a
nerve cell's excitability?

<u>Solution</u>: An EPSP is an excitatory postsynaptic potential.
An IPSP is an inhibitory post synaptic potential. What are
post synaptic potentials?

Postsynaptic potentials refer to changes in a nerve
cell's charge relative to its environment. Normally, the
inside of a nerve cell is negatively charged as compared to
its surroundings. This is because there is a higher concentration of positive charges outside the cell than inside it.
These positive charges cannot pass through the semi-
permeable membrane of the cell. However, if a nerve cell
is stimulated, this situation changes. The stimulation may
be external, or it may come from within, for example, from
another nerve cell. If the stimulus makes the nerve cell
less negative, as would occur if the membrane now begins
to allow positive charges to pass through, we say an excitatory postsynaptic potential has occurred. It is considered excitatory because if it is large enough, it may cause
the neuron to fire; i.e., conduct the impulse along its
axon.

If, on the other hand, the stimulation causes the nerve
cell to become more negative or hyperpolarized, we say an
inhibitory postsynaptic potential has occurred. This stimulation is considered inhibitory because it will now take
a larger excitatory stimulation to cause the cell to become sufficiently positive in order to fire.

In summary, an EPSP causes the nerve cell to become
less negative, thus making it more likely that it will
fire. An IPSP causes the cell to become more negative,
thus making it less likely that it will fire.

● **PROBLEM** 18-26

Compare and contrast the excitatory postsynaptic potential
(EPSP) and the action potential. What is the relationship
between them?

<u>Solution</u>: Both an EPSP (excitatory postsynaptic potential),
and action potentials, are caused by changes in the permeability of the nerve cell membrane. In both cases, these
changes result in a depolarization--the cell becomes less
negative than it was originally. Finally, the occurrence
of activation is followed in both cases by the cell potential returning to its baseline level of -70 millivolts.

The EPSP, however, consists of a much smaller degree
of depolarization than the action potential: the cell becomes only about 10 millivolts more positive. In contrast,
during an action potential, the cell actually becomes more
positive relative to its outside. During an action potential, for example, the cell's charge relative to its surroundings may become +30 millivolts!

Another difference lies in the fact that an action potential comes in one size only, whereas EPSPs can be 'graded'. This means they can be large, up to a +10 millivolt change in the cell's charge, or small, depending on the strength of the stimulus.

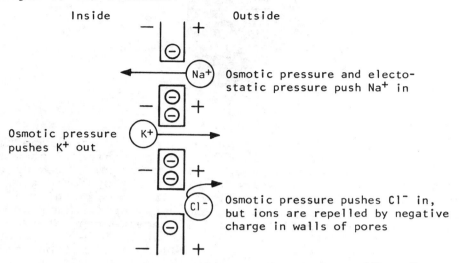

Inside   Outside

Osmotic pressure and electo-static pressure push Na^+ in

Osmotic pressure pushes K^+ out

Osmotic pressure pushes Cl^- in, but ions are repelled by negative charge in walls of pores

An EPSP results from an influx of sodium and an efflux of potassium.

The important relationship between the two is the following: An EPSP which is large enough to reach a certain threshold value, will cause an action potential to be produced in the nerve cell. Usually, an EPSP of +10 millivolts will be sufficient to generate an action potential.

● **PROBLEM** 18-27

What are absolute and relative refractory periods? When do they occur?

Solution: There is a period of time immediately after a cell has fired when the nerve cell will not respond to any new stimulation; this is called the 'absolute refractory period'. It occurs when the nerve cell is still responding to previous stimulation, for instance, when it is conducting an action potential.

When the nerve cell has finished responding to past stimulation, it may be again responsive to new stimulation. However, it takes a much stronger stimulus to get the neuron to fire. This is called the "relative refractory period". During this period, the nerve cell can respond if a strong enough stimulus is provided. The length of the absolute and relative refractory periods varies from nerve to nerve.

● **PROBLEM** 18-28

Describe the anatomy of the synaptic region.

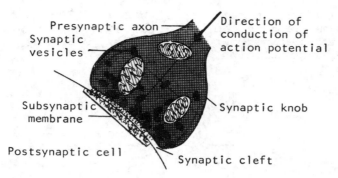

Presynaptic axon
Synaptic vesicles
Direction of conduction of action potential
Subsynaptic membrane
Synaptic knob
Postsynaptic cell
Synaptic cleft

A synapse.

Solution: The synaptic region includes the end of one nerve cell called the presynaptic cell, the beginning of the next cell called the postsynaptic cell, and the small region of space in between them, which is called the synaptic gap. The membrane of the nerve cell which is sending information across this gap is called the presynaptic membrane. The membrane of the cell which will receive the information is called the postsynaptic membrane. This is because from the point of view of the travelling information, this membrane occurs after the synapse.

The presynaptic membrane covers the terminal button, a knoblike projection at the end of the presynaptic cell's axon. The terminal button contains the means for communicating with the post-synaptic cell--chemical substances called neurotransmitters, which are stored in tiny membrane-bound vessels called synaptic vesicles. It is these chemicals that cross the synaptic gap to the postsynaptic nerve cell and effect changes in the permeability of the postsynaptic membrane, changes which will alter the postsynaptic neuron's tendency to fire.

Thus we see that the synaptic region consists of the extremities of two nerve cells plus the region in between them. Since there is no physical contact between presynaptic and postsynaptic neurons, the synaptic region is considered a functional connection.

● **PROBLEM** 18-29

What happens to neurotransmitters once they have "done their job?"

Solution: Once a neurotransmitter has exerted its effect on the membrane of a receiving nerve cell, it must be somehow deactivated in order that the nerve cell can return to its 'resting state'. Deactivation can be accomplished in two ways--through a method called re-uptake, or through enzyme action.

If a neurotransmitter is deactivated through re-uptake, it is simply reabsorbed into the presynaptic terminal it came from. Probably, it is then packaged once again into synaptic vesicles, and ready for reuse.

When enzyme action is used to deactivate the neurotransmitter, it is actually broken down by specific enzymes
near the synapse. It then must be somehow rebuilt and reabsorbed into the nerve cell in order to be ready for use
again.

● **PROBLEM** 18-30

Outline the general course of events that takes place
during interneuron communication.

Solution: Nerve cells are separated from each other by a
small region called the synaptic gap. Once an action potential has been conducted to the ends of a nerve cell, how is
the information conducted across this gap to a nearby cell?
This process of communication between neurons is called
synaptic transmission.

The first event in synaptic transmission is the arrival of the action potential at the terminal buttons
(knoblike projections at the ends of the axon). Its arrival causes tiny membrane-bound vessels called synaptic
vesicles, located within the terminal buttons, to release
chemical substances which they store into the synaptic gap.
These substances, called neurotransmitters, then travel
across the gap to neighboring nerve cells.

When the transmitters come in contact with the cell
membrane of a neighboring cell, the transmitters cause the
membrane to change its permeability to positive sodium ions
(from being impermeable to them to allowing them to enter
the cell). This change in membrane permeability will now
alter the charge of the entire cell relative to its environment. The neuron becomes more positive relative to its
exterior as positive charges are let into the cell. If
the potential of the cell, i.e., its charge relative to
its surroundings, reaches its action potential, the cell
will fire. Thus the neurons have succeeded in communicating
with each other.

● **PROBLEM** 18-31

What are spatial and temporal summations? How do they
contribute to the production of an action potential?

Solution: We know that in order for an action potential
to be produced, a nerve cell's charge relative to its outside must be raised from about negative 70 millivolts to
negative 60 millivolts. Negative 60 millivolts is called
the 'threshold value'. This value can be reached if one
stimulus of great enough intensity is given to the nerve
cell. Or, a number of smaller stimuli can be added together in order to reach threshold. The two types of sum-

mation that can occur are spatial summation and temporal
summation.

   In spatial summation, stimulations that occurred close
to each other in space on the nerve cell are added up (summated). For instance, if a nerve cell is slightly stimulated by two axons that are lying side by side, the effects of these two stimulations may be added together, and
threshold may be reached this way.

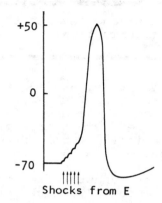

Shocks from E

Temporal summation can occur if subthreshold depolarizations
are present in rapid succession.

   In temporal summation, stimulations that occurred close
to each other in time are added up. For instance, if nerve
A was stimulated by nerve B twice in a short period of time,
the effects of these stimulations may be summated, and
threshold reached in this manner. If threshold is reached,
then an action potential will be produced in that cell.

● **PROBLEM** 18-32

What are the three basic functional units that are involved whenever we respond to a stimulus, and how are they
connected?

Solution: At least three structures are involved whenever
we respond to a stimulus. These are the receptor cell, an
association neuron at some level of the central nervous
system, and finally, an effector cell.

   Receptor cells are those cells that receive the stimulus from the environment and convert the physical stimulus
into an electrical message. This information now travels
through 'afferent nerves' to the spinal cord. Association
neurons in the spinal cord may refer the information to the
brain for further processing, or they may pass the information directly to 'efferent nerves' which innervate the appropriate effector, usually a muscle or gland. The effector effects a response; that is, if it is a muscle, a movement will probably occur, and if it is a gland, a hormone
or enzyme will probably be produced or released.

The reflex arc is the simplest example of the above described pathway. In the classic knee-jerk reflex, a proprioceptor receives the information that the knee has been hit and sends it by afferent nerves to the spinal cord. As this is a simple reflex, the brain is not involved, and the information is relayed by efferent nerves directly to the leg muscle, which then effects the kicking response generally observed.

● **PROBLEM** 18-33

What is sensory transduction and why is this process basic to the study of physiological psychology?

Solution: Our brain can only "understand" messages which are carried in an electrical form called 'electric impulses'. But if this is so, how can we, for example, feel a touch on the arm? A touch is a physical action--not an electric impulse! Thus the question of how information from our environment can be translated into a message our brain "understands" is a crucial one in psychology. We realize that the appropriate information does reach the brain. The basic question, then, is "How?"

The process whereby a physical stimulus from the environment is transformed into electrical activity which the brain understands is called 'sensory transduction'. This process takes place at the receptor cells of each sensory system. For example, in the visual system, the receptors are two types of cells called rods and cones. As light, the physical stimulus, hits these receptors, chemical changes take place within the cells. (In rod cells, the chemical rhodopsin is converted to retinene and opsin). These chemical changes effect electrical changes which can be sensed by the nervous system, and a message concerning the stimulus involved is then sent to the brain.

In summary, we have seen that in order for physical information from our environment to be translated into electrical activity "understood" by the brain, the process of sensory transduction is required. Study of this process is crucial to physiological psychology since it is at this level that our nervous system relates to our environment; it is by this process that the changes necessary to tell our brain "what's going on" take place.

● **PROBLEM** 18-34

What are the four basic types of sensory receptors? Give an example of each.

Solution: Information from the environment (e.g., Is it light or dark outside, did something just fall on your foot, etc. . .) enters our body through units called sensory receptors. Four basic types of sensory receptors can be distinguished.

First, there are receptors that relay information about stimuli that originate outside the body: these are the exteroceptors. Exteroceptors are classified as distant when the source of stimulation is far removed from the receptor, as when you see a star. They are classified as contact exteroceptors when the source of stimulation is in actual physical contact with the receptor, an example being the taste buds in your mouth--you do not taste food until it makes actual contact with the receptors on the tongue.

In direct contrast, interoceptors are sensitive only to internal stimulation that originate within the body itself. They are usually located in the walls of internal organs. In the stomach, for example, they are sensitive to stomach distention (stretching). These receptors are hypothesized to play a role in satiety.

Proprioceptors, located in muscles, tendons, and joints, are sensitive to movements of the muscles, tendons, or joints, such as flexion, when a limb is bent. These provide what we call our "kinesthetic sense" or sense of motion; they are of much importance in performing complex coordinated activities and in helping us maintain our balance.

The fourth class of receptors is concerned with the vestibular senses--those of balance and orientation of the body and head in space. It includes the hair cells of the semicircular canals in the ears, which provide us with information regarding our head position.

In summary, the following four classes of receptors were distinguished: exteroceptors, which deal with stimuli originating outside the body, interoceptors which deal with stimuli originating within the body, proprioceptors which are sensitive to movement of muscles, tendons, or joints, and vestibular receptors, concerned with balance and orientation of head and body in space.

● **PROBLEM** 18-35

What is a receptive field? Give an example of a typical ganglion cell receptive field and explain how it works.

Solution: The receptive field of a nerve cell is the area of sensory surface from which that nerve cell's activity can be influenced. Our skin is an example of a sensory surface. It contains nerve cells which respond to touch. However, a nerve cell on the left hand will not respond to a touch on the right hand. Rather, each nerve cell responds only to information from a particular area of the skin. This area is the receptive field of that nerve cell.

Nerve cells can respond by either increasing or decreasing their activity. If a nerve cell's activity is in-

creased, this is called an "on" response; if its activity
is decreased, the stimulus has produced an "off" response.
Ganglion cells of the retina generally have "on-off"
receptive fields arranged in the following way. Stimulation of the center of the receptive field produces an "on"
response. Stimulation of the edges, on the other hand, produces an "off" response. This is called a "center-
surround" receptive field.

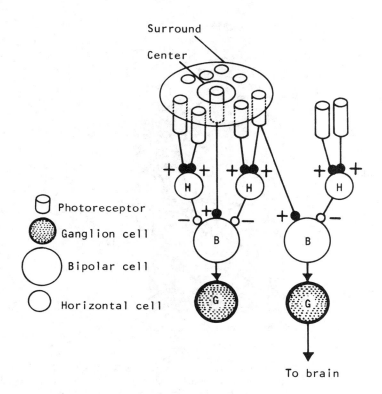

A neural model that can account for the existence of a ganglion cell with a center-on, surround-off response.

Consider how such a system would work in the case of
a light passing from one side of the retinal field to the
other. If the area of the field outside the ganglion's
receptive field is stimulated, the activity level at the
ganglion cell will not be affected. As the stimulation hits
the outskirts of the receptive field, the ganglion's activity will decrease. When the center of the receptive field
is stimulated, the ganglion cell's activity increases markedly. It then decreases below baseline level as the moving light once again hits the outskirts of the receptive
field. Finally, the ganglion cell's activity returns to
baseline when the stimulation does not fall upon that
cell's receptive field. Other types of receptive fields
also exist; this one is the most common.

HORMONES AND THE ENDOCRINE SYSTEM

Compare the modes of action of the nervous and endocrine systems.

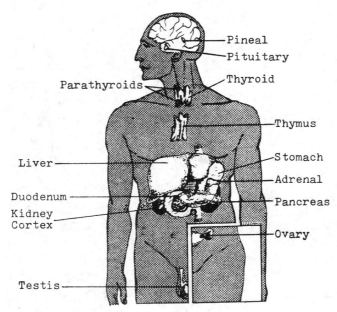

The major endocrine organs in man.

Solution: The activities of the various part of the body of higher animals are integrated by the nervous and endocrine systems. The endocrine system consists of a number of ductless glands which secrete hormones. The swift responses of muscles and glands, measured in milliseconds, are typically under nervous control. Nerve impulses are transmitted along pathways consisting of neurons. The hormones secreted by the endocrine glands are transported by the bloodstream to other cells of the body in order to control and regulate their activities. Nervous stimulation is required by some endocrine glands to release their hormones, particularly the pituitary gland. The responses controlled by hormones are in general somewhat slower (measured in minutes, hours, or even weeks), but longer lasting than those under nervous control. The long term adjustments of metabolism, growth and reproduction are typically under endocrine regulation.

    We already mentioned that hormones travel in the blood and are therefore able to reach all tissues. This is very different from the nervous system, which can send messages selectively to specific organs. However, the body's response to hormones is highly specific. Despite the ubiquitous distribution of a particular hormone

via the blood, only certain types of cells may respond
to that hormone. These cells are known as target-organ
cells.

The central nervous system, particularly the hypothalamus plays a critical role in controlling hormone
secretion; conversely hormones may markedly influence
neural function and behavior as well.

● **PROBLEM** 18-37

Define a hormone. How would you go about proving that
a particular gland is responsible for a specific function?

Solution: The endocrine system constitutes the second
great communicating system of the body, with the first
being the nervous system. The endocrine system consists
of ductless glands which secrete hormones. A hormone is
a chemical substance synthesized by a specific organ or
tissue and secreted directly into the blood. The hormone
is carried via the circulation to other sites of the body
where its actions are exerted. Hormones are typically
carried in the blood from the site of production to the
site(s) of action, but certain hormones produced by neuro-
secretory cells in the hypothalamus act directly on their
target areas without passing through the blood. The
distance travelled by hormones before reaching their target
area varies considerably. In terms of chemical structure,
hormones generally fall into two categories: steroids and
amino acid derivatives. The latter ranges in size from
small molecules containing several peptides to very large
proteins. Hormones serve to control and integrate many
body functions such as reproduction, organic metabolism
and energy balance, and mineral metabolism. Hormones also
regulate a variety of behaviors, particularly sexual behaviors.

To determine whether a gland is responsible for a
particular function or behavior, an investigator usually
begins by surgically removing the gland and observing the
effect upon the animal. The investigator would then
replace the gland with one transplanted from a closely
related animal, and determine whether the changes induced
by removing the gland can be reversed by replacing it.
When replacing the gland, the experimenter must be careful
to ensure that the new gland becomes connected with the
vascular system of the recipient. This must be done so
that secretions from the transplanted gland can enter the
blood of the recipient. The experimenter may then try
feeding dried glands to an animal from which the gland
was previously removed. This is done to see if the hormone
can be replaced in the body in this manner. The substance
in the glands will enter the blood stream via the digestive
system and be carried to the target organ by the circulatory
system. Finally, the experimenter may make an extract of
the gland and purify it to determine its chemical structure.
Very often the chemical structure of a substance is very
much related to its function. Studying the chemical

structure may enable the investigator to deduce a mechanism by which the gland-extract functions on a molecular level. The investigator may also inject the purified gland-extract into an experimental animal devoid of such a gland, and see whether the injection effected replacement of the missing function or behavior. Some hormonal chemicals have additive effects. The investigator may inject a dosage of the purified gland-extract to an intact animal to observe if there was any augmentation of the particular function or behavior under study.

● **PROBLEM** 18-38

What is a pheromone, and how does it differ from a hormone?

Solution: The behavior of animals may be influenced by hormones - organic chemicals that are released into the internal environment by endocrine glands which regulate the activites of other tissues located some distances away. Animal behavior is also controlled by pheromones-substances that are secreted by exocrine glands into the external environment. Pheromones influence the behavior of other members of the same species. Pheromones represent a means of communication and of transferring information by smell or taste. Pheromones evoke specific behavioral, developmental or reproductive responses in the recipient; these responses may be of great significance for the survival of the species.

Pheromones act in a specific manner upon the recipient's central nervous system, and produce either a temporary or a long-term effect on its development or behavior. Pheromones are of two classes: releaser pheromones and primer pheromones. Among the releaser pheromones are the sex attractants of moths and the trail pheromones secreted by ants, which may cause an immediate behavioral change in conspecific individuals. Primer pheromones act more slowly and play a role in the organism's growth and differentiation. For example, the growth of locusts and the number of reproductive members and soldiers in termite colonies are all controlled by primer pheromones.

● **PROBLEM** 18-39

The pituitary gland has been called the master gland. Is this term justified? Where is the gland located and what does it secrete?

Solution: The pituitary gland, also known as the hypophysis, lies in a pocket of bone just below the hypothalamus. The pituitary gland is composed of three lobes, each of which is a functionally distinct gland. They are the anterior, intermediate and posterior lobes. The anterior and posterior lobes are also known as the adenohypophysis and neurohypophysis, respectively.

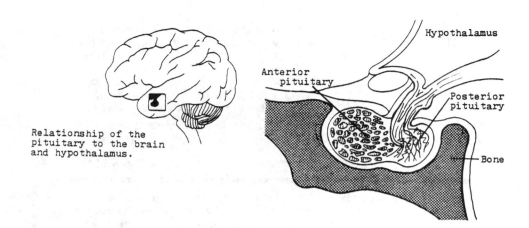

Relationship of the
pituitary to the brain
and hypothalamus.

Hypothalamus

Anterior
pituitary

Posterior
pituitary

Bone

In man, the intermediate lobe is only rudimentary
and its function remains unclear. It contains two
substances known as melanocyte stimulating hormones (MSH)
which are known to cause skin darkening in the lower
vertebrates.

The anterior lobe is made up of glandular tissue
which produces at least six different protein hormones.
Evidence suggests that each hormone is secreted by a
different cell type. Secretion of each of the six hormones
occurs independently of the others.

One of the hormones secreted by the anterior pituitary
is known as TSH (thyroid - stimulating hormone), which
induces secretion of thyroid hormone from the thyroid
gland. Thyroid hormone is a term which includes two
closely related hormones, thyroxine and triiodothyronine.
Another hormone secreted by the anterior pituitary is ACTH
(adrenocorticotrophic hormone), which stimulates the
adrenal cortex to secrete cortisol. The anterior pituitary
is also responsible for the release of the gonadotropic
hormones, FSH (follicle-stimulating hormone) and LH
(luteinizing hormone). These hormones primarily control
the secretion of the sex hormones (estrogen, progesterone
and testosterone) by the gonads. FSH and LH differ from
TSH and ACTH in that, besides controlling the secretion of
other hormones, they regulate the growth and development
of the reproductive cells (sperm and ovum). There are two
hormones secreted by the anterior pituitary that do not
affect other hormonal secretions. One of these is called
prolactin, which stimulates milk production by the mammary
glands of the female shortly after giving birth. The
other hormone is called growth hormone, which plays a
critical role in the normal processes of growth.

The posterior lobe of the pituitary gland is actually
an outgrowth of the hypothalamus and is true neural tissue.
The posterior pituitary differs from the anterior pituitory
with respect to embryological origin as well as types of
hormones secreted. It releases two hormones called oxytocin
and vasopressin. Oxytocin principally acts to stimulate
contraction of the uterine muscles as an aid to parturition.
Emotional stress may also cause the release of this hormone,
and is frequently the cause of a miscarriage.

Vasopressin, also called antidiuretic hormone, stimulates the kidney tubules to reabsorb water and some specific salts.

It should now be clear why the pituitary is called the master gland; it secretes at least nine hormones, some of which directly regulate life processes while others control the secretion of other glands important in development, behavior and reproduction.

● **PROBLEM** 18-40

Removal of the pituitary in young animals arrests growth owing to termination of supply of growth hormone. What are the effects of growth hormone in the body? What is acromegaly?

Solution: The pituitary, under the influence of the hypothalamus, produces a growth-promoting hormone. One of the major effects of the growth hormone is to promote protein synthesis. It does this by increasing membrane transport of amino acids into cells, and also by stimulating RNA synthesis. These two events are essential for protein synthesis. Growth hormone also causes large increases in mitotic activity and cell division.

Growth hormone has its most profound effect on bone. It promotes the lengthening of bones by stimulating protein synthesis in the growth centers. The cartilagenous center and bony edge of the epiphyseal plates constitute growth centers in bone. Growth hormone also lengthens bones by increasing the rate of osteoblast (young bone cells) mitosis.

Should excess growth hormone be secreted by young animals, perhaps due to a tumor in the pituitary, their growth would be excessive and would result in the production of a giant. Undersecretion of growth hormone in young animals results in stunted growth. Should a tumor arise in an adult animal after the actively growing cartilagenous areas of the long bones have disappeared, further growth in length is impossible. Instead, excessive secretion of growth hormone produces bone thickening in the face, fingers, and toes, and can cause an overgrowth of other organs. Such a condition is known as acromegaly.

● **PROBLEM** 18-41

When an adult mouse or bird is castrated, its sexual behavior virtually disappears. Compare the effects of castration of highly developed primates with the less developed animals.

Solution: In simple behavior, animals respond to a particular stimulus in the environment with an appropriate response. However, few animals respond so automatically; stereotyped behavior can be modified. Sometimes the

750

animal does not respond; sometimes it responds differently than expected. Its actions often depend on other controlling factors, such as hormone levels and previous experience. This question involves the use of these two factors in modifying sexual behavior.

Hormones modify behavior by affecting the level of an animal's motivational state. They alter the animal's physiology, which can then alter behavioral patterns. For example, the breeding term in birds is initiated by physiological changes in the reproductive organs which produce the sex hormones. These sex hormones cause the development of special breeding plumage which subsequently affects reproductive behavior. The male hormones also induce courtship displays like bowing and cooing upon sight of the female. The female responds to these courting displays by the release of its own reproductive hormones which affect egg production. Eventually nest building occurs and copulation results. In each step of this reproductive behavior, hormones lead to behavior acts which cause further release of other hormones directing further behavior.

However, as animals have evolved, there is less hormone-directed behavior, and more learned responses. Learning is the change in behavior as a result of experience. Only higher animals with larger and more complex brains demonstrate the process of learning. Learning affects man's behavior, very little of which is stereotyped. In man, hormones play a minor role in modifying behavior; learning plays a major role.

When a mouse is castrated (testes removed), it can no longer produce any male reproductive hormones. As in the bird, these hormones are necessary for the reproductive behavior of the mouse. Removal of the hormones thus causes the sexual behavior of the mouse to decline and eventually disappear. The mouse apparently cannot learn its sexual behavior. In higher primates such as man, castration does not affect the ability to perform the sexual act, provided the male is sexually mature and experienced. This is because the behavior has been learned through experience.

RESEARCH METHODS IN PHYSIOLOGICAL PSYCHOLOGY

● PROBLEM 18-42

Methods of studying the brain. Discuss the four basic methods of research in physiological psychology.

Solution: Physiological psychologists are particularly interested in the relation between nervous system structure and function, and the behavior of the organism. The following four research methods are the basic techniques used for studying this relationship. They are: brain changes, lesions, electrical recordings, and brain stimulation.

In using the method of studying brain changes, the brain is analyzed for structural or chemical differences before and after a particular behavioral manipulation. Also, chemical and structural differences occurring between two experimental groups, each of which underwent a different behavioral manipulation, can be observed in using this method of study. In order to index structural differences that may have occurred as a result of the experimental manipulation, changes in size or weight of parts of the brain are usually measured. In order to index chemical changes, that may have occurred as a result of the chemical manipulation, we measure the amounts of various chemicals in the brain, usually neurotransmitters such as acetylcholine. This method has not given us much information; however, the evidence suggests that the cerebral cortex of rats raised in an enriched environment where 'toys' and contact with other rats is provided, is heavier relative to the rest of the brain than that of littermates raised alone, the 'impoverished condition'.

The method of lesioning involves damaging a part of the brain and can be used to determine both structure and function of various brain parts. To study brain structure, part of a neuron is damaged, and the slowly dying neuron is traced, using appropriate dyes. In "retrograde degeneration", the cell body of a neuron is damaged in order to discover to which axon that cell body corresponds, which is indicated by which axon dies. In "antegrade degeneration", the area of the axon furthermost from the cell body is lesioned in order to discover to which cell body it corresponds. In using the lesion method to study the functions of the various parts of the brain for example, if the thalamus is destroyed and the animal cannot perform on visual tasks, an experimenter may conclude that this area is important in vision. However, this method has a drawback. The effect may be simply due to the fact that pathways which pass through the destroyed area were interrupted, while the area lesioned was not involved at all. Thus, incorrect conclusions are possible in using this method.

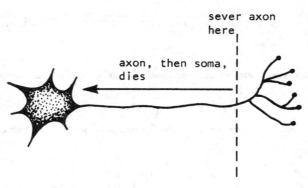

sever axon
here

axon, then soma,
dies

Retrograde degeneration

752

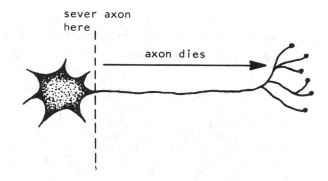

sever axon here

axon dies

Antegrade degeneration

There are three techniques used in the method of electrical recording: microelectrode recording, the method of evoked potentials, and electroencephalography. Microelectrode recording involves the use of fine wires called electrodes whose tips' widths are smaller than the width of a cell. These are inserted into single neurons in order to record the electrical activity of the neuron. Generally, a 'baseline activity' is established followed by presentation of specific stimuli. In this way it is sometimes possible to find what stimulus the neuron responds maximally to, and thus what its function is.

In the method of evoked potentials, thicker electrodes called macroelectrodes are used, and the activity of a group of neurons is recorded. Specific sense organs are usually stimulated, and the activity of the region being studied is recorded. This method was used to map the skin sensory area: Specific parts of the skin were touched in order to determine which cortical areas responded maximally to stimulation of which areas of skin.

Electroencephalography is the crudest recording method. Here electrodes are attached to the skull and electrical activity of the entire brain is recorded. The recording obtained is called an electroencephalogram (EEG). It has been found that certain EEG patterns are associated with specific states of the organism, e.g., when you are awake yet relaxed, your EEG will register tall and wide waves called alpha waves.

The fourth method used by biopsychologists is that of stimulation. A part of the brain is stimulated, usually electrically, and the subject is either observed and the experimenter rates the behavior on relevant dimension, or the subject is simply asked to report how he feels. The motor cortex, the area of the brain dealing with specific movements, was mapped using this method; stimulating particular areas produced particular movements. It was also found that stimulation of certain areas can be pleasureful, and "reward centers" have been mapped in this way.

Discuss three methods used to produce lesions in experimental animals.

Solution: Lesions are damaged or destroyed parts of the body (usually nervous tissue). Physiological psychologists produce lesions in the brains of experimental animals in order to learn more about brain function. These lesions are usually produced through aspiration, passing electric current through an area, or by chemical means.

Aspiration involves suctioning away part of the brain tissue, usually part of the outer layer (the cerebral cortex). Through the use of special instruments, it is possible for very small and precise brain areas to be removed in this way.

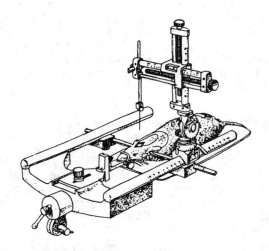

Stereotaxic apparatus

The use of electric current to destroy a brain area usually involves stereotaxic surgery. This type of surgery makes use of a stereotaxic instrument and an atlas of the brain. The atlas provides psychologists with the precise position of any brain area relative to a fixed and easily located point. The stereotaxic instrument holds the subject's head in a particular position, and then allows a fine wire called an electrode to be moved the appropriate distance in the proper direction in order to reach the desired brain area. Electric current passed through the electrode then destroys the tiny region at the electrode's tip. This method of lesioning is called the electrolytic method.

Sometimes chemicals, such as potassium chloride, are used to make certain areas of a brain temporarily nonfunctional--temporary lesions. The advantage of this method is that brain structure is not altered in the process.

However, since it is difficult to prevent the spread of chemicals into nearby areas, precise localization cannot be done. This method has been very useful in studying certain brain areas.

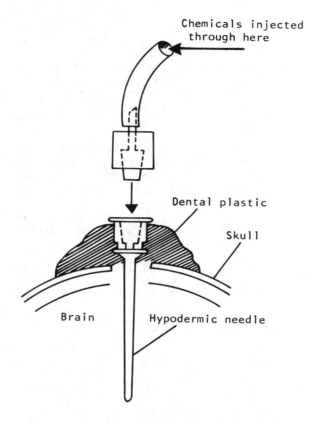

A chronic intracranial cannula. Chemicals can be infused into the brain through this device.

SHORT ANSWER QUESTIONS FOR REVIEW

Choose the correct answer.

1. The region at the base of the brain which is
   highly involved in most emotional and physiological motivation is the   (a)   medulla   (b)
   rhinencephalon   (c)   pituitary gland   (d)
   hypothalamus

   d

2. The main path of communication from the higher
   to the lower centers of coordination is the
   (a)   medial lemniscus   (b)   column of Burdach
   (c)   spinal lemniscus   (d)   pyramidal tract

   d

3. The location of the "motor area" of the brain is
   in the   (a)   precentral gyrus   (b)   occipital
   lobe   (c)   pons   (d)   thalamus

   a

4. Which of the following is not part of the limbic system?   (a)   septal area   (b)   amygdala
   (c)   the pons   (d)   the cingulate gyrus

   c

5. One important function of the midbrain is the
   control of   (a)   emotions   (b)   postural
   adjustments   (c)   digestive activities   (d)
   none of the above

   b

6. Impulses are transmitted to specific sensory
   areas in the cerebral cortex by the   (a)
   thalamus   (b)   limbic system   (c)   reticular
   formation   (d)   amygdala

   a

7. Hormones or autacoids are secreted by   (a)
   involuntary action   (b)   endocrine glands
   (c)   ductless glands   (d)   all of the above

   d

8. Two kinds of change from the resting state
   during neural transmission of an impulse are
   (a)   electrical and chemical   (b)   spontaneous
   and stimulated   (c)   sodium and potassium
   (d)   summation and subtraction

   a

9. Which of the following is not a method for
   studying the nervous system?   (a)   degeneration
   of fibers   (b)   embryological development
   study   (c)   evoked potential   (d)   all of the
   above are methods

   d

10. One of the chemicals responsible for the firing
    of a neural impulse is   (a)   actomyosin   (b)
    acetylcholine   (c)   acetylcholinesterase
    (d)   a and b

    b

11. During the absolute refractory period, the

neuron (a) is hyperpolarized (b) cannot be
restimulated (c) can be restimulated only by
very strong impulses (d) can be restimulated
by mild impulses   d

12. Which of the following are not innervated by
    the autonomic nervous system? (a) leg muscles
    (b) pupillary muscles (c) adrenal glands
    (d) heart muscles   a

13. Endocrine glands are distinguished from other
    glands in that they (a) secrete substances
    that regulate metabolic reactions (b) se-
    crete larger amounts of chemical substances
    (c) secrete chemical substances directly into
    the bloodstream (d) all of the above   c

14. Which of the following does not occur by means
    of a process of depolarization? (a) synaptic
    transmission (b) neural firing (c) muscle
    innervation (d) hormonal release   d

15. The central-peripheral distinction is based on
    the variable of structure and the somatic-
    autonomic distinction is based on (a) loca-
    tion (b) complexity (c) function (d)
    specificity   c

16. Which of the following is not associated with
    the functions of the hypothalamus? (a) moti-
    vation (b) regulation of body heat (c)
    memory (d) sexual behavior   c

17. The involvement of the entire cortex in learning
    is known as (a) aphasia (b) equipotentiality
    (c) preservation (d) agnosia   b

18. The best method of mapping brain pathways
    involves the use of (a) electroencephalogram
    recordings (b) evoked potentials (c)
    microelectrode recordings (d) a and c   b

19. Hyperpolarizing postsynaptic potentials
    (IPSPs) (a) raise the membrane potential to
    a level exceeding the threshhold of excitation
    (b) raise the membrane potential so that it
    approaches the threshhold of excitation (c)
    cause the adjacent neuron to stop firing (d)
    b and c   a

20. The sodium-potassium pump functions to (a)
    move both sodium and potassium ions out of the
    cell (b) move both sodium and potassium ions

SHORT ANSWER QUESTIONS FOR REVIEW

into the cell   (c)   move sodium out of the cell
and potassium into the cell (d)   move sodium
into the cell and potassium out of the cell

c

21. Action potentials result from: (a) a drop
in membrane resistance to sodium and chloride
ions (b) a transient drop in resistance to
sodium ions followed by a drop in resistance
to potassium ions (c) an efflux of sodium
ions, influx of potassium ions (d) an efflux
of sodium and chloride ions, an influx of
potassium ions

b

Fill in the blanks.

22. Neurons send messages (impulses) along their
_____.

axons

23. Nerve fibers running from receptors to the
central nervous system are called _____.

afferent

24. Most of the function of the left cerebral hemis
phere has to do with the _____ side(s) of
the body.

right

25. The emergency reactions of fight, fright and
flight are triggered by means of the _____
system.

sympathetic

26. The autonomic nervous system is divided into
the _____ and _____ components.

sympathetic
para-
sympathetic

27. The basic unit of the nervous system is the
_____.

neuron

28. The three major parts of the neuron are the
_____, _____, and _____.

dendrites
soma
axon

29. Sensory organs such as eyes, ears, nose and
skin, are known as _____.

receptors

30. The endocrine gland considered to be the master
controller of growth patterns and of the action
of other organs is the _____ gland.

pituitary

31. The major brain center for coordination and
posture is the _____.

cere-
bellum

32. The ability to recognize a familiar object is
controlled by the _____ lobes.

frontal

SHORT ANSWER QUESTIONS FOR REVIEW

33. The study of the relationship between mental processes and the physical phenomena is called _____.

psychophysics

34. From an evolutionary point of view, the oldest part of the brain is the _____.

hindbrain

35. The lobe of the cerebral hemisphere concerned with audition is the _____ lobe.

temporal

36. The surface layer of the cerebrum is the _____.

cortex

Determine whether the following statements are true or false.

37. The cerebral cortex (gray matter) is most fully developed in man.

True

38. The heart is composed of smooth-muscle tissue.

False

39. Karl S. Lashley, as a result of his 1920 and 1930 experiments on the cortex of the brains of rats and other animals, found that the greater the amount of cortex removed from the brain of the rat, the more difficult learning seemed to be.

True

40. The importance of the associative areas of the brain seems to be about the same in man and the lower animals.

False

41. The thalamus is often referred to as the basal ganglion.

True

42. Broca's area is primarily involved in the motor control of speech.

True

43. The left and right cerebral hemispheres are separated by the central fissure.

False

44. The phenomenon of the excitation of a muscle inhibiting the firing of its antagonistic muscle is called reciprocal innervation.

True

45. The nervous system is the major integrating mechanism of the body since it controls the muscles and the circulation of the blood as well as the secretion of various glands.

True

46. In higher animals, transmission of nerve impulses is usually two-way.

False

759

SHORT ANSWER QUESTIONS FOR REVIEW

47. A nerve is not a single neuron, but rather a bundle of axons or elongated dendrites belonging to many neurons.

    True

48. The neurons comprising the peripheral nervous system lie outside of the spinal cord and brain; these neurons synapse on the sense receptors and muscles.

    False

49. The autonomic nervous system includes efferent nerves which go to the skeletal or striated muscles.

    False

50. The midbrain regulates breathing and heart rate.

    False

51. The forebrain consists of cerebrum and its covering, cerebral cortex, the thalamus, and the limbic system.

    True

CHAPTER 19

TESTING AND MEASUREMENT

THE NATURE OF PSYCHOLOGICAL TESTS

What is a psychological test? What are the steps that one should follow in designing a test?

Solution: A psychological test may be defined as a "sample of behavior." That is, a psychological test is designed to extract information about a person in the form of test responses in a short period of time. Test responses are viewed as samples of behavior and from these samples the examiner attempts to gain some insight into, to form a profile of, the subject. In the case of an intelligence test the examiner may obtain a score (IQ) for the subject and make predictions based on this information as to how well the subject will perform in relevant situations. If the subject's IQ is relatively high it is expected that he will behave quite "intelligently." The examiner's job is to make accurate generalizations about the subject's usual behavior on the basis of a small sample of behavior (the test results).

There are four basic steps in test construction which should be followed in constructing most tests. First of all, the examiner should identify and analyze the characteristics of the subject matter to determine what content should be tested. Often this is done in accordance with a specific theory pertaining to that subject matter. On a test that measures anxiety, a theory about anxiety may be used to derive test content. The second step is to construct items that represent a reasonable portion of the behavioral domain of interest. Intelligence tests should test each individual aspect of intelligence in proportion to its importance in the construct as a whole. This is why the IQ tests have "subtests"; verbal ability or mathematical ability alone will not be an adequate reflection of a person's intelligence. The third step is to assess the reliability and validity of the test. Content validity is built into the test; an analysis of the subject matter or content of the test was undertaken before the construction of test items. The examiner therefore, will seek to establish criterion-related validity. He will correlate the test with some objective criteria that is an appropriate measure of the trait or ability the test is supposed to be measuring. If the test is either invalid or unreliable or both, the test must be revised. The fourth and final step is to formulate a strategy for making decisions about people based on test scores. That is, the examiner decides how he will go about generalizing profiles of individuals based on their test scores.

● **PROBLEM** 19-2

What variables should be taken into consideration when a test is administered?

Solution: Since the basic rationale of testing involves generalization from the behavior sample observed in the testing situation to behavior manifested in other, nontest situations, it is important to identify any test-related biases which may limit or impair the generalizability of test results.

It is important to prepare all test examiners in advance. They should be familiar with or have memorized all verbal instructions. Materials needed in the testing procedure should be accessible. If any apparatus is used it should be checked for proper functioning and calibration. In group testing, all test blanks and answer sheets should be arranged and counted in advance. If the test is being timed the clock or watch being used should be checked for accuracy.

The examiner should always make an effort to establish a "rapport" with the subject. The term "rapport" refers to the examiner's efforts to arouse the subject's interest in the test and to elicit his cooperation. Often this entails a commitment on the subject's part to concentrate carefully in the case of ability testing or to reveal personal feelings in the case of projective testing. The examiner must endeavor to motivate the subject. It is especially difficult to establish a rapport with very young children because they are often shy, distractible, and negativistic. If the examiner uses verbal praise to motivate a child on a nationally administered test, this must be a standard procedure. The test results would lose their meaning if one examiner motivated with verbal praise and another motivated with the offer of candy. Often a game approach to a test is the best way to establish rapport with young children. It is often helpful to assure a subject that he is not expected to answer all the questions because there is insufficient time. This helps to alleviate the threat of a loss of prestige if the subject does not complete the test.

Many of the practices designed to enhance rapport serve also to reduce test anxiety. Test anxiety is a problem that all examiners must deal with. High test anxiety can significantly lower a subject's score. It is important to inspire confidence in the subject in order to minimize the problems of frustration or fear of failure due to anxiety. It has been found, however, that the relationship between anxiety and test performance is not linear. A small amount of anxiety actually improves test performance. If there is too much anxiety, however, test performance is negatively affected.

(If the level of anxiety is extremely low it may be that the subject does not care about the test and thus his performance may suffer.)

The type of examiner used often has a strong effect on test results. It appears that "warm" examiners elicit better results than "cold" examiners. With Black children, Black examiners usually elicit better results than white examiners. Female examiners sometimes elicit better results than male examiners. The examiner's expectations of a subject's performance often affects the subject's performance in the direction of the expectation. This is often called the "self-fulfilling prophecy."

Another situational variable that affects test performance includes the subject's experience prior to the test. If he had an emotionally depressing experience as opposed to a pleasant experience, he will do comparatively poorly. Separate answer sheets can often be a problem with young children. They often do extremely poorly if they cannot mark their answers next to the question in the test booklet. It is the examiner's responsibility to alleviate confusion, frustration, lack of cooperation or confidence, mistrust, or any other interfering situational variable. If these interfering variables are not controlled, then there may not be a uniformity of procedure and the test may not be "standardized." Unstandardized tests are of little value in comparing people nationwide.

● **PROBLEM** 19-3

What is the distinction between an aptitude test and an achievement test?

Solution: It is not true that achievement tests measure solely the effects of learning and that aptitude tests measure solely "innate capacity" independent of learning. The distinction between aptitude and achievement tests is not absolute; it is a loose distinction.

Examiners usually apply the term aptitude to tests which measure the effects of learning under uncontrolled or unknown conditions. Moreover, the people who are taking aptitude tests have not usually undergone a uniform prior experience as have people who are taking "achievement tests." An example of a uniform prior experience is a geometry class; the New York State Regents Examination in geometry is an achievement test given to all who have undergone the uniform prior experience of taking a geometry class in a New York State public high school. The Scholastic Aptitude Tests' (SAT) math section is a math aptitude test because it is administered to students nationwide with a variety of unknown mathematical backgrounds.

The respective uses of achievement and aptitude tests are also different. Aptitude tests serve to predict subsequent performance, e.g., to determine if an individual will profit from the education at a particular college, if someone will perform well in a particular training program, etc. Achievement tests, on the other hand, are usually administered after training in order to evaluate what the individual has gained through training.

Since achievement tests and aptitude tests have different uses, they are usually validated in different ways. It is most appropriate to use content validity to assess an achievement test because having content validity assures that the test will be measuring an adequate and representative sample of the material covered during training. Criterion-related validity is used to determine if a test will accurately reflect future performance. Therefore, aptitude tests are assessed by criterion-related validity; that is, the test results are checked with a future measure of the same behavior which the test is designed to measure. For example, the SAT is designed to predict college performance; therefore, SAT scores are checked against college grades to make sure that high SAT scores mean that an individual will probably have high college grades.

It must be remembered, however, the distinctions between achievement and aptitude tests are not strict. Achievement tests can be used to predict performance. The College Board's (CEEB) Achievement Tests in specific subjects, physics, for example, will predict an individual's future performance in college physics with some degree of accuracy, even though the test was not designed to predict future performance but past achievement.

● **PROBLEM** 19-4

What are some of the characteristics of cross-cultural tests? Name four examples of popularly administered cross-cultural tests.

Solution: Traditionally, cross-cultural tests have tried to eliminate those factors or characteristics not of interest which differentiate between two cultures. One example of such a characteristic is language. We may presume that the administrator of the test knows that the two cultures have different languages. Language differences are not of interest, the examiner is trying to measure some other variable (intelligence, perhaps). The examiner's concern, then, is that he wants to make sure that language does not affect his measure of intelligence.

There are two ways to deal with the problem of language. The first way is to translate a given test into the language of the target population. Translated tests have two problems, however. First, the translation may not be equivalent to the original. Second, the translated tests should be standardized on a new sample of speakers of that language. The second way to deal with the problem of language is to completely eliminate language from the test.

When educational backgrounds differ widely and perhaps some groups of examiners are inferior in reading skills it is best to eliminate reading and other verbal skills from the test.

Different cultures often differ with regard to the value attached to speed of performance; in some cultures the tempo of daily life is slower and there is less concern with accomplishing tasks as quickly as possible. These cultural differences may be attributable to climate differences or perhaps to differences between urban and rural environments. Therefore, cross-cultural tests often try to eliminate the influence of speed by allowing long time limits and putting no premium on faster performance.

The most important factor that cross-cultural tests differ on is test content. Certain tests may require that the examinee be familiar with the function of objects that are absent in his culture or which have different uses or values in his culture. Persons reared in certain cultures lack the experience to respond correctly to these items. Therefore, examiners who are interested in developing cross-cultural tests are careful about the nature of the test content.

The Leiter International Performance Scale is an individually administered performance scale which almost completely eliminates instructions, both spoken and pantomime. The examiner's comprehension of his task is considered as part of the test. The Leiter scale consists of a response frame with an adjustable card holder. The examiner administers the test by sliding a particular card with printed pictures on it onto the response frame. The examinee is given a set of blocks with printed pictures on them and is supposed to choose the blocks with the proper response pictures and insert them into the correct frame. Among the tasks included in the Leiter scale are: matching identical colors, shades of gray, forms, or pictures; copying a block design; picture completion, number estimation, analogies, series completion, recognition of age differences, spatial relations, footprint recognition, similarities, memory for a series, and classification of animals according to habitat. The Leiter Scale has no time limit. The scale is scored in terms of the ratio of mental age (MA) over chronological age

$$\frac{\text{mental age}}{\text{chronological age}}$$

However, it should be noted that the Leiter Scale IQ does not always correlate highly with the Stanford-Binet and the Wechsler IQ's; it is probable that the Leiter IQ is a measure of different intellectual characteristics.

R. B. Cattell developed the Culture Fair Intelligence Test, a paper-and-pencil test available in three levels each level having a varying number of subtests. The highest level consists of the following four subtests: series, classification, matrices, and conditions. For the series subtest, the examinee selects the item that completes the series. In classification, the examinee marks the item in each row that does not belong. The matrices subtest requires that the subject mark the item that completes the given matrix, or pattern. The subject's task in the conditions subtest is to insert a dot in one of the alternative designs so as to meet the same conditions indicated in the sample design. Unfortunately, Cattell's Culture Fair Intelligence Test does not completely compensate for cultural disadvantages. In cultures different from the one in which the test was developed, performance was considerably below the original norms. Moreover, Black children of low socioeconomic level did no better on this test than on the Stanford-Binet.

The "Progressive Matrices" were developed by Raven and were designed to measure Spearman's "g" factor, i.e., innate generalized intellectual ability. The test consists of 60 matrices (designs), of varying complexity, from which a part has been removed. The subject's task is to choose the missing insert from a set of eight alternatives. The matrices are grouped in five series. The earlier series require accuracy of discrimination; the later, more difficult series involve analogies, permutation and alternation of pattern, and other logical relations. The test is only moderately successful in predicting future academic achievement. Studies in a number of non-European cultures have shown that the test is probably not suitable for groups with very dissimilar backgrounds.

In the Goodenough Draw-a-Man Test the subject (the test is designed for use with children) is simply instructed to "make a picture of a man; make the very best picture that you can." Emphasis is placed on the child's accuracy of observation and on the development of conceptual thinking, rather than on artistic skill. Credit is given for the inclusion of individual body parts, clothing details, proportion, perspective, and similar features. A total of 73 scorable items were selected on the basis of age differentiation, relation to total scores on the test, and relation to group intelligence test scores. Test scores are translated into standard scores with a mean of 100. Again, these test scores should not be confused with IQ. Unfortunately, it has been found that performance on this test is more dependent on differences in cultural background than was original assumed. The search for a perfectly "culture-free test" is probably futile. It may be impossible to create a test free of all of the possible biasing variables.

What are the advantages and disadvantages of cross-cultural tests?

Solution: Recently, there has been much concern about the fairness of applying available intelligence tests to culturally disadvantaged groups. Culturally disadvantaged means that an individual is not assimilated into or knowledgeable about the culture he is living in. He often comes from another, different culture or is segregated from those cultural groups that dominate the society as a whole. It seems unfair to judge these individuals on the basis of their performances on tests that are inherently "culturally biased." There appears to be no question that IQ tests, achievement tests, and aptitude tests are culturally biased. The mere fact that one needs to be fairly proficient in English language skills to do well on these tests is evidence of cultural bias.

Thus, the advantage of developing cross-cultural tests is that it is possible to compensate for the disadvantages many individuals have been subjected to and to measure innate abilities, including general intellectual ability. In this way it is possible to compare people from different cultures fairly on the basis of innate ability.

The disadvantage of cross-cultural tests is that the predictive and diagnostic value of the intelligence test is often lost. The most valuable characteristic of the IQ test, especially the Stanford-Binet, is its ability to predict accurately an individual's future academic achievement. There is little gained by administering culture-fair tests if they do not provide useful information. Educators are primarily interested in using IQ tests to identify those students who will have difficulty succeeding within the system, i.e. within the culture. A poor score on an IQ test suggests that an individual may need special assistance if he is to succeed within the culture. Notice that this says little about innate intelligence. The culturally biased information is in a very real sense necessary information for succeeding within the culture. IQ tests, especially the Wechsler series, can also help to pinpoint specific problem areas for individuals. Culture-fair tests may be able to measure some innate ability but this measure is useless in a society where success is dependent on cultural assimilation and knowledge.

Thus, the problem is not with IQ tests per se; the problem is with their interpretation. IQ test scores should not be interpreted as being indicative of inherent, unchangeable intellectual differences. IQ scores do predict success within the society. They can, however, be increased in disadvantaged children by intervention programs.

OBJECTIVE PERSONALITY TESTS

> What is the Q-technique?

	Very Characteristic					Neutral					Not Characteristic
Pile No.	0	1	2	3	4	5	6	7	8	9	10
No. of statements.	2	4	6	12	14	20	14	12	6	4	2

Example of a Forced Q-Sort Distribution of Self-Referent Statements

Solution: The Q-technique is a method of eliciting a person's own analysis of aspects of his personality. It is a kind of self-report. In the Q-sort, which is the most popular of the various Q-techniques, the subject is given a packet of self-referential statements and he is asked to sort them into piles, usually a specified number of piles (13), on the basis of whether the statement is very characteristic or very uncharacteristic of him. It is expected that the sorting will approximate a normal distribution; there will be relatively few very characteristic and very uncharacteristic of him and thus a plurality of statements will fall in the center; i.e., they will be considered to be fairly neutral statements in terms of the subject's personality. Examples of Q-sorts that Rogers has used are the self-sort in which the subject is asked to sort the cards in accordance with his current self-image and the ideal-sort in which the subject is asked to sort the cards in accordance with the type of person the subject would most like to be. Since the Q-sort is a self-report, its reliability is low because it is expected that the subject will try to deceive the researcher (either consciously or unconsciously). This is called "defensive sorting"; i.e., the subject gives a distorted picture of himself in order to "defend" himself. The subject may also base his decisions on social desirability, i.e., which characteristics are considered as socially desirable. Another criticism of self-reports is that even if the subject is not being deceptive, does his internal frame of reference accurately perceive his personality? Rogers' contention is that therapists are most helpful when they try to work with the patient on his own terms and try to understand his internal frame of reference even if it is not grounded in reality.

What is the Minnesota Multiphasic Personality Inventory (MMPI) and what is it designed to measure?

Sample MMPI Profile (Psychogram)

The Minnesota Multiphasic Personality Inventory

Starke R. Hathaway and J. Charnley McKinley

Scorer's Initials_____

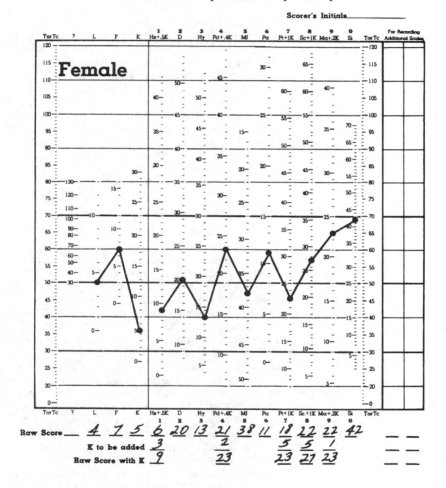

Raw Score___ *4 7 5 6 20 13 21 38 11 18 22 22 42*

K to be added *3   2   5 5 1*

Raw Score with K *9   23   23 27 23*

Solution: The Minnesota Multiphasic Personality Inventory (MMPI) is a self-report personality test. It was originally designed to discriminate between "normals" and people in psychiatric categories. It is now also used to assess an individual's personality.

The MMPI consists of 550 statements to which the subject is asked to answer true, false, or cannot say in respect to himself. If the subject responds that he "cannot say" too many times, his test record is considered invalid. Examples of typical statements on the MMPI include:

"I do not tire quickly."

"I am worried about sex matters."

"I believe I am being plotted against."

"I am sure I am being talked about."

"I get mad easily and then get over it soon."

"I wish I could be as happy as others seem to be."

The statements on the MMPI are divided into ten scales based on psychiatric categories. These scales are as follows: hypochondriasis, depression, hysteria, psychopathic deviate, masculinity-femininity, paranoia, psychasthenia (troubled with excessive fears and compulsive tendencies to dwell on certain ideas), schizophrenia, hypomania (tending to be physically and mentally overactive), and social introversion. In addition to these scales there are three validity scales which represent checks on lying, carelessness, misunderstanding, etc. The lie scale consists of statements in which a particular answer (either true or false) is socially desirable but also extremely unlikely. For instance, "I never lie." The test is considered invalid for individuals who score too highly on any of these validity scales.

Each statement on the MMPI, except for those on the validity scales, is rated plus (+) or minus (-) on one or several scales. A plus means that answering "true" indicates that the subject agrees with the answer to that question given by most individuals who have been diagnosed as having a particular disorder. Many of the items are not "crazy" items. Their meaning is derived empirically without concern for the manifest meaning of the item. For example, the item "I would like to ride a horse" discriminates between several classifications, yet clinicians have no completely satisfactory explanation for why this would be so. The number of plusses and minuses on each scale is tallied and a profile is constructed for the individual. The profile should be interpreted with great care. The MMPI has a high degree of empirical validity. The items (statements) were originally selected on the basis of whether or not they differentiated between normals and people who were specifically diagnosed as depressives, schizophrenics, paranoics, etc. Statements were elminiated if they were unuseful in differentiation. Thus, the MMPI is considered to have a high degree of criterion-related validity (which is quite important for a personality inventory). However, despite the fact that the test is standardized, the standardization sample may be quite uncharacteristic of the general population today (most of the standardization was done in Minnesota in the 1950's).

● **PROBLEM** 19-8

What is the CPI? How is it different from the MMPI?

Solution: The California Psychological Inventory (CPI)
as developed by Gough (1957) is an objective personality
inventory developed for use with less clinical less deviant
groups of subjects than the MMPI. There are several forms
of the test for various age groups of subjects. Most of the
CPI was developed using the method of "contrasted groups"
(i.e., like the MMPI), however four of the subscales were
constructed using the method of internal consistency analysis. Some of the representative scales include a Self-
control scale, Responsibility, well-being, Flexibility,
Achievement via Independence, Tolerance, and Intellectual
efficiency. The items are not designed to measure gross
psychopathy, but to measure more minor forms of maladjustment, especially those common among adolescents and young-
adults.

PROJECTIVE PERSONALITY TESTS

● PROBLEM 19-9

What are the advantages and disadvantages of projective
testing?

Solution: Many psychologists argue that responses on a
projective test may provide more valid and reliable personality data on a particular individual. Answers to questionnaires can be "faked" for the purposes of avoiding damage
to the self-esteem. Moreover, since theoretically many impulses are censored by the ego, they are not available to
consciousness; these aspects of the personality will not
be able to be determined on a questionnaire because there
is no means of "symbolic expression." Repressed impulses
can find a means of expression only symbolically (e.g.,
dreams, parapraxes). Projective testing allows symbolic
expression of conflicts and impulses. Tests like the
Thematic Apperception Test (TAT) allow the subject to
create an entire story, in theory symbolically representing
his conflicts. Often subjects are told that a particular
projective test is one of imagination or artistic ability
so that the subject becomes "task-centered" rather than
"self-centered." The subject is less inhibited and the
responses are not distorted by "ego censorship."

Unlike an objective questionnaire, the projective
test is unstructured. The subject truly has to search and
think of an original answer; he cannot usually respond with
conventional and stereotyped answers. Moreover, on a projective test the subject has the advantage of being able to
modify and expand on his answers.

Some psychologists claim that projective tests also
have the advantage of being pan-cultural because they demand no literacy or academic skills. Unfortunately, this
may not be true. Associations typically used to interpret
data are applicable only to people who are part of the culture in which these associations were originally derived.
An answer which is frequent and "normal" in one culture may

be infrequent and bizarre in another.

Other psychologists argue that projective tests provide a view of the total functioning individual whereas
many objective tests measure only one trait. Projective
tests claim to maintain the integrity and organization of
the total personality (the Gestalt). However, there are
objective tests, the MMPI, for example, which provide data
on many different traits and yield diagnoses in a form similar to the projective tests.

One of the most serious disadvantages of projective
tests is the possibility of examiner bias. Often examiners
have pre-established views of subjects because of case-
history reports. As a result they may produce interpretations which corroborate their pre-established opinions.

The interpretations of projective tests are open to
much deserved criticism. The associations that an examiner
makes between a given response and a given diagnosis may not
be empirically supported. There is no scientific or statistical proof that these associations correlate with instances
of particular diagnoses. Although psychologists have amassed
a great deal of data on the frequencies of various responses,
infrequent responses are by no means necessarily "crazy" responses, nor do particular responses reliably discriminate
between normal and disturbed individuals. Thus, the standardized interpretations are often no more than common sense,
unscientific speculations. Many of the projective tests
cannot be said to be standardized in any rigorous way.
Projective tests are in essence no better and no worse
than the clinician who evaluates the responses. They may
be quite useful to the experienced and insightful clinician, but of little use to the inexperienced tester.

One of the presumed advantages of the projective tests
is that the subject is not aware of the purpose of the test
and thus he lets down his defenses and his responses are
undistorted. He does not "fake" his responses. Currently,
the Rorschach and TAT tests are so well known that it is
unlikely that a subject would not know that his personality
was being assessed. It is likely that he would be even
more defensive than on a questionnaire like the MMPI.

● **PROBLEM 19-10**

What are the assumptions concerning an individual's personality behind projective testing?

Solution: The fundamental assumption behind projective
testing is that there are unconscious and therefore deeper
and more complex elements of the personality that cannot
be determined and measured by objective techniques but can
be determined by projective techniques. Individuals are
often not aware of these unconscious aspects of their personality and thus in self-report personality inventories
(e.g., MMPI) they do not reveal any information about these
aspects of their personalities. Since projective testing

allows the subject to freely associate to the stimuli presented, it is assumed that the responses are expressions (projections) of unconscious desires, conflicts, and impulses. The subject "projects" into the stimulus material his needs and attitudes. It is assumed that when the individual's mind is "free to wander" then it will "fix" on those issues that are most important. Projective examiners often try to conceal the purpose of these tests so that the subjects will not be defensive.

A defensive attitude on the part of the subject will prevent free expression of unconscious elements. The most conflictual impulses will be censored.

Another basic assumption of projective methods is that the production of responses depends largely upon basic personality factors. An appropriate analysis of the productions can reveal the personality structure of the individual.

While most psychologists agree that there are unconscious or "deeper" aspects to the personality, not all psychologists assume that these aspects can be determined and/or measured. Behaviorists and Learning Theorists continually stress that only observable behavior is scientifically meaningful, anything said about the "unconscious" is purely speculatory. Some psychologists (e.g., Allport) think that if there are unconscious aspects of the personality, they are unimportant anyway; these psychologists stress the importance of current behavior patterns.

● **PROBLEM** 19-11

What is the Rosenzweig Picture-Frustration Study (P-F) study?

Solution: The Rosenzweig Picture Study was derived from Rosenzweig's theory of frustration and aggression which emphasized different types of aggression and different ways of expressing aggression.

The test consists of a set of cartoons in which one person frustrates another. The first person says something which provokes aggression or frustration in the second person. There is a blank space in which the second person responds to the aggression of the first person; the examinee fills in what the second person, the frustrated person, would respond. Theoretically, this allows the examinee to project his feelings of aggression or frustration onto the second person. The responses that the examinee attributes to the second person are classified according to type and direction.

There are three types of response to aggression. Obstacle-dominance is the type of response to aggression in which the frustrating object is emphasized; that is, the obstacle is dominant. Ego-defense is the type of response to aggression in which attention is focussed on the protection of the frustrated person; that is, the ego is defended.

Need-persistence is the type of response to aggression which concentrates on the constructive solution of the frustrating problem. The type of response that the examinee selects for the second cartoon figure is assumed to be an indication of his particular psychological problems or lack thereof. Specifically, these responses may help the examiner to gain some insight into the examinee's personality.

The direction of the response to aggression actually yields more information about the examinee than the type of response. The direction of the response may help the examiner learn about the examinee's concept of self. These can be three possible directions of the response to aggression. The response can be extrapunitive; that is, the aggressive response is turned outward toward the environment. An intropunitive response turns the aggression inward on the subject. The impunitive response turns off the aggression in an attempt to gloss over or evade the situation. Often, the latter direction of response is considered to be the most mature. If someone deliberately provokes another person it is probably often best to evade the situation and thereby provoke no further hostility.

The test is scored by computing the percentage of the examinee's responses that fall into the above designated categories. These percentages are compared to the normative percentages; the normative percentages refer to the percentage of a population sample's responses which fall into a particular category. With this information a group conformity rating (GCR) can be computed showing the examinees tendency to give responses that agree with the responses of the standardization sample.

The P-F method seems to be a fairly robust measurement of attitudes and feelings concerning aggression. It can also be used to investigate a variety of interesting problems. For instance, the P-F study can be used to assess attitudes towards minority groups, opinions on the prevention of war, and consumers' responses to products.

● **PROBLEM** 19-12

What is the Thematic apperception Test, how is it scored and its results interpreted?

Solution: The Thematic Apperception Test (TAT) was designed by Murray and Morgan in 1935 to determine the major themes of concern for a particular individual by allowing him to respond freely to the vague and ambiguous pictures presented on the TAT cards. Theoretically, the themes expressed in the responses reflect the subject's concerns. The TAT consists of 31 cards, one blank and 30 with pictures of people in ambiguous poses involved in ambiguous actions. The cards usually show some interpersonal involvement between two or three people. Some of the cards are specifically designed to be presented to a particular sex and age group. The subject's task is to provide a setting for the action in the picture, what the future outcome will be, and the feelings of the characters.   The subject is given as much time as he wants to respond and his responses are recorded verbatim, sometimes by a tape recorder.

Example of a TAT Picture

Traditionally, the TAT's are interpreted according to the needs of the "hero" (the figure in the picture around whom the subject assumes the action revolves) and the presses of the environment. Some of the needs that are typically expressed by subjects are affiliation, autonomy, achievement, and understanding. Scorers usually take into account characteristics of the story (style, originality, length, organization, and continuity), recurrent themes (revenge, struggle, failure, success, domination, and submission), choice of "hero," the description of the specific interrelationships, and the handling of authority and sex relationships. In a picture in which there are three figures, a middle-aged man, a middle-aged woman, and a young man, it is expected that the interrelationships will be described as that of a set of parents with their son. In this situation it is important to note which figure is selected as the authority figure, etc. The content of the response is central to TAT interpretation. Needs are determined directly from content; they are not inferred. Whatever the subject chooses to discuss is considered to be important to him. This differs from the interpretation of the Rorschach test in which the subject's characteristics are inferred from the determinants and location of his response and not strictly according to the content.

775

Unfortunately, the TAT has not proven to be an especially useful diagnostic tool, but it is still often used
in research, especially in the area of achievement motivation.

● PROBLEM 19-13

What are the experimental uses of the Thematic Apperception
Test?

Solution: One of the underlying theoretical principles of
the TAT is that the subject's present motivational and emotional condition will affect his responses in an unstructured test situation. Therefore, it would be possible, in
many cases, to use the TAT to discriminate between two
groups. For instance, if an experimenter were looking for
a group with a high need for achievement and a group with a
low need for achievement, he might be able to use the TAT
to discriminate between these two groups. Another usage
of the TAT might be to ascertain whether a particular experimental manipulation was having the desired effect (a
"manipulation check"), that is, if an experimenter wanted
to create a situation that was frustrating to the subject,
he might use the TAT to determine whether or not he was successful in frustrating the subject. Leon Festinger, a prominent social psychologist, designed an experiment in which
some subjects should experience thirst, hunger, and pain
more acutely than other subjects. He used the TAT to determine whether those subjects actually did experience more
thirst, pain, and hunger. Of course, all of these experimental uses are based on the assumption that a person's
emotions and motivations will come to light in his TAT responses. That is, it would be expected that a frustrated
individual would give responses on the TAT that would
normally be interpreted as being indicative of frustration.

● PROBLEM 19-14

What is the Rorschach Inkblot Test? How is it scored and
how are the results interpreted?

Solution: The Rorschach Test consists of ten inkblots which
were selected by Herman Rorschach in 1942 as being particularly effective in eliciting a richness of diagnostic material. The subject is presented with the cards one at a
time in a specified order and is offered the ambiguous instructions: "Tell me what you see? What might this be?"

The subject is allowed as much time as he wants and is
permitted to move the card in any direction and view it from
any perspective. The examiner notes how much time elapses
between presentation of the inkblot and the response, and
observes any significant behavior. After the subject has
responded, the examiner questions him on his responses. In
order to score the test it is necessary to know where each
item was seen in the blot and what aspects of the blot de-

A set of inkblots similar to those employed by Rorschach

termined the subject's response. There are three different aspects to each response: location, determinant, and content. Location refers to the area of the blot that the subject responded to. The determinant refers to the characteristic of the blot that determined the subject's response (form, color, shading, and movement). The content categories refer to what was seen in the blot: animal or human, male or female, real or imaginary, etc. The examiner tabulates the total number of responses and the total in each category.

The interpretation of test results is usually left in the hands of well-trained clinicians, the interpretation is supposed to provide information on how a subject solves problems, the subject's intellectual level, and his emotional stability. Traditionally, certain responses are associated with certain characteristics; for instance, using the whole blot in a response is associated with intellectual ambition. Unfortunately, the validity of these associations have never been adequately supported and currently the test is of questionable diagnostic value.

● **PROBLEM** 19-15

What is the word association test? What is the sentence completion test?

Solution: Both the word association test and the sentence completion test are referred to as verbal projective techniques because both stimulus materials and responses are verbal in nature. The administration of these two tests presupposes a minimum reading level and thorough familiarity with the language in which the test was developed. Therefore, both these tests are inappropriate for children, illiterates, and people who are from foreign cultures.

The word association test was developed by Galton in 1879. It was originally known as the "free association test." The procedure is simple; the examinee is presented with a series of disconnected words one at a time and is asked to respond by giving the first word that comes to his mind. Originally, the early experimental psychologists used this test to explore thinking processes in accordance with their doctrines of associationism. Associationism refers to the belief of some early psychologists that learning involves an association between processes in the brain. These processes in the brain supposedly represent stimulus events experienced by the individual. The word association test was designed to explore these associations.

The clinical use of the word association test was stimulated by the pschoanalytic movement. Carl Jung (1910) selected words which represented common "emotional complexes" and analyzed the responses with reference to reaction time, content, and physical expressions of emotional tension. Rapaport developed another test (1946) which consisted of a 60-word list. Most of the 60 words on the list were selected because of their psychoanalytic significance. It was believed that these stimulus words would be helpful in eliciting responses that would be indicative of internal psychological conflict.

Kent and Rosanoff (1910) had a different approach to the word association test. The test consists of 100 neutral words which were chosen because they tend to elicit the same reaction from most people unlike the words that were chosen by Rapaport (Rapaport chose his words because they would help to elicit specific individual responses which would help to identify a person's internal conflicts). For instance, the word "dark" is usually responded to with "light". "Table" usually elicits the response "chair". Frequency tables were prepared which indicated how often a particular common response occurred for one stimulus in a standardization sample of 1000 normal adults.

The Kent-Rosanoff test is scored fairly simply. An "index of commonality" is computed by determining how often the examinee's responses appeared in the frequency table. Any responses not found in the tables are designated "individual". When psychotics and normals are compared, it is often found that psychotics obtain much lower indexes of commonality than normals and also give more "individual" responses. Thus, the Kent-Rosanoff test may be helpful as a psychiatric screening instrument.

The sentence completion test is another verbal projective technique. The sentence completion test permits an almost unlimited variety of responses. Examples of the opening words of the test sentences might be: My ambition . . .; Women . . .; What worries me . . .; My mother . . . . Each sentence fragment is usually specifically selected to explore a specific personality domain.

The Rotter Incomplete Sentences Blank consists of 40 sentence stems. The examinee's instructions are, "Complete these sentences to express your real feelings." The exam-

inee's responses are rated on a 7-point scale of adjustment/
maladjustment. The ratings are based on the test manual's
instructions for scoring. Some argue that the scoring for
this test is fairly objective, more so than other projective
tests.

● PROBLEM 19-16

What is the Draw-a-Person Test (DAP)?

<u>Solution</u>: The Draw-a-Person Test is referred to as an ex-
pressive projective technique because it has both diagnostic
and therapeutic purposes. That is, the subject not only
reveals his emotional difficulties but also relieves them
through the free self-expression possible with the DAP.

The procedure for administering the DAP is simple; the
examiner provides the subject with paper and pencil and asks
him to draw a person. The examiner then notes the subject's
comments, the sequence in which various parts are drawn, the
subject's attitude, etc. After the examinee has completed
the first drawing he is asked to draw a person of the opposite sex from that of the first drawing. The drawings are
usually follwed by an inquiry in which the subject is asked
to tell a story about the two persons he drew as if they
were "characters in a play or novel." The examiner also
elicits information about the subject's family, friends,
peers, employers, teachers, and all other possible significant people in the subject's environment. This information
helps in the interpretation of the drawings.

The scoring of the DAP is essentially qualitative (unlike the Goodenough Draw-a-Man test used in intelligence
testing, which is scored quantitatively). That is, the
examiner in the Draw-a-Man test has a checklist of 73 features which should be included in the drawing; the subject
is given a deviation IQ on the basis of how many of the
checklist features were included in his drawing. The qualitative scoring of the DAP means that the examiner prepares
a personality description based on the analysis of various
features contained in the drawing. The examiner concerns
himself with the absolute and relative size of the male and
female figures, their position on the page, quality of lines,
sequence of parts drawn, stance, front or profile view,
position of arms, depiction of clothing, and background and
grounding effects. The examiner also notes and interprets
the omission of specific body parts, disproportions, amount
of details, erasures, symmetry, etc. Every major body part
is considered to have some psychological significance and its
omission or distortion is always noted.

Many unsupported generalizations have been made about
the significance of certain features in the drawings. For
instance, Machover, who designed the DAP, contends that
"disproportionately large heads are indicative of organic
brain damage" or "The sex given the proportionately larger
head is the sex that is accorded more intellectual and social authority." The validation studies done on the DAP do

779

not support Machover's contentions. The DAP may seem interesting, however at this point it probably is best not to use
it as a sole and final diagnostic tool.

INTELLIGENCE TESTS

● **PROBLEM** 19-17

What are the Bayley Scales of Infant Development?

Solution: The Bayley Scales of Infant Development do not
measure IQ; IQ is a measure of adult and child intelligence.
Infant intelligence is either qualitatively different from
adult intelligence or infant intelligence is at least manifested differently from adult intelligence. Adult intelligence is presumed to be manifested in academic achievement;
obviously, infant intelligence cannot be measured on the
basis of academic achievement. Since the Bayley Scales do
not yield an IQ it is not possible to make predictions
about subsequent ability levels. IQ tests are validated
against future academic criteria; the Bayley scales are not.

The Bayley Scales are used to assess an infant's current developmental status and to discriminate between mentally retarded children and normals. The assessment is
carried out by determining if the infant engages in normative behavior for his age. There are three scales of assessment: the Mental Scale, the Motor Scale, and the Infant
Behavior Record.

The Mental Scale tests such functions as perception,
memory, learning, problem solving, the beginnings of verbal
communication, and rudimentary abstract thinking. Bayley
and her associates observed infants through longitudinal
investigation in order to determine when, on the average,
certain characteristics developed. For example, at what
age does an infant recognize familiar faces? Or, at what
age does a child begin to vocalize two-word sentences?
After extensive research Bayley and her associates composed
a schedule of mental development with which they could test
infants.

Bayley followed Arnold Gesell's schedule of infant
motor development in constructing the Motor Scale. The
Motor Scale provides measures of gross motor abilities,
such as sitting, standing, walking, and stair climbing , as
well as manipulating skills of hands and fingers. Specific
motor skills do develop at specific times and it is important to notice an interruption in motor development. Often
retardation of motor development is the first sign of mental
retardation. The intellectual signs of mental retardation
are often not observable until early childhood (2½-4 yrs).

The Infant Behavior Record is a rating scale completed
by the examiner after the other two parts have been administered. It is designed to assess various aspects of personality development, such as emotional and social behavior,

attention span, persistence, and goal directedness. The Infant Behavior Record is a good measure of how well an infant is being socialized and the degree to which the infant's environment is socially and emotionally enriched.

The method of scoring the Bayley scales closely approximates checking a list of behaviors or characteristics to see if they are present or not. The Mental and Motor scales yield separate development indexes, expressed as standard scores with a mean of 100 and standard deviation of 16. (This score should not be confused with the IQ which also has a mean of 100. It should be noted that an infant's score on the Bayley scales is an inaccurate predictor of later intellectual ability.)

● **PROBLEM** 19-18

What is the Wechsler Adult Intelligence Scale (WAIS)?

Solution: The Wechsler Adult Intelligence Scale (WAIS) is the most important and commonly used individually administered intelligence test for adults. It was constructed for adults and thus the test items are often more appropriate for adults than the items from the Stanford-Binet which was designed for children.

The WAIS consists of 11 subtests which comprise 2 subscales: General Information, General Comprehension, Arithmetic Reasoning, Similarities, Digit Span, and Vocabulary comprise the Verbal subscale and Digit-Symbol Substitution, Picture Completion, Block Design, Picture Arrangement, and Object Assembly comprise the performance subscale.

The General Information and General Comprehension subtests test the subject on his knowledge and understanding of information acquired in the American culture. An effort is made to avoid testing specialized or academic knowledge. The General Comprehension subtest is designed to measure practical judgment and common sense.

The Arithmetic Reasoning subtest is a straightforward measure of elementary arithmetic ability. However, the problems are presented orally and are to be solved without the aid of paper and pencil. On the similarities subtest the subject is asked to explain in what way two given objects are similar. The subject's memory is tested on the Digit Span test in which he is asked to repeat a string of three to nine digits read to him by the examiner. In the second part he is asked to repeat a list of two to eight digits in reverse order. The Vocabulary subtest presents 40 words both visually and orally and the subject is asked to define the words orally.

In the Digit-Symbol substitution subtest nine symbols are paired with nine digits; the subject uses this as a key to fill in as many symbols as he can under the numbers on the answer sheet in 1½ minutes.

781

The Picture Completion subtest consists of 21 cards each containing a picture with some part missing; the subject's task is to tell what is missing from the picture. On the Picture Arrangement subtest the subject is given 8 sets of cards one at a time. Each set of cards can be rearranged such that the pictures on the cards represent the proper sequence of a story.

The two remaining subtests require the subject to understand the relationships between three-dimensional objects and their two-dimensional representations. On the Block Design subtest the subject is shown cards containing designs in red and white. His task is to assemble a set of blocks whose sides are painted red, white, and red-and-white in accordance with the design on the card. The Object Assembly test requires that the subject assemble cutout pieces to make a flat picture of familiar three-dimentional objects.

Each subtest on the WAIS is scored separately so that areas of weakness are quickly identified. People who are at a cultural disadvantage are also easily identified by poor performance on the General Information, General Comprehension, and Vocabulary subtests. An individual's final test results are broken up into three scores: verbal, performance, and total.

The three WAIS scores are converted to deviation IQ scores for ease of comparison. The mean is set at 100 and the standard deviation is 15. The correlations between Stanford-Binet IQ's and WAIS IQ's are not so high as one might hope: younger individuals and brighter individuals tend to score higher on the Stanford-Binet whereas older individuals and people of lesser intelligence score higher on the WAIS. One reason brighter individuals do better on the Stanford-Binet and people of lesser intelligence do better on the WAIS is that the WAIS does not have adequate "floor" and "ceiling" scores and thus discriminates poorly among people at the high and low ends of the distribution. At this point it is unclear why older people do better on the WAIS and younger people do better on the Stanford-Binet.

The WAIS is considered to have high reliability and though the validity findings are good, the WAIS is not as good a predictor of future academic performance as the Sanford-Binet.

● **PROBLEM** 19-19

What are the Wechsler Intelligence Scale for Children (WISC) and the Wechsler Preschool and Primary Scale of Intelligence?

Solution: Both the Wechsler Intelligence Scale for Children (WISC) and the Wechsler Preschool and Primary Scale of Intelligence (WPPSI) are adaptations of the Wechsler Adult Intelligence Scale (WAIS). The WISC is normally administered to children from the ages of 6½-16½ and the WPPSI is normally administered to children from the ages of 4-6½ years. Both the

WISC and the WPPSI are divided into subtests for the purpose of easy evaluation of specific problems.

The WISC subtests are the same as the WAIS subtests except that the Digit Span subtest is not always given and on the Performance Scale a Mazes subtest is substituted for the Coding subtest. The Mazes subtest consists of nine paper-and-pencil mazes of increasing difficulty, to be completed within designated time limits and scored in terms of errors. The Coding subtest is the WISC counterpart of the WAIS Digit-Symbol Substitution subtest.

The WPPSI subtests differ somewhat from the WAIS subtests. There is no Digit Span subtest but sometimes a Sentences subtest is given as a supplementary test. On the Sentences subtest, the child is asked to immediately repeat a sentence orally presented to him by the examiner; thus, the Sentences subtest also serves as a memory test similar to the Digit-Span subtest.

The performance scale substitutes the Animal House subtest for the Digit-Symbol Substitution test. The child is given a key which pairs an animal with a colored cylinder which is referred to as the animal's house. The child is to insert the correctly colored cylinder in the hole beneath each animal on the board . The Geometric Design test requires the copying of 10 simple designs with a colored pencil. The Picture Arrangement and Object Assembly subtests from the WAIS are elminated. The Mazes subtest of the WISC is permanently included.

There were special efforts made to eliminate items from the WISC and the WPPSI that would be unfamiliar to certain groups of children; moreover, there were more female and black subjects in the pictorial content of the subtests. Thus, some attempt was made to eliminate the cultural bias of the test.

As in the WAIS the subtests of the WISC and WPPSI can be scored separately for the purpose of identifying individual problem areas. The subtest scores are added and then converted to deviation IQ's with a mean of 100 and a standard deviation of 15.

The reliability coefficients for both the WISC and the WPPSI are very high. At the present time there is no validity data except from age differentiation; that is, older children obtain higher scores in accordance with theories of intelligence. Therefore, at this point the WISC and WPPSI cannot be used to estimate future academic achievement.

● **PROBLEM** 19-20

What is the Stanford-Binet Intelligence Scale?

Solution: The Stanford-Binet Intelligence Scale is a substantially revised version of an intelligence test first

constructed by Alfred Binet in 1905. Binet's original test,
constructed for the purpose of separating intellectually normal children from intellectually subnormal children, was
first revised by Terman, a psychologist from Stanford University, in 1916 (thus the name Stanford-Binet). In 1937,
two parallel forms of the Stanford-Binet test were constructed; the best items of these two forms were combined in
order to construct the 1960 revision of the Stanford-Binet
test which is used currently and referred to as Form L-M.
The Stanford-Binet intelligence scale is used almost exclusively with children.

The Stanford-Binet test is individually administered by
a trained examiner. In total, there are twenty sets of subtests for twenty levels of ability; each set consists of 6
subtests except the Average Adult Level, which contains
eight subtests. There is a separate set for every half year
from ages 2-5, for every year from 6-14, and for four adult
levels. The items on the subtests for each age level are
selected so that the children of that age or older can pass
them, but younger children cannot. Obviously, in actuality
there are children below a specific age who pass items designed for that age level. The accompanying figure illustrates the percentage of children below three years, and older
than three years who pass a three-year-old level item:

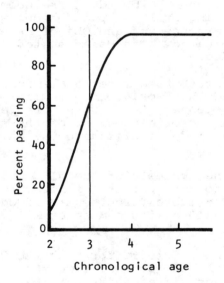

Chronological age

Most children of average intelligence at a given age will
pass an item designed for that age group.

The method of scoring the Stanford-Binet test is complicated. First, the examiner determines the child's basal age.
Basal age is defined as the highest level in which the subject
passes all the subtests. Testing is then continued until the
level is reached at which all the subtests are failed; this
is called the ceiling age. The mental age of the subject is
determined by adding to his basal age further months of
credit for every subtest passed beyond the basal age. Each
subtest from age-levels 7-14 corresponds to two months of
credit; there are 48 subtests in levels 7-14. If an indi-

vidual has a basal age of level 6, a ceiling age of Average
Adult level, and he passes 36 of the 48 subtests between
levels 7-14 then his mental age is 12 years. Since passing
36 tests corresponds to 72 months of credit or 6 years of
credit the subject has a mental age of 12, i.e., the basal
age of 6 plus 6 years of additional credit. IQ's are no
longer computed as ratio's (mental age divided by chronological age); they are computed on the basis of standard
scores; these IQ's are referred to as deviation IQ's. There
are charts with which one can determine the deviation IQ for
an individual by entering the mental age and chronological
in years and months.

The items on the Stanford-Binet are scored on an all-or-
none basis; there are no subjective judgments involved. For
example, on the vocabulary subtest an 8-year old must define
eight words to pass whereas the average adult must define 20
words to pass. Many of the subtests are the same for almost
all ages with the exception of the passing requirement. In
the administration of the Stanford-Binet, these subtests are
given only once and the individual's performance determines
the year level at which they are credited.

The Stanford-Binet test is well-known for its high
reliability and its high predictive value. The Stanford-
Binet is very accurate in the prediction of future academic
achievement and thus it may be best thought of as largely a
measure of scholastic aptitude or achievement and not of
intelligence per se.

● **PROBLEM 19-21**

Describe IQ. What is an IQ supposed to indicate? Trace
the development of the IQ test from its beginnings.

Solution: Intelligence is difficult to define. There are
several theories which attempt to describe it and these have
much in common. However, there is still disagreement, especially over the question of whether intelligence is a single
function or a complex made up of several distinct abilities.
Some psychologists argue that intelligence can only be defined as that which intelligence tests measure. But here
again there is disagreement since other psychologists have
pointed out that there are several different intelligence
tests and no individual receives the same score on one particular test throughout his life.

IQ stands for intelligence quotient, and this has long
been assumed to provide a reliable index for determining
one's mental ability. The first attempt to measure IQ was
in 1905 when the French psychologists Alfred Binet and
Theophile Simon devised what has come to be called the Binet-
Simon Scale. The scale consisted of a list of questions that
became increasingly difficult as the list went on. School
children were asked to answer the questions in order and the
point at which they could no longer answer determined their
mental age. The use of this test became widespread and several countries adopted it.

When Lewis M. Terman at Stanford University adapted the test for use in the United States, he rewrote large portions of it. In addition, he revised the method for expressing the test's results. By dividing the individual's test age or mental age by his actual age and multiplying this number by 100 (in order to avoid decimal fractions), he arrived at that person's IQ. Hence, Terman took into account the individual's intelligence in relation to others his own age. This new test became known as the Stanford-Binet test and was published in 1916. Since that time, it has been the most widely used of all intelligence tests.

A "normal" IQ is considered to be about 100, and 98 percent of the people who take this test fall in the range between 60 and 140. A person who scores below 60 is considered mentally inept or feebleminded. Someone who scores above 140 is considered a "genius."

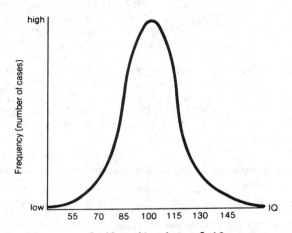

The normal distribution of IQ scores

There have been several refinements on the Stanford-Binet test since its inception. One is the addition of performance portions in which the individual is asked to perform a certain task. This is included to enable infants and preschoolers who cannot read or write to take the test. Refinements have also been made in the statistical procedures used to determine test results. Testing adult intelligence has also been a problem, since intelligence appears to stop developing after about age 16. The Stanford-Binet test allowed for this by using 16 as a cutoff age, in other words, anyone 16 years or older is considered to be 16.

The Stanford-Binet test has stimulated heated criticism and debate. Some argue that IQ only indicates that person's performance ability on taking the test. However, it has been found that IQ tests do have some value in that they can predict how well an individual may do in school and in some jobs, for example. But because intelligence is so complex and related to so many other factors, one should be wary of depending too much on a single score as an indicator of success or failure.

What is Guilford's model of intelligence?

Solution: Guilford's concept of intelligence is based on a multiple-factor theory, which means that Guilford describes intelligence as consisting of a specific set of traits or factors. He does not believe that intelligence is a unitary characteristic. In order to describe this set of traits, Guildford has used a theoretical model called the "structure-of-intellect" model. The model helps to describe these traits or factors of intelligence by classifying them along the model's three dimensions. The three dimensions were selected on the basis of factor analytic research; that is, all intellectual traits can be described in terms of these three dimensions. These three dimensions are operations, contents, and products.

The dimension of operations helps to describe a particular intellectual factor by specifically describing what a person does when he is using that particular intellectual factor. The various operations are cognition, memory, divergent production, convergent production, and evaluation.

The operations are performed on some specific kind of content. The dimension of contents describes the nature of materials or information on which operations are performed. That is, an operation, for example, memory, has to work on a specific kind of information or material. The content of this information or material can be either figural, symbolic (letters, numbers), semantic (words), or behavioral (information about other people).

The dimension of products describes the end result of the operations. More specifically a product is the form in which information is processed. Products are classified into units, classes, relations, systems, transformations, and implications.

There are 120 (5 operations x 4 contents x 6 products) categories or cells in Guilford's three-dimensional theoretical "structure of intellect model." It is expected that at least one factor of intelligence exists for each category or cell; however, there may be many factors of intelligence for any one cell. Thus, there are at least 120 factors comprising intelligence. Each factor of intelligence is described in terms of all three dimensions. For example, verbal comprehension corresponds to the cognition (operation) of semantic (content) units (product). Another intelligence factor is memory (operation) for symbolic (content) units (products); that is, the ability to memorize and recall a string of numbers.

Of the 120 factors of intelligence that must exist according to Guildford, 98 have been identified. Guilford has devised a specific test to measure each factor; a vocabulary test is considered the best measure of verbal comprehension. Guildord's method of assessing intelligence includes specifically measuring each separate factor of intelligence; in this way he can account for unique and individual differences in intelligence. Even people who are not proficient in verbal skills because of a particular cultural background are able to be assessed on the basis of other, nonverbal, factors. Needless to say, Guilford is not a proponet of the method of tapping an underlying "generalized intellectual ability" through IQ testing.

● **PROBLEM** 19-23

What is the difference between IQ (intelligence quotient) and intelligence?

Solution: Psychologists do not agree on a definition of intelligence. Almost all do agree, however, that it is a psychological construct, i.e., intelligence is a trait that is inferred on the basis of behavioral observation. Some people are observed to learn more quickly, seem to be better at tasks which require abstract conceptualization, read faster and retain more information, have better memories, are capable of expressing their ideas more comprehensively, etc. These people are referred to as intelligent.

In addition to the characteristics observed above, the various definitions of intelligence stress that intelligence is an ability or capacity to profit from experience, learn new information, adjust to new situations, to deal "effectively" with the environment, to succeed in activities that are difficult and complex, to undertake activities that have "social value," the ability to adapt to a goal, the ability to act purposively under stress, the ability to survive and advance in a particular culture, and the ability to understand and deal with symbols. Intelligence has also been equated with creativity, social success (defined economically and politically), and with academic success. Many psychologists believe that the trait "intelligence" is not a unitary characteristic, i.e., not a generalized intellectual ability, but rather a set of abilities and processes and therefore intelligence is determined by a large set of factors and cannot be accurately represented by a single test score such as an intelligence quotient (IQ).

Intelligence is not the same as IQ. IQ is best seen as a score on an intelligence test. However, though the IQ is popularly equated with intelligence, it can be either an accurate or an inaccurate indicator of intelligence, depending on one's definition of intelligence. If intelligence is equated with academic achievement, then the IQ is a good way to measure intelligence since the IQ tests are usually validated against criteria of academic achievement. However, if intelligence is viewed as equal to economic/political success and with the carrying out of goals that have social value, then the IQ does not reflect intelligence at all.

IQ tests mostly measure verbal skills. Intelligence is not necessarily synonymous to verbal skills. If it is presumed that intelligence is an innate generalized intellectual ability, it does not follow that the ability is going to be reflected by an IQ score. After all, many innately intelligent people have not had the opportunity to learn or to fully develop their verbal skills, especially if they do not live in the Western Hemisphere.

The IQ is presented as an expression of an individual's intellectual ability level at a given point in time, in relation to his chronological age. Various IQ tests differ in content and thus the meaning of IQ scores on different tests is not necessarily the same. It must be remembered that IQ tests are most useful and accurate as a reflection of prior educational achievement and as a predictor of subsequent educational performance because the tests are validated against the criteria of academic achievement.

In 1904 Alfred Binet was asked by the French government to construct a test that would distinguish between normal children and children with severe learning disabilities. Binet conceived of intelligence as the relationship of mental ability and chronological age.

Binet believed that children developed specific abilities at specific ages. Thus, at age nine, the average child may develop the ability to learn certain arithmetic functions. If a child is capable of learning these arithmetic functions at age 6, then he is considered to be more intelligent than the child who could not learn them until the age of 9. The mental age of a child is determined according to what test level he could pass. If the highest test level that a child could pass was the test level that all average nine year olds passed and no average eight year olds passed then the child was presumed to have a mental age of nine.

For each age up to 15 years, there is a set of characteristic abilities that develop in the normal child. If they developed earlier than average, the child is more intelligent than the average child; if the abilities develop later, then the child is considered to be of below average intelligence. The IQ, for children (but not adults) was computed by dividing the mental age (M.A.) by the chronological age (C.A.) and multiplying the quotient by 100 in order to eliminate decimals.

$$I.Q. = \frac{M.A.}{C.A.} \times 100$$

A boy with a mental age of 8 and chronological age of 5 has an IQ of 160:

$$I.Q. = \frac{M.A.}{C.A.} \times 100 = \frac{8}{5} \times 100 = 160.$$

An IQ of 160 is considerably above average.

IQ's are currently computed on the basis of standard scores. The scores are so arranged that the mean IQ for the adult population is 100 and the standard deviation is 16 (therefore, 68% of the population is considered to have IQ's between 84 and 116).

IQ and intelligence should not be confused. The IQ is a test score that has predictive value with respect to academic achievement. Intelligence is a psychological construct that is useful in describing an individual's behavior. The IQ is representative of intelligence only when one believes that the abilities, processes, and characteristics of which intelligence consists are adequately represented on the IQ test.

● **PROBLEM** 19-24

Is the IQ a stable measure of intelligence?

Solution: Stability of IQ refers to the consistency of 2 or more IQ scores for one individual. There are two significant variables to be considered in the question of IQ stability. These are the interval between the initial test and the retest and the age of the individual. The shorter the interval between test and retest, the more stable the IQ. The age of the individual in question is important because the older the person is at the time of the initial IQ test, the more accurate will that IQ score be. Intelligence continues to change both qualitatively and quantitatively during development and the greatest changes occur early in development. Therefore, the difference in intelligence between a 3-year-old and a 4-year-old is greater than between a 14 year old and a 15 year old.

In general the IQ is a fairly stable measure of intelligence. In a Swedish study, Husen (1951) found a correlation of .72 between the best scores of 613 3rd grade boys and the test scores of the same individuals ten years later. The Fels Research Institute (Sontag, Baker, & Nelson, 1958) conducted a study and found a correlation of .83 between the Stanford-Binet scores of the same individuals at three and four years of age. At age 12 the scores had a correlation of .46 with the scores from age 3. Bradway, Thompson, and Cravens (1958) conducted a study and found that initial IQ's had a correlation of .65 with 10-year retests and .59 with 25-year retests. It should be noted that the stability of the IQ is effectively the same as its reliability. Despite whatever faults the IQ tests may have, they do have impressive reliabilities.

One explanation for the increasing stability of the IQ with age is provided by the cumulative nature of intellectual development. An individual's intellectual skills at any one age include all the skills and knowledge acquired at an earlier age plus all newly acquired skills and knowledge. Predictions of IQ from age 10 to 16 would thus be more accurate than from 3 to 9, because scores at 10 represent more than half of the skills present at age 16 whereas scores at age 3 include a much smaller proportion of the skills and knowledge present at age 9. J. E. Anderson refers to the phenomenon of the increasingly close relationship between IQ scores at different ages as age increases as the 'overlap hypothesis'.

Prerequisite learning skills also contribute significantly to the general stability of the IQ because they play an important role in subsequent learning. The more progress a child has made in the acquisition of intellectual skills and knowledge the better will he profit from subsequent learning experiences and the more stable his IQ. One reason behind childhood intervention programs (e.g., Headstart) is that they help to provide children with prerequisite learning skills.

Environmental stability, i.e. whatever intellectual advantages or disadvantages that an individual had at one stage in his development tend to persist, also accounts for the stability of IQ between tests. However, when there is a large upward or downward shift in the IQ it is usually attributable to a major environmental change. These IQ changes mean, of course, that the child is developing at a faster or a slower rate than that of the normative population on which the test was standardized.

Drastic changes in family structure (divorce, loss of parents), adoption into a foster home, and severe or prolonged illness all have negative effects on a child's intellectual development. In general, children from culturally disadvantaged environments tend to experience a downward shift in IQ whereas children from culturally enriched environments experienced a relative gain in IQ.

Parental concern with a child's educational achievement and with his general welfare is quite important in accounting for shifts in IQ. Without parental concern, children are unmotivated to achieve and to acquire intellectual skills and knowledge.

During the preschool years, emotional dependency on parents seems to have a negative effect on intellectual development and seems to be the principal condition associated with IQ loss. During the school years, IQ gains are associated with high achievement drive, competitive striving, and curiosity about nature, that is, those attributes which are characteristic of an independent child. All of the above traits, including emotional dependency, can probably be attributed to parental attitudes and child-rearing practices.

Emotional stability in general tends to have a beneficial effect on IQ. One study showed that accelerators (people who had a high positive change in IQ) had better coping mechanisms than decelerators (people who had a high negative change in IQ). That is, accelerators had an objective, constructive, realistic approach to dealing with problems and frustrations whereas the decelerators approached problems and frustrations with defense mechanisms. Defense mechanisms are characterized by withdrawal, denial, rationalization, and distortion.

It can be seen that though the IQ is a reasonably stable measure of intelligence and usually a good predictor of future intellectual performance, one must consider an individual's emotional and motivational characteristics to be sure of the accuracy and relevancy of any individual IQ score. Environmental factors are also important in considering the probable nature of an individual's future intellectual development. The purpose of determining the stability of an individual's IQ is to be able to anticipate whatever problems he might encounter in his intellectual development. When problems are anticipated it is often possible to develop intervention programs and to perhaps alter the course of an individual's intellectual development.

● **PROBLEM** 19-25

Name and describe three theories of intelligence.

Solution: The two-factor theory of intelligence was developed by Charles Spearman (1904, 1927). Spearman maintained that all intellectual activities share a single common factor which he called the general factor, or "g". In addition to "g" there are numerous specific, or "s" factors each being strictly specific to a single activity. Positive correlation between any two intellectual functions, like mathematical ability and reading, is attributable to "g". Spearman claims that a two-factor theory implies that the aim of psychological testing should be to measure the amount of each individual's "g". Both Raven's Progressive Matrices and Cattell's Culture Fair Intelligence Test were constructed as measures of "g".

Multiple-factor theory accounts for another theory of intelligence. Here intelligence is viewed as consisting of a set of traits or factors. These traits are organized by group factors. A group factor is a factor that is common to a group of activities; a group factor may account for success in a number of related activities. For example, a verbal factor is a group factor that accounts for varying degrees of success on a vocabulary test, verbal analogies test, and a reading comprehension test. Thurstone was one of the leading exponents of multiple-factor theory. Thurstone proposed about a dozen group factors which he designated as "primary mental abilities". These are: verbal comprehension, word fluency, number, space, associative memory, perceptual speed, and induction or general reasoning.

A third theory of intelligence is referred to as a hierarchical theory of intelligence. Its proponents are Burt, Vernon, and Humphreys. Hierarchical theory is basically an alternative method of organizing the factors that determine intelligence. Spearman's g-factor is placed at the top of the hierarch. Two broad group factors, verbal-educational and practical-mechanical, are at the next level. On the next level there are other more specific group factors. Finally, on the last level there are a multiplicity of specific factors. Thus, the hierarchical theory of intelligence is basically an extension of Spearman's two-factor theory.

What role does factor analysis play in the description of intelligence?

Solution: Psychologists have used factor analysis in an attempt to identify underlying intellectual traits. However, the traits that were identified may not really be underlying entities or causal factors; they may be more accurately referred to as descriptive categories. That is, traits may be seen as a means of expressing correlation among behavior measures.

When psychologists first began to explore intelligence they found, through factor analysis, that the results of several subtests in a battery were highly correlated with each other. This indicated that some trait or generalized ability might account for success in various activities or functions. However, the existence of these "hypothesized" underlying traits or abilities is still tenuous. The names of the traits "uncovered" by factor analysis have been used to establish categories which are useful in describing intelligence.

What is the difference between early childhood intelligence and adult intelligence?

Solution: Some psychologists claim that early childhood intelligence is qualitatively different from adult intelligence because infants (young children) do not possess the same abilities as adults. Others feel that intelligence is an innate ability and that it is only quantitatively different in adulthood. Actually, it is probably more the case that the way intelligence is measured in early childhood differs from the way it is measured in adulthood. In early childhood, i.e., infancy, the child has no verbal or numerical skills and therefore intelligence is measured on the basis of sensorimotor or cognitive abilities. The examiner measures the child's eye-hand coordination, attention span, response to the human voice, his interest in exploratory behavior, locomotor coordination (standing, walking, climbing stairs), memory, manipulatory skills, etc. For slightly older children, drawing tests are administered. It is assumed that drawing tests reflect the child's ability to observe and recall objects and people in his environment as well as providing an index of manipulatory skills.

With adults intelligence is assessed almost exclusively through verbal, numerical, and abstract reasoning measures. It is assumed that in adults intelligence will be manifested through verbal, numerical, or abstract reasoning skills. Very young children are not able to utilize symbols in communication or in thought and thus do not have verbal, numerical, or abstract reasoning skills. Their intelligence is manifested through cognitive and sensorimotor skills. The "intelligent" infant (some psychologists are wary about applying the term "intelligent" to infants) is usually more active, engages in exploratory behavior more frequently, and in general responds to his environment with more interest and awareness. Thus, early childhood intelligence is assessed in terms of motor, cognitive, and sometimes social development. Social development refers to the young child's appropriate responsiveness to human figures. That is, can a particular child distinguish between a frown and a smile? As it stands, psychologists can either regard early childhood intelligence as qualitatively different from adult intelligence because it consists of different abilities or they can regard intelligence as an innate generalized ability and in infancy this innate generalized ability is manifested differently than in adulthood.

PERSONALITY, DEMOGRAPHICS, AND INTELLIGENCE

● PROBLEM 19-28

Is there a relationship between intelligence and personality?

Solution: Intelligence is most often measured through IQ tests and performance on IQ tests is influenced by achievement drive (or achievement motivation according to Atkinson), persistence, value system, emotional stability, and other characteristics that are part of the psychological construct, "personality". In the evaluation and understanding of the results of an intelligence test it is necessary to consider the influence of personality variables. Thus, in order to determine if an IQ score will accurately predict an individual's future academic achievement and intellectual development it is necessary to know if the individual's IQ score truly reflects his potential or his current intellectual development and academic achievement. If a child is "depressive" and therefore is poorly motivated then his performance on the IQ test may be impaired. The resultant IQ score may not reflect his true ability. The depressed child is often "uncooperative" in test situations. Similarly, an individual may not place any value on academic achievement or intelligence and therefore may not take the IQ test seriously. In order to evaluate the accuracy of the IQ score in measuring intelligence, the examiner must know the effects of intervening personality variables. The IQ score may deflate or even inflate the true extent of an individual's true intelligence. Moreover, even if the IQ score is accurate, an individual's personality may affect his future behavior in such a way as to prevent the accurate prediction of academic achievement based on the IQ score (the IQ score is usually used for the purposes of prediction). For example, in certain ethnic groups academic achievement is valued highly and therefore an individual belonging to that ethnic group may score near the mean on an IQ test but then perform above average in future academic achievement. Personality variables will always affect test behavior. So, even though there may not be a direct relation between intelligence and personality, it is almost certainly the case that personality affects test-taking behavior and therefore resultant scores may not be "accurate." It is not the same to say that depressive people are less intelligent as it is to say that depressive people often receive lower intelligence test scores.

One important relationship between personality and intelligence is the effect of high intelligence or high IQ on personality. More intelligent individuals tend to be more successful and success positively affects emotional adjustment, interpersonal relations, and self-concept. However, it is possible that only those intelligent people who are emotionally well adjusted, have a high self-concept, and who have good interpersonal relations are successful. It may not be possible to determine cause and effect in this case. The true relationship between intelligence and personality is uncertain. The definitions of the two terms are imprecise and research methods are relatively inadequate in this field of investigation.

● **PROBLEM 19-29**

What is the relationship of creativity to intelligence?

Solution: Psychologists and educators have come to recognize that creativity and intelligence are not synonomous. Creativity is certainly not measurable by standard IQ tests.

Thurstone has observed that creativity is influenced by many non-intellectual, temperamental characteristics. Moreover, Thurstone observed that creativity is encouraged by a receptive attitude (as contrasted to a critical attitude) toward novel ideas. Ideational fluency, inductive reasoning, and certain perceptual tendencies all seem to play a role in creativity.

Barron (1958, 1969) was curious to know how highly creative people differed from their equally intelligent colleagues. Barron assembled two groups of people from four professions: science, architecture, literature, and mathematics. One group consisted of those individuals who were regarded as "highly creative" by their fellow professionals. The other group consisted of people in the same professional field but who were not regarded as "highly creative." There was no significant difference in IQ between the two groups. Barron found that creative people were more likely to to able to integrate diverse stimuli, to be high in energy, to be able to think of many different words quickly, to be dominant and assertive, to be impulsive, to be interested in music, art, literature, and social service activities, to prefer complex to simple stimuli, to be generally effective in performance in different kinds of situations, and to be less susceptible to social influence in making decisions.

It is clear that there are aspects to creativity that cannot be measured on intelligence tests. Tests of divergent production, i.e., the ability to generate a variety of solutions to one problem, remain the best psychometric method of assessing creativity. The question remains of whether or not the creative person must also be intelligent. That is, are creative people by necessity intelligent or is it possible to be a creative genuis in one field and have a normal or subnormal general intellectual ability? Evidence to date seems to suggest that it is rare that creative people are not also highly intelligent. Currently, psychologists believe that creativity is usually attributable to a combination of innate talent, intelligence, and certain personality traits that are difficult to assess until the creativity is manifested in a concrete way. Intelligence, then, is probably necessary, but not sufficient for creativity.

● **PROBLEM** 19-30

If two subcultural groups have different mean IQ's (e.g., Blacks and whites) can it be concluded from that evidence that heredity is the most important and influential determinant of intelligence?

Solution: The answer to the above question is "no". The difference in the means between two subcultural groups is more likely attributable to environmental factors. It is important to emphasize this point. Much racism and discrimination is justified on the grounds that whites are more intelligent than Blacks, as evidenced by the difference in mean IQ scores. A botanical example may help illustrate the fallacy of concluding heredity accounts for the differences in mean IQ's for different groups. If a farmer has 100 seeds from the same plant and plants 50 of them in an area with poor growing conditions and 50 in an area with good growing conditions then the 50 plants which grew under better conditions will probably have a larger mean size. Even though all the seeds had the same genetic background, the extreme difference in environment exercised a strong enough effect to discount the importance of genetic factors in determining the ultimate size of the plants. In the case of Blacks and whites, it is probably the case that as a group the genetic factors that determine intelligence are the same. However, the average Black environment is relatively impoverished if compared to the average white environment. This difference probably accounts for the difference in mean IQ between the two groups. It is important to remember, however, that the difference in mean IQ between Blacks and whites could be due to genetic factors; this is still an unlikely but possible explanation.

Even though mean IQ's are different for Blacks and whites, it does not follow that any conclusions can be made about individual differences. There are many individual

Blacks who have higher IQ's than most whites. Given one Black and one white it is absurd to assume that the white person is always the more intelligent. Fourteen per cent of the Black population has a higher IQ than the mean for the white population. Of course, all of these group differences are on IQ tests. It is questionable if the IQ test measures "intelligence" at all. It has become apparent that IQ tests discriminate against people who are not well assimilated into white culture.

● **PROBLEM** 19-31

Can intelligence tests be used for diagnosing psychopathology?

Solution: Wechsler has described a number of diagnostic uses for his intelligence tests. First of all, he claims that the amount of scatter (variance) or the discrepancy among the various subtest scores is higher for the psychopathological (psychopathological meaning being mentally disturbed) than for normals. Wechsler also maintains that various score patterns, i.e., lower scores in performance than in verbal etc., can be associated with particular clinical syndromes such as schizophrenia, brain damage, anxiety states, and delinquency.

Decades of research have failed to produce data that corroborates Wechsler's claims for his intelligence test. Wechsler failed to take into account several methodological requirements in making his claims.

First of all, before Wechsler can claim that there is scatter among the subtest scores he must determine what the minimum statistically significant difference between subtest test scores would be. The reason for doing this is that the test scatter may be attributable to normal chance factors (error variance) rather than to specific individual differences (e.g., psychopathology). It may in fact be normal for subtest scores to differ by 10-15 points.

Another point that Wechsler failed to consider was that statistical analysis shows that differences of 15 points or more between only two subtests will occur on the average of five times in every normal person's record (there are 55 possible inter-test differences). Therefore, unless a person has more than 5 or 6 large inter-test differences it is not possible to determine if he is psychopathological.

Wechsler also failed to cross-validate his original findings. When Wechsler compared a pathological sample's test scores to a normal sample's test scores he did not recognize that the differences he found could easily have been attributable to sampling error. When other researchers submitted Wechsler's findings to cross-validation they discovered that Wechsler's initial findings were invalid.

Another problem with Wechsler's contentions is that there are other conditions that could have accounted for

797

atypical variations among subtest scores besides psychopathology. Such variations may result not only from pathology but also from differences in educational, occupational,
cultural, or other background factors. For example, language handicap due to cultural deprivation could account for
lower verbal than performance scores.

The diagnostic categories that Wechsler used in his
studies were imprecise, unreliable, and somewhat crude.
Designations like brain damage and schizophrenia are associated with varied behavior and thus are not always useful
in identifying typical test patterns.

All in all, it has not proven possible to make psy-
chiatriatic diagnoses on the basis of intelligence test
scores. Since psychopathological behavior is not consistent
or specifically identifiable it may not be possible to
associate a clinical syndrome with specific test behaviors.
Moreover, the relationship between intelligence and personality is elusive at best and it does not seem possible at
this time to state with any certainty how personality characteristics interact with intelligence.

oose the correct answer.

. As an assessment technique, informally conducted
interviews (a) may lead to unreliable judgments
(b) tend to put subjects at ease (c) are better than any other technique (d) none of the
above

    a

. The personality assessment technique in which
the subject provides self-appraisal by his responses to questions and statements is (a) the
rating scale (b) the personality inventory
(c) the introspection profile (d) the Rorshach Test

    b

. Of the following which is not true of self-
report personality measures? (a) subjects rate
simple behavioral statements as true or false
(b) the measures usually have extensive norms
(c) subjects are given little freedom in responding (d) most of the measures provide accurate behavioral prediction

    d

. Which of the following is not characteristic of
the MMPI? (a) it was developed within a particular theoretical framework (b) it is composed
of nine trait scales (c) it contains validity
scales (d) it is oriented around abnormal behaviors

    a

. Response sets, which can bias results from self-
report scales, reflect (a) the ambiguity of
the test items (b) the extensive number of
items, making valid responses unlikely (c) a
wish to appear in a good light (d) none of the
above

    c

6. The Thematic Apperception Test supposedly reflects (a) how one organizes ambiguous stimuli
(b) one's overall level of extroversion-introversion (c) interpersonal conflicts and themes
(d) one's relative ranking on several trait
scales

    c

7. The personality test which is sometimes jokingly
referred to as the sane man's MMPI is (a)
Gough's CPI (b) Edward's Inventory (c) the
Lowenfeld Mosaic Test (d) Taylor's MAS

    a

8. Which of the following is not a projective test?
(a) TAT (b) Strong (c) Blacky (d) Rosenzweig P-F

    b

SHORT ANSWER QUESTIONS FOR REVIEW

9. Terman and Oden, in their study investigating
    high IQ children through adulthood, found   (a)
    that, as adults these people were markedly infe-
    rior physically to average people of the same age
    (b) that, as adults, these people were superior
    in most ways to average adults of the same age
    (c) that, as adults, these people were equal in
    most ways to average adults of the same age   (d)
    that a surprisingly small number of them entered
    college   b

10. A questionnaire made up of such items as "I would
    willingly admit members of X-group to my club, to
    my country, or to kinship by marriage," would
    probably be yielding data to form   (a)   a Lickert
    scale (b)   a Thrustone attitude scale   (c)   Gutt-
    man scale (d)   a Bogardos social distance scale   d

11. A psychological theoretician in the process of
    developing a theory would be most interested in
    test measures in terms of their   (a)   construct
    validity (b)   face validity (c)   predictive
    validity (d)   concurrent validity   a

12. Of the following, the most useful for studying
    pupil-pupil relationships is the   (a)   Rorshach
    Test (b) Sociogram (c) Anecdotal record (d)
    MMPI   b

13. The most highly developed tests for observation
    diagnosis in intelligence testing is/are the
    (a) Binet tests (b) Goodenough Draw-a-man
    test (c) Valentine Intelligence tests (d)
    Wechsler scales   d

14. Of the following tests, the most suitable for
    determining the I.Q. of most 12 year old cere-
    bral palsied children is the   (a)   Stanford-
    Binet (b) WISC (c) Arthur Performance Scale
    (d) Raven Progressive Matrices   d

15. One name for a test which is not biased with
    respect to factors in the environment in favor
    of one group over another is   (a)   achievement
    test (b) culture-fair test (c) socioeconomic
    test (d) random sample test   b

16. Intelligence tests measure   (a)   innate ability
    (b) performance (c) educational level (d)
    none of the above   b

17. Cross-sectional studies differ from longitudinal
    studies in that the former   (a)   are more time-

800

SHORT ANSWER QUESTIONS FOR REVIEW

consuming and expensive (b) are not susceptible
to changing generational experiences (c) are
more susceptible to experimental error (d) use
data from samples of varying age levels

d

8. In a factor analysis, separateness of factors is
assessed by (a) degree of correlation (b)
task analysis (c) similarity of distribution
(d) B and C

a

9. Tests of intelligence for infants mainly measure
(a) maturation (b) innate ability (c) mental age (d) none of the above

a

0. It is important to select a random sample of the
population for purposes of standardization (a)
because items need to be verified for future
testing (b) in order to develop unbiased items
and age norms (c) to ensure that items are sufficiently interesting (d) to ensure that all
items measure only intellectual capacity

b

Fill in the blanks.

1. A group mental test and an individual mental test
are administered to a student at the same sitting
The resulting validity correlation, is a form of
criterion validity called _____ validity.

concurrent

2. "The Measurement of Adult Intelligence" was
written by _____ .

Wechsler

3. The mental age divided by the chronological age,
times 100, is the _____ .

intelli-
gence
quotient

4. A test that measures what a person has already
learned in prior training is a(an) _____ test.

achievement

5. The observer's or measurer's biases or prejudices having no effect on observation or measurement is called _____ .

objectivity

6. A summary of obtained results on a test battery
is called the subject's scoring _____ .

profile

7. _____ refers to testing which is characterized
by consistent administration and the use of established norms in the assessment of scores.

Standardi-
zation

8. The Rorshach and TAT tests are types of _____
tests.

projective

SHORT ANSWER QUESTIONS FOR REVIEW

29. The capacity of a test to measure what it sets out to measure is called its _____ .

validity

30. The consistency with which a result will be obtained when either identical or equivalent forms of a test are used is called _____ .

reliability

31. A test of the capacity to learn a particular skill and to learn within a specific area of knowledge is called a/an _____ test.

aptitude

32. A child with an IQ of 100 would have a mental age which was _____ its chronological age.

equal to

33. The Thematic Apperception Test was developed by _____ .

Henry Murray

34. A question to which the choice alternative responses are "yes", "no", and "I don't know" is an example of a/an _____ question.

fixed alternative

35. Increasing test length, _____ reliability.

increases

Determine whether the following statements are true or false.

36. Psychologists use both structured and unstructured tests in trait assessment.

True

37. Stern's intelligence quotient (IQ) is a way of expressing mental development in relation to age

True

38. The average IQ falls in a range between 110 and 120.

False

39. All people with IQ's measured at 53-69 are mentally retarded.

False

40. Children with IQ's of 140 and above have higher suicide and divorce rates than average, and are not generally successful during their lifetimes.

False

41. There is controversy as to whether intelligence is a general ability or is a composite of abilities.

True

42. The Stanford-Binet intelligence quotient correlates perfectly with academic success.

False

43. There is an almost perfect correlation between intelligence test scores and success in school.

False

SHORT ANSWER QUESTIONS FOR REVIEW

4. In general, measures of personality have been
   very successful.

   False

5. There are many personality inventories that are
   used to measure the personalities of individuals.

   True

6. Face validity is more essential to establish for
   a personality test than construct validity.

   False

7. The projective hypothesis holds that personality
   is expressed in the task of making sense of ambiguous stimuli.

   True

8. The responses to the Rorschah Inkblot Test are
   recorded, but not scored.

   False

9. The "hero" in a thematic test response is a person who is described as performing unusual feats
   of daring and valor.

   False

10. Even their critics agree that personality inven-
    tories are more sensitive than projective tests
    and more flexible than open-ended individual in-
    terviews.

    False

11. The task of the psychologist in the clinical
    model of personality assessment is to reconstruct
    the characteristics of the unique, living person
    from the fragments and bits of the test evidence.

    True

803

CHAPTER 20

METHODOLOGY AND STATISTICS

THE EXPERIMENT

● PROBLEM 20-1

What is an experiment?

Solution: An experiment is a test of a theory. A theory is basically a set of coherent and explanatory "laws" that are used to make empirical predictions. In psychology, theories are used to predict behavior. An hypothesis is a generalization derived or deduced from a theory. The hypothesis is usually a verbal statement which makes a prediction. When someone sets out to test an hypothesis he must design a real, practical situation which attempts to test the prediction made by the hypothesis. This is an experiment.

If an experiment fails it means that the prediction made from the hypothesis is incorrect or at least inaccurate. The theory must then be revised. Actually, it is nearly impossible to unequivocally prove or disprove theories because they can only be tested indirectly, through their postulates. Theories can only at best be supported, never proven. Some theories, like psychoanalysis, are strongly criticized by their opponents on the basis of their untestability. It is probably not possible to design an experiment that will convincingly and effectively test the hypotheses derived from the general theory of psychoanalysis.

The experiment is the crux of scientific psychology. It is probably the only effective way of establishing psychological principles and of gathering data which can tell us something about the human mind. The experiment is an objective research tool that is very valuable, however, this does not mean that it is the only tool. There are many areas of psychology that cannot be explored through experimentation; clinical investigation remains one of the best tools for understanding personality and psychopathology.

Distinguish between an independent and a dependent variable, and between an experimental and a control group.

Solution: A variable is any characteristic that varies. It can be a measurement, an outcome, or a determinant in classifying people or events. In an experiment, an independent variable is one which the investigator manipulates. It is the variable of interest. The experimenter tries to hold all other variables in check so he can clearly see the effect of the independent variable on behavior. A dependent variable is called such because it is dependent on the independent variable. In other words, the independent variable affects the outcome of the dependent variable (usually the subject's response). For example, if a psychologist wished to find out the relationship between intelligence and social class, he might administer intelligence tests to two groups of subjects--one consisting of individuals from a low socioeconomic background and another consisting of persons from a high socioeconomic background. Here, social class is the independent variable, the variable of interest. By administering intelligence tests to the two groups, the investigator can determine if there is any relationship between socioeconomic level and intelligence level. The dependent variable is the measure of performance, the type of behavior displayed as a result of the independent variable "dependent" on the independent variable. In our example, therefore, the dependent variable is the test scores. The experimenter tries to determine if there is any relationship between the dependent variable and the independent variable.

If the results of an experiment are represented graphically, it is customary to let the horizontal axis (also called the abscissa or x axis) to represent the independent variable and the vertical axis (also called the ordinate or y axis) the dependent variable.

Some experimental procedures involve the use of a "control group." An experimental group consists of subjects who receive some special treatment during the experiment. In this case, the purpose of the experiment is to find out whether the treatment (independent variable) has any effect on the outcome (dependent variable). However, it is possible that other factors or variables might interfere in the experiment making it difficult, sometimes impossible to assess the effect of the independent variable. If there is reason to suspect this might happen, and there is always at least the possibility, a control group is employed. A control group is identical to the experimental group in all possible relevant ways, except that the control group receives no special (the independent variable) treatment. The control groups acts as a standard against which the treatment effects of the experimental group can be determined.

What is an experimental control? Why is it important to have
experimental control?

Solution: An experimental control is a way of taking into
account the possible effect of an extraneous independent
variable that is not considered in the hypothesis being
tested. Since there may be many independent variables present in an experimental situation it is essential to know
which of the variables are actually affecting the dependent
variables. There may be many "invisible" but highly relevant
variables. The experimenter should always attempt to discover and "control for" the possible effects of variables not
of interest.

If an experimenter wanted to test the effect of a new
drug on a laboratory rat's pain threshold he might give one
group of rats injections of the drug and leave an identical
group of rats untreated. He would then test the mean pain
thresholds of the two groups to determine if there is a significant difference between the experimental (drug) and control groups. However, even though the experimenter may find
a significant difference he cannot be sure that the difference
is attributable to the effect of the new drug. He must have
a third group of rats that is given injections of some innocuous substance, for example, water. Otherwise, he cannot be
certain that the difference in pain thresholds is attributable
to the drug or to the experience of the injection. There
should not be a significant difference between the mean pain
threshold of the untreated group and the group that received
the innocuous injections if the experimenter is to conclude
that the significant difference between the untreated group
and the group injected with the drug is attributable only to
the drug.

An experiment should usually have at least two groups.
One group should be experimentally manipulated and the other
group should be a control group. This is essential in order
to be certain that any changes which take place in the experimentally manipulated group would not have occurred naturally.
For example, if an educator wanted to test the effect of a
new remedial reading program on 5th graders, it is not sufficient to know that before the program the mean reading level
of the subjects was 3.1 and after a year program it was 4.8.
It is possible that those 5th graders' reading levels would
have risen even in the absence of the experimental program.
The educator must use two groups; both groups should have the
same initial mean reading level and the same reading problems.
One group, however, should not be included in the program.
In this way it is possible to assess the effect of the program. If after a year, the group which was included in the
program has a mean reading level of 4.8 and the group not
included has a level of 3.9, and if this difference was
statistically and reliably significant, then it could be concluded that the remedial reading program was effective.

The conclusions based on many (especially early) psychological experiments may be invalid because of the absence of control groups and other experimental controls. Without controls many studies are essentially useless because it is not possible to be certain about the real cause of the change, if there is one, in the experimental group.

● **PROBLEM** 20-4

What is a "placebo" and how is it utilized by researchers? What is the "double blind" technique?

Solution: A placebo is a sugar pill (normally) which is made to look exactly like a drug under study. The purpose of a placebo is to provide a comparison between the actual effects of a drug and any effects which are the result of thinking that one is taking a drug which should result in some change in the individual's state. In fact, placeboes often do cause cognitive, behavioral, and even physiological changes. Physicians have been known to "treat" hypochondriacs with placeboes.

Suppose that a pharmaceutical company wants to test a new drug which it believes reduces anxiety. Now suppose that out of 100 people who were given the drug, 80 report that they are less anxious as a result of taking the drug. Miracle drug? Maybe, but what if we give another 100 subjects placeboes, sugar pills that look like "our drug" and tell them that it is a new anxiety-reducing compound. What if 90 people report feeling less anxious? We would have to conclude that the drug's effect occurs because of people's expectations and that the drug is essentially worthless. The placebo is, if anything, more effective.

The double-blind technique is a method of experimentation where neither the subject nor the experimenter knows whether the subject is in the experimental or control group until the completion of the study. Used most often in drug research the double-blind technique assures that neither the experimenter nor the subject can affect the results. Biases are reduced. In double-blind studies there are 2 possible control groups (often both are used in the same study): A placebo group and/or a group given a second drug already in use for comparison with the drug being tested.

HYPOTHESIS TESTING

● **PROBLEM** 20-5

What is meant by the term "hypothesis testing"?

Solution: A statistical hypothesis is some assertion about a population. This hypothesis is tested by selecting a sample from the population and calculating the validity of the asser-

tion for the sample. The results are then generalized to the
population as a whole, this generalization being expressed as
a probability that the generalization is true.

In statistics, all phenomena are described by some
numerical characteristic. Thus, the distribution of males in
the U.S. can be described in terms of average height, weight,
income, number of children, years of college, etc. Notice,
however, that it would be difficult to describe them as
clever, useful, etc. without a prior definition of terms.

Thus, when conducting a test of a hypothesis it is
necessary to i) know exactly which population is being sampled
and (ii) describe the population characteristics numerically.
Suppose an investigator concludes on the basis of testing
100 dogs that they can be trained to kill rabbits; this does
not mean that it is necessarily true for all dogs. The composition of the sample must be checked to ensure that it is
representative of the total population of interest (all dogs).
If the sample contained a large percentage of Doberman
Pinschers and only a few cocker spaniels, then the validity of
the test and, therefore, the hypothesis is questionable.

The two hypotheses tested in statistics are called the
null (H_O) and alternative (sometimes called the Affirmative)
hypotheses (H_A). An investigator usually conducts an experiment in order to show that an existing theory should be modified in some way. The null hypothesis asserts that no modification is required, i.e., that the population characteristics (parameters) have not changed or that the parameters
of 2 samples are the same and thus both samples can be said
to come from the same population. The alternative hypothesis
states that the change has occurred and, (hopefully), specifies the new population parameters. For example, it is now
believed that the males born after the Second World War are
taller than their pre-1945 counterparts. This conclusion
was reached after several Census surveys. The null and alternative hypotheses in this case would be

H_O: The average height has not changed   (1)

H_A: The average height has changed and is
       greater than before.   (2)

Note that no numerical values have been specified and so we
do not yet have a statistical test. Assuming that the average height before 1945 was 5'8" (1) and (2) become

H_O: The average height (μ) = 5'8"   (3)

H_A: The average height is greater than 5'8"   (4)

Note that the null hypothesis (3) specifies a unique value
to the population. It is called a simple hypothesis. The
alternative hypothesis (4) is actually composed of several
hypotheses (the average height is 5'9", 5'10", 6', 112'4",
etc.) It is therefore called a composite hypothesis.
Ideally, for statistical analysis, both the null and alter-

native hypotheses should be simple, i.e., assign a unique value to the population parameter. For example:

$$H_O = \mu = 5'8'' \tag{5}$$

$$H_A = \mu = 5'10'' \tag{6}$$

In the social sciences most statistical hypotheses are of the form (3), (4).

The actual process of determining which hypothesis is true consists of the following steps: i) carry out the experiment using a random sample selected from the parent population. ii) record the data and calculate the desired sample statistics (sample statistics correspond to population parameters) iii) use the theory of statistics to determine whether to accept or reject the null hypothesis.

For step i) a random sample may be part of a process. For example in an experiment to determine g, the gravitational constant, using a pendulum, the time (t) of the pendulum's swing needs to be found. An experimenter may record thirty or so values of (t). The population here is an ideal one. If we imagine the experimenter patiently repeating his experiments forever, the resulting average time would be the population parameter. In psychological research, the average time taken for a pigeon to peck at a button may be found by taking a sample of 30 pigeons. The population from which this sample comes is the set of all pigeons which could conceivably be captured and subjected to the experiment.

● **PROBLEM 20-6**

Discuss the meaning of the term significant difference.

Solution: The concept of significant difference arises when statistical inferences are made. The theory of statistical inference is concerned with predicting population parameters (i.e., characteristics) on the basis of a random sample selected from the population.

Assume that a psychologist is interested in determining the time taken by college students to memorize a list of nonsense syllables. He collects a sample of students from college A and conducts the experiment. If he repeats the experiment by taking another random sample from college B, then the statistics calculated from the samples (a statistic is a numerical function of the sample) will almost always vary because of sampling variability .

Here the investigator is faced with a difficulty, namely, what caused the variability? There are two possible explanations: 1) The variation was random (some students may have been sleepy, some may have been uninterested etc; the word random covers all factors that the investigator cannot control and feels are not important for his particular purpose or interest). In this case, the students from college

809

A and college B belong to the same population (in terms of ability to memorize nonsense syllables). 2) The two samples come from different populations, i.e., the average time taken by students in college A is different from that of students in college B.

The investigator must decide, on the basis of the difference in samples, whether 1) or 2) is true. If the difference is so large that it would rarely occur because of sampling variability alone, this difference signifies that the two samples are from different populations (meaning simply differing on an identifiable dimension, here perhaps a representative group of very bright students enrolled in college A (which is a prestigeous institution) and another population of not so bright students representative of students at college B). Such a large difference is called a significant difference.

Other examples of samples that may produce significant differences are the following:

1) A random sample of American males and a random sample of American females will usually show a significant difference in height. This means that males and females belong to two different populations as far as height is concerned, i.e., they are normally distributed with different means.

2) Two random samples of daily traffic accidents in two major American cities may or may not show a significant difference. If the samples do indeed belong to different populations, the populations will be "Poisson distributed" with different means (comparatively rare events such as traffic accidents or number of misprints in a book are elements of populations whose probabilities are given by the Poisson distribution which is a distribution with a high frequency of one or a few of the events of interest and a decreasing frequency of more than a few events, etc.).

Just how large a difference must be in order to qualify as "significant" depends on the sample size and how certain the investigator must be before he is willing to admit that the difference is meaningful and not random. The actual computations to determine significant differences are covered in the theory of mathematical statistics.

● **PROBLEM** 20-7

What does it mean if the heritability index for a particular trait is high?

Solution: A high heritability index, .70 for example, for a trait like IQ would mean that 70% of the variance found in the scores in the population are attributable to genetic factors. The problem with heritability indexes is that they are often computed from unreliable data. Thus, people often tend to draw conclusions from heritability indexes that are invalid. There are three limitations to the use of heritabil-

ity indexes in making conclusions about people and populations. First, the concept of heritability is applicable to
populations, not individuals. That is, if the heritability
index of a trait is high, then we still do not know anything
for certain about an individual who has that trait. For instance, if the heritability index for schizophrenia is very
high, we still do not know anything about the etiology (cause)
of a particular individual's schizophrenia. Regardless of
the size of the heritability index, the individual's schizophrenia could have resulted from the genetic background or
from extreme experiential deprivation.

Second, heritability indexes are only valid for the
population on which they were obtained originally. Any change
in either hereditary or environmental conditions would
alter the heritability index. A corollary of this limitation
is that the heritability index from one population cannot be
applied to another population for the purposes of comparison.
If it is determined that the heritability index for intelligence in a population of whites is .6, it cannot be concluded
that it is also .6 for Blacks.

The third limitation of the heritability index is that
it does not indicate the degree of modifiability of the trait.
Even if the heritability index is 1.0 it does not follow that
the environment does not and cannot contribute to the development of the trait. Some traits are modifiable through environmental intervention. Thus, psychologists have to be
very cautious of the problems in drawing conclusions from
small and often unreliable information provided by the heritability index.

OBSERVATION AND FIELD RESEARCH

● PROBLEM 20-8

What roles do observation and introspection play in psychology?

Solution: Both introspection and observation are methods
for obtaining psychological data. Introspection is the older
method. Introspection had its beginnings when psychology and
philosophy were closely related. Scientific psychology, however, has largely abandoned the use of introspection. Observation is still used and is a highly regarded method of obtaining data.

Introspection involves examining one's own thoughts and
feelings and making inferences based on this examination.
Introspectionist's believe that since they are human beings
themselves, they can make statements concerning other people's
internal experiences (feelings, ideas) by generalizing their
own experiences. It was thought that if a psychologist could
arrive at a clearer understanding of his own psychological
functioning, he would also understand human functioning in

general more clearly. William James, one of the most influential of the early psychologists, made extensive use of introspection. James believed that through introspection he could discover many instincts that would account for human motivation. Recent research has questioned James' findings. Currently, scientific psychologists seldom use introspection as a method for collecting or analyzing data.

Introspection, however, has always played an important role in psychoanalysis. Freud developed many of his early theories of dream interpretation, personality dynamics, and psychopathology through his own intensive self-analysis. Freud used the knowledge he acquired about himself to help develop more general theories that would be applicable to the general population. Psychoanalysts still use introspection as a means of directing or guiding their analysis of human behavior. This is one reason why psychoanalysis is sometimes considered to be closer to philosophy than to scientific psychology.

Observation, or naturalisitc observation, has always been a tool of science. In fact, the first requirement of a good scientist is that he must also be a good observer. Observation is a well respected and scientific method for accumulating information. The procedures of observation are simple but must be followed rigorously. The observer simply observes the people and environment he is interested in and records each and every detail with absolute precision. However, observation must be directed. The observer must have a question or set of questions in mind before he undertakes observation. There are millions of observations that one can make and therefore it is important that the observer focus his attention on a particular aspect of behavior. Jean Piaget, a renowned child psychologist, is one of the principal advocates of the method. His procedure for studying the acquisition of knowledge in children included observation of how children's responses to the same questions change qualitatively as they develop. One must caution, however, that the kinds of questions we ask will constrain to some extent what kinds of answers we will produce. Psychologists, like all scientists must remember that where we look determines what we will find.

● **PROBLEM** 20-9

Distinguish between a longitudinal study and a cross-sectional study.

Solution: A longitudinal study is an extended examination of the same subject or subjects over a (usually long) period of time. As an example of this type of study consider a psychologist who wishes to observe language development and uses a single child as his subject over a number of years. This would be considered a longitudinal study.

A cross-sectional study is one in which different subjects at different developmental levels are compared. For

example, instead of using a longitudinal approach, a researcher could investigate language development by comparing
the linguistic ability of different groups of children at
different stages of development.

The obvious advantage of a cross-sectional study over a
longitudinal study is that it is much less time-consuming.
But there are occasions when a longitudinal approach is necessary. For example, if a researcher wants to determine whether
intelligence test scores change with age or remain stable,
he could best accomplish this using a longitudinal study of a
single individual (or group) where he could observe the individual at different periods over a number of years. He
could not do this using a cross-sectional study. In addition
there is sometimes a problem in interpreting cross-sectional
data. For example were we to study possible changes in intelligence test scores with age by the cross-sectional method,
we would assume that the "older" group in our sample once had
test scores which were comparable to our "younger" group.
This, of course, may be an erroneous assumption. It is possible that for some reason our "older" group's test scores
were once significantly higher or lower than our "younger"
group. Comparisons and conclusions are thus not meaningful.
The longitudinal method is clearly the better one in this
instance.

● **PROBLEM** 20-10

What are the advantages and disadvantages of group testing?

Solution: There are several obvious advantages to group
testing that individual testing does not have. First of all,
a group test can be administered to many people at once reducing the cost and time of administration. Moreover, since
group tests can test many people at once, and thus more people
over time, they characteristically provide more reliable
norms.

The scoring in group testing is more objective than in
individual testing. The answers are usually multiple choice
and the tests can be scored by computer. In addition, since
examiners are basically untrained, the cost of administration
is reduced.

However, there are disadvantages to group testing. For
instance, the examiner has much less opportunity to establish
rapport, obtain cooperation, and maintain the interest of
examinees. The conditions of group testing do not allow the
examiner to note individual problems like illness, fatigue,
or anxiety which may interfere with test performance. Moreover, group tests do not normally allow for the examinee to
respond creatively or expansively. Criticisms have been
made against the use of multiple-choice items, analogies,
similarities, and classification items as being too restrictive on the examinee. Some argue that such items penalize
the brilliant and original thinker who is able to see the
more subtle implications of the alternatives. The latter

argument has not been supported. Item analysis and validity
findings have shown group tests to be successful at discriminating between bright and average people. Another criticism
of short answer and multiple choice exams is that they do not
allow the examiner to explore the reasoning behind incorrect
answers which is an important consideration if the examiner
wants to diagnose specific problems and establish remedial
programs.

Another problem with group testing is that it is in some
cases inefficient. That is, all individuals are tested with
the same items even though their ability level may be much
higher or lower in which case they would have to be tested
with more precision. Available testing time could be more
effectively utilized if each examinee concentrated on items
appropriate to his ability level. If this is done it precludes the examinee from becoming bored working on the easier
items or frustrated working on the more difficult items.

Obviously, both individual and group tests have their
respective places in evaluation. Group tests are indispensi-
ble to large scale group comparisons, whereas individual tests
and personal evaluations may be more useful for important
and difficult decisions.

● **PROBLEM** 20-11

Discuss the advantages and disadvantages of doing field
research and laboratory research with human subjects.

Solution: The advantages of field research stem from the
fact that field research focuses on real people involved
in real-world situations. Much of what we know about
"human behavior" comes from laboratory studies using college sophomores. Critics have argued that the behavior
of college students may be very different from that of
people in general. The famous psychologist E. C. Tolman
has gone so far as to suggest that "college students may
not be people." Thus by doing field research we are able
to study many different kinds of people. As a result,
conclusions about how "people" behave can be made with more
assurance.

There are, in addition, limitations on what one can
manipulate in the laboratory. For instance, we cannot
terrify the subject because of ethical considerations. Nor
can we exactly recreate real life situations in a psychology experiment. The "impact" of the situation is less
than it would be outside of our laboratories. Field
studies, on the other hand, by definition have real life
impact on our subjects. The reactions of people under
study are more natural. The subject cannot be said to behave in a certain way because he knows that a psychologist
is watching; the subject does not know that he is being
studied and as a result cannot be suspicious. The "manipulation" is natural, not artificial. Field studies, then,
involve "real people," study more natural situations, and
can be said to have more impact than laboratory studies.

814

While field studies involve situations with more "impact," there is also less "control." Laboratory studies are designed to be controlled situations. The experimenter knows exactly what is going to happen; he has control over the laboratory environment. The laboratory experiment allows the experimenter to manipulate the variables he is interested in and to exclude (control for) variables he is not interested in. Subjects can be assigned randomly to condition, hopefully reducing the effects of individual differences. Suppose one wanted to study the effects of darkness on how fast people walk. Field research might involve timing how fast people walk down a street in the morning and then at night. What would you conclude if the results indicated that the average speed of walking was much greater at night? Does darkness make people walk faster? Perhaps, but it could also be that people who walk fast are more likely to venture out at night and that people who walk slowly (e.g., the elderly) do not like walking the streets at night. This would be an instance of "self-selection," a potential confound inherent in field research. The laboratory study avoids this problem by random assignment to condition. The elderly, for example, would be required to walk down a dark hallway half the time and down a lighted hallway half the time.

Subjects are thus not allowed to select which situation (condition) they will be in; differences between the groups can then be said to be the result of the different situations and not due to individual differences.

Notice that in our example the experimenter has more control in the laboratory. He avoids the problem of self-selection. He is more in control of the environment (in the field other factors, variables may intrude, e.g., more horn honking by cars at night may be the cause of faster walking, the field researcher cannot eliminate this possibility). The laboratory experimenter, however, may find that he can only obtain college sophomores as subjects. He may have to conclude that "college students walk faster in darkness," rather than "people walk faster in darkness." In addition notice that by obtaining more control, our laboratory experimenter sacrifices the impact and reality of the field study. Is walking down a dark hallway really the same as walking down a dark street? Notice also that the subject now knows that he is being studied. He may act much differently as a result of knowing that he is in an experiment.

Both field and laboratory studies have their advantages and disadvantages. Both are useful research tools. There is, in essence, a basic tradeoff between impact and control: field studies generally have high impact but little control and laboratory studies have relatively less impact but much more control. Most phenomena worth understanding should probably be investigated both in the laboratory and in the field given the advantages and disadvantages of the two methods.

TEST CONSTRUCTION

What does it mean to standardize a test? What are norms and why is it important to establish norms?

Solution: Standardization of a test implies that there is a uniformity of procedure in administering and scoring the test. Without standardization it is impossible to compare the test results of different individuals. Every aspect of the test and the testing environment must be strictly controlled. Thus, there must be detailed instructions for administering the test, including time limits, oral instructions, and methods of answering students' questions. In a test situation, the examiner wants there to be only one independent variable--the individual being tested; otherwise, he cannot be certain that the difference in test scores among individuals is attributable to true individual differences rather than to chance factors in the testing environment. For instance, perhaps an individual receives a higher score on the SAT because the exam proctor allowed more time for the test's completion than is normally allowed.

The method of scoring a standardized test is also strictly controlled. This is one reason why the College Board tests have only multiple choice questions. In the case of multiple choice questions, scoring is quick, simple, and objective. It is almost impossible to satisfactorily standardize an essay question test especially if the test is nationwide. It cannot be expected that two graders will evaluate an essay in exactly the same way. (There are, however, ways to minimize the problems of essay scoring by providing precise outlines of what the scorer should look for in an answer.)

When an individual takes a test, a spelling test for example, he receives a raw score; in the case of a spelling test the raw score will probably be the number of words spelled correctly. This raw score has no objective value. Not only is it necessary to know how many words there are on the test (15 out of 30 words spelled correctly is better than 5 out of 30 words spelled correctly; i.e., percentages a more useful for test evaluation than raw scores) in order to evaluate the raw score but it is also necessary to know how everyone else in this individual's category or "comparison group" (age, grade, educational level, field of specialization, cultural background) has done. That is, a norm must be established. If the individual got a raw score of 30 (out of 60 words) and the average performance is 55 words correct, he did relatively poorly. However, if he got a raw score of 30 and the average performance of people in his category is 12 words correct, he did relatively well. A test score can only be interpreted in relation to a norm.

On nationwide tests that are eventually administered

to millions of people it is necessary to establish national norms. A standardization sample that is statistically representative of the population that will eventually be taking the test is tested and the norms for the test are in reference to this sample, the mean score for this sample is considered to be the average score for the population. All of the statistical information about the test is usually in reference to the performance of the standardization sample. Of course, statisticians are always interested in how well a new sample's performance compares to the performance of the original standardization sample. It is very important, especially on intelligence tests, not to judge an individual's performance on a test by the established norms if the individual is not represented in a standardization sample. For example, a Black person's IQ according to the Wechsler Adult Intelligence Scale (WAIS) cannot be evaluated if there were no Blacks in the original standardization sample. One of the major criticisms of the Minnesota Multiphasic Personality Inventory (MMPI), a personality test used nationally, is that since the original standardization sample consisted largely of male, white farmers from rural Minnesota in the 1950's, the norms established are not applicable to the general population.

Norms are the only way to evaluate tests. The idea of absolute scores having absolute values (that is, 90 out of 100 is always a good score) is often untenable. A person's test score is good or bad only in relation to how everyone else does on the test.

● **PROBLEM** 20-13

What is factor analysis and why is it important to the construction of psychcmetric tests?

Solution: Factor analysis is a complex statistical procedure which is used to identify a small number of underlying mental factors or psychological traits for the purpose of simplifying the description of behavior by reducing the number of categories normally used. Usually, the investigator begins his study by administering a large number of tests (e.g., 20) to many individuals (e.g., 300). Normally, it would be possible to describe an individual by giving his scores on the 20 tests but this can often become unwieldy and confusing. The investigator sets up a table of correlations (correlation matrix) in which he can show the extent to which each test correlates with every other test. A correlation shows the relationship between two variables; specifically, the correlation coefficient is a measure of how well one score can predict another score. A correlation coefficient of 1.0 is perfect and means that whatever an individual scores on Test A he will score on Test B. A correlation coefficient of -1.0 is also perfect but indicates that the score on Test A will be opposite of the score on Test B. Thus, if a test is scored from 0-100 points and person A's scores have a correlation

817

of -1.0 with person B's scores then if A gets 100, person B will get 0. A correlation of 1.0 or -1.0 is only a theoretical possibility in the behavioral sciences. Tests do not often even have a correlation of 1.0 with themselves. That is, the second time they are administered the results are only at best very close to the original scores. Normally, investigators find that correlations of point 0.6 and above are helpful in prediction.

If two tests are highly correlated it is not necessary to administer both because the score on one will predict the score on the other. The technique of factor analysis enables the investigator to examine all the intertest correlations and to derive factors accounting for most of the relationships among the tests. If there are tests of vocabulary, analogies, and sentence completion and they intercorrelate highly then the investigator can hypothesize a "verbal comprehension" factor. The investigator can usually derive about five factors from twenty tests. These five factors are frequently as useful as the twenty were in describing behavior. These five factors will not be "pure," however. Each test will be determined by all five factors to a different extent. The extent to which the score on each test appears to be determined by a particular factor is called the loading of a test on that factor. Thus, the analogies test may have a loading of .72 on the verbal comprehension factor and a loading of .20 on a numerical ability factor. Loading is actually the correlation of the test with the factor and thus the maximum loading is 1.0. The loading therefore is a measure of how well the factor predicts the score on a particular test. After the investigator has completed the factor analysis, he usually selects a specific test to be a measure of a particular factor and thus the loadings are actually the correlations of that one test, which represents a factor, with the other tests. The investigator manipulates the factor loadings until his results are psychologically meaningful.

The purpose of psychometric tests is to provide useful information about people. The MMPI would be useless if the results were presented as a list of the subjects' responses. In order to describe behavior usefully it is necessary to organize data by establishing meaningful categories in which people can be placed. An intelligence test is substantially more useful if the scores are broken up into numerical ability, verbal comprehension, and abstract reasoning subscores instead of giving the number of questions right and wrong. The Scholastic Aptitude Test (SAT) is broken up into two factors which describe the individual's aptitude. Factors are a useful way of consolidating information about people into comprehensive categories.

● **PROBLEM** 20-14

What is item analysis and why is it essential to test construction?

<u>Solution</u>: Item analysis is a method of analyzing indi-
vidual items on a particular test for the purpose of discovering problems and failures in the instructor's teaching,
the student's studying, and for the purpose of improving
test construction. An examiner begins an item analysis by
taking each individual item on the test (e.g., a multiple
choice test) and then tabulates not only the number of
people who got the question right or wrong but how many
people selected each particular alternative. Moreover,
the examiner usually makes a special tabulation for the
purpose of comparing the top 25% and the bottom 25% of the
final score distribution. The examiner would like to be
sure that a higher percentage of those who are in the top
25% pass an item than those who are in the bottom 25%.
The examiner makes these tabulations for the purpose of
determining how difficult an item is, whether a particular
item distinguishes between the better and poorer students,
and whether all the choices possible for a particular
multiple-choice problem are attractive enough to continue
being included (an alternative answer is considered unattractive and therefore unfunctional if no one selects it).

A tabulation might look like this.

<u>Question</u>:   "Who was the seventeenth president of the United
States?"

Choice	Upper 25%*	Lower 25%*
A. A. Lincoln	1	3
B. A. Johnson	21	11
C. U. Grant	3	8
D. L. Johnson	0	3
E. G. Ford	0	0

*The number out of 25 who selected a particular choice.

Choice B is correct. This is a good item because it discriminates well between the upper and lower 25%. 32 people
out of 50 passed the item which is a reasonable percentage.
The only problem with the item is that no one selected
choice E and therefore it is a bad or unattractive choice.
It should be discarded in favor of a different choice.

The reason item analysis is important is because it
provides the examiner with feedback on the effectiveness of
his test and of his teaching method. If a large percentage
of a class, or the entire class misses a particular item
then the examiner (i.e., the teacher) can assume that either
the item was bad (i.e., it was ambiguous or the choice
designated as correct by the examiner was perhaps not correct) or the item covered a point or topic that the teacher
failed to explain adequately. The examiner has the choice
of revising the item, eliminating the item, or improving
his teaching depending on the cause of so many people miss-

ing the item.

Sometimes a test has a particular purpose and the items
have to be specifically selected to meet that purpose. For
instance, a test may be used for the purpose of selecting
people for openings in a particular skilled occupation. If
the employers can take only 20% of the applicants then the
items should be selected such that approximately 80% of
the applicants miss most of the items. If this is done
then only approximately 20% of the applicants would pass
and these would be the people best suited for those
skilled positions. If the goal of a test is to determine
if an individual has achieved mastery in a particular
subject area, i.e., acquired the basic knowledge or skill
needed to advance to the next level of learning, then the
percentage passing the majority of the items should probably be 80% or 90%. It is expected that almost all who
have taken the test will pass. In this situation we are
dealing with people who were in a course of instruction
that was designed to teach them essential skills or knowledge. Of course, if the test is designed to determine
what skills or knowledge have yet to be learned then it is
more useful if the items are made to be more difficult in
order to better test the limits of the student's prior
knowledge.

Sometimes an examiner takes the correlation between
an item and the whole test to determine if the test has
internal consistency; i.e., is the test homogeneous. Often
items are rejected if they have a low positive or negative
correlation with the test. These are probably the same
items that would also be rejected because they fail to discriminate in the proper direction between good and bad
students.

Item analysis is essential to test construction because without it it is more difficult to design tests to
particular purposes. It is often desirable to know the
difficulty of each individual item and how attractive or
unattractive its choices are before selecting a set of
items that are appropriate to the goals of the test.

TEST VALIDITY AND RELIABILITY

● PROBLEM 20-15

What is validity?

Solution: Validity is really the central concern in test
construction. The question of validity is whether the
test measures what the examiner wants it to measure and
how well it measures it. Many tests can be highly reliable (give the same score on repeated measurements) but
nevertheless invalid. It should be pointed out that validity is not always absolute, all or none. A test is considered invalid only for a particular purpose. Validity

depends on the focus of the question one wants answered. For example, a particular test, like an IQ test, may be invalid as a measure of innate intelligence while it may be completely valid as a tool to measure educational achievement in a particular culture. Validity should be established on the basis of specific empirical evidence. Some of the better personality tests, for example, the MMPI (Minnesota Multiphasic Personality Inventory) base their validity on clinical evidence. In the MMPI a particular statement, if answered "true", is, for example, considered to be symptomatic of schizophrenia only if schizophrenics tend to answer "true" to that statement. One of the major criticisms of "projective tests" like the Rorschach Inkblot Test is that the examiner's associations between certain types of answers and certain diagnostic categories is not based on empirical evidence (it is largely subjective, not empirical). As a result many consider projective tests like the Rorschach Inkblot Test to have little validity and to be almost useless, as a method for assessing personality.

● **PROBLEM** 20-16

What is construct validity?

Solution: Construct validity is the extent to which a test measures a theoretical construct or an underlying trait. It also raises the question of what a test score reveals about an individual; will the test score help the examiner to understand the examinee by providing meaningful information about his personality or intellectual characteristics?

Construct validity is a complex and often elusive concept. It is difficult to understand fully what a psychological construct is. A psychological construct is a word or term that represents a set of consistent data about a person. It is an inferred conception of a person. Psychological constructs help to organize a person's behavior into meaningful categories. Intelligence is a psychological construct. There is no behavior which can be defined as intelligence. Intelligence is inferred; it is used to explain why some people do better than other people on specific tests. People often do not agree on what intelligence is because people do not agree on what tasks require intelligence. Like all psychological constructs, intelligence has no tangible existence; it accounts for a cluster of behaviors but is not itself a behavior. It is neither a system nor a process. In essence a construct is a description of an assumed underlying relationship among a group of hypothetically related behaviors.

Thus an intelligence test does not really measure intelligence but measures a person's ability to perform certain tasks which the examiner believes require intelligence (the underlying construct which describes how the various tasks are related). In order to evaluate construct validity it is necessary to determine what behaviors are theoretically consistent with the construct being measured. For instance, if a test was designed to measure the strength of an individual's motivation to achieve (achievement motivation), the test results should be consistent with a theory of achievement motivation. Thus, a person who scores high on achievement motivation ought to do well in college (in relation to his scholastic aptitude). If he does not do well in college one of two things must be true. Either the test has poor construct validity and does not measure achievement motivation or the theory of achievement motivation is inaccurate; perhaps there is no such thing as "achievement motivation." When an examiner wishes to assess the construct validity of a test he must do so in accordance with a theory of human behavior. The test score should be able to predict behavior in accordance with a particular theory. Correlational analysis is the usual procedure for determining construct validity. The nature of the trait or construct indicates what other measures the test should be related to. A newly developed group intelligence test should correlate highly with the old, individually administered, Stanford-Binet. The test should not only correlate positively with other tests which are assumed to measure the same trait or construct, but ideally it should also have no significant correlation with tests that do not measure these traits. These two processes are referred to as convergent validation and discriminant validation, respectively.

In accordance with a theory a test with construct validity should support predictions of group differences. College students should score higher on a test of achievement motivation than high-school dropouts (discriminant validity). A test with construct validity should also support theoretical predications about response to experimental treatments or interventions. An individual who takes a test designed to measure anxiety should have a higher score following an anxiety-inducing session than otherwise (convergent validity).

● **PROBLEM 20-17**

What is criterion related validity?

Solution: Criterion-related validity refers to the effectiveness of a test in predicting an individual's behavior in specified situations. This is done by comparing performance on the test with an independent measure of validity, i.e., a criterion. If the test in question is, for example, the Scholastic Aptitude Test, then a suitable criterion would be future college grades. There are two types of criterion-related validity, concurrent and predictive.

Predictive validity is related to tests employed for the prediction of future outcomes, e.g., "Is Mrs. Brown likely to become neurotic?" Predictive validity is most useful when applied to tests designed to select and classify personnel: hiring job applicants, selecting students for admission to college or professional school, or assigning military personnel to training programs.

The concept of concurrent validity is concerned with tests employed for diagnosis of an existing status, e.g., "Is Mrs. Brown neurotic?" Sometimes concurrent validity is used as a poor substitute for predictive validity in instances where there is no time to evaluate a future criterion. The usual purpose of a test with only concurrent validity is to provide a simpler and quicker substitute for the criterion data. It is important to remember that when a test has concurrent validity, the criterion, by definition, is available for use by the examiner. The examiner uses the test only if it is more efficient in decision-making than the criterion.

The criteria themselves should have four qualities. These are: relevance, reliability, availability, and freedom from bias. A criterion is considered to be relevant if the same factors determine success on it as determine success on the test. School grades in mathematics are relevant criteria for a mathematics aptitude test because success in a school subject is determined by basically the same factors as success on an aptitude test for that subject. The reliability of the criterion refers to its stability as a measure. A criterion would have no value if it was inconsistent in its ratings of one individual over a short period of time.

The availability of the criterion is a practical but important consideration. It is most desirable if a criterion score can be derived with a minimum of difficulty, expense, and time. Freedom of bias means that there should be no "criterion contamination."

One of the serious problems encountered in assessing validity is criterion contamination. Criterion contamination results when the criterion is no longer independent from the test results. This most often occurs when a supposedly objective rater is biased by test scores. (In this case the "objective rating" is considered the actual criterion measurement). For example, if an individual performs very poorly on a mathematics aptitude test and a teacher is aware of these results then the teacher's future rating of the individual's mathematical aptitude (the criterion) may be negatively affected. Under these or similar circumstances the teacher's rating, i.e., the criterion with which the aptitude test is supposed to be validated, is contaminated. It is essential that the rater be absolutely ignorant of the original test scores when the purpose of the rating is to validate the test scores.

The type of criterion an examiner selects usually depends on the nature of the test he is trying to validate. Basically, there are six types of criteria in common use. Intelligence tests are usually validated against some index of academic achievement (school grades, achievement tests and teachers' ratings). One of the criticisms of intelligence tests is that since they are validated according to an index of academic achievement it cannot be said with certainty that the test measures intelligence per se; there is no obvious criterion that can be used to measure innate intelligence.

Special aptitude tests are usually validated against one of two criteria. For example, in an Air Force pilot-selection test the criterion is performance in basic Flight training. Another criterion often used is the job performance record of the individual. However, this criterion would probably not be used for an Air Force pilot-selection test because it is too dangerous to wait and see if an individual will be successful in combat (luckily this can usually be determined in specialized training). Performance in specialized training is often preferred as a criterion to job performance because there is a greater uniformity of conditions possible during training. An individual's job performance record may also be used as a criterion to validate intelligence and personality tests.

Validation by the method of contrasted groups involves a criterion which is based on the expected difference in performance of two groups. For an intelligence test it is expected that a group of institutionalized mentally retarded children will have significantly lower scores than normal school children. An intelligence test that could not produce this pattern of results would be invalid. On a personality test designed to assess social skills or traits the test performance of salesmen may be compared to the test performance of engineers. It might be expected that salesmen would be particularly socially adept because their job entails a great deal of social interaction. A personality test claiming to measure social adeptness might be considered invalid if it did not produce higher scores for salesmen than engineers.

The fifth criterion commonly used for validation (also for item selection) is psychiatric diagnosis. We might reasonably hope that a psychiatric diagnosis based on prolonged observation and a detailed case history would support the findings of a personality test. Unfortunately, often this is not the case. It has been found that "projective tests" like the Rorschach Inkblot, the Thematic Apperception Test, and even "empirical tests" like the Minnesota Multiphasic Personality Inventory (MMPI) which are designed to make diagnoses of individuals are often poor substitutes for professional psychiatric diagnoses.

The sixth and last kind of criterion measure commonly used is a previously available test. This type of validation is usually used to validate a shorter, more easily administered test against a longer version. For example, a group administered multiple choice answer intelligence test may be validated against the older and longer, individually administered Stanford-Binet test. If its results correlate highly with the Stanford-Binet then it might be useful to use the new test in many situations.

Criterion-related validity is often referred to as

empirical validation because a test's results are being compared with something empirical or objective. One of the major criticisms of projective tests, like the Rorschach Inkblot Test, is that they are not empirically validated and therefore cannot be said to be assessing anything with certainty. It is essential in all tests that claim to have predictive value to compare results with an empirical criterion; it is important to establish criterion-related validity.

● **PROBLEM** 20-18

How does face validity differ from content validity?

Solution: Content validity is a measure of the extent to which a test measures an adequate sample of the behavioral domain that the examiner is interested in. A behavioral domain simply refers to all of the possible actions and characteristics of a particular behavior. Reading is a behavior and its domain includes spelling, vocabulary, and comprehension. The important question is: does the content of the test adequately represent the content of what is being measured? For example, does an arithmetic test's content adequately represent content in addition, multiplication, division, and subtraction or is it too heavily loaded with division problems to the exclusion of addition problems? This type of validity is most commonly used to evaluate achievement tests. In constructing an achievement test for a particular subject it is desirable to fully describe all characteristics and aspects of that subject so that in effect the content validity is built in. This is usually done by a systematic evaluation of the course syllabi, textbooks, and by consultation with experts on the subject. Once the content and scope of the subject is precisely determined test specifications are drawn up. Some content areas may be more important than others; there should be more items covering these important sub-topics. When an achievement test is constructed in this manner it is likely that there will be a high degree of content validity. Another indication of content validity on an achievement test (e.g., reading) is to see if a higher number of students in the higher grades pass a particular item.

An important aspect of content validity is the importance of the exclusion of irrelevant factors from the test. In a proficiency test in mathematics, for example, the examiner does not want the results to be unduly influenced by the ability to understand verbal instructions. Those who were more proficient in verbal skills might have an advantage irrelevant to what we are attempting to measure.

The concept of content validity as applied to personality and aptitude tests may be inappropriate, or at least deceiving. This is because these tests are not intended to measure any specific behavior domain. These tests measure abstract traits or constructs (intelligence, neuroticism) and should be validated against empirical measures, i.e., an intelligence test must discriminate among people of different levels of intelligence. There is no well defined content from which test items can be drawn.

Face validity refers to the extent that the test looks like it measures what it purports to measure. Arithmetic, reading, spelling, and vocabulary tests have a high degree of face validity. An analogies test used to measure the ability to make abstract associations has less face validity. Projective tests (TAT, Rorschach, Draw-A-Person) have practically no face validity. The lack of face validity in these tests is in fact a deliberate attempt to prevent the subject from becoming defensive and "faking good."

● **PROBLEM** 20-19

What is cross-validation and why is it important?

Solution: When the original sample of individuals upon whom a set of test items is validated is small and when the test items have been selected from a large number of possible alternatives, it is necessary to cross-validate; i.e., it is necessary to independently determine the validity of the entire test on additional samples of subjects. Often, a test is hypothesized to have a particular predictive value and in a preliminary validation study, it may be found that the test is in fact highly predictive. However, since the initial validation sample is usually fairly small, the chance of there being an error in the validation study is large. Statistical analyses become increasingly more accurate as the number of people in the sample increases. If a sample in a study is too small, then often statistics are of no use in analyzing the data and the conclusions that are arrived at may be attributable to chance factors. A good example of the need and importance of cross-validation is found in an investigation of the possible uses of the Rorschach inkblot test (Kurtz, 1948). The investigators were attempting to determine whether the Rorschach test responses could be used to select sales managers for life insurance companies. Eighty managers were chosen from several hundred employed in various life insurance companies. Forty-two had been previously rated as being satisfactory and thirty-eight as unsatisfactory. All eighty managers were given the Rorschach test and their test records were scrutinized. A scoring key was developed based on whether certain patterns were reported more often by the very satisfactory group as compared to the unsatisfactory group. The scoring key was reapplied to the original group of eighty and seventy-nine of the eighty were correctly classified as belonging to either the satisfactory or unsatisfactory group. Thus, the correlation between test score and the criterion was close to +1.0. However, when the test was cross-validated on a new sample of 41 managers the scoring key was practically useless in classification. The correlation between criterion and test score was a negligible

826

0.02. These results indicate that the original finding, that seventy-nine out of eighty managers could be correctly classified, could probably be attributed to chance factors.

It is likely that whatever it was in the Rorschach responses that discriminated between the satisfactory and unsatisfactory managers was unique to those eighty managers. These responses were not traits which could be generalized to all insurance managers. The basic flaw in the study was that the experimenter selected those responses which discriminated between the two groups as his "target responses" and then used the very same responses to see whether the test discriminated between the two groups. It is obvious that the responses would discriminate between the groups because they were chosen because they discriminated in the first place! What the experimenter should have done was to ascertain whether those Rorschach responses discriminated solely on the basis of whether the manager was satisfactory or unsatisfactory. The basis for the discriminatory power of those Rorschach responses was probably not any trait associated with being a good manager or a bad manager.

Thus, before a psychologist draws conclusions and publishes findings he should be certain that his test or experimental procedure can be cross-validated. Too often psychologists (and other scientists) are content with superficially validated data and do not submit these data to a more rigorous analysis of validity.

● **PROBLEM** 20-20

What is reliability and why is it important to test construction?

Solution: Reliability refers to the consistency of scores an individual obtains when reexamined. Reliability is a measure of the extent that differences between different individuals' scores represent true difference in characteristics and not "error variance." Error variance refers to the proportion of the total variance of test scores attributable to errors in test construction. Variance simply means the difference in scores among individuals. People will often score differently on the same test. It is important to know what the difference is attributable to.

When an examiner knows the reliability value for a test he can predict the range of fluctuation likely to occur in a single individual's score due to chance, and irrelevant factors by computing the error of measurement.

A test is not useful if an individual's scores are not reproduceable. Two reasons why a test may not be reliable are poor test construction, and lack of control of the test environment. An example of poor test construction is the testing of an inadequate sample of behavior. A vocabulary test would be unreliable if it consisted of only one word because the individual might be able to guess the correct definition and not six weeks later when retested. Moreover knowing the definition of one word is not indicative of having a good vocabulary. An example of poor control of the test environment is inconsistent instructions. On a hearing test the examiner could say to the subject on one occasion, "Tell me when you think you hear the tone" and on the second occasion he could say "Tell me when you're sure you hear the tone." The instructions are different and therefore the results will be unreliable. The examiner must be certain that his instructions are consistent.

● **PROBLEM** 20-21

Name and describe four types of reliability.

Solution: The four types of reliability most commonly re- ferred to are: test-retest, split-half, alternate or par- allel form, and scorer reliabilities.

Test-retest reliability is measured by administer- ing the same test to the same individual on a second occa- sion and determining the extent to which the score fluctu- ates. (The reliability is measured by the reliability coefficient which is the correlation between the two scores.) This seems like a reasonable method, but there are many problems with it. First of all, if the interval between the tests is too long then the behavior being sampled would be expected to change due to any number of factors including education and maturation or development. If the interval between tests is too short then there will be practice effects (i.e., the subject may have an improved score since he had the practice of taking the first test) or the subject might remember some of his answers from the first test (whether they were right or wrong) and thus the results would not be independent. The reliability coefficient, then will be spuriously high. Moreover, there may be variations in the test conditions that cannot be controlled (weather, sudden noises) which may account for most of the variance.

Alternate or parallel form reliability avoids many of the problems encountered in test-retest reliability. The problem of practice effects is reduced (as is the problem of the subject remembering his answers from the first test). In alternate-form reliability a subject is tested with one form of the test on the first occasion and with a comparable, but different form on the second occasion. The reliability coefficient is represented by the correlation between the score on the first form and the score on the second form. The use of alternate-form reliability allows the examiner to obtain a measure for two different types of reliability. He will obtain not only the measure of the consistency in an individual's score over time, but also a measure of con- sistency in response to different item samples. That is, the examiner has a way of determining if the two forms are actually equivalent; if they are, scores on the second form should not deviate too much from the scores on the first form. Alternate-form reliability also has the advan- tage of reducing error variance due to content sampling.

Error variance due to content sampling refers to the problem of the subject being particularly familiar or unfamiliar with a particular test's content. It is often important to know to what extent scores on a test depend on factors specific to the particular selection of items. Thus, on a vocabulary test, the subject may, by chance happen to know most of the words and his score may not be indicative of the true extent of his vocabulary. In alternate-form reliability, the examiner obtains two samples of the subject's behavior and can thus be more certain that there is less error variance due to content sampling.

Alternate forms of tests should be constructed independently and should contain the same number of items as the first form. Obviously, the range and level of difficulty of the items should be equal. Instructions, time limits, and other testing conditions should also be the same. The period of time between the administration of the two forms must also be specified. If the two tests are administered successively then the advantage of obtaining consistency of scores over time is lost. When the two forms are administered successively there is also the problem of fatigue. The subject may become tired by the time he takes the second form and thus may not do as well. The reliability may therefore be spuriously low. The problem of practice effects was only reduced, not eliminated. Certain problems may involve general principles which if learned once will result in the subject being able to apply them more easily on a second form. In general, however, alternate-form reliability is a desirable quality.

Split-half reliability involves the examiner obtaining two scores for the subject with one administration of a test. The correlation between these two scores is the reliability coefficient. Usually, the examiner uses the scores on the odd and even items as the two scores. This procedure is preferred to comparing the scores on the first and second halves of the test because it reduces the problems of fatigue, boredom, and practice effects which might occur during the second half of the test. Thus, the score on the second half might be either spuriously high or spuriously low. Moreover, tests are often constructed such that the items increase with difficulty from beginning to end. (The reasoning is that this prevents a subject from "getting stuck" on an early item and being unable to reach those items that he could answer successfully.) Thus, if the scores from the first and second halves were compared, the scores on the second half might be spuriously low due to the greater difficulty of the second half of the test. Clearly then, splitting the test according to odd-even items is preferable. The split-half reliability coefficient is often called the coefficient of internal consistency because the comparison of the two halves of the test indicates whether the items on the test have an underlying consistency.

Scorer reliability is used when the scoring on the test is subjective, as in projective testing or tests of creativity. In this case it is essential to know whether

the scoring technique is sufficiently well-defined so that
two scorers can arrive at the same conclusions.

THE NORMAL DISTRIBUTION

● **PROBLEM** 20-22

Explain the importance of the normal distribution in empirical research.

Solution: The normal distribution is the most important
distribution in the theory of statistics. Hence some
knowledge of its properties is essential for psychologists.
The normal distribution is also referred to as the Gaussian
curve in honor of C. F. Gauss, the German mathematician
who first stated its properties.

Fig. 1 shows the typical bell-shaped curve which characterizes the normal distribution. The figure is to be interpreted as follows: x = μ is the most common value in the
population (μ denotes the mean or average). As x increases
(goes to the right) the frequency with which x occurs
(f(x)) decreases. Similarly, as x decreases, f(x) decreases. Since f(x) may be thought of as the probability
of x, this means that extreme values of x are rare.

Fig. 1

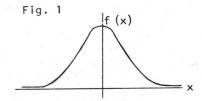

Many natural phenomena are distributed normally. For
example heights and weights of people follow the normal
distribution. This means that in the U.S. (where the average height of males above 25 years is 5'9") most males will
fall within 5'8" to 5'10" height. Heights such as 5'2" or
6'6" will occur with much less frequency.

The following are the important properties of the
normal distribution. 1) Every population that is normally
distributed is completely characterized by two population
parameters: the mean μ and the variance σ^2. This means
that given any element in the population we can find the
probability with which that element will occur .

In any normal distribution, the various population
values are distributed as in Fig. 2. 68% of the population falls within ±1 (plus or minus one) standard deviations of the mean (the standard deviation is the square
root of the variance). 95% of the population falls within
±2 standard deviations of the mean. 99.5% falls within
±3 standard deviations of the mean.

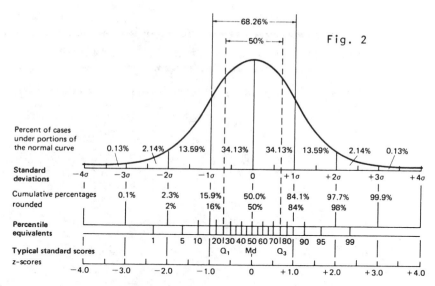

Fig. 2

For example, the Stanford-Binet Intelligence Test
has a mean of 100 and standard deviation of 16. This
means that 68% of the people who take the test will score
between 84 and 116.

A very important aspect of the normal distribution is
its use in theoretical statistics with what is referred to
as the Central Limit Theorem. Consider the following procedure. Assume that an investigator is interested in taking samples from a normal distribution. He takes a random
sample (of size greater than 30) and calculates the sample
mean $\bar{X}$. He then takes another random sample and repeats
the above computation. He would expect the two sample
means to vary slightly. If he repeatedly takes random
samples from this distribution what can he say about the
sample means? They form a new distribution with a mean
and a variance. According to the Central Limit Theorem
the sample means are normally distributed. Even more surprising, we need not assume that the investigator is taking samples from a normal distribution. Any distribution
(Poisson, Binomial, etc.) which has a finite variance and
a mean will have, as its distribution of sample means,
a normal distribution.

This means that an investigator who is conducting an
experiment (say on response time of pigeons to auditory
stimulation) can use the normal distribution to make probability statements concerning mean response time. If he
takes sample groups of 30 pigeons and calculates the average
response time for each group, he can calculate i) the average of the average times, μ ii) the variance of the average
times, $\sigma_{\bar{X}}^2$. He can then state that in the future, 68% of
average response times will fall within $\pm\sigma_{\bar{X}}$ of μ, 95%
within $\pm 2\sigma_{\bar{X}}$ etc.

831

What is the standard deviation of a distribution?

	Set A (ages of 10 people at a college dance)			Set B (ages of 10 people at the park)	
X	*X − X̄ (x)*	*x²*	*X*	*X − X̄ (x)*	*x²*
22	2	4	36	16	256
22	2	4	32	12	144
21	1	1	28	8	64
21	1	1	24	4	16
20	0	0	20	0	0
20	0	0	20	0	0
19	−1	1	16	−4	16
19	−1	1	12	−8	64
18	−2	4	8	−12	144
18	−2	4	4	−16	256
	$\Sigma x = 0$	$\Sigma x^2 = 20$		$\Sigma x = 0$	$\Sigma x^2 = 960$

$$\sigma^2 = \text{variance} = \frac{\Sigma x^2}{N} = \frac{20}{10} = 2.00$$

$$\sigma = \text{standard deviation} = \sqrt{\sigma^2} = \sqrt{2.00} = 1.414$$

$$\text{or } \sigma = \sqrt{\frac{\Sigma x^2}{N}} = \sqrt{\frac{20}{10}} = 1.414$$

$$\sigma^2 = \text{variance} = \frac{\Sigma x^2}{N} = \frac{960}{10} = 96.0$$

$$\sigma = \text{standard deviation} = \sqrt{\sigma^2} = \sqrt{96} = 9.798$$

$$\text{or } \sigma = \sqrt{\frac{\Sigma x^2}{N}} = \sqrt{\frac{960}{10}} = 9.798$$

Computation of the variance and standard deviation for two
sets of scores

Solution: Statistical analysis is used to more succinctly
characterize many bits of data by one or two numerical ag-
gregates. The most important statistical measures are
i) measures of central tendency ii) measures of variation.
The mean, median and mode of a distribution are examples
of i). The range, variance, and standard deviation are
examples of ii).

In order to obtain accurate information concerning a
distribution it is necessary to know measures of both type
i) and ii). The most common measures used to describe a
distribution are the mean and the variance. The square
root of the variance is the standard deviation (The square
root of x is $\sqrt{x}$; e.g., $\sqrt{9} = 3$ $\sqrt{100} = 10$ $\sqrt{53.29} = 7.3$)

What is the variance? As a measure of variation it
measures the deviations of scores about the mean. For
example, let a distribution be given by 1, 3, 7, 9, 10.
The mean is

$$\frac{1 + 3 + 7 + 9 + 10}{5} = \frac{30}{5} = 6 .$$

One measure of deviation would be to subtract each observation from the mean and add the resulting numbers. This
gives

$$(1-6) + (3-6) + (7-6) + (9-6) + (10-6) =$$

$$-5 - 3 + 1 + 3 + 4 = 0.$$

Let another distribution be 3, 4, 8, 9, 16. The mean is

$$\frac{3 + 4 + 8 + 9 + 16}{5} = \frac{40}{5} = 8.$$

The sum of deviations from the mean is

$$(3-8) + (4-8) + (8-8) + (9-8) + (16-8) =$$

$$-5 -4 + 0 + 1 + 8 = 0.$$

A measure of deviation that always gives zero is not very useful. Hence a new measure, the variance, is defined. The variance of a distribution is calculated by the following procedure:

i) Find the mean of the distribution

ii) Subtract each observation from the mean

iii) Square the results

iv) Add the squared deviations from the mean

v) Divide by the total number of observations.

For the first distribution, the variance is

$$(1-6)^2 + (3-6)^2 + (7-6)^2 + (9-6)^2 + (10-6)^2/5 =$$

$$\frac{25 + 9 + 1 + 9 + 16}{5} = \frac{60}{5} = 12.$$

Thus the variance measures the average spread of the observations around the mean. But since the terms were squared it is preferable to take the positive square root. The standard deviation of the above distribution is $12 = \sqrt{3.46}$.

For the second distribution, the variance is

$$(3-8)^2 + (4-8)^2 + (8-8)^2 + (9-8)^2 + (16-8)^2 =$$

$$\frac{25 + 16 + 0 + 1 + 64}{5} = \frac{106}{5} = 21.2$$

The standard deviation is 4.60. Comparing the two distributions one can state that the first distribution is more concentrated around the mean (has smaller variance) than the second.

● **PROBLEM** 20-24

What is a Z-score?

Solution: Z-scores are used when we wish to compare the test scores of different individuals. The term 'Z-score' is derived from the use of the standard normal, or Z-table in computing the scores. The Z-table in turn is derived from the normal distribution. Hence to answer the question, it is first necessary to understand the normal distribution.

It has been empirically observed that when many people take a test, the scores will most often be normally distributed. This means that there is a mean score around which most people will cluster, the more extreme scores being comparatively rarer. Now, a normal distribution is completely specified by i) its mean ii) its variance. That is, given any two elements from a population which is normally distributed, it is possible to state which element is more likely to occur in the population.

The probability of an element occurring in a normal population characterized by a mean and a variance is found by a complicated formula. Whenever the mean or the variance changes the probabilities will have to be re-calculated. All normal distributions share the bell-shaped curve property; given the difficulties in calculation, it would be useful to find a linear transformation that related all normal distributions.

In fact, any normal distribution with mean μ (mu) and variance σ^2 (sigma squared) can be converted to the standard normal distribution with mean 0 and variance 1. More accurately, the probability of X in the distribution with mean μ and variance σ^2 is equivalent to the probability of Z in the distribution with mean 0 and variance 1. The transformation from X to Z is given by

$$Z = \frac{X - \mu}{\sigma} .$$

Standard normal probabilities have been calculated and hence, given X, its Z probability can be found.

As an example, suppose a student scored 630 on a standardized test with mean 450 and variance 22500. The scores on a standardized test follow a normal distribution. Find Z.

$$Z = \frac{630-450}{\sqrt{22500}} = \frac{180}{150} = 1.2$$

We can find the area under the curve from the left-hand end (the "tail") to 1.2 in Fig. 1, by using a table of standard normal probabilities. In such a table, standard deviation units are given on the left-hand and upper parts of the table while the probabilities are given in the main body. The total area under the curve is equal to 1.

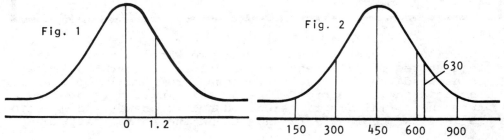

Fig. 1

Fig. 2

630

0   1.2

150   300   450   600   900

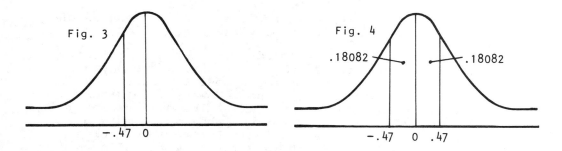

Fig. 3

Fig. 4

.18082 · · .18082

−.47 0

−.47 0 .47

A Z score of 1.20 corresponds to a probability of .88493. This means the student scored in the 88th percentile. It also means that the area under the normal curve from the left-hand tail to 1.2 is .88493.

Fig. 2 shows the original normal distribution. As noted before, computing the probabilities from Fig. 2 would be very difficult but the final answer would be the same--viz. .88493.

Another example, suppose a student scored 380 on the same test. His Z score is

$$Z = \frac{380 - 450}{150} = - .47$$

To interpret this score, remember that the normal distribution is symmetrical. This means that the area under the curve from −.47 to 0 is the same as the area from 0 to −.47. From the standard normal distribution table, the area under the curve from the left hand tail to .47 is .68082. Since the distribution is symmetrical, the area from the left hand side to 0 is .5. Thus the area under the curve from 0 to .47 is .18082 and the area from −.47 to 0 is .18082. Thus the area from the left hand side to −.47 is .5 − .18082 = .31918. This means that the student was in the 31st percentile of students who took the test.

● **PROBLEM** 20-25

What is a random sample? Why is the selection of a random sample important?

Solution: In many scientific studies and in industrial research, it is necessary to describe a population of subjects by one or two numerical characteristics. For example, a 60 watt light bulb is evaluated according to the number of hours it emits light. Suppose the manufacturer of these light bulbs wishes to know how long his bulbs burn. One method of finding out is to test each bulb individually. However, at the end of this experiment there will be nothing left to sell! Another method consists of the following procedure: i) select a certain number of bulbs for testing ii) assume that these bulbs are representative of the total population iii) Describe the results of the test by representing the data by measures of central tendency and measures of variation.

Random sampling is concerned with step i). How are the bulbs to be selected so that they mirror the parent population? The manufacturer could test the first 100 bulbs coming off the assembly line. However, this sample may not reflect the population. The bulbs may have been handled by only one shift of workers who may be more or less efficient than the next shift. Furthermore, bulbs that are produced later in the day may show the effects of machine wear and tear. Thus a sample, in order to adequately represent the population must satisfy the criteria below:

1) Equal chance. A sample meets the criterion of equal chance if it is selected in such a way that every observation in the entire population has an equal chance of being included in the sample.

2) Independence. A sample meets this criterion when the selection of any single observation does not affect the chances for selection of any other.

A sample that satisfies 1) and 2) is known as a random sample. Samples that are not random are called biased samples.

The conditions for randomness can be violated in ways that are not immediately apparent. A classic example of mistaken sampling occurred in the Presidential race between F. D. Roosevelt and A. Landon in 1936. A magazine called the Literary Digest predicted a victory for Landon based on questionnaires sent to its readers and all telephone subscribers. This sample, however, was biased. In 1936 only the middle and upper income segments of society had telephones; they were also predominantly Republican and formed a minority of the total population. Thus the condition of equal chance was violated and the sample was biased. The prediction turned out to be wrong, Roosevelt won. A biased sample often yields inaccurate predictions. Often the best way to obtain a random sample is to assign a number to each individual in the parent population and then select the sample group by using a Table of Random Numbers.

PROBLEMS AND APPLICATIONS IN STATISTICS

● **PROBLEM** 20-26

Differentiate between descriptive statistics and inferential statistics.

Solution: Statistical methods can be divided into two groups: descriptive statistics and inferential statistics.

Descriptive statistics are used, as the name implies, to describe situations, data. Examples of descriptive statistics include measures of central tendency (mean, median, and mode) and measures of dispersion. Inferential statistics, on the other hand, are statistics such as tests of significant differences (T-tests, χ^2, analysis of variance) and measures of sampling error used to draw conclusions from the data, to make "inferences," to test hypotheses.

● **PROBLEM** 20-27

a) What is a distribution? b) What is central tendency?
c) Define the terms mean, median, mode, range, and variability.

Solution: A distribution is a set of scores from a population or a population sample. For instance, if a class of 100 students takes a test, the 100 scores of the students will form a distribution. This distribution can always be represented graphically for the purposes of clarification and analysis.

Sometimes, the examiner may divide the distribution into intervals. For instance, if the possible test scores range from 0-100 he can make 10 intervals (0-9, 10-19, 20-29, etc.) and thus simplify the graph. The y-axis (vertical) will indicate the number of students who fall into each interval. The intervals are on the x-axis (horizontal). This type of distribution is called "discrete" because the scores can take on only specific values and only a limited number of cases can fall into an interval. The graphical representation of a discrete distribution is called a histogram.

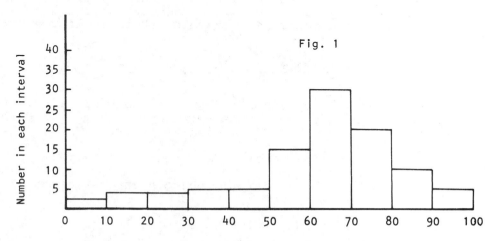
Fig. 1

In figure 1, the total number of scores is 100. From the histogram observe that 30 subjects scored between 60-70. Similarly, 20 scored between 70-80 and 15 between 50-60. The histogram may be translated into tabular form as follows:

Score	# of subjects
0 - 9	2
10 - 19	4
20 - 29	4
30 - 39	5
40 - 49	5
50 - 59	15
60 - 69	30
70 - 79	20
80 - 89	10
90 - 100	5

It has been empirically observed that scores tend to cluster around the middle values of a distribution and become rarer as the extreme values are approached. For example, consider the heights of males in the U.S. within a given age bracket (say 25-45). It is found that most of the people in this distribution are within an inch or two of 5'9", the central value.

Fig. 2 illustrates the above example.

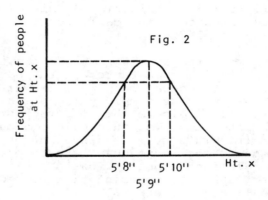

Fig. 2

The mean of a distribution is the arithmetic average. It is obtained by adding up all scores and dividing by the number of subjects. For example, the mean of the numbers 1, 2, 3, 4, 5 is

$$\frac{1 + 2 + 3 + 4 + 5}{5} = \frac{15}{5} = 3.$$

As a more complicated example from frequency distributions (intervals) consider the table representing Fig. 1. Here the mean is found by the following procedure

i) Find the mid-point of each scoring interval

ii) Multiply the number of subjects in each interval by this mid-point

iii) Add and divide by 100 (the total number of subjects).

The mode of a distribution is that value (or interval) which occurs most frequently. The term "mode" comes from the French word meaning fashionable. As an example consider Fig. 3.

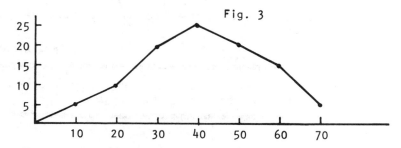

Fig. 3

Assume that this distribution represents the numbers of
ladies buying dresses at given prices. For example, 5
women bought dresses that cost $10.00. Note that 25 women
bought 40 dollar outfits. This is the mode of the distribution since no other priced dress attracted so many
customers. The median of a distribution is that value
which divides the distribution into exactly two halves.
That is, 50% of the scores lie below the median and 50%
of the scores lie above the median. As an example, the
median of: 1, 2, 4, 9, 12, 13, 28 is 9 since 3 scores
fall below and 3 scores above 9. If the number of scores
is even, the median is the average of the two middle
scores. Thus the median of the distribution 1, 2, 2, 6,
7, 8 is

$$\frac{2 + 6}{2} = 4.$$

When graphed data are present the calculation of the median
is more complicated. (A distribution is composed of
grouped data when each score has more than one subject;
e.g., the distribution in Fig. 1.) The range of a distribution is the difference between the largest and smallest
values in the distribution. In Fig. 1, the range is
(100-0) = 100. The range of the distribution 1, 2, 3, 4,
5 is (5-1) = 4.

The mean, median and mode are known as measures of
central tendency. There are also measures of variation in
a set of data. The range is a measure of variation since
it gives the limits within which the elements of a distribution are confined. Another measure of variability is the
variance (the sum of squared deviations from the mean divided by the number of elements in the distribution).

To illustrate why it is useful to know both a measure
of central tendency and a measure of dispersion (variability) consider two groups of people both with mean weights
of 150 lbs. Knowing only the measure of central tendency
we may erroneously assume that the two groups are very
much alike with regard to weight. We may, however, be very
wrong. The first group may be composed of individuals who
weigh 140, 145, 150, 155, 160 lbs. The second group, on
the other hand, may consist of individuals who weigh 100,
125, 150, 175, 200 lbs. Certainly these two groups are
very different, even though the mean weight of each is the
same (150 lbs.). The variance of the second group is much
greater. It is, then, most useful to know both parameters
of the distribution: a measure of central tendency (mean,
median, or mode) and a measure of dispersion (the variance

or standard deviation). (Sometimes it is also very useful to know the range.)

● **PROBLEM** 20-28

Find the mean weight of the sample of rats that weighed 2 lbs., 3 lbs., 6 lb.s, 8 lbs., and 9 lbs.

Solution: The mean weight is the arithmetic average.

Let $X_1 = 2$, $X_2 = 3$, $X_3 = 6$, $X_4 = 8$, $X_5 = 9$.

Therefore,

$$\bar{X} = \frac{\Sigma X_i}{\eta} = \frac{X_1 + X_2 + X_3 + X_4 + X_5}{5} = \frac{2 + 3 + 6 + 8 + 9}{5}$$

$$= \frac{28}{5} = 5.6 \text{ lbs.}$$

● **PROBLEM** 20-29

What is the value of the median for the numbers 5, 8, 12, 3, 9?

Solution: In ascending order, the values are

$$3, 5, 8, 9, 12.$$

We have a sample of 5. The median is the middle or third value 8.

● **PROBLEM** 20-30

Find the median of the sample 34, 29, 26, 37, 31, and 34.

Solution: The sample arranged in order is 26, 29, 31, 34, 34, and 37. The number of observations is even and thus the median, or middle number is chosen halfway between the third and fourth number. In this case the median is

$$\frac{31 + 34}{2} = 32.5$$

● **PROBLEM** 20-31

Find the mode of the sample 14, 19, 16, 21, 18, 19, 24, 15, and 19.

Solution: The mode is another measure of central tendency.

It is the observation or observations that occur with the greatest frequency. The number 19 is observed three times in this sample and no other observation appears as frequently. The mode of this sample is 19.

● **PROBLEM 20-32**

Find the mode or modes of the sample 6, 7, 7, 3, 8, 5, 3, 9.

Solution: In this sample the numbers 7 and 3 both appear twice. There are no other observations that appear as frequently as these two. Therefore 3 and 7 are the modes of this sample. The sample is said to be "bimodal."

● **PROBLEM 20-33**

Discuss and distinguish between discrete and continuous values.

Solution: The kinds of numbers that can taken on any fractional or integer value between specified limits are categorized as continuous, whereas values that are usually restricted to whole-number values are called discrete. Thus, if we identify the number of people who use each of several brands of toothpaste, the data generated must be discrete. If we determine the heights and weights of a group of college men, the data generated is continuous.

However, in certain situations, fractional values are also integers. For example, stock prices are generally quoted to the one-eighth of a dollar. Since other fractional values between, say, 24.5 and 24.37 cannot occur, these values can be considered discrete. However, the discrete values that we consider are usually integers.

● **PROBLEM 20-34**

The IQ scores for a sample of 24 students who are entering their first year of high school are:

115	119	119	134
121	128	128	152
97	108	98	130
108	110	111	122
106	142	143	140
141	151	125	126

(a) Make a cumulative percentage graph using classes of seven points starting with 96 - 102.
(b) What scores are below the 25th percentile?
(c) What scores are above the 75th?
(d) What is the median score?

Solution:

Interval	Interval Midpoint	Frequency	Cumulative Frequency	Cumulative Percentage
96-102	99	2	2	8.34
103-109	106	3	5	20.83
110-116	113	3	8	33.33
117-123	120	4	12	50.00
124-130	127	5	17	71.00
131-137	134	1	18	75.00
138-144	141	4	22	91.33
145-151	148	1	23	96.00
152-158	155	1	24	100.00

The frequency is the number of students in that interval. The cumulative frequency is the number of students in intervals up to and including that interval. The cumulative percentage is the percentage of students whose IQ's are at that level or below.

$$\text{Cumulative Percentage} = \frac{\text{Cumulative Frequency}}{24} \times 100 \text{ \%} .$$

We will plot our graph using the interval midpoint as the x coordinate and the cumulative percentage as the y coordinate.

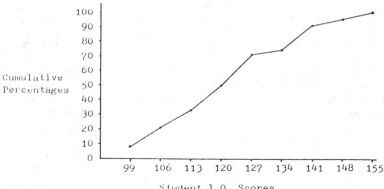

Student I.Q. Scores

(b)   The 25th percentile is defined to be a number that is exactly greater than the lowest 25 % of the scores. We want to know the score that is at least greater than (.25)24=6 other students. The 6 lowest scores are 97, 98, 106, 108, 108 and 110. We cannot use 111 as a 25th percentile since another student has that score so we use 110.5.

(c)   The 75th percentile is the score which exceeds the lowest 75% of the population but is less than the top 25 % of scores. We want the score below 6 students and above 18. The 6 highest scores are 152, 151, 143, 142, 141, 140. The next highest is 134. As our 75 % percentile we can take any value between 134 and 140. We will take 137, the average of 134 and 140.

(d) The median is the value which half of the values of the population exced and half do not. There are 12 values ≤ 123

842

and 12 values $\geq$ 124. Therefore we take as our median 123.5, the average of these two values. The median is the 50th percentile.

● **PROBLEM** 20-35

The following data is a sample of the accounts receivable of a small merchandising firm.

37	42	44	47	46	50	48	52	90
54	56	55	53	58	59	60	62	92
60	61	62	63	67	64	64	68	
67	65	66	68	69	66	70	72	
73	75	74	72	71	76	81	80	
79	80	78	82	83	85	86	88	

Using a class interval of 5, i.e. 35 - 39,

(a) Make a frequency distribution table.
(b) Construct a histogram.
(c) Draw a frequency polygon.
(d) Make a cumulative frequency distribution.
(e) Construct a cumulative percentage ogive.

Class Interval	Class Boundaries	Tally	Interval Median	Frequency
35 - 39	34.5 - 39.5	/	37	1
40 - 44	39.5 - 44.5	//	42	2
45 - 49	44.5 - 49.5	///	47	3
50 - 54	49.5 - 54.5	////	52	4
55 - 59	54.5 - 59.5	////	57	4
60 - 64	59.5 - 64.5	/// ///	62	8
65 - 69	64.5 - 69.5	/// ///	67	8
70 - 74	69.5 - 74.5	/// /	72	6
75 - 79	74.5 - 79.5	////	77	4
80 - 84	79.5 - 84.5	///	82	5
85 - 89	84.5 - 89.5	///	87	3
90 - 94	89.5 - 94.5	//	92	2

We use fractional class boundaries. One reason for this is that we cannot break up the horizontal axis of the histogram into only integral values. We must do something with the fractional parts. The usual thing to do is to assign all values to the closest integer. Hence our above class boundaries. The appropriate histogram follows.

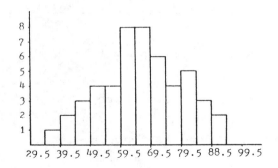

843

We now construct a frequency polygon as follows:

Plot points (x_i, f_i), where x_i is the interval median and f_i, the class frequency. Connect the points by successive line segments.

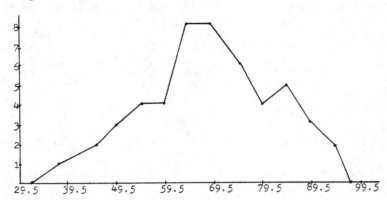

Accounts Receivable

Interval	Interval Median	Frequency (f_i)	Cumulative Frequency	Cumulative Percentage
35 - 39	37	1	1	2
40 - 44	42	2	3	6
45 - 49	47	3	6	12
50 - 54	52	4	10	20
55 - 59	57	4	14	28
60 - 64	62	8	22	44
65 - 69	67	8	30	60
70 - 74	72	6	36	72
75 - 79	77	4	40	80
80 - 84	82	5	45	90
85 - 89	87	3	48	96
90 - 94	92	2	50	100

The cumulative frequency is the number of values in all classes up to and including that class. It is obtained by addition. For example, the cumulative frequency for 65 - 69 is 1 + 2 + 3 + 4 + 4 + 8 + 8 = 30. The cumulative percentage is the percent of all observed values found in that class or below. We can use the formula -

$$\text{cumulative percentage} = \frac{\text{cumulative frequency}}{\text{total observations}} \times 100 \text{ \%}.$$

For example, Cum. per. (65-69) $= \frac{30}{50} \times 100 \text{ \%} = 60 \text{ \%}.$

We construct the cumulative percentage ogive by plotting points x_i, f_i) where x_i is the interval median and f_i is the cumulative percentage. Finally we connect the points with successive line segments.

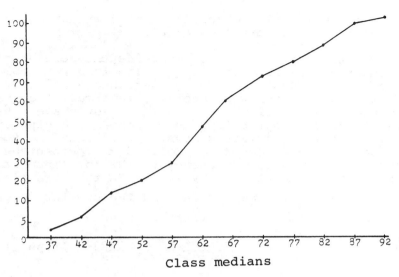

Class medians

● PROBLEM 20-36

In the following chart, make 2 additional columns and fill in the cumulative frequencies and cumulative percentages. Also draw a histogram and a cumulative frequency diagram.

Relative Frequency Distribution of 100 Sixth-Grade Students and their Weights

Class	Frequency (f_i)	Relative Frequency	Percentage Distribution
59-61	4	4/100	4
62-64	8	8/100	8
65-67	12	12/100	12
68-70	13	13/100	13
71-73	21	21/100	21
74-76	15	15/100	15
77-79	12	12/100	12
80-82	9	9/100	9
83-85	4	4/100	4
86-88	2	2/100	2
	100		100%

Solution: The relative frequency of a class is found by dividing the class frequency by the total number of observations in the sample. The results, when multiplied by 100, form a percentage distribution. The class relative frequencies and the percentage distribution of the weights of 100 sixth grade students are given in the above table.

The relative frequency of a class is the empirical probability that a random observation from the population will fall into that class. For example, the relative frequency of the class 59-61 in the table is 4/100, and therefore, the empirical probability that a random observation falling in this interval is 4/100.

The table allows us to determine the percentage of the observations in a sample that lie in a particular class. When we want to know the percentage of observations that is above or below a specified interval, the cumulative frequency distribution can be used to advantage. The cumulative frequency distribution is obtained by adding the frequencies in all classes less than or equal to the class with which we are concerned. To find the percentage in each class just divide the frequency by the total number of observations and multiply by 100 %. In this example, $\frac{x}{100} \times 100 \% = x \%$. Now we can find the cumulative percentages by taking the cumulative frequencies.

$$\text{Cum. percentage} = \frac{y \text{ cumulative frequency}}{\text{total observations}} \times 100 \% =$$

$$= \frac{y}{100} \times 100\% = y\%.$$

Cumulative Frequency and Cumulative Percentage Distribution of the 100 Sixth-Grade Students

Class	Frequency (f_i)	Cumulative Frequency	Cumulative Percentage
59-61	4	4	4
62-64	8	12	12
65-67	12	24	24
68-70	13	37	37
71-73	21	58	58
74-76	15	73	73
77-79	21	85	85
80-82	9	94	94
83-85	4	98	98
86-89	2	100	100 %
	100		

The data in a frequency distribution may be represented graphically by a histogram. The histogram is constructed by marking off the class boundaries along a horizontal axis and drawing a rectangle to represent each class. The base of the rectangle corresponds to the class width, and the height to that class' frequency. See the accompanying histogram depicting the data on the table in the beginning of the problem. Note that the areas above the various classes are proportional to the frequency of those classes.

Often a frequency polygon is used instead of a histogram. In constructing a frequency polygon, the points (x_i, f_i) are plotted on horizontal and vertical axes. The polygon is completed by adding a class mark with zero frequency to each end of the distribution and joining all the points with line segments. The frequency diagram for the data in this problem follows:

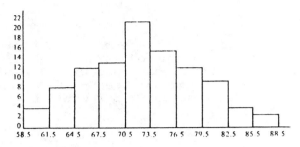

Frequency Histogram of the Weights of the 100
Sixth-Grade Students

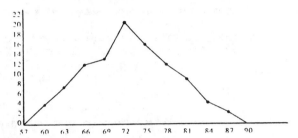

Frequency Polygon of the Weights of 100 Sixth-Grade
Students

A frequency polygon may also be constructed by
connecting the midpoints of the bars in a frequency
histogram by a series of line segments. The main advantage of the frequency polygon compared to the frequency
histogram is that it indicates that the observations in
the interval are not all the same. Also, when several
sets of data are to be shown on the same graph, it is
clearer to superimpose frequency polygons than histograms,
especially if class boundaries coincide.

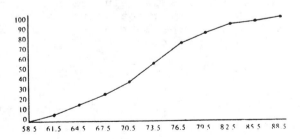

Class Boundaries

Cumulative Frequency Graph of the Weights of 100 Sixth-
Grade Students

It is often advantageous and desirable to make a graph
showing the cumulative frequency within a sample. The
data for such a graph depicting the cumulative frequency
of the weights of the 100 sixth grade students are found
in column three of the table in the solution. The graph,
called an ogive, is illustrated below. To avoid the
confusion of less than or greater than, the class boundaries are plotted on the horizontal axis rather than the

interval medians.

A cumulative frequency graph makes it easy to read such items as the percentage of students whose weights are less than or greater than a specified weight. If the cumulative percentage had been plotted, the graph would appear the same as above but would be called a percentage ogive.

● **PROBLEM 20-37**

Find the mode of the sample 14, 16, 21, 19, 18, 24 and 17.

Solution: In this sample all the numbers occur with the same frequency. There is no single number which is observed more frequently than any other. Thus there is no mode or all observations are modes. The mode is not a useful concept here.

● **PROBLEM 20-38**

The number of home runs the Boston Red Sox hit in eight consecutive games were 2, 3, 0, 3, 4, 1, 3, 0.

(a) What is the mean number of home runs hit?
(b) What is the median?
(c) What is the mode?

Solution: (a) The mean number of home runs hit is the average per game.

$$\overline{X} = \frac{\Sigma \; x_i}{n} = \frac{2 + 3 + 0 + 3 + 4 + 1 + 3 + 0}{8} = \frac{16}{8} = 2.$$

(b)   The median is the middle value. Since we have an even numbered sample we take the value halfway between the two central values, the fourth and fifth. We must put the data in ascending order,

$$0, \; 0, \; 1, \; 2, \; 3, \; 3, \; 3, \; 4 \; .$$

The median will be 2.5, the value which is halfway between 2 and 3.

(c)   The observation 3 appears most often, three times, and is the mode.

● **PROBLEM 20-39**

Given the following set of ungrouped measurements

3, 5, 6, 6, 7, and 9,

determine the mean, median, and mode.

Solution: The mean is the average value of the measurements,

$$\bar{X} = \frac{\sum_i x_i}{n} = \frac{3 + 5 + 6 + 6 + 7 + 9}{6} = \frac{36}{6} = 6.$$

The median is the middle value. Since we have an even number of measurements, we take as the median the value halfway between the 2 middle values. In this case the 2 middle values are both 6 and hence the median is

$$\frac{6 + 6}{2} = 6.$$

The mode is the most common value. Therefore, it is 6, the same as the mean and the median.

● **PROBLEM 20-40**

Consider the distribution of the previous problem. Let us add 2 relatively high values in order to observe the differential effect on the three measures of central tendency. Use the following eight ordered values: 3, 5, 6, 6, 7, 9, 16, 20.

Solution: (a) First the mean.

$$\bar{X} = \frac{\sum_i x_i}{n} = \frac{3 + 5 + 6 + 6 + 7 + 9 + 16 + 20}{8} = \frac{72}{8} = 9.$$

We have 8 (an even number) observations. The median will be halfway between the two middle ones, the fourth and fifth. Halfway between 6 and 7 is 6.5. The mode is still easily found. The only value that appears more than once is still 6.

Comparing the measures of central tendency for the data of the last two problems, we find that the measure which is most affected by the addition of extreme measurements is the mean; the measure which is only somewhat affected is the median; the measure which is unaffected is the mode.

● **PROBLEM 20-41**

For this series of observations find the mean, median, and mode.

500, 600, 800, 800, 900, 900, 900, 900, 900, 1000, 1100

Solution: The mean is the value obtained by adding all the measurements and dividing by the numbers of measurements.

$$\bar{X} = \frac{\sum_i x_i}{n}$$

$$\bar{X} = \frac{500+600+800+800+900+900+900+900+900+1000+1100}{11}$$

$$\overline{X} = \frac{9300}{11} = 845.45.$$

The median is the observation in the middle. We have 11, so here it is the sixth, 900.

The mode is the observation that appears most frequently. That is also 900, which has 5 appearances.

All three of these numbers are measures of central tendency. They describe the "middle" or "center" of the data.

● **PROBLEM 20-42**

Nine rats run through a maze. The time each rat took to traverse the maze is recorded and these times are listed below.

    1 min., 2.5 min., 3 min., 1.5 min., 2 min.,
       1.25 min., 1 min., .9 min., 30 min.

Which of the three measures of central tendency would be the most appropriate in this case?

Solution: We will calculate the three measures of central tendency and then compare them to determine which would be the most appropriate in describing these data.

The mean, $\overline{X}$, is the sum of observations divided by the number of observations. In this case,

$$\overline{X} = \frac{1 + 2.5 + 3 + 1.5 + 2 + 1.25 + 1 + .9 + 30}{9}$$

$$= \frac{43.15}{9} = 4.79.$$

The median is the "middle number" in an array of the observations from the lowest to the highest.

    0.9, 1.0, 1.0, 1.25, 1.5, 2.0, 2.5, 3.0, 30.0

The median is the fifth observation in this array or 1.5. There are four observations larger than 1.5 and four observations smaller than 1.5.

The mode is the most frequently occurring observation in the sample. In this data set the mode is 1.0.

    mean, $\overline{X}$ = 4.79

    median = 1.5

    mode   = 1.0

The mean is not appropriate here. Only one rat took

more than   4.79 minutes to run the maze and this rat took 30 minutes. We see that the mean has been distorted by this one large observation.

The median or mode seem to describe this data set better and   would be more appropriate to use.

● **PROBLEM 20-43**

A family had eight children. The ages were 9, 11, 8, 15, 14, 12, 17, 14.

(a) Find the measures of central tendency for the data.
(b) Find the range of the data.

Solution: (a) The mean is the average age.

$$\bar{X} = \frac{\Sigma \ x_i}{n} = \frac{9 + 11 + 8 + 15 + 14 + 12 + 17 + 14}{8}$$

$$= \frac{100}{8} = 12.5 \text{ years.}$$

The median is the middle value. To find it, first we must arrange our data in ascending order;

8, 9, 11, 12, 14, 14, 15, 17.

We have an even number of measurements, eight.

The median will be the midway point between the fourth and fifth observations, 12 and 14. The median is 13.

The mode is the most common age. Only one age, 14, appears more than once. 14 must be the mode.

(b)   Often we want to know how spread out the observations of data were . The range of the sample is a quantity which measures dispersion. We define the range to be the difference between the largest and smallest observations in our sample. In this case, R   = 17 - 8 = 9.

● **PROBLEM 20-44**

Find the range of the sample composed of the observations: 33, 53, 35, 37, 49.

Solution: The range is a measure of dispersion of the sample and is defined to be the difference between the largest and smallest observations.

In our sample, the largest observation is 53 and the smallest is 33. The difference is 53 - 33 = 20 and the range is 20.

The range is not a very satisfactory measure of dispersion as it involves only two of the observations in the sample.

When is it preferable to use the mode or median rather than the mean to describe central tendency?

Solution: Suppose a class of 15 students obtained the following scores in a mid-term exam: 48, 49, 68, 69, 71, 73, 73, 73, 75, 75, 76, 77, 78, 97, 99. The mean arithmetic average is

$$\frac{1100}{15} = 73.3.$$

The mode, the score which occurs most frequently, is 73 and the median, the "middle" score is 73. In this case there is hardly any difference between the three measures of central tendency.

Now suppose another class of 15 students obtains the scores: 46, 46, 46, 47, 47, 49, 56, 58, 58, 59, 62, 92, 95, 97, 99. The mean in this case is

$$\frac{957}{15} = 63.8.$$

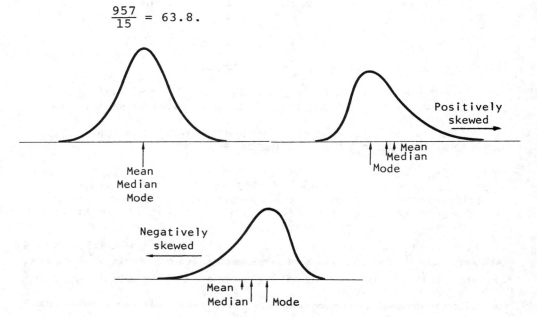

Location of the mean, median, and mode in symmetrical, positively-skewed and negatively-skewed distributions.

However, most of the students scored below 63. Thus the mean here is not a good measure of central tendency. A better measure is the median (the median is that value in the population which is greater than 50% and less than 50% of the remaining values, the "middle score." Here the median is the 8th score, i.e., 58. The mean was not a good estimator of central tendency in this case because a few bright students raised the arithmetic average, mean of the class by obtaining almost the maximum number of points. In collegiate slang, they "raised the curve." Finally, an example of a population where the mode is the best measure of central tendency. Suppose our students scored as follows: 80, 80, 80, 80, 80, 80, 80, 80, 80, 80, 80, 80, 80, 0, 0. What score best represents the performance of the group? What is the best measure of central tendency? Clearly it is the score that occurs most frequently, the mode, in this example--80. (Notice that in this example the median is also 80, however 80 is better chosen by observing that it occurs with overwhelming frequency, the fact that it is also the "middle" score is secondary.) The mode is most useful in situations where measures of the dependent variable are usually very similar (if not identical), but that occasionally a measurement varies drastically (in our example perhaps the two zeros are the result of not answering the questions in the prescribed manner). In a situation where there is greater variance among scores, for example: 50, 70, 71, 72, 73, 74, 75, 76, 76, 76, 90, it is probably preferable to use the mean (74) rather than the mode (76). Notice that the presence of extreme scores (50 and 90) makes the mean an undesirable measure of central tendency.

● **PROBLEM** 20-46

What are the most important sampling statistics? What distributions do they belong to?

Solution: Statistics is concerned with making inferences about population parameters on the basis of random samples chosen from populations. Sampling statistics are approximations of the population parameters. For example, the sample mean is said to approximate the population mean. The most important sampling statistics are the sample mean and the sample variance. To illustrate the meanings of these terms, consider the following example. A psychologist selects a sample of 32 rats and records the time they take to complete a maze. The times are

χ (Time)	f(x) # of rats	xf(x)
29	1	29
31	1	31
32	2	64
33	2	66
34	3	102
35	4	140
36	5	180
37	5	185
38	4	152
39	2	78
40	2	80
41	1	41

The sample average (mean) is found by adding up the

xf(x) column and dividing by 32. Thus, x (mean) = 35.9.
The computation of the sample variance is more involved
but can be found to be 7.6 using the formula

$$s^2 = \frac{\Sigma f_i (x_i - \bar{x})^2}{n-1}$$. Where each value (x_i) is subtracted

from the mean $(\bar{x})$ and squared, each of these squared
values are summed and the total is divided by the number
of values (rats) giving the variance (7.6). In the
absence of prior research the psychologist assumes that
the times are normally distributed. Thus the population
consists of all the rats that could conceivably run
through the maze and the population is described by
the average time and variance.

What can the psychologist say about the parent
population on the basis of the sample and calculated
sample statistics? He cannot definitely assert that the
population mean and variance are 35.9 and 7.6. Different
samples would no doubt yield different sample means
and sample variances. Thus the best he can do is give
an interval within which the population mean is most
likely to fall (and similarly for the population variance).
In order to make such a statement he must know something
about the population of sample means and the population
of sample variances, i.e. their distributions.

If the psychologist were to take an infinite
number of samples, then, according to the Central Limit
Theorem, the distribution of the sample means will
approximate a normal distribution with mean μ and

variance $\frac{\sigma^2}{N}$ (where N is sample size). The sampling

distribution of the sample variance is more complicated.
It is known as the Chi-Square distribution. We say that

the statistic $\frac{(n-1)s^2}{\sigma^2}$ has a χ^2 distribution with n-1

degrees of freedom. The χ^2 values can be found from a

table. Since $\frac{\Sigma (x_i - \bar{x})^2}{n-1} = s^2$ is calculated from the sample,

this enables us to make probability statements concerning
σ^2, the population variance.

Thus the sample mean of a sample of size η taken from

a population with mean μ and variance σ^2 has a normal

distribution with mean μ and variance σ^2/n. The sample

variance (the ratio $(n-1)s^2/\sigma^2$) from the same population

has the χ^2 distribution with n-1 degrees of freedom.

Given the values 4, 4, 6, 7, 9 give the deviation of each from the mean.

Solution: First find the mean.

$$\overline{X} = \frac{\Sigma\ x_i}{n} = \frac{4 + 4 + 6 + 7 + 9}{5} = \frac{30}{5} = 6.$$

$X - \overline{X}$ = the deviation from the mean.

We will provide the deviations in tabular form.

X	$X - \overline{X}$
4	4 - 6 = - 2
4	4 - 6 = - 2
6	6 - 6 = 0
7	7 - 6 = + 1
9	9 - 6 = + 3

Find the variance of the sample of observations 2, 5, 7, 9, 12.

Solution: The variance of the sample is defined as

$$s^2 = \frac{\Sigma\ (X_i - \overline{X})^2}{n}$$. This is an average of the squared deviations from the sample mean, $\overline{X}$.

$$\overline{X} = \frac{\Sigma\ x_i}{n} = \frac{2 + 5 + 7 + 9 + 12}{5} = \frac{35}{5} = 7$$

and $$s^2 = \frac{(2-7)^2 + (5-7)^2 + (7-7)^2 + (9-7)^2 + (12-7)^2}{5}$$

$$= \frac{25 + 4 + 0 + 4 + 25}{5} = \frac{58}{5} = 11.6.$$

A couple has six children whose ages are 6, 8, 10, 12, 14, and 16. Find the variance in ages.

Solution: The variance in ages is a measure of the spread or dispersion of ages about the sample mean.

To compute the variance we first calculate the sample mean.

$$\overline{X} = \frac{\Sigma X_i}{n} = \frac{\text{sum of observations}}{\text{number of observations}}$$

$$= \frac{6 + 8 + 10 + 12 + 14 + 16}{6} = \frac{66}{6} = 11.$$

The variance is defined to be

$$s^2 = \frac{\sum\limits_{i=1}^{n} (X_i - \overline{X})^2}{n}$$

$$= \frac{(6-11)^2 + (8-11)^2 + (10-11)^2 + (12-11)^2 + (14-11)^2 + (16-11)^2}{6}$$

$$= \frac{25 + 9 + 1 + 1 + 9 + 25}{6} = \frac{70}{6} = 11.7.$$

● **PROBLEM** 20-50

From the sample of data 5, 8, 2, 1, compute the standard deviation of the sample.

Solution: The degree to which numerical data tends to spread about an average value is usually called dispersion or variation of the data. One way to measure the degree of dispersion is with the standard deviation. We define it as

$$s = \sqrt{\frac{\sum\limits_i (X_i - \overline{X})^2}{n}} \quad .$$

It gives a feeling for how far away from the mean we can expect an observation to be. Sometimes the standard deviation for the data of a sample is defined with n - 1 replacing n in the denominator of our expression. The resulting value represents a "better" estimate of the true standard deviation of the entire population. For large n (n > 30) there is practically no difference between the 2 values. Let us find the mean for our sample.

$$\overline{X} = \frac{\Sigma X_i}{n} = \frac{5 + 8 + 2 + 1}{n} = \frac{16}{4} = 4 \quad .$$

X_i	$X_i - \overline{X}$	$(X_i - \overline{X})^2$
5	5 - 4 = 1	$1^2 = 1$
8	8 - 4 = 4	$4^2 = 16$
2	2 - 4 = -2	$(-2)^2 = 4$
1	1 - 4 = -3	$(-3)^2 = 9$

$$\Sigma (X_i - \overline{X})^2 = 1 + 16 + 4 + 9 = 30$$

$$n = 4$$

$$s = \sqrt{\frac{\Sigma (X_i - \overline{X})^2}{n}} = \sqrt{\frac{30}{4}} = \sqrt{\frac{15}{2}} = \sqrt{7.5} = 2.74.$$

Find the standard deviation of the sample of measurements 1, 3, 7, 10, 14.

Solution: We first compute,

$$\overline{X} = \frac{\Sigma X_i}{n} = \frac{1 + 3 + 7 + 10 + 14}{5} = \frac{35}{5} = 7,$$

the sample mean. Next we compute the standard deviation, s, a measure of dispersion about the sample mean.

$$s = \sqrt{\frac{\sum\limits_{i=1}^{n} (X_i - \overline{X})^2}{n}}$$

$$= \sqrt{\frac{(1-7)^2+(3-7)^2+(7-7)^2+(10-7)^2+(14-7)^2}{5}}$$

$$= \sqrt{\frac{36 + 16 + 0 + 9 + 49}{5}} = \sqrt{22} = 4.69.$$

A survey asking for the number of times toast is burned during one week was distributed to eight randomly selected households. The survey yielded the following results:

$$2, 3, 0, 3, 4, 1, 3, 0.$$

What is the range, variance and standard deviation for this data set?

Solution: The range is the difference between the largest and smallest observations is 4 - 0 = 4.

The variance is the mean   or average squared deviation from $\overline{X}$. To compute the variance of this sample we use the formula

$$s^2 = \frac{\Sigma X^2 - n\overline{X}^2}{n} \quad .$$

To facilitate the computation we use the following table,

X	X^2
2	4
3	9
0	0
3	9
4	16
1	1
3	9
0	0
$\Sigma X = 16$	$\Sigma X^2 = 48$

Thus $\quad \overline{X} = \dfrac{\Sigma X}{n} = \dfrac{16}{8} = 2 \quad$ and

$$s^2 = \frac{48 - 8(2)^2}{8} = \frac{48 - 8(4)}{8} = \frac{16}{8} = 2 \ .$$

The standard deviation is

$$s = \sqrt{s^2} = \sqrt{2} = 1.414.$$

● **PROBLEM** 20-53

What is the relative measure of skewness for the data listed below? This data represents the waist measurements of six randomly selected chocolate rabbits.

3 inches,   2 inches,   3.7 inches,   5 inches,
2.7 inches,   3 inches.

<u>Solution:</u>   The relative measure of symmetry is defined to be $\quad a_3 = \dfrac{m_3}{s^3} \quad$ where s^3 is the standard deviation cubed and m_3 is the third moment.

The third moment is defined as;

$$m_3 = \frac{\Sigma (X_i - \overline{X})^3}{n} \ .$$

We have encountered other examples of moments. The first moment is

$$m_1 = \frac{\Sigma (X_i - \overline{X})^1}{n} \ .$$

We can see that this moment has only one value.

$$m_1 = \frac{\Sigma (X_i - \overline{X})^1}{n} = \frac{\Sigma X_i}{n} - \frac{n\overline{X}}{n} = \frac{\Sigma X_i}{n} - \overline{X}$$

but $\quad \overline{X} = \dfrac{\Sigma X_i}{n} \quad$ thus $\quad m_1 = 0$.

The second moment is $\quad \dfrac{\Sigma (X_i - X)^2}{n} \quad$ or the sample

858

variance.

The fourth moment is defined as

$$m_4 = \frac{\Sigma(X_i - \overline{X})^4}{n} \ .$$

The measure of symmetry has the following interpretation, if $a_3 = \frac{m_3}{s^3}$ is equal to zero, the distribution is symmetrical. If $a_3 < 0$ then the distribution is negatively skewed. If $a_3 > 0$ the distribution is positively skewed.

To calculate the measure of symmetry we use the table below:

X_i	$\overline{X}$	$(X_i - \overline{X})$	$(X_i - \overline{X})^2$	$(X_i - \overline{X})^3$
3	3.23	- .23	.053	- .012
2	3.23	- 1.23	1.51	- 1.86
3.7	3.23	.47	.22	.103
5	3.23	1.77	3.13	5.54
2.7	3.23	- .53	.28	- .148
3	3.23	- .23	.053	- .012

$$\Sigma(X_i - \overline{X})^2 = 5.246 \qquad \Sigma(X_i - \overline{X})^3 = 3.611$$

$$s^2 = \frac{\Sigma(X_i - \overline{X})^2}{n} = \frac{5.246}{6} = .8743$$

$$s = \sqrt{s^2} = .9351$$

$$s^3 = .817$$

$$m_3 = \frac{\Sigma(X_i - \overline{X})^3}{n} = \frac{3.611}{6} = .6018$$

and $a_3 = \frac{m_3}{s^3} = \frac{.6018}{.817} = .73659$.

The distribution of the chocolate rabbits' waist measurements is skewed to the right or positively skewed.

● **PROBLEM** 20-54

What are two ways to describe the form of a frequency distribution? How would the following distributions be described?

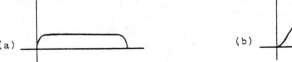

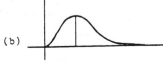

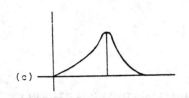 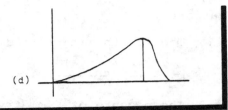

(c)　　　　　　　　　　　　　(d)

Solution:　　　The form of a frequency distribution can be described by its departure from symmetry or skewness and its degree of peakedness or kurtosis.

If the few extreme values are higher than most of the others, we say that the distribution is "positively skewed" or "skewed" to the right.

If the few extreme values are lower than most of the others, we say that the distribution is "negatively skewed" or "skewed" to the left.

A distribution that is very flat is called "platykurtic" and a distribution that has a high peak is called "leptokurtic".

(a) This curve is quite flat indicating a wide dispersion of measurements. Thus it is platykurtic.

(b) This distribution has extreme values in the upper half of the curve and is skewed to the right or positively skewed.

(c) This frequency distribution is very peaked and is　　　leptokurtic.

(d) The extreme values of this distribution are in the lower half of the curve. Thus the distribution is negatively skewed or skewed to the left.

● **PROBLEM** 20-55

Find the degree of skewness of the distribution representing these data.

Class Limit	Frequency	Class Midpoint
49-54	6	51.5
55-60	15	57.5
61-66	24	63.5
67-72	33	69.5
73-78	22	75.5

Solution:　　　We compute our measure of skewness $a_4 = \frac{m_3}{s^3}$ from the following table. First compute the mean, $\overline{X}$.

$$X = \frac{\Sigma f_i X_i}{\Sigma f_i}$$

$$= [6(51.5) + 15(57.5) + 24(63.5) + 33(69.5)$$

860

$$+ 22(75.5)] \div 100$$

$$= 66.5.$$

In tabular form we see;

Class	Frequency f_i	Class Mark X_i	$\overline{X}$	$(X_i - \overline{X})$	$f_i(X_i - \overline{X})^2$	$f_i(X_i - \overline{X})^3$
49–54	6	51.5	66.5	− 15	6(225)=1350	− 20250
55–60	15	57.5	66.5	− 9	15(81)=1215	− 10935
61–66	24	63.5	66.5	− 3	24(9)=216	− 648
67–72	33	69.5	66.5	3	33(9)=297	891
73–78	22	75.5	66.5	9	22(81)=1782	16038

$$\Sigma f_i = 100 \qquad \Sigma f_i (X_i - \overline{X})^2 = 4860$$

$$\Sigma f_i (X_i - \overline{X})^3 = -14904 .$$

It is now possible to compute the standard deviation, s, and the third moment, m_3.

$$s = \sqrt{s^2} = \sqrt{\frac{\Sigma f_i (X_i - \overline{X})^2}{\Sigma f_i}} = \sqrt{\frac{4860}{100}}$$

$$= \sqrt{48.60} = 6.97$$

$$s^3 = (6.97)^3 = 338.675$$

$$m_3 = \frac{\Sigma f_i (X_i - \overline{X})^3}{\Sigma f_i} = \frac{-14904}{100} = -149.04$$

$$a_3 = \frac{m_3}{s^3} = \frac{-149.04}{338.675} = -.44 .$$

The distribution from which these observations are drawn is slightly negatively skewed.

● **PROBLEM** 20-56

What is the correlation coefficient and where is it useful?

Solution: Correlation analysis measures the degree of linear association between two characteristics, say x and y. For example, it is generally found that the height and weight of a person are positively correlated.

This means that the taller people are, the more they will weigh. Studies also show that intelligence affects college grades; they are said to be positively correlated.

Typically in correlational research the characteristics being studied are set and cannot be manipulated by the investigator. Thus, each element in the sample (or population) has two characteristics and we are trying to find out if there is any association between these characteristics.

Fig. 1 shows how long rats with prior training took to traverse a maze. As training time increased, travel time decreased and vice-versa. The variables, training time and travel time, are inversely (negatively) correlated. Here, the variable 'training time' could be controlled by the investigator.

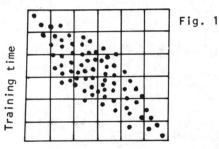

Fig. 1

Training time

Travel time

The correlation coefficient is denoted by r, when referring to the sample and e (the Greek letter rho) when referring to the population. Statisticians have devised many methods of computing r for two sets of data. A property of r necessary for its interpretation is that r always lies between +1 and -1.

What does a value of r = +1 indicate? Since the correlation coefficient indicates the degree of linear association between two variables, r = 1 means that x and y are perfectly correlated. That is, as x increases y increases by a proportionate amount.

Fig. 2 graphically demonstrates perfect correlation. Note that all the observations fall on the same straight line (hence a perfect "linear relation").

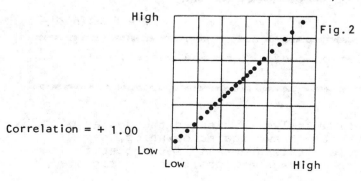

High

Fig.2

Correlation = + 1.00

Low

Low   High

When r = -1, there is a perfect negative correlation and the association between x and y is of the inverse type.

In Fig. 3, the line on which all the observations fall has a negative slope showing that as y decreases, x increases by a proportionate amount.

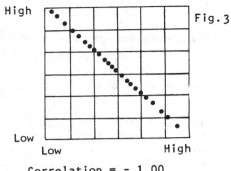

Fig. 3

Correlation = - 1.00

Finally, in Fig. 4, when r = 0, there is no correlation between x and y and they are said to be independent.

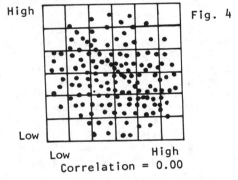

Fig. 4

Correlation = 0.00

Note that increases in y are sometimes accompanied by decreases and sometimes by increases in x. Thus there is no linear association between them.

Students of statistics are always warned against confusing correlation and causation. Correlation is a mathematical technique for showing whether elements in two sets of data are associated with each other while the idea of causality is a remnant of Medieval Scholastic philosophy ('every event has a cause': this implies that every event is the effect of some cause). It is perfectly possible for two phenomena to be correlated without one causing, or being caused by, the other. Thus the sale of Swiss watches has been correlated to the incidence of reported toothaches in Italy but no one would argue that one variable was the cause of the other (unless for some reason Italians like to eat Swiss watches). Similarly a study found that as the number of high school teachers in a district increased, so did the number of alcoholics. Again, teachers did not cause the increase in liquor intake: both variables were subsequently found to be explained by a rise in per capita income in that district.

Correlation analysis is used to determine which independent variables account for variation in a given dependent variable. The task of prediction is then taken over by the use of "regression analysis," a much more complicated statistical tool.

● **PROBLEM** 20-57

What are standard scores and percentiles and why are they important?

Solution: A standard score is a way of expressing an individual's raw score on a test in terms of its distance from the mean score of a tested group. The distance from the mean score is expressed in terms of the standard deviation of the distribution. The standard deviation is a measure of the variability or spread of scores in a group, that is a score of 1 corresponds to whatever score is 1 standard deviation above the mean. A score of -1.7 is whatever score is 1.7 times the standard deviation below the mean. A score of 0 corresponds to the mean. Therefore if the mean in a distribution was 100 and the standard deviation was 10 a standard score of 1 would correspond to a raw score of 110. A standard score of -1.7 would correspond to a raw score of 83. The examiner needs to know only the standard score in order to interpret an individual's performance. He wants to know where the individual stands in relation to the rest of the examinees; he does not need to know the raw score. From statistical tables the examiner can tell exactly what percentage of the people scored above and below the individual in question.

Percentiles are a way of expressing scores in terms of the percentage of persons in the standardized sample who fall below a given raw score. For example, if a raw score of 70 is in the 90th percentile, then 90 percent of the sample obtained raw scores below 70. Percentage scores are not the same as percentiles. A percentage score refers to the percentage of problems answered correctly; percentages are expressed in terms of raw scores and percentiles are derived scores. A derived score, e.g. a percentile, gives the examiner information about an individual's relative standing in a group. Raw scores cannot be interpreted in the same manner.

Standard scores and percentiles are important in that they help the examiner compare different individuals on the same test and the same individual on different tests. A standard score of 1.0 always means the same thing; it always corresponds to doing better than average (in fact, it always means that an individual's score is in the 84th percentile and therefore 84% of the examinees scored lower than he did). Regardless of the type of test taken a score expressed in terms of percentiles

864

or in terms of the standard deviation (standard scores) always has the same relative meaning vis a vis group comparisons.

SHORT ANSWER QUESTIONS FOR REVIEW

Choose the correct answer.

1. All of the following are averages commonly used
   in interpreting data except (a) mean (b)
   median (c) frequency (d) mode   c

2. When is it preferable to use the median rather
   than the mean of a distribution of scores? (a)
   when extreme scores would affect the average
   disproportionately (b) when the standard deviation is also needed (c) when the data is taken
   from ratio scales (d) when the mean does not
   fall squarely on an integral value   a

3. The reliability coefficient is a measure of (a)
   whether or not the test is measuring what it is
   supposed to measure (b) whether or not the
   trait being tested is related to other traits
   in the individual (c) how consistently the
   subject will maintain his position within the
   sample group on an equivalent test (d) none
   of the above   c

4. What percent of the scores in a distribution
   fall between the median and the third quartile?
   (a) 33 (b) 25 (c) 65 (d) 50   b

5. Which of the following is not a characteristic
   of ideal scientific observations? (a) being
   repeatable (b) having a visual component (c)
   being verifiable (d) A and C   b

6. A few extreme scores in a distribution (a)
   will affect the value of the median more than
   that of the mean (b) will affect the value of
   the mean more than that of the median (c) will
   affect the values of the mean and median equally
   (d) will affect the value of the mode more than
   that of the mean   b

7. If the reliability coefficient of a test is .16
   then the validity coefficient between the test
   and the independent criterion which it is index-
   ing cannot be greater than (a) .04 (b) .16
   (c) .40 (d) .016   c

8. In the T-score distribution of derived scores,
   (a) the mean is set at 100 and the standard deviation at 10 (b) the mean is set at 0 and the
   standard deviation at 10 (c) the mean is set at
   75 and the standard deviation at 15 (d) the
   mean is set at 50 and the standard deviation at
   10   d

866

SHORT ANSWER QUESTIONS FOR REVIEW

9. The pattern of sampling variability is known if the sampling is (a) random (b) from two related populations (c) the result of experienced judgment (d) none of the above

a

10. You have statistically tested the difference between two means in your experiment. You would have the most confidence in them if you found the differences to be on what significance level? (a) .05 (b) .1 (c) .01 (d) .001

d

11. Which of the following is not a measure of the variability of a set of scores? (a) average deviation (b) standard deviation (c) deviation ratio (d) square root of variance

c

12. The theory of statistical regression would predict that (a) fathers of short stature are likely to have somewhat taller sons (b) fathers of average height are likely to have sons who are somewhat shorter (c) a certain proportion of the population will exhibit atavistic behavior (d) a certain proportion of the population will exhibit repressed behavior

a

13. The term "non-parametric" statistics refers to a variety of statistical procedures which (a) require at least an interval scale if their use is to be valid (b) make no assumptions regarding the form of the population-distribution (c) make assumptions about the reliability of the data (d) require normally distributed data

b

14. Random assignment of a different number to each person in a group is an example of (a) an ordinal scale (b) a ratio scale (c) a nominal scale (d) an interval scale

c

15. The prime objection to introspective observations in psychology is that they (a) involve too many people (b) are not verifiable (c) are irrelevant to psychology (d) its based on logic

b

16. Scientific findings are always (a) ultimate truths (b) simple correlations (c) tentative statements (d) consistent

c

17. The median may be regarded as a(n) (a) additive measure (b) rank measure (c) ratio measure (d) none of the above

b

18. The case in which scores in one distribution decrease as scores in the other increase is best

represented by a correlation coefficient of   (a)
-1.0   (b)   +1.0   (c)   0   (d)   +3.0   a

19.   Given a sample mean, a range of values within
which the parametric mean must lie can be computed.   This is the   (a)   parametric deviation   (b)
variability range   (c)   mode   (d)   confidence
interval   d

20.   Which of the following characterizes a control
group?   (a)   it does not receive the experimental
treatment   (b)   it serves as a baseline   (c)   it
is necessary in a double-blind experiment   (d)
all of the above   d

21.   As the standard deviation of a distribution gets
smaller, one should expect the individual scores
of the distribution   (a)   will cluster closer
about the mean   (b)   will remain the same in
amount of scatter about the mean   (c)   will scatter more widely about the mean   (d)   none of the
above   a

22.   A frequency distribution will often approach the
normal distribution as   (a)   the number of scores
included gets very large   (b)   the number of
scores gets very small   (c)   more variables are
included in the frequency distribution   (d)   certain scores are elminated from the distribution   a

23.   If a distribution had 20 scores, what would be
the percentile ranking of the score that fell in
the 15th position from the bottom? (a)   15th
percentile   (b)   50th percentile   (c)   75th percentile   (d)   300th percentile   c

24.   Inferential statistics are used primarily to
(a)   avoid the use of random samples   (b)   describe the characteristics of large groups of
data   (c)   infer the mean and standard deviation of the sample   (d)   make generalizations
to the world-at-large   d

25.   When trying to establish a difference between
two groups, one usually assumes that   (a)   one
will not need to resort to inferential statistics   (b)   there is no difference between the
groups   (c)   the difference between the two
groups is very large   (d) one will be able to
specify the exact difference in the general
populations   b

26.   A significant correlation means that (a)   a high

SHORT ANSWER QUESTIONS FOR REVIEW

correlation is more likely to exist between
significant variables (b) the likelihood of
getting a correlation that large is very large
(c) a relationship is likely to exist between
the two variables in the general population
(d) all of the above

c

Fill in the blanks.

27. A study which followed a group of subjects over
a period of several years would be a _____ study.

longi-
tudinal

28. If the raw score is 25, mean = 20 and standard
deviation = 4 the z-score is _____.

+ 1.25

29. That value of a variable which occurs most often
is called the _____ .

mode

30. The "learning capacity" of a subject is an
example of a(n) _____ variable.

inter-
vening

31. Those variables that scientists manipulate in
order to produce effects are _____ variables.

inde-
pendent

32. The sum of all scores divided by the number of
scores is the _____ .

mean

33. Measurements describing an entire population are
_____ .

para-
meters

34. Scales in which the units are equal in size are
_____ scales.

interval

35. If each element in a population has an equal
chance of being chosen for a sample, the sampling
is _____ .

random

36. Graphically presented material in which a bar
represents the number of cases in an interval
of measurement is a _____ .

histo-
gram

37. The measure usually used to determine the variability of a set of scores around the mean value
is the _____ .

standard
deviation

38. The number of standard deviation units a score is
from its mean is called the _____ score.

standard

39. The _____ procedure is used to ensure that experimental bias will not occur and entails both

869

SHORT ANSWER QUESTIONS FOR REVIEW

the experimenter and subjects not knowing which
subjects are in the control and which in the experimental groups. double-blind

40. The hypothesis of "no difference" is called the
_____ hypothesis. Null

41. A transformed score that represents how many
standard deviations above or below the mean a
particular score lies is called a _____ score. Z

Determine whether the following statements are true
or false.

42. A frequency distribution is obtained by recording the number of cases of a sample scoring within each classification interval. True

43. An acceptable test must meet all of the following criteria: discrimination, reliability and
validity. True

44. The normal curve is the basis for much of the
measurement in psychology because it has a
number of valuable properties and statistical
procedures have been worked out for it. True

45. The normal curve is symmetrical, showing the same
slope to the left of its high point as it does
to the right. True

46. Central tendency may only be found by determining the mean. False

47. Standard deviation is the difference between
the highest and lowest scores. False

48. Sixty eight percent of the cases will be between
the score at one standard deviation above and
one standard deviation below the mean. True

49. Percentile scores represent the proportion of
items one gets correct on a test. False

50. The correlation coefficient is a procedure for
determining whether there is a relationship between measures and the degree of relationship. True

51. Correlations may be used to determine cause and
effect. False

52. Reliability indicates the relationship between
test scores and something we wish to predict

SHORT ANSWER QUESTIONS FOR REVIEW

from these scores.

False

53. In general, we do not accept an observed difference between two groups as significant unless the probability of obtaining that difference from procedures of random sampling is low.

True

54. All of the elements in which an investigator is interested define the population of a study.

True

55. The basic aim of the case history approach is to discover important variables associated with the behavior of a single individual.

True

56. An example of a covert psychological variable would be sex.

False

CHAPTER 21

EXPERIMENTAL

FORMAT AND GUIDELINES FOR WRITING REPORTS

Writing the Experimental Report.

An experiment in all areas of psychology is regarded as complete when the results are shared with the scientific community so that other investigators interested in the same topic can have access to the results. Precise and detailed guidelines for professional paper writing and publication can be found in the Publication Manual of the American Psychological Association, 1974, Washington, D.C. The following general information on the preparation of experimental papers has been adopted from the Publication Manual.

Experimental results are usually published in one of approximately 15 American Psychological Association (APA) scientific journals and fall into one of three categories: 1) experimental reports, 2) review articles and 3) theoretical articles. Because experimental reports are by far the most common, they are the focus of the information presented here. Due to the enormous quantity of research and experimentation occuring in the field of psychology, certain specific style conventions have been adopted by the APA and must be followed in any manuscript submitted for publication. This is one of the reasons that the accepted form for these reports is now taught to beginning students. It is also helpful to be familiar with the form of psychological journal articles to facilitate research and study efforts.

The traditional experimental report must consist of definite sections presented in an established order. They are: Title, Author's Name, Institutional Affiliation, Abstract, Introduction, Method, Results, Discussion, References and, if needed, Appendix and Footnotes.

Included here you will find a sample experimental report lay-out. A summary of the guidelines for each particular section follows.

The Title: The title should be placed on a separate page
along with the institutional affiliation and the date of
submission of the article. The title should summarize
(concisely) the main idea of the study. Because the
title is used for library and cross-reference listing, it
is important that it be as clear and succinct as possible
and that it describe accurately the nature of the study.
It is recommended that the title be no longer than 12 to
15 words in length and in the form of a statement. No
abbreviations are to be used. It is also advised to avoid
such phrases as "a study of" or "an experimental investigation of" as these are redundancies that are not necessary
for describing the study. Remember that your title should
tell the reader immediately whether your paper is relevant
to his research interests or not.

Author's Name: A writer should always use the same form
of his or her name when submitting articles. If more
than one person contributed to the implementation and
conception of the experiment, each contributor should be
listed.

Institutional Affiliation: The name of the institution at
which the experiment took place is included under the
author's name. If the writer has no institutional affiliation, the city and state of residence is to be cited.

Abstract

        The abstract is presented on a separate sheet
of paper (i.e. the second page of the report). The abstract is a self-contained summary of the contents and
purpose of the study. It includes only conclusions and
information that appear in the main body of the report.
Because the abstract is also used for reference and listing
purposes and is printed as-is by abstracting services,
it should be a condensed, clear summary of the article.
Because it is so difficult to write, some authors prefer
to leave it until the rest of the article is finished to
make the writing easier. An experimental report abstract
must include the basics of the design, test instruments
or data gathering procedures. If any drugs are used the
full names are to be included. Major findings stated in
a summary fashion should be listed including statistical
significances, if any. Inferences and comparisons should
also be reported.

        The recommended length for an experimental ab-
stract is 100 to 175 words (approximately 12-20 typewritten
lines). A theoretical or review article abstract should
include the central thesis of the topics covered (the nature and content of the theoretical discussion) as well
as the sources used and the conclusions drawn. Recommended
length is 75 to 100 words (6 to 12 typewritten lines).
A well-written and comprehensible abstract increases the
audience that will be attracted to reading it. In summary
the abstract should include the following:

1. Object of investigation (1-3 sentences)

2. Description of process (5-7 sentences)

3. Statement of results (1-3 sentences)

4. Conclusions and implications (1-2 sentences)

(Sometimes it is acceptable to have Title, Author(s), Affiliation and the Abstract all on page 1. This is often the case for laboratory reports in psychology courses. This is not done when the report is to be submitted for review for a journal.)

Introduction

The main purpose of the introduction is to state the question that is asked by the study and the rationale for asking it. The specific problem is described and the research strategy for investigating it is outlined. This section is not, never, labeled "Introduction" as it is self-explanatory. The other sections of the report are, however, labeled. In writing the paper, assume a professional audience, yet do not make the language so technical that only specialists in that particular area can understand the problem, procedures and results. The psychological community as a whole should be the audience to whom the report is written.

The relationship of the problem to the existing work in the field is discussed in the introduction. Authors must acknowledge the contribution of others to the problem under study. It is necessary to show continuity from the past to the present work and by so doing to demonstrate the logic used in arriving at your hypothesis. If you summarize earlier works, include only major conclusions, but, again, do not sacrifice clarity for brevity. Be sure to state controversial issues fairly, even though your paper may go on to support one of them against the other.

It is in the introduction that you will make the formal statement of your hypothesis as well as describing the major independent (IV) and dependent (DV) variables. In a theoretical paper, you will state the theoretical propositions, the relevant arguments and data supporting them, as well as how your design and hypothesis relate to the issue involved.

Put simply when writing the introduction ask yourself, "What results do I expect?" "Why do I expect these results?" "What will I be manipulating?" Then state your problem. Discuss the background material. Tell what you are going to do. Remember that "you have not done the experiment yet" as you write your introduction. Do not refer to your results here!

Method

This is the main body of the report. It is here that you describe how the experiment was conducted. Be careful to include only information that is essential for understanding and replicating the study. This is perhaps the most important point. The procedure must be described with enough detail that another experimenter can replicate just what you have done, yet it must not be too lengthy or complicated that it includes nonessential information that makes the report cumbersome or confusing to read and understand. Usually the method section includes subsections to aid with the clarity of the presentation. The three usual subsections are 1) subjects, 2) apparatus or materials, 3) procedure. If the procedure is complicated a fourth section "design" can be added.

Subjects. Answer the questions "Who participated? How many participated?" "How were they selected?" Include sex and age. Include payments given, promises made, geographical location and institution used. Do not forget to mention any subjects that did not complete the study and why. When using animals include genus, species, strain number and other specific identification material. Include all relevant details of their handling and other treatment.

Apparatus (or Materials). All aspects of the equipment you used are included in this section. This includes all instruments, devices, questionnaires or quizzes. Specialized equipment should include the manufacturer's name and model number. Standard laboratory equipment such as furniture and stopwatches need not be described in detail. If the apparatus used is particularly complex and the understanding of its nature is necessary to explain the study, a picture can be included. (When manuscripts are being submitted for publication as few figures as possible are recommended due to the extra cost of printing them.)

Procedure. This is the "how" section of the report. It is here that you discuss how the IV was manipulated, how the DV was recorded, etc. Summarize each step in the research. This includes instructions, control features in the design such as randomization or counterbalancing. Standard testing procedures need not be described in detail since most people are familiar with them. If animals are used, include schedules of reinforcement. Summarize any instructions you give, except if their exact nature is vital to the experiment, then report them verbatim. If the experiment is complicated, sometimes a "Design" subsection is included. To further help in simplifying your organization of this section, arrange your material in these steps: 1) design, 2) steps in conducting and 3) method for measuring subject's behavior.

Results

To begin the results section, report your findings in a summary statement. Then go on to add the detail that supports your conclusions. Be sure to include results that run counter to your hypothesis. These can be important to other researchers. Do not include a theoretical or extended discussion of the results or their implications in this section. Raw data should be presented in a summary form. Use tables and graphs if this is the clearest way to present your material (which it often will be). All graphs, photographs, pictures and drawings are referred to as "figures" and all tables as "tables". Always explain the figures and tables in the text and remember to use as few as possible. Line graphs have become increasingly popular in psychological journals because they show the data in such a way that they can be more quickly grasped, whereas the table form of presentation usually requires time-consuming careful study. Of course, some data must be presented in a table form. For tests of significance (t, r, etc.) include the values of the test, degrees of freedom, probability level, direction of the effect. Assume a professional knowledge of statistics in your presentation.

Discussion

Here is the place to evaluate and interpret your results. Ask yourself "What have I contributed to the resolution of the original problem?" Emphasize the theoretical implications of the results. Include negative findings and your reasoning in explaining them in light of your hypothesis but do not take too much space in excusing results that go against your hypothesis. This is a natural and expected part of experimentation. This section is a good place to make suggestions for improvement of research methodology. What you see as crucial uncontrolled variables, and additional problems not covered by the study that need consideration in future work may also be included. Whatever speculation you make should follow closely to already existing theory and be kept to a minimum. If (and only if) the discussion is brief it can be included with the results to give you a "Results and Discussion" section. Although the abstract is meant to take the place of the summary, it can aid with the integrity of the article to end it with a brief formal statement of the problem, results and conclusions.

References

List all of the references cited in the text. Precise guidelines for the reference section are in the Publication Manual. Put reference listings in alphabetical order, regardless of the order of presentation in the text. A typical listing would include in the following order:

For articles:

Author's Last Name, First and Middle Initial. Name of the article. Name of the Journal (standard abbreviations acceptable), year, vol. number, pages.

For books:

Author's Last Name, First and Middle Initial. Name of Book. Place Published: Publisher, year, page or chapter numbers, (if necessary).

With a questionable or unusual reference, it is advisable to check the Publication Manual or to look through the reference sections of articles in any of the APA journals as they all follow the standard form recommended by the APA.

Appendix

An appendix is rarely used and is advisable only for complex material that is necessary for the replication or understanding of the study that would detract from the main body of the text were it included there. Examples of possible appendix materials might be:

1. Computer programs specifically designed for the research.

2. An unpublished test and its validation.

3. Complex mathematical proofs.

4. A list of stimulus materials (such as those used in word lists)

Do not include anything in this section for its own sake or for general interest. The main purpose of the experimental or theoretical report is to communicate your work in a clear, concise manner to a scientific audience. Keeping this goal in mind should help you with the organization and writing.

SAMPLE EXPERIMENTAL REPORTS

<u>Title</u>

(12-15 words. Summarizes main idea simply and concisely)

<u>Author's Institution</u>

(or city and state if no institutional affiliation)

<u>Date of Submission</u>

<u>Abstract</u>

Summary of contents and purpose of study. Self-contained.

Experimental report:

(100-175 words)

Include problem, methods, results, conclusions, subject population, describe research design, test instruments or data gathering procedures. Summarize findings including statistical significances. Report inferences and comparisons.

(Theory or Review:

(75-100 words)

Include the central thesis, the nature of the theoretical discussion, sources used and conclusions.)

(Introduction) - Do not use the heading "Introduction"; start immediately with the text.

Problem under study and the point of the study. Include hypothesis and major variables.

Method

How was the study conducted? Enough detail for replication. Include the following subsections.

<u>Subjects</u>. Who participated?

<u>Apparatus</u>. Equipment and tests used

<u>Procedure</u>. Summarize each step of research

<u>(Design)</u>. Use a design section only for complicated procedures.

Results

Summarize the data gathered and your treatment of them.

Discussion

Evaluate and interpret results.

References

Alphabetically include all references made in the text only.

Appendix

To be used rarely. Only for complex or lengthy material essential for the replication or understanding of the study.

Note: Though the sample reports which follow are single-spaced, experimental reports should normally be double-spaced. Ask your instructor.

LEARNING PRINCIPLES

Training Mice to Leap Over a Barrier Using Termination of
Electric Shock as Reinforcement

Jack Scientist and Carol Curious

Smythesville University

Abstract

This experiment was designed to see how quickly
and consistently mice could be trained to leap a barrier
using the termination of electric shock as a reinforcement and to determine what conditions would be most
conducive to this type of training.* 45 out of 50 animals
learned to make the response. In most cases training
was immediate. To test for best conditions we used the
variable of current intensity. Five groups of five mice
were subject to a high current of .5 ma. and the other
five groups of five were subject to a lower current of .3
ma. The high current group responded more quickly during
the first 50 trials. Because of the speed with which the
learning took place little data were collected concerning
the difference in the original non-conditioned response
and the conditioned one. The learning curve was restricted to the first few trials. Redesign using a less
aversive stimuli may produce results more conducive to
studying original response to aversive stimuli.

Many writers have recently suggested that aversive stimuli play an important role in human behavior.
Most of the studies conducted to date, however, have
dealt mainly with avoidance training and punishment.
The subjects in these studies can avoid being stimulated
by making an appropriate response before the stimulus
is presented. In order to investigate the more basic
question of how behavior is influenced by direct negative
stimuli we wished to have stimuli that could be directly
manipulated by the experimenter rather than being assigned
to the learned or conditioned responses of the subjects.
The simple model of escape training seemed ideal for our
purposes. With this model, escape is possible only after
the stimulus has been administered. In the literature
review it was difficult to locate many studies that
dealt directly with this problem (Jones, 1942, Marrow,
1958, Sims, 1952, Zinger, 1970). We therefore, found
it necessary to design an appropriate program to measure
the learning responses of the subjects. We designed
this experiment to demonstrate the influence of one
variable--the amount of electric shock current administer-
ed--on the learning of a response that ends this shock.

---

*The reader should note that this experiment and
its results are hypothetical.

The animals we used were white mice. The response required
was that of jumping over a wall.

Method

Subjects. All Ss were male white mice approximately
2 years old at the start of the experiment. Ten other
Ss were not included in the results because of a defect
in their shock grids.

Apparatus. The Ss were placed in a box of Plexi-
glass 1/8" thick, 8" wide x 20" long x 15" deep. The
top was hinged and latched to permit insertion or removal
of the animal. The floor was a grid composed of 18 steel
rods, 1/4" in diameter, placed at intervals of 1" from
center to center. The grid was 6" above the bottom of
the box.

The wall over which the animal had to jump was
made of stainless steel 1/4" thick, 3" high, and 8" in
length. It was mounted on the grid floor midway in the
box. The grid was equipped with 2 pressure switches,
one for each side of the grills. This was defined as
the response. The experimental box was enclosed in a
sound-resistant and lightproof chamber made of plywood
12" wide x 24" long and 20" deep that could be opened
from the top.

The current used to shock the animals was induced
by a transformer with a 600 v output and was regulated
by a grid potential of a 6SK7 tube. The experiment
was conducted by an electronic and relay network and the
onset, duration, and termination of each shock and each
pressure on the opposite side of the grill were recorded
on a constant-speed polygraph.

Procedure. The mice were kept with the rest of the
department mice until the experiment began. They were
normally kept five to a cage and given continuing access
to food and water. They were then assigned at random
to ten groups of five each. Five groups were subjected
to the current of .5ma and five to the .3ma. We placed
the five cage mates into their boxes and administered
the shock. For the next 60 minutes each jump to the other
side of the cage was followed within approximately 1/2
second by termination of the shock. The shock remained
off for 20 seconds before it was again administered,
this time to the opposite side of the grill. The same
procedure was repeated the next day.

Results and Discussion

Only 5 of the 50 animals failed to become conditioned. In most cases, the mice made the response
shortly after the first application of the response
and continued to respond so quickly that it was impossi-

ble to measure any difference between the original responding and the conditioned response.

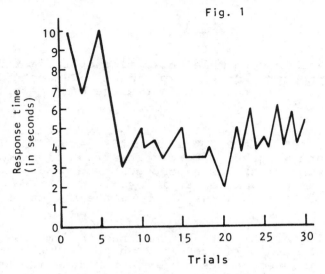

Fig. 1

The learning curve was restricted to the first
few trials as shown in Fig. 1. The groups that received
the stronger shock showed quicker response times than
the other groups. An analysis of reciprocals of the
response time shows that the difference between high
and low current groups has a chance probability less
than .01. This shows that our results should be reliable.

We intend to design a further experiment using
less aversive stimuli to facilitate the collection of
data concerning the nature of the original response.

References

Jones, J. K. Resistance to extinction in mice. Our
    Journal, 1942, 42, 88-100.

Marrow, M. L. Use of food to maintain avoidance behavior.
    Psychology, 1958, 84, 543-580.

Sims, A. L. An automatic shock-grid apparatus. J. of
    Mice, 1952, 24, 432-465.

Zinger, S. A. Punishment in learning. Learning Today,
    1970, 18, 114-123.

HUMAN LEARNING

Extinguishing a Response in Young Children
Through the Withdrawal of Positive Reinforcement

John M. Analyst

Helimingdale College

Abstract

Children were taught to push a button to receive
gumdrops. Later this response was punished by turning
off a cartoon they were watching for five seconds.* This
effectively extinguished the response. The control S's
who were not punished for pushing the button showed much
less extinction of the button pushing response even when
no candies were forthcoming. In later sessions the control
S's showed considerable spontaneous recovery while the
punishment S's did not. From these results it was concluded that the withdrawal of positive reinforcement is
an effective punishment method, though generalization of
this conclusion to more complex behavior was questioned.

Traditionally, there have been two ways in which
punishment has been defined: 1) as the introduction of
a negative reinforcer for a response and 2) as the withdrawal of a positive reinforcer for a response. While
a great deal of research has been conducted concerning the
former (Baller, 1970), the latter has received very little
treatment in the literature. The only experiments to
date dealing with this approach to punishment are those
by Elmsworth (1952) with chimpanzees and by Smith (1961)
who used it to facilitate backward conditioning in adolescents. Because the withdrawal of positive reinforcement
may play a large part in the learning histories of many
children, it seems of primary theoretical and practical
importance.

It has been demonstrated that negative punishment
stimuli have a very weak effect in altering the responses
to which they are directed. Harrows (1965) concluded
that "punishment is ineffective over the long term for
shaping desired responses". It has also proven difficult
to make a distinction between the administering of
negative reinforcement as, for instance, with a spank,
and the withdrawing of positive reinforcement such as
affection and approval. It may well be the withdrawal
of the positive reinforcement that plays the greatest
role in shaping behavior. This study is designed to
investigate the effect of withdrawing a positive reinforcement on learned behavior in an unambiguous reinforce-

_____

*The reader should note that this experiment and
its results are hypothetical.

ment environment, that is, when no other positive
reinforcement is offered for different behavior.

Method

Subjects. Kindergarten children from Romulus Elementary School were used for the experiment. All S's
were experimentally naive. 20 children started the
experiment. By the end of the experiment, 5 of the children had been lost either through illness, family vacation,
or moving from the area. One child was randomly eliminated
to give even-numbered control and study groups. The
children were normal in intelligence and were from
middle income families. The average age of the 7 children
in the control group was 5 years 8 months, and that of
the 7 in the study group was 5 years 10 months.

Apparatus. The experiment was conducted in a Barnum
workshop on wheels in the school parking lot. The workshop was a 26' model. The workshop consisted of two
rooms. One was a playroom and the other a one-way observation booth for the experimenter. In the playroom was
a screen, a table, two chairs, a windup top; a special
candy dispensing box was on the table next to one of
the two chairs. The film was operated by the experimenter and was a 20-minute color cartoon from Happytime
Films entitled "Jose the Horse Goes to Hay". The candy
dispensing box was 2' long x 1' high x 6" wide and
was equipped with a button on the side nearest the child
and a slot out of which the gumdrops could be dispensed.
Every button press produced a doorbell chime for 2
seconds. If the experimenter so desired the button press
would also turn the cartoon off for 5 seconds.

Procedure. A young man, Mr. B was the only person
to deal with the children. Mr. B. had known the children
for a number of months and was accustomed to dealing
with them. They had been informed in advance that this
playroom would be arriving and were looking forward to
visiting it. The first visit was designed to familiarize
the children with the environment and each child was
brought into the laboratory, shown to the chair and
shown the cartoon. Mr. B simply retired to another chair
in the corner where he read a book. As soon as the cartoon ended Mr. B came for the child and they left. The
second visit the child was asked if he or she wanted to
do something different this time and was shown the gumdrop
machine. Mr. B. explained, "This is a candy machine".
He then went again to the corner. Each child soon began
to push the button on the machine. The following reinforcement schedule (fixed ratio) was used: 1, 2, 4, 6,
9, 11, 15. As soon as the last gumdrop was received,
Mr. B. came and told the child it was time to go.

On the next visit, the child was asked if he or
she wanted to go again. This time the film was started
immediately. S was allowed to push the button as much
as desired. Mr. B went again to the corner. In the con-

trol group the button pressing produced the doorbell
chime, but no candy. In the punishment group, each time
the button was pushed, the cartoon went off for five
seconds. The next visit was arranged to allow for spontaneous recovery. Mr. B asked each child if he or she
wanted to see the cartoon again. At this visit the
button pushing neither produced candy nor stopped the
film. At the last session, the child was allowed to
either play with the windup top or the candy machine.
This was designed to test for the strength of the learned
response with no punishment. Each visit occurred one
week after the previous visit and all occurred in the
morning.

Results

All the button pressing responses were recorded
on the Wearever Recorder. From these results it was
apparent that the stopping of the cartoon significantly
affected the button pressing response. Also this reduction
appears to be permanent. During the spontaneous recovery
session, control S's showed considerable interest in the
candy box, while the punishment group made only one or
two responses. In the last session, the control group
still showed interest in the box, while all those children in the punishment group went directly to the windup
top. Figure 1 shows the response of the two groups
during the 2nd, 4th, and 6th session.

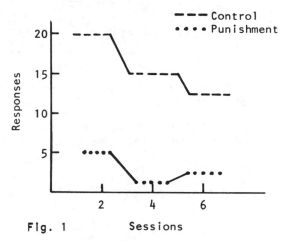

Fig. 1

Discussion

These results have demonstrated that the interruption of a cartoon that a child is watching can serve
as a powerful punishment. It will effectively reduce
a recent previously learned response. The hypothesis
that the removal of a positive reinforcer has punishing
effects is strengthened by the data. At least, this is
true with young children and in situations similar to
the one in which the experiment took place. Admittedly,

885

it is assumed that the cartoon is a positive reinforcement. This has been tested elsewhere and shown to be true (Beeman, 1964).

It is also worth considering that the response strength of the new button-pushing behavior was probably quite weak compared to the normal, everyday behavior patterns of a child. The candies the child received were sufficient for setting up a reinforcement pattern, but it is under question whether they can be considered a strong reinforcement for a well-fed child. In real life situations, the reinforcement schedule followed by the experimenter--consistent and immediate--is unlikely to take place. It is more usual that punishment is administered to a child some time after the undesirable action, or inconsistently, or even incomprehensibly.

In spite of these questions, the data do support the theory that withdrawal of positive reinforcement can be effectively used to repress a response in young children.

References

Baller, J. K. Punishment and reward in children, A Journal, 1970, 19, 225-241.

Beeman, G. The effect of a cartoon on learning schedules, J. of Animation, 1964, 8, 543-567.

Elmsworth, K. L. Positive reinforcement as a control of behavior in chimpanzees, Primate Monthly, 1952, 12, 226-287.

Harrows, S. P. A study of reward and punishment, A Journal, 1965, 2, 112-128.

Smith, L. L. The facilitation of backward conditioning in a group of adolescents, Learning Today, 2, 45-61.

COGNITION

● **PROBLEM** 21-3

Concept Formation as a Function of the Concept
Problem in Chimpanzees

Ronald S. Rhesus

University of Anywhere

Abstract

Using a 9-window illuminated-box (Kelly, 1961)
the concept forming ability of three chimpanzees already
trained to press a bar for food was tested over 150 hours
of training time.* Following the methodology of Sterns
(1972) 15 positive and 15 negative stimulus patterns were
presented accompanied by a 50-response variable-ratio
schedule of reinforcement for bar pressing in response
to 2 concepts. The two concepts presented were of different levels of abstractness. The common element of the
first problem (a row of illuminated bottom windows) had
a specific spatial location, while the common element of
the second problem (any three illuminated windows) did
not. This level of abstractness proved to be a determining factor in the ability of the chimpanzees to retain
discrimination. All chimpanzees learned to discriminate
between the two concepts with a high degree of accuracy.
However, in the problem requiring response to specific
stimulus patterns (any three windows), when the patterns
were changed but the concept kept constant, the performance dropped off markedly, which was not the case in
the problem requiring discrimination based on response
to the common element (bottom windows). Since the nature
of the concept problem played such a large role in determining performance, further study of the nature of complex
discriminations in chimpanzees was recommended.

The complex behavioral process of concept formation has received a great deal of attention in recent
years (Farrington, 1972; Jeralds, 1969; Harris, 1973).
Here we use the term "concept formation" to mean learning
to respond to a class of stimuli on the basis of some
common physical characteristic. Concept formation has
been demonstrated and tested in both animals (Kelly,
1961) and humans (Mauns, 1973). In a recent experiment
by Harris (1973) it was discovered that the degree of
abstractness of a concept was an important determinant
of whether or not it could serve as reinforcement for
the chimpanzee.

It was decided to further test this hypothesis
by varying the degree of abstractness of concepts

---

*The reader should note that the experiment and
results reported here are hypothetical.

presented in a similar learning environment to see the qualitative or quantitative effect such a variance would have on performance. Because so little work has been conducted on the specific characteristics of various concepts, we further decided to vary the degree of abstractness by including a concept for which the common element was a specific spatial location and a concept for which the common element was a specific stimulus pattern. It is predicted that the more abstract quality of the second concept will impede the performance of the chimpanzees.

Method

Subjects. The three subjects were food-deprived chimpanzees, each at 85-90% of body weight at the start of the experiment. Subject 1 was a 6-year-old male; experimental history: spatial discrimination (Jones, 1974), play (Marlborough, 1975). Subject 2 was a 5-year-old male; experimental history: visual deprivation (Hines, 1976). Subject 3 was a 6-1/2-year-old male; experimental history: word lists (Serif, 1976). The food reinforcements on which all three animals had been previously trained were 8-gram Purina Lab Chow pieces. The same food was used as reinforcement during the experiment. Diet supplement of vitamins, oranges and milk was also provided.

Apparatus. A nine-window Kelly illuminated box (Kelly, 1961) was used for the entire experiment. The chambers in which the experiments took place were 24 x 36 x 38 inch concrete cubicles with plywood doors, and expanded metal floors. The Kelly box was installed on one wall. It consists of nine small Plexiglas windows arrayed in a 3" x 3" square and a bar press device below where food reinforcement comes via a chute.

All experimental results were automatically recorded on the Harris Recordograph Lab Model 63. The experimental manipulations were all automatically timed and carried out by the standard laboratory program unit.

Procedure. Stimulus patterns were programmed by illuminating some of the windows while leaving the others dark. A sequence of 30 successive stimulus patterns--15 positive and 15 negative--was presented. The reinforcement schedule during the presentation of the positive stimulus patterns was a 50-response variable-ratio schedule. (The number of times the chimpanzee had to push the bar to receive food varied randomly from 1 to 100 with a mean of 50.) The positive stimulus patterns stopped with reinforcement. When the negative stimulus patterns were presented, extinction was begun. That is, responses were not reinforced at all. The negative stimulus patterns terminated when the bar had not been pressed for one minute. Between each experimental session a one-minute rest period was given. The experiment was considered over after 50 reinforcements had been delivered.

888

The two concept problems were investigated through the following procedure. The first concept that was held constant through various manipulations of the sequence pattern was the illumination of the bottom row of windows. The second concept was the illumination of any three windows in positive stimulus patterns; two or four windows were illuminated in negative stimulus patterns.

Initially on each of these problems, the animals were repeatedly exposed to one sequence of stimulus patterns. If the animal's behavior showed no consistent trend, the stimulus patterns were presented in a different sequence, but none of the specific stimulus patterns was changed. After 20 experimental sessions on the new sequence, six positive and six negative stimulus patterns were changed. The concept was never changed during this training period.

Results

The animals developed clear discriminations on both the concept problems. Neither discrimination was affected by changing the sequence in which the stimulus patterns were presented. However, the discriminations made were qualitatively different. Figure 1 demonstrates the results for the two concepts:

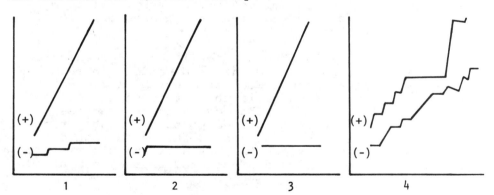

Fig. 1

Cumulative response curves with effect of changing specific stimulus patterns. 1 & 2 are from the first concept problem. 3 & 4 are from the second concept problem.

The response curves show the overall record after 100 hours of the experiment on the first sequence of patterns. The animals responded at increasingly higher rates during the positive patterns, and soon rarely responded during negative response patterns. For the first concept problem, when the stimulus patterns were presented in a new sequence no disruption in the performance occurred. When six negative and six positive patterns were reversed there was still no disruption-- the concept continued to be recognized.

For the second concept problem the performance
was also not disrupted when a new stimulus was presented.
When, however, six negative and six positive patterns
were changed, this altered the performance significantly
even though the concept was not changed. High rates of
responding to the negative patterns occurred and a great
deal of pausing occurred when the positive patterns were
presented.

Discussion

The results indicate that the abstractness of
the problem does contribute to the ability to form a
concept. That is, the nature of the concept problem is
vital in determining whether or not a concept will be
learned. At this point it seems necessary to determine
what the maximum number of stimuli is to which a chimpanzee can respond effectively. Apparently the number
presented in this experiment exceeded its cognitive
capacities. It had to respond in the second concept
problem to at least 12 specific stimulus patterns presented in a successive manner to recognize the concept.
The first concept, on the other hand, seemed to be
grasped quickly and effectively and this learning was
not altered or disturbed by altering other aspects of
the presentation. The characteristic of common spatial
location appears to be a quality of concept for which
a chimpanzee is well equipped cognitively. It is more
concrete and less abstract than the characteristic of
the second problem.

This finding throws a new light on previous conclusions concerning complex discriminations in chimpanzees. What looks like a complex discrimination may
actually be quite simple, if the nature of the concept
is thoroughly examined. The degree of abstractness
involved in the concept is an important variable that
must be investigated. Studies in this area should be
scrutinized carefully and the basis of the discrimination
assessed before results are accepted as they now stand.

References

Farrington, C. B. Cognitive Life. New York: Primate
      Press, 1972, 12, 125-141.

Harris, B. Concept formation in white-tail pigeons.
      J. of Exp. Cognition, 1973, 12, 185-189.

Hines, J. P. The effect of visual deprivation on the
      learning ability of adult chimpanzees. J. of Animal
      Learning, 1976, 25, 512-425.

Jeralds, P. E. An analysis of number concept formation
      in horses. Horse Today J., 1969, 33, 135-148.

Jones, H. Spatial discrimination abilities in the chim-
    panzee. Primates of Our Time, 1974, 3, 155-173.

Kelly, W. A. A new technique for the measurement of
    concept formation. Exp. J. of Life, 1961, 21,
    195-209.

Marlborough, A. Q. Is play an instinct? Primate Forum,
    1975, 5, 344-352.

Mauns, S. M. The nature of human conceptualization.
    Our Life. 1973, 24, 438-460.

Serif, W. M. Linguistic learning in chimpanzees. Pri-
    mates of Our Time, 1976, 22, 845-862.

SENSATION

Preferred Audio Stimulation Variation

H. James Baritone

Tenorsville State University

Abstract

To test the general hypothesis that people tend to prefer a moderate amount of stimulus variation in their environment, five tape recorded sequences of tones ranging from a minimal to a great range in frequency, duration and loudness were used.* In phase one of the study, the recordings were rated by forty-five college students to determine the perceived "amount of variation and change". As was expected, the tones were ordered as they would have been according to objective criterion. During phase two of the experiment, forty-seven different students listened to the tapes and were asked to rate them on a five point scale from "very unpleasant" to "very pleasant". The experimental hypothesis was confirmed as ratings indicating greater pleasantness were given to the sequences with moderate stimulus variations. The recordings with the least and greatest variations were least preferred.

A number of studies have demonstrated that people find environments aversive either when they are complete-ly predictable with very little stimulus variation (Hil-degard, 1969; Jones & McCloughlin, 1972) or when they contain too great an array of unexpected, novel, or varia-ble stimuli (Mills, 1971; Jackson, 1969). The bulk of this work has been conducted with visual, tactile, and audio deprivation or overload. Little systematic study of the individual sensory systems has taken place.

The present study was designed to test specifical-ly the preferred range of stimulation in the audio system. The research carried out by Barnes & Vickland (1967) testing for the relation between preference for complex-ity in music and education and social factors, and that of Hildegard (1973) on aversive noise levels are two studies that have addressed themselves to the character-istics of sound which make it pleasant or unpleasant.

Varying the three dimensions of sound: frequency, duration, and loudness, we devised tape recordings of different complexities (from simple to complex) in an attempt to confirm the hypothesis that the auditory system prefers a moderate range of stimulus variation.

*The reader should note that the experiment and results reported here are hypothetical.

Method

Subjects. The subjects were forty-five undergraduates, all of whom had volunteered for an experiment in experimental psychology. Twenty-six males and 19 females participated in the first phase. In the second phase, forty-seven different students who had volunteered with the first group, served as subjects.

Apparatus. 5 tape recordings of two minutes each were made of pure tones varying in frequency, duration, and loudness. The tones were combined in a random order with the required variation in the characteristics necessary for the different levels of complexity. A .03 second interval between each of the tones was maintained on all of the recordings. The five sequences were combined in three different random series to provide testing for 15 different orders. Table 1 presents the number and range of variations in the sequences.

Table 1: Number and range of variations in frequency, duration and loudness in recordings

	Frequencies	Duration	Loudness
1	2 (350 - 450)	2	medium
2	4 (300-550)	3	medium-low
3	8 (280-680)	5	low-medium
4	12 (200-800)	6	low-high
5	16 (100-2000)	8	low-high

Procedure. To obtain subjective verification of the objective levels of stimulus variation represented in the 5 tone sequences, subjects were asked to rate the tone sequences on "amount of variation and change" ranging from "very little" to "very great" variation. An eight point scale was used. As was expected the ratings conformed to the objective criterion used for making up the sequences. Scores on the sequences were as follows: 1) 1.3; 2) 2.8; 3) 5.6; 4) 6.8 and 5) 7.9. These mean ratings were used as the core index of variation when the findings from phase two were plotted.

During phase two of the study, the different subjects listened to the recordings and were asked to rate each piece on a five-point scale ranging from "very unpleasant" to "very pleasant". The mean ratings from this study were plotted against the ratings for variation in stimulus from phase 1.

Results

Figure 1 shows the relationships found between the pleasantness ratings and the variation ratings.

Fig. 1

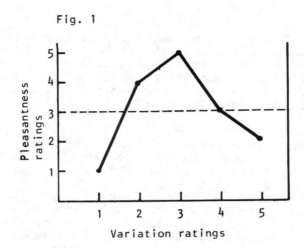

The experimental hypothesis was confirmed. The ratings indicate that the greatest pleasantness was experienced listening to the sequences with a moderate amount of variation. The sequence with the lowest level of variation actually received the lowest score and that with the highest amount of variation received the second lowest score.

These are mean scores. There were in fact individual departures from the norm. Three of the subjects rated the first sequence the highest and two rated the fifth highest. Yet, the vast majority preferred the tone arrangements with a moderate amount of variation.

Discussion

Further work remains to be conducted to determine whether previous training or exposure to more complex music results in a preference for it. It has been suggested by Harrill (1974) that moderate variation from the range of stimulation to which we are accustomed is that which is most preferred, rather than any objective standard of moderation. It is therefore necessary to subject these findings to even further testing which would include the level of musical sophistication of the subjects.

The majority of people are musically naive and this may bias our conclusions and lead us to believe that there is an objectively moderate level that is applicable to all. The same study using graduate music students as subjects might result in a very different pattern of results.

References

Barnes, E. A. and Vickland, P. Education and social factors in musical preference. Cochlea Research, 1967, 4, 57-72.

Harrill, I. R.   The case against objective sensory
    moderation levels. The Five Senses Review, 1974,
    53, 232-240.

Hildegard, T. G.   Sensory deprivation and affect. Jour-
    nal, 1969, 18, 115-128.

Jackson, S.   Novel stimuli as reinforcing. J. of Experi-
    ments, 1969, 11, 432-451.

Jones, T. and McCloughlin, G. P.   Motivational components
    of deprivation. Behavior Tomorrow, 1972, 32,
    543-565.

Mills, M. M.   Aversive levels of stimulation in the
    rat. Rodent Weekly, 1971, 13, 25-39.

PERCEPTION

Limits on Recall of Unfamiliar Material
in Visual Perception

I. C. Vision

Wellington State College

Abstract

To explore the parameters of visual memory, 20 subjects were presented with a matrix of 12 letters and numbers for 50 msec. and asked to recall as many of the letters and numbers as possible.* To provide a test for the hypothesis that icons or persistent images are produced in the visual process, a second phase of the experiment was conducted. A similar matrix was presented to the subjects, and immediately afterward a light flashed indicating which of the 3 rows (of 4 symbols each) was to be reported. The general recall limit was found to be about 4 to 5 letters. However, in the condition indicating a particular line, any letter or number in any line was perfectly recalled. As the light signal was delayed, performance declined rapidly back to the original level of 4 or 5. It was concluded that the icon or physical image had lasted long enough for the subject to direct his or her attention to it in order to report the correct answer. To do this the enrire matrix must be contained within the sensory capacity.

What are the sensory limits of the visual processing system? This question has been explored in tachtiscopic experiments by Burns (1968), Miller (1970) and Wiland (1971) to such an extent that we now know that the threshold for visual recognition is approximately 1/4 of a second. However, the more detailed operations of the visual recognition system have not been systematically explored.

There have been a number of theories set forth supporting the theory that the visual system processes information by first forming a persistent image or "icon" that is subsequently encoded and finally stored for later retrieval. It has not been demonstrated whether this iconic process is purely sensational or if it involves the work of higher mental processes or perception (Field, 1961; Merns, 1969; Jacobson & Jenson, 1965; Hall, 1971).

---

*The reader should note that this is an hypothetical experiment with fabricated results. Interested readers are referred to Sperling, G. 1963. A model for visual memory tasks. Human Factors, 19-31 for the actual experiments in this area.

To explore both questions, we devised a two-phase tachtiscopic experiment to determine the limit of visual memory for unfamiliar material at a single glance, and to measure the extent to which the contents of immediate visual memory could be determined. By directing the attention of the subjects to specific areas of the visual material after the presentation of that material, the presence of a visual picture or icon could be determined if the quality of this memory differed from that which occurred with general recall alone.

Method

Subjects. Twenty college sophomores from the Wellington men's dormitory system volunteered for this experiment. All subjects were instructed that the experiment concerned visual perception. None had previously participated in any scientific experiment.

Apparatus and Procedure. All visual material was presented on a tachtiscope. Each image was flashed for 1/4 second (including the colored light flashed to indicate which line of the matrix to be recalled).

The matrix presented to the subjects was similar to the following:

```
D  8  C  4
2  S  9  T
W  5  X  7
```

All subjects were shown 5 different matrixes and after each one asked to recall as many of the letters and numbers as they could.

The subjects were then given a fifteen minute rest period. After the rest period another 5 matrixes were shown to the subjects. This time the subjects were instructed that they would be asked to recall the figures and letters by row and informed that lights of different colors would come onto the screen immediately following the presentation of the matrix to indicate which of the three rows should be recalled. Within 50 msec. after the presentation of the matrix a red light was flashed to indicate that the first row was to be reported, a yellow light for the second row and a green light for the 3rd row across.

Rows were randomly selected for each of the subjects.

This procedure was repeated increasing the amount of time between the presentation and the light flash up to 500 msec.

Results

In the initial presentation, the mean number of responses from any given matrix for all the subjects was 4.4 letters or figures. Only one subject recalled as many as 6 items and only one as few as three.

The results of the second phase of the experiment indicated a much greater capacity for recall, particularly with regard to the detail of the presentation. In every case the subjects were able to recall the entire line in the exact order it was presented regardless of what line was chosen for recall. As the amount of time between the presentation and the light flash increased, the quality of recall decreased until about 500 msec. at which time the recall level was the same as the original level (about 4 to 5). Apparently the recall capacity immediately after presentation was 12, and not the 4 to 5 that it appeared to be with a general report from the subject.

Discussion

It appears that a visual image does persist in the mind of the subject after the tachtiscopic image disappears. It is the presence of this icon that enables the subject to direct his attention to whatever line he is requested to recall and produce it perfectly. By the time this is done, the image has faded sufficiently that the subject no longer can call upon it to produce the rest of the matrix. For a brief period of time the icon does, however, exist in the sensory capacity. This experiment also tells us that the limits on the visual memory system are not merely sensory. As the sensory system does record the entire image. The limits on visual memory must be due to a process further along than the sensory recording stations. Because it takes time to record the information on the sensory screen for more permanent use, what has not been encoded immediately after only a single glance is lost. The colored light indicated to the subject to encode that particular line first and by the time that was done the other lines had faded from iconic memory.

Thus the effect of attention is to indicate to the observer what part of a display to encode first. The mystery of iconic store needs to be further investigated. What effect does familiarity have on the encoding process? Does attention increase the speed of the encoding only or does it effect the quality of the sensory image? These and many other questions remain to be answered.

References

Burns, J. The effects of coding on visual memory. Review of Exp. Psych., 1968, 14, 28-43.

Field, P. Visual memory. Bulletin of Exp. Psych. 1961,
     18, 251-263.

Hall, P. V. The role of the iconic store in visual
     memory. Review of Today's Research, 1971, 34,
     342-351.

Jacobson, T. P. and Jenson, V. The iconic image. J. of
     American Perceptual Science, 1965, 14, 114-132.

Merns, P. T. Information processing in the visual system.
     J. of Visual Perception, 1969, 11, 28-46.

Miller, M. Selective attention and visual memory. J. of
     Visual Perception, 1970, 18, 45-61.

Wiland, C. A measure of visual memory capacity. Visual
     Science, 1971, 41, 289-391.

MOTIVATION

Brain Stimulation Current Intensity Selection
in the Rat

Maureen A. Mause

Marysville State College

Abstract

To test the self-stimulation regulatory ability
of two groups of rats with electrodes implanted in
different sections of the brain, a first group of ten
animals had an anterior electrode placed in the cingulate
cortex and a second group of ten had a posterior electrode implanted deep in the midbrain tegmentum.* Over
a three-week period of time both groups of rats were
trained on the current regulating device for five hours
every day. Five-minute periods of self-stimulation were
alternated with five-minute rest periods throughout the
entire training period. The performance of the cingulate
group was consistently poor and typically this group
would self-stimulate to intensity levels producing punishment level convulsions. The tegmentum group self-
regulated perfectly selecting a level of 13 to 15 ma.
after a very short adaptation period. These results
support James' hypothesis that the rostral positive reinforcing sites have fewer negative cell blocks surrounding
them to mitigate the effect of the positive cell groups.

By now it is well established that animals will
work to stimulate certain portions of the brain with
electric current (James 1962). Because self-stimulation
has such promising possibilities for use as a tool in
understanding the action of many variables on the central
nervous system such as drugs, food or drink deprivation,
mating behavior--all of which effect the rate of self-
stimulation to particular areas of the brain--it was
determined to further test the hypothesis set forth by
James (1965) that the rostral brain areas (including the
septum and the cingulate cortex) contain more inhibiting
or negatively reinforcing areas than do the caudal sites
(including the hypothalmus and the midbrain tegmentum)
by testing the self-regulatory abilities of two groups
of rats with electrodes planted in one of these two
areas.

Other work in this area has been conducted by
Smith and Jackson (1968) to determine the optimal
stimulation for learning maze running in rats and by
Mans (1966) in his investigation of color blindness in

---

*The reader should note that both the experiment
and results reported here are hypothetical.

pigeons. Mapping studies by Fields (1967) have supported the theory that the negative and positive reinforcing cell groups exist and are reciprocally inhibitory so that temporary increases in the negative structure's threshold level may be brought about by prolonged stimulation to the positive sites. Additionally there is much evidence supporting the theory that animals seek self-regulation based on a preferred moderate energy of stimulation (Henderson, 1954, 1961; Williams, 1963).

Method

Subjects. Ss were male albino rats all about one year old with bipolar electrodes (0.01" platinum wires, twisted together and insulated) permanently implanted in either the cingulate cortex (10 animals) or the midbrain tegmentum (10 animals).

Apparatus. Animals were trained in a James self-regulatory box (1963) with two levers, one of which increased the amount of current delivered and the other of which decreased the stimulating current. Eighteen current steps were available up to approximately 50 ma. A current level could be maintained by alternating between the two levers. A continuous record of the amount of current selected was recorded on a potentiometer. A cumulative response recorder and impulse counters simultaneously gave records of the self-stimulation rate. The stimulating current came from a pulse-pair generator as used by Harris (1972). A brain-shock reward was a train of pulse pairs 50 to 100 cy/sec in frequency and fixed in duration at 0.25 or 0.5 sec. Optimal values of frequency and duration varied for different animals and were selected experimentally.

Procedure. During the conventional preliminary training session all rats were trained to operate either lever to receive a mildly reinforcing shock. After the self-stimulation rates had been determined the rats were required to push one of the two levers to receive the reinforcing shock. Most rats learned to do this in one three-hour session. During the next session, the training was directed at learning to regulate the current. At the beginning of this session the experimenter facilitated the learning by raising the current when it was quite low and lowering it when it had reached convulsive levels. After the training sessions, five-minute periods of rest were alternated with five-minute periods of self-stimulation. During the rest periods the stimulator light was turned off. This provided an exact test of regulating ability as the rats had to reestablish the optimal stimulation level after each rest period.

Results and Discussion

All of the rats with the tegmentum implantation

learned to self-regulate at the preferred level of 12-15 ma., whereas the typical response of those animals with the cingulate cortex electrode was to self-stimulate to maximum intensity or until convulsive behavior began. This supports the hypothesis that intermediate intensities are preferred because the stronger current spreads to negative reinforcing areas which have an inhibitory effect. The rats with cingulate implantations continued to favor increased stimulation even to the point of punishment because the positive reinforcing sites are larger in this area.

Similar experiments with animals in which frequency and intensity of current have been varied (Jacobs, 1965) have demonstrated that when the frequency is increased, the rat with an electrode in the midbrain tegmentum will select a current with a lesser intensity, and decreases in the frequency will lead the rat to select a higher intensity shock. That the animals tended to compensate for frequency changes by changing the intensity levels also points to the conclusion that self-regulation is based on a preferred energy of stimulation.

Further experimentation on the negative or positive reinforcing effects of various areas of the central brain structures answering such questions as "What effect do drugs have on the self-regulation activity of the trained rat?" "Does food or drink affect, facilitate, or inhibit the learning of self-regulatory behavior?" "Is amount of current an important determinant in producing rewarding stimulation in the cingulate cortex?" Detailed testing of the various areas of the brain using the self-regulatory method can eventually yield a central structure map of reinforcing areas that will be invaluable in scientific use.

References

Fields, A. B. Mapping cell groups. Cell Journal, 1967, 5, 101-110.

Harris, C. D. The pulse-pair generator in research. Laboratory Equipment, 1972, 7, 140-145.

Henderson, E. F. Preferred stimulation in rats. Journal of Rat Studies, 1954, 2, 90-101.

Henderson, E. F. Moderate self-stimulation in rats. Journal of Rat Studies, 1961, 9, 14-25.

Jacobs, G. H. The role of frequency and intensity variations in self-stimulation of rats. Rat Quarterly, 1965, 91, 15-18.

James, Z. Z. Electric current as reinforcer in rats. Rodent Digest, 1962, 14, 80-88.

James, Z. Z. Rostral brain areas in the rat. <u>Rat Studies Monthly</u>, 1963, <u>5</u>, 67-69.

James, Z. Z. The self-regulatory box. <u>Journal of Rat Studies</u>, 1963, <u>11</u>, 40-44.

Mans, M. M. Color blindness in pigeons. <u>Journal of Pigeon Studies</u>, 1966, <u>13</u>, 14-17.

Smith, S. S. and Jackson, J. J. Maze running in rats. <u>Journal of Rat Studies</u>, 1968, <u>15</u>, 90-95.

Williams, W. W. Thermo-regulation in rats. <u>Rat Digest</u>, 1963, <u>15</u>, 5-15.

INFORMATION PROCESSING

Further Exploration of the Spatial-Motor Function of the Right Hemisphere

Joseph Casey

Mills Institute, New York, N. Y.

Abstract

To test the theory that the right hemisphere of the cerebrum has principal control of spatial-motor functions, a series of tests were carried out on 6 patients with a lesion in the corpus callosum.* The three spatial-motor tests administered were: 1) the matching of blocks with a picture design, 2) drawing a cube in three dimensions, and 3) repairing a torn piece of paper. These tasks were presented to each side of the brain. In all six cases, the performance of the left hand (controlled by the right hemisphere) was superior to the performance of the right hand. In the case of repairing the paper the right hand could not perform the task at all. The evidence is mounting supporting not only the theory that there are two "independent" brains in each human, but that one of them controls language acquisition skills; the other, spatial and motor skills. Our findings support the prevailing view that the right hemisphere contains spatial-motor control mechanisms.

Numerous questions have arisen since the discovery that the two hemispheres of the brain have separate and apparently independent functions. Initial work done with patients who had undergone surgery on the corpus callosum to prevent epileptic seizures (Wells, 1965) revealed that these patients favored the right side of the body (which is controlled by the left hemisphere) for a long time after the operation. Subsequent testing identified the main features of the bisected-brain syndrome.

When information was presented to the left hemisphere the patient responded normally. However, when similar information was presented to the right hemisphere, the patients were often unable to respond. The capacities of the two different sides were tested by presenting visual or tactile information to one side only and asking the patient for a verbal or written response describing what had been presented. At first it appeared that the right half of the brain had been damaged. Further testing requiring nonverbal responses proved the predominance of the right hemisphere. For example, when a

---

*The reader should note that the experiment and results reported here are hypothetical.

picture of a spoon was presented, the patient was able
to feel around with the left hand and locate a spoon.
He was also able to pick out a saucer when presented with
a cup and a group of ten objects that contained no cup,
demonstrating that the right side of the brain also contains conceptual ability.

We wished to further investigate the qualities
of the right side of the brain. It has been suggested
(Hals, 1970) that higher motor functions cannot be carried
out by patients with damage to the right side of the
brain and that, even though normal speaking ability
remains, the ability to do creative work is greatly
diminished in patients with right side brain damage.
Musical ability is also thought to be connected with the
right hemisphere (Morris & Stevens, 1972).

This brings us to our main question: how can we
precisely measure the special functions that reside in
the right and not the left hemisphere? We designed three
tests of spatial-motor ability and administered them to
both halves of the brains of six split-brain patients.
We hypothesized that the performance of the right half
of the brain would excel that of the left.

Method

Subjects. All six patients had undergone the operation to split the corpus callosum as a method for relieving uncontrollable epilepsy. The operation consists
of cutting the corpus callosum and other commissure
structures connecting the two halves of the cerebral
cortex. All operations took place at Mills Institute.
All subjects were male between the ages of 30-50, and had
undergone the operation within 2-4 years of the experiments.

Apparatus. The standard testing table used in split-
brain research (Howard, 1973) was utilized. The central
point on the viewing screen was highlighted in red to
facilitate keeping the gaze fixed upon it during the
experimentation. The patient was instructed to keep his
or her gaze fixed on the central point on the viewing
screen so that the information presented on one side of
the screen did not fall onto the visual field of the other
side of the brain, thereby confusing the results.

A picture design of 8 2" sq. blocks piled into
three rows was one of the stimulus objects; a picture of
a three-dimensional cube was another; the third object
presented to the patients was two pieces of paper--one
of which was 8-1/2" x 11" and another of which was a
small two inch square that had been cut off the bottom
of the 8-1/2" x 11" page.

Procedure. Subjects were first familiarized with
the testing table and screen and well-practiced with
fixing their gaze on the central point of the screen.

905

A number of visual and tactile tests were administered for approximately one hour before the three stimuli described above were administered. The picture of the 8 blocks was flashed on the screen to the right hemisphere and the subject was asked to reassemble the blocks before him to resemble as closely as possible those in the picture. Five minutes were allotted for this task.

After 5 minutes a three-dimensional cube was flashed on the screen to the left hemisphere and the subject was asked to draw the cube as it appeared on the screen. Five minutes was again allotted for this task. Finally, the subject was given the torn piece of paper and the missing piece from it in the left hand and provided with scotch tape and asked to reassemble the paper.

A 15 minute rest period was taken after which the exact procedures described above were again administered except that each test was presented to the opposite side of the brain and the opposite hand as in the first series.

Results

All 6 of the subjects arranged the blocks correctly with the left hand; no subject could manage this task with the right hand. The drawings of the three-dimensional cube with the left hand, though shaky (all of these men were right-handed), resembled a cube--that is contained a three-dimensional element. All of the drawings executed with the right hand were primitive and lacked any concept of three-dimensionality. The paper repair task was carried out successfully by the left hand, though clumsily; while the right hand could not seem to figure out how to put the two pieces of paper together.

Discussion

From our studies it appears that the right hemisphere is capable of mental functions of a "high order". Because of our predominantly verbal orientation we have long believed that its functions were minimal and secondary to the dominant left hemisphere. It appears that the left hemisphere does excel in what has been called verbal activity or linguistic thought (Wendel, 1975). However, the right hemisphere excels in non-language or nonverbal functions.

It is important to remember that these studies were carried out on adults. Evidence exists that up to about the age of four the right hemisphere is about as proficient in handling language as the left (Pauling, 1968). In other words, in the young child each hemisphere is about equally developed with respect to language and speech function. We are thus faced with the interesting ques-

tion of why the right hemisphere at an early age, and
stage of development, possesses substantial language
capacity whereas at an adult age it possesses a poor
capacity. One hypothesis is that the systems that allow
for language capacity connected with the particular
functions of the right hemisphere are somehow disconnected
or inhibited and only the left hemisphere is allowed to
develop. Because of the creative and conceptual abilities in the right hemisphere, this question deserves our
careful attention and study as it may represent a key
to better training for creativity at an early age.

References

Hals, P. Two modes of thinking. Psychology Tomorrow,
    1970, 28, 115-124.

Howard, F. Exploring the functions of the two-sides of
    the brain. Modern Thought, 1973, 34, 13-28.

Morris, F. A. & Stevens, R. P. An exploration of right
    hemisphere functions. Physiology Quarterly, 1972,
    5, 255-261.

Pauling, K. Neurological evidence of an equal relation
    between the hemispheres of children. Child Play,
    1968, 211, 112-119.

Wells, H. A. Corpus callosum lesions for control of
    epileptic seizures. Southwest J. of Medicine,
    1965, 14, 675-689.

Wendel, J. Left hemisphere dominance in verbal ability.
    Southwest J. of Medicine, 1975, 58, 351-367.

PHYSIOLOGY

● PROBLEM 21-8

Thermal Behavior in the Rat

James Farenheit

Des Moines, Iowa

Abstract

The question under study was what factors lead
to the initiation of thermoregulatory behavior in the rat.*
The hypothesis that the body temperature has to descend
to a certain critical point before heat becomes reinforcing was tested in the following manner. 14 pairs
of white rats were used. One member of each pair was
placed into a cold room for 16 hours before the experiment and its partner was kept at room temperature. Rats
were then placed into the test apparatus which consisted
of a cold chamber containing a key which when pressed
turned on an infrared heat lamp for a few seconds. Rats
that had been exposed to normal room temperature waited
a mean of 4.41 hours before starting to work for heat
at a steady rate. But rats that had spend the preceding
hours in the cold waited only a mean of 1.89 hours
(t=2.40, df=13, p<.05). This supported the hypothesis
that there is a critical point at which the heat becomes
reinforcing. The precooled rats started pressing sooner
because their body temperature was lower when they began
the experiment.

Quantitative information on the role of behavior
in thermoregulation is rare, although one can point to
numerous examples of its importance as one of the principle mechanisms by which organisms regulate body temperature. It has been shown by Heller (1965) that rats
placed in a heat regulatory apparatus will make few
responses for the first few hours and then will apparently
spontaneously begin to press a lever to receive heat
reinforcement and continue pressing the lever at a
steady rate. A question raised by this research is why
does the rat's behavior change so quickly? It is known
that rats placed in a cold chamber tend to lose body
temperature at a progressive rate. It was therefore
hypothesized that the body temperature might have to
drop to a certain point before the heat from the lamp
becomes reinforcing.

This has been tested by Layman & Green (1971) in
a study of cold acclimatization. Although animals
acclimatized to cold show numerous structural and biochemical changes, perhaps the most dramatic difference

*The reader should understand that this is an hy-
pothetical experiment. The experiment and its results are
fictional.

between acclimatized and normal rats lies in their resistance to cold after their fur has been removed. Nonacclimatized rats die at low temperatures, while the body temperature of the acclimatized rats never falls to a lethal level. If the period of time before the rats begin to work at a steady rate for heat is a function of the rate at which body temperature falls in the cold, then acclimatized rats should wait longer than normal rats do to begin pressing. This is supported by the results of the Layman and Green experiments.

We proposed to further test this hypothesis by using normal rats that had not been acclimatized but merely had their body temperature cooled and comparing their behavior with that of normal rats. If the hypothesis is correct that there is a critical point at which the body's need for heat becomes reinforcing, the precooled rats should begin pressing for heat before the rats kept at normal room temperatures.

Method

Subjects. 14 pairs of male, albino rats, all approximately one year old were used for the experiment.

Apparatus. The heat reinforcing apparatus consists of a Plexiglas cylinder containing a plastic lever attached to a telegraph key. The duration and intensity of the burst of heat from the red-bulb infrared lamp above the chamber is controlled by a timer and a variable transformer. This apparatus was kept in a refrigerated room at approximately 1 degree C. The Mindo recorder used to record the events occuring in the heat reinforcing chamber was located in a separate room.

Wire mesh cages 2' x 2' x 3' were used for the precooled rats and the control rats.

Procedure. The fur of all the rats used in the experiment was removed by clipping before the experimental sessions to insure that the rats could not maintain a normal body temperature in the cold environments in which they were placed. From the 14 pairs one member of each pair was randomly selected and placed in a wire mesh cage in the cooled room. His partner was placed in a wire mesh cage and kept in an adjoining room at room temperature. Six hours later both rats of the pair were placed in test chambers and exposed for 12 hours to the cold room temperature.

The heat lamp was set at 300 watts and each burst of heat lasted three seconds. After each burst of heat the temperature rise in the skin surface of the rats was 3 degrees C. Each time the lever was pressed, the lamp came on. Lever presses made while the lamp was on had no effect.

Results

The usual behavior of a rat placed in the heat reinforcing chambers is that it spends a few minutes exploring its surroundings and usually strikes the lever with enough force to trigger the lamp. After this initial activity, the rat usually spends the next few hours huddling and shivering making very few other responses. However, at some point, the rat begins to press the lever quite suddenly at a steady and substantial rate and maintains that rate for many hours.

This is precisely what occurred with all of the rats. The rats that had been exposed to room temperatures before being placed into the chamber did not begin to work for a steady heat rate until 4.41 hours had passed. The rats that had spent the preceding six hours in the cold room started pressing the key after only 1.89 hours. Analysis of this data by the t-test showed the difference to be significant at the .05 level ($t = 2.40$, $df = 13$, $p < .05$).

Discussion

It appears that the precooled rats start pressing earlier because they reach the critical temperature level before the normal rats. Though this evidence favors the view that a definite relationship exists between body temperature and working for an exteroceptive source of heat, concrete evidence for this view is still lacking. It is now essential to measure body temperature at the same time that the rats begin to work for heat to determine definitely that this view is correct and also to chart the exact point at which the temperature reaches the reinforcing level.

The work presented here provides further incentive to continue the work being done (Morril, 1975) to develop a suitable skin temperature recorder, one that will record the subcutaneous temperature, rather than simply the surface as development of this information could prove invaluable in understanding the relation of temperature to behavior.

References

Heller, R. J. Heat reinforced behavior. Physiology and Our Times, 1965, 185, 773-792.

Layman, P. T., and Green, J. Behavior in the cold after acclimatization. Science and the Laboratory, 1971, 4, 112-123.

Morril, W. A temperature recording device. Methods in the Laboratory, 1975, 43, 987-1003.

SOCIAL PSYCHOLOGY

Using Three-Dimensional Objects to Test the Effect
of Group Pressure on Conformity

H. G. Agree
and
Anne M. Yes
William A. Morris College

Abstract

Modeled on the work on conformity by Barris (1965)
in which he used judgments of lines of different lengths,
this experiment was conducted to ascertain if the judgment
of three-dimensional unambiguous objects would also be
highly influenced by group opinion. Similar, but different
sized, paired stimuli were presented to 24 groups of 15
persons. Each person was asked for a judgment as to the
relative size of the objects. Only one person in each of
the groups was actually a subject. 24 college freshmen
served as the subjects. The 14 other group members were
also college students, but they were confederates, prein-
structed as to the nature of the experiments and the responses they were to give. In half of the groups all the
confederates reported that the smaller item in a pair was
the larger. In the other half of the groups, all but one of
the confederates claimed that the smaller item was the
larger. 80% of the subjects in the unanimous group conformed with the group opinion. In the groups with one deviate confederate the percentage conforming to the majority
dropped to 26%. It was concluded that in unambiguous stimulus situations the pressure to conform is greater than in
ambiguous situations, but that with even minimal support,
the chances of an individual basing judgments on his or her
own perceptions rather than the opinion of others is
greater.*

The startling findings concerning the tendency of
the average person to conform with an obviously incorrect
judgment offered by a group (Barris, 1965; Holmes, 1967) has
led to a renewed interest in the field of conformity (James
& Sheffield, 1970; Harringson, 1969). Most of the
studies to date have used somewhat ambiguous stimuli to test
the parameters of conforming behavior.

According to the work of Holmes (1968) with lines
and circles, the more ambiguous the difference in the sizes
of the stimuli presented, the more likely the subject is to
follow the group opinion. In the situations where the dif-

---

*Readers should note that the experiment described
here is ficticious. See Asch, S. E., 1956 Studies of independence and submission to group pressure. Psychological
Monographs, Vol. 7, Series No. 416 for actual research on
this topic.

ference between the stimuli is greatest, the amount of conforming behavior drops from 65 to 30%. All research to date
has been conducted with two-dimensional impressions presented
on a screen. It has been suggested (Ayes, 1971) that this
manner of presentation tends to suggest to the subjects that
some kind of manipulation of the stimuli is occurring as
part of the experiment and that this biases the conformity
results. This experiment is designed to eliminate this factor by using only three-dimensional objects as stimuli. It
is further designed to determine if reducing the ambiguity
of the stimuli would reduce the tendency to conform. It is
hypothesized that it would.

Method

Subjects & Apparatus. The subjects were 24 college
freshmen at William A. Morris College, experimentally naive
according to the Flescher Testing Questionnaire. They had
all volunteered in their dormitories for an experiment in
perception. They were paid $3.00 per hour for their par-
ticipation. The confederates were taken from the same group
and paid similarly. The experiments took place in the
William A. Morris College Experimental Psychology Department
conference room. All group members sat around a 12' long
table. The objects were presented on a platform approximately 15' from the table.

Three paired objects were shown to each group.
They were 1) Indian rubber plants--one 7' high, the other
5' high; 2) Bicycles--one 4' high x 6' long and the other
3' high x 5' long, the bicycles were identical otherwise;
3) pictures of the Mona Lisa in a plain gold frame, one 18"
x 30" and the other 26" x 40". Screen & slide projector
were standard Kawleen laboratory models.

Procedure. Confederates were instructed to arrive 2
hours earlier than the subjects for the experiment. The
true nature of the study was explained to them. A sample
judging session was held during which they were instructed
as to appropriate responses. They were then sent out of
the building for a 1/2 hour break and asked to return at the
time scheduled for the other participants to arrive.

Subjects and confederates together were all instructed by the experimenter that they were going to participate
in an experiment in perception, principally to study individual differences in visual perception. The Miller Visual
Acuity Register was adminsitered to the group. This required approximately 15 minutes to complete. After these
tests were collected by the experimenter, pictures of a
number of perceptual illusions were presented on the screen
and each group member was asked to judge the illusion and
verbally report his or her opinion. The illusions that were
presented were the Ponzo illusion, a Mueller-Lyer figure and
the Herring illusion. No prompting was given to the confederates for this section of the experiment. It was conducted
mainly to reduce any suspicion that might come from simply
presenting the objects themselves and to establish more

firmly the "mind-set" that the experiment was concerned with the measurement of different perceptual phenomena. This portion of the experiment required about 20 minutes.

Finally, the group's attention was directed to the platform on which were the rubber plants and each member was again asked to make a judgment about the size of the two plants and to offer that judgment orally. The subjects in every case were either the last person or the next-to-last person called upon as the confederates went in turn counter-clockwise around the table giving their judgment. The judgments offered by the confederates varied from one word replies to "right is smaller" to longer phrases such as, "well, I'm not sure, it is quite hard to tell from here, but I'll take a shot at it--I think the one on the right is shorter."

Actually, the difference in the sizes of each of the objects was evident and readily discernable from the distance of 15'.

In half of the 24 groups all of the confederates reported that the larger plant was the smaller one. In the other half of the groups one confederate (the 7th speaker in all cases) said that he or she thought the smaller plant was the smaller.

A curtain was pulled by the experimenter so that the plants could be replaced by the bicycles. The same judgment procedure that occurred with the plants was carried out with the bicycles. Once more the curtain was pulled and the bicycles replaced by the pictures of Mona Lisa.

A brief questionnaire was administered after this part of the experiment with a few questions about the nature of perception and also a key question to determine if the subject had any idea of what the experiment was actually about.

Results and Discussion

In the groups with unanimous but erroneous support of the judgment that the smaller object was the larger, 80% of the subjects also stated that the smaller was the larger. The group with one deviant answer, the subjects supported the majority opinion only 26% of the time. Table 1 shows the number of subjects responding for each of the three object-pairs.

Table 1. No of S's conforming out of 24 S's

Objects	A Plants	B Bicycles	C Pictures
No. of S's Conforming	22	18	20

The results are surprising and do not support the
hypothesis that unambiguous stimuli will produce less pressure for conformity than stimuli that are more easily perceived (or perhaps conceived) to be of different sizes. The
reverse appears to be the case. The unambiguous situation
may be the most threatening to the individual who finds himself perceiving differently from the rest of his peers. He
may, more than in the ambiguous perceptual situation, question his perception; or a more likely explanation, value the
anonymity and invisibleness that accordance with the group
offers rather than the distinctiveness and attention that being
the single deviant voice brings.

These results force us to question the current explanations of the role of ambiguity in conforming behavior.
Though currently believed to be a major factor in the tendency to adopt individual opinion to the group standard,
perhaps it now must be investigated more carefully. The
evidence from the group with one dissenter makes an important contribution to theoretical concerns surrounding peer
support and forces us to question the very nature of conformity.

References

Ayes, M. P. Experimental controls in conformity research.
        J. of Exp. Research, 1971, 53, 546-575.

Barris, J. P. Conformity behavior in a small group.
        Behavior Today, 1965, 3, 245-253.

Harringson, H. H. Small groups and the individual attitude.
        J. of Learning & Attitudes, 1969, 92, 111-120.

Holmes, C. The tendency to conform using perceptual cues
        as attitude measure. J. of Learning & Attitudes,
        1967, 83, 214-234.

Holmes, C. Ambiguous perceptual cues: their judgment in a
        group setting. Astral Attitudes, 1968, 14, 45-62.

James, A. P., and Sheffield, W. Individual judgment and
        the group norm. Groups, 1970, 24, 118-132.

DEVELOPMENT

● PROBLEM 21-10

A Comparison of Social Responsiveness in
Male and Female Infants

Marion Miles and Fay Jones

Greenley Institute for Childhood Research

Abstract

It has long been asserted by practitioners in the
field of child development that female infants are more
socially mature than male infants and this difference has
been noted to continue through adolescent years.* To test
the hypothesis that female infants are more socially responsive than males, observational ratings of responsiveness
both motor and verbal to social and nonsocial stimuli were
made for 14 infants between the ages of three to six months.
Smiling, frowning, moving toward or away from the object,
crying, yelling or other productions of sound were all used
as measures of responsiveness. Social stimuli were both
familiar and strange human faces. Nonsocial, spatial-motor
were glittering, rotating balls attached on a string across
the top of the crib. The social responsiveness scores of
the females differed from those of the males significantly
at the .05 level. The males scored higher on the responsiveness to the nonsocial stimuli at a level significantly
higher than the females.

The ongoing controversy concerning the innate psychological differences in the sexes rests on much inference
and little fact. From verbal reports (Noring, 1968) and
from the subjective impressions of parents (whose impressions hold little scientific interest because of the socially biased attitudes they may already have which influence
their perceptions), female infants are more gregarious, more
socially oriented than are their male counterparts. Though
much weight has been given to these observations, this assertion has not yet been systematically studied.

There is some evidence (Pollin & Norton, 1972) that
the nervous system in the female infant is more fully developed than that in the male. It has been suggested (Montagne,
1974) that the observed differences in the sociability of
the two sexes in infancy is due to this physiological difference. The argument that the male child must work harder
in the "female hormonal environment" than the female infant,
who goes through gestation in and environment completely
compatible to her own endocrine system, also has been offered as an explanation for the differing levels of develop-

---

*The reader should note that the experiment and
results reported here are hypothetical.

ment at birth. No definite relationship between the level
of neurological development and sociability has been definitely established.

Though this question is too complex for us to attempt to fully answer, we have designed this experiment in
order to test the assertion that female infants are more
sociable than male infants. Using responsiveness to two
types of stimuli--human faces and plastic play toys--we
sought to measure the difference in responsiveness of the
two sexes before the age of six months to social and spatial
motor stimuli. This age range was selected as it is generally considered (Barnes, 1974) that after this age the effects of the confounds of the social environment begin to
become indiscernible from innate tendencies.

Method

Subjects. 14 infants--7 males and 7 females ranging in
age from three to six months participated in the study.
Their mothers were all participants in the Childhood Development Study being conducted at the Greenley Institute and
had been coming to the Institute for tests once a week since
the third month of their pregnancy. The socio-economic
status of this group of women was principally middle class
and upper middle class as many were the wives of professors
or researchers connected with the Institute.

The adults selected to serve as the stimuli for the
children were in every case the mother, the father and two
assistants to the experimenter, one a male and one a female.
These last two individuals were unfamiliar to the infants.

Apparatus. Each child was tested in a standard hospital
crib equipped with a hand bar across the top that could
slide from the front to the back of the crib. A crib toy,
the "Sparkling Ball" by Delight Toys was used as the nonsocial, spatial-motor stimuli in each case.

Procedure. All of the infants were familiar with the
laboratory setting as each had visited at least twice before
the experiment began. Some had been to the laboratory as
many as six times before the start of the study. During the
first session each infant was visited for 5 minutes by the
mother, left for 5 minutes with the toy; visited for 5 minutes by the strange male, left for 5 minutes with the toy;
visited for 5 minutes by the father; left for another 5 with
the toy and finally visited for 5 minutes by the strange female.
The order of these visits was varied in each of the four sessions and randomly assigned to the different infants.

During the visits none of the visitors spoke to the
children. They were, however, instructed that it was fine
to make facial expressions and gestures toward the infant.
Throughout these experimental sessions, three trained observers observing through a one-way window recorded the
reactions of the children. The Jameson Response Scale (1969)
was used for keeping track of the reactions of the child to

each of the experimental situations. This scale has four major responsiveness variables: expression, vocalization, movement, and eye contact. Analysis of the ratings of the observers gives a numerical rating of degree of responsiveness ranging from 0 to 100.

The four sessions took place over a two week period for each of the infants. All the sessions were held in the morning.

Results

The mean social responsiveness score for the female infants was .78 while that for the males was .32. An analysis of variance performed on the responsiveness data indicated that the difference between the social responsiveness of the female infants and the male infants was significant at the .01 level. Typically when someone visited the female infants their reaction was notable. They either began smiling, gesturing, vocalizing excitedly or, occasionally, particularly with the strange faces, they would show disturbance at the visitor and on a number of occasions started to cry. The reaction of the male infants was markedly different. The overall response to the visitors was typically a mild indifference--except to the mother for whom the responsiveness rating for the males was .72 (for the females .94). Much movement or face-making on the part of the visitor was necessary to evoke even a mild degree of responsiveness from the males. As compared to the female group, a much lower percentage of male infants began crying when faced with a stranger. The human face simply did not seem to be of much interest to the males.

The response to the "Sparkling Ball" toy was greater among the boys. They demonstrated a .65 level of responsiveness to this toy. The girls, on the other hand, responded to the toy at a .43 level. The difference in these two response rates is significant at the .05 level.

Discussion

These data support the hypothesis that females demonstrate a greater propensity toward social responsiveness during first few months than do males. We cannot say and have not tried to answer the question of what the cause of this difference may be. The relative level of development of the nervous system has been mentioned as a possibility deserving further study.

It certainly cannot be denied that socialization practices further enhance the difference in the interests of the two sexes. "Girls are interested in people; boys are interested in things" is a cliche of which we are all aware. It may be that without the reinforcement of our socialization practices, the female interest in things and the male interest in social stimuli would become more equal as the

917

physiological development of the two sexes equalizes in the late teens. Unfortunately, we have no way of controlling for socialization practices until the age of 18 or 21. We are therefore left with speculation, speculation that is based, nonetheless on the fact that at birth the two sexes begin responding to different aspects of the world. As unpleasant as it may seem to our democratic principles, the sexes appear to be tuned from their earliest days to attend to different parts of the environment.

References

Barnes, C. The early effects of socialization. Journal of Early Development, 1974, 34, 567-582.

Jameson, S. O. Responsiveness in infants. Tests and Measurements Quarterly, 1969, 14, 345-352.

Montagne, W. The neurological antecedents of sociability. Neurological Review, 1974, 4, 234-246.

Noring, P. T. Sex differences in sociability. Journal of Sex Differences, 1968, 14, 535-541.

Pollin, T. J. & Norton, P. W. Nervous system development in infants. Childhood Research, 1972, 31, 114-128.

GLOSSARY

GLOSSARY

A-B variable – A variable that describes the effectiveness of therapists with schizophrenic or neurotic patients. "A" therapists work best with schizophrenics, and "B" therapists work best with neurotics.

Ability – Possessing the necessary skills to perform a specific act at the present time, as opposed to aptitude (having the potential to perform with additional training).

Ability tests – Subdivided into tests of aptitude and achievement, ability tests are designed to measure individual differences in knowledge and skills to determine what a person can do.

Ablation – Removal of a body part for the purpose of studying it.

Abnormal behavior – Behavior which creates a problem for the individual and/or for society. Abnormal behavior is often maladaptive to the individual's functioning in society.

Abortion – A spontaneous or induced expulsion of the fetus usually prior to the twentieth week of pregnancy.

Abreaction – A term used by Breuer and Freud to describe a patient's expression, sometimes violent, of a repressed emotion during hypnosis. This release of strangulated affect is synonymous with catharsis.

Abscissa – The x-axis, or horizontal axis of a graph. The independent variable is plotted on the abscissa.

Absolute refractory period – A brief period toward the end of neural stimulation during which the nerve cannot be restimulated.

Absolute threshold – The lowest level of intensity of a stimulus at which its presence or absence can be correctly detected 50 percent of the time.

Abstract intelligence – The ability to deal effectively with ideas expressed in symbols such as words, numbers, pictures, or diagrams.

Accommodation – 1. In vision, the changes of lens shape or curvature that produce sharpened retinal images of objects at varying distance from the eye. 2. In Piaget's system, the adaptive modification of the child's cognitive structures in order to deal with new objects or experiences. (See Assimilation.)

Acculturation – The learning of behaviors and attitudes one is expected to adopt as a member of a particular culture.

Acetylcholine – An acid that acts as an excitatory substance to facilitate neural transmission at many synapses and neuromuscular junctions.

Achievement motivation – The need, or drive, to perform a task successfully as judged against standards of excellence. The concept predominates in the expectancy value theory of motivation.

Achievement test – The part of an ability test designed to assess what an individual has already learned through prior training.

Achromatic – Without hue or saturation, varying only on the brightness dimension. For example, the black, gray, and white series.

Achromatism – Total color blindness due to congenital absence of cone cells.

Acoustic stimulus – A sound wave arising from the vibrations around an object in the air. Sound waves are generally referred to as acoustic stimuli only when they are audible.

Acquisition – The gradual strengthening of a response through learning as it is incorporated into the behavioral repertoire.

Acquisition curve – The graphic representation of the acquisition process in which response strength is displayed on the vertical axis and amount of practice on the horizontal.

Acrophobia – A neurotic fear of heights.

Act – A single unit in the continuous stream of behavior.

ACTH (adrenocorticotrophic hormone) – A hormone secreted by the pituitary gland in response to stress, causing the adrenal cortex to secrete corticosterone.

Acting out – 1. The performance in a new setting of behavior learned from and appropriate to another social situation. 2. In psychoanalysis, the carrying out of repressed impulses; the manifest behavior that is often symbolic of earlier stages of the individual's life.

Action decrement – The tendency of an organism not to repeat the action just completed.

Action potential – The nerve impulse; the changes in electrical potential along a nerve fiber that constitute the nerve impulse as it travels through the axon.

Action-specific energies (Lorenz) – Motivating energies that impel only very specific sequences of behavior; motivating energy for instinctual behaviors.

Active analytic psychotherapy – The form of psychoanalysis developed by Wilhelm Stekel in which the therapist takes a directive role as educator.

Active avoidance learning – A learning task in which the subject must make a prescribed response in order to avoid an aversive stimulus.

Active learning – Learning procedures that stress recitation and performance as opposed to simple reading of materials.

Actualization – The desire to realize one's own potential; in Maslow's theory of motivation, the highest level in the human need hierarchy.

Acuity – Sharpness of perception. Usually visual acuity, the ability of the eye to see spatial detail.

Adaptation – 1. A reduction in the sensitivity of a sense organ due to continued stimulation from the same source. 2. Behavioral or anatomical changes which enhance the possibility of survival. 3. In Piaget's system, the process of cognitive growth which modifies psychological structures to suit the environment.

Adaptation level – The level of stimulation to which an individual has already adapted and against which new stimulus conditions are judged.

Addiction – A state of dependence upon a drug or chemical in which discontinued use of the substance results in extreme psychological and/or physiological reactions.

Adipsia – A condition resulting from the destruction of the lateral hypothalamus that causes the victim to stop drinking.

Adjective checklist – A technique, used in the assessment of adult emotions, in which the subject is presented with a list of emotion words and is then instructed to check off those that are most appropriate to his feelings.

Adler, Alfred – A personality theorist who emphasized social factors in personality development. Founder of the school of Individual Psychology, he broke away from Freud in 1911.

Adolescence – The period from the onset of puberty to adulthood (11 to 19 years of age).

Adrenal cortex – The outer layer of the adrenal gland that secretes several hormones, including corticosterone, in response to emotional arousal.

Adrenal gland – A gland of the endocrine system that produces many hormones; especially important in regulating bodily responses to stress.

Adrenal medulla – The inner core of the adrenal gland that secretes the hormones epinephrine and norepinephrine into the bloodstream.

Adrenal steroids – Hormones secreted into the circulatory system by the adrenal cortex during emotional arousal.

Adrenaline – Also called epinephrine; a substance produced by the adrenal gland which is related to increases in general arousal.

Affect – A synonym for emotion; sometimes employed as a quantitative term to express a person's emotional capacity and degree of reaction to given situations.

Affective component – The emotional or feeling aspect of an attitude.

Affective feedback – The feelings of pleasantness or unpleasantness following an organism's responses.

Affective psychosis – Psychotic behavior characterized by extremes of mood. The most common include depressive reactions or manic-depressive reactions.

Affective state – The emotion of an individual at a specified point in time; can include negative, positive, or neutral feelings.

Afferent nerves – Nerves carried by the dorsal root which relay sensory impulses (information about the environment) to the central nervous system; sometimes used synonymously with sensory nerves.

Afferent neuron – A neuron carrying information to the central nervous system.

Affiliation – The need to associate with others; also, the quantity and quality of group memberships and friendship bonds.

Affirmation rule – In concept learning, a rule specifying that all items with a particular attribute are instances of the concept.

Afterbirth – The placenta and other membranes that are expelled from a woman's body following the birth of a child.

Aftersensation – Most often in vision (afterimages), the continuation of a sensation even after the removal of the stimulus.

Age equivalent – 1. In testing, a score conversion in which a test score is assigned the age value for which that score is the average score. 2. In development, the average age at which a child reaches a particular developmental stage.

Age norms – Norms based upon large samples of children at each age.

Aggression – Hostile action or feelings, especially those caused by frustration, which may result in harm or injury to another person.

Aggressive drive – One of the inherited instincts proposed by Freud and thought to give rise to the destructive components of human behavior.

Agoraphobia – A strong fear of open places; often referred to as a form of neurosis.

Albinism – The congenital absence of hair, eye, and skin pigmentation. An albino is color-blind.

Alcoholism – A substance-use disorder marked by compulsive drinking and inability to control drinking behavior.

Alexia – A form of aphasia, usually caused by brain damage, in which one has an inability to read or understand written or printed language.

Algorithm – A method for attacking a problem which is assured of success; often involves repetitive operations which survey the possibilities at each step.

Alienation – The state of feeling separated or withdrawn from one's culture and/or social and personal relationships; the central theme of existential philosophy.

All-or-none law – The principle that the axon of a neuron fires either with full strength or not at all to a stimulus, regardless of its intensity, provided the stimulus is at least at the threshold value.

Allele – One of a pair of genes located at corresponding positions on a pair of chromosomes. Each pair contains the genetic code for a particular trait, with one allele often dominant (i.e., the determinant of the trait).

Allport, Gordon – American psychologist who studied the development of personality. He favored a dynamic trait model.

Alpha rhythm – A wave pattern, found in the EEG during periods of relaxed alertness, which has a frequency of 8 to 12 cycles per second.

Alpha waves – A particular brain wave pattern that occurs when the subject is in a state of "relaxed wakefulness." People can be taught to control the presence of alpha waves through biofeedback training.

Altered state of consciousness – State that occurs when the overall functioning of the mind takes on a pattern that is qualitatively different from normal.

Alternation – Experimental method used in the study of thinking in which the subject is required to alternate responses in a pattern (such as left-right-left-right or left-left-right-right).

Altruistic behavior – Behavior that benefits others and is not directly rewarding to the self.

Amacrine cells – Retinal cells believed to be of importance in summation effects. They interconnect bipolar or second order neurons.

Ambiguity – The possibility that a given stimulus can elicit more than one definition response.

Ambivalence – The bipolarity of feeling; the state of being drawn to or away from two mutually antagonistic goals at the same time.

American Psychological Association (APA) – The major and official professional organization for psychologists in the United States.

American Sign Language – The gestural language used by the deaf in North America.

Amnesia – The inability to recall events in one's past, sometimes including one's identity, often as a result of physical or psychological trauma. In the absence of physical trauma, amnesia is often attributed to neurotic dissociation of threatening aspects of one's past sometimes restricted to one severely traumatic event.

Amniocentesis – The removal of fetal cells from the fluid of the amniotic sac to test for the presence of abnormal chromosomes.

Amniotic fluid – A dark, watery fluid that fills the amniotic sac during pregnancy. The sac lines the uterus and contains the developing child.

Amphetamine – A class of drugs which stimulate the central nervous system. Chemically all amphetamines contain $C_9H_{13}N$. Use can become addictive.

Amplitude – The intensity or loudness of sound, measured in decibels.

Amygdala – A part of the limbic system, the system where emotion is organized, located between the hypothalamus and pituitary gland which becomes active whenever we encounter anything new or unexpected.

Anal character – In psychoanalytic personality, one characterized by stinginess, orderliness, and compulsive behavior because of an infantile fixation on the anal region.

Anal stage – The second of Freud's stages in which libidinal interest and conflicts center on excretory functions and toilet training. This stage usually occurs between the ages of 8 and 18 months.

Analog computer – A computer that operates on continuous signals of varying voltages.

Analysis of variance – A statistical test appropriate for analyzing reliability from experiments with any number of levels on one or more independent variables.

Analytical psychology – The term applied to the form of psychoanalysis developed by Carl Jung.

Anaphrodisiac – Having to do with a lack of sexual feeling.

Anchorage effect – Resistance to attitude change because of particularly strong beliefs or group support.

Androgens – Substances associated with male sex hormone activity in vertebrates, produced mainly by the testes and to a small extent by ovaries and the adrenal cortex.

Androgyny – Having psychological characteristics expected of members of both sexes.

Anecdotal record – A written report describing an incident of an individual's behavior. Theoretical conclusions based solely on anecdotal reports are often suspect. They do, however, often serve as the basis for actual research.

Anechoic chamber – An enclosure, the walls of which are especially absorbing of sounds.

Angell, James – One of the founders of Functionalism.

Anger – An acute emotional reaction characterized by strong impulses in the autonomic nervous system which may occur when the attainment of a goal is blocked. Often induced by frustration.

Anima – According to Jung, an archetype representing the feminine characteristics as opposed to the animus, or male archetype.

Animism – The belief held by young children to the effect that nonliving objects have some of the characteristics of living beings, such as will and intention.

Anisocoria – A pathological condition in which the pupils of the two eyes are of unequal diameter.

Anomalous color defect – Anomalous dichromatism and trichromatism. In dichromatism only two colors are seen (most often blue and yellow). In trichromatism weakness in the red-green region is observed.

Anomy – A term employed by Bull to describe the earliest stage in the development of mortality. Refers to the absence of a moral orientation.

Anorexia – (nervosa: self starvation) Extreme loss of appetite accompanied by pathological and dangerous weight loss.

Anosmia – Complete absence or serious deficiency in the sense of smell.

Anoxemia – An oxygen deficiency which interferes with normal metabolism.

Anoxia – A condition in which the brain does not receive enough oxygen to allow it to develop or function properly.

Antabuse – Drug that causes intense nausea if a person drinks alcohol while the chemical is in the bloodstream. Used as a method of controlling the pathological drinking behavior of alcoholics.

Antecedent-consequent research – Research strategy that studies subjects of the same age to determine how different environmental conditions affect performance.

Anthropomorphism – The attribution of human characteristics to subhuman species. Anthropomorphic explanations often attribute conscious thought, etc., to animals or to inanimate objects (most common in children).

Anticipation – A technique for testing learning and memory that requires the subject to indicate the learned material in a determined order.

Anticipation learning – A form of rote-learning procedure in which the subject tries to give the next item in the list during each trial. Affords a running account of the subject's progress.

Antidepressant – A drug which elevates the mood and relieves depression. Most antidepressants are "set-point" drugs which, like aspirin, have no effect on an individual unless he or she is in an abnormal state (e.g., has a headache). People who are not depressed do not feel better after taking antidepressants (just as aspirin will not change the temperature of someone who already has a temperature of 98.6°F.)

Antipsychotics – These drugs are used with major psychotic disorders such as schizophrenia. The drugs have a calming effect and seem to alleviate schizophrenic symptoms such as delusions and hallucinations. Some examples are chlorpromazine and reserpine (also known as "major tranquilizers").

Antisocial behavior – Behavior characterized by a failure to act according to societal standards and the absence of anxiety about such behavior; also called psychopathic or sociopathic behavior.

Anvil – A small bone in the middle ear located between the hammer and stirrup (synonym: incus).

Anxiety – Feeling of dread and apprehension without a specific and realistic fear of some threatening object.

Anxiety reaction – A form of neurosis characterized by vague feelings of anxiety. Often called free-floating anxiety because it is not attached to any specific stimulus. Physiological symptoms of anxiety reactions include heart palpitations, tremors, nausea, and shortness of breath.

Apathy – Extreme indifference to situations that normally arouse a response. In extreme cases (depression), complete and total indifference to one's surroundings.

Aphagia – Condition in which an animal refuses to eat, ignores food, and starves to death unless treated. Aphagia has been produced experimentally by surgical removal of the lateral hypothalamic nucleus.

Aphasia – Loss or impairment of the ability to express or receive linguistic communications, resulting from cerebral damage to the parietotemporal cortex.

Aphonia – Loss of speech resulting from emotional or laryngeal disorders.

Apoplexy – A cerebral hemorrhage or blocked blood vessel causing a loss of consciousness and motor control.

Apparent motion – An illusion in which objects either appear to move but, in fact do not, or appear to move in directions contrary to their actual movement.

Appetitive behavior – Behavior directed toward some positive goal (from the Latin, *petere*: to seek).

Applied psychology – Any branch of psychology that employs psychological principles for solution of practical problems.

Approach-approach conflict – The conflict in which a person or organism is motivated toward two gratifying goals or stimuli that are incompatible.

Approach-avoidance conflict – A conflict situation in which one is both attracted to and repelled by the same goal. For example, one may want to go to college, but be fearful of the work that would be involved.

Approach-withdrawal systems – The organization of behavior patterns according to whether the response is toward or away from objects and events.

Aptitude test – An ability test designed to appraise, to predict, what the individual can learn to do if he receives appropriate education or job training.

Aquaphobia – Fear of water.

Aqueous humor – A fluid behind the cornea of the eye.

Arachnoid – The middle protective tissue layer of the central nervous system between the pia mater and dura mater.

Archetype – According to Jung, a symbolic representation of a universally meaningful concept based on the experiences of all one's ancestors in the inherited "collective unconscious."

Arithmetic mean – The common average, obtained by adding together all of the scores in a set and dividing by the number of scores.

Arousal – Increased alertness and attention accompanied by changes in the central and autonomic nervous systems and increased muscle tension.

Arousal jag – An increase in arousal, followed by a decrease in arousal; the decrease and its anticipation are reinforcing.

Arousal potential – The capacity of stimuli, or of their characteristics to cause or raise arousal.

Arousal theory – A motivational theory that assumes man needs to maintain arousal at an optimal level for specific behavior. Arousal theory explains behavior involved in risk-taking, gambling, curiosity, and learning.

Artificial insemination – An artificial breeding procedure often employed in animal husbandry and sometimes with humans. This procedure obviates the necessity for a physical union between a pair of opposite-sexed individuals.

Asch situation – A test of the effectiveness of a group on an individual's judgment in which the subject is falsely led to believe that his perceptions are different from those of the majority.

Assertion-structured therapy – The term applied to the system of psychotherapy developed by E. Lakin Phillips in which the behavioristic therapist models assertive behavior patterns for the client.

Assertiveness training – Teaching someone to express emotions, feelings, and beliefs in an "open" or forthright way.

Assessment – The evaluation of a person with respect to some psychologically meaningful characteristic, trait, or disposition.

Assimilation – In Piaget's theory, the taking in of new information. Assimilation ultimately results in the accommodation of a schema to the new information.

Association – The functional relationship between two psychological phenomena or concepts based on prior learning.

Association cortex – Largest portion of the cerebral hemispheres, most highly developed in humans. The more complex functions like perception, language, and thought are centered here.

Association, Laws of – Principles formulated to account for functional relationships between ideas: similarity, contiguity, contrast, coexistence, succession, and causality.

Association theory – Asserts that all behaviors are the result of accumulations of stimulus and response associations.

Associationism – In psychophysics and cognition, the theoretical approach that complex ideas are the result of associations between simple elements. In learning theories, synonymous with the S-R connection (stimulus with response).

Associative attribute – In Underwood's theory of memory, one of the attributes of a memory. It consists of items to which that memory is linked associatively. For example, returning to one's hometown may facilitate the recall of memories long "forgotten."

Associative cortex – Areas of the cortex outside the primary sensory and motor areas.

Associative thinking – Uncontrolled thinking which is not directed to any goal, e.g., daydreaming. Also a train of thoughts, each one leading to another.

Asthma – A disorder characterized by increased airway resistance caused by constriction in the bronchioles, often aggravated or precipitated by psychological stress.

Asymptote – In a learning curve, the point at which performance has approached near maximum and begins to level off. The value of the dependent variable at which no further effects of the independent variable occur.

Atavism – A genetic carryover from an older phylogenetic ancestor.

Atmosphere effect – Refers to errors made in reasoning or behavior that are the result of the atmosphere surrounding the problem, namely, the subject's attitude or the way the problem is presented. Affirmative premises tend to create an affirmative atmosphere and, thus, imply an affirmative conclusion.

Attachment – The normal relationship of a child to parents and other significant individuals; usually develops during the first six months of postnatal development.

Attention – The selective focusing upon certain aspects of the environment to the neglect of others.

Attention-rejection – A way of classifying emotions according to the degree of orientation to the event the emotion produces.

Attention span – The number of elements or amount of material that can be perceived in a single brief exposure; the length of time a person focuses on a given object or task.

Attenuation – Weakening of the relationship between two measures because of the unreliability of either or both. Also the reduction in amount or degree of the stimulus.

Attitude – A fairly stable and lasting predisposition to behave or react in a characteristic way (positive or negative) toward individuals, objects, events, or institutions. Attitudes include feeling, thinking and behavioral components.

Attitude scale – Devices employed to measure the degree or strength of attitudes or opinions.

Attitude system – A cluster of attitudes which share common or similar concepts, beliefs, motives, and habits.

Attribute – A perceived characteristic of some object or person. As a verb, it means to infer that an individual has certain characteristics. Also a fundamental or characteristic property of anything.

Attribute identification – Learning to identify the relevant attributes is a component task of concept learning.

Attribution – Ways of assigning causality to the behaviors or cognitions of other people or oneself.

Audition – The sense of hearing.

Auditory canal – Sometimes referred to as the external auditory meatus. The tubular passage which connects the external ear with the middle ear.

Auditory localization – Identifying positions from which sounds emanate; often a function of the slight discrepancy between the times at which the signal reaches each ear.

Augmented sensory feedback – Synonymous with biofeedback. The control through conditioning of internal processes.

Authoritarian personality – Personality type characterized by, among other traits, high ethnocentrism, conservatism, antidemocratism, and prejudice.

Authoritarians – Those people who score high on the California F-Scale. Normally, such people exhibit certain antidemocratic personality characteristics and are often prejudiced against minorities; they consistently exhibit their need to establish authority.

Autism – A nearly total withdrawal from reality and escape into fantasy—perceiving the world in terms of wishes.

Autistic – A term referring to psychological processes that do not correspond to reality and are strongly determined by a person's needs. Also refers to a severe mental illness of early childhood, involving extreme withdrawal and isolation, absorption in fantasy, and profound defects in thought and language.

Autogenic – Originating within the self.

Autokinetic effect – Apparent movement of a small spot of light seen against a dark background in a completely dark room.

Automatic action – A well-practiced response that occurs "automatically" when its appropriate stimulus is presented.

Autonomic conditioning – The eliciting of responses of the autonomic nervous system, including salivation, galvanic skin response, gastric motility, etc.

Autonomic nervous system (ANS) – The peripheral nervous system that controls the function of many glands and smooth-muscle organs. It is divided into the sympathetic and parasympathetic systems.

Autonomy – Self-determination, a need to be self-determining.

Average – The arithmetic mean, the median, and the mode are all measures of central tendency referred to as "the average."

Aversions – Stimuli that give rise to avoidance behavior.

Aversive behavior – Behavior aimed at avoiding unpleasant consequences.

Aversive conditioning – Instrumental conditioning in which an aversive stimulus can be prevented by making an appropriate response.

Aversive stimulus – Any stimulus the organism judges to be noxious or unpleasant.

Aversive therapy – A technique that pairs unpleasant (aversive) stimuli with inappropriate behavior.

Avoidance-avoidance conflict – A conflict between two unattractive alternatives, for example, a child given the alternative to eat spinach or go to bed without supper.

Avoidance conditioning – A form of learning in which the behavior change is motivated by the threat of punishment.

Avoidance response – Any response an organism makes in order to keep from experiencing an anticipated aversive stimulus.

Axillary hair – Armpit hair.

Axon – The elongated part of a nerve cell body which carries the nerve impulse away from the cell body toward another nerve fiber or neural structure.

Babbling – The relatively meaningless speech patterns comprising repetitive sequences of alternating consonants and vowels that infants repeat in the first six months of life.

Babinski reflex – A reflex present in the newborn child, but disappearing later in life. It involves fanning the toes as a result of being tickled in the center of the soles of the feet. Adults normally curl their toes inward rather than fanning them outward.

Backward conditioning – In classical conditioning, a trial in which the onset of the UCS occurs before the onset of the CS. The procedure is often unreliable.

Balance theory – The theory which argues that people prefer and seek consistency with respect to their belief systems and avoid inconsistent and incompatible belief systems.

Balanced Latin square – An experimental design in which each subject is exposed to each experimental condition and employs a counterbalancing scheme in which each condition is preceded and followed equally often by every other condition.

Bales analysis – A technique for describing social groups by making functional analyses of the types of communications between the group members, with the aid of a computer which is programmed to score 164 different categories.

Band wagon – A propaganda technique in which the propagandist's view is made to appear the majority view which causes more and more people to associate themselves with the "majority opinion."

Barbiturate – A class of drugs that depress the central nervous system inducing drowsiness and muscular relaxation. Barbiturates are highly addictive substances (e.g., nembutal, seconal, and phenobarbital).

Barrier – Any environmental or psychological obstacle which interferes with one's needs.

Basal age – The highest year level at which a subject passes all the subtests of an intelligence test, used in conjunction with intelligence tests to compute mental age.

Baseline – A measurement of frequency of a certain variable prior to experimental treatment.

Basic anxiety – In Horney's theory, the anxiety that arises out of the helplessness and insecurity of childhood. The child may feel helpless and alone in a hostile world.

Basic research – Research performed solely to acquire knowledge which is often not "theory guided."

Basilar membrane – The cochlear membrane at the base of the cochlear canal on which is found the Organ of Corti. The basilar membrane is important in pitch perception.

Behavior – The term is usually employed to refer to anything a human being does: any act or succession of acts which are objectively observable. Some psychologists would also include conscious phenomena such as cognitions, perceptions, and judgments.

Behavior chain – Learning related behaviors in sequence in which each response serves as a stimulus for the next response.

Behavior control – The ability one person has to control another's inputs.

Behavior disorder – A general term referring to one of the various categories of psychopathology. Any behavior which is not socially acceptable.

Behavior modification – The application of scientifically derived principles (usually from learning) to the control of human behavior. Both classical and operant conditioning may be employed.

Behavior rating scales – Scales that are used to measure certain classes of observed behavior from which emotions or cognitions may be inferred.

Behavior therapy – The application of learning theory in treating behavioral disorders.

Behavioral arrest – Immobility resulting from severe conflict.

Behavioral genetics – The study of the influence of heredity on behavior.

Behavioral model – Model of psychopathology in which all behavior, normal or otherwise, is a product of learning about the environment.

Behavioral sink – When severely overcrowded conditions lead to pathological responding, despite environmental conditions that are otherwise normal.

Behavioral vacillation – Repeated cycles of movement toward and then away from a goal, characteristic of approach-avoidance conflicts.

Behaviorism – A system of psychology, founded by John B. Watson, which studied observable, measurable stimuli and responses only, without reference to consciousness or mental constructs which the system argues have no real utility. The objective is to predict the response evoked by certain stimuli.

Behavioristic theory – A general term for those theories of learning concerned primarily with the observable components of behavior (stimuli and responses). Such theories are labeled S-R learning theories and are exemplified in classical and operant conditioning.

Bel, decibel – A bel is a unit of auditory intensity relative to the auditory threshold; a decibel is one tenth of a bel. The decibel scale is often used as a scale of auditory loudness. Sounds of different pitch, but of the same decibel level often appear not to be equally as loud.

Belief prejudice – Beliefs which involve stereotyping: over-generalization and classification based upon rigid and biased perceptions of an object, group, class, or individual.

Belonging – Thorndike's assumption that connections between items in learning are more readily formed if they are related in some way a priori.

Beta – 1. A statistic in signal detection theory related to the criterion adopted by the observer. Beta is a measure of response bias and is independent of the observer's actual ability to detect a signal's presence. 2. In weight, the weights of multiple correlation predictors which yield the best prediction in multiple regression equations.

Beta rhythm – An EEG rhythm with a frequency from 13 to 25 hertz and a low amplitude that occurs during states of alertness.

Beta waves – Relatively low amplitude brain waves.

Between group variance – A measure of the dispersion among groups in an experiment.

Between-subject design – An experimental design in which each subject is tested under only one level of each independent variable.

Bias – In research, a factor that distorts data. In attitude, an internalized predisposition of affect because of the environment.

Biconditional rule – In concept learning, a rule that states that a given item is an instance of the concept if it possesses a given attribute, but only if it also possesses a second attribute.

Bilingualism – The ability to speak and understand two languages.

Binary – A term referring to a system with only two possible states. Binary numbers usually have only two values: 0 and 1.

Binocular depth cues – Cues to depth perception based upon the simultaneous functioning of two eyes.

Binocular disparity – The minor difference between the two retinal images when viewing a solid (3-dimensional) object. It is caused by the separation of the two eyes with a consequent difference in the visual angle. Binocular disparity is important in depth perception.

Biofeedback – The use of a device to reveal physiological responses that are usually unobservable. Biofeedback experiments typically inform the subject about his heart rate, respiration rate, EEG activity, or similar responses in order to enable him to achieve some degree of control over the responses. Biofeedback is now often used in psychotherapy in teaching individuals to control their own physiological states (e.g., to reduce anxiety and its symptoms).

Biological rhythms – Regular, repeating patterns of activity of various lengths or cycles.

Bipolar cell – Neuron in the retina connecting rods or cones to ganglion cells.

Bipolar disorder – A mood disorder in which there are recurrent and severe fluctuations of affective state between elation and depression. Formerly called "manic-depression."

Birth order – The position that a child occupies in the family (for example, first, second, or third born).

Birth-order effects – Various consistencies in personality that seem to be tied to whether a person was the first-born child in his family, the second-born, etc.

Birth trauma – The damaging effect on the psyche of the transition from uterine to extrauterine environment. In the Rankian literature, the birth trauma is treated as the fundamental anxiety experience out of which most subsequent neurotic conditions of the individual grow. The term is also used to refer to physical damage occurring at birth.

Black box – A term used by psychologists when referring to the organism's processing information (the stimulus) before acting (the behavior). The black box thus encompasses all cognitive processes including emotion, preference, and thoughts which are believed to mediate between stimulus and subsequent response.

Blind spot – The area in the retina where the optic nerve exits to the brain; no vision is possible here because there are no receptors.

Bloch's law – The inverse, linear relation between the duration of a visual target and threshold.

Block design – Dividing experimental subjects into homogeneous categories on a predetermined variable so that the categories can be treated as one unit.

Block sampling – 1. Sampling by geographic area. 2. The grouping of people or elements to be sampled into categories representative of the population.

Body language – A term referring to nonverbal and often unconscious communication by means of gestures, postures, expressions, etc.

Body-type theory – An attempt to predict personality by identifying the shape of the body and the characteristics that supposedly accompany that shape. Now thought to have little value as such systems are extreme oversimplifications at best.

Brain bisection – A longitudinal division of the brain between the two hemispheres. The procedure may be used to alleviate epileptic seizures and to study brain functions.

Brain lesions – Structural or functional alterations of the brain caused by injury; lesions can be produced by electrical coagulation of an area, by chemical means, by surgical removal of tissue, or by disease.

Brain stem – A part of the brain which regulates incoming and outgoing signals; it contains an area which influences the degree of general activity of an animal.

Brain waves – Rhythmic and spontaneous electrical discharges by the brain.

Brightness – That aspect of color perception that has reference to the black-white dimension correlated chiefly with wave amplitude.

Brightness constancy – Observation that objects maintain their brightness even though the amount of light reflected from them changes.

Broca's area – One of the areas of the cerebral cortex, located in the frontal lobe, which is important for the motor aspects of speech. Located in the inferior frontal gyrus in the left cerebral hemisphere of righthanded individuals and in the right hemisphere for left-handed people.

C factor – A variable, in some factor analyses of intelligence tests, which includes cleverness and quickness in thinking.

California F-Scale – The California Fascism Test, a test designed to measure authoritarianism, which isolates a personality type whose main characteristics are a rigid adherence to middle-class morality, deference to authority, and a dominating attitude.

Cannon-Bard theory – A theory of emotion that holds that bodily reaction and emotional experience occur simultaneously because they are both controlled from the same place in the mid-brain. It challenged the James-Lange theory of emotion (see James-Lange).

Cannula – A small tube inserted into some area of the brain in order to chemically stimulate that area or to extract some substance from that area.

Card stacking – A propaganda technique that involves the selective use of evidence in making an argument. Also designing an argument or experiment procedure such that it is almost certain, or at least "unfairly" likely, that any conclusion except the desired one will ensue.

Cardiac arrhythmias – Disorders involving heart rate.

Cardiograph – A device used for recording the rate and amplitude of the heartbeat.

Cardiovascular – Pertaining to the heart and blood vessels.

Case study (case history method) – It is an intensive investigation of a particular instance, or case, of some behavior which does not infer any cause and effect relationship but uses a combination of objective descriptive methods such as biographical data, psychological testing, and personal interviewing.

Castration anxiety – In Freudian theory, the fear experienced by a male child that he will be castrated by his father in reprisal for his sexual attraction to his mother. In the female child, the thought that she once possessed a penis but lost it by castration.

Catatonia – Generally, any reaction in which there is a complete withdrawal characterized by an inhibition of movement, speech, and responsiveness to the environment.

Categorization – The act of placing stimulus input in categories. According to Bruner, recognizing an object means placing it into an appropriate category.

Categorized list – Words used in memory experiments that are related in some taxonomic, associationistic, or other meaningful way.

Catharsis – Synonymous with abreaction.

Cattell, James – Personality theorist interested in trait measurement; developed the "factorial theory of personality."

Causation – The relation in which a given event produces the effect.

Ceiling – The maximum score set by the items in a test. A test that had items practically all of which could be answered by the average fifth grader would have a ceiling at the fifth grade level.

Ceiling age – The year level at which a subject fails to pass any subtests of an intelligence test.

Cell body – The mass, composed of cytoplasm, surrounding the nucleus of a cell not including any projecting fibers, which is responsible for the life processes of the entire cell; especially the cytoplasm around the nucleus of a neuron exclusive of the axons and dendrites (also called soma).

Centile – A method of ranking scores by computing the percentages of scores in a distribution that lie above and below a certain point in the distribution on a scale of 1 to 100.

Centile rank – A measure of relative position in a group indicating what percentage of the norm group had poorer performance than the individual being measured.

Central nervous system (CNS) – The brain and spinal cord.

Central tendency – A typical measure summarizing a set of scores that reveals a middle representative value such as the mean, median, and mode.

Centralist position – The theory that behavior is explained best by reference to processes in the brain, as opposed to the peripheral structures.

Centrality of an attitude – The degree to which an attitude affects a person's thinking and behavior; the relevancy of an attitude.

Centration – The tendency to center attention on a single feature of an object or situation.

Cephalocaudal – Refers to the sequence of body growth in which development occurs first at the head and then moves downward through the rest of the body, part by part. Also, pertaining to the dimension of the body between the head and tail.

Cerebellum – The cerebellum or "little brain" lying at the rear of the medulla which is responsible for the control of coordination and posture. It receives fibers from the kinesthetic and vestibular pathways and also has interconnections with the cerebrum.

Cerebral cortex – The outermost half-inch layer of the cerebral hemispheres, it contains motor, sensory, and intellectual processes. It is made up of gray tinted cells and thus is sometimes called gray matter. (Also known as the neocortex of the new brain.)

Cerebral hemispheres – The largest parts of the brain in humans and other higher mammals, they are the seat of the more complex functions like language, numerical ability, and abstract thought, in addition to being responsible for sensation, some aspects of bodily movement, and many other functions.

Cerebral palsy – A type of paralysis caused by a lesion in the brain; frequently it is a congenital defect.

Cerebrotonia – In Sheldon's personality typology, one of the three primary temperamental states characterized by fast reactions, social inhibition, rigid bearing, sensitivity, hypersensitivity to pain, resistance to alcohol and the tendency to be a "loner." It is associated with the ectomorphic body build.

Cerebrum – The largest and most highly developed part of the nervous system in higher animals. It is divided into the right and left cerebral hemispheres which are connected to each other by the corpus callosum. It occupies the entire upper area of the cranium and is involved in the regulation of sensory processes, thought formation, and motor activity.

Cervix – The small circular opening to the womb (uterus) that dilates considerably during birth.

Cesarean birth – Delivery through a surgical incision into the mother's abdomen and uterus.

CFF (critical flicker frequency) – The frequency at which a flickering stimulus (e.g., light), when going on and off rapidly, appears to be steadily on.

Chaining – Type of instrumental conditioning whereby one learns to exhibit a series of behaviors in order to obtain reinforcement in which each response serves as a stimulus for the next response.

Chemical senses – Those classifications of experiences, such as taste and smell, whose stimuli are chemical and which react with receptors in such a manner as to produce nervous impulses.

Chemotherapy – A medical therapy involving the use of drugs to try to treat abnormal behavior or personality patterns.

Chi (square) – Chi refers to the Greek letter c which is employed in the chi square, a statistical test. The chi square determines whether a distribution is significantly different from the expected or theoretical distribution.

Childhood – In humans, by convention, from two to eleven years of age.

Choleric – A temperament characterized by Hippocrates as prone to anger and outrage.

Chromatic color – A color having hue (wavelength) and saturation.

Chromosomes – Structures within the nucleus of a cell which contain the genes. Human cells contain 23 pairs of genes for a total of 46.

Chronological age (CA) – Length of life; distinguished from "mental age."

Chronoscope – An instrument which measures speed of reaction.

CIE chromaticity diagram – A three-dimension model that reflects the main principles of additive color mixture.

Ciliary muscles – The circular mass of smooth muscles within the eye that are responsible for accommodation of the lens.

Circadian rhythms – Cyclical patterns of change in physiological functions such as hunger, sleep, or body temperature occurring at approximately 24 hour intervals.

Circular reaction – A type of behavior pattern observed in early infancy that involves repetitive behaviors that are self-stimulating, e.g., thumb-sucking.

Clairvoyance – A form of extrasensory perception in which one is aware of the past, present, or future without the use of sense organs.

Class – 1. A grouping of objects or people according to an a priori scheme. 2. In biology, a taxonomic category between Phylum (or Subphylum) and Order (or Subclass). 3. In statistics, a grouping of values into a single category.

Class interval – The arbitrarily selected range of scores within a given division of a measurement scale or frequency distribution.

Classical analysis (or psychoanalysis) – Psychoanalytic theories and practices based on the earlier Freudian period with emphasis on unraveling the unconscious blockings of the libido. Also used to refer to the hypotheses and techniques of Freud and his followers as opposed to all others.

Classical conditioning – (also known as Pavlovian or Respondent or Type S conditioning) A form of learning in which an originally neutral stimulus repeatedly paired with a reinforcer elicits a response. The neutral stimulus is the conditioning stimulus (CS), the reinforcer is the unconditioned stimulus (UCS), the unlearned response is the unconditioned response (UCR), and the learned response is the conditioned response (CR).

Claustrophobia – A fear of closed spaces.

Client-centered therapy – Treatment of mental illness in which the patient is responsible for working out his problems; nondirective therapy. Generally associated with Carl Rogers.

Clinical case history – Records or data from therapy situations; used to identify behaviors and to suggest problems that need to be studied.

Clinical investigation – An experimental technique involving the use of a laboratory or clinic, usually in order to administer tests or provide experiences that require elaborate or non-portable equipment.

Clinical psychiatrist – A physician (M.D. degree) whose training emphasizes the treatment of mental disorders using both psychotherapeutic and medicinal treatments.

Clinical psychologist – A psychologist (either M.A. or Ph.D. degree) whose training emphasizes the assessment, treatment, research, and prevention of mental disorders.

Clinical psychology – A branch of psychology concerned with the assessment and treatment of mental illness and with researching its causes.

Cloning – The process of reproducing identical individuals from selected cells of the body. Cloning ordinarily involves replacing the nucleus of one egg cell with a cell from the body of the individual who is being cloned (reproduced).

Closure (Gestalt Law) – The tendency to perceive gaps as being filled in, usually completing a figure.

Cloze technique – A procedure in which words are deleted from verbal passages, and subjects are required to identify the missing words.

Cochlea – The bony, coiled structure in the ear containing the receptor organ for hearing. The cochlea contains three tubes: the scala vestibular, scala media, and scala tympani.

Cochlear microphonic – Electrical activity recorded from the cochlea of the ear that, up to relatively high frequencies, closely matches the frequency and amplitude of the stimulus.

Codability – Ease with which a stimulus can be assigned a language label.

Coding – The transformation of data from one form into another so that it can be communicated over some channel. In information theory, the transformation of messages into signals.

Coding system (Bruner) – A concept referring to a hierarchical arrangement of related categories.

Coefficient of contingency – A correlational measure used when the distributions are on nominal scales.

Coefficient of correlation – A numerical index of the degree of relationship between two variables.

Cognition – A concept including all forms of knowing, perceiving, imagining, reasoning, judging, and thinking.

Cognitive component – The part of an attitude revealing the beliefs a person has about a stimulus.

Cognitive consistency – Attitude formation and change that stresses the motive to attain consistency between one's various beliefs, emotions, and behaviors. Also, such a state of consistency or congruity.

Cognitive development – Changes in sensory, perceptual, and intellectual performances with age.

Cognitive dissonance (Festinger) – An uncomfortable psychological conflict between beliefs and behavior. Also the motivational position that the individual will take to reduce the dissonance.

Cognitive psychology – An approach to psychological phenomena that focuses upon hypothetical cognitive structures (representations of experience) rather than upon responses.

Cognitive style – One's individual approach to perceiving and thinking about events or the world.

Cognitive theory – Approach to personality that emphasizes the cognitive processes such as thinking and judging and is thus highly rational in its outlook. Such theories have been developed by George Kelly and Edward Tolman.

Coherence – The quality of systematic and predictable connection; consistency.

Cohesiveness – The overall attractiveness of a group for its members. The quality of "hanging together," as applied to social groups perceptual phenomena, traits, or items learned.

Colic – A syndrome characterized by a distention of the abdomen, apparently resulting in severe pain and causing a baby to cry violently and continuously; also, used loosely to describe the symptoms of infants who have regular or prolonged bouts of paroxysmal crying during their first few months.

Collative variables – Employed by Berlyne to describe those properties of stimuli most likely to increase arousal in an organism. Such characteristics of stimulus objects as novelty, surprise, complexity, and ambiguity are collative variables.

Collective unconscious – In Jungian psychoanalytic theory, one of the two parts of one's unconscious mind which is inherited and common to all members of the species. It houses the archetypes and contains racial memories and psychic material.

Color – The quality dimension of light. The hue of a visual stimulus, determined by the wavelength of the light.

Color blindness – Inability to experience the colors of the spectrum in the same fashion as would a normal member of the same species.

Color circle – A circular arrangement of hues in which sectors of complementary colors are opposite and in which saturation of color is represented by the radial distance from the center.

Color constancy – The tendency to perceive an object as of the same hue under wide variations of illumination.

Color solid – A geometric 3-dimensional representation of the hue, brightness, and saturation of color.

Combinativity (compensation) – A term which refers to changes compensating each other.

Common fate (factor of uniform density) – A Gestalt principle that elements in perception which function, change, or move in the same direction will be apprehended together.

Communication – 1. The transmission of messages. 2. The transfer of energy from one place to another in an organism or system. 3. Any message or signal which does not always require language. 4. A psychotherapist's information as given by a patient.

Communication net – The channels of communication in a group; the number of channels compared to the number of potential channels is the conductivity of the communication net.

Communication network – The pattern of open and closed channels of communications among the members of a group.

Community mental health – Approach to mental health that emphasizes the prevention of mental illness and the need for broader and more effective mental health services based within communities including community support systems.

Comparative psychology – The branch of psychology which compares behavioral differences among the species on the phylogenetic scale to discover development trends.

Comparison level – In social exchange theory, the standard by which one evaluates what he deserves which is usually based on the average of past experiences.

Comparison level for alternatives – The experience level below which the individual will attempt to seek alternate interactions. An individual engaged in a social interaction or relationship above his comparison level for alternatives will continue the interaction.

Compensation – Emphasizing a behavior or trait to account for or cover up some perceived deficiency in other areas. Also a defense mechanism in which one behavioral act is substituted for another behavioral act in an attempt to alleviate anxiety.

Competence – 1. Appropriateness. 2. The view that a person is responsible for his actions.

Competence motivation – The motive to develop those skills necessary to effectively manipulate the environment.

Competition – Trying to get the best in a situation, a mutual striving between individuals or groups for the same objective.

Complementarity – The tendency for people to be attracted to each other because they possess opposite qualities, and thus fulfill each other's needs.

Complementary colors – Two hues that when mixed in proper proportion yield an achromatic additive mixture, i.e., gray.

Complex concept – A concept that represents more than one stimulus property simultaneously.

Compliance – Performance of an act at another's request, regardless of one's own attitudes.

Compound schedules – Partial reinforcement schedules in which a response is reinforced according to the requirements of two or more schedules that operate at the same time.

Compromise formation – In psychoanalysis, behavior representing a fusion or accommodation between a repressed force or impulse and the repressive forces of the psyche, such that the behavior may become manifest without censorship of the ego.

Compulsion – 1. An irrational and unwanted repetition of an activity which arises when one can no longer control an anxiety or attempts to satisfy an obsession. 2. The forcing of an individual to act against his own wishes.

Computer-assisted instruction (CAI) – The use of a computer to store and select material to be presented in a learning program.

Computer program – A set of directions, or algorithm, telling a computer exactly what to do.

Computer simulation – Programming a computer to "behave" in exactly the way specified by a theory. More generally, programming a computer to do something an organism or system does.

Conative component – The part of an attitude revealed by the actions a person takes in response to a stimulus.

Concentrative meditation – Meditation that involves "one-pointedness" of the mind limiting one's attention to a specific object for some period of time.

Concept – l. A general idea or meaning. 2. An idea which combines several elements to form a notion, abstract properties, or relationships.

Concept formation – The process of finding the common element in a set of events or objects. Abstracting a quality or property of an object or event and then generalizing that quality or property to appropriate objects or events.

Conception – The beginning of human life which occurs with the union of a sperm cell with an egg cell.

Conceptual problems – Problems that can be solved by recognizing or learning the concept the solution is based on, by the use of systematic strategies.

Conceptual replication – An attempt to demonstrate an experimental phenomenon with an entirely new paradigm or set of experimental conditions. Typically new independent and dependent variables are selected which are thought to have the same underlying meaning (concept) in the experimental situation.

Concordance – In genetics, having the same trait(s) as a relative under study, usually an identical or fraternal twin.

Concordance rate – Probability that one of a pair of twins will show a given characteristic, given that the other twin has the characteristic.

Concrete operational period – The third of Jean Piaget's stages of cognitive development (from seven to eleven years of age). The child's thoughts become organized, with understanding of time, space, and logic, but he can apply them only to concrete situations.

Concurrent schedules – Partial reinforcement schedules in which two or more responses are made to satisfy two or more schedules at the same time.

Concurrent validity – A measure of how well a test measures what it was designed to measure by comparing the test results of the experimental group with test results of those people who are already in the field for which the test was designed.

Condensation – A dream process that disguises material by having one aspect of a dream, such as a person, actually represent or be a composite of several things in real life.

Conditional rule – In concept formation, if an item has one specified property, then it must also have another property in order to be an instance of the concept.

Conditioned emotional responses – Emotional reactions which result from being classically conditioned to stimuli in the environment.

Conditioned inhibition – The suppression of a conditioned response by pairing it with a neutral stimulus without any reinforcement so that the neutral stimulus becomes a signal for no reinforcement and the conditioned response is suppressed.

Conditioned reflex – A learned response elicited by a conditioned stimulus. Also called conditioned response.

Conditioned reflex therapy – The term applied to the system of psychotherapy developed by Andrew Salter in which clients learn to be assertive to overcome inhibitions. The six basic techniques used are feeling-talk, facial talk, contradiction and attack, using "1," express agreement, and improvisation.

Conditioned reinforcer – Something that, through association with the primary reinforcer, becomes a reinforcer itself.

Conditioned response (CR) – In classical conditioning, the response elicited by the conditioned stimulus. It usually resembles its corresponding unconditioned response.

Conditioned stimulus (CS) – An originally neutral stimulus that, through repeated pairings with an unconditioned stimulus becomes effective in eliciting the conditioned response.

Conditioning – The process of evoking a specific response other than one that would have been produced naturally by presenting a particular stimulus.

Conditioning, classical – (See Classical conditioning.)

Conditioning, instrumental – (See Operant conditioning.)

Conduct disorder – A disorder of childhood or adolescence involving a pattern of violating age-appropriate social norms or the basic rights of others through aggressions, theft, deceitfulness, and violating rules.

Conduction – 1. Pertaining to the transmission of sound waves. 2. The transmission of a nervous impulse from one area in the nervous system to another.

Cones – The cone shaped photoreceptor cells located in the retina particularly the fovea, which are responsible for color and high acuity vision.

Confabulation – The act of filling in memory gaps with statements that make sense but that are untrue. The person believes his statements to be true.

Confederates – In research, collaborators of the experimenter who pose as subjects. Their true identity is unknown to the other subjects.

Confidence interval – A statistic which specifies at some known probability level, the range within which the population mean must lie given a known sample measure.

Conflict – A term referring specifically to behavioral indecision as a result of the positive or negative qualities of goal situations. Conflicts may be approach-approach, involving equal temptation to strive for two incompatible goals; avoidance-avoidance, involving the struggle to avoid unpleasant consequences although doing so will incur other unpleasant consequences; or approach-avoidance, in which a single behavior has both pleasant and unpleasant consequences.

Conflict frustration – Frustration of a motive because it is in conflict with some other motive.

Confluence – 1. In perception, the fusing of perceptual elements. 2. The flowing together of motives or responses. 3. As developed by Adler, the merging of several instincts into one.

Conformity – The tendency to change or develop attitudes and behavior in accordance with peer pressure; to acquiesce to group norms.

Confounding – Simultaneous variation of a second variable with an independent variable of interest so that any effect on the dependent variable cannot be attributed with certainty to the independent variable; inherent in correlational research.

Confusion error – A classification error in which an instance of one category is thought to be an instance of another; it is often assumed that these errors are not random but depend on the degree to which the two categories have similar characteristics.

Congenital – A characteristic acquired during development in the uterus and not through heredity; existing at or dating from the time of birth.

Congruence (Rogers) – Term meaning what is experienced inside and what is expressed outwardly are consistent.

Conjunctive concepts – A concept which is defined by several attributes, usually all of which must be present.

Conjunctive rule – In concept formation, the rule that all examples of a concept must have one or more attributes in common.

Connectionism – The doctrine that the activity of the central nervous system is to connect stimuli and responses. Intelligence may also be viewed as a neural bond, dependent upon the number and availability of connections.

Connector cells – Cells in the brain and spinal cord that transmit nerve impulses from the afferent cells to the efferent cells.

Connotation – That aspect of the meaning of a word which refers to its associations and emotional implications.

Conscience – 1. The sense of right and wrong in conduct; that is, an individual's system of moral values. 2. As developed by Freud, the part of the superego that contains the moral values, attitudes, and rules which one acquires from parents. The conscience is internalized to govern behavior.

Conscious – 1. Awareness. 2. That which is attainable through introspection. 3. In Freudian theory, the images, thoughts, and ideas of which one is aware. The portion of the mind which is aware of the immediate environment.

Consciousness – The sum total of a person's mental experiences; one's complete awareness.

Consensual validation (Sullivan) – The process whereby a person reaches a more realistic point of view by comparing his thoughts and feelings with those of his associates. The corrective experience for an individual's parataxic distortions.

Conservation – 1. Piaget's term implying that certain quantitative attributes of objects remain unchanged unless something is added to or taken away from them. Such characteristics of objects as mass, number, area, volume, and so on, are capable of being conserved. For example, at a certain level of development one realizes that the amount of water is not changed by pouring it into glasses of different shapes. 2. Concerning memory or retention.

Conservative focusing – A systematic approach to solving conceptual problems in which the subject uses a positive instance of the concept as focus and then compares it with other single instances, each differing in one and only one dimension from his or her focus. By this method, irrelevant dimensions are eliminated (one at a time) until only the relevant dimension remains.

Consistency principle – The underlying view of cognitive dissonance and balance theories. The basic premise is that people strive to be consistent in their behavior. In this connection, attitudes held by a particular individual are mutually supportive and do not conflict with each other. Also, it is a tendency to segregate liked objects from disliked objects and to structure thoughts in simple black-and-white terms.

Consolidation theory – The postulate that short-term memories are converted into long-term memories. Consists of two stages – reverberating circuits and structural changes. In order for any experience to be permanently stored, it must be strengthened because of retroactive inhibition and retrograde amnesia.

Consonance – 1. Harmonious tone combinations. 2. In cognitive dissonance theory, when one idea or belief implies another in some psychological sense.

Conspecific recognition – Recognizing members of one's own species; discrimination of members of one's own species from members of other species.

Constancy – The tendency to perceive the properties of objects as unchanging in spite of changes in the retinal image; accomplished by integration of information from several sensory mechanisms.

Constancy hypothesis – As developed by the structuralists and behaviorists, the view that there is a one-to-one correspondence between stimulus and response, regardless of surrounding conditions.

Constancy of internal environment – As developed by Cannon, the tendency for metabolic processes (such as, levels of heat, blood sugar, and blood pressure) to remain constant.

Constant error – A continuous one-directional error, such as always underestimating.

Constellation – 1. In psychoanalysis, a group of emotionally charged ideas. 2. Any complex.

Constitutional factors of aggression – Relatively enduring dispositions and physiological traits, whose foundations are organic or hereditary, that are related to aggressive behavior; distinguished from environmental and learning factors.

Constriction – 1. In perception, a decrease in the diameter of the pupil of the eye. 2. Being overly determined by external factors. 3. In testing, poor form responses (F responses) on the Rorschach Test. 4. Any contraction or shrinking.

Construct – 1. A concept, trait, or dimension which represents relationships between variables in the formulation of theories. Empirical constructs are based on observed facts or data and represent measurable variables. Hypothetical constructs are verified indirectly. These constructs are inferred to have real existence. 2. A scientific model. 3. A piece of apparatus.

Construct validity – The extent to which a particular item in a test is a true measure of some abstract trait or concept that can only be verified indirectly.

Contact analog display – An integrated visual display that is arranged so that the information one receives is analogous to what one would get from direct visual contact.

Contact comfort – The satisfaction in many young organisms from having something warm and soft to cling to.

Contact desensitization – A technique of behavior therapy which involves physical contact during systematic desensitization.

Content – 1. As developed by Guilford, the raw material of intellectual activity such as thoughts and feelings. 2. As developed by Piaget, the term for uninterpreted behavioral data relating to one's behavior. 3. The material in a test, the material in consciousness, or the material expressed by a patient in an analytic session.

Content validity – The extent to which a particular instrument samples the behavior it is supposed to measure or predict.

Context – 1. Conditions which surround a mental process and thus alter its meaning. 2. The related verbal or perceptual material which clarifies the meaning of a word, phrase, or statement.

Contextual learning – The derivation and assimilation of meaning for a new item from the surrounding context.

Contextual stimuli – In adaptation, level theory of motivation. The background simulation against which the individual makes his judgments.

Contingency – 1. In instrumental conditioning, a situation in which reinforcement is not delivered unless certain responses are made. 2. An expression which indicates a meaningful relationship between two variables.

Continuation – The perceptual tendency to see objects in the form of some continuous pattern, e.g., a line or curve.

Continuity – A law of perceptual organization that states that incomplete contours tend to become closed.

Continuity theory – The theory that learning occurs by incremental increases in the strength of S-R bonds.

Continuous culture – A culture that does not clearly demarcate passage from one period of life to another. Contemporary Western societies are usually continuous.

Continuous reinforcement – A schedule of reinforcement in which every correct response is followed by reinforcement.

Contour – In perception, the boundary of a perceptual figure.

Contrast – 1. The perceptual effect of a specific visual area, caused by the difference between the area and its surroundings. 2. The stressing of a difference between two sensations by the immediate successive juxtaposition of two stimuli. 3. The intensified perception of differences between any stimuli by bringing them into juxtaposition.

Control – An experimental condition identical to other conditions in the experiment, but lacking the independent variable, (the experimental treatment), thus allowing different results in the other conditions to be attributed solely to the independent variable.

Control group – The group of subjects in an experiment which is statistically equivalent in all respects to the experimental group, except that it does not receive the treatment of the independent variable (the experimental treatment). Thus the control group can be used as a comparison to the experimental group to ascertain whether subjects were affected by the experimental procedure.

Control variable – A potential independent variable that is held constant in an experiment.

Convergent hierarchy – According to mediational theory, a hierarchy of different external stimuli, all of which can elicit the same response. Seen as the basis for forming concepts.

Convergent thinking – As termed by Guilford, thinking which results in a unique correct solution to a problem.

Converging operations – A set of related lines of investigation that all support a common conclusion.

Conversion reaction – A neurotic reaction which reduces anxiety by inactivation of part of the body; the psychological problem is converted into a physical one which prevents anxiety-provoking behavior. The underlying psychological conflict is transformed into a sensory or motor symptom, such as blindness or paralysis.

Converted score – A score expressed in some type of derived unit, such as an age equivalent, grade equivalent, percentile, or standard score.

Convulsion – An involuntary seizure involving rapid spasmodic contraction of the voluntary muscles.

Cooperation – Working with or assisting someone else in an attempt to reach a mutually satisfying goal.

Cornea – The transparent outer coating of the eye that allows light to pass through to the interior.

Corneal-reflection technique – A technique for studying eye movement which involves photographing light reflected from the cornea.

Corpus callosum – The structure consisting of a large group of nerve fibers that connect the left and right hemispheres of the cerebrum, allowing the hemispheres to communicate with each other.

Correlation – A statistical term that describes the relationship between two variables in such a way that change in one is associated with change in the other. (See Correlation coefficient for more detail.)

Correlation coefficient – A statistical index expressing the degree of relationship between two variables. The range of possible values is from +1.00 to –1.00. The numerical size of the correlation is an expression of the strength of the relationship. The sign of the correlation coefficient is an indication of the direction of the relationship. A positive correlation indicates that a change in one variable is associated with a change in the other variable in the same direction. A negative correlation indicates an inverse relationship between the two variables. A correlation of .00 represents no relationship between the variables.

Correlational approach – Research method used to discover the degree of relationship between two or more variables by analyzing how well one variable helps predict the value of another. Testing, interviewing, surveying are often combined under the general heading of correlational approach.

Cortex – The outer layer of any organ.

Cortical lobes – The four somewhat arbitrarily designated divisions of the cortex: frontal, parietal, occipital, and temporal.

Corticosteroid – A group of chemicals produced by the metabolism of cortisone and other chemical secretions of the adrenal cortex. These chemicals have been shown to increase during acquisition of a conditioned emotional response. Also known as adrenal steroids.

Cortisone – A hormone secreted by the adrenal cortex in response to stress, serving to reduce inflammation.

Cotwin control method – The use of twins in an experiment. One twin serves in the control condition and the other twin serves in the experimental condition.

Counseling psychology – The branch of psychology dealing with personality, marital, and vocational problems.

Counterbalancing – An experimental procedure used to eliminate the effect of irrelevant variables, confounding, by systematically varying the order of conditions in an experiment. For example, the effect of practice on variable X may be eliminated by presenting X at the beginning, middle, and end of a series.

Counterconditioning – The weakening or elimination of a conditioned response by the learning of a new response that is incompatible with, and stronger than, the one to be extinguished. It is used in therapy to replace unacceptable responses with acceptable ones.

Countermovement – An attempt to resist social change.

Cranial nerves – The twelve pairs of nerves which have their origin or termination within the ventral surface of the brain.

Creativity – A process of thought resulting in new and original ideas that are useful solutions to problems.

Crespi effect – A disproportionate increase or decrease in performance of a learned response as compared to the increase or decrease of the reinforcement.

Cretinism – A physiologically caused form of mental retardation and other abnormalities resulting from a prenatal thyroid insufficiency.

Crisis – 1. A point in a person's life which has great psychological significance for the individual. 2. A turning point characterized by a marked improvement or a marked deterioration.

Crisis intervention – A major feature of the primary prevention approach to mental health, whereby someone is always on call to help people handle a crisis in effective ways.

Criterion – 1. An absolute standard of performance used to evaluate a subject's performance on a test. 2. An outside measure against which a test can be validated.

Criterion of mastery in learning – The level of performance at which practice is terminated.

Critical period – As developed by Binet, the period early in life during which imprinting is possible. Any limited period in development in which the organism is especially susceptible to a given developmental process.

Cross-cultural studies – The observance of the effect of the same environmental conditions on behavior in different cultures.

Cross-sectional research – A research strategy that

tests at a given period of time a sample of persons or variables that are representative on several dimensions of the population as a whole. Age and ability level are two frequently used variables.

Cross-validation – A technique for determining the validity of a procedure by testing it for a second time on another sample after its validity has been demonstrated on a first sample. Cross-validation is important when items or test weights have been chosen from a large number of possible alternatives, and when the original sample was small.

Crossing-over – A process in which genes that were previously linked become unlinked or linked with a different set of genes due to the detachment of a chromosome part and possible reattachment to a new chromosome during cell division.

Crossover interaction – When the effect of one independent variable on a dependent variable reverses at different levels of a second independent variable.

Crystallized intelligence – Intelligence used in the application of already-learned materials which is usually considered to be rigid or unchanging.

Cue – In motivational theory, any distinctive property of a stimulus that can serve to determine the direction or nature of a response; an obscure secondary stimulus.

Cue-dependent forgetting – Inability to remember learned information due to retrieval failure. Cues present during learning are not present during recall.

Cultural relativity – The belief that the behavior and the personality of an individual can only be understood and evaluated within the context of the culture in which he or she originated.

Culturally biased – An adjective expressing the relative dependence of a concept or a test on cultural influence.

Culture – The total set of values, expectations, attitudes, beliefs, and customs shared by the members of one group which characterize them as a group and distinguish them from other groups.

Culture-fair tests – Tests that try to eliminate bias by using items that should be equally well-known to all subjects taking the test, regardless of their cultural or subcultural background.

Culture-free test – A test for which the solutions do not depend on any specific culture. All items that depend upon cultural factors have been eliminated.

Cumulative frequency – A sum of all the cases falling below a specified score, achieved when each new case up to a specified criterion is added to the preceding total. The cumulative percent is the accumulated percent of cases falling below a specified score.

Cumulative record – A continuous and complete tally or record of appropriate or satisfactory instrumental responses made in a given time period.

Cumulative recorder – An instrument for recording and displaying the complete sequence of responses over time.

Curiosity – The motivation to seek out and respond to novel stimuli, sometimes regarded as one of the primary drives.

Curve of forgetting – The graph plotting the percentage of learned materials retained as a function of time since the absolute amount forgotten for each subsequent time interval decreases over time, which means most retention loss occurs soon after acquisition.

Cutaneous senses – The senses whose receptors are located in the skin. These are usually classified as cold, hot, pain, and pressure.

Cybernetics – The science of communication and control theory that is especially concerned with the comparative study of automatic control systems.

Cycle of motivation – A proposal explaining many motive situations as a sequence of need, instrumental response, goal, and relief; the cycle often repeats itself.

Cytoplasm – The protoplasmic material surrounding the nucleus of a cell, exclusive of the material in the nucleus.

d' – A statistic in signal detection theory related to the sensitivity of the observer.

d reaction test – A reaction time test in which a subject must not make a response until he has identified which of two stimuli has been presented. For example, a subject is asked to push a lever when the green light appears and not when the red light appears.

Dark adaptation – A process of increasing sensitivity to light whereby the retina becomes over a million times more sensitive resulting from the reduction or complete absence of light energy reaching the eye, attributable to a resynthesis of a rod stimulating substance which is broken down under bright light. The DA curve has two segments, one for rod and one for cone vision.

Data – A collection of statistics, facts, or information obtained by observation, experimentation, or computation on a dependent variable.

Day-residues – Apparently trivial but unconsciously important events of the day that play a part in dream content.

Death instinct (Thanatos) – In psychoanalytic theory, the instinct for destruction and death and when fused with pleasure, inward and outward directed drives for pain. Like the life instinct, Eros, it originates from the libido, which is the source of all energy in the individual.

Decay theory of STM – A view that holds that without rehearsal or representation, the traces of an experience fade with time until the experience is forgotten completely.

Decentration – Jean Piaget's term for the ability to shift the center of one's attention.

Decerebrate – An animal whose cerebral cortex has been removed.

Decibel (db) – A logarithmic unit for measuring physical sound intensity.

Decile – In a ranked distribution, a division containing one-tenth of the cases. The first decile is the score value below which one tenth of the cases fall. The fifth decile is the same as the median, or the 50th percentile.

Deduction – The logical process of reasoning from the general to the particular.

Deep structure – The meaning transmitted by words used in a language.

Defense mechanism – As termed by Freud, the unconscious process by which an individual protects himself from anxiety. Defense mechanisms discussed by Freud include repression, rationalization, reaction formation, projection, isolation, introjection, regression, and thought dissociation. These mechanisms are often termed ego defenses.

Deferred imitation – As espoused by Piaget, the ability of a child to imitate behaviors long after the child has seen them. This occurs in the preoperational stage after representation has been attained.

Degrees of freedom (df) – The number of values free to vary if the total number of values and their sum are fixed.

Deindividuation – Relative anonymity of individual characteristics and identifications in certain social situations such as mobs and crowds.

Deiter's cells – Elongated cells, found in the outer portion of the organ of Corti, which anchor the hair cells.

Déjà vu – An illusion of familiarity in a strange place or experience. For example, some features in a new city may be similar to those features which have already been experienced. From the French "already seen."

Delay of reinforcement – A period of time between the response and reinforcement in a contingency situation.

Delayed conditioning – In classical conditioning, a trial in which the onset of the conditioned stimulus precedes the unconditioned stimulus, with the conditioned stimulus staying on at least until the unconditioned stimulus has occurred.

Delayed instinct – An instinct which does not manifest itself immediately after birth.

Delinquency – Antisocial acts committed by persons who are legal minors, usually in a repetitive fashion.

Delta waves – A wave of 1–3 Hz of high voltage found in the EEG which is characteristic of low arousal and deep sleep.

Delusion – A belief or thought that a person maintains as true despite irrefutable evidence that it is false, e.g., believing that one is being persecuted; this is characteristic of psychotic reactions.

Delusions of grandeur – The false belief that one is a great or powerful person.

Demand characteristics – Those cues available to subjects in an experiment that may enable them to determine the purpose of the experiment, or what is expected by the experimenter.

Dementia – The deterioration of intellectual and emotional processes; usually associated with senility and psychoses.

Demographic – Pertaining to characteristics of populations; used loosely to refer to such characteristics as sex, age, social class, ethnic background, and so on.

Dendrite – A neural fiber that transmits electrical impulses toward the cell body of a neuron.

Denial – A defense mechanism in which there is minimization of the importance of a situation or event or of unacceptable impulses or feelings.

Denotation – The literal meaning of a word; its definition.

Denotative meaning – That aspect of meaning that has reference to the describable characteristics of an object.

Deoxyribonucleic acid (DNA) – An extremely complex molecule, assumed to be the basis of all life, composed of phosphates, bases, and sugars.

Dependence – 1. A relationship of causality between two occurrences such that a change in one produces a change in the other. 2. A reliance on others for ideas, emotions, and opinions.

Dependent influence – A change in a person's attitudes or behaviors that occurs because of the social characteristics of a model or group.

Dependent variable – The factor the experimenter wants to measure, which may be affected by the independent variable.

Depersonalization – 1. In psychopathology, a condition in which one experiences a loss of personal identity. 2. In existentialism, the feeling attributed to man as being insignificant in a vast world.

Depolarization – The process by which the electrical charge of a neuron reverses and becomes positive during the passage of an action potential.

Depression – A state of extreme sadness and dejection. As a psychological disorder it is accompanied by lowered sensitivity to certain stimuli, reduction of physical and mental activity, and difficulty in thinking.

Depressive reactions – A state in which the person responds to life's disappointments with excessive emotionality and withdrawal, usually precipitated by an event such as the loss of a loved one.

Deprivation – The loss or removal of something desired or loved. In developmental psychology, a significant reduction of stimulation or opportunity.

Depth-oriented therapy – Any form of psychotherapy which professes to treat the unconscious sources of an individual's problems. The Freudian and Jungian systems of psychoanalysis exemplify depth psychology.

Depth perception – The ability to perceive three dimensionality and the awareness of distance between an observer and an object.

Derived lists – Learning materials arranged so that subsequent lists are systematically related to original lists by taking every other item in order, every third item, every fourth item, etc.

Descartes, René – Seventeenth-century French philosopher and mathematician. He is important in the history of psychology for his views on the interaction of mind and body.

Descriptive research – Research involving the collection and objective reporting of data about a particular characteristic of the subjects under study without any attempt at identifying causal relationships. Techniques include introspection, observation, surveys and clinical investigation.

Descriptive statistics – Measures or techniques that allow a summary portrayal of collected data including measurements of central tendency, variability, and correlation.

Desensitization – A form of behavior therapy in which the individual is reconditioned so that previously aversive stimuli no longer elicit anxiety responses.

Desurgency – As developed by R. B. Cattell, a factor analysis personality trait which is characterized by anxiety, agitation and isolation.

Detached affect – An idea separated from its emotional counterpart.

Detachment – 1. According to Horney, a neurotic characteristic involving a lack of feeling for others and a tendency to view one's problems in an objective fashion without any emotional attachment. 2. The development of independent behavior which often occurs when an adult of high attachment status is close by.

Detection theory – A theory which accurately assesses the subject's sensory capacities. It is a psychophysical method of studying the process of motivation, stimulus probability, and extraneous stimuli on the decision regarding the presence or absence of a given stimulus or a change in stimulus value. It employs such factors as hits, misses, correct rejections, and false alarms. Also known as signal detectability theory, theory of signal detection, and decision theory.

Deterioration index – As measured by the Wechsler-Bellevue tests, an approximation of the amount of loss of mental abilities due to age. The mental abilities tested are digit span, digit symbol, block design, and similarities.

Determinism – In general, the philosophical doctrine that for every effect there is a cause. As applied to psychology, the view that all behavior is related to an antecedent event, and all of man's motivation is subject to forces over which he has no volitional control.

Detour problem – A problem solving situation in which one has to learn to take a roundabout route to a goal instead of trying to approach it directly.

Deuteranope – A color-vision defective individual who sees shades of gray instead of red and green, possibly because of insensitivity to blue-green light.

Development – The total progressive and continuous change whereby an individual adapts to his environment via the processes of growth, maturation, and learning; qualitative growth.

Developmental age – A measure of the degree of a person's physiological or cognitive maturity. This includes such factors as dental maturity and skeletal maturity, and the ability to think or behave in a particular manner, contrasted with chronological age.

Developmental psychology – The area within psychology that is concerned with discovering the principles of behavioral change in the individual from conception to death. All the topics in psychology such as personality, learning, and cognition as they relate to the dimensions of growth and maturation. In its broadest sense, developmental psychology includes the periods of infancy, childhood, adolescence, and adulthood.

Developmental scale – Reports of average or typical behavior for a particular age group based upon data collected from large groups of individuals for the purpose of measuring the level of development a child has attained.

Deviance – Departure from what is considered to be correct, normal and proper. In statistics, the departure from the norm or mean.

Deviant case analysis – Investigation of similar cases that differ in outcome in an attempt to specify the reasons for the different outcomes.

Deviation – 1. In statistics, the difference between a score and a reference point such as the mean or median. If the mean is 40 and a score is 25, the deviation of that score from the mean is -15. 2. A departure from what is considered normal, correct, or proper. 3. In optics, the bending of light rays from a straight line.

Deviation IQ – A standard score on an intelligence test in which the mean is set at 100 and the standard deviation at 15 or 16. It expresses the extent to which the individual deviates from the average score obtained by his peers. The meaning of the deviation IQ is similar to that of the conventional IQ, namely, the value obtained on the Stanford-Binet.

Dewey, John – Dewey was one of the founders of the functionalistic movement in psychology and education. He wrote one of the first textbooks in the field.

Diagnosis – The process of determining the nature of an abnormality or disease using information gained from tests, interviews, and other observations.

Diagnostic test – A test that is utilized to determine the nature and source of an individual's difficulties or skills, in contrast with survey tests, which give a general appraisal of an area of achievement.

Diastolic blood pressure – The lowest pressure recorded from an individual during a cardiac cycle which is the period of ventricular dilation during which the ventricle fills with blood (contrasted with systolic blood pressure).

Diathesis – Genetic predisposition to a particular psychotic disorder or disease.

Diathesis-stress theory – Theory of what causes schizophrenia; states that schizophrenia develops when there is a genetic predisposition (diathesis) present and there are environmental factors (stress) that trigger the disorder.

Dichotic listening – A test of attention in which two separate messages are delivered simultaneously, one to each ear.

Dichromat – A color-defective individual whose full range of color experience can be produced by the mixture of two (rather than the normal three) primary colors. Most common is red-green blindness; blue-yellow blindness is rarer.

Difference threshold (or jnd) – Given an initial level of stimulation, the DL is the minimally effective stimulus difference which is correctly reported by the subject as being different. By convention a 75 per cent judgment rate has been adopted.

Difference tone – A sound heard when two tones are sounded simultaneously. The pitch of the difference tone is the difference in frequency between the two original sounds.

Differential extinction – The selective gradual diminishing of one response while another is being maintained.

Differential psychology – The field of psychology which concerns itself with individual differences in reference to their consequences, causation, and magnitude among groups.

Differentiation – 1. In development, the process of cells developing into specialized tissues. 2. The change in a psychological field from homogeneity to heterogeneity. 3. In conditioning, the process by which an organism is trained to respond to only certain stimuli, that is, to discriminate between stimuli. 4. In mathematical psychology, the process of obtaining a differential.

Difficulty index – A numerical value used to express the difficulty of a test item. In the United States, the difficulty index, also called the facility index, is usually the percent getting the item correct.

Diffraction – The bending of light waves as they pass over the edge of an object.

Digit-span test – A test of short term recall in which the subject repeats a random series of digits following a single presentation.

Digital computer – A computer that operates on two-valued signals, typically +1 and 0, as contrasted with an analog computer.

Dilation – An increase in the diameter of the pupil of the eye.

Dimming effect – The intensification of an afterimage by reducing the intensity of the field upon which it is projected.

Dioptric power – The ability of a lens to bend, or refract, light.

Dipsomania – A continuous craving for alcohol.

Direct aggression – An attack or aggressive behavior which is projected upon the source of frustration.

Direct analysis – The term applied to the system of psychotherapy developed by John Rosen. Rosen contends that the therapist must identify with the unhappy patient.

Direct replication – Repeating an experiment as closely as possible to determine whether or not the same results will be obtained.

Directed thinking – Thinking that is governed by a goal or thinking that occurs for a purpose, such as problem solving.

Directional hypothesis – A prediction that a specific change in the conditions of an experiment will result in a particular change in the outcome of the experiment.

Directive counseling – The treatment of mental illness in which the patient is given positive advice and direct suggestions as to what activities and attitudes he should adopt. Also the counselor suggests the area of personality to be explored.

Directive psychotherapy – As developed by Frederick Thorne, a system of therapy in which the therapist assumes an active role for the purpose of breaking down resistance.

Discontinuous culture – A culture with clear demarcations between various states or stages. For example, discontinuous cultures often mark the passage from childhood to adulthood by elaborate ritual and ceremony.

Discriminated operant – An instrumentally learned response that is reinforced only if made in the presence of a particular stimulus.

Discrimination – 1. The ability to recognize the distinctive features of similar but nonidentical things. 2. The process of distinguishing differences between stimuli. 3. In learning, differentiation, the ability to withhold a behavioral response except in the presence of a specific stimulus.

Discrimination index – A graphic or numerical expression of the extent to which a test or test item differentiates between subjects having or not having the trait being tested.

Discrimination learning – Learning to distinguish between two or more different stimuli, or between the presence and absence of a stimulus. In general, any learning in which the task is to make choices between alternatives.

Discriminative stimulus (S_D) – A signal presented only when reinforcement is present or is to follow, thereby controlling the occurrence of the response.

Disinhibition – 1. The temporary restoration of an extinguished response that is manifested when the conditioned stimulus is presented in a novel way. 2. A loss of self-control upon overindulgence in alcohol or while under the influence of drugs. 3. In modeling, observing a response and learning

that the response is appropriate to a given situation.

Disinhibition of aggression – A reduction in the self-control or inhibition of aggressive behaviors in response to environmental stimulation or aggression-eliciting events.

Disjunctive concept – A complex concept based upon the simultaneous consideration of two or more stimulus properties, but in which the presence of any one stimulus property is adequate to qualify the stimulus as an instance of the concept.

Disjunctive rule – In concept formation, a rule which specifies that any object having a particular attribute is an example of a given concept.

Disowning – The process developed by Carl Rogers, whereby an individual avoids being aware of experiences and needs which have not been symbolized and which are inconsistent with the self. Disowning is similar to repression and dissociation in the Freudian and Sullivanian theories, respectively.

Dispersion – A measure that shows the scatter of a group of scores in a distribution. The common measures of dispersion are the range, average deviation, standard deviation, variance, and the semi-interquartile range.

Displaced aggression – Aggressive behavior oriented away from the source of frustration to other "safer" targets.

Displacement – The process or result of shifting an idea, activity, or emotional attachment from its proper object to another object. It may be a rechanneling of instinctual energy from an unacceptable object to one that is of neutral value to society (Freudian defense mechanism). It is also a dream process by which material is disguised. It involves changing the affective emphasis of something in a dream so that if it is very important in real life, it is seemingly unimportant in the dream or vice versa.

Displacement activity – In ethology, seemingly irrelevant behavior made in the presence of two simultaneous but incompatible releaser stimuli; vacuum activity.

Displacement theory – The view that forgetting from short-term memory is due to a distortion of items from a temporary store by the occurrence of new items.

Display design – The study of effective presentation of information in a man-machine system.

Dissociation – 1. A defense mechanism in which there is a separation of activities and psychological processes which may then function independently. An extreme form would be the multiple personality. It is also present in amnesia, fugue, and schizophrenia. 2. In Sullivanian theory, the process by which one excludes from awareness certain aspects of his experience which lead to acute anxiety. It is similar to Freudian repression and Rogerian disowning.

Dissociative disorders – A group of disorders involving the abandonment of the sense of self-consistency characteristic of normal functioning. Dissociative behavior is evident in sleepwalking (somnambulism), amnesia, fugue, and multiple-personality (dissociative identity disorder).

Dissonance – 1. In cognitive dissonance theory, when one idea or belief a person holds contradicts another cognition he or she also holds. 2. The unpleasant effect produced by two notes which are sounded simultaneously and do not blend into a mellifluous sound.

Distal effect – A response which changes the environment in some way.

Distal receptors – Sense receptors that allow man to apprehend sensation that emanates from a distance. Vision and hearing are the two most important distal receptors, or distance senses.

Distal stimulus – A stimulus as it emanates from environmental objects such as a doorbell.

Distal variable – A variable which originated as a stimulus in the environment which is mediated via a proximal stimulus (a stimulus acting on our sense organs).

Distinctiveness – The tendency of some items to "stand out" from the context in which they occur. Distinctiveness is one factor determining how well material can be learned.

Distorting lenses – Lenses utilized to present an illusory set of stimuli to the retina by the bending of an image achieved by changing orientation, line formation, or color.

Distortion – 1. In psychoanalysis, the cognitive alteration or disguising of unacceptable impulses so that they can escape the dream censor. 2. In perception, the changing in orientation of a stimulus to the retina.

Distortion theory – A theory of forgetting that maintains information is not entirely forgotten but becomes distorted with the passage of time.

Distracting task – A task that is assigned to the subject of a memory experiment between the time of presentation of the material to be learned and the time of recall or recognition, thus interfering with the rehearsal and processing of that material into memory.

Distractor – A term sometimes used to designate the incorrect response options provided in a multiple-choice item.

Distributed learning – The spacing of learning trials into several time periods instead of one long learning session.

Distribution – An array of the instances of a variable arranged so that different classes of the variable are ordered in some manner and the frequency of each class is indicated.

Distributive analysis and synthesis – The phrase applied to the characteristic procedures of psychobiological therapy. This view emphasizes the importance of obtaining a clear and full understanding of the patient's own views of his or her problems.

Disuse theory – The theory of forgetting that states that memory lapses are due to lack of use of what has been learned.

Divergent hierarchy – According to mediational theory, a hierarchy of responses all of which can be elicited by a single stimulus. Seen as the basis for problem solving in most situations.

Divergent thinking – Guilford's term for the type of thinking that produces several different solutions for a problem. Divergent thinking is assumed to be closely related to creativity, and the term is often used interchangeably with it.

Dizygotic – Developing from two different fertilized eggs.

Dizygotic (or fraternal) twins – Twins who develop from two separate eggs.

Dogmatism scale – A questionnaire designed to measure rigidity and inflexibility in thinking.

Dominance – A term used to refer to the fact that in many animal groups there is a "pecking order," usually related to strength. Animals high in the "pecking order" usually have first access to food and mates.

Dominant gene – The gene that takes precedence over other related genes in determining genetic traits. The presence of a dominant gene means that the characteristic which is controlled by that gene will be present in the individual.

Dominator module theory – In perception, the view that brightness vision is communicated through a special dominant receptor and that color vision is mediated by receptors which control the response of the dominant receptor.

Double approach-avoidance conflicts – A conflict in which there are two goals, with each goal having an attraction and a repulsion.

Double-bind theory – In the etiology of schizophrenia, the hypothesis that traces the origins of schizophrenia to situations in which a parent gives conflicting messages to an offspring. Thus, the child is "damned if he does and damned if he doesn't."

Double blind – An experimental technique in which neither the experimenter nor the subject knows who is in the experimental and control groups. The double blind technique is used to control for demand characteristics and other extraneous variables.

Down's syndrome – A congenital form of mental retardation which is caused by the failure of the 21st pair of chromosomes to separate properly when an egg or sperm is formed. Characteristics of the disease are a limited intelligence, a flat face, a skin fold at the corner of the eyes, a broad nose, and a protruding tongue.

Dream – An experience that occurs during the sleeping state, drugged state, or hypnotic state that involves a more or less coherent awareness of imagery, scenes and events.

Dream analysis – The process, originally used by Freud, of deciphering the meaning of a dream. Based on the idea that dreams are symbolic representations of our impulses and conflicts, and that by understanding the symbols, we can learn about ourselves.

Dream processes – Various methods used to disguise material so that when it is presented in a dream, it is not too emotionally threatening.

Drive – A goal-directed tendency of an organism based on a change in organic processes; any strong stimulus that impels an organism to action. For example, the hunger drive results from the need for food.

Dualism – 1. A philosophical position, as developed by Plato, which holds that mind and matter are two fundamentally different substances. 2. In psychology, the idea that the mind and the body are separate entities.

Ductless glands – Endocrine glands that release their hormones directly into the bloodstream.

Dura (dura mater) – The outer protective tissue layer of the central nervous system.

Dyad – Two persons interacting with each other.

Dynamic culturalists – The term applied to the psychoanalytic theories and practices of those who deviate from the teachings of Freud by placing less emphasis on the instinctive and more emphasis on the changing social sources of human behavior.

Dynamic lattice – As developed by R. B. Cattell, a graphic representation of the interrelations between goal seeking and motives.

Dynamic model – Model of psychopathology in which abnormal behavior reflects a "dynamic" battle or conflict between parts or aspects of a person's personality rather than any physical or organic

deficiencies.

Dynamism – A relatively enduring and consistent mode of behavior used in interpersonal relations, drive satisfaction, and alleviation from psychological stress.

Dynamometer – An instrument utilized for measuring the strength of muscular response, such as a hand-grip.

Dyscontrol – A personality dimension, scored on the Emotions Profile Index, which measures tendencies to act impulsively.

Dyslexia – An inability to read which is usually characterized by a specific reading impairment, such as reversing similar letters or numbers.

Dyssocial character – Individual who has no personality disorganization, but rather has values that conflict with the usual mores of the society; cultural deviant.

Eardrum (tympanic membrane) – The beginning of the middle ear separating the outer ear and auditory canal. The sound reaching the eardrum sets in motion the three bones of the middle ear.

Early childhood – The second period of postnatal development; from approximately age two to age six.

Early training project – A preschool project developed by Gray and Klaus emphasizing enriched and distinctive stimulation for children from impoverished backgrounds.

Ebbinghaus, Hermann – A pioneer psychologist in the field of learning. He devised the nonsense syllable and the completion test.

Ebbinghaus curve of retention – As developed by Ebbinghaus, a curve which displays the retention of nonsense material.

Echoic memory – Information stored briefly as an auditory image of a stimulus.

Echolalia – A perfunctory repetition of words or phrases by mental patients.

Echopraxia – An automatic imitation of movements by another. This reaction is sometimes found in catatonics.

Eclectic – A psychologist who uses the theories and techniques of several approaches or models, rather than specializing in one.

Eclecticism – In general, the selection and organization of a variety of approaches from many sources. In psychotherapy, an approach which uses various methods depending upon the patient and other circumstances.

Ecological – Pertaining to the study of biological

forms, both among species and between species and their environment. According to Lewin, pertaining to those aspects of an individual's environment which are important parts of his or her life space.

Ectomorph – One of Sheldon's somatotyping classifications; ectomorphs are frail and are inclined to a long, stringy, and skinny body. They are associated with cerebrotonia; that is, they are assumed to be restrained in movement, concerned with privacy, sensitive, and socially inhibited.

Edging – In reference to the Rorschach test, a tendency of an individual to turn the cards edgewise.

Educable mentally retarded (EMR, IQ score 52-70) – This group of individuals is considered capable of being educated. The intellectual level as adults is comparable to that of the average 8- to 11-year old child. Socially, EMRs approximate the adolescent, however, they lack imagination, inventiveness, and judgment. Many, with proper guidance, can function in society and support themselves. Also called mildly retarded.

Educational psychology – A science that is concerned primarily with the application of psychological knowledge to problems of education.

Educational quotient – The ratio of educational age to chronological age, multiplied by a factor of 100.
$$EQ = \frac{EA}{CA} \times 100$$

Edwards personal preference schedule (EPPS) – A test, employing a forced choice technique, which is designed to measure the needs proposed by Murray's theory of personality.

E – F scale – A subscale of the Minnesota Multiphasic Inventory of Personality which measures authoritarianism and ethnocentrism.

Effect, law of – As developed by Thorndike, the view that, all other things being equal, an animal will learn those habits which lead to satisfaction and will not learn those habits which lead to annoyance.

Effectance motivation – The concept of competence (that is, effectively interacting with the environment).

Effective-habit strength – As developed by Hull, the strength of a learned reaction as a function of the number of reinforcements.

Effectors – Neural cells that are directly involved in glandular or muscular behavior.

Efferent nerves – Nerves that transmit impulses from the central nervous system to the end organs.

Effort syndrome – An anxiety neurosis characterized by palpitations and circulatory disorders.

Ego – In the structural model of psychoanalytic theory as proposed by Freud, the largely conscious mental institution which mediates between the demands of the id and demands of the environment. The ego is sometimes called the executive agency of the personality because it controls action, selects the features of the environment to which a person will respond, and decides how the person's needs can be satisfied.

Ego-analysis – A form of psychoanalysis which emphasizes the strengths and weaknesses of the ego. There is little concentration on deeply repressed processes, and it is shorter than conventional psychotherapy.

Ego ideal – In Freudian theory, the image of the self that a person consciously and unconsciously strives to become, and against which the person judges him- or herself.

Ego-involvement – Perception of a situation in terms of its potential effect on one's self-concept.

Ego psychology – Erikson's theory of personality development which emphasizes ego development. Ego psychology is an eight-stage theory requiring a successful coping at each stage for proper development.

Egocentric speech – Piaget's term for speech that does not take into account the point of view of the listener. The three basic manifestations of egocentric speech are repetition, monologue, and collective monologue.

Egocentrism – Lack of differentiation between one's own point of view and that of others. As used by Piaget, it refers to the early adolescent's failure to differentiate between what he and others are thinking about. Young children's thinking is heavily egocentric.

Eidetic imagery – Ability to retain an image of a picture or a scene with great clarity for a fairly long period of time. Sometimes called "photographic memory."

Eigenwelt – In existential psychology, the term which refers to man's relationship with himself.

Einstellung – A set; an attitude. Learned habits and preparatory outlooks toward a problem or direction which may be geared by preceding events which often are factors in thinking.

Electra complex – A Freudian stage occurring around the age of 4 or 5 years, during the phallic stage, when a girl's awareness of her genital area leads her to desire her father and to become jealous of her mother. This corresponds to the Oedipus complex in the male.

Electroconvulsive shock (ECS) – A form of psychotherapy used in the treatment of manic depressive psychosis and schizophrenia. An electrical current is passed through the brain resulting in convulsions and a short period of unconsciousness. Also called electroshock therapy.

Electrode – A small insulated wire that is surgically implanted into an area of the brain in order to artificially stimulate that area.

Electroencephalogram (EEG) – An instrument used to measure the electrical activity of the brain.

Electromagnetic spectrum – The variety of changes occurring in electrical and magnetic fields measured in terms of wavelength or frequency of vibrations.

Electromyogram (EMG) – A record of the electrical activity of a muscle usually recorded from the surface of the skin.

Elicited response – A response brought about by a stimulus. The expression is synonymous with respondent.

Eliciting effect – That type of imitative behavior in which the observer does not copy the model's responses but simply behaves in a related manner.

Ellipsis – The omission of ideas in free association.

Embryo – The second stage of prenatal development, beginning around the first week after conception and terminating at the end of the sixth week.

Embryonic period – The second of the three stages of gestation, from the third to the sixth week, at the end of which many body systems are in operation and the embryo begins to resemble the human form.

Emergency reaction – As developed by Walter Cannon, a term describing the reactions of fight or flight of an animal to dangerous situations. These reactions include increased heart rate, increased blood flow to the muscles, inhibition of digestion and expansion of the air sacs in the lungs.

Emitted response – A response not elicited by a known stimulus, but simply emitted by the organism. An emitted response is an operant.

Emmert's law – The principle that the perceived size of an image on the retina varies directly with the perceived distance of the object that presumably is projecting the image.

Emotion – A complex state of the organism, usually marked by a heightened state of arousal and the feelings accompanying that condition. Includes such human feelings as fear, rage, love, or desire.

Emotional meaning – Connotative meaning as opposed to denotative meaning. Meaning suggested by a term or symbol beyond its explicit or referential meaning.

Empathic understanding – Rogerian concept referring to the importance that a therapist actively understand the immediate feelings of his client.

Empathy – 1. The acceptance and understanding of the feelings of another person, but with sufficient detachment to avoid becoming directly involved in those feelings. 2. In Sullivanian theory, a kind of vague, biologically derived process whereby the infant senses the emotions of the mothering one through "contagion and communion."

Empirical – That which is based on the observation of events occurring in an experiment or in nature, as distinguished from that founded on opinion, beliefs, or reasoning.

Empirical key – A scoring key, typically for a measure of personality. The items to be weighted and the manner in which they are weighted are based on data showing the extent to which the items do, in fact, differentiate different groups of individuals.

Empirical study – An arrangement of conditions such that observations can be made systematically.

Empirical testing – Testing that relies on observation or experimentation for its answers.

Empiricism – 1. The philosophical view that experience is the source of knowledge. John Locke, George Berkeley, David Hume, David Hartley, and James Mill were empiricists. 2. The psychological view that behavior depends upon learning, experience, and objective observations. There is a strong emphasis on operational definitions and on relating theories to experimental findings.

Empty nest syndrome – Restlessness, anxiety, and depression in middle-aged parents whose children have left home; formerly said to be due to a woman's menopause and the loss of ability to bear children.

Enactive mode – The most primitive (or basic) way that humans convert immediate experiences into a mental model, as proposed by Bruner. It is based upon action or movement and is nonverbal.

Encephalitis – Any type of infection of the brain that causes inflammation.

Encounter group – A form of group psychotherapy focused on personal growth, more effective interpersonal communication, and open expression of feelings. The aim is a more direct encounter with one's own feelings toward others, and vice versa. Openness, honesty, emotional expression, and sensitivity is encouraged.

Enculturation – The process of adapting to a new culture.

Endocrine glands – A group of ductless glands which secrete hormones directly into the bloodstream.

Endocrine system – The functioning order of glands

which produce hormones, it is central in the control and regulation of behavior and interacts closely with the nervous system.

Endogenous control – Control that comes from within the body.

Endomorph – One of Sheldon's somatotyping classifications. Endomorphs are described as soft and rotund. They are viscerotonic and are believed to love comfort and eating, be relaxed and slow in movement, and social.

Engineering psychology – A branch of psychology which concentrates on the relationships between people and machines.

Engram – A hypothetical physiological change corresponding to something learned; also called a memory trace.

Entropy – 1. In psychoanalysis, the extent to which psychic energy cannot be transferred once it has been invested in an object. 2. The number of possible outcomes an event may have. 3. In social psychology, the tendency for social progress to diminish, because each new change uses up energy which is not available for the succeeding change.

Environment – The totality of significant aspects of an individual's surroundings. Includes all experiences and events that influence an individual's development. The three basic subcategories of environment are postnatal, prenatal, and cellular.

Environmental factors – Those factors that act as stimulating forces on the organism.

Environmental-mold trait – A personality trait, developed by R. B. Cattell, which has been evolutionized through environmental influences.

Environmentalism – The belief that emphasizes environmental differences as the cause for individual differences. Holds that heredity has only a minor role in behavior.

Enzyme – A complex protein substance that acts as a catalyst in regulating chemical reactions in the body.

Epigenesis – The hypothesis that new traits emerge during embryonic development. These are traits not contained in the original fertilized cell. Rather, they develop out of prenatal environmental and intracellular influences.

Epilepsy – Epilepsy refers to a general condition characterized by convulsions. The various convulsions associated with epilepsy are petit mal, grand mal, and psychomotor.

Epileptoid personality – A compilation of personality traits which are believed to be associated with epilepsy, including stubbornness, irritability, and uncooperativeness.

Epinephrine – (See adrenaline.)

Episiotomy – A small cut made in the perineum to facilitate the birth of a child. An episiotomy prevents the tearing of membranes and ensures that once the cut has been sutured, healing will be rapid and complete.

Episodic memory – Retention of specific events which we have ourselves experienced, like dates, names, events.

Epistemic behavior – A label employed by Berlyne to describe behavior designed to gather information.

Epistemology – That branch of philosophy concerned with the acquisition and validity of people's knowledge about the world.

Equilibration – 1. The balance between what is taken in, assimilated, and what is changed, accommodated. Equilibration is the mechanism for cognitive growth and development. 2. The achievement of balance between two opposing forces.

Equilibrium – As developed by Piaget, a term referring to a balance between assimilation and accommodation. The concept of equilibration is of primary importance to Piaget's explanation of motivation. He assumed that an individual constantly interacts with his or her environment through assimilation and accommodation to achieve a state of equilibrium.

Equity norm – The rule of social exchange which says that a person's outcomes should be proportionate to his or her inputs to the group.

Equivalent form – One of two or more forms of a test that have been built to the same specifications to measure the same attribute or attributes, and that consequently have approximately the same statistical characteristics.

Erg – As developed by R. B. Cattell, an innate predisposition of certain response activities to certain stimuli.

Erikson, Erik – A noted child psychoanalytic psychologist. He coined the term "identity crisis."

Erogenous zone – An area of the body which, when stimulated, gives rise to sexual feeling.

Eros – A Greek word meaning love, employed by Freud to describe the life instinct present at birth that includes all drives for self-preservation. Early in his career, Freud classified 'Eros' as the sex instinct.

Error of measurement – 1. The amount by which any specific measurement differs from the individual's hypothetical "true" score in the quality being measured. Since no measurement procedure is perfectly exact, each has included in it some component of error. 2. An error due to the unreliability of an instrument.

Erythrolabe – A pigment in retinal cones that absorbs light mostly in the red region of the spectrum.

Escape conditioning – A form of learning in which the proper response ends noxious stimulation.

Escape response – Any response made by an organism in order to get away from an already-present aversive stimulus.

ESP – (See extrasensory perception.)

Essential hypertension – A disorder characterized by high blood pressure of unknown origin.

Este's statistical model of learning – In learning theory, the view that all stimuli are composed of a large number of elements and that only a small percentage can be effective at any given time.

Estrogen – A female sex hormone secreted by the ovaries, which maintains sexual characteristics and the reproductive functions.

Ethical model – Model of psychopathology in which psychopathology comes from guilt over immoral behavior; assumes that individual has responsibility for his or her behavior.

Ethology – The study of organisms and their behavior in their natural habitats.

Eugenics – A form of genetic engineering that selects specific individuals for reproduction. The term was coined by Galton and is really an expression of the belief that individuals should be selected for breeding purposes in order to enhance racial characteristics.

Eunuch – A castrated male.

Euphoria – A psychological state of well-being and heightened motor activity. When pathological it may be characteristic of manic states.

Eustachian tube – The valved tube connecting the middle ear and mouth which provides an equilibrium of atmospheric pressure between the outside and middle ear.

Evaluation – The complete process of comparison and determination of the relative importance of a phenomenon and the appraising of the extent to which certain objectives have been achieved.

Evoked potential – A very small change in voltage recorded from the cerebral cortex of the brain following stimulation of one of the sense modalities.

Evolution – 1. In general, the orderly development of a theory, system, or body. 2. The process of orderly changes in the phylogenetic species which have been brought about by environmental and genetic changes with survival of the best-adapted mutants. Evolutionary proc-esses are assumed to be responsible for the present variety and distri-bution of life forms.

Evolutionary biology – Study of living organisms stressing the importance of understanding the similarities and differences between animals.

Ex post facto – Literally, "after the fact"; refers to conditions in an experiment that are not determined prior to the experiment but only after some manipulation has occurred naturally.

Excitation – General level of arousal or a state of activity stemming from arousal; stimulation resulting from the firing of nerve cells; agitated emotional state; generalized in Salter's theory to refer to a state in the individual in which he or she is ready for vigorous action.

Excitatory postsynaptic potential (EPSP) – Depolarizing effects of synaptic transmission on the postsynaptic neuron.

Excitatory potential – As developed by Hull, the strength of a tendency to respond.

Excitatory tendency – The ability of a stimulus to evoke a response.

Exhibitionism – A sexual variant form of behavior which involves the intentional exposure of the genitals to unsuspecting people under inappropriate conditions.

Existential analysis – The term applied to the system of psychotherapy which combines some of the teachings of existential philosophy with some of the theories and practices of psychoanalysis. The goal is to restore to the individual a sense of freedom and responsibility for his or her own choices.

Existential model – An explanation of abnormal personality patterns that stresses the influence of present events rather than past experiences.

Existential neurosis – Feeling a loss of meaning in life even though one is a successful member of society.

Existential therapy – A type of psychotherapy developed by Rollo May and other existentialists, it emphasizes the here-and-now, or human's present being, and the uniqueness and separateness of each individual.

Existentialism – A philosophical-psychological movement characterized by a preoccupation with existence. Existential philosophers describe the human condition in such terms as abandonment, loneliness, despair, and alienation. These feelings are purported to result from the individual's lack of knowledge about his or her origin and eventual end. Hence the term existentialism, since the only knowable reality is existence. A philosophy which adheres to the idea that at any moment in time humans are in a state of growth toward whatever they will to become.

Exocrine glands – Glands with ducts that secrete fluids onto the body's surface or into its cavities.

Exogenous control – Control that comes from outside the body.

Exorcism – Ritual used to drive out evil spirits.

Expansion gradient – The less dense part of a visual path (texture gradient) which appears to be closer.

Expectancy – 1. The probability of an occurrence. 2. A learned anticipation by an organism that a certain response to a stimulus will result in the occurrence of a specific situation. 3. An attitude characterized by attentiveness and heightened muscular tension.

Expectancy table – A table showing, for each level of a predictor test, the frequency of different levels of success in some outcome variable.

Experience – Learning, or the effects of the environment on development.

Experiential therapy – The term applied to the system of psychotherapy developed by Carl Whitaker and Thomas Malone. The emphasis is placed on matters of maturity. The goal is to increase the ease in the exchange of energies within an individual.

Experiment – A scientific investigation carried out under controlled conditions for the purpose of observing a specific variable.

Experimental control – Holding constant extraneous variables in an experiment so that any effect on the dependent variable can be attributed to manipulation of the independent variable.

Experimental group – In a scientific experiment, those subjects who respond to an independent variable that is "specially" manipulated by the experimenter; the responses of the experimental group can then be compared with the responses of the control group.

Experimental method – Research procedure in which the psychologist manipulates one variable and tests to see what effects the manipulation has on a second variable. Controls are used to eliminate the effects of all extraneous variables. This procedure can establish a cause-and-effect relationship between manipulated and unmanipulated variables.

Experimental neurosis – The result of an experimentally induced conflict in which an animal in a difficult discrimination situation is unable to respond. At a critical point the animal finally "breaks down," exhibiting indiscriminate, restless behavior.

Experimental psychology – A field of psychology that studies behavior by performing experimental research. Problem areas investigated are learning, perception and sensation, memory, motivation, and the underlying physiology of behavior.

Experimenter bias – The effect that an experimenter may unknowingly exert on results of an experiment, usually in a direction favoring the experimenter's hypothesis.

Experimenter effect – The effect on subjects' behavior that is attributable to the experimenter's expectations about how the subjects should perform. Also called the Rosenthal effect.

Exploratory behavior – A global term describing behavior that has no specific goal object, but rather seems to be directed solely toward the examination or the discovery of the environment. The term frequently denotes curiosity-based activities.

External auditory meatus - The canal leading from the outside of the ear to the tympanic membrane.

External inhibition – The temporary suppression of a conditioned response that is manifested when the CS is accompanied by a novel stimulus.

Externalization – 1. The arousal, via learning, by external stimuli of a drive which previously was aroused by internal stimuli. 2. In development, the process of differentiating between self and not self. 3. The projection of one's own psychological processes to the environment, characteristic of paranoid or hallucinatory states.

Extinction – In classical conditioning, the gradual disappearance of the conditioned response. This occurs with repeated presentation of the conditioned stimulus in the absence of the unconditioned stimulus. In instrumental conditioning, the elimination of a learned behavior resulting from withholding all reinforcement of that behavior.

Extirpation – Removal of some part of the nervous system to determine the effect on behavior.

Extraneous variable – A condition that may affect the outcome of an experiment but is irrelevant to the experiment.

Extrasensory perception – Alleged ability to get information about ideas or objects through some means other than the usual sensory channels. This phenomenon includes telepathy, clairvoyance, and precognition.

Extra-specific aggression (inter-specific aggression) – Fighting or other aggression directed at a member of a different species; i.e., aggression between organisms from different species.

Extraversion – One of the types of personality proposed by Jung in which the predominant interest is in social interaction and the external world.

Extrinsic motivation – Motivation based on material rewards, not inherently internalized.

Extrinsic rewards – Candy, money, and similar objects that can be given to organisms with the effect of increasing the frequency of behaviors that precede them.

Extrovert – A person characterized by more attention to external stimuli than to internal thoughts and feelings; more spontaneous, distractible, and changeable in mood than the introvert. Introversion-extroversion is one of the major dimensions in Eysenck's theory of personality.

F-minus-K index – A measuring of a subject's attempt to fake a socially desirable score on the Minnesota Multiphasic Personality Inventory.

Face validity – From an intuitive standpoint, the test items should look as if they are related to what is supposedly being measured. That is, there should be a reasonableness or plausibility of test tasks in terms of measuring what the test is supposed to be measuring.

Facial talk – A method used by Salter in his system of conditioned-reflex therapy to help a patient to overcome inhibitions by learning to show emotions on his or her face.

Factitious disorders – Disorders in which an individual deliberately produces psychological or physical symptoms in an attempt to be seen by others as sick and be able to assume the role of "patient." Sometimes actual physical symptoms are exaggerated or self-inflicted, but often physical or psychological symptoms are made up.

Factor – An element in a causal explanation.

Factor analysis – This refers to a variety of statistical techniques whose common objective is to represent a set of variables in terms of a smaller number of hypothetical variables, called factors. In psychology, these factors represent intellectual or personality traits. For example, one could account for the intercorrelations among tests of multiplication, division, and subtraction with a factor called number.

Factor analytic approach – Trait theory approach used by Cattell that seeks to understand personality by summarizing the dimensions of personality.

Factor rotation – A process usually associated with factor analysis which involves the manipulation of the axes in a centroid analysis so that they will pass through the maximum number of correlations.

Factorial design – An experimental design in which each level of every independent variable occurs with all levels of the other independent variable.

Fading – An instrumental conditioning technique that gradually introduces or removes a stimulus so that ongoing behavior is not disrupted.

Fading theory – A theory of forgetting that maintains items of information can no longer be remembered when the "memory trace" associated with them has disappeared.

Fallopian tubes – Tubes linking the ovaries and the uterus. Fertilization ordinarily occurs during the egg's passage through the fallopian tubes.

False alarm – In signal detection theory, the trial in which the signal is not present, but the subject says he sees the signal. Also called a false positive report.

False negative report – A report that a signal or event was not present when in fact a signal was actually presented, usually associated with signal-detection theory. Also called a miss.

Family therapy – Psychotherapy with members of a family meeting together with the therapist.

Fantasy – Creative imagination of a complex object or event, existent or non-existent, in concrete symbols or images, usually in the pleasant sense of a wish-fulfillment.

Fate control – The ability a person has to control one's own or another's outcomes.

Fear – A primary emotional response to a specific object or situation perceived as dangerous, and which the individual believes he or she cannot control.

Feature extraction – Identification of the most important aspects of a total stimulus configuration.

Fechner's law – A rule that relates any level of intensity of stimulation with a level of experience by the law $S = K \log I$, where S is physical stimulation, K is Weber's constant, and I is the stimulus. This states that physical stimulation increases logarithmically as experience increases arithmetically.

Feedback – 1. Information received by an individual on the effects of some previous action which is to be used by the individual to regulate further output. 2. In neuropsychology, the afferent impulses from proprioceptive receptors which give rise to motor movements. 3. In a man-made system, a means of controlling input by connecting the system to output, such as, a thermostat.

Feral children – Children raised by animals in social isolation, i.e., with only animal contact.

Ferry-Porter law – The relation between the apparent brightness of a flickering light, with a frequency greater than the critical flicker-fusion frequency, and the duration and intensity of the "on" portion of the light-dark cycle.

Fertilization – The union of sperm and ovum.

Fertilized ovum stage – The first stage of prenatal development beginning at fertilization and ending at approximately the second week; also called the zygote stage.

Fetal growth – The development of the fetus in the uterus.

Fetal stage – The third period in prenatal development, from approximately the seventh week until delivery; in a full-term pregnancy of thirty-eight weeks, the last thirty-two weeks.

Fetish – Maladaptive preference for an object or nonsexual part of the body, rather than a person, as a source of sexual satisfaction.

Fetus – The term for the embryo during the final stage of prenatal development which begins approximately 6 weeks after conception and lasts until birth.

Fiber tract – A group of axons located within the central nervous system.

Field dependent – Type of personality involving dependency on external reference points for the formation of perceptions.

Field independent – Type of personality involving an emphasis on internal reference points for the formation of perceptions.

Field research – Observation of behavior in its natural setting where subjects typically do not know that they are in an experiment.

Figural aftereffect – A change in the apparent shape or location of a visual figure following inspection of another figure, because there is a tendency to maintain constancy in the figure-ground relationship.

Figure-ground – A principle of Gestalt psychology that holds that we organize our perceptions into figure and background. The figure gives the appearance of solidity or three dimensionality and the background is not clearly shaped or patterned.

Filtering – A hypothetical perceptual process involving selective attention that prevents unimportant signals from reaching awareness. New, unusual, or important signals, however, are processed into consciousness, implying that the stimulus meaning can be discriminated by this process.

Fissure – A major indentation in the cerebral cortex. Smaller indentations are called sulci.

Fixation – 1. In psychoanalytic theory, the failure of psychosexual development to proceed normally from one stage to the next, so that an individual's libidinal energy must in part be expended to satisfy motives appropriate to an earlier stage. 2. In perception, the point at which the eyes are directed. 3. In behavior, an inability to reject an incorrect stimulus or extinguish an incorrect response for a correct response. 4. In personality, a relatively strong and enduring emotional attachment for another person.

Fixed-action pattern (FAP) – Unvarying sequences of movement, keyed by a releaser, sign, or stimulus, which are species-specific.

Fixed alternative – In a test or questionnaire, when a person must choose an answer from among a few specified alternatives.

Fixed-interval schedule – A reinforcement schedule in which a reinforcement is delivered after every response that follows a specified and constant time period since the previous reinforcement.

Fixed-ratio schedule – A plan of partial reinforcement in which the subject is rewarded each time a set number of correct responses have occurred.

Fixed schedule – An intermittent schedule of reinforcement in which the reinforcement occurs at fixed intervals of time, an interval schedule, or after a specified number of trials, a ratio schedule.

Flesch index – A gauge of the reading difficulty of a passage.

Fluid intelligence – Intelligence that can adjust to new situations; usually considered as flexible or adaptive thinking.

Focal stimuli – Stimuli which are the focus of attention; in adaptation-level theory of motivation, they represent one factor determining the adaptation level.

Focus gambling – An approach to solving conceptual problems in which the subject varies two or more attributes in each comparison with the focus; it sometimes produces quicker solutions but it can also backfire, causing slower problem solving.

Focused attention – Attending to one aspect of a stimulus while ignoring all other parts.

Fontanelles – The soft areas of connective tissue on the skull of the newborn. They allow some flexibility in the skull during labor and growth.

Forced-choice (item) – A pattern, used in rating scales, in which the individual is required to select one of a set of statements as most descriptive and perhaps another as least descriptive. In preparing the sets of statements, the attempt is usually made to have all the statements in a set approximately balanced for acceptability or desirability, but quite different in what they signify about the person.

Forebrain – The frontmost division of the brain, encompassing the thalamus, hypothalamus, and cerebral hemispheres. This part of the brain is responsible for higher processes in humans.

951

Forgetting – The loss of retention or the inability to retrieve a stored memory.

Formal group – A gathering of people in which formal titles, rules, hierarchy, and other designations are significant.

Formal operational period – The fourth stage of cognitive development as proposed by Piaget, it occurs during early adolescence, as the teenager learns to conceive of events beyond the present, to imagine hypothetical situations, and to develop a complex system of logic.

Fourier analysis – A mathematical procedure for breaking down complex waves into simple sine waves.

Fovea – A small indentation in the center of the retina into which most of the cone cells are packed. Form and color vision are centered here.

Frames – Systems of rules, understandings, and expectancies operative in repetitive social situations, such as waiting rooms.

Fraternal twins – (See dizygotic twins.)

Free association – 1. In psychoanalytic therapy, the reporting of whatever comes to the mind of the individual being analyzed. 2. In testing, a word-association test where no restrictions are put on the nature of the subject's response.

Free-floating anxiety – Anxiety reactions that have no referent in the environment.

Free recall – A technique for testing memory that requires the subject to reproduce learned items, but not in any specific order.

Free-response rate – Rate at which an organism responds in an operant situation.

Free-running rhythm – A rhythm that does not derive its regularity from an entraining stimulus.

Free will – The philosophical view that behavior is ultimately directed by volition, that humans are capable of independent choice and action.

Frequency – The number of times something occurs within a given length of time. The number of vibrations or cycles per second reaching a given point in space; often refers to a dimension of sound.

Frequency distribution – Classifying data in a graphical format for a group of individuals in which the possible score values are arranged in order from high to low, and the number of persons receiving each score is indicated.

Frequency of usage – A count of how often a particular event occurs in some block of time or sequence of behavior, most commonly how often a particular word occurs in a text.

Frequency polygon – A graphic representation of a frequency distribution in which the number of cases in each score category is plotted, and the successive points are connected with straight lines.

Frequency principle – A physiological law stating that a neuron will fire more rapidly to stronger stimuli than weaker ones, generating more action potentials per given period of time.

Frequency theory – A theory of pitch discrimination that assumes that pitch is dependent upon the rate at which the whole basilar membrane vibrates.

Freud, Sigmund – Founder of psychoanalytic theory.

Freudian slip – An error in speaking or writing which unintentionally reveals the speaker's or writer's true meaning.

Frigidity – Lack of any enjoyment from sexual intercourse with a partner; also termed arousal insufficiency.

Frontal area of the brain – The part of the cerebral cortex lying in front of the central sulcus.

Frontal lobe – The area of the cortex in front of the central sulcus and above the lateral fissure.

Frontal lobotomy – Surgical severing of the connections between the frontal lobe and the rest of the brain. Usually restricted to the prefrontal region, it is done only to treat severely psychotic patients.

Frustration – An unpleasant state of tension engendered by being blocked from attaining a goal or gratification; also, the process of blocking motivated behavior; also, the emotional response to blocking the goal.

Frustration-aggression hypothesis – A theory proposed by Dollard and Miller, according to which the only cause of aggression is frustration. Further, that frustration always leads to some kind of aggressive reaction, whether explicit or implicit.

Frustration tolerance – The general resistance of an individual to anxiety in frustrating situations without undue psychological harm.

Fugue state – A defense by actual flight; that is, a neurotic dissociative reaction in which a person has amnesia for the past, but avoids the anxiety associated with such loss of identity. This is accomplished by developing a new identity and fleeing from the intolerable situation. An individual's activities during the fugue could range from spending a great deal of time in movie theaters to starting a completely new life.

Functional autonomy – As developed by Allport, a situation in which a response which was made originally to satisfy some motive becomes intrinsically motivating.

Functional disorder – A malfunction or pathological condition without a known organic cause.

Functional fixedness – In problem-solving, a tendency or mental set in which one considers only the common uses of objects, rather than the possibilities for novel or unusual functions.

Functional invariant – As termed by Piaget, those aspects of human interaction with the environment that are unchanging as the individual develops. The functional invariants of adaptation are assimilation and accommodation, since the processes of assimilating and accommodating remain constant as the child develops.

Functional psychoses – Psychotic reactions that are provoked by psychological or experiential influences and have no demonstrable bodily origin.

Functionalism – Early school of psychological thought which emphasized how conscious behavior helps one adapt to the environment and the role learning plays in this adaptive process. This school of thought held that the mind should be studied in terms of its usefulness to the organism in adapting to its environment.

Functioning – As termed by Piaget, the processes by which an organism adapts to its environment. These processes are known as assimilation and accommodation.

Fundamental – 1. In audition, the lowest frequency in a compound tone. 2. In perception, hues that make up the primaries for any given theory of color vision. 3. In industrial psychology, a skill needed before further skills can be learned.

"G" factor – Spearman's construct for a hypothetical factor, presumably measured by a test of general intelligence, which affects performance on a variety of different tasks (as opposed to specific aptitudes).

Galvanic skin response (GSR) – A change in the electrical resistance of the skin as detected by a sensitive galvanometer. The GSR has been correlated with emotional states, strain, and tension.

Gamete – The mature reproductive cell; specifically, the sperm or the egg.

Ganglion – A cluster of nerve cell bodies that can be located outside of the central nervous system or in the subcortical regions of the brain.

Ganglion cells – Neurons in the retina connecting bipolar cells to relay areas in the brain; axons of ganglion cells form the optic nerve.

Ganzfeld – A homogeneous visual field.

Gastrointestinal system (g.i.) – Extends from the lips to the anus, including the stomach and intestines.

Gene – An area within a chromosome composed of deoxyribonucleic acid that determines hereditary traits.

General adaptation syndrome (GAS) – A pattern of physiological responses to extreme stress including increased autonomic activity and longer-term endocrine activity.

General habit – The learned tendency which results in a person's maintaining the same relationship between corresponding stimuli and responses in a class of situations.

General intelligence – A trait postulated to account for the positive relation found between many different kinds of tests of abilities and achievement.

General motive – Motives, which have in common an abstract goal, that involve diverse activities and situations.

Generality of results – The issue of whether or not a particular experimental result will be obtained under different circumstances, such as with a different subject population or in a different experimental setting.

Generalization – 1. The application of a response to a whole class or group after having been conditioned to respond in that way to a limited portion of the class or group. 2. Of or relating to forming an idea or judgment which is applicable to an entire class of objects, people, or events.

Generalized reinforcement – A form of secondary reinforcement that is not specifically related to any single need state, such as praise, smiling, and thanks.

Generative grammar – As developed by Noam Chomsky, the concept that linguistic utterances are learned through general rules which allow for great variety and originality in linguistic production.

Generativity – In Erikson's personality theory, the positive outcome of one of the stages of adult personality development, specifically, the ability to do creative work or to contribute to the raising of one's children. The opposite of stagnation.

Genetic model – The point of view that present behavior and development is to be understood in terms of heredity and developmental history.

Genetic opportunity – The likelihood of having an experience which influences a given trait as a function of the expression of another genetic trait not related to the first. For example, the genetic trait of skin color influences the opportunity to have experiences which may influence IQ test performance.

Genetic transmission – The processes involved in passing genetic material from one generation to the next.

Genetics – The study of the transmission of hereditary characteristics as it relates to evolutionary theory.

Genital period – In Freudian psychoanalytic theory, the final psychosexual stage beginning with puberty at approximately the age of 11, during which sexual interest is shifted from autoeroticism to heterosexuality by involvement with normal adult modes of sexual gratification.

Genitalia – A term referring generally to sex organs.

Genotype – A person's genetic makeup composed of both dominant and recessive genes.

Geriatric – A specialization in the treatment of diseases of old age.

Germ cells – Reproductive cells during any stage of their development. In the female, the egg; in the male, the sperm.

Germinal period – The first two weeks of the prenatal period, during which the blastula forms.

Gerontology – The science of old age, including geriatrics, psychology, sociology, and anthropology.

Gestalt – The term has no exact equivalent in English. The approximate English equivalents are configuration, meaningful organized whole, structural relationship, and theme.

Gestalt psychology – Founded by Max Wertheimer, the basic premise is that "the whole is greater than the sum of its parts." Gestalt psychology not only contends that stimuli are perceived as whole images rather than as parts built into images, but also maintains that the whole determines the parts instead of the parts determining the whole. The theory originally focused on perception, however, it is applicable to a broad range of areas.

Gestalt therapy – A distinctive formal theory of personality in which therapeutic techniques are based on existential philosophy and emphasize the here and now awareness of personal sensations and feelings. The goal is to enable a person to form meaningful configurations of personality.

Gestation – The prenatal phase of life lasting an average of 266 days in humans.

Gland – A bodily structure whose function is to manufacture chemicals, called hormones, that are secreted into the bloodstream and regulate bodily activities. The two general types are endocrine glands and exocrine glands.

Goal – In motivation, the satisfier of a motive condition.

Goal gradient – The tendency for motivation to increase or decrease as the organism approaches the goal.

Goal specificity – The desire to satisfy a motive condition with a particular reinforcement rather than with any satisfying reinforcement.

Gonad – The primary sex gland: ovaries in the female and testes in the male.

Good form – A Gestalt principle of organization which asserts that figures or patterns are perceived in such a way as to be as uniform as possible.

Goodenough Draw-a-Man Test – A test of intelligence in which one is asked to draw the best possible picture of a man; primarily used with children up to age 11.

Grade equivalent – A score conversion in which a test score is assigned the grade value for which it is average.

Grade norm – A standard of performance which represents the average performance of a given population.

Graded potential – The sum of the excitation and inhibition at a given synapse; generator potential; receptor potential.

Gradient of stimulus generalization – Mathematical curve that illustrates the degree of generalization between various stimuli. Generally, the closer the stimuli to the conditioned stimulus, the greater the response.

Graphic rating scale – A rating scale in which the rater indicates his rating by making a mark at some point along a line. Selected points on the line are characterized by evaluative adjectives or descriptions of the quality of behavior represented.

Gray matter – A general term for the neural tissue found in the brain, spinal cord, and ganglia, comprised of cell bodies.

Group-centered therapy – The term applied to the system of group therapy developed by Carl Rogers and associates in which the individuals in the group rather than the therapist has the primary role in the therapeutic relationship.

Group factors – 1. Psychological factors postulated to account for interrelations of groups of tests; typically numerical, clerical, verbal, spatial, etc. 2. In factor analysis, any factor that is manifested in at least two tests that constitute the correlation matrix.

Group pressure – The effect that the opinions, feelings, exhortations, or behavior of groups has on a single individual.

Group therapy – Any therapy in which more than one patient is present in the therapy setting at the same time.

Grouping – The tendency to perceive objects in

groups, rather than as isolated elements; determined by proximity, similarity, good form, and continuity.

Growth – Ordinarily refers to such physical changes as increasing height or weight; quantitative growth.

Growth curve – A statistical curve derived from plotting weight and height against chronological age for comparison of an individual child's growth pattern with the average rate of growth.

Growth therapies – Therapies aimed at helping an individual achieve maximum self-actualization.

GSR – (See Galvanic Skin Response.)

Habit – An acquired response that becomes fixed and relatively automatic through constant repetition.

Habituation – Decreased response to a stimulus because it has become familiar. It is often a condition resulting from repeated use of a drug and characterized by a desire for the drug; little or no tendency to increase the dose; and psychological, but not physical, dependence.

Hair cells – Receptor cells possessing cilia (tiny hairs) such as the auditory receptor cells located in a membrane in the cochlea that are stimulated by vibrations in the cochlear fluid.

Hallucination – Perception of an external object, often bizarre in nature, in the absence of stimulation.

Hallucinogenic drugs – A group of drugs also known as psychedelic drugs and psychotogenic drugs that produce hallucinations and often provoke highly imaginative thought patterns and/or unusual and mixed perceptions.

Halo effect – The tendency, when rating an individual on one characteristic, to be influenced by another characteristic of his personality, e.g., physically attractive people are more likely to be judged as intelligent than unattractive people.

Haptic system – The perceptual system whereby object properties are perceived through active touch. It includes the tactile sense as well as proprioception.

Hawthorne effect – Generally, the effect on subjects' performance attributable to their knowledge that they are serving as experimental subjects or being treated in a special manner. Sometimes, the tendency for people to work harder when experiencing a sense of participation in something new and special.

Head-turning reflex – A reflex elicited in the infant by stroking his cheek or the corner of his mouth. The infant turns his head toward the side being stimulated.

Hedonic – The motivation to seek pleasure and avoid pain.

Hedonic tone – The affective quality of an emotion; degree of pleasantness or unpleasantness of an emotion; a basic dimension of all emotions.

Hedonic value – The value of a stimulus or an experience on a scale from pleasant to unpleasant.

Hereditary factors – Those inherited biological factors that are involved in the development of the structure and function of the body.

Heredity – The biological transmission of genetic traits from parent to offspring.

Hering theory – Theory of color vision postulating six primaries, black-white, red-green, and blue-yellow, in three opponent process pairs.

Heritability – A statistical concept which reflects the percentage of variability in a trait that is associated with differences in the genetic composition of the individuals in the group. The capability of being inherited.

Hermaphrodite – An animal or plant having both male and female reproductive organs.

Hertz (Hz) – A frequency measurement of cycles per second. One Hz equals one cycle per second, etc.

Heterogeneous – Dissimilar; characteristic of groups, sets of data, or individuals who show differences or dissimilarities.

Heteronomy – An intermediate stage in Bull's scheme of moral development in which the individual responds to situations primarily by their effect on him- or herself. Also, pertaining to activities originating outside the self or the guidance of one individual by another (e.g., hypnosis).

Heterophemy – Speaking or writing the opposite of what is intended.

Heteroscedasticity – The quality or condition of a matrix in which the arrays show significantly different standard deviations.

Heterosexuality – An attraction toward members of the opposite sex.

Heterozygous – Refers to an individual who has both one dominant and one recessive gene for a given trait.

Heuristic – A principle or strategy used in problem solving which serves as a device for shortening the solution process; often used when there are many different ways to solve a problem; a solution is not guaranteed.

Hierarchical model of intelligence – The view that intelligence is hierarchically structured with general intelligence, group factors, specific factors, and, finally, specific information in an interdependent system.

Hierarchization – A term used in linguistics to suggest that in the course of development, the child's linguistic abilities build upon and elaborate upon constructions made at earlier phases of development.

Hierarchy of needs – A proposal by Abraham Maslow that arranges motives in an order of importance; those lower in the hierarchy must be satisfied before the higher ones can be satisfied. The lower motives being food, shelter, etc., progress to "self-actualization" as the motive highest in the hierarchy.

Hierarchy of skill – A task that displays several levels of organization or structure. Performance curves often show interesting evidence of such structure.

Higher-order conditioning – A form of classical conditioning in which the previously trained conditioned stimulus now functions as an unconditioned stimulus to train a new conditioned stimulus.

Higher-order interaction – Interaction effects involving more than two independent variables in multifactor experiments, often making interpretation difficult.

Hindbrain – Phylogenetically, the oldest portion of the brain. It contains the medulla, cerebellum, pons, and base of the reticular formation. Also known as the rhombencephalon.

Histogram – A graphic representation of a frequency distribution in which the cases falling in each score category are represented by a bar whose size is proportional to the number of cases. Since each bar is the full width of the score category, the bars make a continuous "pile" showing the form of the frequency distribution.

Hit – The correct detection of a signal that has been presented; usually associated with signal-detection.

Holophrases – A term used in linguistics to describe the phenomenon wherein a young child will use a single word in the sense of a phrase or sentence. "Johnny" can mean "Pick Johnny up" or "Give Johnny some water," and so on.

Homeostasis – A state of optimal organismic balance brought about by internal regulatory mechanisms.

Homeostatic mechanisms – Mechanisms for achieving homeostasis.

Homogeneous – Highly similar; coming from the same background. For example, a homogeneous culture is one in which all members have had highly similar experiences.

Homosexual – A person who has overt sexual inter-

ests in or receives sexual satisfaction from members of the same sex.

Homosexual panic – In a heterosexual individual, the fear arising from homosexual thoughts or the suggestion that one might have such thoughts.

Homozygous – Refers to an individual whose two genes for a given trait are both either dominant or recessive.

Hope of failure – A desire for failure; not as well investigated as hope of success or fear of failure or success.

Horizontal decalage – A term introduced by Piaget to describe the fact that conservation of different quantities occurs at different times, even though all conservations require the same mental operations for their attainment. For example, number conservation is routinely observed to appear before length conservation.

Hormone – A chemical manufactured and secreted into the bloodstream by an endocrine gland, which may then activate another gland or help to regulate bodily functioning and behavior.

Hospitalism – A medical name for the syndrome (configuration of symptoms) associated with the inability of infants to survive in children's homes or hospitals. Symptoms of hospitalism include listlessness, inability to gain weight, unresponsiveness, and eventual death.

Hostility – Angry, hateful, or destructive behavior against another. Also, the motive behind this behavior.

Hue – That aspect of color experience referred to by color names, e.g., blue or yellow. Hue is the psychological correlate of wavelength.

Human engineering – The applied field of psychological specialization concerned with the design of equipment and the tasks performed in the operation of equipment.

Humanism – In psychology, a movement in personality and clinical psychology that focuses uniquely upon human experience, rather than abstract conceptions of human nature. There is an emphasis on positive, constructive human capacities.

Humanistic psychology – Psychology based on humanistic principles (see Humanism).

Humanitarianism – Concern with the welfare of people.

Hunger – A drive state or tissue need based on the deprivation of food; also, the feelings associated with such deprivation.

Huntington's chorea – A disorder characterized by progressive mental and physical deterioration and death, usually after the age of 20 or 30. Huntington's chorea is caused by a dominant gene and is always fatal.

Hydraulic drive model of motivation – A belief that motives or tensions behave like fluid under pressure that must break out or find release when the pressure builds up and becomes too great.

Hypermania – A manic-depressive state of excitement characterized by ravings, continuous movement, and disorientation as to time and place.

Hyperopia – Farsightedness. The inability to see near objects clearly because the image is focused behind the retina instead of on it.

Hyperphagia – Condition in which an animal eats abnormally large amounts of food and shows no satiation of hunger, produced experimentally by destruction of the ventromedial hypothalamic nucleus.

Hypertension – A condition of abnormally high blood pressure.

Hypnagogic imagery – Imagery that occurs as one is dropping off to sleep. It may be visual, auditory, or somesthetic, and is more vivid in some people than in others.

Hypnagogic state – State of consciousness experienced when passing from wakefulness to sleep.

Hypnoanalysis – Psychoanalysis carried on while the patient is under hypnosis.

Hypnosis – A technique (or group of techniques) for inducing an altered state of consciousness. It is characterized by increased suggestibility, relaxation or alertness, and possible distortion of reality.

Hypochondriasis – A neurotic reaction in which a person is excessively concerned with his or her physical health or welfare.

Hypomania – A manic-depressive state of excitement that is characterized by great enthusiasm and grandiose planning without any reality orientation.

Hypothalamus – A group of nuclei in the forebrain that controls the involuntary functions through the autonomic nervous system. It helps to control many basic drives and emotional processes, including sleep, thirst, temperature, sex, and hunger. It also controls much of the endocrine system's activities through connections with the pituitary gland.

Hypothesis – A testable statement that offers a predicted relationship between dependent and independent variables.

Hypothesis theory – Describes problem solving as a matter of formulating, selecting, and testing hypotheses about possible solutions until the correct one is found.

Hysteria – A form of neurosis in which patients manifest variable sensory, motor, vasomotor, visceral, and mental symptoms. These symptoms include paralyzed limbs, deafness, blindness, and other pathological conditions for which no anatomical or physiological causes could be found.

Iconic memory – A transient visual memory of a stimulus lasting about 0.5 seconds.

Iconic mode – As developed by Bruner, a method of converting immediate experience into mental models by using images in the form of sensory information.

Id – According to Freud, the id is the most fundamental component of personality, comprised of drives, needs, and instinctual impulses. It is unable to tolerate tension, is obedient only to the pleasure principle, and is in constant conflict with the super-ego.

Ideal self – The way a person would like to be, which may not match the way one actually is.

Idealism – A philosophical doctrine that affirms the pursuit of ideas and ideals rather than actuality or reality.

Idealized self-image – As developed by Horney, a pattern of perfectionist strivings and godlike fantasies which constitute the core of a neurosis. The idealized image is a false and exaggerated estimate of one's true potentialities and abilities, and it is derived more from fantasy than from reality.

Identical twins – Two individuals who have developed as a result of the splitting of an already fertilized egg; thus, both individuals have identical chromosomal patterns. Also called monozygotic twins.

Identification – 1. In psychoanalytic theory, the internalization of a conscience through contact with one's parent of the same sex, creating a superego; also, a defense mechanism in which one incorporates the image of an object or individual into the psyche, taking the demands of an object or individual into the psyche and acting as if they were one's own. This is also called introjection. 2. In social psychology, the process through which someone is persuaded to a particular attitude because one has internalized the persuader's attitude. Also, the process by which people acquire a sense of personal definition from their reference group memberships. 3. According to Erikson, it is the process through which the infant learns a conviction of his or her self. This process is dependent on the mother's predictability and consistency in her relationship with the infant.

Identity – 1. A logical rule specifying that certain activities leave objects or situations unchanged. 2. The individual self.

Identity crisis – As proposed by Erikson, a period

when one's sense of self and direction in life becomes clearer. It is marked by much confusion, experimentation, and emotionality. It generally occurs first during adolescence and may reoccur once or more often during adulthood.

Idiographic – The approach to personality study that emphasized those aspects of personality unique to each person.

Idiosyncratic – Unique to a particular person or situation.

Idiot savant – A person with marked skill or talent in some specific activity, such as art, music, or calculations, although his or her general intellectual level is low.

Illumination – In problem solving, one stage in which the answer seems to come in a flash of insight. The elements of the problem suddenly appear in a new relationship to each other. Since an emotional feeling often accompanies this experience, it is also called the "Aha!" experience or insight.

Illusion – A distorted or false perception of an object, or an object or event that induces a false perception. One can experience illusions with respect to movement or perspective.

Image – 1. A mental representation of an object or event. 2. As developed by Titchener, one of three elements of consciousness; the other two are affective states and sensations. 3. The component of dreams.

Imagery – A characteristic of verbal material that tends to evoke images or internal symbolic representations; the representations themselves.

Imagination – The creation of objects that have only a mental existence without the aid of sensory data.

Imaginative play – Play activities that include make-believe games. These are particularly prevalent during the pre-school years.

Imitation – The modeling of one's actions on those of another; one of the fundamental ways a child learns.

Immature birth – A miscarriage occurring sometime between the twentieth and the twenty-eighth week of pregnancy, and resulting in the birth of a fetus weighing between 1 and 2 pounds.

Immediate memory – Continuation of the stimulus image for about a second after the stimulus has disappeared; sensory memory.

Implicit behavior – The convert movement of muscles which cannot be detected without the aid of instrumentation. Some examples are glandular secretions or the movements of the larynx at the time of speech. Some believe that thinking could be reduced to implicit subvocal behavior.

Implosive therapy – As developed by Stampfl and Levis, a type of behavior therapy in which anxiety-arousing stimuli are presented in imagination while the patient is encouraged to experience as intense anxiety as possible. The therapist deliberately attempts to elicit a massive flood or implosion of anxiety. With repeated exposure in a safe setting, no objective danger is apparent, the stimulus loses its power to elicit anxiety, and the maladaptive behavior is extinguished.

Imprinting – In ethology, a social learning mechanism akin to learning, whereby animals of certain species, especially fowl, become "emotionally attached" to whatever stimulus they are first exposed to shortly after hatching or birth. The attachment is manifested by the animal's persistent following after the imprinted object. Imprinting occurs very early in life and is somewhat resistant to later modification.

Impulsive – A personality characteristic manifested in a greater concern with the rapid solution of problems than with their correct solution. There is an underlying need for immediate gratification rather than a need for a best possible solution.

Incentive motivation – An explanation for human behavior referring to the belief that it is the reinforcing property of the outcome of behavior that determines whether or not the individual will behave. It is the incentive value of a behavioral outcome that determines its occurrence or nonoccurrence.

Incidence – The frequency with which any condition or event occurs.

Incidental learning – Learning which takes place without the set or instruction to learn, as opposed to intentional learning.

Incongruence – As developed by Carl Rogers, the state of behaving in ways that are different from the way we see ourselves or the way we feel. The disharmony experienced can result in anxiety or psychopathology.

Incremental theory – Any theory that regards development as an additive series of qualitatively similar steps.

Incubation – A phase of problem solving during which the person puts aside the problem and engages in irrelevant activity, yet unconscious processes seem to be working on the solution.

Independence – 1. An attitude characterized by a reliance upon one's own perceptions and past experience to guide behavior. 2. In statistics, no causal or correlational relationship exists between the variables under study.

Independent influence – A change in a person's attitudes or behaviors that occurs because a perceived message itself, rather than the sender of the message, is persuasive.

Independent variable - In psychological research, the condition that the psychologist manipulates. By convention, it is plotted on the Y axis.

Individual differences - Refers to the fact that all individuals vary and are different from other individuals, even though they may have some things in common.

Individual psychology - The term applied to the system of psychotherapy developed by Alfred Adler. Its emphasis is on the uniqueness of individual personality. Once the particular lifestyle of the individual is fully understood, the job of the therapist is to re-educate the patient toward healthier experiences and goals.

Individual test - Psychological tests given to only one subject at a time.

Induced movement - Apparent movement of a stationary object that is induced by movement of a surrounding frame.

Induction - 1. Discipline that is based on reasons. Most effective if tailored to the child's cognitive level. 2. In logic, reasoning from the particular to the general. 3. In physiology, the arousal of activity in one area as a result of the spread of activity from an adjoining area.

Industrial psychology - A branch of psychology that studies ways of improving efficiency in industry, both in terms of human beings and machinery. This area devises methods of selection, training, counseling of personnel, and psychological engineering.

Infancy - The period from birth to two years of age.

Infantile autism - Psychotic patterns of behavior shown by children under age ten characterized by poor communication, no desire for personal contact, and a desire for status quo.

Inference - A guess about unobservable processes that is based on data.

Inferential statistics - Measures or techniques that allow for the analysis or evaluation of relationships that exist within a sample of data or between samples of data. Such analysis is useful in making predictions.

Inferiority complex - As developed by Adler, the concept that a person may experience feelings of deficiency that are reinforced in such a belief by others in society.

Inflection - A method of communication involving raising and lowering the voice and placing accents in certain spots during a verbal exchange.

Influence - A change in a person's attitude or behavior that is induced by another person or group.

Informal group - A gathering of people in which there are no formal rules or titles; however, unwritten guidelines may exist.

Information - A set of facts or ideas that are obtained through learning; in information theory, a quantitative property of items that enable the items to be categorized in some meaningful manner. The bit is the unit of information.

Information-processing theory - Theory of problem solving which refers to the way a person receives information from the environment, operates on it, integrates it with other information available in memory, and uses it as a basis for deciding how to act.

Informational feedback - The stimuli that follow an organism's responses and show it the effect of its responses.

Infrared rays - An invisible part of the electromagnetic spectrum with wavelengths that are longer than visible red; experienced as heat.

Ingratiation - Behaving in a friendly, positive manner toward another with the aim of manipulating that person in order to serve one's own purpose.

Inheritance - The genetic composition of an organism.

Inhibition - 1. In general, a reduction of response due to suppression or restraint. 2. In physiology, a decrease in the firing of a neuron. 3. In psychoanalytic theory, the process by which the superego intervenes with the instinctual impulses of the id, thus preventing those impulses from reaching consciousness.

Inhibitory-disinhibitory effect - Imitative behavior that results in either the suppression (inhibition) or appearance (disinhibition) of previously acquired deviant behavior.

Inhibitory postsynaptic potential (IPSP) - Hyperpolarization of the membrane of a postsynaptic neuron which decreases the probability of neural firing.

Innate - Present at birth; inborn; due to heredity; not learned.

Innate releasing mechanism - An internal mechanism of an organism's nervous system triggering a fixed action pattern (instinctive pattern) when a releasing stimulus is presented.

Inner ear - The part of the ear that contains the cochlea (hearing), semicircular canals, utricule, and the saccule (balance).

Inner speech - Internal representations of verbal stimuli, thought to be a process in memory and thinking.

Innervation - The supply of neurons to a muscle or gland.

Inoculation effect – When first exposure to mild arguments creates a set for a person so that later, stronger arguments can be resisted.

Insanity – A legal but not psychological term denoting the inability to distinguish between right and wrong or to know what one is doing.

Insight-oriented therapy – Type of psychotherapy that emphasizes change in motivation and knowledge. It focuses on increasing self-knowledge or insight of which the subject was unaware.

Instinct – An invariant sequence of complex behaviors that is observed in all members of a species and that is released by specific stimuli in the apparent absence of learning. Innate behaviors that are unaffected by practice.

Instrumental behavior – Activity that usually achieves some goal or satisfies a need.

Instrumental conditioning – (See Operant conditioning.)

Instrumental response – Behavior leading toward a goal.

Insulin – A hormone secreted by the islands of Langerhans in the pancreas. It is involved in the utilization of sugar and carbohydrates in the body. Also used in insulin shock therapy.

Insulin shock therapy – An early form of shock therapy that utilizes insulin-induced comas to treat mental disorders.

Integration – 1. The process by which parts are unified into a whole, as in the coordination of several neural impulses into a unified whole. 2. In personality, the state in which the traits of an organism work smoothly together in a coordinated whole.

Intellectualization – A Freudian defense mechanism whereby the individual emphasizes the intellectual or rational content of his or her behavior in order to exclude any of the emotional connotations of that behavior.

Intelligence – Intelligence is a difficult term to define with any precision. Generally, it is a trait postulated to underlie abilities to make judgments, solve abstract problems, succeed in academic activities, etc. Operationally, it is that which is measured by intelligence tests.

Intelligence quotient (IQ) – An index for expressing the results of an intelligence test. The intelligence quotient is an indicator of the individual's standing in relation to his own age group. Originally, quotients were computed by the ratio

$$100 \left(\frac{\text{Mental age}}{\text{Chronological age}} \right)$$

Currently, practically all intelligence quotients are standard scores, designed so that the average individual receives an intelligence quotient of 100 and the standard deviation in the group is 15 or 16.

Intelligence tests – Tests designed to measure intelligence, usually consisting of a series of aptitude tests that predict academic ability.

Intensity – Strength or amount of energy in a stimulus or response.

Interaction – 1. An experimental result that occurs when the levels of one independent variable are differentially affected by the levels of other independent variables. 2. A relationship between systems such that events taking place in one system influence events taking place in the other.

Interaction-oriented group – A group whose primary goal is to provide opportunity for social interaction.

Interest tests – Tests which focus on occupational and educational interests and assess an individual's selection of activities that he or she would like to engage in.

Interference – 1. The obstruction of learning something new caused by previously or subsequently learned material; a theory of forgetting, invoking the above process. 2. In cognition, a decrease in the amplitude of a sound or light wave because two waves occurring simultaneously are out of phase.

Intermittent reinforcement – Any pattern of reinforcement which is not continuous. It may vary according to ratio or interval.

Internal clock – A hypothetical physiological mechanism that regulates the cyclic variations recorded from many physiological systems.

Internal consistency – Degree of relationship among the items of a test, that is, the extent to which the same examinees tend to get each item right. Measures of reliability based upon a single testing are really measures of internal consistency.

Internal inhibition – A hypothetical process postulated by Pavlov to account for extinction. The special term given to the type of extinction in which the CS does not simply lose its effectiveness in eliciting the CR, rather it actively inhibits the CR.

Internalization – The process by which the individual's moral behaviors become independent of external reward and punishment.

Interpersonal attraction – Issue of friendship and romantic involvement, and attitudes of liking; subject of social psychological research.

Interpersonal relations – The often reciprocal interactions between two or more persons, or the characteristic pattern of such interactions. Most commonly employed in Sullivan's writings.

Interpolated task – A task used to fill the interval between the study of material and its recall in memory experiments.

Interposition – A monocular depth cue in which one object appears closer to the viewer because it partly blocks the view of another object.

Interquartile range – The middle 50 percent of the distribution of values. It falls between the first and the fourth quartiles.

Inter-role conflict – When an individual is confronted with expectations based upon at least two different roles that cannot be fulfilled simultaneously.

Inter-stimulus interval (ISI) – The time between two successive stimuli measured from the onset of the first to the onset of the second, usually the time between the onset of the CS and the onset of the UCS.

Intertrial interval – The delay after the feedback and before the start of the next stimulus presentation.

Interval scale – Numbers arranged to order a variable in such a way that equal changes in the variable are represented by equal differences in the numbers.

Interval schedules – A reinforcement schedule in which reinforcement is delivered after a response that has been made at the end of a given time period.

Intervening variable – Factor that stands between and provides a relationship between some stimulus in the environment and some response on the part of an organism.

Intervention programs – A global term referring to educational programs, which are typically remedial in nature. Many intervention programs have been organized at the preschool level to supplement the backgrounds of culturally deprived children.

Interview – A conversation between investigator and subject for the purpose of obtaining factual information, for evaluating one's personality, or for therapeutic purposes.

Intra-role conflict – When an individual is confronted with two or more expectations, which arise from only one role but cannot be fulfilled simultaneously.

Intraverbal responses – Verbal responses that are related to other verbal responses; word associations; facts known through verbal chains.

Intrinsic rewards – A form of reward that results from the activity itself because the activity is interesting, pleasurable, and rewarding.

Introjection – A defense mechanism in which the ego protects itself against an impulse from the id that is anxiety-producing by identifying itself with another person.

Introspection – The attempt of describing one's own private, internal state of being, including one's thoughts and feelings.

Introversion – As developed by Jung, the personality dimension describing an orientation inward toward the self. An introvert is self-directed and concerned with his or her own thoughts, avoids social contact, and tends to turn away from reality. At the two extremes are the extroverts and introverts.

Intuitive judgment – A decision based upon statistical data and other information, and the feelings of the psychologist giving the test.

Intuitive thought – One of the substages of the preoperational period, beginning around age 4 and lasting until age 7 or 8. Intuitive thought is marked by the child's natural ability to solve many problems and also by his or her inability to respond correctly in the face of misleading perceptual features of problems.

Invariance – 1. The degree to which given relationships among properties of objects, events, or individuals are unaffected by specified changes in the conditions under which those things are observed. 2. The characteristic of an afterimage retaining its size, despite changes in the distance to which it is projected.

Inverse relationship – The relationship indicated when an increase in one variable is paralleled by a decrease in another variable; a negative correlation.

Iodopsin – A photosensitive pigment found in cone cells that apparently is involved in color vision.

Ipsative test – A test yielding multiple scores, in which the sum of scores for all individuals is the same. Thus, an individual who is high on some scales of the test must be low on others. A test in which the individual's profile is expressed in relation to his or her own overall average, rather than in relation to some outside group.

Ipsilateral – On the same side, often used in describing brain-to-body relationships; the opposite of contralateral.

IQ – (See Intelligence quotient.)

Iris – The colored part of the eye containing the pupil (a group of muscles that regulates the amount of light entering the eye).

Irradiation – An increase in the number of muscles coming into play in a localized reflex, due to an increase in the strength of stimulation.

Irregular verbs – Verbs that take idiosyncratic modification, rather than regular endings, to show change of tense: eat-ate, run-ran, etc.

Irrelevant dimensions – The stimulus dimensions that do not provide defining information about the concept.

Isolation – The defense mechanism whereby the affect connected with a painful past event is dissociated from the memory or thought of the event.

Isomorphism – The Gestalt hypothesis that there is a point-for-point correspondence between a stimulus and its representation in the cerebral cortex.

Item analysis – Study of the statistical properties of test items. The typical qualities of interest are the difficulty of the item and its ability to differentiate between more capable and less capable examinees. Difficulty is usually expressed as the percent getting the item right, and discrimination is exposed as some index comparing success by the more capable and the less capable students.

James-Lange theory of emotion – A theory proposing that emotion-producing stimuli generate physical reactions, which in turn are perceived as felt emotions.

Jensen hypothesis – The controversial argument advanced by Jensen on the basis of some evidence regarding heredity and environment. With respect to intelligence, the most influential environmental factors are prenatal, and racial and social class differences in intelligence test scores cannot be accounted for by differences in environment alone. Hence, genetic factors are assumed to be responsible for some of the observed differences in intelligence among different racial groups.

jnd (just noticeable difference) – The smallest difference between two stimuli that can be detected reliably (by convention, 50% of the time).

Jump stand – An experimental device developed by K. S. Lashley to test visual discrimination and discrimination testing. The subject, usually a rat, must choose which of several doors to jump through to obtain a reward.

Jung, Carl Gustav – (pronounced yung) Swiss psychoanalyst who broke with Freud in 1913 and founded the School of Analytical Psychology. Jung rejected the central importance of libido as a sexual energy and emphasized the meaning of art, religion, history, mythology, anthropology, and literature in his complex theory of personality.

Just noticeable difference – (See jnd.)

Justification – The use of rationalizations to achieve a feeling of equity; real equity is not achieved.

Juvenile era (Harry Stack Sullivan) – The stage in a child's development which begins when he or she shows a need for playmates and lasts until the emergence of a need for an intimate relationship with another person of comparable status at preadolescence.

Karyotyping – The process of photographing chromosomes and analyzing them into the pairs that are characteristic of the species.

Kinesthesis – The sense of movement and bodily position, as mediated by receptors in the muscles, tendons, and joints.

Kinship (anthropology) – Relationship between two or more persons based upon common descent and genetic similarity.

Knowledge of results (Kb) – Any information about the effect of a response; also called feedback.

Koffka, Kurt – One of the founders of Gestalt psychology.

Köhler, Wolfgang – One of the founders of Gestalt psychology.

Korsakoff's psychosis – A mental disorder brought on by alcoholism and characterized by a memory disturbance in which there is an inability to form new associations.

Krause end bulb – An encapsulated neural ending located at the junction of mucus membranes and dry skin, thought to be a receptor for cold.

Kuder-Richardson reliability – Reliability estimated from data available from a single test administration, using the average score on the test, its standard deviation, and difficulty indices for the separate items.

Kymograph – A device, now rarely used, for recording the strength of a response on a moving drum.

Labor – The process during which the fetus, the placenta, and other membranes are separated from the woman's body and expelled. The normal termination of labor is birth.

Labyrinth – The area in the head containing the organs of the middle and inner ear.

Laguno – Downy, soft hair that covers the fetus. Laguno grows over most of the child's body some time after the fifth month of pregnancy and is usually shed during the seventh month. However, some laguno is often present at birth, especially on the infant's back.

Landolt ring – A figure in the shape of a C, or a ring with a small gap, used in the laboratory assessment of visual acuity.

Language – No universally acceptable definition is available. Used loosely, it can mean anything from simply "a communication system" to "a learned arbitrary set of symbols passed along from one generation to the next in a culture."

Language acquisition device (LAD) – Innate biological mechanism common to all humans which operates on language data provided by parents and other speaking organisms, and produces a given language structure. The basic mechanism for language acquisition.

Lashley jumping stand – Device used to study discrimination learning. (See Jump stand.)

Latency – The length of time between stimulation and response.

Latency stage – In psychoanalytic theory, a stage of personality development in which sexual expression is repressed and channeled into other activities; about ages 6 to 12.

Latent content (of dreams) – Unconscious wishes or impulses that seek expression through dreams; the symbolic meaning of a dream.

Latent learning – Learning that appears to occur in the absence of reinforcement, facilitating performance in later trials when reinforcement is introduced.

Later childhood – The third period of postnatal development; from approximately age six until age twelve (the onset of puberty).

Law of effect – A proposal by Thorndike which suggests that behavior which is satisfying or pleasing is "stamped in," while behavior that leads to annoyance or unpleasantness is "stamped out." In general, the principle that reinforcement is necessary for, or facilitates, learning.

Law of least effort – The tendency to choose an act which accomplishes the goals of the organism and which requires the least expenditure of energy.

Law of similarity – One of the laws of organization which states that things similar to each other tend to be grouped as part of the same entity.

Laws of association – Classic treatment of knowing and thinking which held that associations arose from three sources: similarity, contrast, and contiguity in space or time.

Laws of organization – Rules by which perceptions are integrated and made coherent. Gestaltists believed that these rules reflected brain functioning.

Learned helplessness (Seligman) – The acceptance of what seem to be the unalterable consequences of a situation on the basis of previous experience or information, even if change may now be possible.

Learned motives – Conditions that result from experience and initiate, guide, and maintain behaviors; often called social motives.

Learning – The acquisition of any relatively permanent change in behavior traceable to experience and practice.

Learning curve – A graphic representation of the change in performance as a function of time or number of trials.

Learning set – An acquired ability to learn more rapidly in new learning situations because of previously learned responses.

Learning strategies – Methods for forming concepts and for acquiring and using information about the environment. Children gradually develop more sophisticated and efficient strategies.

Learning to learn – A gradual improvement, via positive transfer, in learning to solve problems of the same type as previously solved. Thought by some to account for "insight learning."

Lens – Transparent structure in the eye that changes shape to focus the optic array on the retina at the back of the eye.

Lesbianism – Homosexuality among women.

Lesion – Damaged or destroyed part of the body. Lesions are often made in the nervous system by cutting out or electrically burning tissue in order to study the physical and psychological effects that occur.

Level of aspiration – A self-imposed standard against which a person judges his or her own performance.

Level of confidence (level of significance) – In statistics, the confidence that the null hypothesis can be rejected. It is the probability that the desired result could occur by chance.

Level of tension – As a dimension of emotion, the level of activity to which the individual is impelled in his or her anticipation of affective change.

Leveling – Cognitive style whereby one ignores differences and emphasizes similarities in perceiving the world.

Lewin, Kurt – Founder of Field Theory in social psychology.

Libidinal gratification – The gratification of sexual impulses. Within the context of Freud's theory, these need not necessarily involve what the layman considers to be the sexual regions of the body.

Libido – The name given in Freudian theory to the instinctual or id energy that is the source of all psychological energy. Sometimes used to refer specifically to sexual motivation.

Life cycle – Regularly occurring episodes and events throughout the life period from conception to death which have impact upon the total development of the person.

Life space – A term employed by Lewin to describe the individual's interpretation of his or her environment. The life space includes the individual, his or her personal goals and aspirations, the alternatives necessary to obtain those goals, and the barriers that obstruct this action.

Life style – In Adler's writings, an individual's characteristic and pervasive pattern of behavior for gaining status and dealing with feelings of inferiority.

Light adaptation – A decrease in sensitivity to light resulting from an increase in light energy reaching the eye.

Limbic system – A group of anatomical structures surrounding the brain stem; thought to be involved with motivated behavior and emotion.

Linear program – Any programmed learning situation that progresses in the same way for each subject.

Linguistic-relativity theory – A theory of thinking that states that the form and structure of a language are the determinants of the ways of thought. (See Worfi hypothesis.)

Live modeling – One organism copying a behavior of another organism that is physically present and observed.

Lobotomy – Type of psychosurgery that involves severing the connections between the frontal lobes and the rest of the brain. It has been used to treat extremely hyperemotional mental patients but is infrequently used today.

Locus of control (Rotter) – A personality construct which is dependent upon whether the individual perceives rewards as being contingent upon his or her own behavior.

Logarithmic scale – A scale in which the intervals are based on logarithms instead of on the original numbers.

Logical positivism – The position in philosophy that in science meaningful statements must be operationally defined. The consequence of this position is to deny mentalistic concepts.

Logical syllogism – Three-step argument which consists of two premises, assumed to be true, and a conclusion that may or may not follow from these premises.

Long-term memory – Memory for learned material over a relatively long retention interval (generally an hour or more). A hypothetical memory system for permanent storage of learning.

Longitudinal study – An investigation conducted over a fairly long period of time, using the same subjects throughout; the study may be used to determine how age, the independent variable, affects behavior.

Looming – A perceptual phenomenon occurring when an object appears to be directly approaching the observer because of a symmetrical increase in size.

Loudness – The psychological attribute corresponding to amplitude of a sound wave.

Love-withdrawal – Discipline based on threatened loss of love (showing anger or hurt, isolating, or threatening to leave the child.) Excessive use may lead to anxiety, dependency, and inhibitedness.

LTM – (See Long-term memory.)

Lucid dream – Special type of dream during which the dreamer is aware that he or she is dreaming and possesses his or her normal ability to think and reason.

Luminosity – The effective brightness of light, with intensity constant, a result of the varying sensitivity of the visual system to different wavelengths of light.

Mach bands – Visual contours that appear where there is no corresponding physical discontinuity in light intensity.

Machiavellianism – A personality characteristic, measured by the Mach scale, in which one tends to manipulate other people for one's own ends.

Macula – Generally, an anatomical structure shaped like a spot; the central region of the retina; a receptor organ in the inner ear that responds to gravitational pull.

Magazine training – The establishment of conditioned reinforcers by periodically providing reinforcement no matter what the subject is doing.

Magnitude estimation – A psychophysical method in which the observer judges the intensity of the stimulus in some numerical ratio to a standard stimulus.

Main effect – When the effect of one independent variable is the same at all levels of another independent variable.

Major gene determination – A hereditary process whose outcome is determined by the presence or absence of a single dominant or recessive gene.

Malleus – The outermost of the three bones in the middle ear that transmits vibrations from the eardrum to the cochlea. Sometimes referred to as the hammer.

Mand – A verbal utterance under the control of the state of deprivation of the speaker. A basic form of verbal behavior in Skinner's system.

Mandala – 1. A model of the cosmos, based on concentric shapes; often includes images of deities. 2. In Jung's theory, a magical circle that represents self-unification efforts.

Mania – Psychotic affective reaction involving speeding up of thought processes and motor behavior and exaggerated feelings of optimism.

Manic depression – A mood disorder in which there are recurrent and severe fluctuations of affective state between elation and depression. Currently called "bipolar disorder."

Manifest Anxiety Scale – The most widely used paper-and-pencil test to measure anxiety.

Manifest content (of dreams) – In psychoanalysis, dream materials that are recalled by the dreamer; concrete objects and events of the dream.

Manipulative drive – A tendency to explore and utilize new objects in the environment independent of their immediate utility.

Mantra – A word or phrase to be recited, contemplated, or sung, especially as a part of meditation.

Marasmus (also called anaclitic depression) – The label given to the condition brought about by maternal deprivation. Results of marasmus include retarded development, depression, and occasionally death. The progressive atrophy of tissue because of nutritional disease is also common.

Marathon – In psychotherapy, a group session of exceptionally long, uninterrupted duration, usually eight or more hours.

Marbe's law – The generalization that the latency of a response in word association increases as the popularity or commonness of the response decreases.

Marijuana – A psychoactive substance prepared from the flowers or leaves of the Indian hemp plant Cannabis sativa, the active ingredient being THC.

Masochism – The turning of any sort of destructive tendencies inward upon oneself.

Massed practice – Bunching learning trials close together without rest periods. Adversely affects performance and sometimes retention.

Mastery test – A test that is being used to determine whether pupils have mastery of some unit that has been taught. In a mastery test, one is not really concerned about differences between individuals.

Matched groups design – An experimental design in which subjects are matched on some variable assumed to be correlated with the dependent variable and then randomly assigned to conditions.

Matched sampling – A technique for selecting subjects in which an experimenter makes sure that each group in the experiment contains the same number of subjects who possess a certain characteristic that might influence the outcome.

Maternal behavior – Behavior concerned with giving birth to young and providing postnatal care.

Maturation – A developmental process defined by changes that are relatively independent of a child's environment. While the nature and timing of maturational changes are assumed to result from genetic predispositions, their manifestation is at least partly a function of the environment.

Mature birth – The birth of an infant between the thirty-seventh and forty-second week of pregnancy.

Maze-bright – An adjective describing those rats able to learn to run through mazes very easily.

Maze-dull – An adjective describing the rat who has a great deal of difficulty in learning how to run a maze.

Mean – A measurement of central tendency that is computed by dividing the sum of a set of scores by the number of scores in the set, otherwise known as the arithmetic mean or average.

Meaningfulness – In verbal learning, the number of associations evoked by material that is being learned.

Means-end analysis – Problem solving process in which one tests for difference between the present situation and a solution situation and continues to perform operations until no difference is detected. Applicable whenever there is a clearly specifiable problem situation and a clearly specifiable solution.

Measurement – The assignment of numbers to events on the basis of rules.

Mechanical problem – Lowest level of problems studied by psychologists. All mechanical problems have specific, known solutions which can be found relatively automatically by following a simple series of steps. They may emphasize perceptual or verbal factors.

Mechanistic – A theoretical point of view which holds that all things in the universe, including living organisms, may be best understood as machines.

Median – A measure of central tendency; the middle score of a distribution, or the one that divides a distribution in half.

Mediated association – Association between two items via another item. Thus, if A is associated with B and B is associated to C, A is mediately associated with C.

Mediation – A term used to describe the processes assumed to intervene between the presentation of a stimulus and the appearance of a response. Mediation is often assumed to be largely verbal.

Mediational response – According to mediational theory, an internalized version of an external response which is formed during the learning process and manipulated in the thinking process. May be located in the nervous system, muscles, and glands, or may be thought of as purely a theoretical construct.

Mediational theory of thinking – Holds that as a consequence of external stimulus-response associations, the individual may form internal miniaturized versions of these stimuli (mediational stimuli) and responses (mediational responses) which serve as the connecting link between the environment and the way one responds to it.

Medical model – A model of psychopathology in which pathological behaviors are viewed as symptoms of a disease.

Medical therapies – Therapies that involve the use of physical procedures to try to treat abnormal personality problems.

Meditation – Concentration technique used to purify the ordinary state of consciousness by removing illusions and to facilitate the production of states of consciousness in which truth is more directly perceived.

Meditational process – A hypothetical process that bridges the gap between stimuli and responses.

Medulla (medulla oblongata) – The lowest and most posterior part of the brain which is connected to the spinal cord. It contains several kinds of nuclei, especially those concerned with breathing, heartbeat, and blood pressure.

Meiosis – The division of a single sex cell into two separate cells, each consisting of 23 chromosomes rather than 23 pairs of chromosomes. Meiosis, therefore, results in cells that are completely different.

Melancholia – A mental state of extreme depression often accompanied by bodily complaints, hallucinations, and delusions.

Memory – The term designating the mental function of recalling what has been learned or experienced; the physical retention of information.

Memory drum – An electromechanical device used to present materials for verbal learning experiments.

Memory trace – A hypothetical physiological change in the nervous system during learning. Also called engram. Gestaltists hold that the trace undergoes systematic change and reorganization.

Memory trace change theory – The theory that forgetting is due to qualitative changes in the memory trace over time.

Menarche – The girl's first menstrual period. An event which transpires during pubescence.

Menses – A monthly discharge of blood and tissue from the womb of a mature female. The term refers to menstruation.

Mental age (MA) – A term applied to both items and scores on intelligence tests. For an item, the age level is that age at which 50-70 percent of children pass the item. For an individual, it is the age group of children who would pass the same items he or she has passed.

Mental chronometry – The attempt to measure mental functions by subtracting simpler tasks from more complex ones.

Mental health – A state of personality that shows self-actualization, ability to withstand stress, and high productivity; the absence of symptoms of mental illness. (Freud: The ability to love and work.)

Mental illness – A state of personality in which behavior is statistically infrequent, violates societal norms, or impairs functioning.

Mental retardation – A designation for exceptional subjects whose IQ scores are below the -2 standard deviations from the mean of a normal probability distribution of intelligence test scores, generally a score below 68.

Mental set – The tendency to respond in a given way regardless of the requirements of the situation. Sets sometimes facilitate performance and sometimes impair it. (Impairment is referred to as "functional fixedness.")

Mentalistic – Subscribing to the principle that mental processes are distinct from physiological processes and that conscious processes can be exposed by introspection; explanations of psychological processes in terms of the operation of the mind.

Mentally gifted – Persons with IQ scores substantially above average.

Mescaline – A hallucinogenic drug obtained from the peyote cactus.

Mesomorph – A body type in Sheldon's system characterized by muscular build. A mesomorph has the personality characteristics of somatotonia: assertiveness, love of adventure and risk, physical courage, etc.

Metabolism – A general term referring to chemical and physical processes in the body cells including the assimilation of food, the storage and utilization of energy, the repairing of tissues, and the disposal of cellular wastes.

Methadone – A drug used in treatment of heroin addiction, which prevents withdrawal symptoms and blocks the heroin "high" but still is addictive.

Method of adjustment – A psychophysical method in which the observer sets the stimulus to some predetermined limit, e.g., just detectable.

Method of constant stimuli – A psychophysical method in which the stimuli are presented relative to a standard, the observer judging between them.

Method of limits – A psychophysical method in which stimuli are presented in ascending and descending series, the observer reporting when he or she can detect stimulation.

Method of locations – A method of facilitating memory by associating new items to be recalled with specific familiar locations or places. Also called the method of loci.

Method of successive approximations – Shaping by reinforcing behavior that successively approximates a desired behavior.

Midbrain – One of the parts of the cerebrum lying beneath the forebrain situated between the forebrain and the hindbrain. Also known as the mesencephalon, it is the primary location of the reticular formation.

Middle childhood – An arbitrary division in the sequence of development beginning somewhere near the age of 6 and ending at approximately 12.

Milieu therapy – A type of therapy that tries to incorporate the social standards of a culture or community into the hospital or treatment setting.

Minimal social situation – A laboratory game which simulates social exchange.

Minimum age of viability – The youngest age at which the fetus can survive outside the womb. Currently this age is about 6 months.

Minimum principle – In perceptual organization, the organization that is perceived in an ambiguous stimulus is the one which keeps changes, discontinuities, and differences to a minimum; simplicity of organization is a determinant of what will be seen.

Minnesota Multiphasic Personality Inventory (MMPI) – A widely used empirically derived paper-and-pencil personality test designed to provide a measure of a subject's similarity to various psychopathological groups.

Minority group – Describes a cultural, social, ethnic, or religious group existing within a larger cultural group.

Mitosis – The process of cell division by which the body produces new cells in order to maintain growth and good health, each cell being nearly identical to the original.

Mixed-motive game – A laboratory game in which the distinction can be made between players who cooperate to achieve profits and players who compete to achieve profits.

Mixed-motive group – A group in which members share some common goals but also have some opposing goals.

Mnemonics – Memory aids or systems for learning materials.

Modality effect – Different effects on retention often produced by visual and auditory presentation; auditory presentation usually produces better memory for the last few items in a series than does visual presentation.

Mode – The score value that occurs most frequently in a given set of scores.

Model – A physical, mathematical, or heuristic representation of a process, an object, or an event.

Model status – The standing or position accorded the model by the observer.

Modeling – In social learning theory, a form of learning in which the subject imitates the actions or reactions of another person. In behavior modification therapy, a technique based on imitation and perceptual learning.

Monitoring task – A form of dichotic listening where observers are not required to verbalize a message as it is presented.

Monochromator – An instrument for producing light of a very narrow wavelength band.

Monocular cues for depth – Cues for depth perception derived from information in the optic array that is available to either eye alone; interposition, size perspective, linear perspective, shading, aerial perspective, texture gradients.

Monotonic relationship – Relationship between two variables in which an increase on one variable is accompanied by a consistent increase or decrease on the other variable.

Monozygotic – Developing from the same fertilized egg; identical twins resulting from the division of a single fertilized egg.

Moods – Transient states, sometimes called affects; they refer to the perception by an individual of internal feelings associated with emotions.

Moral anxiety – Feelings of guilt.

Moral realism – The immature orientation in all the areas of moral judgment studied by Piaget. An attitude that the morality of an act is inherent in that act and can be perceived immediately by an observer as an objective fact.

Moral relativism – The mature orientation in all the areas of moral judgment studied by Piaget. Morality and rules are seen as something that is flexible and subject to consensus, rather than fixed.

Moro reflex – An automatic response shown by most normal infants to a startling stimulus, it involves throwing the arms to the side, extending the fingers, and then curving the hands back to the midline.

Morpheme – The smallest part of a word that conveys meaning and cannot be further subdivided without destroying the meaning; the units into which phonemes are arranged to make a language.

Mosaic hypothesis – The postulation of a simple one-to-one correspondence between perceptual experience and physical stimulation; the basic weakness, according to Gestalt theorists, in the system of Structuralism.

Motion parallax (relative motion) – The apparent movement of stationary objects occurring when the observer changes position.

Motivated forgetting theory – The theory that holds that forgetting is due to a person's motivation, e.g., a desire to avoid certain memories, which are therefore repressed. Freud argued for this theory of forgetting.

Motive – A condition or tension that initiates, guides, and maintains behavior.

Motor – Refers to information being carried out from the central nervous system. Efferent is a synonym.

Motor area – An area of cerebral cortex around the central fissure controlling voluntary movements of the skeletal muscles.

Motor learning – Learning in which the primary elements are the control of bodily movements through various cue systems, e.g., visual, auditory, and kinesthetic cues.

Motor nerves – The bundles of neurons that conduct impulses from the central nervous system to muscles and glands.

Motor sequence – The series of events involving the development of posture, crawling, and walking in infants. These events tend to occur in a set order and at approximately the same age in most infants of a particular culture.

Motor theory – An early stimulus-response theory of thinking espoused by behaviorists proposing that thinking always involves muscular or glandular activity of some kind. According to this theory, most human thought is basically subvocal speech activity.

Motor units – Groups of motor neurons, many of which comprise a muscle or glandular terminal.

Movement parallax – The difference in the rate of motion over the retinal surface of images projected by objects at different distances from a moving observer; motion parallax.

Multiple approach-avoidance conflict – A situation in which a subject must choose between two (or more) stimulus situations, each of which has both positive and negative values (double bind).

Multiple personality – An extremely rare form of dissociation in which a person displays two or more relatively distinct personalities, each with its own set of memories. The second personality often exhibits traits repressed in the first.

Multiple schedules – Partial reinforcement schedules that require the subject to satisfy two or more independent schedules that are presented successively, each cued.

Multiple therapy – Any form of psychotherapy in which two or more therapists simultaneously participate.

Muscle spindle – Receptors in muscles that signal muscular stretching.

Mutation – A change in, or deformation of, a gene, causing a modification in the character that the gene determines.

Mutual satisfaction – A leadership style in which policies are made by the group, with the leader simply acting as a focal point for carrying out their wishes.

Myelin – A white fatty substance which covers many axons, usually surrounding the axon in a bead-like arrangement.

Myelin sheath – The fatty, or lipid, substance that surrounds the axons of some neurons. The greater the degree of myelinization, the greater the speed of transmission of neural impulses. The sheath is whitish in color.

Myoneural junction – The meeting point between neural axons and muscle fibers. Also called the neuromuscular junction.

Myopia - Nearsightedness; deficient acuity for distant objects.

Mysticism – A belief in a spiritual meaning or reality that is neither apparent to the senses nor rationally obvious.

N – Symbol used to represent the number of cases in the group being studied.

Naive realism – The philosophy that perceptual experience is a mirror of the objective world.

Name calling – The propaganda technique giving an object a name with either pleasant or unpleasant connotations.

Narcissistic – Self-centered, egotistical gratification-oriented; characteristic of the infant and of persons whose personalities retain infantile features.

Narcotherapy – The treatment of mental illness, particularly personality disorders, by giving sleep inducing drugs, e.g., sodium amytal. The patient is encouraged to discuss his difficulties, and interpretations are given afterwards.

Narcotic drugs – Drugs that can be used as painkillers, opiates, such as heroin or morphine.

Nativism – Encompasses the notion that there are innate ideas, such as space and time perception, as well as the notion that the capacity for intelligence is inherited.

Nativist – One who emphasizes the role of heredity in the behavior of mature individuals rather than to the specific experiences in the course of development.

Natural childbirth – Refers to the birth of a child in which a mother employs no anesthetics (or very little) to relieve pain. Physical exercises, exercises in relaxation, and mental preparation are advocated for the mother prior to the birth of the child.

Natural selection – The theory Darwin posed to explain evolution by which traits that aid the organism to survive and propagate their own kind recur in future generations, while those that are unsuitable do not; "survival of the fittest."

Naturalistic observation – A method for research in which subjects are observed in their natural setting, rather than in the laboratory. The researcher attempts to be as unobtrusive as possible.

Nature – That side of the nature-nurture issue which represents the influence of heredity.

Nature-nurture controversy – The question of determining the relative contribution of heredity and environment to the development of the individual.

Need – Any deficiency which an organism feels is necessary for its welfare. It may be learned or innate; an animal drive or physiological motive.

Need achievement (McClelland) – An indicator of motivation; concern with improvement of performance; aggressive and ambitious people possess a higher need for achievement than more passive and less ambitious people.

Need for affiliation – Concern for establishing, maintaining, and cultivating relationships with people, often assessed by means of the content analysis of TAT stories.

Need for power – Concern with having or attaining status, reputation, and influence, often assessed by means of analyzing the content of TAT productions.

Need-reduction theory – The theory that reinforcement is based on reduction of primary physiological drives through consummatory behavior.

Negative acceleration – A decrease in the rate of growth or change in a function with time or practice; a curve of diminishing returns, characteristic of learning and forgetting.

Negative afterimage – After staring at a colored stimulus for a period of time, a person sees the same stimulus in complementary colors against a neutral background.

Negative instances – All stimuli in a population which do not have those characteristics that illustrate a given concept. For example, if mammal is the concept, then reptiles are negative instances.

Negative reinforcement – In operant conditioning, where reinforcement is paired with or contingent upon the termination of an aversive stimulus. Thus the absence of the stimulus condition strengthens or maintains a response.

Negative skew – When most of the scores of a distribution are found at the upper end of the measurement scale and the tail of the distribution is predominantly on the left; skewed to the left.

Negative transfer – The inhibitory effect of prior learning upon new learning.

Negative transfer of training – When the learning of one task increases the difficulty of learning a second task.

Neobehavioristic theories – A division in learning theory that includes those theoretical positions that, although they are still concerned with stimuli and responses as the fundamental data of psychology, they do take into account the events that intervene between stimuli and responses.

Neocortex – The outer, highly developed, convoluted covering of the brain. It is the most recently evolved neural tissue.

Neo-Freudian – Refers to a large number of psychologists who agree with some of Freud's ideas but have amended his theory to develop their own, more modern theories. Also called "neoanalytic," the category includes Horney, Erikson, and Fromm.

Neo-Freudian analysis – The psychoanalytic theories and practices of therapists who claim to have revised, rather than to have rejected, the teachings of Freud. These practices emphasize social factors, insecurity, and interpersonal relationships in the causation of neuroses.

Neonate – The newborn infant.

Nerve – A bundle of axons from many neurons. Outside of the central nervous system, it runs from one point in the body to another and carries nerve impulses; used synonymously with neuron.

Nerve impulse – A change in polarity in the membrane of a nerve fiber that is propagated along the length of the fiber when its initial segment is stimulated above threshold; an action potential.

Nervous breakdown – Popular term typically used to describe a person whose emotional problems are so severe that he or she can no longer cope with home or work responsibilities and requires hospitalization; not a description of a physical nervous condition.

Nervous system – The brain and spinal cord, plus all of the neurons traveling throughout the rest of the body. It is a communication system, carrying information throughout the body.

Neurasthenia – A neurotic reaction in which the person is constantly tired and feels vaguely unwell. It is no longer included in the standard psychiatric nomenclature.

Neurilemma – A thin covering of Schwann cells over the myelin sheath in neurons of the peripheral nervous system necessary for the regeneration of injured fibers.

Neurohumor – A chemical substance emitted at the tips (terminal button) of neural fibers that participates in transmission of impulses across the synaptic junction; transmitter substance; neurotransmitter.

Neuron – The basic structural unit of the nervous system, composed of a cell body, an axon, and one or more dendrites; its function is to send and receive messages.

Neurosis – Any of several less severe personality disturbances instigated and maintained for the purpose of contending with stress and avoiding anxiety; characterized by anxiety and rigid and unsuccessful attempts to reduce it.

Neurotic – Person who is experiencing a neurosis. (See Neurosis.)

Neurotic anxiety – In Freud's theory the fear that the impulses of the id will get out of control; in learning theory, conditioned fear.

Neurotic depression – A mild depressive reaction, usually in response to some environmental stress. The patient is quite dejected and inactive physically and mentally.

Neurotic need (Horney) – A strategy employed by an anxious person to find a solution to the problems of disturbed human relationships and to cope with his or her feelings of isolation and helplessness; it takes the form of a compulsive demand for certain behavior on the part of others.

Neurotic paradox – Refers to the fact that the neurotic person persists in his or her maladaptive behavior despite its self-defeating nature and the resulting unpleasant consequences.

Neurotic reactions – Behavior patterns produced by high levels of conflict and frustration that are repetitious and maladaptive.

Neutral transfer – Lack of transfer of any training effects from prior learning to present learning.

Noise – In detection theory, the term used to describe any extraneous stimuli; the background of stimulation in which the signal is embedded.

Nominal realism – The belief held by young children that names are identical with the properties or objects that they name; by naming an object it is made real.

Nominal scaling – The assignment of numbers to groups as names, used to distinguish between logically separated groups, e.g., Team Numbers 1, 2, 8, 20.

Nomothetic – Approach to personality study that involves looking for traits common to all persons.

Nonconformity – When a person responds in a manner contrary to a group's opinions or expectations.

Noncontingent reinforcement – Reinforcement that is not dependent on a response made by the organism.

Noncontinuity theory – The theory that learning occurs on one trial or not at all.

Nondirective therapy – A form of therapy originated by Carl Rogers in which the therapist serves mainly to reflect the feelings expressed by the patient, accepting them without evaluation; client-centered therapy.

Nonintellective behaviors – Behaviors that are not specifically cognitive or intellectual in nature, but rather involve such things as social, emotional, and physically oriented actions.

Nonreactive – Term to describe observations that are not influenced by the presence of the investigator; unobtrusive methods.

Nonreversal shift – A type of discrimination learning in which the subject, who has been reinforced for selecting one value of a dimension, is now reinforced for selecting stimuli on the basis of another dimension. For example, the subject who has been taught to select black animal figures and reinforced for doing so is now reinforced for selecting animal figures regardless of their color.

Nonsense syllable – A syllable, usually with three letters, constructed to be as devoid of meaning as possible, used often in verbal learning experiments. There are two varieties: consonant-vowel-consonant syllables and consonant trigram syllables.

Nonverbal communication – Communication by means other than words. Often termed body language.

Norepinephrine – An excitatory neurotransmitter substance found in the brain and in the sympathetic division of the autonomic nervous system.

Norm – A representative standard for performance or behavior; an established rule for identifying desirable behavior.

Norm group – The group with which an individual is being compared.

Normal curve – A mathematically defined curve that is bell-shaped and in which the mean, median, and mode are all in the same interval; it is the graphic representation of the normal probability distribution.

Normal distribution – The distribution is bell-shaped, that is, symmetrical with a piling up of cases in the middle, steep shoulders, and flat tails. It is thought to approximate the distribution of many biological and psychological characteristics. Its mathematical formula is derived from the laws of probability.

Normative developmental research – Research strategy that compares the behavior of children at different ages in a particular situation. It tends to be used by psychologists who stress the role of maturation in development and aims to chart behavioral norms for different ages.

Normative test – A test in which the individual's performance is expressed in relation to that of some norm or reference group, as contrasted with an ipsative test.

Nuclear family – A family consisting of a mother, a father, and their offspring.

Nucleus – Structure containing genetic material found in the center of most cells. Also, a cluster of cell bodies of neurons in the central nervous system.

Null hypothesis – States that the independent variable will have no effect on the dependent variable.

Null result – An experimental outcome where the dependent variable was not influenced by the independent variable.

Nursery school – A preschool institution that accepts children at an early age and that emphasizes child care and emotional and social development.

Nurture – The side of the nature-nurture issue that reflects the influence of the environment, socialization, education, and training on the development of an organism.

Nystagmic eye movements – Rapid involuntary movements of the eye followed by a slow return to normal fixation, as in the following of a moving target.

Obesity – Corpulence; fatness. The condition of being 20% or more overweight.

Object – A relatively stable aspect of the environment with relatively consistent meanings. It can also mean a goal.

Object concept – Piaget's expression for the child's understanding that the world is composed of objects that continue to exist quite apart from his or her perception of them.

Object conservation – A child's ability to ignore irrelevant transformations (e.g., the child knows that when water is poured from a wide, short glass into a tall, thin glass the volume is the same, is conserved).

Object permanence – A term in Piaget's theory of development which refers to a child's belief that an object continues to exist even though it is no longer visible.

Objective – Having an existence independent of the observer, existing in fact or physical reality; unbiased.

Objective psychotherapy – The term applied to the system of psychotherapy developed by Benjamin Karpman in which the patient receives a memorandum based on his or her answers to autobiographical questions.

Objective test – A test made up of structured response items that provide both a specific problem and a limited set of choices from which the student must select his or her answer.

Objectivity – When judgments made are free from bias or the influence of personal feeling.

Observational methods – Research techniques based on simply observing behavior without trying to manipulate it experimentally; field or natural setting research.

Obsession – An idea, often irrational or unwanted, usually associated with anxiety, that persists or frequently recurs and cannot be dismissed by the individual.

Obsessive-compulsive reactions – Neurotic reactions in which undesirable thought and activity patterns are repeated in a ritualistic way.

Obstetrics – The medical art and science of assisting women who are pregnant, both during their pregnancy and at birth; midwifery.

Occipital area (or lobe) of the brain – The part of the cerebral cortex lying at the back of the head involved in vision.

Oddity problem – A problem in which the solution lies in choosing the stimulus item which is unlike the others. If two circles and one square are presented, the square is the correct choice.

Oedipal conflict (complex) – Proposed by Freud, this

is the attraction a boy has for his mother and its accompanying anxiety and guilt. In the female Electra conflict, it is her attraction for her father and the resulting anxiety and guilt.

Ogive – A curve that is loosely described as S-shaped.

One-tailed test – Test that places the rejection area at one end of a distribution. Events falling in the other end of the distribution are ignored as being spurious.

Ontogenetic (genetic) – Pertaining to development within the members of a species.

Opening-up meditation – An attempt to produce continuous attention to all aspects of the stimulus environment.

Operant – The label employed by Skinner to describe a response not elicited by any known or obvious stimulus. Most significant human behaviors appear to be operant. Such behaviors as writing a letter or going for a walk are operants, if no known specific stimulus elicits them. ("Operating" on the environment so as to produce a result.)

Operant conditioning – A type of learning involving an increase in the probability of a response occurring as a result of reinforcement. Much of the experimental work of B. F. Skinner investigates the principles of operant conditioning. Also referred to as Instrumental conditioning. (See Classical conditioning.)

Operant conditioning chamber – An apparatus used for experimental testing of instrumental conditioning; several varieties exist, the best known being the "Skinner box."

Operant level – The rate at which a response is emitted prior to the introduction of a reinforcement schedule.

Operation – According to Jean Piaget, a process that changes its object.

Operational definition – A definition of a concept in terms of the operations that must be performed to demonstrate the concept; a definition by concrete example.

Opinion – The verbal expressions of a belief, often still open to modification.

Opponent process theory – A theory of color vision holding that there are three kinds of visual receptors, one for brightness and two for color (red-green and blue-yellow), and that any color experience results from a combination of excitation and/or inhibition of these color receptors.

Optic array – A pattern of observable light energy, reflected from the surface of an object, that enters the eye.

Optic chiasm – A structure on the base of the brain that transmits the impulses from the receptors in the eye to the brain. In man, half of the optic fibers cross to the opposite hemisphere at the optic chiasm thus providing information from both eyes to each hemisphere.

Optic disc – The area of the retina where all the nerve impulses leave the eye to form the optic nerve and where there are no rods or cones, creating a "blind spot" on the retina.

Optical resolving power – The ability of the lens in the eye to focus the optic array sharply on the retina and not in front of or behind it.

Oral stage – In the genetic model of psychoanalytic theory, the first stage of psychosexual development, in which libidinal interest and conflicts center on the mouth—on sucking, eating, biting, and so on.

Order effect – An effect on behavior attributable to the specific sequence of experimental conditions to which subjects are exposed.

Ordinal scale – Numbers arranged to correspond to the increase or decrease in the variable being measured; a set of ranks. The relative distances between the elements need not be, and usually are not, equal.

Ordinate – The y-axis, or vertical axis, of a graph. By convention the dependent variable is plotted on the ordinate.

Organ of Corti – The lining on the basilar membrane of the inner ear that contains the hair cells which are the receptors for hearing.

Organic disorder – An emotional problem resulting from biological causes, usually from impairment of brain functioning.

Organic psychoses – Psychotic reactions having a demonstrable bodily origin, e.g., brain injury or neurological disease.

Organism – A form of life exhibiting integration and coordination of function that has the capacity for self-maintenance. In psychology, the term is often used to refer to the higher animals including human beings.

Organization – The process of cognitive growth that, according to Piaget, integrates one psychological structure with another.

Orientation reaction (response) – The initial response of humans and other animals to novel stimulation. Also called the orienting reflex or orienting response. Components of the orientation reaction include changes in EEG patterns, in respiration rate, in heart rate, and in galvanic skin response.

Orthogenetic – Refers to Heinz Werner's theory of the sequence of development that takes place in the same direction and through the same stages in every organism despite differing external conditions. Also, pertaining to that which encourages desirable development.

Orthogenetic principle – The generalization that the psychological development of individuals is characterized by increasing differentiation among the subparts of their personalities and by increasingly complex organizational structures among those parts.

Orthographic attribute – In Underwood's theory of memory, the attribute of a memory relating to the physical shape of the remembered item.

Oscilloscope – An electronic device for displaying waveforms on a cathode ray tube screen. It is widely used in studying nervous impulses.

Osgood's transfer surface – A three-dimensional representation, first formulated by Charles Osgood, representing positive and negative transfer as a function of stimulus and response similarity.

Osmotic pressure – A difference in the concentration of fluids on either side of a semipermeable membrane.

Ossicles – Three tiny bones in the middle ear that transmit the sound vibrations from the eardrum to the cochlea.

Ossification – The process of bone formation, starting from a few locations and spreading outward from those locations.

Otolith organs – Sense organs in the inner ear that are sensitive to changes in the tilt of the head, involved in maintaining equilibrium.

Out-of-body experience (OOBE) – An experience during which a person feels that he or she is located at a point other than where the physical body is and still feels a normal state of consciousness.

Ovaries – The reproductive organs in females; they are also endocrine glands that secrete hormones (including estrogens) regulating sexual cycles and behavior and supporting pregnancy.

Overlearning – The amount of practice occurring after a performance criterion has been reached, resulting in no mistakes in a given number of trials.

Overloading – The presentation of material to one sense modality at such a high rate that the person cannot absorb it; stimulus overload.

Overt – Outward or external. Capable of being observed. Not concealed physically or psychologically.

Overtones (Partials, Harmonics) – Components of a complex periodic sound wave that are multiples of the fundamental, or lowest, frequency. The pattern of overtones determines the timbre of a musical instrument.

Ovum (*pl.* ova) – The sex cell produced by a mature female approximately once every 28 days. When mature, it consists of 23 chromosomes as opposed to all other human body cells (somatoplasm), which consist of 23 pairs of chromosomes. It is often referred to as an egg cell.

Pacinian corpuscle – A tactile receptor found below the skin, in the joints, and in other deep tissues. It consists of a nerve fiber inside of a capsule; the capsule moves under pressure, activating the fiber.

Pain – The drive aroused by noxious stimulation, especially at high intensity levels. The actual mechanism for pain detection remains a mystery.

Paired-associate learning – Learning a list of paired items such that one member of the pair can be recalled given the other member as a stimulus.

Paleocortex – Parts of the cerebral cortex considered to be old, with respect to evolution.

Palmar reflex – The grasping reflex that a newborn infant exhibits when an object is placed in his or her hand.

Pancreas – Produces the hormone insulin and thus regulates the use of sugar in the body. Below-normal production of insulin by this gland leads to diabetes mellitus, or too much sugar in the blood.

Paper-and-pencil tests – Psychological tests that use written or check-type answers only.

Papilla – A small, nipple-shaped protuberance. Papillae are located on the skin, the tongue, and the nasal mucosa, and contain receptors for touch, taste, and smell.

Paradigm – A pattern or model. In psychology, the term is often used to apply to an accepted procedure for investigating some phenomenon, such as the paradigm for studying transfer of training.

Paradigm clash – Conflict between two radically different views of the nature of the physical or psychological world.

Parallel attention – Sensory processing when several stimuli are attended to simultaneously.

Parallel forms – Two alternative forms of a test that yield equivalent results.

Parameters – Measurements describing a population. Parameters are usually inferred from statistics, which are measurements describing a sample.

Paranoia – A psychotic reaction in which there are delusions of persecution or grandeur with no withdrawal or impairment of other intellectual functioning.

Paranoid schizophrenia – Subtype of schizophrenia in which paranoid tendencies predominate, characterized by delusions of persecution, suspicion of others, and delusions of grandeur.

Parapraxis – A minor error in behavior, such as a slip of the tongue or pen, memory blockings, small accidents, misplacing articles, etc.

Paraprofessional – The designation of a person with relatively little training who works to help individuals confront personal problems.

Parapsychology – Study of topics that are related to psychology (such as ESP, clairvoyance, telepathy, and psychokinesis) but are not fully accepted as belonging under the heading of psychology.

Parasympathetic nervous system – A division of the autonomic nervous system which functions to maintain and conserve bodily resources.

Parataxic distortion (Sullivan) – Any attitude toward another person based on fantasy or identification of that person with other figures. The Freudians call this transference.

Parathyroid – A gland of the endocrine system that controls nervous tissue excitability by regulation of calcium and phosphorus levels in the body.

Paresis – A mental disorder caused by syphilitic infection of the brain.

Parietal lobe – The area of the cortex from the rear of the central fissure to the central back of the brain.

Part learning – Learning by dividing the materials into subsections or units, learning each unit separately, then combining at the end. Distinguished from whole learning.

Partial reinforcement – A reinforcement schedule in which less than 100 percent of all correct responses are rewarded.

Partial reinforcement effect – The finding that responses conditioned under partial reinforcement are more resistant to extinction than are those conditioned under continuous reinforcement.

Passive avoidance learning – A learning task in which the subject must refrain from making a prepotent response in order to avoid an aversive stimulus.

Passiveness – A personality trait characterized by overdependency, lack of assertiveness, and lack of autonomy.

Pathology – The science of diseases and disorders; the abnormality of structure and function characteristic of a disease.

Pavlovian conditioning (classical conditioning) – Process in which an originally neutral stimulus repeatedly paired with a reinforcer comes to elicit a response.

Peak experience – According to Maslow, the most important experiences humans have. They may involve much tension and excitement or deep peace and relaxation. They generally are marked by total involvement in the present.

Peck(ing) order – A dominance hierarchy established in a group of fowl, such as chickens; sometimes refers to any dominance hierarchy.

Pedophilia – Characterized by an individual who is sexually aroused by children.

Peer group – Those who are members of one's social group, especially in cultures in which membership is determined by age or status, and by whom one is treated as an equal.

Peer-group influence – The attachment to and the effects of age mates; increasingly important as a child grows older.

Penetrance – A characteristic of a gene that refers to the extent to which the traits it is responsible for will be expressed in the face of environmental variations.

Penis envy – A Freudian concept referring to the repressed envy that a young girl is assumed to have for males, since they have a penis.

Perceived locus of causality – A judgment as to whether the source of another's behavior lies in one's own motivations (internal locus) or in the nature of the situation in which one is placed (external locus).

Percentile – The score value below which a specified percent of cases falls. Thus, the 50th percentile on an examination is the raw score below which 50 percent of examinees fall.

Percentile band – A range of percentile values within which the true percentile for an individual may be expected to lie. Usually the band extends one standard error of measurement above and below the percentile rank corresponding to the obtained score.

Percentile norms – A system of norms based on percentiles within a specific reference group.

Perception – The reception of information through sensory receptors and interpretation of that information so as to construct meaningfulness about one's world.

Perceptual constancies – The tendency for our experience of objects to remain relatively constant in spite of changing stimulus conditions.

Perceptual defense – Failure to recognize stimuli that are threatening because of their relation to unconscious conflicts.

Perceptual deprivation or isolation – A condition in which patterned stimulation is reduced; sensory deprivation.

Perceptual displacement – Perceiving an event as having occurred at some other time or place than its actual occurrence, usually as a consequence of the structure of its context.

Perceptual learning – The effects of past experience on current perception, usually as a result of sensorimotor changes.

Perceptual segregation – The tendency to organize one's perception into figure and ground, or focus and margin.

Perceptual selection – The tendency to focus upon only part of the potentially available stimuli.

Perceptual vigilance – Heightened sensitivity to stimuli that are threatening because of their relation to unconscious conflicts; related to perceptual defense.

Performance – The responses or behavior exhibited by an organism, which may or may not reveal what the organism has learned.

Performance test – A test, most often an intelligence test, in which ability is primarily evaluated in terms of motor skills.

Perilymph – The fluid filling the inner ear that responds to bone displacements from the ossicles.

Period – The time required for any oscillation to make a complete cycle.

Period of the embryo – The second of the three principal stages of gestation, during which the blastocyst is implanted in the uterine wall. From the second to the eighth week of gestation.

Period of the fetus – The third of the three principal stages of gestation, from the eighth week until birth, during which body systems advance and the fetus grows rapidly.

Peripheral nervous system (PNS) – Those nerves outside the central nervous system; it has two subdivisions, the somatic and autonomic systems. It contains all the neurons connecting to muscles, glands, and sensory receptors.

Peripheral skin temperature – The skin temperature of the hands and feet.

Peripheralist position – The theory that thinking is explained best by reference to speech or other muscular movements, as opposed to central (cortical) processes.

Persona (Jung) – The mask of conscious intentions and fulfillments of social requirements of the individual behind which one hides (from oneself as well as others); the more deeply rooted components of personality; the role which a person plays.

Personal construct – In Kelly's personality theory, a hypothetical learned process that determines how one construes a particular set of events.

Personal equation – The correction of an observation for the observer's time error.

Personal responsibility – Seeing an outcome as due to one's own efforts or skills (or lack of), rather than due to luck, chance, fate, or the actions of others.

Personal space – The physical distance surrounding a person; often considered by the person as his or her "own." The invasion of this space by another who is not on special terms can make the person feel uncomfortable.

Personal unconscious – In Jung's theory of personality, the part of personality that holds memories and repressed desires.

Personality – The unique organization of relatively enduring characteristics possessed by an individual as revealed by his or her interaction with this environment.

Personality assessment – Administering and evaluating a variety of tests (and perhaps interviews) in order to develop an understanding of an individual's personality.

Personality disorders – A classification of abnormal personality patterns characterized by the person's inability to act in accordance with societal standards, although not to the extent of neurosis or psychosis.

Personality impression – A characterization by one person of the invariant affects, intents, and abilities that are peculiar to another individual.

Personality inventories – Personality assessment procedures that use many statements or questions by which a person may evaluate oneself.

Personality test – Tests of personality undertaken to appraise the individual's typical or habitual way of acting and thinking, as distinct from his or her ability to perform.

Personality trait – A combination of perceptual, conceptual, motivational, and acting tendencies which gives rise to relatively stable, consistent behavioral dispositions in a class of situations.

Personification – A type of projection in which an individual attributes favorable or unfavorable qualities to another person as a result of his or her own unconscious conflicts.

Perspective – A monocular depth cue in which perception of distance is based upon previous knowledge of size-distance and shape-slant relationships.

Perspective theory – Explanation of how physically equal stimuli are perceived as unequal by proposing that one uses perspective clues to judge depth and then uses this depth information in perceiving size.

Perversion – Sexual conduct that deviates from normally accepted sexual behavior.

Phallic stage – In psychoanalytic theory, the third stage of psychosexual development, lasting from age $1\frac{1}{2}$ to 6, in which primary gratification is obtained through stimulating the genitalia.

Phallic symbol – A symbol representing some aspect of sexual experience and generally having an elongated, pointed, or upright shape.

Phantom limb – Term applied to sensory experiences seeming to arise in a limb, or part of a limb, that has been amputated.

Phase – A point in a waveform that recurs in a cyclic manner.

Phenomenal field – Everything experienced by an individual at any moment, including awareness of the self. Objects physically present but not perceived are not part of the phenomenal field, and objects not physically present but thought about are.

Phenomenalistic causality – Belief held by young children that events that occur together cause one another. For example, a little boy may scratch his head and win a game; thereafter he may believe that scratching his head will always help him to win games.

Phenomenological point of view – The hypothesis that an individual's behavior may be entirely understood and explained in terms of his or her phenomenal field (all that he or she experiences at a given moment).

Phenomenological report – A subject's description of his or her own behavior or state of mind; also called subjective report.

Phenomenology – The study of the experience of objects and events, in contrast with the study of the objects and events themselves. Sometimes contrasted with behavioristic approaches to psychology.

Phenomenon – An event, occurrence, or happening.

Phenotype – The observable properties or characteristics of organisms resulting from the influence of the genotype and the environment.

Pheromone – A chemical secreted by one member of an animal species that communicates usually through the sense of smell with another member of the species; often used as trail or territory markers or in sexual signaling.

Phi phenomenon – The apparent movement that occurs when two or more visual figures are successively illuminated as in stroboscopic motion.

Phlegmatic – A temperamental characteristic in Hippocrates' system. The phlegmatic person is apathetic and sluggish.

Phobia – An intense, compelling, and irrational fear of something; according to analytic theory, it involves displacement of anxiety onto a situation that is not dangerous or only mildly dangerous.

Phobic reaction – A neurotic reaction characterized by fear of situations, e.g., crowds or high places.

Phone – In the science of phonology, the actual sound made by a speaker on any particular occasion.

Phoneme – The smallest unit of sound that has meaning in the language, generally consisting of a single sound such as a vowel.

Phonology – The study of the system of speech sounds within and across languages.

Photographic memory – Uncommonly vivid imagery as though the subject were actually perceiving; common in childhood but usually disappears during adolescence; eidetic imagery.

Photon – A quantum of radiant energy. It is the stimulus that excites photoreceptive cells, rods being able to detect the presence of only one photon.

Photopic – Pertaining to visual functioning under conditions of relatively high-intensity illumination; cone vision.

Phrase – In grammar, a group of words that can function as a unit in grammatical structure.

Phrenology – An obsolete system developed by Franz-Joseph Gall for identifying types of people by examining their physical features, especially the configuration of "bumps" on their skulls.

Phylogenetic development – The evolutionary development of the species from its origins to its present state. Phylogeny is contrasted to ontogeny in the sense that it refers to the development of a species rather than to the development of an individual.

Physiological psychology – A branch of psychology which studies the physiological, or bodily, foundations of behavior.

Physiological responses – Any bodily changes, as in heart rate, occurring in response to stimuli.

Piaget's theory – A theory of cognitive development that describes changes in the cognitive abilities of children. The four stages described by Piaget are sensorimotor, preoperational thinking, concrete operations, and formal operations.

Pigment – A substance that absorbs certain wavelengths of light and reflects others. The light reflected accounts for the color of the pigment.

Visual pigments, contained in the rods and cones, absorb the light that ultimately results in visual experience.

Pilomotor response – The response of hair cells to stimulation in which they stand up, producing the effect called goose pimples; also termed piloerection.

Pineal gland – A gland located in the center of the brain whose functions are obscure.

Pitch – The psychological attribute of sounds that corresponds approximately to the fundamental frequency of the waveform.

Pituitary – An endocrine gland located at the base of the brain consisting of an anterior portion that controls other glands and growth and a posterior portion that is involved in metabolism. Because it regulates other glands it is sometimes referred to as the "master gland."

Pivot grammar – A form of grammar found among young children—usually consists of a single "pivot" word and a class of "open" words that can be joined with the pivot—e.g., "Bobby go."

Place theory – A theory of pitch discrimination that holds that specific places on the basilar membrane respond to different frequencies.

Placebo – A chemically inert material that has the same appearance as an active drug; allows psychologists to test the effects of the expectations of subjects who believe they are actually taking a drug; by analogy, the "placebo effect" is any situation in which subjects believe they are experiencing a manipulation by the experimenter when in fact they are not.

Placenta – The disk-shaped mass of tissue that serves as a two-way filter between the bloodstreams of the mother and the embryo.

Placental stage – The third and final stage of labor, during which the placenta and the attached membranes and cord (the afterbirth) are expelled from the uterus.

Plateau – In a learning curve, a period of little or no change in performance preceded and followed by periods of performance improvement.

Plato – Greek philosopher and early proponent of dualism who first divided the mind into rational and irrational elements.

Play therapy – A technique for the treatment of mental illness in children in which they are given an opportunity to express their otherwise forbidden feelings and desires in a permissive playroom situation.

Pleasure centers – Areas in the brain which, when electrically stimulated, produce very strong, pleasurable sensations. May be involved in determining what is rewarding for animals in everyday life.

Pleasure principle – A concept originated by Freud, it is the idea that humans strive to avoid pain and seek pleasure. It is on this principle that the id operates, seeking immediate gratification.

Polar adjectives – Adjectives having opposite meanings; used in the semantic differential procedure.

Polygenetic determination – The determination of a trait through the interaction of a number of genes, rather than through major gene determination.

Polygraph – An instrument used to record various physiological measures such as galvanic skin response, heart rate, etc. The lie detector is a common form of a polygraph.

Pons – A part of the hindbrain containing large bands of nerve fibers connecting the lobes of the cerebellum, pathways going to and from higher centers, and many vital nuclei.

Population – The entire group from which samples may be chosen.

Population genetics – The application of genetic principles to the study of the pattern and frequency of traits throughout an entire population or species.

Positive acceleration – A value that changes by larger and larger steps as a function of time or trials. In learning curves, a curve of increasing returns.

Positive instances – All stimuli in a population which have the characteristics that illustrate a given concept. For example, if flying animals is the concept, birds are positive images.

Positive regard – In Roger's theory of personality, the concept of acceptance by others; may be unconditional (unrestricted) or conditional (restricted).

Positive reinforcement – A type of event in which the presence of a stimulus condition strengthens or maintains a response.

Positive skew – When most of the scores of a distribution are found at the lower end of the measurement scale used.

Positive transfer – The facilitory effect of prior learning on present learning.

Possession state – State in which the subject feels as if his own personality or soul has been taken over or displaced by some nonphysical entity.

Posthypnotic effects – Behavior caused by suggestions given to the subject while he or she is hypnotized but which occur after the subject has been brought back to a normal state of consciousness.

Postmature birth – The birth of an infant after the forty-second week of pregnancy.

Postnatal – Following birth.

Postpubescent stage – The third stage of puberty, at which time the sex organs are capable of adult functioning.

Postsynaptic neuron – A neuron that receives the information (transmitter substance) from the axon of a presynaptic neuron.

Post-traumatic stress disorder – Inability to successfully cope with stress, brought on by a single traumatic incident or by prolonged, intense stress from which there is no escape, such as battle stress in war.

Postural reflexes – Those reflexes involved in keeping the body upright without conscious control.

Power – In modeling, potential influence. In social relations, the ability to influence others.

Power (of a statistical test) – The probability of rejecting the null hypothesis in a statistical test when it is in fact false.

Power assertion – Discipline based on the physical or material superiority of the parents.

Power law – The principle that sensation increases as some power of the physical stimulus. $S = aI^K$ where S is sensation, I is intensity of the physical stimulus and a and K are empirically derived constants.

Power test – A test given with ample time, designed to appraise how well the individual can perform, rather than how fast he or she can work.

P-O-X model (Heider) – Descriptive model used to diagram relationships according to balance theory; P (person) has an orientation toward O (another person); P also has an orientation toward X (usually an object); and P perceives O as having an orientation toward X. The nature of the orientations determines whether a balanced state exists.

Practice effect – The systematic change in scores on a test, ordinarily a gain, resulting from previous practice with the test.

Preadolescence – The period in the development of the individual that follows the juvenile period and ends with the beginning of genital sexuality.

Precipitating factors – Stimuli that actually initiate or trigger behavioral patterns.

Precognition – An alleged ability to predict events in the future without the benefit of sensory information.

Preconceptual thought – The first substage of the period of preoperational thought, beginning around age 2 and lasting until 4. It is so called because a child has not yet developed the ability to classify and therefore has an incomplete understanding of concepts.

Preconscious – In Freudian theory, the ideas, thoughts, and images a person is not aware of at a given moment but which can be brought into awareness with little or no difficulty. Any thought that happens to be conscious at a given moment is preconscious both before and after that particular moment.

Predicaments – Regularly occurring events during the life cycle, such as birth, entering school, or marriage, which may have a possibility of producing a crisis or disorder.

Prediction (actuarial) – Prediction of a trend or average tendency of a group of subjects, as opposed to prediction of the behavior of an individual.

Prediction (clinical) – Prediction of the behavior of an individual.

Predictive validity – The degree to which a test measures what it is supposed to measure.

Predispositions – The background characteristics of a person that serve to influence personality patterns, particularly hereditary characteristics which favor the development of a particular trait.

Prefrontal lobotomy – A form of psychosurgery in which the connections between the prefrontal areas of the cerebral cortex and the thalamus are cut. This once popular procedure results in permanent brain damage, an inability to inhibit impulses, and an unnatural tranquility and shallowness.

Pregenital stages – In psychoanalysis, the stages of the infantile period that precede the phallic phase during which the libido seeks satisfaction from the anal and oral regions.

Prehension – A term denoting the ability to grasp.

Preimplantation period – The first of the three stages of gestation, during which all cells are exact replicas of the zygote and are not attached to the wall of the uterus.

Prejudice – Negative attitude, which is emotionally, rigidly, or inflexibly felt and acted on, that is held toward members of another group.

Premack principle – In operant conditioning, the principle that given two behaviors which differ in their likelihood of occurrence, the less likely behavior can be reinforced by using the more likely behavior as a reward.

Premature birth – Refers to the delivery of a fetus before the normal gestation period has been completed; between the 29th and 36th week of pregnancy.

Prenatal development – The period of development beginning at conception and ending at birth during which the zygote differentiates and grows.

Preoperational period – The second of Piaget's stages of cognitive development (from two to seven years of age), characterized by the child's development of symbolic representation. During this time children are still confused in their use of language and explanations of causality.

Preparedness – An evolutionary concept regarding the organism's readiness to learn; used to try to explain why some learning occurs easily while other learning may be quite difficult.

Prepubescent stage – The first stage of puberty, during which the secondary sex characteristics begin to develop but the reproductive organs do not yet function.

Presbyopia – Deficient visual acuity in old age, attributable to loss of flexibility of the tissues of the lens, resulting in decreased ability to accommodate.

Presumptive symptoms – The initial, highly probabilistic signs of pregnancy frequently noted by prospective mothers. These include cessation of menses, morning sickness, changes in the breasts, and occasionally an increase in the frequency of urination.

Presynaptic neuron – The neuron whose axon releases transmitter substance into the synaptic cleft thereby transmitting information across the synapse to the postsynaptic neuron.

Prevention services – Community-based services that are designed to identify and reduce stress factors in the community.

Primacy effect – In verbal learning, the tendency to recall items at the beginning of the list better than items in the middle. There is little proactive interference at this point.

Primal therapy – A "pop" therapy technique emphasizing the release of "frozen" pain often through the primal scream.

Primary circular reaction – An expression employed by Piaget to describe a simple reflex activity such as thumb sucking.

Primary drives – The behaviorally activating concomitants of physiological need states; in some motivational models, the innate motives on which all others are based.

Primary emotions – Emotions directly involved in goal-oriented behavior, related to gratification or frustration of our motives; joy, anger, fear.

Primary gain – For neurotic behavior, the immediate reduction of anxiety.

Primary group – A reference group with which a person spends a great deal of time, which exerts a major influence on his or her behavior, beliefs, and standards.

Primary mental abilities – Major components of intelligence. Group factors posited by the Thurstones as a result of factor analyses.

Primary prevention – Programs and services designed to change the behavior of persons and organizations in order to reduce rates of occurrence of disorder and promote psychological well being.

Primary process – The characteristic functioning of the id, whereby there is immediate and direct satisfaction of an instinct. Primary process thinking is the dominant mode for the young child and persists in the unconscious in adult life and manifests itself chiefly through dreams, humor, and pathology.

Primary receptive area – An area of the cerebral cortex that receives afferent information from a sense organ by relatively direct routes.

Primary reinforcement – A stimulus that is reinforcing in the absence of any learning. Such stimuli as food and drink are primary reinforcers, since presumably an organism does not have to learn that they are pleasurable.

Primary stimulus generalization – The generalization of responses exhibited toward a primary stimulus to similar stimuli.

Principle of least interest – In a dyadic relationship, when the person with the least involvement establishes the conditions and the other accepts them in order to maintain the relationship.

Prismatic lenses – Lenses made in the shape of a prism that distort color and line in a perceptual field.

Proactive interference – In learning, the negative influence of previously learned material on the recall of new material. When the influence is on the learning of the new material, it is called negative transfer.

Probability – An estimate of the likelihood that a particular event will occur.

Probability matching – In a discrimination task where each stimulus alternative has a finite probability of being correct, the tendency of subjects to respond to each stimulus with a probability that approximates the probability that the stimulus is correct.

Process schizophrenia – A form of schizophrenia for which the symptoms are slow in onset, beginning at a relatively early age, and for which the prognosis is relatively poor.

Product-moment correlation (r) – A correlational measure used when the distributions are on either interval or ratio scales.

Proficiency test – A measure of current level of skill in some aspect of a job or of an educational program. The term is used with almost the same meaning as achievement test but with somewhat more implication of a job-oriented skill.

Profile – Graphic representation of a set of scores for an individual, organized so that the high and low scores can be identified. In order for scores to be meaningfully displayed in a profile, they must be converted to some common score scale, such as standard scores or age or grade equivalents.

Prognosis – The probability of recovery.

Prognostic test – A test designed to predict progress in achieving skill or knowledge in some area.

Program – A compilation of statements used in a teaching machine for automated instruction; the statements that control the operation of a computer.

Programmatic reasoning – Reasoning using already-existing systems of thought.

Programmed learning – A learning method based on operant conditioning, it involves taking the student through a set of learning materials in small steps and requires mastery of each step before proceeding to the next. Reinforcement is immediate and usually positive.

Projection – A Freudian defense mechanism whereby the individual protects his ego from the recognition of an undesirable id impulse by relocating the impulse in another person.

Projective technique – A method of investigation or observation in which the subject is encouraged to respond in his own way to relatively nebulous stimuli, and the investigator then interprets the subject's response. The assumption is that the subject will project his or her true feelings, thoughts, or beliefs.

Projective test – A relatively unstructured test designed so as to enhance the likelihood that the test-taker's motives and conflicts, and style of dealing with them, will be revealed in his or her responses.

Prolactin – A hormone secreted by the pituitary gland that stimulates the production of milk in female mammals and brooding in birds.

Propaganda – An organized attempt to change attitudes in a desired direction.

Proposition – In psychological jargon it refers to a statement that can be either true or false.

Proprioceptors – Receptors that sense position and movement of the limbs and the body in space. The principal proprioceptors are Pacinian corpuscles, muscle spindles, Golgi tendon organs, semicircular canals, utricles, and saccules.

Pro-social aggression – Aggressive behaviors which may be harmful to the target person but that are generally sanctioned in the society as contributing to social order.

Prosody – Modes of expression, intonations, accents, and pauses peculiar to a particular language.

Protanope – A dichromat with a red-green deficiency (colorblindness) due to a relative insensitivity to red light.

Protocol – The original notes or records of an experiment from which scientific data may be extracted.

Proximity – A Gestalt law of organization which asserts that elements which are close to one another will tend to be perceptually organized together.

Proximo-distal trend – The tendency for the central portions of the body to develop before and more quickly than the peripheral portions.

Pseudoconditioning – A temporary elevation in the amplitude of the conditioned response following a conditioning series that is not due to association between the conditioned stimulus and unconditioned stimulus. Apparently the conditioning series sensitizes the subject to respond.

Psilocybin – A hallucinogenic drug found in a certain type of mushroom.

Psyche – The mind or the organized totality of all mental processes or psychological activities.

Psychedelic – In reference to drugs, it denotes any drug whose primary effect is to induce an altered state of consciousness characterized by intensified sensory experience, distorted perceptions, hallucinations, and mood changes.

Psychiatrist – A physician (M.D.) with specialized training in the treatment of mental illness.

Psychiatry – A specialty of medicine that is concerned with the diagnosis and treatment and prevention of abnormal personality patterns.

Psychic determinism – The assumption that there is either a conscious or unconscious cause behind every mental process, including errors, dreams, and slips of the tongue.

Psychic energy – In Freud's system, the energy, like physiological energy, that is involved in psychological processes. It is organized into instincts, or motives.

Psychoactive drugs – Any of a number of drugs that can cause subjective or psychological effects for a person.

Psychoanalysis – A method of treatment of mental illness developed by Freud stressing motivational processes in behavior and the importance of early experience in the development of the adult personality. It attempts to uncover repressed material from the unconscious mind by free association and dream analysis.

Psychoanalyst – Any therapist who treats mental illness according to psychoanalytic theories.

Psychoanalytic theory – The complex personality theory developed by Freud and his followers which emphasizes unconscious ideas, motives, and conflicts and which stresses the biological-sexual basis of personality development.

Psychobiologic therapy – The term applied to the system of psychotherapy developed by Adolf Meyer which emphasizes environmental manipulative and supportive approaches.

Psychodrama – A method of therapy originated by Moreno, in which patients act out plays about their conflicts in which the roles are those of significant people in their lives.

Psychodynamic – A term referring to processes that motivate behavior, particularly unconscious processes.

Psychokinesis – Making physical events happen in a desired manner with no physical intervention, such as moving objects by using only thought processes.

Psycholinguistics – The study of the learning, use, and understanding of language.

Psychological abnormality – A failure to meet one or more of the criteria of adjustment.

Psychological hedonism – The belief that people act to obtain pleasure and avoid pain.

Psychological testing – The use of some measurement technique to try to assess a behavioral characteristic.

Psychology – The scientific study of behavior and the systematic application of behavior principles.

Psycholytic therapy – A type of psychotherapy that uses small doses of LSD or other psychedelics during regular therapeutic work.

Psychometric test – Any device designed to obtain a quantitative assessment of an individual's psychological attributes.

Psychopath – A very general term for an individual who is not deterred from committing immoral or antisocial acts by the anxiety that normally accompanies such behavior; attributable to inadequate socialization.

Psychopathology – The branch of psychology concerned with the investigation of mental disorders.

Psychopharmacology – The study of the psychological effects of drugs.

Psychophysics – The study of the relationship between physical stimulation and the conscious sensations it provokes in a person.

Psychophysiology – The study of the relationship between behavior and bodily changes, usually in humans; psychobiology, physiological psychology.

Psychosexual stages of development – A Freudian term describing child development as a series of stages based on the focus of libidinal energy. The sequence of the stages is oral, anal, phallic, latent, and genital.

Psychosis – A severe psychological disorder characterized by gross distortion of reality or by loss of reality testing, inability to distinguish between reality and fantasy, hallucinations, and/or delusions.

Psychosocial crises – In Erikson's theory of personality development, a series of stages at which critical choices must be made in regard to one's relationship to other people and to society in general.

Psychosomatic disorder – A physical disorder that has a psychological cause.

Psychosurgery – A medical therapy involving the surgical destruction of brain tissue with the aim of reducing or eliminating psychological symptoms or maladaptive behavior.

Psychotherapy – Any of several techniques employing psychological, rather than physiological, methods for treating personality disturbances.

Psychotherapy by reciprocal inhibition – The system of psychotherapy developed by Joseph Wolpe which employs conditioning to overcome a maladaptive habit by forming a new and antagonistic habit in the same stimulus situation.

Psychotic – A person who is experiencing a psychosis.

Psychotic episode – A sudden experience, generally triggered by some specific stimuli in the environment, during which a person develops a psychosis.

Psychotomimetic drug – Any drug that produces a state of being similar to a psychosis.

Puberty – The period of adolescence during which an individual reaches sexual maturity and acquires secondary sexual characteristics.

Pubescence – The period in late childhood or early adolescence during which secondary sexual characteristics begin to develop.

Public opinion poll – A technique in which a sample from a population is asked a few questions regarding attitudes toward a particular topic.

Punishment – The presentation of an unpleasant stimulus or removal of a pleasant stimulus for the purpose of eliminating undesirable behavior.

Pupil – The aperture in the eye, surrounded by the iris, through which light passes.

Pupillary reflex – An involuntary change in the size of the pupil as a function of brightness or darkness. The pupillary reflex is present in the neonate.

Pure line – A breeding line of animals that are relatively homogenous genetically.

Pure tone – A sinusoidal sound wave composed of only one frequency.

Purity – A psychological sensation corresponding to the degree of mixing of different wavelengths in one light stimulus; increasing the degree of mixing reduces the purity of a color experience; saturation.

Purkinje shift – A change in the perception of color brightness as levels of illumination change. As illumination decreases, the subjective brightness of the extremes of the visible spectrum (particularly the red) also decreases.

Q-sort – A personality questionnaire in which the subject or rater sorts a large number of statements into piles that range from "highly typical" to "highly atypical."

Quartile – A score value that separates one quarter of a group from the next. There are three quartiles. The first or lower quartile separates the lowest quarter of the group from the upper three-fourths. The second quartile is the same as the median. The third or upper quartile separates the top quarter of the group from the rest.

Quickening – The name given to the first movements of the fetus in utero that the mother can feel; does not occur until after the fifth month of pregnancy.

Race – A large subdivision of a species; in humans, these divisions are based on common ancestry and visible or somatic characteristics, but they still contain a deeply arbitrary nature.

Random – Occurring by chance; in a haphazard manner.

Random error – Chance errors. Such errors form a normal distribution about the mean of the measurements.

Random groups design – When subjects are randomly assigned to conditions in a between subjects design.

Random sample – A sample of cases drawn from some larger population in such a way that every member of the population has an equal chance of being drawn for the sample.

Random schedule (variable schedule) – An intermittent schedule of reinforcement. It may be either interval or ratio and is characterized by the presentation of reward at random intervals or on random trials.

Range – The range of a set of scores is the difference between the highest and the lowest score in a set of scores; the distance between the highest and lowest data points.

Rank-difference correlation – A correlation measure used when the distributions are on ordinal scales. Also called the rank-order correlation.

Rapid eye movement (REM) – One component of paradoxical sleep, characterized by rapid eye movements, an EEG like that of light sleep, and difficulty in waking. Dreams are thought to occur in this stage of sleep.

Rapport – A reciprocally comfortable and unconstrained relationship between two or more persons, especially between therapist and patient or between tester and testee.

Rating scale – A pencil-and-paper measuring device by which a person rates the personality traits, performance, and any number of characteristics of another person.

Ratio scale – An interval scale beginning with a true zero point. Only on such a scale are ratios meaningful.

Ratio schedules – Partial reinforcement schedules in which the reinforcement delivered is based upon the number of correct responses made.

Rationalization – A defense mechanism whereby one interprets and defends his or her behavior in terms of some motive other than the one actually responsible for the behavior; an intellectualized explanation or excuse.

Raw score – A score expressed in the units in which it was originally obtained, that is, pounds, inches, or points earned on a test. Raw scores are often transformed into "normal form" for ease of interpretation and comparison.

Reactance – The tendency to resist being manipulated by other people. As a theory, the position that if opportunity to choose an object is limited, its attractiveness will be increased (Jack Brehm).

Reaction formation – A Freudian defense mechanism whereby the individual behaves in a manner opposite to his or her inclinations. Reaction formation is illustrated by an individual who intensely desires someone but is unable to obtain that person, and consequently, shows evidence of disliking that person. Results from unconscious or repressed desires or traits.

Reaction time (RT) – The minimum time between a stimulus and a response.

Reaction type – A psychiatric diagnostic classification in terms of the preponderating symptom.

Reactive – Term used to describe observations that are influenced by, contaminated by, or maybe, in part, a reaction to the detected presence of the investigator. More generally, phenomena (including neurosis and psychosis) precipitated by adverse conditions or occurrences in the environment.

Reactive schizophrenias – Schizophrenic reactions in which the onset of symptoms is relatively sudden; sometimes called acute schizophrenias.

Readiness – A concept in development referring to one's state of being ready to learn a particular skill.

Real self – The concept of I, me, or myself as one really is; one's own awareness of his or her existence.

Realistic-group-conflict theory – Theory of prejudice stating that if two groups are in conflict with each other, members of each group will tend to develop prejudice against members of the other group.

Reality anxiety – In Freud's theory, reality anxiety is anxiety for which there is a realistic cause, i.e., fear; objective anxiety.

Reality principle – The process by which the ego becomes aware of the demands of the environment and works out an adjustment between these demands and the basic needs of the id, in a socially and psychologically accepted manner. The reality principle utilizes the secondary process.

Reappearance hypothesis – The notion that copies of images are stored in memory and that remembering consists of making these copies reappear.

Recall – A method for measuring retention of material previously learned, The material must be reproduced, verbally or in writing, either exactly in the order in which it was given (serial recall), or in any order desired by the subject (free recall).

Recency effect – The tendency to recall or incorporate into cognitive schemes material that was recently learned rather than earlier material; such a tendency is depicted by a serial position curve.

Reception paradigm – A procedure in concept learning wherein the experimenter presents the subject with stimuli which the subject must learn to categorize without error.

Receptive field – Area of the retina corresponding to a single cell in the visual cortex.

Receptive language – What is understood from words that are used.

Receptor – A specialized structure for transducing particular stimulus energy into a form processable by the nervous system.

Recessive gene – The gene in a pair of dissimilar genes that does not usually affect the process of development (the phenotype), but does affect the genotype of the individual and may be transmitted genetically to the next generation.

Reciprocal inhibition – Learning to decrease the presence of a response like anxiety by increasing the presence of an incompatible response like relaxation while the original anxiety-producing stimulus occurs.

Reciprocal innervation – The relaxation of a muscle when the one antagonistic to it is excited.

Reciprocity norm – 1. The rule of social exchange that people should help and not hurt those who have helped them. 2. (Piaget) The child's acquired belief that punishment should be logically related to an offense.

Recognition – A test of memory in which the subject must indicate which one of a set of items was previously experienced, or is the correct answer. In contrast to recall, the spontaneous generation of the correct answer is not necessary.

Recollection redintegration – The reinstatement of a memory upon the appearance of an element, a part, of the entire memory.

Reconnaissance (Sullivan) – The part of therapy characterized by the collection of biographical information about the patient through intensive interrogation.

Reconstruction – The notion that memory consists of an abstraction and coding process and that recall involves decoding and elaboration and not simply the recovery of, for example, "photographs" of the memory from a storage space.

Reconstructive therapy – Any psychotherapy that professes to effect major changes in the personality of a patient.

Redintegration – Remembering the whole event on the basis of partial cues; recollection.

Redirection – An organism's inappropriate responding in the presence of a single releaser stimulus.

Reductionism – The point of view that the explanation of events at one level (for example, psychological) is best accomplished by reference to processes at a "lower" or more basic level (for example, physiological).

Redundancy – The extent to which stimuli are predictable and repetitious. In assertion structured therapy, circular and self-defeating behavior developed as a result of the individual's persisting in assertions which meet with disconfirmation.

Re-educative therapy – Systems of psychotherapy which are believed to help the individual to handle problems more effectively than personality reconstruction would. Contrasted with reconstructive therapies.

Reference group – A group to which a person belongs, or identifies with, that influences his or her attitudes, standards, proper conduct, etc.

Referent – The object or thing to which a word refers.

Reflective – A personality predisposition exhibiting a tendency to evaluate alternatives and to delay decisions in order to avoid errors.

Reflex – An automatic response to a stimulus dependent on unlearned neural connections; exhibiting reflexive behavior.

Refraction – The bending of light rays when they pass from one medium to another, as through a lens.

Refractory period (phase) – Time interval, usually following a response, during which almost no stimulus will produce another response.

Regression – A defense mechanism of neurotic behavior, symbolic of returning to an earlier period of development.

Regression to the mean – The tendency for extreme measures on some variable to be closer to the group mean when remeasured, due to unreliability of measurement.

Regularization – The tendency of young children to learn the rules of grammar before they learn the exceptions and to deal with the exceptions as if they followed the rule; some examples are "feets," "runned," "bringed." Often taken as evidence of innate language ability.

Rehearsal – The repetition of a verbal input.

Reinforcement – A stimulus occurring after a response that increases the probability of the response.

Reinforcement schedule – A rule specifying the occasions on which reinforcements will be delivered.

Relational concept – A complex concept based upon the relationship between two features of a stimulus situation rather than having any absolute basis.

Relearning – A measure of retention in which the time or trials necessary for the second learning of a task are compared to the time or trials necessary for original learning.

Releaser – A concept in ethology, referring to highly specific stimuli that release fixed action patterns, or complex sequences of instinctive species-specific behavior.

Relevant attributes – Characteristics of a stimulus that make the stimulus a positive instance of a given concept. Also, characteristics of a stimulus or environment of interest to the researcher.

Relevant dimension – Stimulus dimension along which a concept is defined. For example, color is a relevant dimension along which the concept red is defined; size is not a relevant dimension for the concept red.

Reliability – The degree to which a test score remains stable over repeated measurements.

Reliability coefficient – The correlation coefficient between two equivalent measurements. The measurements may be two applications of the same test at different points in time, or the application of two equivalent forms of a test.

REM sleep – A stage of sleep in which brain waves are recorded that look very much like those recorded when the subject is awake and in which rapid eye movements occur. Dreaming occurs in this stage.

Reminiscence – A rise in performance of learned behavior beyond the level at which it was learned, which follows a rest after learning. It is thought to be due to a loss of work inhibition.

Repeatability – The attribute of observations that appear regularly under the same experimental conditions.

Repeated learning – Relearning material previously learned back to the point of mastery. Normally reduces subsequent forgetting.

Replication – Repeating an experiment precisely as it was conducted before; replication is usually necessary before any empirical findings are scientifically acceptable.

Representational thinking – Characteristic of the second stage in Piaget's system. The child develops representations for things that one can do. From about one-and-a-half to four years old.

Repressed emotions – According to the psychoanalytic tradition, a person who has an emotion without being conscious of it—the existence of such unconscious emotions can only be inferred through indirect means; for example, gestures, facial expressions, tone of voice and dreams.

Repression – A defense mechanism in which painful memories or frustrations are prevented from reaching the conscious level.

Research – A systematic attempt to discover by means of experimental investigation.

Residual stimuli – Stimulation carried over from recent experience that influences adaptation level.

Resistance – Opposition by a patient to the orders, actions, recommendations, or suggestions of the therapist.

Resistance to extinction – A measure of learning in which the number of unreinforced responses, before the response disappears in extinction, is used as the index of response strength in acquisition.

Respondent (Skinner) – A response elicited by a known specific stimulus. Unconditioned responses of the type referred to in classical conditioning are examples of respondents.

Response – Any measurable behavior. Sometimes specific to behavior elicited by a stimulus.

Response amplitude – A measure of the magnitude or intensity of a response as measured on a predetermined dimension.

Response chaining – Putting several responses together into one integrated behavior.

Response competition – The association of two (or more) responses to the same stimulus, which will only evoke the more strongly associated of the two.

Response discrimination – Learning to give only one particular response in a given situation.

Response generalization – Responding to the original stimulus not only with the original response, but with other similar responses.

Response integration – Unitizing or knitting together a complex response to be learned.

Response probability – The frequency with which a response occurs relative to the number of opportunities for its occurrence.

Response-produced cues – Cues that result from a response and that act as stimuli for the next response in a chain.

Response specificity – Change in one response system that is not seen in another.

Response strength – (See Response amplitude.)

Resting potential – The nonactivated state of a neuron, in which the inside of the cell is slightly negative in potential when compared to the outside.

Retarded – A general term describing abnormally slow development, or those people who have not developed either physically or intellectually as rapidly as normal.

Retention – Memory for material previously learned. The persistence of a learned behavior or experience after a temporal interval.

Retention interval – The period of time between acquisition of a response and the correct retrieval

of that response from storage.

Reticular activating system (RAS) – A network of nerve fibers spread throughout the brain that acts as a general activating system responsive to sensory stimulation.

Retina – The layer of photosensitive cells at the back of the eye containing the receptors and other neural structures responsible for vision.

Retinal disparity – The slight difference in stimulus patterns produced on the two retinas of the eyes from one object; an important depth cue, also referred to as "binocular disparity."

Retinal receptive field – The small areas on the retina which, when stimulated, give rise to electrical activity in a single neuron in the visual cortex.

Retrieval – The process of bringing materials from storage.

Retrieval cue – Information presented at the time of a memory test to aid recall.

Retrieval failure – A theory of forgetting which suggests that forgetting is caused by failure in the retrieval process and not in "loss" of the stored material itself.

Retroactive inhibition (interference) – Difficulty in recalling learned information because of something learned after the information one is trying to recall.

Retrograde amnesia – Forgetting of past events (i.e., before the amnesia) caused by physiological or psychological trauma.

Retrospective study – An investigation involving recollected data reported by people who were significant in a person's life. Errors in recollection often result in unintentional "retrospective errors."

Reverberating circuit – The first stage posited by consolidation theory; consists of short-lived electrical events occurring in the brain. These circuits are capable of maintaining activity after the initial impulse has died out.

Reversal (ABA) design – Small n design in which a subject's behavior is measured under a baseline (A) condition; then an experimental treatment is applied during the B phase and any changes in behavior are observed; finally, the original baseline (A) conditions are reinstituted to ensure that the experimental treatment was responsible for any observed change during the B phase.

Reversal learning – A discrimination-learning procedure in which the roles of the "correct" and "incorrect" stimuli are switched after the subject has reached a criterion performance level.

Reversal shift – A solution shift where all stimuli are reassigned to their opposite response categories.

Reversibility (Piaget) – A property of mental operations such that an operation proceeding in one direction may also proceed in the opposite direction. It is responsible for the development of conservation of various quantities.

Reward – An object, stimulus, event, or outcome that increases the probability of a learned behavior; reinforcement.

Rewrite rules – Set of rules in a transformational grammar specifying what a sentence consists of and how it can be rewritten; a way of describing a language. Rewrite rules specify structure but not meaning.

Rh factor – A substance present in the red blood cells of most people that causes antigenic reactions when the mother's blood is Rh negative and the fetus' blood is Rh positive.

Rhodopsin – The photosensitive pigment found in the rod cells of the retina of the eye involved in dark adaptation.

Ribonucleic acid (RNA) – Large molecules concerned with protein synthesis, possibly implicated in memory storage.

Ricco's law – The inverse linear relationship between the area of a visual target and its threshold.

Rigidity – The characteristic of continuing to perform a task in a stereotyped fashion even after better methods become possible. A personality trait characterized by inability to change one's attitudes, opinions, or manner of adjustment.

Risky shift – A group decision that is more venturesome than what could have been predicted from the responses of any one individual in the group or the mean response of the group.

Rites of passage – The procedures whereby a child becomes an adult member of his or her culture. Also called puberty rites. Often ritualistic and ceremonial in more primitive cultures.

RNA – (See Ribonucleic acid.)

Rods – The visual receptors that function primarily in dim or dark conditions; they are located toward the periphery of the eye and operate only in a black-and-white dimension.

Role – A person's function in a group; the set of behaviors expected of a person serving a particular function in a group.

Role consistent or role appropriate – Behavior that is consistent with what is expected on the basis of a role; the individual may or may not be comfortable with the behavior.

Role playing – Technique involving the acting out of specific roles in order to work through problems.

Rorschach Ink Blot Test – A projective personality test consisting of 10 cards, each containing a bilaterally symmetrical ink blot. The subject is instructed to tell what the blot reminds him or her of.

Rote learning – Learning verbatim; learning "by heart"; sometimes, learning without understanding.

Saccadic eye movement (saccade) – An abrupt point-to-point dart of the eye as it moves from its original fixation point to a new one.

Sadism – The compulsive tendency to vent aggression and destructiveness on another person; overt sexual satisfaction may or may not be derived from this behavior.

Safety needs (Maslow) – A term to describe the individual's need to maintain an orderly and predictable environment—an environment not threatening in either a physical or psychological sense.

Saliency – An inherent quality of some properties of stimuli that makes those properties more noticeable than others. The relative prominence or distinctiveness of some parts of the cognitive field over others.

Sample – A set of elements drawn from a population; the attempt should be made to make the sample as representative as possible of the population when the sample is to be used as the data base for research.

Sample bias – Any procedural variable that can cause a sample to be nonrepresentative of its population.

Sample error – The error caused by sample bias which occurs when a sample is nonrepresentative.

Sampling – Selection of subjects from a population; in general, the experimenter attempts to make the sample as representative of the population as possible.

Sampling techniques – Procedures for selecting a small number of cases from a large population such that the sample that results is representative of the larger population.

Sanguine – One of the four temperaments in Hippocrates's system of personality types. A sanguine person is warm and confident. Once thought to be due to the predominance of healthy blood.

Sanity – The condition of "normalcy" with respect to behavior as defined by society.

Saturation – One of the three attributes of color experience, saturation is the psychological correlate of purity, or number of different wavelengths in the color mixture. More wavelengths result in less saturation.

Savings – The measure of retention (or forgetting) by measuring the time or number of trials needed to relearn something as opposed to the time originally taken to learn the material.

Scale – Any series of values, objects, or magnitudes according to which a phenomenon can be quantified. In science there are nominal, ordinal, interval, and ratio scales.

Scale attenuation effects – Difficulties in interpreting results when performance on the dependent variable is either nearly perfect (a ceiling effect) or nearly lacking altogether (a floor effect).

Scanning – Strategy for solving conceptual problems which uses a hypothesis-testing approach. Successive scanning involves testing possible solutions one at a time. Simultaneous scanning involves testing more than one hypothesis at a time.

Scapegoat theory – Theory that prejudice is a displacement of aggression and thereby serves as an outlet for personal feelings of hostility and aggression.

Scattergram (scatterplot) – A pictorial way of displaying the correlation between two variables by plotting on a graph.

Schachter-Singer theory (1962) – A theory of emotionality that holds that emotions are differentiated by their cognitive content, rather than by physiological responses.

Schedules of reinforcement – Ways of arranging partial reinforcement according to either a time interval or the number of responses made by the subject.

Schemes (also schema or schemata action) – Systems that allow the child to test out the characteristics and properties of things in the physical world.

Schizoid personality – A type of personality characterized by withdrawal, avoidance of others, and often eccentricity.

Schizophrenia – Group of psychotic disorders in which there are severe disturbances in thought processes and emotions as well as a marked distortion of reality; often characterized by emotional blunting, disturbances in interpersonal relationships, depersonalization, and preoccupation with inner fantasies.

Scholastic tests – Aptitude tests used to predict future performance in academic pursuits.

School psychology – A branch of psychology which specializes in testing, counseling, and guiding students.

Scoring profile – The presentation of a summary of the results collected from the administration of a test battery, as in a personality profile.

Secondary appraisal – A reinterpretation of the causes of an emotion; may change the explanation from the one that was first proposed.

Secondary circular reaction – Infant responses that are circular in the sense that the response serves as a stimulus for its own repetition, and secondary since the responses do not center on the child's body, as do primary circular reactions.

Secondary drives – Drives acquired through the contiguity of previously neutral stimuli and primary drives; drug addiction, for example.

Secondary elaboration – Process of forming manifest dream content into a more cohesive unit through combining or creating elements.

Secondary gain – For neurotic behavior, other positive consequences in addition to the relief from tension or anxiety; as when being ill results in attention or relief from work.

Secondary group – A reference group with which a person has less contact than a primary group but which influences his or her behavior in some situations.

Secondary process – The characteristic functioning of the ego in which it fulfills id impulses by indirect routes while at the same time meeting the demands of the external environment; the reality principle.

Secondary reinforcers – Originally neutral stimuli that come to function as reinforcers as the result of their learned association with primary reinforcers or through exchange for a reward, as in token economy therapy.

Secondary sexual characteristics – Physical features—such as growth of beard in males and enlarging of breasts in females—that appear during puberty as indicators of sexual maturity.

Secondary stimulus generalization – Stimulus generalization based upon the subject's knowledge of language or some other type of symbol.

Sector therapy – The system of psychotherapy developed by Felix Deutsch to change defensive attitudes and to discriminate present realities from past experiences. The therapist focuses on symptoms and conflicts revealed by the patient's own words.

Security – In Sullivanian terminology, a state of belonging, of being accepted, and of being nonapprehensive about future satisfaction of one's needs.

Sedative – Drug that reduces anxiety by inducing muscle relaxation, sleep, and inhibition of the cognitive centers of the brain.

Segmentation – In speech perception, the process of dividing the acoustic wave into meaningful units.

Pauses are perceived between segments, although they may not necessarily be present in the wave itself.

Selection paradigm – A procedure in concept learning; subjects select the stimuli which are classified by the experimenter until the subject can define the concept.

Selective attention – A sensory state in which an organism attends to certain aspects of the environment while ignoring others.

Selective breeding – Planned matings between individuals having certain genetic backgrounds, with the aim of getting offspring of a particular genotype.

Selective inattention – Not being guided in behavior by an aspect of the situation that is perceived. Doing so avoids the anxiety of unpleasant or discrepant information.

Selective learning – Selection of a dominant response in response competition by means of selective reinforcement.

Self – That which is perceived as one's own conscious being; the individual revealed through introspection as the persistent center of psychological processes; the ego or I.

Self-actualization (Maslow) – The process or act of developing one's potentiality, achieving an awareness of one's identity and fulfilling oneself; the highest level of need.

Self-arousal – In modeling, a motive condition that arises out of the observation and retention of the behaviors of others and brings the individual closer to some action or cognition.

Self-concept – The definition of oneself including the person's mental image of his or her physical self, expectations about his or her behavior, and the attitudes and other cognitions that define the person's meaning.

Self-dynamism (Sullivan) – Pattern of the enduring motivations toward satisfaction and toward security that form the self-system.

Self-esteem needs – Maslow's term used to describe the individual's desire for others to hold him or her in high regard and also the desire to maintain a high opinion of his or her own behavior and person.

Self-fulfilling prophecy – When an expectation appears to lead to or cause the anticipated behavior. In research, an experimenter's expectations may inadvertently get his subjects to act in a particular way, ensuring that the prediction comes true.

Self-image – The personality as viewed by the self; self-concept.

Self-reinforcement – In modeling, the satisfaction of standards that have been established by observing others' behaviors.

Self-stimulation – Generally, stimulation of oneself; also a procedure whereby a human or animal may administer electrical stimuli to areas of his or her own brain (intra-cranial self-stimulation).

Self theory – Approach to personality that focuses on the individual as a whole, unified self. It takes a fairly positive view of humans and is a part of the humanistic approach to psychology.

Semantic differential – A rating-scale approach to connotative meaning developed by Osgood. Each adjectival concept is rated on a series of bipolar scales like good-bad.

Semantic generalization – Transfer of a response from one word as it was initially learned to another word that is meaningfully related to the first.

Semantic memory – Retention of rules, knowledge of our language, and other material not specifically related to particular places, times, or events.

Semantics – The study of the relation of words, signs, and symbols to what they mean or denote.

Semicircular canals – Three fluid-filled canals in the inner ear, which contain receptors responsive to acceleration resulting from body rotation. They are partly responsible for maintaining equilibrium and posture.

Semi-interquartile range (Q) – One half of the difference between the upper and lower quartiles. The semi-interquartile range provides an index of the variability of a set of scores.

Sensation – The simplest form of experience resulting from stimulation of a sense organ; a feeling.

Sense modality – A category of perceptual experience which depends on a particular kind of energy affecting a particular type of receptor.

Sensitivity – The range over which a test measures differences.

Sensitivity training – Group experience aimed at improving human relations, skills, and honesty and understanding of oneself and others; also called T-group.

Sensitization – An outcome of repeated stimulation whereby a particular response temporarily becomes easier than usual to elicit; an increase in sensitivity to some stimulus.

Sensorimotor – The knowledge possessed by a child during Piaget's first stage of development which extends until age two. A child acquires object constancies, the independent existence of objects and representations of the world during this period.

Sensorimotor period (or stage) – The first stage of development in Piaget's classification. It lasts from birth to approximately age 2 and is so called because the child understands his world primarily through his contact and physical manipulation of it.

Sensorimotor play – Play activity involving the manipulation of objects or execution of activities simply for the sensations that are produced.

Sensory – Refers to information being brought into the central nervous system; pertaining to the sense organs. Afferent is a synonym.

Sensory adaptation – The process of adjustment to unusual levels of stimulation by either an increase or decrease in sensitivity in that receptor.

Sensory cortex – Areas of the cerebral cortex that are the highest level receiving stations for sensory information.

Sensory deprivation – A situation in which an experimental subject is placed in a condition of reduced stimulation, either in intensity or variety. Subjects in prolonged conditions of sensory deprivation experience restlessness, impaired perceptual and cognitive functioning, and hallucinations.

Sensory gating – A brain process that reduces the input into certain sensory systems while allowing other systems to remain fully functioning.

Sensory memory – One of several hypothesized memory stores. In sensory memory the input is stored in relatively raw form and for brief periods of time.

Sensory nerves – The bundles of neurons that conduct impulses from the receptors to the central nervous system; also termed afferent nerves.

Sensory overload – Excess stimulation; extremely high levels of a stimulus that may result in pain, improper assimilation of information, and temporary or permanent impairment.

Sensory storage – The very brief retention of a signal in its unprocessed sensory form; also termed very short-term memory.

Septal region – A portion of the limbic system of the forebrain that is thought to be involved in the inhibition of emotional behavior.

Sequential attention – Sensory processing in which single units of information are treated in succession as opposed to simultaneous attention.

Serendipity – The experience of finding one thing while looking for another. Not an infrequent occurrence in science.

Serial act – A sequence of acts that occurring in such a way that the stimuli produced by each act serve as cues for the successive act.

Serial anticipation – A learning method in which the subject is given a series of items to memorize in order and is asked to predict, as each item in the list comes up, what the next item will be.

Serial learning – Learning in which materials or operations are presented in a particular order that must be followed.

Serial position curve – A graphic representation of retention as a function of the input position of the information; usually memory is better for the first items (primacy effect) and the last items (recency effect) than for those in the middle.

Seriation – The ordering of objects according to one or more empirical properties.

Serotonin – An inhibitory neurotransmitter found in the brain and believed to play a role in sleep and emotion.

Servo system – A closed-loop system in which behavior of one part affects, through feedback, all other parts of the system.

Set – A predisposition to respond in a particular way; in problem solving, a tendency to persist in solving a problem according to a particular procedure.

Sex chromosomes – Chromosomes contained in sperm cells and ova responsible for determining the sex of the offspring. Sex chromosomes produced by the female are of one variety, X; those produced by the male may be either X or Y.

Sex definition – Definition of an individual as male or female by physical criteria.

Sex differentiation – Increasing differences in physical development of males and females before or after birth; differential treatment of individuals on the basis of sex.

Sex-linked characteristic – A hereditary characteristic determined by a gene carried on the X or the Y chromosome, which also determines sex; red-green colorblindness is an example of such a characteristic.

Sex role – A set of expectations for behavior and characteristics held for a person on the basis of sex.

Sex-typed behavior – A behavior in which males and females do differ or are expected to differ; actual differences are not necessarily the same as expected differences.

Sexual deviation – Sexual behavior which is in violation of accepted norms regarding method or target.

Sexual dimorphism – When the males and females of a species are of dissimilar size, shape, or coloration.

Sexual impotence – Inability of the male to engage in sexual intercourse.

Sexual instinct – Refers to sexual craving or erotic desire.

Shadowing – A procedure used in studies of attention, in which the subject must repeat word for word a message as it is being presented.

Sham rage – Ferocious, undirected rage behavior provoked by very mild stimulation; experimental condition produced by surgical removal of the cerebral cortex.

Shape constancy – The tendency to perceive an object as of constant form in spite of change in the contours of the retinal image.

Shaping – In operant conditioning, the procedure whereby the desired behavior is gradually "put together" by reinforcing the series of successive steps that culminate in the final response.

Shaping behavior – Modifying behavior by reinforcing only those responses that tend toward the direction desired by the experimenter.

Sharpening – The cognitive process of accentuating certain details and dropping others in memory, so that objects and events become more clearly defined in the recall than they were in the original experience.

Shock therapy – The treatment of mental illness by the administration of some agent causing convulsions and coma. Such agents include insulin, metrazol, and electric current (electroconvulsive therapy, ECT) applied to the brain.

Short-term memory (STM) – One of several hypothetical memory stores. STM has a persistence on the order of 30 seconds but can be prolonged by rehearsal. It is of limited capacity, about 7 items (bits).

Shuttle box – Device with two compartments separated by a door, used to study learning and motivation.

Sibling rivalry – Jealousy or competition between brothers and/or sisters (siblings), which often develops in a child upon the birth of a new brother or sister due to competition for parental attention.

Sign stimulus – A stimulus that triggers one phase of an instinct.

Signal – A stimulus pattern which serves as a basis for a particular response; stimuli that can be used for communication.

Signal detection theory – A psychophysical method in which the observer is placed in varying conditions, e.g., variation in frequency of stimulus presentation, and asked to state if a particular stimulus is present.

Significance level – Probability that an experimental finding is due to chance, or random fluctuation, operating in the data; the p value.

Significant difference – A difference between two statistics which is so great that it is quite unlikely that it could have occurred by chance. The cutoff point is usually at the .05 or .01 level of confidence.

Similarity – Gestalt law of organization, which says that elements that are similar to one another will tend to be grouped together.

Simple schizophrenia – Subtype of schizophrenia characterized by withdrawal, indifference, and apathy, but seldom any delusions or hallucinations.

Simulation – In psychology, the attempt to use a computer program to duplicate the processing (thinking) stage in problem-solving.

Simultaneous conditioning – A classical conditioning procedure where the conditioned stimulus and the unconditioned stimulus occur at the same time.

Simultaneous contrast – The effect on brightness or color produced by presenting in close proximity, and at the same time, complementary visual stimuli, usually resulting in the detection of a greater contrast.

Sine wave – A sound pressure wave with regular cyclical properties; any complex waveform may, through Fourier analysis, be analyzed into a series of sine waves.

Single-blind control – An experimental situation in which the subjects are unaware of how or when the variables are manipulated by the experimenter, but the conditions are known to the experimenter.

Situational attribution – The judgment that situational constraints, rather than an actor's typical motivations, have shaped his or her behavior in a particular situation.

Situational instigators of aggression – Stimuli or events in the environment that increase the probability that aggressive behavior will occur.

Situational test – A test for studying behavior or personality based upon the simulation of a natural life situation, as opposed to artificial laboratory situations.

Size constancy – The tendency to perceive an object as of the same size in spite of variations in retinal image size, which occur when we move away from an object.

Skeletal muscles – Striated muscles under voluntary control that move the trunk and limbs.

Skew – When the scores of a distribution occur with greater frequency at one end of the distribution.

Skewed distributions – Nonsymmetrical frequency

distributions. A distribution is skewed in the direction of the longer tail.

Skin resistance (GSR, PGR) – Sometimes called the galvanic skin response or psychogalvanic response, it reflects a sudden decrease in the electrical resistance of the skin, usually due to increased sweating.

Skinner box – Experimental apparatus employed by Skinner in much of his research with rats and pigeons. It is a cagelike structure, equipped, usually with a lever, to allow the animal to make a response and the experimenter to reinforce or punish it for the response.

Small n design – Research design utilizing a small number of subjects.

Smell – Sense that deals with the reception of chemical stimuli in the olfactory organs.

Smooth muscles – Muscle tissue innervated by the autonomic nervous system which shows no striations and is not under voluntary control; found in the blood vessels and the gastrointestinal system. (Synonym: involuntary muscles.)

Snellen chart – A series of letters varying in size, used for the clinical assessment of visual acuity.

Social attitude – Combination of feelings, beliefs, and action tendencies toward classes of persons or objects that are directly or indirectly social in nature.

Social change – A significant alteration of social structure.

Social class – A group of people, differentiated from other members of society in terms of income, housing, values, privileges, and prestige, who associate with other members of the group socially and are perceived by themselves and others as belonging to a distinctive social level.

Social comparison – The process of determining one's own standards or standing on the basis of the behavior of others or using the behavior of others for purposes of evaluating one's own behavior, particularly in situations of uncertainty.

Social development – The development of a child's ability to interact with others. A consideration of social development frequently includes such topics as games, morality, the learning of language, and the learning of socially appropriate and inappropriate behaviors.

Social exchange theory – Interpersonal attraction can be analyzed in terms of rewards and costs of each event or type of interaction.

Social facilitation – Phenomenon in which the mere presence of other persons, as an audience or as coworkers, without any verbal exchange, increases individual performance.

Social interaction – Communication among individuals who both send and receive messages, verbally or by gestures.

Social interference – When the presence of others appears to hinder performance of a particular response.

Social learning – Acquiring patterns of behavior that conform to social expectations. Learning what is acceptable and what is not acceptable in a given culture.

Social learning theory – Attempt to explain personality in terms of learning, based on the assumption that much of what we call personality is learned behavior involving imitation. Social learning therapy tries to restructure maladaptive behavior using this theory.

Social motive – A motive whose satisfaction requires the presence of at least one other person and often involves status or companionship.

Social movement – An attempt by a large group of people to cause social change.

Social psychology – A psychology that draws upon the social sciences; a study of the effect on individual behavior of the real or implied, immediate or past, presence of others.

Social responsiveness – The extent to which a person responds to subtle social pressures and the presence of other people.

Social stimulus value – The effect of the external aspects of personality (appearance and behavior patterns) and other situational variables on the behavior and attitudes of others.

Social structure – A description of the ways in which the persons in a given society are ranked and related to one another.

Social system – A group of participants united through stable patterns of interaction and interdependent organizational structures.

Socialization – The complex process of learning those behaviors that are appropriate within a given culture as well as those that are less appropriate.

Society – A group of people living in one area who have developed patterns of interaction for getting along with one another.

Sociogram – A pictorial or graphic representation of the social structure of a group.

Sociometry – Technique for describing the structure of social groups by showing the patterns of preferences and aversions among the members.

Socionomy – An intermediate stage in Bull's scheme of moral development in which the individual begins to accept external social rules and incorporates them into an internal system for determining morality.

Somatic – Refers to the body.

Somatic nervous system – The part of the peripheral nervous system that innervates the skeletal muscles and peripheral sense organs.

Somatic therapy – Any of several forms of therapy for mental illness involving physical treatment including drugs, shock therapy, etc.

Somatoform disorders – A group of disorders that involve real motor or sensory deficits that nevertheless have no neurological or medical basis.

Somatotonia (Sheldon) – A temperamental characteristic associated with mesomorphy. The somatotonic individual is restless, aggressive, noisy, competitive, and active.

Somatotype – W. H. Sheldon's system of grouping body types into the categories of endomorph (soft and rounded), mesomorph (well-muscled), and ectomorph (thin and frail), each of these somatotypes correlating with certain personality types.

Somesthesis – Perceiving stimulation of the body surface.

Sone scale – A scale of auditory loudness based on direct loudness judgments. It is a logarithmic scale because the auditory system is forced to compress the broad range of intensities it can perceive.

Sound localization – The capacity to determine where a sound is coming from. It is dependent upon time of arrival, intensity, and phase differences between the signals perceived by the two ears.

Source traits (Cattell) – The personality traits that are the basic causes of one's overt, or surface, behavior.

Space perception – The ability to see depth.

Spaced practice – Practice in which trials are separated by sufficient amounts of time to dissipate fatigue.

Specific factor – Reliable component of a test score specific to the test itself, that is, not correlating with other tests.

Spectral – Pertaining to the visible band of wavelengths within the range of electromagnetic radiation.

Spectral sensitivity curve – The curve representing the perceived brightness of equal intensities of light of various wavelengths.

Speed-accuracy tradeoff – In reaction time experiments, the ability of the responder to substitute changes in the percentage of correct responses for changes in speed of responding.

Speed tests – Psychological tests in which the time limit for completion is considered a crucial variable.

Sperm cell – The sex cell produced by a mature male. It is haploid, like the egg cell (ovum) consisting of 23 chromosomes rather than 23 pairs of chromosomes.

Spermatogenesis – Development of sperm, the male reproductive cell.

Spike potential – The large amplitude change in electrical potential that constitutes the "neural impulse"; the magnitude of the spike follows the all-or-none law.

Spinal cord – That portion of the central nervous system located in the vertebral column. It is the main neural pathway for somatic information traveling to and from the brain and capable of reflex action interchanges.

Split-brain experiments – Research conducted when the corpus callosum has been severed, creating two entirely separate hemispheres which function independently.

Split-half reliability – Determining the reliability of a test by dividing the test items into two arbitrary groups and correlating the scores obtained on the two halves of the test.

Spontaneous recovery – In classic conditioning, the reoccurrence of an extinguished response following a rest period between extinction and retesting, and with no retraining.

Spontaneous remission – Recovery from abnormal personality patterns without any therapy. This phenomenon has always confounded attempts to assess the effectiveness of therapy.

Spreading depression – Procedure that involves chemically preventing part of the brain from functioning.

Stages of development – Periods in the development of a child when his or her mental operations can be characterized in a particular way and certain phenomena can be observed.

Stages of sexuality (Freud) – The developmental periods through which the individual is pushed by the libido toward the achievement of mature sexuality. The first period is the oral stage. The second is the anal stage. The third period is the phallic stage, during which interest is first focused on the penis or clitoris, but soon fastens upon the parents.

Standard deviation – A measure of the variability or spread of scores in a group. The standard deviation is the square root of the average of the squared deviations from the arithmetic mean of the group.

Standard error of the mean – An estimate of the amount that an obtained mean may be expected to differ from the true mean due to chance; s (for populations), s (for samples).

Standard error of measurement – A measure of the size of errors that are likely to result from the application of a particular measurement procedure. It is the standard deviation of the distribution of errors.

Standard score – A relative score that indicates the score's relation to the norm in terms of the number of standard deviations from the mean.

Standardization – The establishment of norms or standards for administering, scoring, and interpreting a psychological test. It usually involves administering the test to a large group of people representative of those for whom the test is intended.

Standardization group – Persons chosen to be tested with a new test; their scores determine the norms for the test when it is given to other persons drawn from the same population.

Standardized test – A test that has been published for general use. The most distinctive feature is a set of norms established on the basis of preliminary tryout and analysis of the test on a general reference population.

Stanford-Binet test – A revision of the Binet intelligence test made by psychologists at Stanford University, it is an individual test using age level subtests. It is the most widely used children's intelligence test.

Stapes – The third of the three tiny bones in the middle ear that conduct the sound vibrations from the eardrum to the cochlea.

Startle pattern – A primitive pattern of emotional responses to any sudden, unexpected stimulus which produces reflexive responses of the head, neck, face, and arms as well as the visceral system.

State anxiety – Momentary, consciously perceived feelings of apprehension and tension.

State dependent learning – Ability of the learner's internal physiological state to affect learning; the more similar this state is during learning and recall, the better recall will be.

Statistical judgment – Decisions based solely on statistical (or numerical or data-based) information.

Statistics – The discipline that deals with the collection, analysis, interpretation, and presentation of numerical data.

Status – A position in a social structure that is defined by the privileges and responsibilities of the persons having that position.

Status envy – Hypothesis that a person will identify with the person who is a rival for resources which he covets but cannot control.

Stereogram – A set of two pictures taken from two different points of regard so that retinal disparity is simulated. Viewing a stereogram in a stereoscope results in stereoscopic vision.

Stereoscope – An instrument for presenting one visual stimulus to the right eye and a different stimulus to the left eye; used in the laboratory for investigating the perception of depth.

Stereotype – A set of relatively rigid, oversimplified, or overgeneralized beliefs about a group of people.

Stereotyped behavior – Making the same response(s) over and over, regardless of environmental change; occurs in situations involving high frustration levels.

Stimulant – A substance that increases physiological activity and alertness.

Stimulation needs – A class of motives in which a person seems to require certain levels of sensory or perceptual stimulation, as shown by stimulation deprivation studies.

Stimulus – Any event in the physical environment capable of affecting an organism; specifically, anything that can activate a sensory neuron.

Stimulus control – State of learning in which the organism is responding only to the discriminative stimulus in an operant situation.

Stimulus discrimination – Learning to respond differently to various stimuli that may have some similarities.

Stimulus generalization – The elicitation of a learned response by a stimulus similar to, but not identical with, the conditioned stimulus.

Stimulus satiation – Loss of interest in a stimulus after continued exposure to it, as measured by a reduction in exploration, inspection, or choice of that stimulus in competition with a fresh alternative.

Stimulus-seeking – Tendency of isolated subjects to provide self-stimulation and to value and be rewarded by external stimuli introduced into the situation.

STM – (See short-term memory.)

Stranger anxiety – A development in the third quarter of the infant's first year in which unfamiliar people are frightening and separation from familiar people is distressing.

Stratified sampling – A technique for selecting subjects in such a way that nonoverlapping subgroups are sampled in proportion to each group's representation in the total population.

Stress – Psychological state of an organism when there is a disparity between its ability to cope comfortably with demands of the environment and the level of such demands.

Stroboscopic – Illusion or effect; apparent motion produced by presentation of stimuli at successive intervals, too short for the visual system to record as separate events; e.g., motion pictures.

Stroop effect – Difficulty in attending to or responding to a given stimulus due to an inability to block responses to irrelevant features in the stimulus situation; a response competition phenomenon.

Structural change – The second stage of learning posited by consolidation theory; consists of a relatively permanent change in neurophysiological activities.

Structural hypothesis – The third and last theory of the psyche proposed by Freud, in which he distinguished three functionally related structures of the psyche: the id, the ego, and the superego.

Structuralism – Early school of psychological thought originated by Wundt which held that psychology should attempt to analyze psychological phenomena into its components and determine how the components are synthesized; the primary method was introspection.

Structure – Term employed by Piaget to describe the organization of an individual's capabilities, whether they be motor or cognitive.

Structured test – A test that permits the selection of only particular given response alternatives.

Subject representativeness – Determination that samples are considered true or valid indices of the characteristics of the entire population.

Subject variable – Characteristics of people that can be measured or described, but cannot be varied experimentally (e.g., height, weight, sex, I.Q., etc.).

Subjective – Accessible only to private experience and unverifiable by others; dependent upon individual interpretation; nonstructured; used in contrast with objective.

Subjective orientation – Moral judgment of an act based on the intentions of the person who committed the act.

Subjective report or test – One in which the responses or answers are nonstructured or creative, resulting from open-ended questions.

Subjectivity – When judgments are affected by bias, prejudice, or personal feeling.

Sublimation – A defense mechanism in which an acceptable activity is substituted for an unacceptable activity or motive.

Subliminal perception – The supposed understanding or interpretation of stimuli which occurs at a level slightly below the threshold value.

Subliminal stimulation – Stimulation that falls below some psychophysical threshold but that still has a measurable behavioral effect.

Subtractive method – Donder's technique to estimate the amount of time required for various mental operations by subtracting one component from another.

Subvocal activity – Behavior of speaking to oneself (moving the muscles of the voice apparatus at very low levels without speaking overtly). According to the motor theory of thinking, subvocal activity is the basic behavioral component of thinking.

Sucking reflex – The automatic sucking response of a newborn child when the oral regions are stimulated. Nipples are particularly appropriate for eliciting the sucking reflex.

Suicide – The deliberate taking of one's own life.

Superego – In Freudian theory, the part of the personality developing out of the ego during childhood. It contains values, morals, and basic attitudes as learned from parents and society.

Superstitious behavior – Responses made by an organism in an operant situation that are not necessary for reinforcement but that have become associated with it nonetheless, due to reinforcement following an arbitrary movement.

Suppression – In psychoanalysis, the conscious act of keeping an impulse or memory just below the level of awareness, in the preconscious, because it is likely to provoke anxiety or other negative consequences.

Supraoptimal motivation – Motivation at such a high level that performance is impaired.

Surface structure – In linguistics, the arrangement of words in a language at the level of interpersonal communication.

Surface traits – In Cattell's approach to personality, the typical behaviors of an individual, as opposed to the underlying source traits that are the basic causes of the behavior; postulated to account for the correlations observed among tests of personality.

Surrogate mother – Term used by Harry Harlow to describe a wire or a terry cloth covered figure that he used as a substitute, or surrogate, for a monkey's real mother.

Survey research – Technique of obtaining a limited amount of information from a large number of people, usually through random sampling by asking a fixed set of questions to all of n.

Surveys – Opinion-polling; usually done with a sample taken from some predetermined population.

Sutures – The places where the skull bones become fused together.

Syllables – Sound uttered at a single effort of voice. The smallest speech units to which the receiver usually attends.

Syllogism (syllogistic reasoning) – A logical form that consists of two premises and a conclusion based on the two premises.

Symbol – Any specified stimulus that has become a commonly understood representation for some object, event, action, or idea.

Symbolic – The final stage in the development of a child's representation of his or her world. The term is employed by Bruner to describe a representation of the world through arbitrary symbols. Symbolic representation includes language as well as theoretical or hypothetical systems.

Symbolic learning – In modeling, learning a behavior without actually observing it; verbal descriptions are used to establish the modeled response.

Symbolic mode – The most sophisticated method for converting immediate experiences into mental models. As proposed by Bruner, it involves using words and sentences as symbols of objects, events, and states of affairs.

Symbolization – Dream process that disguises material in the dream so that something in the dream represents or stands for something else in real life.

Symmetry – A law of perceptual organization that states that balanced figures are usually perceived from exposure to ambiguous or complex stimuli. Balanced figures are aesthetically pleasing.

Sympathetic nervous system – A part of the autonomic nervous system, it prepares the organism for emergencies, making much bodily energy available for use.

Synapse – The space between the terminal button of an axon and the membrane, or dendrites, of another neuron. Transmitter substance flows across this space completing the circuit.

Synaptic space – Small gap separating the ends of the axon and dendrite in a synapse.

Synaptic vesicles – Membranous packets found in the terminal buttons of neurons from which transmitter substance is discharged into the synaptic cleft.

Syncretic – Refers to a developing organism's behavior, its qualities being fused though striving toward being separate and distinct.

Syncretic reason – A type of semilogical reasoning characteristic of the classification behavior of the very young preschooler. It involves grouping objects according to egocentric criteria, which are subject to change from one object to the next. In other words, the child does not classify on the basis of a single dimension, but changes dimensions as he or she classifies.

Syndrome – A group of symptoms that go together and (usually) characterize a particular disease or condition.

Synesthesia – A condition in which stimulation in one sensory modality arouses imagery in a different modality.

Syntactic boundary – The edges of constituents of sentences.

Syntactics – The study of the rules of language, particularly of sentence production.

Syntax – The grammar of a language consisting of the rules that govern the arrangement of words as elements in a sentence showing their interrelationships and dependencies; sentence structure.

System of psychology – Any particular body of theories of psychology used in the organization or interpretation of all of behavior.

Systematic desensitization – Type of behavior therapy developed by Wolpe to help people overcome fears and anxiety. It involves step-by-step classical conditioning in which an anxiety-producing stimulus (CS) is paired with relaxation (UCS).

Systematic replication – Repeating an experiment while varying numerous factors considered to be irrelevant to the phenomenon to see if it will survive these changes.

2 + 2 phenomenon – Adoption of a prejudiced attitude from an erroneous conclusion about facts. Logical error based on unquestioned acceptance of an erroneous or deceiving premise.

T-group – A sensitivity training encounter group.

T-score – A score on a test which is transformed to a score on a scale with a fixed mean and standard deviation.

T-test – The ratio of a statistic to its standard error. It is generally stated in terms of the probability or p value.

Tabula rasa – In reference to the mental content of a newborn, the empiricist notion that the mind is initially a "blank tablet" to be inscribed upon by experience.

Tachistoscope (T-scope) – An apparatus for presenting visual stimuli for brief, controlled periods of time.

Tact – A verbal utterance under the control of events in the world rather than specific needs of the speaker. A basic form of verbal behavior in Skinner's system.

Task-oriented group – A group whose primary goal is to perform a specific task, such as producing something, solving a problem, providing ideas, or reaching a consensus. Such a group concentrates on performing the task rather than on factors unrelated to the group's goal, e.g., social relations within the group.

Taste – The sense that deals with the reception of dissolved chemical stimuli through the papillae on the tongue.

Taste buds – Receptors for taste; located on the surface of the tongue. They are not neurons, but they synapse directly onto sensory neurons.

TAT (Thematic Apperception Test) – A basic projective measurement technique in which the subject is asked to tell a story about each of several relatively ambiguous pictures; often used in the measurement of aspects of achievement motivation.

Teaching machines – Devices that present material to be learned in a series of single statements, to each of which the learner must respond for reinforcement.

Tectum – The upper portion (roof) of the midbrain, comprising the inferior and superior colliculi.

Tegmentum – The lower portion of the midbrain located beneath the tectum.

Telepathy – An alleged phenomenon whereby one person can communicate with another without benefit of the known sensory channels or known forms of physical energy.

Temperament – A general term used to refer to an individual's disposition, energy level, and social orientation. An aspect of personality.

Template matching – A theory of pattern recognition which suggests that patterns are recognized by being matched to internally stored templates.

Temporal conditioning – A classical conditioning procedure in which the UCS occurs at regular intervals; these regular intervals are treated as the CS.

Temporal lobe – The area of the cortex in front of the occipital lobe and below the lateral fissure.

Temporal maze – An apparatus for studying temporal order rather than spatial sequences.

Temporal summation – The compounding of the effects of several subthreshold depolarizations that occur one right after another to produce an action potential.

Tension reduction – A view of reinforcement or reward which holds that reduction in stimulation from the attainment of a goal is the basic condition for reinforcement.

Teratogens – Environmental agents that produce abnormalities in the developing fetus.

Terminal buttons – The ends of an axon which form the synaptic knob and which release transmitter substance into the synaptic cleft.

Terminal response theory – The theory that reinforcement is based on response termination. Since the subject stops responding, what was done last is preserved until the next time the same stimulus is presented.

Terminal threshold – The maximum stimulus intensity which will still produce a sensation.

Territorial instinct – An organism's innate desire or drive for complete control of the physical area in which it lives.

Tertiary circular reaction – An infant's response that is circular in the sense that the response serves as the stimulus for its own repetition, but where the repeated response is not identical to the first response. This last characteristic, the altered response, distinguishes a tertiary circular reaction from a secondary circular reaction.

Test – Any form of measurement that yields quantitative data.

Test anxiety – An increase in anxiety brought on by a testing situation.

Test battery – The combination of several different psychological tests into a series presented to a subject.

Test norms – Data collected in the course of validating a test that enable a test user to compare a person's score with the scores for the population of which that person is a part.

Test-retest reliability – Reliability estimated by giving the same test on two occasions and finding the correlation between the scores for the two administrations. Since the test is unchanged, differences from test to retest reflect either change or inconsistency of the individual from one occasion to another.

Testes – Reproductive organs in males; endocrine glands that secrete many hormones which regulate sexual behaviors and characteristics.

Testimonials – A propaganda technique that uses statements from respected persons as to the worth of some person or thing.

Testosterone – A male sex hormone secreted by the

testes, which is responsible for many male primary and secondary sexual characteristics.

Textual response – Reading; saying what one sees written. Also, a scoring category in the Rorschach Inkblot Test for responses based on the texture of the inkblot.

Texture gradient – The change in the appearance of texture based upon distance from the viewer; a monocular depth cue. The apparent increase in density and loss of separateness of the elements in a perceptual field, with increasing distance.

Thalamus – One of the main structures of the diencephalon of the forebrain. It contains nuclei that relay information to the cerebral cortex.

Thanatos – A Greek word meaning death, employed by Freud in his later writings to describe what he calls the death wish or death instinct. It is used in contrast with the word Eros.

Thematic Apperception Test – (See TAT.)

Theory – A set of general principles that explains existing related facts and permits the prediction of new facts.

Therapist – An individual who conducts treatment procedures; the agent who provides psychotherapy.

Theta – Relatively high amplitude brain waves; 4-7 Hz.

Thinking – The cognitive manipulation and reorganization of percepts, concepts, habits, motives, and rules.

Thirst – A postulated drive related to water deprivation; the sensations arising from water deprivation.

Threshold – A statistically determined point on a stimulus continuum at which there is a transition in a series of sensations or judgments.

Thymus – An endocrine gland located in the lower neck region involved with the lymphoid system and immunological reactions.

Thyroid – An endocrine gland located in the neck region that regulates metabolic rate and activity levels.

Timbre – The attribute of tonal sounds which is the correlate of waveform complexity. The characteristic tone quality of a voice or a musical instrument, their patterns of overtones (harmonics).

Time perspective – Organized concepts of past and future compared with the present.

Tip-of-the-tongue phenomenon (TOT) – When retrieval (usually verbal) from long-term storage seems almost possible, but cannot quite be accomplished.

Toddler – A nontechnical label sometimes used to describe the child between the ages of 18 months and $2^1/_2$ years.

Toilet training – Training the child to defecate and urinate in the proper place at appropriate times.

Token – A secondary reinforcer that can be exchanged for a primary reinforcer, e.g., as in a "token economy." Chips may serve as "money," for example, on a hospital ward or in a halfway house. Participants "earn" their tokens and exchange them for primary reinforcers (privileges, food, etc.) in the "economy" (e.g., the ward).

Trace – In theories of memory, the hypothetical residual effect of stimulation used to explain memory.

Trace conditioning – A classical conditioning procedure in which the onset and cessation of the CS occurs before the UCS is presented.

Trace-dependent forgetting – Loss of learned information due to the loss of a memory trace.

Tract – A bundle of neural fibers within the central nervous system, analogous to a nerve.

Trait – In respect to personality, a relatively persistent and consistent characteristic or attribute that serves to distinguish one person from another.

Trait anxiety – Anxiety proneness; the predisposition to respond with high state anxiety when under stress.

Trait cluster – Group of traits that tend to go together, so that a person who has one of the traits will probably have all of them.

Trait theory – An attempt to categorize personality using the presence or absence of several characteristics.

Tranquilizer – Any of several drugs that relieve anxiety without inducing sleep.

Transcendental meditation – One type of concentrative meditation, as taught by the Maharishi Mahesh Yogi. Its basis is the use of a mantra.

Transduction – The conversion of energy from one form to another, stimulus energy into action potentials as accomplished in a rod or cone cell, for example.

Transductive reasoning – Semilogical reasoning that proceeds from particular to particular, rather than from particular to general or from general to particular. One example of transductive reasoning is the following: Cows give milk. Goats give milk. Therefore goats are cows.

Transfer index – A measure of the ability to apply what one has learned previously to new situations. It is based upon performance in discrimination learning tasks but is presumably independent of overall learning ability.

Transfer of training – The effect of earlier learning on present learning: transfer is positive if the earlier learning makes present learning easier; it is negative if the earlier learning makes present learning more difficult.

Transference – A psychoanalytic theory describing the stage of therapy in which the patient begins to respond to the analyst as though the analyst were some significant person (e.g., mother or father) in the patient's past.

Transformational grammar – Rules of grammar specifying how large units of language, such as sentences, can be modified to express different meanings.

Transmitter substance – A chemical, secreted by axon terminals, which excites or inhibits an adjacent neuron. Transmitters are responsible for synaptic action.

Transposition – The tendency to recognize common patterns in stimulus configurations made up of different elements.

Transverse presentation – A crosswise presentation of the fetus at birth, instead of the normal headfirst presentation.

Trauma – Damage or injury to the psyche; an experience or set of experiences that inflicts serious physical or psychological injury.

Tree diagram – A visual way of describing the phrase structure of a sentence.

Trephining – Cutting a hole in the skull; an operation used in ancient times to remove the evil spirits that supposedly caused mental illness.

Triad – Three persons interacting with one another.

Trial and error – A method of problem solving in which a sequence of acts is performed until one act produces the goal. This method involves a minimum understanding of the relationship between the factors involved.

Trichromatic theory – The Young-Helmholtz theory of color vision which posits the existence of three basic receptor types, each maximally sensitive to a limited region of the visible spectrum.

Tritanope – A dichromat with a blue-yellow deficiency. This form of color blindness is rare.

Trucking game (Deutsch and Krauss) – Decision making game used in research on cooperation and competition. Subject is asked to make a decision between cooperating for a steady reward or competing for a large but risky reward.

True prevalence – The presence of treated as well as untreated persons with mental disorders in a community.

True score – The hypothesized underlying ability of an individual on the attribute measured by a test. An obtained test score is considered to result from this true level of ability modified by an error of measurement that characterizes that particular test.

Truncated range – The amount of dispersion (or range) of scores on one variable may be small due to a small number of subjects, which may lead to low correlations.

Truth-table strategy – A systematic procedure for solving rule-learning problems.

Two-phase movement – An act in which the initial movements are preparatory and perhaps opposite to the ultimately desired movement.

Two-tailed test – A test that places the rejection area at both ends of a distribution.

Tympanic membrane – The eardrum, separating the middle ear from the external auditory canal.

Type – In personality theory, a group of individuals having certain characteristics in common. Typologies are usually based upon a very limited set of categories and thus are not generally and completely accepted by most psychologists.

Type 1 error – The probability that the null hypothesis is rejected when it is in fact true; equals the significance level.

Type 2 error – Failure to reject the null hypothesis when it is in fact false.

Type R learning – A Skinnerian expression for operant conditioning. It is so called since both reinforcement and a response are involved in the learning.

Type S learning – A Skinnerian expression for classical conditioning. It is so called since stimuli are involved in classical conditioning.

Ultradian rhythms – Biological rhythms with cycles shorter than about 24 hours; may be as short as microseconds.

Ultrasonic – Referring to vibrations whose frequency is above the upper limit of human hearing, greater than approximately 20,000 Hz.

Ultraviolet – Electromagnetic radiation whose wavelength is below that of violet light, i.e., below about 380 nanometers.

Umbilical cord – A thick cord that runs from the fetus, at the point that will become the navel, to the placenta. It transmits nourishment and oxygen from the mother to the growing fetus and carries away the fetus' waste products.

Umweg learning – Detour learning. The subject must

learn to move away from a goal in order to get around a barrier that prevents direct access to the goal.

Unconditioned positive regard (Rogers) – Concept involving the idea that a therapist must care about his or her client without any conditions put on the caring, even when the client reveals things that the therapist is uncomfortable about.

Unconditioned response (UCR) – In classical conditioning, the response elicited automatically, without any training, by the presentation of the unconditioned stimulus (UCS).

Unconditioned stimulus (UCS) – In classical conditioning, a stimulus that can elicit a response in the absence of conditioned learning.

Unconscious – A division of the psyche, the contents of which are at least temporarily (and usually permanently) unknown to the individual. According to Freud, this part of the psyche contains repressed material which is often the cause of human actions.

Unconscious motives – Information that is held in memory and continues to influence responding but is not recognized at a conscious level.

Undoing – Ego-defense mechanism whereby the individual engages in a ritual which is intended to abolish the effect of a previously committed act.

Unimodal – Having only one peak or mode, as opposed to bimodal or multimodal.

Unlearned motives – Innate conditions that initiate, guide and maintain behaviors.

Unlearning – The hypothesis that subsequent learning interferes with earlier learning by dissolving the earlier associations; a deliberate attempt to erase undesirable habits.

Unstructured test – A test that allows responses to vary widely to reveal personality.

Uterus – A relatively sophisticated term for what is frequently called the womb; the organ in the mother where fetal development takes place.

Utricle – A saclike structure within the inner ear which contains receptors sensitive to gravitational pull.

Vacuum activity – Occurrence of behavior in the absence of appropriate stimuli and considered by ethologists to be the result of a high drive state; displacement activity.

Vagus nerve – The tenth cranial nerve, with fibers extending to the heart, lungs, thorax, abdominal viscera, external ear, larynx, and pharynx.

Validity – The degree to which a test measures what it is supposed to measure as determined by a criterion.

Value – An abstract concept, often merely implicit, that defines what ends or means to an end are desirable; a general motive relating to one's behavior or goals.

Variability – The extent to which scores in a set of scores are spread out from the average score in the group; common measures are the range and the standard deviation.

Variable – A property, measurement, or characteristic which can take on two or more values; variables can be independent or dependent.

Variable interval schedule – A schedule of reinforcement in which the first response following a given interval of time is reinforced. The length of the time period, however, is changed from trial to trial.

Variable ratio schedule – A schedule of intermittent reinforcement in which every nth response is reinforced, with n varying from trial to trial.

Variable schedules – Partial reinforcement schedules that can change in ratio or interval, usually around some average value.

Variance – Measure of dispersion of scores around some measure of central tendency; the standard deviation squared.

Vasoconstriction – Reduction in the diameter of blood vessels by contraction of the smooth muscles surrounding these blood vessels.

Vasodilation – Increase in the diameter of blood vessels by relaxation of the smooth muscles surrounding these blood vessels.

Vasomotor activity – The activity in the smooth muscles of blood vessels which affects the degree of vasoconstriction and vasodilation of the small blood vessels.

Ventricles – The hollow spaces within the brain which form a continuous channel for the flow of cerebrospinal fluid; includes the lateral, third, and fourth ventricles.

Verbal IQ – A special score given by the Wechsler IQ tests as a measure of the ability to deal effectively with words, based on the subtests of information, comprehension, digits forward and backward, arithmetic, similarities, and vocabulary.

Verbal learning – The learning of language, lists of words, and wordlike material.

Veridical – Corresponding to objective reality or physical measurement.

Verifiability – The ability of a theory or group of results to be tested by observation or experimentation for veridicality; the ability of an experiment to be repeated yielding similar results.

Verification – The testing and application of hypothesis or theory as the solution to a problem.

Vertical decalage – Term used by Piaget to suggest developmental differences in cognitive ability; that different stages of child development reflect actual differences in cognitive functioning rather than arbitrary divisions along a continuum.

Very short-term memory – Memory for events presented for a very brief time (e.g., 50 milliseconds) which lasts only a second or so; sensory memory including iconic and echoic memory.

Vestibular sacs – Sense organs for perception of balance; enlargements at base of semicircular canals that respond to tilt, the utricle and saccule.

Vestibular sense – The perception of balance; the function of the three semicircular canals, the utricle and the saccule.

Vicarious learning – The experience of observing and understanding another's response and the consequences of that response.

Vicarious reinforcement – Reinforcement that results from observing someone else being reinforced.

Viennese School – The followers of Freud's teachings of psychoanalysis.

Viscerotonia (Sheldon) – A temperamental characteristic associated with the endomorphic body build; a cheerful person seeking a passive, accepting environment.

Visual acuity – Ability to discriminate fine detail in a patterned stimulus.

Visual cliff – An apparent but not actual drop-off designed to test depth perception in infants. It consists of a glass floor over a patterned surface which terminates and immediately continues, but at some distance below the glass. Through the glass a "cliff" is perceived.

Vocal tract – The entire assembly of the organs of speech including the larynx, pharynx, tongue, teeth, lips, nasal passages, and mouth.

Vocational tests – Aptitude tests used to predict future performance in a job or career.

von Restorff effect – The tendency of items that are distinct in some way from the other items in a list to "stand out" and thus be more easily learned.

WAIS – (See Wechsler Adult Intelligence Scale.)

Warm-up – Any of a number of experiences that serve to prepare an organism for performance of a response.

Watson, John B. – Early twentieth-century American psychologist and founder of behaviorism.

Wavelength – The distance between successive peaks in a periodic waveform.

Weber fraction (DI/I) – The ratio of the threshold increment to the baseline intensity. It is part of Weber's law that a jnd increases with the magnitude of the baseline.

Wechsler Adult Intelligence Scale (WAIS) – An intelligence test, administered individually, and primarily concerned with the assessment of intelligence in adults.

Wechsler-Bellevue – Intelligence test battery, in adult and children's versions, composed of tests for different abilities. Divided into performance tests and verbal tests, it yields a point score which can be converted into an IQ.

Wernicke's area – An area within the temporal lobe of the brain that is involved in language perception. It has connections to memory areas of the brain, and damage to the area results in Wernicke's aphasia in which language has syntax but no meaning.

Wertheimer, Max – One of the founders of Gestalt psychology.

White matter – Neural tissue in the brain and spinal cord consisting of axons that are whitish due to the light-colored myelin sheath covering them.

White noise – Noise often used in experimentation consisting of a flat spectrum of energy at all frequency levels.

Whole learning – Learning the entire set of materials as a unit rather than by parts.

Whorfian hypothesis – The assumption that the form of expression in a language directs the form of thought processes that develop.

Will therapy – The term applied to the system of psychotherapy developed by Otto Rank in which the patient is encouraged to assert him- or herself and achieve independence, as in the birth trauma.

Within-group variance – A measure of the dispersion among subjects in the same group in an experiment as contrasted with the variance which occurs as a result of different experimental conditions.

Within-sex variation – The dispersion of scores for subjects of only one sex.

Within-subject design – An experimental design in which each subject is tested under more than one level of the independent variable.

Word association – A projective technique for eliciting responses to single words. A word is presented and the subject is directed to respond with the first word it makes him think of.

Word-association norms – Tables of the frequency of occurrence of various responses to stimulus words for particular populations such as school children, college students, neurotics, etc.

Work inhibition – A buildup in fatigue due to continuous effort.

Wundt, Wilhelm – The founder of structuralism, he also started the first experimental laboratory of psychology at Leipzig.

X chromosome – The chromosome responsible for sex determination. The XX chromosome combination in humans results in a female.

X-axis – The abscissa or horizontal axis in a graph. By convention the independent variable is plotted on the abscissa.

XXY pattern (Klinefelter's syndrome) – A genetic abnormality once believed to be related to criminal or aggressive behavior.

Y chromosome – A chromosome responsible for sex determination. In humans, a Y chromosome paired with an X results in a male.

Y-axis – The ordinate or vertical axis on a graph. By convention the dependent measure is plotted on the ordinate.

Yantra – A visual pattern that can be used in meditation.

Yerkes-Dodson law – A statement that performance is a curvilinear function of arousal or motivation, showing first an increase and then a decrease as arousal or motivation is increased.

Young-Helmholtz theory – Theory of color vision holding that there are three kinds of color receptors (cones), each for a different primary color, and that any color experience involves a combination of stimulation of the three types of receptors.

Ypsilanti project – A preschool project based heavily on instructional methodology derived from Piaget.

Z score – The difference between the obtained score and the mean, divided by the standard deviation.

Zeigarnik effect – Better recall of uncompleted than completed tasks, provided that the subject is concerned with the outcome of the task.

Zeitgeber – An event that is indicative of the passage of a particular period of time and that helps to maintain the periodicity of certain physiological functions. Daylight or a new moon is an example of such an event.

Zipf's law – The observation that the frequency of usage of a word in a text times its rank order equals a constant (f x r = C).

Zygote – A fertilized egg cell.

APPENDIX

APPENDIX

USEFUL DIMENSIONS IN LABORATORY WORK

Length

1 meter (m) = 3.28 feet (ft) = 39.37 inches (in.)
            = 100 centimeters (cm) = 1000 millimeters (mm)
            = 10^6 micrometers (μm), or microns (μ)
            = 10^9 nanometers (nm), or millimicrons (mμ)
            = 10^{10} Ångstrom units (Å)
1 foot = 12 in. = 30.48 cm
1 inch = 2.54 cm

Volume

1 liter (l) = 1.0567 quarts (qt) = 1000 milliliters (ml)
           = 1000.03 cubic centimeters (cc or cm^3)

Weight

1 gram (g) = .0022 pound (lb) = .035274 ounce (oz)
            = 1000 milligrams (mg) = 10^6 micrograms (μg)

Angle

1 degree (°, deg) = 60 minutes (min) = 3600 seconds (sec) = 0.0175 radian (rad)

Photometry

1 millilambert (mL) = 0.929 footlambert (ft L) = 3.183 candles per square meter (c/m^2)
            = 10 apostilbs

Frequency

1 cycle per sec = 1 cps = 1 Hz = 360°/sec = 2 π rad/sec

Time

1 second (sec) = 1000 milliseconds (msec) = 10^6 microseconds (μsec)

Temperature

Degrees centigrade (°C) = 5/9(n°F − 32) = n°K − 273
Degrees fahrenheit (°F) = 9/5n°C + 32
Degrees kelvin (°K) = n°C + 273

π = 3.1416

e = 2.71828

RANDOM NUMBERS

Line\Col.	(1)	(2)	(3)	(4)	(5)	(6)	(7)	(8)	(9)	(10)	(11)	(12)	(13)	(14)
1	10480	15011	01536	02011	81647	91646	69179	14194	62590	36207	20969	99570	91291	90700
2	22368	46573	25595	85393	30995	89198	27982	53402	93965	34095	52666	19174	39615	99505
3	24130	48360	22527	97265	76393	64809	15179	24830	49340	32081	30680	19655	63348	58629
4	42167	93093	06243	61680	07856	16376	39440	53537	71341	57004	00849	74917	97758	16379
5	37570	39975	81837	16656	06121	91782	60468	81305	49684	60672	14110	06927	01263	54613
6	77921	06907	11008	42751	27756	53498	18602	70659	90655	15053	21916	81825	44394	42880
7	99562	72905	56420	69994	98872	31016	71194	18738	44013	48840	63213	21069	10634	12952
8	96301	91977	05463	07972	18876	20922	94595	56869	69014	60045	18425	84903	42508	32307
9	89579	14342	63661	10281	17453	18103	57740	84378	25331	12566	58678	44947	05585	56941
10	85475	36857	53342	53988	53060	59533	38867	62300	08158	17983	16439	11458	18593	64952
11	28918	69578	88231	33276	70997	79936	56865	05859	90106	31595	01547	85590	91610	78188
12	63553	40961	48235	03427	49626	69445	18663	72695	52180	20847	12243	90511	33703	90322
13	09429	93969	52636	92737	88974	33488	36320	17617	30015	08272	84115	27156	30613	74952
14	10365	61129	87529	85689	48237	52267	67689	93394	01511	26358	85104	20285	29975	89868
15	07119	97336	71048	08178	77233	13916	47564	81056	97735	85977	29372	74461	28551	90707
16	51085	12765	51821	51259	77452	16308	60756	92144	49442	53900	70960	63990	75601	40719
17	02368	21382	52404	60268	89368	19885	55322	44819	01188	65255	64835	44919	05944	55157
18	01011	54092	33362	94904	31273	04146	18594	29852	71585	85030	51132	01915	92747	64951
19	52162	53916	46369	58586	23216	14513	83149	98736	23495	64350	94738	17752	35156	35749
20	07056	97628	33787	09998	42698	06691	76988	13602	51851	46104	88916	19509	25625	58104
21	48663	91245	85828	14346	09172	30168	90229	04734	59193	22178	30421	61666	99904	32812
22	54164	58492	22421	74103	47070	25306	76468	26384	58151	06646	21524	15227	96909	44592
23	32639	32363	05597	24200	13363	38005	94342	28728	35806	06912	17012	64161	18296	22851
24	29334	27001	87637	87308	58731	00256	45834	15398	46557	41135	10367	07684	36188	18510
25	02488	33062	28834	07351	19731	92420	60952	61280	50001	67658	32586	86679	50720	94953
26	81525	72295	04839	96423	24878	82651	66566	14778	76797	14780	13300	87074	79666	95725
27	29676	20591	68086	26432	46901	20849	89768	81536	86645	12659	92259	57102	80428	25280
28	00742	57392	39064	66432	84673	40027	32832	61362	98947	96067	64760	64584	96096	98253
29	05366	04213	25669	26422	44407	44048	37937	63904	45766	66134	75470	66520	34693	90449
30	91921	26418	64117	94305	26766	25940	39972	22209	71500	64568	91402	42416	07844	69618
31	00582	04711	87917	77341	42206	35126	74087	99547	81817	42607	43808	76655	62028	76630
32	00725	69884	62797	56170	86324	88072	76222	36086	84637	93161	76038	65855	77919	88006
33	69011	65795	95876	55293	18988	27354	26575	08615	40801	59920	29841	80150	12777	48501
34	25976	57948	29888	88604	67917	48708	18912	82271	65424	69774	33611	54262	85963	03547
35	09763	83473	73577	12908	30883	18317	28290	35797	05998	41688	34952	37888	38917	88050
36	91567	42595	27958	30134	04024	86385	29880	99730	55536	84855	29080	09250	79656	73211
37	17955	56349	90999	49127	20044	59931	06115	20542	18059	02008	73708	83517	36103	42791
38	46503	18584	18845	49618	02304	51038	20655	58727	28168	15475	56942	53389	20562	87338
39	92157	89634	94824	78171	84610	82834	09922	25417	44137	84813	25555	21246	35509	20468
40	14577	62765	35605	81263	39667	47358	56873	56307	61607	49518	89656	20103	77490	18062
41	98427	07523	33362	64270	01638	92477	66969	98420	04880	45585	46565	04102	46880	45709
42	34914	63976	88720	82765	34476	17032	87589	40836	32427	70002	70663	88863	77775	69348
43	70060	28277	39475	46473	23219	53416	94970	25832	69975	94884	19661	72828	00102	66794
44	53976	54914	06990	67245	68350	82948	11398	42878	80287	88267	47363	46634	06541	97809
45	76072	29515	40980	07391	58745	25774	22987	80059	39911	96189	41151	14222	60697	59583
46	90725	52210	83974	29992	65831	38857	50490	83765	55657	14361	31720	57375	56228	41546
47	64364	67412	33339	31926	14883	24413	59744	92351	97473	89286	35931	04110	23726	51900
48	08962	00358	31662	25388	61642	34072	81249	35648	56891	69352	48373	45578	78547	81788
49	95012	68379	93526	70765	10592	04542	76463	54328	02349	17247	28865	14777	62730	92277
50	15664	10493	20492	38391	91132	21999	59516	81652	27195	48223	46751	22923	32261	85653

AREAS UNDER THE NORMAL CURVE

An entry in the table is the proportion under the entire curve which is between $z = 0$ and a positive value of z. Areas for negative values of z are obtained by symmetry.

z	Second decimal place of z									
	.00	.01	.02	.03	.04	.05	.06	.07	.08	.09
0.0	.0000	.0040	.0080	.0120	.0160	.0199	.0239	.0279	.0319	.0359
0.1	.0398	.0438	.0478	.0517	.0557	.0596	.0636	.0675	.0714	.0753
0.2	.0793	.0832	.0871	.0910	.0948	.0987	.1026	.1064	.1103	.1141
0.3	.1179	.1217	.1255	.1293	.1331	.1368	.1406	.1443	.1480	.1517
0.4	.1554	.1591	.1628	.1664	.1700	.1736	.1772	.1808	.1844	.1879
0.5	.1915	.1950	.1985	.2019	.2054	.2088	.2123	.2157	.2190	.2224
0.6	.2257	.2291	.2324	.2357	.2389	.2422	.2454	.2486	.2517	.2549
0.7	.2580	.2611	.2642	.2673	.2703	.2734	.2764	.2794	.2823	.2852
0.8	.2881	.2910	.2939	.2967	.2995	.3023	.3051	.3078	.3106	.3133
0.9	.3159	.3186	.3212	.3238	.3264	.3289	.3315	.3340	.3365	.3389
1.0	.3413	.3438	.3461	.3485	.3508	.3531	.3554	.3577	.3599	.3621
1.1	.3643	.3665	.3686	.3708	.3729	.3749	.3770	.3790	.3810	.3830
1.2	.3849	.3869	.3888	.3907	.3925	.3944	.3962	.3980	.3997	.4015
1.3	.4032	.4049	.4066	.4082	.4099	.4115	.4131	.4147	.4162	.4177
1.4	.4192	.4207	.4222	.4236	.4251	.4265	.4279	.4292	.4306	.4319
1.5	.4332	.4345	.4357	.4370	.4382	.4394	.4406	.4418	.4429	.4441
1.6	.4452	.4463	.4474	.4484	.4495	.4505	.4515	.4525	.4535	.4545
1.7	.4554	.4564	.4573	.4582	.4591	.4599	.4608	.4616	.4625	.4633
1.8	.4641	.4649	.4656	.4664	.4671	.4678	.4686	.4693	.4699	.4706
1.9	.4713	.4719	.4726	.4732	.4738	.4744	.4750	.4756	.4761	.4767
2.0	.4772	.4778	.4783	.4788	.4793	.4798	.4803	.4808	.4812	.4817
2.1	.4821	.4826	.4830	.4834	.4838	.4842	.4846	.4850	.4854	.4857
2.2	.4861	.4864	.4868	.4871	.4875	.4878	.4881	.4884	.4887	.4890
2.3	.4893	.4896	.4898	.4901	.4904	.4906	.4909	.4911	.4913	.4916
2.4	.4918	.4920	.4922	.4925	.4927	.4929	.4931	.4932	.4934	.4936
2.5	.4938	.4940	.4941	.4943	.4945	.4946	.4948	.4949	.4951	.4952
2.6	.4953	.4955	.4956	.4957	.4959	.4960	.4961	.4962	.4963	.4964
2.7	.4965	.4966	.4967	.4968	.4969	.4970	.4971	.4972	.4973	.4974
2.8	.4974	.4975	.4976	.4977	.4977	.4978	.4979	.4979	.4980	.4981
2.9	.4981	.4982	.4982	.4983	.4984	.4984	.4985	.4985	.4986	.4986
3.0	.4987	.4987	.4987	.4988	.4988	.4989	.4989	.4989	.4990	.4990

CRITICAL POINTS OF THE t DISTRIBUTION

The first column lists the number of degrees of freedom (ν). The headings of the other columns give probabilities (P) for t to exceed the entry value. Use symmetry for negative t values.

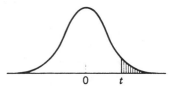

df \ P	.10	.05	.025	.01	.005
1	3.078	6.314	12.706	31.821	63.657
2	1.886	2.920	4.303	6.965	9.925
3	1.638	2.353	3.182	4.541	5.841
4	1.533	2.132	2.776	3.747	4.604
5	1.476	2.015	2.571	3.365	4.032
6	1.440	1.943	2.447	3.143	3.707
7	1.415	1.895	2.365	2.998	3.499
8	1.397	1.860	2.306	2.896	3.355
9	1.383	1.833	2.262	2.821	3.250
10	1.372	1.812	2.228	2.764	3.169
11	1.363	1.796	2.201	2.718	3.106
12	1.356	1.782	2.179	2.681	3.055
13	1.350	1.771	2.160	2.650	3.012
14	1.345	1.761	2.145	2.624	2.977
15	1.341	1.753	2.131	2.602	2.947
16	1.337	1.746	2.120	2.583	2.921
17	1.333	1.740	2.110	2.567	2.898
18	1.330	1.734	2.101	2.552	2.878
19	1.328	1.729	2.093	2.539	2.861
20	1.325	1.725	2.086	2.528	2.845
21	1.323	1.721	2.080	2.518	2.831
22	1.321	1.717	2.074	2.508	2.819
23	1.319	1.714	2.069	2.500	2.807
24	1.318	1.711	2.064	2.492	2.797
25	1.316	1.708	2.060	2.485	2.787
26	1.315	1.706	2.056	2.479	2.779
27	1.314	1.703	2.052	2.473	2.771
28	1.313	1.701	2.048	2.467	2.763
29	1.311	1.699	2.045	2.462	2.756
30	1.310	1.697	2.042	2.457	2.750
40	1.303	1.684	2.021	2.423	2.704
60	1.296	1.671	2.000	2.390	2.660
120	1.289	1.658	1.980	2.358	2.617
∞	1.282	1.645	1.960	2.326	2.576

TABLE OF χ^2

Degrees of Freedom df	P = .99	.98	.95	.90	.80	.70	.50	.30	.20	.10	.05	.02	.01
1	.000157	.000628	.00393	.0158	.0642	.148	.455	1.074	1.642	2.706	3.841	5.412	6.635
2	.0201	.0404	.103	.211	.446	.713	1.386	2.408	3.219	4.605	5.991	7.824	9.210
3	.115	.185	.352	.584	1.005	1.424	2.366	3.665	4.642	6.251	7.815	9.837	11.341
4	.297	.429	.711	1.064	1.649	2.195	3.357	4.878	5.989	7.779	9.488	11.668	13.277
5	.554	.752	1.145	1.610	2.343	3.000	4.351	6.064	7.289	9.236	11.070	13.388	15.086
6	.872	1.134	1.635	2.204	3.070	3.828	5.348	7.231	8.558	10.645	12.592	15.033	16.812
7	1.239	1.564	2.167	2.833	3.822	4.671	6.346	8.383	9.803	12.017	14.067	16.622	18.475
8	1.646	2.032	2.733	3.490	4.594	5.527	7.344	9.524	11.030	13.362	15.507	18.168	20.090
9	2.088	2.532	3.325	4.168	5.380	6.393	8.343	10.656	12.242	14.684	16.919	19.679	21.666
10	2.558	3.059	3.940	4.865	6.179	7.267	9.342	11.781	13.442	15.987	18.307	21.161	23.209
11	3.053	3.609	4.575	5.578	6.989	8.148	10.341	12.899	14.631	17.275	19.675	22.618	24.725
12	3.571	4.178	5.226	6.304	7.807	9.034	11.340	14.011	15.812	18.549	21.026	24.054	26.217
13	4.107	4.765	5.892	7.042	8.634	9.926	12.340	15.119	16.985	19.812	22.362	25.472	27.688
14	4.660	5.368	6.571	7.790	9.467	10.821	13.339	16.222	18.151	21.064	23.685	26.873	29.141
15	5.229	5.985	7.261	8.547	10.307	11.721	14.339	17.322	19.311	22.307	24.996	28.259	30.578
16	5.812	6.614	7.962	9.312	11.152	12.624	15.338	18.418	20.465	23.542	26.296	29.633	32.000
17	6.408	7.255	8.672	10.085	12.002	13.531	16.338	19.511	21.615	24.769	27.587	30.995	33.409
18	7.015	7.906	9.390	10.865	12.857	14.440	17.338	20.601	22.760	25.989	28.869	32.346	34.805
19	7.633	8.567	10.117	11.651	13.716	15.352	18.338	21.689	23.900	27.204	30.144	33.687	36.191
20	8.260	9.237	10.851	12.443	14.578	16.266	19.337	22.775	25.038	28.412	31.410	35.020	37.566
21	8.897	9.915	11.591	13.240	15.445	17.182	20.337	23.858	26.171	29.615	32.671	36.343	38.932
22	9.542	10.600	12.338	14.041	16.314	18.101	21.337	24.939	27.301	30.813	33.924	37.659	40.289
23	10.196	11.293	13.091	14.848	17.187	19.021	22.337	26.018	28.429	32.007	35.172	38.968	41.638
24	10.856	11.992	13.848	15.659	18.062	19.943	23.337	27.096	29.553	33.196	36.415	40.270	42.980
25	11.524	12.697	14.611	16.473	18.940	20.867	24.337	28.172	30.675	34.382	37.652	41.566	44.314
26	12.198	13.409	15.379	17.292	19.820	21.792	25.336	29.246	31.795	35.563	38.885	42.856	45.642
27	12.879	14.125	16.151	18.114	20.703	22.719	26.336	30.319	32.912	36.741	40.113	44.140	46.963
28	13.565	14.847	16.928	18.939	21.588	23.647	27.336	31.391	34.027	37.916	41.337	45.419	48.278
29	14.256	15.574	17.708	19.768	22.475	24.577	28.336	32.461	35.139	39.087	42.557	46.693	49.588
30	14.953	16.306	18.493	20.599	23.364	25.508	29.336	33.530	36.250	40.256	43.773	47.962	50.892

The degrees of freedom are listed on the left and the levels of significance across the top. The entries are the values of χ^2 that must be exceeded for those degrees of freedom to achieve that level of significance.

SQUARES, SQUARE ROOTS, AND RECIPROCALS

n	n^2	$\sqrt{n}$	$\sqrt{10n}$	$1/n$	n	n^2	$\sqrt{n}$	$\sqrt{10n}$	$1/n$
1	1	1.000	3.162	1.00000	51	2601	7.141	22.583	.01961
2	4	1.414	4.472	.50000	52	2704	7.211	22.804	.01923
3	9	1.732	5.477	.33333	53	2809	7.280	23.022	.01887
4	16	2.000	6.325	.25000	54	2916	7.348	23.238	.01852
5	25	2.236	7.071	.20000	55	3025	7.416	23.452	.01818
6	36	2.449	7.746	.16667	56	3136	7.483	23.664	.01786
7	49	2.646	8.367	.14286	57	3249	7.550	23.875	.01754
8	64	2.828	8.944	.12500	58	3364	7.616	24.083	.01724
9	81	3.000	9.487	.11111	59	3481	7.681	24.290	.01695
10	100	3.162	10.000	.10000	60	3600	7.746	24.495	.01667
11	121	3.317	10.488	.09091	61	3721	7.810	24.698	.01639
12	144	3.464	10.954	.08333	62	3844	7.874	24.900	.01613
13	169	3.606	11.402	.07692	63	3969	7.937	25.100	.01587
14	196	3.742	11.832	.07143	64	4096	8.000	25.298	.01562
15	225	3.873	12.247	.06667	65	4225	8.062	25.495	.01538
16	256	4.000	12.649	.06250	66	4356	8.124	25.690	.01515
17	289	4.123	13.038	.05882	67	4489	8.185	25.884	.01493
18	324	4.243	13.416	.05556	68	4624	8.246	26.077	.01471
19	361	4.359	13.784	.05263	69	4761	8.307	26.268	.01449
20	400	4.472	14.142	.05000	70	4900	8.367	26.458	.01429
21	441	4.583	14.491	.04762	71	5041	8.426	26.646	.01408
22	484	4.690	14.832	.04545	72	5184	8.485	26.833	.01389
23	529	4.796	15.166	.04348	73	5329	8.544	27.019	.01370
24	576	4.899	15.492	.04167	74	5476	8.602	27.203	.01351
25	625	5.000	15.811	.04000	75	5625	8.660	27.386	.01333
26	676	5.099	16.125	.03846	76	5776	8.718	27.568	.01316
27	729	5.196	16.432	.03704	77	5929	8.775	27.749	.01299
28	784	5.292	16.733	.03571	78	6084	8.832	27.928	.01282
29	841	5.385	17.029	.03448	79	6241	8.888	28.107	.01266
30	900	5.477	17.321	.03333	80	6400	8.944	28.284	.01250
31	961	5.568	17.607	.03226	81	6561	9.000	28.460	.01235
32	1024	5.657	17.889	.03125	82	6724	9.055	28.636	.01220
33	1089	5.745	18.166	.03030	83	6889	9.110	28.810	.01205
34	1156	5.831	18.439	.02941	84	7056	9.165	28.983	.01190
35	1225	5.916	18.708	.02857	85	7225	9.220	29.155	.01176
36	1296	6.000	18.974	.02778	86	7396	9.274	29.326	.01163
37	1369	6.083	19.235	.02703	87	7569	9.327	29.496	.01149
38	1444	6.164	19.494	.02632	88	7744	9.381	29.665	.01136
39	1521	6.245	19.748	.02564	89	7921	9.434	29.833	.01124
40	1600	6.325	20.000	.02500	90	8100	9.487	30.000	.01111
41	1681	6.403	20.248	.02439	91	8281	9.539	30.166	.01099
42	1764	6.481	20.494	.02381	92	8464	9.592	30.332	.01087
43	1849	6.557	20.736	.02326	93	8649	9.644	30.496	.01075
44	1936	6.633	20.976	.02273	94	8836	9.695	30.659	.01064
45	2025	6.708	21.213	.02222	95	9025	9.747	30.822	.01053
46	2116	6.782	21.448	.02174	96	9216	9.798	30.984	.01042
47	2209	6.856	21.679	.02128	97	9409	9.849	31.145	.01031
48	2304	6.928	21.909	.02083	98	9604	9.899	31.305	.01020
49	2401	7.000	22.136	.02041	99	9801	9.950	31.464	.01010
50	2500	7.071	22.361	.02000	100	10000	10.000	31.623	.01000

FACTORIAL n, n! = 1·2·3·....·n

n	n!	n	n!	n	n!
0	1 (by definition)	40	8.15915×10^{47}	80	7.15695×10^{118}
1	1	41	3.34525×10^{49}	81	5.79713×10^{120}
2	2	42	1.40501×10^{51}	82	4.75364×10^{122}
3	6	43	6.04153×10^{52}	83	3.94552×10^{124}
4	24	44	2.65827×10^{54}	84	3.31424×10^{126}
5	120	45	1.19622×10^{56}	85	2.81710×10^{128}
6	720	46	5.50262×10^{57}	86	2.42271×10^{130}
7	5040	47	2.58623×10^{59}	87	2.10776×10^{132}
8	40,320	48	1.24139×10^{61}	88	1.85483×10^{134}
9	362,880	49	6.08282×10^{62}	89	1.65080×10^{136}
10	3,628,800	50	3.04141×10^{64}	90	1.48572×10^{138}
11	39,916,800	51	1.55112×10^{66}	91	1.35200×10^{140}
12	479,001,600	52	8.06582×10^{67}	92	1.24384×10^{142}
13	6,227,020,800	53	4.27488×10^{69}	93	1.15677×10^{144}
14	87,178,291,200	54	2.30844×10^{71}	94	1.08737×10^{146}
15	1,307,674,368,000	55	1.26964×10^{73}	95	1.03300×10^{148}
16	20,922,789,888,000	56	7.10999×10^{74}	96	9.91678×10^{149}
17	355,687,428,096,000	57	4.05269×10^{76}	97	9.61928×10^{151}
18	6,402,373,705,728,000	58	2.35056×10^{78}	98	9.42689×10^{153}
19	121,645,100,408,832,000	59	1.38683×10^{80}	99	9.33262×10^{155}
20	2,432,902,008,176,640,000	60	8.32099×10^{81}	100	9.33262×10^{157}
21	51,090,942,171,709,440,000	61	5.07580×10^{83}		
22	1,124,000,727,777,607,680,000	62	3.14700×10^{85}		
23	25,852,016,738,884,976,640,000	63	1.98261×10^{87}		
24	620,448,401,733,239,439,360,000	64	1.26887×10^{89}		
25	15,511,210,043,330,985,984,000,000	65	8.24765×10^{90}		
26	403,291,461,126,605,635,584,000,000	66	5.44345×10^{92}		
27	10,888,869,450,418,352,160,768,000,000	67	3.64711×10^{94}		
28	304,888,344,611,713,860,501,504,000,000	68	2.48004×10^{96}		
29	8,841,761,993,739,701,954,543,616,000,000	69	1.71122×10^{98}		
30	265,252,859,812,191,058,636,308,480,000,000				
		70	1.19786×10^{100}		
31	8.22284×10^{33}	71	8.50479×10^{101}		
32	2.63131×10^{35}	72	6.12345×10^{103}		
33	8.68332×10^{36}	73	4.47012×10^{105}		
34	2.95233×10^{38}	74	3.30789×10^{107}		
35	1.03331×10^{40}	75	2.48091×10^{109}		
36	3.71993×10^{41}	76	1.88549×10^{111}		
37	1.37638×10^{43}	77	1.45183×10^{113}		
38	5.23023×10^{44}	78	1.13243×10^{115}		
39	2.03979×10^{46}	79	8.94618×10^{116}		

NUMBER OF PERMUTATIONS $P(n,m)$

This table contains the number of permutations of n distinct things taken m at a time, given by

$$P(n,m) = \frac{n!}{(n-m)!} = n(n-1)\cdots(n-m+1)$$

n\m	0	1	2	3	4	5	6	7	8	9	10
0	1										
1	1	1									
2	1	2	2								
3	1	3	6	6							
4	1	4	12	24	24						
5	1	5	20	60	120	120					
6	1	6	30	120	360	720	720				
7	1	7	42	210	840	2520	5040	5040			
8	1	8	56	336	1680	6720	20160	40320	40320		
9	1	9	72	504	3024	15120	60480	1 81440	3 62880	3 62880	
10	1	10	90	720	5040	30240	1 51200	6 04800	18 14400	36 28800	36 28800
11	1	11	110	990	7920	55440	3 32640	16 63200	66 52800	199 58400	399 16800
12	1	12	132	1320	11880	95040	6 65280	39 91680	199 58400	798 33600	2395 00800
13	1	13	156	1716	17160	1 54440	12 35520	86 48640	518 91840	2594 59200	10378 36800
14	1	14	182	2184	24024	2 40240	21 62160	172 97280	1210 80960	7264 85760	36324 28800
15	1	15	210	2730	32760	3 60360	36 03600	324 32400	2594 59200	18162 14400	1 08972 86400

n\m	11	12	13	14	15
8					
9					
10					
11	399 16800				
12	4790 01600	4790 01600			
13	31135 10400	62270 20800	62270 20800		
14	1 45297 15200	4 35891 45600	8 71782 91200	8 71782 91200	
15	5 44864 32000	21 79457 28000	65 38371 84000	130 76743 68000	130 76743 68000

FOUR PLACE COMMON LOGARITHMS
Log₁₀ N or Log N

N	0	1	2	3	4	5	6	7	8	9	Proportional Parts								
											1	2	3	4	5	6	7	8	9
10	0000	0043	0086	0128	0170	0212	0253	0294	0334	0374	4	8	12	17	21	25	29	33	37
11	0414	0453	0492	0531	0569	0607	0645	0682	0719	0755	4	8	11	15	19	23	26	30	34
12	0792	0828	0864	0899	0934	0969	1004	1038	1072	1106	3	7	10	14	17	21	24	28	31
13	1139	1173	1206	1239	1271	1303	1335	1367	1399	1430	3	6	10	13	16	19	23	26	29
14	1461	1492	1523	1553	1584	1614	1644	1673	1703	1732	3	6	9	12	15	18	21	24	27
15	1761	1790	1818	1847	1875	1903	1931	1959	1987	2014	3	6	8	11	14	17	20	22	25
16	2041	2068	2095	2122	2148	2175	2201	2227	2253	2279	3	5	8	11	13	16	18	21	24
17	2304	2330	2355	2380	2405	2430	2455	2480	2504	2529	2	5	7	10	12	15	17	20	22
18	2553	2577	2601	2625	2648	2672	2695	2718	2742	2765	2	5	7	9	12	14	16	19	21
19	2788	2810	2833	2856	2878	2900	2923	2945	2967	2989	2	4	7	9	11	13	16	18	20
20	3010	3032	3054	3075	3096	3118	3139	3160	3181	3201	2	4	6	8	11	13	15	17	19
21	3222	3243	3263	3284	3304	3324	3345	3365	3385	3404	2	4	6	8	10	12	14	16	18
22	3424	3444	3464	3483	3502	3522	3541	3560	3579	3598	2	4	6	8	10	12	14	15	17
23	3617	3636	3655	3674	3692	3711	3729	3747	3766	3784	2	4	6	7	9	11	13	15	17
24	3802	3820	3838	3856	3874	3892	3909	3927	3945	3962	2	4	5	7	9	11	12	14	16
25	3979	3997	4014	4031	4048	4065	4082	4099	4116	4133	2	3	5	7	9	10	12	14	15
26	4150	4166	4183	4200	4216	4232	4249	4265	4281	4298	2	3	5	7	8	10	11	13	15
27	4314	4330	4346	4362	4378	4393	4409	4425	4440	4456	2	3	5	6	8	9	11	13	14
28	4472	4487	4502	4518	4533	4548	4564	4579	4594	4609	2	3	5	6	8	9	11	12	14
29	4624	4639	4654	4669	4683	4698	4713	4728	4742	4757	1	3	4	6	7	9	10	12	13
30	4771	4786	4800	4814	4829	4843	4857	4871	4886	4900	1	3	4	6	7	9	10	11	13
31	4914	4928	4942	4955	4969	4983	4997	5011	5024	5038	1	3	4	6	7	8	10	11	12
32	5051	5065	5079	5092	5105	5119	5132	5145	5159	5172	1	3	4	5	7	8	9	11	12
33	5185	5198	5211	5224	5237	5250	5263	5276	5289	5302	1	3	4	5	6	8	9	10	12
34	5315	5328	5340	5353	5366	5378	5391	5403	5416	5428	1	3	4	5	6	8	9	10	11
35	5441	5453	5465	5478	5490	5502	5514	5527	5539	5551	1	2	4	5	6	7	9	10	11
36	5563	5575	5587	5599	5611	5623	5635	5647	5658	5670	1	2	4	5	6	7	8	10	11
37	5682	5694	5705	5717	5729	5740	5752	5763	5775	5786	1	2	3	5	6	7	8	9	10
38	5798	5809	5821	5832	5843	5855	5866	5877	5888	5899	1	2	3	5	6	7	8	9	10
39	5911	5922	5933	5944	5955	5966	5977	5988	5999	6010	1	2	3	4	5	7	8	9	10
40	6021	6031	6042	6053	6064	6075	6085	6096	6107	6117	1	2	3	4	5	6	8	9	10
41	6128	6138	6149	6160	6170	6180	6191	6201	6212	6222	1	2	3	4	5	6	7	8	9
42	6232	6243	6253	6263	6274	6284	6294	6304	6314	6325	1	2	3	4	5	6	7	8	9
43	6335	6345	6355	6365	6375	6385	6395	6405	6415	6425	1	2	3	4	5	6	7	8	9
44	6435	6444	6454	6464	6474	6484	6493	6503	6513	6522	1	2	3	4	5	6	7	8	9
45	6532	6542	6551	6561	6571	6580	6590	6599	6609	6618	1	2	3	4	5	6	7	8	9
46	6628	6637	6646	6656	6665	6675	6684	6693	6702	6712	1	2	3	4	5	6	7	7	8
47	6721	6730	6739	6749	6758	6767	6776	6785	6794	6803	1	2	3	4	5	5	6	7	8
48	6812	6821	6830	6839	6848	6857	6866	6875	6884	6893	1	2	3	4	4	5	6	7	8
49	6902	6911	6920	6928	6937	6946	6955	6964	6972	6981	1	2	3	4	4	5	6	7	8
50	6990	6998	7007	7016	7024	7033	7042	7050	7059	7067	1	2	3	3	4	5	6	7	8
51	7076	7084	7093	7101	7110	7118	7126	7135	7143	7152	1	2	3	3	4	5	6	7	8
52	7160	7168	7177	7185	7193	7202	7210	7218	7226	7235	1	2	2	3	4	5	6	7	7
53	7243	7251	7259	7267	7275	7284	7292	7300	7308	7316	1	2	2	3	4	5	6	6	7
54	7324	7332	7340	7348	7356	7364	7372	7380	7388	7396	1	2	2	3	4	5	6	6	7
N	0	1	2	3	4	5	6	7	8	9	1	2	3	4	5	6	7	8	9

FOUR PLACE COMMON LOGARITHMS
Log$_{10}$ N or Log N

N	0	1	2	3	4	5	6	7	8	9	Proportional Parts								
											1	2	3	4	5	6	7	8	9
55	7404	7412	7419	7427	7435	7443	7451	7459	7466	7474	1	2	2	3	4	5	5	6	7
56	7482	7490	7497	7505	7513	7520	7528	7536	7543	7551	1	2	2	3	4	5	5	6	7
57	7559	7566	7574	7582	7589	7597	7604	7612	7619	7627	1	2	2	3	4	5	5	6	7
58	7634	7642	7649	7657	7664	7672	7679	7686	7694	7701	1	1	2	3	4	4	5	6	7
59	7709	7716	7723	7731	7738	7745	7752	7760	7767	7774	1	1	2	3	4	4	5	6	7
60	7782	7789	7796	7803	7810	7818	7825	7832	7839	7846	1	1	2	3	4	4	5	6	6
61	7853	7860	7868	7875	7882	7889	7896	7903	7910	7917	1	1	2	3	4	4	5	6	6
62	7924	7931	7938	7945	7952	7959	7966	7973	7980	7987	1	1	2	3	3	4	5	6	6
63	7993	8000	8007	8014	8021	8028	8035	8041	8048	8055	1	1	2	3	3	4	5	5	6
64	8062	8069	8075	8082	8089	8096	8102	8109	8116	8122	1	1	2	3	3	4	5	5	6
65	8129	8136	8142	8149	8156	8162	8169	8176	8182	8189	1	1	2	3	3	4	5	5	6
66	8195	8202	8209	8215	8222	8228	8235	8241	8248	8254	1	1	2	3	3	4	5	5	6
67	8261	8267	8274	8280	8287	8293	8299	8306	8312	8319	1	1	2	3	3	4	5	5	6
68	8325	8331	8338	8344	8351	8357	8363	8370	8376	8382	1	1	2	3	3	4	4	5	6
69	8388	8395	8401	8407	8414	8420	8426	8432	8439	8445	1	1	2	2	3	4	4	5	6
70	8451	8457	8463	8470	8476	8482	8488	8494	8500	8506	1	1	2	2	3	4	4	5	6
71	8513	8519	8525	8531	8537	8543	8549	8555	8561	8567	1	1	2	2	3	4	4	5	5
72	8573	8579	8585	8591	8597	8603	8609	8615	8621	8627	1	1	2	2	3	4	4	5	5
73	8633	8639	8645	8651	8657	8663	8669	8675	8681	8686	1	1	2	2	3	4	4	5	5
74	8692	8698	8704	8710	8716	8722	8727	8733	8739	8745	1	1	2	2	3	4	4	5	5
75	8751	8756	8762	8768	8774	8779	8785	8791	8797	8802	1	1	2	2	3	3	4	5	5
76	8808	8814	8820	8825	8831	8837	8842	8848	8854	8859	1	1	2	2	3	3	4	5	5
77	8865	8871	8876	8882	8887	8893	8899	8904	8910	8915	1	1	2	2	3	3	4	4	5
78	8921	8927	8932	8938	8943	8949	8954	8960	8965	8971	1	1	2	2	3	3	4	4	5
79	8976	8982	8987	8993	8998	9004	9009	9015	9020	9025	1	1	2	2	3	3	4	4	5
80	9031	9036	9042	9047	9053	9058	9063	9069	9074	9079	1	1	2	2	3	3	4	4	5
81	9085	9090	9096	9101	9106	9112	9117	9122	9128	9133	1	1	2	2	3	3	4	4	5
82	9138	9143	9149	9154	9159	9165	9170	9175	9180	9186	1	1	2	2	3	3	4	4	5
83	9191	9196	9201	9206	9212	9217	9222	9227	9232	9238	1	1	2	2	3	3	4	4	5
84	9243	9248	9253	9258	9263	9269	9274	9279	9284	9289	1	1	2	2	3	3	4	4	5
85	9294	9299	9304	9309	9315	9320	9325	9330	9335	9340	1	1	2	2	3	3	4	4	5
86	9345	9350	9355	9360	9365	9370	9375	9380	9385	9390	1	1	2	2	3	3	4	4	5
87	9395	9400	9405	9410	9415	9420	9425	9430	9435	9440	0	1	1	2	2	3	3	4	4
88	9445	9450	9455	9460	9465	9469	9474	9479	9484	9489	0	1	1	2	2	3	3	4	4
89	9494	9499	9504	9509	9513	9518	9523	9528	9533	9538	0	1	1	2	2	3	3	4	4
90	9542	9547	9552	9557	9562	9566	9571	9576	9581	9586	0	1	1	2	2	3	3	4	4
91	9590	9595	9600	9605	9609	9614	9619	9624	9628	9633	0	1	1	2	2	3	3	4	4
92	9638	9643	9647	9652	9657	9661	9666	9671	9675	9680	0	1	1	2	2	3	3	4	4
93	9685	9689	9694	9699	9703	9708	9713	9717	9722	9727	0	1	1	2	2	3	3	4	4
94	9731	9736	9741	9745	9750	9754	9759	9763	9768	9773	0	1	1	2	2	3	3	4	4
95	9777	9782	9786	9791	9795	9800	9805	9809	9814	9818	0	1	1	2	2	3	3	4	4
96	9823	9827	9832	9836	9841	9845	9850	9854	9859	9863	0	1	1	2	2	3	3	4	4
97	9868	9872	9877	9881	9886	9890	9894	9899	9903	9908	0	1	1	2	2	3	3	4	4
98	9912	9917	9921	9926	9930	9934	9939	9943	9948	9952	0	1	1	2	2	3	3	4	4
99	9956	9961	9965	9969	9974	9978	9983	9987	9991	9996	0	1	1	2	2	3	3	3	4
N	0	1	2	3	4	5	6	7	8	9	1	2	3	4	5	6	7	8	9

NATURAL OR NAPIERIAN LOGARITHMS
$\log_e x$ or $\ln x$

x	0	1	2	3	4	5	6	7	8	9
1.0	.00000	.00995	.01980	.02956	.03922	.04879	.05827	.06766	.07696	.08618
1.1	.09531	.10436	.11333	.12222	.13103	.13976	.14842	.15700	.16551	.17395
1.2	.18232	.19062	.19885	.20701	.21511	.22314	.23111	.23902	.24686	.25464
1.3	.26236	.27003	.27763	.28518	.29267	.30010	.30748	.31481	.32208	.32930
1.4	.33647	.34359	.35066	.35767	.36464	.37156	.37844	.38526	.39204	.39878
1.5	.40547	.41211	.41871	.42527	.43178	.43825	.44469	.45108	.45742	.46373
1.6	.47000	.47623	.48243	.48858	.49470	.50078	.50682	.51282	.51879	.52473
1.7	.53063	.53649	.54232	.54812	.55389	.55962	.56531	.57098	.57661	.58222
1.8	.58779	.59333	.59884	.60432	.60977	.61519	.62058	.62594	.63127	.63658
1.9	.64185	.64710	.65233	.65752	.66269	.66783	.67294	.67803	.68310	.68813
2.0	.69315	.69813	.70310	.70804	.71295	.71784	.72271	.72755	.73237	.73716
2.1	.74194	.74669	.75142	.75612	.76081	.76547	.77011	.77473	.77932	.78390
2.2	.78846	.79299	.79751	.80200	.80648	.81093	.81536	.81978	.82418	.82855
2.3	.83291	.83725	.84157	.84587	.85015	.85442	.85866	.86289	.86710	.87129
2.4	.87547	.87963	.88377	.88789	.89200	.89609	.90016	.90422	.90826	.91228
2.5	.91629	.92028	.92426	.92822	.93216	.93609	.94001	.94391	.94779	.95166
2.6	.95551	.95935	.96317	.96698	.97078	.97456	.97833	.98208	.98582	.98954
2.7	.99325	.99695	1.00063	1.00430	1.00796	1.01160	1.01523	1.01885	1.02245	1.02604
2.8	1.02962	1.03318	1.03674	1.04028	1.04380	1.04732	1.05082	1.05431	1.05779	1.06126
2.9	1.06471	1.06815	1.07158	1.07500	1.07841	1.08181	1.08519	1.08856	1.09192	1.09527
3.0	1.09861	1.10194	1.10526	1.10856	1.11186	1.11514	1.11841	1.12168	1.12493	1.12817
3.1	1.13140	1.13462	1.13783	1.14103	1.14422	1.14740	1.15057	1.15373	1.15688	1.16002
3.2	1.16315	1.16627	1.16938	1.17248	1.17557	1.17865	1.18173	1.18479	1.18784	1.19089
3.3	1.19392	1.19695	1.19996	1.20297	1.20597	1.20896	1.21194	1.21491	1.21788	1.22083
3.4	1.22378	1.22671	1.22964	1.23256	1.23547	1.23837	1.24127	1.24415	1.24703	1.24990
3.5	1.25276	1.25562	1.25846	1.26130	1.26413	1.26695	1.26976	1.27257	1.27536	1.27815
3.6	1.28093	1.28371	1.28647	1.28923	1.29198	1.29473	1.29746	1.30019	1.30291	1.30563
3.7	1.30833	1.31103	1.31372	1.31641	1.31909	1.32176	1.32442	1.32708	1.32972	1.33237
3.8	1.33500	1.33763	1.34025	1.34286	1.34547	1.34807	1.35067	1.35325	1.35584	1.35841
3.9	1.36098	1.36354	1.36609	1.36864	1.37118	1.37372	1.37624	1.37877	1.38128	1.38379
4.0	1.38629	1.38879	1.39128	1.39377	1.39624	1.39872	1.40118	1.40364	1.40610	1.40854
4.1	1.41099	1.41342	1.41585	1.41828	1.42070	1.42311	1.42552	1.42792	1.43031	1.43270
4.2	1.43508	1.43746	1.43984	1.44220	1.44456	1.44692	1.44927	1.45161	1.45395	1.45629
4.3	1.45862	1.46094	1.46326	1.46557	1.46787	1.47018	1.47247	1.47476	1.47705	1.47933
4.4	1.48160	1.48387	1.48614	1.48840	1.49065	1.49290	1.49515	1.49739	1.49962	1.50185
4.5	1.50408	1.50630	1.50851	1.51072	1.51293	1.51513	1.51732	1.51951	1.52170	1.52388
4.6	1.52606	1.52823	1.53039	1.53256	1.53471	1.53687	1.53902	1.54116	1.54330	1.54543
4.7	1.54756	1.54969	1.55181	1.55393	1.55604	1.55814	1.56025	1.56235	1.56444	1.56653
4.8	1.56862	1.57070	1.57277	1.57485	1.57691	1.57898	1.58104	1.58309	1.58515	1.58719
4.9	1.58924	1.59127	1.59331	1.59534	1.59737	1.59939	1.60141	1.60342	1.60543	1.60744

$\ln 10 = 2.30259$	$4 \ln 10 = 9.21034$	$7 \ln 10 = 16.11810$
$2 \ln 10 = 4.60517$	$5 \ln 10 = 11.51293$	$8 \ln 10 = 18.42068$
$3 \ln 10 = 6.90776$	$6 \ln 10 = 13.81551$	$9 \ln 10 = 20.72327$

EXPONENTIAL FUNCTIONS e^x

x	0	1	2	3	4	5	6	7	8	9
.0	1.0000	1.0101	1.0202	1.0305	1.0408	1.0513	1.0618	1.0725	1.0833	1.0942
.1	1.1052	1.1163	1.1275	1.1388	1.1503	1.1618	1.1735	1.1853	1.1972	1.2092
.2	1.2214	1.2337	1.2461	1.2586	1.2712	1.2840	1.2969	1.3100	1.3231	1.3364
.3	1.3499	1.3634	1.3771	1.3910	1.4049	1.4191	1.4333	1.4477	1.4623	1.4770
.4	1.4918	1.5068	1.5220	1.5373	1.5527	1.5683	1.5841	1.6000	1.6161	1.6323
.5	1.6487	1.6653	1.6820	1.6989	1.7160	1.7333	1.7507	1.7683	1.7860	1.8040
.6	1.8221	1.8404	1.8589	1.8776	1.8965	1.9155	1.9348	1.9542	1.9739	1.9937
.7	2.0138	2.0340	2.0544	2.0751	2.0959	2.1170	2.1383	2.1598	2.1815	2.2034
.8	2.2255	2.2479	2.2705	2.2933	2.3164	2.3396	2.3632	2.3869	2.4109	2.4351
.9	2.4596	2.4843	2.5093	2.5345	2.5600	2.5857	2.6117	2.6379	2.6645	2.6912
1.0	2.7183	2.7456	2.7732	2.8011	2.8292	2.8577	2.8864	2.9154	2.9447	2.9743
1.1	3.0042	3.0344	3.0649	3.0957	3.1268	3.1582	3.1899	3.2220	3.2544	3.2871
1.2	3.3201	3.3535	3.3872	3.4212	3.4556	3.4903	3.5254	3.5609	3.5966	3.6328
1.3	3.6693	3.7062	3.7434	3.7810	3.8190	3.8574	3.8962	3.9354	3.9749	4.0149
1.4	4.0552	4.0960	4.1371	4.1787	4.2207	4.2631	4.3060	4.3492	4.3929	4.4371
1.5	4.4817	4.5267	4.5722	4.6182	4.6646	4.7115	4.7588	4.8066	4.8550	4.9037
1.6	4.9530	5.0028	5.0531	5.1039	5.1552	5.2070	5.2593	5.3122	5.3656	5.4195
1.7	5.4739	5.5290	5.5845	5.6407	5.6973	5.7546	5.8124	5.8709	5.9299	5.9895
1.8	6.0496	6.1104	6.1719	6.2339	6.2965	6.3598	6.4237	6.4883	6.5535	6.6194
1.9	6.6859	6.7531	6.8210	6.8895	6.9588	7.0287	7.0993	7.1707	7.2427	7.3155
2.0	7.3891	7.4633	7.5383	7.6141	7.6906	7.7679	7.8460	7.9248	8.0045	8.0849
2.1	8.1662	8.2482	8.3311	8.4149	8.4994	8.5849	8.6711	8.7583	8.8463	8.9352
2.2	9.0250	9.1157	9.2073	9.2999	9.3933	9.4877	9.5831	9.6794	9.7767	9.8749
2.3	9.9742	10.074	10.176	10.278	10.381	10.486	10.591	10.697	10.805	10.913
2.4	11.023	11.134	11.246	11.359	11.473	11.588	11.705	11.822	11.941	12.061
2.5	12.182	12.305	12.429	12.554	12.680	12.807	12.936	13.066	13.197	13.330
2.6	13.464	13.599	13.736	13.874	14.013	14.154	14.296	14.440	14.585	14.732
2.7	14.880	15.029	15.180	15.333	15.487	15.643	15.800	15.959	16.119	16.281
2.8	16.445	16.610	16.777	16.945	17.116	17.288	17.462	17.637	17.814	17.993
2.9	18.174	18.357	18.541	18.728	18.916	19.106	19.298	19.492	19.688	19.886
3.0	20.086	20.287	20.491	20.697	20.905	21.115	21.328	21.542	21.758	21.977
3.1	22.198	22.421	22.646	22.874	23.104	23.336	23.571	23.807	24.047	24.288
3.2	24.533	24.779	25.028	25.280	25.534	25.790	26.050	26.311	26.576	26.843
3.3	27.113	27.385	27.660	27.938	28.219	28.503	28.789	29.079	29.371	29.666
3.4	29.964	30.265	30.569	30.877	31.187	31.500	31.817	32.137	32.460	32.786
3.5	33.115	33.448	33.784	34.124	34.467	34.813	35.163	35.517	35.874	36.234
3.6	36.598	36.966	37.338	37.713	38.092	38.475	38.861	39.252	39.646	40.045
3.7	40.447	40.854	41.264	41.679	42.098	42.521	42.948	43.380	43.816	44.256
3.8	44.701	45.150	45.604	46.063	46.525	46.993	47.465	47.942	48.424	48.911
3.9	49.402	49.899	50.400	50.907	51.419	51.935	52.457	52.985	53.517	54.055
4.	54.598	60.340	66.686	73.700	81.451	90.017	99.484	109.95	121.51	134.29
5.	148.41	164.02	181.27	200.34	221.41	244.69	270.43	298.87	330.30	365.04
6.	403.43	445.86	492.75	544.57	601.85	665.14	735.10	812.41	897.85	992.27
7.	1096.6	1212.0	1339.4	1480.3	1636.0	1808.0	1998.2	2208.3	2440.6	2697.3
8.	2981.0	3294.5	3641.0	4023.9	4447.1	4914.8	5431.7	6002.9	6634.2	7332.0
9.	8103.1	8955.3	9897.1	10938	12088	13360	14765	16318	18034	19930
10.	22026									

EXPONENTIAL FUNCTIONS e^{-x}

x	0	1	2	3	4	5	6	7	8	9
.0	1.00000	.99005	.98020	.97045	.96079	.95123	.94176	.93239	.92312	.91393
.1	.90484	.89583	.88692	.87810	.86936	.86071	.85214	.84366	.83527	.82696
.2	.81873	.81058	.80252	.79453	.78663	.77880	.77105	.76338	.75578	.74826
.3	.74082	.73345	.72615	.71892	.71177	.70469	.69768	.69073	.68386	.67706
.4	.67032	.66365	.65705	.65051	.64404	.63763	.63128	.62500	.61878	.61263
.5	.60653	.60050	.59452	.58860	.58275	.57695	.57121	.56553	.55990	.55433
.6	.54881	.54335	.53794	.53259	.52729	.52205	.51685	.51171	.50662	.50158
.7	.49659	.49164	.48675	.48191	.47711	.47237	.46767	.46301	.45841	.45384
.8	.44933	.44486	.44043	.43605	.43171	.42741	.42316	.41895	.41478	.41066
.9	.40657	.40252	.39852	.39455	.39063	.38674	.38289	.37908	.37531	.37158
1.0	.36788	.36422	.36060	.35701	.35345	.34994	.34646	.34301	.33960	.33622
1.1	.33287	.32956	.32628	.32303	.31982	.31664	.31349	.31037	.30728	.30422
1.2	.30119	.29820	.29523	.29229	.28938	.28650	.28365	.28083	.27804	.27527
1.3	.27253	.26982	.26714	.26448	.26185	.25924	.25666	.25411	.25158	.24908
1.4	.24660	.24414	.24171	.23931	.23693	.23457	.23224	.22993	.22764	.22537
1.5	.22313	.22091	.21871	.21654	.21438	.21225	.21014	.20805	.20598	.20393
1.6	.20190	.19989	.19790	.19593	.19398	.19205	.19014	.18825	.18637	.18452
1.7	.18268	.18087	.17907	.17728	.17552	.17377	.17204	.17033	.16864	.16696
1.8	.16530	.16365	.16203	.16041	.15882	.15724	.15567	.15412	.15259	.15107
1.9	.14957	.14808	.14661	.14515	.14370	.14227	.14086	.13946	.13807	.13670
2.0	.13534	.13399	.13266	.13134	.13003	.12873	.12745	.12619	.12493	.12369
2.1	.12246	.12124	.12003	.11884	.11765	.11648	.11533	.11418	.11304	.11192
2.2	.11030	.10970	.10861	.10753	.10646	.10540	.10435	.10331	.10228	.10127
2.3	.10026	.09926	.09827	.09730	.09633	.09537	.09442	.09348	.09255	.09163
2.4	.09072	.08982	.08892	.08804	.08716	.08629	.08543	.08458	.08374	.08291
2.5	.08208	.08127	.08046	.07966	.07887	.07808	.07730	.07654	.07577	.07502
2.6	.07427	.07353	.07280	.07208	.07136	.07065	.06995	.06925	.06856	.06788
2.7	.06721	.06654	.06587	.06522	.06457	.06393	.06329	.06266	.06204	.06142
2.8	.06081	.06020	.05961	.05901	.05843	.05784	.05727	.05670	.05613	.05558
2.9	.05502	.05448	.05393	.05340	.05287	.05234	.05182	.05130	.05079	.05029
3.0	.04979	.04929	.04880	.04832	.04783	.04736	.04689	.04642	.04596	.04550
3.1	.04505	.04460	.04416	.04372	.04328	.04285	.04243	.04200	.04159	.04117
3.2	.04076	.04036	.03996	.03956	.03916	.03877	.03839	.03801	.03763	.03725
3.3	.03688	.03652	.03615	.03579	.03544	.03508	.03474	.03439	.03405	.03371
3.4	.03337	.03304	.03271	.03239	.03206	.03175	.03143	.03112	.03081	.03050
3.5	.03020	.02990	.02960	.02930	.02901	.02872	.02844	.02816	.02788	.02760
3.6	.02732	.02705	.02678	.02652	.02625	.02599	.02573	.02548	.02522	.02497
3.7	.02472	.02448	.02423	.02399	.02375	.02352	.02328	.02305	.02282	.02260
3.8	.02237	.02215	.02193	.02171	.02149	.02128	.02107	.02086	.02065	.02045
3.9	.02024	.02004	.01984	.01964	.01945	.01925	.01906	.01887	.01869	.01850
4.	.018316	.016573	.014996	.013569	.012277	.011109	.010052	$.0^290953$	$.0^282297$	$.0^274466$
5.	$.0^267379$	$.0^260967$	$.0^255166$	$.0^249916$	$.0^245166$	$.0^240868$	$.0^236979$	$.0^233460$	$.0^230276$	$.0^227394$
6.	$.0^224788$	$.0^222429$	$.0^220294$	$.0^218363$	$.0^216616$	$.0^215034$	$.0^213604$	$.0^212309$	$.0^211138$	$.0^210078$
7.	$.0^391188$	$.0^382510$	$.0^374659$	$.0^367554$	$.0^361125$	$.0^355308$	$.0^350045$	$.0^345283$	$.0^340973$	$.0^337074$
8.	$.0^333546$	$.0^330354$	$.0^327465$	$.0^324852$	$.0^322487$	$.0^320347$	$.0^318411$	$.0^316659$	$.0^315073$	$.0^313639$
9.	$.0^312341$	$.0^311167$	$.0^310104$	$.0^491424$	$.0^482724$	$.0^474852$	$.0^467729$	$.0^461283$	$.0^455452$	$.0^450175$
10.	$.0^445400$									

INDEX

INDEX

Numbers on this page refer to **PROBLEM NUMBERS**, not page numbers

Numbers on this page refer to **PROBLEM NUMBERS**, not page numbers

Numbers on this page refer to **PROBLEM NUMBERS**, not page numbers

Numbers on this page refer to **PROBLEM NUMBERS**, not page numbers